S0-ASM-850

5 PILLARS
OF THE VISUAL WORKPLACE

5 PILLARS OF THE VISUAL WORKPLACE

The Sourcebook for 5S Implementation

Hiroyuki Hirano

JIT Management Laboratory Company, Ltd.
Tokyo, Japan

Translated by Bruce Talbot

New York

 Additional copies of this book are available from the publisher. Discounts are available for multiple copies through the Sales Department (800-394-6868). Address all other inquiries to:

Productivity Press
444 Park Avenue South, 7th Floor
Nw York, NY 10016
United States of America
Telephone: 212-686-5900
Telefax: 212-686-5411
E-Mail: info@productivitypress.com

Cover design by William Stanton
Graphics by Productivity Press (India) Private Ltd. (Madras, India) and Rohani Design (Edmonds, Washington)
Composition by Rohani Design
Printed and bound by Sheridan in the United States of America

Library of Congress Cataloging-in-Publication Data

Hirano, Hiroyuki
[5S shidō manyuaru. English]
5 pillars of the visual workplace : the sourcebook for 5 S implementation / Hiroyuki Hirano.
p. cm.
Translation of: 5S shidō manyuaru.
Includes index.
ISBN: 1-56327-047-1
1. Factory management. 2. Office management. I. Title.
TS155.H48513 1995
658.5--dc20 94-30624
CIP

10 09 08 07 06 20 19 18 17 16

Contents

Publisher's Message

The book before us is *5 Pillars of the Visual Workplace: The Sourcebook for 5S Implementation*. I consider Hiroyuki Hirano, the author, to be a genius and the 5S's to be the most important step for productivity improvement and safety today. Let me explain what I mean.

Products and processes today involve very close tolerances. Variability must be fully controlled. The physical work environment is critical in the drive for high quality, low cost, and speedy delivery. Think about the Indy 500 in which, thanks to precise teamwork and organization, a car can be serviced in the pits in only 14 seconds. The computer industry has created "clean-room" work environments to produce the required precision and purity in production. Now growing consumer demand for quality products is forcing people from other industries to rethink their workplaces.

Will product improvements see the light of day (or night) in filthy plants? Can we expect people in dismal environments to work at their maximum potential? Can uncluttered minds with fresh ideas function in cluttered work-places? The answer is obvious — and the solution so simple.

Organization, Orderliness, Cleanliness, Standardized Cleanup, and Discipline are needed. This is what Mr. Hirano calls the "5S's" — simple activities that can be difficult to implement. And this is what is required for companies to survive in the years ahead. Americans too often expect high drama from an idea when what is needed is simplicity — and a solid foundation to sustain good work.

In 1988 Productivity Press published what we considered to be the best companywide introduction to the Just-in-Time (JIT) production system. It was a picture book entitled *JIT Factory Revolution: A Pictorial Guide to Factory Design of the Future*. One of numerous books written by Hiroyuki Hirano, a top international consultant, it sparked the interest of Auburn University's Dr. JT Black. His invaluable editing transformed Mr. Hirano's textbook for Japanese factory workers into an educational and eye-opening "before and after JIT plant tour" for American workers as well.

A few years later, in 1990, we published its counterpart, also written by Mr. Hirano — the most comprehensive and detailed manual for setting up a complete JIT program. The *JIT Implementation Manual: The Complete Guide to Just-in-Time Manufacturing*'s one thousand pages examined how to plan, implement, monitor, and standardize each of the eleven principal types of JIT improvements. Encyclopedic in scope (and known in Japan as the "JIT Bible"), it was packed with hundreds of illustrations and useful forms.

A primary focus for both JIT books was to build a companywide foundation for making improvements in both factory and office. It is this foundation for making improvements that Mr. Hirano calls the 5S's — the Japanese "S" words (*seiri, seiton, seisō, seiketsu, shitsuke*) that we call Organization, Orderliness, Cleanliness, Standardized Cleanup, and Discipline.

Mr. Hirano recalls a JIT axiom that says: "Good workplaces develop beginning with the 5S's. Bad workplaces fall apart beginning with the 5S's." The first part refers to the thorough implementation of the 5S's that we need in order to lay the groundwork for subsequent improvements. The 5S's are the foundation blocks — or workplace "pillars" — upon which we can establish flow production, visual control, standard operations, and other JIT building blocks. Working through the process properly will, in a few years, turn a factory into a close approximation of the JIT production system.

On the other hand, it only takes a moment for a workplace to begin falling apart. This process also begins with the 5S pillars — in this case, shaky pillars that collapse. Mr. Hirano says that there is no such thing as a factory that manufactures well without a strong 5S foundation. And I agree.

As business leaders and managers, we demand the best from the people who work for and with us. But in order to get it, we must provide the best working environment. It is possible. In fact, as opposed to how factories used to look, I have seen U.S. factories that are amazingly clean. Omark Industries, for instance, produces saw chains. Their production processes involve abrasives, oil, cutting debris, and so forth — not to mention incredible noise. And their factory is spotless! I even saw open offices situated next to cutting operations — and it was quiet enough to work. This is because the Omark people — all of them — have worked and continue to work hard to improve their operations and procedures.

I regard this manual as a gift to America. We should sell it for five hundred dollars but have decided that it's more important to disseminate the information. No doubt people will still complain about the price, but, believe me, it is a fraction of what it costs in Japan. Productivity Press people have invested enormous time and resources on Mr. Hirano's material — and we stand behind its value to consultants, managers, and interested workforce.

In acknowledgment of the efforts of many, I wish to thank a few people: Bruce Talbot (Nevada City, California), translator; Bill Berling (Elletsville, Indiana), freelance editor; Cheryl Rosen, project editor; Karen Jones, managing editor; Catchword, Inc. (Portland), index; William Stanton, production manager and cover designer; Productivity Press (India) Private Ltd. (Madras, India) and Rohani Design (Edmonds, Washington), illustrations; and Rohani Design, composition.

Finally, I wish to thank Mr. Hiroyuki Hirano and colleagues at the JIT Management Laboratory Ltd. in Tokyo for working with us these past years. They have spent years investigating and training people in factories worldwide. Their generosity in sharing with us their experience, information, and materials is a tribute to friendship and the pursuit of manufacturing excellence.

Norman Bodek

Preface

The 21st century is no longer afloat in the distant future. The new century is coming tomorrow. And today's corporate managers are asking themselves how to ensure their companies' survival. With future challenges in mind, many are gearing up by promoting ambitious companywide "rationalization" efforts.

Watching these eager survival campaigns unfold, I feel that the 1990s may become known as the 20th century's final battle for survival. Which consumer electronics companies will survive? Which auto companies will go belly up before the end of the century? How will Japanese companies fare amidst the global competition? How will American and European companies do? And what about Asia's newly industrialized economies such as the Republic of Korea and Taiwan?

The following question is the one I hear most often from top managers: "What kind of rationalization policy should I adopt to make sure my company survives into the approaching century?" Without hesitation I answer, "The 5S's" [the Japanese "S"-words that we call the five pillars of the visual workplace]. The questioner frequently meets this response dubiously and asks another question: "You mean seiri and seiton and all that stuff?" They wonder how such an elementary concept can be an adequate rationalization policy.

When I meet this kind of resistance, I know there is little point in sticking around to elaborate. More than likely, these top managers are the type who visit their factories and clerical offices only a few times a year. Knowing very little about the 5S's, on the rare occasion of inspecting company facilities they have only the vaguest idea about what occurs there. With such limited knowledge and understanding, they tend to overvalue superficial appearances and undervalue their content. Knowing this, their subordinates prepare for such inspections by tidying up the sites, adding a new coat of paint here, and straightening up the shelves there. Following the inspection tour, everyone congratulates themselves on a job well done. The show is over.

This kind of company is unlikely to survive into the next century. And there is nothing I can tell their top managers except "be careful." Companies that fail to implement the 5S's will likewise fail in their attempts to implement large-scale rationalization. They will be out-distanced quickly by those companies that succeed.

A company is like a living organism. When its environment changes abruptly, it must also change — or perish. The 5S's comprise the basic civilization that protects corporate organisms from the ravages of the changing environment. Not only are the 5S's the foundation upon which a company must stand to survive, they are also part of a company's unique corporate culture. No matter how you envision it — companies truly intent on finishing this century ahead of competition must make the 5S's their first step.

After working for many years in the field of factory improvement, I assure the reader that this book is full of two things: (1) my enthusiasm for tearing down the walls of old, inefficient systems and (2) the know-how I have garnered in implementing the 5S's in various workplaces. As such, it is intended as a practical and comprehensive manual.

The 5S's have broad application. They apply not only to factories but to clerical and sales offices as well. Specifically, this book has been written for three categories of readers:

1. people active in the rationalization of factories, clerical offices, and sales offices
2. top managers who are ultimately responsible for their companies' survival
3. professional rationalization consultants

Chapters 1 and 2 describe cases where the 5S's are not implemented thoroughly. By showing their importance in such cases, I hope to impress upon the reader just how fundamental they are to corporate survival.

Chapters 3 and 4 define the 5S's and advise the reader on how to introduce them in their companies. Several case studies illustrate the establishment of 5S promotion organizations.

Chapters 5 through 12 present detailed descriptions and illustrations of the 5S's — *seiri* (Organization), *seiton* (Orderliness), *seisō* (Cleanliness), *seiketsu* (Standardized Cleanup), and *shitsuke* (Discipline) — and their related techniques. Chapters 5 and 6 focus respectively on Organization and Orderliness and emphasize the application of these two housekeeping principles in clerical and sales-office situations. Chapters 7, 8, and 9 describe tools and techniques for making Organization and Orderliness more visible; namely, the red-tag strategy and the signboard strategy. Chapter 10 focuses on Cleanliness. Chapter 11 examines Standardized Cleanup, the optimal state of affairs that occurs when the first three "S's" are implemented and maintained properly. Chapter 12 provides an in-depth discussion of Discipline, historically the least discussed of the 5S's. As a summation, Chapter 13 presents management reports from four Japanese companies of various sizes and dispositions regarding their individual 5S implementation campaigns.

I want to close by emphasizing that the 5S's and this manual are not to be used simply as a way to tidy up the superficial aspects of factory or office. As noted in the book title, these five pillars are the foundation for any company wishing to ensure long-term survival. As such, they deserve to be implemented with utmost care and thoroughness.

I will be happy indeed if this book helps companies establish a firm foundation in the visual workplace of today and tomorrow.

Hiroyuki Hirano

Illustrations

1

Why Are the 5S's Necessary?

Factories are living organisms. Organisms move and change in a flexible relationship with their environment.

In the business world, client specifications are always changing, new technologies are continually being developed, and generation after generation of new products appear on the market. Meanwhile, sales competition grows harsher each year as companies strive to manufacture more sophisticated products at lower cost.

Challenged with living amidst such severe conditions, factories are desperate to find ways to ensure their survival. As living organisms, if they do not adapt to their changing environment, they perish. To survive, factories must learn from the environment; they must destroy former organizational concepts and customs that no longer apply and build up more appropriate and stronger organizations.

However, many of these concepts and customs are ingrained into every part of the production, clerical, and sales divisions. With such deep roots, they are not easily uprooted and replaced. To use another biological metaphor, these deeply ingrained concepts and customs are like fat that has been finely marbled into every part of the body. Every ounce of this fat is pure waste, and overweight companies are the least likely to win the marathon race for survival into the next century.

Photo 1-1. A Fat Factory

The 5S's are introduced as they relate to various examples of organizational obesity. The examples are actual case studies. While it may amuse readers to think of factories and offices as fat, the intended purpose of these metaphors is to impress upon the reader that *every company is fat to some degree and every company can do something about it.*

The Phantom Pallet Shortage

As one factory superintendent looked out over his factory, staffed by some 400 workers, he could not hide his pride and exuberance. "Wow! What a change!" he shouted. He then confided that the recent factory improvement resulted from a recent red-tag strategy campaign.

I rarely hear factory superintendents mention the *red-tag strategy.* But students of factory improvement seem to agree that the red-tag strategy is the essential first step toward eliminating waste.

Red-tagging means sticking red "tags" or pieces of paper on everything in the factory that is waste — or that appears to contribute to waste. Since we address red-tagging as a "strategy," we therefore declare an enemy. In this case, the enemy is waste.

Factories are like people — they sweat and get dirty. People deal with this problem by bathing. The red-tag strategy was devised as a way to periodically wash off the factory's accumulated oil, dirt, and grime.

Let us look more closely at what we mean by "grime" in a factory.

Let us begin with inventory. Most factories accumulate unnecessary inventory that is either stored in the warehouse or stacked up between stations on the production line. At some factories, items received and stuck away ten years ago still gather dust on warehouse shelves. People often regard open floor space or shelf space in the factory as perfect for inventory storage. This is where things need to be adorned with red tags.

Next, we can look at machinery and other equipment. Just about every factory has a machine or two that are no longer used but considered too valuable to scrap. So they sit there — taking up space.

The red-tag strategy means tagging every unneeded item that clogs up the factory. (There is one exception to this rule: No matter how useless, people are not to be red-tagged!)

At one point, the aforementioned factory superintendent told me that just before launching their red-tag strategy, he received some requisition forms to order more pallets. He said the factory managers were complaining of a terrible pallet shortage.

When I asked what he did about it, he said, "What could I do? I sent in their order for another 300 pallets."

I responded, "Huh? You really did that?"

He then explained that when they began their red-tag strategy, he figured they would need about a thousand red tags. However, they actually required almost 3,000. He said, "The whole factory was turning red. I think we eliminated one-third of our inventory. We still hadn't received the 300 pallets ordered, but when the red-tagging was over, we were left with about 300 extra pallets!"

Obviously, the resulting glut of pallets indicated the amount of waste in the factory. Regardless of its form, waste is waste. It is appalling to think of the money this factory wasted on pallets.

The Inventory that Time Forgot

I remember a conversation with another factory superintendent. He looked at me and spoke as if making a grave confession.

"This is nothing to be proud of. It's something the red-tagging strategy revealed, and it came as a big surprise to us. We found some parts inventory in the warehouse that had sat there for 20 years!"

I was speechless. My mind's eye pictured this factory boss wearing a victory crown seated atop the back seat of a big convertible in a confetti-showered parade announcing his achievement as the world's record holder in inventory waste. Finally, I managed to remark, "Twenty years! Amazing!"

"Well, as I said, it was a big shock for us, too. We figured the order form must have specified the wrong parts and no one ever noticed."

A typical mistake. Instead of specifying the name of a frequently used part, the person filling out the order form probably wrote down the name of a rarely used part, which ended up forgotten on the shelves. In recognition of human errors, the factory should have had a confirmation step in the parts-ordering procedure.

The amazing thing is that those parts could sit on the shelf for 20 years without anyone bothering to find out why they were there — not even the person who ordered them! Finally, a red-tag campaign discovered inventory that time forgot.

Trying to understand how such a mistake was possible, I imagined the person who made the faulty order wondering where the parts were: "That's strange. I ordered some parts, but they never came. Hmmm... Maybe they forgot to deliver them. I'd better check."

I then pictured the order clerk picking up the telephone and saying, "OK, so you figure the order never came in or it was lost somewhere. I guess I'll just re-order."

It is sad that such a situation is so easy to imagine.

If we're looking for someone to blame, we need to include others. What about the delivery clerk or the warehouse workers? They might have noticed something strange and just shrugged it off.

People who should pay close attention to these kinds of mistakes are on the factory floor. However, if the factory is cluttered with piles of unneeded inventory, workers are unlikely to discover the error even though they might notice that "something is strange."

Piles of inventory waste reflect a factory manager's greatest fear: that factory operations might grind to a halt someday because some essential part is not in stock.

To quote yet another factory superintendent: "Production people, procurement people, and warehouse people are never concerned about having too much of anything. As long as there are no shortages, they are happy." Or, as an assembly-line supervisor put it, "Nothing is worse than having to stop the line."

Obviously, these people are concerned with little else.

What about Yellow Tags?

Some people find it hard to red-tag anything, knowing that it is tantamount to declaring it useless. I remember an instance in which a factory group leader took a few dozen red tags to his workers and left after instructing them to stick them on unneeded items in their workshop.

When the group leader returned later, he exclaimed, "What? You guys haven't tagged a single thing! What happened?"

Someone answered, "We had a look around and talked it over, but we couldn't find anything that wasn't really needed."

Incredulous, the group leader again left but soon returned with the workshop's production schedule for the next month. He pointed to a stack of parts and said, "What about these?"

"We're not using them this month, but we will be next month."

"I see." Then the workers gasped with surprise as the factory leader slapped a red tag onto the stack of parts. "Now, how about this stuff?"

"Those are seasonal supplies. We'll definitely use them next season." (The worker emphasized the word "definitely.")

"Hmmm." Slap — another red tag.

This triple action of question, answer, and red-tag repeated itself for quite a while in that workshop.

When people use the same machines every day for years to turn out products and earn their wages, like most craftspeople, they become attached to the tools of their trade. Little wonder that they are reluctant to red-tag them.

Don't think of red-tagging as putting an old dog to sleep. It should be more like tipping a waiter or waitress for a job well done. And no sentimentalism — if the item is not needed, tag it. Since this is often easier said than done, it may be better to ask the supervisors — not the shop-floor workers — to do the red-tagging.

Which reminds me of another red-tag campaign, where both tags and workers turned yellow. A factory manager had assigned a workshop supervisor the task of red-tagging his workshop; he in turn asked the workers to do it. Later, when the manager returned, he found yellow tags everywhere, but not a single red one.

"What's going on here?" exclaimed the manager.

"Well, the thing is," said the supervisor nervously, "they were having trouble deciding whether certain things were needed or not, so we came up with the idea of using yellow tags to mark those items."

"Look," responded the manager, "there are only two options — needed and unneeded. You went and asked the shop workers to do the red-tagging, but they have customized this equipment themselves and are attached to it. Naturally, they don't want to get rid of it. That's why I asked you to do it."

The Mysterious Bacteria Murder

Early one morning at a pharmaceutical plant, a plant worker cried out, "Oh, no! All the bacteria are dead!"

Pharmaceutical plants use bacteria as an essential tool to biologically treat waste fluids. However, bacteria are living organisms and require a support environment. For plants needing very specific types of bacteria, it can easily take months or years to cultivate the types that suit their needs. One can understand the worker's dismay upon discovering that the precious bacteria had all died overnight.

The whole plant was thrown into confusion and an investigation was launched. The final analysis showed that the direct cause of the bacteria's death was intrusion of a cyanide compound into the waste fluid. The primary question: How did cyanide enter the waste fluid?

Shortly before this incident, plant managers had introduced a program of improvement activities that included implementing the 5S's. They kicked off the 5S's with a red-tag campaign. All of the plant's obvious waste and unneeded items were red-tagged. During this red-tag cleanup, some overzealous housecleaners decided to avoid the cost of properly disposing of a 20-year-old stock of cyanide-compound solution by pouring it down the drain. As the plant began looking roomier and cleaner, someone discovered that all the bacteria were dead. Ironically, an employee's eagerness to clean out the plant resulted in the waste-cleaning bacteria being cleaned out also. The hapless employee was never revealed. In fact, the investigation team was unsure whether to track down the culprit since it was obviously a case of good intentions and bad consequences.

A Windowless Wall

There are various methods to move parts and products through production lines. A method that we call "shish-kebab production" moves goods from one production process to the next in lots. "One-piece flow production" is another method in which goods flow along in a steady stream of separate units. Still another method, called "load-and-shoot production," is all too common among factories that follow monthly schedules. Typically, during the first half of the month factory workers take it easy and concentrate on stockpiling parts. However, during the second half of the month everyone busily fires off products in quick succession as delivery deadlines draw near.

In one instance, at a manufacturer of office equipment, assembly-line workers complained that the fluorescent lamps were not bright enough to work by. The managers checked it out and agreed. They added more lights and hung them lower — and therefore closer to the line. The workers were satisfied with the improvement and the problem was seemingly resolved.

However, although the assembly work proceeded beautifully, toward the end of the month I noticed that cardboard boxes were stacked up to the ceiling next to the assembly line. So I asked a department chief working on the line what the boxes were for.

"They are empty boxes for the finished products."

"You mean this big wall is nothing but empty boxes?"

Warily, the department chief responded, "Yes, that's right."

"When did you build that wall of boxes?"

"We did it during the first half of the month before we started the assembly work."

In other words, the factory workers filled up their idle hours during the first half of the month by assembling and stacking boxes for use when the assembled products were finished. Since assembly operations were in progress at the time, the wall of boxes was receding from the ceiling. Gradually, light began streaming in from a window formerly blocked by the wall of boxes. At that point, I remarked to the department chief that without the empty boxes there would be plenty of light from the window and no need to install additional lighting. With a quick nod of agreement, the section chief went over and switched off some of the fluorescent lights.

The Rowboat Factory

One way to manufacture products is to group goods together in lots (or shish-kebab chunks) that are passed down the production line (or skewer). As mentioned earlier, this method is nicknamed "shish-kebab" production.

I recall visiting one automotive parts manufacturing plant where the workers on diecast line A especially liked large shish-kebab lots. When introducing just-in-time (JIT) production to the plant, they switched from shish-kebab to one-piece flow production. At that time, I was at the diecast factory to help them establish a direct link between the diecast machine and the processing line, which was the next process.

Photo 1-2. A Filthy Diecast Factory

I saw that factory and knew it was one of the filthiest places I had ever visited. The pillars and walls were covered with a deep underlayer of soot and a slimy top layer of oil. When I touched the wall, it was as sticky as flypaper; when I took my hand away, slime hung from my fingers like melted cheese. The floor had puddles of wax and water all over it, and my shoes made splashing sounds as I walked. And never had I seen so much oil, aluminum scrap, mold lubricant, soot, burrs, and water spread so thickly on factory equipment.

Restraining myself from leaving, I queried the factory superintendent if the workers ever complained about working around such filth. He answered in the affirmative, saying that they had even asked for boots to enable them to walk around the place more easily. When I asked what he was going to do about it, he said the workers had a good point and management would be supplying them with boots very soon.

Hearing this, I understood at once how the factory had been allowed to get so filthy. The factory superintendent did not realize that handing out boots would not rectify the real problem. In fact, it would probably make things worse, since wearing boots would make workers less likely to notice the oil and water on the floor. Boot-clad workers might let conditions slide until the water got knee-high — at which point they might ask the factory superintendent for rowboats! Still failing to get the point, the factory superintendent would honor their request. Soon we would have the world's first aluminum automotive parts-forging factory staffed by workers in rowboats.

Using a Wide Room like a Narrow Hall

Many Japanese companies establish their head offices and sales divisions in major cities, such as Tokyo and Osaka, to facilitate sales activities and information handling.

For example, I had a client with its head office in Tokyo. This electrical equipment manufacturing company rented four floors of a 12-floor building, each floor capable of accommodating 100 clerical workers. However, as the company grew, clerical people complained that office areas were becoming overcrowded. In turn, management considered renting another floor or two.

Coincidentally, the company's factory had just initiated a rationalization plan to improve its responsiveness to customer needs. Already the factory had achieved particularly impressive results by using the red-tag strategy.

Hearing of this success, the company president thought, "I wonder if the red-tag strategy could help us solve our space problem without having to rent additional space?" Interestingly, he ran into some pretty stubborn resistance.

The clerical staff's objections went like this: "We don't move around all kinds of material and parts like in the factory, so red-tagging won't help." Or "We've already established Organization (*seiri*) and Orderliness (*seiton*) here and there just isn't enough space." However, the president was not swayed by these negative attitudes and ordered everyone to give red-tagging a try.

With some grumbling at first, the slow-moving managers and salespeople finally got into the act. To begin, they marked off an area on each desktop (called a "public display area") where the person could keep stationery and supplies. This public display quickly revealed the following: While most people had four or five pens and two or three erasers in their desks, others had enough stationery supplies to open a small store!

The next step was to gather up the extra supplies. Clerical workers were told (1) to order the minimum amount of items needed, (2) to keep these supplies on top of their desks in the designated areas, and (3) to always return

Photo 1-3. Red-tagged Items in Locker

the items to the same place on the desk. A new rule was made: Stationery supplies were no longer allowed inside desk drawers. As a result, there was enough surplus to meet everyone's stationery needs for three or four years.

Next came a red-tag campaign on documents and files. They began with those kept in individual desks. Workers were asked to remove (1) all documents and files not used during the past month and (2) anything else not needed to calculate the next year's budget. They were also told to eliminate any duplicate copies of company records.

Similar measures were then carried out for locker contents. All unneeded and duplicate items were tossed out.

As a result, mounds and mounds of documents and files — and even empty lockers and unused chairs — were set aside for disposal. It took at least three four-ton truckloads to haul it all away in the end.

After cleaning out and organizing the offices, all four floors looked spacious. There was no longer a need to consider renting additional floors. The president proudly noted, "Since the red-tag campaign, I haven't heard a single complaint about crowded conditions."

In the final analysis, conditions are only as crowded as the people who work there allow them to become — even in management and sales divisions!

A Tale of Needless Suffering

One day a section chief in the sales division yelled, "Hey, where'd you put that report you just finished?"

A sales worker replied, "I gave it to you already."

"You did? That's strange. I've been looking for it and can't find it."

The sales worker insisted that he had handed the report to the section chief — whose desk was cluttered with various papers. The chief stood up and put some papers on his chair while looking through stacks of others. He mumbled, "I have to present that report at the managers' meeting tomorrow morning!" This prompted the sales worker to come and help in the search.

The section chief looked through papers on the desk behind his desk. He also asked if anyone else had seen the report, but everyone thought the section chief had it. The section chief then checked his desk drawers and even in his locker. Still nothing.

Wearing an expression of frustration mixed with despair, the section chief asked the sales worker, "How long did it take to write up that report?"

The sales worker and a co-worker looked at each other and answered, "About three hours."

It was then 5 PM. With the section chief's help, they redid the report from scratch. It took over four hours.

Thanking the two workers for staying late, the chief added that in preparation for tomorrow's meeting he would take the new report home to review. He then picked up his briefcase and, opening it, gasped.

In it was a file folder containing the missing report. Thoroughly embarrassed, the section chief again — this time, awkwardly — thanked his subordinates for their overtime efforts. Their *useless* overtime efforts.

When Reference Material Becomes Immaterial

Computers are useful tools. They can record vast amounts of information and perform calculations with lightning speed. They also make recorded information almost instantly accessible. This explains why so many companies invest in computers and want their money's worth in return.

As a result, data-processing departments are often swamped with requests for processing reference charts, forms, and other materials. The materials typically requested might include process-specific load survey charts for manufacturing managers, vendor-specific accounts-payable spreadsheets for accountants, and client-specific order data for sales managers.

As part of their duties, the data-processing staff must organize the data required for the requested materials and often must customize the software to generate the desired forms. Usually, the bulk of the requested materials is due by the end of the month, which makes the data-processing department a frantic place during this period.

It was during just such a busy period that the following incident occurred. Someone in data processing forgot to send some regular monthly materials to the manufacturing department. Naturally, when the beginning-of-the-month due date passed, one would expect the manufacturing department to notice the omission and file a complaint against the data-processing department. However, the data-processing person did not notice his mistake until the middle of the month, partly because the manufacturing staff likewise had not noticed the omission, or at least had failed to say anything about it.

Wondering how to make up for his mistake, the data-processing person discussed the matter with his section chief. The chief was puzzled by the situation and remarked, "Instead of asking them whether to send the late materials, let's find out if they actually use the information." The staffperson admitted that he had no idea — his only concern was getting the requested materials to the requesters.

The section chief reviewed recent trends in the data-processing department. There had been a steady increase in the amounts and types of materials requested by various departments — over 200 different types of materials were being prepared and sent each month. However, he was perplexed to discover that no department had ever canceled a request for monthly materials.

He decided to conduct an experiment. He would see which computer-generated materials were actually being used and which were not — and red-tag the latter. The experiment involved generating all requested materials by the deadline and then holding onto the materials until the requesters asked for them. Once a certain time period had passed without word from the requester, the section chief red-tagged the materials as unnecessary and ordered their cancellation.

This was a very successful experiment. Of the 200+ types of materials, only 70 drew responses from requesters when they were late. In other words, two-thirds of the materials were not even missed.

The section chief concluded that this was normal because organizational needs change as conditions change. While requesters informed them of their needs by ordering certain things, they rarely bothered to cancel obsolete materials. This resulted in a workload for the data-processing staff that just kept growing. However, materials that are no longer needed are immaterial to productivity and must be eliminated.

TWELVE TYPES OF RESISTANCE TO THE 5S'S

Any company introducing the 5S's is likely to encounter various kinds of resistance, whether from the shop-floor or clerical staff. I group such resistance into the twelve types shown in Figure 1-1.

Resistance 1. What's So Great about Organization and Orderliness?

This direct resistance toward 5S implementation is like asking "Why make such a fuss over something so obvious?" or "You're treating us like kids ordered to clean their rooms." But the fact remains that 5S implementation is needed

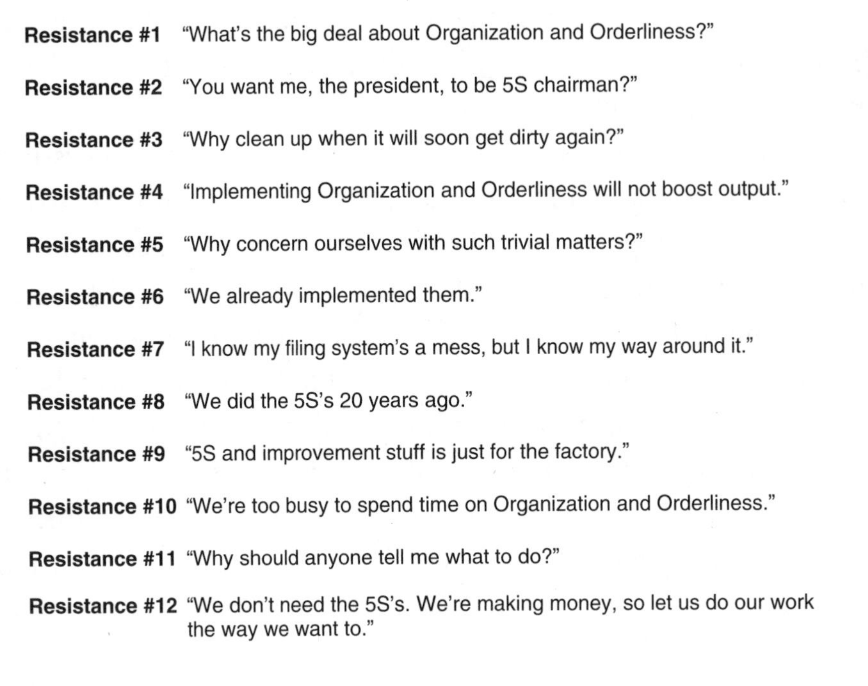

Resistance #1	"What's the big deal about Organization and Orderliness?"
Resistance #2	"You want me, the president, to be 5S chairman?"
Resistance #3	"Why clean up when it will soon get dirty again?"
Resistance #4	"Implementing Organization and Orderliness will not boost output."
Resistance #5	"Why concern ourselves with such trivial matters?"
Resistance #6	"We already implemented them."
Resistance #7	"I know my filing system's a mess, but I know my way around it."
Resistance #8	"We did the 5S's 20 years ago."
Resistance #9	"5S and improvement stuff is just for the factory."
Resistance #10	"We're too busy to spend time on Organization and Orderliness."
Resistance #11	"Why should anyone tell me what to do?"
Resistance #12	"We don't need the 5S's. We're making money, so let us do our work the way we want to."

Figure 1-1. Twelve Types of Resistance to the 5S's

when the factory or office is not neat and organized. This particular resistance stems from the humiliation people feel when they think they are being treated like children. Therefore, the key is to eliminate such humiliation before implementing the 5S's.

Resistance 2. Why Should I, the President, Be 5S Chairman?

More times than I care to recall, company presidents have said something like: "You don't really expect me to get involved in something as trifling as Organization and Orderliness?" Instead, they want to assign the 5S chairmanship to a middle manager. "After all," they add, "I have more important things to do — like manage the company's sales and business policies."

I would be the first to agree that sales and business policies are important. However, believe it or not, the 5S's are even more important as a foundation of corporate strength. Obviously, some presidents don't believe this — but were the company's 5S foundation to be destroyed, they would soon find out what I mean. Nor do many presidents understand how difficult it can be to implement the simple 5S's. 5S implementation requires leadership, and top management must abandon its vain preconceptions and get personally involved.

Resistance 3. Why Clean When It Just Gets Dirty Again?

Factory people tend to accept dirtiness as an inevitable condition in their workplace. They argue that cleaning it up would do little good since it would soon get dirty again. When employees are indifferent to making and maintaining improvements, it is not surprising that defect rates remain high and productivity low. Acceptance of unclean conditions in a workplace must be eliminated.

Resistance 4. Implementing Organization and Orderliness Will Not Boost Output.

This objection is heard most often in busy factories. Usually, it is spouted by shop-floor people standing in a pigsty asserting that "our job is to make things." Some workers — and their managers — judge productivity by how much they move and sweat. This is fine at the athletic club, but not in the factory. In a factory motion is often a form of waste. Everyone must learn the important difference between "moving" and "working."

Resistance 5. Why Concern Ourselves with Triviality?

The culprits here are typically middle managers such as leaders of teams, sections, or departments. I've heard these people say that dirt is a minor problem while standing on a factory floor drenched with oil or covered with a thick layer of machining chips.

Any manager who treats the 5S's as trivial is really trivializing productivity and efficient management activity. After all, any manager who can stand on an oil-drenched floor and call dirt a minor problem is someone who might absentmindedly toss a cigarette butt onto that floor and cause a fire.

Managers who fail to promote neatness and order end up with a sloppy and undisciplined work force. For this reason, we must eliminate managerial disregard for the 5S's.

Resistance 6. We Already Implemented Organization and Orderliness.

Some managers only consider the superficial and visible aspects of the 5S's. They think that rearranging things a little and putting them into neat rows is all there is to it. Their factories tend to undergo a "makeover" just prior to the company president's inspection tour — floors are swept, walls painted, and objects lined up neatly. However, such Orderliness only scratches the surface of what the 5S's are all about.

When the unsuspecting president enters the made-over factory, he is duly impressed and says something like "Wow, now I call that clean!" Usually never seeing behind the veneer of superficial Organization and Orderliness, he leaves the factory with a false impression.

Resistance 7. My Filing System Is a Mess — but I Know My Way Around It!

Some people are able to work around piles of papers and files. In fact, the sheer volume of the mess reassures them of their productivity.

I encounter people who actually get upset when I suggest that they clear off their desks. They mutter something like "Please leave me alone — I work better this way" and return to the comfort of their mess. Such people tend to be loners who avoid contact with others and like having a wall of books and papers around them. Theirs is a different world from the one that results from standardization and 5S implementation. The first step in standardizing clerical operations is to open up such private messes so that books and files are easily accessible to anyone who needs them.

Resistance 8. We Did the 5S's Years Ago.

This type of comment is heard most often from people who think the 5S movement is a fad. If they attempted 5S implementation once 20 years ago, they don't see why they should do it again.

The 5S's are not a passing fashion. They actually are the fertilizer on the field of making improvements. They are the foundation of long-term corporate survival. People who don't know this should be informed; people who think they don't need to know it should get off their high horses. When I hear someone say they did the 5S's 20 years ago, I am tempted to ask, "Has it also been 20 years since you took a bath?"

Resistance 9. 5S's and Related Improvements Are Just for the Factory.

In some companies, while the manufacturing people energetically implement the 5S's and other improvement and rationalization measures, the clerical and sales people assert that such measures have nothing to do with their kind of work. They do not realize that allowing documents and memos to litter desktops is the same as allowing dirt and cutting debris to litter factory floors. This is why 5S implementation must be a companywide program

Resistance 10. We're Too Busy to Spend Time on Organization and Orderliness.

In some workplaces, Organization and Orderliness are the first things ignored when things get busy. Soon we find jigs and tools left out, parts and materials piled in inconvenient places, and oil and grime building up on the machinery and floors. The excuse is always that "we're too busy for that." Are these people too busy to take showers and brush their teeth? What they're really saying is that they don't want to keep the place neat and clean, and this is their excuse. The truth is that their excuses are no more valid than their attitude toward cleanliness.

Resistance 11. Who Are They to Tell Me What to Do?

Most 5S implementations run into human-relation problems early on. Someone might understand how important the 5S's are but object to taking orders from the 5S promotion people. Once human relations become tangled up, it takes a long time to smooth them out. Consequently, it pays to form 5S promotion teams with members skilled at applying the 5S's to human relations.

Resistance 12. We Don't Need the 5S's — We're Making Money, So Just Let Us Do Our Work!

It can be difficult to implement the 5S's or other improvement programs at companies that are currently profitable. If you point out that it is more efficient to keep only one box of parts on hand at each process, you will likely be countered with something like "Yes, but we're doing alright, and this is the way we like to do it." Generally, such people fail to recognize how many processes are involved in making a product. Instead of emphasizing the productivity of individual processes, we should look first at the overall production flow. Production has a rhythm, and this rhythm gets upset when workers care only about their individual processes. A poor rhythm has a negative impact on inventory and conveyance management, which in the end creates more waste, such as the extra time needed to find certain items. By allowing operators to do things their way, we grant a selfish kind of freedom that hurts everyone in the long run.

These types of resistance occur at every factory in the early stages of 5S implementation. If we ignore such resistance and plow ahead with 5S implementation, the result will likely be nothing more than superficial improvements. Instead, we must get everyone to truly understand just how necessary the 5S's are while incorporating 5S implementation into ongoing improvement activities. This is how to lay a solid foundation for overall improvement.

THE NEED FOR THE 5S'S

"Why must we implement the 5S's?"

This is a simple question that can be difficult to answer. You can talk about things like productivity and quality until you are blue in the face — and you will still find that some people do not understand why the 5S's are necessary. When straightforward explanations get you nowhere, I suggest that you try the following.

First, simply say, "People take showers and baths to get clean, right? It's a lot like that."

Or you may even want to answer the question with a question: "Why do you take showers and baths?" This puts the ball back in the other person's court.

After all, people practice the 5S's in their personal lives without even noticing it. Their daily routine of bathing, dental care, and so on are all personal-hygiene types of 5S implementation. Likewise, we practice Organization and Orderliness when we keep things like waste baskets, dish towels, and tissues in convenient places.

Suppose we see a man at a restaurant who has just eaten and is about to pay the check. Unconsciously, he reaches into his pocket where he always keeps his wallet. He would be shocked if he discovered that it was not there. This is an instance of how people practice Organization and Orderliness in their daily lives.

Few factories are as standardized with 5S routines as is the daily life of an orderly person. Moreover, nowhere in Japan are the ubiquitous "Organization-Orderliness" signs more eye-catching than in factories where these activities are least practiced. This is no doubt because of the contrast between the message on the sign and the mess on the floor beneath the sign. Unfortunately, these signs are such a common sight in Japanese factories and offices that they become mere formalities — like a welcome mat at the door.

Sadly, only a handful of factories and offices actually practice what they preach. Organization and Orderliness become empty words. At best, they are expressions of hope, inasmuch as people recognize how things could be better if the concepts were truly put into practice. When companies pursue them, it is usually only to rearrange messy piles into neater piles, after which everyone congratulates themselves on a job well done.

This is where the 5S's come in as a more thorough version of the popular "Organization-Orderliness" concept.

The 5S's include the familiar Organization and Orderliness as well as the Japanese words for Cleanliness, Standardized Cleanup, and Discipline.

People in some companies add other "S's" — for instance, Habits and Stability. Regardless of how inventive the word plays become, implementing seven S's is unlikely to make your factory any cleaner than implementing five. The important thing is thorough implementation.

The 5S's remain the basic formula and Organization and Orderliness are still the foundation for achieving zero defects, cost reductions, safety improvements, and zero accidents.

In most factories, the need to look for things — such as parts, carts, jigs, and tools — is taken for granted. The more people have to search for things, the lower their productivity slips. And in this era of product diversification, this rings all the more true.

Five minutes spent looking for things is no big loss in the context of a one-hour changeover operation. However, those five minutes become critical when attempting to implement single-digit changeover or Shigeo Shingo's SMED system (single-minute exchange of die).

The same goes for offices. How much time do people in your offices spend looking for files, papers, pencils, and staplers?

Consider the following:

- A neat and clean factory or office will have higher productivity.

- A neat and clean factory or office will produce fewer defects.
- A neat and clean factory or office will meet deadlines better.

Thorough implementation of the 5S's affords many direct and indirect benefits. What I call the essential benefits are listed in Figure 1-2.

Benefit 1. Zero Changeovers Bring Product Diversification

The trend toward product diversification accelerates with each passing day. Companies that continue to practice "shish-kebab production" are

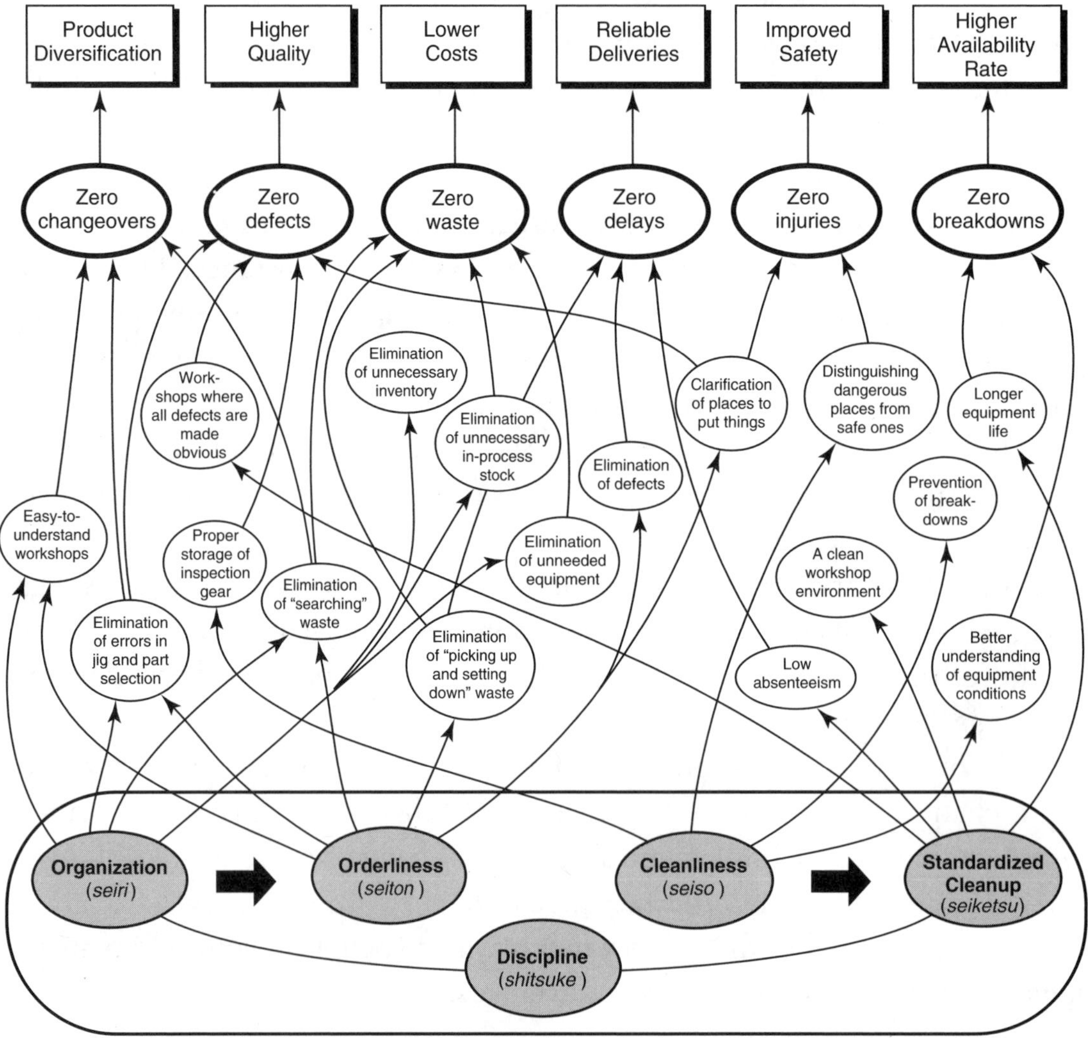

Figure 1-2. Benefits of the 5S's

finding themselves unable to keep up with this trend. To remain competitive, they must reduce to zero the extra time taken for retooling and other changeover operations, increase the frequency of changeover, and become more adaptive to product diversification.

- The orderly arrangement of dies, jigs, and tools eliminates a major form of waste ("searching" waste).
- Clean equipment and a neat workplace help raise operational efficiency.
- Thorough implementation of the 5S's makes workshops simple and logical enough for observers to understand with ease.
- Don't use non-specified jigs for the sake of convenience.

Benefit 2. Zero Defects Bring Higher Quality

Defects result from many causes, including attaching the wrong parts and using the wrong jig. Organization and Orderliness prevent these kinds of errors. Further, keeping production equipment clean reduces equipment-operation errors and enables faster retooling. These and other 5S effects all add up to fewer defects.

- Defects are harder to discover when the workplace is a mess.
- Taking things from and then returning them to designated locations will help eliminate part and tool selection errors.
- Clean equipment tends to operate normally and without defects.
- A clean and well-organized workplace makes workers more conscious of the way they are making things.
- Proper maintenance and storage of quality-assuring inspection tools and measuring instruments is a prerequisite for zero defects.

Benefit 3. Zero Waste Brings Lower Costs

Factories and offices are virtual storehouses of waste. In Japan, a television slogan states that people who spend a lot of time talking on the telephone or carrying around too many papers cannot get much work done. And I agree completely. Big telephone talkers fail to implement Organization and Orderliness to shorten their phone conversations. People burdened with too many papers fail to implement Organization and Orderliness by filing or discarding unnecessary papers. Long telephone conversations and armloads of papers are two forms of waste, and too much waste can prevent us from getting any productive work done. This applies to both factories and offices.

- Eliminate too much "stand-by waste" in in-process inventory and warehouse inventory.
- Eliminate "too-much-to-carry waste" in handling documents or other materials.
- Eliminate overly abundant (unneeded) storage places (warehouses, shelves, cabinets, lockers, etc.).
- Eliminate "stand-by waste" in waiting for conveyance equipment (pallets, carts, forklifts, etc.).
- Eliminate waste arising from unneeded desk supplies (too many pencils, erasers, etc.)
- Eliminate waste arising from unneeded allocation of space and equipment.
- Eliminate wasteful motion in searching, side-stepping, etc.
- Eliminate non-value-added actions (picking up, putting down, counting, carrying, etc.).

Benefit 4. Zero Delays Bring Reliable Deliveries

People who carry too many things mix useful and useless things. Shuffling through useless papers to find what is important is a waste. Clearly, these people have failed to implement Organization and Orderliness in their minds. In the same way, sloppy thinking results in sloppy actions.

The same holds true in the factory. Factories that lack thorough 5S implementation tend to produce defects no matter what they do to prevent them. Deadlines whiz by while everyone is busy reworking defective products. It is indeed hard to meet delivery deadlines in the face of problems like wasteful motion and too many errors and defects.

- When errors and defects are eliminated, deliveries can go out on time.
- We need good work environments and smooth, highly visible operations.

- Absenteeism is lower at 5S workshops.
- Work is more efficient in waste-free workshops.

Benefit 5. Zero Injuries Promote Safety

Injuries can be expected when items are left protruding into walkways, when stock is piled high in storage areas, or when equipment is covered with grime, swarf, or oil.

Other common events at factories that fail to implement the 5S's include confusion due to a lack of outlined storage sites, head-on collisions when forklifts turn corners without warning, hand injuries when operators attempt to fix stalled equipment without cutting the power first, injuries when tall stacks of inventory fall over unexpectedly, head injuries when crane hoist handlers forget to wear helmets, and hand injuries when press operators forget to press the safety switch before handling the press. "Safety First" is a good concept — once the 5S's are in place.

- We can discover mechanical failures and hazards immediately when equipment is kept in spotless condition.
- Maintain well-defined places to put things, plenty of uncluttered aisles, and rest areas.
- Place things in a safe manner to prevent breakage, etc.
- Clearly mark fire-extinguishing equipment and emergency exits in case of fires, earthquakes, or other emergencies.

Benefit 6. Zero Breakdowns Bring Better Maintenance

Equipment should be routinely wiped and polished. Its condition should be evaluated as part of regular daily upkeep. When daily maintenance tasks are integrated with daily cleaning tasks, equipment will be ready for use and result in an improved "availability" ratio.

- Trash, dirt, and dust can lead to major equipment breakdowns and shorter equipment life.
- It is easier to see how equipment is running when the workshop is free of shavings, filings, and oil leaks.

- Nip breakdowns in the bud by maintaining and checking the equipment daily.

Benefit 7. Zero Complaints Bring Greater Confidence and Trust

Factories that practice the 5S's are virtually free of defects and delays. This means they are also free of customer complaints about product quality.

- Products from a neat and clean workshop are defect-free.
- Products from a neat and clean workshop cost less to make.
- Products from a neat and clean workshop arrive on time.
- Products from a neat and clean workshop are safe.

Benefit 8. Zero Red Ink Brings Corporate Growth

Companies cannot grow without the trust of customers. The 5S's provide a strong, solid base upon which to build successful business activities.

- People from 5S workplaces gain the respect and trust of their communities.
- Customers are happy to buy from manufacturers that have eliminated waste, injuries, breakdowns, and defects.
- Factories with a solid 5S foundation are more likely to grow.

2

Foundation for Corporate Survival

Consider the following 5S slogan: "Behind all workplace successes and failures are the 5S's."

As noted in Chapter 1, thorough implementation of the 5S's is the starting point in the development of improvement activities to ensure corporate survival. Improvements must begin with eliminating everything that is no longer necessary and making the remaining needed items easily accessible.

In this sense, the 5S's are the foundation upon which we lay other improvement-related blocks — such as flow production, visual management, and standard operations. We can eventually build up enough blocks to enable one-piece flow and Just-In-Time (JIT) production.

With hard work, it can take one or two years for any company to establish JIT production capable of providing the kind of quick turnaround that can respond to today's trends toward product diversification and shorter delivery deadlines. On the other hand, only one or two weeks is needed to destroy a JIT production system. When 5S implementation grows too weak to support the other improvement activities built upon it, the whole complex edifice of JIT production can come crashing down.

I sincerely believe that one can judge a factory's production strength by looking at its 5S conditions.

HOW THE 5S'S RELATE TO CORPORATE SURVIVAL

Some people consider the 5S's to be simply a matter of cleaning up. In factories or offices where the 5S's are implemented by such people, 5S conditions are so superficial and fragile that it takes little in the way of a problem or abnormality to create chaos and confusion.

While cleaning up is an important part of 5S implementation, I would emphasize that the importance of how clean things appear is secondary to the importance of everyone's attitude toward cleaning and 5S implementation.

In today's increasingly complex business environment, the 5S's relate to corporate health and survival. For example, in factories the 5S's must be in place prior to any successful development of JIT production or Total Productive Maintenance (TPM); in offices, prior to any major improvement campaigns.

For many companies, the development of JIT production requires nothing less than a revolution in corporate organization — a wholesale abandonment of the type of organization that may have been in place for decades. This revolution is a revolution in awareness among all employees, and the foundation for workplace improvement is the 5S's.

Figure 2-1 outlines a companywide program for developing JIT production.

5S'S ARE THE FOUNDATION FOR IMPROVEMENT

Any company improving its shop-floor operations with a view toward establishing JIT production must have the 5S's as its foundation. As explained in Chapter 1, the 5S's are Organization, Orderliness, Cleanliness, Standardized Cleanup, and Discipline.

Within this 5S foundation, the two most crucial elements are Organization and Orderliness. The success of improvement activities depends upon them.

You can bet that if you see a factory filled with equipment operators in stained uniforms who do not mind working amidst dirt, debris, and oil, you are looking at a factory that produces far too many defective goods, that misses far too many delivery deadlines, and that suffers from low productivity and morale. It is obvious that such a factory has failed to implement Organization and Orderliness.

In Japan, the average factory is only 30 percent factory. The other 70 percent is warehouse — for equipment, materials, and other unnecessary items posing as obstacles for the real production activities to work around.

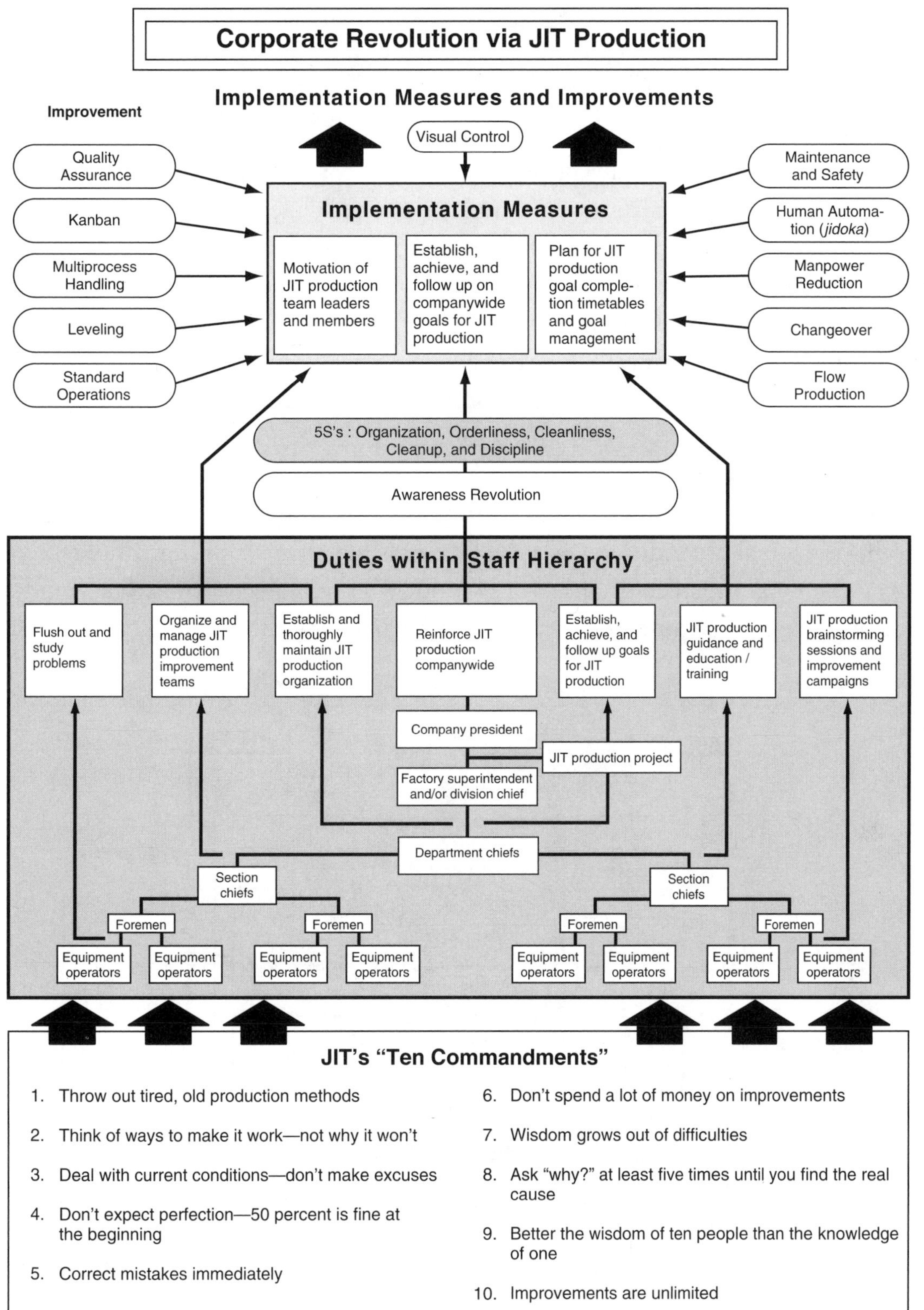
Corporate Revolution via JIT Production
Implementation Measures and Improvements
Improvement
Visual Control
Quality Assurance
Kanban
Multiprocess Handling
Leveling
Standard Operations
Maintenance and Safety
Human Automation (jidoka)
Manpower Reduction
Changeover
Flow Production
Implementation Measures
Motivation of JIT production team leaders and members
Establish, achieve, and follow up on companywide goals for JIT production
Plan for JIT production goal completion timetables and goal management
5S's : Organization, Orderliness, Cleanliness, Cleanup, and Discipline
Awareness Revolution
Duties within Staff Hierarchy
Flush out and study problems
Organize and manage JIT production improvement teams
Establish and thoroughly maintain JIT production organization
Reinforce JIT production companywide
Establish, achieve, and follow up goals for JIT production
JIT production guidance and education / training
JIT production brainstorming sessions and improvement campaigns
Company president
JIT production project
Factory superintendent and/or division chief
Department chiefs
Section chiefs
Section chiefs
Foremen
Foremen
Foremen
Foremen
Equipment operators
JIT's "Ten Commandments"
1. Throw out tired, old production methods
2. Think of ways to make it work—not why it won't
3. Deal with current conditions—don't make excuses
4. Don't expect perfection—50 percent is fine at the beginning
5. Correct mistakes immediately
6. Don't spend a lot of money on improvements
7. Wisdom grows out of difficulties
8. Ask "why?" at least five times until you find the real cause
9. Better the wisdom of ten people than the knowledge of one
10. Improvements are unlimited

Figure 2-1. Companywide Promotion of JIT Production

People working in this kind of factory consider the search for parts, dies, and tools a part of their jobs. Veteran workers who know where to look for missing items are highly valued.

How can any improvement campaign be effective when it takes place among such conditions? It simply cannot. That is why we must begin with Organization and Orderliness and make it perfectly clear where items needed for production are to be kept and in what amounts.

Improvements are not born of placards and posters. They are hands-on activities that must take place on the shop floor. Many factories display large "Organization-Orderliness" signs even as spare parts and garbage abound. The lack of Organization and Orderliness implementation at any particular factory may be due to poor discipline or because no one knows how to implement them.

When implementing Organization and Orderliness, the most important thing is to make conditions as visual as possible. Even children understand that when you organize things, you sort out what you need from what you do not need. Likewise, one does not get too far in life without being taught that

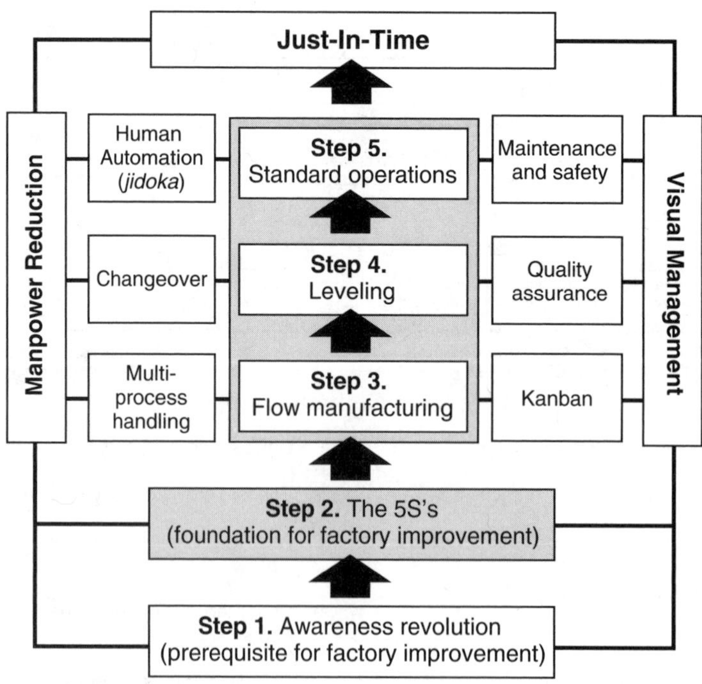

Figure 2-2. Improvement Steps for Establishing the JIT Production System

Orderliness has to do with putting everything in its place. Indeed, Organization and Orderliness should be taught in factories in a manner that ensures that everyone, even new or temporary employees, can easily understand how to implement them.

We call this "visual Organization and Orderliness." The main strategy for implementing visual Organization is called the "red-tag strategy," while that for implementing visual Orderliness is called the "signboard strategy." These strategies will be discussed in Chapters 8 and 9.

Figure 2-2 illustrates the improvement steps used when establishing JIT production. Like the "awareness revolution," the 5S's are implemented before making improvements. Both are basic building blocks for establishing improvement activities. For simplicity's sake, we will limit our discussion to the JIT production functions that are grounded in the 5S's.

Step 1. Awareness Revolution: Prerequisite for Factory Improvement

The awareness revolution means throwing out fixed ideas that belong to outdated production methods and embracing the new concepts of JIT production.

Key Points

1. Think of the current way of making things as the worst possible way.
2. The awareness revolution should begin in the minds of top managers.
3. Managers and supervisors must transform the old system by making shop-floor improvements.
4. Instruct operators in new methods at every opportunity, including routine meetings and special seminars.
5. Because factory revolutions always meet with resistance, it is important to instill and emphasize a basic spirit of improvement making.

Step 2. The 5S's: Foundation for Factory Improvement

5S implementation begins with clearing out everything that is no longer needed and organizing needed items so that everyone knows where to find them and return them. This also includes making a habit of keeping the workplace clean.

Key Points

1. Make Organization and Orderliness activities as visual as possible, so that everyone can see how to maintain the proper conditions.
2. Promote 5S implementation on a companywide basis.
3. Because they pave the way for discovering waste and other problems, make 5S implementation a part of any improvement campaign.

Step 3. Flow Production

Flow production entails producing products unit by unit in pace with the tact time (and in a well-regulated manner that follows the sequence of processes).

Key Points

1. Lay out production equipment according to the sequence of processes.
2. Have production lines follow a U-shaped cell pattern.
3. Make products one unit at a time.
4. Train operators in multiple skills to enable multi-process handling adapted to the sequence of processes.
5. The production line moves in pace with the tact time.
6. Operators stand while working.
7. Gradually re-equip the factory with small and inexpensive machines and special-purpose machines.

Step 4. Production Leveling

Product types and output volumes should be leveled to minimize variation among different shifts and to promote a smoother production flow.

Key Points

1. Use tact times to calculate monthly and daily output requirements.
2. Create a tact table based on the tact time.
3. Shorten the times required for changeover and parts replacement.
4. Design a smoother production flow.

5. Keep information moving in small units and implement frequent conveyance and transportation trips.

Step 5. Standard Operations

Standard operations are defined as the work methods which are most conducive to establishing an effective combination of operators, materials, and machines to create quality products promptly, cheaply, and safely.

Key Points

1. The three basic elements of standard operations are:
   - tact time
   - operation sequence
   - standard stock-on-hand
2. Standard operations use the following operation forms:
   - part-specific capacity worktables
   - work summary tables
   - work instruction sheets
   - standard operation combination sheets
   - standard operation sheets
3. Make improvements based on the tables and perform standard operations according to the sheets just mentioned.

3

Overview of the 5S's

About ten years ago, markets in the industrialized nations underwent a change. Consumers began reaching the satisfaction point with regard to functional features in products and were becoming more interested in distinctive ("personalized") features. With this shift in demand, markets that had previously been "seller's markets" (geared toward manufacturer preferences) became "buyer's markets" (geared toward consumer preferences). This same trend has caused the emphasis in supply-side activities to shift from supplying goods to supplying services.

The 5S approach arose from the need to meet the changing times and to support the resulting corporate restructuring. It developed via 5S campaigns undertaken at various progressive companies in recent years.

In Japan, the 5S approach has become so familiar that it is hard to find a factory or office that has not borrowed at least some of its ideas. Unfortunately, many Japanese companies pay it little more than lip service. Few have actually used this approach to build the foundations for corporate survival.

One cannot judge a factory's 5S environment by how often supervisors remind everyone of the 5S's. Judgment only comes from observing the factory itself. In most factories where I see "Organization-Orderliness" signs on display, they are little more than decoration. In fact, as more people hear about Organization and Orderliness, fewer really come to understand them.

The truth is that Organization and Orderliness are not words to just discuss. Neither are they meant to be printed on posters and banners. Organization and Orderliness are activities — things to be done.

With this in mind, let us renew our understanding of the 5S's, our five pillars of the visual workplace. (See Figure 3-1).

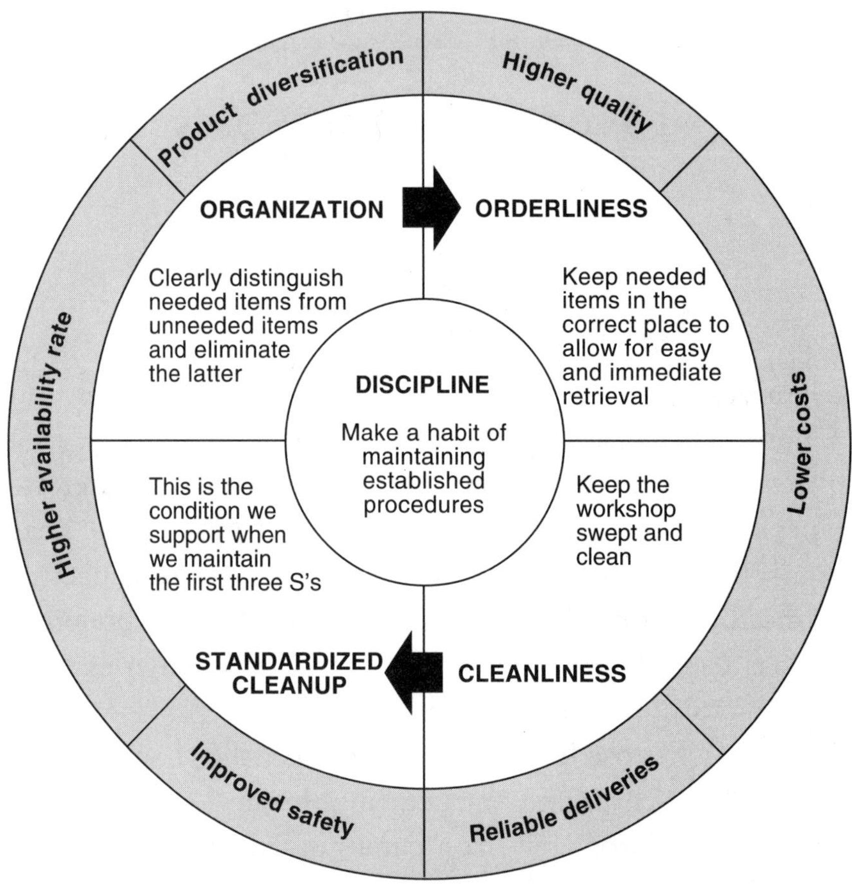

Figure 3-1. Meaning of the 5S's

PILLAR 1. ORGANIZATION

This simple word is often misunderstood. Organization does not simply mean lining things up in rows or into neat stacks. That is just forming lines. When done properly, Organization is expansive enough to include the organization of job assignments, outside orders, and so on.

When the factory experiences a lull in orders, managers should be able to easily determine which workers are still needed and make the necessary personnel changes. Only in terms of factory equipment does basic Organization mean arranging things in neat rows and stacks.

Be sure you understand the full meaning of this word — and remember:

Organization means clearly distinguishing between (1) what is needed and to be kept and (2) what is unneeded and to be discarded.

Surprisingly, this simple concept is easily misunderstood. At first, it may be difficult to distinguish between what is needed and what is not. My suggestion is "when in doubt, throw it out."

People tend to hang onto parts, thinking that they may be needed for the next order. They see an inappropriate machine and think that they will use it somehow. Meanwhile, inventory and equipment start to accumulate and get in the way of everyday production activities. This leads to a massive buildup of waste factorywide.

The following types of waste lead to errors and defects:

- Unneeded inventory incurs extra inventory-related expenses.
- Unneeded documents and materials require additional warehouse space and shelving.
- More lockers, shelves, etc. are needed just to store unneeded items.
- Unneeded conveyance requires extra pallets and carts.
- Extra manpower is needed to manage the growing inventory.
- It gets harder to sort out larger amounts of needed inventory from larger amounts of unneeded inventory.
- Greater amounts of stocked items become obsolete due to design changes, limited shelf life, etc.
- Quality defects result from unneeded in-process inventory and machine breakdowns.
- Unneeded equipment poses a daily obstacle to production activities.
- The presence of unneeded items makes designing equipment layout more difficult.

Red-tagging is a visual method of Organization that makes identifying waste easier. (The red-tag strategy is presented in Chapter 8.)

PILLAR 2. ORDERLINESS

In Japan, Orderliness is a word frequently used — but rarely understood. It is more than an orderly appearance or pattern, which means it is not just lining things up.

Orderliness always accompanies Organization. Once everything is organized, only what is necessary remains. Next, we must clarify where these things belong so that anyone can immediately understand where to find them and where to return them. Orderliness means standardizing how needed things are kept.

Orderliness means organizing the way needed things are kept so that anyone can find and use them easily.

It is worth repeating that everyone should be able to easily understand how things are kept in the factory. This is important. We should avoid situations in which people have to "learn the ropes" or ask a veteran worker before understanding where things go.

The signboard strategy is a visual Orderliness method that helps operations run smoothly by enabling anyone to understand where things go. (The signboard strategy is presented in Chapter 9.)

PILLAR 3. CLEANLINESS

This is the kind of cleaning that most people carry out in their own homes. Unfortunately, in Japan, where public littering is common, cleaning often stops at home. At the workplace — where many of us spend more time than at home — people ironically tend to ignore the need for Cleanliness.

Cleanliness means sweeping floors and keeping things in order.

In a factory, Cleanliness is closely related to the ability to turn out quality products. The basics are simply sweeping floors and wiping off machinery.

Cleanliness also entails saving labor by finding ways to prevent dirt, dust, and debris from piling up in the workshop. For example, with regard to oil leakage and debris from cutting and drilling machines, in order to restore the workplace's original clean state it is necessary to go beyond cleaning and make improvements.

Cleanliness should be integrated into daily maintenance tasks to combine cleaning checkpoints with maintenance checkpoints. The equipment operator is usually the person who best understands how well the equipment is operating. And often, only when the operator wipes dirt from the machine does he or she notice that it is leaking oil or that a burning smell is coming from the control panel. Rather than allow separation between the operator's work and the maintenance technician's work, we should involve everyone in developing better maintenance activities.

PILLAR 4. STANDARDIZED CLEANUP

Standardized Cleanup differs from Organization, Orderliness, and Cleanliness. These first three pillars can be thought of as activities, as something we "do." In contrast, Standardized Cleanup is not an activity — it is a state:

Standardized Cleanup means that Organization, Orderliness, and Cleanliness are being maintained.

While relating to each of the first three pillars, Standardized Cleanup relates most strongly with Cleanliness. It results when we keep machines and their surroundings free of debris, oil, and dirt. It is the condition that exists after we have practiced Cleanliness for some time. We can also improve the state of "Standardized Cleanup" by devising ways to prevent dirt and grime from accumulating in the first place. This creates a workplace with an even stronger 5S foundation.

PILLAR 5. DISCIPLINE

Discipline refers to social and safety conventions, such as friendly greetings among coworkers and wearing work uniforms, name tags, and helmets. All of these contribute to safety, a clean work environment, and a positive work attitude. The first four S's can be implemented thoroughly without difficulty if the workplace is one where the employees maintain Discipline. Such a workplace is likely to enjoy high productivity and high quality.

Discipline is not to be taken lightly. It is, in fact, a pivotal factor for the production system as a whole.

Discipline means always following specified (and standardized) procedures.

I have heard factory supervisors lament that great amounts of time and effort spent in organizing and cleaning were spent in vain because employees lacked the discipline to maintain 5S conditions. While managers can organize as many 5S campaigns and 5S contests as they want, without Discipline the 5S's will not last long.

The key to maintaining Discipline is not in a particular tool, such as a 5S checklist. Discipline is best taught by example; in other words, by the disciplined behavior of factory bosses and managers who are committed to establishing and maintaining the 5S's. The foreman should be called to the workshop if just one screw is left lying on the floor. Rather than reprimanding the worker who left the screw on the floor, we should call the foreman to task for allowing the attitude that it is alright to leave debris on the floor. The person ultimately responsible for any 5S backsliding is not the individual worker — it is the manager.

Managers who do not accept responsibility for maintaining the 5S's are not entitled to complain if their workers feel the same way.

4

Introducing the 5S's into the Workplace

The methods used to introduce the 5S's will differ between companies. Even within a single company, methods will differ among the various divisions (for instance, manufacturing, sales, and management). Let's look at some ways to introduce the 5S's:

- Example 1: Introduce the 5S's to build a foundation for introducing Just-in-Time (JIT) production.
- Example 2: Introduce the 5S's to build a foundation for Total Productive Maintenance (TPM), with particular emphasis on combining cleaning activities with maintenance activities.
- Example 3: Use the 5S's to breathe fresh air and enthusiasm into a stale Total Quality Control (TQC) program.
- Example 4: Introduce the 5S's as a first step toward the future implementation of JIT production and/or TQC.
- Example 5: Introduce the 5S's by emphasizing the red-tag strategy as the solution to an inventory glut.
- Example 6: Introduce the 5S's in the manufacturing division as an experiment. If successful, then introduce them elsewhere (e.g., the sales division).
- Example 7: Introduce the 5S's as a way to maximize efficiency in sales warehousing and other sales tasks.

- Example 8: Introduce the 5S's to help evaluate current operations and to build a strong foundation for introducing a computer-based system.

In this chapter, we shall focus on the two or three primary types of 5S introduction.

5S INTRODUCTION STEPS

Even though the steps may vary according to circumstances, we can still apply a standard set of introduction steps to most cases. These steps are shown in Figure 4-1.

With factories, the 5S's are usually intended to support something else, such as a JIT production system. In these cases, we should envision the outline shown in Figure 4-1 as fitting into the "5S" position of the outlined steps for companywide promotion of JIT production illustrated earlier in Figure 2-1. (See Chapter 2.)

The steps shown in Figure 4-1 need no such larger context in cases where the 5S's are being introduced to non-manufacturing divisions, such as sales and clerical divisions.

Step 1: **Establish a 5S Promotion Organization**

There should always be some kind of organization in charge of promoting 5S implementation. This organization should be led by some of the company's top managers and should operate companywide.

Step 2: **Establish a 5S Promotion Plan**

5S implementation is never-ending, but for Organization's sake it is best to schedule implementation activities one year at a time.

Step 3: **Create 5S Campaign Materials**

Top managers should be involved in creating materials that enlist companywide cooperation in the company's 5S campaign.

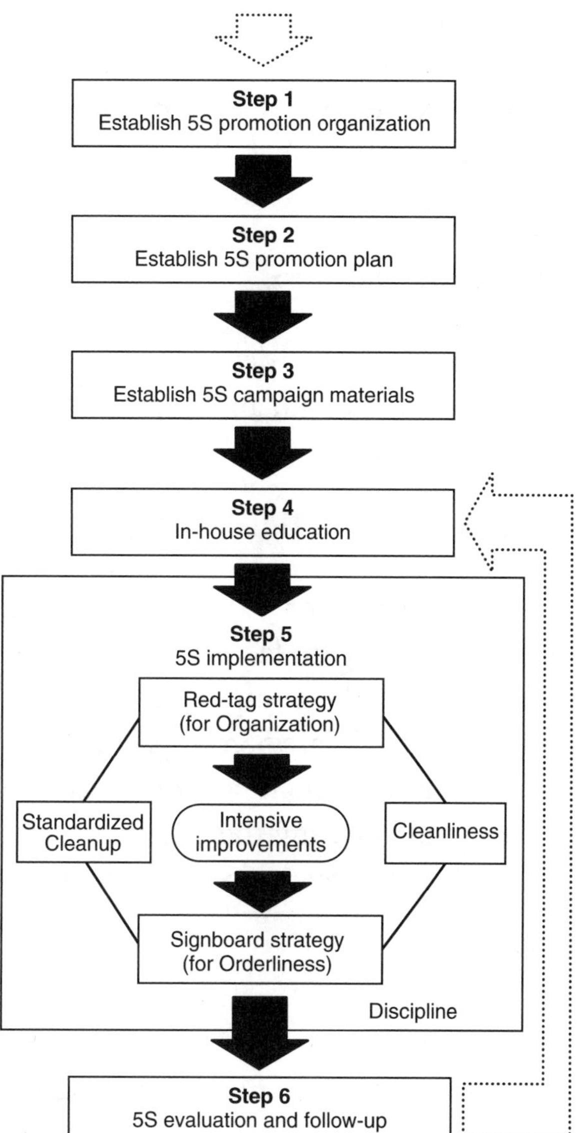

Figure 4-1. 5S Introduction Steps

Step 4: In-house Education

In-house education is needed to answer the first question on everyone's lips, namely "What does 5S mean?" It is also needed to teach the importance of the 5S's for ensuring the company's long-term survival.

Step 5: 5S Implementation

5S implementation activities are what firmly establishes all five S's in the company. Such activities include "visual 5S" methods such as red-tagging for visual Organization and the signboard strategy for visual Orderliness.

Step 6: 5S Evaluation and Follow-up

To prevent 5S conditions from deteriorating, periodic 5S evaluations should be initiated to check, maintain, and improve 5S conditions. Repeating steps 4 and 5 will also help improve 5S conditions.

ESTABLISHING THE 5S PROMOTION ORGANIZATION

Terms such as "5S campaign" or "5S strategy" are used to describe the implementation of 5S activities in factories and offices. However, before launching into such activities, the company should establish some kind of organization to promote and facilitate 5S campaigns on a companywide basis.

The organization's aims and methods may vary depending upon the company's purposes for implementing the 5S's. Nevertheless, the goal will be the same — to promote companywide 5S implementation.

A Basis for Survival

Figure 4-2 outlines the structure of a 5S promotion organization designed to facilitate the introduction of JIT production as a way to revolutionize the factory.

This 5S promotion organization is characterized by its inclusion of the 5S's within a wider plan for developing a JIT production system. With the 5S's as a foundation, this company will be prepared to reform its entire organizational structure.

Promotion Headquarters

The role of leading the company into the reform process falls squarely on the shoulders of top management. As a result, the promotion headquarters should be staffed entirely by upper-level managers — with the company president as the company's promotion chief.

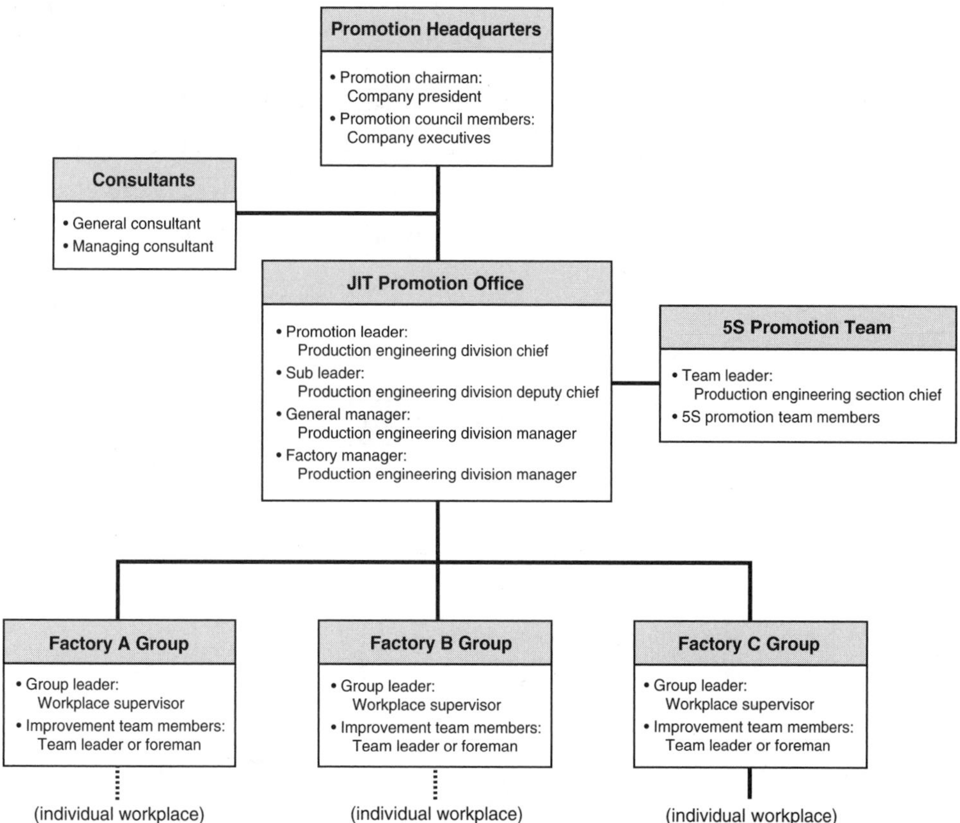

Figure 4-2. 5S Promotion Organization as a Step Toward Introducing JIT Production

JIT Promotion Office

The JIT promotion office directs the promotional and instructional activities. The staff generally includes (1) managers who understand how information and goods flow through the company and (2) production engineers with at least a basic grasp of industrial engineering (IE) techniques.

5S Promotion Team

The 5S promotion team functions as a subcommittee of the JIT promotion office. It handles such tasks as on-site 5S education, discipline training, 5S standardization, guidance in 5S techniques, and provision of 5S tools.

Groups at Individual Factories

The factory superintendent is the central figure in the JIT promotion group at each factory, as shown in Figure 4-3. This group oversees the JIT production improvements within each factory's organization. Of course, these efforts begin with 5S implementation to lay the groundwork for later improvements.

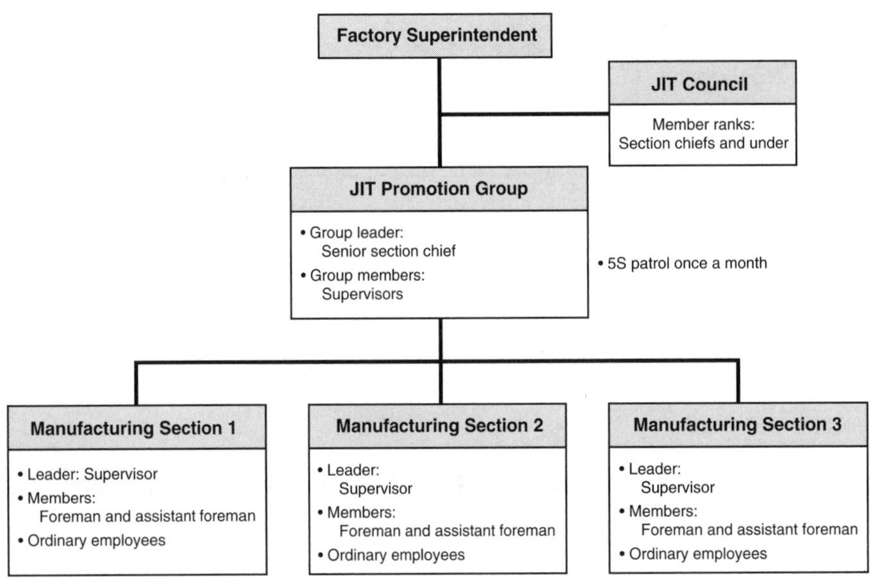

Figure 4-3. One Factory's JIT Promotion Groups

Promoting the 5S's, TQC, and TPM

Some companies have formed a promotion organization that combines TQC (one of quality control's earliest movements) with TPM and the 5S's.

Instead of calling this a "5S/TQC/TPM" organization, we simply refer to it as "5ST" and call its threefold approach the "5ST" strategy. (See Figure 4-4.)

By simultaneously implementing these three strategies for long-term survival, the company can avoid the confusion that tends to arise when the 5S's, TQC, and TPM are implemented separately. The 5ST organization outlined in Figure 4-4 is designed to establish centralized control over all three

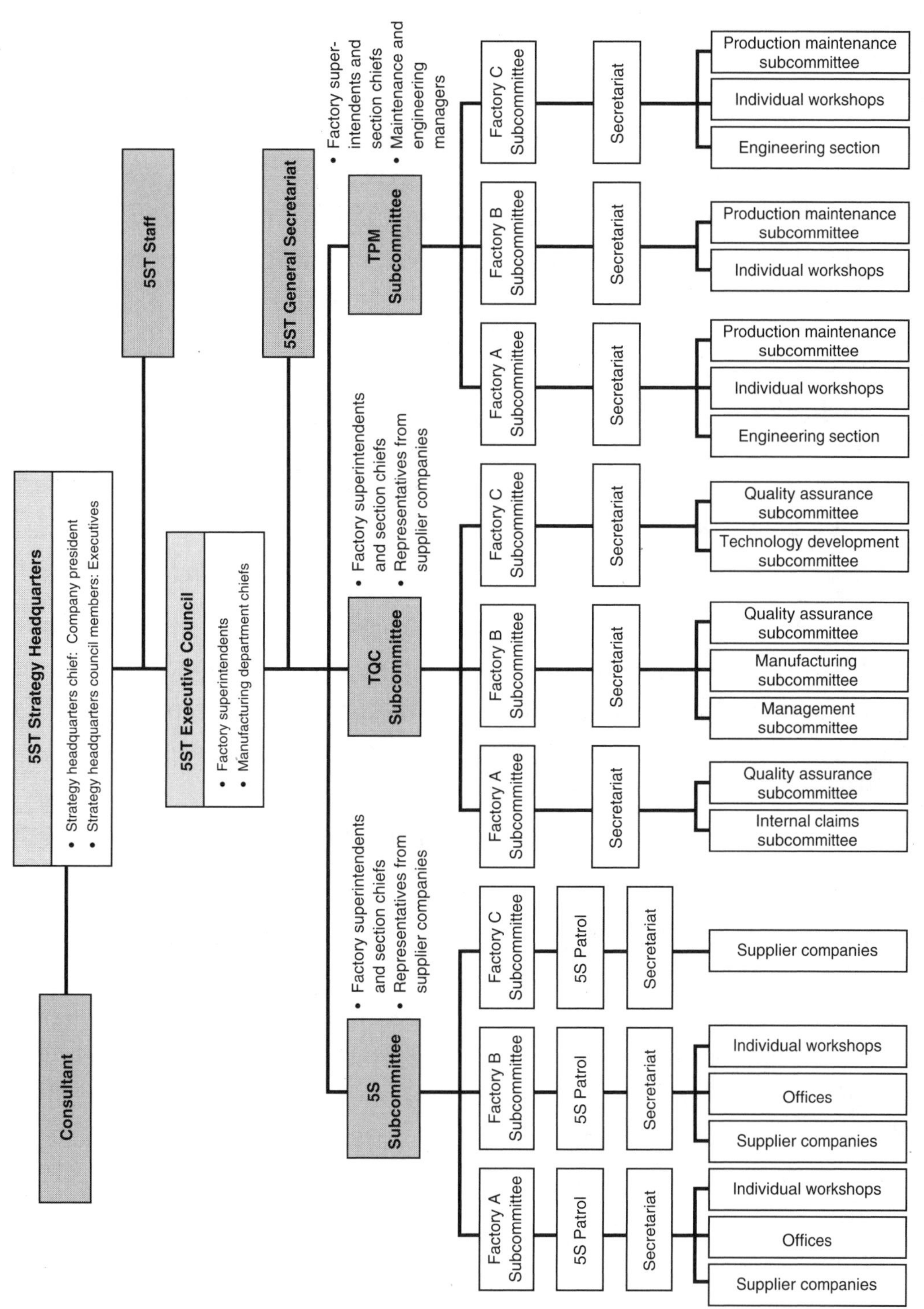

Figure 4-4. "5ST" (5S/TQC/TPM) Promotion Organization

strategies. This creates an integrated strategy for long-term corporate survival that is an important option to consider. A brief description of the parts of this organization follows.

5ST Strategy Headquarters

Centralized control is maintained over 5S, TQC, and TPM promotion at 5ST strategy headquarters under the acronym "5ST." The company president serves as the chief with high-ranking executives as council members.

5ST Staff

The 5ST staff is responsible for creating an outline for 5ST promotion. This includes such factors as the overall 5ST approach, introduction methods, and technical considerations. As such, the 5ST staff functions as the "brain trust" for the 5ST strategy headquarters.

5ST Executive Council

The 5ST executive council is responsible for executing the outline drafted by the 5ST staff and approved by the 5ST strategy headquarters. To do this, the 5ST executive council develops a 5ST strategy plan and assigns duties for its implementation and evaluation.

Council membership includes factory superintendents and manufacturing department chiefs.

Major Subcommittees (5S, TQC, and TPM Subcommittees)

The members of these subcommittees are responsible for carrying out the 5ST strategy plan at the factory level. They draft their own more detailed, factory-level versions of this plan and then implement and evaluate the plan.

All three subcommittees have similar functions and a common purpose — to help ensure the company's survival.

5S Patrols

No matter how successful 5S implementation has been, you can bet that, if left alone, 5S conditions will soon begin to deteriorate. To prevent this from happening, 5S patrols are given the job of inspecting workplaces to check up on 5S conditions.

A Compact 5S Promotion Organization in a Small Factory

Figure 4-5 outlines a compact 5S promotion organization. This small company wisely chose to ensure a solid 5S foundation before carrying out implementation measures for JIT and TPM.

The structure of this organization is based not so much on logical necessity as on emphasizing 5S implementation as the all-important first step in all parts of the company. To avoid confusion, they used only simple names for the groups within their 5S organization.

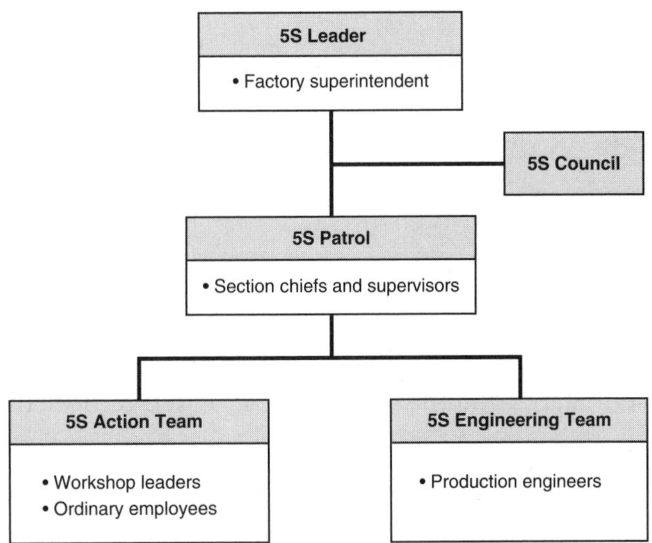

Figure 4-5. Compact 5S Promotion Organization

5S Leader

Within this organization, the top-ranking job goes to the factory superintendent or manufacturing division chief. Because the company is small, the number of people in each part of the 5S promotion organization must be minimized.

5S Patrol

The patrol members are mainly the section chiefs and supervisors who answer directly to the factory superintendent or manufacturing division chief. The 5S patrol makes weekly or biweekly inspection tours to check up on 5S conditions and suggest remedial measures when conditions have begun to deteriorate.

5S Council

The 5S council members are the people who have the most detailed understanding of 5S implementation. They function as the "brain trust" for the 5S leader and the 5S patrol.

5S Action Team

The 5S action team, which consists of workshop leaders and ordinary employees, is responsible for the nuts and bolts of 5S implementation. The team members study 5S theory while putting it into practice in making 5S-oriented improvements.

5S Engineering Team

The 5S engineering team lends its support to the 5S action team when the latter encounters technical problems (for example, when remodeling equipment).

Promotion Organization for the Clerical 5S's

In most respects, the 5S promotion organization for sales and clerical offices is the same as that for factories. One significant difference is that, due to the relative lack of case histories in clerical 5S campaigns, 5S promotion staff are encouraged to be imaginative in their approach to implementing the 5S's.

Different companies use different names for their 5S campaigns. I encourage companies to come up with something catchy. The company whose 5S promotion organization is outlined in Figure 4-6 coined the term "J5" to refer to their 5S campaign for clerical work. (The "J" comes from the Japanese word for clerical work.)

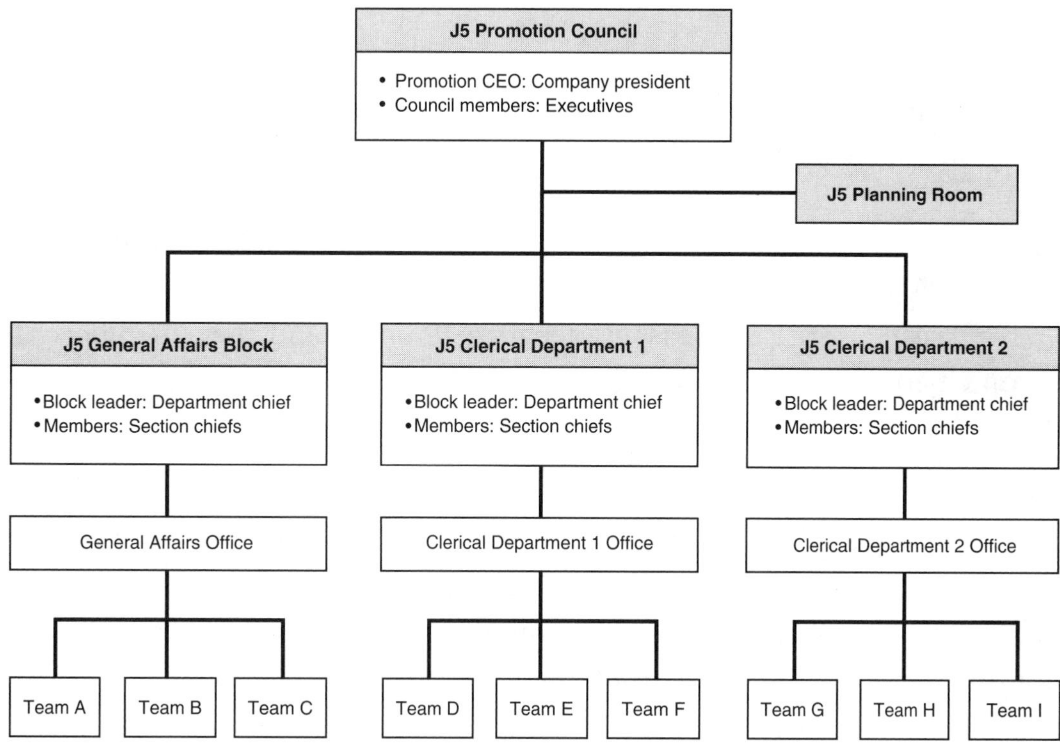

Figure 4-6. Promotion Organization for 5S's in Clerical Work

J5 Promotion Council

The company president leads the J5 campaign. He chairs the meetings of the J5 promotion council, which is responsible for (1) establishing a companywide program of 5S implementation and (2) officiating at J5 meetings and evaluating the 5S implementation work of each J5 block.

J5 Planning Room

At this company, the J5 planning room was established within the business planning office with the business planning chief serving as the J5 planning chief. This planning room serves as a general secretariat for the entire J5 campaign. Its duties include the scheduling of J5 implementation activities, training programs, and result evaluations.

J5 General-Affairs Block

Following the 5S campaign schedule made by the J5 planning-room staff, the J5 blocks are responsible for executing and managing 5S implementation activities. The block for the general-affairs office is called the J5 general-affairs block. Those for the two clerical departments are called the J5 clerical-department blocks 1 and 2.

The leaders of these blocks are department chiefs and their members are section chiefs.

General-Affairs Office

An office is attached to each block and named after it. These offices (for example, the general-affairs office) handle the clerical needs of each block. These generally include keeping the minutes of meetings, writing and distributing 5S newsletters, and arranging for meetings.

Team A

These teams are formed around workplace groupings, such as sections and work teams. The teams select their own leaders and implement and evaluate 5S activities.

We have briefly examined four different types of 5S promotion organizations. In all four examples, it may appear that the organization has been developed to suit the purposes of 5S promotion. However, a closer look reveals that these organizations are closely patterned after the company's managerial hierarchy, with top executives always at the top of the 5S promotion organization. While the names given to the various parts of the 5S promotion organization differ from their counterparts in the managerial hierarchy, the ways in which people are grouped are the same.

The 5S's are intended as a foundation for revolutionizing every workplace in the company. Such a revolution must be carried out from within the workplaces themselves. Consequently, it is very important that the 5S promotion organization be firmly rooted in the existing organizational hierarchy.

5S CAMPAIGN PROMOTION

The company's top executives are responsible for companywide deployment of the 5S campaign. The company president is the 5S promotion headquarters chief. Once the general outline of the company's 5S promotion organization has been worked out, the various 5S promotion teams and the 5S planning room can begin to implement specific projects.

How does the 5S promotion staff go about promoting the 5S's? In answering this question, we will follow the 5S introduction steps shown in Figure 4-1.

Establish a 5S Promotion Plan

All too often people still unclear on the 5S concept ask: "If we implement the 5S's for six months, is that enough?" Usually I respond with another question: "Would you stop taking a shower after six months?" The point is that, like bathing, the 5S's are ongoing activities that should continue as long as the company exists.

This does not mean that the 5S's remain the same — after all, companies change, too. As new products are brought out that require new equipment layouts and new staff assignments, today's 5S activities become outdated. Continual improvements are essential to keep 5S activities in pace with changing conditions.

This is why 5S promotion plans should only cover periods of one or two years.

Figure 4-7 shows a sample 5S promotion plan. Although formally prepared by the company's 5S staff, the plan's original framework was prepared by a consultant before the company had established its 5S promotion organization.

5S Campaign Materials

Once the 5S promotion organization and the 5S promotion plan have been established, it is time to announce the start of the 5S campaign. This news can be spread via a memo or newsletter (although such print media

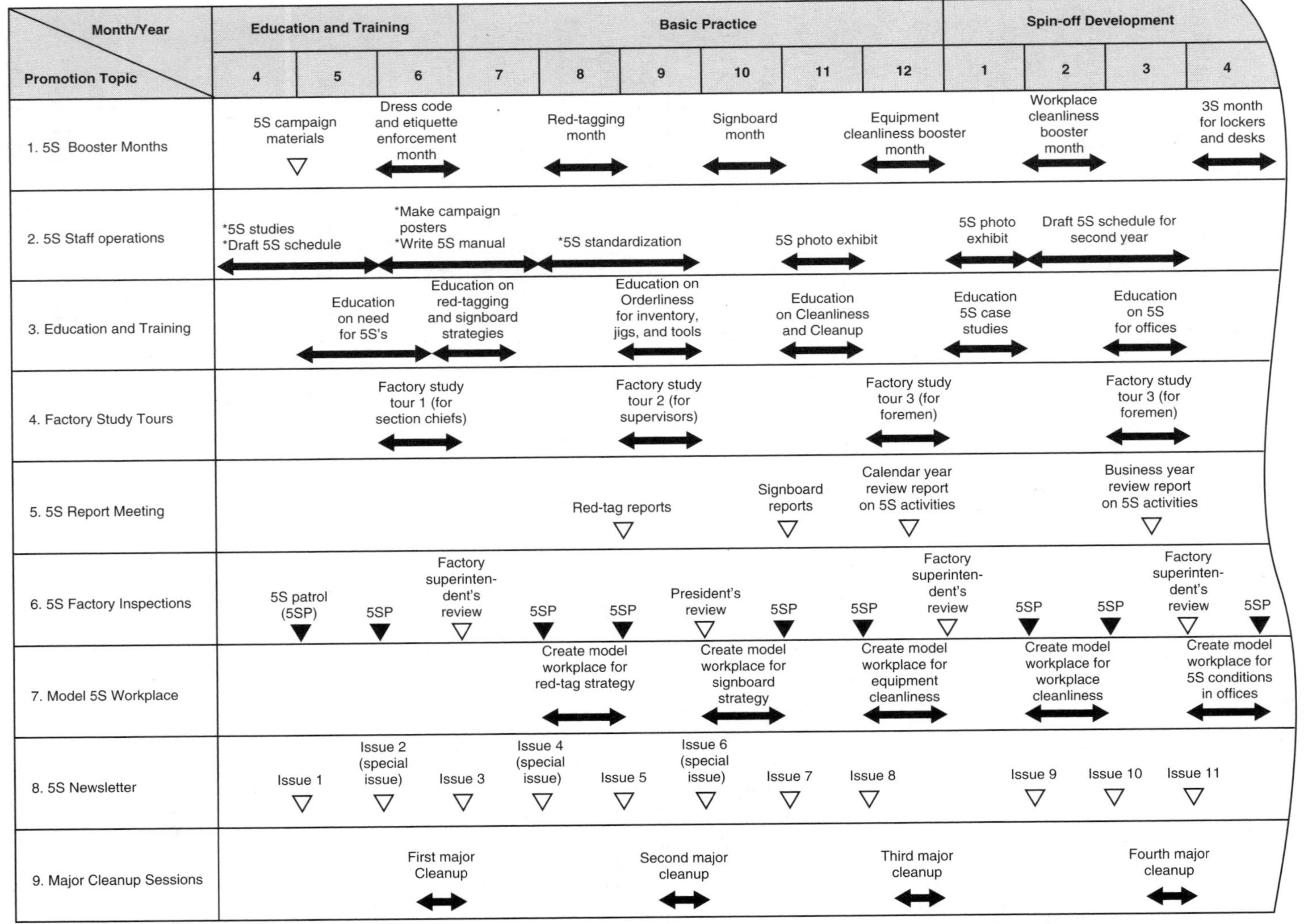

Promotion Topic \ Month/Year	Education and Training			Basic Practice						Spin-off Development			
	4	5	6	7	8	9	10	11	12	1	2	3	4
1. 5S Booster Months	5S campaign materials ▽		Dress code and etiquette enforcement month ⟷		Red-tagging month ⟷		Signboard month ⟷		Equipment cleanliness booster month ⟷		Workplace cleanliness booster month ⟷		3S month for lockers and desks ⟷
2. 5S Staff operations	*5S studies *Draft 5S schedule ⟷		*Make campaign posters *Write 5S manual ⟷		*5S standardization ⟷			5S photo exhibit ⟷		5S photo exhibit ⟷	Draft 5S schedule for second year ⟷		
3. Education and Training		Education on need for 5S's ⟷	Education on red-tagging and signboard strategies ⟷			Education on Orderliness for inventory, jigs, and tools ⟷		Education on Cleanliness and Cleanup ⟷		Education 5S case studies ⟷		Education on 5S for offices ⟷	
4. Factory Study Tours			Factory study tour 1 (for section chiefs) ⟷			Factory study tour 2 (for supervisors) ⟷			Factory study tour 3 (for foremen) ⟷			Factory study tour 3 (for foremen) ⟷	
5. 5S Report Meeting						Red-tag reports ▽		Signboard reports ▽	Calendar year review report on 5S activities ▽			Business year review report on 5S activities ▽	
6. 5S Factory Inspections	5S patrol (5SP) ▼	5SP ▼	Factory superintendent's review ▽	5SP ▼	5SP ▼	President's review ▽	5SP ▼	5SP ▼	Factory superintendent's review ▽	5SP ▼	5SP ▼	Factory superintendent's review ▽	5SP ▼
7. Model 5S Workplace					Create model workplace for red-tag strategy ⟷		Create model workplace for signboard strategy ⟷		Create model workplace for equipment cleanliness ⟷		Create model workplace for workplace cleanliness ⟷		Create model workplace for 5S conditions in offices ⟷
8. 5S Newsletter	Issue 1 ▽	Issue 2 (special issue) ▽	Issue 3 ▽	Issue 4 (special issue) ▽	Issue 5 ▽	Issue 6 (special issue) ▽	Issue 7 ▽	Issue 8 ▽		Issue 9 ▽	Issue 10 ▽	Issue 11 ▽	
9. Major Cleanup Sessions			First major Cleanup ⟷			Second major cleanup ⟷			Third major cleanup ⟷			Fourth major cleanup ⟷	

Figure 4-7. 5S Promotion Plan

make it difficult for the company president and other 5S leaders to show their enthusiasm). At this stage, the main purpose of 5S campaign publicity is not so much to announce the beginning of the 5S campaign as it is to show the enthusiasm of 5S leaders. It is better to have face-to-face meetings between 5S leaders and company employees.

The best format for such meetings can be the regular monthly meeting where attendance is mandatory. Ideally, the company president should address the meeting and describe the company's current conditions, its goals, and its plan to use the 5S's to lay a foundation for achieving those goals.

If the company is too large to hold meetings attended by everyone, have the president and other 5S leaders hold a meeting for all managers, at which 5S publicity is combined with 5S instruction. If this meeting is videotaped, it can be replayed at individual factory workshops and sales offices. Additional instruction and comments should be provided by the factory superintendent or other managers who attended the original meeting.

The following examples illustrate the approaches that four company presidents took when addressing their employees:

Example 1: From a President Drowning in Red Ink

"Our business environment has grown much harsher, and our company has been in the red for the past two years. Many other companies like ours are being required by their client factories to cut costs — and those who cannot meet such requirements will not survive. We can and will survive by strengthening our company to meet cost-reduction needs.

"To do this, we need everyone to help root out the waste that is companywide. 5S activities are extremely important because they lay the foundation for thoroughly eliminating waste. As president, I will do my utmost to make this a stronger company. However, to succeed I need everyone's help."

Example 2: From a President Faced with Declining Profits Due to Product Diversification

"In the past few years we have expanded our range of product models more than tenfold. Such diversification has complicated our in-house operations and forced our factories to operate under increasingly chaotic conditions. The future outlook is for even greater diversification. This means that we must offer an even wider range of products, making profits even harder to achieve.

"We cannot buck this trend and survive. To survive these changes, our company must move away from the mass-order, mass-production, and mass-sales format adhered to previously. Our first order of business is to establish the 5S's. This will allow us to stay afloat while being washed by the sea of change. Our company's destiny depends upon our success in establishing the 5S's — and I ask for your total cooperation."

Example 3: From the President of a Company Lacking a Strong Foundation to Support Rapid Expansion

"As a result of everyone's tireless efforts, our company has achieved a several-fold increase in sales over the past few years. I am very pleased with this success. However, it has not been easy to maintain stable operations during this rapid-growth period. People are having trouble finding the information they need and our product warehousing system is a mess. I see people everywhere spending a lot of time searching for needed documents or products.

"Obviously, sales expansion is very important — but so is operational strength. To lay the foundation for future growth, we need to thoroughly implement the 5S's. I will personally be involved in our 5S campaign, and I ask for your cooperation in making it a big success."

Example 4: From the President of a Company that Has Not Changed with the Times

"Our company has maintained its traditional ways for so long that they are dragging us down. While other companies undertook radical rationalization measures, we wasted time thinking about what to do without doing anything. And now we are several years behind our competitors in rationalization and other areas.

"It is time for us to change. We will do it via a thorough companywide 5S campaign that will establish a foundation for all of the necessary changes. In particular, we must adhere to 5S rules and provisions and develop stronger habits and discipline.

"I cannot implement the 5S's alone. I need your help. Please join me now to ensure that our company has a future."

In-house Education

Generally, people in Japan do not recognize the importance of the 5S's. When average factory or office workers hear their president speak of "Organization" and "Orderliness," their reactions are usually along the lines of "Why is he or she going on about that again?" That is why employees must learn the importance of the 5S's in concrete terms. Along with information, employees must be full of enthusiasm. This makes the entire company a receptive environment for 5S implementation.

In-house 5S education might include the following activities:

- **Slogans.** The 5S leaders can solicit slogan suggestions from everyone — even part-time and temporary employees — and display the best ones on banners and in in-house bulletins.
- **Posters.** Eye-catching posters that contain slogans and 5S information can be hung in the company cafeteria, meeting rooms, individual worksites, and other places where they are likely to be noticed.
- **In-house bulletins.** All employees can read the company's in-house bulletin to find out why the 5S's are needed and how they will be implemented.
- **5S news.** A newsletter devoted to 5S-related topics can be published by the 5S secretariat and distributed to all employees.
- **Outside consultants.** To improve 5S education, hold 5S seminars for the company's upper and middle managers.
- **Videos and books.** 5S books and videos can be circulated throughout the company.
- **Single-point 5S lessons.** In their daily meetings with subordinates, have supervisors incorporate what they have learned about the 5S's as short, single-point lessons.

These activities are useful ways to carry out in-house 5S education. When conducting such educational activities, please heed the following points.

Point 1: Make 5S Education Continuous

5S education should never be thought of as something that ends with the conclusion of the 5S introduction phase. Instead, it is a vital part of the discipline-building process and should be continuous.

Point 2: Don't Be a Perfectionist

Any company that takes a perfectionist approach to 5S implementation will be disappointed. Taking Organization as an example, we should never expect to find a perfectly organized workplace. Neither should we expect signboards to be put to their fullest possible use. Instead of looking for 100 percent compliance with 5S directives, simply go to the workplaces and confirm that the 5S's are being implemented.

Point 3: The Primary Place for 5S Implementation Is the Individual Workplace

Whenever a company announces its establishment of a 5S promotion organization, some employees misinterpret the news to mean that "the 5S promotion people will be doing the 5S implementation." However, the main players in 5S implementation are the people in the factories and offices —only they can create and maintain 5S conditions.

Point 4: Encourage Independent Thinking

Because factory and office workers are the primary players in 5S implementation, the role of 5S promotion teams and 5S planning-room staff is to support and guide employee efforts. It is important to encourage every employee to be inventive and to take the initiative in establishing 5S conditions in their workplaces.

Point 5: Encourage Motivation and Skill-building

5S activities should do more than make workplaces cleaner. They should motivate employees to maintain 5S conditions, build discipline, and improve their skills.

5S Implementation

In most cases, the momentum for 5S implementation dies out after the first attempt at the red-tag strategy. This strategy calls for clearly labeling all unneeded items with large red tags as part of Organization. Such items generally include jigs, tools, and obviously useless items. Once the results of

5S Checklist (for offices)	Workplace: General affairs section	Evaluator: Kazuo Yamagawa			
	Score: 25/100	Previous Score: 24/100	Date: Nov. 14, 1994		

5S	Check Item	Check Description	Score 0	1	2	3	4
Organi-zation (6/20)	1. Are there any unneeded items in the lockers?	Are any papers, drawings, or meeting notes in the locker unnecessary?		○			
	2. Are there any unneeded items on people's desks?	Are there any machines or other equipment	○				
	3. Are there any unneeded items on floor?						
	4. Are there any unneeded it… clearly indicated as such?						
	5. Are there clear criteria for … what is needed and what i…						
Orderli-ness (7/20)	6. Are place indicators in use…						
	7. Are item labels in use?						
	8. Are amount labels in use?						
	9. Are divider lines in place f… and temporary storage site…						

5S Checklist (for factories)	Workplace : Assembly section 1	Evaluator: Kazuo Yamagawa			
	Score: 31/100	Previous Score: 28/100	Date: Nov. 7, 1994		

5S	Check Item	Check Description	Score 0	1	2	3	4
Organi-zation (10/20)	1. Are there any unneeded materials or parts?	Are there any unneeded items in the warehouse or in-process inventory?			○		
	2. Are there any unneeded machines or equipment?	Are there any machines or other equipment not being used?			○		
	3. Are there any unneeded jigs, tools, or dies?	Are there any jigs, tools, dies, cutting bits, or spare parts not being used?				○	
	4. Are all unneeded items clearly indicated as such?	Can items marked as unneeded be recognized immediately?			○		
	5. Are there clear criteria for determining what is needed and what is not?	Where are the criteria for determining what is needed and what is not ?		○			
Orderli-ness (9/20)	6. Are place indicators in use?	Do signs indicate storage places (such as address signs, etc.)?			○		
	7. Are item labels in use?	Are all shelved items labeled and entered on an inventory list?				○	
	8. Are amount labels in use?	Do signs indicate maximum and minimum inventory amounts?					
	9. Are divider lines in place for walkways and temporary storage sites?	Are floor markers easy to see (i.e., thick white lines)?					

Figure 4-8. 5S Checklists

the red-tag strategy are announced, people feel that 5S implementation is over and they tend to rest on their laurels.

The truth is that at this point the 5S's have just begun. Once red-tagging has removed unnecessary items from the workplace, it is not time to straighten up the remaining items and continue as before. It is time to make improvements. For example: In a factory, this is the time to improve equipment layout and operation methods. In an office, it provides the opportunity to redesign the workplace and review work procedures.

Once we have improved the layout in the factory or office and have removed waste from the old operation methods, we can start figuring out how the necessary items should be kept to make them as easily accessible as possible. Once these things are accomplished, we can move on to the signboard strategy and other ways to implement Orderliness.

5S Evaluation and Follow-up

Maintaining 5S conditions is like a stretched rubber band. Once released, it returns to its original shape. 5S leaders use terms such as "collapsed" or "broken down" to describe 5S conditions that have returned to their original state due to lack of 5S evaluation and follow-up.

The strongest force in maintaining 5S conditions is Discipline (the fifth "S"). When there is sufficient discipline in a workplace, outside evaluators are not needed to correct 5S conditions. Instead, the people in the workplace have the discipline to value the 5S's in their work lives and to maintain 5S conditions. That is why building discipline is considered the most effective way to prevent 5S breakdowns. External evaluations and follow-through are also important — but not as important as Discipline.

Companies should use the same companywide set of standards for 5S evaluations. Often, they make use of standard 5S evaluation tools, such as the 5S checklist shown in Figure 4-8 or 5S evaluation sheets. Such evaluations can be conducted by 5S patrols during their routine inspection activities.

After all workplaces in the company have been evaluated for 5S conditions, they should be ranked according to their evaluation scores. Those with top-ranking scores should receive some kind of award. All workplace rankings should be publicized companywide so that people can tell how well their workplaces are progressing.

We will now examine some primary ways to maintain 5S conditions.

Establish an Organization for Maintaining 5S Conditions

5S promotion organizations are established to carry out 5S implementation during the introduction phase. Once this phase is over, many companies allow 5S promotion to slack off. However, the fact is that at this stage the 5S's are more important than ever. As noted previously, we rely primarily upon employee discipline to prevent 5S conditions from deteriorating. Nonetheless, when such deterioration is evident we also need other means of stopping it. Companies should establish some kind of organization (such as 5S patrols or reviews by 5S promotion teams) to help maintain 5S conditions.

Make the 5S's Part of Normal Working Procedures

Once the 5S introduction phase is over, reminders will not be enough. It is therefore important to incorporate 5S principles into standard work procedures. In this way Organization, Orderliness, Cleanliness, and Standardized Cleanup become part of the natural way of doing things. The flow of operations in factories and offices should follow 5S principles and help maintain 5S conditions — making verbal or written reminders unnecessary.

Devise Tools for Maintaining 5S Conditions

This should be considered part of the implementation work that 5S promotion teams and other 5S staff do. 5S tools may include 5S slogan displays, 5S posters, 5S badges, 5S patrols, 5S report meetings, 5S awards ceremonies, and single-point 5S lessons.

Total 5S

One indication that 5S conditions are about to break down is when we hear employees remark that "putting up signboards is the 5S staff's job" or that "this 5S stuff should be done by the 5S promotion team."

It is worth repeating that the maintenance of 5S conditions depends upon the positive support and cooperation of individual employees. As in TQC, any 5S campaign must be a total companywide campaign. Successful 5S implementation depends upon whether or not individual workers take the trouble to incorporate the 5S's into their own work methods. In production-engineering terms, this means achieving "line integration of the 5S's."

5S Maintenance Is a Hands-on Activity

The truth is that companies depend upon the behavior of individual employees. We must not lose sight of this fact when devising tools for maintaining 5S conditions. In other words, 5S maintenance is a hands-on activity. Rather than pointing out at a general meeting that workshop X has a dirty floor, go to that workshop yourself and talk to them about the dirty floor. Keeping 5S maintenance hands-on and direct is also an important key for building discipline.

Cultivating Discipline Is an Ongoing Effort

It is no exaggeration to say that the 5S's begin and end with Discipline. Discipline cannot be created through lip service. Instead, we build it up by incorporating 5S maintenance into our work methods, by keeping 5S maintenance hands-on and direct, and by keeping the 5S's firmly rooted in the factory and office through effective ongoing 5S education.

QUESTIONS AND ANSWERS ABOUT 5S INTRODUCTION

I have selected three representative questions from among the many I am asked about introducing and maintaining the 5S's. These questions follow along with my responses.

Five Points about Caring and Succeeding

Question: While I personally understand the importance of the 5S's in our corporate-restructuring plans, could you teach me some ways to get everyone else more concerned about them?

You might explain the importance of the 5S's by using a sports analogy. In almost every physical sport, athletes regard running as a fundamental part of their training. Likewise, the 5S's are fundamental to how well a company performs in the business arena. Indeed, the 5S's are of basic importance not only to corporate activities but to other types of activities as well.

The term "5S" is an acronym, which makes it easy to remember and talk about. However, the actual implementation and maintenance of the 5S's is not that simple. Some companies never get beyond the initial stages of the 5S introduction phase. Others give up just as 5S conditions are finally getting established in their factories. To help companies avoid such failures, I have formulated the five key points shown in Figure 4-9.

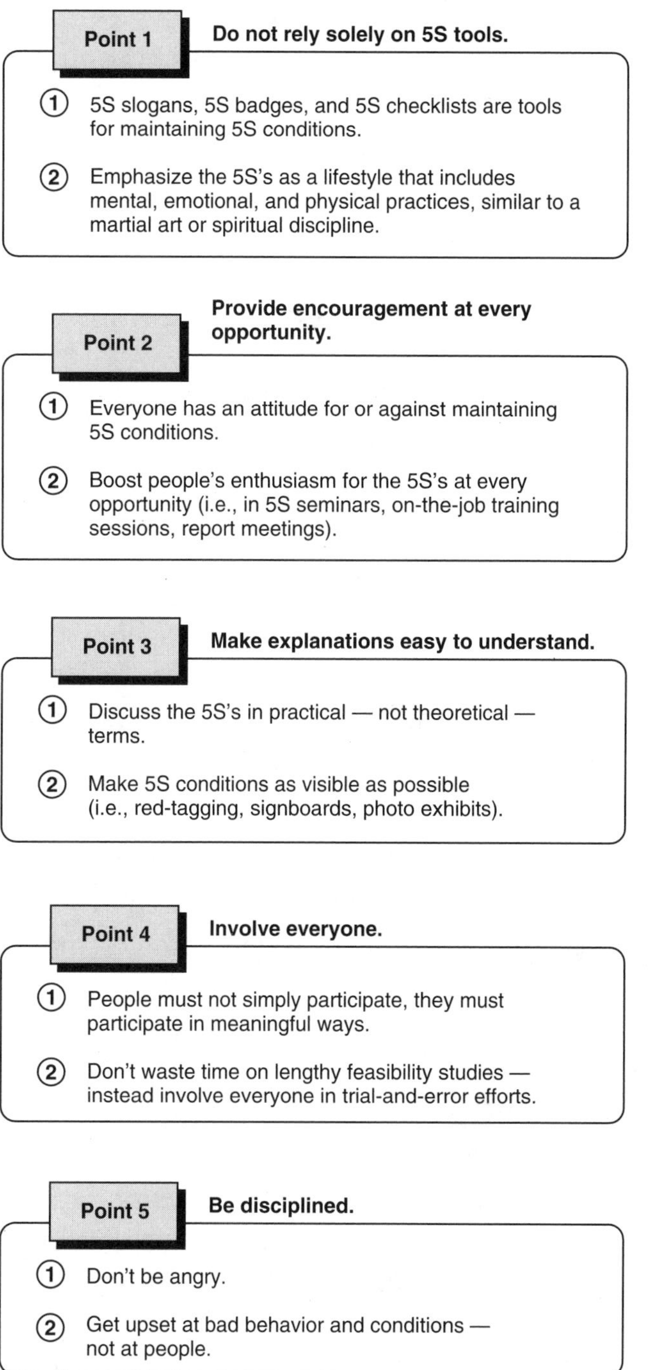

Figure 4-9. Five Key Points for 5S Success

Point 1: Do Not Rely Solely on 5S Tools

5S slogans, 5S badges, and 5S checklists are some of the tools available for maintaining 5S conditions. But these alone are not enough. Maintaining 5S conditions should be taught as a lifestyle — a way of working that includes mental, emotional, and physical practices similar to a martial art or a spiritual discipline.

The martial-arts analogy is a useful one. To learn judo or kendo, one must learn more than techniques. One must also learn a moral code and a new way of living. This is why Discipline is so crucial to 5S success.

Point 2: Provide Encouragement at Every Opportunity

Everyone has some kind of feeling about the work they do. Motivating people to work involves encouraging them to share their positive feelings about the work to be done. Without encouragement, people will be divided by their different feelings rather than united by enthusiasm. Providing encouragement is a key part of leadership.

Strong corporate leaders generally do not need to give reasons. When they tell subordinates to do something, it gets done. However, how well it is done depends in part upon the employee's emotional responses. When a leader gives a directive, will the response be positive ("Great"), ambiguous ("OK, if you say so"), or negative ("I'd rather not, but I'd better")? To get positive responses to 5S implementation, leaders need to follow through by providing encouragement at every opportunity. This can include 5S seminars, on-the-job training sessions, report meetings, and awards ceremonies.

Point 3: Make Explanations Easy to Understand

Avoid theoretical discussions. When people start thinking in abstract terms, they tend to lose sight of the all-important practicalities. The 5S's do not require theoretical underpinnings. If someone asks why the 5S's are necessary, instead of giving an abstract answer, just answer: "Why is bathing necessary?" Always try to keep 5S discussions simple and to the point.

To keep the 5S's uncomplicated, always remember that the 5S's are simply about (1) making conditions free of dirt and waste (and "conditions" means the workplace right in front of your nose) and (2) having clearly visible means of maintaining those conditions. These means include the 5S tools mentioned earlier (such as red-tagging, signboards, divider lines, and 5S photo exhibits).

Point 4: Involve Everyone

It is not hard to find "group activities" in which only a few people in the group actually do anything. The passive participants might as well be elsewhere.

Improvement activities require everyone's active participation. All employees should be ready to red-tag unneeded items and wipe up dirt wherever they find it. If 5S groups have only a few active members, you can bet that 5S conditions will eventually collapse.

Point 5: Discipline Comes First

Put simply, Discipline means adhering to what has been decided. Everyone agrees on the virtues of discipline, but few people know how to cultivate it.

For managers, the answer is simple: Correct mistakes. If you go to a workshop and find the floor dirty, immediately raise a fuss about it. Show that the dirt really upsets you. However, when reprimanding the guilty party, take care to show that your anger is with the poor conditions or behavior — not with the person. Managers who can do this will find Discipline on the rise in their workplaces.

Various Approaches to the 5S's

Question: Some books about JIT and TPM discuss the 5S's. Are these the same 5S's?

While I understand the 5S's in connection with JIT production, I cannot claim to know exactly what is meant in other contexts such as TPM. My guess is that they are basically talking about the same thing. On the other hand, I have read authors who discuss the 5S's in a way that suggests that they merely include the term because of its name recognition.

Some companies have undertaken 5S campaigns ambitious enough to include as many as eight "S's". I recall one such case where the sixth "S" was Habit, the seventh was Stability, and the eighth was Safety. I think it is absurd for companies to compete over how many "S's" they can add to their formula. In fact, I warn against having more than five. This is because the greater numbers weaken the impact of the two most important ones — Organization and Orderliness. They also downplay the importance of Cleanliness, Standardized Cleanup, and the all-important Discipline.

Eight Tips for Firmly Establishing the 5S's

Question: Our company is not doing well in establishing the 5S's as a foundation for improvement. Can you recommend some ways to help workers understand and practice the 5S's?

If a company fails to firmly establish the 5S's, the improvement road ahead will be a bumpy one. Unfortunately, I have heard many managers report difficulties in establishing the 5S's among their employees. It bears repeating that the 5S's are the starting point for making improvements. Without them, improvements have little or nothing to build upon.

How to help workers understand and practice the 5S's is not so much a technical question as it is an admission that problems exist in the 5S introduction campaign. Therefore, I will respond by listing eight tips to aid your search for those problems and thereby help your company firmly establish the 5S's. (See Figure 4-10.)

Tip 1: The President Is Ultimately Responsible

A lot of people think of the 5S's as common sense applied to common everydayness — and that they therefore merit someone else's attention. Sometimes even company presidents think this way. They may be the titular heads of their own 5S campaigns — but they pass down all real responsibility to their subordinates. This is the worst possible thing a president can do. Presidents cannot expect their companies to get behind the 5S's unless they practice it publicly themselves.

Tip 2: Every 5S Policy Decision Requires Company Authorization

5S implementation will not work if the various corporate sections proceed in different ways. Neither will 5S implementation work if the 5S staff does most of the policy making. 5S slogans, displays, posters, and policy decisions should be the product of companywide efforts, allowing everyone to recognize his or her role in firmly establishing the 5S's.

Tip #1 The president must take ultimate responsibility.

- Don't place this responsibility with subordinates.

Tip #2 Every 5S policy decision requires company authorization.

- Informal, improvised 5S policymaking does not work.

Tip #3 Promote companywide participation.

- 5S introduction does not work when only some employees get involved.

Tip #4 Explain the 5S's until everyone understands them.

- Thorough 5S implementation requires thorough understanding.

Tip #5 Be persistent and meticulous.

- Don't give up on something just because it is difficult.

Tip #6 Be quick and ruthless when red-tagging and making signboards.

- Long, drawn-out red-tagging and signboard strategies die of inertia.

Tip #7 Have the president participate in 5S patrols.

- Top managers are especially needed when a 5S patrol discovers mistakes made by middle managers.

Tip #8 The 5S's are the company's road to survival.

- Without them, there is little hope for improvement.

Figure 4-10. Eight Tips for Establishing the 5S's

Tip 3: Promote Companywide Participation

Again, it will not do to have only a few people doing most of the work. The 5S staff should consult with middle managers before making any major decisions, just as they do in other companywide campaigns (such as TQC and TPM). This does not mean that all employees need to be involved in all aspects of 5S implementation. It means that all employees should be ready to take part whenever they are needed to assist in 5S implementation — especially in their own workplaces.

Tip 4: Explain the 5S's Until Everyone Understands

Teach the meaning and importance of the 5S's at every opportunity — during seminars, training sessions, and routine meetings — so that no one is left wondering why the 5S's are needed to make improvements.

Tip 5: Be Persistent and Meticulous

Unfortunately, Organization and Orderliness have become buzzwords in Japan. People recognize these words without understanding them. Make sure that people in your company understand what Organization means.

For example: When using red tags to eliminate unneeded items, make sure that people doing the red-tagging really understand the criteria for determining what to tag. Likewise, regarding Orderliness and the signboard strategy, people should know how to quickly and confidently set up signboards containing the right information. Concerning Cleanliness, people should understand how to make divider lines. When implementing Standardized Cleanup, they should have a manual that specifies the standards of their workplace and how to maintain them.

Tip 6: Be Quick and Ruthless when Red-Tagging and Making Signboards

I will keep emphasizing the ongoing nature of the 5S's until people no longer ask me when they can stop. In particular, red-tagging and signboards are two 5S strategies that should be repeated several times a year — companywide and intensively. If a red-tag campaign is strung out too long, people will lose interest or want to hide things rather than get rid of them. It is best to be quick and ruthless when red-tagging.

Tip 7: Have the President Participate in 5S Patrols

The president should personally inspect factory and office workplaces and remark on whatever good and bad points he or she discovers. I have found that, as if by magic, word of a presidential inspection is often enough to transform dirty workplaces into ones that sparkle. (Another tip: Do not have the president stick to the same schedule or route when inspecting workplaces.)

Tip 8: **The 5S's Are the Company's Road to Survival**

The 5S's build up a company's foundation for improvement. Take advantage of opportunities to emphasize this fact. For example: Exhibit "before" and "after" workplace photos. Hold meetings to report on 5S benefits. Methods like these help everyone to recognize the real physical connection between the 5S's and the company's long-term survival.

5

The First Pillar: Organization

We learn from early on about getting things organized. As children, we were told to organize our toys and books. Our parents were the supervisors who pointed out what needed organizing and how well (or poorly) we accomplished the task.

Strictly speaking, this kind of organizing is not the same as that practiced as part of the 5S's. When children organize their toys and books, they usually just line them up or store them somewhere — without sorting out what is necessary (and to be kept) from what is unnecessary (and to be discarded).

Making a clear distinction between the necessary and the superfluous is a key part of Organization in the context of the 5S's. One could even say that "discard" is the key word.

THE NEED FOR ORGANIZATION AND ITS ESSENTIAL POINTS

Organization, the first pillar of the visual workplace, is the 5S component that corresponds to the Just-in-Time (JIT) principle of "only what is needed, only in the amounts needed, and only when it is needed." In other words, Organization means removing from the workplace all items that are not needed for current production (or clerical) operations.

Factories and offices are full of items that are not required for current operations. These include many items that are no longer needed for any reason. As these unneeded items accumulate, the following types of problems and waste tend to arise without our knowing it:

1. The factory becomes increasingly crowded and hard to work in as unneeded inventory and machinery accumulate and take up space.
2. Valuable factory space is increasingly taken up by unneeded items and is therefore not being used productively (in a value-adding way).
3. People have to walk and work around obstacles posed by unneeded items, which increases nonproductive motion waste.
4. When unneeded items clutter up parts and tool storage sites, more time is wasted in searching for required parts and tools.
5. Fewer items being managed are actually necessary. It thus becomes easier to omit needed items from orders, to make operational errors, or to overlook missing items.
6. Unneeded inventory and machinery cost money to maintain and eat into profits.
7. Excess inventory undergoes age-related deterioration and eventually becomes useless.
8. Design changes render excess existing inventory obsolete. Or, if the existing inventory must be used to save money, the company loses some of its flexibility and competitiveness.
9. Unneeded inventory means money wasted on extra inventory management.
10. Excess stock-on-hand in the factory tends to hide other types of problems (i.e., poor operational strength, unbalanced processes, production of defective goods, equipment breakdowns, missing items, delayed deliveries, and slow changeover).
11. Even unneeded items must be accounted for when taking inventory. This creates unnecessary work for inventory managers.
12. Unneeded items and equipment pose obstacles for redesigning the equipment layout and make it harder to improve the process flow.
13. Unneeded papers and files take up valuable office space and lead to cramped, uncomfortable office environments.
14. Lockers, shelves, and cabinets built to contain unneeded items put walls between employees in the same workplace, thereby hindering communication.

15. Even when items are well labeled, mixing up needed items with unneeded ones makes more things to search through ("searching waste").
16. Wordy reports take longer to read and are usually more difficult to understand.
17. Introducing superfluous information and materials at meetings slows down decision making and causes confusion among managers.
18. Keeping unneeded clerical supplies in desks raises costs.
19. Office productivity declines when desks are cluttered with unneeded items.
20. Having unneeded inventory and documentation around becomes the accepted norm. This sloppiness makes it easier for defective products and confidential information to escape the company.

When Organization Means "Get Rid of It!"

Often, in Japan when people are asked to implement Organization, they simply line things up without discarding anything. Perhaps this is because of the strong tradition of frugality in Japan and the tendency to place sentimental value on tools and other familiar objects.

I recall visiting one workplace where the place most in need of Organization was the desk drawer of the manager who had been ordering everyone else to organize their things. Among the items in this drawer were order-reception notices for old orders and proposals for old product models that he kept "just in case a similar new model comes out."

Organization does not mean throwing out only the items that you are sure to never need. Neither does it mean simply arranging things into neat, straight patterns.

Organization means leaving only the bare essentials: *When in doubt, throw it out.*

In Japan, companies also use the word "Organization" when describing the need to reduce personnel or scale back on farming out work to other companies. This is the kind of Organization we should apply to unneeded items in workplaces. After all, companies do not implement Organization for personnel by lining employees up in neat rows. When implementing the difficult task of "personnel Organization," companies must sort out the employees who are currently needed from those who are not. The key word is "currently." Everyone understands that the company bases its layoff decisions on current personnel needs under current conditions. This is the same criterion one should apply to items that are not currently needed. Defining and strictly applying this criterion is the most important part of implementing Organization.

From another perspective, we can view Organization as sorting things we will be using from things that we will not be using. The latter category actually includes three kinds of things, as shown in Figure 5-1.

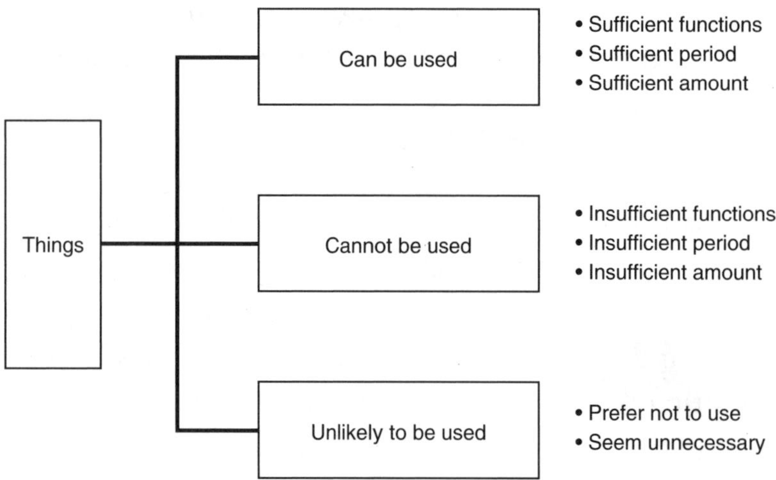

Figure 5-1. Categorizing Things Being Used and Not Used

If the item in question (1) has all of the required functions and (2) is available at the required time and (3) in the required amount, then we should keep it as a "thing that can be used." If the item is clearly lacking in any of the three criteria of functions, timing, and amount (e.g., a defective machine that does not provide all required functions), we should judge the item as a "thing that cannot be used." Lastly, there may be a few items that meet the criteria as a "thing that can be used" but are still unlikely to be used for some other reason (such as inferior operability, a tendency to break down occasionally, or a temporary lull in demand for the item). We can call such items "things unlikely to be used."

Generally, "things that cannot be used" and "things unlikely to be used" should be discarded as unneeded.

The following are some pointers on how unneeded items tend to accumulate in factories and offices. Please keep these in mind when implementing Organization.

At Storage Sites for Parts and Inventory

- Unneeded and defective items tend to accumulate in the left and right corners next to the warehouse entrances and exits.
- Look in the shadow of partitions and pillars.
- Look under desks and shelves and in bottom drawers of desks and filing cabinets.
- Look in boxes that have not been labeled.
- Look under the eaves of warehouses.
- Look where there are large piles of miscellaneous objects.
- Look near the bottom of tall stacks of items. (See Photo 5-1.)

Photo 5-1. Materials Stacked High at Storage Sites

At Storage Sites for Jigs, Tools, Cutting Bits, Dies, Inspection Gear, Etc.

- Look for unneeded items in miscellaneous piles, especially at the top and bottom of piles.
- Look for jigs, tools, and cutting bits locked away in lockers.

Photo 5-2. A Messy Pile of Spare Parts

Photos 5-3. Parts Stored Directly on Floor

- Look for old rags and small parts that are left scattered around.
- Look for age-deteriorated items, such as broken or rusted items.
- Look for items with no clearly designated storage place and that tend to get put down anywhere. (See Photo 5-2.)
- Look through tool boxes whose contents do not immediately appear to be clearly sorted.

- Look for dies that are filthy with accumulated oil or dust.
- Look behind rows of dies.
- Look for drill bits that are left loose in desk drawers.

Floors, Walkways, and Work Areas

- Rooms or floor spaces not designated for any particular purpose tend to be collection sites for unneeded or unusable items. (See Photo 5-3.)
- Items tend to be left along walls or behind pillars.
- Look for items near factory entrances and exits and along walkways near restrooms.
- In assembly plants, look for unneeded items left underneath conveyor belts.
- Look in shelves and desk drawers near worktables.
- Look for jigs, tools, bits, and rags hidden beneath machinery.
- Investigate any piece of equipment with a thick layer of dust on it.
- Investigate any piece of electrical equipment whose power cord is either broken or unplugged.
- Look through shelves, corners, and desktops located between manufacturing or assembly processes.
- Look through any pile of goods not labeled or that is labeled "defective."
- Look for small pieces of parts and materials near machines or materials storage sites. (See Photo 5-4.)
- Look for empty floor space or storage space.

Walls, Signs, and Management Boards

- Look for outdated posters and slogan signs.
- Look for outdated notices and memos.
- Look for unused management boards and production schedule boards.

Outdoor Sites

- Look for piles of defective or unneeded items near exterior walls.

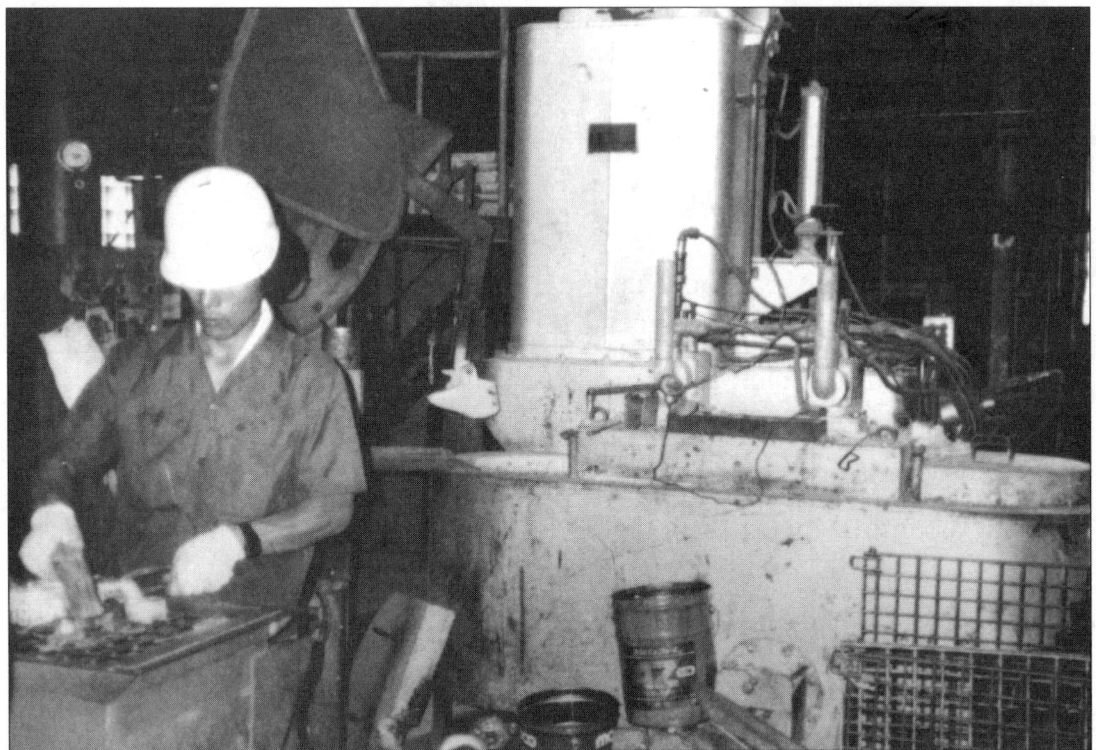

Photo 5-4. Spare Parts Accumulated Next to the Equipment

- Look for items left lying near trash disposal sites or around the boiler room.
- Look in detached buildings and sheds whose contents are not clearly designated.

Offices

- Look toward the back of drawers in individual employees' desks.
- Look in the center and right top drawers of desks to find unneeded writing supplies.
- Look for disorganized paper piles on desktops. Also look through any cardboard boxes kept under the desk.
- Look around and through lockers, shelves, and cabinets to find unneeded papers, files, and drawings.
- Look for sample goods left in room corners or near desks.

- Look through cabinets, blackboard stands, and other areas in meeting rooms for spare or unneeded goods.
- Look through cabinets and lockers located in office corners.

ORGANIZATION IN THE FACTORY

It takes five "M's" to run a factory: Manpower, Materials, Machines, Methods, and Money.

Organization has long been applied to these essential five factors. However, rationalization and other types of improvement made in manpower, work methods, and investments of money are considered as separate from the 5S's. Therefore, we shall discuss implementing the 5S's with regard to the remaining two factors — materials and machines.

Organization Applied to Inventory

Various terms are used to describe the types of items we find in factories. The names change depending upon where the items are on the continuum that begins with raw materials and ends with finished products. For example, there are raw materials, parts, semifinished goods, subassembly goods, and

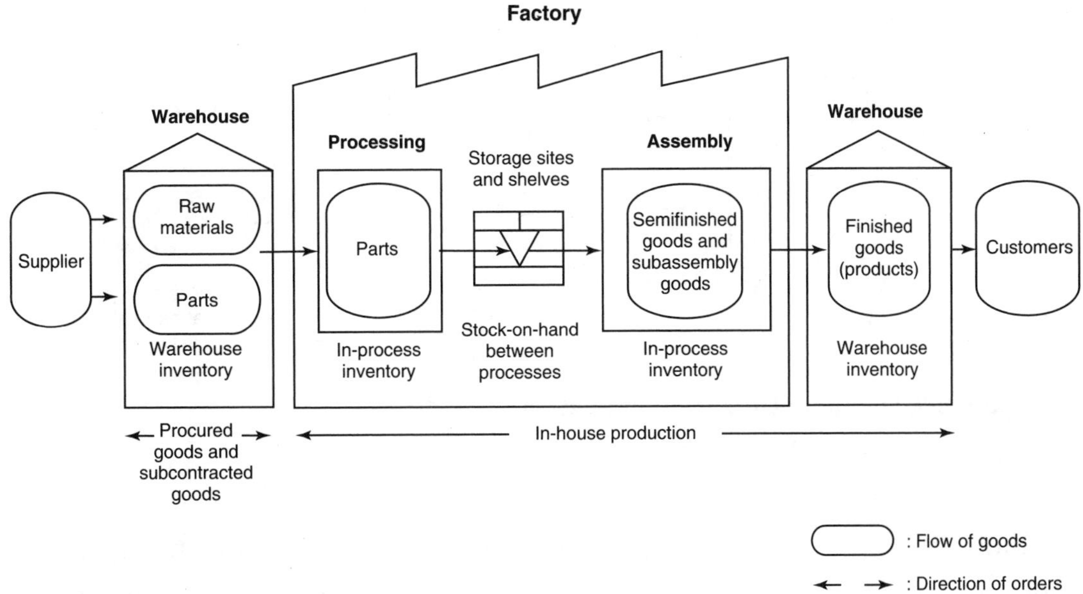

Figure 5-2. Names for Factory Items

finished products. Depending upon the company's ordering system, distinctions may also be made among procured goods, subcontracted goods, and in-house goods. Materials can also change names depending upon their location (for example, warehouse inventory, in-process inventory, and stock-on-hand between processes). (See Figure 5-2.)

The most general term for such items is "inventory," especially when the items are resting in place rather than moving. Obviously, warehouse items are called inventory, but we also refer to items temporarily stored in and between processes as in-process inventory.

Ideally, factories should be able to turn out products in a way that does not require the accumulation of inventory. Many of the improvements made today in work methods and equipment layout are aimed toward this ideal.

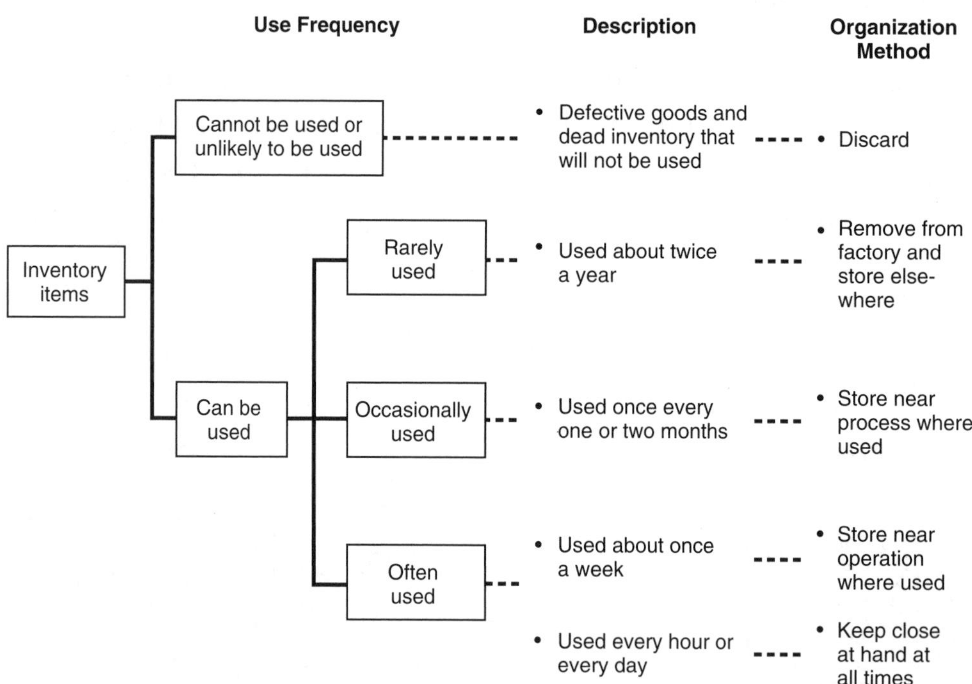

Figure 5-3. Inventory Organization System

However, once a factory accumulates some inventory, it must be organized. Most factories use the system outlined in Figure 5-3 to organize their inventory.

First, we divide inventory items into (1) items that cannot be used and items unlikely to be used and (2) items that can be used.

Items that Cannot Be Used/Items Unlikely to Be Used

These items may include defective goods and inventory rendered "dead" due to design changes. All such items must be discarded.

Items that Can Be Used

Items that can be used are broken down by use frequency into three main categories.

1. **Rarely used items**

   These include seasonal items, special-order items, or items used only once or twice a year. Sometimes called "long-term retained goods," these items should be kept somewhere separate from the production facility where they will be used.

2. **Occasionally used items**

   These items are used once every month or two. They include parts for low-demand products that are still produced on a regular albeit infrequent basis, as well as special-order and other particularly expensive parts. It is best to store these items in an out-of-the-way place (such as a corner) near the process where they will be used.

3. **Frequently used items**

   Within this category, different storage sites should be used depending upon the frequency of use (such as weekly or daily). Items used only once a week should be stored in a storage compartment near the machine or work area where they will be used. Items used every day or every hour should be kept close at hand within the work area.

The most important point in this breakdown of inventory types is to identify and discard all items that either cannot be used or that are unlikely to be used. In this regard, it helps to have a clear-cut and obvious method of item selection. We call this "visual Organization." The primary visual Organization method described in this book is the red-tag strategy. (See Chapter 8.)

Organization Applied to Production Equipment

We apply Organization to machines, tools, jigs, dies, and other factory equipment the same way we apply it to inventory items. However, it can cost a considerable amount of money to relocate or discard large equipment units. Therefore, even though large equipment units clearly may be unneeded, they may have to remain in place until their costs as obstacles and space-takers exceed their disposal costs. In such cases, it is a good idea to clearly label such equipment as "frozen" or "out of commission" so that everyone knows what it is and why it is there.

Another good idea: Always install large equipment units on rollers so that they can later be moved more easily and cheaply.

For production equipment as for inventory items, the recommended visual Organization method is the red-tag strategy, which enables everyone to easily see which equipment units are needed and which are not.

ORGANIZATION IN OFFICES

In Japan, it is safe to say that if a company has a factory with a management division, it also has a head-office division and a sales division. This is the standard organizational format used by nearly every manufacturing company in Japan. The essential operation factors of such companies are summarized in the formula: 3M + 1MS + I [(Manpower/Money/Method) plus (Materials and Services) plus Information].

"Rationalization" is the term generally applied to improvements made in manpower allocation, services, financial investments, and clerical work methods. Here, we shall see how Organization can be used with information.

The kinds of information used in offices include documents, files, books, drawings, reports, and business cards. In the past, virtually all information was on paper ("hard copy"). With the recent computerization trend, however, information is gradually shifting toward other media, such as magnetic tape, magnetic disks, and microfilm.

Whether on paper or computer data-storage media, all information can be described as "records." It used to be that the amount of information in a particular corporate office was small enough for one person to keep organized in his or her head. This method of organizing naturally emphasized frequently used information while it discarded rarely used information.

Today's record-keeping methods lack this self-cleansing tendency. Therefore, unless we organize the information kept on paper and in data-storage devices, it will continue to accumulate indefinitely. This is especially problematic in the current "information explosion" era — when people produce and disseminate vast amounts of information via computers, photocopiers, fax machines, and other office-automation devices.

When dealing with information, the best approach is not to sort out needed information from unneeded information. Instead, find ways to prevent unneeded information from being collected or produced in the first place.

Besides accumulating indefinitely, information also tends to lose its value. In short, yesterday's information may be useless today. Products and parts in factories have also undergone a trend toward shorter marketability periods (or product life cycles) — but the life cycle of information in offices is generally much shorter still.

Figure 5-4 graphs the use frequency of documents stored in a company's clerical division. As shown, documents created over six months ago have a use

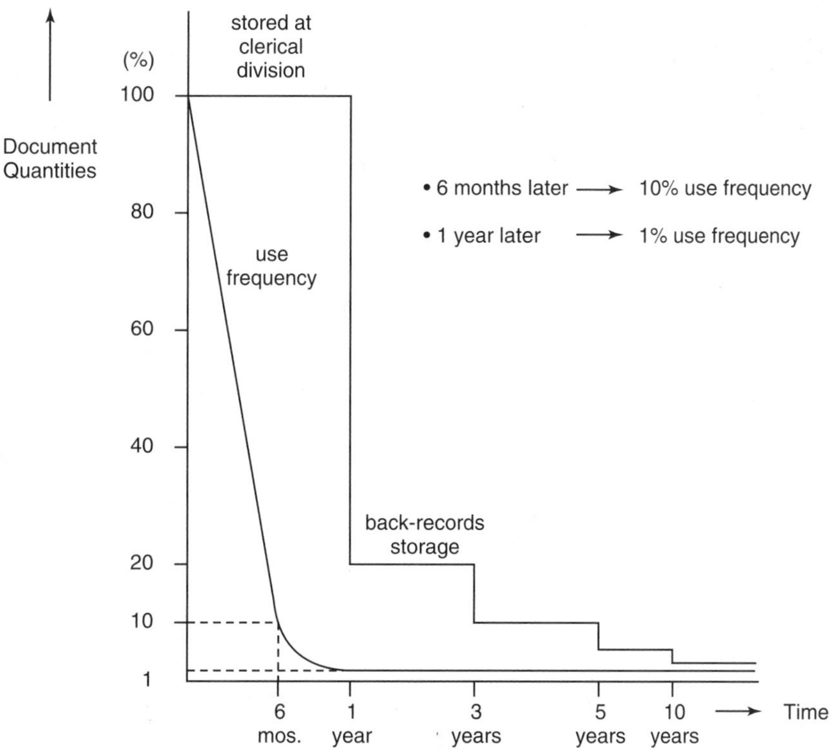

Figure 5-4. Document Usability Trend (Source: NAREMCO)

frequency of only 10 percent and those created over a year ago have a use frequency of only 1 percent.

One year after documents are generated, their use-frequency rate drops to a mere 1 percent. However, as long as they have any use frequency at all, they should be accessible. By throwing out the information, we run a small but significant risk of not having it on hand when it is needed. Therefore, all information is kept available.

The key — and the first priority — is to avoid generating useless information. Next, we need clear criteria by which to judge when to discard a document. When armed with good criteria, we can throw away old documents without worrying that some might be needed again someday.

To get a general idea of how much documentation is expendable, let us look at some statistics from a few major Japanese companies. (See Table 5-1.)

Table 5-1. Examples of Document Discard Rates

Year	Company	No. of employees involved	Discard amount (in tons)	Discard amount per employee (per year) (kg)
1978	TDK	600	100	166
1980	Kawasaki Steel Corp. (head office)	1,600	170	106
1982	Mitsui Engineering & Shipbuilding	1,300	140	106
1983	Taisho Marine & Fire Insurance Co.	1,300	210	161

The amount of documents discarded by a company depends on many factors, including the company's age, the building's age, and the type of business. As a rule of thumb, Japanese companies discard 100 kilograms (220 pounds) of documentation per employee per year. Moreover, statistics have shown that the amount of discarded documentation corresponds to roughly half of that generated. In other words, about twice as many documents are generated each year as get discarded.

Organization for Documents

In addition to a daily routine of Organization for documents, companies should implement special companywide document Organization campaigns about twice a year. Such campaigns should be aimed at minimizing the amount of documents and other written materials kept on hand. Figure 5-5 shows a flow chart for one such campaign, called the "Document Cleanup Campaign."

As noted, we might expect to discard about five out of every ten pages of documents. Of the five pages that are kept, three pages will be transferred to remote storage and the other two will be kept available for use.

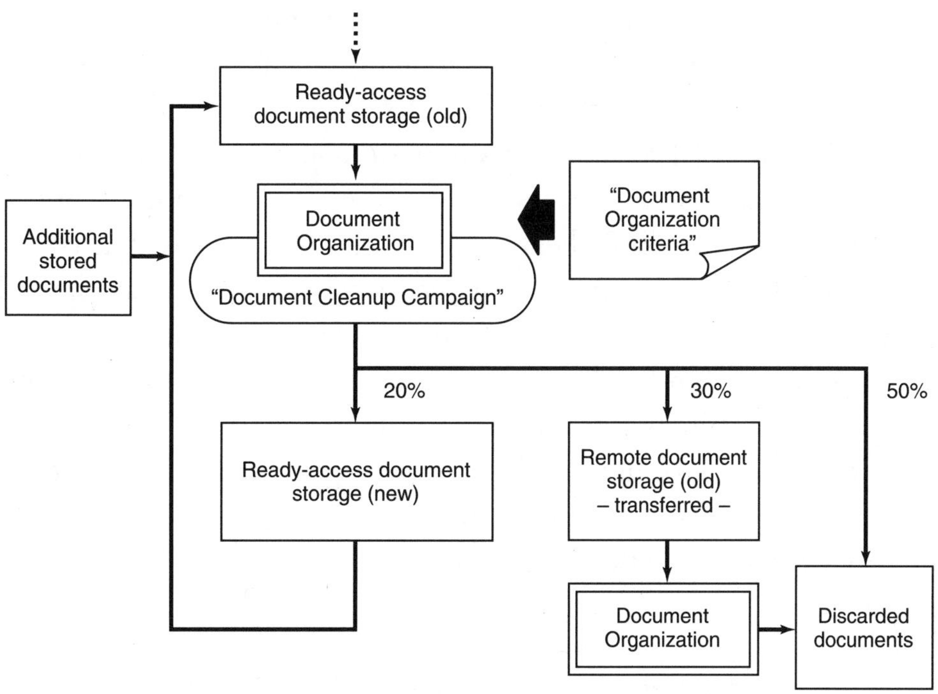

Figure 5-5. Process Flow of Organization for Documents

Obviously, some criteria are needed to determine which documents stay handy, which go to remote storage, and which will be discarded. The criteria for discarding documents must be carefully selected because discarded documents are, by definition, irretrievable. However, the person who knows best whether or not a document should be discarded is usually the person storing it. This makes it difficult to come up with a good companywide set of criteria.

To help determine such criteria, some suggestions can be made. For example, we can ask if this document has been used in the past month? If the answer is no, we would then ask if this document will be needed during the year-end flurry of paperwork. If the answer to this question is still no, we would finally ask if this document is at least two years old. A positive response should be evidence enough that the document in question is no longer needed and can safely be discarded.

It is relatively easy to regulate document Organization based on expected results. In other words, before people are asked to implement Organization for documents, they are told the goal in terms of how many documents each person should have after discarding the unneeded ones. There are various ways to measure quantities of documents (for instance, by number of pages, number of binders, or by stack thickness in inches/feet or centimeters/meters).

In Japan, a stack of 100 standard-size photocopy papers happens to be one centimeter thick, so that a three-centimeter binder can hold up to 300 sheets, a five-centimeter binder 500 sheets, and so on. This means that twenty full five-centimeter binders equals one meter of stacked documentation. If the company's document containers are in standard sizes, documentation can be counted in terms of binders (three or five centimeters), cardboard boxes (45 centimeters), file cabinets (55 and 85 centimeters), and so on. In this way, Japanese companies have figured that the average clerical worker stores from one to one and a half meters of documentation.

The following are some words of advice concerning the transfer of documents from ready-access storage to remote storage.

1. Clearly separate the ready-access storage and remote storage sites.
2. Clearly label all remote-storage documents.
3. Determine storage periods in advance.
4. Have labels on all storage containers describe the contents, the storage period, and the person in charge.
5. Establish and enforce clear rules for remote storage.

Figure 5-6 shows an example of an Organization chart for documents.

Dec. 1, 1994

Organization Chart for Documents

Document Cleanup Campaign Headquarters

It's time for the year-end "Document Organization" campaign. By this, we mean discard unneeded items. To meet our goal, we need everyone to discard whatever they no longer need. (Please submit your completed Document Organization chart by December 20th.)

Goal: 1.3 meters of documents per person

Department			Dept. chief	
No. of persons in dept.			Total meters	
Discarded amount	This campaign: m		Previous campaign: m	
Remote storage amount	This campaign: m		Previous campaign: m	
Ready-access storage amount	This campaign: m		Previous campaign: m	
Description	Open cabinet	85 cm	This campaign: m	Previous campaign: m
	Closed cabinet	55 cm	This campaign: m	Previous campaign: m
	Binder	5 cm	This campaign: m	Previous campaign: m
	Cardboard box	45 cm	This campaign: m	Previous campaign: m
Documents per person = amount of documents / no. of people			m	

• Total/goal comparison: 1. less than goal 2. about the same 3. more than goal

• Measures to be taken:

Figure 5-6. Organization Chart for Documents

Organization for Business Cards

In Japan, where business cards are routinely exchanged whenever business-people first meet, applying Organization to them is an important task. Unfortunately, few people organize their collection of business cards rationally.

In fact, about half of the business cards that people receive are useless from the beginning. They are exchanged merely as a formality with neither party

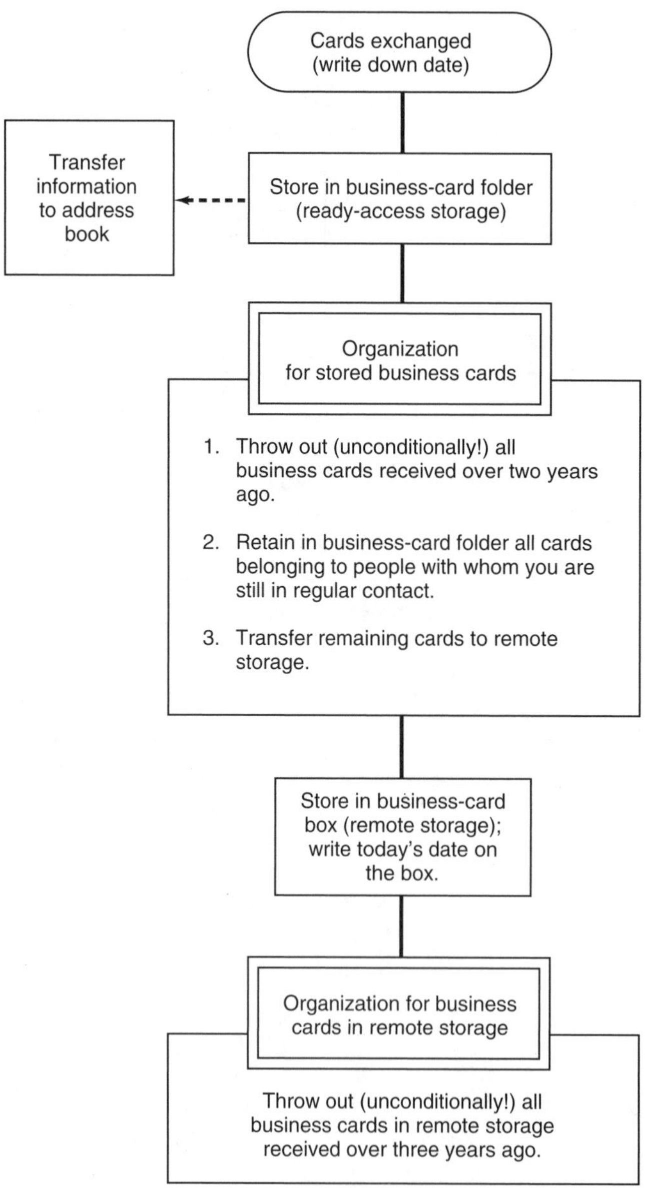

Figure 5-7. Organization for Business Cards

intending to use the card at a later date. Only the most ambitious salespeople manage to follow up on 60 or 70 percent of the business cards they receive.

It pays to apply to business cards the same "ready-access storage" and "remote storage" Organization system that was described previously for organizing documents. It does not take long for a businessperson in Japan to accumulate a fat folder full of business cards. While such folders may function well as souvenir albums of past business meetings, they are hardly practical for daily use.

Figure 5-7 outlines a system for applying Organization to business cards. At the first opportunity after receiving a business card, the recipient should write down the date of the meeting at the top of the card.

If the meeting was a promising one, the business-card recipient later transfers the card's information into a pocket-size address book and then stores the business card in a folder (for ready-access storage).

Implement business-card Organization about once a year. First, throw out all business cards received over two years ago. (The majority of Japanese employees change ranks or even departments within their company in two years' time. And if you have regular contact with someone, you already will have that person's new business card after any such job transfer.)

Next, quickly look over the remaining business cards in the folder. Pull out those belonging to people with whom you still have regular contact. (Remember: These are not cards to be discarded or placed in remote storage, but those needed for ongoing business relationships.)

Now put the extracted cards aside and empty the folder of the remaining cards. Then return the extracted cards to the folder. Gather the remaining cards into a stack and place them into a storage box (for remote storage) and write today's date on the box.

During your annual Organization of business cards, check all of the storage boxes and throw out the contents of any boxes dated over three years ago. Do not worry about whether you may need one of those cards again some day — you already checked the cards and returned important ones to the ready-access folder before transferring cards to the storage boxes.

Organization for Stationery Supplies

Why do stationery supplies tend to accumulate? The answer is simple — because there are desk drawers to hold (and hide) them.

Busy office workers tend to stash pens and other supplies in drawers when they are hastily cleaning up their desks. When they need a pen, they do not always take time to check their desk drawers but instead grab a new one from the supply closet. Before they know it, there are several pens rolling around their desk drawers.

So, what is the best way to prevent such accumulation of stationery supplies? Again, a simple answer — do not put them in desk drawers.

Instead of putting them into drawers, design a desktop sheet of cardboard or thick paper that outlines spaces for all necessary stationery supplies. Such a storage system is faster to use than drawers — we can immediately see what we need and where to return it when we are done. Figure 5-8 illustrates this kind of desktop outline sheet.

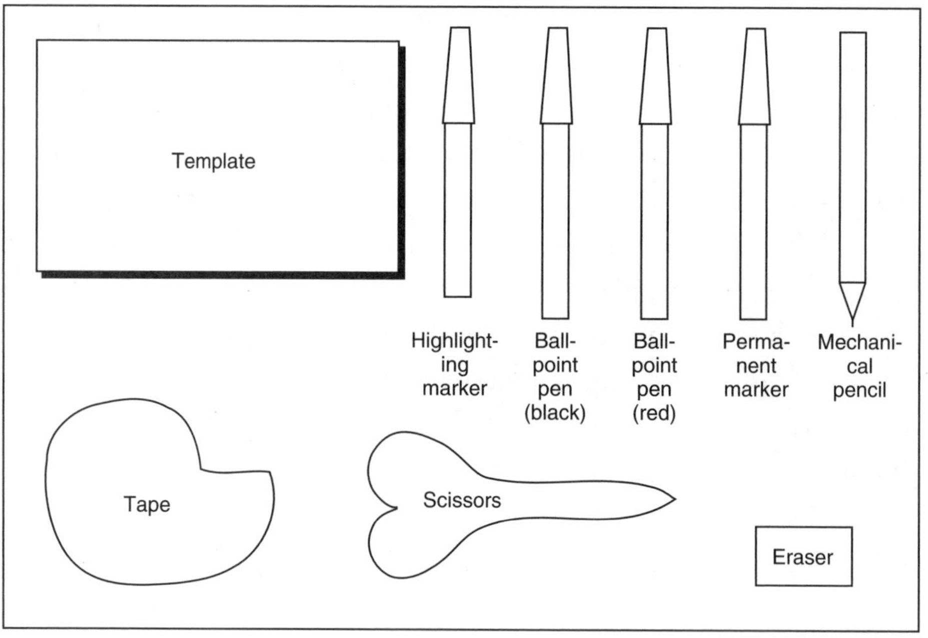

Figure 5-8. Space Outline Sheet for Stationery Supplies

Figure 5-9 shows a flowchart of steps for implementing the Organization of stationery supplies.

First, office workers pick up and fill in an Organization chart for stationery supplies. (See Figure 5-10.) For example, an employee enters the

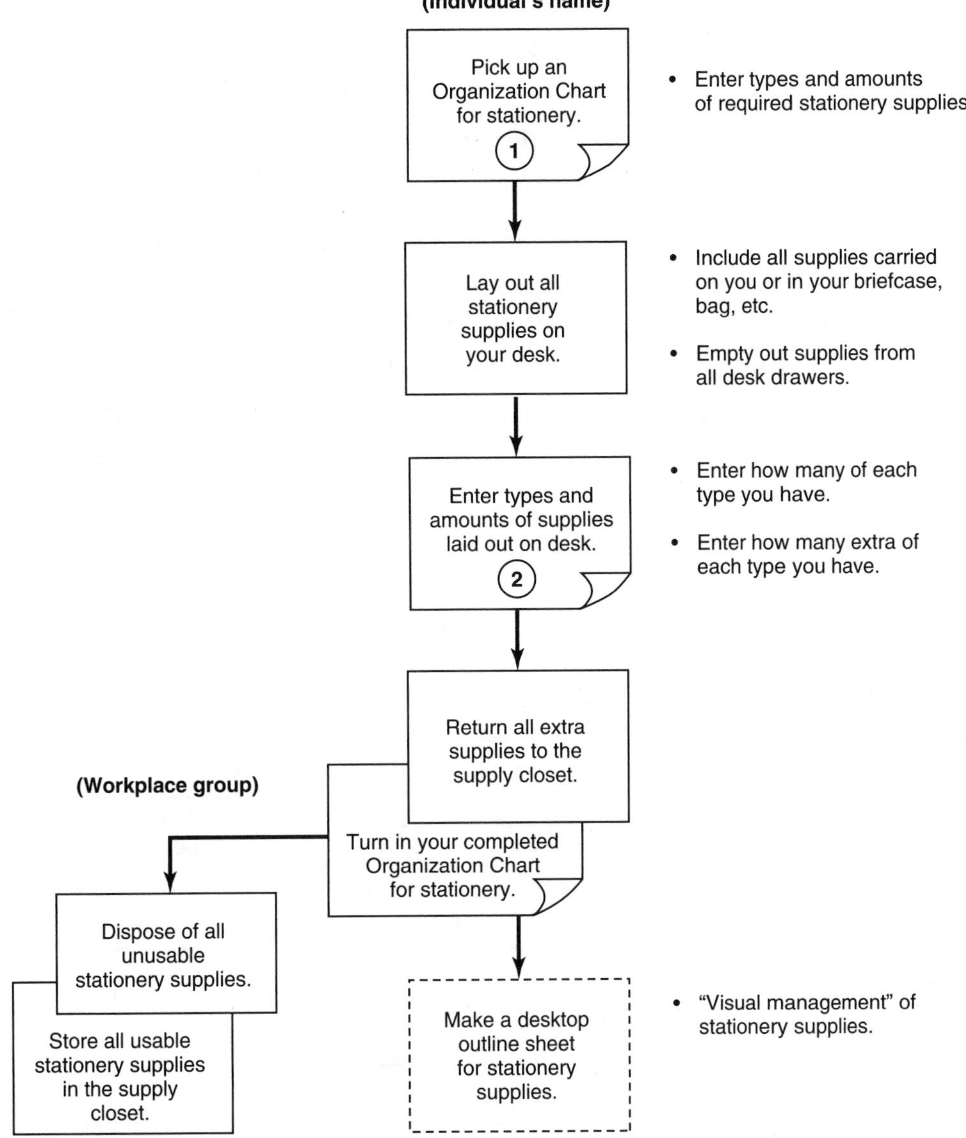
(Individual's name)
Pick up an Organization Chart for stationery.
1
• Enter types and amounts of required stationery supplies.
Lay out all stationery supplies on your desk.
• Include all supplies carried on you or in your briefcase, bag, etc.
• Empty out supplies from all desk drawers.
Enter types and amounts of supplies laid out on desk.
2
• Enter how many of each type you have.
• Enter how many extra of each type you have.
Return all extra supplies to the supply closet.
(Workplace group)
Turn in your completed Organization Chart for stationery.
Dispose of all unusable stationery supplies.
Store all usable stationery supplies in the supply closet.
Make a desktop outline sheet for stationery supplies.
• "Visual management" of stationery supplies.

Figure 5-9. Flowchart of Organization System for Stationery

information asked for on the chart, including the minimum number of each type of stationery item she needs. Next, she would put out on her desk every stationery item in her possession, including those from her jacket pockets, briefcase, and desk drawers. She adds up all of these and enters the totals onto the corresponding spaces on the Organization chart. Then she subtracts the minimum required numbers from these totals to determine how many extra stationery items she has. She returns all extra items to the person in charge of stationery supplies. That person determines which items are still usable and which are not, then stores the former and discards the latter.

Meanwhile, the office worker returns to her desk and sets up a sheet with spaces outlined for all of the minimum required stationery items. Strictly speaking, this sheet is an Orderliness device rather than an Organization device. (Other Orderliness devices will be described in Chapter 6.) Applying this and other "visual management" methods to documents, stationery supplies, and operational procedures is an important part of 5S implementation in offices. This in turn is fundamental to substantial improvement of clerical operations.

<table>
<tr><td rowspan="3">Organization Chart for Stationery</td><td colspan="2">Division:</td><td colspan="2">Manager:</td></tr>
<tr><td colspan="2">Manufacturing management</td><td colspan="2">Sakuma</td></tr>
<tr><td colspan="2">Name: Hoshino</td><td>Date:</td><td>February 1, 1994</td></tr>
<tr><td>Item description</td><td>Minimum amount required</td><td>Current amount</td><td>Amount to be returned</td><td>Comments</td></tr>
<tr><td>1. Pencil</td><td>1</td><td>7</td><td>6</td><td></td></tr>
<tr><td>2. Mechanical pencil</td><td>1</td><td>3</td><td>2</td><td></td></tr>
<tr><td>3. Eraser</td><td>1</td><td>4</td><td>3</td><td></td></tr>
<tr><td>4. Ballpoint pen (black)</td><td>1</td><td>6</td><td>5</td><td></td></tr>
<tr><td>5. Ballpoint pen (red)</td><td>1</td><td>2</td><td>1</td><td></td></tr>
<tr><td>6. Permanent marker (black, thick point)</td><td>1</td><td>3</td><td>2</td><td></td></tr>
<tr><td>7. Permanent marker (black, fine point)</td><td>1</td><td>2</td><td>1</td><td></td></tr>
<tr><td>8. Permanent marker (red, thick point)</td><td>1</td><td>3</td><td>2</td><td></td></tr>
</table>

Figure 5-10. Organization Chart for Stationery

6

The Second Pillar: Orderliness

Orderliness should never be implemented without its partner, Organization. No matter how well you arrange items, Orderliness can have little impact if many of the items are unnecessary. Organization demands boldness and ruthlessness in discarding unneeded items.

Neither of these two pillars amount to much alone. However, when they are combined as the "Organization/Orderliness strategy" their true worth can be realized. This means that Organization and Orderliness should be implemented together.

We can define Orderliness as "arranging needed items so that they are easy to use and labeling them to make their storage sites easily understood by anyone." The key word in this definition is "anyone."

THE NEED FOR ORDERLINESS AND ITS ESSENTIAL POINTS

Once Organization has been implemented in a workplace to clear away the unnecessary items, it is time to begin implementing Orderliness for the remaining items. Each item must be arranged so that anyone can see where it is kept, can easily pick it up, use it, and return it to its proper place. In other words, Orderliness designs production or clerical activities in a way that minimizes waste. This includes "searching waste," "waste due to difficulty in using items," and "waste due to difficulty in returning items."

Both factories and offices have more than their share of "searching" work. For example, it is not unusual for a three-hour changeover routine to include 30 minutes of searching. This might include a whole parade of searches — for a forklift, for a monkey wrench, for a backplate, for a hex wrench, for a cart, and for a die. When attempting to radically reduce changeover time (for example, from three hours to just ten minutes), there is clearly no room for 30 minutes of searching waste.

The following are some problems we can expect to find in factories or offices where Orderliness is not implemented thoroughly.

1. Only the parts supply clerk understands where certain materials and parts are kept. (See Photo 6-1.)
2. Only the person who regularly performs the changeover operation knows where to find the tools and jigs needed for that operation.
3. No one knows where to find the die needed for the next product.
4. No one knows what happened to the screwdriver used in an assembly operation.
5. The person sent to get a cart could not find it.
6. Someone finally found the wrench underneath a machine.
7. No one can find the key to the locked cabinet containing needed tools.
8. No one knows where to find some needed documents.
9. Someone gives up on finding a needed template after looking in vain for half an hour. (See Photo 6-2.)
10. Some desk drawers are crammed full of pencils, markers, erasers, and other stationery supplies.
11. Brooms are found leaning against machines and walls.
12. Some document files are not labeled.
13. Things are left protruding into walkways, causing someone to trip and get injured. (See Photo 6-3.)
14. Someone gets hurt when standing in front of a door that is hastily opened from the other side.
15. The storage site of certain parts has been switched since yesterday, but the operator does not notice and picks up the wrong part.

Photo 6-1. Disorderly Parts Storage Space

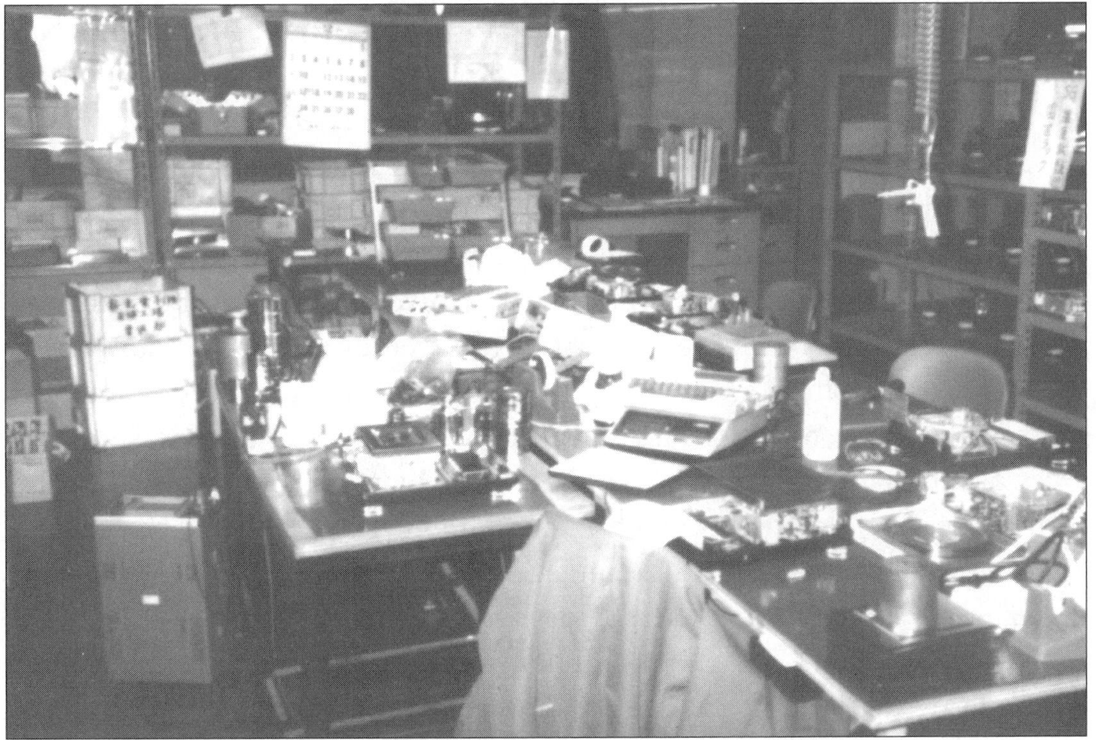

Photo 6-2. Messy Desks and Shelves

Photo 6-3. Disorderly Piles Line the Wall

Orderliness Means Standardization

Standardization is indeed an important theme for factories and offices.

How much can we expect from a workshop where only operator A knows how to operate machine A and only operator B can operate machine B? Not much. By contrast, can we reasonably expect more from a workshop where any operator — even one newly trained — can operate the machinery? Yes, we can, and the reason is called "machine standardization."

When specific people are needed for specific operations, how can a factory or office hope to expand its range of operations? When anyone, veteran or rookie, can readily take over operations from anyone else, then the factory or office has room for expansion. We call this "operation standardization."

Factories and offices are full of things needing standardization (for example: machinery, operations, clerical tasks, managerial tasks, vouchers, slips, and other types of information). To get along together, people even need to standardize their behavior — although a certain amount of individuality should be retained.

Among all of these types of standardization, Orderliness is the most fundamental — standardizing where things are kept. (See Figure 6-1.)

When we think "standardization," we should also think "anyone." Machinery standardization means anyone can operate the machinery. Operation standardization means anyone can perform the operation.

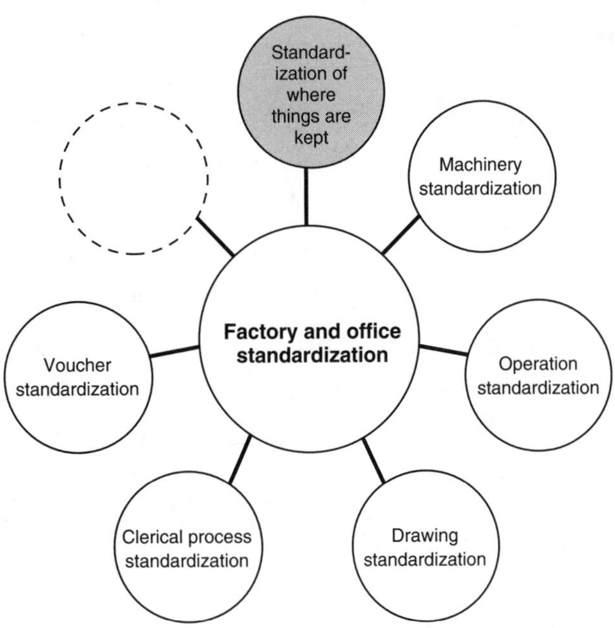

Figure 6-1. Orderliness Related to Various Standardizations

In this context, we think of Orderliness — the foundation of standardization — as arranging things so that anyone can understand where an item is kept, can easily and quickly pick it up and use it, and can easily and quickly return it to its proper place.

Understanding where things are kept (meaning "at a glance") brings us to the concept of visual control. In Chapter 9 we will examine the "signboard strategy," a principle tool for visual Orderliness in which anyone can see at a glance where things are kept.

When we take standardization to the point where it becomes a form of visual control, there is only one place to put each item and we can tell right away whether a particular operation is proceeding normally or abnormally. For instance, when there is only supposed to be one workpiece stored between processes, there should be a sign at the storage site saying "one-piece storage." If we happen to see two or three pieces stored there, one glance at the sign tells us that something is wrong. Usually, we can trace the problem to its source, which could be a missing part, a defective product, or a machine breakdown. Once we identify the problem, write it down on a chart, and immediately make a corrective improvement, we are practicing visual Orderliness (or visual control). And it is hard to overstate its importance.

ORDERLINESS IN THE FACTORY

The conditions for Orderliness incorporate three basic elements: what, where, and how many. Signs and labels should clearly display information on all three elements so that we can see what types of items should be kept there, exactly where they should be kept, and how many of them there should be. Signboards are one type of sign used for this purpose. Indeed, the signboard strategy is a key method in this connection that we shall examine later. For now, let us consider other types of Orderliness methods.

Please refer now to Table 6-1, which lists typical targets for Orderliness.

Table 6-1. Orderliness Targets

Category	Orderliness Target
Spaces	Floors, walkways, operation areas, walls, shelves, warehouses
Products	Raw materials, procured parts, parts for machining, in-process inventory, assembly parts, semi-finished products, finished products
Equipment	Machines, equipment, jigs, tools, cutting bits, gauges, dies, carts, conveyance tools, work tables, cabinets, chairs

Painting Strategy

5S implementation usually begins with the red-tag strategy (described in Chapter 8). The red-tag strategy is a method for removing all unneeded items from the workplace, leaving only what is truly needed for current operations. Later the signboard strategy is implemented as a method for clearly displaying where to keep these needed items.

The painting strategy is another method that can be implemented for floors and walkways at about the same time as the signboard strategy. (See Figure 6-2.)

Divider Lines

The first step in the painting strategy is to mark off the factory's walking areas ("walkways") from its working areas ("operation areas"). We put down divider lines to mark off these areas.

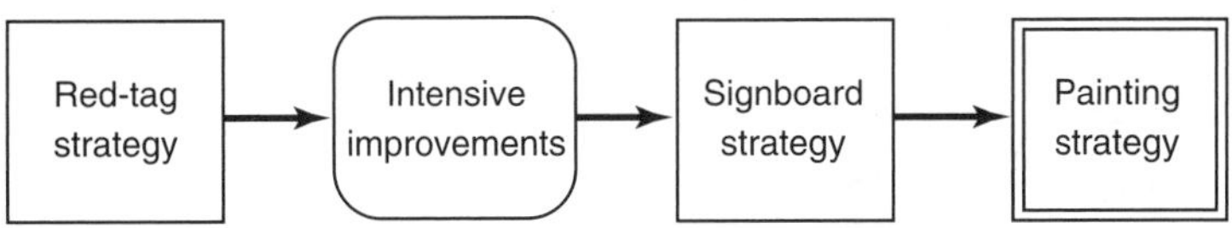

Figure 6-2. Steps before the Painting Strategy

First, we should put down divider lines that mark off walkways and operation areas. Before that, however, we must determine the exact size and location of the operation areas, while being sure to leave enough space for the walkways. (See Photo 6-4.)

Photo 6-4. Divider Lines for Walkway and Operation Areas

When mapping out the operation areas, we should keep in mind certain factors. One is the greater operability afforded by U-shaped cell designs (a flow-production equipment layout method in which processes are grouped into U-shaped cells). Another factor is the efficient positioning of in-process inventory. Key considerations when mapping out walkways are safety and ensuring a smooth flow of goods.

I have seen many factories with floors that are bumpy or full of holes. When possible, it is a good idea to invest in repairs to level out such floor surfaces.

Walkway layout is partly determined by the operating area layout. Given this restriction we should still strive to avoid having a lot of twists and turns in the walkways. (See Figure 6-3.) The more twists and turns you have, the greater the risk of collisions and other accidents. This is particularly true when forklifts are driven in the factory — a potential hazard that requires great care in route layout.

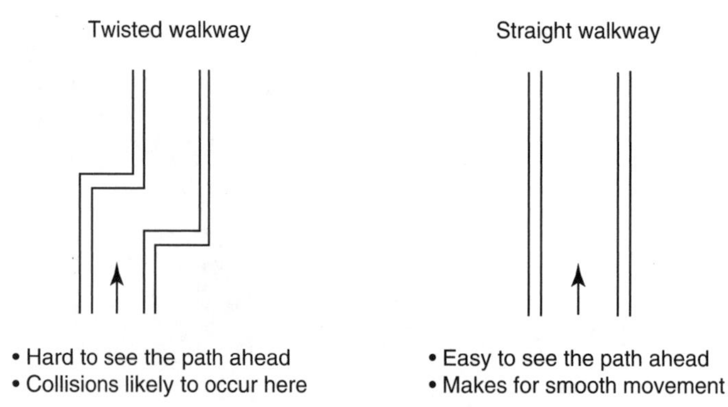

Figure 6-3. Good and Bad Walkway Layouts

This we call the "painting strategy" because paint is the material generally used for the divider lines. However, acrylic sheets are the material of choice for some factories because they can be bought in large sheets, cut into strips of any width, show up as clearly as paint does, tend not to peel off like tape does, and are easy to clean. Were it not for their relatively high cost, acrylic sheets would probably be used more.

As for colors, it is best to use bright ones that show up clearly even in poorly lit areas. For example:

- operation areas: green
- walkways: fluorescent orange
- divider lines: yellow

Many factories use white for divider lines. However, this lacks distinctiveness when white is also being used to mark off storage sites for in-process inventory, worktable sites, and corners. I suggest using yellow for general divider lines.

These divider lines should be between 5 and 10 centimeters wide. Three centimeters wide is not visible enough and 15 centimeters wide is a waste of space. The most common width is 7 centimeters.

In factories where many small items are being handled (i.e., the semiconductor industry), common divider line widths are 5 and 7 centimeters. By contrast, in large outdoor work areas (i.e., construction sites with heavy machinery) 10-centimeter divider lines are often used to mark off operation areas for cranes or other large machines.

Table 6-2. Divider Lines Used in Painting Strategy

Category	Subcategory	Color	Width	Comments
Floors	Operation area	Green		
	Walkway	Orange		Fluorescent orange
	Rest area	Blue		
Lines	Area divider lines	Yellow	10 cm	Solid line
	Entrance and exit lines	Yellow	10 cm	Broken line
	Door-range lines	Yellow	10 cm	Broken line
	Direction lines	Yellow		Arrow
	Place markers (for in-process inventory)	White	5 cm	Solid line
	Place markers (for operations)	White	5 cm	Corner lines
	Place markers (for ashtrays, etc.)	White	3 cm	Broken line
	Place markers (for defective goods)	Red	3 cm	Solid line

Divider lines can make the difference between life and death in factories that use large, potentially hazardous machinery. In such factories, I heartily recommend frequent "Don't Cross the Line" campaigns.

Table 6-2 lists the types of divider lines used at one factory. Each factory should determine a system of divider lines to suit its particular needs.

Door-range Lines and Aisle-direction Lines

Nearly everyone at some time has been bumped by a door being opened. Putting down door-range lines, like the one shown in Photo 6-5, is a good way to prevent such an accident.

Photo 6-6 shows how lines can be used to mark aisle directions.

Place Markers for In-process Inventory, Etc.

After putting down divider lines between walkways and operation areas, we can start putting down lines in the operation area to mark places for certain items, such as in-process inventory and carts. These lines can outline the entire item or just mark the item's corners. (See Photo 6-7.) Because place markers for

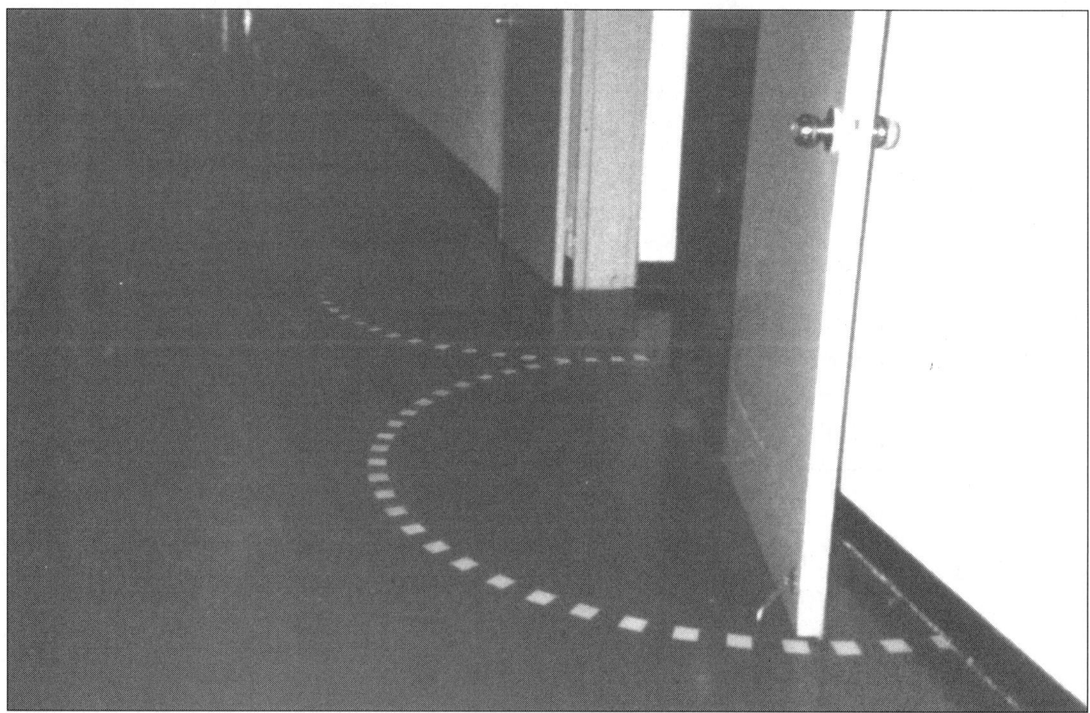

Photo 6-5. Door-range Line

Photo 6-6. Aisle-direction Line

Photo 6-7. Corner Lines for In-process Inventory

Photo 6-8. Place Markers for Cart Storage Area

Photo 6-9. Place Markers for Worktables

in-process inventory tend to change frequently as improvements are made, it is best to mark these places with an inexpensive material that is easy to remove.

A good idea for cart storage is to mark each cart with a number. Then mark its storage space with the same number in a way that makes it easy to see if the carts are parked correctly. (See Photo 6-8.)

Place markers are useful for more than on-site storage. For example, as we see in Photo 6-9, worktables can benefit from having place markers. Specifically, one could have a place marker for items to be worked on, another place marker for finished items, and place markers that show where to keep tools.

Tiger Marks

Accidents can occur easily in factories when someone inadvertently allows equipment to cross over operation area lines and protrude into walkways. These events pose serious safety hazards. Figure 6-4 shows how

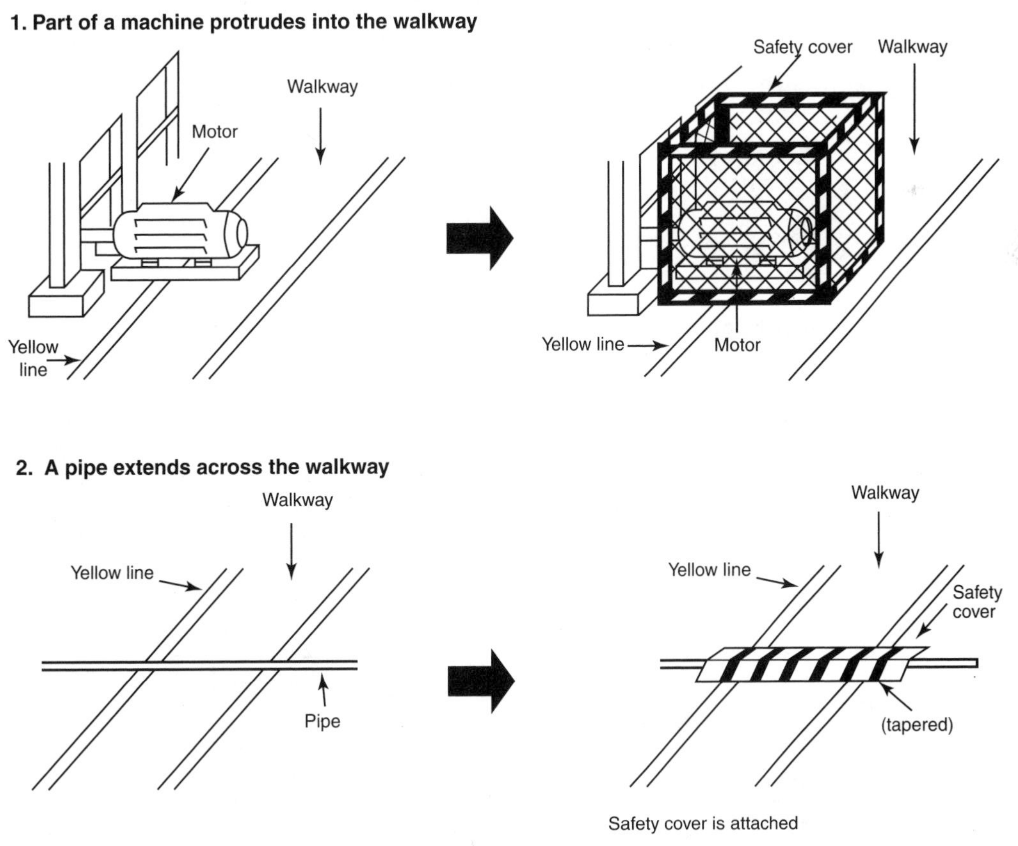

Figure 6-4. Tiger Marks

"tiger marks" (yellow-and-black striped lines) can be used to help prevent such accidents.

Obviously, the most effective preventive measure is to make it impossible for equipment to protrude into walkways. When such protrusions cannot be avoided, however, tiger marks are an extra safety assurance.

Orderliness in the Warehouse

While signboards are a primary tool for Orderliness in warehouses, several other techniques deserve consideration.

First In, First Out (FIFO)

In many factories inventory stacks up all over the place. The worst way to stack inventory, as we see in Figure 6-5, is to stack different types of items on top of each other. If you need something from the bottom of the stack, you must first move everything on top of it. This situation creates a lot of waste.

However, as the figure shows, even having stacks of the same type of items can pose problems. They are not easy to move and, more important, the first item stacked will not the first one removed.

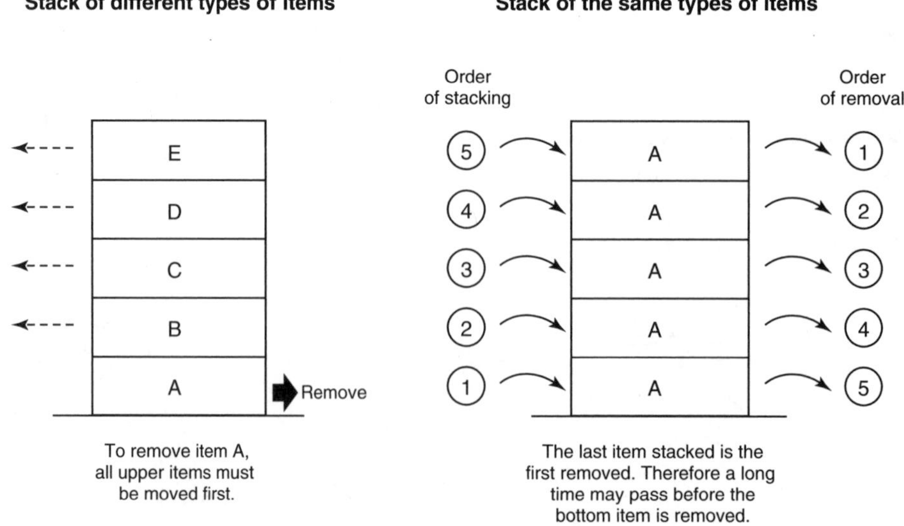

Figure 6-5. Stacked Inventory Items

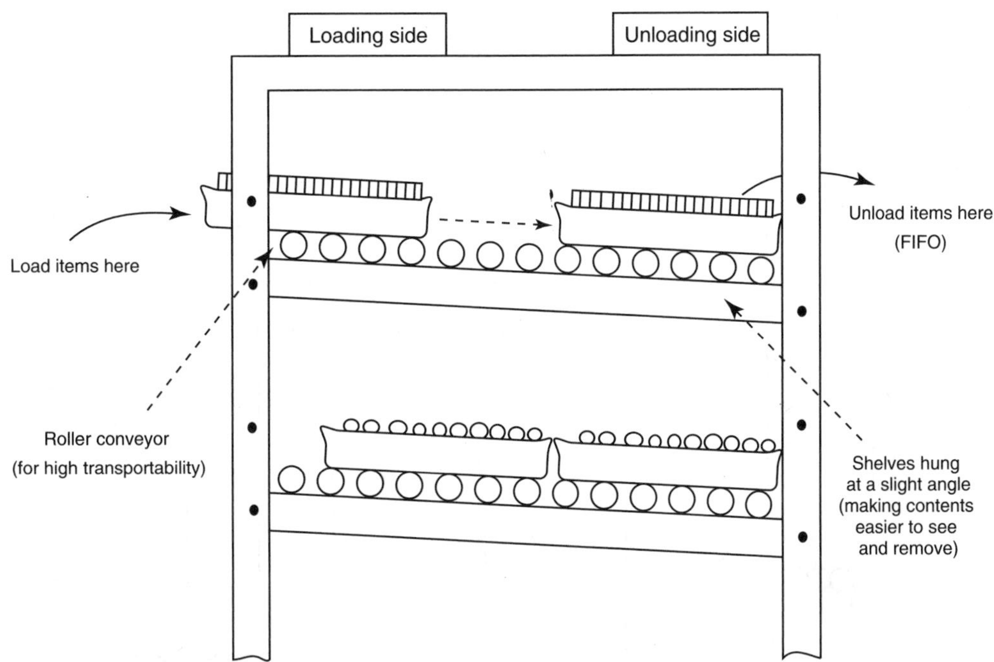

Figure 6-6. Inventory Storage Shelves Using FIFO Method

What we find in Figure 6-5 is called "last in, first out" (LIFO). Figure 6-6 illustrates the "first in, first out" (FIFO) method applied to shelved inventory items. Using FIFO rather than LIFO helps to prevent rust and other age-related deterioration from turning inventory items into defective goods.

Efficient Use of Conveyors

Whether we call it "inventory" or "in-process inventory," the fact is that these items are at rest in some part of the factory. We call this condition "retention." If an item is retained, it must be moved later — and its conveyance is a form of waste. Obviously, it would be best to eliminate all conveyance of retained goods. When this is not possible, the next best thing is to make inventory, in-process inventory, and other retained items as easy to convey as possible.

Figure 6-7 presents a "conveyance readiness index" that compares the conveyance readiness of items retained using various storage methods.

Stacking items on the floor has the lowest conveyance readiness index value of 0. This is because prior to being moved these items must be loaded

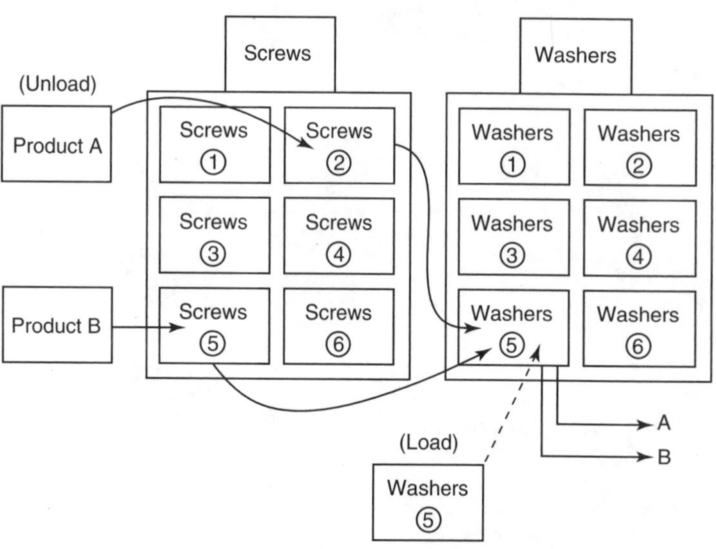

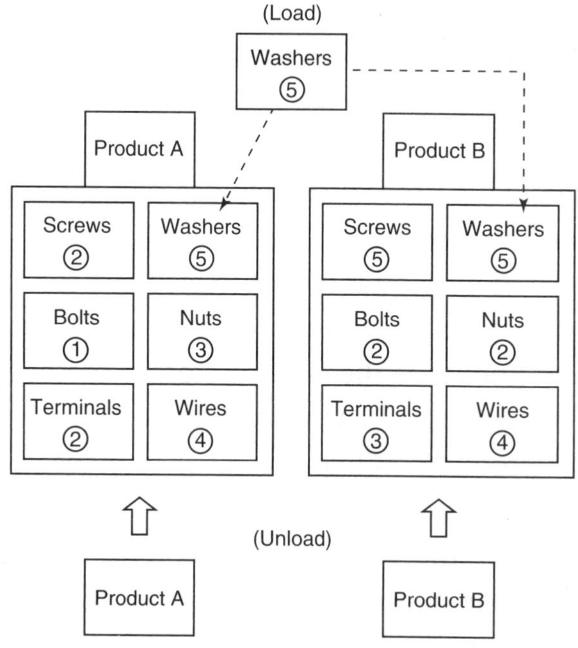

Figure 6-8. Function-based Method and Product-based Method

ments of parts. "Marshaling" is the term used to describe the supply of ready-made "parts kits" for specific products. Usually, marshaling is done at the start of assembly lines, where trays of marshaled parts are fed one at a time to the line as we see in Figure 6-9.

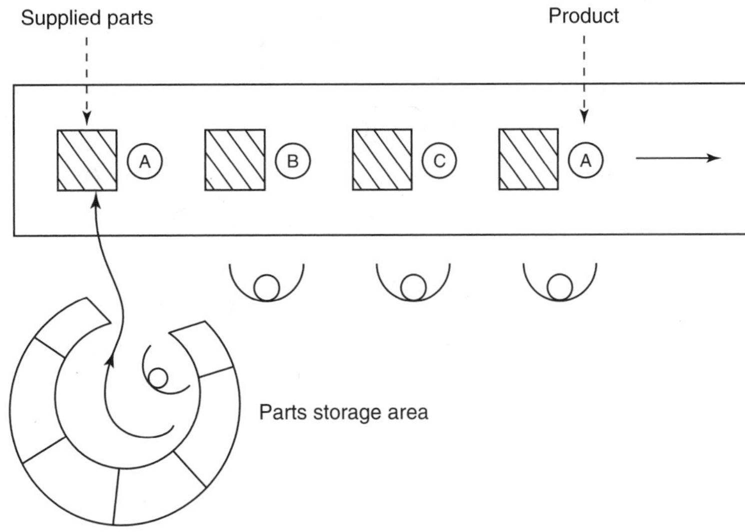

Figure 6-9. Marshaling

Marshaling has two advantages:

1. It reduces reaching motion in assembly work.
2. It reduces defects that stem from the use of missing, defective, or incorrect parts.

However, it has the disadvantage of requiring an additional sorting operation sometime between the time the supplier manufactures the parts and the assembly worker receives them.

Orderliness for Jigs and Tools

Jigs, tools, dies, and the like differ in character from materials and parts in that these items must be put back where they came from after each use.

We know that materials and parts are picked up from somewhere, used to make a product, and then packaged and shipped off as part of the product. In contrast, jigs and tools are picked up, used, and then put back for later use. This makes a big difference when we compare jig-and-tool storage with part-and-material (inventory) storage.

We can greatly reduce the frequency with which shop supervisors and production managers throw up their arms and yell "this place is a mess" by making it easier to return jigs and tools to their proper places after each use.

I am not ignoring the importance of making jigs and tools easy to use. However, I wish to stress that it is equally important to make jigs and tools easy to put back after use. In terms of Orderliness, the proper replacement of jigs and tools concerns us most.

We can distinguish among several stages (or degrees) in which Orderliness for jigs and tools is easily disrupted. We can call this concept "stages in the development of Orderliness for jigs and tools" as shown in Figure 6-10.

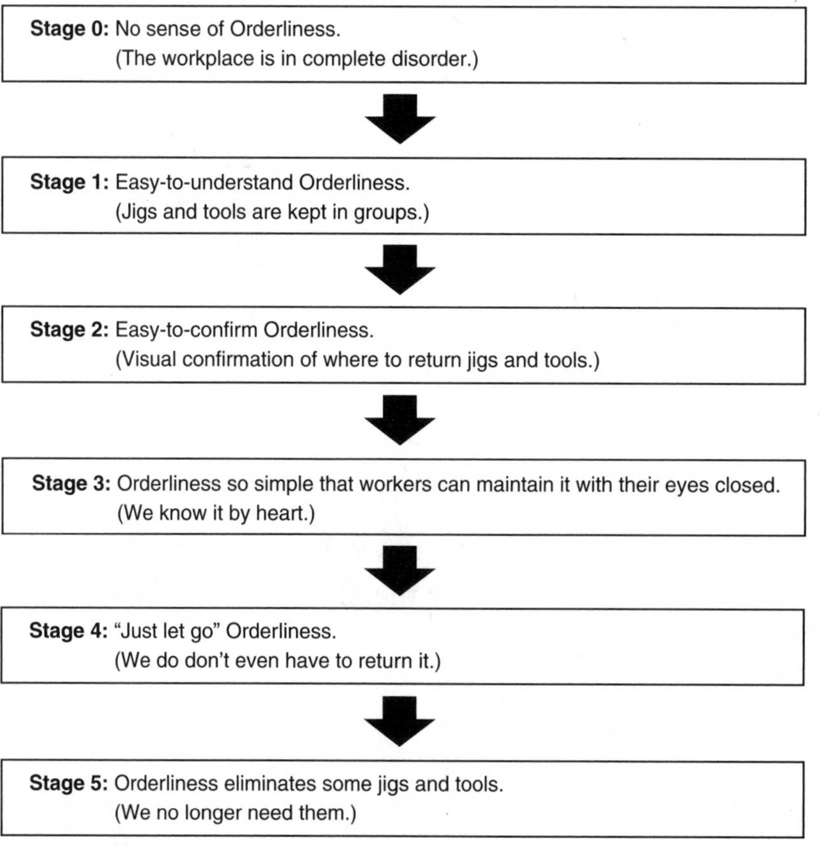

Figure 6-10. Stages in Development of Orderliness for Jigs and Tools

Stage 0: No Sense of Orderliness (Complete Disorder)

The staff in this workshop has not considered the value of making it easier to put things back. When they need a jig or tool, they search for it. When they are finished with it, they put it down anywhere. At some workshops like this, operators dislike sharing and even have their own sets of tools.

Stage 1: Jigs and Tools Are Kept in Groups (Easy-to-Understand Orderliness)

In this workshop, jigs, tools, cutting bits, rags, and even parts are all kept in the same general area. This way, whenever workers need something, they at least know where to start searching. Eventually, the workshop staff tires of this situation and decides to keep the tools in one place, the jigs in another, and so on. This makes it slightly easier to pick up and return items. (See Photo 6-11.)

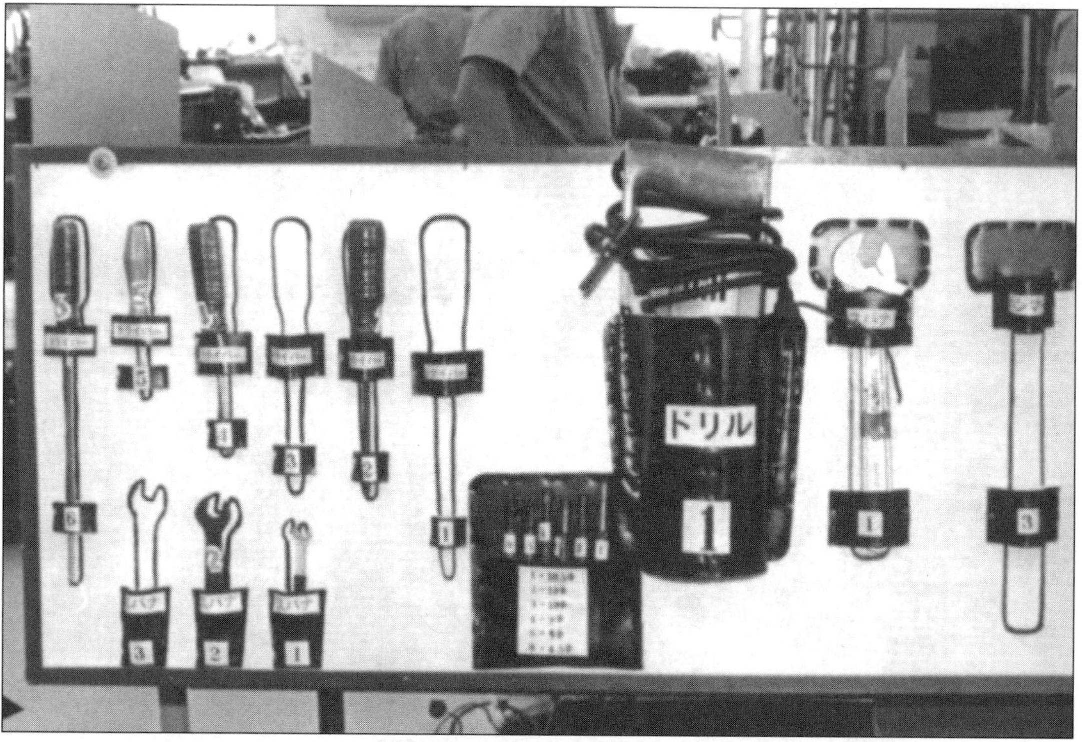

Photo 6-11. Tools Stored in Groups (Stage 1) with Outlines (Stage 2)

Stage 2: Visual (Easy-to-Confirm) Orderliness of Where to Return Jigs and Tools

At this stage, the workshop staff seeks visual confirmation of where to return jigs and tools after using them. In this case, they have chosen the following methods for doing this.

- **Signboards**

  Signboards show what goes where in a way that anyone can understand. Here, the "what" is the tool or jig to be put back and the "where" is the location of the storage site. (See Photo 6-12 and Figure 6-11.)

- **Color-coding Orderliness**

  Color-coding can be used to show clearly which jigs and tools are to be used for which purpose. We call this "color-coding Orderliness." For example, if different jigs and tools are used for different machines, we can assign a different color to each machine and then match the machine colors with color labels on the corresponding jigs and tools. (See Figure 6-12.)

Photo 6-12. Signboard for Parts Storage

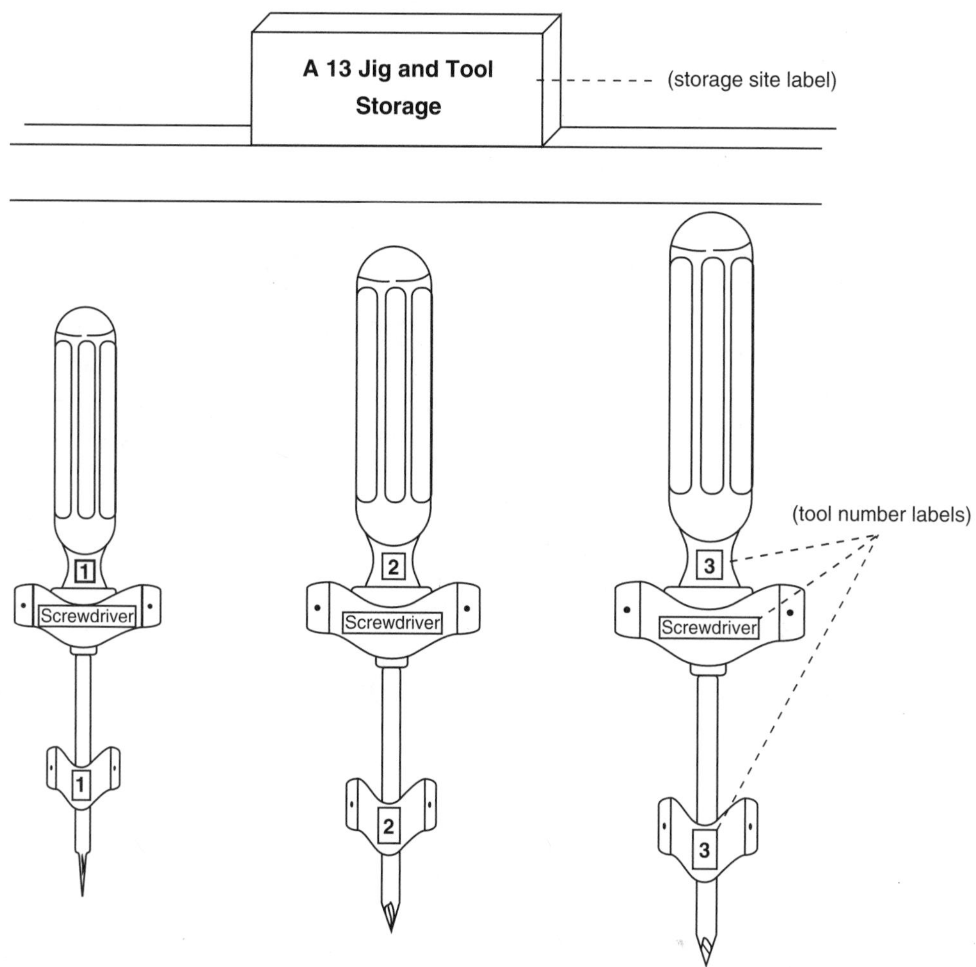

Figure 6-11. Signboard for Tools and Jigs

• Outlining Orderliness

If it is unclear where to return certain jigs or tools, we cannot expect Orderliness to be maintained for long. Outlining is a good way to show at a glance exactly what goes where. Outlining simply means drawing outlines of jigs and tools in their proper storage positions. For example, when you want to return a tool, the outline provides an additional indication of where it belongs. (See Photo 6-11.)

In some restaurants, I have seen place mats for children that outline the plate, fork, spoon, and knife to show where each properly belongs. Outlining tool storage sites applies this same idea.

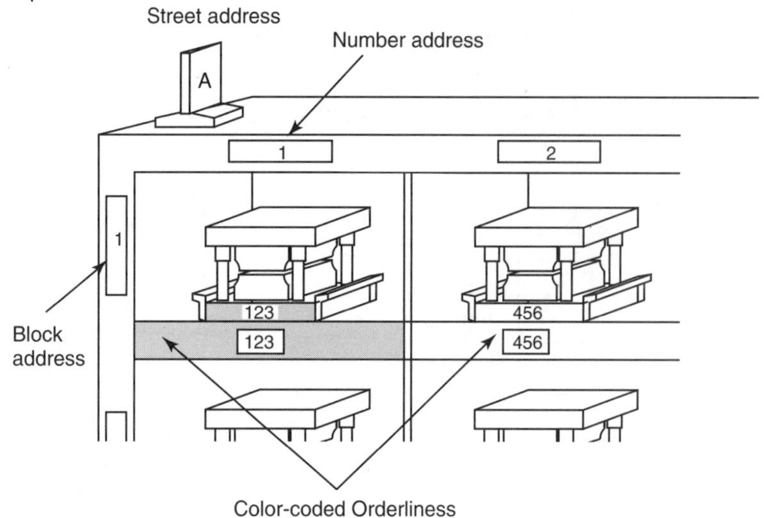

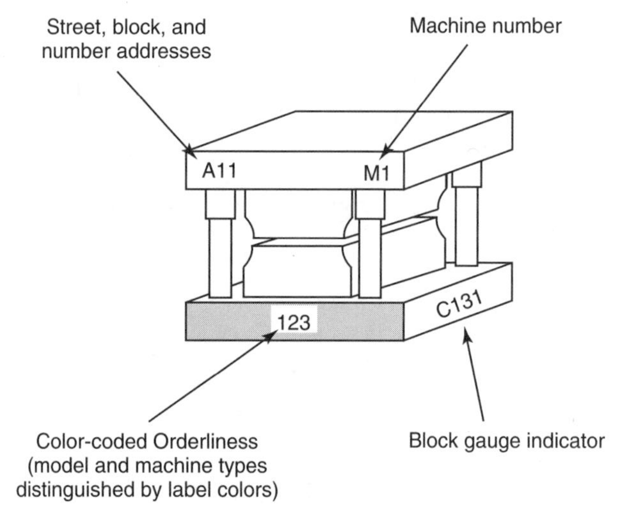

Figure 6-12. Color-coded Orderliness for Dies and Die Storage

Stage 3: Orderliness So Simple that Workers Know It by Heart

The lazy part of us would prefer to just set down a tool without having to visually find and check its proper storage site. Hence, the following method:

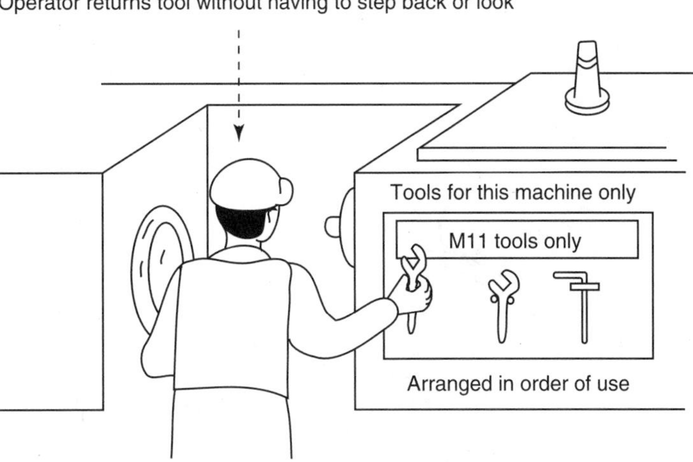

Fig. 6-13. Tools Kept Close at Hand

- **Keep storage sites for jigs and tools as close as possible to their places of use**

It is more difficult to learn tool storage sites by heart if jigs and tools are kept some distance away from where they are used. In fact, when possible keep them close to their place of use and stored in a manner that enables users to put them back correctly without even having to look. This is especially true for jigs and tools used in changeover operations.

If several tools are used in a changeover operation, store them in the same sequence as they are used. (See Figure 6-13.) This is an example of how the 5S's can make all the difference in achieving single-minute exchange of die (SMED).

- **Make the receiving hole bigger**

In Orderliness we encounter the same problems that face someone trying to thread a needle. The main difficulty is the smallness of the hole. If it were larger, putting a thread through it would be easy.

Consider another example. What happens when we try to pour salad oil from one long-neck bottle into another, as shown in Figure 6-14? Most of us know that to avoid a mess we need to make the receiving hole bigger. To do this, we use a funnel.

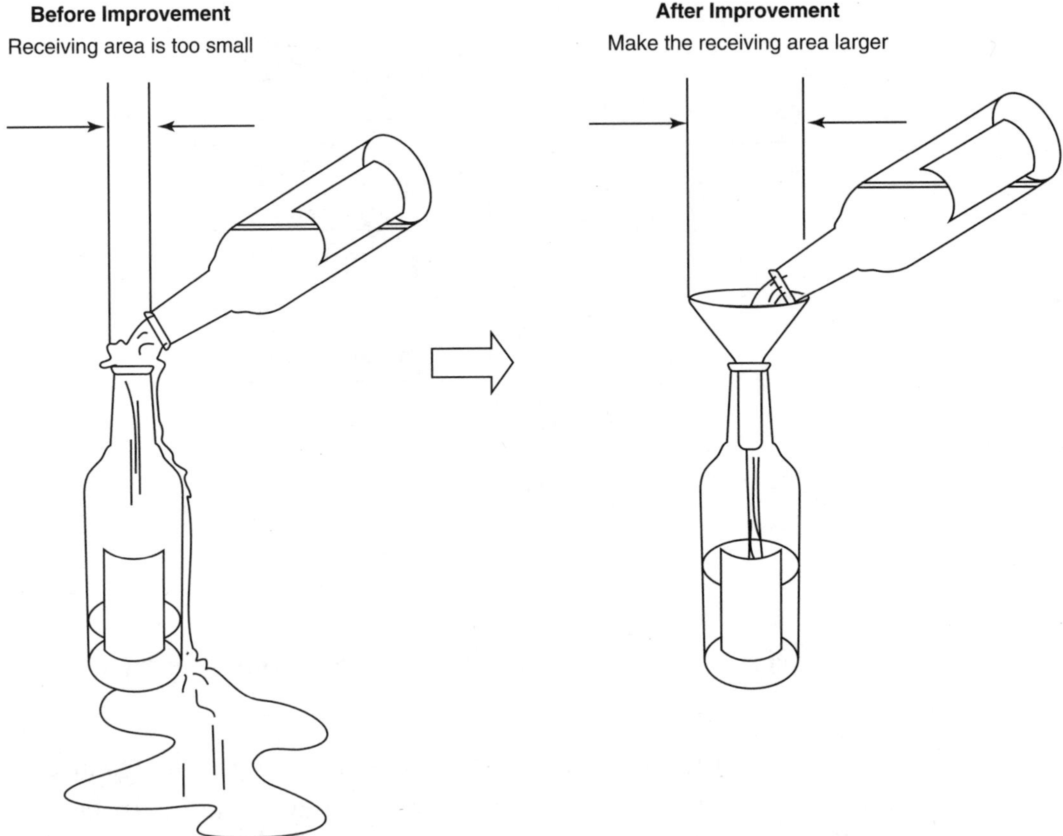

Figure 6-14. Fix This Mess

There is no reason not to apply such kitchen wisdom to the workplace. Figure 6-15 shows how Orderliness can be applied to the storage of brooms and mallets. Here, we see four steps in Orderliness implementation. Each step makes the "hole" (or device) for holding the tool bigger and easier to use, requiring less attention. Again, the easier it is to replace things, the easier it becomes to maintain Orderliness.

Stage 4: "Just Let Go" Orderliness (We Don't Even Have to Return It)

In some workshops, when operators finish, they simply let go of their tools. This method is taken from our daily lives. In Japan, where small fish-markets and greengrocers are still in abundance, some merchants keep their

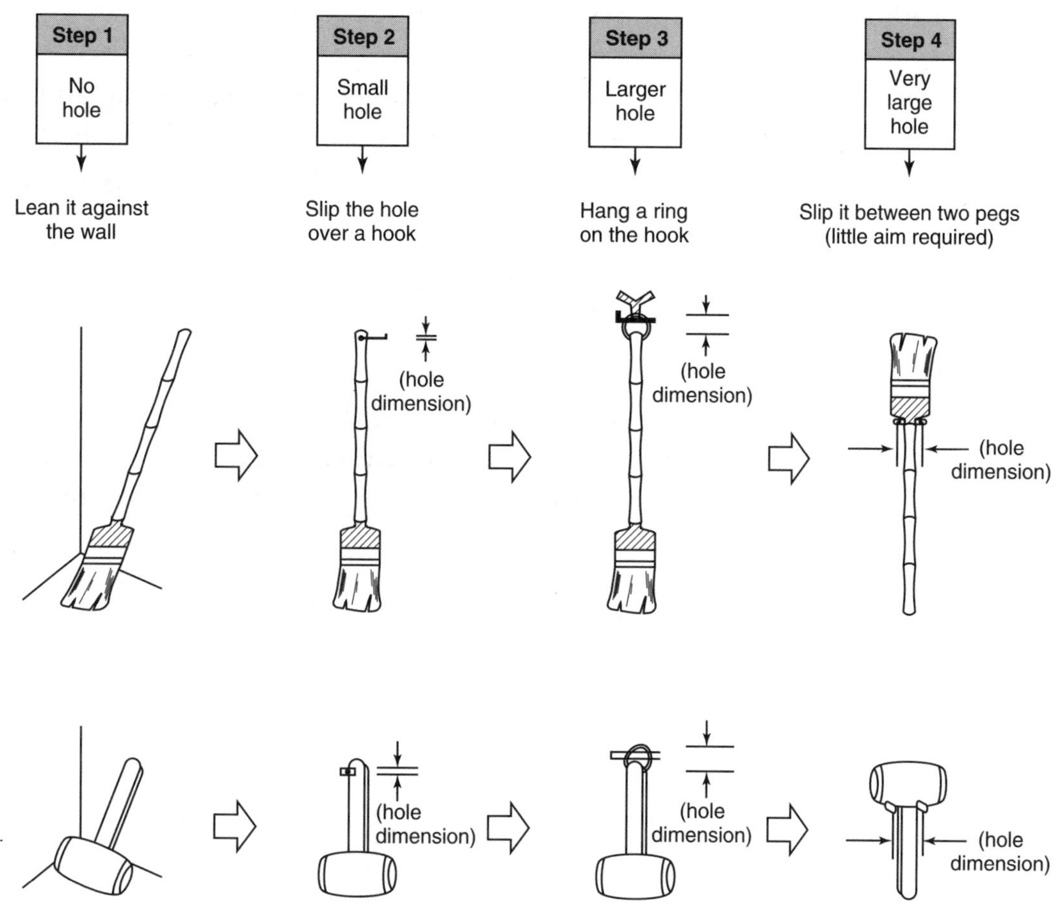

Figure 6-15. Implementing Orderliness for Brooms and Mallets

money buckets on an elastic cord suspended from the ceiling. When they receive money from a customer, they reach up for their buckets, put in the money, retrieve any required change, and then release them. The buckets instantly spring back to their former positions. No one has to think about it.

We find this idea often used in assembly lines; for example, in an automobile assembly line in which tools are suspended overhead like the money buckets. Consumer electronic product assembly plants often suspend electric screwdrivers in this manner.

Generally, this "just let go" Orderliness requires some kind of balance or suspension device to keep the tools as close as possible to their place of use.

Stage 5: Orderliness that Eliminates the Need for a Jig or Tool

People are never satisfied. After all, what is easier than just letting go of a tool after using it, knowing it will be there when you next reach for it? The only thing simpler would be to somehow eliminate the need for the tool in the first place.

- **Unification of tools**

  We can reduce the number of jigs and tools needed by eliminating tool variety (in other words, by unifying the tools). Figure 6-16 shows an improvement that reduces two pneumatic (or electric) tools to one. Obviously, the key to tool unification is design unification.

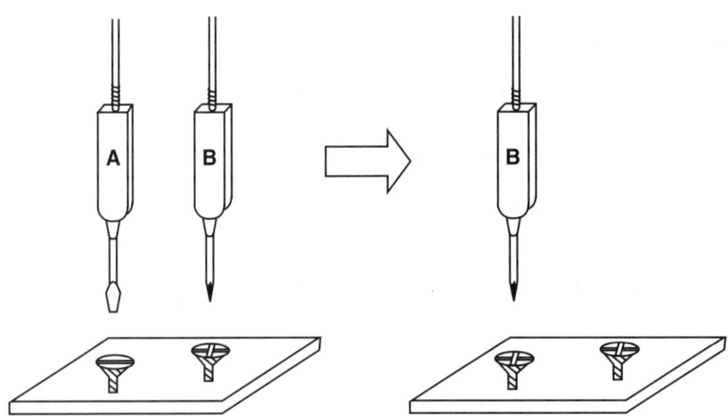

Figure 6-16. Combine Electric Screwdrivers

- **Look into jig and tool functions**

  The best kind of Orderliness eliminates the need for Orderliness. After all, Orderliness must always be maintained.

  The key to eliminating the need for tool Orderliness is to eliminate the need for the tool in question. In other words, think about how to do the same operation without using a tool. We can begin by asking (1) why must this tool be used, (2) what are its basic functions, and (3) is there another way to perform that function without a tool. These questions can lead to the discovery of tool-free alternatives. (See Figure 6-17).

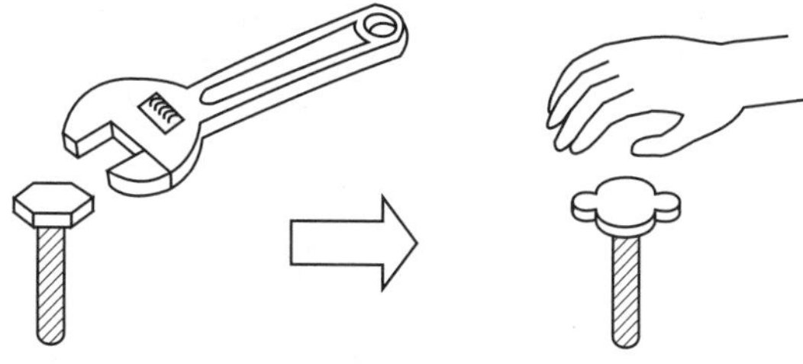
"How can we eliminate the need for this wrench?"

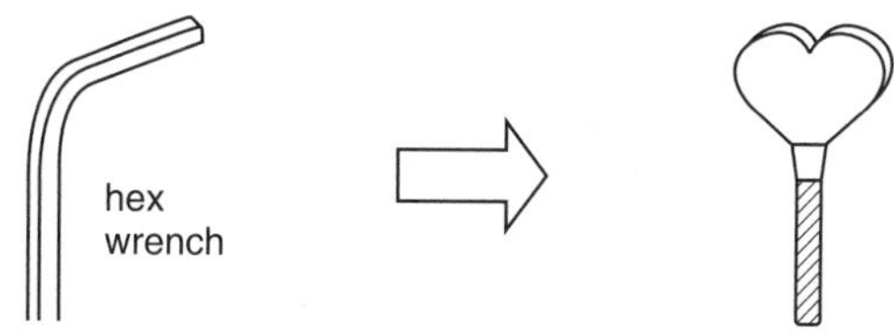
"How can we eliminate the need for this hex wrench?"
hex
wrench

Figure 6-17. Ways to Eliminate the Need for Tools

Following this line of questioning will reveal the tool's basic functions. If the tool's basic function is to rotate an object, perhaps there is a way to rotate the object without using a tool. For example, there are some screw- and bolt-fastening operations in which we can replace screwdrivers and wrenches with grips or handles that enable turning by hand to work as efficiently as turning by tool.

Orderliness for Cutting Tools

Figure 6-18 illustrates a variety of cutting tools while the following are some Orderliness suggestions concerning these tools.

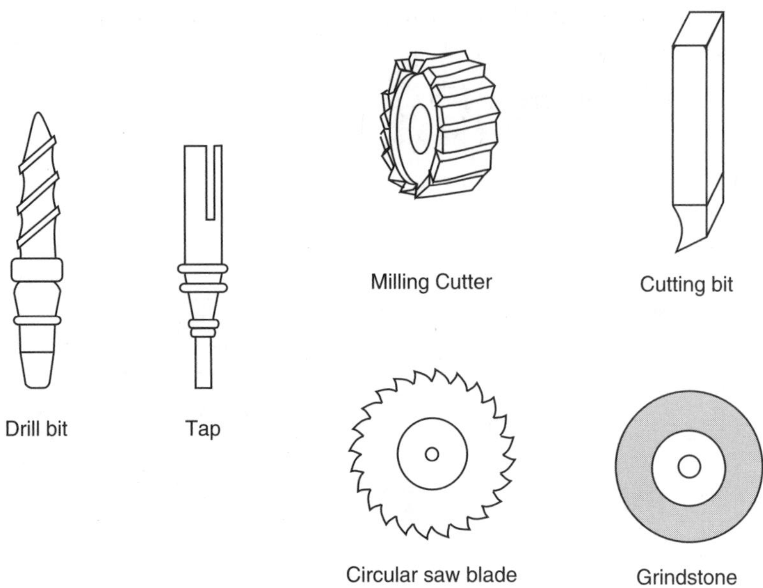

Figure 6-18. Types of Cutting Tools

Storage Location of Cutting Tools

There are two types of cutting-tool storage locations: centralized and decentralized.

- **Centralized location**

  All cutting tools are kept at the same centrally controlled storage site. This works best if the cutting tools are used infrequently.

- **Decentralized location**

  Cutting tools are stored at several sites, each of which usually holds only cutting tools that are used frequently and/or only those that are used for a particular machine.

Placement of Cutting Tools

After designating the location of cutting-tool storage sites, decide the method of cutting-tool placement at those sites. As with the placement of parts, our two basic options are function-based and product-based methods.

- **Function-based method**

  Sort out cutting tools according to function and group together those with the same or similar functions. This method is best suited for unit production systems (job-shop production).

- **Product-based method**

  Sort out cutting tools according to the products on which they will be used. Place them in separate groups for each product, preferably at a location that is incorporated into the line. This method is best suited for repetitive production.

In addition, Photo 6-13 shows a method in which the cutting tools are loaded into a mobile cart that is preset for use in changeover operations. When cutting tools need to be changed as part of changeover, the operator simply brings the cart containing the required tools to the changeover site. In such cases, the floors need to be level enough to allow easy passage of heavy carts. Also, tools must be placed in the cart in a way that prevents them from banging against (and damaging) each other.

Photo 6-13. Cutting Tools Set Up and Stored on Mobile Carts

Storage of Cutting Tools

When storing cutting tools, care must be taken to protect their cutting edges. The cutting edges of drills, taps, and so on should not be allowed to touch each other. To prevent contact, we can use a storage system like the one shown at the left of Figure 6-19. It includes an anti-rust oiling mechanism and grooves that separate the cutting tools.

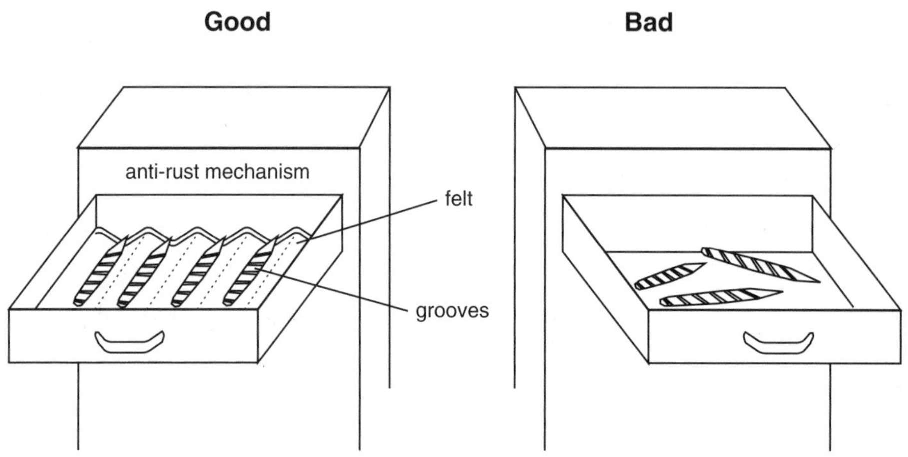

Figure 6-19. Good and Bad Storage for Cutting Tools

Orderliness for Measuring Tools

Figure 6-20 illustrates various types of measuring tools. Because most measuring tools are used to make precise measurements, they require the utmost care in handling and storage. For example, they should always be stored in a manner that prevents the accumulation of dirt, dust, or rust. (See Photo 6-14.)

Orderliness for Lubrication

Lubrication technicians migrate regularly. A good way to prevent errors along the lubrication route is to apply color-coding Orderliness, giving each type of lubrication task its own color.

To begin color-coding Orderliness for lubrication, we must first identify the different types of lubrication tasks. Next, we assign a different color for each type. Finally, we make sure that all lubrication sites and their corresponding lubrication tools receive the correct color coding. (See Figure 6-21.)

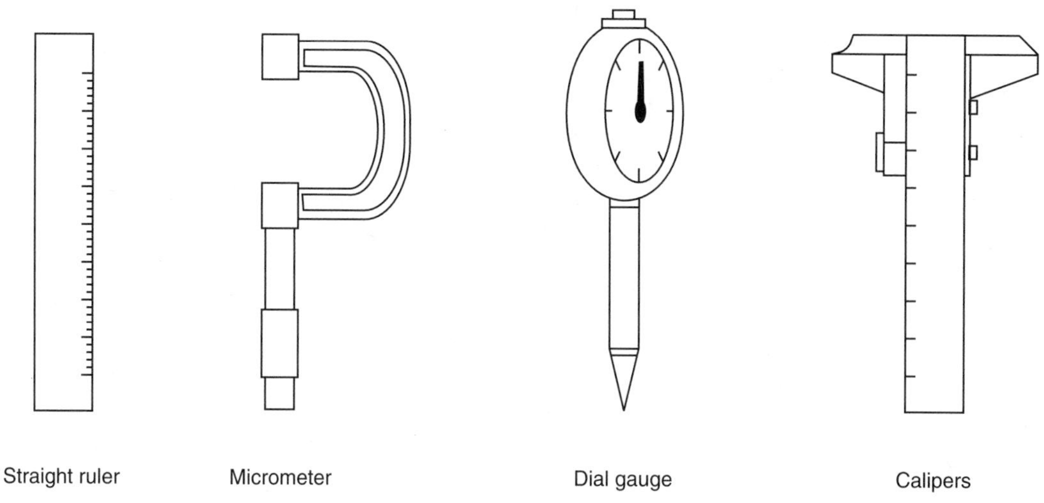

Figure 6-20. Types of Measuring Tools

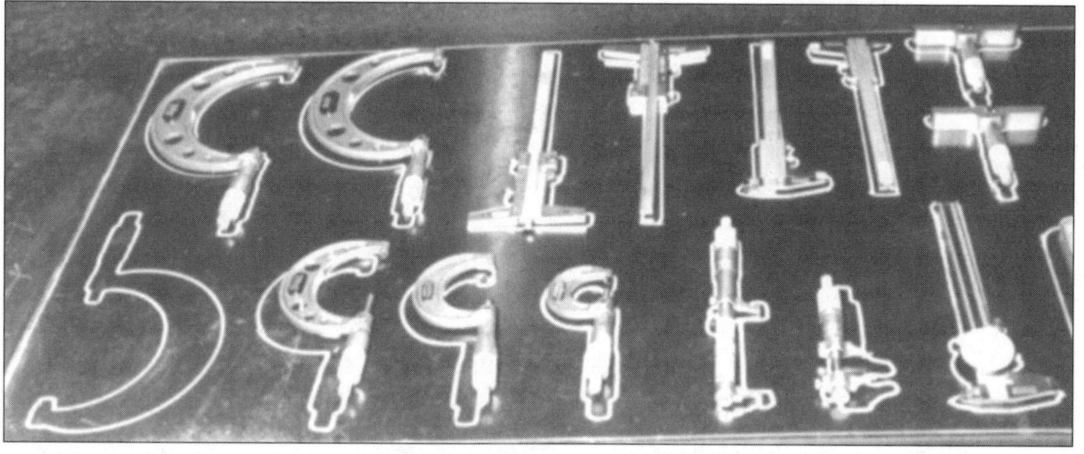

Photo 6-14. Storage of Measuring Tools on Rubber Mats

Creating a Waste-free Workshop with Principles of Motion Economy

Generally, we use the term "operation improvements" to describe measures that remove waste from human motions. By this I mean motion waste inherent in the way people move their trunks, feet, arms and hands, and so on.

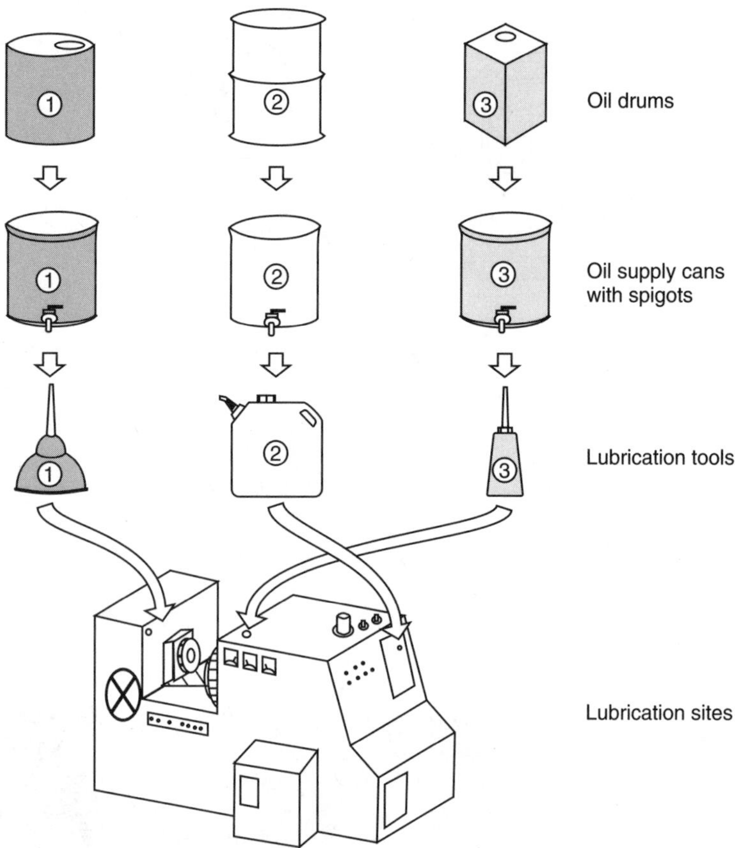

Figure 6-21. Color-coded Orderliness for Lubrication

When manufacturing products, we must make a series of finely coordinated motions. Obviously, it would boost our efficiency greatly if we could remove all nonessential motion from the motions we make. However, even more important is the question of why motion waste occurs, a simple question that we should always bear in mind. By asking "why" we can find methods of manufacturing that approach the zero-waste mark.

For example, consider conveyance operations. There are various ways we can improve such operations — for instance, by using carts to prevent wasteful motions in picking up and putting down things. Again, we should ask the all-important question: "Why does conveyance occur?"

Another example is a production line that consists of separate processes — like small islands in a river. Parts and materials are conveyed between these "islands" by carts (like river boats). Asking why conveyance is needed leads us to consider other options — for instance, linking the processes together to eliminate cart conveyance completely. This type of linkage is called "line integration" (arranging production equipment in the order of processes to enable one-piece, zero-defect manufacturing).

We have just distinguished between two types of operation improvement. "Motion improvement" removes motion waste from an operation while "radical improvement" goes to the root of the waste by finding a way to eliminate the operation itself. All improvement activities should make "radical improvement" the first priority. (See Figure 6-22.)

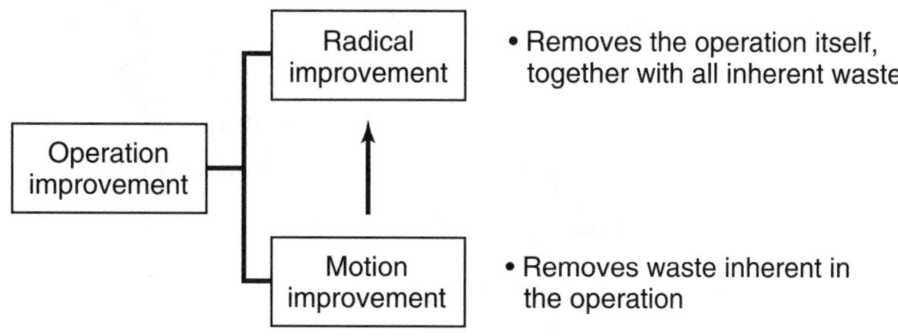

Figure 6-22. Radical Improvement and Motion Improvement

When seeking to remove waste from human motions, I recommend that you first study the principles of motion economy. These principles can be split into three groups: principles concerning the use of the body, principles concerning the layout of the workplace, and principles concerning tools, jigs, and machines.

Principles Concerning the Use of the Body

These principles help us to either eliminate or reduce the motions that operators make.

- *Principle 1:* **Start and end each motion with both hands moving at once.**

  When beginning an operation, both hands should move simultaneously, and likewise when finishing the operation.

- *Principle 2:* **Both arms should move symmetrically and in opposite directions.**

  As when swimmers do the breast stroke, the arms should move in opposite directions, following the same timing and moving in symmetry.

- *Principle 3:* **Keep trunk motions to a minimum.**

  On assembly lines, if any parts are placed behind the assembly workers, the workers must move their feet to turn around to get them. If all parts are kept beside the workers, they need only twist to pick them up. If all parts are in front of and above them, they need only use their arms and shoulders to reach them. Finally, if all parts are kept directly in front of them and slightly to the left and right sides, they need only move their hands and forearms to pick them up. The progression of motion improvement is therefore feet ➔ hips (twisting) ➔ shoulders ➔ forearms ➔ fingers. If you observe a worker's motions from the side, you can quickly discover which kinds of motions are being made to do the work.

- *Principle 4:* **Use gravity instead of muscle.**

  The more you must use your muscles when working, the more fatiguing the work becomes. When moving objects, always try to use gravitational force rather than muscle power.

- *Principle 5:* **Avoid zig-zagging motions and sudden changes in direction.**

  Motions should be continuous, gentle, and flowing.

- *Principle 6:* **Move with a steady rhythm.**

  All work operations should have a rhythm. Operations that do not have a natural rhythm are more likely to produce defects or result in injuries. Instead, there should be a smooth, steady rhythm in pace with the cycle time.

- *Principle 7:* **Maintain a comfortable posture with comfortable motions.**

  Bending over, sitting too high or too low, and other unnatural postures and motions will destroy the work rhythm and inevitably create motion waste.

- *Principle 8:* **Use the feet.**

  Some motions are made easier with a foot switch, especially when the hands are already occupied.

Principles Concerning Workplace Layout

- *Principle 9:* **Keep materials and tools close and in front.**

  To minimize operator motions, place materials and tools used in an operation as close as possible to their place of use. (See Figure 6-23.)

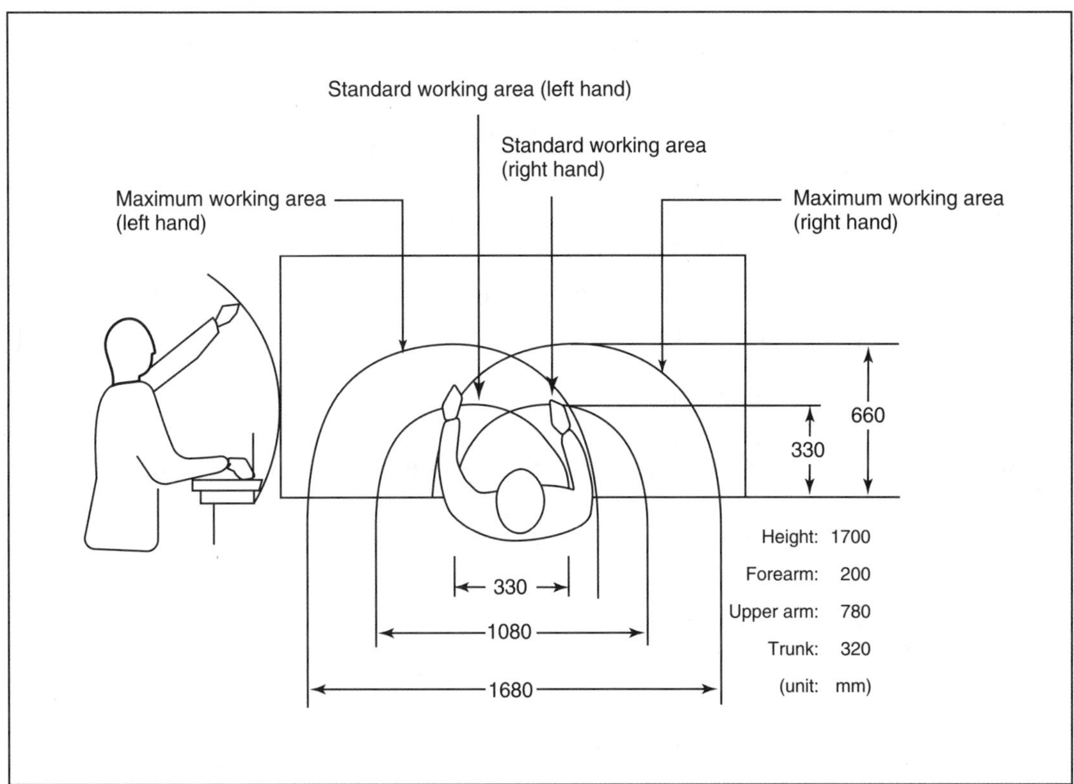

Figure 6-23. Working Area

- *Principle 10:* **Arrange materials and tools in the order of their use.**

  Keep materials and tools close to the operator and arranged according to operation sequence. To make this layout possible, parts must occupy a small area, which means they must be restocked frequently. This in turn requires the support of well-maintained 5S conditions.

- *Principle 11:* **Use inexpensive methods for moving things.**

  Use inexpensive methods for feeding in and sending out materials.

- *Principle 12:* **Keep operators at a proper height for the work to be done.**

  The operators should be seated or standing at a comfortable, relaxed height relative to the worktable and machinery.

- *Principle 13:* **Maintain a work-friendly environment.**

  Maintain environmental factors such as lighting, ventilation, heating, and air conditioning at comfortable levels to facilitate work.

Principles Concerning Jigs, Tools, and Machinery

- *Principle 14:* **Use the feet to good purpose.**

  Help minimize hand motions by devising ways in which the feet can be used to operate machinery.

- *Principle 15:* **Unify tools.**

  If there are two tools, try to combine their functions into one tool.

- *Principle 16:* **Make materials and parts easy to pick up.**

  To make them easy to pick up, keep materials and parts in front of and slightly below the operator's reach. The same goes for parts containers and tools.

- *Principle 17:* **Make handles and grips in efficient, easy-to-use shapes and positions.**

  The operator should be able to use handles and grips without having to shift his or her torso. The shapes and positions of such devices should also be designed for efficient, easy use.

In theory, while operator motions should add value to the product, this is never the case in practice. Only a small percentage of operator motions are actually value-adding motions. The goal of motion improvements is to reduce the number of non-value-adding motions and thereby raise overall work efficiency. This field of improvement studies is called "motion study."

Motion study can be defined as research whose purposes include eliminating wasteful motions from work, determining the most comfortable and economical work motions, methods, sequences, and combinations, and promoting work standardization.

To make work motions more economical (or value-adding), improvements resulting from motion study make liberal use of the principles of motion economy to eliminate waste, inconsistency, and irrationality. Work-method improvements should also go beyond work motions to include improvements in the layout of parts and materials, jigs and tools, and other work environment factors.

Improving the Layout of Parts

Figure 6-24 shows an improvement in which plastic sheets used in packaging are moved from a rack behind the operator to a hook in front of the worker and above the production line. This improvement eliminates four seconds of motion waste from each unit of packaging work.

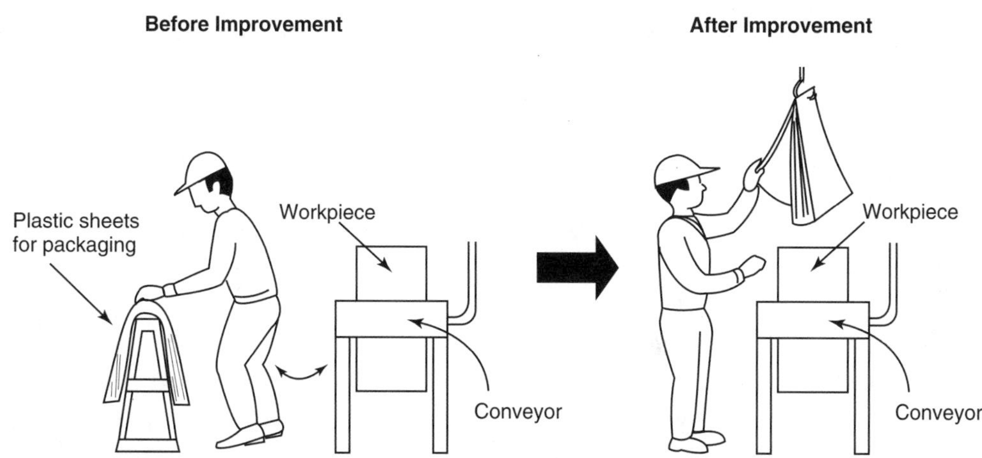

- Plastic sheets kept on rack behind the operator.
- Operator forced to turn around each time he needed a plastic sheet.
- Turning motion required four seconds.

- Now plastic sheets are hung on hook in front of operator.
- The operator does not have to turn around.
- Four seconds of motion waste eliminated.

Figure 6-24. Improvement in Parts Layout

Improving the Retrieval of Parts

Figure 6-25 shows an improvement in picking up parts as part of assembly work. Before this improvement, the worktable was so large that the assembly worker had to stretch to pick up parts. Also, the parts boxes were laid flat at table level, making it difficult to reach inside them.

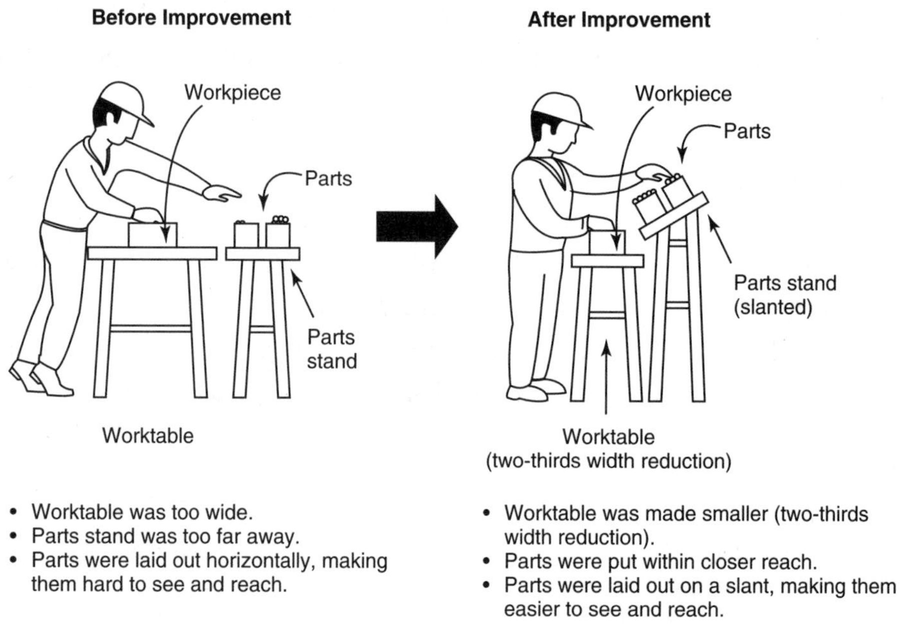
Before Improvement
Workpiece
Parts
Parts stand
Worktable
After Improvement
Workpiece
Parts
Parts stand (slanted)
Worktable (two-thirds width reduction)
• Worktable was too wide.
• Parts stand was too far away.
• Parts were laid out horizontally, making them hard to see and reach.
• Worktable was made smaller (two-thirds width reduction).
• Parts were put within closer reach.
• Parts were laid out on a slant, making them easier to see and reach.

Figure 6-25. Improvement in Picking Up Parts

After the improvement, the decreased width of the worktable enabled the assembly worker to reach the parts without overstretching his arm. Furthermore, the parts boxes were set on an inclined surface to make their contents more accessible.

Similar improvements can be made in conveyor-based assembly operations. Putting parts containers at an angle toward the operator makes it easier for the operator to pick up parts from the containers. When motions are easier to make, they are generally more efficient as well.

From One- to Two-handed Motion

Figure 6-26 shows an improvement that changes the assembly of a telephone's push-button set from a one-handed motion to a two-handed motion.

Before the improvement, there was no jig to secure the workpiece. The operator used his left hand to hold while using his right hand to insert push buttons one at a time into their places.

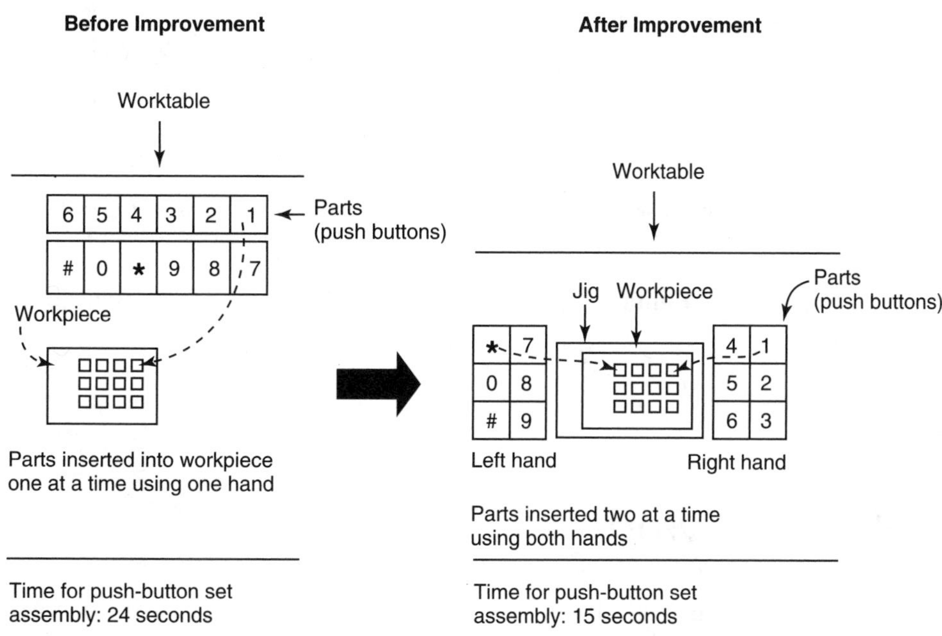

Figure 6-26. Improvement from One-handed to Two-handed Work

After the improvement, a jig holds the workpiece in place, freeing the left hand to join the right one in two-handed assembly of the push-button set. The positions of the parts and the set (workpiece) were also improved to help eliminate assembly errors.

From Checking Standards to Checking Actual Conditions

Figure 6-27 shows an improvement made in a pressure-gauge display. Before the improvement, the person checking the gauge had to check the manual for standard pressure values for each machine. After the improvement, the standard value was indicated on each machine's pressure-gauge display, thereby eliminating the need to check the manual and speeding up gauge readings.

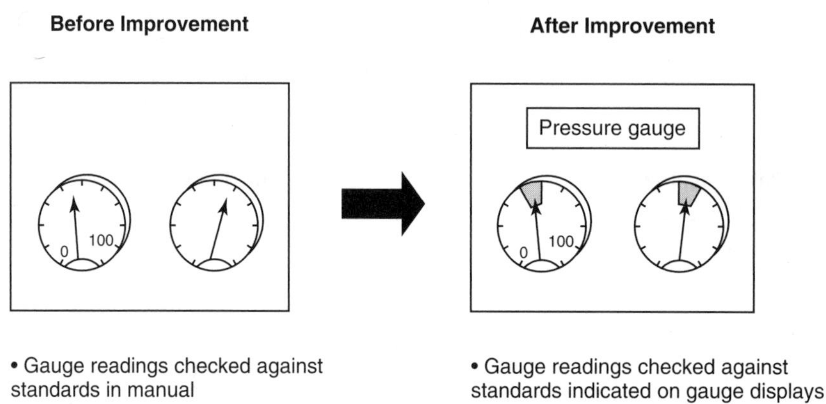
Before Improvement
After Improvement
Pressure gauge
0
100
0
100
• Gauge readings checked against standards in manual
• Gauge readings checked against standards indicated on gauge displays

Figure 6-27. Eliminating the Need to Check Manual for Standards

ORDERLINESS IN THE OFFICE

There is no substantial difference between Orderliness for factories and Orderliness for offices. In both situations, the idea is first to get rid of the unneeded items cluttering up the place (Organization), and then to put the remaining necessary items into efficient order (Orderliness). In factories and offices alike: Organization and Orderliness are implemented together.

Orderliness is meaningless unless everyone is assured of understanding where things are kept and how to use them. Let us look at "five keys" to Orderliness in the office.

- *Key 1:* **Eliminate searching waste.**

  In offices, a lot of time is wasted in searching for documents, markers, staplers, and other materials used in office tasks. The first priority is therefore to eliminate this waste.

Table 6-3. Folder Method Versus Binder Method

	Folder Method	Binder Method
Advantages	Folders come in smaller units. • More easily managed according to frequency of use. • Smaller storage units require less management. • Easier to find. • Folders provide smaller units for sorting, transferring, discarding. Folders do not need fastening. • No hassle with hole punches and binder clips. • Documents can be picked up and returned more easily. Cost advantages: • Folders cost less. • Folders take up less space.	Because they are fastened, documents tend to stay in order better. Binder size discourages private acquisition.
Disadvantages	Folders get out of order easier than binders. Because of their size, folders are more apt to be kept in people's desks.	Binders are bulky. • Less manageable (i.e., sorting according to frequent use). • Larger storage units require more management. • Used less. (Because documents are fastened into binders people are more reluctant to remove them.) • Documents in binders cannot be sorted, transferred, or discarded easily. (It requires fastening and unfastening.) • Because they take time to dispose of, useless documents accumulate. Documents must be fastened into binders. • Requires time-consuming hole punching or clipping. • Documents in binders are harder to find and put back. Cost disadvantages • Binders cost more. • Binders take up more space.

- Inserting documents into file folders is easier and faster than fastening them into binders — there are no paper punches or clips to bother with.
- When looking through folders, the folder labels guide you to specific documents. Documents can then be removed without having to loosen binder fasteners.

A second advantage is that folders can be managed in more detail.

- Listing specific document titles on folders makes the documents more accessible and easier to classify or otherwise manage.
- Documents can be managed in more detail throughout the series of

storage steps, from document generation to ready-access storage, transfer, remote storage, and disposal.

A third advantage of the folder method is cost.

- Folders cost less than binders.
- Folders take up only slightly more space than the documents they are holding. In contrast, a binder whether full or half empty takes up the same amount of space.

Table 6-3 lists the relative advantages and disadvantages of the folder method and the binder method.

File Generation Methods

Between the time a document is generated and discarded, smooth office operations depend upon document accessibility during storage phases. Therefore, the method for generating files should take into account making filed documents easily accessible.

- **File-folder capacity of 100 sheets is okay, but 70 sheets is better.**

  If you think storage efficiency is increased by filling folders to capacity, try pulling out a stuffed folder with one hand. One spill will convince you otherwise. Moreover, it is more time-consuming to find and return specific documents that are filed among a huge batch of other documents. That is why the rule of thumb for file-folder capacity is 100 sheets — but 70 sheets is better.

- **File-folder labels are like addresses.**

  Every file folder in storage should be labeled. Proper labeling is the key to locating the file later on — and how well we do it helps determine how much searching waste there will be.

  Suppose you are looking for a one-sheet document in a storage system containing several thousand documents. How can anyone other than the person who filed the document hope to avoid looking through every document? The answer is to assign "addresses" to file cabinets — just as houses have city, street, and number addresses. These addresses will lead to the right file cabinet. Once there, you can find the file by looking at the folder labels.

Be sure to label file folders descriptively. Avoid vague or abstract folder titles such as "miscellaneous," "other," "XXX-related," or "general."

- **Assign each file folder its own storage period.**

  Organize file folders so that each folder contains documents related to the same title. This makes documents easier to search through — although no easier to discard. When sorting out documents to discard as part of the process of transferring older and infrequently used file folders to remote storage, we would still have to look at each document in each file folder and judge whether or not to discard it. This is too troublesome for many people and why useless documents tend to accumulate in such large numbers.

  We must approach this problem in two steps. First, find a way to make the documents easy to locate and search through. After that, we must find a way to make them easier to discard. The answer is to label file folders specifically so that everyone can see what they contain. The second step is to assign each file folder a limited storage period, after which its contents will be discarded.

File Organization Methods

A key principle of Orderliness for documents is to make them easy to find. The file organization method selected can make a big difference in work efficiency — the key being how we organize file titles. The following are some recommended methods.

- **Region-based organization**

  Figure 6-31 shows how file folders can be organized by region (i.e, a regional breakdown of suppliers or customers). Obviously, this method works best when the files contain documents that describe either region-based activities or activities that are easily broken down by region. For example, the documents may concern region-based subsidiary companies with their sales territories, region-based suppliers, or region-based distribution networks.

  This concept can be extended or broken down further into other types of territorial definitions (i.e., countries, states, counties, and cities).

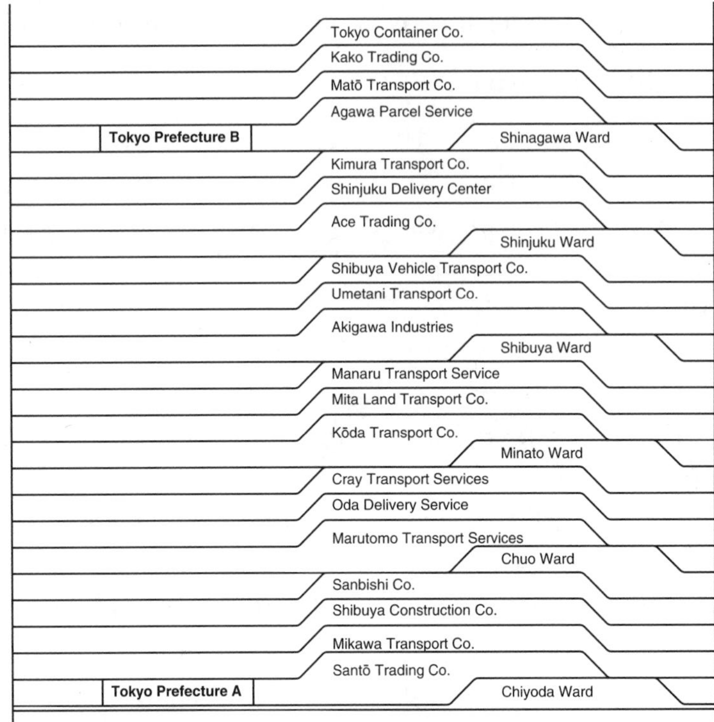

Figure 6-31. Region-based File Organization

- **Subject-based organization**

This does not mean using territory names as subjects but rather using categories of file folder titles as subjects. Often, subject categories can be taken directly from categories already defined and used within the company's management organization as shown in Figure 6-32.

No matter how complex the array of folder titles, they usually can be grouped conveniently under the company's existing organizational categories (i.e., division, department, section). This method is useful because subcategories can be made as general or specific as needed.

Another argument in favor of this kind of file organization is that it tends to group together folders that have been filed under vague or inaccurate titles. As a general rule, I suggest (1) that a list of standard folder titles be made for each section in the company and (2) that everyone follows these standards when titling and filing new folders.

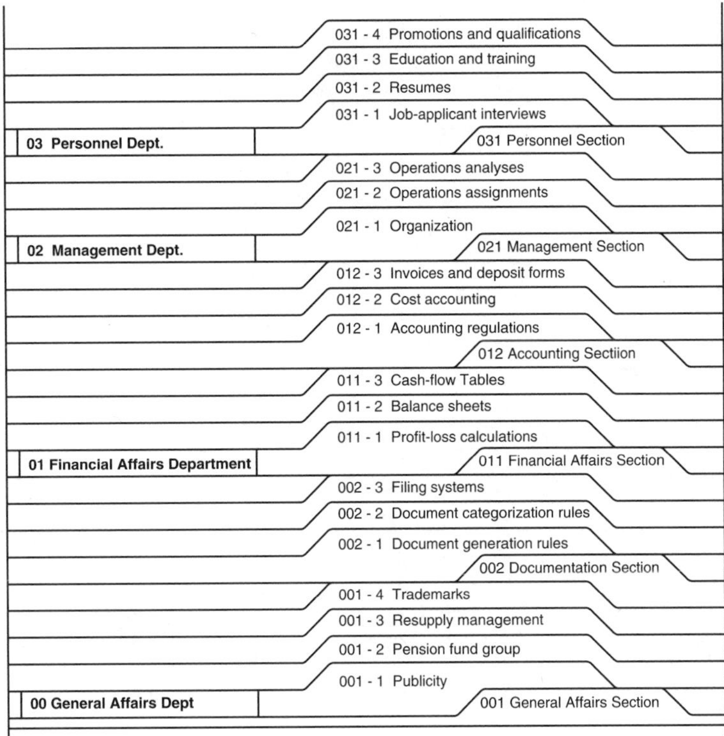

Figure 6-32. Subject-based File Organization

- **Alphabetical organization**

The alphabetical organization method is the most popular filing system. Figure 6-33 illustrates this method. In this example, client company names are filed in alphabetical order. If a particular letter ("A") happens to have a lot of client files in it, the section can be further divided into two or more subsections ("Aa to Al" and "Am to Az").

- **Code-based organization**

When using this method, instead of directly indexing files under their descriptive titles or company names, we first assign a code number to each file and then index the codes in numerical order. This indirect method requires the use of a chart or manual to match codes with file descriptions.

In some instances, companies use alphanumeric codes (codes that contain numbers and letters) rather than more simple numeric

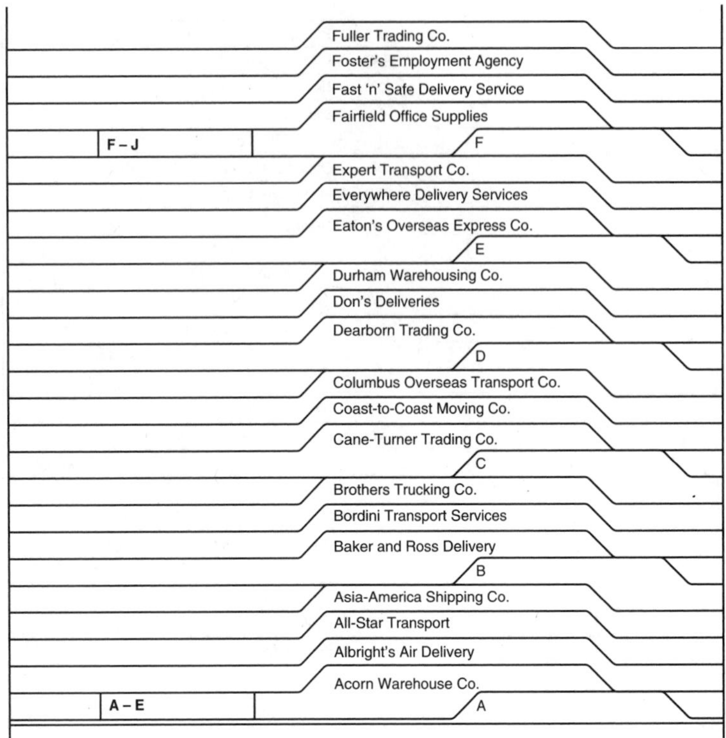

Figure 6-33. Alphabetic Organization

codes. In either case, code-based file organization lends itself more easily to computerization. The advantage of strictly numeric codes, as shown in Figure 6-34, is that they can be entered quickly from the ten-key pad of a computer keyboard.

The disadvantage of any kind of code-based system is that the file contents are not immediately discernible. However, this can be an advantage when the files are of a confidential nature (e.g., files containing classified documents at a company or patient records at a hospital).

Document Storage

Once a document has been generated, distributed, and put into storage, it is managed as part of a file unit during the various storage phases. Figure 6-35 illustrates this flow — from ready-access storage (which may include

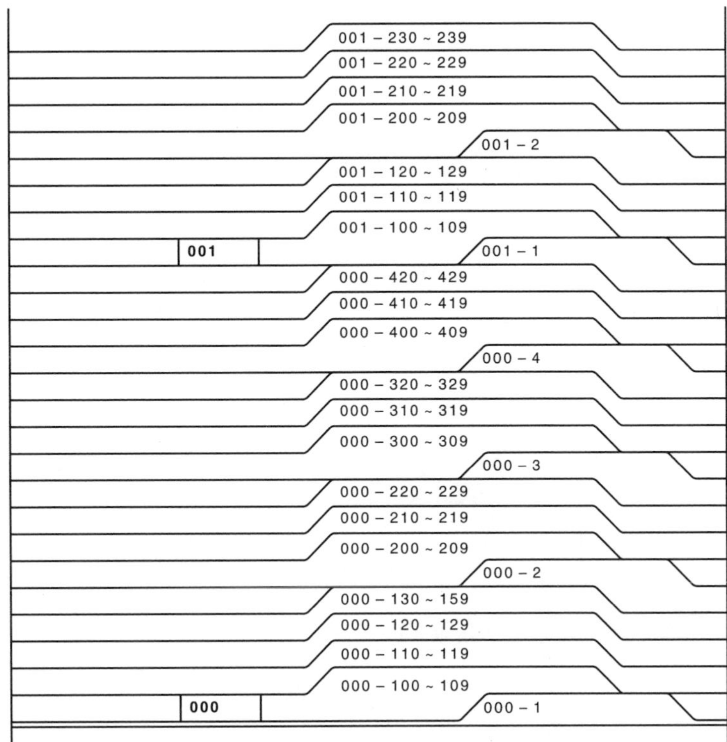

Figure 6-34. Code-based Organization

"active" and "inactive" sections) to remote storage in cardboard boxes and, ultimately, disposal.

The most important rule when transferring documents to remote storage is to mark each storage container with a storage-limit date. The following are some suggestion points regarding remote storage.

- *Point 1:* **Keep ready-access and remote storage in clearly separate locations.**

  As mentioned earlier, on the average we can expect only 1 percent of stored documents to be needed after one year in ready-access storage. After two years of storage very few documents are of any potential use to the company. For this reason it is good practice to transfer documents once a year from ready-access storage to remote storage.

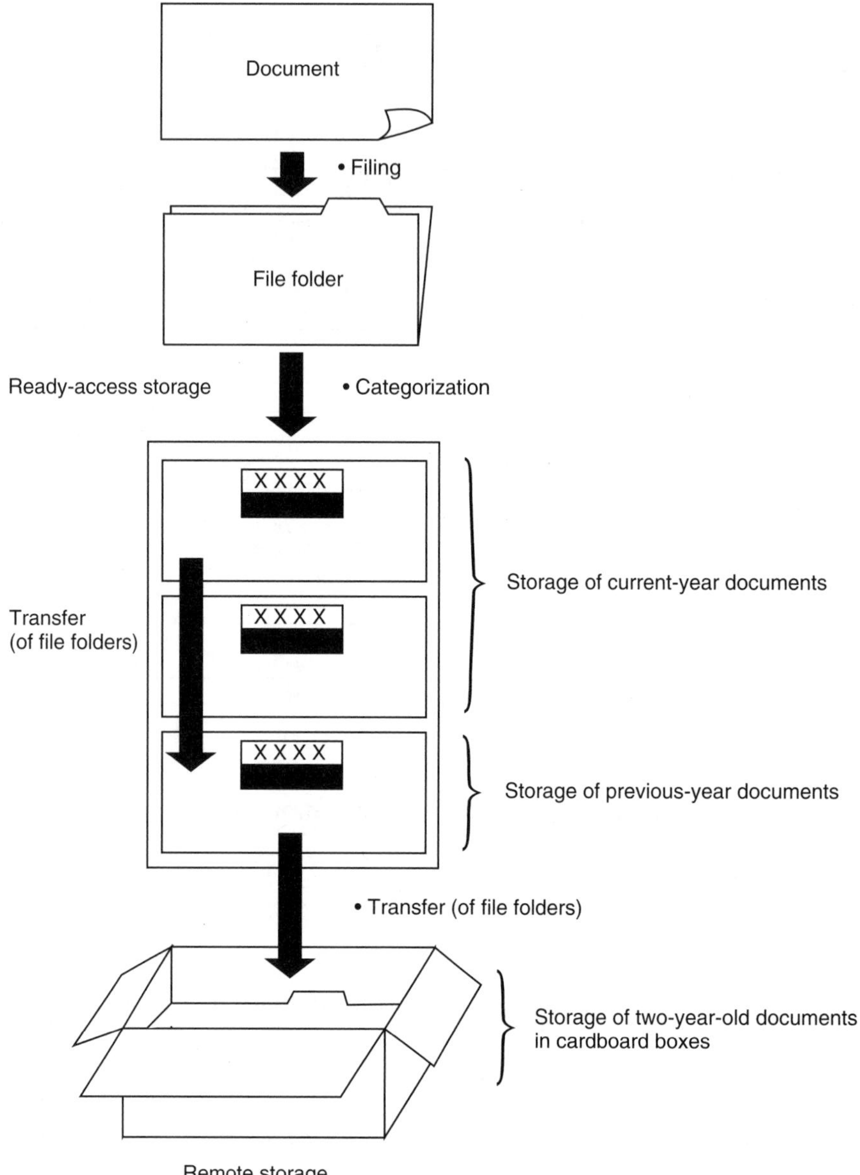

Figure 6-35. Flow of Document Storage

The location for remote storage should be a document archive area in a remote corner of the building (i.e., the basement) or in a separate building (i.e., a detached warehouse). Three factors to consider when choosing a separate place for remote storage are: (1) security, (2) easy manageability of stored documents, and (3) accessibility of stored documents if needed.

• *Point 2:* **Establish storage-limit dates.**

Mark all stored documents with storage-limit dates. Dates for some items will be determined by company regulations or legal requirements. Those for other items will be determined by other criteria.

Documents whose storage limits are determined by company regulations or legal requirements include personnel lists, wage-payment ledgers, and accounting records. Criteria differ for other types of documents, such as reports, minutes of meetings, and planning proposals. Furthermore, the section of the company that generated a particular document may require a different storage-limit date than the section that received the document.

I recommend three steps for determining storage limits for such non-regulated documents:

First, remove duplicate documents. Several sections of the company keep their own copies of daily logs, meeting minutes, and other documents in their ready-access filing systems. Therefore, before moving documents to a single remote storage location, we should check for and discard duplicates of documents.

Next, ascertain storage-limit differences between document senders and receivers. When the section of the company that generated a particular document requires a different storage-limit date than the section that received the document, both storage limits must be taken into account.

Finally, establish each file folder's ready-access storage limit and remote storage limit. Determine in advance how long each file folder will remain in ready-access storage (usually within the section that stored the document). Also determine how long it will remain in remote storage (usually separate from the section that stored the document).

• *Point 3:* **Discard remote storage items by the boxload.**

Once documents have passed through the ready-access stages in folders and are ready for transfer to remote storage, transfer them to cardboard boxes. Do not treat them as separate documents. (See Figure 6-36.) Be sure that all remote storage boxes are clearly marked with a storage period (i.e., one year, three years, five years, permanent) before transferring file folders into them. Discard each box in its entirety when the end of the storage period arrives.

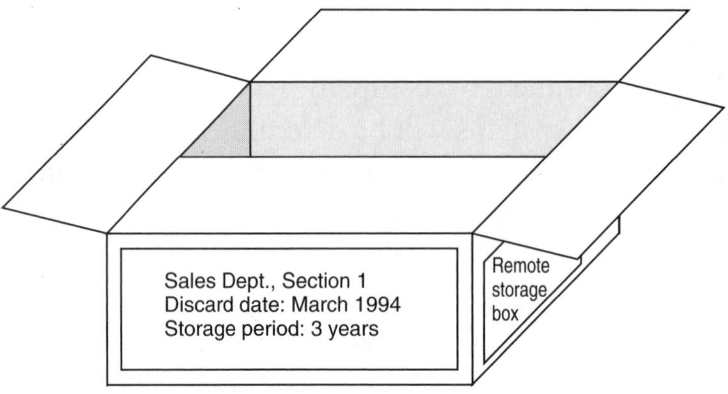

Figure 6-36. Cardboard Boxes for Remote Storage

- *Point 4:* **Discard boxes at the end of the storage period.**

  Check at least every six months to see if any boxes in remote storage have passed their discard dates. It is also a good idea to review the contents of all boxes marked "permanent storage" to see if some can be discarded safely.

Orderliness for Vouchers

The basic points in Orderliness for vouchers are the same as for documents. However, in recent years vouchers have replaced ledger books in many corporate accounting systems. This means that Orderliness for vouchers impacts how well the company's accounting system works. Consequently, we should recognize the following differences between vouchers and documents:

1. Vouchers usually have more detailed categories and greater format structure to allow for expandability.
2. Many vouchers are from sets containing several carbon copies. These copy sheets tend to be thinner and more fragile.
3. Vouchers tend to circulate more frequently than documents. They also tend to be stored temporarily at several places.
4. Due to greater circulation, vouchers should always be accessible for quick retrieval.

5. A voucher storage system must be comprehensive enough to accommodate and account for all target vouchers.

We should select file organization and storage methods that suit the particular characteristics of target vouchers. Figure 6-37 shows a file organization method used for itemized account vouchers.

Vouchers that are held onto briefly before being passed on should be kept in a small folder that either sits on the desktop or in one of the desk's side drawers. This allows a person to retrieve such vouchers with minimal wasted motion.

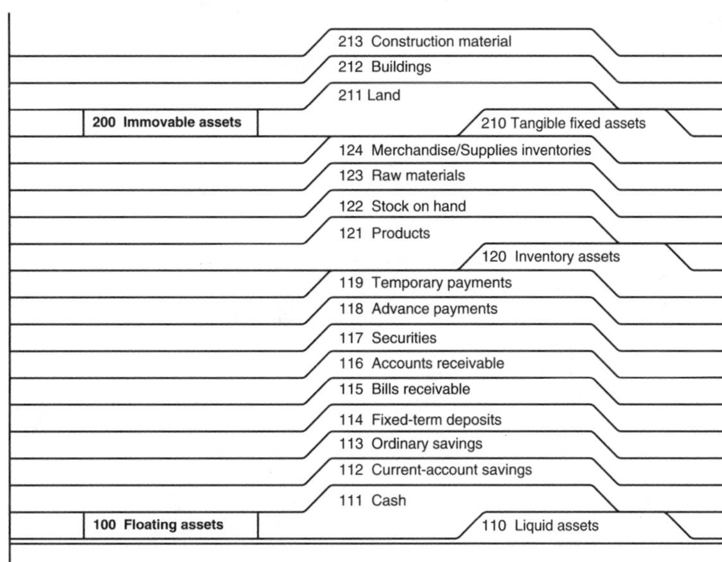

Figure 6-37. Organization of Itemized Account Files

Orderliness for Business Cards

Again, Orderliness principles for business cards are basically the same as for documents. However, like vouchers, there are a few differences:

1. Business cards are much smaller than most documents.
2. In Japan they may contain information on both sides.
3. Business cards function as reminders of certain people or meetings.

In view of these differences, it is a good idea to file business cards in folders or books with transparent sheets that display several cards on a page and make retrieval easy. Office supply stores offer various types of business-card folders. Select one that best accommodates these points and your particular needs.

Generally, business cards are organized alphabetically, either by the last name of the person named in the card or by the name of that person's company.

Orderliness for Stationery Supplies

Stationery supplies should be distributed to people only in the amounts requisitioned. Users should follow the basic principle of not keeping unneeded supplies on hand. Similarly, supplies used every day should not be stored in desk drawers. This is because they are not visible (or countable) and time is wasted searching for them.

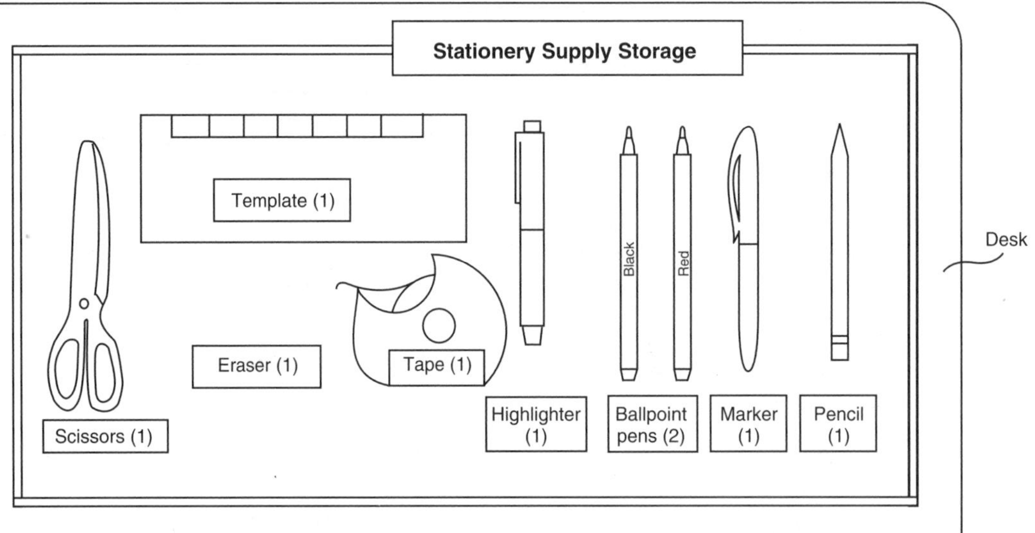

Figure 6-38. Desktop Organizer

Instead, keep stationery supplies for daily use on the desktop so that anyone can see at a glance their locations and quantities. To do this, we can use the outlining or "template" technique introduced earlier in this chapter.

Many people use cups or small boxes to hold writing tools and stationery supplies. However, such devices prevent us from seeing quantities at a glance. I recommend the template method illustrated in Figure 6-38. Make sure that all outlined spaces are marked with the names and amounts of the items stored there.

7

Visual Organization and Visual Orderliness

In factories and offices alike, everything should be easy to understand at a glance. To achieve this, rationalization measures and improvement activities should be aimed in part at making the flow of goods, the identification of abnormalities, and various other aspects of factory or office operations visible enough so that anyone can quickly and easily understand what is happening.

As mentioned in earlier chapters, the 5S's are the foundation for making improvements. The most fundamental of these 5S pillars are Organization and Orderliness. Therefore, it is no surprise that "visual" Organization and "visual" Orderliness are the most important ingredients of making 5S conditions visible.

RED-TAG AND SIGNBOARD STRATEGIES

The primary methods used to implement visual Organization and visual Orderliness are the red-tag strategy (for Organization) and the signboard strategy (for Orderliness).

People in factories where visual Organization and visual Orderliness have not yet been established are unable to give positive answers to questions such as: "Do you know exactly what things your factory needs and does not need?" and "Can you tell just by looking around where each type of item is stored and in what amount?" However, once the red-tag strategy and signboard strategy are implemented, a factory's problems, waste, and abnormalities become as clear as day.

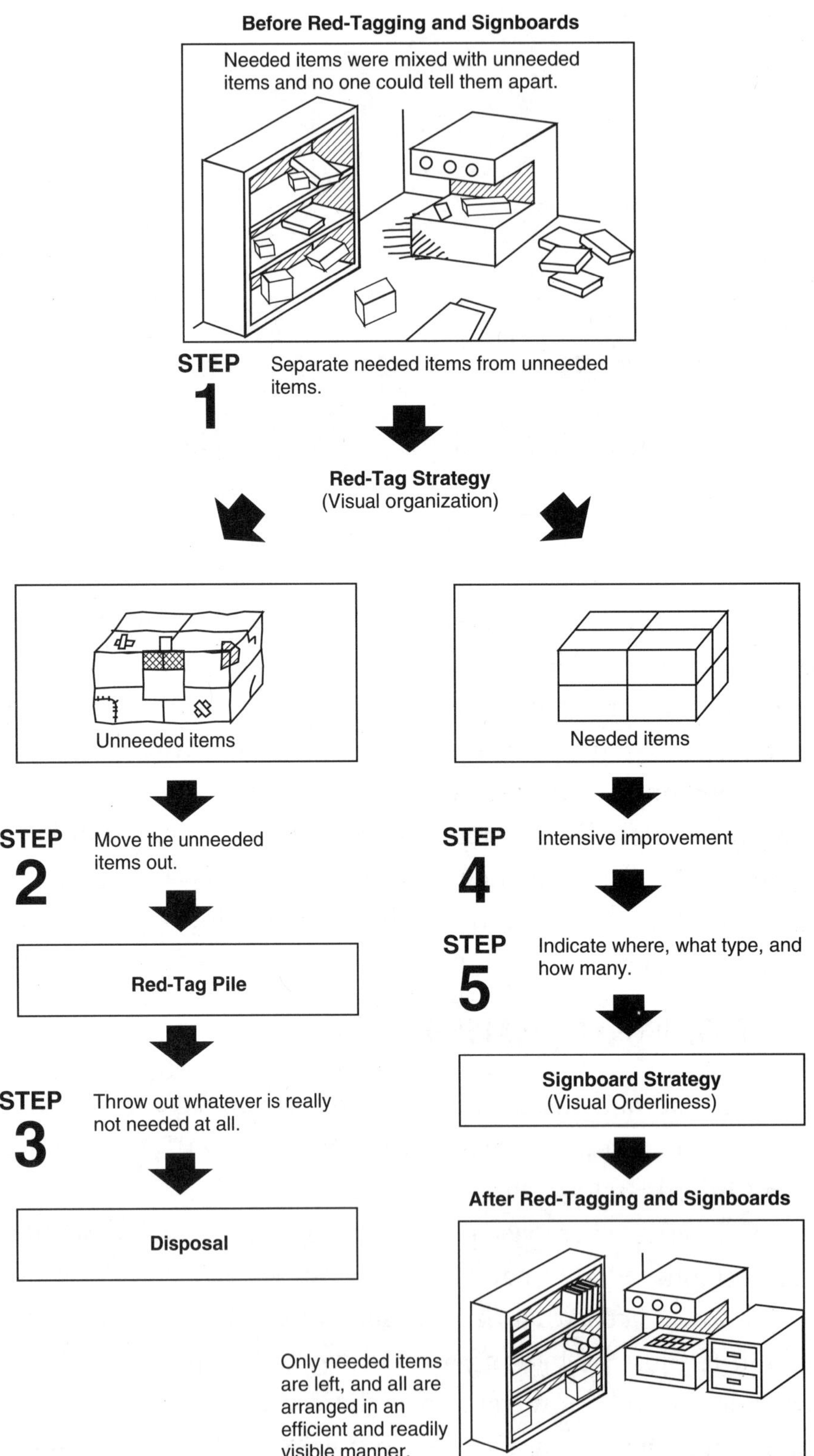

Figure 7-1. Steps in Red-Tag and Signboard Strategies

The first step is to implement visual Organization by carrying out the red-tag strategy on a companywide basis. This clears away everything that is not needed.

First, divide all items into two categories: "currently needed" and "not currently needed." Then divide the latter items into "items to store" and "items to discard."

Meanwhile, only currently needed items remain in the factory. Now it is time to clearly establish which items go where and in what amount. The way to do this is via the signboard strategy (visual Orderliness).

A factory that has implemented both the red-tag and signboard strategies should contain nothing but currently needed items, all of which are kept in clearly marked places that enable anyone to see at a glance what goes where and in what amount.

Figure 7-1 outlines the steps in implementing the red-tag and signboard strategies.

Step 1. Separate Needed from Unneeded Items

Factories and offices contain all sorts of items, from machines and parts to dies and documents. Many of these are not actually needed for current production or clerical activities. For example, some items may be kept in case a certain type of order is received for which they are needed. In another instance, some parts may be left over from a discontinued product model.

At storage sites we always find unneeded items mixed in with needed items. Therefore, our first task is to separate them — by attaching red tags to all unneeded items to make their status immediately clear to anyone.

Step 2. Transfer Unneeded Items

After red-tagging unneeded items, we should move them out of the workplace (the factory workshop or office section) to a storage site reserved for red-tagged items. This will leave only currently needed items in the workplace, which may now seem rather empty.

Step 3. Discard All Truly Unneeded Items

Now it is time to go through all of the red-tagged items at their storage site to determine which items are not needed at all and can be discarded.

Step 4. Carry Out Intensive Improvements

Once the red-tag strategy is implemented, there should be nothing left in the factory except items currently needed for production. This generally means a 20 to 30 percent reduction in the amount of inventory. However, inventory is always tied in with how things are made. As shown in Figure 7-2, although we may experience reductions, if we continue to use the same production and goods-distribution methods, inventory levels will eventually climb back to their original levels.

Therefore, as soon as the red-tag strategy is implemented, we must carry out intensive improvements to change both how products are made and how goods flow in the factory. Only with such intensive efforts can we maintain a streamlined inventory. When post-red-tagging conditions are met, production becomes healthier and more efficient — and waste and other problems associated with unneeded items are eliminated.

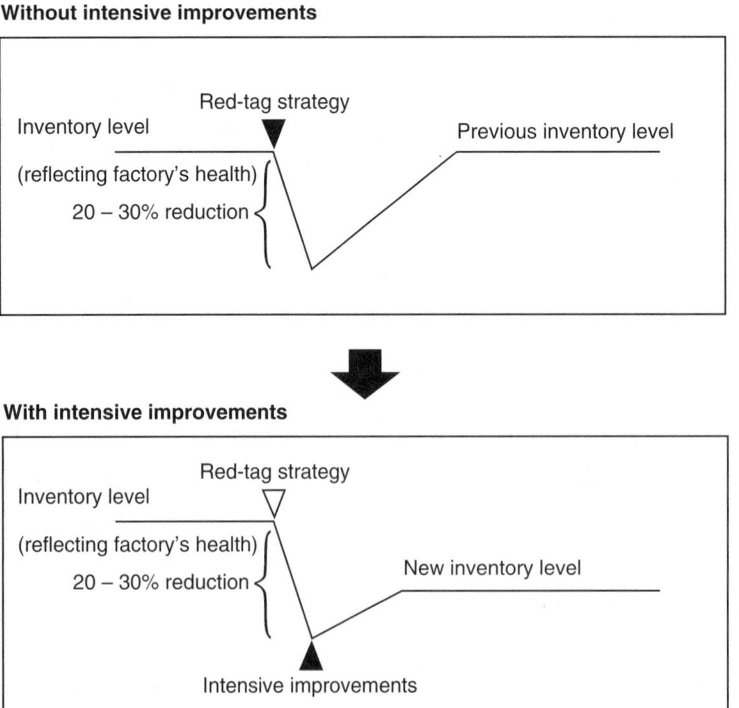

Figure 7-2. Timing of Red-Tag Strategy and Intensive Improvements

Step 5. Clearly Show What Goes Where and in What Amount

When implementing improvements, we should expect to see changes in equipment layout, which means changing the production-line layout. When changing the production line, we must also determine where to place inventory so that it supports maximum production efficiency. Once these storage sites are determined, we can hang signboards that clearly indicate what goes where and in what amount. This is the signboard strategy.

8

The Red-Tag Strategy

Recent years have witnessed a rapid increase in the number of factories and offices that have implemented the red-tag strategy. To lay the foundation for making improvements, these same factories and offices usually have implemented all 5S's. Companies have learned that — at little cost — these efforts can bring big rewards, such as substantially reduced inventories, higher productivity, and improved clerical efficiency. Furthermore, attaching red tags to unneeded items is a simple task that anyone can perform, which is another reason why companies have so willingly implemented it.

This recent wave of red-tag strategy implementation has reached from Japan to Korea and even to France. Indeed, the red-tag strategy is gaining popularity in many countries as an effective tool for "visual Organization."

In this chapter we will examine the red-tag strategy and steps needed for its implementation, several red-tag case studies, and some questions and answers.

WHAT IS THE RED-TAG STRATEGY?

Recently I attended a tape-cutting ceremony to mark the completion of a factory to be staffed by a hundred people. Everything in the brand-new factory sparkled. It was refreshing to see. Unfortunately, I thought, it will only take a year or two for it to become as dirty as other typical factories.

Some might say that wherever there are people there is dirt. How could it be different in a factory? However, I would argue that at least people know how to wash off dirt that accumulates. The challenge is to find a bathing substitute for the factory.

The best "factory bath" known to me is the 5S's: Organization, Orderliness, Cleanliness, Standardized Cleanup, and Discipline.

People are used to treating unnecessary things in the factory — vouchers, operations, equipment, and the inventory those things require — as personal possessions. That is why it is so important to look around us and determine what is really needed and what is not.

This is where the red-tag strategy comes in. Every strategy is aimed at conquering a specific enemy. Obviously, the enemy confronted by red-tagging is waste and other ills that we create.

It is not always easy to identify waste in the factory. Workers seldom know how to separate items needed for current production from unnecessary items. Even conservative-minded factory managers can look factory waste right in the face and not recognize it.

We need a simple method to bring such ills to the surface and to enable even the most tunnel-visioned manager or company president to differentiate between what is needed and what is not. The red-tag strategy happens to fit the bill. (See Figure 8-1.)

STEPS IN THE RED-TAG STRATEGY

Once red-tagging is underway, we suddenly find red tags everywhere. And a factory full of red-tagged items is nothing to be ashamed of — there can never be too many red tags. In fact, when this strategy is carried out well, the whole factory will look red.

Why use the color red? First of all, red is conspicuous. Second, red is the color of stoplights. Finally, the Japanese word for "red" also means "dirt."

The criteria for attaching red tags to items differ from factory to factory. Typically, red tags are attached to all items that will not be needed for the next month's production schedule. At stricter factories, the "need period" for items is the next week's schedule.

In some cases, when nobody can tell for sure whether a particular item will be needed or not during the next week or month, some factories will use yellow tags to mark these items. I personally disapprove of yellow tags because they open the door to indecision. I prefer to use only red tags that keep things clear and simple.

Item name

Quantity

Date

Reason

No.

RED TAG

Category	1. Equipment 2. Jigs and tools 3. Measuring instruments 4. Materials 5. Parts 6. In-process inventory		7. Quasi products 8. Finished products 9. Quasi materials 10. Office products 11. Paper, pens, etc.
Item name			
Manufacturing No.			
Quantity	Units	Value	$
Reason	1. Not needed 2. Defective 3. Not need soon 4. Scrap material 5. Use known		6. Other
Disposal by:	Department / Division / Section		
Disposal method:	1. Discard 2. Return 3. Move to red-tag storage site 4. Move to separate storage site 5. Other		Disposal complete (signature)
Today's date:	Posting date:		Disposal date:
Red-tag file number			

Figure 8-1. Examples of Red-Tag Forms

Figure 8-2 shows the steps for carrying out a red-tag strategy.

Step 1. Launch the Red-Tag Project

Optimally, red-tagging is something that happens every day. But even factories that devote a few minutes daily to red-tagging still need to carry out companywide red-tag campaigns at least once or twice a year.

Implement each campaign as a distinct red-tag project. The person with final responsibility for the project should be a top manager — the company president, the manufacturing division chief, or the factory superintendent.

What is the red-tag strategy ?
It is a means of implementing organization by labeling all unneeded items with conspicuous red tags.

Step 1: Launch the red-tag project.
- Members: Employees in manufacturing, materials, management, and accounting divisions.
- Period: 1 to 2 months
- Key point for JIT consultant: Help the factory employees understand how to identify what items are not needed.

Step 2: Identify red-tag targets.
- Inventory: Raw materials, parts, in-process inventory, and products.
- Equipment: Machines, miscellaneous equipment, jigs, tools, carts, desks, chairs, dies, vehicles, fixtures, etc.
- Space: Floor and shelving.

Step 3: Set red-tag criteria.
- Set the criteria for determining what is needed and what is not.
  Example: Do not tag items needed for the next month's production schedule; tag all other items.

Step 4: Make the red tags.
- To be eye-catching, red tags should be as large as a standard piece of typing paper.
- For inventory items, red-tag teams should write down the item's name, quantity, retention period, reason for retention, etc.

Step 5: Attach the red tags.
- People from indirectly related divisions should come to the workshop, listen to a description of current conditions, and be objective in attaching red tags to all unneeded items.
  - Look with a critical eye.
  - Don't let the workshop's own workers decide where to stick red tags. They tend to think everything is necessary.
  - Be merciless when attaching red tags!
  - If in doubt, red-tag it!
- Red-tagging should be done intensively over a short time period.

Step 6: Evaluate the red-tag targets.
Inventory:
- Divide red tags into two types: (1) "dead stock" and (2) "retained stock."
- Set the "need period" for service parts according to the product life of corresponding products. Keep service parts in the warehouse for the appropriate need period.
- Create and execute a schedule for disposing of dead stock. The schedule should indicate quantity, value, and disposal period.
- Make a list of all unneeded inventory to facilitate understanding and for use in accounting.

Equipment:
- Basic principle: Whatever gets in the way during improvement activities should either be moved or disposed of.
- Follow the company's disposal application procedure to dispose of unneeded equipment.
- If equipment in the way during improvement activities is an off-the-book asset, simply get rid of it, since there are no applications to fill.

Make signboards (Visual Orderliness)

Figure 8-2. Steps in Red-Tag Strategy

Project members should come from every division in the company. It is especially important to actively involve the accounting department in the disposal of unneeded warehouse stock and equipment.

Figure 8-3 outlines a project organization for the strategy.

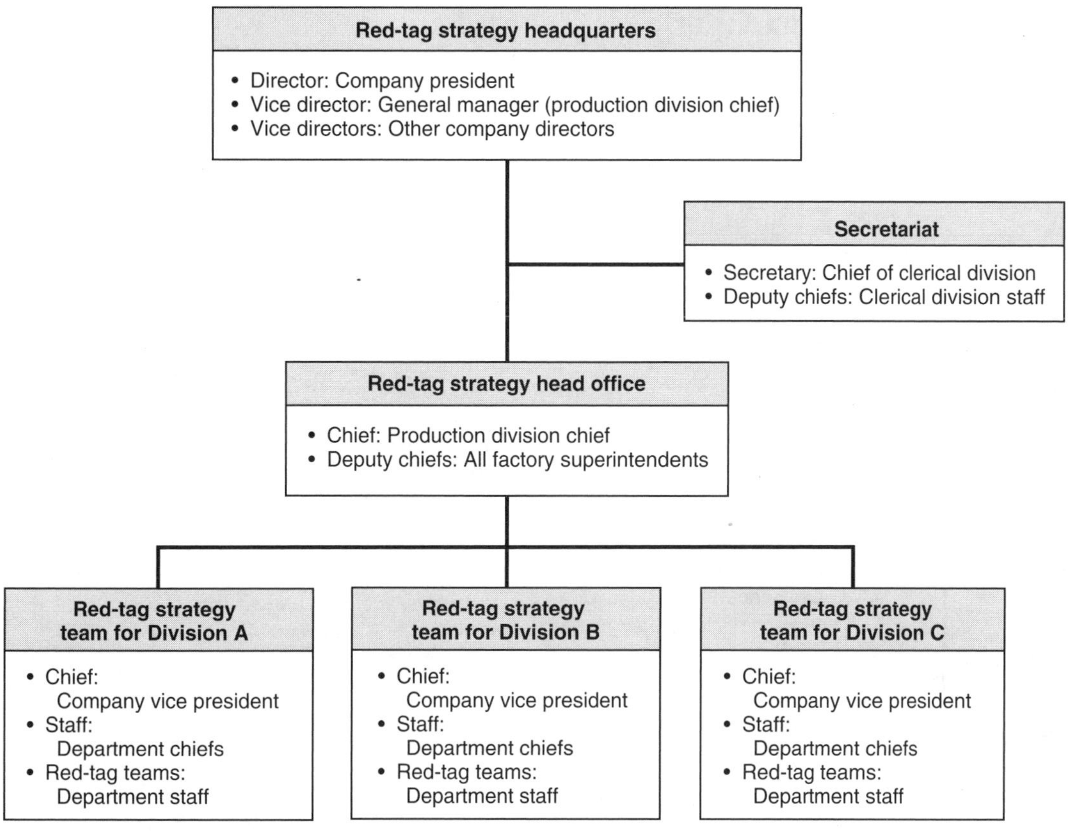

Figure 8-3. Project Organization for Red-Tag Strategy

Step 2. Identify Red-Tag Targets

In the manufacturing area, the main targets for red tags include inventory, equipment, and space.

Inventory can be divided into warehouse inventory and in-process inventory. Warehouse inventory has its own subdivisions: material warehouse, parts warehouse, product warehouse, and so on. We must be especially careful to target all inventory that lacks a specified location (i.e., inventory that piles up along aisles or on factory shelves).

In the clerical division, we must target all unnecessary paperwork, along with superfluous desks, lockers, and the like.

The point is to make it immediately obvious what is needed and what is not. That is what the red-tag strategy is all about.

Figure 8-4 outlines red-tag targets.

Step 3. Set Red-Tag Criteria

The most difficult thing about red-tagging is differentiating what is needed from what is not.

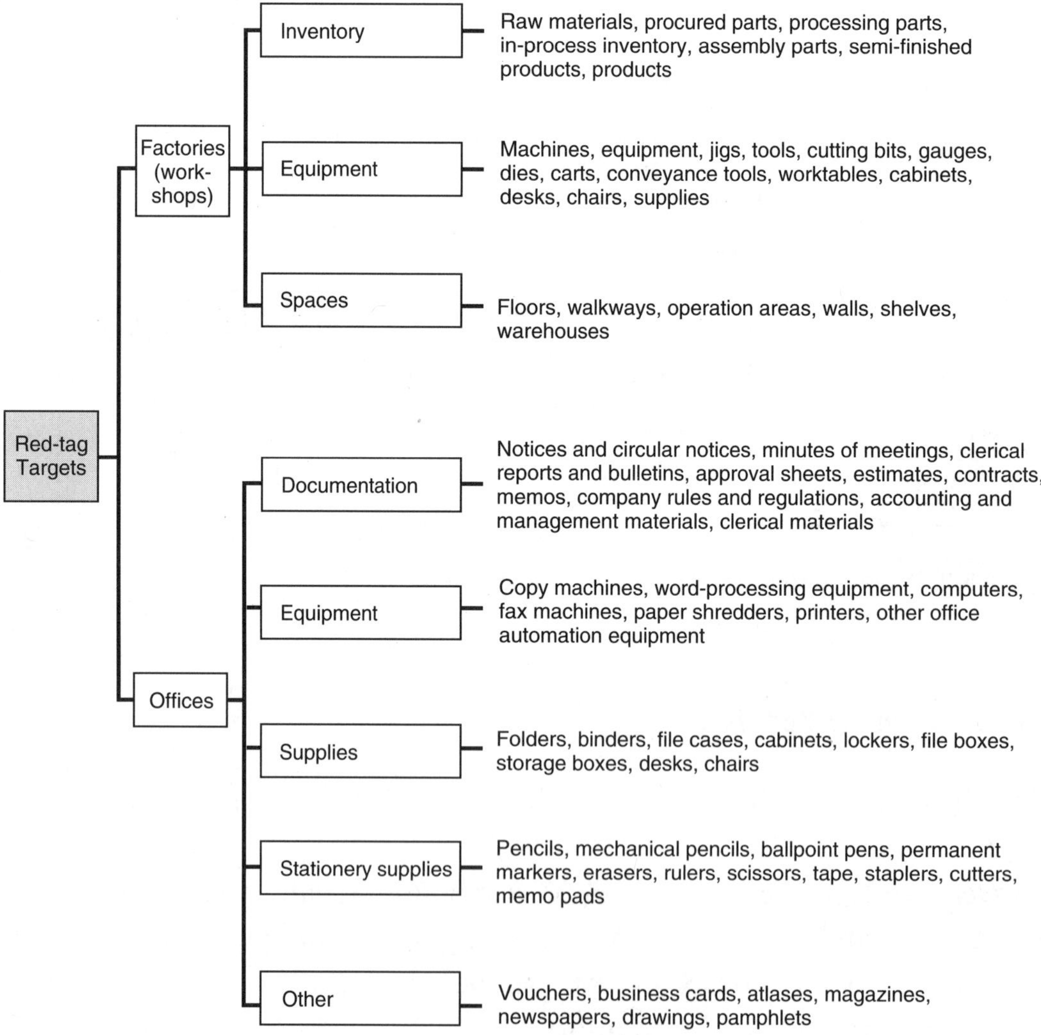

Figure 8-4. Red-Tag Targets

If a red-tag team member asks someone who works in the workshop whether a particular item is needed, the answer is almost always "yes." Even items such as parts and machines that are used once every two or three years will be judged as necessary by the workshop staff. They will look at parts that have been rendered obsolete by equipment changes and say, "Let's hang onto those. We'll find a way to use them sooner or later."

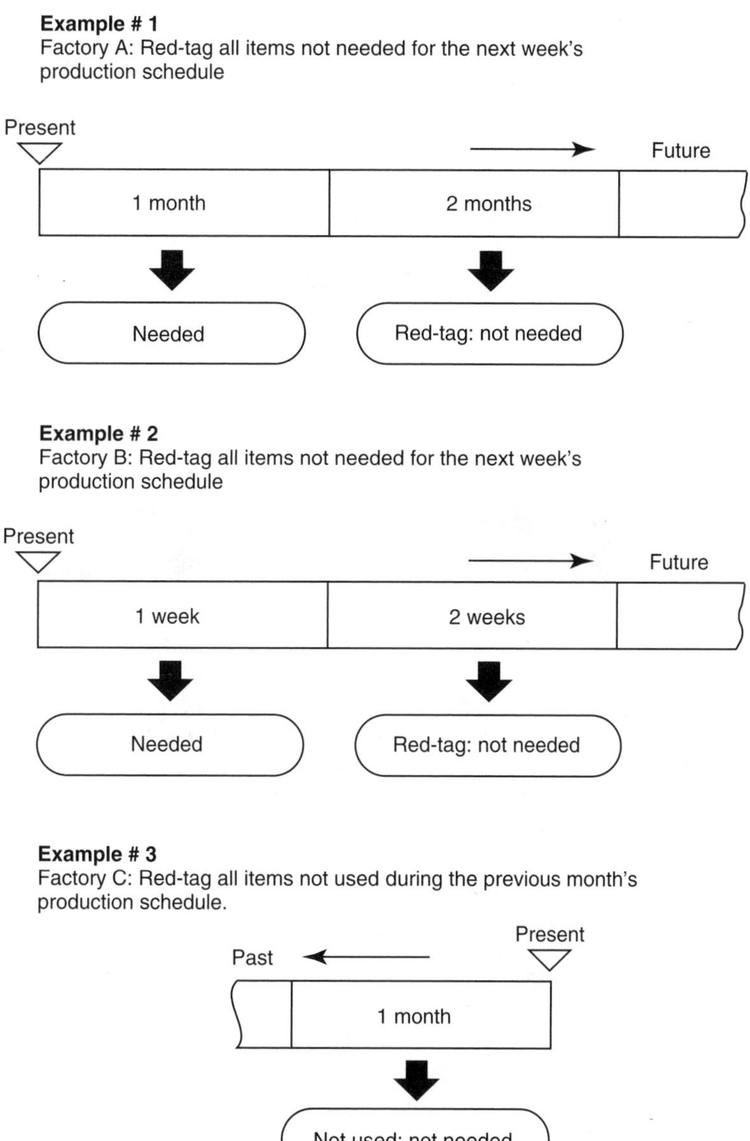

Figure 8-5. Examples of Red-Tag Criteria

All too often, we run into people who exclaim, "Throw it away? What a waste." This sentimental attachment to things waxes especially strong when the things were built or customized by the workshop staff themselves.

The truth is that people are naturally reluctant to throw away anything familiar. How do we get around this? In general we accomplish this by establishing clear-cut criteria for deciding what is needed and what is not. The most common criterion is the next month's production schedule. Whatever is needed for that schedule is retained. Whatever is not required for the schedule is superfluous and can be hauled away.

Some factories may adopt a stricter criterion by using the next week's production schedule instead of the next month's. However, at the average factory, this one-week criterion would result in almost everything being red-tagged. It is best to stick to the one-month production schedule criterion.

Figure 8-5 shows some examples of red-tag criteria.

In factories (like factory C in Figure 8-5) that produce the same types of products month after month, it is safe to say that types of materials, parts, and equipment not used during the previous month will be unneeded next month

RED TAG

Category	1. Raw material 2. In-process stock (3.) Semi-finished goods 4. Products	5. Machine and other equipment 6. Dies and jigs 7. Tools and supplies 8. Other	
Item name:	DOOR		
Manufacturing No.:	PX-180X		
Quantity:	2 UNITS	Value:	$ (total)

Figure 8-6. Example of a Red Tag

also. With regard to managing inventory items, I suggest that someone in the factory make a list of unshipped inventory items and red-tag everything on the list. These items should receive the same treatment as the types of items not used in the factory during the previous month.

Step 4. Make the Red Tags

The material used for red tags does not matter. Use red paper, thick red tape, or whatever else works. The key is to make sure the red tags attract attention. (See Figure 8-6.)

Whatever the material chosen, laminate it with plastic or another material to protect it during repeated use. In offices, it is a good idea to use round red stickers.

Red paper is easy to use for red tags. In any case, the purpose is to make eye-catching memos. The kind of information we should put on the red tags is described next.

- **Category.** Provide a general idea of the type of thing to which the tag has been attached (e.g., a warehouse item or machine). Major categories include raw materials, in-process inventory, products, equipment, jigs, tools, dies, and fixtures.
- **Item name.** Write the name or number of the item to which the red tag has been attached.
- **Quantity.** Indicate the number of items included under this red tag.
- **Reasons.** Describe why you attached a red tag. If the item is an inventory item, give only the main reason ("unneeded," "defective," or "not needed soon").
- **Division.** Write the name of the division responsible for managing the red-tagged item.
- **Date.** Enter the red-tagging date.

Step 5. Attach the Red Tags

Be sure the entire red-tagging team thoroughly understands the criteria for differentiating unneeded items from needed items. Then send them to the workshops.

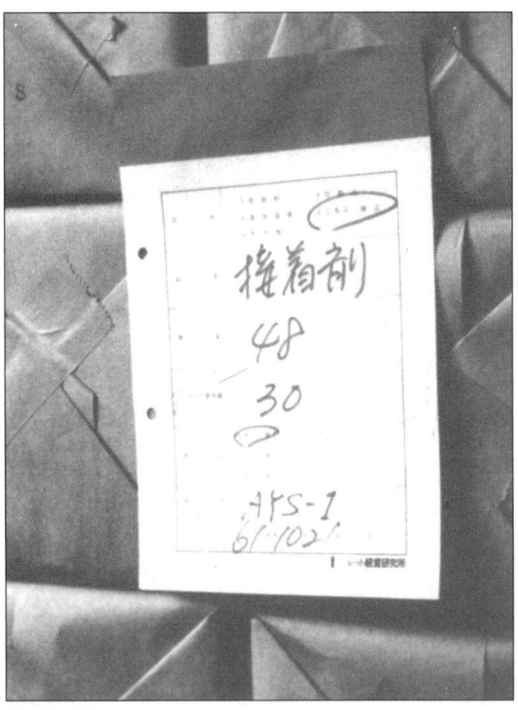

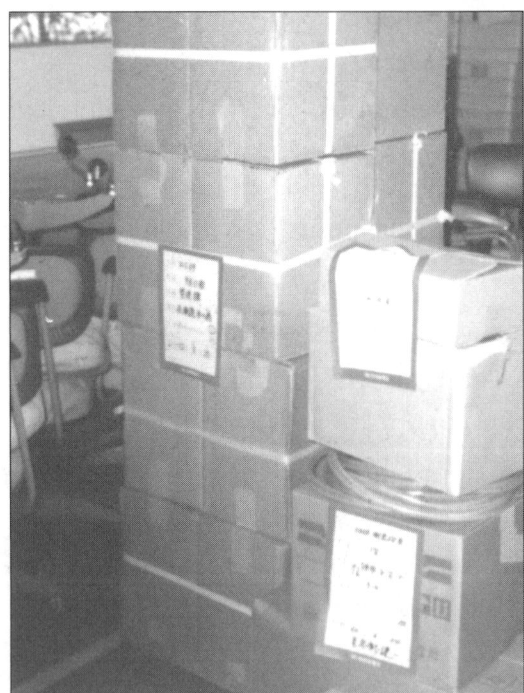

Photo 8-1. Red-tagged Items

It is better if the people who attach the red tags are not from the workshop being examined. Instead, let managers or people from other work areas do the red-tagging. They will be less hindered by sentimental resistance.

Photo 8-1. (continued)

The best way to carry out red-tagging is to do the whole factory quickly — if possible, in one or two days. Stringing out the project period any longer than necessary will lower morale. In short, it is important to regard red-tagging as a swift and powerful event.

Photo 8-1 shows various ways in which items can be red-tagged.

Step 6. Evaluate the Red-Tag Targets

The final step in red-tagging — evaluating red-tag targets — is very important.

First, we should examine the targets in the inventory categories to clarify the types of unneeded warehouse items and how they were warehoused. This will help us decide what to do with the items. Figure 8-7 shows the major types of unneeded warehouse items and the corresponding disposal methods.

After analyzing the unneeded items to understand them better, we are ready to apply the "unneeded inventory items list," the basic tool for reducing unneeded items. Figure 8-8 shows a sample list.

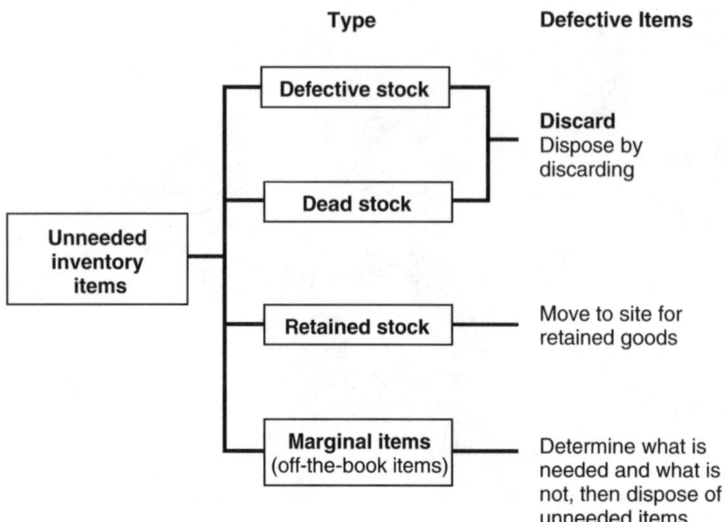

Figure 8-7. Types and Disposal Treatments of Unneeded Inventory Items

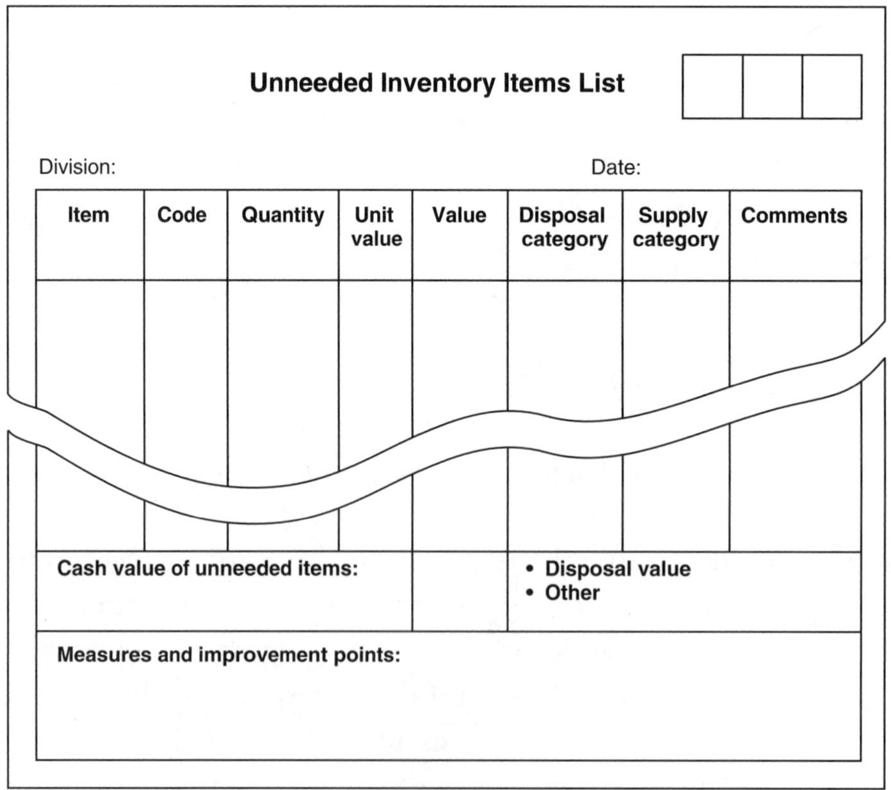

Unneeded Inventory Items List

Division: Date:

Item	Code	Quantity	Unit value	Value	Disposal category	Supply category	Comments
Cash value of unneeded items:					• Disposal value • Other		
Measures and improvement points:							

Figure 8-8. Unneeded Inventory Items List

As a target for red-tagging, equipment is as important as warehouse inventory. We should remove all red-tagged equipment from areas where daily production activities take place. However, large equipment and equipment attached to the floor may be expensive to move. To avoid undue expenses, it is sometimes better not to move such equipment unless it interferes with daily production activities or prevents workshop improvements. Until such a time, label unneeded and unwieldy equipment with a "freeze" red tag. (See Photo 8-2.)

Photo 8-2. Equipment with "Freeze" Tags

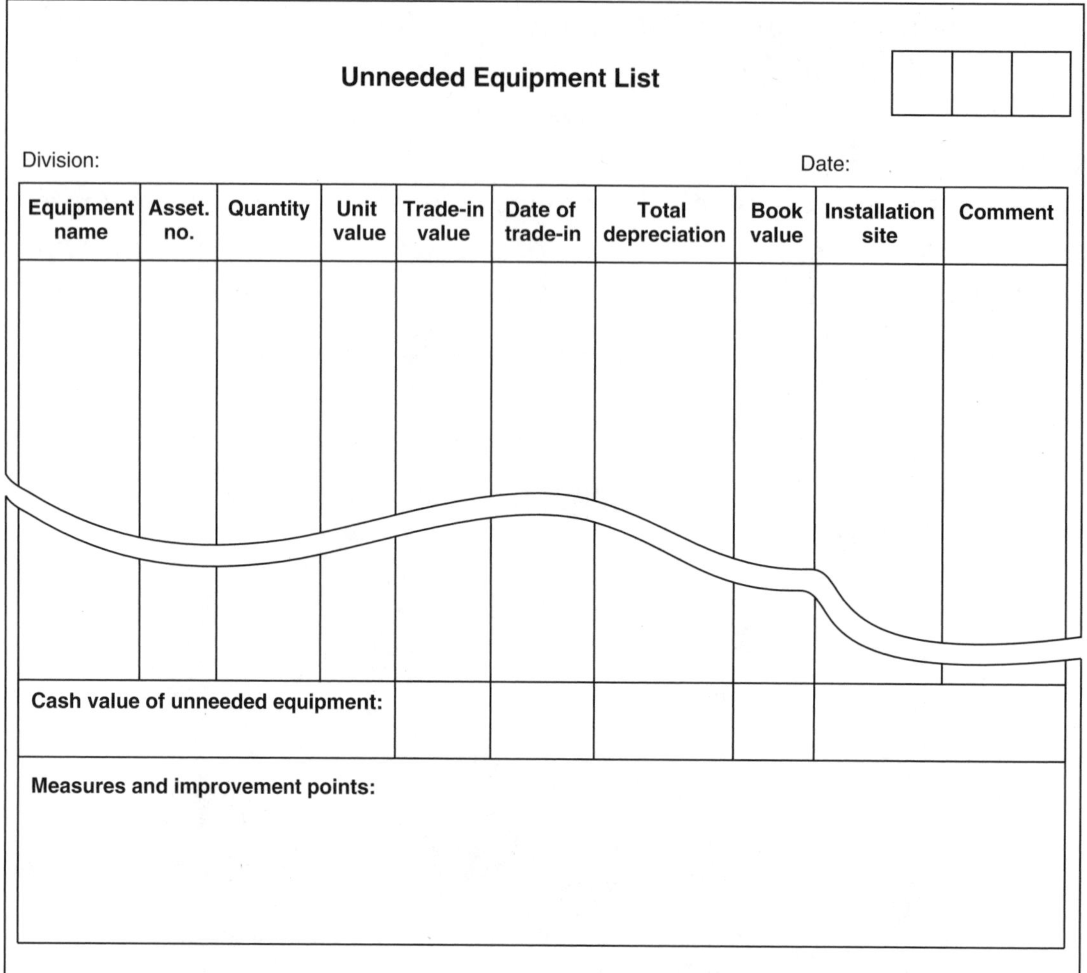

Unneeded Equipment List

Division: Date:

Equipment name	Asset. no.	Quantity	Unit value	Trade-in value	Date of trade-in	Total depreciation	Book value	Installation site	Comment
Cash value of unneeded equipment:									
Measures and improvement points:									

Figure 8-9. Example of Unneeded Equipment List

Figure 8-9 shows an example of the "unneeded equipment list" that we need to draw up and use when deciding how to dispose of red-tagged equipment.

When implementing the red-tag strategy, we move red-tagged items from the production line to a more remote storage site. Afterward, we suddenly find the factory dotted with empty spaces — a sign of real progress. Now we can change the layout of equipment and worktables to take advantage of the added space. Photo 8-3 shows some dramatic space-saving results of the red-tag strategy.

Factory managers who thought they needed to build a new factory to turn out new products have discovered — via the red-tag strategy — plenty of space in the old factory.

Photo 8-3. Empty Space Resulting from the Red-Tag Strategy

RED-TAG COMPUTERS

Wide-variety, small-lot production with short delivery deadlines.

For years we have heard, spoken, and dreamt of this kind of production. Meanwhile, this new wave of diversification has grown stronger, as have the accompanying demands for shorter delivery schedules and lower costs.

Mass production is long gone, and a new era of production centered on small lots of many product models has dawned. This new era encompasses all manufacturing industries, industries that must now find a new production system to provide the key for changing from volume-oriented to model-oriented production.

This radical change is what we call "factory revolution." And making things remains the foundation of production. However, everything above that foundation — product variety, shorter delivery schedules, information-intensiveness, and overall speed — has changed dramatically.

In the days of mass production, factories had only a handful of products to manage. They could afford to take their time in deliveries. Indeed, many such factories shipped products only once a month on regularly scheduled shipping days.

Today, product diversification and small lots require that factories handle a broader assortment of product models — all with increasingly shorter life cycles. This trend has brought an upsurge in the amount of information needed by factories about each of their products.

When the variety of products increases in a factory, the factory must deal with hundreds or even thousands of additional parts. Wider product variety also means an exponential increase in the variety and volume of order-related data and parts-management data.

In this light, how can factories still manage to shorten their delivery times?

Even when factories ship only once a month, they must manage the shipments in two ways: as dealer-based deliveries and as time-based deliveries. This alone requires a vast volume of information. In other words, the switch to diversified, small lots and shorter delivery schedules has engendered revolutions in both factory and information management.

With further expansion of information expected in the future, people are rightfully concerned about how they will handle it all. This trend is making computers an indispensable part of every factory.

This brings up our current subject: red-tag computers.

When managers see all kinds of items being red-tagged and disposed of, they want to know all the details: "We need specific accounts of how parts and products are affected by this reduction of inventory! And we need to know how these things are being disposed of in each factory division!"

RED-TAG STRATEGY: Red-Tag List

	Category	Number of red-tagged items	Total units covered by red tags	Value
1.	Equipment	11	12	
2.	Jig and tools	11	18	
3.	Measuring instruments	10	10	
4.	Materials	10	8,431	
5.	Parts	1,022	6,692,659	
6.	In-process items	6	126	
7.	Quasi products	97	201,238	
8.	Finished products	19	7,655	
9.	By-product materials	60	645	
10.	Office materials	1	1	
11.	Documentation materials	4	21	
	(Total)	1,251		

Figure 8-10. A Computer-generated Red-Tag List

As a way to come up with all of these analytical reference data, I would propose the following:

Red tags themselves are an important type of data because they indicate the factory's superfluous items. But how can we put these data to good use?

One way is to remove the red tags from items just before they are disposed of and enter the data written on the red tags into a computer. To facilitate computerized data processing, data (such as item category, item name, reasons for red-tagging, and company division) should be converted to codes before being entered.

Figures 8-10 and 8-11 show examples of red-tag-related data lists output by a computer. Figure 8-10 shows a general "red-tag list" and Figure 8-11 a more detailed "reason-specific red-tag list."

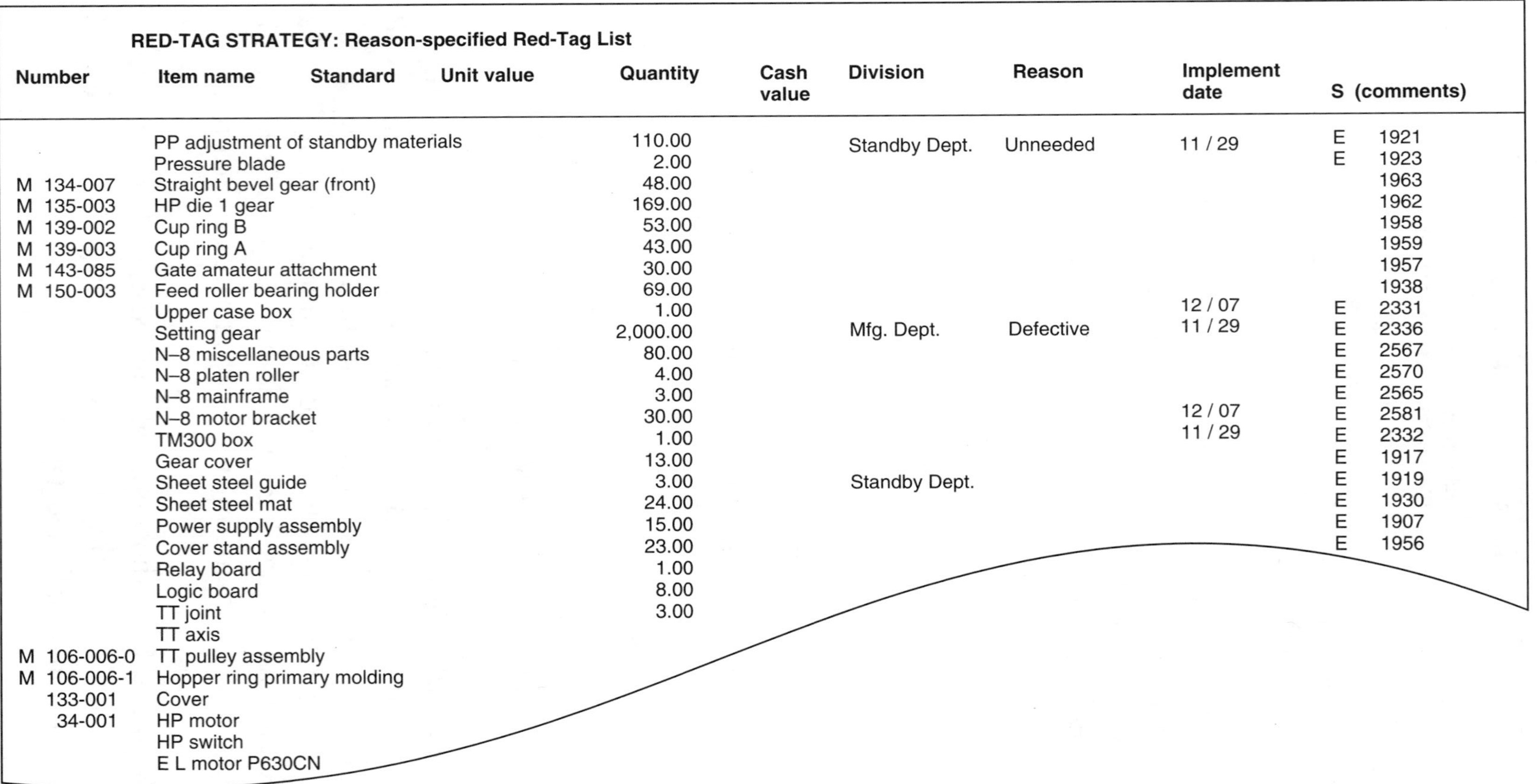

RED-TAG STRATEGY: Reason-specified Red-Tag List

Number	Item name	Standard	Unit value	Quantity	Cash value	Division	Reason	Implement date	S	(comments)
	PP adjustment of standby materials			110.00		Standby Dept.	Unneeded	11 / 29	E	1921
	Pressure blade			2.00					E	1923
M 134-007	Straight bevel gear (front)			48.00						1963
M 135-003	HP die 1 gear			169.00						1962
M 139-002	Cup ring B			53.00						1958
M 139-003	Cup ring A			43.00						1959
M 143-085	Gate amateur attachment			30.00						1957
M 150-003	Feed roller bearing holder			69.00						1938
	Upper case box			1.00				12 / 07	E	2331
	Setting gear			2,000.00		Mfg. Dept.	Defective	11 / 29	E	2336
	N–8 miscellaneous parts			80.00					E	2567
	N–8 platen roller			4.00					E	2570
	N–8 mainframe			3.00					E	2565
	N–8 motor bracket			30.00				12 / 07	E	2581
	TM300 box			1.00				11 / 29	E	2332
	Gear cover			13.00					E	1917
	Sheet steel guide			3.00		Standby Dept.			E	1919
	Sheet steel mat			24.00					E	1930
	Power supply assembly			15.00					E	1907
	Cover stand assembly			23.00					E	1956
	Relay board			1.00						
	Logic board			8.00						
	TT joint			3.00						
	TT axis									
M 106-006-0	TT pulley assembly									
M 106-006-1	Hopper ring primary molding									
133-001	Cover									
34-001	HP motor									
	HP switch									
	E L motor P630CN									

Figure 8-11. A Computer-generated Reason-specific Red-Tag List

RED-TAG EPISODES: LAUGHING AND LEARNING

People working in a factory year after year can watch dirt and grime gradually accumulate without really noticing. The red-tag strategy directly battles such dirt and grime.

Many humorous "war stories" are born of these battles against dirt. The following eight red-tag episodes offer lessons that may be applicable to your own situation.

Twenty Years of Inventory

One plant supervisor recalled how bad the inventory situation had been at his factory. "It was nothing to be proud of. I was shocked by what we found. For instance, we discovered a part that had sat in the warehouse for 20 years!"

It seems that somehow the wrong part name was assigned when the order was made. Until the factory carried out a red-tag campaign, the part sat unnoticed in the warehouse. Apparently, even the person who originally ordered the part failed to notice the mistake.

The factory superintendent reflected, "We were never especially concerned with superfluous parts in the warehouse. As long as nothing was missing, we felt that all was well. The red-tag strategy showed us where we were wrong."

LESSON: Just as we watch for missing parts, so must we watch for excess inventory!

Twice Red-tagged

At another factory, March was designated "red-tag month." Unexpectedly, however, their red-tag project lingered on into April. I asked someone at the factory what happened.

He said, "March is also our company's audit month. People thought the factory would look horrible to the auditors if red tags were stuck all over the place, so we removed them."

The audit was completed at the end of March. In April, the factory workers replaced the red tags. Obviously, these people do not really understand what red-tagging is all about.

LESSON: **Be sure that everyone completely understands the red-tag strategy!**

Red-tagging People

In another factory, people had already red-tagged unneeded inventory, equipment, and space.

The red-tag project leaders exhorted everyone, "Don't hold back! Tag everything that deserves it!"

Later, it was discovered that someone had stuck a red tag on the desk belonging to the chief of the manufacturing department. The department chief in question took it as a bad joke.

I would suggest that red-tagging desks may be called for in certain situations. However, even in jest, never stick a red tag on someone's back where it would seem like the proverbial "kick me" sign.

LESSON: **Don't red-tag people unless you want to be red-tagged yourself!**

Too Many Pallets

When a factory was suffering a pallet shortage, they ordered 300 pallets to fill the gap.

However, a red-tag project was carried out before the new pallets arrived. The project achieved inventory cutbacks that resulted in a 300-pallet surplus.

The factory superintendent asked everyone, "What will we do when we get those new pallets?" With a wry smile, he answered his own question: "I know. We'll turn this place into a pallet factory!"

LESSON: **An appetite for more pallets is a sure symptom of a gluttonous production system.**

A Yellow-Tag Flop

Factories are mysterious entities. It is not always easy to tell what will be needed for production from one month to the next. One factory sought to appease peoples' reluctance to red-tag certain items by allowing yellow tags to be used for items of doubtful necessity. When the red-tag campaign was completed, the factory was full of yellow tags and nary a single red tag. As a result, the campaign was a big flop.

LESSON: Yellow tags only go half the distance!

Red-Tag Stickers

Red-tag project members at a major household electronics manufacturer decided on the convenience of having red-tag forms on adhesive-backed paper, thereby eliminating the need for rolls of cellophane tape. However, these large red-tag stickers were expensive — each one cost over a dollar.

When the factory superintendent saw the fancy stickers, he put a red-tag sticker on the whole roll and announced, "I'm red-tagging these needlessly expensive red-tag stickers!"

LESSON: Improvements — including red-tagging — should be inexpensive. The more money we spend, the less we use our ingenuity to find solutions.

People Should Attach Four Red Tags Apiece

I once visited a factory where people were disappointed with the results of their red-tag project. I figured that with 300 employees, each tagging at least four things, there would be about 1,200 red-tagged items.

When I got to the factory, I asked the superintendent how many items were red-tagged.

"Oh, I guess about 40 or 50," he replied.

No wonder they were disappointed!

LESSON: A red-tag project is not real unless members attach at least four red tags apiece.

Show No Mercy!

At another factory, people had set up a red-tag project, had made the red tags, and were ready to start attaching them to unneeded items. The red-tag team distributed red tags to workshops throughout the factory and instructed workers to stick them on everything that was not needed.

A week later, the red-tag team received nearly every red tag back from the workshops. People had the same excuse for returning them: "There are no unneeded items in our workshop."

LESSON: Everyone must understand and use the same criteria for deciding what is needed and what is not.

LESSON: Everyone in the target workshop will agree that they need everything. Instead, let managers or workers from other areas do the red-tagging. (One tip is to avoid the production engineering staff because they tend to feel sentimental about the workshops they know so well.)

As these episodes illustrate, red-tagging reaches into the hearts of factories and can bring striking changes. It is an important strategy.

The only thing that can produce greater results and boost improvement higher than red-tagging is visual Orderliness — the signboard strategy.

CASE STUDY: THE RED-TAG STRATEGY AT COMPANY S

The following case study of red-tag strategy implementation occurred at company S.

Finding Oneself Amid Waste

Company S's production division sponsored a meeting of the production management subcommittee on February 24. Their intention was to concentrate on the 5S's and lay the foundation for factory improvements. They recognized the need for top manufacturing management's understanding and support — but so far no progress had been made.

The production division chief addressed the meeting in a loud voice: "I want us to implement the 5S's and get ready to start improving the factory. Let's make March our '5S month.'"

This suggestion was considered a prime directive and employees inaugurated their 5S month by kicking off a red-tag campaign. In turn, on March 1 the production division chief sent the memo shown in Figure 8-12 to every manufacturing department in the company.

The production management division would be active only in the overall promotion and organization of the red-tag project. Details would be handled by the factory people themselves using their know-how and ingenuity.

MEMORANDUM

To: All Manufacturing Divisions
Re: 5S Implementation

Date: March 1
Issued by: Production management division chief

1. Main Objectives
(1) To lay the groundwork for flow production
(2) To reduce inventory and raise efficiency in capital turnover

2. 5S Month
March has been designated 5S Month.

3. Main 5S Activities
(1) Attaching red tags (Organization)
By March 10, red tags must be attached to the following target items if they have not been used for one month or their status has otherwise remained unchanged.
(2) Red-tag target items
- Empty space
- Equipment (carts, dies, etc.)
- Shelved items (materials, in-process inventory, quasi products)
- Other unneeded items (desks, shelves, other furnishings, etc.)

Figure 8-12. 5S Implementation Memo at Company S

At one company factory, employees figured they would need 500 red tags. However, once they started tagging things they ran out. They ended up using over 1,500 red tags — three times their original estimate.

Because of red-tagging, people finally came to realize how much dirt and waste they were working around.

Anticipatory Large-Lot Production

The key to survival in today's highly competitive manufacturing world is to produce a wide variety of products in small lots and with short delivery times. In addition, the products must reflect high quality and low cost.

Founded in 1954, company S is currently one of Japan's top manufacturers of stainless steel sinks and other kitchen fixtures and furnishings. To encourage employees to meet the competitive challenge, company S's president came up with the "CSS" strategy ("company S's survival").

Part of this strategy was to set up a comprehensive computer-based sales/production system to help company S promptly identify current market needs and distribute this information to the proper manufacturing divisions. In this way, they were trying to beef up their information-related strengths by putting more information into the company "brains" and making that information more accessible.

However, brains are not enough. A company must have a quick and agile body that can provide prompt "hardware" responses to the "software" (information) it receives from the computer system.

This all boils down to a radical change in the character of the large lot-oriented factories. Obviously, making such a change is an enormous project requiring more than incremental factory improvements. Many people — not liking the idea — will be reluctant to follow along. Such radical improvement will require that improvement teams put in long hours after work, day after day. First, they must reeducate the workers. Then they must overhaul the factory layout and change the production methods.

This is nothing short of a "factory revolution."

Factory improvement is an underlying assumption of factory revolution. Carrying out the 5S's is the only way to lay the foundation for factory improvement and to set the stage for the revolution.

It is easy to find manufacturing people in Japan who are familiar with the 5S's. In fact, as mentioned earlier, many Japanese factories display signs and banners showing the first two (and most basic) of the 5S pillars — Organization and Orderliness. However, few factory people have a clear idea of how to actually establish them.

Company S understood what red-tagging meant and adopted the following basic policy points:

Properly arrange items by removing currently unneeded items. Then make them orderly in all directions: horizontal, vertical, perpendicular, and parallel.

This simple statement is all a company needs to ignite sparks of awareness in its factories.

Ready for Improvement!

Company S's inventory is now one-third what it was six months ago. Not only did they get their large and small factories involved in red-tagging, they also enlisted the participation of several subcontractors.

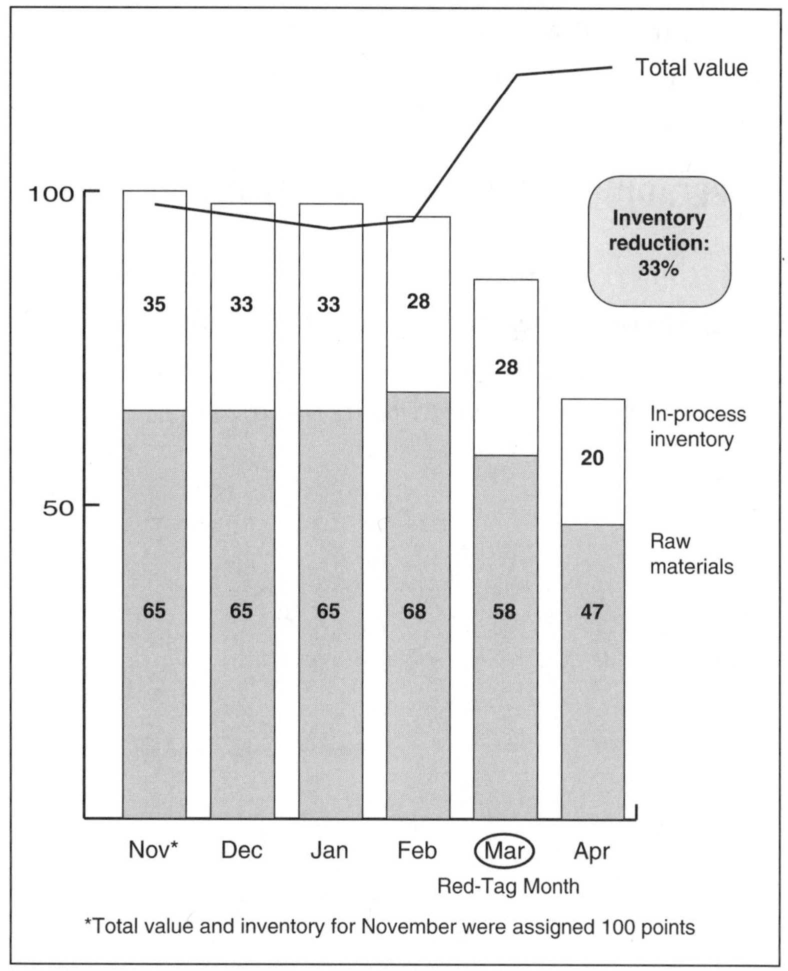

Figure 8-13. Achieving a 33 Percent Inventory Reduction

As a result, some factory managers reported that implementing the 5S's was enough to boost productivity 20 percent. This productivity increase was probably due to the elimination of the need to search for parts and tools and the removal of conveyance-related waste. Another reason was that factories became conducive to visual control.

Company S's factories now had too many pallets and carts and their inventory levels had dropped dramatically. In the case of the large factory that received the most attention, red-tagging resulted in a one-third inventory reduction over the level recorded just six months earlier. (See Figure 8-13.) People were amazed at how spacious their factories had become after red-tagging. In fact, they felt a little disoriented without the familiar clutter.

As 5S implementors, if we can get this far, we are halfway there. The stage is set for factory improvement and everyone is anxious for the curtain to rise and for improvements to begin.

CASE STUDY: SPREADING THE NEWS ABOUT RED-TAG IMPLEMENTATION

Figure 8-14 shows the memo that company A management sent to employees in all divisions regarding the implementation of their red-tag strategy. Figures 8-15 and 8-16 show the "red-tag strategy checklist" and the "red-tag strategy report form" referred to in the memo.

MEMORANDUM

TO: All divisions (division chiefs and department chiefs) November 24, 1993
RE: **Implementation of Red-Tag Strategy**

You all know that the Operations Division and others have successfully carried out red-tag strategies. However, because there are still a lot of space-wasting unneeded items in various workplaces, we are undertaking the following additional red-tag strategy in order to lay the foundation for JIT improvement. We hope we can count on your cooperation in this effort.

1. Objective
Remove space-wasting unneeded items from workplaces and lay the foundation for JIT improvement.

2. Implementation period
February 13-24: Red-tag strategy period
February 28: Report on red-tag strategy results

3. Red-tag targets
Equipment, production, inventory items, etc.

4. Criteria for red-tagging
Attach red tags to all equipment, inventory items, etc. that will not be required under March's production schedule.

5. Organization
(1) Head office
CEO for overall red-tag strategy: President
Vice-CEOs: Managing director and factory superintendent
Secretary: Operations division chief
(2) Operations division and other divisions
CEOs for red-tag strategy: Each division chief
Vice-CEOs: Each department chief
Division and department chiefs will set up a red-tag strategy promotional organization within each division.

6. Implementation method
(1) Members of the red-tag strategy promotional organization will attach red tags individually to items judged as unneeded based on reasons other than those listed in the red-tag criteria used by the division concerned. They will also notify the relevant departments of the number of items red-tagged in this way.
(2) While waiting for an investigative team to study the red-tagged items, division employees will sort out items and start arranging for their disposal.
(3) Regarding shelving or other immovable assets: Separate items for which disposal applications have already been made. Then clear out as many of them from the workshop as possible.
(4) Main tasks in red-tag strategy (see diagram).

Figure 8-14. Memo to All Division and Department Heads

		CEO (head office) Vice-CEO (head office)	Secretary-general	Red-tag strategy executive officers in each division	Red-tag strategy promotion team	Division members
Develop red-tag strategy		Issue general instructions for red-tag strategy.	After consulting with CEO and vice-CEOs, issue more detailed instructions.	Act as person responsible within operation division based on executive officers' policies.	Act as the team that carries out specific red-tag activities.	Investigate disposal of red-tagged items.
Main tasks		←	Same	Make sure everyone understands the red-tag strategy and then establish the strategy's general direction.	Review their own workplaces, related workplaces, and various warehouses. Use appended checklist for reviews.	Dispose of red-tagged items from their own division. For items from other divisions, consult with division staff first, then attach white tags to items that cannot be disposed of or that must be moved to temporary storage. Determine disposal method for all other items.
Report results			↑	←	←	Fill out appended report form.

7. Long-term storage
Contact the secretary-general's office to receive instructions regarding storage sites for parts that cannot be disposed of. Store items to be disposed of during this business term separately from items to be disposed of after this term.

8. Disposal of administrative materials
Consult with the General Affairs Department before disposing of administrative materials.

9. Other
The red-tag strategy promotion team should work with the head office in dealing with any problems that arise after the red-tagging has been completed.

Figure 8-14 (continued)

Red-Tag Strategy Checklist

	Target	Checkpoints
Clerical	File cabinets, books, documents	Dispose of all books and documents for which the specified storage period has expired. Bundle up all documents that require incineration. Leave necessary files alone or put them into storage.
	Signs and other posted items	Remove and dispose of all outdated or otherwise old items.
	Desks, tables, etc.	Organize what is on top of, inside or underneath, and next to all desks. Leave only items necessary to the current operation on the desktop. (Minimize the number of documents, tools, and other small articles kept there.)
	Fixtures and machines	Dispose of all unneeded items.
Workplace	Inventory items	All quasi-products, finished products, in-process inventory, testing materials, etc. that fall outside of the red-tagging criteria.
	Equipment	Items that fall within the red-tagging criteria and that are not expected to be needed, off-the-book items, etc.
	Worktables	Items that fall outside of the red-tagging criteria or that are rendered unnecessary by a layout revision or other reason.
	Jigs and measuring instruments	Unneeded shared or individually used items and defective items.
	Tools	Unneeded items stored in boxes or on shelves.
	Wires, cables, etc.	Return all materials that cannot be disposed of to the distribution department or store them in a common storage site.
	By-product materials	Store or dispose of unneeded bolts, nuts, clamps, chemicals, etc.
	Shelving and boxes	Dispose of all shelving and boxes that are unnecessary and/or detract from productivity.
	Drawings	Check what is not being used currently and what is being stored in duplicate.
	Other	Be sure to dispose of whatever does not seem to be needed.
Warehouse	Retained goods	Items related to management or design that are of questionable need in schedules, off-the-book items, items that are removed from equipment and stored, items that have never been used, etc.
	Books, files, wires, steel plates, metal fittings, etc.	Review all of these and dispose of all unneeded items.
	Equipment	Dispose of all items not expected to be used, old and worn items, and outdated items.

Figure 8-15. Red-Tag Strategy Checklist

TO: Operation Division Chief

Red-Tag Strategy Report Form

Date:
Department name:
Signature:

Machines, devices, etc.	Name and processing number
Remove inventory items from workplace	
Disposed of, filed, or placed in library	
Other	

Make space, include areas with equipment for which a current-term removal application has been made	Note the factory name and the number of floors in the factory

Figure 8-16. Red-Tag Strategy Report Form

ESSENTIALS FOR PROMOTING THE RED-TAG STRATEGY

Table 8-1 lists the general steps for promoting the red-tag strategy.

Step 1. Establish Red-Tag Teams

The departmental productivity council is responsible for establishing red-tag teams.

1. Red-tag teams should comprise employees from production engineering, quality control, and other departments, all of whom are judged competent to make red-tag decisions.
2. If possible, there should be enough participants to carry out red-tagging for all target sites at the same time. Teams should have about five members.
3. Once teams are established, clear divisions of duties for specific red-tag target sites should be made for team members. Members should also be able to objectively carry out other red-tag duties.

The departmental productivity council is responsible for assigning responsibilities for Organization in red-tagged areas.

Table 8-2 shows the persons responsible for implementing Organization.

Step 2. Attach Red Tags

Establish red-tag targets as shown in Table 8-3.

Next, define your terms. (See Table 8-4.)

Table 8-5 shows the procedures for ranking red-tagged items to be organized.

As shown in Tables 8-6, 8-7, 8-8, and 8-9, we next establish standards for red-tagging items in the various work areas.

- red-tag standards for factories (based on the production schedule)
- red-tag standards for warehouses
- red-tag standards in tool and jig room, die workshop, and measuring instrument room
- red-tag standards related to construction, power equipment, maintenance, R&D centers, and general affairs

Table 8-1. Steps in Red-Tag Strategy Promotion

Activity	Team	Targets
Establish teams	Headquarters productivity council	
Attach red tags	Red-tagging teams	All factory workshops and appropriate management and clerical sections
Transport and collect unneeded and useless items	Persons responsible for Organization in red-tagged areas	All factory workshops and appropriate management and clerical sections
Storage and disposal of unneeded and useless items	Headquarters productivity council	Persons responsible for Organization in red-tagged areas
Report and follow-up on disposal results	Headquarters productivity council	Persons responsible for Organization in red-tagged areas

Table 8-2. Persons Responsible for Organization

Red-tagged Target	Persons Responsible for Organization
Inventory Items	Chief of production management department
Equipment and space	Chief of production engineering department
Equipment and measuring instruments	Chief of quality control department
Support for disposal	Chief of production department

Table 8-3. Establish Red-Tag Targets

Target	Description
Inventory	Raw materials, assembly parts, in-process inventory, semi-finished goods, and other items related to manufacturing
Equipment	Machines, equipment, tools, measuring instruments, carts, supplies, utilities, and pallets
Space	Operation areas, walkways, shelves, and storage spaces

Table 8-4. Define Terms

Needed/Unneeded	Term	Description	Red Tag?
Needed items	Needed items	Items needed now or very soon for current production activities	NO
Unneeded items	Unneeded items	Usable items seldom used or not appropriate in their current storage site; also surplus items	YES
	Useless items	Useless items; to be disposed of, sold, or returned to their source	

Table 8-5. Ranking Items to Be Organized

Rank	Rank Division	Use Period
A	Useless items; not used	Items or spaces that either will not be used for the next year or have not been used during the previous year
B	Unneeded items; seldom used	Items or spaces that either will not be used for at least the next 6 months or have not been used during the previous 6 or more months
C	Unneeded items; occasionally used	Items or spaces that either will not be used for the next 3-6 months or have not been used during the previous 3-6 months
D	Unneeded items, not to be used for a while	Items or spaces that either will not be used during the next 3 months or have not been used during the previous 3 months

Note: Use periods for each rank are subject to change (e.g., when change is required by the company's inventory management regulations or when otherwise deemed necessary).

Table 8-6. Standards for Factory Red-Tagging

Target	Red-Tagging Standard
Warehouse	Items unlikely to be used in the next month
Equipment	Equipment units unlikely to be used in the next month
Spaces	Spaces unlikely to be used in the next month

Table 8-7. Standards for Warehouse Red-Tagging

Target	Red-Tagging Standard
Warehouse	Items that will not be used in the next 3 months or have not been used during the past 3 months
Equipment	Equipment units that will not be used in the next 3 months or have not been used in the past 3 months
Spaces	Spaces that will not be used in the next 3 months or have not been used in the past 3 months

Table 8-8. Standards for Red-Tagging in Tool and Jig Room, Die Workshop, and Measuring-Instruments Room

Target	Red-Tagging Standard
Warehouse	Items that will not be used in the next 3 months or have not been used in the past 3 months
Equipment	Equipment units that will not be used in the next 3 months or have not been used in the past 3 months
Spaces	Spaces that will not be used in the next 3 months or have not been used in the past 3 months

Table 8-9. Standards for Red-Tagging Items Related to Construction, Power Equipment, Maintenance, R & D Centers, and General Affairs

Target	Red-Tagging Standard
Warehouse	Items unlikely to be used in the next 6 months
Equipment	Equipment units unlikely to be used in the next 6 months
Spaces	Spaces unlikely to be used in the next 6 months

Note 1: Adjust the above target items and standard periods based on the standards of each relevant division or department.

Note 2: In principle, if uncertain whether to include a particular item as a red-tag target, consider the item a red-tag target.

At this stage, we are ready to attach red tags.

The red-tag teams will work over a three-day period. ("D" is the start day, "D-day + 1" is day 2, and "D-day + 2" is day 3.)

1. Determine the red-tag schedule.
   - Determine details of the red-tag schedule beforehand.
   - Complete all red-tag activities within the scheduled three days.
2. Gather information prior to red-tag implementation.
   - Each red-tag team member must gather all necessary information (production schedule, dead inventory list, etc.) for his or her duties (location and target items) before beginning red-tag implementation.
3. Categorize red-tag target items.
   - Red-tag target items should be categorized with the cooperation of operators and supervisors at each workplace.
   - Operators and supervisors should actively help to organize items at their workplace.
4. Attach red tags.
   - When attaching red tags to items, enter the target location, date, red-tag campaign number (for each department, person, or serial number), the relevant standard and item category, item number, item name, amount, and quantitative unit. If the red tag is not self-adhesive, use tape, glue, or pins to attach the tag. The method used must be approved by the relevant supervisor.
5. Create red-tag lists.
   - Issue red-tag lists and red tags at the same time. The lists should have entry spaces for the red-tag campaign number, item categories, item numbers (or control numbers), item names, amounts, and quantitative units.
6. Assign to red-tagged items an Organization ranking.
   - When attaching a red tag, people must write on the red-tag list the item's Organization ranking and the name of the Organization person responsible for that item or space. Omit nothing — if some items are difficult to judge, seek help from the relevant supervisor.

7. Compile red-tag lists.
   - ➤ Have red-tag teams gather the attached red-tag lists, enter page numbers, and immediately send the originals to the chief of the departmental productivity council.
   - ➤ The council chief should then send copies of the lists to people in charge of Organization for the listed items so that Organization implementation can begin.

Step 3. Collect and Transport Unneeded and Useless Items

The primary collection site for red-tagged items should be specified by the departmental productivity council according to Organization targets and rankings.

Regarding the operation of exempt areas:

- The departmental productivity council should specify and operate any exempt areas to help ensure successful red-tag campaign results (i.e., removal of waste from workplaces).
- Within the specified timetable, the promotion team and other departmental staff will transport all red-tagged items (unneeded and useless items) from exempt areas by the end of the Organization period (D-day + 3).
- Appoint separate red-tag teams to work the exempt areas. They should handle the red-tagged items using the same procedures applied to other areas.
- To ensure successful Organization activities in the exempt areas, have a departmental promotion team lend its support for the following activities.

Lastly, we are ready to collect and transport the red-tagged items.

- Have each promotion team collect the red-tagged items at the specified locations.
- Collect all red-tagged items at the primary collection site within 48 hours (two working days) of the red-tag implementation.
- Determine the Organization rankings and assignments for all red-tagged items before transporting them to the primary collection site.

- Once red-tagged items arrive at the primary collection site, make individual weight, number, volume, and floor-space requirements/ measurements according to each Organization target and ranking.

Step 4. Store and Dispose of Unneeded and Useless Items

Treat unneeded and useless items according to their Organization ranking as shown in Table 8-10. These treatment methods are reviewed in Table 8-11. Treatment procedures follow:

1. For the disposal and sale of these items:
   - ➤ Collect at primary collection site (by D-day + 5).
   - ➤ Make approval list of items for disposal or sale (by D-day + 10).
   - ➤ Measure (weight or volume of) items for disposal or sale (by D-day + 12).
   - ➤ Dispose of or sell items (by D-day + 30).
2. For returns, loaners, location changes, and Orderliness:
   - ➤ Have them collected at the primary collection site (by D-day + 5).
   - ➤ Store them at their specified site (by D-day + 10).
   - ➤ Have loaned items put to use.
3. Once these treatment procedures are completed as specified, enter the treatment date and method in the "Treatment result" column.

Step 5. Report and Follow Up on Disposal Results

Have the red-tag teams provide departmental productivity councils with summary reports of red-tagging campaigns and their results.

Once all red-tagged items have been treated, the departmental productivity councils can compile a treatment result report that includes the following:

- a list of red-tagged items
- a breakdown of red-tagged items by Organization ranking
- the weight (or volume or value) of scrapped and sold items
- documents generated during treatment of red-tagged items

Table 8-10. Treatment of Items According to Organization Ranking

Organization Rank	Treatment
Useless A	Dispose of, sell, return, lend out
Unneeded B	Return, lend out, change location, apply Orderliness
Unneeded C	Return, change location, apply Orderliness
Unneeded D	Change location, apply Orderliness

Table 8-11. Treatment Methods

Treatment	Description
Dispose of	Dispose of as scrap or incinerate items that are useless or unneeded for any purpose.
Sell	Sell off to other companies items that are useless or unneeded for any purpose.
Return	Return items to their previous owner (if the item is an unprocessed claim item from a supplier company) or to where they were previously.
Lend out	Send items to other sections of the company that can use them.
Change location	Move items to another specified storage site.
Apply Orderlinesss	Return items in better order or apply Orderliness to improve storage method and then store the items.

Each departmental productivity council should hold a meeting to present this report, copies of which should go to the productivity subcommittee.

The productivity subcommittee will compile the reports from each department and present them to the productivity promotion council. Unneeded items that can be reused will be registered at certain storage sites and receive top priority for later use. Inventory managers will carry out thorough follow-

Table 8-12. Red-Tagging Categories for Production Facilities

No.	Description	Category
Inventory		
1	Excess inventory (more parts and materials than required for the current product model)	Unneeded
2	Items left over after production halt due to change in production schedule or problems concerning materials or quality factors	Unneeded
3	Spare attachments and other parts being stored with no current demand	Unneeded
4	Items used for custom-order products	Useless
5	Items discontinued due to design or specification changes	Useless
6	Items with material defects	Useless
7	Items with processing defects	Useless
Equipment		
1	Items not required for production	Unneeded
2	Machines, equipment, jigs, tools, dies, etc. needed for production but: (a) unrelated to the product model currently in production (b) currently out of operation due to breakdown repairs, routine maintenance, or improvement repairs. (c) broken, worn-out, and abandoned equipment	 Unneeded Unneeded Useless
Other (supplies, desks, etc.)		
1	Cleaning equipment: equipment that is unneeded or otherwise in surplus	Unneeded
2	Desks: Extra desks (more than needed by managers and supervisors)	Unneeded
3	Signs: More than required (not yet targeted for Organization implementation)	Unneeded
4	Material storage boxes: Empty boxes or boxes misappropriated for personal use	Unneeded
5	Pallets: Empty pallets or more than are needed for current operations	Unneeded
6	Other: Items in work areas, rest areas, lavatories, etc. that are unused or otherwise in surplus	Useless

up operations (e.g., reviewing volumes of orders and payments, reviewing payment cycles) and work to maintain Organization at workplaces. As part of their 5S activities, the departmental productivity councils will evaluate and inspect these conditions.

References to Use During Red-Tag Implementation

Table 8-12 presents red-tagging categories for production facilities. Table 8-13 shows what to look for when identifying unneeded and useless items.

Table 8-13. What to Look for When Identifying Useless and Unneeded Items

Target	No.	What to Look For
Jig storage shelves	1	Jigs that are unused or cannot be used, and extra jigs
	2	Miscellaneous goods other than jigs
	3	Items piled on the top and bottom shelves
Tool boxes, drawers, lock-equipped cabinets, lockers	1	Hammers, wrenches, knives, other surplus tools
	2	Micrometers, calipers, dials, gauges, other surplus measuring instruments
	3	Rags, gloves, oil cans, other surplus consumables
	4	Magazines, books, other personal property
Floors	1	Items left in corners
	2	Equipment, large jigs, carts, other items not being used
	3	In-process inventory, materials, and scrap piles left due to poor quality or other problems
	4	Parts, defective goods, etc. left under conveyors, next to windows or pillars, or below machines, worktables, or shelves
Parts storage shelves and storerooms	1	Materials that have not been moved for a long time (long-term inventory or other retained goods)
Outdoors	1	Materials (useless inventory) that have not been moved for several months
	2	Carts and pallets
	3	Scrap piles
	4	Dies and jigs
Near the desks of supervisors and inspection staff	1	Defective goods and other ignored items
	2	Surplus inventory from parts replacements (not yet returned)
	3	Drawings not being used
	4	Excess rags or other consumables
	5	Other unneeded odds and ends

QUESTIONS AND ANSWERS ABOUT THE RED-TAG STRATEGY

The two questions presented here reflect many of the doubts commonly associated with the proper implementation of the red-tag strategy. The following answers should help to dispel these doubts.

Five Keys to a Successful Red-Tag Strategy

Question: We tried implementing the red-tag strategy once but it did not work very well. Are there keys to ensure its success?

At most factories, the red-tag strategy is the hands-on tool used to implement Organization. At some factories, the red-tag strategy followed by the signboard strategy have reduced inventory by one-third while raising productivity by a factor of 1.2.

Generally, companies that are unsuccessful with the red-tag strategy are companies that have been unsuccessful with other strategies — like small-group activities and employee suggestion systems. Their problem is a basic weakness evidenced by low employee motivation and half-hearted cooperation.

Until this fundamental problem is resolved, they cannot reasonably hope for much success in the red-tag strategy. At any large company, responsibility for such a problem lies squarely on the shoulders of management.

The red-tag strategy deserves at least a moderate amount of cooperation and effort. In Figure 8-17, I list five keys to a successful red-tag strategy.

Key 1: Teach the Importance of the 5S's.

The 5S's are every factory's key for long-term survival. Their proper implementation brings immeasurable benefit to quality, productivity, and delivery lead time. Therefore, it is essential that everyone — from top managers to shop-floor operators — understands the importance of the 5S's.

Key 2: Be Sure Everyone Understands What Organization Means.

Put bluntly, Organization means eliminating whatever is not needed. Simply rearranging unneeded goods into neater piles is not Organization. If people have done this, they require retraining.

Key 3: The Company President Should Lead the Red-Tag Promotion Council.

The initial question ("We tried implementing the red-tag strategy once...") reveals a lack of confidence — as if it was attempted by just a few people as a quiet experiment. The red-tag strategy will not succeed unless the company president gets behind it and personally leads the red-tag promotion council. The red-tag strategy organization must be rooted in the company's managerial hierarchy and receive the support of the entire company.

Key 4: **Have the Red Tags Attached by People With No Direct Relationship to the Target Items.**

Actual red-tagging should be done by teams of management-division people who have no direct connection with the target items. If the people who work with (or near) the target items were to do the red-tagging, their emotional reaction would be to resist throwing out unneeded items such as jigs that they made or machines that they have used in the past.

Figure 8-17. Five Keys for Success in the Red-Tag Strategy

Key 5: **Establish and Use 5S Patrols.**

Organization is followed by Orderliness and the rest of the 5S's: Cleanliness, Standardized Cleanup, and Discipline. As 5S implementation proceeds, 5S patrols should be formed to periodically patrol workplaces and check 5S conditions against a 5S checklist. It also helps to have the company president make personal inspections every once in a while. Such patrols and inspections give powerful reminders to people who have allowed themselves to backslide in maintaining 5S conditions.

Five Suggestions about Red-Tag Implementation

Question: After implementing the red-tag strategy several months ago, we found that the actual number of items tagged was much lower than expected. Have you any suggestions about the actual work of red-tagging items?

It is unusual that red-tagging should fail to produce an abundance of red-tagged items. Of ten companies who reported their red-tag results to me, eight said they red-tagged many more items than they thought they would. One factory actually red-tagged close to 30 10-ton trucks; another ended up with two large empty rooms.

The main stumbling block when red-tagging items is the fear that you will move out needed items whose absence tomorrow will cause production to grind to a halt.

My advice is to adhere firmly to the red-tagging criteria and let tomorrow take care of itself. I would also offer the following five suggestions about red-tagging.

Suggestion 1: **If in Doubt, Red-Tag It!**

Do not be hesitant or fearful when red-tagging items. If you are unsure whether an item is needed or not, red-tag it anyway. Don't think, "Maybe they need this." Instead think, "I don't see why they need this." And remember that I adamantly oppose "yellow-tagging" items that are in doubt.

Suggestion 2: **Finish Red-tagging in One or Two Days.**

Avoid spending a week or ten days on red-tagging. The longer the process takes, the more unpleasant it will be for everyone concerned.

Also, if a workplace is warned in advance of a red-tagging campaign, some people may hide unneeded items that they want to keep. Therefore, red-tagging should be done with little or no advance notice and should be completed within a day or two.

Suggestion 3: **Set a Target Number of Red Tags to Be Used.**

Instead of handing them out as needed, determine in advance approximately how many red tags each workplace should use. While factors vary (such as the age of the factory), my experience shows that we can expect an average of four red tags per workshop employee. In other words, a workshop with 30 employees should need about 120 red tags.

Suggestion 4: **Apply One Red Tag per Item.**

When finding a shelf full of odds and ends, it is tempting to attach one red tag for the whole shelf. However, this can lead to confusion when it is time to dispose of the shelved items. Avoid this temptation and be meticulous enough to attach individual tags to individual items.

Suggestion 5: **Tag Excessive Amounts of Needed Items.**

We obviously want to red-tag types of items that are unneeded. However, we should also red-tag some types of items that are needed — if there are excessive amounts of them. Required amounts can be calculated based on the red-tagging standards. Everything in excess of these amounts should be red-tagged and removed along with unneeded items.

9

The Signboard Strategy

Signboards are found in every town and city. Shops have big signboards in front and sometimes small ones to indicate the shop's address. Some signs jut out over the street and can be seen from far away. Ordinary address and nameplate signboards are found at residences.

These signboards may be an eyesore in some areas, but what if they were all removed? How would we know which store is which or who lives where? How would the mail carrier make deliveries? Only people who have lived in the area a long time would know.

The same principle applies to factories and offices. Without signboards of one kind or another, only veteran employees would know where to find things. Others would be at a loss in their own workplace. To turn a factory into a workplace where everyone can see at a glance what goes where, we need signboards.

This chapter examines the following topics:

- what the signboard strategy is
- how to implement it
- case studies in visual Orderliness
- a case study in promoting the signboard strategy

WHAT IS THE SIGNBOARD STRATEGY?

The following simple two-step procedure is all it takes to lay the foundation for achieving zero defects and eliminating waste:

1. Clearly separate what is needed from what is not.
2. Remove all unneeded items from daily production activities.

Now only needed items remain — and the natural thing to do is arrange and use these needed items in the most efficient way. While we are at it, we should post signboards that indicate the kind of machines we are using and

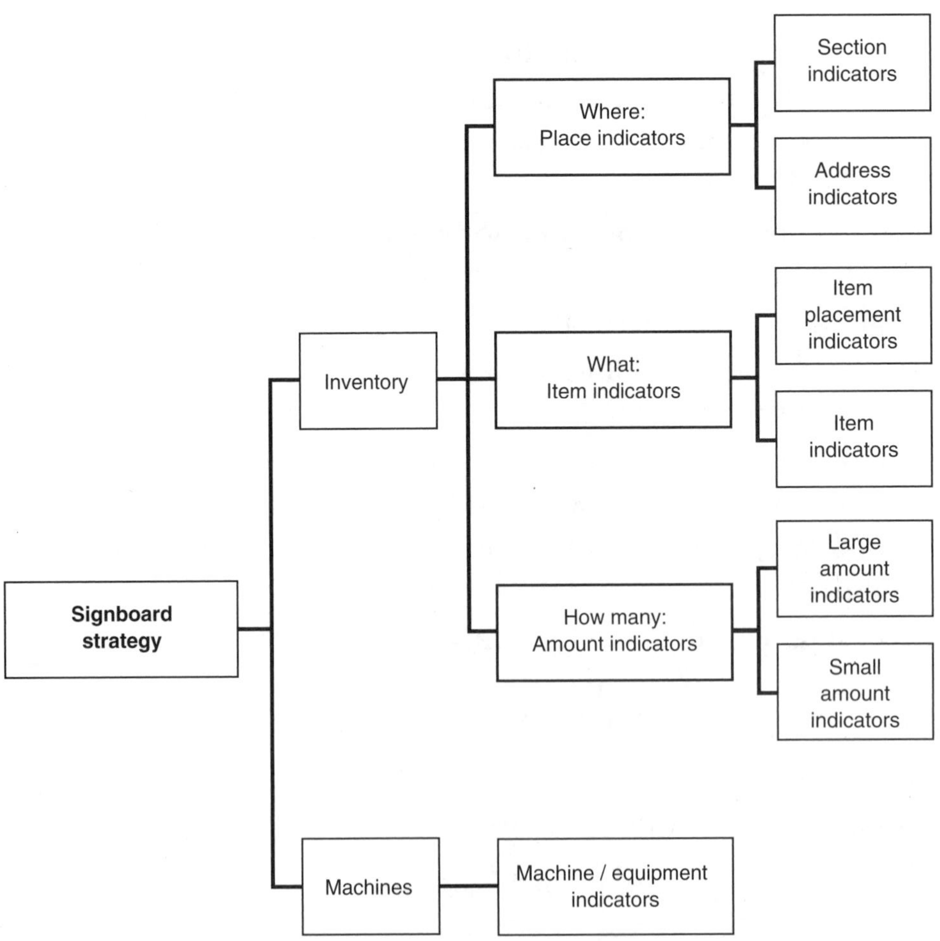

Figure 9-1. Overview of Visual Orderliness Using the Signboard Strategy

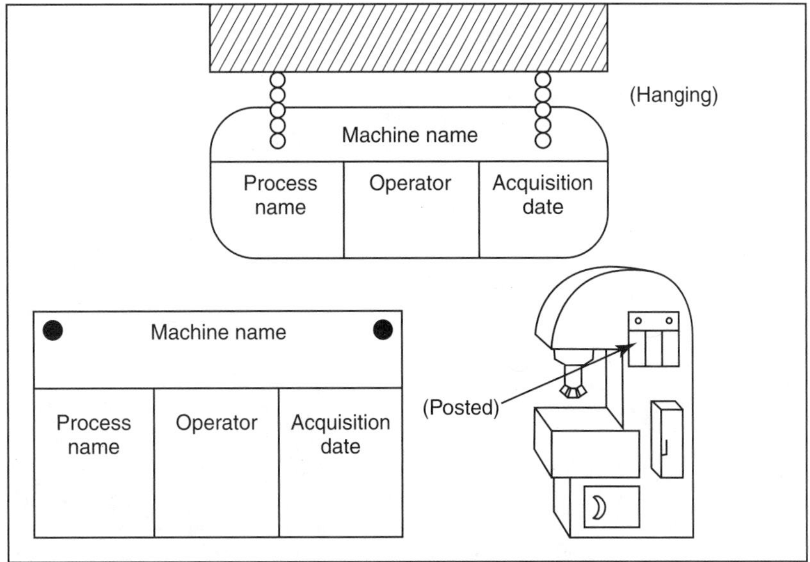

Figure 9-2. Examples of Machine/Equipment Signboards

"where," "what," and "how many" inventory items are to be kept. In other words, make everything obvious and visible. The signboard strategy is a tool that makes Orderliness a more visual process.

Figure 9-1 presents an overview of visual Orderliness using the signboard strategy.

Of these signboards, the most important ones are inventory signboards that clearly indicate where each inventory item belongs and in what amount. This way anyone can understand the inventory layout. Signboards should only be used for items that are needed for current production purposes. Therefore, the signboard strategy should always be preceded by the red-tag strategy. If not, we will end up wasting time posting signboards over unneeded items.

Before taking a closer look at how to apply the signboard strategy to inventory items, let us study the machine/equipment signboard example shown in Figure 9-2.

We simply write down the name of the machine, the process name, the operator or other person-in-charge, and the machine's acquisition date. Then we hang the signboard from the ceiling or post it against a wall or on the machine itself.

Display the workshop name, line name, cell name, and other important information clearly, as shown in the examples in Photo 9-1.

Photo 9-1. Signboards Indicating Workshop and Cell Names

What is the signboard strategy?
It is a method for clearly indicating where (location), what (item names), and how many (quantity) necessary items go where as we make the factory more orderly.

Step 1: Determine locations

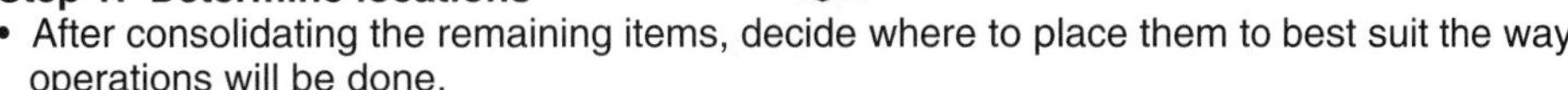

- After consolidating the remaining items, decide where to place them to best suit the way operations will be done.
- Note: Be sure to put frequently used items as close as possible to the operators for easy retrieval.

Step 2: Prepare locations
- Organize shelving and cabinets in their specified places.
- Note: Use your ingenuity (e.g., make parts easier to remove from shelves and cabinets or set up a first-in first-out stocking system).

Step 3: Indicate locations
- Make and post (or hang) signboards that clearly indicate where each item belongs.
- Note: Use either a place name/diagram signboard or an address signboard to indicate where things belong.

Step 4: Indicate item names
- Make and post (or hang) signboards that clearly indicate item names and the name/number of the shelf or cabinet where items will be kept.
- Note: Use a shelved item signboard or other place-specific item signboard.

Step 5: Indicate amounts
- Indicate the number of inventory items covered by each signboard.
- Note: Indicate both maximum and minimum amounts.

Step 6: Make Orderliness a habit
- Make Orderliness a habit so that the workplace does not lapse into disorder.
- Notes:
  (1) Make Orderliness easy to maintain.
  (2) Maintain discipline.
  (3) Make the 5S's a daily habit.

Figure 9-3. Signboard Strategy Procedure

STEPS IN THE SIGNBOARD STRATEGY

After we have carried out the red-tag strategy, the factory should contain only those items needed for current production. The question now is what to do with the remaining items (remembering that items needed for current production are not necessarily the most efficient).

After red-tagging, factories will show empty space on the floor and on shelves. It is time to consolidate what is left and make any necessary changes to the equipment layout or production flow pattern. Once operations are redesigned, we are ready to move the remaining inventory and in-process items to the most efficient and orderly sites.

Figure 9-3 illustrates the signboard strategy procedure.

Step 1. Determine Locations

As soon as the red tag strategy is completed, we must make improvements to consolidate both the equipment layout and the production flow. Then we are ready to ask where things should be placed to best suit the new layout.

When determining locations, make sure to place often-used items as close as possible to the operator's position and place seldom-used items farther away from the line. Keep easily portable items about waist-high on the shelves and keep harder-to-carry items on the upper and lower shelves.

Step 2. Prepare the Locations

Once we know where we want to place something, we still need to prepare the site. We can use some of the cabinets, shelving, boxes, pallets, or other containers that became superfluous following the red-tag strategy.

While doing this, if we find that we need additional cabinets or shelves or whatever, do not rush out and buy more. Instead, take this golden opportunity to reconsider the containers we are using and try to think of smaller ones that will do just as well. We should also consider whether to reduce lot sizes or whether to customize unneeded items to serve as the kind of cabinet or shelf needed.

We might also want to set up a system that lets us extract items in "first-in first-out (FIFO)" order, or use labor-saving roller conveyors or other clever devices.

Step 3. Indicate Locations

After deciding where to put things, we need location indicators — in other words, signboards that show the place and address of the item concerned.

Location indicators can be modeled after the postal system's address approach. No matter where in the world we send a letter, if that letter indicates our return address, it can be returned to us. The factory's address system should be at least as comprehensive as the postal address system. The factory system should include both "town" and "street" addresses that indicate where in the factory the item belongs as well as what specific address within that area. Because address numbers are often duplicated among different areas, we must be sure to specify the area and not just the number.

An address system and a map are all a person should need to find anything in the factory.

Section and address indicators can be separate signboards, as shown in Figure 9-4. In this example, the section signboards indicate which set of shelves (A, B, C, etc.) the items are on and the address signboards show the part of the shelf (1, 2, 3, etc.).

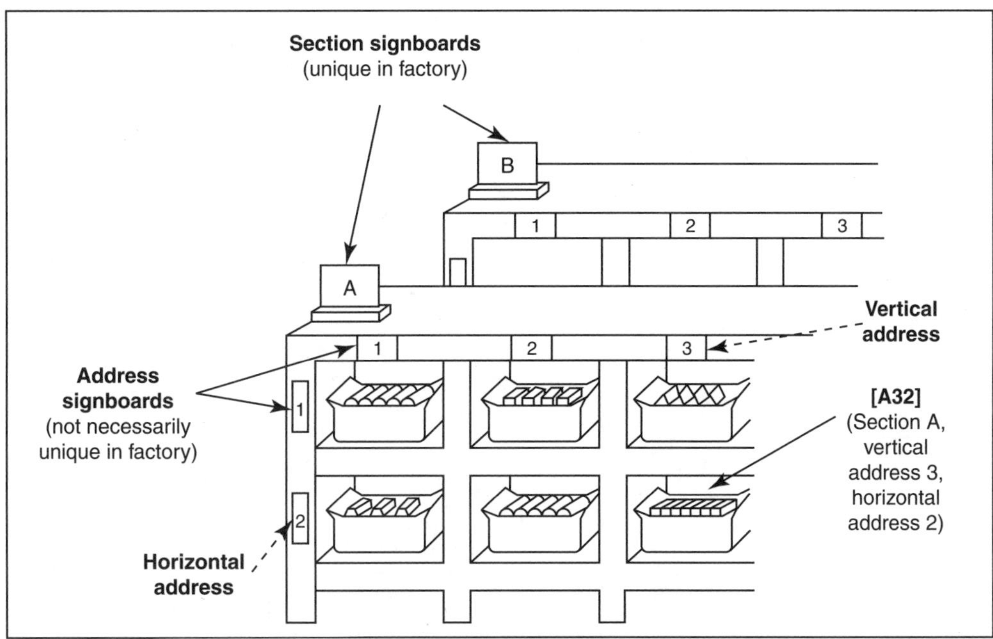

Figure 9-4. Location Indicators

In this example, the address consists of a vertical address number and a horizontal address number. Once we set up such a system, we can give an item to a brand-new employee in the factory and simply say, "Take this to address A32 on the shelves" — and trust that the item will get put in the right place. This is what we mean by making things visible so that anyone can understand them.

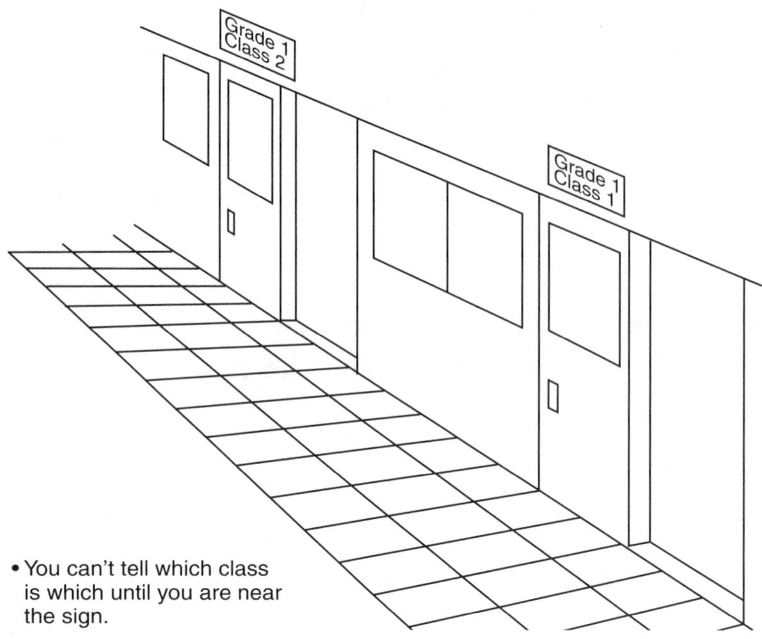
Grade 1
Class 2
Grade 1
Class 1
• You can't tell which class is which until you are near the sign.

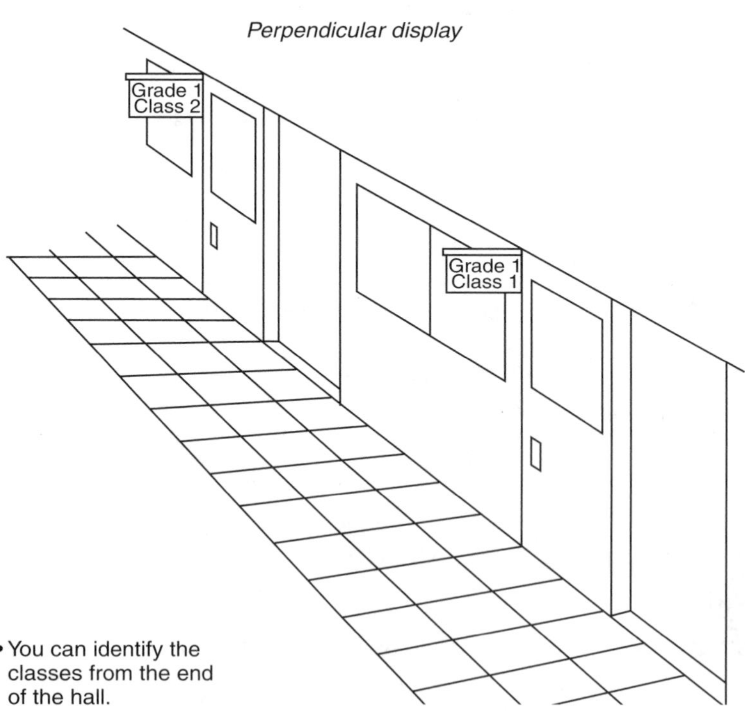
Perpendicular display
Grade 1
Class 2
Grade 1
Class 1
• You can identify the classes from the end of the hall.

Figure 9-5. Parallel Versus Perpendicular Display of Signboards

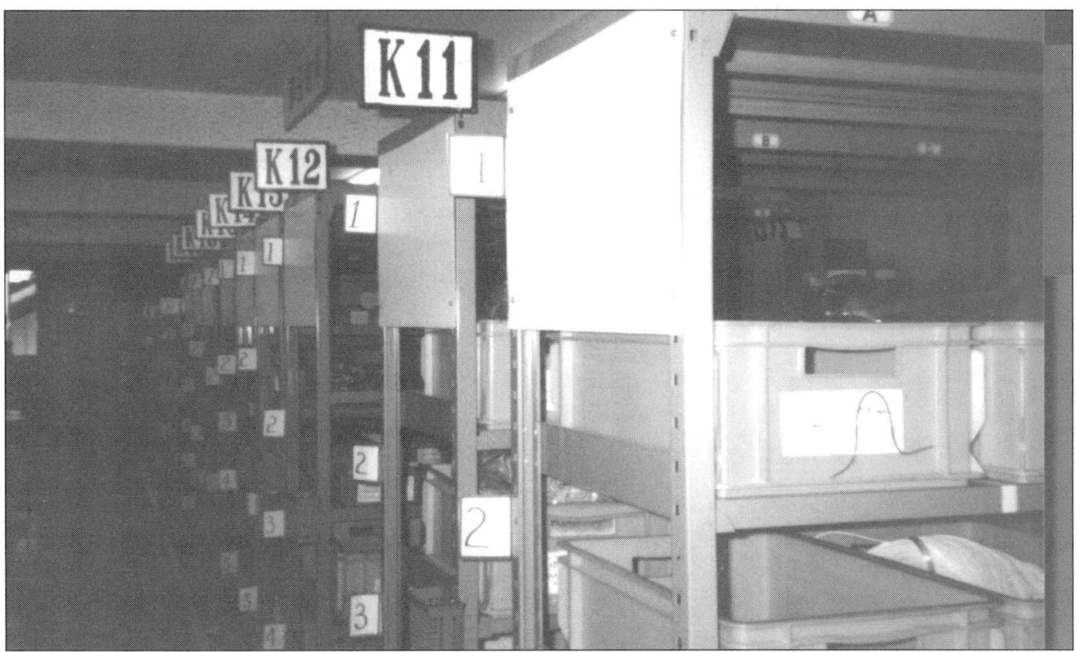

Photo 9-2. Section and Address Signboards for Shelves

Section signboards are best placed perpendicular to walkways. The reason for this is obvious in Figure 9-5, where room signs are shown in parallel and perpendicular arrangements. It is much easier to find a particular room when its sign juts out over the walkway. By contrast, when the room signs are laid flat against the wall, we must approach each door to find out which room it is. This greatly reduces the effectiveness of the signs.

Photo 9-2 shows a signboard system that includes section signs, address signs, and even more detailed signs.

Obviously, it would be a waste to use such a good signboard system only for shelves. In warehouses and throughout factories, this type of signboard system can be effectively used to indicate locations. In particular, factories that manufacture large products on a made-to-order basis need location signboards to keep track of inventory. Figure 9-6 shows an example of the use of vertical and horizontal address signboards.

Step 4. Indicate Item Names

After setting up the shelf addresses, we still need to indicate what kinds of items go there. For this, we use item indicators.

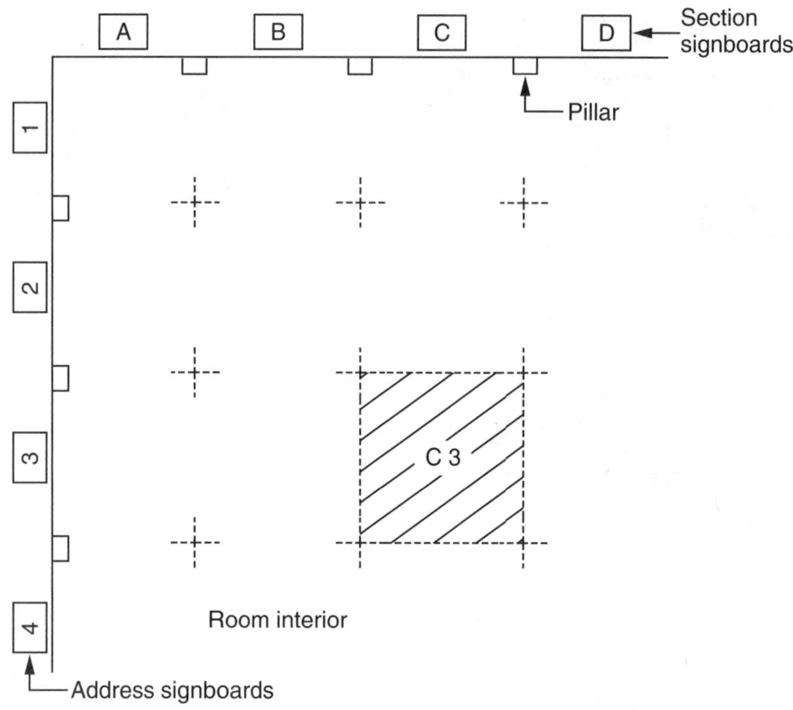

Figure 9-6. Location Signboards in a Large Room

Examples of such indicators abound in high-rise apartment complexes and parking lots. Figure 9-7 compares a well-managed parking lot with a poorly managed one.

Let us assume that a new parking-lot attendant is starting his first day on the job. He finds that all of the parking spaces have people's last names on them. He sees a car with the license-plate number 90R 3G56 in the space marked as Smith's but cannot tell whether or not the car is parked correctly. The old attendant knew which car belonged to whom — but the new one is at a loss.

If the lot was organized and managed as shown in the bottom half of Figure 9-7, the new attendant would know right away if a car was parked in the wrong space. In this lot, all parking spaces include item placement indicators that show what specific item belongs in each space. In this case, the items (automobiles) are identified by their license-plate numbers. The license plate on the car parked in Smith's space matches the number shown on the item placement indicator in that space. The new attendant knows immediately that the car is parked

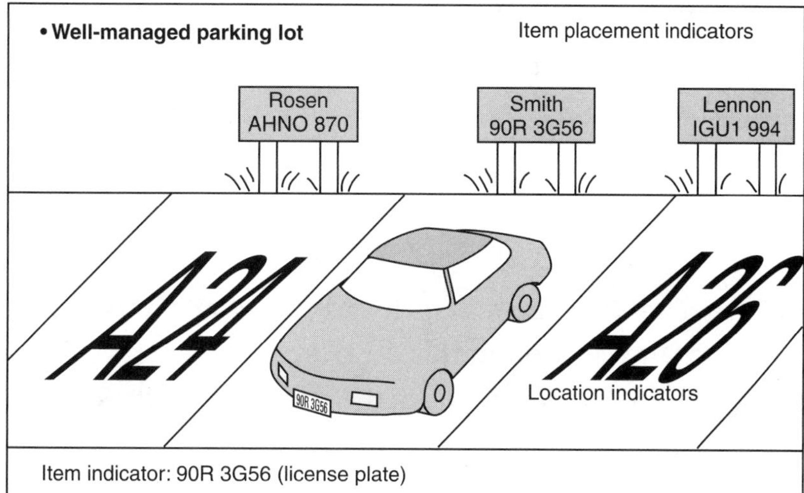

Figure 9-7. Well-Managed and Poorly Managed Parking Lots

correctly. All over the lot, one glance is enough to see whether the numbers on the license plates and on the item placement indicators match.

The same goes for factories. Figure 9-8 shows how item placement indicators and item indicators can be used for shelf slots in factories.

The item placement indicators show exactly what item belongs in what place while the item indicators identify each item. If we take this item indicator and include various other data (such as data used to maintain the "pull" production system, operation instructions, and/or delivery instructions), this simple signboard becomes a full-fledged kanban.

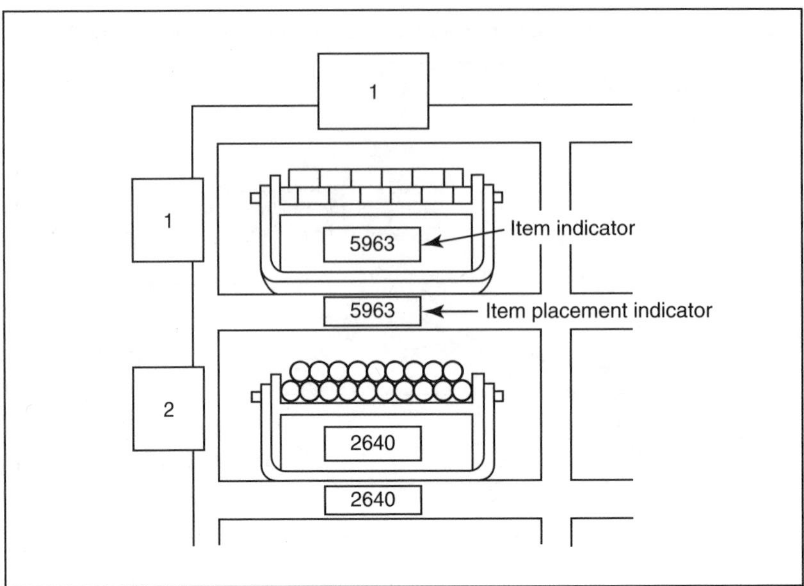

Figure 9-8. Item Indicators

Photo 9-3 shows a storage area in disorder. I would wager that the only people who know their way around this mess are the people who work directly with it every day. In fact, I would bet that even some of those people do not know where everything is kept. How could we call such a place an efficient workplace? Consider your own workplace. Does it have anything in common with this one?

Photos 9-4 through 9-7 show storage sites that use signboards. Photo 9-4 shows a product storage site, Photo 9-5 a materials storage site, Photo 9-6 a parts storage site, and Photo 9-7 a voucher storage site.

Step 5. Indicate Amounts

Unless we keep tabs on their amounts, inventory items tend to pile up. The best reason to have amount indicators is that they limit the number of shelves and other storage spaces to be used for inventory items. When exact amounts cannot be indicated, we should at least indicate the minimum and maximum amounts. Color coding is a good way to clearly distinguish between minimum and maximum amount indications. (See Figure 9-9.)

Photo 9-3. A Disorderly Workplace

Photo 9-4. Product Storage Site

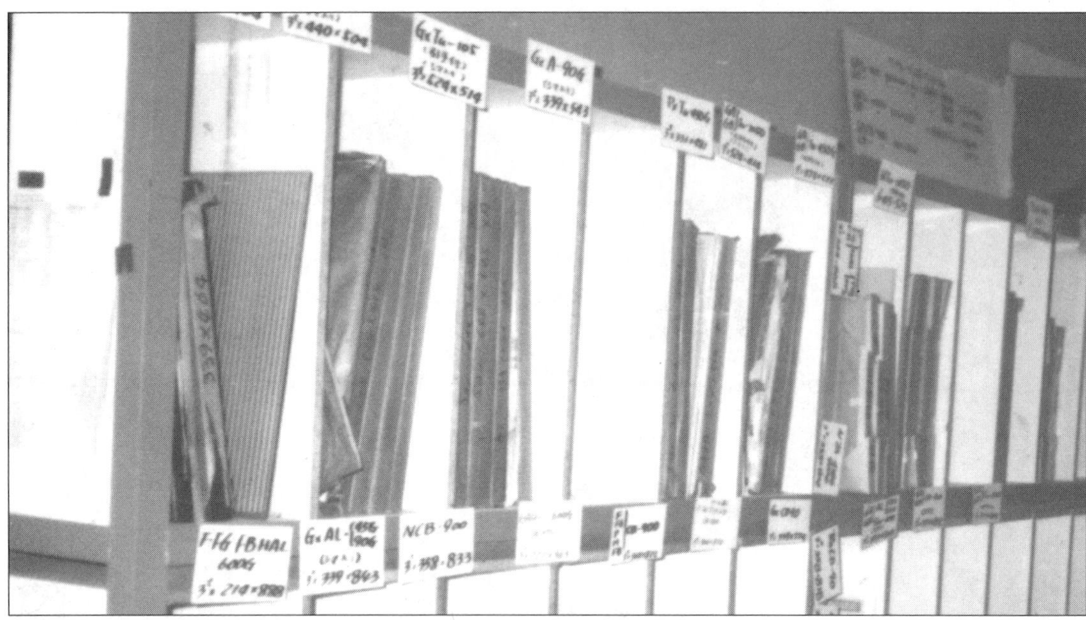

Photo 9-5. Materials Storage Site

Photo 9-6. Parts Storage Site

Photo 9-7. Voucher Storage Site

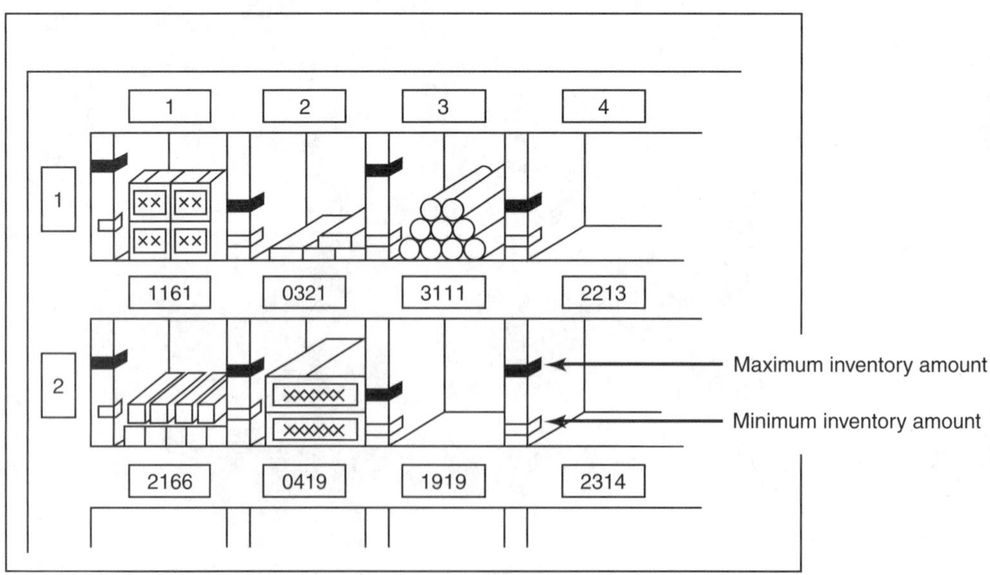

Figure 9-9. Amount Indicators

This system enables anyone to spot misplaced items right away. Again, this brings us back to a basic tenet: *Abnormalities, waste, and all other problems in the factory must be made visible so that they can be recognized at a glance.*

One method of dealing with in-process inventory that has been stacked (on pallets, for example) is to use insertable poles and apply red tape or paint on the pole to mark the maximum stacking height. (See Figure 9-10.)

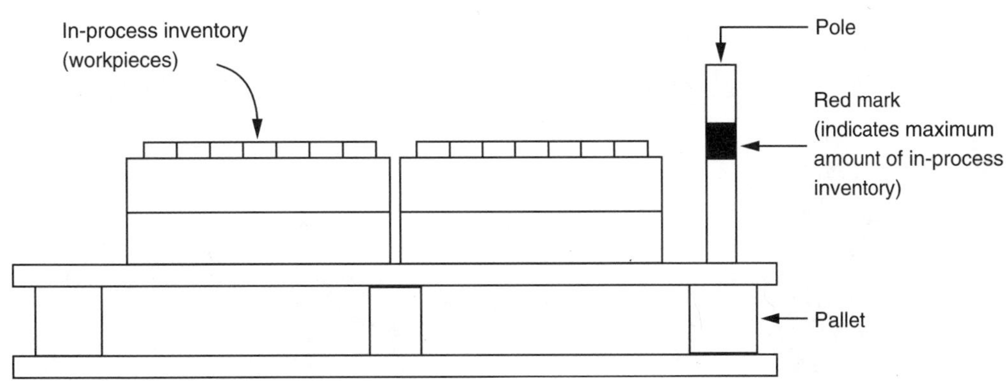

Figure 9-10. Maximum Stacking Height Indicator for In-process Inventory

Stacking workpieces directly onto the floor along the wall, as shown in Photo 9-8, is not recommended; a pallet or cart should be used. However, at least in this case a signboard is displayed and a red line indicates the maximum amount to be stacked there.

Step 6. Make Orderliness a Habit

Orderliness means standardizing the new way we place things as a result of Organization. Orderliness should clarify what goes where and in what amount and should make all abnormalities and problems immediately obvious to everyone. The key to maintaining Orderliness is to respond to problems as soon as they arise by identifying the causes and making the appropriate improvements.

The three most important things to do to prevent backsliding on Orderliness are: (1) make Orderliness easy to maintain, (2) be disciplined, and (3) make the 5S's a daily habit.

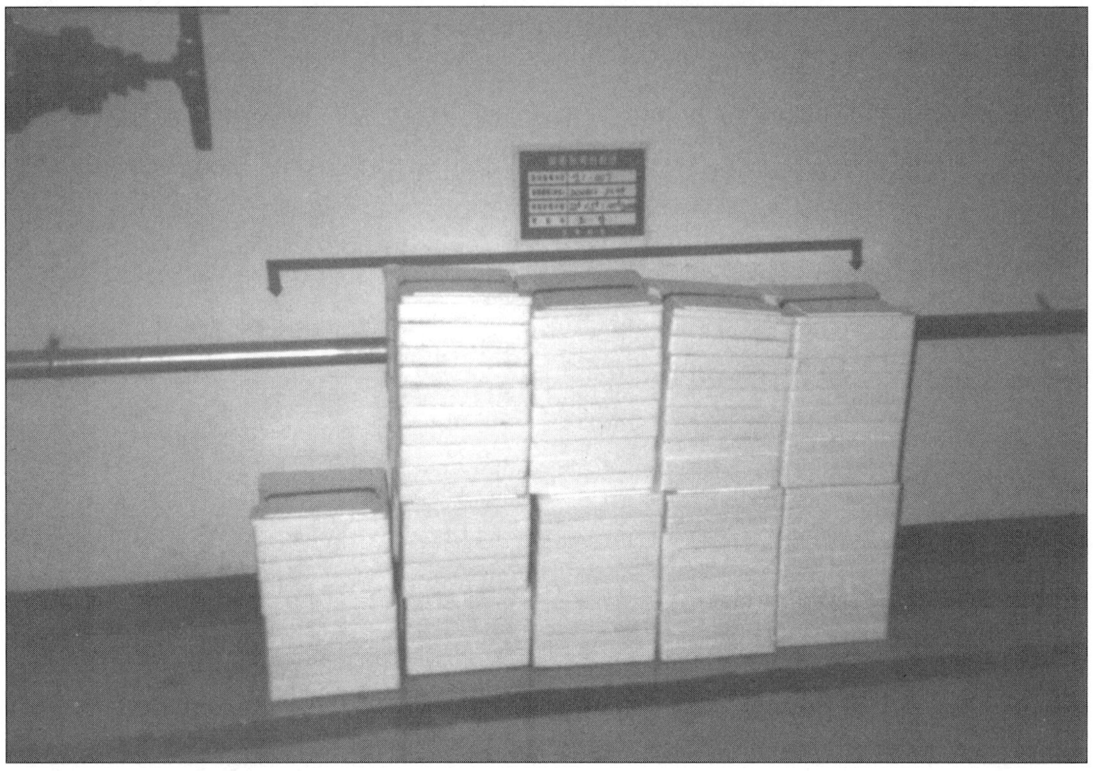

Photo 9-8. Maximum Stacking Height Shown on Wall

To sum up the most important points of the signboard strategy:

When implementing the signboard strategy for inventory, we use location indicators to show where (specific places) items go, item indicators to show what (specific items) goes in those places, and amount indicators to show how many (specific amounts) belong there.

Table 9-1 presents the three "specifics" that comprise the core of visual Orderliness as practiced via the signboard strategy.

Table 9-1. The Three "Specifics" of Visual Orderliness

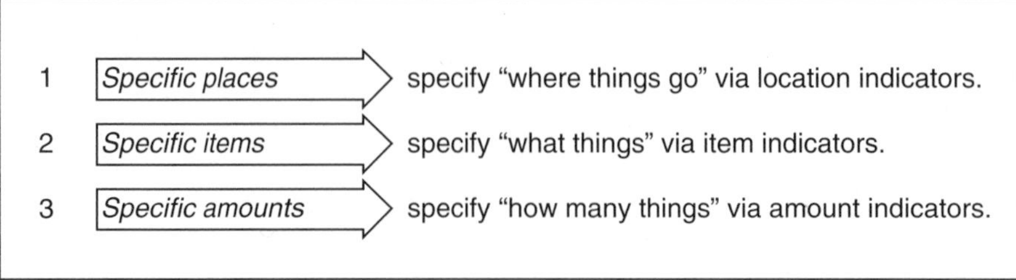

1	*Specific places*	specify "where things go" via location indicators.
2	*Specific items*	specify "what things" via item indicators.
3	*Specific amounts*	specify "how many things" via amount indicators.

Pattern for a basic signboard

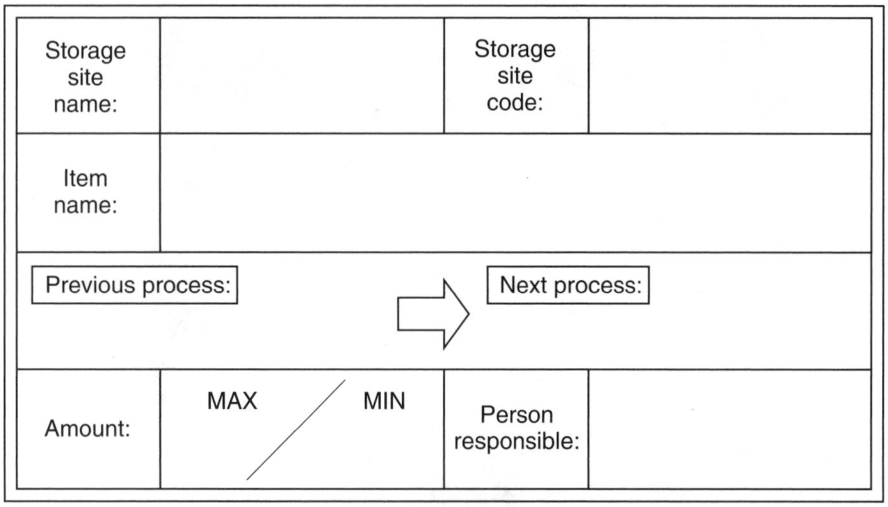

Storage site name:		Storage site code:	
Item name:			
Previous process:	⇨	Next process:	
Amount:	MAX / MIN	Person responsible:	

Figure 9-11. Signboard for In-process Inventory Storage Site

We have considered the use of signboards for general inventory. However, what about the in-process inventory that is kept temporarily between processes, sometimes amounting to nothing more than a single workpiece on a worktable? Here, too, we should use signboards to make it immediately clear to everyone which in-process inventory items go where and in what amounts.

Figure 9-11 shows a sample format for signboards used at storage sites for in-process inventory, procured parts, and the like. Note how the "three specifics" (specific places, specific items, and specific amounts) are fundamental to this signboard format.

The signboards should be the same for items stored between processes and for carts that carry items to and from storage sites and processes. Photo 9-9 shows a simple signboard used for carts. Again, the "three specifics" are the key ingredients.

CASE STUDIES IN VISUAL ORDERLINESS

Orderliness means standardizing how you keep things. And standardization means enabling anyone to see the difference between normal and abnormal. Visual Orderliness means enabling anyone to see at a glance the difference between normal and abnormal.

Photo 9-9. A Signboard on a Cart

With this in mind, let us look at the household electronic parts-storage shelves shown in Photo 9-10. If possible, view it from the Orderliness perspective of the 5S's.

If I were to give this electronic parts-storage system a score, it would be 25 on a scale of 100. I got this score after subtracting points for the following reasons.

1. "G1" is obviously a section indicator, but the address indicators are not so obvious. What do the vertical columns mean? And what do the horizontal rows mean? (Subtract 15 points.)
2. There are item indicators on the boxes, but there are none on the shelves. How do people know where to put things back? (Subtract 15 points.)
3. There are absolutely no amount indicators. We are not told how many items each box can hold. (Subtract 15 points.)

4. The boxes are too big — we cannot see what is inside them. (Subtract 10 points.)

5. The most serious problem concerns the boxes stored on the top shelf. Only the people who put the boxes there have any idea what is in them. They are likely to become dead inventory. They are also evidence that 5S conditions have begun to deteriorate. (Subtract 20 points.)

A storage system that may look fine to an unpracticed eye turns out to be full of problems when viewed from the 5S perspective.

Photo 9-10. Storage Area for Electronic Parts

Photo 9-11. Parts Shelves at an Automotive Assembly Plant

Photo 9-11 shows a parts-storage area at an automobile plant. Let us see how this system differs from the electronic parts-storage system shown in Photo 9-10. Primary differences are:

1. The shelves are lower. (In fact, the shelves at the household electronics assembly plant should be lower because most of the employees there are women.)
2. The parts boxes at the auto plant are smaller. This suggests that the boxes are pulled out and returned more often than are boxes at the household electronics plant.
3. Each shelf has detailed indicators, making it easy to see what goes where.
4. The section-indicator signboards at the auto plant are all inside the white line on the floor. (At the household electronics plant, they protrude across the line, albeit at a height.) This can be an important safety difference when tall objects are being moved in the area.

5. The auto plant's boxes are small enough for us to see what they contain.
6. The biggest difference is in the way the parts are stored and retrieved. At the auto plant, each set of shelves has an "input" sign on top of its left side and an "output" sign on top of its right side. What do you suppose that means? In Chapter 6, we discussed it as the FIFO system ("first in, first out"), the most efficient way to store and retrieve storage items.
7. At the auto plant, shelves have roller conveyers in them to allow the storage boxes to slide easily from the "input" to the "output" side.

Again, an educated comparison of the two shelf storage systems reveals several important differences. Having made this comparison, we can see how the auto plant's system is superior in several ways to the system used by the household electronics manufacturer. I suggest that you maintain this 5S perspective while reviewing and scoring your own company's shelf storage system.

CASE STUDY: ESSENTIALS FOR PROMOTING THE SIGNBOARD STRATEGY

Here, we are using the term "signboard strategy" broadly to cover all activities undertaken as part of the Orderliness component of 5S implementation. Accordingly, the signboard strategy includes the steps outlined in Table 9-2.

Table 9-2. Eight Steps of the Signboard Strategy

No.	Activity	Group
1.	Training and lectures about signboards and Orderliness	Productivity subcommittee Headquarters productivity committee
2.	Organization of signboard strategy promotion teams	Headquarters productivity committee
3.	Drafting a schedule	"
4.	Listing needed items	"
5.	Designating storage sites	"
6.	Place markers and signboard installation	Productivity subcommittee Headquarters productivity committee
7.	Signboard (Orderliness) improvement activities	Headquarters productivity committee
8.	Evaluation	Productivity subcommittee Headquarters productivity committee

Step 1. Set Up Training for Signboards (Orderliness)

The productivity subcommittee should sponsor Orderliness lectures for managers from the headquarters productivity council. In turn, they should appoint managers from each division to instruct their subordinates in Orderliness.

The productivity subcommittee should also assist in instructing ordinary employees in each division about Orderliness and the signboard strategy.

Step 2. Organize Signboard-Strategy Promotion Teams

Structure the signboard-strategy promotion teams around the same teams who promoted the red-tag strategy.

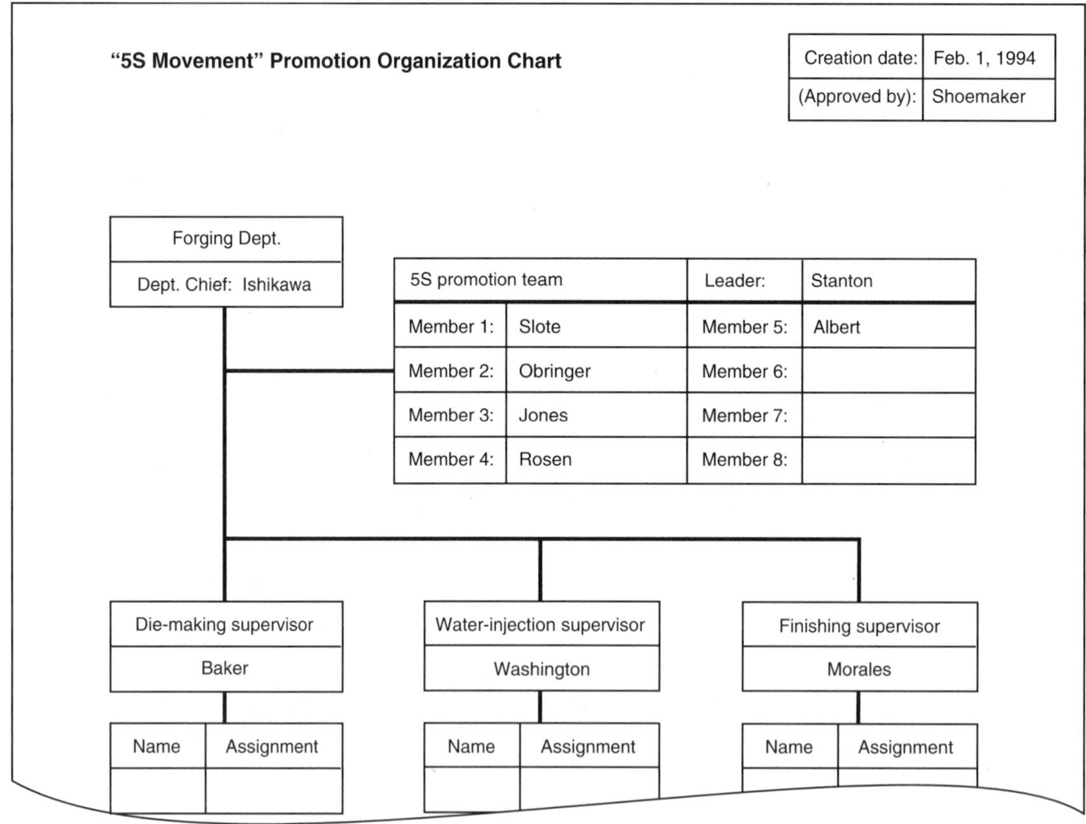

Note: As with the red-tag strategy, the promotion teams are managed based on the company's existing management hierarchy.

Figure 9-12. Promotion Organization for 5S Movement

Structure these teams in a way that encourages maximum participation from everyone in carrying out the signboard strategy. They should include shop-floor supervisors and group leaders as well as section and department managers. Give the higher-ranked managers executive roles within the teams and place the others in charge of drawing up lists and providing support for Orderliness tasks.

An Organization chart for promoting the "5S Movement" is shown in Figure 9-12.

Step 3. Draft a Schedule

Have each promotion team draft its own daily schedule for display on its own schedule sign.

Table 9-3. 5S Promotion Schedule

No.	Activity	Scheduled Date
1.	Training and lectures about signboards and Orderliness	D + 10
2.	Organizing signboard strategy promotion teams	D + 15
3.	Drafting a schedule	D + 20
4.	Listing needed items	D + 30
5.	Designating storage sites	D + 30
6.	Placing markers and installing signboard	D + 45
7.	Signboard (Orderliness) improvement activities	D + 45 ~
8.	Evaluation	D + 60

All members should participate in drafting the daily schedule. Allow plenty of time for discussion and concensus-building to help foster a sense of group solidarity and commitment.

Table 9-3 presents a typical promotion schedule.

Table 9-4. Sample List of Targets (Needed Items)

Category	Subcategory	Description
Inventory Items	• Raw materials	Parts for assembly, sheet metal, etc.
	• Secondary materials	Lubricants, consumables, etc.
	• In-process inventory	Inventory stored in and between processes
	• Products	Semi-finished and finished products
Equipment	• Machines	Fixed equipment and mobile equipment
	• Jigs and dies	Jigs, fixed tools, dies
	• Tools	Work tools
	• Measuring instruments	Measuring tools and gauges
	• Conveyance carts and vehicles	Work vehicles and conveyance vehicles (carts, forklifts, etc.)
	• Work supplies	Tool boxes, parts boxes, shelves, measuring-instrument boxes, safety equipment, stationery supplies, drawings, signs, worktables, books, chairs, etc.
Spaces	• Floors	Operation areas and walkways
	• Space inside of work supplies	Space inside containers for tools, parts, measuring instruments, drawings, and documents
	• Walls and empty room space	Walls and empty space in rooms
	• Rooms	Rest areas, other rooms

Step 4. List Needed Items

A sample list of needed (target) items is shown in Table 9-4.

A separate list is then drawn up for needed inventory items. (See Figure 9-13.) The types of needed inventory items include medium and large items that take up lots of floor space as well as small items that require shelves, boxes, and worktables.

The following instructions refer to Figure 9-13:

Size	Storage site	Listing method
Medium and large products	Floor spaces, on pallets	Create separate list for each type of item
Small products	Shelves, boxes, worktables	Use time-unit method for each process (e.g., list showing how many days' worth of assembly parts)

Sample List

List of Needed Inventory Items (1)				Div./dept./process:	MANUFACTURING DEPT. (PARTS SUPERVISOR)			
				List by:	STANTON	Date:	1 FEB 1994	
No.	Item name (number)	Inventory category	Storage site name (or code)	Amount/ storage containers	Inventory amount		Comment	
					Max.	Min.		
1.	ST RELAY BOARD (M211-311)	SECONDARY	PARTS STORAGE ROOM (A10)	1	12	4		
2.	Y JIG ASSEMBLY (M260-913)	"	"	1	12	4		
3.	AP MOTOR (M260-610)	"	"	1	12	4		
4.	COUPLING A3 (M250-131)	"	"	1	12	4		

Figure 9-13. List of Needed Inventory Items

1. Enter the page number in the parenthesis after the form title.
2. In the box marked "division/department/process" enter the name of the relevant line, work group, or process.
3. The inventory categories to be entered are: raw materials, secondary materials, in-process inventory, and products.
4. Use the most commonly used names when listing item names. Enter specifications when necessary under a separate column. (For example, if under "item name," you have entered "log," then under "specifications" enter "24C 20-phi X 3m.")
5. Under the "amount/items stored" column, enter the amounts in terms of the units in which the items are stored (i.e., the number of pallets, boxes, drums, etc.).

6. Under the "maximum" part of the "inventory amount" column, for each item enter the maximum number that can be stored in the designated storage space. Determine this based on the needs of both the previous and next processes.

This is one of the most important tasks in the signboard strategy. The foundation required to enable the previous and next processes to mutually maintain no more than the maximum number of inventory items is the revolutionary just-in-time (JIT) concept — only what is needed, only when it is needed, and only in the amount needed.

An example of a needed inventory list is given in Table 9-5.

Table 9-5. Example of Needed Inventory List

Unit		Maximum Quantity	
Storage unit	No. of unit	No. of storage units	Total amount
pallet	5	3 pallets	15 EA
drum	180 L	2 drums	360 L
EA	1	10 EA	10 EA
box	20	10 boxes	200 EA
•	•	•	•
•	•	•	•

Next, two types of needed equipment lists are required: one public and the other personal. Make a public list for each factory (or each department, workshop, or line). Make a personal list for each set of equipment used by an individual worker (such as work tools, measuring instruments, jigs, and supplies). An example is shown in Figure 9-14.

Instructions for what goes in the "list title" parentheses and the "department/ division/process" box are the same as for the needed products list described previously.

The "equipment category" column should include the following:

- machines
- jigs and dies

- measuring tools and gauges
- work vehicles and conveyance vehicles
- work supplies

Sample List

Needed Equipment List (1)						Div./dept./ process:	MANUFACTURING DEPT. 2 (WINDING AND SETUP)				
						List by:	WASHINGTON		Date:	1 FEB 1994	
No.	Equipment name	Equipment category	Asset No.	Quantity	Unit price	Acquisition price	Acquisition date	Depre-ciation	Book value	Installation site	Comments
1.	HAND PRESS 3	MACHINES	M0126	1		$45	3/30			SETUP SITE	
2.	HAND PRESS 4	"	M0127	1		$45	3/30			"	
3.	30-TON PRESS 2	"	M0264	1		$50	4/10			"	
4.	30-TON PRESS 3	"	M0265	1		$50	4/10			"	
5.	WORKTABLE	SUPPLIES		6		$55	4/10			"	UNLISTED

Figure 9-14. Example of Equipment List

Under "equipment name," enter the equipment name and the control number used within the department. (If there is no control number, assign one.) In the "asset number" column, enter the code from the company's fixed asset list. If no such number exists, leave this column entry blank and enter "unlisted asset" in the "comments" column.

Targets for the needed space list include rooms, parts of rooms, and indicators such as signs.

Make a separate needed space list for each factory. Be sure it is comprehensive and complete. The "manager responsible" is the person in charge of maintenance and security (locks). "Area" means the effective interior area inside the walls (width times length). Figure 9-15 shows an example.

Sample List

Needed Space List (1)			Div./dept./ process:	PRODUCTION DEPT. 1		
			List by:	GAFFNEY	Date:	1 FEB 1994

No.		Space used	Manager responsible	Area (in square meters)	Comments
1.	ASSEMBLY LINE A	PRODUCTION DEPT. 1 (ASSEMBLY)	BAZZANI	45	EXCLUDING WALKWAY
2.	ASSEMBLY LINE B	"	SANTI	37	
3.	ASSEMBLY LINE C	"	BOLIVER	49	
4.	ASSEMBLY PARTS STORAGE 1	PRODUCTION DEPT. 1 (ASSETS)	SUZUKI	125	EXCLUDING WALKWAY
5.	" 2	"		64	

Figure 9-15. Example of Needed Space List

Step 5. Designate Storage Sites

Describe the storage sites of the inventory items and equipment the same way they are described in the current layout diagram.

If you are making a new layout, make a 1/50th size reduction and use it for improvements in the new layout.

Step 6. Install Place Markers and Signboards

To make area descriptions for spaces (storage areas), follow this precedure:

- If the storage space is on the floor in part of the storage area, mark off and identify the space.
- If the storage space is on carts, pallets, or other devices, clearly mark off the areas where those devices are stored.
- Mark off all walkways related to the areas in question.
- Use standard area divisions. (See Table 9-6.)

Table 9-6. Signboard for Standard Area Divisions

Category	Color	Line Width
Walkway line	Yellow	10 cm
Storage area for needed item	White	5 cm
Storage area for defective or useless items	Red	5 cm

To make signboards:

- Once all target items have been listed, make signboards to be used companywide.
- Have the signboards made from metal, acrylic, adhesive-backed paper, coated board — or whatever works best for the ambient conditions. (You may want to discuss this with the relevant manager or productivity subcommittee.)

Next, attach the signboards at target locations:

- Place signboards for inventory items, equipment, and spaces wherever they are needed for the sake of Orderliness. Discuss the specific contents and allocation of signboards beforehand with the relevant managers or supervisors.
- Once the signboards are hung, select the best one for standardized use throughout the company.
- Fill in the signboards and then attach name tags. See the examples illustrated in Tables 9-7, 9-8, and 9-9.

Table 9-7. Signboard (Example #1)

Inventory items

Storage site	Storage site code
Product name	
Previous process ➡	Next process
Max./min.	Person responsible

Table 9-8. Signboard (Example #2)

Equipment

Part name (standard)	
Control no. (acquisition date)	
Asset no.	
Management dept. (person responsible)	

Table 9-9. Signboard (Example #3)

Spaces

__________ room

Management dept.	
Manager (tel.)	

To any items listed as unneeded, useless, or surplus, attach red tags under the supervision of the promotion team leader (i.e., a supervisor or manager). Then carry out the same treatment steps described in Chapter 8's discussion of the red-tag strategy.

Step 7. Maintain Ongoing Improvement Activities

Maintain an ongoing improvement program for the signboard strategy by employing the following activities:

- At least once a month, take photos to document Organization and Orderliness conditions. They will be helpful when confirming subsequent improvements.
- Use memos to keep the people responsible continually aware of problem points that have yet to be addressed.
- Set up a suggestion system to help dig up improvement ideas.
- Draft improvement case study reports.

Step 8. Evaluate

Evaluation is critical and essential — no less here than in any other area of the company:

- Set up an evaluation and certification system to evaluate the results of Orderliness activities.
- Display an outline of Organization/Orderliness essentials. Also, report on activity results (particularly, successful case studies) to help promote standardization of improvements.

10

The Third Pillar: Cleanliness

Here's what I do when I inspect a factory for 5S conditions — I visit the men's restroom. The restroom is always a good indicator of 5S conditions. I look around. Are there any unneeded items? Are the toilet paper, soap, and other needed items all kept in clearly designated places? Are the windows dirty or the windowsills dusty? No one likes cleaning restrooms, and for this very reason they provide at-a-glance evidence of how well 5S conditions are being maintained throughout the factory.

Cleanliness is the third pillar and the 5S component that emphasizes the removal of dirt, grime, and dust from the workplace. As such, we can define Cleanliness as "keeping everything swept and clean."

THE NEED FOR CLEANLINESS AND ITS ESSENTIAL POINTS

Cleanliness for factories and offices is a lot like bathing for human beings. It relieves stress and strain, removes sweat and dirt, and prepares the body and mind for the next day.

Both Cleanliness and bathing are important for physical and mental health. Factories that do not implement Cleanliness suffer the following types of symptoms:

1. Windows are so dusty and dirty that very little sunlight filters through even on a sunny day.

2. Some areas are poorly lit and work there tends to get done less efficiently.
3. Walkways are dark and therefore hazardous.
4. Defects are less obvious in dark, messy factories.
5. Customers' trust is undermined when they see dirty floors and puddles of water or oil.
6. Puddles of oil and water cause slipping and injuries.
7. People must avoid the oil and water puddles as they work.
8. Machines are so dirty and oily that it is hard to observe their oil-level and air-volume gauges.
9. Machines do not receive sufficient check-up maintenance and tend to break down frequently.
10. Machine breakdowns not only cause problems at subsequent processes but eventually lead to late deliveries.
11. Machines that do not receive sufficient maintenance tend to operate incorrectly at times, which can be hazardous.
12. Swarf scattered on the floor can result in more damage-related defects.
13. Having swarf around can endanger people's eyes.
14. Equipment that is not kept clean tends to produce more defective goods.
15. A factory where swarf, shavings, dirt, and dust are allowed to build up is bound to suffer from low morale.
16. Cluttered desktops in offices make implementing Organization and Orderliness impossible and work less efficient.
17. It is difficult to start the day with fresh ideas when one's desk is littered with eraser bits, useless papers, and leftover work from the previous day.
18. The will to work hard weakens when office floors and walls are filthy.

Cleanliness can play an important part in aiding work efficiency and safety. It is also tied in with employee morale and their awareness of improvements. When you visit another company's factory or office, I suggest you go to the restroom and look around. Its condition will illustrate the state of the company's improvement-consciousness.

Cleanliness Means Inspection

When we think of Cleanliness, we should imagine someone standing with a broom in one hand and a dustcloth in the other. Sweeping and wiping are the two fundamental activities of Cleanliness.

The Cleanliness phases listed in Figure 10-1 are built upon this foundation.

To prevent equipment breakdowns, it is essential that all three phases are thoroughly implemented.

PHASE 1: **Daily Cleanliness — Making things clean**

Make Cleanliness a part of daily duties (e.g., sweep and wipe away dirt, grime, and dust daily).
- Sweep, mop, and wipe floors, walkways, and shelves until they shine.
- Scrub away grit and swarf that has become caked onto oily equipment surfaces until the equipment shines.

PHASE 2: **Cleanliness Inspections — Using your senses**

Once Cleanliness takes root as a daily practice, we can help maintain conditions by using our senses to detect slight defects or other abnormalities in the various equipment units.
- Pay close attention not only to the main section of each machine but also its moving parts and drive chain.
- Check for proper amounts of oil, air, ventilation, etc.

PHASE 3: **Cleanliness Maintenance — Making improvements**

Once someone discovers a defect, the operator in charge of that particular machine should be given first chance to immediately make a repair or improvement. If the operator fails, then it's time to call a maintenance technician. This is "Cleanliness maintenance."
- If the operator is able to quickly fix or improve the slight defect, this should be considered part of the operator's "Cleanliness inspection" duties (phase 2).
- If the operator finds it difficult to fix or improve the defect quickly, he/she should stick a maintenance card onto the defect site and send out a maintenance-request kanban.

Figure 10-1. Three-Phase Cleanliness to Prevent Equipment Breakdowns

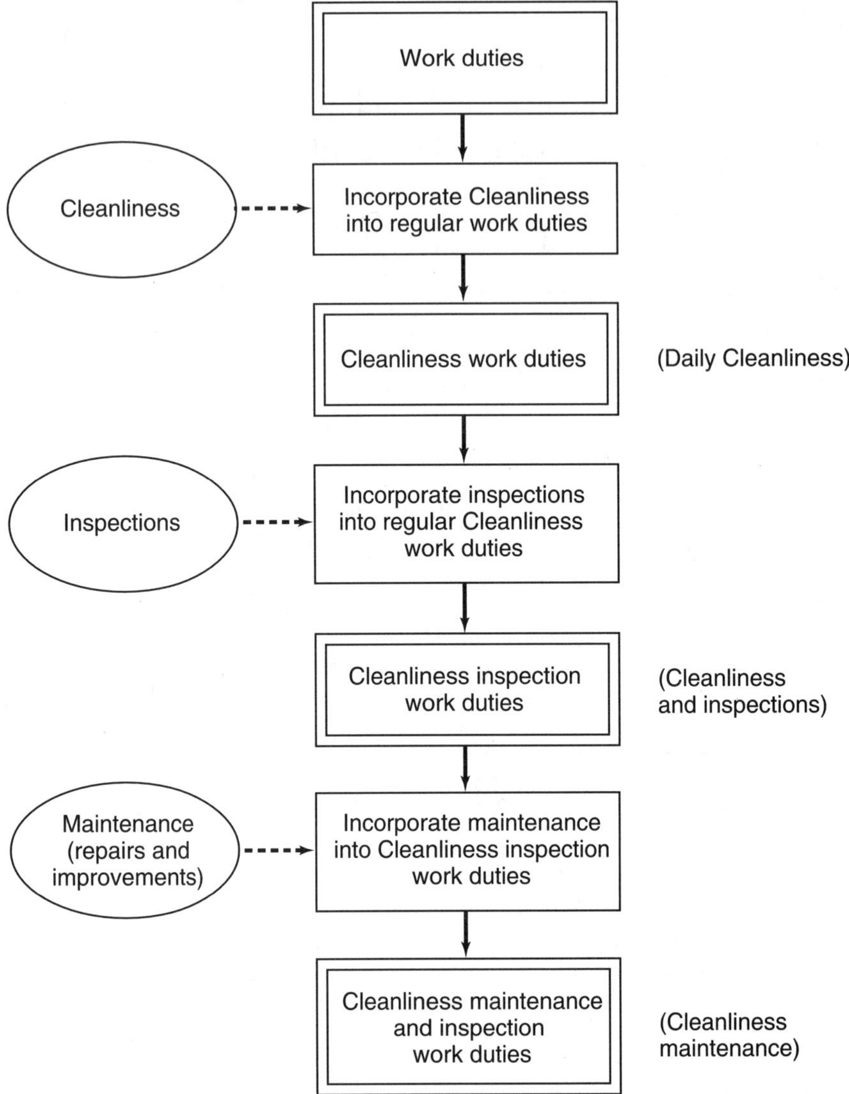

Figure 10-2. Flowchart of Cleanliness Key Points

Phase 1 is "daily Cleanliness" for things like floors, walkways, machines, and other equipment. These things should be cleaned and scrubbed until they shine like new. This can also be called the "make it shine" strategy that is done daily, and whose two fundamental activities are sweeping and wiping. In addition to daily cleaning, companywide cleanup days should be held regularly two to four times a year. These major cleanups help everyone turn Cleanliness into a regular work habit.

Phase 2 goes a step farther by encouraging people to train their senses on the cleaned-up equipment to detect abnormalities. This is called "Cleanliness inspections — using your senses." The ability to detect slight defects in equipment is a key part of maintenance activities that help prevent equipment breakdowns. Cleanliness inspections also deserve to become a firmly established part of daily work habits, along with other Cleanliness duties.

Finally, in phase 3 the operators themselves are given the opportunity to fix or improve upon slight defects or other abnormalities that have been discovered in their equipment. Their task is to make "instant improvements," which means an immediate repair or improvement. If the task proves too difficult for the operator, only then should he or she resort to calling in a maintenance specialist. Called "Cleanliness maintenance," this is also something that needs to become part of everyday work and cleaning habits.

Figure 10-2 shows a flowchart of key Cleanliness points.

DAILY CLEANLINESS

The 5S's begin with Organization — getting everything that is not needed out of the workplace. This is followed by Orderliness — putting the remaining needed items into good order so that they can be easily found and used by anybody. But what good are Organization and Orderliness if the materials we use are dirty and the equipment we depend upon frequently breaks down?

One of the more obvious purposes of Cleanliness is to turn the workplace into a nice, bright place for everyone. Another key purpose is to keep everything in top condition so that when someone needs to use something, it is ready to be used. This is why companies should abandon the inadequate tradition of annual "year-end" or "spring" cleanings. Instead, cleaning should become a deeply ingrained part of daily work habits.

Steps in Cleanliness

Repeatedly sending out reminders to clean up is not enough to ensure thorough implementation of Cleanliness or its incorporation into daily work habits. Instead, daily Cleanliness should be taught as a set of steps and rules, which employees should learn to maintain with discipline. Figure 10-3 lists these Cleanliness steps.

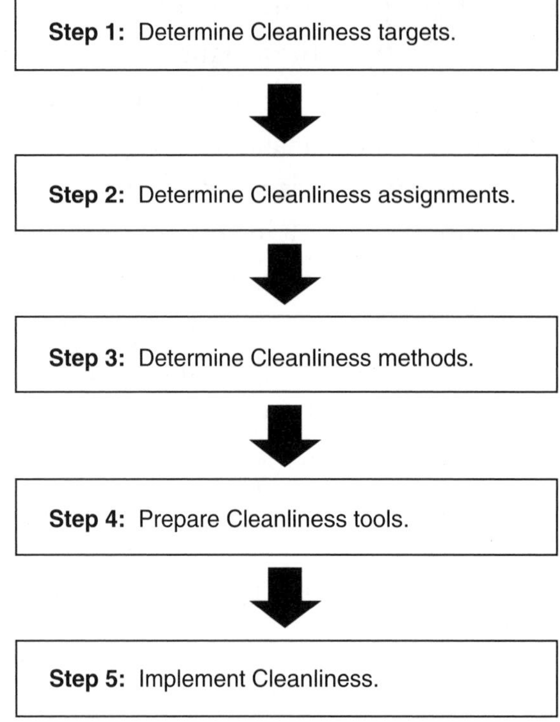

Figure 10-3. Cleanliness Steps

Step 1: Determine Cleanliness Targets.

We start by determining the targets for Cleanliness. Basically, Cleanliness targets consist of three categories: warehouse items, equipment, and space. A further breakdown of each category follows.

- **Warehouse items** include raw materials, procured parts, subcontracted parts, parts made in-house, assembly components, semi-finished products, and products.
- **Equipment** includes machines, welding tools, general tools, cutting tools, measuring instruments, dies, wheels and casters, conveyance tools, work tables, cabinets, desks, chairs, and spare equipment.
- **Space** refers to floors, work areas, walkways, walls, pillars, ceilings, windows, shelves, closets and rooms, and lights.

Step 2: Determine Cleanliness Assignments.

Workplace Cleanliness is the responsibility of everyone who works there. To begin with, we divide each factory or office into specific "Cleanliness" areas. Next, we assign these areas to individuals, beginning with the highest manager and continuing to the lower managers. Finally, we assign specific areas with its equipment to individual operators.

- **5S assignment map**

  It does no good to determine Cleanliness assignments if the assignments are not carried out. One good way to make sure this happens is to take an existing factory layout map and turn it into a "5S assignment map." Have it show all of the "Cleanliness" areas and name the persons responsible for each area.

- **5S schedule**

  So far, there may have been little trouble in dividing up the factory or office into Cleanliness areas and assigning specific areas and machines to individuals. However, things get more complicated when an area or machine is used by many people (i.e., meeting rooms, rest areas, lavatories, and libraries). For such areas, it is usually best to draft a 5S schedule in which people who use the area take turns cleaning it. The people may change from day to day, but the assignment is still a daily one.

  When a group is involved, it is easy for individuals to forget which day is theirs. One way to prevent this is to use the "tag team" concept. Pass a "Cleanliness tag" from person to person as a reminder that the next day is his or her turn.

Step 3: Determine Cleanliness Methods.

Daily Cleanliness activities should include not only what is required at the end of the work shift but also "Cleanliness inspections" before the shift starts. These activities are the foundation of Cleanliness. It is important to establish times for them and to carry them out with skill and enthusiasm so that they eventually become a natural part of the workday.

- **Five-minute Cleanliness**

Except for the semiannual major cleanup campaigns, Cleanliness is something that is practiced daily and does not require a lot of time. In fact, it is better to break down Cleanliness activities into smaller time segments (e.g., "five-minute Cleanliness").

By dividing Cleanliness time into short segments, we can assign specific tasks to each segment on the assumption that they will be carried out quickly and efficiently. Once people know exactly what is expected of them during a five-minute Cleanliness segment, they will be motivated to do it.

- **Determine Cleanliness procedures**

Unless people know exactly what to do, they are likely to spend most of a five-minute segment just getting ready to clean. To use the time efficiently, people need specific procedures to follow.

For example, let us suppose the Cleanliness target for the five-minute segment is a cutting machine. The machine can be divided into several areas requiring cleaning and checking (e.g., the cutting section, rotary section, saw table, control section, hydraulic section, overall exterior, surrounding floor area, local storage sites). Some of these areas may not require daily cleaning and can be scheduled out in a cycle of two days, four days, or one week. In such cases, make a Cleanliness checklist for each day and keep it in a visible place.

Figure 10-4. Mop-equipped Cart and Forklift

- **Cleanliness targets and tools**

  Determine Cleanliness targets for each Cleanliness participant. If the workplace is a machining shop, Cleanliness targets will mainly be machines. If it is an office, Cleanliness targets will likely be desks, floor areas, windows, and so on. After listing and assigning all of the Cleanliness targets, allocate the Cleanliness tools required for the targets:

  - ➤ Cleanliness starts with a thorough sweeping using brooms — especially in machining shops and other workplaces where cutting swarf or other processing debris collects on floors.
  - ➤ A mop is similar to a broom but functions more as a rag for wiping floors. Figure 10-4 illustrates how mops can be attached to vehicles such as carts and forklifts to turn them into Cleanliness tools on wheels.
  - ➤ Rags are the main tool for cleaning worktables, office desks, and equipment surfaces. Use damp rags on surfaces that collect dust or grime. Dry rags are better for polishing and wiping up oily areas.

Step 4: **Prepare the Cleanliness Tools**

Having determined at step 3 what Cleanliness tools are needed and in what amounts, apply Orderliness. Store the tools in places where they can be easily picked up and returned. (See Photo 10-1.)

Step 5: **Implement Cleanliness**

When implementing Cleanliness, make it a habit to start by grabbing a broom or rag. (By the way, I try to follow my own advice as you can see in Photo 10-2.) The following are some suggestions regarding Cleanliness implementation.

- Be sure to sweep away dirt from floor cracks, wall corners, and around posts and pillars.

Photo 10-1. Storage Site for Cleanliness Tools

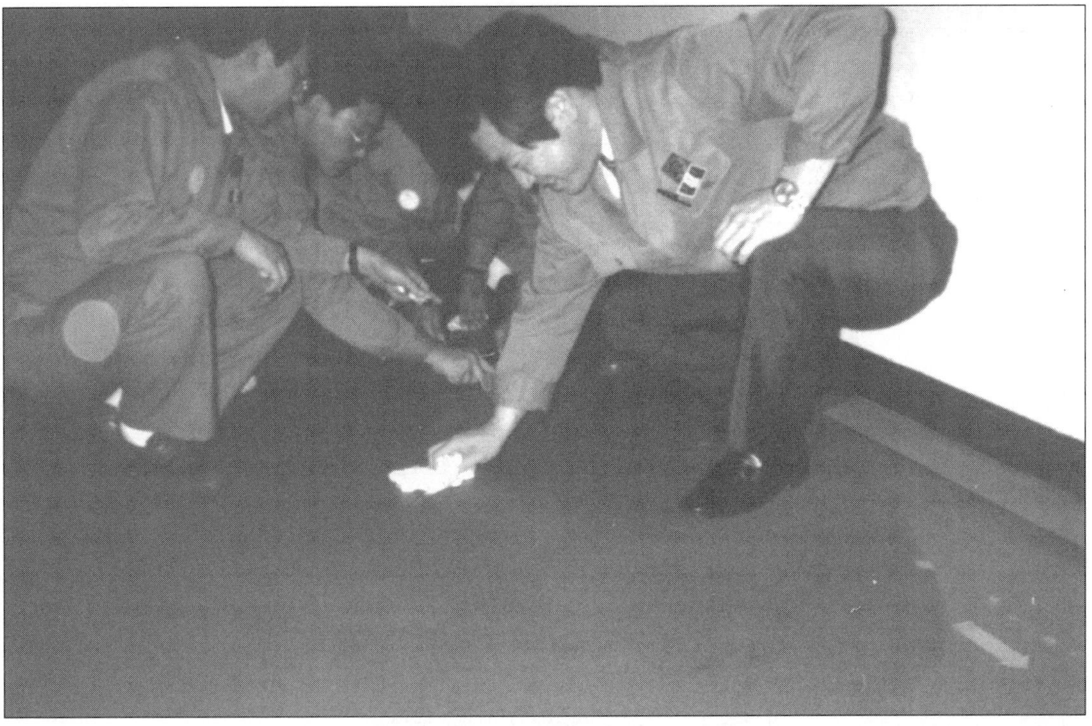

Photo 10-2. The Author Takes Cleanliness to the Floor

- Wipe off dust and dirt from walls, windows, and doors.
- Be thorough about cleaning dirt, scraps, swarf, oil, dust, rust, shavings, sand, paint, and other foreign matter from all surfaces. Try to restore to the surface's original state.
- Use cleansing or polishing agents when simple sweeping or wiping is not enough to remove dirt or stains.
- Cleanliness is an activity that everyone should take part in — especially the people who work with the machines or other Cleanliness targets.

Checkpoints for Cleanliness Implementation

Figure 10-5 lists some checkpoints concerning Cleanliness implementation for inventory items, equipment, and floor areas.

① Inventory Items

No.	Checkpoint	Check off
1.	Have you removed all dirt and dust from products, parts, and/or materials?	☐
2.	Have you removed rust that accumulates on parts that have been cut or rinsed?	☐
3.	Have you removed dirt from inventory storage shelves?	☐
4.	Have you removed dirt from in-process inventory storage sites?	☐
5.	Have you removed dirt from pallets used to move inventory items?	☐

② Equipment

No.	Checkpoint	Check off
1.	Have you removed dust and oil from the vicinity of the equipment?	☐
2.	Have you removed water, oil, and trash from underneath the equipment?	☐
3.	Have you removed dirt, dust, and oil that builds up on top of the equipment?	☐
4.	Have you removed oil stains or finger smudges from equipment sides and control section covers?	☐
5.	Have you removed dirt from glass displays, such as in oil level gauges or pneumatic pressure gauges?	☐
6.	Have you removed all equipment covers and lids and wiped away the dirt inside?	☐
7.	Have you removed dirt, dust, and oil from pneumatic pipes and electrical cables?	☐
8.	Have you removed dirt, dust, and oil from limit switches and all other switches?	☐
9.	Have you removed dirt and dust from light bulbs and tubes? (Use a soft cloth for this.)	☐
10.	Have you removed oil and grime from steps and other graded surfaces? (Use a damp cloth for this.)	☐
11.	Have you removed dust and grime from jigs and cutting tools?	☐
12.	Have you removed oil stains from dies?	☐
13.	Have you removed dust and dirt from measuring instruments?	☐

③ Spaces

No.	Checkpoint	Check off
1.	Have you removed sand, dirt, dust, and trash from floor spaces and walkways?	☐
2.	Have you removed water and oil puddles from floor spaces and walkways?	☐
3.	Have you removed dust and dirt from walls, windows, and ledges?	☐
4.	Have you removed finger smudges and dust from window panes?	☐
5.	Have you removed dust and dirt from ceilings and beams?	☐
6.	Have you removed dust from light tubes and bulbs?	☐
7.	Have you removed dust from light fixtures (stands, shades, etc.)?	☐
8.	Have you removed dust and dirt from shelves and worktables?	☐
9.	Have you removed oil and trash from stairwells?	☐
10.	Have you removed dirt and grime from the bottoms and corners of pillars and walls?	☐
11.	Have you removed trash and empty containers from the vicinity of the building?	☐
12.	Have you washed the building's exterior walls?	☐

Figure 10-5. Cleanliness Implementation Checkpoints (for Inventory Items, Equipment, and Floor Areas)

CLEANLINESS INSPECTION

Machine or equipment breakdowns frequently are caused by age-related deterioration. Once daily Cleanliness and periodic major cleanups become a habit, we can start incorporating inspection procedures into our Cleanliness procedures. This turns "Cleanliness" into "Cleanliness inspection."

Even when equipment in the workplace appears to function normally, the following types of problems and undesirable conditions may exist:

1. Oil leaks from the equipment onto the floor.
2. Cutting swarf accumulates on machines and on the floor.
3. Machines are so dirty that operators avoid touching them.
4. Dirt and grime leak from clogged ducts.
5. Gauge displays and other indicators are too dirty to be read.
6. Areas around oil inlet sites are dirty.
7. Oil in the oil tanks is murky.
8. Oil and air leak from hydraulic and pneumatic devices.
9. Nuts and bolts are either loose or missing.
10. Some machines make strange noises.
11. Some machines have strange vibrations.
12. Dust or grime accumulates in optoelectric sensors, limit switches, and other devices.
13. Motors overheat.
14. Sparks flare from power cords.
15. V-belts are loose.
16. Some V-belts are broken while others carry the increased burden.
17. Broken gauges are left unrepaired.
18. Cardboard is inserted into cracks as a temporary fix.

This list might easily result from just one observation of a machine shop. All of these conditions fall into the category of "strange phenomena" in machines or other equipment.

Generally, when machines or other equipment begin to emit strange sounds or vibrations, the operators — not the maintenance people — notice it first. Operators often sense the following types of abnormalities:

- motors that emit growling or buzzing sounds
- rotary mechanisms that emit scraping or scratching sounds
- rotary mechanisms that emit loose, "clunk, clunk" sounds
- pulleys that emit slapping sounds due to loose belts
- motors or control panels that emit a burning smell
- the leftover odor of cleanser in an area that usually has no distinctive odor
- rotary or friction mechanisms that emit a burning smell and/or smoke
- any unusually strong vibration felt when touching the machine
- a change in the sounds that usually accompany the normal vibration of machinery

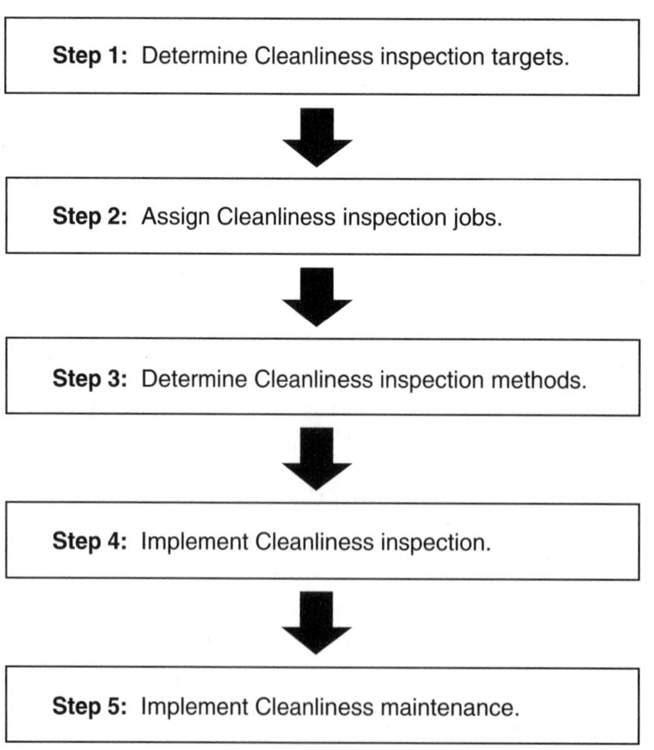

Figure 10-6. Steps in Cleanliness Inspection

It is important to take advantage of operator sensitivity toward equipment. That is why we incorporate the five senses in Cleanliness inspection.

Figure 10-6 outlines the steps in Cleanliness inspection.

Step 1. Determine Cleanliness Inspection Targets

The targets for Cleanliness inspection are basically the same as the equipment-related targets noted earlier with regard to Cleanliness duties. These include machines, equipment, jigs, tools, cutting tools, measuring instruments, and so on.

Step 2. Assign Cleanliness Inspection Jobs

In principle, the people who carry out Cleanliness inspection on a particular machine should be the same people who operate the machine. When one person operates several machines (as in multi-process handling), it is a good idea to also involve line supervisors and group leaders in Cleanliness inspection duties.

Once Cleanliness inspection job assignments are determined, they should be written up (1) on a large signboard for the workshop or (2) on small signs attached to each target machine.

Step 3. Determine Cleanliness Inspection Methods

Once Cleanliness inspection targets and job assignments have been determined, it is time to examine methods. First, list all of the inspection check items and combine them to make a "Cleanliness inspection checklist."

Table 10-1 shows a list of Cleanliness inspection points related to target mechanisms while Table 10-2 shows a list related to target phenomena.

Step 4. Implement Cleanliness Inspection

When actually implementing Cleanliness inspection, the key is to use your senses to detect abnormalities. For example:

- Look closely at how the machine works and watch for slight defects (e.g., oil leakage, debris scattering, deformation, wear, warping, mold, insufficient amounts, missing items, lopsidedness, inclinations, color changes).

Table 10-1. Cleanliness Inspection Points Related to Target Mechanisms

Mechanism	No.	Point	Main Response: Clean	Main Response: Lubricate	Main Response: Replace	Main Response: Restore
Hydraulic systems	1.	Is there any dirt or dust in the oil inlets?	○			
	2.	Do the oil level indicators show adequate levels?		○		
	3.	Can the oil level indicators be clearly seen?	○			
1. Hydraulic fluid tank ↓	4.	Are there any cracks in the hydraulic fluid tank?				○
	5.	Is the bottom of the hydraulic fluid tank dirty?	○			
2. Hydraulic fluid pump ↓	6.	Is the hydraulic fluid dirty?			○	
	7.	Is there enough hydraulic fluid?		○		
3. Control valve ↓	8.	Is the correct type of hydraulic fluid being used?			○	
	9.	Is the intake filter dirty?	○			
4. Actuator	10.	Is the pump making any strange noises?				○
	11.	Is the pump unusually hot?				○
	12.	Is there any oil leaking from the control valve?			○	○
	13.	Is there any oil leaking from pipe joints?			○	○
	14.	Is there any oil leaking from the actuator (hydraulic cylinder)?			○	○
Air compression systems	15.	Is the air filter dirty?	○			
	16.	Is the oil in the oiler dirty?			○	
1. Three-point setting ↓	17.	Is the oil level in the oiler adequate?		○		
	18.	Does the oiler drip at a suitable rate?		○		○
2. Control valve ↓	19.	Is there any air leakage from the control valve?			○	○
	20.	Is there any air leakage from the pipe joints?			○	○
	21.	Does the control valve make any strange noises?			○	○
3. Actuator ↓	22.	Is the control valve's locknut loose?				○
	23.	Is there any air leakage from the actuator (air cylinder)?			○	○
4. Exhaust line	24.	Is the air cylinder's fastening bolt loose?				○
	25.	Is there any clogging in the exhaust line?			○	○
Lubrication system	26.	Is there any dirt or dust in the oil inlets?	○			
	27.	Do the oil level indicators show adequate levels?		○		
1. Oil inlets ↓	28.	Can the oil level indicators be clearly seen?	○			
	29.	Are there any cracks in the oil tank?				○
2. Tank ↓	30.	Is the bottom of the oil tank dirty?	○			
	31.	Is the oil in the tank dirty?			○	
	32.	Is there any oil leakage from the tank or pipe joints?			○	○
3. Oil pipes ↓	33.	Are oil levels adequate?		○		
	34.	Is the correct type of oil being used?			○	
4. Lubrication sites	35.	Is there any clogging in the oil pipes?			○	○
	36.	Is there any dust or dirt at lubrication sites?	○			
	37.	Are the lubrication tools dirty?	○			

Table 10-1. (cont.)

Mechanism	No.	Point	Main Response: Clean	Main Response: Lubricate	Main Response: Replace	Main Response: Restore
Friction-bearing mechanisms Rotary mechanisms Drive mechanisms	38.	Is there any dirt or grime in the friction-bearing mechanism?	○			
	39.	Are there any foreign fragments or dents in the friction-bearing mechanism?			○	
	40.	Does the friction-bearing mechanism make any strange noises?	○		○	○
	41.	Is there any dirt or grime in the rotary mechanism?	○			
	42.	Does the rotary mechanism rotate in a lopsided manner?			○	○
	43.	Does the rotary mechanism make any strange noises?	○		○	○
	44.	Are any of the fastening bolts loose?				○
	45.	Are any of the V-belts or chains loose?			○	
	46.	Does the pulley make any strange noises?			○	○
	47.	Are there any dents or scratches in the table bed?			○	
	48.	Is there any backlash in the cogwheels?			○	○
	49.	Is the table bed level?			○	○
Electrical systems	50.	Are the warning lamps dirty?	○			
	51.	Are any of the warning lamps burnt out?			○	
	52.	Do any of the control panels have broken doors or lids?			○	○
	53.	Do any of the doors or lids have broken or missing insulating seals?			○	
	54.	Are any of the wires in the control panel broken, torn, or shorted?	○		○	○
	55.	Are any of the contact points dirty or damaged?			○	○
	56.	Are any of the printed circuit boards bent, loose, or dirty?	○			○
	57.	Are any of the fastening bolts loose?				○
	58.	Is the NC machine's tape reader dirty?	○			
	59.	Are any of the switches dirty or damaged?	○			
	60.	Are any of the photo cells dirty?	○			
	61.	Have any of the timers or relays exceeded their warranty periods?			○	
	62.	Are any of the ground connections loose?				○
	63.	Do the ground connections have adequate insulation?				○
Jigs and tools Cutting tools Measuring instruments	64.	Are any of the jigs and tools dirty?	○			
	65.	Is there any looseness or backlash in the jigs and tools?			○	○
	66.	Do the jigs and tools have the specified precision?			○	○
	67.	Is there any foreign matter on the cutting tools?			○	○
	68.	Do any of the cutting tools seem on the point of breaking?				○
	69.	Are the measuring instruments (micrometers, dial gauges, etc.) dirty?	○			
	70.	Do the measuring instruments have the specified precision?			○	

Table 10-2. Cleanliness Inspection Points Related to Target Phenomena

No.	Phenomena	Point	Main response
1.	Dirt and grime	Dust, grime, dirt, rust, chips, shavings, swarf, etc.	Cleaning
2.	Oil	Oil leakage, oil stains, oil depletion, oil shortage, incorrect oil type, oil clogging	Add oil, change oil, clean and repair
3.	Temperature, pressure	Overheating, insufficient heating, excess pressure, insufficient pressure, abnormal coolant temperature, off-standard control devices	Repair to restore original state
4.	Looseness, slack	Loose or missing bolts, loose or missing nuts, slack belts, broken welds	Tighten, replace, and repair to restore original state
5.	Damage	Broken or cracked hoses, broken meters, cracked glass, damaged switches, broken wires, damaged mechanical arms, vibration in rotary mechanisms.	Replace and repair to restore original state

- Listen closely for changes in the sounds the machine makes (e.g., sporadic sounds, odd sounds).
- Use your nose to detect burning smells or other unusual odors (e.g., burning rubber, cleansing agents).
- Touch the machine where it is safe during operation and during downtime to detect deviations from normal conditions (e.g., strange vibrations, wobbling, looseness, excessive heat, shifting).

We should be sensitive to equipment abnormalities. However, when feeling around for unusual conditions, we must be as careful as a doctor making a diagnosis. Inspection is not simply a visual activity.

The following are additional points concerning the implementation of Cleanliness inspection.

Have Equipment Operators Perform Cleanliness Inspection

Do not assign Cleanliness inspection duties to maintenance staff. Instead make operators responsible for taking care of their own machines.

Carry Out Cleanliness Inspection Systematically

Establish separate systematic routines for implementing hydraulic systems, pneumatic systems, lubrication systems, and so on. Draw up and use a Cleanliness inspection checklist.

Take Care of Slight Defects Immediately

Once they discover any slight defects, operators should try to (1) fix them at once (restore to the original state of the equipment) or (2) improve upon them (make it better than its original state).

Use Maintenance Cards

Whenever an operator discovers a slight defect and either restores the condition or makes an improvement, he or she should put up a "maintenance card" and set up a maintenance kanban. (Maintenance cards should be attached to the parts of the machines or equipment where maintenance is required. The card should stay there until the maintenance is completed. It can also be used as a maintenance approval card.)

Figure 10-7 shows an example of how Cleanliness inspection checklists, maintenance cards, and maintenance kanban can be used. In this example, there is just one central Cleanliness inspection checklist.

Cleanliness inspection checklists should be incorporated into daily cleaning, maintenance, and checking work for mechanical equipment as part of the overall production maintenance program. These central checklists enable group leaders and other shop-floor supervisors to easily and quickly check on equipment inspection conditions for each equipment unit. They also help them determine exactly where and when any abnormalities have occurred. After confirming such inspection, repair, or improvement work, supervisors then return the maintenance kanban to the corresponding machines as they make their patrols.

Step 5. Implement Cleanliness Maintenance

Slight defects discovered during Cleanliness inspection are subjected to "instant maintenance." This means that the person who discovers the problem takes immediate action to repair or improve it. If that person is unable to take

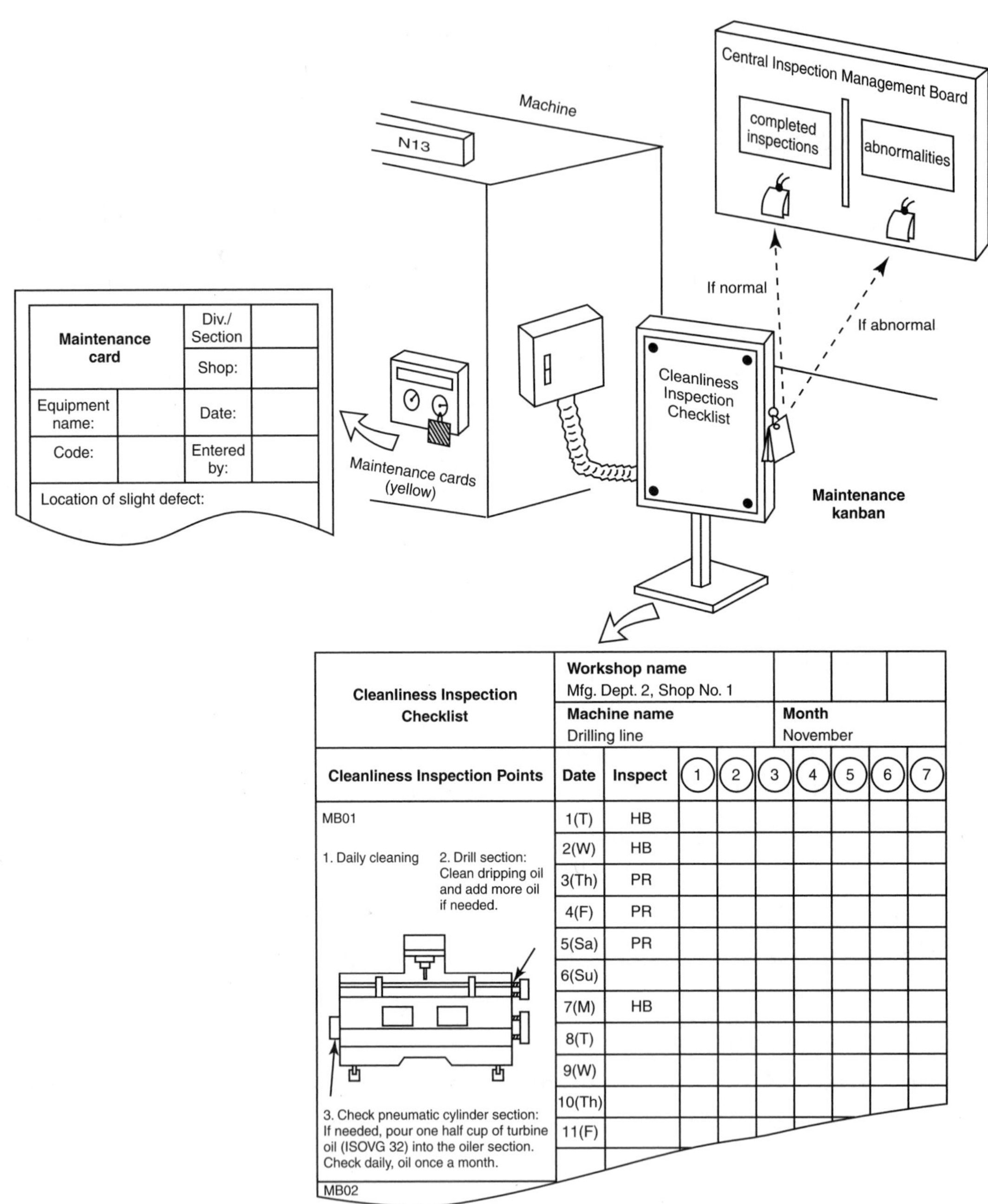

Figure 10-7. Cleanliness Inspection Checklist, Maintenance Cards, and Maintenance Kanban

corrective action, he or she should issue a maintenance kanban to request the services of a maintenance technician.

CLEANLINESS MAINTENANCE

All equipment abnormalities or slight defects should be fixed or improved. Figure 10-8 outlines two ways to do this.

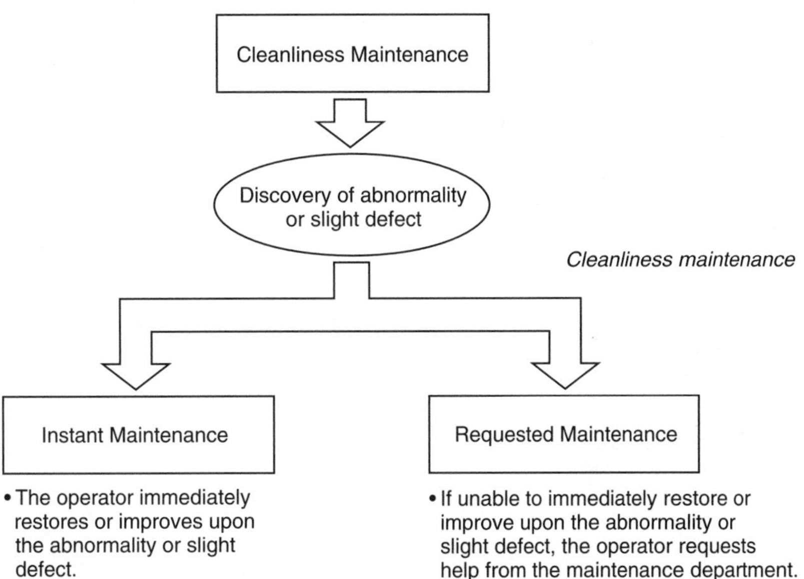

Figure 10-8. Two Methods for Cleanliness Maintenance

Instant Maintenance

If an operator discovers an abnormality or slight defect in a machine during Cleanliness inspection, he or she should immediately fix or improve the discovered problem. This “instant maintenance” requires that operators be able to determine clearly what level of maintenance work they can handle.

Requested Maintenance

If operators discover abnormality or slight defect during Cleanliness inspection and determine that it is too difficult for them to restore or repair, they attach a maintenance card to the site of the problem and issue a maintenance kanban to request help from the maintenance department.

Maintenance Item Checklist			Division:	Production Engineering Div. (Maintenance)			
			Manager:	O'NEAL		Date:	FEB 1994
No.	Machine name (code)	Maintenance item and description	Requested Dept.	Request date	Maintenance technician	Maintenance date	Confirmation
1.	LATHE 3 (L230-023)	MISSING LID ON OIL CUP (REPLACE)	LATHE TECHNICIAN	1/29	LARUE	2/1	✓
2.	LATHE 6 (L230-026)	CRACKED GLASS IN AIR PRESSURE GAUGE AT 3-POINT SETTING (REPLACE)	"	2/1	"	2/2	✓
3.	PRESS 2 (P160-012)	OIL LEAKAGE IN CONTROL VALVE (REPAIR LOOSE VALVE)	PRESS TECHNICIAN	2/2	"	2/3	✓
4.	LATHE 7 (L230-027)	BROKEN BULB IN WARNING LAMP (REPLACE)	LATHE TECHNICIAN	2/2	"	2/4	✓
5.	DRILL PRESS 4 (D120-044)	MOTOR OVERHEATING (REPLACE)	DRILL TECHNICIAN	2/3	"	2/4	✓
6.	DRILL PRESS 6 (D120-046)	BROKEN REVERSE LIMIT SWITCH (REPLACE)	"	2/3	"	2/5	✓
7.	BLANKING UNIT 1 (B001-001)	UNSTABLE PRESSURE CONTROL VALVE	CUTTING TECHNICIAN	2/4	"	2/6	✓

Figure 10-9. Maintenance Item Checklist

In cases of requested maintenance, it is also a good idea to require that operators enter the requested maintenance item onto a checklist such as the one shown in Figure 10-9. These checklists are an aid to planning maintenance activities, including maintenance item assignments and scheduling.

Once a requested maintenance item has been taken care of and its result confirmed, the item should be checked off in the "confirmation" column on the far right in the checklist. The maintenance card should then be retrieved from the machine where it is attached.

11

The Fourth Pillar: Standardized Cleanup

Standardized Cleanup, the fourth pillar of our visual workplace, differs from Organization, Orderliness, and Cleanliness. This is because it refers not to an activity but to a standardized state or condition at a certain point in time. Specifically, we may define it as "the state that exists when the first three pillars — Organization, Orderliness, and Cleanliness — are properly maintained."

THE NEED FOR STANDARDIZED CLEANUP AND ITS ESSENTIAL POINTS

A room, factory, or city block in which Organization, Orderliness, and Cleanliness are maintained is a clean room, a clean factory, or a clean city block.

When considering a clean city block in this "Standardized Cleanup" sense, we not only mean that the area has been swept and washed clean of debris and dirt. We also infer that it is well laid out and that the neighborhood houses are well maintained. In other words, Standardized Cleanup is a combination as well as a culmination of Organization, Orderliness, and Cleanliness. It is the condition that exists when these three pillars are properly maintained.

Therefore, the need for Standardized Cleanup derives from the need for Organization, Orderliness, and Cleanliness as a unified whole. The need for it also derives from the following types of problems that result when it is not maintained:

- Conditions revert to their previous undesirable levels even after a companywide 5S implementation campaign.
- At the end of the day, people must deal with piles of unneeded items left over from the day's production that lie scattered around the production equipment.
- Tool storage sites tend to get mixed up and must be put back in order at the end of the day.
- Cutting swarf constantly falls onto the floor and must be swept up.
- Puddles of cleaning fluid and rinse water must be mopped up regularly.
- The entire floor must be swept free of litter every two or three days.
- Even after implementing Organization and Orderliness, it does not take long for office workers to start accumulating more stationery supplies than they need. This makes inspection patrols necessary.

These problems and others reveal backsliding from gains made via Organization, Orderliness, and Cleanliness. The basic purpose of Standardized Cleanup is to prevent such setbacks, to help make maintaining the first three S's a daily habit, and to ensure that they are maintained in their fully implemented state.

Standardized Cleanup Means Preventing Dirt

The foundation of Cleanliness is sweeping and wiping. The foundation of Standardized Cleanup is making sure that Organization, Orderliness, and Cleanliness are being maintained and incorporated into everyday activities.

However, that's just the first level. How can Standardized Cleanup go beyond just the maintenance of conditions established by the first three S's?

Obviously, to maintain Cleanliness, it is fundamental to 5S implementation that activities such as mopping up oil-stained floors and sweeping away scattered swarf become habitual. However, we can also take Standardized Cleanup to a higher level of implementation by asking the following types of questions:

1. **Question:** Why mop the floor every day?

   Answer: Because oil collects on the floor.

Question: Why does oil collect on the floor every day?

Answer: Because...

2. **Question:** Why sweep the floor every two or three hours?

   Answer: Because swarf gets scattered there.

   Question: Why does swarf get scattered there?

   Answer: Because...

This simple line of questioning can help solve many kinds of problems even in the most complex factories. It is called the "five why's" — we ask "why" until we identify the underlying causes. Combine it with asking "how" to find a way to make improvements once the final "why" is answered, and it is known as the "5W1H approach."

Let us suppose that in your factory people are mopping up oil from the floor every day and sweeping away scattered swarf every two or three hours.

Dirt and other forms of contamination naturally tend to disperse. They usually begin in a relatively small area and, over time, spread out. For instance, contaminants from individual buildings or ships can pollute large stretches of rivers or seas. Dirty exhaust from a single industrial smokestack can pollute a big chunk of the sky. Once such widespread pollution has occurred, it becomes very difficult and expensive to take corrective action. It is much easier, safer, and cheaper to deal with the problem at its source.

The same principle applies to oil and swarf on the floor. The longer you let it spread, the bigger the mess becomes. People get oily swarf stuck on their shoes and track it to other areas. Or, a forklift comes by and leaves long, oily tire tracks. Eventually, the oil and swarf get spread throughout the factory.

This is where 5S implementation comes in. Anyone who has participated in 5S implementation can tell you that the initial cleanup is hard work indeed. To minimize the drudgery of cleaning up, the key is to treat contamination problems at their source. Instead of mopping up oil puddles, repair whatever it is that is leaking oil on the floor.

In a factory, when something leaks oil or scatters swarf onto the floor, we need to find out what that something is and exactly where the oil or swarf comes from. It is not enough to put an oil pan under a leaky machine. This solution goes only half way — it permits the oil leak to continue. This is far from the true meaning of Standardized Cleanup, which requires treating dirt, oil, or other contamination at the source. Of course, treating dirt at its source is the same as preventing dirt.

Figure 11-1 shows three levels of 3S conditions, two of which correspond to the two levels of Standardized Cleanup just described. The first level is "3S habituation" to maintain 3S conditions. Activities at this level include the following:

- reimplementing Organization whenever unneeded items begin to accumulate
- reimplementing Orderliness whenever people begin to leave things in unspecified places
- cleaning floors whenever they begin to get dirty

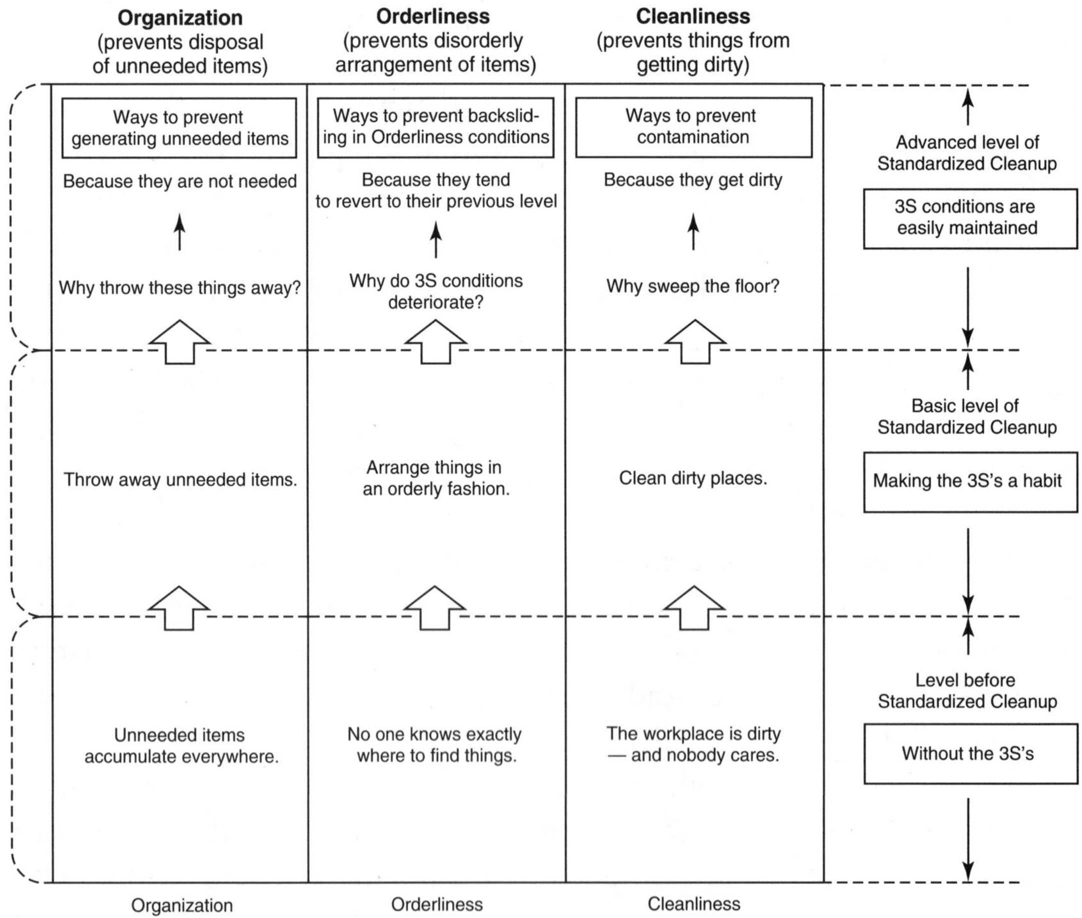

Figure 11-1. Three Levels of 3S Conditions

This is Standardized Cleanup at its basic level. At its advanced level, we apply the 5W1H approach, asking "why" about the causes of dirt, dust, oil, and other contamination until we can identify their sources and take preventive action. This helps to establish 5S conditions that do not deteriorate.

For example:

1. **Question:** Why clear away those things?

   Answer: Because they are not needed.

   Resolution: Find a way to prevent the generation of unneeded things.
2. **Question:** Why do 3S conditions deteriorate?

   Answer: Because they tend to revert to their previous level.

   Resolution: Find a way to prevent conditions from reverting to their previous level.
3. **Question:** Why sweep the floor?

   Answer: Because it is dirty.

   Resolution: Find a way to prevent floors from getting dirty.

Standardized Cleanup only exists as long as 3S conditions are maintained. This makes 3S deterioration actually 4S deterioration.

The key to maintaining 4S conditions is the fifth "S" pillar — Discipline. After that come the wisdom and ingenuity of the workplace staff who must devise ways to prevent 4S deterioration. The 5W1H approach is a good aid to their creative thinking.

THREE WAYS TO MAKE ORGANIZATION, ORDERLINESS, AND CLEANLINESS A HABIT

Discipline is vital to making Organization, Orderliness, and Cleanliness a habit and to maintaining Standardized Cleanup. I strongly advise people to avoid the assumption that using simple checklists and other 5S tools is enough to maintain 5S conditions. Chapter 12 will be devoted to Discipline. For now, we will discuss it only as it relates to 3S habituation. Figure 11-2 illustrates how Discipline is fundamental to making the 3S's a habit.

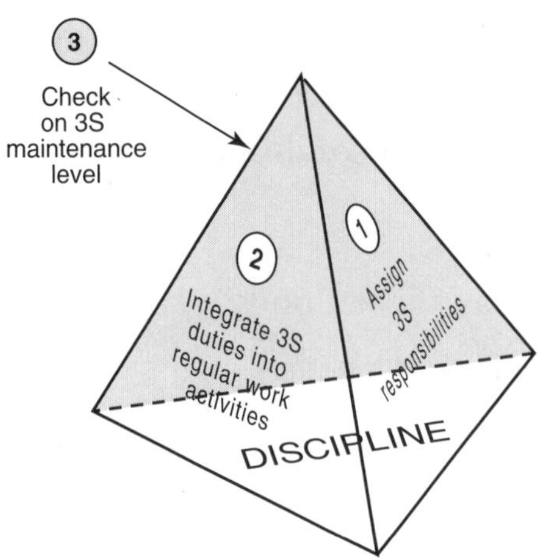

Figure 11-2. Three Ways to Make the 3S's a Habit

First, we must determine who is responsible for what with regard to maintaining 3S conditions. Next, to prevent backsliding and omissions, we need to integrate 3S maintenance duties into regular work activities. Finally, we need to check on how well 3S conditions are being maintained. This is a cycle of methods that gets repeated, based on the QC movement's famous Plan-Do-See cycle.

1. Assign 3S Responsibilities

When it comes to maintaining 3S conditions, unless everyone knows exactly what they are responsible for doing and exactly when, where, and how to do it, neither Organization, Orderliness, nor Cleanliness has much meaning. It is essential that people be given clear job assignments based on their own workplaces.

A useful tool is the 5S map, which was introduced in Chapter 10. 5S maps show how the workplace is divided into sections and list the names of the people responsible for maintaining 5S conditions in those sections. This makes 5S job assignments visible at a glance.

Figure 11-3 shows another variation on the theme of 5S maps, in which divider lines and arrows are used to show who is responsible for what areas in the workplace.

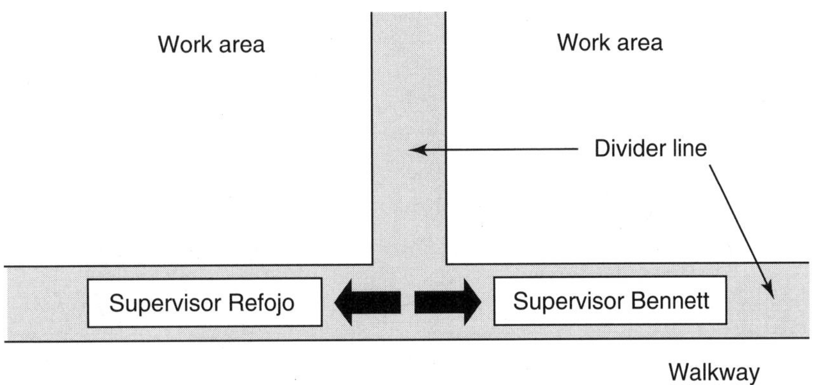

Figure 11-3. Alternative 5S Map Method

Similarly, clear instructions should be given to the people who deliver goods from outside suppliers. The delivery sites should be clearly marked and a 5S map posted to show where each supplier's goods are to be unloaded. At each unloading site, signboards such as the one shown in Figure 11-4 will make it clear whose things go where and in what amount. The suppliers should be made responsible for maintaining 3S conditions at their own unloading sites and encouraged to join in full 5S implementation.

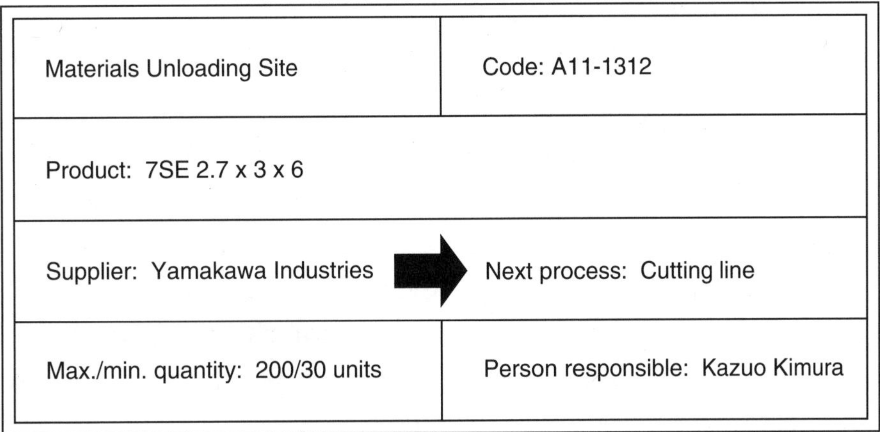

Figure 11-4. Unloading-Site Signboard for Suppliers

5S Job Cycle Chart	Div./Dept./ Section	Production Div. 1, Assembly Dept. A		
	Entered by:	COMARELLA	Date:	1 FEB 1994

No.	5S Job	Organization	Orderliness	Cleanliness	Cleanup	Discipline	Job Cycle A	B	C	D	E	F
1.	Red-tag strategy (occasional, companywide)	○									○	
2.	Red-tag strategy (repeated)	○					○					
3.	Place indicators (check or make)		○						○			
4.	Item indicators (check or make)		○						○			
5.	Amount indicators (check or make)		○						○			
6.	Sweep around line			○				○				
7.	Sweep within line			○				○				
8.	Sweep around worktable			○				○				
9.	Sweep on and under worktable			○				○				
10.	Sweep work areas and walkways											

Figure 11-5. 5S Job Cycle Chart

Once job assignments are determined, it helps to use a "5S job cycle chart." Use this chart to list the 5S jobs to be done in each area and to set a frequency cycle for each job (for example, daily or weekly).

In the example shown in Figure 11-5, 5S duties are sorted out according to the first three S's and the scheduling cycle. In the figure, code letters are used for the various cycle periods: A is for "continuously," B for "daily (mornings)," C for "daily (evenings)," D for "weekly," E for "monthly," and F for "occasionally." Each 5S job assignee can then use such charts as 5S checklists. This particular chart shows clearly who is responsible for each job, which area, what to do, and when to do it — making it a good start for 3S habituation.

2. Integrate 3S Duties into Regular Work Duties

If people carry out 3S maintenance duties only when they see 3S conditions slipping, that is evidence enough that the 5S's have not yet taken root. Maintenance must become a natural part of everyone's regular work duties. In other words, the 5S's — centered on maintaining 3S conditions — must be part of the normal work flow. We sometimes refer to this as "5S line integration" or establishing a 5S flow.

Most of us practice this sort of thing in our daily routine. We wake up in the morning, go to the bathroom to wash, shave, and brush our teeth, then head downstairs for breakfast. Such habits are part of our normal morning work flow. Likewise, at the end of the workday, factory workers straighten up their workshops, remove their work uniforms, and go home. Such habits, learned at first, later become automatic.

The visual 5S's and the five-minute 5S's are two approaches that help make 5S maintenance work part of the everyday work routine.

The Visual 5S's

Described in detail in Chapter 12, the visual 5S approach makes the level of 5S conditions clearly discernible at a glance. Obviously, this is helpful in factories that handle a great variety and number of materials. However, it is also true in offices, where the main "material" is information.

The three salient points regarding the visual 5S's are that

- anyone should be able
- to distinguish between abnormal and normal conditions
- at a glance.

In addition, abnormalities that are immediately visible deserve an immediate response.

As a factory example, consider a drill-press process where Orderliness has been applied so that the position and amount of each finished workpiece is clearly indicated. As an additional visual aid, the place where the last batch item goes can be marked with a thick red line to indicate that it is time to stop and send the batch to the next process. (See Figure 11-6.)

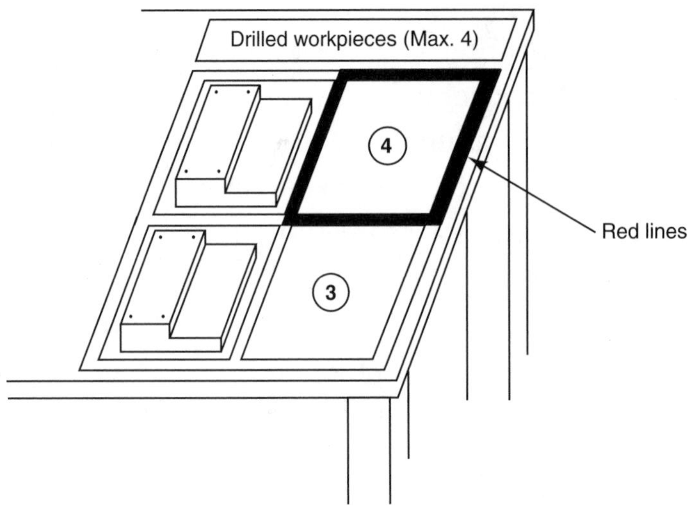

Figure 11-6. Visual 5S Method for Indicating Maximum Batch Size

The Five-Minute 5S's

When using the visual 5S approach, instant visibility can act as a trigger for taking immediate 3S action (Organization, Orderliness, Cleanliness) against the discovered abnormalities (i.e., overproduction, disorder, and contamination).

However, we must also deal with the question of how skillfully and efficiently such 3S actions are carried out. Instead of allotting two hours for removing all of the swarf from the floor, we can set up a 30-minute or a one-hour Cleanliness procedure that accomplishes the same task. In a sense, we can apply the same efficiency-boosting approach that changes 30-minute changeover procedures into a SMED changeover. (This "single-minute exchange of die" refers to changeovers that take nine minutes or less.)

The term "five-minute 5S" is a loose one — the actual time can be three minutes, six minutes, or whatever. The point is to make the 3S work brief, effective, and habitual.

Figure 11-7 shows a "five-minute 5S signboard" that was made as part of a "one-minute 1S" campaign.

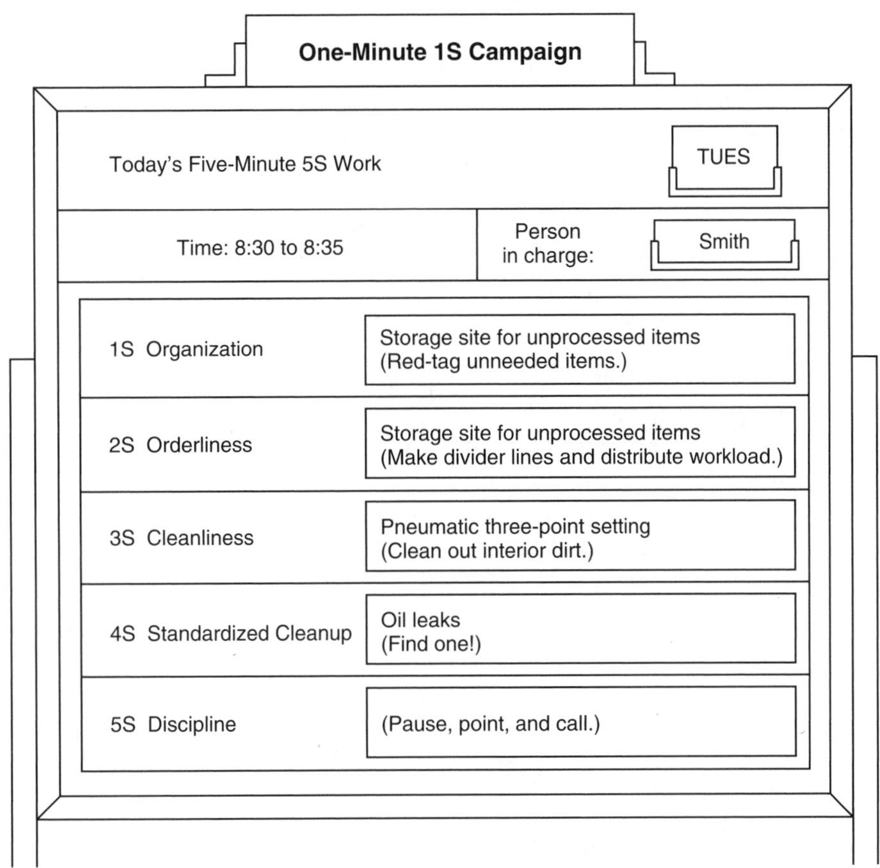

Figure 11-7. "Five-Minute 5S Signboard" as Part of "One-Minute 1S Campaign"

3. Check on 3S Maintenance Level

Even after we have assigned 3S jobs and have incorporated 3S (or 5S) maintenance into the everyday work routine, we still need to evaluate how well the 3S's (or 5S's) are being maintained. For this, we can set up a 5S patrol (described further in Chapter 12). These 5S patrols are similar to the QC patrols used in the Quality Control movement, except that the 5S focus is more specific and they patrol more often.

Figure 11-8 presents a "five-point Standardized Cleanup-level checklist" that is used by 5S patrols in a factory. To evaluate the Standardized Cleanup level, the evaluator ranks the Organization, Orderliness, and Cleanliness levels

Five-Point Standardized Cleanup-level Checklist		Dept.: Assembly Dept. 1	FEB. 15, 1994			
		Assigned area	Entered by: YAMAGUCHI		Page 1/1	
No.	Process and checkpoint	Organization Level	Orderliness Level	Cleanliness Level	Total	Previou total
1.	WORK AT LINE A, PROCESS 1	1 2 3 (4) 5	1 (2) 3 4 5	1 (2) 3 4 5	8	6
2.	"	1 (2) 3 4 5	1 2 (3) 4 5	1 2 (3) 4 5	8	6
3.	"	1 (2) 3 4 5	1 (2) 3 4 5	1 (2) 3 4 5	6	5
4.	"	1 (2) 3 4 5	1 2 (3) 4 5	1 (2) 3 4 5	7	7
5.	"	1 2 (3) 4 5	1 2 (3) 4 5	1 2 3 (4) 5	10	6
6.	"	1 2 3 (4) 5	1 2 3 (4) 5	1 2 3 (4) 5	12	8
7.	AVERAGE AND TOTAL FOR LINE A	1 2 (2.6) 3 4 5	1 2 (2.8) 3 4 5	1 2 (2.8) 3 4 5	(50)	(38)

Figure 11-8. Five-point Standardized Cleanup-level Checklist

on a scale of 1 to 5. Such checklists can be made for specific workshops and/or production processes. Some examples are shown in Tables 11-1, 11-2, 11-3, and 11-4.

Table 11-1. Five-Point Check for Organization

Description / Points	1	2	3	4	5
Needed and unneeded items are mixed together at the workplace.	○	×	×	×	×
It is possible (but not easy) to distinguish needed/unneeded items.	×	○	×	×	×
Anyone can easily distinguish needed/unneeded items.	×	×	○	○	○
All unneeded items are stored away from the workplace.	×	×	×	○	○
Completely unneeded items have been disposed of.	×	×	×	×	○

Table 11-2. Five-Point Orderliness Check for Inventory and Stock-on-Hand

Description \ Points	1	2	3	4	5
It is impossible to tell what goes where and in what amount.	○	×	×	×	×
It is possible (but not easy) to tell what goes where and in what amount.	×	○	×	×	×
General location signs show what goes where.	×	×	○	○	○
Location indicators, item indicators, and divider lines enable anyone to see at a glance what goes where.	×	×	×	○	○
A FIFO system and specific indicators show what goes where and in what amount.	×	×	×	×	○

Table 11-3. Five-Point Orderliness Check for Jigs and Tools

Description \ Points	1	2	3	4	5
It is impossible to tell what goes where and in what amount.	○	×	×	×	×
It is possible (but not easy) to tell what goes where and in what amount.	×	○	×	×	×
There are location and item indicators for all jigs and tools.	×	×	○	○	○
Various techniques (i.e., color coding, outlining, easy replacement methods) are used to facilitate replacing things properly.	×	×	×	○	○
Jigs and tools are unified and, when possible, eliminated.	×	×	×	×	○

Table 11-4. Five-Point Cleanliness Check

Description \ Points	1	2	3	4	5
The workplace is left dirty.	○	×	×	×	×
The workplace is cleaned once in a while.	×	○	×	×	×
The workplace is cleaned daily.	×	×	○	○	○
Cleanliness has been combined with inspection.	×	×	×	○	○
Cleanliness (dirt-prevention) techniques have been implemented.	×	×	×	×	○

THREE WAYS TO DEVELOP "UNBREAKABLE" STANDARDIZED CLEANUP

When we find that tools have not been put back correctly, we immediately take care of them. When we find an oil puddle on the floor, we immediately mop it up. Making these actions habitual is the unchanging foundation of Standardized Cleanup. However, at least for a while, the fact remains that we will find tools in the wrong places and floors dirty.

To take Standardized Cleanup to a higher level, we must ask "why?" Why do unneeded items accumulate (despite Organization)? Why do tools get put back incorrectly (despite Orderliness)? Why do floors get dirty (despite Cleanliness)? When we ask "why" repeatedly, we eventually find the source of the problem and can address that source with a fundamental improvement. Such improvements can help us develop "unbreakable" Standardized Cleanup which, by definition, means:

- unbreakable Organization
- unbreakable Orderliness
- unbreakable Cleanliness

Prevent Unneeded Items from Accumulating (Preventive Organization)

The red-tag strategy described in Chapter 8 is our main means of implementing Organization for unneeded items. By sticking red tags on all unneeded items in the factory or office, this strategy is a "visual Organization" method that enables anyone to see at a glance which items are no longer needed. Ordinarily, red-tag strategies should be implemented on a companywide basis once or twice a year.

However, we should note that the red-tag strategy is an after-the-fact approach that deals with unneeded items that have accumulated. No matter how often we implement this strategy, unneeded items will accumulate in the interim. Such "post-facto" Organization is similar to "post-facto" maintenance in which maintenance work is done once something has broken down.

Nowadays, smart companies are shifting from "post-facto" maintenance to "preventive" maintenance, in which machines are maintained in a way that prevents them from breaking down. In the same way, companies can switch from post-facto Organization to preventive Organization. Instead of waiting until unneeded items accumulate, we find ways to prevent their accumulation. We could also call this approach "unbreakable" Organization because once Organization has been implemented, the condition of being free of unneeded items becomes an "unbreakable" condition.

To achieve unbreakable Organization, we must prevent unneeded items from even entering the workplace. In other words, we must allow only needed items to enter. These words — "only what is needed" — have a familiar ring to anyone acquainted with the Just-in-Time (JIT) philosophy and program.

For example, to prevent the accumulation of unneeded inventory, we must find a way to procure and produce only those materials that are needed, only when they are needed, and only in the amount needed. Similarly, with regard to documentation, we must find a way to generate, photocopy, and distribute only those documents that are needed, only when they are needed, and only in the amount needed. The former is the basic principle of JIT production; the latter is the basic principle of JIT clerical operations.

Figure 11-9 outlines the steps in applying the JIT production approach to prevent the accumulation of unneeded inventory.

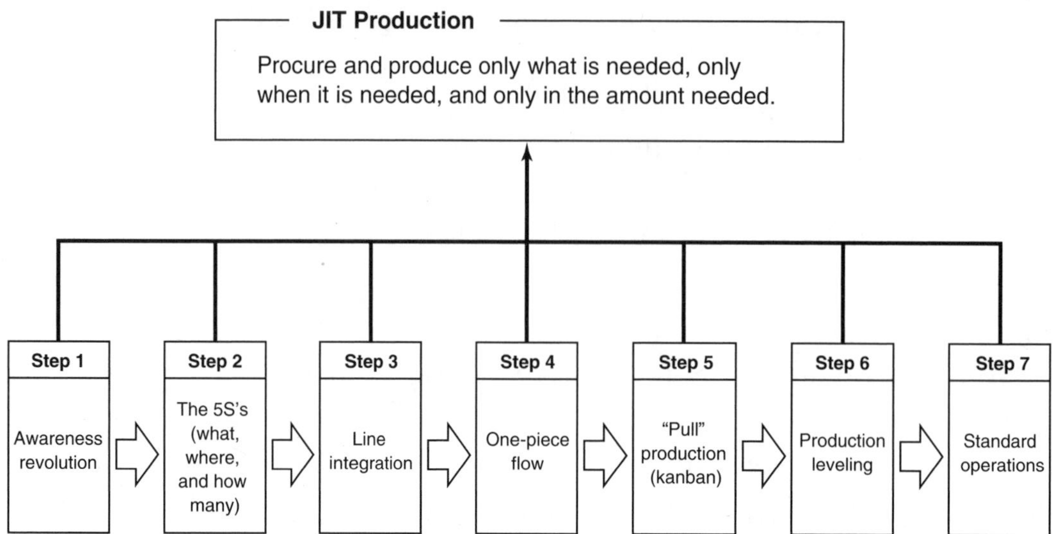

Figure 11-9. Steps in Applying JIT to Prevent the Accumulation of Unneeded Inventory

Step 1: The Awareness Revolution

We should begin by understanding that JIT production means producing only nondefective products, one at a time, and delivering them on time to the customer. It is important to note that this is a clear departure from production based on predicted orders, lot orders, or other types of lot production.

Step 2: The 5S's (What, Where, and How Many)

To prevent the production of unneeded items, proper identification and control of inventory and stock-on-hand are stressed. This means strictly maintaining inventory so that the people responsible always know what is needed, where it is to be kept, and how many are needed.

Step 3: Line Integration

Line integration includes arranging production equipment according to the sequence of production processes and eliminating conveyance waste. The best way to do this is by using small, inexpensive, special-purpose production equipment.

Step 4: One-Piece Flow

This step involves changing production operations from lot-production-based operations to one-piece production-based operations. At this level goods are produced one unit at a time via a production flow through line-integrated machinery.

Step 5: Pull Production (Kanban)

"Pull production" means that downstream processes control production at upstream processes (for instance, between suppliers and factories and between processes within a factory) to prevent the production of excess goods. This type of production usually includes kanban as a key tool for controlling production.

Kanban are often tags or pieces of paper that carry information needed to maintain JIT production. They include "withdrawal kanban" that downstream processes use to order goods from upstream processes and "production kanban" that provide work instructions.

Step 6: Production Leveling

At the production planning stage, rather than plan production based on lots, we spread out the variety and amounts of goods to be produced as evenly as possible. This balance enables an even level of high productivity throughout the factory as well as JIT scheduling.

Step 7: Standard Operations

"Standard operations" means regulating processing times and the amounts of inventory between processes and between machines within a process to prevent the accumulation of excess parts and the production of excess products.

Prevent Things from Having to Be Put Back (Preventive Orderliness)

Inasmuch as order has no meaning without chaos, Orderliness also implies its opposite (that is, the disorderly placement of things). Preventive Orderliness means keeping Orderliness from "breaking down." Whether in factories or offices, Orderliness must be applied to everything — from inventory to tools and from documents to stationery supplies — to eliminate the inefficiency that results from the lack of orderly control of such items.

To achieve preventive Orderliness, we must somehow prevent order from lapsing into chaos. There are two ways to do this: (1) make it difficult to put things in the wrong place and (2) make it impossible to put things in the wrong place.

Action / Target		Organization (without discarding)	Orderliness		Organization (discarding)
		Replenishment (generating)	Use	Return	Discard
Inventory		○	○	△ (Return unused inventory)	△ (Dead inventory and defective goods)
Equipment	Machines	○	○	×	○
	Carts and other conveyance tools	○	○	○	○
	Jigs, tools, and dies	○	○	○	○
Documentation		○	○	○	○
Space		○	○	×	×

Figure 11-10. Orderliness-breaking Actions

The first method relies heavily on discipline and visual Orderliness. Clearly visible storage sites indicate at a glance what goes where and in what amount.

When it is obvious what goes where and in what amount, it is also obvious when things are not put back properly. As people practice returning things, such visual Orderliness becomes habitual. This condition is "Orderliness that is difficult to break."

However, there is still a big difference between Orderliness that is difficult to break and Orderliness that is unbreakable. Why settle for the former when the latter is possible? But how do we achieve unbreakable Orderliness?

We begin by asking: "Why?" Why is Orderliness "breakable?" We might respond that it is because people use things. But using things does not of itself cause Orderliness to be disrupted as long as the user puts them back properly. Therefore, the answer is because people make mistakes when putting things back.

Figure 11-10 tabulates Orderliness-breaking human actions regarding such things as inventory, equipment, documentation, and space.

As shown in the figure, carts and other conveyance tools, jigs, tools, dies, and documentation are all things that are usually returned after use. However, when inventory (which is generally not returned) gets ordered in a batch from its storage site, the entire batch may not be used. The unused items will need to be returned to their storage site.

Once we have identified the types of items that must be returned somewhere, the question is how to achieve "unbreakable Orderliness" by making it impossible to return them to the wrong place. What if we could somehow eliminate the need to return them at all?

Let us examine three techniques by which we can eliminate this need: suspension, incorporation, and use elimination.

Suspension

Photo 11-1 shows the suspension technique. An elastic cord or weighted pulley device is used to suspend tools from an overhead rack. When the operator finishes using a tool, he or she merely releases it and it automatically returns to its proper storage place.

While this techniques does not eliminate the need to return items to a specific place, it does effectively eliminate the need for people to return them.

People may make mistakes in returning things — but suspension devices do not. This technique achieves unbreakable Orderliness.

Photo 11-1. Unbreakable Orderliness: Tools Suspended from an Overhead Rack

Incorporation

In every factory, goods are moved and operations are carried out according to a regular pattern or flow. This is particularly true of processes or factories that have developed standard operations. Except when major problems occur, such as when parts are missing or are defective, the flow of goods and operations does not change.

In the present context, "incorporation" means creating a smooth flow of goods or operations in which (1) jigs, tools, and measuring instruments are smoothly integrated and (2) such devices are used without having to be returned.

Photo 11-2 shows an example where a measuring instrument has been incorporated into a cutting process for a certain automobile part. The instrument is used to inspect the parts as they emerge from the cutting machine. The inspection procedure is an example of "mistake-proofing" (or *poka-yoke*). The incorporation of the measuring instrument means that its storage place is also its place of use. It is therefore used (for full-lot inspection) without having to be put back anywhere.

Photo 11-2. Incorporating a Measuring Instrument into the Process Flow

Use Elimination

Suspending or incorporating jigs, tools, or measuring instruments effectively eliminates the need to return them after each use. However, these items are still being used. From an industrial-engineering (IE) perspective, we can say that an "improvement" has been made in their use in order to achieve unbreakable Orderliness.

Asking "why" helps us reach beyond such improvements. Why must the jig, tool, or measuring instrument be used? Answer: because it serves a necessary function. The next question is: Is there some way to serve the same function without using the jig, tool, or measuring instrument? This takes us beyond the IE realm and into that of value engineering (VE), which constitutes a more radical change than simply making improvements. If you recall from Chapter 6, Orderliness that eliminates the use of a particular jig, tool, or measuring instrument is in fact unbreakable Orderliness.

Three techniques for achieving unbreakable Orderliness are the following:

- **Tool unification**

  Tool unification (or tool commonization) means combining the functions of two or more tools into a single tool. As such, it is an approach that usually reaches back to the design stage. For example, we can reduce the variety of die designs to unify dies, or make all fasteners that require a screwdriver conform to the same kind of screwdriver, flat-tip or Phillips.

- **Tool substitution**

  Tool substitution means using something other than a tool to serve the tool's function, thereby eliminating the tool. For example, it is sometimes possible to replace ordinary wrench-turned bolts with hand-turned butterfly-grip bolts, thereby eliminating the wrench.

- **Method substitution**

  If we substitute ordinary wrench-turned bolts with hand-turned butterfly-grip bolts, we have eliminated the wrench but we have not eliminated the method (bolt fastening). Bolt fastening is just one way to fasten things. Fastening pins, clamps, and cylinders can also be used for this purpose.

  We may find we can improve efficiency even more by replacing the wrench-turned bolt-fastening method with another method, such as a cylinder method. This is "method substitution."

Prevent Things from Getting Dirty (Preventive Cleanliness)

Standardized Cleanup is related to all of the first three "S" pillars — Organization, Orderliness, and Cleanliness. However, it is most strongly and directly related to Cleanliness. Cleanliness is mainly a matter of cleaning up dirt, oil, and other contaminants that accumulate in and around factories and offices. Standardized Cleanup is basically a matter of maintaining the clean conditions achieved through Cleanliness. At a higher level, it involves preventing contamination — not just maintaining the routine of cleaning up contamination as it occurs. This higher level of Standardized Cleanup creates a higher level of 5S conditions in the factory or office.

For example, consider the simple but effective prevention device shown in Figure 11-11. Side panels are added to a fingernail clipper to prevent the scattering of fingernail clippings. In Figure 11-12, we see a different kind of panel serving a similar purpose for a drill press. In this example, the panel eliminates swarf scattering close to its source (the drill bit), thereby eliminating swarf-cleaning (Cleanliness) work. This is the key when installing such preventive devices: The closer you can get to the source of the contamination, the better you will be able to implement Standardized Cleanup.

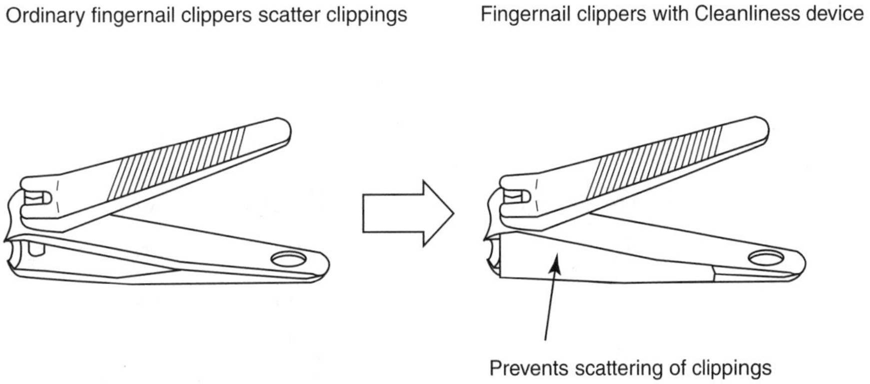

Figure 11-11. Cleanliness Device for Fingernail Clippers

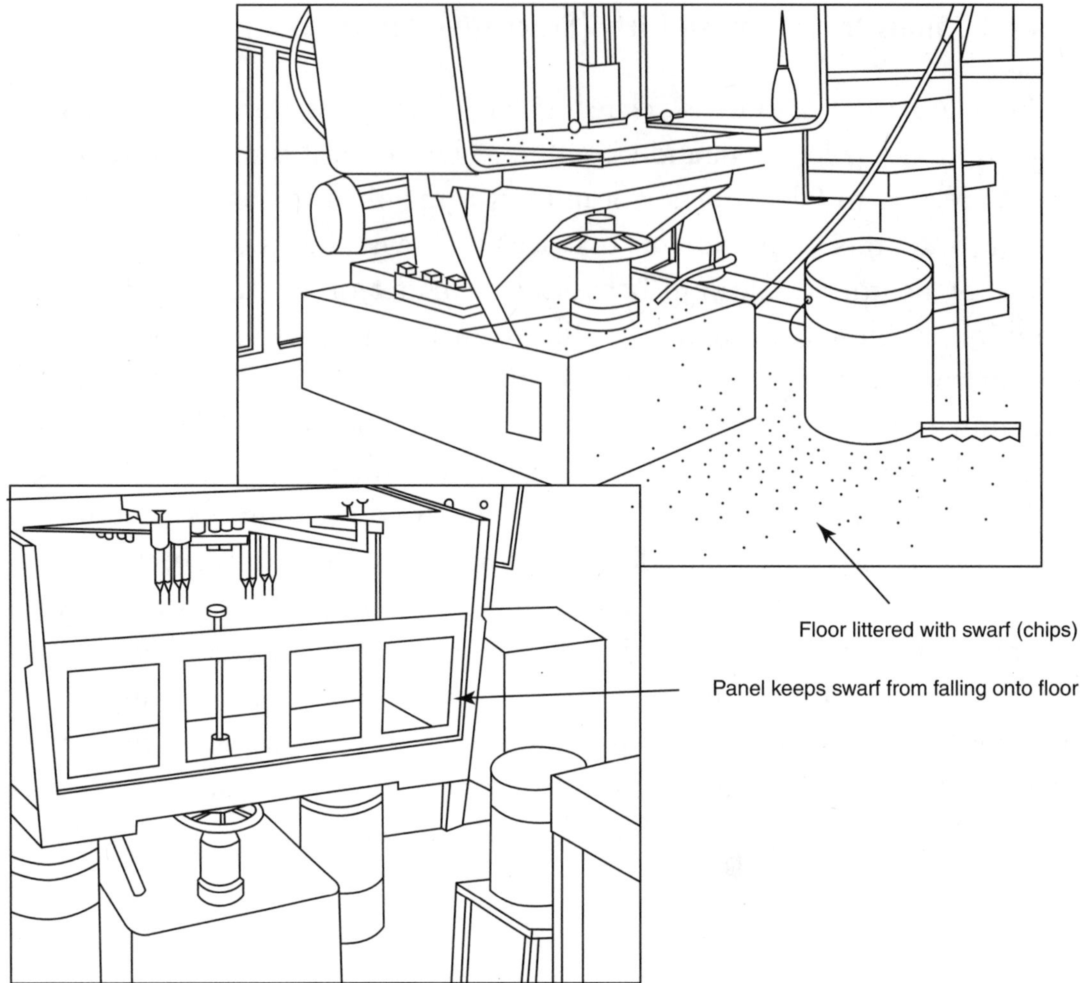
Floor littered with swarf (chips)
Panel keeps swarf from falling onto floor

Figure 11-12. Cleanliness Device for Drill Press

A few years ago, the Japanese National Railways was privatized and renamed the Japanese Railways. Photo 11-3 shows an improvement made following the privatization. Previously, booths where ticket punchers worked had to be swept out every two or three hours due to the steady accumulation of punched ticket pieces on the booth floors. Privatization seemed to provide a boost for "workplace wisdom" that generated the improvement shown in the photograph.

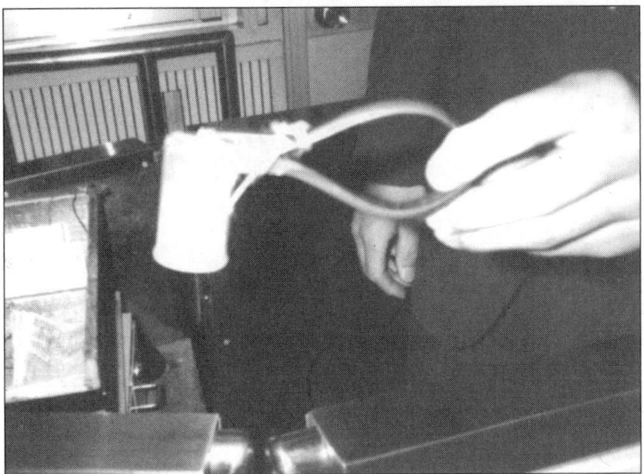

Photo 11-3. Ticket Punch Equipped with a Device to Prevent Ticket Debris

Instead of allowing debris to drop to the floor, the punches now incorporate empty plastic film containers to catch the ticket pieces. This improvement effectively eliminated the need for frequent floor sweeping and is an example of preventive Cleanliness.

12

The Fifth Pillar: Discipline

The fifth 5S pillar is Discipline. Within the context of the 5S's, Discipline is defined as "making a habit of properly maintaining correct procedures."

THE NEED FOR DISCIPLINE AND ITS ESSENTIAL POINTS

What would happen to the 5S's without Discipline? The list of possibilities is endless, but a few come to mind:

1. No matter how often the 5S's were implemented, 5S conditions would fall apart in no time and the workplace would be dirty and chaotic again.
2. Unneeded items would begin piling up the minute Organization implementation is completed.
3. No matter how well planned Orderliness implementation is, tools and jigs would not get returned to their designated places after use.
4. No matter how dirty equipment became, little or nothing would be done to clean it.
5. People would neglect to wear safety helmets and someone would eventually sustain a head injury.
6. Items would be left protruding into walkways, eventually causing someone to trip and get injured.

7. Oil puddles on the floor would sooner or later cause someone to slip and fall.
8. Someone would get injured by using a drill without first removing his or her work gloves.
9. Dirty machines would start to malfunction and produce defective goods.
10. "Clean rooms" would become dirty enough to cause product defects.
11. Dirt from the floor would spread to press dies and cause diecasting defects.
12. Lack of care in handling freshly painted products would cause painting defects.
13. Because parts storage sites would be poorly organized, people would sometimes select the wrong part and make a defective product.
14. Dark, dirty, disorganized workplaces would lower workers' morale.
15. Customers would become disgusted by the company's dirty factories and disorganized offices.

These 5S-related problems and others are likely to occur in any factory or office that lacks Discipline. Of course, the problems would not be limited to the 5S's. Discipline stands at the core of every type of work a company is involved in — from making products to selling the products to customers.

Discipline is essential for any company that hopes to succeed by implementing the 5S's. Consider common courtesy, which is a basic part of Discipline: Would a company where people do not even say "good morning" to each other be a company capable of successfully carrying out such things as an improvement suggestion system, small-group activities, or Total Quality Control?

Discipline Includes Knowing How to Give and Receive Criticism Gracefully

A common lament among factory supervisors, company presidents, and other top managers is: "No matter how hard we try to maintain 5S conditions, they always revert to their previous state." This is followed by a string of complaints, concluding with, "I guess there's just not enough Discipline in this company."

At this time I usually say, "With all due respect, I think you've got it wrong. The problem is not that your employees lack discipline. The problem is that you and other managers do not correct them when they slack off."

Knowing how to give and receive criticism gracefully is both an art and an essential part of Discipline. Correcting another person's work habits does not have to be an emotional affair. It should be an act of reasoning in which we seek to elicit understanding in the person being corrected.

Let us consider three key points:

Point 1: Be Compassionate, Not Passionate

For example, if 5S conditions begin to slip at a workplace, the supervisor should not show anger when reprimanding the employees responsible. After all, the workplace is a reflection of management.

People who are unclear about how to care for things will find that their efforts to maintain Standardized Cleanup in the workplace will be half-hearted at best. Like a mirror, the workplace does not lie. It faithfully reflects the attitudes and intentions of managers, from the top brass to the shop-floor supervisors.

When managers criticize employees thoughtlessly or arrogantly, they put the blame on others for whatever the problem is. This one-sidedness will be reflected in the workplace as resentment. Instead, managers should discover exactly why the workplace is failing to meet expectations. Perhaps they themselves have failed to do something. In other words, managers should be as strict with themselves as they are with their employees.

This is what I mean by being compassionate instead of passionate. By keeping one's own responsibilities in mind, one can turn anger into sympathy and rage into reason.

Point 2: Take Care of the Problem Immediately

Suppose you are a supervisor. During your morning rounds, you find that cutting tools at a certain workshop have been thrown together messily rather than put away properly. You do not mention it to anyone at the time. However, at an afternoon meeting, you tell the workshop's group leader that the workshop is failing to put away the cutting tools properly. The group leader says OK. But for all you know, his "OK" may be no more significant than a politician's promise.

Workplaces are like children. What happens now can easily be forgotten in a few hours. It often takes a strong action for something to be really learned and remembered.

Supervisors patrolling 5S conditions should take immediate action when they discover any slacking-off. They should talk about the matter at once with those responsible, pointing out their errors while also reflecting on management's possible mistakes.

Point 3: Employees Should Be Criticized by Their Workplace Leaders

When managers or supervisors find problems in 5S conditions, they should not reprimand the equipment operators or other workers directly. For instance, when employees throw debris on the floor, it is because they think it is OK to do so. And the person responsible for this attitude is the workplace, group, or team leader.

To use an analogy, when siblings quarrel among themselves, the parent often scolds only the older one, saying, "You should know better." Likewise, when managers notice backsliding on 5S conditions, they should address the people who should know better — the workplace leaders. If there are paper scraps on the floor, the manager should pick some up, walk over to the workplace leader, and ask why workplace employees think it is OK to throw paper on the floor.

When the person directly responsible for making a mess is an equipment operator, it is the workplace leader's job — not the supervisor's — to correct the operator. Anyone being corrected should be made to understand exactly why such action is being taken. In Japan, when the reprimand is over, the person on the receiving end apologizes. The person doing the criticizing gracefully accepts the apology, and both consider the matter settled with no hard feelings.

To sum up, we can say that Discipline means "compassionate criticism performed immediately by the workplace leader."

FIVE WAYS TO DEVELOP DISCIPLINE

Factory superintendents and company presidents have no reason to bemoan poor 5S conditions or their company's lack of discipline. Instead they should find out how companies can build up discipline and then put those discipline-building techniques into action. Complaining about its lack is no way to cultivate discipline — and, like Rome, discipline is not built in a day. Discipline is part of a company's culture and history.

When a factory or company lacks discipline, the finger of blame is pointed correctly at top management. Before praising or criticizing anyone for discipline or a lack thereof, managers should strive to implement the measures outlined in Figure 12-1.

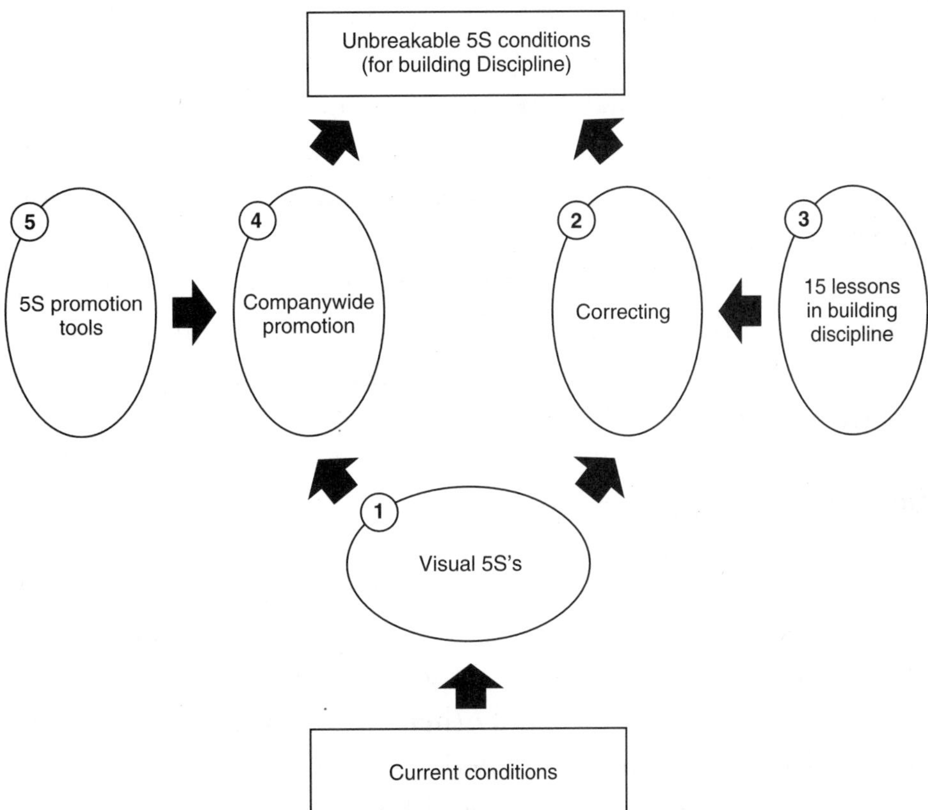

Figure 12-1. Five Measures for Building Discipline

1. The Visual 5S's

There are many things that should be made visible at factories and offices, from the flow of goods and/or information to operation and management methods. The general term for this practice is "visual control," which means that anyone should be able to tell at a glance whether current conditions are normal or abnormal.

The same goes for the "visual 5S's." Anyone should be able to see at a glance whether or not Organization, Orderliness, and Cleanliness conditions are being maintained. Red-tagging, signboards, and divider lines are all visual 5S techniques.

2. Correcting Others

Thorough implementation of the visual 5S's includes not only being able to tell immediately whether current conditions are normal or abnormal. It also includes taking immediate action when abnormal conditions are found. This means asking the person in charge "Why is this abnormal?" or "Why have 5S conditions deteriorated?" If the cause is a lack of discipline, some reprimands are in order.

Positive criticism contains two main elements — skill and proper method. When both elements are practiced, the workplace staff will feel motivated to work at the best of its abilities. In this way, the company benefits from skillful, constructive criticism.

3. Lessons in Building Discipline

Criticism should take place as soon as 5S conditions begin to fall apart. Its purpose is to build up discipline — not to put people down. Therefore, let the methods of correction be instructive rather than destructive.

Company managers should apply their longer work experience to teach subordinates how to do things correctly. As already noted, this instructive criticism should exhibit compassion and be performed immediately by the workplace leader.

4. Companywide Promotion

5S implementation will go nowhere if only a handful of people or only one or two company departments are involved. Success requires companywide 5S development and promotion.

When a company launches a “5S campaign” or “5S month,” the top managers should be visibly involved as leaders, working to enlist everyone’s cooperation and enthusiasm.

5. 5S Promotion Tools

Effective companywide 5S implementation is a big task requiring powerful tools. These 5S promotion tools need not be expensive. In fact, such simple tools as 5S badges and 5S newsletters can be quite effective in building companywide participation.

THE VISUAL 5S’S

To survive in today’s harsh business environment, companies in all fields are having to pursue rationalization and cost-cutting measures.

Imagine a factory full of hard-working employees that shows little improvement. The managers wonder if rationalization measures have been taught improperly throughout the company or if improvement methods were not learned well enough. So they take action by setting up new training programs and holding seminars taught by consultants.

But even then, the factory still experiences little improvement. Next, the managers think, “Maybe there’s something wrong with our promotion organization. Maybe we don’t have the right project team members.” So they rearrange the promotion organization — but even this makes no significant difference.

The problem at such factories lies not so much in their improvement methods or in their promotion organizations. Rather it lies in their failure to search out and understand the sources of waste and inefficiency. Waste and other problems in factories are half resolved once they are understood. Once we understand the problems and sources of waste, we need only apply our knowledge and experience in making corrective improvements.

Much of the waste, abnormalities, and other problems in factories remain hidden or obscure. The way to make them clear and obvious to everyone is through visual control.

There is no such thing as a problem-free factory. Some companies or factories are better than others and some merely think they are better than others. But regardless of degree, they all have something in common — endless problems. The best companies stand out because they recognize their problems quickly and waste no time in resolving them. Once one problem is solved, another appears and is immediately pursued.

At the worst factories, people do not even recognize problems. They might treat them as nonexistent or try to work around them. Unresolved problems are gradually accepted as the norm and sink deeper into the factory's character. Meanwhile, new problems pop up — many caused by old, unresolved problems.

Every factory is awash with problems. The key difference between the good ones and the bad ones is that the former are able to recognize and

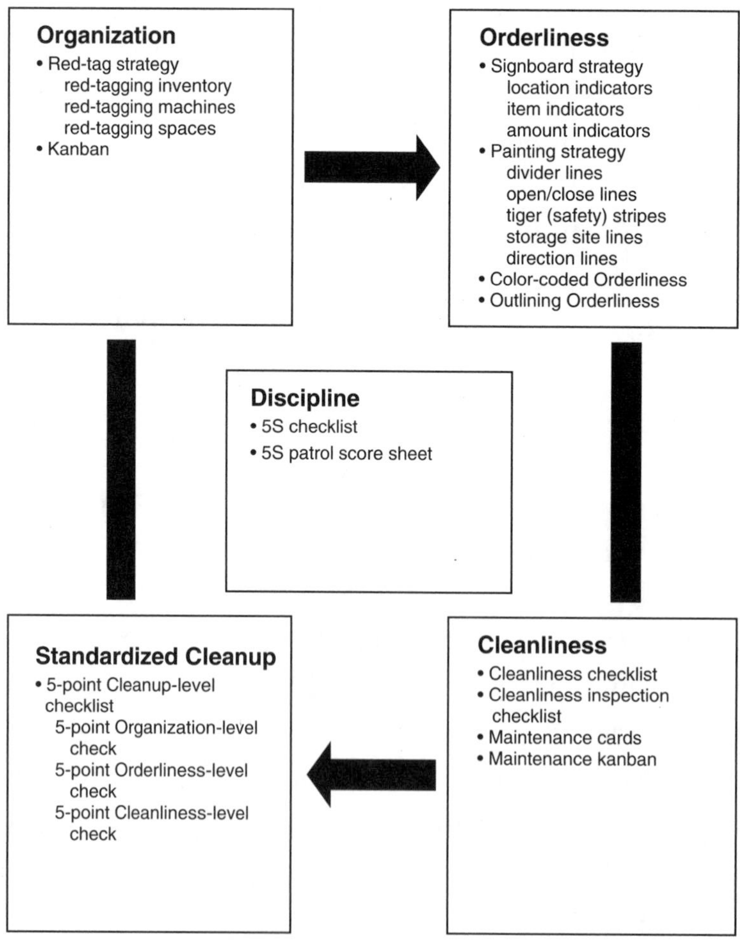

Figure 12-2. The Visual 5S's

resolve problems as they occur. In other words, good factories possess a method for recognizing and resolving problems right away. This method is "visual control."

When visual control is applied to the 5S's, the result is referred to as the "visual 5S's." Figure 12-2 outlines the visual 5S's — visual Organization, visual Orderliness, visual Cleanliness, visual Standardized Cleanup, and visual Discipline. We will examine them one at a time.

Visual Organization

There are two key methods for visual Organization. The first is the red-tag strategy, whose purpose is to eliminate all currently unneeded items. The second is kanban, whose purpose is to prevent unnecessary procurement and production.

The Red-Tag Strategy

Not everything we find in factories and offices is needed for current operations. Many materials, parts, machines, and jigs in factories and many papers and documents in offices are simply unnecessary.

Even if people want to get rid of the unneeded items, they may find it difficult to distinguish what is needed from what is not. This is where the red-tag strategy comes in. By attaching red tags to unneeded items, we make it clear to everyone.

Kanban

Kanban are tags, slips, or vouchers for maintaining just-in-time (JIT) production. Kanban "requests" are used by downstream processes to order goods from upstream processes, enabling products to be "pulled" downstream.

While red tags are tools that enable factories and offices to clear out all currently unneeded items, kanban enable them to avoid buying or manufacturing unneeded items. Thus, kanban are tools for "preventive Organization," eliminating the step of discarding unneeded items.

The kanban are attached to materials or parts, as shown in Photo 12-1. When the material or part is about to be used, its kanban is removed and sent as a request to buy or make one more of the same item. This is an ordering

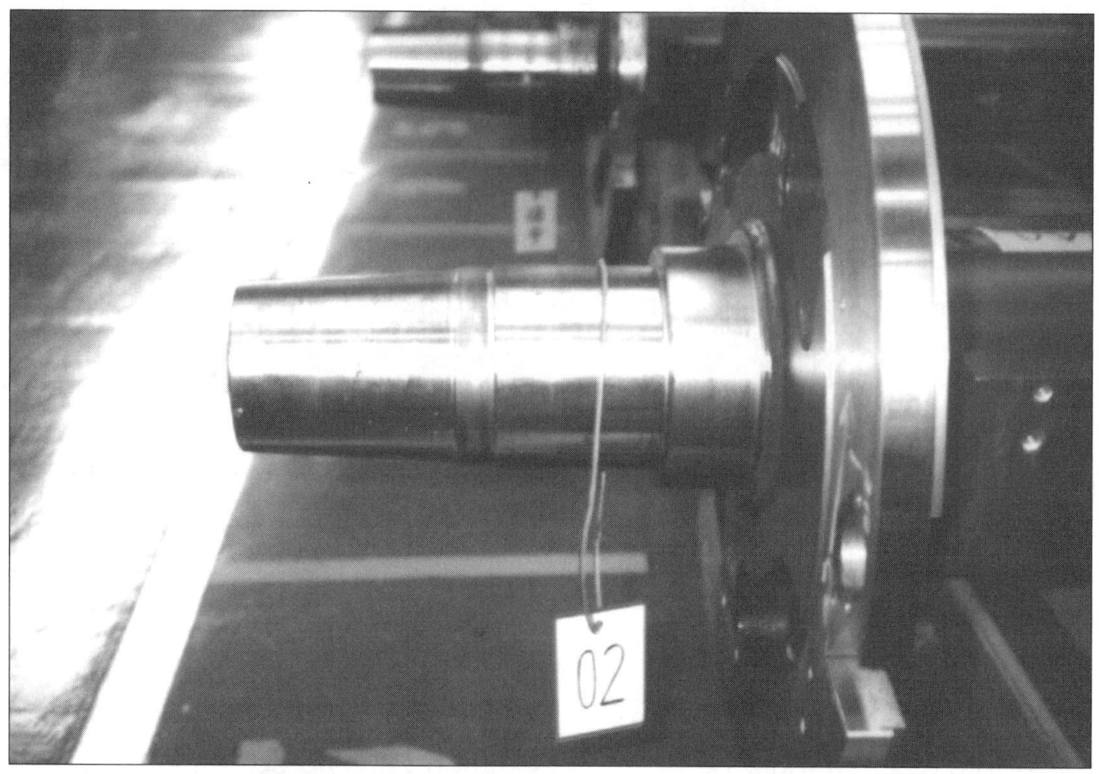

Photo 12-1. Withdrawal Kanban

system that prevents the production of unneeded items — and is understandable at a glance.

Visual Orderliness

The needed items that now remain in the factory or office still must be made obvious to everyone. This is where visual Orderliness and its strategies come in. First, the signboard strategy indicates exactly what goes where and in what amount. Next, the painting strategy identifies walkways, working areas, and so on.

Signboard Strategy

If Organization has been implemented thoroughly, nothing should remain in the factory or office except currently needed items. We must now make it easy for anyone to see where these needed items belong and in what amounts. The strategy for doing this uses signboards to indicate locations, items, and amounts.

Painting Strategy

Factories use various types of machines, from production equipment to carts, forklift, and cranes. Given these conditions, divider lines are an essential tool to maintain safety, regulate the flow of goods, and ensure high productivity. The purpose of these divider lines is not so much to divide but to alert people visually to distinctions between areas. The following are types of lines used in the painting strategy:

- **Divider lines and storage-area lines**

  These mark off walkways from work areas or set boundaries among work areas. Generally, these lines are made with white or yellow paint (or tape, etc.). Storage-area lines mark off storage areas for specific items or types of items. (See Photo 12-2.)

- **Open/close lines and direction lines**

  Too often people get hurt when approaching a door that suddenly opens toward them. Open/close lines ("door range lines")

Photo 12-2. Storage Lines and Signboards in Materials Storage Area

in front of doors are a good way to prevent this type of accident. Lines that mark the travel direction on walkways or the flow direction in pipes are other good examples of visual control. (See Photo 12-3.)

- **Tiger stripes**

  The standard colors for these slanted alternating lines are yellow and black. Use these safety lines wherever they can help promote safety (i.e., in front of elevator doors, on the first step in a staircase, on shelves in hazardous work areas).

Color-coded Orderliness and Outlining Orderliness

"Color-coded Orderliness" means designating different colors for specific products or machines. The same colors are then used for the corresponding jigs, tools, and dies.

"Outlining Orderliness" means drawing the outlines of tools in their designated storage sites so one can see at a glance which tool goes where.

Photo 12-3. Door Open/Close Lines and Walkway Direction Lines

Photo 12-4. Slanted Lines for File Binders

Another type of Orderliness line is shown in Photo 12-4. This "slanted" line helps keep reference books or file binders in the correct order on shelves.

Visual Cleanliness

Besides the periodic inspection tasks that are the foundation of maintenance activities, Cleanliness should include daily cleaning and checking tasks. Cleanliness checklists and Cleanliness inspection checklists help us carry out such inspections, cleaning, and checking work more effectively. Cleanliness checklists summarize the Cleanliness checkpoints concerning inventory, equipment, and spaces. Cleanliness inspection checklists, like the one shown in Figure 12-3, are incorporated into daily cleaning, maintenance, and checking work for mechanical equipment as part of the overall production maintanance program.

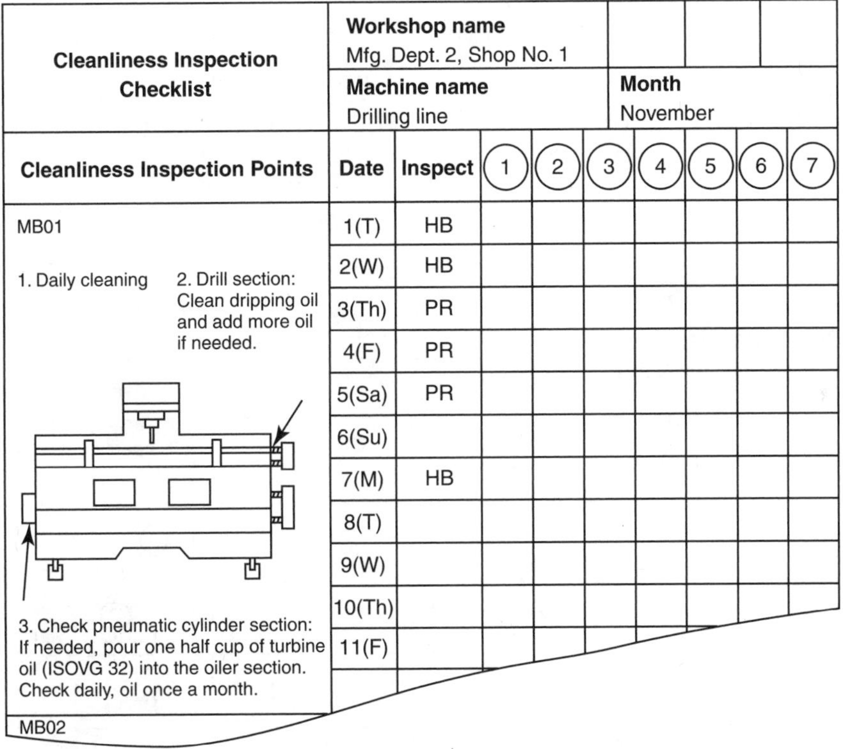

Cleanliness Inspection Checklist	Workshop name Mfg. Dept. 2, Shop No. 1		
	Machine name Drilling line	Month November	

Cleanliness Inspection Points	Date	Inspect	1	2	3	4	5	6	7
MB01	1(T)	HB							
1. Daily cleaning	2(W)	HB							
2. Drill section: Clean dripping oil and add more oil if needed.	3(Th)	PR							
	4(F)	PR							
	5(Sa)	PR							
	6(Su)								
	7(M)	HB							
	8(T)								
	9(W)								
	10(Th)								
3. Check pneumatic cylinder section: If needed, pour one half cup of turbine oil (ISOVG 32) into the oiler section. Check daily, oil once a month.	11(F)								
MB02									

Figure 12-3. Cleanliness Inspection Checklist

In addition to these checklists, maintenance cards are used to mark the exact site where maintenance is required. Maintenance kanban (see Chapter 10) are used to request assistance from the maintenance department.

Visual Standardized Cleanup

Organization, Orderliness, and Cleanliness must be practiced daily to keep factories and offices clean and well organized. Standardized Cleanup is the condition that results when these first three S's are practiced correctly. The five-point Standardized Cleanup-level checklist is useful for evaluating these 3S conditions by ranking them on a scale of 1 to 5. (See Figure 12-4.) Such checklists can be made for specific workshops and/or production processes.

Visual Discipline

We cannot simply look at people and know whether or not Discipline is being maintained. This is because the source of Discipline is in hearts and minds — not in appearances. However, we can expect the presence or absence of Discipline to express itself to some degree in how people behave. In fact, we can judge the level of Discipline by the results of their behavior.

Five-Point Standardized Cleanup-level Checklist	Dept.: Assembly Dept. 1	FEB. 15, 1994		
	Assigned area	Entered by: YAMAGUCHI	Page	1/1

No.	Process and checkpoint	Organization Level	Orderliness Level	Cleanliness Level	Total	Previous total
1.	WORK AT LINE A, PROCESS 1	1 2 3 (4) 5	1 (2) 3 4 5	1 (2) 3 4 5	8	6
2.	"	1 (2) 3 4 5	1 2 (3) 4 5	1 2 (3) 4 5	8	6
3.	"	1 (2) 3 4 5	1 (2) 3 4 5	1 (2) 3 4 5	6	5
4.	"	1 (2) 3 4 5	1 2 (3) 4 5	1 (2) 3 4 5	7	7
5.	"	1 2 (3) 4 5	1 2 (3) 4 5	1 2 3 (4) 5	10	6
6.	"	1 2 3 (4) 5	1 2 3 (4) 5	1 2 3 (4) 5	12	8
7.	AVERAGE AND TOTAL FOR LINE A	1 2 3 4 5 (2.6)	1 2 3 4 5 (2.8)	1 2 3 4 5 (2.8)	(50)	(38)

Figure 12-4. Five-point Standardized Cleanup-level Checklist

We can discern the degree of Discipline in a group of people by looking at their achieved levels of Organization, Orderliness, Cleanliness, and Standardized Cleanup. The five-point Standardized Cleanup-level checklist comes in handy for this purpose.

Because Discipline is largely a matter of the heart, those who are not 100 percent sincere in their practice of Discipline do not go far in cultivating it. In the martial arts, students begin by practicing the most basic forms of movement, and while practicing these forms, they begin to cultivate sincerity and skill. Likewise, in the "art" of the 5S's, we cultivate Discipline by practicing the forms known as Organization, Orderliness, Cleanliness, and Standardized Cleanup.

5S Checklists

5S checklists like the one in Figure 12-5 are used to check 5S levels in the factory as a whole. When a company implements a 5S month of intensive activities, 5S checklists should be used to make weekly evaluations of 5S conditions. They are best used for general inspections of individual workplaces. Some companies sponsor 5S contests and present awards to those workplaces with the highest total score from 5S checklists filled out during the 5S month.

5S Patrol Scoresheets

5S patrols make weekly inspection rounds, filling out 5S checklists as we saw in Figure 12-5. After scoring each workplace, they record the scores on a 5S patrol scoresheet that they later display. (See Figure 12-6.) When improvements are planned, it is important to assign improvement deadlines.

EXPRESSIONS TO AVOID WHEN CRITICIZING OTHERS

Any discussion of Discipline must include a discussion of how to criticize people positively and effectively. There is little Discipline in a factory or office where people's mistakes are not corrected. However, to encourage workplace staff to act autonamously to build discipline, supervisors and managers must be careful in how they criticize others.

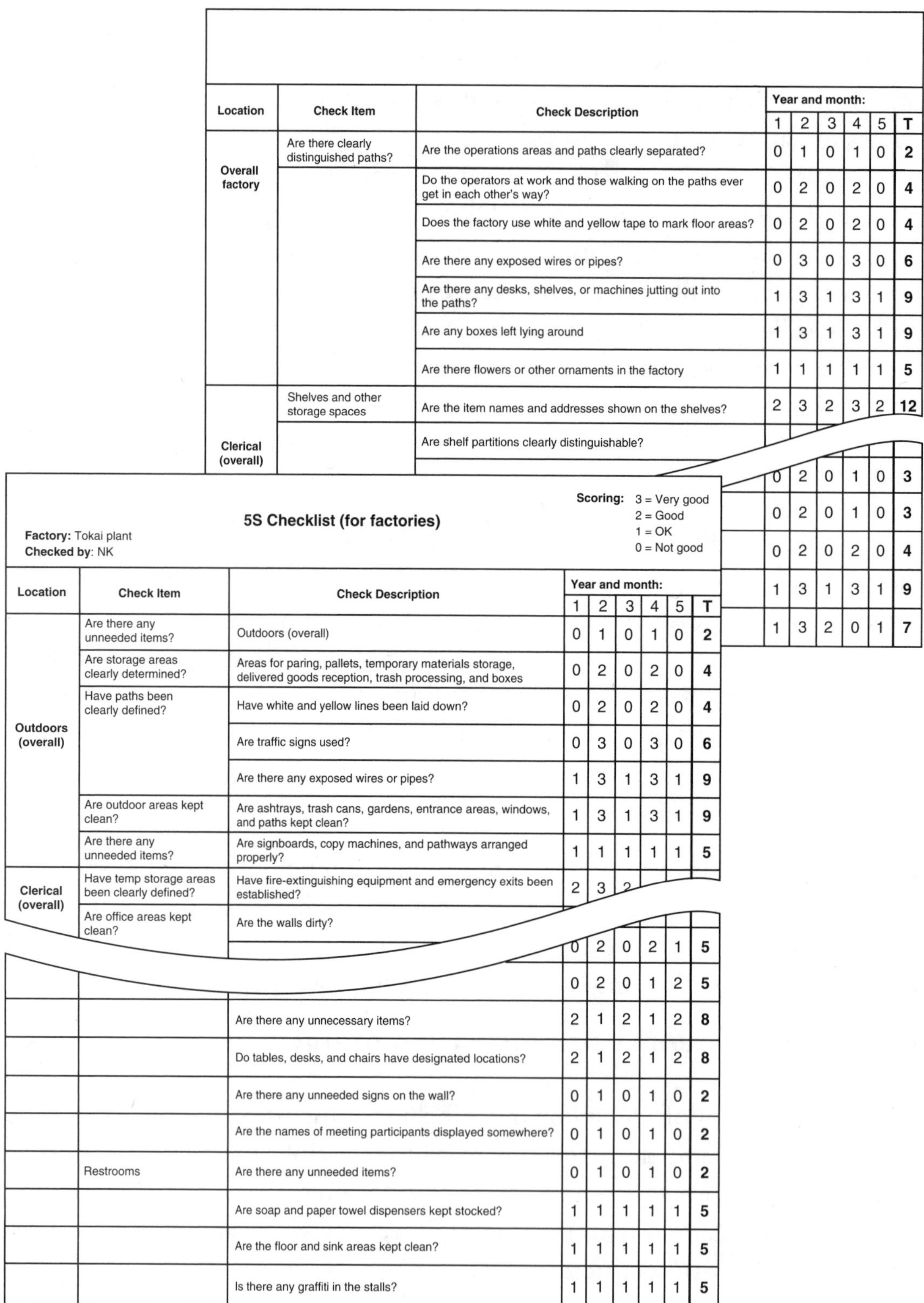

Location	Check Item	Check Description	Year and month: 1	2	3	4	5	T
Overall factory	Are there clearly distinguished paths?	Are the operations areas and paths clearly separated?	0	1	0	1	0	2
		Do the operators at work and those walking on the paths ever get in each other's way?	0	2	0	2	0	4
		Does the factory use white and yellow tape to mark floor areas?	0	2	0	2	0	4
		Are there any exposed wires or pipes?	0	3	0	3	0	6
		Are there any desks, shelves, or machines jutting out into the paths?	1	3	1	3	1	9
		Are any boxes left lying around	1	3	1	3	1	9
		Are there flowers or other ornaments in the factory	1	1	1	1	1	5
Clerical (overall)	Shelves and other storage spaces	Are the item names and addresses shown on the shelves?	2	3	2	3	2	12
		Are shelf partitions clearly distinguishable?						
			0	2	0	1	0	3
			0	2	0	1	0	3
			0	2	0	2	0	4
			1	3	1	3	1	9
			1	3	2	0	1	7

5S Checklist (for factories)

Factory: Tokai plant
Checked by: NK

Scoring: 3 = Very good, 2 = Good, 1 = OK, 0 = Not good

Location	Check Item	Check Description	Year and month: 1	2	3	4	5	T
Outdoors (overall)	Are there any unneeded items?	Outdoors (overall)	0	1	0	1	0	2
	Are storage areas clearly determined?	Areas for paring, pallets, temporary materials storage, delivered goods reception, trash processing, and boxes	0	2	0	2	0	4
	Have paths been clearly defined?	Have white and yellow lines been laid down?	0	2	0	2	0	4
		Are traffic signs used?	0	3	0	3	0	6
		Are there any exposed wires or pipes?	1	3	1	3	1	9
	Are outdoor areas kept clean?	Are ashtrays, trash cans, gardens, entrance areas, windows, and paths kept clean?	1	3	1	3	1	9
	Are there any unneeded items?	Are signboards, copy machines, and pathways arranged properly?	1	1	1	1	1	5
Clerical (overall)	Have temp storage areas been clearly defined?	Have fire-extinguishing equipment and emergency exits been established?	2	3	2			
	Are office areas kept clean?	Are the walls dirty?						
			0	2	0	2	1	5
			0	2	0	1	2	5
		Are there any unnecessary items?	2	1	2	1	2	8
		Do tables, desks, and chairs have designated locations?	2	1	2	1	2	8
		Are there any unneeded signs on the wall?	0	1	0	1	0	2
		Are the names of meeting participants displayed somewhere?	0	1	0	1	0	2
	Restrooms	Are there any unneeded items?	0	1	0	1	0	2
		Are soap and paper towel dispensers kept stocked?	1	1	1	1	1	5
		Are the floor and sink areas kept clean?	1	1	1	1	1	5
		Is there any graffiti in the stalls?	1	1	1	1	1	5

Figure 12-5. 5S Checklist

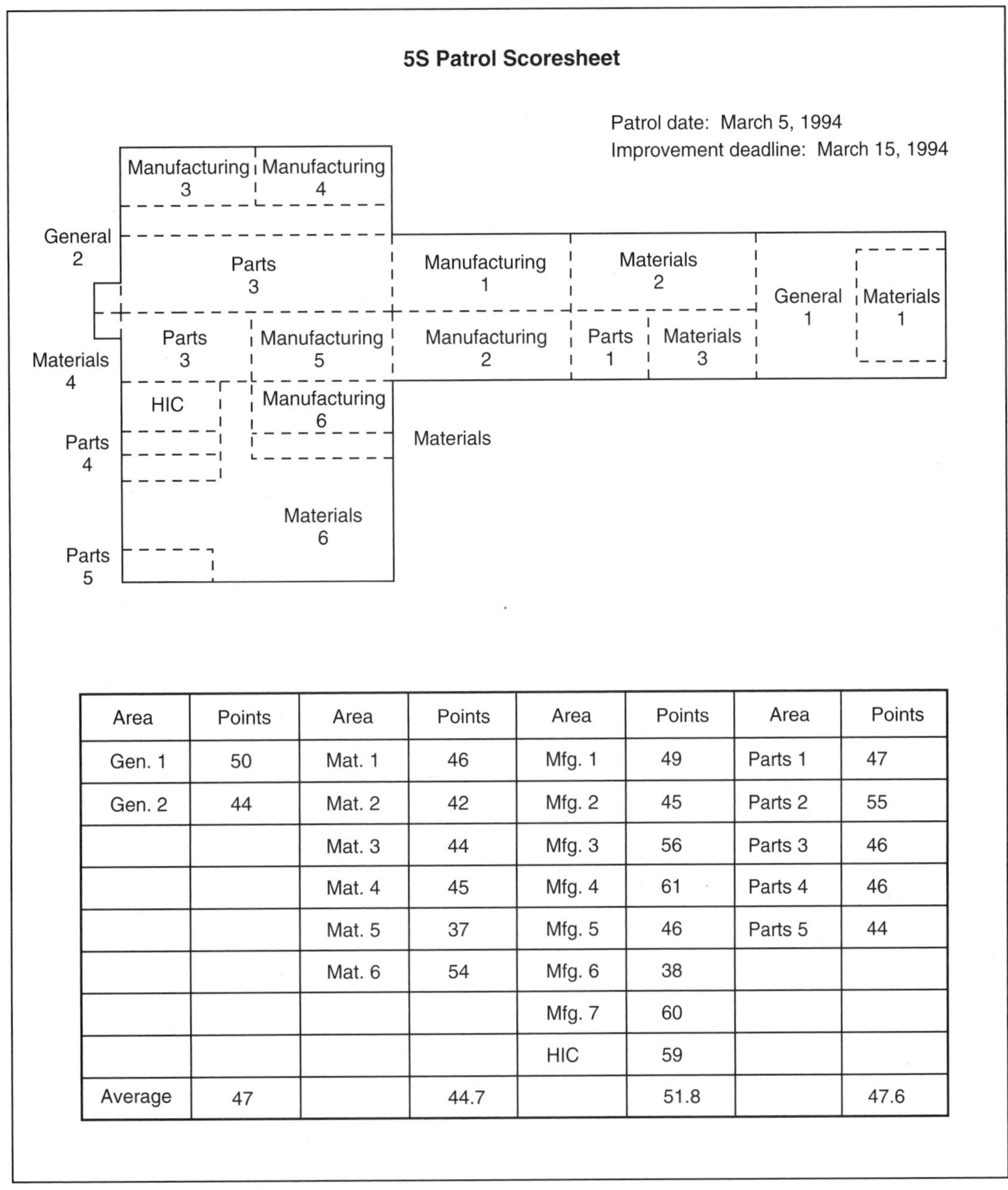

Area	Points	Area	Points	Area	Points	Area	Points
Gen. 1	50	Mat. 1	46	Mfg. 1	49	Parts 1	47
Gen. 2	44	Mat. 2	42	Mfg. 2	45	Parts 2	55
		Mat. 3	44	Mfg. 3	56	Parts 3	46
		Mat. 4	45	Mfg. 4	61	Parts 4	46
		Mat. 5	37	Mfg. 5	46	Parts 5	44
		Mat. 6	54	Mfg. 6	38		
				Mfg. 7	60		
				HIC	59		
Average	47		44.7		51.8		47.6

Figure 12-6. 5S Patrol Scoresheet

A supervisor who is good at correcting others is someone who understands the psychology of the workplace well enough to know what motivates people to try harder. In contrast, a supervisor who bullies and blames subordinates without compassion is likely to use some of the negative expressions listed in Table 12-1.

Table 12-1. Expressions to Avoid when Correcting

1. "Don't you hear what I'm saying?"
   (This insults the other person's intelligence.)
2. "You people are just impossible!"
   (This negates the possibility of improvement.)
3. "I won't put up with any more mistakes!"
   (This discourages people from taking risks to accept challenges.)
4. "Stop this nonsense!"
   (This is a general put-down that teaches nothing specific.)
5. "Can't you remember this one thing?"
   (This insults another's creativity and intelligence.)
6. "If you blow it again, you're fired!"
   (This destroys self-motivation to make improvements.)
7. "This is why (such-and-such) happens!"
   (This invites resentment rather than regret from the other person.)
8. "Everybody knows that — it's just common sense!"
   (This makes appearance seem more important than substance.)
9. "I don't like it, but the boss says so — so that's it!"
   (This leaves reasons unexplained and invites confusion.)
10. "That's none of your business!"
    (This denigrates the other person's value as a member of the company.)
11. "Get to the point."
    (This is a rude interruption.)
12. "Who's to blame for this mistake?"
    (This is like hitting someone who is down.)

1. "Don't you hear what I'm saying?"

This remark is the kind that supervisors and managers use when thoroughly exasperated. It means that they are in charge and everyone else should shut up and listen. Basically, it insults the other person's intelligence and tells him or her not to bother thinking on their own.

2. "You people are impossible!"

Workplaces are conservative places that resist change. Occasionally, however, the staff is prodded into changing something. When they encounter the inevitable problems, the last thing they need to hear from a supervisor is that they are to blame. Such words are counterproductive and discourage further efforts to make improvements.

3. **"I won't put up with any more mistakes!"**

These words should be directed only at oneself. They are counterproductive when directed at subordinates because they encourage people to take the safe and easy route instead of a more effective one. Telling people not to make mistakes is tantamount to telling them not to bother taking risks. It deflates their motivation to try.

Instead, be positive and promote productivity by saying: "Don't be afraid to make mistakes. If you are, you will never make improvements."

4. **"Stop this nonsense!"**

This criticism is too vague to address the problem at hand. People want feedback from their supervisors but this kind only hurts people's sense of pride in themselves and in their workplace.

5. **"Can't you remember this one thing?"**

When new people enter the workplace, they have many things to learn. Sometimes the teacher becomes impatient and says, "Look, don't think about it, just remember it." Similarly, frustrated supervisors use this type of expression when dealing with mistakes made by subordinates — and often what they are supposed to remember does not directly relate to the mistake in question.

Saying "Can't you remember this one thing?" insults the creativity, intelligence, and subjective identity of the workplace staff. One way to avoid making these and other oversights is to use checklists.

6. **"If you blow it again, you're fired!"**

First of all, supervisors are not authorized to fire people by decree, and their subordinates know it. So this expression is usually taken for what it is — an empty threat. Therefore, the more often it is spoken, the less impact it has.

Even if a supervisor says this to someone gullible enough to believe it, the effect will be to frighten that person from doing anything risky for the sake of improvement. Such words gradually drain the vigor and self-motivation from employees.

7. **"This is why such-and-such happens!"**

When people in a workplace make a big mistake, they are naturally discouraged by it. They do not need a supervisor to rub salt in the wound by saying some variation on the above theme. They already understand and regret their mistake.

Further beratement breeds resentment. Supervisors should focus simply on the problem at hand and not mention past mistakes.

8. **"Everybody knows that — it's just common sense!"**

I often run across managers who, from the safety of their desks, pass off other people's comments with condescending remarks like this one.

Telling people to use "common sense" to maintain 5S conditions simply dissuades them from asking questions. Instead, employees will try to keep up appearances without really understanding what they are doing or why. This superficial 5S implementation is unlikely to lead to significant improvements.

9. **"I don't like it, but the boss says so — so that's it!"**

There are bound to be differences of opinion between management — between department chiefs and section chiefs or between section chiefs and supervisors. However, managers should avoid bad-mouthing or complaining about each other in front of staff, which creates confusion about what to do.

10. **"That's none of your business!"**

Some managers say this as a way to cut off discussions they dislike or questions they cannot answer. However, the fact that employees ask questions shows that they are working with their brains — not just their brawn. Managers who stifle such thinking will see energy and enthusiasm quickly disappear from the workplace.

It is not easy to find self-motivated workers. Managers should value and encourage them.

11. "Get to the point."

Many employees rarely speak with managers and may have difficulty expressing themselves when they do. At the same time, managers may be accustomed to using such expressions among themselves (during planning meetings, for example). However, to tell a subordinate to "get to the point" is both rude and chilling. At the very least, it makes employees hesitate to take the initiative in discussing problems with managers.

12. "Who's to blame for this mistake?"

Everybody makes mistakes — and everybody reflects on them and tries to correct them. The bigger the mistake, the more this is true. Therefore, embarrassing someone by pointing him or her out as a target for blame is counterproductive — and invites resentment.

FIFTEEN LESSONS IN BUILDING DISCIPLINE

We have just discussed the importance of being able to correct people while still taking their perspectives into account. Now let us turn to what we actually need to teach about Discipline.

During childhood we typically learn the following Discipline lessons:

- Wash our hands before eating.
- Set the fork on the left of the plate and the knife and spoon on the right.
- Be polite at the dinner table and ask to be excused before leaving it.
- Chew with your mouth closed.
- Do not talk with your mouth full.
- Say "good morning" upon rising and "good night" upon retiring.
- Do not bother other people.

These are a few of the lessons we learn that help us build discipline in our lives. Likewise, veteran employees in factories and offices learn discipline lessons concerning their production or administrative activities. Table 12-2 lists fifteen such lessons.

Table 12-2. Fifteen Lessons for Building Discipline

1. Be polite in addressing others, starting with "good morning."
2. If you have a work uniform, wear it neatly and with pride.
3. Remember: Good workplaces are made and destroyed by 5S conditions.
4. Divider lines can mark the difference between life and death.
5. The "three specifics" are fundamental and must therefore be maintained.
6. Apply Orderliness to disorder and Cleanliness to dirt.
7. Inspect before working.
8. Immediately reprimand any slacking-off on 5S conditions.
9. Know how to correct others and how to receive corrections from others.
10. Address the source of disorder or dirt.
11. Money is limited but wisdom is limitless.
12. Stick to a hands-on, here-and-now approach.
13. For reports: three pages are unsatisfactory, two pages are better, and one page is best.
14. For meetings: three hours are wasteful, two hours are better, and one hour is best.
15. Improvement requires effort and effort requires enthusiasm.

1. Be courteous in addressing others.

It is uplifting to hear people cheerfully saying "good morning" to each other at the factory or office. It gets everyone off to a good start in sharing a day of work together.

Courtesy makes for good relations among employees, which in turn empowers the entire company. In comparing a company like this with one where greetings are either lacking or half-hearted, you will sense the greater power of the former.

2. **If you have a work uniform, keep it clean and wear it with pride.**

   For many manufacturing workers, the work uniform includes a cap or helmet, safety glasses, work clothes, and safety shoes. Wearing these items neatly and consistently is fundamental to quality and safety.

3. **Remember that good workplaces are made and destroyed by 5S conditions.**

   Workplace improvement begins with the 5S's. Maintaining 5S conditions is the only way to achieve long-term rationalization goals (i.e., one- or two-year plans). However, after achieving a goal, if we allow backsliding on 5S conditions, the new rationalized order will begin to collapse. Watch out for danger signs — like people no longer bothering to pick up dropped screws or mop dirty floors.

4. **Divider lines can mark the difference between life and death.**

   Work areas are often hazardous and divider lines can ensure the safety of people who must walk near them. Use yellow or white divider lines to designate walkways from work areas. Teach people who still carelessly cross them that divider lines do make a difference in their personal safety.

5. **The "three specifics" are fundamental and must be maintained.**

   What, where, and how many are basic to any kind of production or clerical work. The idea of clearly indicating what (specific item) goes where (specific places) and in what amount (specific amounts) are called the "three specifics." Properly defining and maintaining them is necessary for any company.

6. **Apply Orderliness to disorder and Cleanliness to dirt.**

   Once the "three specifics" are being maintained and the workplace is clean, people can immediately spot any disorder or dirt that creeps into the workplace. To maintain Standardized Cleanup, we must make it a habit to immediately apply Orderliness to disorder and Cleanliness to dirt.

7. **Inspect before working.**

   Check over the machinery and procedures involved before starting work. Make this an automatic part of the work process.

8. **Reprimand any slacking-off on 5S conditions immediately.**

   Supervisors cannot afford to put off reprimanding people in workplaces where Orderliness conditions begin to falter or where machines or floors are obviously dirty.

9. **Know how to give criticism and and how to receive it.**

   Supervisors must learn to keep their emotions contained when reprimanding others. For their part, people who receive criticism should learn to listen simply and honestly. Under any other conditions, criticism becomes ineffective — if not counterproductive.

10. **Address the source of disorder or dirt.**

    Each of the 5S's is prone to deterioration. When the workplace starts getting disorderly or dirty, we need to ask specifically why this has occurred. To identify the root cause, we can use the "5W1H" approach. (We ask "why" five times or until we identify the source. Then we ask "how" to make a corrective improvement.)

11. **Money is limited but wisdom is limitless.**

    Once we have used the 5W1H approach to identify the source of a problem and are busy devising a corrective improvement, we must remember that the improvement should not be costly. In companies, money may be limited but wisdom is limitless. Rely on employee brain power — not just company money.

12. **Use a hands-on, here-and-now approach.**

    Hands-on, here-and-now. Any company that has lost touch with this approach is doomed. That is how important this lesson is. "Hands-on" means tackling problems in detail, working with the actual physical sources of the problem and not just abstractions such as drawings and statistics. "Here-and-now" means tackling problems as they occur, not at some more convenient time. This approach should be at the core of all company operations and activities and a central principle behind all 5S activities.

13. **When it comes to reports: three pages are unsatisfactory, two pages are better, and one page is best.**

    Begin reports by stating the conclusion and keep the copy to within one page whenever possible. Reports that babble on are like bad TV programs that no one wants to watch.

14. **When it comes to meetings: three hours are wasteful, two hours are better, and one hour is best.**

    I often hear managers complain in tones mixed with pride that they have a whole string of daily meetings to attend. The longer meetings are extended for unnecessary reasons, the more useless they become. ("People meet but don't deliberate on anything; and even if they deliberate they don't decide on anything; and even if they decide they don't do anything; and even if they do something they don't maintain it afterward.")

    Meetings done correctly should only last an hour — and everyone involved should be tired from the effort to be efficient. There is no excuse for a three-hour meeting.

15. **Improvement requires effort and effort requires enthusiasm.**

    Substantive improvements are rarely easy and fun to carry out. To the contrary, I find that when people try to make the improvement easier (usually by spending more money), the results are more fragile. As a rule of thumb, the more effort that goes into an improvement, the more substantial and steady the results will be. Likewise, whenever I see great effort, I also find great enthusiasm — making them almost one and the same.

COMPANYWIDE PROMOTION OF DISCIPLINE

Discipline is too fundamental to be the problem of a particular person or department. In fact, the fundamental importance of Discipline goes beyond the 5S's — it is basic to the survival of the entire company. It should be a major improvement theme at every company. Top managers should lead the way and enlist cooperation and support from everyone.

Table 12-3 lists several sub-themes that can be pursued when promoting Discipline. The major ones we will examine here.

5S Months

Companies should designate two, three, or four months every year as "5S months." During these months, various activities, ranging from 5S seminars to 5S study tours and 5S contests, can be held to further companywide understanding of and enthusiasm for 5S implementation. 5S campaign banners (like the one shown in Photo 12-5) can be displayed.

5S Patrols

5S patrols should be established as part of the 5S promotion organization. The patrol teams carry out inspection patrols about once a week. They use 5S checklists and 5S patrol scoresheets to evaluate 5S conditions at each target workplace. (The results can be used in 5S contests and 5S award competitions.)

Photo 12-5. 5S Campaign Banner

Table 12-3. Companywide Themes for Promoting Discipline

No.	Promotion Theme	Description	Frequency	Effects
1.	5S Months	A month that emphasizes the 5S's. (Allow two to four 5S months a year; each 5S month should include 5S evaluations of each workplace.)	2 to 4 per year	Such companywide efforts broaden and deepen 5S implementation.
2.	5S Days	A day that emphasizes the 5S's. (Allow one to four 5S days a month; each 5S day should include 5S evaluations of each workplace.)	1 to 4 per month	same as above
3.	5S Seminars	Bring in outside experts to lead 5S seminars.	twice a year	This draws fresh opinions and study materials from outside sources.
4.	5S Study Tours	People see how the 5S's have been implemented successfully in other companies.	twice a year	This provides first-hand study and adaptation of other 5S implementation efforts.
5.	5S Patrols	5S patrol teams are established to carry out periodic inspection patrols.	once a week	This helps to stop backsliding on 5S conditions.
6.	5S Model Workplaces	Workplaces that have been especially successful in establishing 5S conditions are recognized.	twice a year	This boosts morale at model workplaces and promotes lateral deployment.
7.	5S Contests	5S contests are held within all workplaces.	twice a year	The spirit of competition is utilized to support 5S implementation.
8.	5S Award System	Awards are presented to outstanding 5S workplaces.	twice a year	same as above
9.	Top Management Inspections	Top managers visit workplaces to inspect 5S conditions and offer advice and encouragement.	2 to 4 times a year	5S implementation becomes a conduit for communication between top managers and employees.
10.	5S Photo Exhibits	5S photographers visit workplaces to photograph 5S conditions for display.	2 to 4 times a year	Workplace photo exhibits draw interested people from other workplaces.
11.	Red-Tag Strategy	This achieves Visual Proper Arrangement by eliminating unneeded items.	2 to 4 times a year	This clears away unneeded items.
12.	Signboard Strategy	Signboards are created to indicate exactly what goes where and in what amount.	2 to 4 times a year	Visual Orderliness is achieved.
13.	5-Minute 5S	A five-minute period each day is devoted to the 5S implementation of Cleanliness.	daily	This helps make 5S maintenance a habit.
14.	1S 1-Minute Campaign	A one-minute period each day is devoted to implementing one of the 5S's. (The emphasis is on consistency — not scope.)	daily	same as above
15.	5S Pep Talks in Morning and Evening	At routine morning and evening meetings, managers spend a minute reviewing the 5S's.	daily	This promotes 5S awareness.
16.	5S Public Announce-ments	The in-house broadcast system is used to communicate brief 5S messages.	daily	same as above
17.	5S Video Presentation	An opportunity to study (via video) 5S conditions at workplaces both in-house and at other companies.	2 to 4 times a year	same as above

Inspections by Top Managers

I suggest that company presidents participate in inspections two to four times a year. Factory superintendents should do the same once a month. In both cases, these top managers should walk from workplace to workplace, checking on 5S conditions. They may want to hand out 5S improvement memos with their written comments or talk with workers about what they find. However, the main point is to give employees a chance to meet and talk with the company's top brass.

5S Photo Exhibits

The 5S promotion organization should include a designated group of photographers. Their assignment is to take photos of workplaces two to four times a year and set up photo exhibits at gathering places such as the company cafeteria. Possible variations on this sub-theme include "mini"

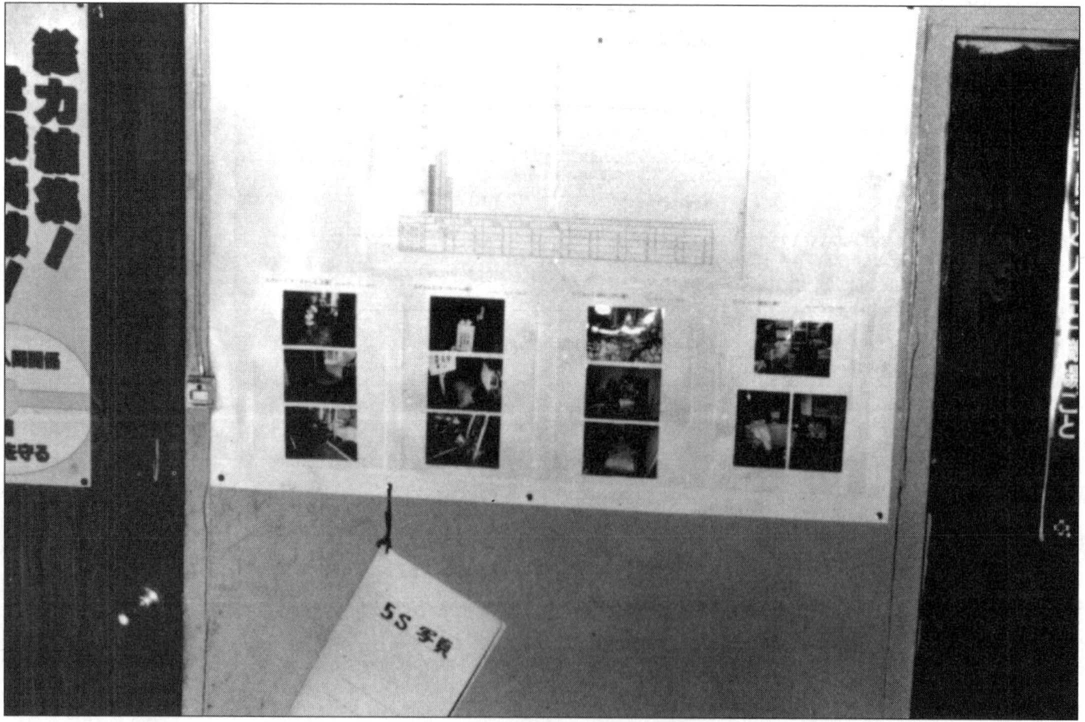

Photo 12-6. 5S Photo Exhibit with a Notebook for Comments

photo exhibits that focus on the people in a particular workplace and 5S focus displays that encourage viewers to add their comments in an attached notebook. (See Photo 12-6.)

5S PROMOTION TOOLS FOR BUILDING DISCIPLINE

Let me explain three main points concerning the promotion, reinvigoration, and habituation of 5S activities. Point 1 is the need to educate everyone

Table 12-4. 5S Promotion Tools

No.	Promotion Tool	Description	Frequency	Effects
1.	5S Slogans	5S slogans can be displayed on banners and buttons.	2 to 4 times a year	This promotes 5S awareness.
2.	5S Badges and Buttons	Badges and buttons that display 5S logos can be worn on the chest or sleeve.	2 to 4 times a year	same as above
3.	5S Maps	5S maps clarify territories assigned to people responsible for maintaining 5S conditions.	continually	This promotes adherence to 5S implementation.
4.	5S Schedules	These are detailed schedules showing who is responsible for specific 5S activities on specific days.	continually	same as above
5.	On-duty Tags	These tags circulate among people on the 5S schedule to remind them when it is their turn.	continually	same as above
6.	5S Job Cycle Charts	These charts facilitate making an exhaustive listing of 5S duties and enable assignment of 5S implementation cycle times.		This helps prevent oversights in 5S duties.
7.	5S News	This is an internal newsletter featuring 5S-related matters.	once or twice a month	This spreads information about internal 5S conditions and activities.
8.	5S Improvement Memos	These are small memos that top managers can write their comments on and hand out at workplaces that they visit.	2 to 4 times a year	This helps convey comments and encouragement from top managers.
9.	5S Posters	These posters display 5S slogans, monthly subthemes, etc.	once or twice a year	This broadens and deepens 5S implementation.
10.	5S Photo Exhibits	Publicize 5S conditions via photo exhibits and comment displays.	2 to 4 times a year	This broadens awareness of 5S conditions in specific workshops and in the company as a whole.
11.	5S Stickers	These adhesive stickers display 5S definitions, slogans, mini-slogans, etc.	2 to 4 times a year	This broadens and deepens 5S implementation.
12.	5S Mini-Slogan Signs	These small signs display 5S definitions, mini-slogans, etc.	weekly	same as above
13.	In-house 5S Articles	Articles about 5S activities are included in the company's regular internal newsletter.	as needed	This broadens and deepens 5S implementation.
14	5S Pocket Manuals	These pocket-size manuals contain 5S-related definitions and descriptions.	continual	same as above

in the company about the 5S's and how they are to be implemented companywide. Top managers must take the lead in setting up the promotion organization and overseeing its administration. Point 2 is that various 5S tools must be employed to lend ongoing support to 5S promotion. Together, they make for stronger, more effective 5S implementation. Point 3 is that 5S implementation is an ongoing process and should become a habit for everyone involved. The base supporting this habituation process is the skill of giving and receiving criticism.

Table 12-4 presents a list of 5S tools that provide essential support for 5S promotion and implementation.

5S Slogans

5S slogans vary widely and are largely employee-suggested. They can be displayed on badges and ribbons worn by people, on posters, stickers, mini posters, and other types of displays. New mini slogans should be displayed each week to help improve everyone's awareness and readiness concerning 5S implementation.

In Japan, slogans are usually written in one of the two rhythmic patterns used in the short poems called haiku. The main point is to make the slogan easy to say and easy to remember. The following are translations of some 5S slogans I have seen:

- **Even factories agree that it feels good to take a bath.** (Factories, like people, get dirty and grimy, so let's give them a bath now and then.)
- **Sometimes it hurts to get rid of what you don't need.** (Organization means getting rid of all unneeded items.)
- **A good tool is a multitool.** (Can that jig or tool be combined with another one?)
- **Stay at the cutting edge of Orderliness for cutting tools.** (Store cutting tools in groups for frequently made products.)
- **Watch out and stay safe — use divider lines.** (Clearly mark off walkways from work areas.)
- **Smart people don't sweep dirt — they prevent it.** (Find out how things get dirty, then treat the cause.)

5S BADGES AND 5S BUTTONS

5S badges and 5S buttons display insignias and slogans that are worn on the chest or sleeve to help raise 5S awareness. (See Photo 12-7.)

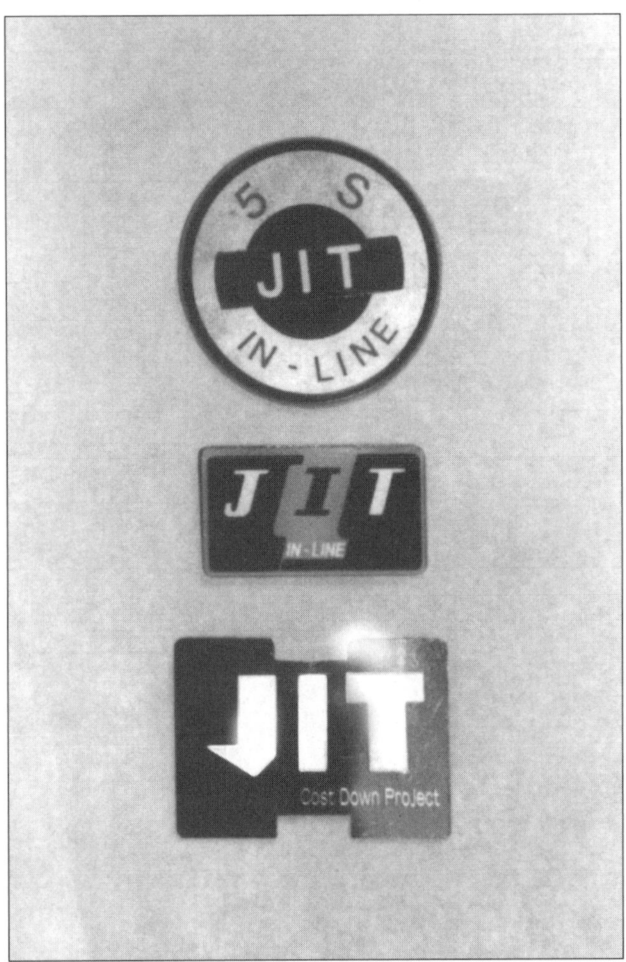

Photo 12-7. 5S Badges

Another good idea is to award special 5S badges to workplaces that have received high scores on their most recent 5S evaluation. This helps to recognize and distinguish the top-performing workplaces.

5S Maps

5S maps showing workplace layouts clarify the territories assigned to the people responsible for maintaining 5S conditions. An example is shown in Figure 12-7.

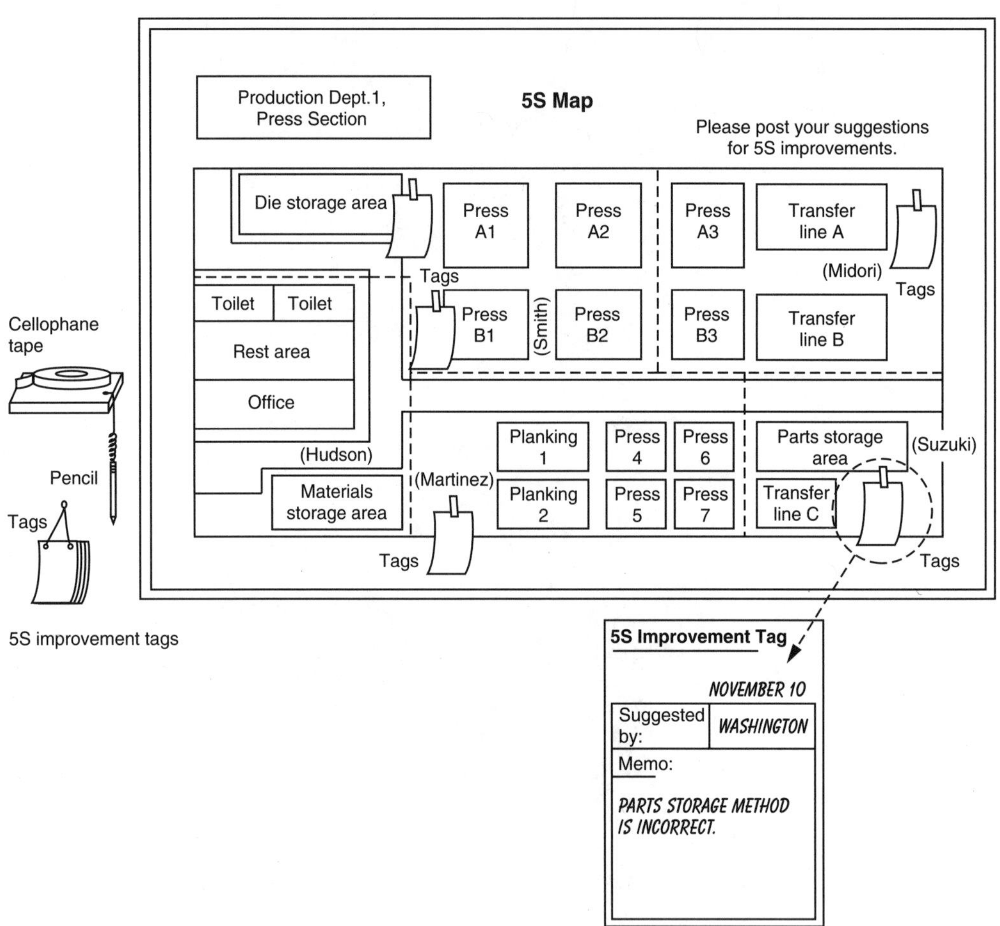

Figure 12-7. 5S Map

Some 5S maps feature 5S improvement tags, which are memo pads attached to the 5S map for use by anyone who notices something in the workplace needing improvement. That someone can be an official inspector (such as a 5S patrol member) or a person walking by. The memo-pad sheets have adhesive backs so that the person suggesting the improvement can stick it at the target site on the 5S map. A workplace employee or supervisor should check the 5S map at least once a day to see if any improvements have been suggested that the workplace staff can address promptly. Once implemented (or rejected as unfeasible), the memo with the suggested improvement is removed from the 5S map.

5S Job Cycle Charts

Job cycle charts facilitate a detailed listing of 5S duties, as shown in Figure 12-8. They also enable the assignment of 5S implementation cycle times for each group of operations. After determining 5S areas and the persons assigned to each area, use this chart (1) to list the 5S jobs to be done in each area and (2) to set a frequency cycle for each job (such as daily or weekly). Afterward, draw up a 5S check chart that lists all operations for each 5S implementation cycle time.

5S Job Cycle Chart	Div./Dept./ Section	Production Dept. 1, Assembly Section A			
	Entered by:	*MIZUNUMA*	Date:	*1 FEB 1994*	

No.	5S Job	5S's: Organization	Orderliness	Cleanliness	Cleanup	Discipline	Job Cycle: Continual	Daily	Weekly	Monthly	One time	Other
1.	Red-tag strategy (one-time, companywide)	○									○	
2.	Red-tag strategy (repeat round)	○					○					
3.	Location indicators (checking and making)		○						○			
4.	Item indicators (checking and making)		○						○			
5.	Amount indicators (checking and making)		○						○			
6.	Clean up around line			○				○				

Figure 12-8. 5S Operation Cycle Chart

5S Newsletter

5S newsletters are in-house news bulletins centered on 5S topics. They typically carry factory reports on 5S conditions and activities making liberal use of eye-catching illustrations and page layouts. Issued once or twice a month, they can be handed out at regular staff meetings, perhaps as part of a "one-minute 5S" segment of the meeting agenda.

5S Posters

5S posters displaying 5S slogans or descriptions of 5S activity themes are posted at various workplaces. New posters are put up about once or twice a year.

5S Photo Exhibits

Official 5S photographers roam the workplaces periodically to take pictures of good and bad examples of 5S implementation and maintenance. The photos are added to 5S photo exhibits and 5S focus displays usually shown in gathering places such as the company cafeteria.

5S Stickers

As illustrated in Figure 12-9, 5S stickers typically define the 5S's or carry messages about their importance. They are posted in places where they will be seen easily and help improve employee awareness.

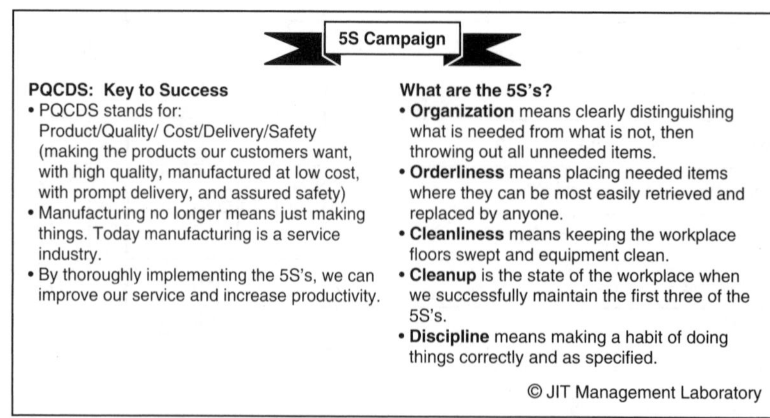

Figure 12-9. 5S Sticker

At one household electronics factory, 5S stickers are attached at eye level in the lavatories and rest areas where people tend to relax for a few minutes. Other common and effective places for their display are on individual desks and bulletin boards, aside operator panels for machines and other equipment, and in the company cafeteria.

5S Mini Slogan Signs

Have employees suggest 5S mini slogans as part of a companywide 5S awareness campaign. These slogans can be drawn and displayed in eye-catching places, such as the lavatory, rest areas, and cafeteria. It is a good idea to put up new mini slogan signs each week.

5S Pocket Manuals

The 5S pocket manual contains 5S definitions and descriptions; it is small enough to fit into the pocket of one's work clothes. Employees — including managers and supervisors — have easy reference to the 5S essentials when they need them. The manual can be used in the following ways:

- as a textbook for "one-minute 5S lessons" during meetings
- as a quick study on 5S definitions and descriptions
- as a reference for confirming checkpoints during 5S implementation

13

Case Studies: Reports from Four 5S Campaigns

Our five pillars for the visual workplace involve much more than simply sweeping the floors or washing windows. The 5S's — Organization, Orderliness, Cleanliness, Standardized Cleanup, and Discipline — are daily activities promoted and performed by everyone from top management to shop-floor employees to build a strong foundation for corporate survival.

This chapter presents four case studies from Japanese companies that have introduced the 5S's. They are in the form of reports to various participants. These reports should enable you, the reader, to create a scenario for introducing the 5S's at your own company.

The topics covered are:

1. a "5S campaign" planning proposal
2. a "5S campaign" for small and mid-sized companies
3. a "5S campaign" for large companies
4. a promotion strategy for a "5S campaign" in the sales division

A "5S CAMPAIGN" PLANNING PROPOSAL

- 5S Campaign Planning Proposal

5S Campaign Planning Proposal

5S	Category	Campaign Description	Main Points	Goals
Organization Orderliness Cleanliness Clean-up Discipline	Activity-related	① Periodic Organization-Orderliness campaigns (For instance, clear out unneeded items once a month.)	Periodic 3S campaigns help make a habit of: • clearing away unneeded items • determining a specific storage site for each item • returning all items to their specific storage sites	○ We implement Organization-Orderliness campaigns to eliminate waste and improve efficiency. (Goals: waste reduction and efficiency improvement)
		② Periodic Cleanliness campaigns (Perform major clean-up once a month.)		○ We implement Cleanliness campaigns to help keep work-places clean. This helps improve quality and prevent defects. (Goals: workplace cleanliness and defect prevention)
		③ Periodic safety and hygiene education (Classes are held every two months.)	○ This provides a regular, periodic stimulus to safety awareness.	○ Periodic classes help improve safety awareness and know-ledgeability. (Goal: to reconfirm safety education in case people forget)
		④ Presentation of 5S activity sheets (Groups present reports describing their 5S activities.)	○ Presented once a month, with scoring system to encourage competition between groups.	○ Group competition promotes better teamwork within groups. (Goal: to recognize that "two heads are better than one")
		⑤ Presentation of improvement proposals (Each group presents one proposal per week.)	○ Evaluate the proposals and award a prize for the best one.	○ This encourages people to abandon old ideas and be flexible in solving problems. (Goals: to encourage dissatisfaction with current conditions and to promote creative thinking)
	Morale-related	① Promote common courtesy (For instance, greeting people when arriving or leaving the workplace)	○ Courtesy improves morale.	○ Courtesy boosts workplace morale and sets the tone for positive behavior. (Goal: to make "good morning" and "good night" the first two steps in Discipline)
		② Address superiors by their work titles.	○ This promotes professional courtesy among employees and encourages respect.	○ Addressing someone as "Supervisor Smith" instead of "Mr. or Ms. Smith" recognizes that person's responsibilities and helps strengthen the team structure at the workplace. (Goal: to promote teamwork)
		③ Have everyone sing or repeat the 5S "anthem" or slogan. (Issue 5S cards with the words.)	○ Have everyone recite the 5S slogan during morning assembly.	○ This improves everyone's 5S awareness. (Goal: to get every-one into the mood for 5S implementation)
		④ Strictly enforce requirement for giving prior notice of absence. (Employees must notify their superior before arriving late, leav-ing early, taking a vacation, etc.)	○ This helps make a habit of notifying immediate superiors about work schedules.	○ This rule promotes communication and teamwork. (Goal: to eliminate the confusion caused by unexplained absences)
		⑤ Be conscientious about communicating via written memos. (Write promptly and clearly.)	○ Verbal instructions are easily forgotten. When possible, send written memos and check up on responses to them.	○ Clearly written memos are less likely to encounter problems. (Goal: to eliminate verbal instructions that risk being misunderstood or forgotten)

A "5S CAMPAIGN" FOR SMALL AND MID-SIZED COMPANIES

- 5S Campaign Implementation Outline (Manufacturing Division)

p. 1/3

5S Campaign Implementation Outline (Manufacturing Division)

1. Purpose
To promote the 5S's in the factory; to improve work efficiency and machine availability that lead to overall productivity improvement

2. Goal
To make the factory the cleanest in the country

3. Item-specific goals and activities

Items	Goals	Activities
Organization and Orderliness	○ Do not allow any items in the workplace that are not being used on a regular basis. ○ Apply the "three specifics" (assign *specific* storage sites for *specific* amounts of *specific* items) in a way that anyone can understand at a glance.	○ Apply Proper Arrangement and Orderliness to the following workplace items: • machine parts • lubrication supplies • tools and supplies • cleaning equipment • in-process inventory and materials
Cleanliness	○ Remove all garbage, dust, and dirt from the workplace.	○ Cleanliness events (part of 5S month) • month-long Cleanliness-boosting events for machines • month-long Cleanliness-boosting events for workplace cleanliness and hygiene ○ Cleanliness pep talks on Monday mornings and between shifts
Standardized Cleanup	○ Standardized Cleanup's goal is to maintain 3S (Organization, Orderliness, Cleanliness) conditions. ○ Devise ways to prevent deterioration of cleanup.	○ Point out deterioration of Standardized Cleanup via routine patrols (including one with the company president). ○ Hold regular weekly meetings among workplace supervisors to devise Standardized Cleanup improvements.
Discipline	○ Cultivate workplaces where people act on their own to maintain Cleanup. ○ Cultivate workplaces where everyone dresses neatly and is courteous. ○ Cultivate workplaces where everyone adheres to prescribed procedures and provides necessary reports and other communications. ○ Cultivate a company where everyone correctly understands the 5S philosophy.	○ Establish well-prepared workplaces • Apply Organization and Orderliness to offices. ○ Events • Cleanliness/hygiene month • 3S month for lockers and desks • month-long promotion of proper dress and courtesy ○ Routine inspection patrols (including president's patrol) • supervisor meetings, evaluations to encourage independent activities, report presentation meetings to boost motivation ○ 5S lesson (a 10-minute 5S lesson at one Monday-morning general meeting per month) ○ Classes sponsored by the 5S promotion council (basic 5S activities, philosophy, and information) ○ Instruction by supervisors • Basically, 5S information is given at the workplace during patrols or meetings, etc.

4. Organization

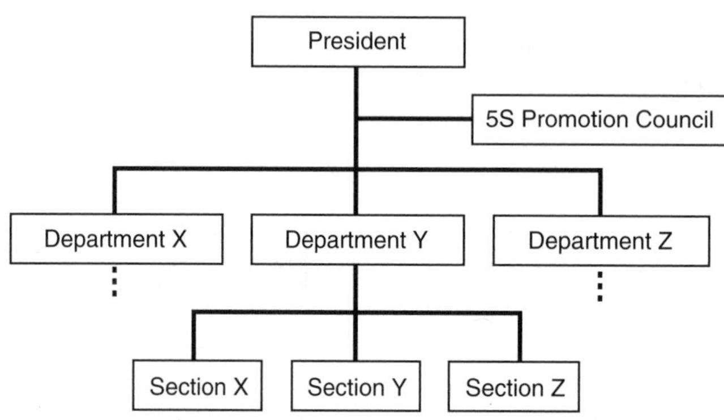

A. 5S Council
The 5S council includes "5S promoters" from various management levels, from the company president down to the section chief level. This council has decision-making authority regarding the delegation of duties concerning the 5S campaign.
The 5S council also formulates policies regarding various 5S activities, plans the 5S activity calendar, and provides implementation instructions to workplaces.

B. 5S Promotion Council
The 5S promotion council works out the details of planned 5S activities and provides instructions and encouragement to make 5S implementation go more smoothly at the workplace level.

p. 3/3

5. 5S Activity Calendar

Date	Routine Patrol	Study Sessions and Meetings		Events	Workplace Organization & Orderliness
		(At classes or morning assembly)	(Promotion Council)		
February/ March	• Routine inspection patrols • Inspection patrols by company president	• Safety (Part 1) • The 5S's (Part 1) • JIT	• Meetings	- - - • Preparation period (3 weeks)	• Apply to machine parts • Apply to lubrication supplies
April	• Routine inspection patrols • Inspection patrols by company president	• Safety (Part 2) • The 5S's (Part 2)	• Meetings	• Month-long promotion of work-place Cleanliness and hygiene (preparing the workplace)	• Apply to offices
May	• Routine inspection patrols • Inspection patrols by company president	• Safety (Part 3) • The 5S's (Part 3)	• Meetings • Factory tour (Part 1)	• Follow up Organization (two weeks) - - - • Preparation period (2 weeks)	• Apply to tools and supplies
June	• Routine inspection patrols • Inspection patrols by company president	• Safety (Part 4) • The 5S's (Part 4)	• Meetings	• Month-long promotion of Cleanliness for machines	• Apply to cleaning supplies
July	• Routine inspection patrols • Inspection patrols by company president	• Safety (Part 5) • The 5S's (Part 5)	• Meetings	• Follow up Organization (two weeks) - - - • Preparation period (2 weeks)	• Apply to in-process inventory and materials
August	• Routine inspection patrols • Inspection patrols by company president	• Safety (Part 6) • The 5S's (Part 6)	• Meetings • Factory tour (Part 2)	• 3S month for lockers and desks	
September	• Routine inspection patrols • Inspection patrols by company president	• Safety (Part 7) • The 5S's (Part 7)	• Meetings	• Follow up Organization (two weeks) - - - • Preparation period (2 weeks)	
October	• Routine inspection patrols • Inspection patrols by company president	• Safety (Part 8) • The 5S's (Part 8)	• Meetings • Report presentations	• Month-long promotion of proper dress and courtesy	
				• Follow up Organization (two weeks)	

A "5S CAMPAIGN" FOR LARGE COMPANIES

- "5S Campaign" Implementation Memo
- "5S Campaign" Promotion Memo

p. 1/4

MEMORANDUM

To: Factory superintendents for each factory
From: Production management division chief

(Copies to: Procurement department chief, engineering department chief, rationalization promotion council, accounting department, auditor's office, and clerical offices)

"5S Campaign" Implementation

During a subcommittee meeting held on February 24, the production management subcommittee was instructed by the production division chief to carry out 5S implementation. Please consider the following outline to be the official notification of this implementation plan. (See the outline chart appended to the end of this memo.)

Re: 5S implementation

1. Main goals
   (1) To create a facility that is able to operate as a flow production facility
   (2) To reduce inventory and increase the efficiency of asset operations

2. Establishment of a 5S implementation promotion month
   March is designated as the 5S implementation promotion month.

3. Main 5S operations (for the immediate future)
   (1) Implement the red-tag strategy (Organization)
   By March 10, attach red tags to all of the following types of target items that have not been used (or changed) for one month or longer.

Red-tag targets:

- Empty spaces
- Equipment (carts, dies, jigs, tools, etc.)
- Inventory assets (raw materials, in-process inventory, semifinished goods)
- Other unneeded items (desks, shelves, lockers, and other supplies)

p. 2/4

Notes

1. Red-tag sizes
   Choose sizes that are appropriate for the target items. (For example, 8.5" x 11" paper is used on idle machines at factory A.)

2. Minimum requirements for data entry on red tags:
   Equipment: name of machine or process
   Inventory assets: item names and amounts

3. Red-tag procurement
   Each workplace is responsible for procuring its own red tags. (Cost estimate for 5" by 7" tags is 4 cents per tag.)

4. Follow-up on red-tag management
   (1) The production division chief, production headquarters chief, and other managers will make an inspection tour in mid-March. (The schedule will be provided in a separate notice.)

   (2) Treatment of red-tagged items
   All red-tagged items must be disposed of or removed to an unneeded item storage site by the end of March.

   (3) Make and use signboards (Orderliness)
   After all unneeded items have been cleared away, make signboards for all needed items and useless items.

      a. Contents of signboards:
         Equipment: name of machine or process
         Other items: storage site and amount to be stored
         Examples:
         - materials storage site
         - machining parts storage site
         - assembly parts storage site
         - useless item storage site (enter item names and amounts on red tags)
      b. Deadline for signboard implementation is the end of April
      c. Signboard examples (see examples appended)

   (4) Recovery (retention) status of raw materials, etc. (color-coded by month)
   Management of this matter is still under consideration. (Opinions on this matter are being sought from all relevant departments.)

Types of Signboards

① Equipment-related Signboard

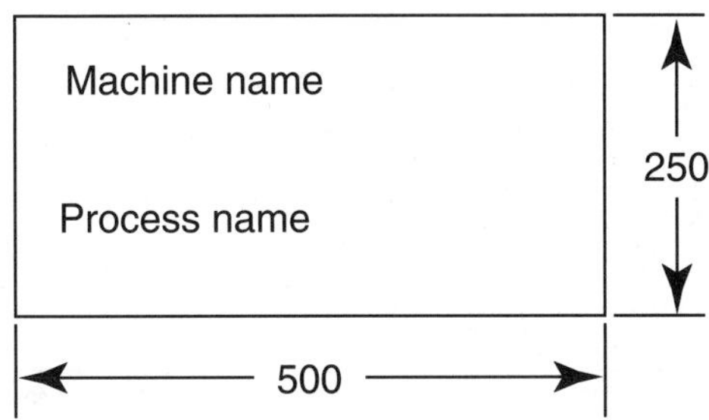

(if placed on top of machine)

② Material-related Signboard

(1) suspended type

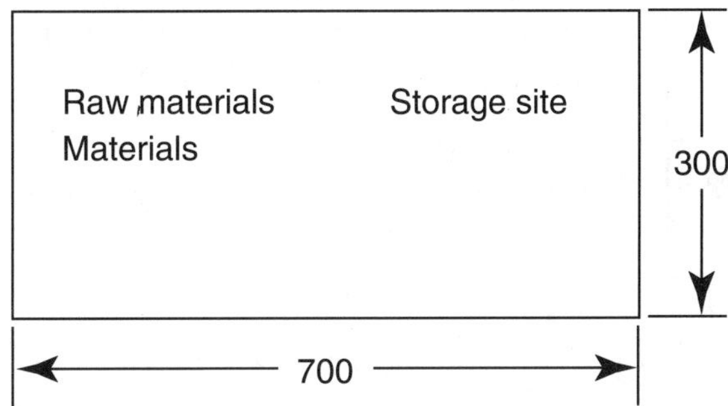

(2) freestanding type

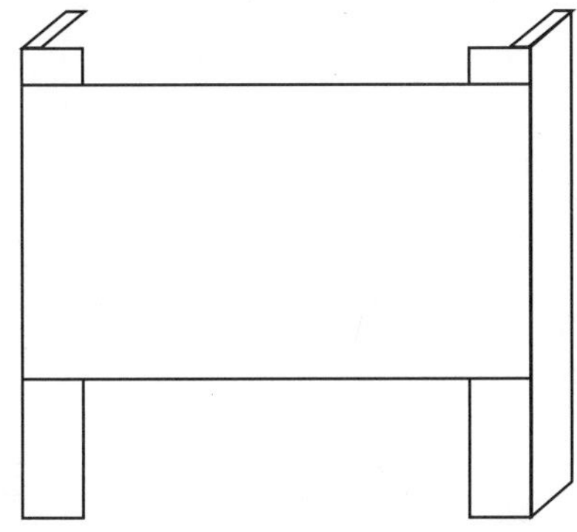

(stand material can be cardboard or plywood)

(dimensional unit = mm)

p. 4/4

(Comments)

5S Implementation Outline

Description by 5S categories

	5S	Description	Schedule and Person Responsible
1	Organization	Attach red tags to all unneeded and useless items in the factory to clearly distinguish between needed and unneeded items.	Target / Person responsible / Deadline: In-process inventory Semi-finished goods Set components Raw materials and parts Service parts
2	Orderliness	(1) Indicate all storage sites clearly; don't allow items to be stored anywhere else. (Use standing signboards.) (2) Set up signboards for machines that show names of machines and processes in production lines	Deadline: end of April Devise suitable methods for each workplace before implementing.
3	Cleanliness	Routinely sweep work areas and walkways.	Upon completion of each shift. Also, during next day's work changeover.
4	Standardized Cleanup	Maintain 3S (Organization, Orderliness, Cleanliness) conditions.	Make a 3S checklist and use it often.
5	Discipline	Make a habit of performing procedures correctly.	Carry out three-minute Discipline lessons at regular morning meetings.

Nested table in row 1:

Target	Person responsible	Deadline
In-process inventory		
Semi-finished goods		
Set components		
Raw materials and parts		
Service parts		

p. 1/2

MEMORANDUM

To: Factory superintendents for each factory
From: Production management division chief

(Copies to: Information department chief, procurement department chief, and engineering department chief)

"5S Campaign" Promotion

The requested Organization implementation via the red-tag strategy (targeted at all retained materials, unneeded equipment, etc.) has been completed by each department as scheduled. The following instructions concern the next stage — Orderliness implementation.

Orderliness Outline

1. Designate and indicate storage sites.
   Determine storage sites for raw materials, in-process inventory, semi-finished goods, and other items, and use signboards to indicate them. (See Figure 13-7.)
   (1) Consult with the engineering department concerning installation cost estimates for storage shelves or other items.
   (2) Draft storage layout diagrams for all inventory assets and submit the drawings to the production management division chief by May 14.
   (3) Make signboards to clearly indicate names of machines and processes on the production line.

2. Determine inventory amounts.
   Review existing inventory amounts for all parts and materials.

3. Send instructions to parts suppliers.
   Send specific instructions to parts suppliers concerning delivery sites and amounts.

4. Orderliness implementation deadline: by the end of May
   Offer guidance to suppliers concerning implementation of Organization and Orderliness at supplier facilities.

p. 2/2

Signboard example for parts storage shelves

- Supplier name
- Part code
- Part name
- Maximum storage amount
- Minimum storage amount

Layout example for parts storage

(Warehouse)

"Company A" press parts, cutting machine parts	"Company B" forging parts casting parts	C	D
walkway			
E	F	G	H

10m

(Establish addresses for all storage sites.)

ONE COMPANY'S PROMOTION STRATEGY FOR 5S CAMPAIGNS IN ITS SALES DIVISIONS

- Essentials for Promoting 5S Campaigns
- Detailed Schedule for 5S Campaign Implementation
- Red-Tag Management Chart
- Signboards
- In-House Promotion Schedule for 5S Campaign
- Management Chart of Red-tagged Items
- 5S Deposited Item Form

ESSENTIALS FOR PROMOTING 5S CAMPAIGNS

1. Name of promotion project: "5S Campaign"

2. Period: February 1 to 28
- Preparation period: January 25 to 29
- Results compilation period: March 1 to 8

3. Objectives:

To thoroughly eliminate waste in inventory management, the goal being a 30 percent reduction in inventory

"Zero waste" means lower costs and higher efficiency.
- Eliminate waste due to excess inventory.
- Eliminate waste due to excess warehouse space, shelves, cabinets, and other storage spaces.

"Zero injuries" means improved safety.
- Design storage methods for safety and prevention of loading errors.

"Zero late deliveries" means strict adherence to deadlines.
- 5S warehouses make it easy to tell when items are missing.

"Zero customer claims" means enhanced customer trust.
- Neat, clean warehouses are less likely to send out defective products.

4. Scope of 5S targets:

This campaign is targeted at warehouse items (merchandise).

5. Implementation themes:

(1) ORGANIZATION means clearly distinguishing between needed and unneeded items and disposing of the latter. It is more than reorganizing existing items neatly.
- Unneeded inventory creates excess inventory management costs.
- Unneeded warehouse space and shelving take up valuable facility space.
- Excess inventory creates excess conveyance, unneeded carts, etc.
- Excess inventory creates excess labor costs.
- Excess inventory makes it more difficult to find needed items.
- Excess inventory creates more dead inventory (due to design changes, age related deterioration, etc.)

(2) ORDERLINESS means arranging needed items so that they are easy to use and labeling them to make their storage sites understandable at a glance. It is more than arranging them neatly.
- Always implement Orderliness as a follow-up to Organization.
- Orderliness conditions are worthless if the storage system can only be understood by experienced people.
- Orderliness should make it easy for anyone to find and return all needed items.

(3) CLEANLINESS means keeping everything swept and clean.
- A warehouse with good Cleanliness conditions will have higher quality items (i.e., less age-related deterioration).
- Cleanliness includes finding ways to prevent the accumulation of dirt and dust.

(4) STANDARDIZED CLEANUP means maintaining the 3S conditions of Organization, Orderliness, and Cleanliness over the long run.

(5) DISCIPLINE means making a habit of properly maintaining correct procedures. It is the foundation for maintaining 5S conditions.

6. Specific implementation methods:

Organization and Orderliness are the 5S's used for making improvements because their implementation makes it easy for anyone to see where waste, abnormalities, and other problems exist in inventory, operations, and other areas. In this sense, they can be referred to as "visual Organization" and "visual Orderliness." The main method used to turn Organization into visual Organization is the red-tag strategy. To turn Orderliness into visual Orderliness we use the signboard strategy:

"Organization + red-tag strategy = visual Organization"
"Orderliness + signboard strategy = visual Orderliness"

Tips for Success in the Red-tag and Signboard Strategies:

(1) Everyone must participate.
(2) Get company authorization.
(3) Ultimate responsibility rests with the company president, factory superintendent, and other top managers (who must take an active role when necessary.
(4) Make sure everyone thoroughly understands their instructions.
(5) Explain things patiently and thoroughly. (Don't neglect details.)
(6) The factory superintendent or company president should make factory inspections personally and point out positive and negative conditions.
(7) Don't stop halfway in establishing the 5S's. (It is all or nothing.)
(8) The 5S's are a bridge to other improvements. (One improvement leads to another.)

"Ten Commandments" for Improvement:

(1) Throw out traditional concepts.
(2) Think of a new method that works. (Don't just criticize methods that fail.)
(3) Don't accept excuses. (Deny the status quo.)
(4) If it's good, do it immediately. (If it's bad, stop immediately.)
(5) Don't seek perfection. (A 60 percent success is good enough.)
(6) Correct mistakes the moment you find them.
(7) Problems give you a chance to use your brain.
(8) Ask "why" five times until you discover the root cause.
(9) The ideas of ten people are better than the knowledge of one.
(10) Improvement knows no bounds.

Definition of the Red-tag Strategy:

People bathe to remove the sweat and dirt that build up on their bodies. This is part of what the 5S's mean for people. The most fundamental of the 5S's are Organization and Orderliness.

This is where the red-tag strategy comes in. The word "strategy" implies an enemy against whom the strategy is to be launched. In our case, the enemy is the waste and dirt that we have allowed to accumulate around us. Such waste can be difficult even for professionals to discover — and is certainly not easy for anyone to see at a glance.

The red-tag strategy is a way (1) to clearly distinguish what is needed from what is not and (2) to eliminate the latter.

Steps in the Red-tag Strategy:

Red-tag teams attach red tags to anything that appears unnecessary. You can't overdo it — so don't be embarrassed. When the warehouse appears to have turned red, we know the red-tag team has been thorough.

Surprisingly, items show up that no one can clearly identify as needed or unneeded. I say tag them: when in doubt, throw it out.

Step 1. Launch the red-tag project.
Step 2. Identify red-tag targets.
Step 3. Set red-tag criteria.
- Set criteria for determining what is needed and unneeded.

Step 4. Make the red tags.
Step 5. Attach the red tags.
- Have people from other work areas listen to a description of current conditions and then objectively red-tag all unneeded items.
  - ➤ Look for target items with a cool, critical eye.
  - ➤ Don't let workplace staff decide what to red-tag. Workplace staff think everything is necessary.
  - ➤ Be merciless when attaching red tags.
  - ➤ When in doubt, red-tag it.
- Red-tag intensively over a short time period.

Step 6. Evaluate the red-tag targets.
- Move red-tagged items to a separate red-tag storage area.
- Divide red-tagged items into two types: (1) "dead stock" and (2) "retained stock".
- To dispose of dead stock, create and execute a schedule that indicates quantities, values, and disposal periods.
- Compose a list of all unneeded inventory to facilitate an understanding of it and to use in accounting.

Signboard Strategy:

Once our red-tag strategy has eliminated unneeded items and left only the needed ones, the task remains of making it easy for people to see at a glance what goes where and in what amount. To do this, hang signboards in every workplace that clearly indicate items, their locations, and quantities. This is the signboard strategy (via visual Orderliness).

Step 1. Determine locations.
- Estimate the overall volume of inventory and allocate a suitable amount of space.
- Divide up the storage space with consideration given to the traffic of incoming and outgoing items.
- Divide up the storage space so that the most frequently used items are the most conveniently placed for storage and retrieval.
- After determining maximum storage amounts for each item, allocate only that much space.

Step 2. Set up location indicators.
- Make and post or hang signboards displaying numbers, words, or codes that identify item groups or warehouse sections.

Step 3. Set up item indicators.
- Make and post or hang signboards that clearly indicate the names of specific types of items.

p. 4/4

Cleanliness:

Step 1. Set up Cleanliness tools.
- Establish specific places where Cleanliness tools (brooms, mops, rags, buckets, etc.) will be kept.

Step 2. Establish and clearly describe Cleanliness methods, steps, and task assignments.

Detailed Schedule for 5S Campaign Implementation

Preparation period (January 25-29):
Prepare for red-tag and signboard strategies.

(1) Explain the gist of the 5S campaign to all employees (at an all-company meeting if possible). Emphasize methods for promoting the campaign.
(2) Establish a specific implementation schedule. Include implementation periods for the red-tag strategy, for returning purchased items, for moving red-tagged items to a separate storage area, for the signboard strategy, etc.
(3) Work out task assignments for everyone involved.
(4) Make a provisional list of red-tag targets based on the inventory list.
(5) Establish the warehouse layout and a separate storage area for red-tagged items.
(6) Other

Implementation period (February 1-12):
Carry out the red-tag strategy intensively on one or two of the days during the above implementation period.

(1) Attach red tags. (Use carbonless duplicate tags.)
(2) Check the results of red-tagging.
(3) Remove the "post card" section from the red tags and use the data to make a management chart (see next page). Send a copy of the management chart to the campaign headquarters (planning management office).
(4) Organize and carry out the return of purchased items.
  • (Designated return periods: February 1-10, 17-18, and 17-22 (deadline).
(5) Move red-tagged items to red-tag storage area.
(6) Revise warehouse layout.
(7) Make and attach signboards.
(8) Cleanliness implementation period (February 22-28)
(9) Patrol by project members.

Results compilation period (March 1 to 9):
Make a red-tag management chart, a red-tag result report, and a proposal for follow-up management. (Include a monthly inventory list of red-tagged items.)

p. 1/1

Red-Tag Management Chart

Organization No.

Red Tag

Location: ______________________ (Size:)

Code No. ☐☐☐☐

Product name:

Description

1. Item category: (1. A/T 2. B/T 3. C/T 4. D/T 5. E/T)
2. Procurement category: (1. In-house 2. Local supplier)
3. Quantity: (______________ pieces, units, other)
4. Value: $______________
5. Treatment:
   (1) Return: Div. 1; Div. 2; Div. 3; Div. 4; Div. 5; Div. 6; Div. 7; Local supplier
   (2) Disposal: Value is fully depreciated; discard
   (3) Dispose of all remaining unneeded items.
6. Reasons for red tagging:
   1. Not needed
   2. Surplus for current products
   3. Surplus from previous products
   4. Products for local clients only
   5. Other

Notes:
(1) Attach/fill out one red tag per target item.
(2) Attach/fill out one red tag per cardboard box (containing the same products in the same size).

Signboards

Orderliness means assigning a specific storage site for each needed item and indicating the sites so that people can easily tell what goes where. (This makes needed items easier to use.)

General warehouse location indicators are shown in Figure A, shelf (address) indicators are shown in Figure B, and product (item) indicators are shown in Figure C.
For warehouse walkway indicators, use white lines to mark off walkways and teach everyone never to cross over the lines. Regarding the allotment of product shelf space, mark storage spaces to indicate maximum and minimum item storage amounts. (Make the product indicators easy to attach and remove so that they can be repositioned whenever necessary.)

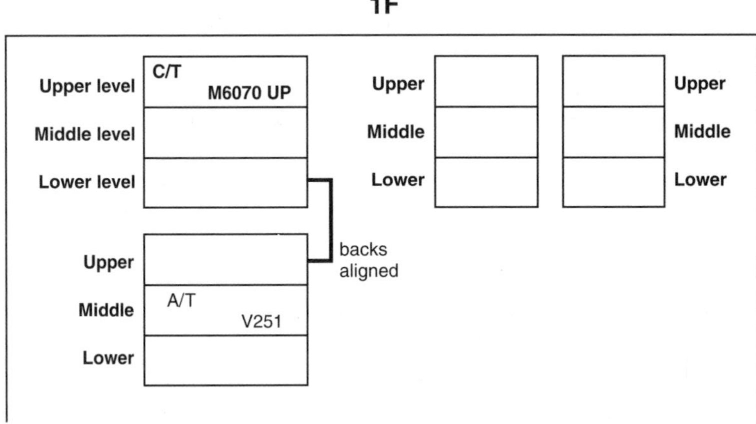

Figure A. Location Indicators

p. 2/2

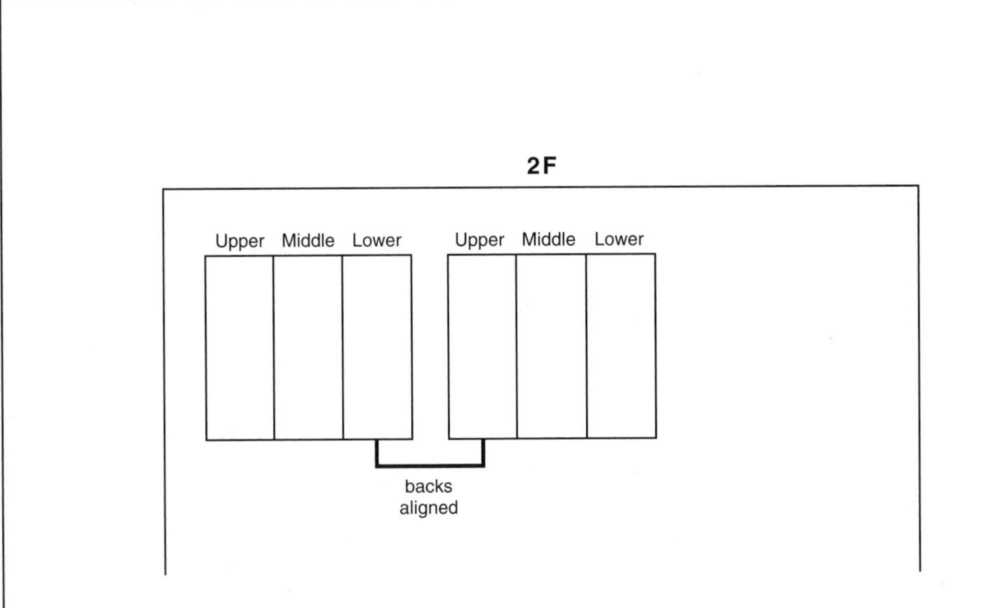

Figure B. Shelf (Address) Indicators

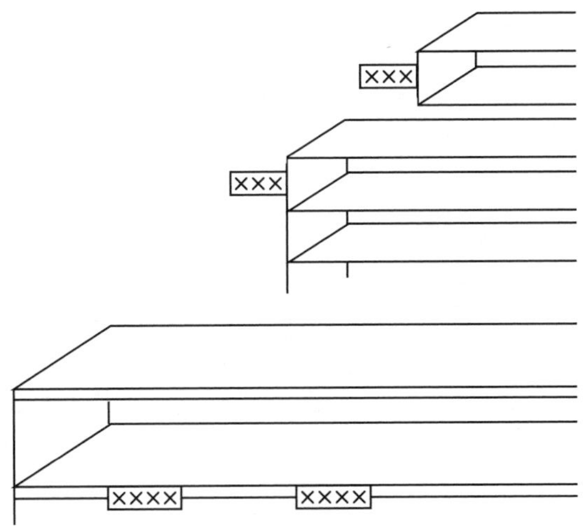

Figure C. Product (Item) Indicators

In-house Promotion Schedule for 5S Campaign

Store name/sales company name: (Manager's signature)

Schedule creation date:__________

1. Names of 5S Campaign Participants:

Period	Task	Person responsible	Scheduled implementation date	To be implemented by:
2. Preparation period: Jan. 25-29	① Explain the 5S's at an all-employee meeting.			
	② Make a provisional list of red-tag targets based on the inventory list (as of Jan. 20).			
3. Implementation period: Feb. 1-12	① Red tag strategy implementation date			
	② Person in charge of red tag team			
	③ Person in charge of checking red-tagged items			
	④ Person in charge of removing postcard sections from red tags			
	⑤ Person in charge of collecting returnable purchased items from red-tagged items			
	⑥ Person in charge of making a list of returnable purchased items			
	⑦ Person in charge of carrying out return of purchased items			
Feb. 17-22	⑧ Person in charge of moving red-tagged items to red tag storage area			
	⑨ Person in charge of confirming completion of above tasks			
	⑩ Person in charge of any required warehouse revisions			
	⑪ Person in charge of rearranging warehouse items according to new layout			
	⑫ Person in charge of confirming completion of above tasks			
	⑬ Person in charge of making signboards			
	⑭ Person in charge of putting up signboards			
	⑮ Person in charge of confirming completion of above tasks			
	⑯ Person in charge of setting up Cleanliness tools			
	⑰ Person in charge of maintaining Cleanliness (after initial Cleanliness implementation)			
	⑱ Person in charge of confirming completion of all of the above tasks			
Feb. 22-28	⑲ Patrols to be carried out by project council members			
4. Results compilation period: March 1-5	① Person in charge of making in-house management chart of red-tagged items.			
March 7-20	② Person in charge of sending management chart of red-tagged items to campaign headquarters (planning management office)			
	③ Person in charge of collecting companywide data at campaign headquarters			

This schedule filled out by: Store/sales branch manager (Jan. 29)
Send copies to branch president (by Feb. 2), who forwards a copy to the campaign headquarters (planning management office).

Management Chart of Red-tagged Items

Store name:

Item	Name of red-tagged product	Quantity	Unit value: $____	Value: $____	Treatment method		Treatment by store	
					Returnable purchased item ($____)	Fully depreciated item (discard)	Treatment by store ($____)	Future treatment methods

5S Deposited Item Form

To: Date:

Store name:

Attach this form to all boxes of items to be returned.

Content descriptions:

Item	Quantity	Item	Quantity

About the Author

Hiroyuki Hirano was born in Tokyo, Japan in 1946. He graduated from Senshu University's School of Economics in 1970 and then joined a large software company to work in the consulting division. There he laid the conceptual groundwork for Japan's first full-fledged production management system. Leaving the software company, he established JIT Management Laboratory Company, Ltd. Using his personal interpretation of the just-in-time philosophy (which emphasizes ideas and techniques for the complete elimination of waste), Mr. Hirano helped bring the JIT production revolution and JIT sales and distribution concepts to dozens of companies in Japan as well as major firms worldwide, such as a French automobile manufacturer and the Republic of Korea's largest corporate conglomerate.

Mr. Hirano's many publications in Japan include *Manual for JIT Consultants, 100 Questions and Answers about JIT, A Graffiti Guide to the JIT Factory Revolution, Visual Just-in-Time Production, The 5S Comic, Factory Rationalization Handbook*, and a nine-part videotape series entitled "JIT Production Revolution: Stages 1, 2, and 3." (These titles are available in Japanese from the publisher Nikkan Kogyo Shimbun-sha.)

Books available in English include *JIT Factory Revolution: A Pictorial Guide to Factory Design of the Future* (Productivity Press, 1987), *JIT Implementation Manual: The Complete Guide to Just-in-Time Manufacturing* (Productivity Press, 1989), and *5 Pillars of the Visual Workplace* (Productivity Press, 1995). Japanese journalist Ichiro Majima has examined several of Mr. Hirano's projects (i.e., the Renault factory) in his fascinating book, *The Shift to JIT: How People Make the Difference* (Productivity Press, 1992).

Index

Contents

Taken from: *A Design Manual,* Fourth Edition, by Shirl Brainard

Preface

Many people want to be an artist when they grow up.

I consider myself very lucky. As a retired teacher of design and color theory, I can now wake up in the morning thinking about a painting to finish or one to begin. As I paint, I practice the design principles in this book. I am now an artist, but, thankfully, not totally grown-up!

With every revision of this book, I have understood how we all must progress and mature with our thinking, our concepts, our perceptions. What I practice now as a painter, I either didn't know or didn't believe when I was younger. I know now that education is a never-ending process . . . one of building information, keeping that information tucked away in some "file drawer" of our brain, and then pulling it out and looking at it anew. And perhaps then having an "Ah ha!" moment.

My mission with this book is to continue teaching and to offer some very basic contributions about design: basic knowledge for the student designer to build on.

I use many illustrations of everyday objects because understanding design is also the seeing of design. My confirmed belief is that students should become acquainted with the designers at work in their field today. And I also believe students have a right to see their instructor's work. While we should look at the masters of art history, we definitely need to remember that some of those in the field of design today will be the next generation of masters.

ACKNOWLEDGMENTS

Fortunately, I'm making art in an extremely energetic art community. I am so grateful to my fellow artists and colleagues, who not only willingly gave their work for this edition but also gave me personal support, sharing their knowledge of diverse fields. They often pointed me in helpful directions. My son Evan Brainard contributed sound advice and his viewpoints from the world of three-dimensional design. Artist Mark E. Mehaffey, artist/writer Wes Pulkka, and artist, teacher, and friend Jim Ferguson gave me some creative ideas. I thank the reviewers of my last textbook for their views and comments. To the museums, galleries, and private companies who gave me reproductions and who helped me find particular artists—a big thank you. I thank the followings reviewers for their helpful suggestions:

Alisa Fox of Ivy Technical State College, IN; Stacy Leeman of Columbus State Community College, OH; Susan Copas of Seward County Community College, KS; Jennifer Clevenger of Radford University, VA; Joan C. Balster of Gloucester Community College, NJ, and Gina Reynoso of Columbus State Community College, OH.

And, finally, to my editors Kimberly Chastain, Amber Mackey, and Jean Lapidus . . . what would I have done without their shoulders to cry on? Thank you.

Shirl Brainard

PART 1 ◆ Introduction to Design

1

What Design Is

- The Design Encounter
- What Is Design Supposed to Mean?
- Do All Designs Have Them?
- Theory
- This Is What *We'll* Do!

The Design Encounter

We are going to explore the fundamental concepts of DESIGN. This book is, in fact, "designed" as "user-friendly," and the information in it is presented in a direct, conversational manner. And because design is all around us in our lives, some illustrations in this text are familiar objects.

Many related studies are connected with design, such as drawing, rendering techniques, or art history, but here we are concerned with ONLY the essence—or skeleton—of DESIGN. Other input and skills *can* and *should* be used to expand and elaborate upon this essence.

The content of this presentation will make us think about and explore ways of approaching our work in the design field.

Design concepts are not new. The Greeks had design standards some 2,000 years ago. Da Vinci made notes on design on many of his innumerable sketches. But the credit for analyzing various forms and structuring our basis for design theory goes to the Bauhaus, a school started in Dessau, Germany, in 1919 by Walter Gropius, an architect. He brought together a group of artisans with various training to lay the groundwork and to teach at this innovative and—eventually—influential school. The main concern of this school was to blend art with industry. Craftsmanship was of prime importance, but so were beauty and function. In formulating this bond, certain criteria emerged that were found to be in all of the classical arts. These criteria were isolated, discussed, and written about. All of the arts shared these standards, which have become the designer's visual vocabulary and circulating terminology over the years.

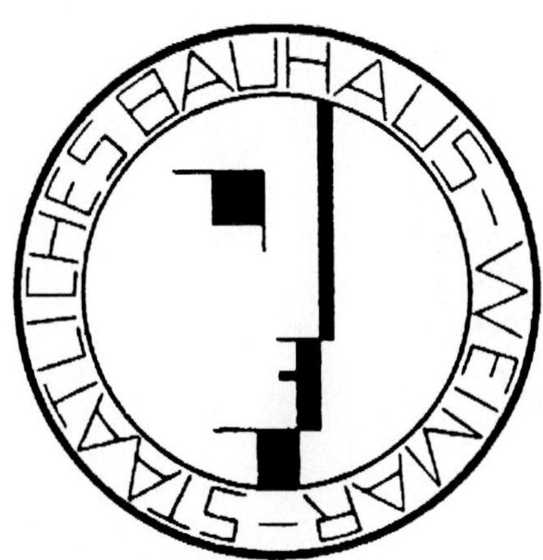

1◆1

The logo of the Bauhaus was considered "modern."

It's interesting to note that many of the practices that were routine at the Bauhaus are being reintroduced at some of the leading design and architectural schools internationally.

What Is Design Supposed to Mean?

A **design** is a creative endeavor to solve a problem. A design is the end result—what you have when the problem is solved. It *is* the solution. **Composition** is the *way* the components, parts, or elements are used or arranged to reach the solution. A design *has* composition.

The very ACT of designing is COMPOSING. Design differs from math or any exacting science because there may be many solutions to a given problem, and that is the challenge (and fun) for the designer.

Design is all around us. We often say that something is well designed, especially if it *functions* well. We understand and are aware of new designs in cars, clothing, and home furnishings, but look around you. The parts that make up these common designs are in nearly everything we know, whether designed by man or nature. These parts or components we call **ELEMENTS:** LINE—SHAPE—TEXTURE—VALUE—COLOR—in a SPACE.

The *ways* these parts are used to compose the design are called **PRINCIPLES**. These principles are: SPACE DIVISION—BALANCE—UNITY—and EMPHASIS. We have to remember as we start this exploration about design that we are not talking about what "art" is. We are speaking about design. Many forms are well designed but they are not art. An example of this is a refrigerator—a refrigerator is a design, but it is not considered art.

Do All Designs Have Them?

Think about the elements: SPACE, SHAPE, LINE, TEXTURE, VALUE, COLOR.

Do buildings have them?
Does a tree have them?
Does a painting have them?
Did your dinner last night have them?
ALL DESIGNS HAVE THEM.

It is easy to agree as we look at different things that, yes, all designs have these parts or elements.

Theory

The study of design is a theoretical study. As in many theoretical studies, the theory and the result of the

practiced theory may be a contradiction! What is a theory? A **theory** is the examination of information, often through a nonscientific analysis. From the information studied, a plausible statement is made—an assumption. I am sure you have heard the statement that a certain idea "is fine in theory, but it doesn't work in practice."

Some time ago there was an article in a newspaper about an airplane powered by microwaves. It was amusing because the plane only flew for a few minutes, but "in theory" it was supposed to be able to fly forever.

The THEORY of design is that if you know the elements and principles of design—*voilà! Magic!* We can design!

However, it takes some forethought and planning. We must approach our ideas (or theories) of design in a systematic way, first things first. I have read design texts that give information about HOW to arrange the parts of a design, before students can identify the parts.

◆ This Is What *We'll* Do!

We'll begin at the beginning. We'll first look at the different design fields and then what our responsibility is in our role as designers. To clarify the process of designing, we'll use the analogy of baking a cake . . . not from a boxed cake mix . . . but an honest-to-goodness cake from scratch! First we gather the ingredients (the ELEMENTS), then we assemble the ingredients and bake the cake using the instructions (the PRINCIPLES). The kind of cake we bake will depend on both factors, as do designs. A memorable artist and teacher said: "There is a certain common sense in procedure which may be basic to all." Robert Henri spoke those words and they are as relevant today as when he spoke them to his students.

1◆3

Robert Henri, SPANISH GYPSY. 1923. Oil on canvas. 32″ × 26″. Private collection.
Courtesy of Owings-Dewey Fine Art, Santa Fe, New Mexico.

1◆2

Ingredients for one kind of "scratch" (not in a box!) cake.
S. Brainard, Photo.

2

The Design Scene

◆ Kinds of Design

There are many kinds of design under the "Design Umbrella." If we look around us with a "new" eye, we see that *everything* that affects our lives was designed by *somebody*.

Design is basically classified into four categories:

1 ◆ FUNCTIONAL DESIGN includes the things in our lives we deem necessary. They *function* or do a task for us. Product design and structural design are included in this category. Product design is the most familiar . . . our automobiles transport us, electronics may be in the equipment we used at our jobs, our clothing covers us and keeps us warm or cool, and a can opener opens our cans. One furniture company has even redesigned one basic office chair in three sizes to accommodate our "growing" workers. Additionally, our homes are "architectural" or "structural" designs, and someone designs the structural steel that is the skeleton of many buildings.

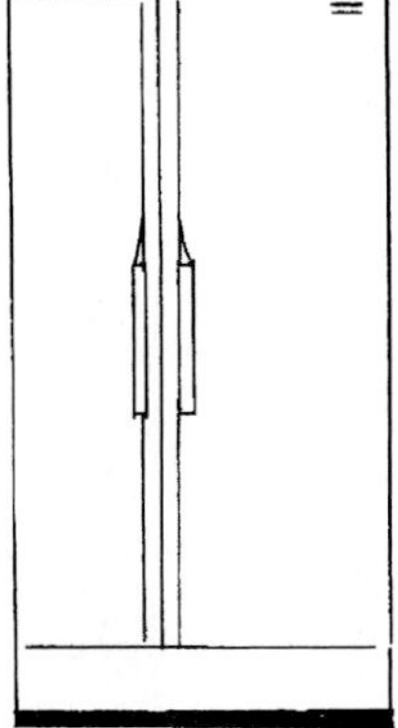

2◆1

Our culture considers a refrigerator a "necessity."

2◆2

Both a product and a functional design, a car is expected to operate reliably. *S. Brainard, Photo.*

2◆3

The "BIG-I" interchange between two state freeways, Albuquerque, NM. Functional design. *S. Brainard, Photo.*

2 ◆ GRAPHIC DESIGN is also functional. It is a *visual* design meant to attract the eye to a product, to advertise or to give information for commercial purposes. Graphic designs include advertisements on TV, magazine displays, or logos that identify businesses or sports teams or sporting events, such as the five colored rings for the Olympics (see Figure 1–1).

2◆4

This logo is an example of graphic design. It advertises the studio and identifies the work of the "restoration of ceramic art and antiquities." *Source: Andy Goldschmidt. Courtesy of Andy Goldschmidt.*

3 ◆ ENVIRONMENTAL DESIGN is also functional, but deals with the OUTDOORS. Such design is inhabited by people or animals and includes public parks and gardens, zoos, and even our private residential landscapes. It also includes areas such as highways or median strips.

Usually the natural environment influences the type of design, as in the American Southwest, where lack of abundant water or rainfall necessitates "xeriscaping" (from the Greek, *xeri*, meaning "no water"). Gardens there will differ greatly from those along coastal areas, like Seattle or San Francisco, where reliable rainfall as well as water vapor creates lush plant growth.

2◆5

"Master Gardeners" created this xeriscaped garden, Sandoval County, NM. *S. Brainard, Photo.*

4 ◆ NONFUNCTIONAL DESIGN encompasses a wide range of decorative arts, including the making of stained or etched glass, jewelry, fine paintings, hand-carved furniture, and so forth. It is usually considered nonfunctional, because it satisfies more of an emotional or aesthetic need than a practical need. A glass in a door frame does not have to be etched. You don't have to have a tie with your shirt. It serves *no functional* purpose.

So why are some things designed to satisfy our aesthetic needs? Do we *need* beauty to survive? It is believed that we humans would not have evolved to our current level if we had not considered these inherent needs. Beauty enhances the quality of our lives. True, beauty is also in the eye of the beholder, and what

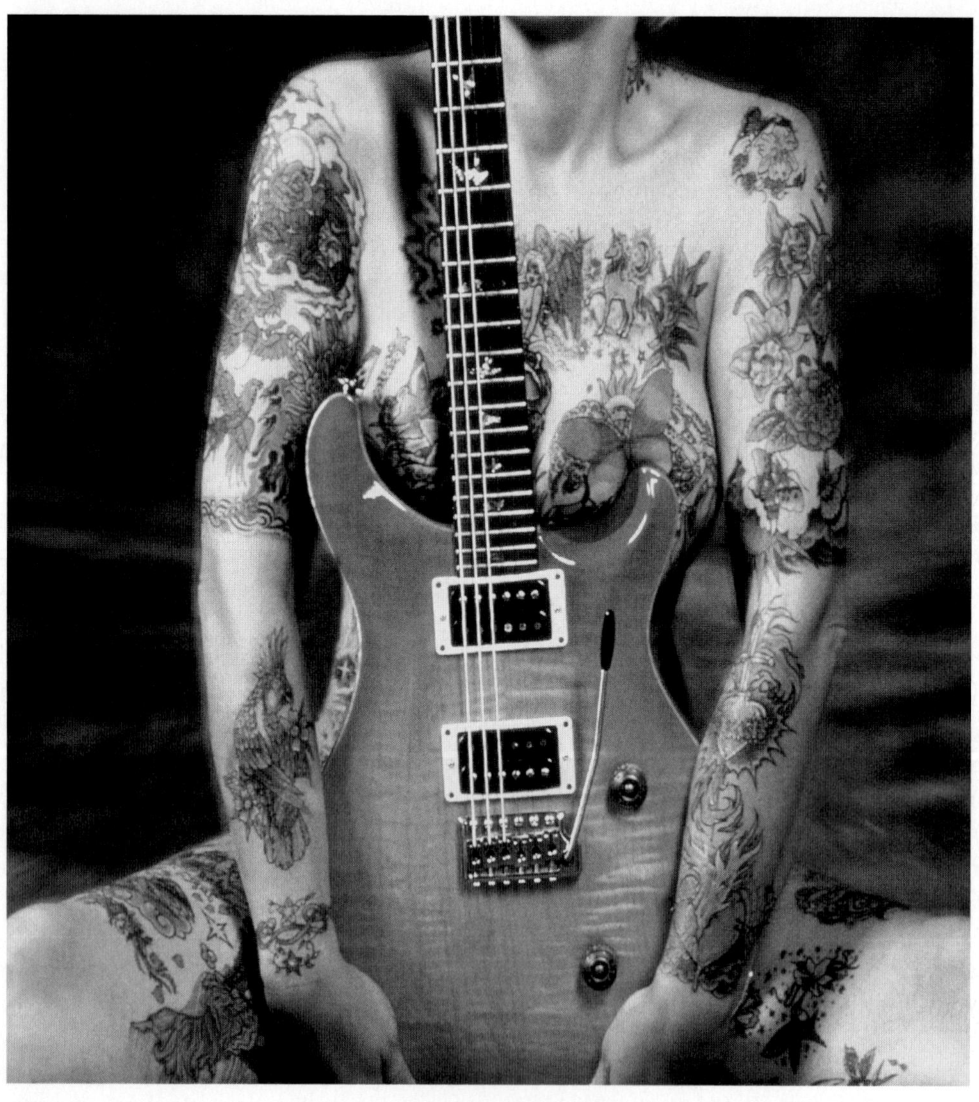

2◆6

Tattoos are a mark of beauty for some people. *SuperStock, Inc.*

beauty is to one culture may not be beauty to another. But since early man, we have decorated ourselves and our environment. This is why some of these designs will overlap—be utilitarian but also attractive, like dinnerware; or be completely nonfunctional but well crafted, like a piece of jewelry. A house may be designed to fit "around" something in the environment—like a long but very narrow lot, or a boulder, or a tree—but will still be a safe, functional yet beautiful structure.

Louis Sullivan, an architect, said, "Form ever follows function," which means that the best design solution will follow the primary need of the problem. So, you see, the form of the building will conform to the problems of the environment, as ski clothing is designed to conform to the physical needs of the athlete as well as climatic conditions of the sport. Have you ever wondered who put the first handle on a vessel and made it become a "cup"? And think about how that cup handle has evolved to become a handle on a "mug." Most cups and mugs are now easier to hold. Did you know that antique cups had small handles for the main reason of propriety only? But some things will just be "pretty," with no reason to be otherwise. . . just because we humans *need* pretty things, like the ribbon bow on a gift.

2◆7

Roger Evans, ENDANGERED SPECIES. Acrylics on wood. 26″ H × 26″ W × 8″ D. An environmental social statement. *Source: Roger Evans. Courtesy: Roger Evans.*

◆ The Role of the Designer

It's important to know the role the designer must play. Designers today, in any field, may have to deal with many issues. One prevalent concern is that someone else may have an idea which the designer must implement, whether it's appealing to his or her creative nature or not. Designers may have their own office with its business practices, or may work for a corporation or collaborate with other designers in industry, marketing, and even manufacturing.

Different kinds of designs have different purposes, as we have discussed. It may be the intention of the fine artist to make social comment through a work of art. This may or may not be a positive, "pretty," or **aesthetic** comment. It is, however, the **content**, and this message was the **intent** of the artist. The viewer may indeed sense that feelings or emotions have been exploited, or even violated. That is, perhaps, exactly what the designer intended. The designer wanted the viewer to be shocked at what he or she saw and felt. If so, the designer was *successful!* Another artist may want the viewer to experience an upbeat mood, a feeling of lightness, warmth, or happiness. The design may be successful in extracting that response from the viewer—or the viewer may not give it a second look.

In the first chapter we talked about the problems of the designer. While the fine artist may face the "problems" of mood or color as his or her objective, the designer of refrigerators has the problem of making the viewer stop, look, and OPEN the refrigerator door, making an evaluation about how this product would work in his or her kitchen. Then the viewer may consider purchasing the product. The role of any functional designer is more restricted than that of the nonfunctional designer. There are very specific messages—or content—directed to often very specific audiences. For instance, adults buy refrigerators, so that design message is not directed to children. Sometimes advertising is directed to children, so that they may coerce parents into buying a product. Sometimes communicating exclusive information is the primary responsibility of the graphic designer. This is the CONTENT of the work. The INTENT is the idea of the problem and its solution.

Designers must also be **original**. A friend told me that when he was in college, his teacher replied when he said he had no new subject to paint, "Yes, everything has been done, but not by you." This is so true. But beginning artists are often intimidated by this concept. So they hope that a "new" subject will appear magically for them to depict. There really are no new images or even new ideas! What may be new, however, are attitudes, tools, or media. Even the basic tenets of design and its components do not change . . . but the terminology (a "tool" of communication) may! So, even though an

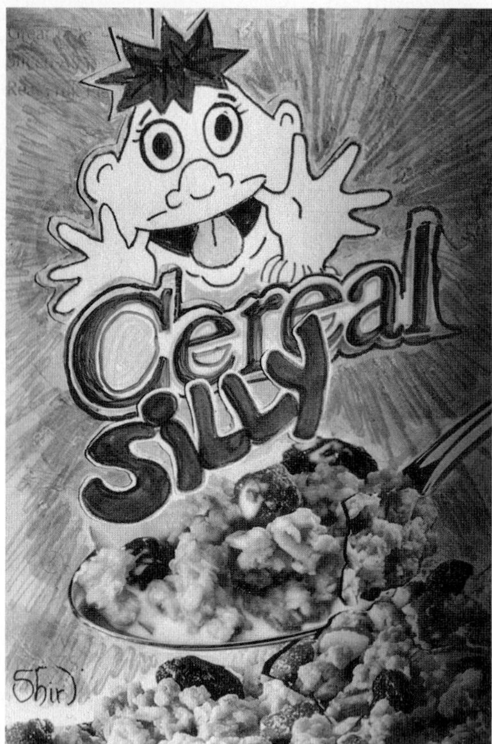

2◆8

A graphic design advertises a product: cereal, geared toward catching a child's eye. *S. Brainard, Photo.*

2◆9

Vebjorn Sand, THE LEONARDO BRIDGE PROJECT, Oslo. Currently a global project to build Leonardo bridges around the world as a tribute to Leonardo da Vinci and as a goodwill art project. This is an example of good design always being good design. *Brickfish Creative Services. Terje Johannsen, Photo.*

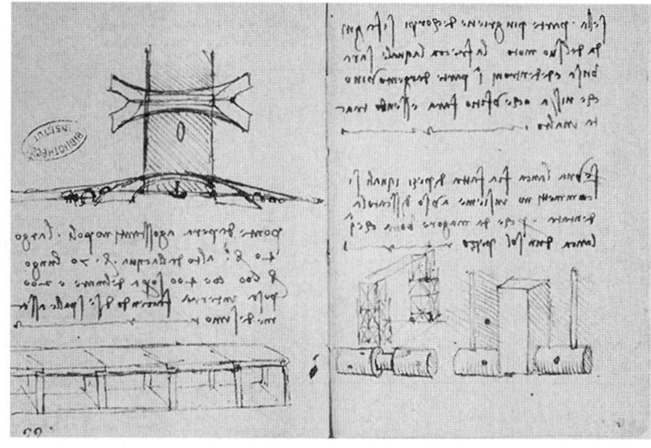

2◆10

Original Leonardo da Vinci drawing with codex of Ponte da Pera a Gosstrantjnopoli bridge. Sketched in 1502 for Sultan Bajazet II of Constantinople. *Brickfish Creative Services.*

artist may be using an image or content that has been used for centuries, the way that idea or image is presented is what is new, creative, and original.

An example of using an "old" design is artist Vebjorn Sand's adaptation of a bridge designed by Leonardo da Vinci. The bridge proves that GOOD design is everlasting.

A version of "redesign," from an article in a contemporary design magazine, tells of a "cooky-shape" contest. YES! Cookies! The winners were a cookie with a slit to enable it to sit on the edge of a cup, and a long cookie to be used as a stirrer—a "dunking" cookie!

Artist Eugène Delacroix said, "What moves men of genius or rather what inspires their work, is not new ideas, but their obsession with the idea that what has already been said is still not enough."

◆ Are You Already a Designer?

Each of us gets up every morning, looks in the mirror, and asks: What am I going to do today? How am I going to function? Am I a businessperson sitting in executive meetings most of the day? Am I a college student going to classes all day? Am I getting married? Will I jog before I do anything else?

What we decide to do will determine our selection of the clothes we will wear. We will also probably choose clothes that we think look well on us, colorwise and stylewise. We dress according to the chosen function for that day, and we try to look our best while doing it. We even think about how our hair should be

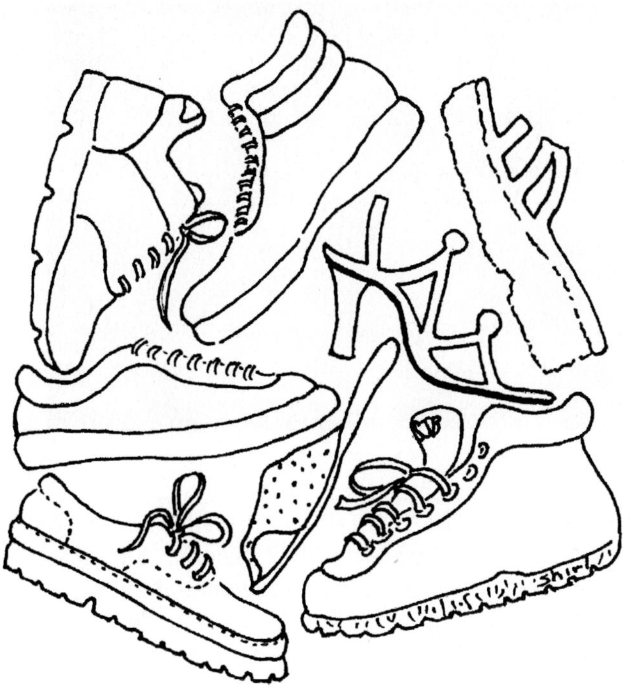

2◆11

Line drawing of shoes. What you will be doing will influence your choice of shoes to wear.

arranged so that it best complements our features. We try, then, to present ourselves as a package, a total, a whole. We are the result of our clothes, hair, makeup, colors, and the like. We design *ourselves* every day. Yes, we are already designers.

You have been introduced to:

DESIGN
COMPOSITION
ELEMENTS
PRINCIPLES

Do you remember the differences among these concepts?

The parts: SPACE SHAPE LINE TEXTURE VALUE COLOR are *composed by using* SPACE DIVISION BALANCE UNITY EMPHASIS = *THE DESIGN!*

On the following pages, you will learn to identify the ELEMENTS in a SPACE and see how the PRINCIPLES have been used to compose or finalize the DESIGN.

◆ Let's Think About Design

Can some areas of design overlap? Can you determine which kind of design are involved in making the following?

Bathtubs	Pots and pans
Earrings	Greeting cards
Chairs	Nuts and bolts
Ships	Tablecloths
Skooters	Plates and cups
Textiles	Wallpaper
Vases	Hair ornaments
Bookcovers	Calendars

Which items can be functional as well as decorative? What one would YOU like to design?

Do you understand how the other design disciplines are connected with your design?

Keyword to remember: SOLUTION.

◆ Review

design ◆ A visual, creative solution to a functional or decorative problem.

composition ◆ The way the parts are arranged.

elements ◆ The parts, or components, of a design.

principles ◆ The ways the parts or elements are used, arranged, or manipulated to create the composition of the design; how to use the parts.

theory ◆ The examination of information that often ends in a plausible assumption or conclusion.

functional design ◆ Design that is utilitarian; necessary.

product design ◆ The design of necessary, functional items in a society.

graphic design ◆ Visual communication design for commercial purposes.

environmental design ◆ Functional designs considering natural surroundings.

nonfunctional design ◆ Design that is decorative or aesthetic. It is not strictly necessary to our functioning as a culture.

aesthetic ◆ A personal response to what we consider beautiful, often based on cultural or educational experience.

content ◆ The message created by the artist. May be functional for consumer purposes; iconography.

intent ◆ What the designer or artist intended with the design; may not have content or message.

original ◆ A primary, inventive form of producing an idea, method, performance, etc.

3

Space

Before we begin looking at the parts, or ELEMENTS, of design, let's remember that we're studying some basic guidelines to help us look at what we see around us with an objective, more informed view.

◆ Kinds of Space

Psychologist Rollo May said: "The first step in the creative process is "Encounter"—the seeing/meeting/perceiving a problem to be solved in a creative way."

SPACE is the first thing we encounter.

Technically, space is not considered an element, but it is so essential to understanding the concept of design that I would like to think of it as a part of our whole.

The page before this one is empty. EMPTY, NOTHING, **negative**, SPACE. **Space** is where we start to solve our design problem. Even if we are designing a **three-dimensional** building or a sculpture with height, width, depth, and volume (or weight), we would use paper for planning our design. That paper is a **two-dimensional** space, having only width and height.

This two-dimensional space is called our **working space**. It gives us an idea where our limitations are—our boundaries. This working space often reflects what is called the **actual space**. The actual space may be a

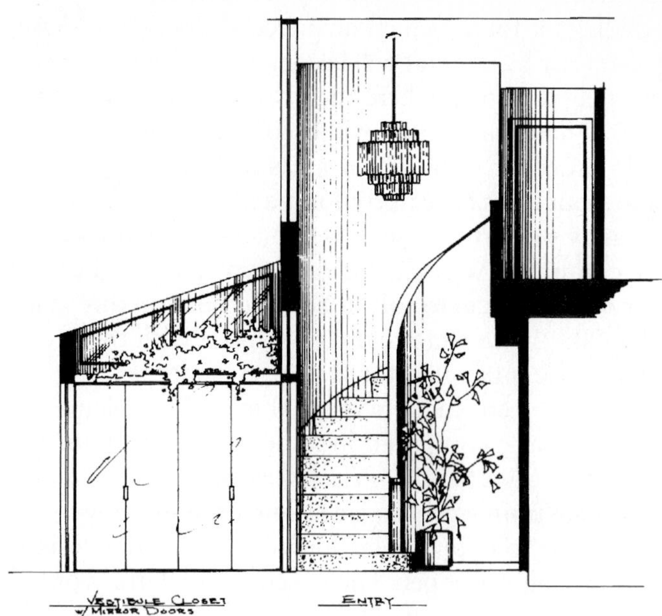

3◆2

The three-dimensional space is planned on a two-dimensional space. *Douglas Richey. A.S.I.D. Interior Design.*

3◆1

Three-dimensional space (a foyer in a private home). *Douglas Richey. A.S.I.D. Interior Design.*

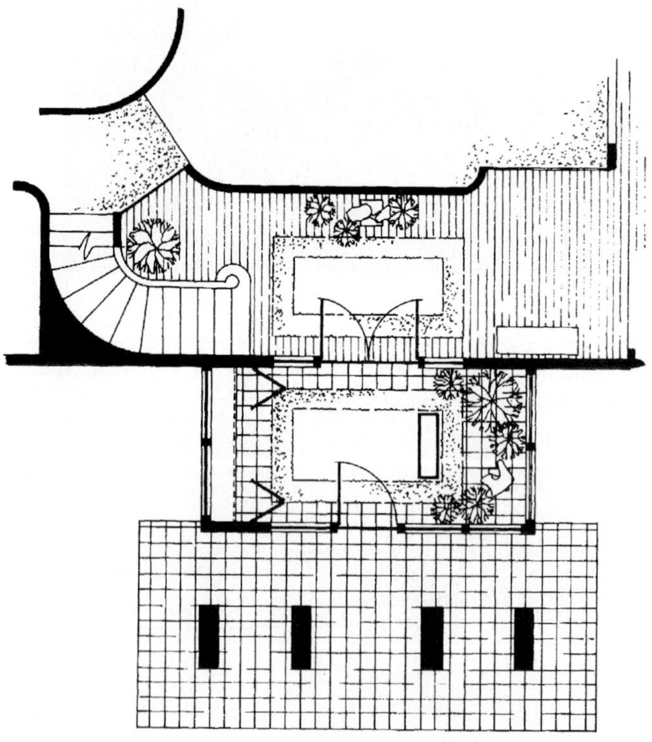

3◆3

Floor design of foyer space (see Fig. 3.2), done on a two-dimensional space. *Courtesy: Douglas Richey, A.S.I.D. Interior Design.*

building lot for which an architect will design a house, several city blocks that will become a city mall, a portion of a magazine page where an advertisement may appear, or an empty canvas that will become a painting.

In order for us to fit our ideas realistically onto this space, our ideas have to conform to the space we have. If we are visual artists—such as painters or printmakers—we can pretty well choose our own space and create our own problem to solve: What do I put on this space now? But if we were that city planner with those city blocks, we must plan for *that* given space.

In this electronic world we think all problems are solved on the computer. In a recent article about the very innovative Santiago Calatrava, who designs sculptural-like train stations, air terminals, and bridges, it's interesting to note that he does all of his initial designs by drawing on paper. The specifications are worked out later on a computer.

The two-dimensional painter, or perhaps the architect will now be confronted by a different kind of space: the ILLUSION of DEPTH or DISTANCE. Because it is something to contend with, we'll be introduced to **pictoral space**: that is, the presentation of a foreground, a middle ground, and a background. We'll look at the most basic and familiar aspects of pictorial space, of "visual" distance. Leonardo da Vinci said that "perspective is the rational law by which experience confirms that all objects transmit their image to the eye in a pyramid of lines."

The usual solution of creating this "visual" distance is by using *linear perspective*, which is not a matter of design as much as a mechanical DRAWING technique. Basic to drawing perspective is the determination of the eye level in relation to the horizon and in relation to the subject. This determination is called the horizon line. A vanishing point is then established:

3◆4

Santiago Calatrava, CUIDAD DE LAS ARTES, Valencia, Spain.
Jose Fuste Raga, Photo. Source: Corbis/Bettmann.

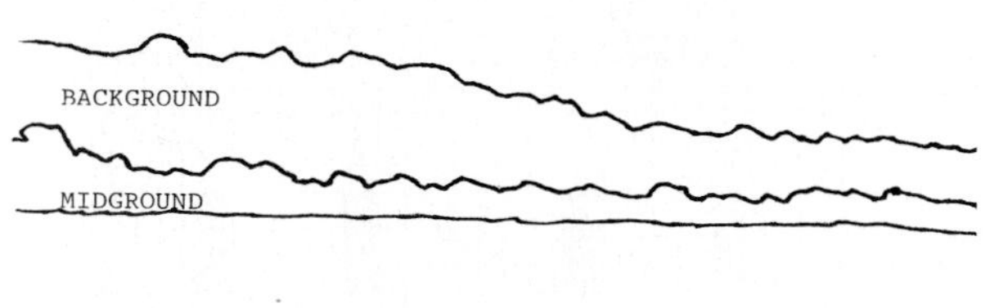

3◆5

Pictorial space (or working space) usually depicts background, middle ground, and foreground, or variations of these three.

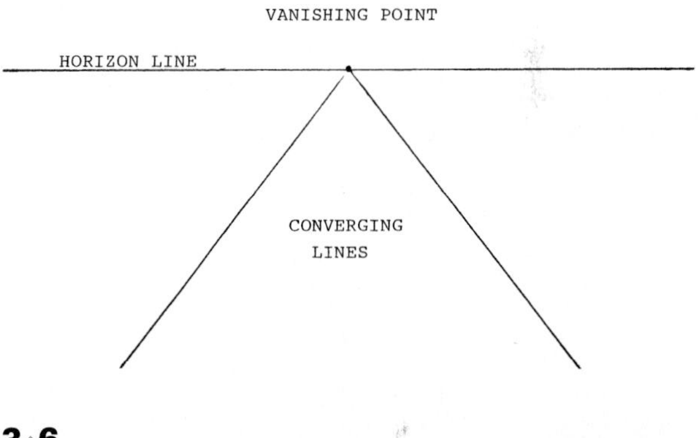

3◆6

Depiction of da Vinci's Pyrapid.

3◆7

Cornfield shows how rows of corn visually converge at a vanishing point. *S. Brainard, Photo.*

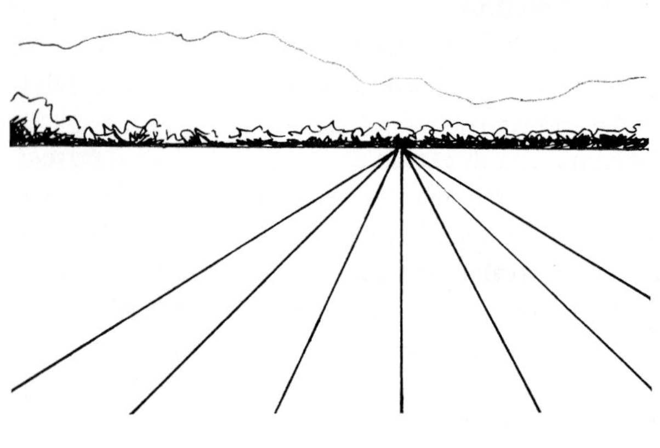

3◆8

Diagram of 3-7.

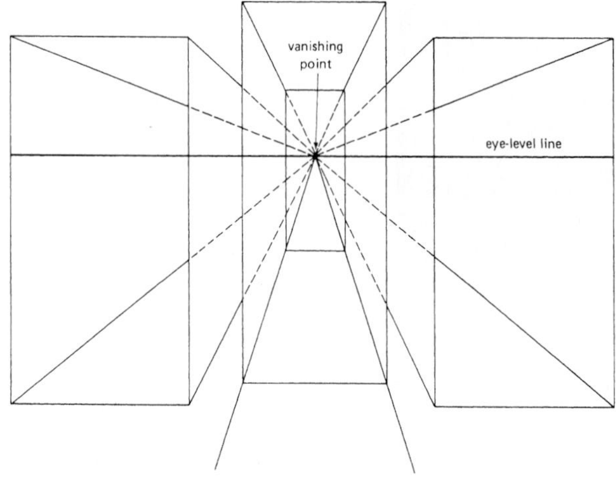

3◆9

Diagram of one-point perspective. All horizontal lines converge at a vanishing point. Verticals remain perpendicular to bottom of space.

This is where subjects APPEAR to disappear into the distance. Depending on the number of subjects and their relative "sides," there MAY be multiple vanishing points.

Other ways to create the feeling of visual distance may include using diminishing sizes, overlapping shapes, changing values (see figure 6–7), or changing uses of color. More about these techniques will be addressed in our discussion of PRINCIPLES. In designing, we help our eyes see what we want them to see.

With some designs we must plan ahead about HOW our actual space may be used. Do we need space for people to move about, such as in a mall or a garden?

3◆10

Dave Wade, A DISTANT THUNDER. Oil. 30″ × 40″. Overlapping and diminishing sizes of the pronghorn give the viewer an illusion of distance. *Source: Dave Wade. A Distant Thunder/Dave Wade.*

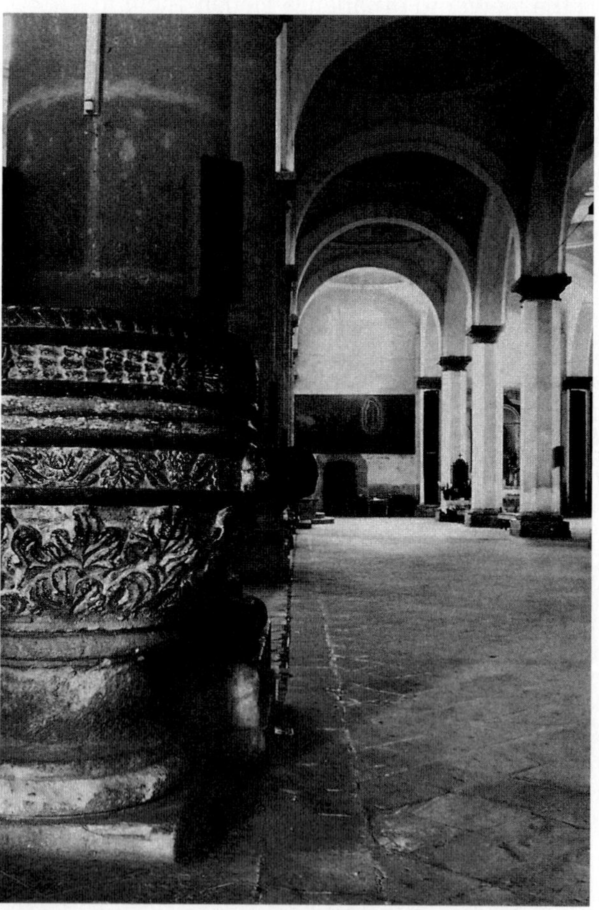

3◆11

Lincoln Draper, BAPTISMAL FONT, CAPILLA REAL, Mexico. Platinum/palladium print. Value changes and almost converging horizontals convey to the viewer the depth of space. *Source: Lincoln Draper.*

Or how about moving around a sculpture? (see 14–A, B, C). Or how about a zoo? Animals must be able to move about in their space. Or consider a kinetic sculpture or a ride in an amusement park? And what about the TIME needed for any of these designs to be realized? Sometimes we must think about the CONCEPT of **time and motion**.

In PLANNING our designs for a given space, we need to know how much space we have . . . and what shape that space is.

The shape and direction of our space is called **format**. If that empty page at the beginning of this chapter is looked at in the usual way, or direction, the book is read, it has a **vertical format**. If you turn the book sideways, this empty page would have a **horizontal format**. Andy Warhol said, "I like painting on a square because you don't have to decide whether it should be longer-longer or shorter-shorter or longer-shorter; it's just a square."

3◆12

Sueellen Ross, TAKING FLIGHT, Mixed media. 12″ × 28″. The horizontal format and empty visual space allows the viewer to experience motion about to happen in a given time. *Courtesy: Sueellen Ross.*

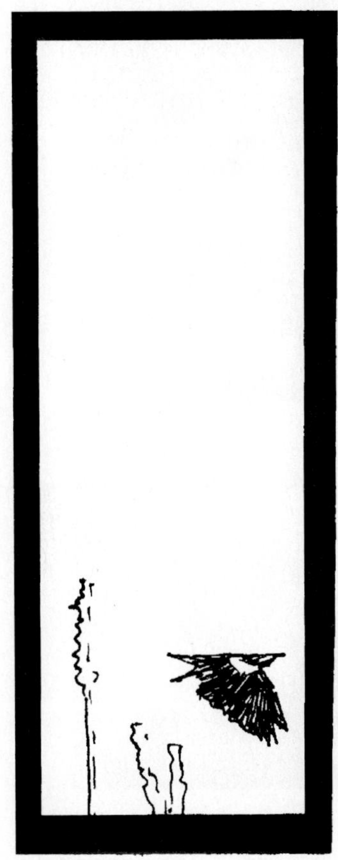

3◆13

Illustration of TAKING FLIGHT by Shirl Brainard. *Source: Shirl Brainard.*

3◆14

Logos for Corrales Bosque Gallery, Corrales, NM. Both horizontal and vertical formats allow this logo to fit various advertisements, letterheads, brochures, etc. *Source: Corrales Bosque Gallery. Courtesy of the Corrales Bosque Gallery.*

3◆15

Logos for Corrales Bosque Gallery, Corrales, NM. Both horizontal and vertical formats allows this logo to fit various advertisements, letterheads, brochures, etc. *Source: Corrales Bosque Gallery. Courtesy of the Corrales Bosque Gallery.*

First, we will talk about two-dimensional design only—that design that is ORGANIZED on a flat surface with only height and width.

◆ Let's Think About Space . . .

Why do we use a two-dimensional surface if we want to design a three-dimensional object?

What does FORMAT have to do with our design?

Is our working space ever our actual space? Give an example.

Why would a given or actual space affect our choice of FORMAT?

Would a "circular" format have a direction?

If you plan the arrangement of your furniture on a piece of paper representing your apartment, what *kind* of space is the paper? What *kind* of space is the apartment—or room, or house?

Can you depict a full three-dimensional scene on paper?

Does there ALWAYS have to be a horizon line in a painting?

Can you imagine the ACTUAL space for a zoo? Can you draw it?

Keyword to remember: SPACE—an empty (NEGATIVE) area where our design will fit.

◆ What Can You Do with Space?

What do you think your answer should be?

◆ Can You Identify . . .?

WHERE the vanishing point may be in figures 4–13, 12–8, and 14–1? *If* figure 3–12 had been on a format like figure 3–13, *how* would that have affected the viewer?

Can you identify these formats by direction or shape name?

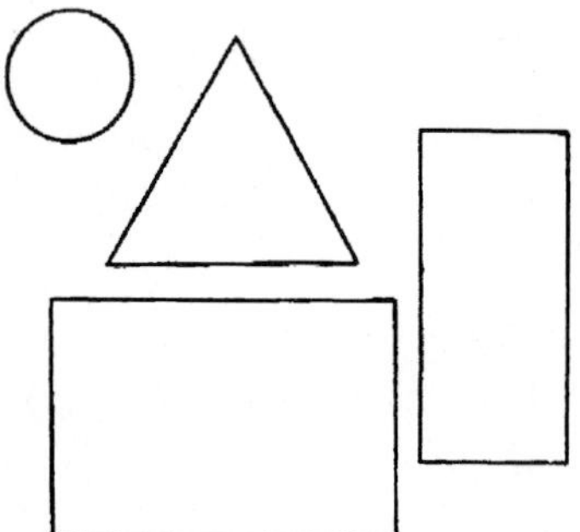

3◆16

Various formats.

◆ Review

space ◆ An empty, negative area where our design will fit.

negative space ◆ Completely empty actual or working space.

two-dimensional space ◆ A flat space; having only height and width.

three-dimensional space ◆ Space having height, width, and depth.

actual space ◆ The real space we have to fill with our design. This space has definite dimensions.

working space ◆ The space that reflects the actual space. The two *may*, but not always, be the same space. This is the space we use to solve our design problem.

format ◆ The shape and direction of our working or actual space. MAY BE HORIZONTAL, VERTICAL, ROUND, or the like.

pictorial space ◆ The illusion of depth or distance on a two-dimensional space.

perspective ◆ The drawing technique of creating the receding, diminishing, or vanishing objects of a three-dimensional nature on a two-dimensional surface.

time and motion ◆ In design, the planning for the ACTUAL space to be used in bodily movement, OR the anticipated illusion of movement in time.

4

Line

- What Is a Line?
- Kinds of Line
- Let's Think About Line . . .
- What Can You Do with Lines?
- Can You Identify . . .?
- Review

THIS IS A LINE

THIS IS A LINEAR SHAPE

4•1

Line and pencil.

What Is a Line?

How do we describe a line? How does it differ from a shape? Can a line be a shape? Can a shape be a line? A **line** is a mark that is longer than it is wide and is seen because it differs in value or color from its background.

As small children, the first thing we draw on a piece of paper with a marker (or crayon, or pencil) is usually a squiggly line. What we experience then is the magic of seeing "something" appear on the paper.

A line is not usually thought of as a shape, but a shape can appear **linear.**

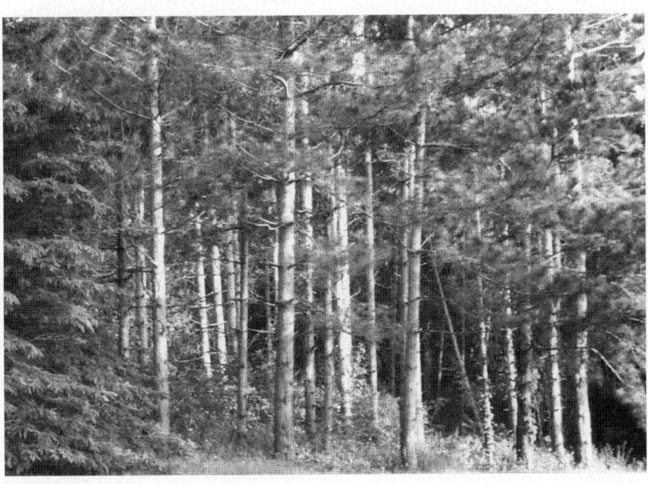

4•2

An example of linear shapes. *S. Brainard, Photo.*

On the following pages, you will see different things that lines can do for us. Again, we use these all the time, but seldom do we think that it is a line being used.

Kinds of Line

LINE AS CONTOUR. We know that in drawing, line can create shapes. As children we probably had our first coloring books to scribble in and to help us begin identifying objects. The coloring books had simple objects drawn by using simple lines—outlines. That same "outline" is called a **contour line,** or a line that defines the outer edges of shapes. We use it constantly to begin our drawings.

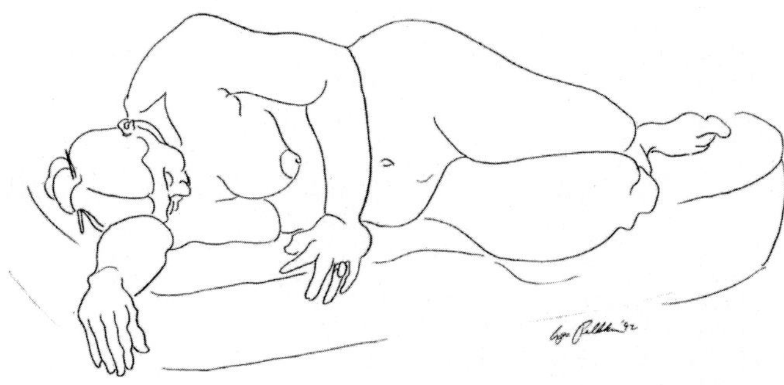

4•3

Wesley Pulkka, RECLINING NUDE. Pencil drawing.
Courtesy: Wesley Pulkka.

But, to quote again from Robert Henri, "In considering lines as a means of drawing, it is well to remember that the line practically does not exist in nature."

Contour lines are also often used in map design to show water depths or land contours—different elevations and shapes of land masses—as well as in architectural renderings and interior drawings to show the shape, size, and position of structures.

LINE AS A SYMBOL. How often when you letter or write do you *think* that you are only using lines? Yet the letter A is made of lines and yet acts as a symbol of communication. It is a symbol of the first letter in our alphabet. Our numbers, too, are made up of a combination of lines to create symbols that mean something to us.

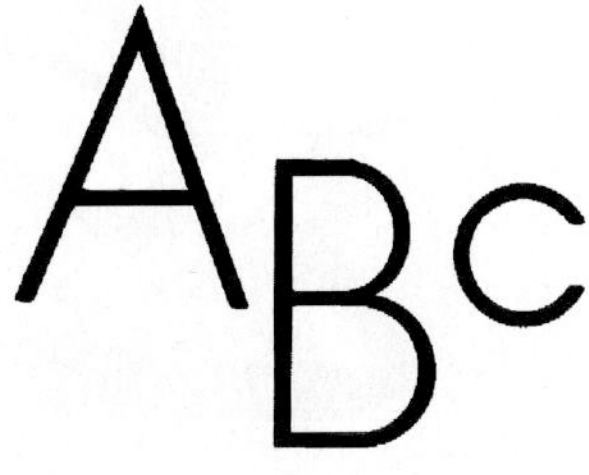

4•4

Our alphabet is made up of lines—they become symbols.

4◆5

Diana Stetson, SUMI INK ON ARCHES 90# HOTPRESS. Calligraphic symbols from the Japanese, Chinese, Sanskrit, and Eskimo languages.

Lines may be **symbolic** in other ways. The manner in which lines or linear shapes are positioned may portray certain sentiments or attitudes. Lines or figures lined up in a straight vertical way give us the feeling of alertness, dignity, even rigidity. Lines used in a horizontal way may make us feel more restful; a feeling of repose or quietude.

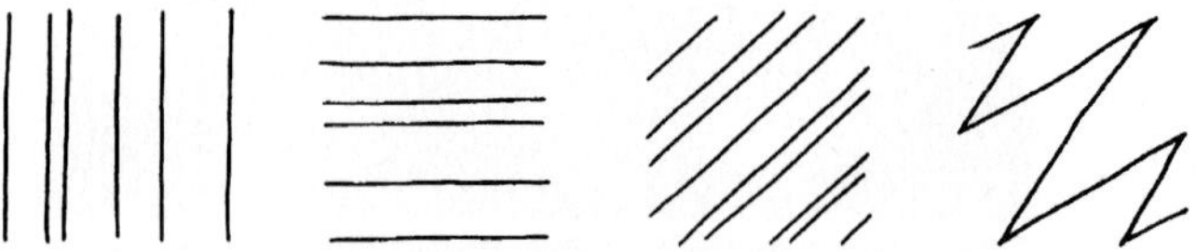

4◆6

Symbolic lines that suggest motion.

Lines on a diagonal create a compromise between rigidity and repose—becoming more interesting than either the horizontal or the vertical. They are relaxed, but not lazy.

But POW! Diagonal lines can also be exciting, dangerous, and even sometimes confusing. These are dynamic but usually too forceful to use in abundance.

LINE AS DIRECTION. Linear shapes are familiar to those of us who drive. What do we know when we see this road sign (see figure 4–7)?

Again, it is a symbol, but one of direction and information. Lines can establish a sense of **direction** or

4◆7

Road sign. *S. Brainard, photo.*

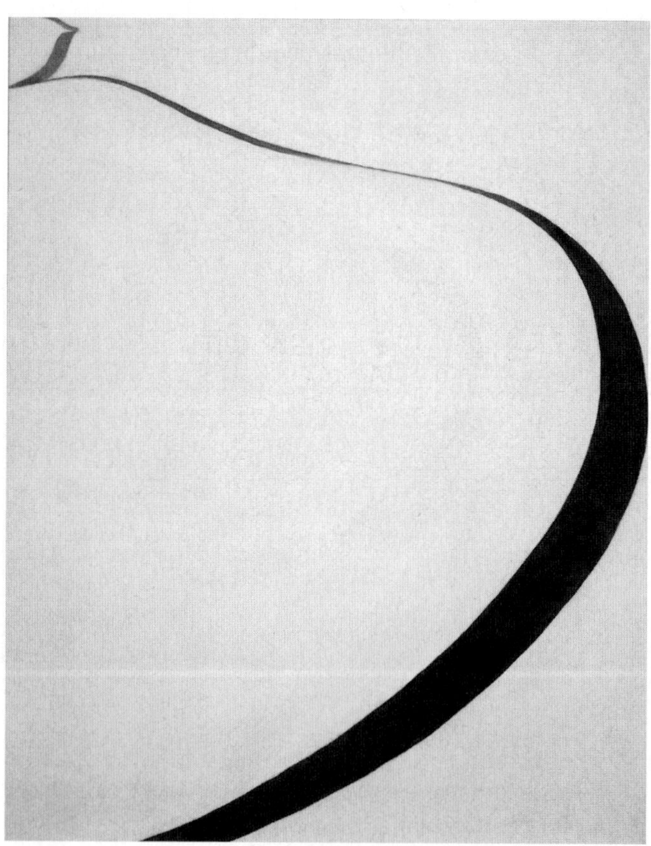

4◆8

Georgia O'Keeffe, WINTER ROAD I. 1963. Oil on canvas, 22″ × 18″; framed, 22 3/16″ × 18 1/4″. National Gallery of Art, Washington, DC. This painting of a road in winter looks like a line and also like the road sign. *Gift of The Georgia O'Keeffe Foundation. Copyright 1998 The Georgia O'Keeffe Foundation/Artists Rights Society (ARS), New York.*

movement within the given space. Think of a kite up in the sky with its tail weaving back and forth in the wind: Our eye sees movement. Think of a fence meandering across a field: Our eye *senses* movement.

LINE AS A BOUNDARY. A line also acts as a **boundary.** Any edges of two shapes that abut or share the same edge can create a visual line. And that line is, therefore, a boundary line separating the two shapes. Think of a fence separating two properties. If we could see it from the air, we would perceive a line instead of the fence itself.

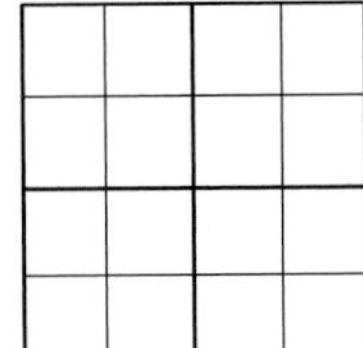

4 ◆ 9

A grid is an example of lines dividing a space into smaller spaces.

4 ◆ 10

Rows of plantings, seen from the air, divide the space of the vineyards. *Max Aguilera-Hellweg, Photo, CHALONE VINEYARDS, Los Angeles, CA.*

IMPLIED LINE. Implied lines are lines that do not physically exist but are visually connected by the eye. An example is this broken line: ---------------

The vacant or negative areas are still perceived by the eye and mind as filled in to complete the line—the implication of a total continual line

4 ◆ 11

Geese in flight create an implied V-shaped line. *S. Brainard, Photo.*

LINE AS VALUE. When we draw black lines close together on a white surface, we are making a darker area relative to the white negative area. Fewer lines would give the visual illusion of a medium-shaded area, and we could control our "shading" process with the number of lines used.

LINE AS TEXTURE. If you pull out one of the hairs from your own head and hold it taut between the

4 ◆ 12

Claudia Nice, TIMBER WOLF. Ink drawing. The play of lines creates the texture of the wolf's coat. *Courtesy: Claudia Nice.*

thumb and forefinger of each hand, you see a line. Put millions of these lines together and you have hair—hair that can be kinky, curly, straight, permed, and going in many directions. It has the sensation of something you can touch or feel. To recreate this feeling of texture with line, you would have to study the hair or lines and watch the many different directions the hairs take individually. Many kinds of textures can be reproduced by the use of line.

◆ Let's Think About Line . . .

When was the last time you used a line—in *any* way? What was it?

Did you create a boundary?
Did you follow a street sign?
Did you divide some kind of space?
Did you fly a kite?
Did you write or add figures manually?
Did you draw in the sand with a stick?
Did you make some shapes?
Did you plan a house?
Did you sew (either with a machine or by hand)?
What else did you do?

Keyword to remember: LINE—a long, thin mark, or images that make you *think* of long, thin marks!

◆ What Can You Do with Lines?

You can make lines . . .

THIN
THICK
LONG
SHORT
VERTICAL
HORIZONTAL
CLOSE TOGETHER
FAR APART
DIAGONAL
ZIGZAG
CURVE . . . AND WHAT ELSE?

You can use lines to . . .

DIVIDE SPACE
MAKE SHAPES
MAKE SYMBOLS
DIRECT THE EYE
CREATE VALUE
CREATE TEXTURE
AND . . .?
LINE IS IMPORTANT!

◆ Can You Identify . . .?

Lines?
Linear shapes?
How this photo makes you feel?
WHY?

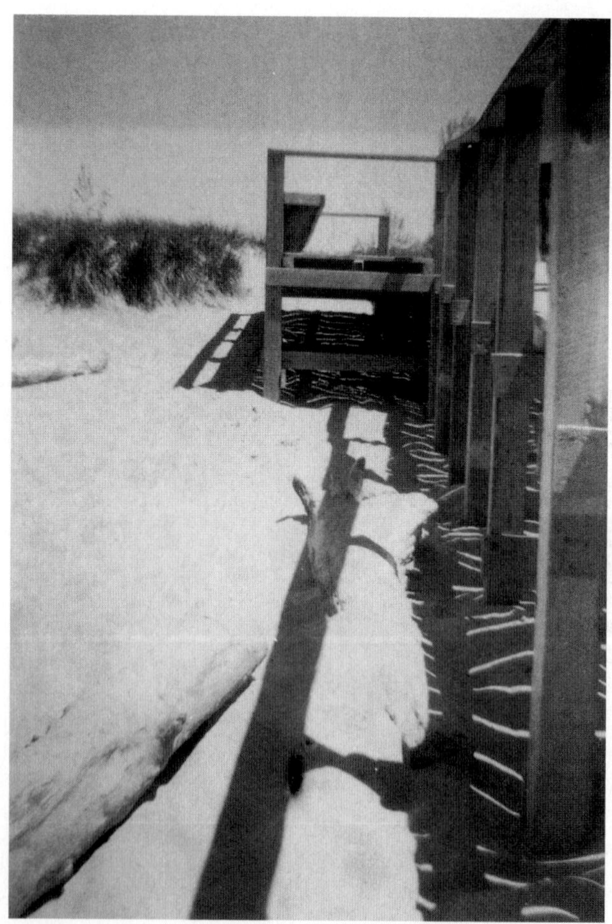

4◆13

Holland Beach boardwalk. *S. Brainard, Photo.*

◆ Review

line ◆ A mark longer than it is wide and is seen because it differs in value, color, or texture from its background.

linear shape ◆ An elongated shape that reminds us of line.

contour line ◆ A line depicting the outer edge of a shape or group of shapes.

symbolic line ◆ A line or combination of lines that stands for, or reminds us of, something within our realm of knowledge.

directional line ◆ A line or lines that direct our visual attention in a specific direction.

boundary line ◆ A line that confines our visual attention. It may serve to separate areas.

implied line ◆ A perceived continuation of images or symbols that implies a line.

5

Shape

- What Is a Shape?
- Kinds of Shapes
- Positive and Negative Shapes
- Let's Think About Shapes . . .
- What Can You Do with Shapes?
- Can You Identify . . .?
- Review

What Is a Shape?

A **shape** is an image in space. This shape may or may not be recognizable. Babies see an undefined blur that changes to a face with color and with a voice that is eventually recognized as a sound that goes with this "shape."

Later, when we are older, someone gives us a crayon and some paper, and with lines we start to draw our small world (remember those lines in the last chapter?). We hook the lines together and they turn into shapes that become someone who is important to us—Mama, the cat, or "Jimmy" (an imaginary friend). To us, the shape we put on our paper is who or what we say it is. The *drawing* of Mama, however, is what becomes the subject of the day, not Mama herself. The family is proud of the drawing, and *voilá!* An artist is born! It does not matter that it is not an exact duplication, or even a near representation, of Mama; it is the essence or the symbolism that has become important.

It is hard for us to accept this symbolism. Why has Picasso's work been so difficult for people to accept? Because it is ugly? We have trouble with Picasso because his faces do not seem like faces we *know.* As we grow older, realistic or representational shapes seem to become more important to us than symbolism.

There is a paradox here.

As we enter the years of curiosity, experimentation, and rebellion, why don't we reject the *images* that are familiar to us in the same way we turn against other familiar things, like our dress, our behavior, or the food we eat? Why don't we experiment with images the way we experiment with other things in our new grown-up life? Instead, we cling to the traditional, to the familiar shapes of "things" we *know.*

"*Things*" are used as sources for kinds of shapes, and the original meaning of the "thing" is no longer as important as the found shape.

Kinds of Shapes

This is a "rose." We know it as a "thing," an object we all recognize. We are now going to try and think of this rose as a **shape,** a source for other shapes, shapes in space.

The rose (an identifying name only) can be the source for many kinds of shapes that the design world puts into categories. One such category is **natural shapes**—shapes as we know them in their natural state, or from the world of nature. These are familiar to us. In other references, you may see them called organic or biomorphic shapes.

These shapes can be altered, simplified, distorted, enlarged, half-hidden . . . anything that changes them . . . and their subject may still be recognized; the

5•1

Kristyn Brainard, GRANDMA & ME. Colored ink drawing. (The author is on the right.)

5•2

"Chicago Peace" rose. Photo. A rose is a natural shape—or a shape found in nature. *Photographer: Goodman. Source: Jackson & Perkins. Photograph courtesy of Jackson & Perkins.*

5◆3

Artist unknown. Chinese paper cutting. This rose is seen as a rose but is not "realistic." It is slightly abstract. *Collection of the author.*

5◆4

Artist Unknown. The "mola" is an art form of reverse appliqué indigenous to the Cuna Indians of San Blas, Panama. This abstract shape of a bird uses geometric shapes. *Courtesy of S. Brainard.*

5◆5

Inlaid jewelry using geometric shapes. *Judith Young/Alan Edgar Jewelry. Source: Judith Young. Courtesy of Edgar/Young Jewelry.*

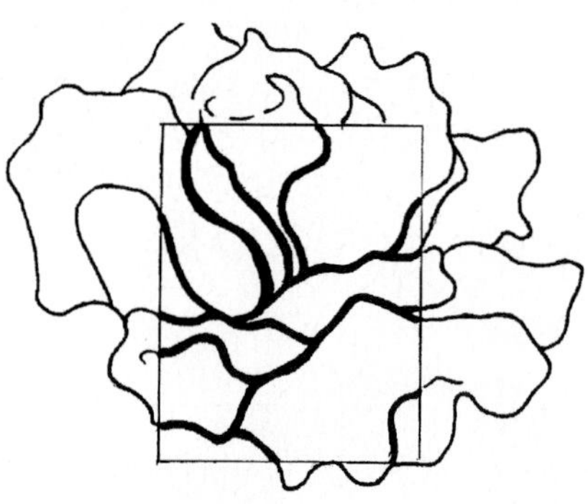

5◆6

The line drawing represents the rose. The portion shown is later enlarged.

essence remains. They are then called **abstracts,** since they are "abstracted," or "pulled from" the original.

Pablo Picasso said "There is no abstract art—you must always start with something."

Sometimes circles, squares, and triangles are used to create an abstraction of a natural shape. These are called **geometric** shapes and are usually thought of as man-made shapes, being more precise and even than shapes in nature. Buildings, for instance, are usually designed from geometric shapes.

If we were to enlarge just one portion of our original shape, it would no longer be recognizable as a rose—just some weird shapes. These new shapes are often called invented, found, or **nonobjective** shapes. There is NO object, no symbol for us to identify: They are just shapes. Enlarging is not the only way to create nonobjective shapes. If you spill a liquid, for instance, it makes a shape. You cannot reproduce that shape by spilling that liquid again, but it could be copied and used as a shape.

Knowing the names or titles of different shapes helps you verbalize more precisely about your own work and makes you sound professional. It will help you to understand an author when you read; to understand other related material, such as videos, or lectures; or, when you visit an art gallery or museum, to identify kinds of art as abstract, nonrepresentational, or representational because of the shapes used.

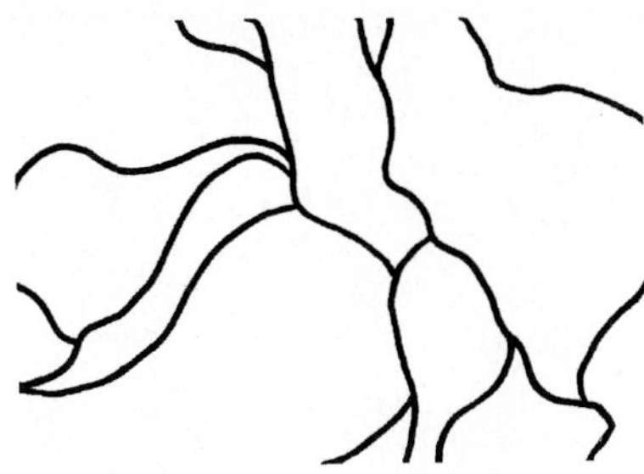

5◆7

The enlarged portion (turned in another direction) produces shapes that do not represent any object or shape. They have become nonobjective shapes.

5◆8

Example of a nonobjective shape. *Source: S. Brainard.*

◆ Positive and Negative Shapes

When we place any of the shapes we have been discussing in our empty space (NEGATIVE SPACE), we call it a **positive shape.** The space left over is still negative space—there is nothing there.

If we place at least two shapes together in this space, touching or almost touching, we create an illusion of a third (or more) shape(s). This illusionary shape is called a **negative shape.** This is more often called the POSITIVE and the NEGATIVE GROUND.

Below is an example of the use of positive and negative shapes. What do you see? Do you see the faces or

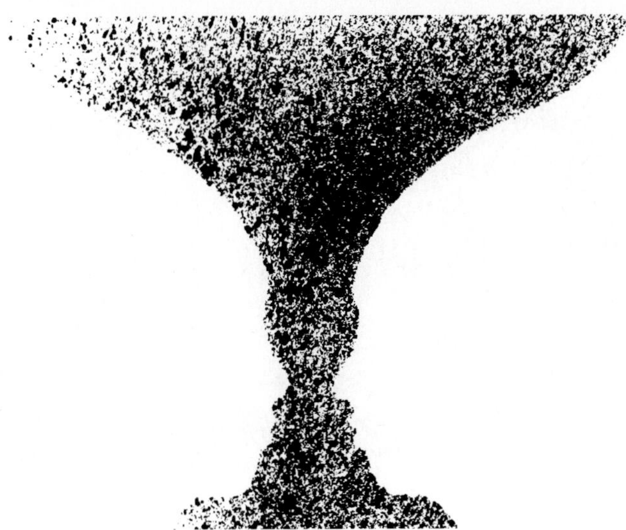

5◆9

What do you see?
Two faces? A vase?
Which is the negative?
Which is the positive?

do you see the vase? Which is the one you are supposed to see? Is there an answer to this question?

Betty Edwards said in *Drawing on the Right Side of the Brain,* "Usually it takes years of training to convince students, in the way experienced artists are convinced, that the negative spaces, bounded by the format, require the same degree of attention and care that the positive forms require."

◆ Let's Think About Shapes . . .

Produce all four kinds of shapes (natural, geometric, abstract, and nonobjective) from one source.

What kind of shape was the original source you used?

Do you really think abstracted shapes are new to man?

What kinds of shapes do you like best?

Do you know WHY you like those shapes?

What are ways you might produce nonobjective shapes?

Would the choice of your shape influence your choice of a format?

WHY?

KEYWORD to remember: SHAPE (an image)—

GEOMETRIC SHAPE
NATURAL SHAPE
ABSTRACT SHAPE
NONOBJECTIVE SHAPE

◆ What Can You Do with Shapes?

You can make them . . .

CUT
TORN
BIG
LITTLE
LONG
SHORT
FAT AND THIN
TOUCH OTHER SHAPES
ALMOST TOUCH
OVERLAP . . . and take them out of the space

and bring them back in to make them . . .

SHARE AN EDGE WITH ANOTHER SHAPE
. . . OR . . .
SHARE AN EDGE WITH THE SPACE
DARK OR LIGHT
RIGID
RELAXED
OPPOSE ONE ANOTHER
PROGRESS ACROSS THE SPACE
ANYTHING YOU WANT . . . as long as they WORK for you!

◆ Can You Identify . . .?

Look at the following abstract figures. Which one do you think was earliest? Which was the most recent? Is the abstract figure new? Can you match the figures with the dates?

A—2500–2000 B.C.	F—Unknown
B—1949	G—680 B.C.
C—Unknown	H—1907
D—25,000–20,000 B.C.	I—2700–2600 B.C.
E—1900s	

(Answers below)
Author/Author's Disclaimer: These line drawings that represent historical art works are for educational purposes only and are not to be considered as "copies" of original art.

Answers
1–B 1949 "La Desesperanto" (Joan Miro)
2–I 2700–2600 B.C. Head of God Abu Tell Asmer
3–F ? Papuan Spirit Figure
4–A 2500–2000 B.C. Cycladic Idol
5–G 680 B.C. Mantiklos "Apollo"
6–E 1900s Folk Art—Michigan
7–C ? Native American (Barrier Canyon, Utah)
8–H 1907 "Les Demoiselles d'Avignon" (Picasso)
9–D 25,000–20,000 B.C. Venus of Willendorf

5◆10

A game.

◆ Review

shape ◆ An image in space.

natural shape ◆ Shapes found in nature; sometimes called organic.

abstract shape ◆ A recognizable image that has been distorted or simplified.

geometric shape ◆ Usually man-made shapes that are precise, exact: triangles, squares, circles, rectangles, and the like.

nonobjective shape ◆ A shape often made accidentally or invented from another source. There is no recognizable object involved.

positive shape ◆ A shape or line placed in a negative or empty space.

negative shape ◆ The implied shape produced after two or more positive shapes are placed in a negative (empty) space.

6

Value

- **What Is Value?**
- **A Matter of Relativity**
- **Let's Think About Values . . .**
- **What Can You Do with Values?**
- **Can You Identify . . .?**
- **Review**

◆ What Is Value?

Value is the range of possible lightness or darkness that can be achieved with the particular **medium** you are employing in your design. It is a surface quality of a shape or line, such as a black line or a black shape. The range is usually thought of as the extremes from black to white and the grays in between. This means that the range available to print a photograph may reach only 18 or 19 values, or possibilities, whereas with mixing pigments for a painting, or inks for printing, it may reach a considerably higher range.

When we draw with a black pencil, we usually add what is generally called "shading," or medium to dark strokes, to give us the required darks and lights that we see. Just as a camera using black and white film, we are making a "value" interpretation of our colored world.

Most students have problems with values, especially in drawing. The reason for this is the relativity of values and the difficulty of learning to see the subtleties of values. Just about every design book has a value chart—and so do we. We explain that the values are relative. But what does "relative" mean?

◆ A Matter of Relativity

Relative means "in comparison to." Next to one of you, I may look short. Next to someone else I may appear tall.

Let's look at the VALUE CHART. When the strip that is medium gray is on the darkest value, the gray looks light, but not as light as white. On the lightest value, it looks quite dark. The gray strip hasn't changed, only its position *compared to other values*. Sometimes when we are drawing, there is no real black. A mid-value or even a medium-dark value may be the darkest, and all other values must relate to this as being the darkest. Once we have trained our eye to these subtle differences, or compared one dark to another, our drawings and

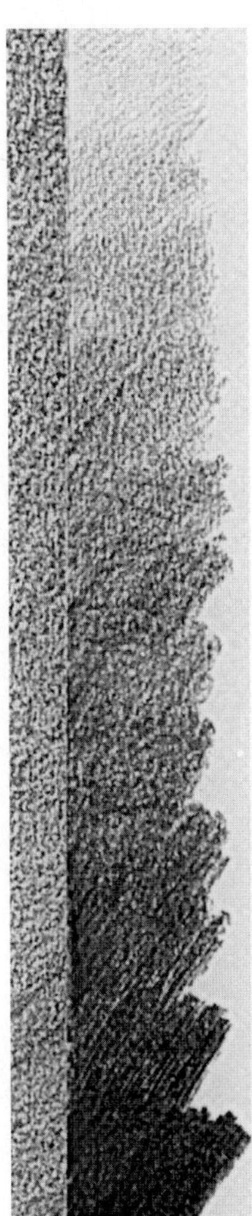

6◆1

This value scale has been rendered in pencil. It indicates the values that can be achieved with this medium. The gray strip to the left shows relative contrast. *Source: S. Brainard.*

6◆2

TEEN GIRL SITTING ON A CHAIR. People are in living color. In a black and white photo, you can see the many values from the darkest dark to the lightest light.
Photographer: Camille Tokerud. Source: Photo Researchers, Inc.

other design works improve. We need to be aware of value **contrasts** and how to use them. White and black alone give you the extreme "highest contrast." Several values added from each direction create what is called a "medium contrast" while values close to one another give us a "low contrast"—or not much contrast. They may all be used and may play an essential role in our design, for they accentuate differences and, through contrasts, make our design more arresting to the viewer.

The most common use of values is to achieve the effect of volume, or the visual effect of the third dimension: that of depth and weight on a two-dimensional surface. Values are important in the creation of a three-dimensional effect, because without "shading" to round out our shapes, they would appear flat. But often we use flat shapes and *want* them to be flat. We would still use contrast in the "push-and-pull" of one value against another to distinguish one shape from another. When we are using gradual value changes to create this three-dimensional effect, it is crucial not to jump quickly from one value to another. This use of values is more prevalent in the fine art field of design than in the field of functional design.

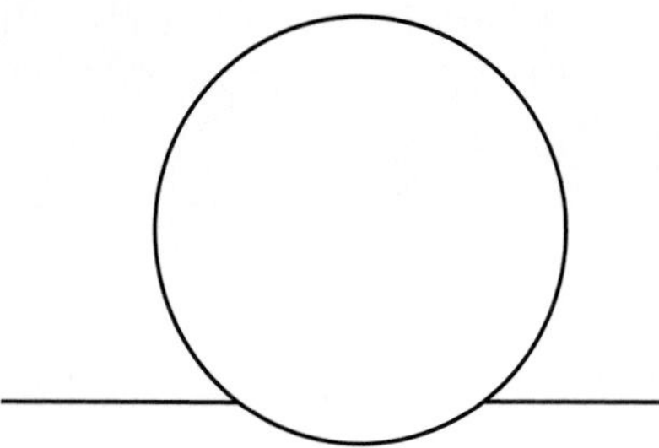

6◆3

A circle with no values or "shading" looks flat, having no volume or depth.

6◆4

The same circle with added values makes the round shape appear as a sphere.

6◆5

Kalon Baughan, MALE FIGURE. 1987. Drawing. Graphite on paper. 18″ × 24″. Adding values gives the head a three-dimensional effect. *Courtesy: Kalon Baughan.*

The portrayal of values plays an important role in evoking certain responses from the viewer. We may want the viewer to perceive a special effect, like an emotional response, by the use of somber, darker values for the shadowy sides of life; or light values for the upbeat parts of our lives. Sometimes we may contrast these values to create emphasis, or to feature something else in the design that needs the attention.

What often seems like a contradiction in the portrayal of representational still lifes or landscape drawing and painting is the special effect of depth or distance. We use darker values to create *depth* but lighter values to create *distance*. Is there a difference? Depending on the subject matter involved, and recognizing particular shapes in the foreground, a dark value can create the perception of depth, or a "measurable distance down or into" a space. In other words, we can make a shape on a surface look as though it goes *into* and *beyond* that surface—or into a "hole"! Conversely, lighter values used in the background of a landscape gives the viewer the sense of

6◆6

Dark values can indicate depth. *S. Brainard, Photo.*

6◆7

Light values can achieve the visual effect of distance. *S. Brainard, Photo.*

greater space in terms of mileage. Darker values are usually used in the foreground to sharpen the details of the foreground.

The use of values is often misunderstood by the novice student. Values are the most intimidating of the elements. In beginning drawing, the student tends to make drawings too light, while the beginning painter usually uses colors that are too dark!

◆ Let's Think About Values . . .

Do values add interest?

Do value contrasts apply only to representational work?

Do you know how to evaluate one value against another?

Can you evaluate value differences?

What would happen if very close values were used in one design?

KEYWORD to remember: VALUE

◆ What Can You Do with Values?

Values Can Be Used:

TO CREATE A CONTRAST

TO ADD INTEREST

TO CREATE A VISUAL FEELING OF VOLUME, OR A THREE-DIMENSIONAL EFFECT

TO CREATE VISUAL DEPTH

TO CREATE VISUAL DISTANCE

TO CREATE EMPHASIS

TO CREATE A MOOD

◆ Can You Identify . . .?

The differences in value between the two photos of bulbs in figures 6–8 and 6–9?

Why does the difference in value make a difference in the way you see the photos? What would you do to correct either one?

6◆8 and 6◆9

BULBS. *S. Brainard, Photos.*

◆ Review

value ◆ The range of possible lightness or darkness within a given medium.

Medium ◆ The kind of material(s) one is working with, such as pigments, film, fabric, pencil, steel, and the like. (plural: media)

Relativity ◆ The degree of comparison of one thing to another. How does *a* compare to *b;* then what is the comparison of *a* to *c*?

Contrast ◆ The result of comparing one thing to another and seeing the difference.

7

Texture

- **What Is Texture?**
- **Rough or Smooth?**
- **Can You Identify . . .?**
- **Let's Think About Texture . . .**
- **What Can You Do with These Textures?**
- **Review**

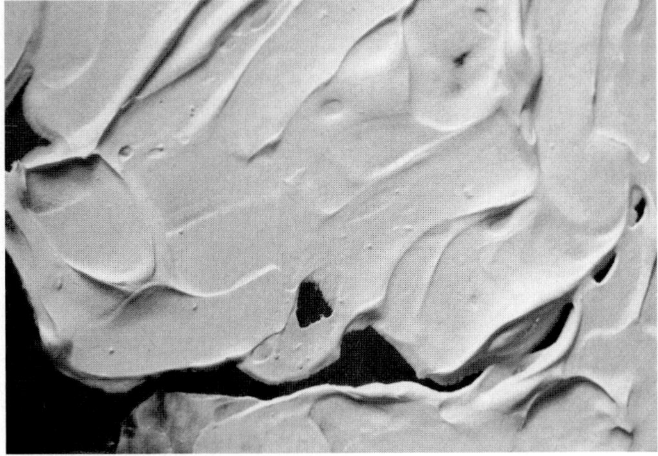

Figure 7◆1

An example of thick paint on a painting. Called "impasto," it is real texture. *Source: S. Brainard.*

◆ What Is Texture?

Texture is the easiest element to describe because it is a visual surface quality. We are familiar with real texture, or a TACTILE surface, meaning "that which can be felt." The element TEXTURE on a two-dimensional surface is usually a **simulated** tactile surface, mentally interpreted as tactile. However, many designs have a real surface texture, which may have been created by the medium or technique used, such as "impasto" painting (using paint thickly, perhaps laid on with a palette knife); or a "collage" (a construction of various materials glued on a two-dimensional surface). Both are examples of work having real texture. Our definition of TEXTURE is "having a simulated or real tactile surface."

Look back at figure 4–12. Can you feel the coat of the animal?

◆ Rough or Smooth?

Texture is often thought of as something that is rough only, or has a structural feeling. But a smooth surface is also a texture.

Think of all the rough surfaces you can feel. Think of the smooth ones you can feel. What kind of textural sensations do you have when you eat? What can you think of as rough-against-smooth textural contrast?

Textures can be created in many ways, the most common ways are by using contrasting lines or values, directional lines, shapes placed close together, or rubbings from actual textural surfaces.

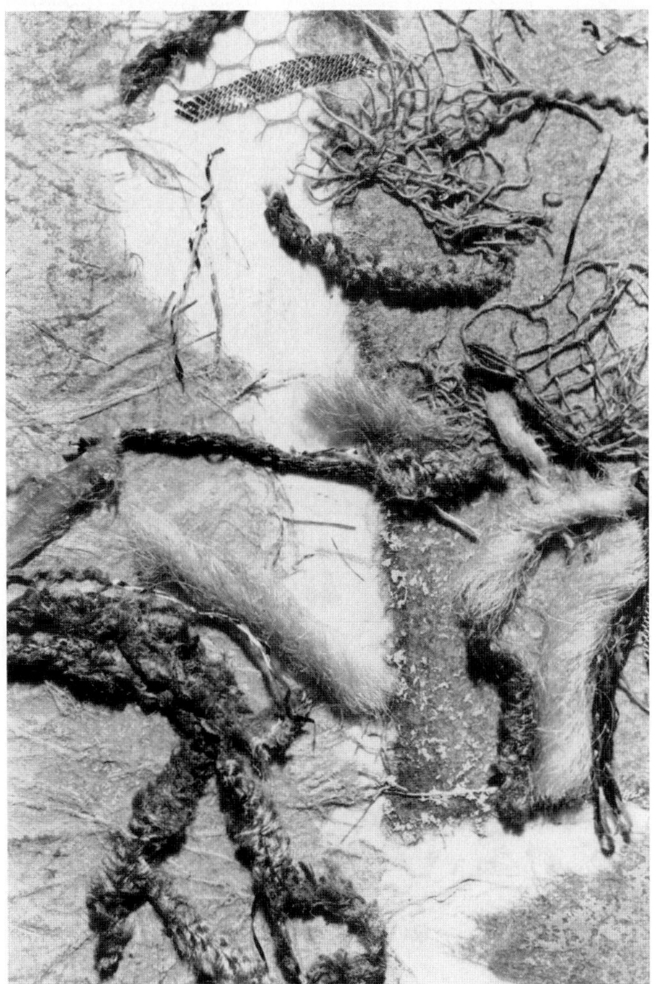

Figure 7◆2

Detail of a collage showing fibers and miscellaneous real textures. *Pat Berret, Photography.*

Figure 7◆3

Nature creates many variations in texture. *Pat Berret, Photography.*

Figure 7•4

Artist unknown. Embroidered linen cloth. The embroidery stitches create a raised surface that contrasts with the weave of the linen cloth. *Collection of the author.*

Figure 7•6

Two pitchers—both glass—show contrasting surface textures *S. Brainard, Photo.*

Figure 7•5

S. Brainard, THE GIFT. Pencil drawing (detail). Simulated texture based on the embroidered cloth. *Source: S. Brainard.*

Figure 7•7

Kalon Baughan, SELF PORTRAIT. Drawing. Graphite on paper. Note texture of hair, skin, muscles, and worn jeans. *Source: S. Brainard.*

Can You Identify . . .?

By its visual quality, can you identify what each of these ten common textures represent?

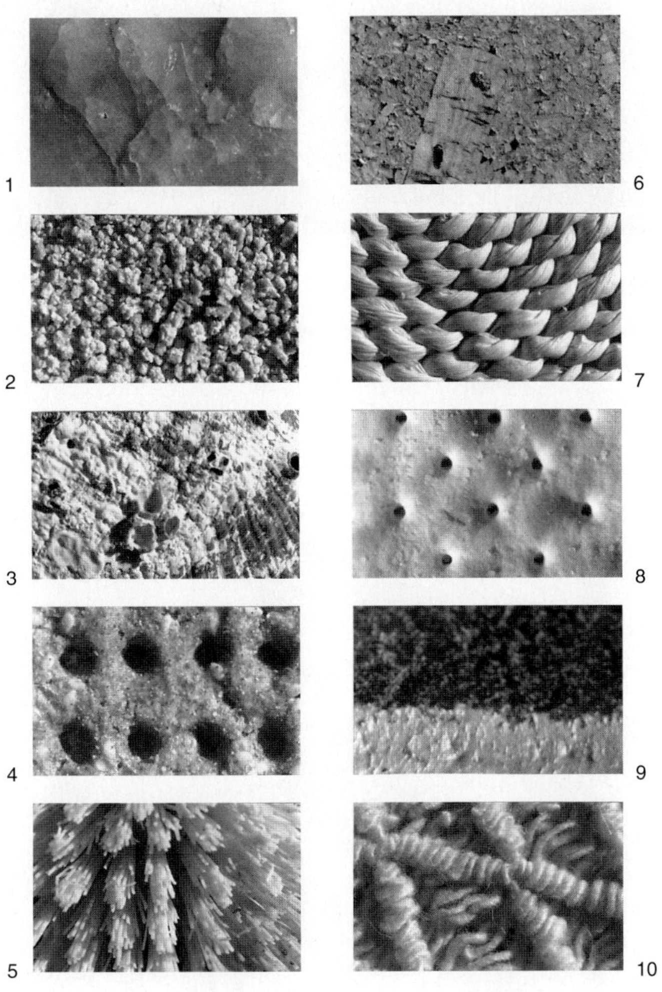

Answers
1. Stone surface (quartz)
2. Cereal
3. Shell Surface
4. Rye cracker
5. Brush bristles
6. Cork
7. Woven hemp
8. Saltine cracker
9. Chocolate cake and frosting!
10. Woven wool

Figure 7◆8

Textures. *S. Brainard, Photo.*

Let's Think About Texture . . .

What are some TEXTURES you like?

ICE CREAM	LEATHER
SATIN	CHOCOLATE CAKE
CORDUROY	A NEW CAR
BRICK	FUR (THIS COULD BE YOUR PET FRIEND!)
RAW LIVER	YOUR HAIR
YARN	SOMEONE ELSE'S HAIR
POLYESTER	CUT GLASS
PLASTIC	WOOD
PLANTS	A PINE CONE

KEYWORD to remember: TACTILE—either simulated or real.

What Can You Do with These Textures?

Can you depict them visually?

Can you produce any of these simulated textures by using *real* textures, perhaps by doing something like rubbings?

Can you do rubbings and have others identify the source?

Review

texture ◆ The quality of being tactile, or being able to *feel* a rough or smooth-type surface.

simulated texture ◆ The real quality of a tactile surface being copied or imitated.

8

Color

- What Is Color?
- Color Wheels
- Color Identity
- Color Perception
- Color Interaction or "Those Lying Colors"
- Color Contrasts
- More Color Contrasts
- Let's Think About This Painting . . .
- Let's Think About Color . . .
- What Can You Do with Color?
- Can You Identify . . .?
- A Preview of Things to Come
- Review

◆ What Is Color?

Color is EVASIVE—
CONTRADICTORY
BEAUTIFUL
SENSUOUS
RELATIVE
DECEPTIVE
CONTRARY
LOVELY
FUN
LIVELY
MYSTERIOUS
AND . . .
PULCHRITUDINOUS!*

*The ultimate in beauty.

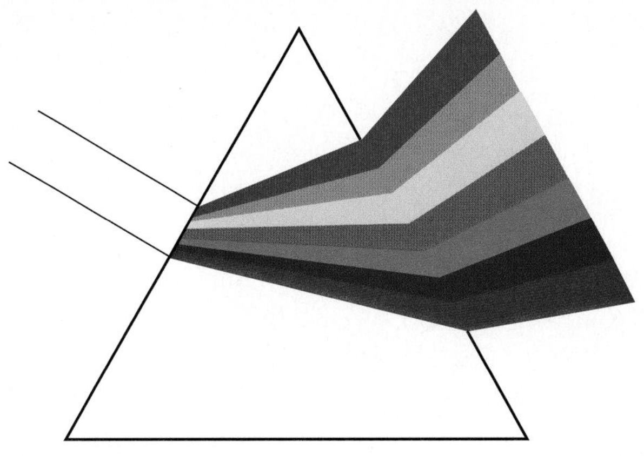

8◆1

A visual spectrum created by white light which has been broken (or refracted) by entering a prism. *(Plate 4.6 Design by Philip Rawson, p. 114.)*

Whole books have been written about color: What it is; what it isn't; comparative analyses; what colors look good with what other colors or color harmonies; how colors affect us mentally, emotionally, and even physically. Color has been used to soothe us, excite us, and label us. The *use* of so many colors is mind-boggling. But we must remember, when speaking of the basic rudiments of design, that *color is another element!* It must be considered as one with the other elements and used as the other elements are used.

Many academic design courses are separated into two areas: DESIGN Theory and COLOR Theory. In this book, we will keep color in perspective, and consider it as only WHAT is necessary in the practice of design.

COLOR IS NICE, BUT, AS FROSTING ISN'T NECESSARY TO A CAKE, COLOR ISN'T NECESSARY TO A DESIGN.

Most of us had a color wheel in our first-grade room in elementary school. This was probably our introduction to color, and we were told that yellow, red, and blue combined to make all the other colors.

Then, later in science class we were told that light made color, and we were shown pictures of sunlight going through a little triangle called a prism, resulting in a rainbow.

I don't know about you, but I was confused!

I thought a lot about theories . . . like, "If a tree fell in the woods would there be a sound?"—OR—"If the light goes out is there still color?"

We now know a lot more about color than we used to know, thanks to the sciences. We know that the physical and natural worlds work hand-in-hand so that we humans can experience the marvel of color.

Let's look again at that prism. This color mixture is the product of light. As the light—light that is produced by the sun—passes through the prisms of nature, as beams of light passing through drops of moisture and dust particles, they are broken up or "diffracted" into different wave lengths, or graduated bands of color. This is called a spectrum or, when viewed in its entirety reflected in the sky, a rainbow.

This mixture of color is called an ADDITIVE mixture.

The science of physics explains an **additive color mixture** as the addition of one light color vibration to another; the more color that is added, the more light you have.

In the 1660s, Sir Isaac Newton (of "apple dropper" and law of gravity fame) experimented with glass prisms, allowing light to pass through them and split up into a range of colors, therefore documenting the physical phenomenon of light. Today, many of us hang tiny glass prisms in our windows, producing little spectrums that dance and play on our walls on a sunny day.

Nature also produces *pigments,* substances that impart color to objects or materials. Every living thing has an *internal* pigmentation. There is "chlorophyll" in green plant life, "carotene" in carrots, "anthocyanine," which produces our red leaves in the fall, and "melanin" in humans, which determines our skin color.

8◆6

Example of *additive* co
Rawson, p. 114.)

8◆7

Example of *subtractive*
Philip Rawson, p. 114.)

Our eyes have abo
and sort out various
"messages" to the b
100 million additiona
darks and lights. Bot
make up the retina
process is unbelievabl
the green tree, the red
pink flamingo! The r
dark green or light gr

It will be easier to r
remember these two c
is used to produce lig
televisions, and theat

8◆2

MOTEL 6-POT-O-GOLD. A double rainbow displays nature's spectrum—twice! *S. Brainard, Photo.*

8◆3

A glass prism hung in a window gives us "rainbows" on our walls. *S. Brainard, Photo.*

8◆4

Albino Gorilla/Barcelc
of pigmentation. *Super*

These are only a fe
goofs with the perce
and a mutation occu
lack a degree of colo
This is called an *al*
albino.

Humans make an
put on the *surface* of

8◆5

Diagram: How we see

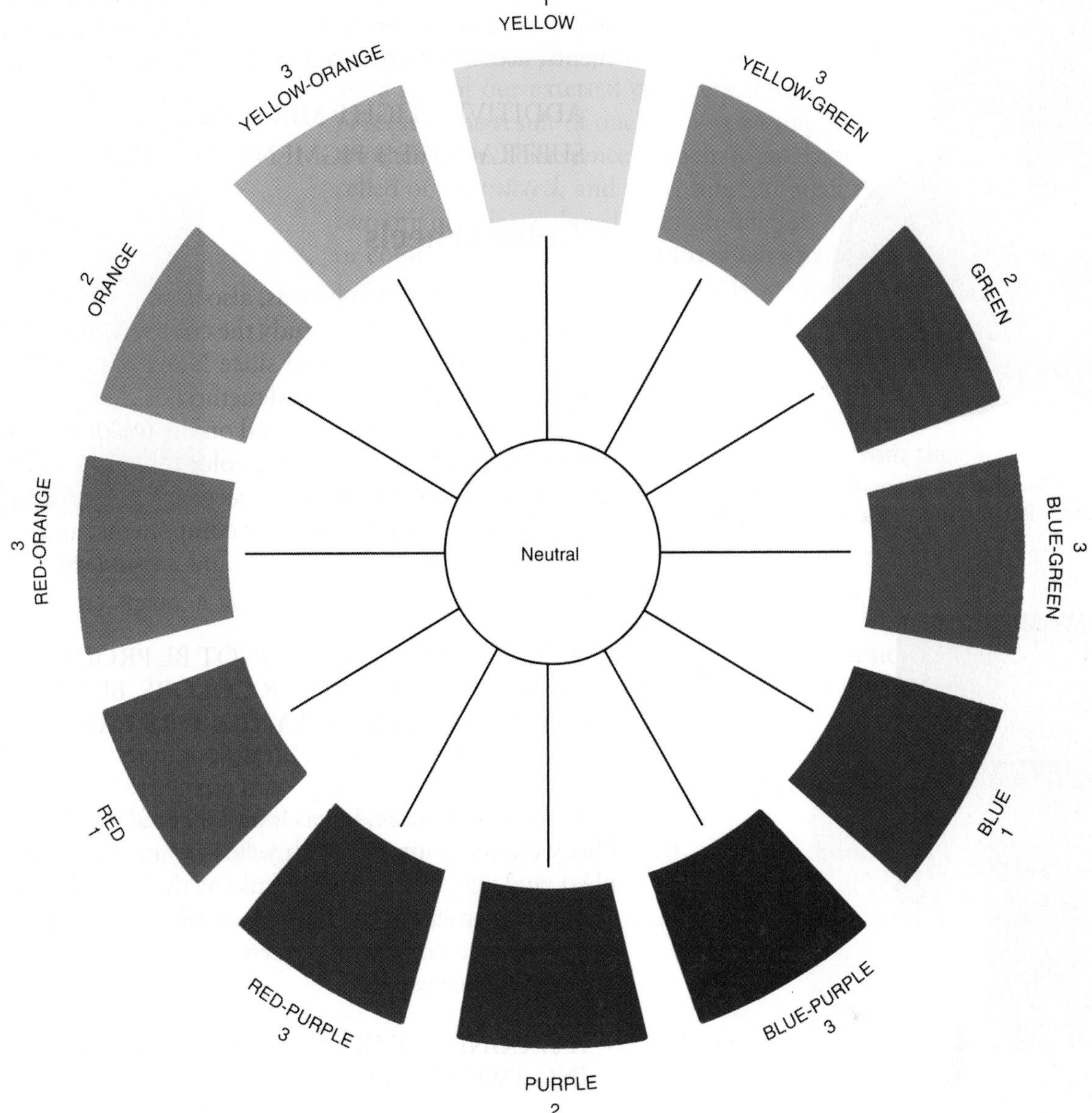

8◆8

Example of one color wheel. *Courtesy Shirl Brainard.*

produced, how we see it, ways to chart it, and the basic colors.

The colors on the color wheel are *technically* called **hues.** COLORS are usually made from changes to these basic hues OR from the actual pigmented source. But we do not call these charts "hue charts"! (It is not uncommon to use the two words synonymously.)

◆ Color Identity

How do we identify all the colors we see?

There are three major properties to each color:

HUE
VALUE
INTENSITY

Let's try and define each.

HUE. Hue is the pure state of a color. A pure hue means the hue has not been changed or altered from its original state; it is virginal.

The easiest way to remember hue is that it is a family with a family name. All the names given a hue such as blue, like "Periwinkle," "Navy," "Cornflower," "Royal," "Indigo," or " Blueberry," tend to describe

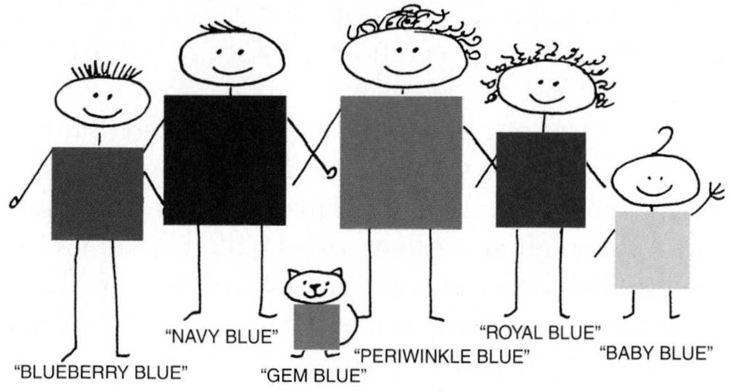

8◆9

The blue (hue) family.

something in our experience that we are familiar with and that we can identify with. They bring to mind an object which has a color that is close to the named color. Each color has many variations. Hue is the same as a family name like "Smith." How do you distinguish one Smith from another? *By first names.* John Smith and Marsha Smith are not unlike Navy blue and Baby blue. Names of colors tend to be fads, usually because of retail businesses, and a color may be one name one year and another name ten years later.

However, the names given to colors help us to mentally describe and identify the colors. Can't you mentally tell the difference between "Raspberry red," "Cherry red," and "Burgundy"? So we will learn to identify colors in a more academic way, using the three parts of a color's identity. To simplify, we will say that the colors on the color wheel represent families—twelve families that we will get to know.

VALUE. Value is the range of darkness or lightness of a color. Value scale relates to color the same as it does to the white-to-black values that we studied earlier. A high value of a color is one closer to white, while a low value is closer to black. Value has to do with HOW MUCH LIGHT—or quantity of light—we see on a color. If our green tree and red barn are observed at dusk when there isn't much light available, they may appear dark green and dark red.

When mixing pigments, *to change the value of a color* we add black to make it darker, white to make it lighter. If it is a darker color, we call it a **shade;** if it is lighter, we call it a **tint.**

We can now have dark hues, medium-dark hues, medium hues, medium-light hues, or light hues. We would say "a high value blue" for light blue hue.

INTENSITY. Intensity is the brightness or dullness of a color. This brightness or dullness has to do with the *kind* of light—or *quality* of light—a color receives. On a bright, sunny day, colors will appear brighter than on a dull, dismal day. Our green tree and red barn at dusk would look dark and *dull* if it were a rainy evening. But

8◆10

An example of dark and light *values* on colors. *S. Brainard, Photo.*

8◆11

A color value chart depicting the same color altered by the addition of white or black to some shades. *Source: S. Brainard.*

just because a color is dark DOES NOT MEAN IT IS DULL, nor is a light color always bright.

A *hue in its pure state is at its brightest.* The colors on the color charts are pure hues. A color cannot be made brighter than its pure state. It can be changed to darker, lighter, or duller.

When a color is at its brightest, it is called HIGH **intensity.** When it is dull or grayish, it has a LOW INTENSITY.

The degree of color purity can be decreased in pigments in three ways. One is by dilution, such as when using watercolor. As more water is added to the pigment, the solution weakens and the color becomes less intense. This is like adding a lot of water to a cup of coffee to make two cups of coffee: The intensity of the color of the coffee, as well as the flavor, has been reduced.

The second way the purity of a color can be decreased in pigments is to add gray, a combination of black and white. If you add a *light* valued gray, the result will be a light, dull color.

The third way to decrease color purity is by adding the color's complement. What is a complement? Let's look at the color wheel again.

The color directly opposite any selected color on the wheel is called its **complement.** This is important information to remember, as complements will be referred to many times in the study of color.

If we choose blue as our color, the color opposite is orange. Orange is the complement of blue. So adding a touch of orange to our blue will LOWER THE INTENSITY of the blue, making it duller. It may also make it a tad lighter! DO YOU KNOW WHY? Look at the *value* of blue. It is darker than orange. The orange being lighter in value will bring up the value of the blue. WE ARE SPEAKING OF COLORS IN THEIR PURE STATE—PLAIN OLD BLUE AND PLAIN OLD ORANGE.

Sometimes colors are dark . . . and bright!

Sometimes colors are light and dull!

Sometimes colors are medium and medium!

Let's refer to our color wheel again. I recommend that we use the color wheel with the yellow at the top and purple at the bottom. In this way, we have a reference not only to the hues, or families of color, and their relative purity—and in this pure state they are all equally bright—but also to their relative values. The yellow at the top is, in its pure state, the lightest hue, with yellow-orange and yellow-green (on either side) a bit darker than the yellow, until as we go down the wheel laterally we come to purple, which is the darkest hue.

Do you remember seeing a gray circle in the middle of that grade school color wheel? That gray represented **neutral,** or what you get when you mix complements together. The thing is, you *never* get gray, you get a "grayed" or dull color—a **tone.**

8◆12

This photo of cottonwood leaves shows a range of *tones* or a scale of bright to dullness of the leaves' colors. At the lowest range, the color becomes a neutral (a brownish color) and is also darker in value. *S. Brainard, photo.*

8◆13

Grant Wood (American 1892–1942), NEAR SUNDOWN. 1933. Oil on canvas. 38 × 66 cm. High-value, low-intensity colors are depicted in this painting. *Spencer Museum of Art, University of Kansas: Gift of Mr. George Cukor. Source: VAGA. © Estate of Grant Wood/Licensed by VAGA, New York, NY.*

What does neutral usually mean? That it isn't this way or that, it's in the middle! This is what a neutral is in colors also. When we use our complement to lower the intensity of a color to the point that neither color is evident, but the mixture is something in between, it is neutral. Our blue, for instance, with enough orange added, wouldn't be blue, but it wouldn't be orange either. It would be neutral.

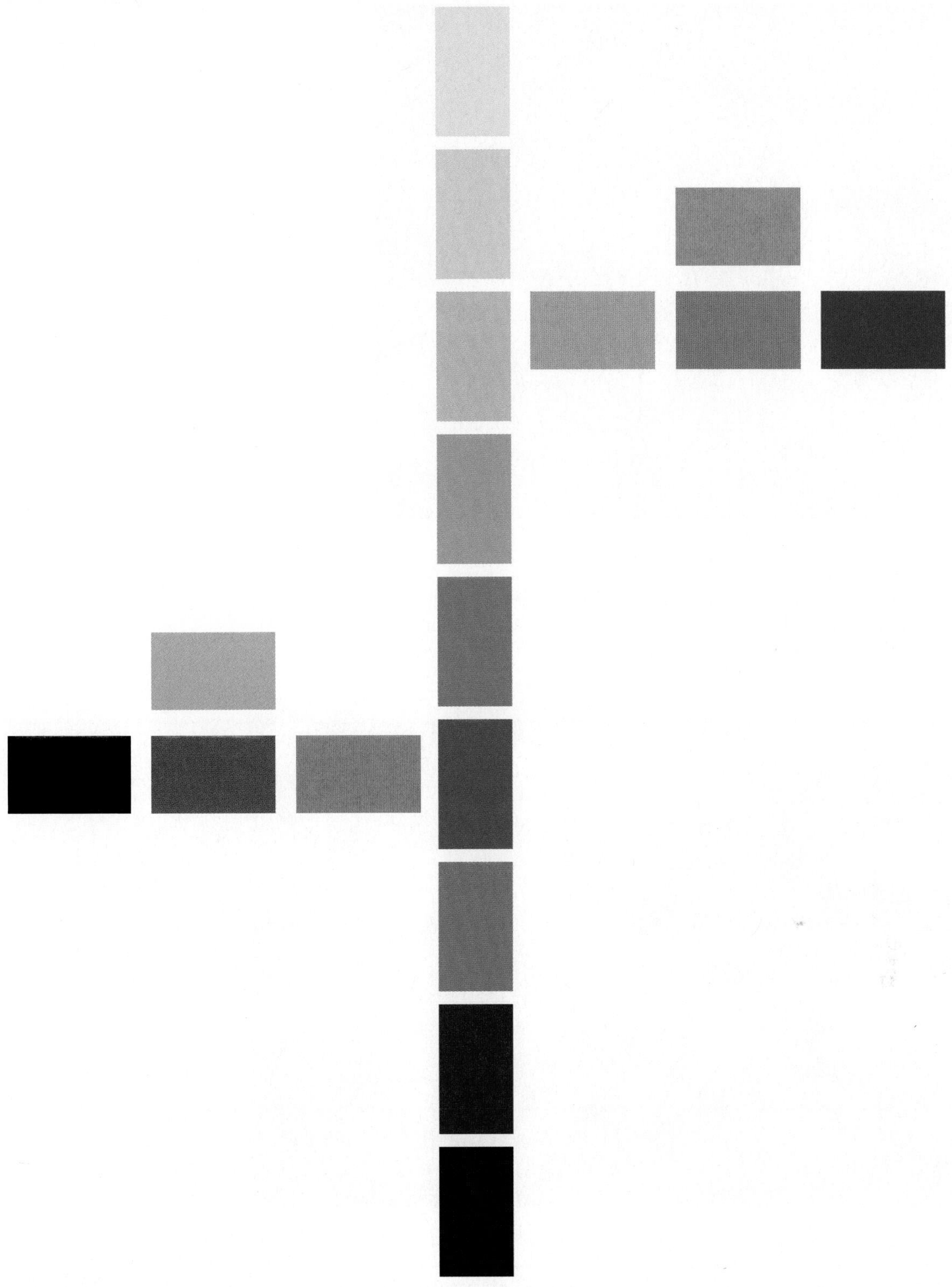

8◆14

A color intensity chart showing how the same hue can be altered to make *tones* by the addition of grays or by the addition of the hue's complement. *Source: S. Brainard.*

8•15

WINTER. This winter scene makes us feel cool perhaps because of our experience with winter and the colors associated with coolness. *S. Brainard, Photo.*

Many colors we know are colors made from neutralizing colors. "Brown" is the lowered intensity of orange, while "khaki" is the lowered intensity of green. Our tans, beiges, taupes, and so on are all neutrals. (These colors may also come from natural pigments.) A technical explanation of gray is that it is produced by mixing a black and white pigment. Gray is achromatic, or without color.

Let's remember: *Intensity is the brightness or dullness* of a COLOR. If the INTENSITY has been modified, it is a *tone*. If it has been changed to the point of no recognition (by its complement), it has become a *neutral*.

There are many colors of one hue. For instance, there may be ten natural sources for a blue pigment. We can add them all into our original family. Then we can change all those blues by value and intensity, and we begin to see how many colors are possible within one family. Then we can mix some of the blues together and get still different blues, and then we can change the value and intensity of those blues . . . WOW!

8•16

Gary Ernest Smith, MAN WITH STRAW BALE. Oil on canvas, 48″ × 36″. What kind of temperate feeling do you experience looking at these colors? *Courtesy: Overland Gallery of Fine Art, Scottsdale, AZ.*

COLOR TEMPERATURE. I am of the opinion that there is a fourth important identification that should be learned, and this fourth identity is **color temperature.**

When we speak of a color being WARM or COOL, we're not referring to an actual physical quality of the

color but an emotional or aesthetic quality. However, when we *experience* actual heat or cold, the colors we associate with either can help us. HOT or WARM reminds us of fire, or sun—red, yellow, orange—but also the bright blue of a very hot flame. These colors are usually *bright,* with perhaps a medium or even dark value. On the other hand, COLD reminds us of ice, snow, or gloomy days that make us feel cold. These colors of association are usually light, maybe white, and, *perhaps,* dull.

We have been taught that the colors on the color wheel—red-purple through the reds, oranges, and yellows to yellow-green—are considered "warm"; while green through purple are the "cool" colors. Each color, however, has its own degree of warmth or coldness as a *pigment.* Remember those ten blues a few paragraphs back? Blue is supposed to look cool. Why, then, does one look warm? The degree of apparent "visual" warmth or coolness depends not only on the individual pigment but also on WHAT OTHER COLOR IS PLACED ALONGSIDE IT. Our blues will all look cooler next to yellows—right? WRONG! If a blue's value is darker and its intensity very bright, and if the yellow's value has become almost white, the yellow will appear cooler!

It takes close observation over time to see these variances. For safety's sake, let's remember the following usual temperate appearances:

WARM—HOT = Bright (high intensity) Medium to dark value

COLD—COOL = Medium (low intensity) High value

◆ Color Perception

This is a good time to discuss **perception,** which plays a HUGE part in color. The viewer's—as well as the designer's—perception of a given color may vary a little, or a lot.

Perception has to do with stimuli to our senses. It also has to do with what we were exposed to as we grew up.

Let's think about our chocolate cake again. In our Western world, and especially in the United States, chocolate cake is very common! In some countries, however, people may be well acquainted with chocolate but *not* with "cake." If I hear "chocolate cake" or see a picture of a chocolate cake, it evokes a taste and smell sensation—and I want some! However, if we have never had a piece of chocolate cake, then this doesn't work. But it doesn't mean that we can't acquire a taste for it—we can . . . and probably will.

If we have never been exposed to a wide variety of experiences, we have a limited number of comparisons. If we've been taught one thing and lived with that information for many years, it is sometimes difficult to quickly adapt to new ideas. This often happens with color. If we haven't developed an awareness of many color variations (and we do take colors for granted), it can be very hard to "see" the differences in 20 different blues.

This often occurs in the classroom as we try to identify colors by "hue, value, intensity, and temperature." Some of us will catch or perceive any slight nuance of modification, while others may be able to identify only one or two changes.

But color perception can be learned, so don't worry. Again, time and practice are the keys.

We could describe one blue from another in this way: "blue hue, medium value, high intensity, and warm," while its partner may be "blue hue, high value, medium-low intensity, and cool."

See how many colors of one hue you can identify in this way. In my classes, we have a BLUE-DAY or RED-DAY and we all wear the same hue. VERY INTERESTING!

◆ Color Interaction or "Those Lying Colors"

We have been thinking of comparisons. We NEVER see one color all by itself. There are always other colors around it, and so one color always relates to another.

Color is the most relative element. Its behavior will change with its environment!

This is very sneaky and deceptive!

You may see a color that looks bright blue and along comes another blue and the first blue looks like a dull . . . green? Or what about that red sweater you bought that you just *knew* would go with your red plaid skirt? That sweater now looks absolutely ORANGE! So, you'll wear the sweater with another plaid skirt that has blue-green, rust, and orange in it. Now the sweater looks RED! We spoke of similar comparisons when talking about color temperature, variations of colors, and the like. It happens all the time!

All of these comparisons have to do with the **interaction** between colors, and this is why color can be deceitful.

Think how you would feel if you owned a successful neighborhood meat market and had the same reli-

8◆17

Example of blue pigments (all blue hue) in their pure state. Does one look warmer than others? If so, *why?* *Source: S. Brainard.*

able customers for years. Your shop has been painted a sterile white all this time and is showing its wear, so you decide to do a little redecorating. Reading somewhere that yellow was a cheery color, you paint your interior a nice, bright yellow . . . and slowly, but surely, your loyal customers leave your store without buying, and many never return. WHY? It was found that the yellow walls made the meat look . . . PURPLE! A "color-fairy" comes along, whispers in your ear to paint the walls a nice "mint" green, and PRESTO! your business shoots upward again!

In human psychology or color consulting, this is a common story. The experience is called seeing an "after-image," and it happens after we have consciously, or unconsciously, stared at a color for a length of time—as we would be apt to do standing in line at a grocery counter. When we suddenly look elsewhere, we see the *complement* of the color we were looking at, often in small geometric shapes.

What is important to realize is that unusual things can and do happen with color, and we should plan for those unexpected events. As a painter myself, I often "mentally" paint while driving, before I physically pick up my brush. We all do masterpieces in our heads, but then it often doesn't come off! When faced with such a failed masterpiece, we have to analyze the basic design, the color. We have to see WHAT went wrong, and make corrections.

The control of color—and good color usage is control—comes not only from the choice of colors we use, but, as with the other elements, from HOW we use them. We have to be careful how our colors act and react together; we must plan their contrasts.

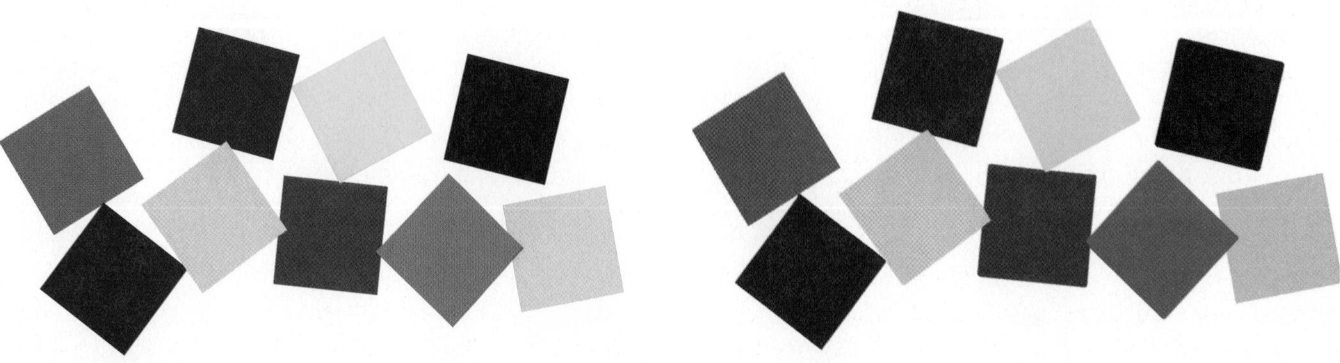

8◆18 and 8◆19

A color's behavior depends on the colors around it. *Source: S. Brainard.*

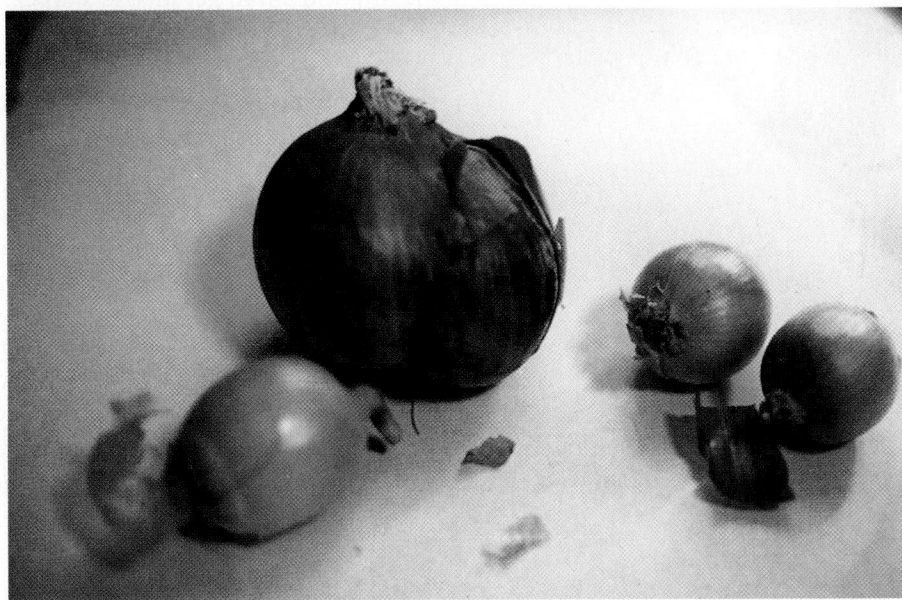

8◆20 and 8◆21

The same onions with different backgrounds. Which appears cooler? *Why?*
S. Brainard, photo.

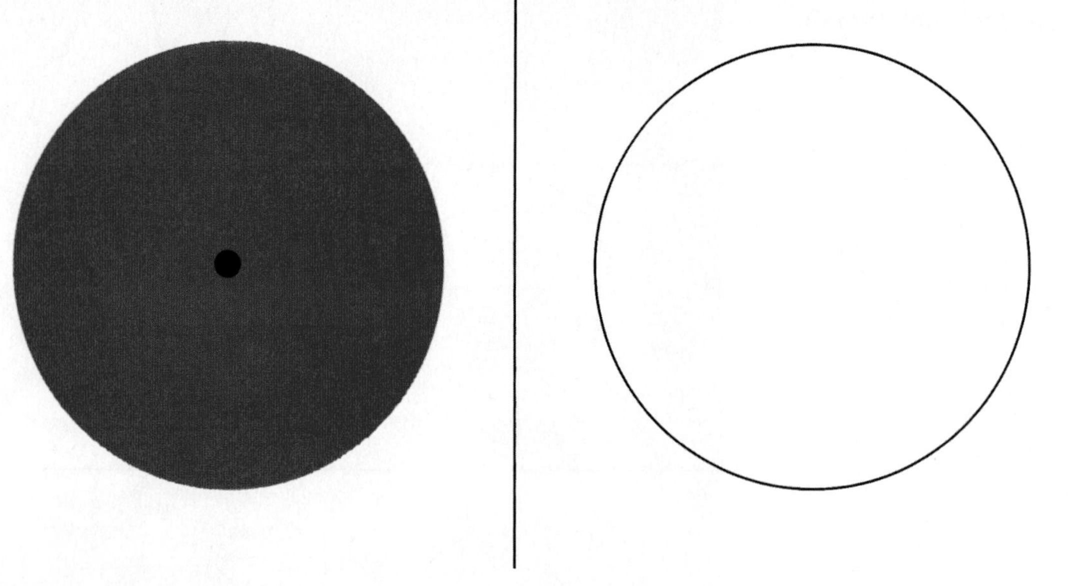

8◆22

Stare at the black dot on the red circle for a full minute–then shift your eyes to the white circle. *What do you see? Source: S. Brainard.*

◆ Color Contrasts

We talked of contrasts in the chapter about value. Remember high contrasts and low contrasts? With color, there are four major **contrasts,** and the capable colorist will carefully consider color placement. Let's look at the contrasts:

DARK/LIGHT—BRIGHT/DULL—
WARM/COOL—LARGE/SMALL

1 ◆ Dark/light is the relative contrast between values of colors. This could be a dark red to a light yellow; a dark red to a light red (which could be pink); or a dark neutral to a light red.

2 ◆ Bright/dull is the relative contrast between intensities of colors. This could be a dull red to a bright red, or a dull red to a bright blue, or a dull neutral—(neutrals are already dull)—to a bright red.

3 ◆ Warm/cool is the relative contrast between temperatures of colors. This could be yellow to blue, or bright blue to pale, light yellow; bright red to pale, light blue, or hot pink to blue-green.

COULD ALL OF THESE CONTRASTS BE IN ONE COMBINATION? Can a dark, bright, warm, sensitive red find happiness with a light, dull, cool, sweet blue? Sure they can!

4 ◆ Large/small is the relative proportion of one color to another, with one color usually dominant. Sometimes one color will dominate other colors; we may remember a "red" painting and know that we observed other colors but not recall what they were. This is an example of contrast of quantity—how much "red"—(and these may be different reds)—compared to the amounts of blue, green, purple, or any other colors.

◆ More Color Contrasts

In the use of color, one solution for unifying color (see UNITY in the section on the PRINCIPLES) is the use of a "color system."

"All colors are the friends of their neighbors and the lovers of their opposites," wrote Marc Chagall. He was speaking of the use of color "systems" ("harmonies," "schemes") or "simultaneous contrasts," as their founder, Michel-Eugène Chevreul, called them.

In the early 1800s, paints were mixed by chemists. Michel-Eugène Chevreul (1786–1889) was one such chemist. He spent his life fascinated by pigments, their properties, and the interaction between the colors these pigments produced. In a scientific journal he gave a report on "**Simultaneous Colour Contrast,**" which evolved into his basic color harmonies, based on the

8◆23

JAPANESE GARDENS. Dark/light contrast.
S. Brainard, Photo.

8◆24

LUNASCAPES, Watercolor by Pauline Eaton. Bright/dull contrast. *Courtesy: Pauline Eaton.*

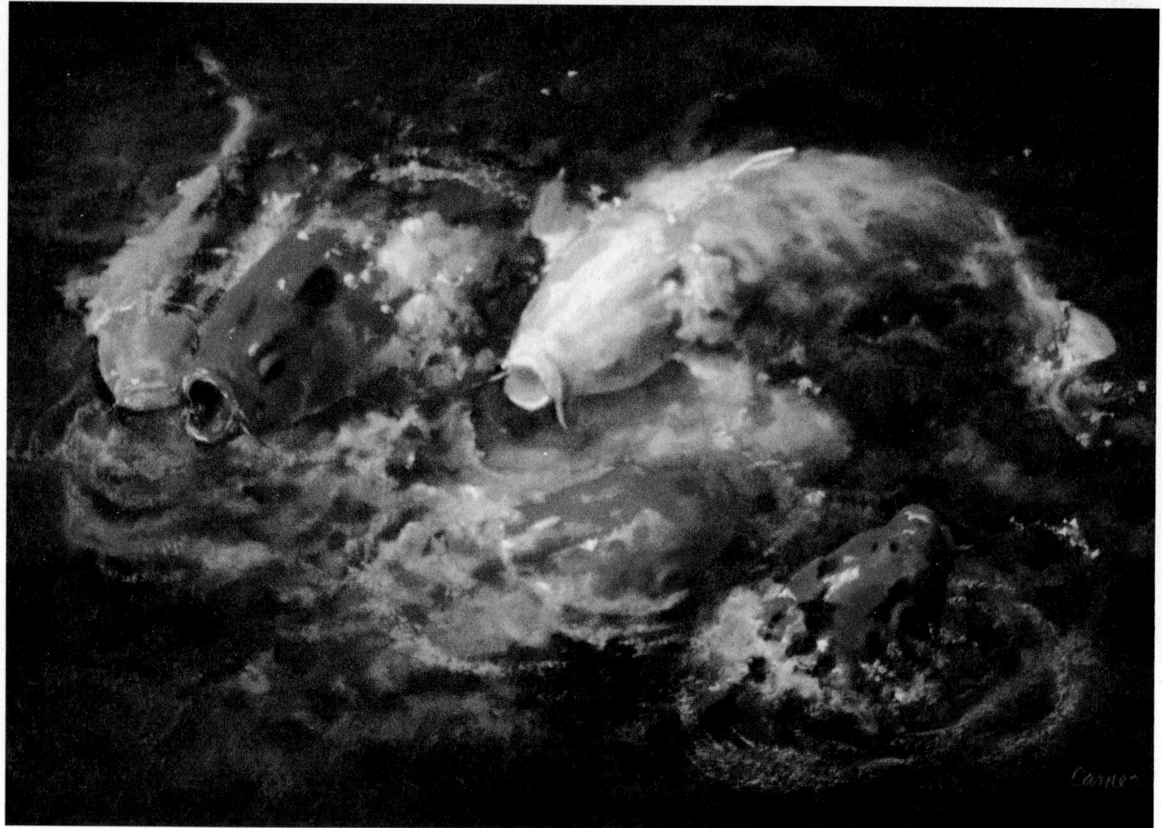

8◆25

Cindy Carnes, KOI. Pastel on sanded p. paper, 24″ × 30″. How many color contrasts do you see in this painting? *Courtesy: Cindy Carnes.*

traditional *pigment* color wheel. (The "light mixture" or "additive" mixture wheel differs from the pigment wheel.)

In 1920, Josef Itten taught these concepts at the Bauhaus (remember the Bauhaus?) and Josef Albers (1888–1976) was one of his students. Both went on to do scientific research about color, resulting in new applied studies about color. Here, we'll look at Chevreul's basic color harmonies, now called "systems" or "schemes."

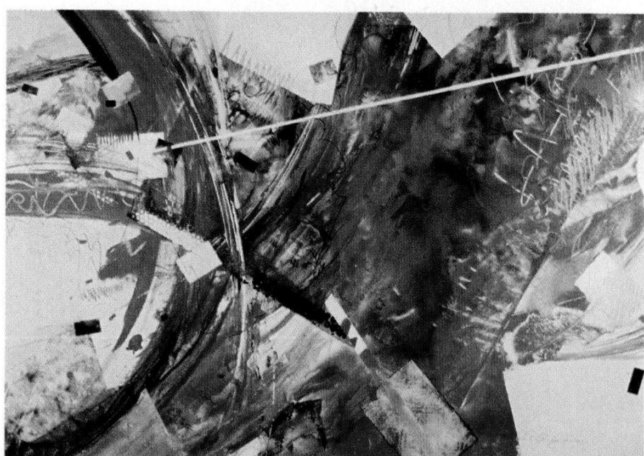

8◆26

Mark E. Mehaffey, VISUAL LAYERS, RED. Mixed water media. Red is the dominant color. *Source: Mark E. Mehaffey.*

8◆27

Nature's complements, purple and yellow wildflowers blanket a field. *S. Brainard, Photo.*

We readily see these select contrasts in many design areas. Look for them in textile/fabric design (clothing, upholstery, bed linens, drapery, and table linens), home decorating (a speciality of interior Design), graphics, and photography (especially in high-end magazines that use free-lance photographers for advertisements).

It may have been in the observation of nature that Chevreul saw some of these color harmonics because the complements are familiar in nature settings, seen in the coloration of the flowers, and in nurseries, gardens, and floral designs everywhere.

The complements have also been used by painters (Cezanne loved them), and that one contrast is used by many painters today, whereas the other contrasts aren't as common. Intensities and values may be changed in any of these contrasts. Often in the use, a contrast will AUTOMATICALLY become a contrast of light and dark, or warm and cool. All of these contrasts make interesting learning exercises for the painter.

1 ◆ COMPLEMENTARY: These *two* hues we've been introduced to earlier. TWO hues that lie directly opposite one another on the traditional color wheel tend to intensify each other visually.

8◆28

Nurseries often use color contrasts with flower displays. *S. Brainard, Photo.*

8◆29

Nature uses complements with flowers, often seen in their stems and/or leaves. This daisylike flower is pale yellow-orange with blue-purple center. *S. Brainard, Photo.*

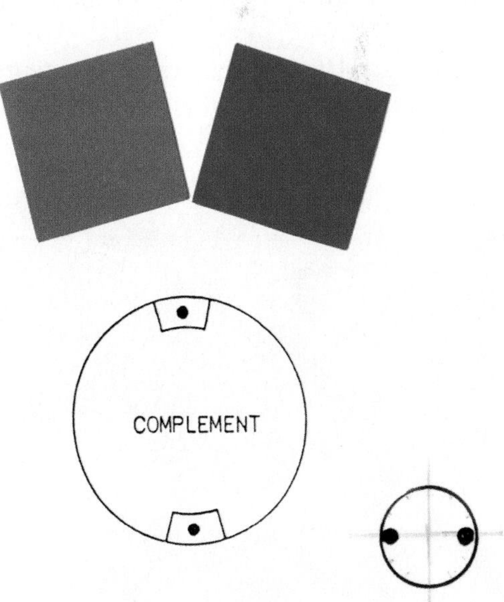

8◆30

Complementary color chart using red-orange and blue-green. *Source: Shirl Brainard.*

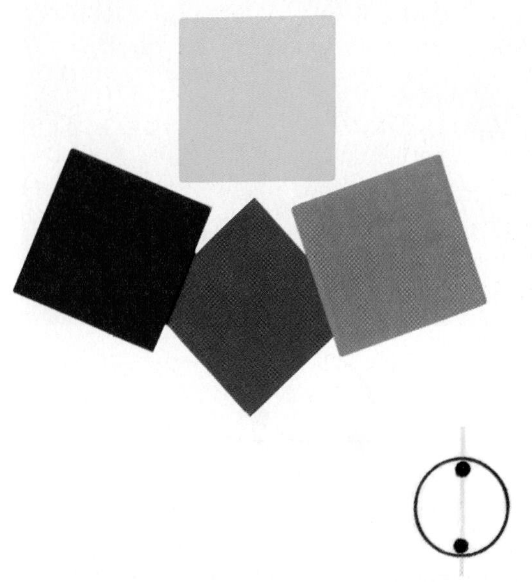

8◆31

Complementary color chart showing a hue and its complement with value changes. *Source: Shirl Brainard.*

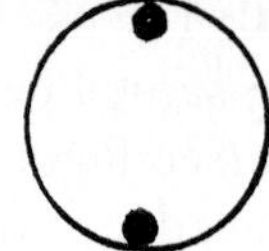

8◆32

James McGulpin, YELLOW SPIDER CHRYSANTHEMUM, oil on canvas. *Source: James McGulpin.*

8◆33

Susan Weeks, UNIFOLIA. Uses complements red-purple and yellow-green. Source: Susan Weeks. *Courtesy of Susan Weeks.*

8◆34

Interior of Corrales Bosque Gallery in New Mexico, with purples and yellows on its walls. Source: Corrales Bosque Gallery. *Courtesy of Corrales Bosque Gallery.*

2 ◆ SPLIT-COMPLEMENT: This is a combination of *three* hues, a chosen hue and the hues on *either* side of its complement. Such a combination produces a dramatic effect.

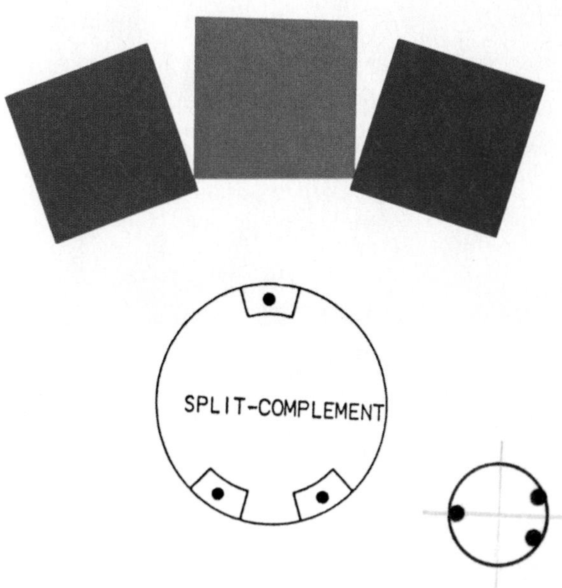

8◆35

Split-complement chart using red-orange, blue, and green. *Source: Shirl Brainard.*

8◆36

Shirl Brainard, A MATTER OF OPINION. Paper collage/water media. Split-complements are red-orange, green, and blue. *Source: Shirl Brainard.*

8◆37

African motif fabric using split-complements red, yellow-green, and blue-green. *Source: Shirl Brainard.*

8◆38

Julie Hopkins, 5 PM. Oil. A split-complement combination of purple, yellow-orange, and yellow-green. *Source: Julie Hopkins. Courtesy of Julie Hopkins.*

3 ◆ MONOCHROMATIC: The use of *one* hue (using different pigments of the same hue), usually with value and intensity changes (see Figure 8–15). Many times a design may be perceived as monochromatic, but on closer scrutiny, other colors are seen. This then, is the *dominant contrast* we spoke of earlier. A truly monochromatic design creates a feeling of calmness or elegance (in an interior), but it can lead to boredom.

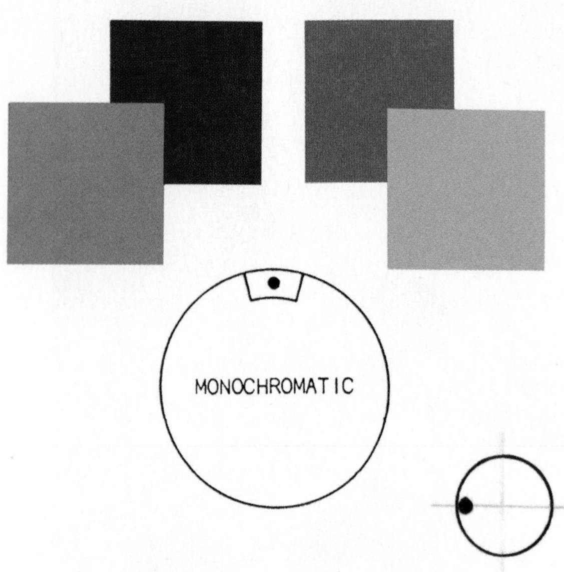

8◆39

Monochromatic chart showing *one* hue with value and intensity changes. *Source: Shirl Brainard.*

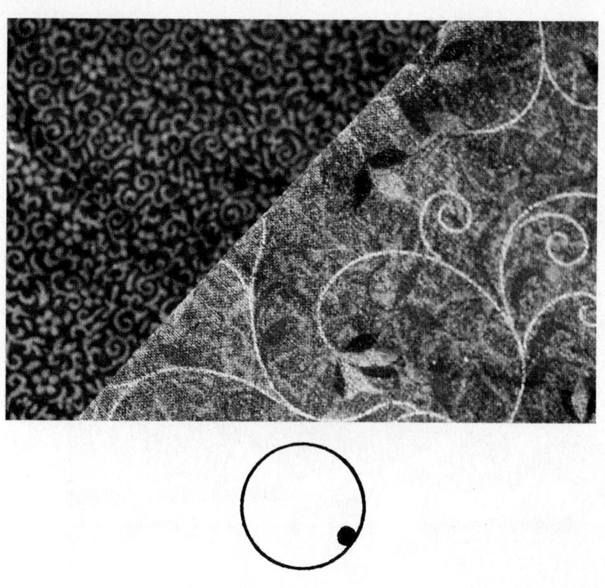

8◆41

Two fabrics, both all blue. *Source: Shirl Brainard.*

8◆40

Susan Weeks, PEARS AS LANDSCAPE. Watercolor. A range of yellow-oranges makes this a monochromatic color system. *Source: Susan Weeks. Courtesy of Susan Weeks.*

8◆42

Stephen Quiller, WINTER RHYTHM, TWILIGHT, SAN JUAN. Watercolor. 21″ × 29″. Various blues make this monochromatic color system. *Source: Stephen Quiller. Courtesy of Stephen Quiller.*

8◆43

Susan Weeks, WINTER THAW. Watercolor. Often a work will *appear* as monochromatic. When looked at closely, however, other colors will be seen to have been used to enhance the *dominant* color. *Source: Susan Weeks. Courtesy of Susan Weeks.*

4 ◆ TRIAD: *Three* hues equal distance from one another on the color wheel. This combination can be energetic.

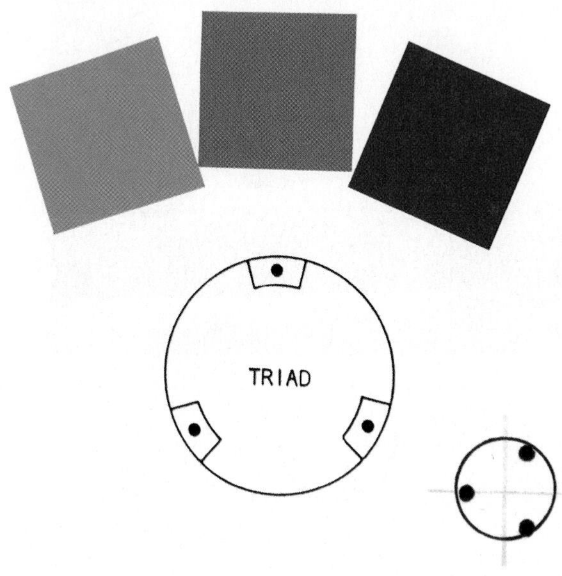

8◆44

Triad chart using red-orange, blue-purple, and yellow-green. *Source: Shirl Brainard.*

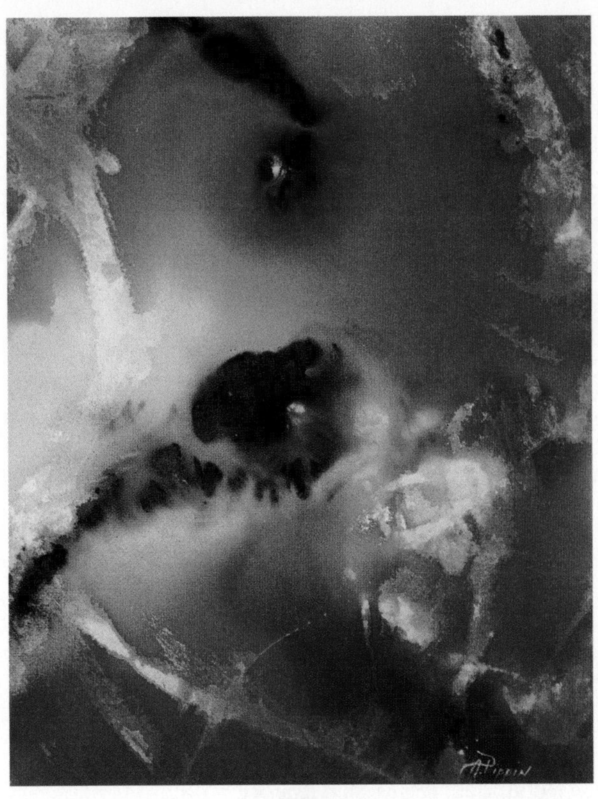

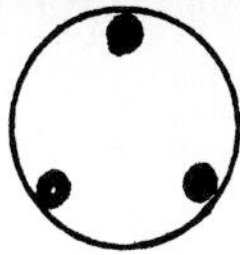

8◆45

Aleta Pippin, IN BLOOM. Red, yellow, and blue make this triad color contrast. *Source: Aleta Pippin. Courtesy of Aleta Pippin.*

5 ◆ ANALOGOUS: Something similar is the meaning of this mixture. Made up of *three* to maybe *five* hues lying next to each other on the color wheel. When *three* to *four* are used, they share one hue in common; if *five* are used, another major hue is involved. This creates a dynamic effect.

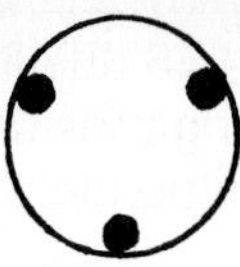

8◆46

Susan Weeks, BELLFLOWER. Watercolor. A triad combination of purple, green, and orange. *Source: Susan Weeks. Courtesy of Susan Weeks.*

8◆48

Nature produces analogous colors in the rose, such as in the "Joseph's Coat" rose, with pale yellow, yellow-orange, orange, red-orange, and red. *S. Brainard, Photo.*

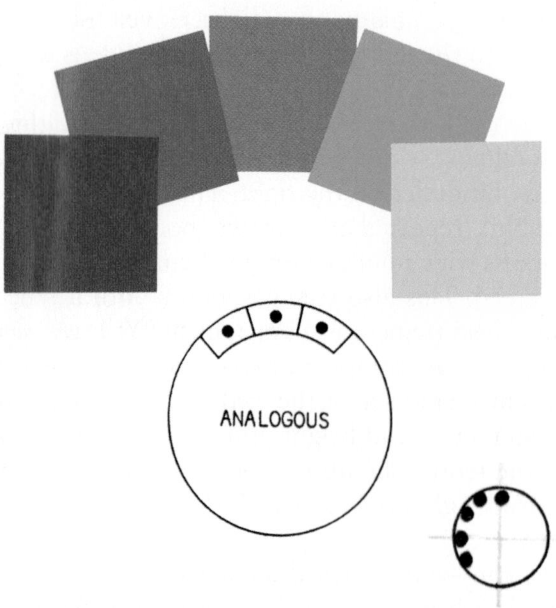

8◆47

Analogous chart with yellow, yellow-orange, orange, red-orange, and red. Five neighbors on the color wheel. *Source: Shirl Brainard.*

8◆49

Single "Joseph's Coat" rose. *S. Brainard, Photo.*

8♦50

James McGulpin, ZINNIAS. Oil on canvas. Analogous combination of yellow-orange, orange, red-orange, red, and red-purple. *Source: James McGulpin.*

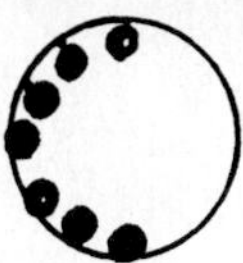

8♦51

Shirl Brainard, SPIRIT OF THE SIPAPU. Acrylic. 18″ × 24″. This analogous painting uses the full side of the color wheel from yellow to purple. *Source: Shirl Brainard.*

These contrasts can be instrumental in creating a successful design.

We can't forget that color, like value or texture, is often on the surface of our shapes and lines and, being mutually supportive, they are *all* arranged to work together in a given space. Theoretically, a good design planned out in a black-and-white value range *should* work as well in a color range, but control is the winning factor in good color usage.

Color is a "part"—another ELEMENT. It can be used in our design like the other elements, and the principles will determine HOW effective that design is.

But—never, never turn your back on COLOR! Even Leonardo da Vinci noted, "Colors appear what they are not, according to the ground which surrounds them." And Josef Albers said, ". . . in order to use color effectively, it is necessary to recognize that color deceives continually."

When an artist has learned the use of color contrasts (as well as other color theories), it often appears to be second nature to a designer, but a thinking process is usually going on in the artist's mind. The painting *Gallo* (or "Rooster") by artist John Nieto (figure 8–52) is an example of this use of color contrasts that we have been talking about.

The rooster itself has very bright, warm colors. There is a light, bright yellow along the back of the bird, with pinky red-purples, reds, red-oranges, and oranges forming the main body. Let's look at this painting, color to color, as a journey through the SPACE that makes up this work. The yellow is lighter, but not brighter, than the red to red-purple next to it, used as background (or negative space). This red-purple is next to a band of blue-purple that runs across the top of the painting. This band is lighter over the bird's head than on the left side, and the right side is darker but still relatively bright. This band moves to the tail, which is blue-green, and changes to a lighter value, to almost white (lower left on tail) and lighter, but a tiny bit duller on the right. This, then, turns to a bright blue (repeated on the lower body of the bird), which meets with a dull, warm, medium-to-dark value yellow-green. This also changes values until it meets its complement (remember complement? Yellow-green and red-purple are complements!) of red-purple, which also runs in a band across the bird's feet. It changes to a very light value and bright pink; then to a red that repeats the red by the upper body background. This band, from right to left, is a dark, dull red (lower right), which is a mid-value, but changes to a lighter—but not light—value toward the left side.

There is a bright, mid-value streak of red-purple (perhaps we would call it fuschia?) on the left of the pink that connects with the foot. This brightness contrasts with duller, mid-value to the extreme dark value, almost black, above it. This very dark blue-purple varies in value, but not intensity, throughout this

8◆52

John Nieto. GALLO. Acrylic on canvas. 44″ × 40″. *Source: John Nieto.*

larger negative space, with a lighter blue-purple next to the breast and legs of the bird.

Did you think there would be so many dark-to-light, dull-to-bright, warm-to-cool contrasts in one work?

◆ Let's Think About This Painting . . .

Look at figure 8–52.

What is the darkest color?

What is the lightest?

What is the brightest?

What is the dullest?

Which color is the warmest?

Which color is the coolest?

Is there a neutral "color"?

Is it warm or cool?

Is a color repeated?

Is there a dominant color?

Is there another color next to its complement?

What would have happened if the white area between the legs (actually, a high-value blue) were not there?

Why do you think the legs are blue and not some other color?

◆ Let's Think About Color . . .

Do you have chromophobia?

Can you verbally describe the difference between:

lilac

purple

lavender

violet

orchid?

Why would you change the intensity of a color?

If you change the value, does the intensity change?

If you change the intensity, does the value change?

Can you describe "pink" by hue, value, and intensity?

Could "pink" have different intensities?

Why would a landscape painter want to know about warm or cool colors?

Why would an interior designer want to know about warm or cool colors?

Can you describe the clothes your colleagues are wearing by hue, value, and intensity? How about temperature?

If you mix two complements, what do you have?

8◆53

John Shannon, A NINE'S PERSPECTIVE. Mixed media.
Source: John Shannon.

What happens if you add white to the above resulting color?

If you use the two complements and the above result together in *one* project, what kind of color system do you have?

If you use red, yellow, and blue in *one* project, what kind of color system do you have?

If you use yellow-green as your chosen hue, what hues would you choose to make a "split complement"?

KEYWORD to remember: COLOR—*relativity; color is an element.*

◆ What Can You Do with Color?

Can color create a focal point? How?

Can color be used as emphasis?

Can color be used to manipulate a viewer's feelings?

Can we divide space with color?

Can color be a negative space?

Can color be a shape?

Can color be a line?

Can color have texture?

Can color have value?

Can we use color to create balance?

Can rhythm be created with color? HOW?

(Refer again to figure 8–52, *Gallo.*)

8◆54

Rick Satava, ONE-OF-A-KIND GLASS JELLYFISH. 6″ × 24″. Colors abound in this glass piece. *Source: Rick Satava. Courtesy of Rick Satava.*

◆ Can You Identify . . .?

1. What kind of shapes are predominant?
2. Is line important?
3. Is there a value contrast?
4. Is there a visual textural area?
5. What color dominates?
6. What do you think the red color does?
7. Do you have any idea "what" balances "what"?

   The line?

   The shapes?

   The color?
8. Do you have any idea HOW the elements are held together or HOW "unity" is established?
9. What is the "focal point"?
10. Numbers 7, 8, and 9 were questions about HOW the elements are used, or composed, using the PRINCIPLES of design, which we'll study next.

◆ A Preview of Things to Come

When we later discuss three-dimensional design, we will see that the element **color** is as important to that type of design as it is in two-dimensional design. Let's preview three illustrations that all depict three-dimensional design and look how color is used in each.

8◆55

Joy Franklin, SUN DANCE CEREMONY. Stained glass, found bone and feathers. 24″ × 24″ × 6″. Artificial or natural light shows the colors in this work. *Private collection. Source: Joy Franklin.*

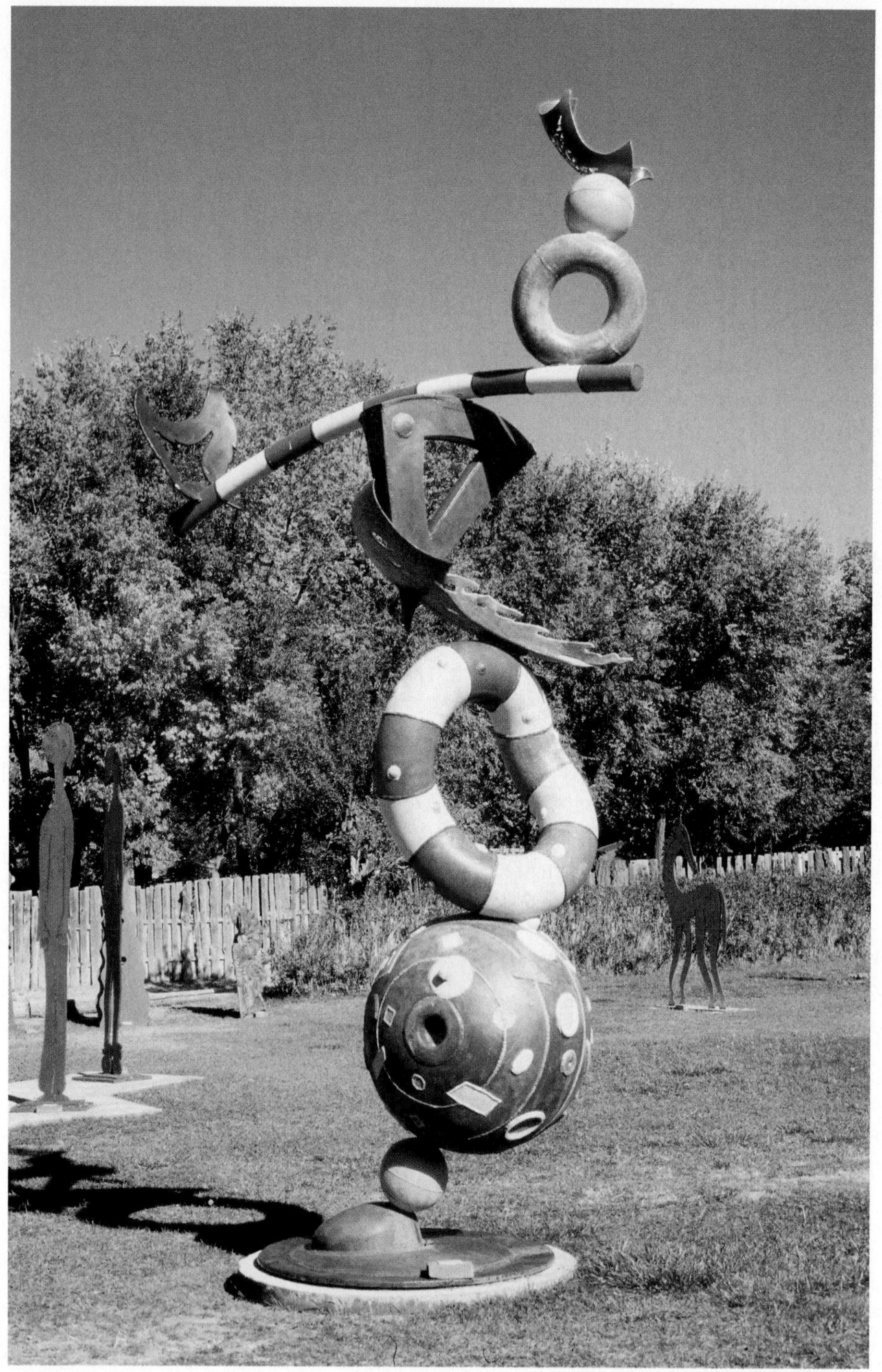

8◆56

Steve Kline, LETTERS FROM HOME. 18″ H × 10″ L × 6″ D. This fun sculpture of welded painted steel is full of color. *Courtesy: Steve Kline. S. Brainard, Photo.*

◆ Review

additive color mixture ◆ The result of diffracted light reflected to our eye from a surface; color produced by light.

subtractive color mixture ◆ The result of pigments mixed together and exerting their force upon one another.

color wheel ◆ A reference chart for colors.

primary colors ◆ Colors that cannot be produced by mixing other colors. Theoretically, all other colors can be produced from the primaries.

secondary colors ◆ Colors produced by mixing two primaries.

tertiary (intermediate) colors ◆ Colors produced by mixing a primary and a secondary color.

hue ◆ A "family" of color; the pure state of a color.

value ◆ The range of possible lightness or darkness within a given medium.

shade ◆ A dark value of a color.

tint ◆ A light value of a color.

intensity ◆ The relative purity of a color; brightness or dullness.

complement ◆ The color directly opposite a selected color on the color wheel.

tones ◆ Neutrals of colors; relative neutral scale.

neutral ◆ The color resulting after two complements have been mixed to the point where neither color is evident.

temperate colors ◆ The apparent psychological or emotional state of warmth or coolness of colors.

perception ◆ The individual response to the sensations of stimuli. Often cultural.

color interaction ◆ The relative differences between colors as they react to one another in different environs.

contrast ◆ The result of comparing one thing to another and seeing the difference.

Simultaneous color contrast ◆ A system of contrasting colors as defined by Michel-Eugène Chevreul using the traditional color wheel.

Color systems (schemes, harmonies) ◆ Synonymous with "Simultaneous color contrast"

Split-complement ◆ Three hues; one hue and the hues on *either* side of its complement.

Monochromatic ◆ One hue with value and/or intensity changes.

Triad ◆ Three hues at *equal* distance from one another on the color wheel.

Analogous ◆ "Alike" hues. Three to five (or more) hues lying next to one another on the color wheel.

9

Space Division & Balance

◆ Use of the Elements

We have now considered all of the design elements. It is as if we were looking at those ingredients for our cake: flour, sugar, butter, eggs, flavoring (chocolate preferred), and so on.

The cake ingredients, like our elements, are not exciting by themselves. They have to be put together and it is HOW they are put together that results in a "WOW" of gratification . . . or . . . an "OHhh . . ." of disappointment.

The *principles* are *how* the elements or components of a design are used or composed. They are considered guidelines only because all these elements can be combined in millions of ways and still be a good design. There is no right or wrong—only designs that work well and those that do not. If the design is successful, all the parts will work together as one total form and will attract and affect the viewer as the designer intended. If it is semisuccessful, the viewer may consider the design momentarily but not as the designer wished. And if it fails to attract the viewer at all, let alone hold the viewer's attention, it can be considered a failure.

As Edgar Whitney, artist, said, "Every time you make conscious choices in design, you sharpen your taste, and good taste is nothing more than information at work."

We will look at how we can manipulate our elements in our space, considering the following principles of design: space division and balance, unity, and emphasis.

◆ Dividing Space

We are now ready to examine how we can combine the parts to create the total effect we call a design.

First, we choose a space to use for our design. One of the first things we do automatically, without realizing what we are doing, is to divide or break up that space.

SPACE IS BROKEN BY NEGATIVE AND POSITIVE SHAPES

The *instant* we draw that horizon line in our pictorial space, we have divided our space into TWO areas. Or when we place one shape into a negative space, we have "broken" the emptiness of that space. Think of it in terms of something tangible, like putting one chair into an empty room. This placement immediately creates a charge of energy in the space. It breaks up the space and makes both the space and the shape more interesting.

As we place a *second* shape into our space, we break up the space even more, and we now have to start thinking about the *relationship* of our shapes to *one another,* the relationship of our shapes *to the space,* as well as to the *negative shapes* that may be formed in the process. The more shapes or lines (which are also

9◆1

TWO STONES. This placement of two stones is practicing the principles of design with only an aesthetic purpose in mind. "It is salutary that in a world rocked by greed, misunderstanding, and fear, with the imminence of collapse into unbelievable horrors, it is still possible and justifiable to find important the exact placement of two pebbles."—*Jim Ede, aesthete and collector. S. Brainard, Photo.*

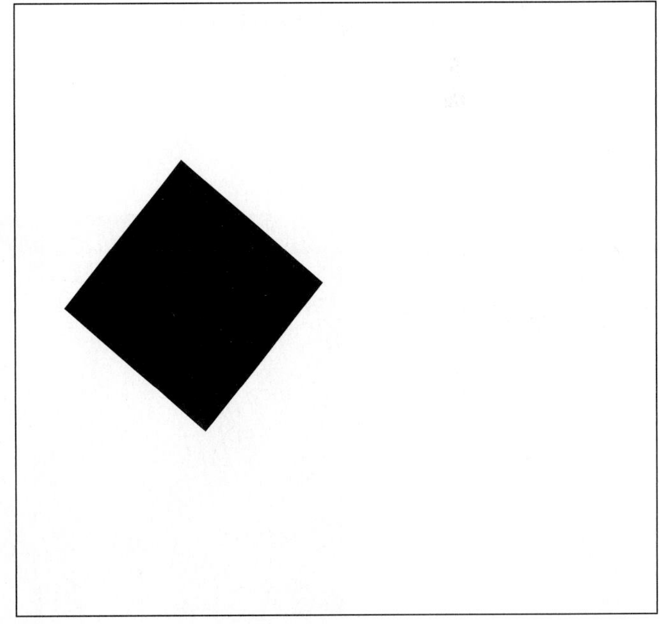

9◆2

Diagram 1. A shape put into a space breaks up the space. This action energizes the space.

positives) that are added to our space, the more complicated this relationship becomes. It becomes a **complex** design, as opposed to a **simple** design, where only a few shapes or images are used.

Balance

When we divide or break up our space, we commit a physical act. Think of it as something we actually DO in our space. We make it happen.

We, as humans, tend to see bilaterally—from side to side rather than up to down. In Western culture, we usually look at a two-dimensional space from left to right. If, then, we place something on the left with nothing on the right, we perceive an **implied axis,** or "a line that really isn't there," down the center of our space, dividing the space in half; we create a design that forces the viewer to make a *mental* division of the space. We are an orderly people and we want those two halves to balance or we feel uncomfortable with the design.

Often viewers don't know WHY they don't "like" a design; they just don't. It doesn't fit their need for harmony and balance even though they may not know it. So balance and **space division** affect one another.

Let's define **balance** as positive and negative spaces or shapes distributed in space by apparent VISUAL weight. We can use any or all of our elements to create balance. We may balance a shape with lines, or lines with value, or many lines together to balance a color, and obviously with shapes to shapes, and the like.

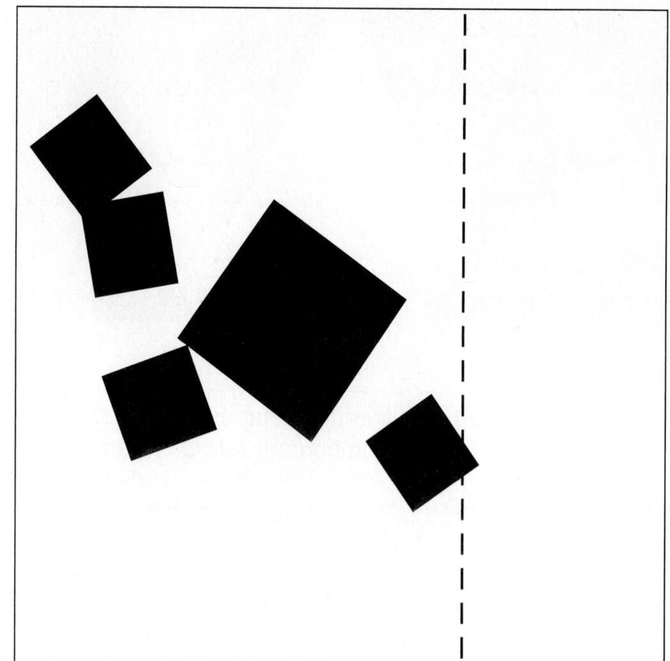

9◆4

Diagram 3.

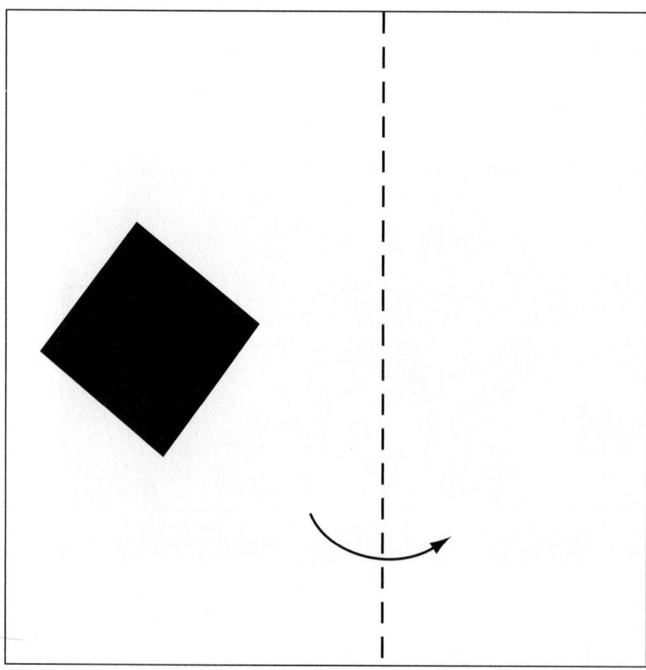

9◆3

Diagram 2.

Kinds of Balance

There are known balance systems we can employ—ways to use our elements to achieve a balanced effect. I think it is important to be aware of several of the most frequently used balance systems and the differences among them.

1. SYMMETRICAL. When we divide our space with that "implied" vertical axis and divide our space equally into halves, the easiest and most common balance system to employ is **symmetrical** or **formal** balance. *Symmetrical balance has the exact identical weight on both sides of the implied axis.* A very technical definition of this balance system says that not only are both sides identical in weight but that they also share *identical imagery in reverse.* This is called "mirror image." Formal balance is instantly understood as it requires little of the viewer. It is exacting, noncasual, and quiet, but it can also be boring.

SYMMETRICAL balance is USUALLY (but not always) found in functional design, and it can be found in buildings, cars, clothing, furniture, and so on.

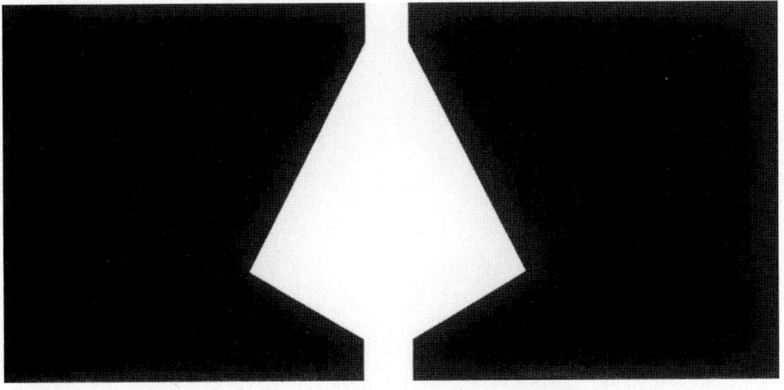

9◆5

Diagram depicting two *identical* shapes in a mirror-image design creates an immediate *formal* balance.

9◆6

Two exactly alike cups in opposite positions create symmetrical balance. *Source: Shirl Brainard.*

9◆7

Eighteenth-century English mahogany high chest. Both sides of the chest are exactly the same but in reverse. An example of *formal balance. Courtesy: Baker Furniture, Grand Rapids.*

9◆8

One of the formal gardens in the Bois de Boulogne, Paris. Max Alexander, Photo. *Source: Dorling Kindersley Media Library. Max Alexander © Dorling Kindersley.*

9◆9

Frank Gehry, architect. CHIAT/DAY ADVERTISING AGENCY BUILDING (1991) in California. Combined with sculptor Claes Oldenburg. Neil Setchfield, *Photo. Source: Dorling Kindersley Media Library. Neil Setchfield © Dorling Kindersley.*

2. ASYMMETRICAL. The second most common type of balance system is **asymmetrical,** or **informal** balance. In this system, the space may be divided in unequal parts and, therefore, the elements must be placed with care to distribute the weight and create the needed balance. The *visual weight* is EQUAL but NOT IDENTICAL. This system is really used more extensively than formal balance or any of the other balance systems. It is more gratifying because it is more casual and more interesting. It is, however, harder for the designer to achieve and also asks more effort from the viewer.

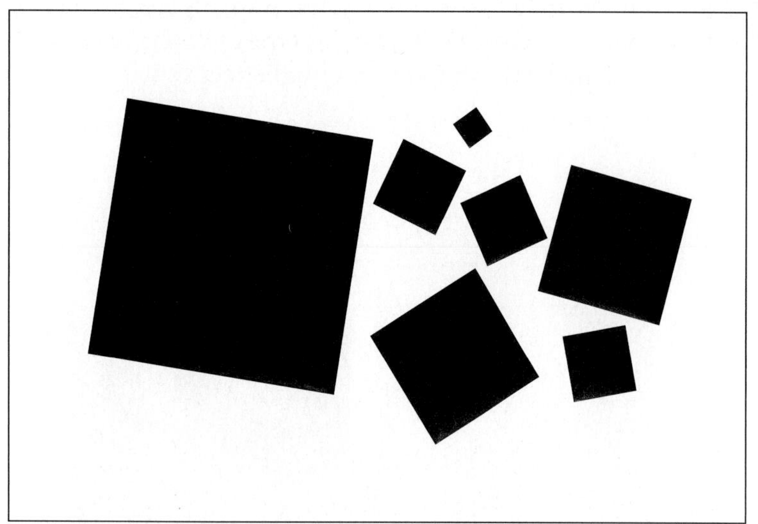

9◆10

Diagram depicting *informal balance.* A large shape and several smaller shapes suggest the same *visual weight* distributed equally.

9◆11

Asymmetrical balance is achieved in this design by the values, the transparency, and the size of the two objects with the cup, which is opaque, making it visually "heavier." *S. Brainard, Photo.*

9◆12

Shirl Brainard, SPIRIT OF THE SIPAPU. 1989. Acrylic on masonite. 18″ × 24″. The elements in this painting have been distributed in order to achieve *informal balance.*

3. APPROXIMATE SYMMETRY. A third system, which is seldom mentioned in design texts but that I feel is important to know about, is **approximate symmetry.** This symmetry makes the distinct technical differentiation between exact SYMMETRY, or "mirror image," and that which is often *perceived* as formal balance and *is not.* The *visual weight appears identical.* I always feel someone is practicing a little deception—leading me to perceive the design as formal—yet I realize it is a kind of informal balance, or a mixture of the two. This approach can relax a design that calls for being somewhat formal because it does not require the exactness or the mirror imagery of a strictly formal system. Often you will notice that this balance system may be called formal or symmetrical in instances where the precise technical difference may not be important. I feel we should be aware of approximate symmetry and be able to use this system. A dying design may be saved by resorting to just this type of variance in order to achieve the maximum visual effect.

9◆13

Rob Douglas's painting, INFINITE STILLNESS 1. Acrylic and raw pigment on panel, 49″ × 60″. *Courtesy of Nuart Gallery, 670 Canyon Road, Sante Fe, NM 87501.*

9◆15

Two similar cups *appear* to be balanced symmetrically. Different values change the apparent visual weight, so they are considered to be in *approximate* symmetry. *Source: Shirl Brainard.*

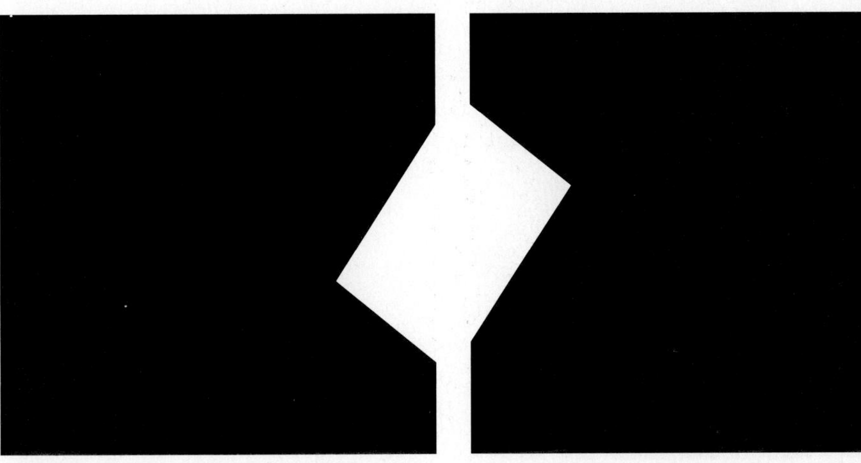

9◆14

Diagram: The shapes are the same but mirror-image reversed. Other shapes may be similar to one another but not the same. At first glance a viewer may "read" that they are the same. This illustrates *approximate symmetry.*

9◆16

Gary S. Griffin, DOORS. Hand-wrought steel. 81″ H × 66″ W × 2 1/2″ D. These doors have two sides that are very similar but are actually different. This design represents *approximate symmetry* balance. *Courtesy: Gary S. Griffin.*

9◆17

Shirl Brainard, STORM. 2000. Mixed media collage. 16″ × 20″.

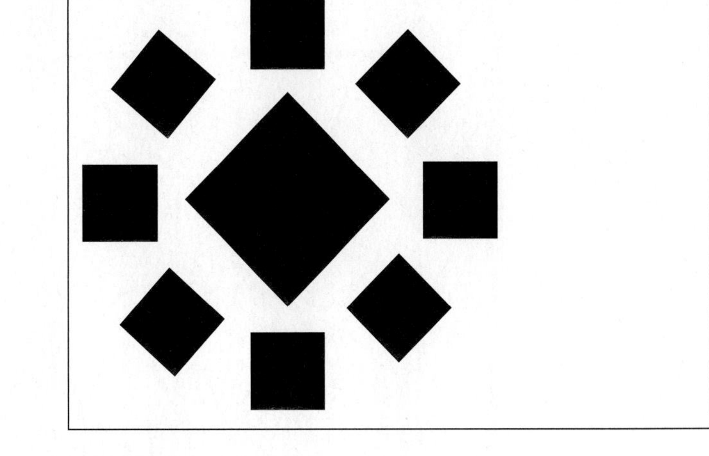

9◆18

Diagram: *Radial balance.* Shapes are arranged around a center or radius. The visual weight of the smaller shapes is collective.

4. RADIAL BALANCE. The last balance system is **radial balance.** This system uses a center or radius. The elements radiate from this center point and the *visual weight* is distributed collectively, creating the feeling of equilibrium.

9◆19

VICTORIAN-STYLE GAZEBO. An architectural form based on *radial balance.*
S. Brainard, Photo.

9◆20

L. Migdale, CIRCLE OF SMILING FACES. Circle of teen friends in Oakland, CA. Faces arranged in a circle balance one another by radiating from the center. *Photographer: Lawrence Migdale. Photo Researchers, Inc.*

A POSSIBLE PROBLEM What happens when we take objects of identical imagery and place one each on each side of our space? Or place different images in each "corner" of our space? We may question whether we are using the space to the best advantage, for one thing. Would you put a different chair in each corner of your living room?

The visual response, again, is a mental division of the space into halves or quarters. The halves that are the same or appear to be the same (symmetrical or approximately symmetrical) can be soothing or boring, depending on the imagery and the function of the design.

The quarters of the room, however, tend to make us see four "squares," or a grid effect. The images lead the eye from one imaginary square to the next. Often this is acceptable and, in fact, is commonly used to unify diverse subjects, as we will examine later. It is

9◆21

Dartboard. *Source: Getty Images, Inc.—Photodisc.*

9◆22

LANTERN TOWER, Ely Cathedral, Cambridgeshire, England. This octagon tower is based on radial balance. *Source: Corbis/Bettman.*

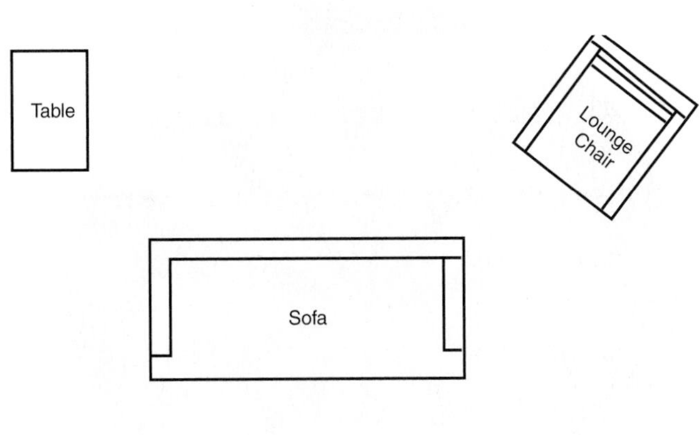

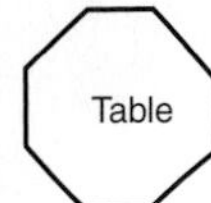

9◆23

Would you put your living room sofa in the center of a room and a chair or table in each corner?

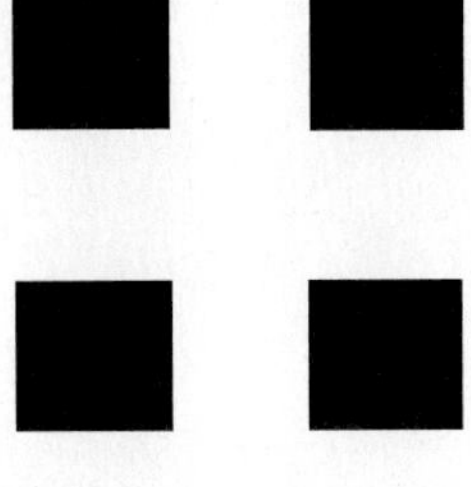

9◆24

Diagram: Grid effect.

an automatic way to unify and balance elements, but its use must be chosen carefully. Simple, all-over patterns—using the repetition of a motif—are based on this balance concept. (We'll discuss "pattern" later.)

But would you use a grid in a room arrangement? Would you design a refrigerator with four equal spaces? What would happen if you designed a landscape painting in this way?

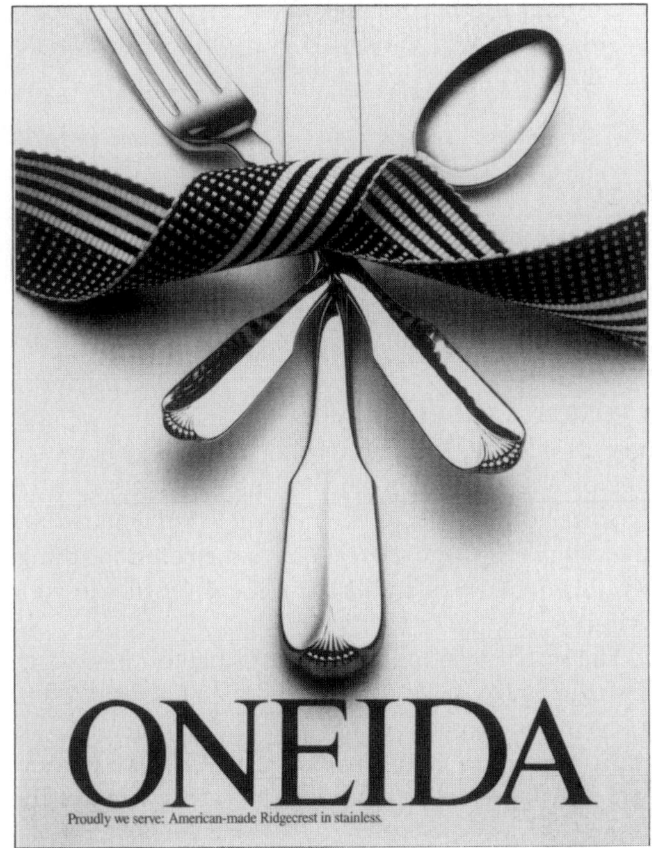

9◆25

Oneida Silversmiths, Stainless steel tableware, Ridgecrest design. *Advertisement Courtesy: Oneida Ltd., Silversmiths.*

Let's Think About Space Division . . .

Why does the division of space affect BALANCE?

Are all designs divided within their space?

Are all the spaces equal?

When might it be possible to have a design divided in equal parts?

Can you see *where* and DIAGRAM *how* the design figure 9–25 is divided?

KEYWORD to remember: SPACE DIVISION—space is divided by POSITIVE and NEGATIVE SHAPES. (Don't forget that lines are positive.)

Let's Think About Balance . . .

To create *balance:*

Do shapes have to be the same *kind* of shapes?

Do shapes have to be the same size?

Do shapes have to be the same value?

Do shapes have to have the same texture?

Do shapes have to be the same color?

Do shapes have to have the exact same visual weight?

What kind of balance would require all of the above?

Can lines be used in a design when you are trying to create balance?

Can shapes and other elements be manipulated to appear to have the same visual weight?

Now let's look at figure 9–26. This somewhat abstracted landscape uses a loosely defined vanishing point. The shadow of the pole serves to divide the wide space of the road. What would have happened to the BALANCE of the painting IF that shadow wasn't there?

9•26

Mark E. Mehaffey, COUNTRY ROAD. Watercolor on paper, 21″ × 29″. Source: Mark E. Mehaffey. *Courtesy of Mark E. Mehaffey. Country Road, WC on paper, 21″ × 29″.*

Figures 9–27, 9–28 is a diagram of how to make some geometric shapes. Prepare some so we can do some "visual thinking" while we physically manipulate the shapes in a given space. You should have three to four values, from very light gray to black. For your spaces, use a sheet of white paper: 8″ × 10″ and 4″ × 5″.

What Would Happen If . . .?

You used your largest black square and largest gray square on either side of an equally divided space on your small space?

Which appears heavier?

What happens if we turn the gray square?

What happens if the gray square were larger?

What happens if you turn the black square?

Keyword to remember: BALANCE—positive and negative shapes distributed in space by *visual* weight to create harmony.

Ideas to Try Dividing Space

Use the following spaces, try and divide each space into three sections, using line.

Do you see you have broken up the space?

Think—the parts have become "shapes."

Think—are any of the divisions equal?

Could two parts, or sections, equal one part?

What Would Happen If . . .?

You add a dark value to one shape?

You add two different values to two sections?

You add many lines to one section?

Is the balance affected?

Ideas to Try for Balance

Using your cutout squares on the biggest paper, experiment with all four balance systems. First, use your space horizontally, then vertically; you will see that there *is* a difference.

Now try using some varied shapes on your smaller space. At first, try only the black squares. It will be easy

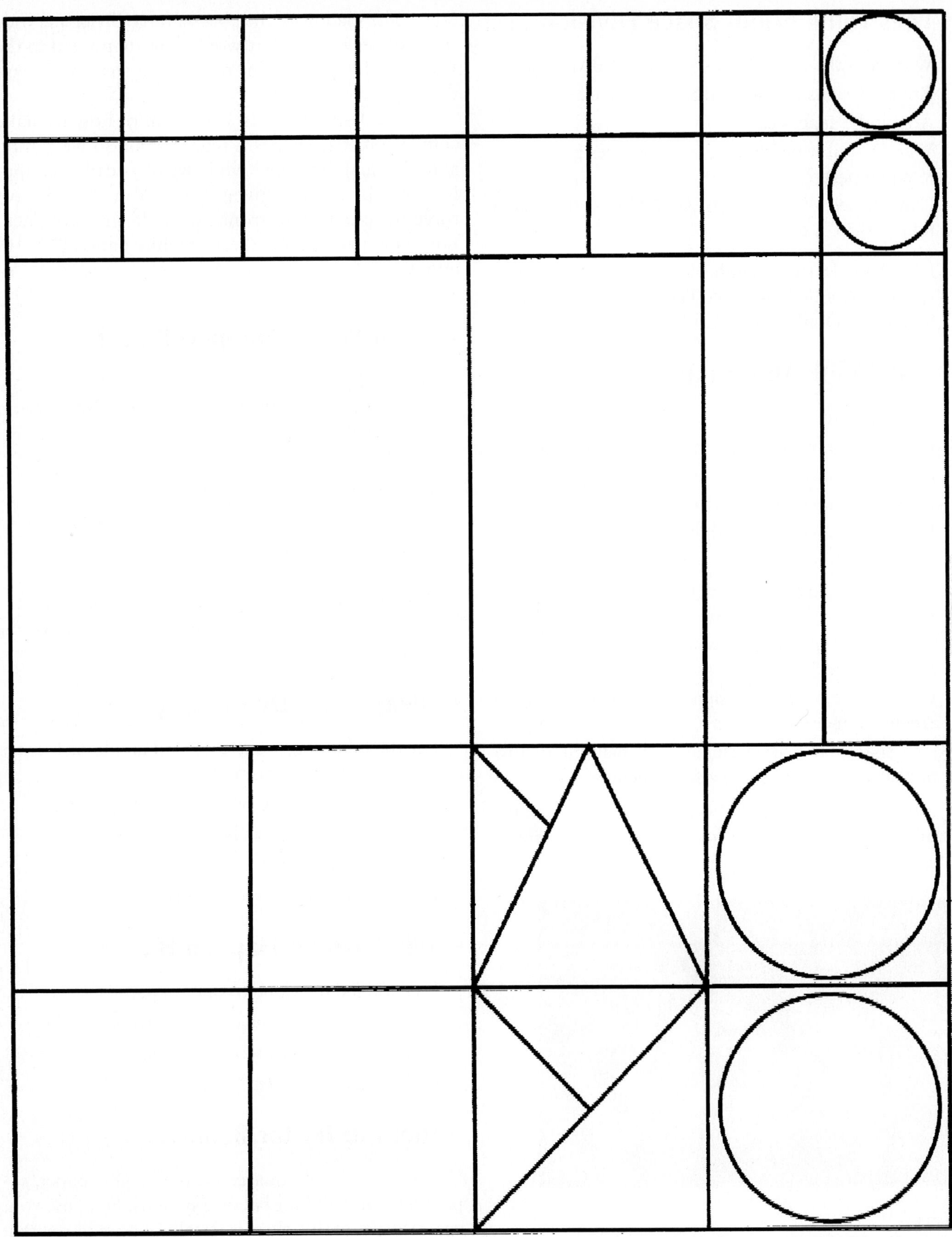

9◆27

Diagram: Geometric shapes for you to copy and use.

9◆28

Spaces to work on.

to create all of the systems. Now try substituting gray values for your black squares. You have changed the value and, therefore, the weights visually. Try other squares of different sizes or textures, or add lines with a pen.

WHAT HAPPENS?

More Ideas to Try for Balance.

Grouping small shapes to counterbalance a large shape.

Grouping small shapes to counterbalance a dark shape.

Trying active textures with darker values, and lightly textured surfaces with lighter values.

Try using irregular shapes, which are usually more heavier than more easily recognized shapes.

Using a bright color to balance less bright colors of a larger mass.

Placing shapes above eye level to add visual weight.

Try placing lines close together. They will appear darker and can help counterbalance a dark-valued solid mass.

◆ Can You Identify . . .?

How is the space divided?

What element is used the most?

What kind of balance system is used?

9◆29

Artist unknown, perhaps a child's work. MOLA. *Courtesy: Shirl Brainard.*

◆ Review

simple design ◆ Few elements used in the space and in the composition. Not difficult for a viewer to comprehend.

complex design ◆ Complicated as opposed to simple. Many elements used, so it is harder to design and comprehend.

implied axis ◆ A "mental" (or psychological) division of space. Usually centered or perceived bilaterally.

space division ◆ Space divided by the use of positive and negative shapes.

balance ◆ Positive and negative shapes distributed in space by apparent *visual* weight to create harmony.

symmetrical (formal) balance ◆ Technically, a mirror image: elements on either side of the implied axis having precisely the same shapes *but in reverse*—and having the identical same visual weight.

asymmetrical (informal) balance ◆ A balance system in which the visual weight on both sides of the implied axis of elements is equal. Elements often cross the axis.

approximate symmetry ◆ A balance system in which our first impression is that of symmetry. Weight may be identical but not a mirror image.

radial balance ◆ Created by repetitive equilibrium of elements radiating from a center point.

10

Unity

The principle of unification seems to be the most difficult principle to grasp. Balance is readily perceived, and we seem to notice more quickly when a design is not balanced. If a design lacks unity, however, it is more difficult to pinpoint WHY, because it is a more subtle problem.

Unification is the blending of flavors; it guides our eye and contributes to our reactions; it pulls the design together and makes us feel its wholeness or effectiveness.

I use the analogy of a party: A group of invited people with nothing in common, no theme, and no host or hostess present equals a very uncomfortable situation. The party needs at least *one* thing that everyone can relate to—one person (a host or hostess), an interest (music, food, a political figure), a theme (costume party, New Year's)—SOMETHING that enables each guest to say to someone else, "I am here for the same reason you are." This unifies the situation.

So let's define **unity** as the effect of having all the elements in harmony with one another, with each element being supportive to the total design.

There are three components or combinations which create unity: *REPETITION, VARIETY,* and *RHYTHM.*

Each of these components contributes to the unity of the composition. We will see how each can be used, and then how important it is that all are used together.

Repetition

Repetition means "to use again."

In music we repeat a note or a theme that acts as a bridge to the time we heard the note before. This repetition unifies the structure of the musical composition.

In a design, we can repeat any of our elements.

We can repeat a shape.

We can repeat a line.

We can repeat a value.

We can repeat a texture.

We can repeat a color.

We can repeat the *size* of a shape or a line!

Repeating an element more than once is an important factor, but again we must plan carefully *how* we repeat and *what* we repeat. When we talked about balance, I mentioned the danger of having more than two images in a space visually dividing that space. At the other extreme, too much repetition of one image might also damage our design, *unless* we have a reason to create the effect of a "pattern," which we will discuss later.

Let's look at figure 10–1, which is a simple design. There are five black squares. Lines divide the rest of the negative space. There is formal balance. The negative spaces between the squares form rectangular shapes that are also repeated. The Large negative space at the top seems to counterbalance the heavier (due to value) shapes on the lower space. The shapes relate to one another because they are an exact repeat of each other.

Variety

Variety, the second part of unity, means "to change the character" of an element. Variety provides the contrast that creates interest. But we have to be careful about variety also. If we have too much, it leads to confusion and we lose the interest factor. Any element can be made different, just as any element can be repeated. Some ways to vary our elements are the following:

Shapes can be varied . . . by kinds, sizes, colors, values, textures, location in the space, alternation, and the like.

Lines can be varied . . . by thickness, thinness, length, salves, straight, curved, and the like.

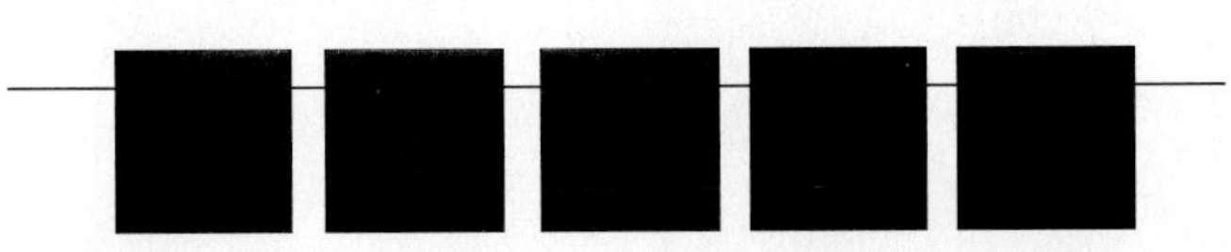

10◆1

Diagram: REPETITION. The space has been broken up by same-size geometric shapes and lines, using formal balance.

10◆2

Diagram: *Variety.* The sizes of the shapes have been altered. The balance is no longer formal. (Do you know what kind it is?)

Values can be varied . . . from dark to light.

Textures can be varied . . . from smooth to rough.

Colors can be varied . . . by their intrinsic nature.

Let's look at figure 10–2. NOW WHAT HAS HAPPENED?

In figure 10–2 we have added different values and sizes. The smaller squares are placed in such a way that they carry the eye from one shape to another. The up and down position contributes to a "beat" in the composition. We have created the last part of our unity: RHYTHM. Now look at figure 10–3.

Rhythm

Rhythm means "a recurrence of movement." In music, the repetition and variety of notes create the rhythm that we remember, identify, and perhaps hum or whistle. In a visual work, RHYTHM is also created by repetition and variety. The way these two components are used gives us movement, both emotional and visual. As our eye travels around the design, we may experience an upbeat feeling, or we may be left with a more subdued sensation—one of calmness, sadness, or perhaps boredom.

The "visual path" our eye follows can be influenced by the *way* chosen elements are aligned or repeated. Windows repeated in a building may take our eye around and through the design; the same could be said for the repetition of a color in a room. The kinds of shapes used and how they are used together will decide the feeling we get from rhythm in a particular setting.

Look at 10–4. This photo of a swing "reads" as static. Why is this "play" object so quiet? Maybe it's naptime, a quiet afternoon. Or, maybe . . . what??

Let's now look at figure 10–5. How did your own feelings change as you looked at this? How does this "read"? There is a difference in the EMOTIONAL quality of the two photos.

10◆3

Diagram: *Rhythm.* More variety and repetition and a more active way of positioning the shapes make the whole design more lively.

10◆4

Swing. Chris Volk, Photo. *Source: SuperStock, Inc. Chris Volk/SuperStock.*

10◆5

Child on swing. Photographer: Nancy Rica Schiff, Photo. *Source: SuperStock, Inc.*

Because this concept of mood, or "emotional quality or movement," is often hard to grasp, let's think about one more example. A penal institution should have good exterior and interior design. It needs to function in a specific way. Architecturally, it could

look decent, acceptable, BUT should it look welcoming? Should it be designed so that many of us would want to go in? Should the interior be so inviting and comfortable you would never want to leave? Churches, on the other hand, are designed to welcome, to enfold, and, once inside, to inspire exultation.

What about a sports car? A sports car's sleek, geometric shapes are aligned in long, tension-filled horizontals. It makes us think of sophistication, money!—speed! Other horizontal alignments, such as a landscape, may make us feel restful, peaceful, or even lazy. Landscape shapes will probably not be angular ones, as in the sports car, but soft, curved shapes undulating horizontally with little or no opposition.

Let's look at figure 10–6. This painting is an excellent example of BALANCE and UNITY using *repetition, variety,* and *rhythm.* It is an informal balance of geometric and natural shapes. The two verticals on the left *balance* the vertical of the figure. The "joining" of those two verticals with the horizontal leading to the circular geometries creates a triangle which is *repeated* and *balances* the bend of the figure's arm resting on his hip. The circular shapes are *repeated* and there is a *variance* in the size as well as in the variety of the two kinds of shapes. The *rhythm* is created with the circular shapes moving (almost) around and around. One may almost hear a "hum" of factory noises. It makes a statement: "This is this man's job . . . however tedious."

Later, in SHAPE RELATIONSHIPS, we'll look at some "rhythmic devices" that can be of help to lead and carry the eye through a design.

10◆6

Joseph Lorusso, CAPTAIN OF INDUSTRY. Oil on panel. Repetition, variety, and rhythm create a unified painting. *Source: Joseph Lorusso.*

10◆7

Diagram of *Captain of Industry. Source; Shirl Brainard.*

◆ Let's Think About Unity . . .

Look at figure 10–8. WHAT HAS HAPPENED? WHAT HAS GONE WRONG? Let's think about what we have studied so far:

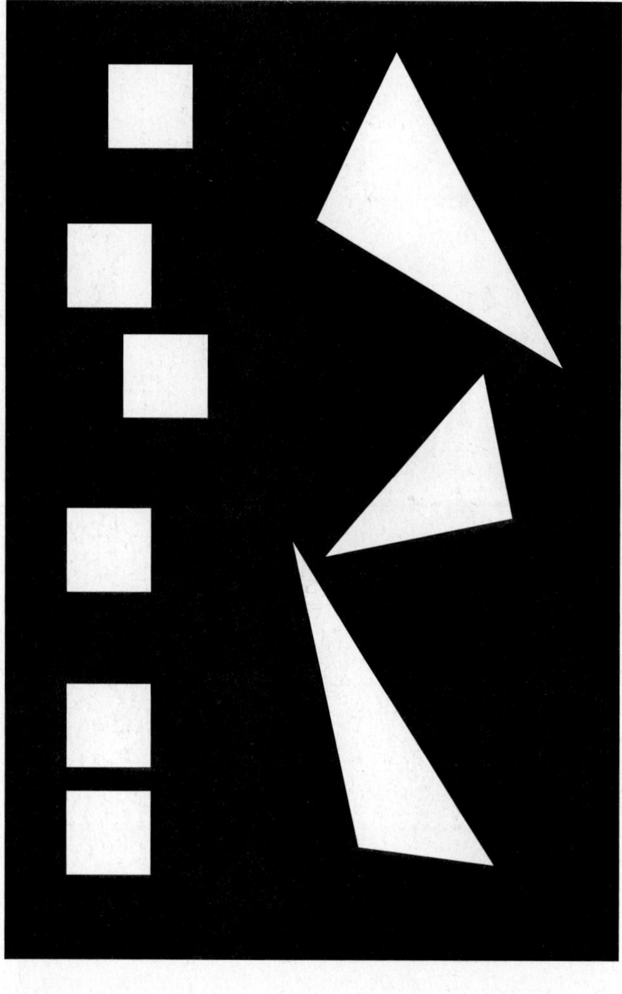

10◆8

Diagram.

We have geometric shapes that are squares and triangles.

We have the darkest value as a background of the shapes.

We have a smooth texture as a surface quality of the shapes.

The more numerous small squares enhance balance by adding visual weight to counter balance the large triangles.

Shapes and sizes have been varied, but not too much.

It has REPETITION, VARIETY, and is RHYTHMIC.

WE HAVE DONE ALL THE THINGS WE HAVE TALKED ABOUT.

WHY DOESN'T IT LOOK GOOD? WHY DOESN'T IT WORK FOR US?

Keyword to remember: UNITY—wholeness

◆ Analysis

In figure 10–8, the space has been visually divided into two parts or halves by the exact repetition of the shapes. The two sides come close to balancing weight-wise, but the eye tends to look at EITHER the squares OR the triangles and not to "flow" through the space, taking in both at once.

◆ What Would Happen If . . .?

the values were changed?

lines were added?

textures were added?

the negative spaces were considered more as "shapes"?

the triangles were located differently?

the squares were intermingled with the triangles?

10◆9

Mortimer Menpes. FIVE STUDIES OF WHISTLER. Drypoint. *A. E. Gallatin Collection, Miriam and Ira D. Wallach Division of Art, Prints and Photographs, The New York Public Library, Astor, Lenor & Tilden Foundation.*

◆ An Idea to Try with Unity

Using your duplicate shapes, see if you can improve this composition. Try all of the above ideas. Which one, or combination, works best?

◆ A Design Analysis

Look at the drawing in figure 10–9.

What kinds of shapes are used?

What do these shapes portray?

Was line used as a contour line to create any shapes?

Was line used in any way that stands out to you?

Are a wide range of values used?

What do these values do to the shapes?

What kinds of textures are portrayed? Smooth? Shiny? Rough?

What kind of balance is used?

Why is this drawing unified?

Has the space been used well?

◆ Review

unity ◆ The effect of all the elements being in harmony with one another, creating the feeling of wholeness.

repetition ◆ The result of repeating or doing the same thing over and over.

variety ◆ The changing of the original character of any element; diversity.

rhythm ◆ A recurrence or movement. A "visual path" for the eye to follow; a "visual beat."

11

Emphasis

- Contrast
- Any Contrast Can Be Made to Work! By the Way . . . What Is an Anomaly?
- Selection
- Let's Think About Emphasis . . .
- Ideas to Try for Emphasis or Focal Point
- Can You Identify . . .?
- Review

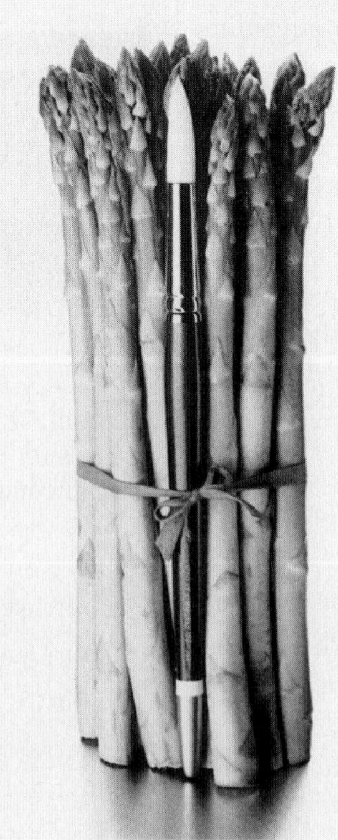

The last principle of design is the creation of emphasis. **Emphasis** *is what we want the viewer to see.* Emphasis is the visual destination of our design journey and should invoke a mental, emotional, or physical response. It is the designer's responsibility to direct the viewer's eye to this area. A quote from Robert Henri: "The eye should not be led where there is nothing to see."

The NAME of the product is an absolute necessity in the instance of a product to be sold. The name IS the emphasis or focal point. In the design of a building, emphasis is perhaps placed on the door, which may be more decorative than the rest of the building so people are drawn to enter there. In a painting, however, the emphasis may be on an *element* only, such as texture or color. Earlier, we discussed the intention of the designer. This emphasis only on an element is a prime example of the difference between functional design, which has content, message, or focal point for the viewer, and nonfunctional design, which considers the creative intention of the artist or designer whether or not there is a message.

11◆1

Stephen Quiller, AUTUMN ASPEN RHYTHM. Watercolor and gouache. 26″ × 20″. This painting emphasizes the abstract quality of the trees with line and geometric shapes. *Courtesy: Stephen Quiller.*

◆ Contrast

Emphasis is created by CONTRAST. If you will remember, CONTRAST was discussed in the chapter on VALUE. It is seeing the difference between one thing compared to another. Some authors of design textbooks give many titles to the ways one might create emphasis, but it all comes down to contrasting one thing to another. It *does* matter how the contrasts are used, as it does with the other principles: One gray square contrasted with another square the same size but of a contrasting value will not create an emphasis. The eye will only go back and forth between them, unable to decide which is the more important. *Perhaps the entire message of the designer is "see the contrast of this square to this square."* But if we want the viewer to see more, we must make more defined contrasts.

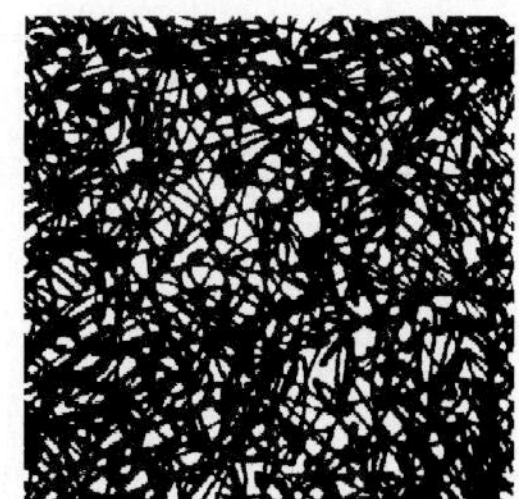

11◆2

Diagram: There is not enough contrast between the two squares for one to be seen more than the other. They tend to compete for attention.

The following are some contrasts that can create emphasis:

Contrast of position or location of an element to other elements.

Contrast of size of shapes to other shapes.

Contrast of size of a shape to the rest of the space.

Contrast of values to other values.

Contrast of shapes to lines.

Contrast of lines to values.

Contrast of textures to other textures.

Contrast of textures to values.

Contrasts between widths, lengths, kinds of line.

Contrast between colors.

Contrast of edges of shapes—torn to cut, and the like to other edges.

Contrast of the "anomaly" to the rest of the design.

◆ Any Contrast Can Be Made to Work! By the Way . . . What Is an Anomaly?

An **anomaly** is a deviation from the normal, or what is considered ordinary. If I go to the beach on a hot day dressed in a muffler, mittens, and winter coat, I am an "anomaly." People would notice me! We all, at one time or another, have felt we were "different" from others in a given circumstance or didn't "fit" into a situation. At that time, we were "anomalies"—or thought we were.

Anomalies very efficiently create emphasis by directing the eye quickly and surely to the area we want the eye to go.

Obviously, several elements can be combined in our effort to create emphasis: A textured area may have a defined color; a shape that is an anomaly to other shapes may also have a contrast of values; and so on. The ideas one can generate with contrasts are endless.

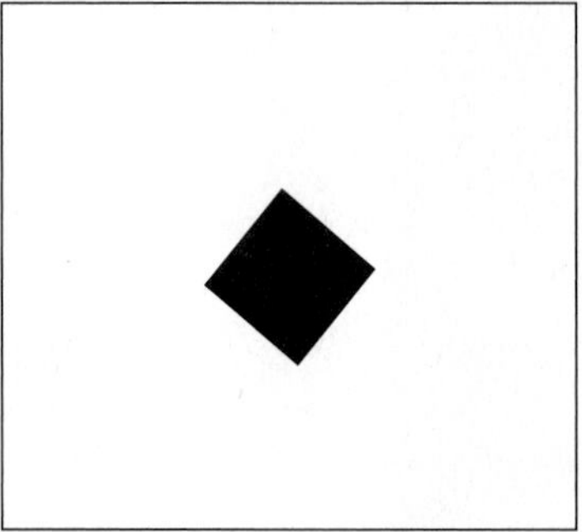

11◆3

Diagram: The size of the shape contrasted with the size of the space makes you see the shape.

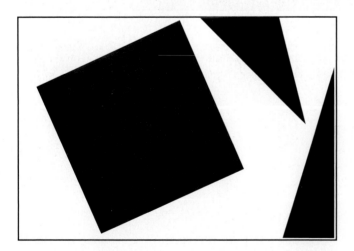

11◆4

Diagram: The same idea–the contrast between size of space to shape. In this example, the shapes are larger than the space.

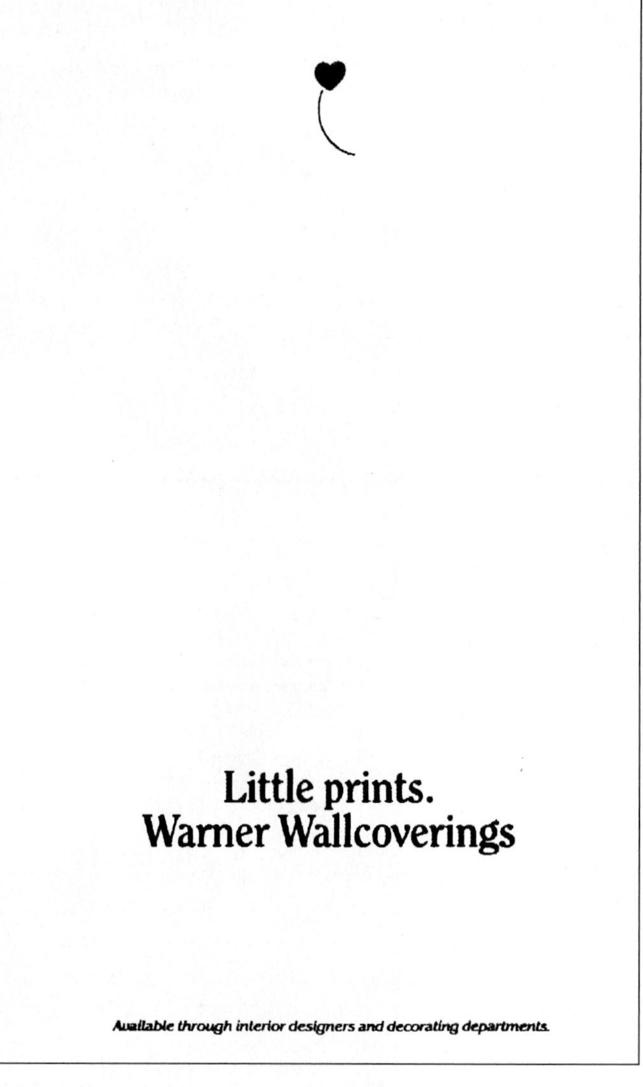

Little prints.

Available through interior designers and decorating departments.

11◆5

Warner Wallcoverings, Advertisement. The little shape in a big space makes the shape seem obvious. Because nothing else competes with the shape, the eye drops to the message. (Note how the little "tail" on the heart also directs the eye to the name.) *Courtesy: Warner Wallcoverings. Chicago.*

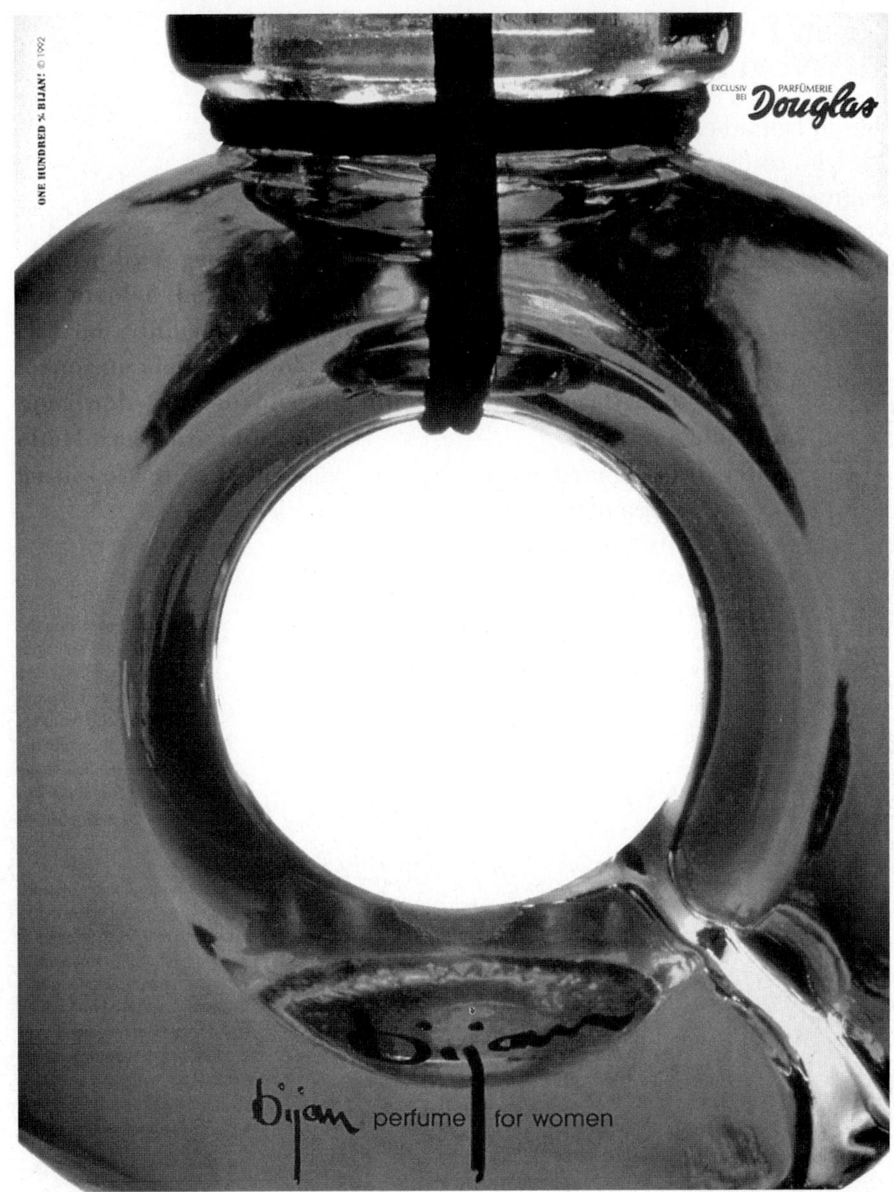

11◆6

A 1993 advertisement for BIJAN perfume. The size contrast makes it impossible not to see the product advertised. *Courtesy: Bijan Fragrances, Inc.*

11◆7

Diagram: The contrast of values indicates a focal point or emphasizes what the viewer is meant to see.

11◆8

NOT A ONE HORSE TOWN (Chicago). The value contrasts—shadowed areas against sunlit areas—make one see the carriage and horse. *S. Brainard, Photo.*

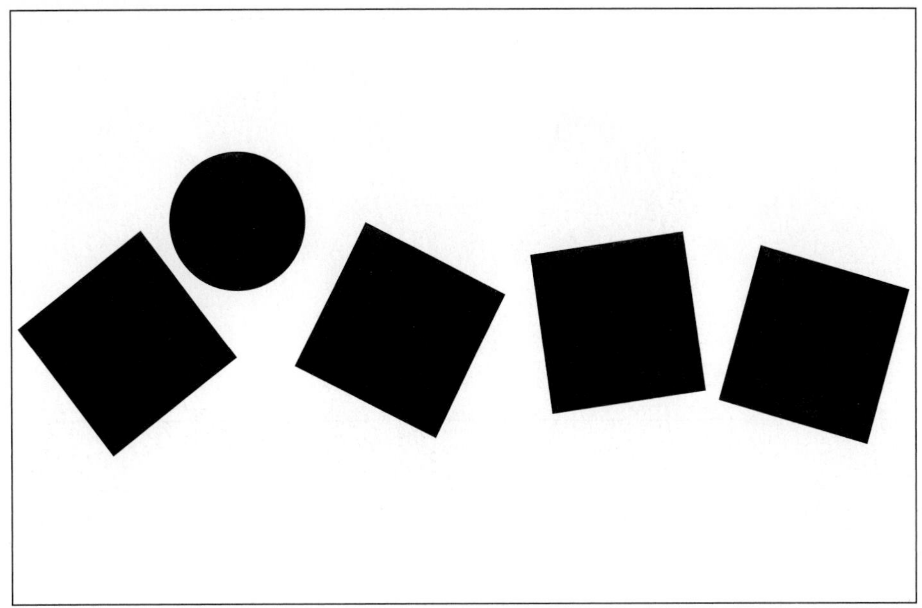

11◆9

Diagram: An *anomaly* is something "out of place." In this example, the circle is "out of place," so it is readily seen.

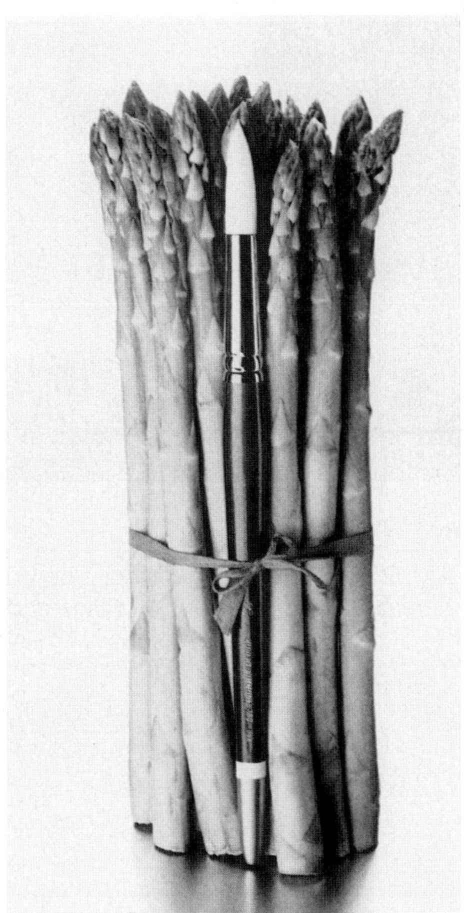

11◆10

Advertisement for brushes. A paintbrush nestled in a bunch of asparagus is an *anomaly.* *Photography: Pat Berret. Permission granted by Daler Rowney, Cranbury, NJ.*

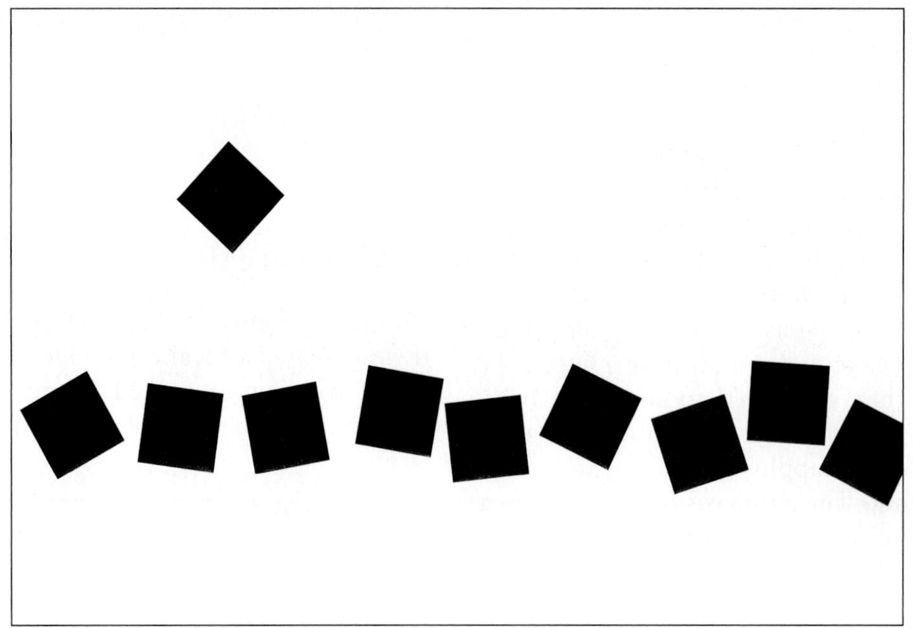

11◆11

Diagram: The contrast of position of one shape to other similar shapes creates emphasis. The eye interrupts its travel to look at that shape.

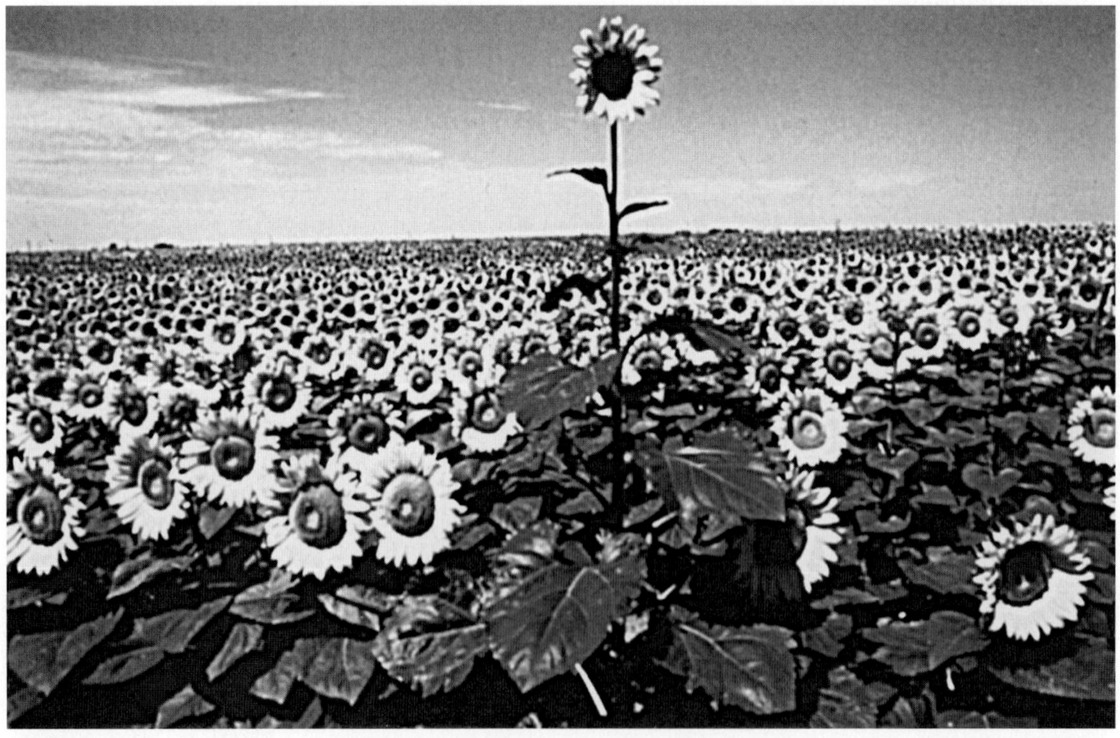

11◆12

Daniel D. Morrison, A SUNFLOWER FIELD. *Photo for Texas Department of Agriculture*

◆ Selection

Emphasis is often a matter of selection. Students (and professionals) often can't decide what they really want the viewer to see. This is especially true in drawing and painting. In designing, we want to direct the viewer's eye by using rhythm (to get the viewer on the visual path) and emphasis (to make the viewer stop and look). We must also pare down the nonessentials.

Once again using baking as our analogy, let's think about our chocolate cake. We already have a fine recipe for our cake, but then we decide to add some nuts. Good . . . they go well together. And how about a banana? Some raisins? Pineapple?

What is happening? The emphasis is no longer on a CHOCOLATE cake. It has become another kind of cake, and although we may have created an excellent new cake, the chocolate *essence*—or CHOCOLATE emphasis—has been diminished.

We must economize so as not to use more than what is needed for an excellent design.

Remember: LESS CAN BE MORE.

◆ Let's Think About Emphasis . . .

What might you emphasize when designing or decorating your living room?

What might you emphasize when designing a refrigerator?

What might you emphasize when designing a garden?

What might you emphasize when you are dressing (designing) yourself?

What do you think a chef might try to emphasize?

What do you think a choreographer might emphasize?

What does tying a yellow ribbon on a tree mean?

What are ways in which we might emphasize our house if we are having a party?

HOW MANY OF THE ABOVE ARE FOCAL POINTS?

Keyword to remember: EMPHASIS—*contrast*

◆ Ideas to Try for Emphasis or Focal Point

Go back to figure 10–12. WHAT WOULD HAPPEN IF you created a focal point? How could you do this?

Use your cutout, valued geometric shapes, or make some more. You might also consider adding line.

CAN YOU MOVE YOUR SHAPES AND LINES AROUND TO CREATE THE CONTRASTS WE TALKED ABOUT?

Did you create an ANOMALY?

Did you tend to use one kind of geometric shape more than any other?

Do you prefer that kind of shape?

Do you know why?

What could this tell you about yourself as a designer?

◆ Can You Identify . . .?

Which figure in figure 10–13 is the focal point? WHY?

Which SHAPE in figure 13–23 is the focal point? WHY?

◆ Review

emphasis ◆ The main element or focal point; what the viewer's eye should see first.

anomaly ◆ Something that is noticed because it differs from its environment.

12

Shape Relationships

◆ Safety Nets

The information we have just studied is essential to a design. Any effective design must include elements, and these elements must be arranged using these particular principles.

But sometimes that isn't enough. Sometimes we get stuck, or we look at our work and it doesn't seem to work. Sometimes we have a "dry period" and need a new direction. We may need a "safety net" or some "device" to help us out.

A **device** is not a design term. It is a word that means "a way" or, as *Random House Dictionary* cites, "a trick for effecting a purpose." This definition describes the following information, which I call "devices."

◆ Shape Relationships

It happens frequently in uneasy design (a design that starts with good ideas but doesn't feel satisfying) that the way our shapes relate to one another or to their space does not work. The devices that can help us the most to correct this are SCALE, PROPORTION, PLACEMENT, and TENSION. We can use these selectively when we need them.

SCALE. Scale refers to the *size* of one shape compared to another or to the space it occupies. Look at the example in figure 12–1. Notice how size affects your reaction to this design.

PROPORTION. Proportion is the relative measurement or dimension of parts to the whole. It is common in drawing to use one part = *X* parts to get good proportional representation . One example of this is the adult figure. We usually use the length of the head as a measurement for the rest of the body: One head length equals eight body parts, or the whole body. Proportion and scale are often confused and sometimes used interchangeably. Let's look at some examples of good proportion and observe how proportioned shapes look with other shapes or spaces. In figure 12–4, example A is a well-proportioned house. Example B is not. Why? In example C, the house in the first example is shown with a tree. What is your conclusion? Example D shows the tree with a person. What is your conclusion?

12◆1

Two men holding a giant pen or pencil. An example of exaggerated scale. *Source: SuperStock, Inc.*

11◆7

Diagram: The contrast of values indicates a focal point or emphasizes what the viewer is meant to see.

11◆8

NOT A ONE HORSE TOWN (Chicago). The value contrasts—shadowed areas against sunlit areas—make one see the carriage and horse. *S. Brainard, Photo.*

◆ Safety Nets

The information we have just studied is essential to a design. Any effective design must include elements, and these elements must be arranged using these particular principles.

But sometimes that isn't enough. Sometimes we get stuck, or we look at our work and it doesn't seem to work. Sometimes we have a "dry period" and need a new direction. We may need a "safety net" or some "device" to help us out.

A **device** is not a design term. It is a word that means "a way" or, as *Random House Dictionary* cites, "a trick for effecting a purpose." This definition describes the following information, which I call "devices."

◆ Shape Relationships

It happens frequently in uneasy design (a design that starts with good ideas but doesn't feel satisfying) that the way our shapes relate to one another or to their space does not work. The devices that can help us the most to correct this are SCALE, PROPORTION, PLACEMENT, and TENSION. We can use these selectively when we need them.

SCALE. Scale refers to the *size* of one shape compared to another or to the space it occupies. Look at the example in figure 12–1. Notice how size affects your reaction to this design.

PROPORTION. Proportion is the relative measurement or dimension of parts to the whole. It is common in drawing to use one part = *X* parts to get good proportional representation . One example of this is the adult figure. We usually use the length of the head as a measurement for the rest of the body: One head length equals eight body parts, or the whole body. Proportion and scale are often confused and sometimes used interchangeably. Let's look at some examples of good proportion and observe how proportioned shapes look with other shapes or spaces. In figure 12–4, example A is a well-proportioned house. Example B is not. Why? In example C, the house in the first example is shown with a tree. What is your conclusion? Example D shows the tree with a person. What is your conclusion?

12◆1

Two men holding a giant pen or pencil. An example of exaggerated scale. *Source: SuperStock, Inc.*

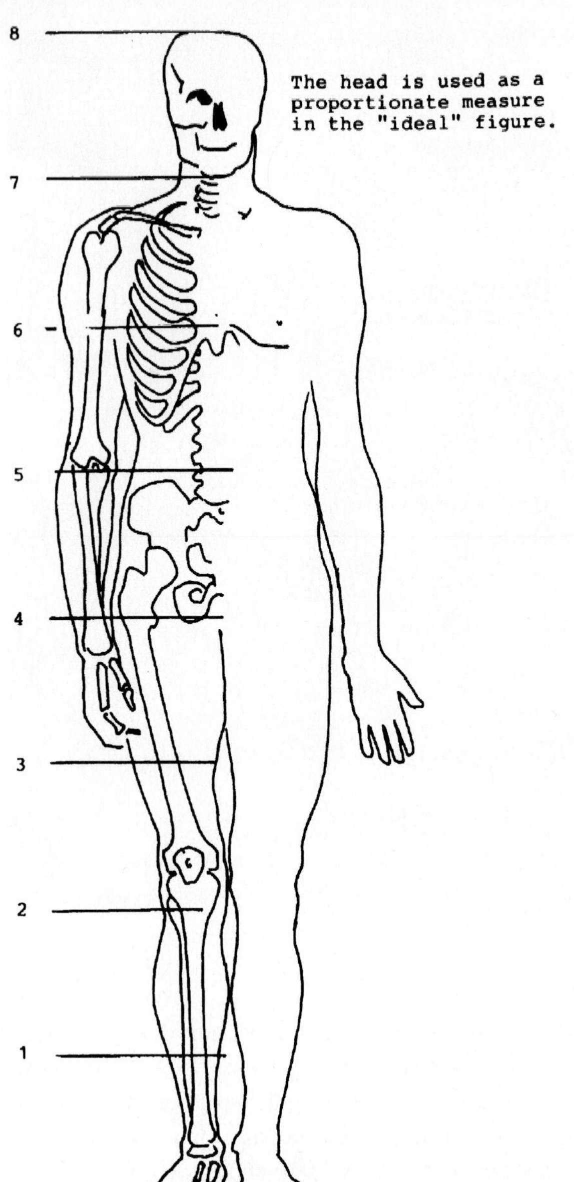

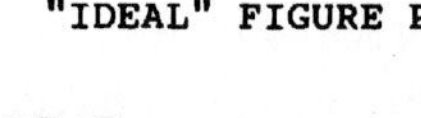

12◆2

Diagram: Shows how the measurement of the head is used to draw an "ideally" proportioned figure.

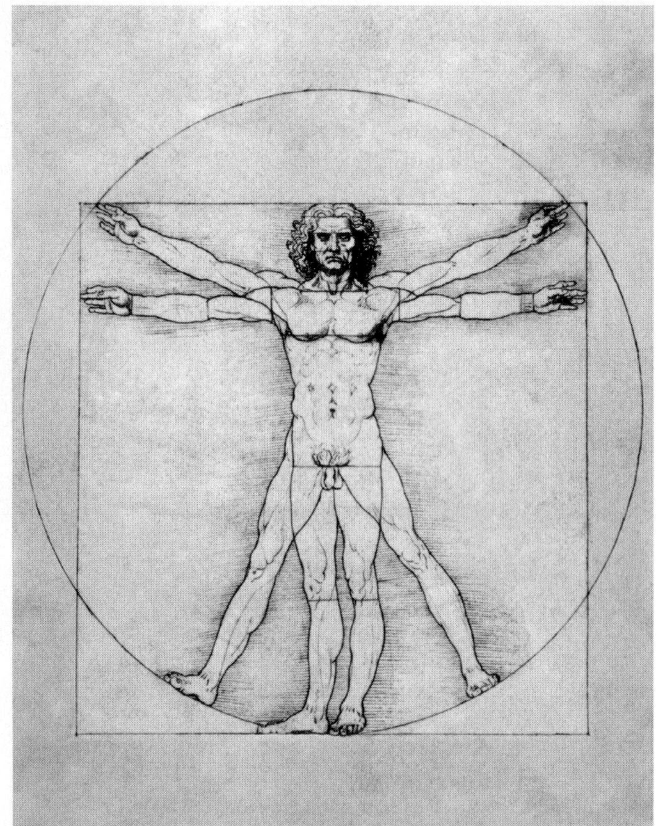

12◆3

Leonardo da Vinci (1452–1519), PROPORTIONS OF THE HUMAN FIGURE. *Source: SuperStock, Inc. Galleria dell' Accademia, Venice/SuperStock.*

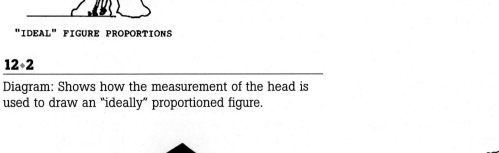

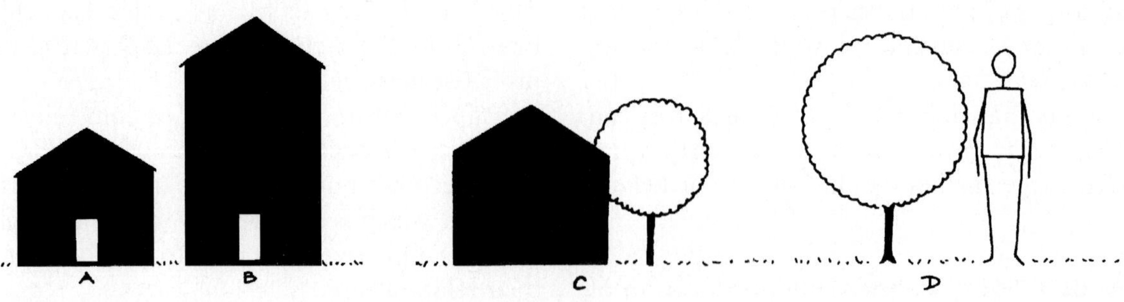

12◆4

Diagram.

12•5

Advertisement for custom-made sofas. A well-proportioned sofa in a well-proportioned room is still not compatible because of a difference in scale. *Courtesy: Century Furniture, Hickory, NC.*

If we change the size of our shapes, we can control the scale and proportion in our design. We can also create more interest because of the variance added to our design. This may be one of the first decisions we have to make, as in the case of refrigerator design. We not only need to have interesting variations in our size relationships of shapes (which can start with space division), but we must consider the actual inner-space usage. A freezer section and the cooling part of a refrigerator are not usually equal. We also have to consider the space into which some of our designs must fit and whether or not they will work in a utilitarian, as well as harmonious, way. Another reason for changing shape sizes is that we can control what the viewer sees in a believable way.

So we can say that changing the sizes of shapes can solve several design problems: scale, proportion, interest, space usage (actual or illusionary), or believable content.

SHAPE PLACEMENT. The **placement** or location of our shapes is important. We have all seen pictorial compositions in which some of the shapes just seem to float, not relating to each other or to the space, and that end up boring the viewer. Let's see what happens when we place our shapes in a more thoughtful way.

In the first example (figure 12–6), the person appears to be the same size as the tree. If we change the shape sizes *and* OVERLAP the shapes (figure 12–7), what do we see now? The viewer either thinks the person is in front of the tree, or that the tree is farther behind the person, but that both the person and the tree are of normal size.

In figure 12–8, we see that several circles differ in size and overlap some of the other circles. In overlapping, some of the circles appear to be parts of other circles, but they are still seen as circles. Isn't this a more interesting design than figure 12–9, where the circles just exist in space?

Shapes that do not overlap or come close together are difficult to control. It's as though the space between them becomes boundless and the shapes are forever floating, which is nice if we want the feeling of being airborne. Otherwise, we need to anchor them through their relationships.

We spoke earlier of "visual" space division—when our eye perceives the space in quarters or halves because of the way shapes are placed and balanced. I

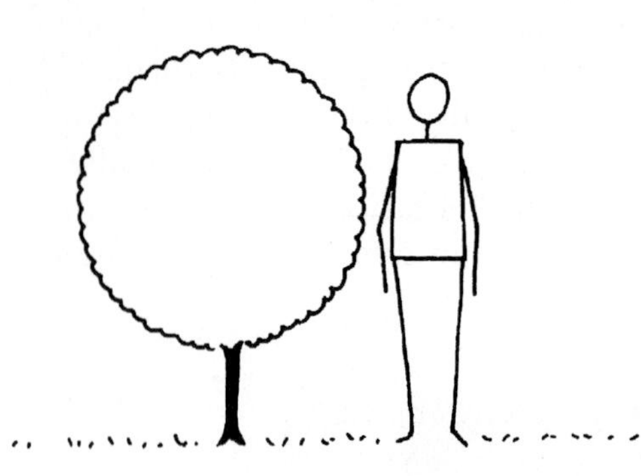

12◆6 and 12◆7

Diagram.

always use the word clump, indicating that our eye seems to move awkwardly (or "clump") from one shape to another. I think many students make the mistake "clumping" their shape because they sense the need for using the space but don't exactly know how. Many times—especially in two-dimensional pictorial designs—students will place their shape of interest in the middle of the space; then, because they instinctively feel a need to do more, they will put other shapes in the "corners." Remember when we talked about this briefly in the chapter about space division and balance?

We can overlap one or more shapes; we can change the size of the shapes; we can move some closer together or even *almost* touch, or yes . . . **touch.** We can cluster or mass many small shapes together. In effect, we "count" them visually, and "weightwise" we "weigh" them as one shape. This is helpful in the principle of balance.

12◆8

Diagram.

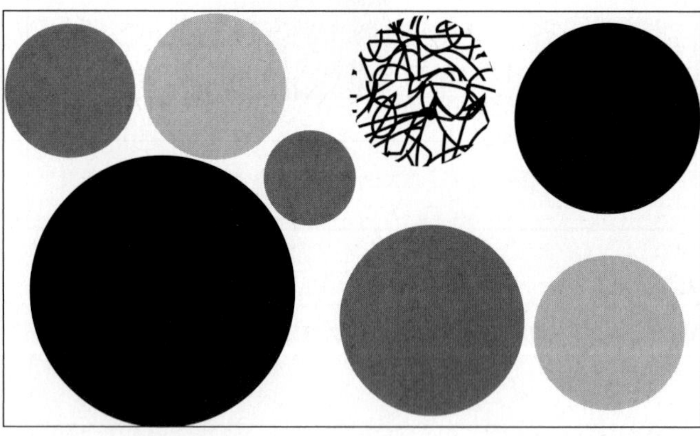

12◆9

Diagram.

The way shapes FIT together is also important. Often when students try to vary their shapes, they create too much variety or create shapes that don't fit together well. If we look at figure 12–10, we see that these three shapes are different. They are geometric shapes. How do we make them work together or FIT together? We use the devices we have been speaking of: overlapping, touching, repositioning. Repositioning simply means playing with the shapes until they all look, feel, and work better together. Try them in different positions: upside down, sideways, half-concealed, cropped, from different views and different angles. An interesting "negative shape" may appear that the eye perceives as an actual shape in the design.

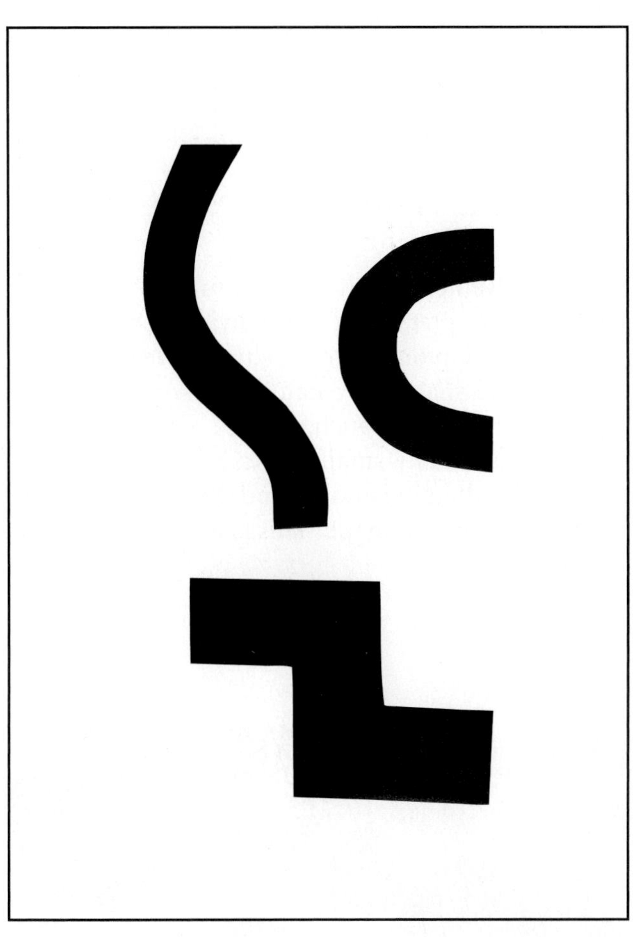

12◆10

What would you do with these three shapes?

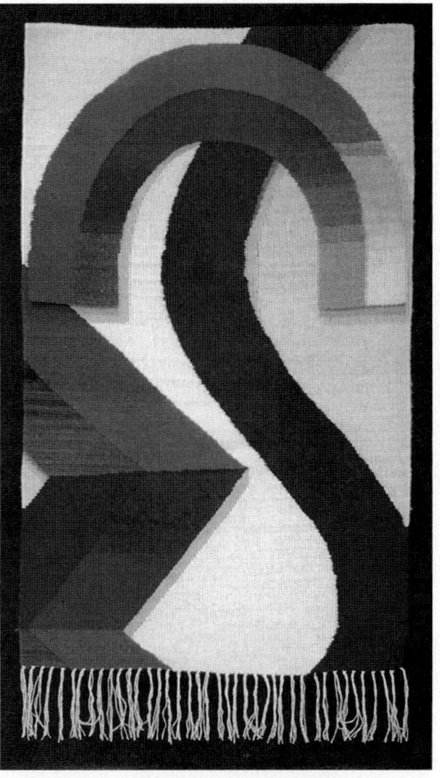

12◆11

Nancy Kozikowski. U.S. SERIES #3. The use of "tension" in a design. Tapestry. 44″ × 30″. Look at how some of the "points" of triangular shapes fit into a curved negative shape. What does the "U" overlapping shape do for the design? *Copyright Nancy Kozikowski Design. Courtesy Dartmouth Street Gallery.*

Cropping. Another device we have already touched on briefly is that of **cropping,** or cutting off part of a shape. This happens automatically when we overlap shapes—the one in back is cropped. Fifty years ago cropping was not an acceptable idea in design, but then we didn't know many of the things about design we now do. Today we know that we can emphasize a shape *more* by cutting off part of it while still retaining its essence. In figure 12–13, part of the body is cropped, emphasizing the midtorso. It also serves to make the viewer *feel* that there is more space than can be seen.

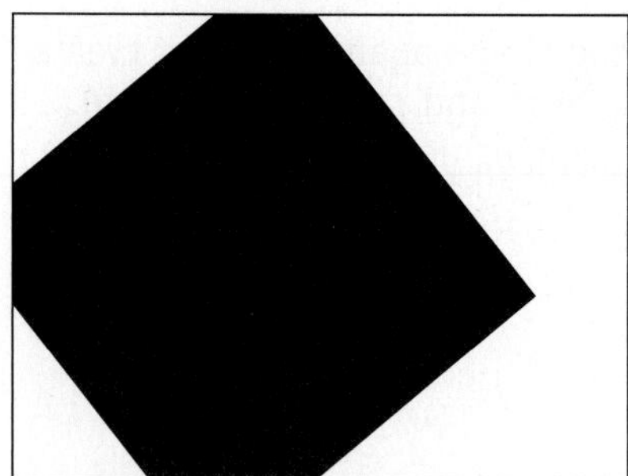

12•12

Diagram: A shape can become more important by "cropping" or cutting off a portion.

Tension. What is tension? **Tension** is OPPOSITION! We get a "tension headache" when someone opposes or goes against what we are doing, or not doing. Even TIME sometimes seems to work against us. Tension in certain compositions can create a liveliness, a vitality, excitement, or energy. Do you recall what I did with the squares when we discussed variety? To give variety to otherwise static squares, I positioned each square at a little angle to the next square. This relieved the monotony of having each square marching solidly across the line to the same beat: DUM—DUM—DUM. By adding a little tension, the squares seem to skip along, DUM—TE—DUM—TA! Tension creates rhythm and mood in a design and, in general, makes that design more arresting to the viewer. Zigzags, verticals, diagonals, and fan shapes are useful in composing upbeat paintings.

Tension is not a new design concept, but the term *Tension* is relatively new. It means a "push-pull" per-

12•13

Wesley Pulkka. ALICE. Ink drawing. *Source: Wesley Pulkka.*

12◆14

The symbol for "yin-yang".

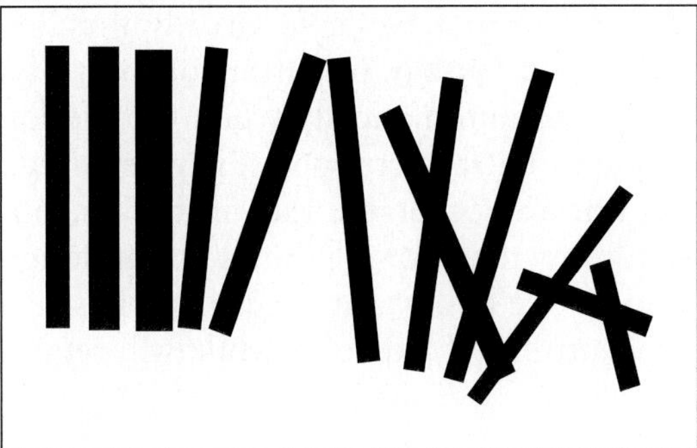

12◆16

Diagram: Juxtaposing one shape against another creates *tension* or the sense of "push and pull" (or yin-yang). Different degrees of the angles determine how active a design can be.

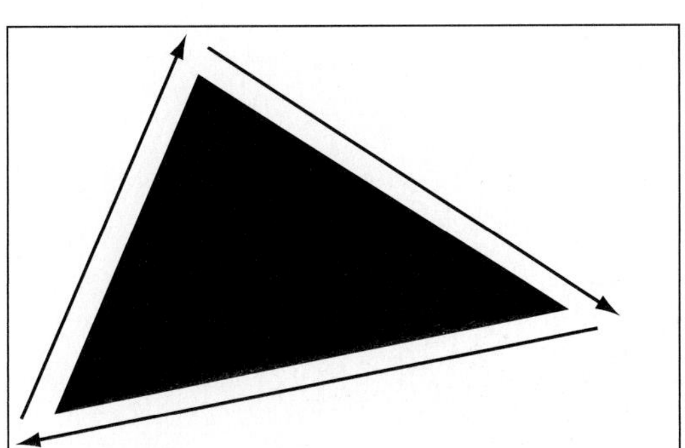

12◆15

Diagram: A triangle is an example of ready-made "tension" as each side opposes the other. Triangles generate energy and action in a design.

12◆17

Mark Mehaffey. SOUTHERN EXPOSURE. Watercolor. 21″ × 29″. By intersecting diagonals, the design has become energized. *Courtesy: Mark Mehaffey.*

ception, created by elements that oppose one another slightly to greatly. Originally it was called "yin-yang," a principle in the Taoist philosophy founded by Lao-Tsu in China. It meant "opposing forces that bring about balance" (or harmony or unity), and it often stands for MALE/FEMALE.

Let's study a design using strong tension. Look at figure 12–18. This painting portrays active street life. Its shapes all oppose one another. Doesn't this say it's an accident about to happen? The composition also forms an upended "square" or shape for a visual path, which we will speak of shortly.

12◆18

David FeBland. INTERSECTION. 1998. Oil on linen. 16″ × 20″. Can you "feel" the tension in this painting? Does it make you wonder if there will be an accident? *Source: David FeBland.*

Rhythmic Devices. The hints given you thus far will help with the placement of shapes and lines. As you move these elements around in your space, you will see that they may be arranged so as to create the "visual path," or rhythm, spoken of earlier.

12◆19

A "visual path": some ways that elements can be arranged to guide the eye through space.

12◆20

Diagram: Elements aligned as a "C."

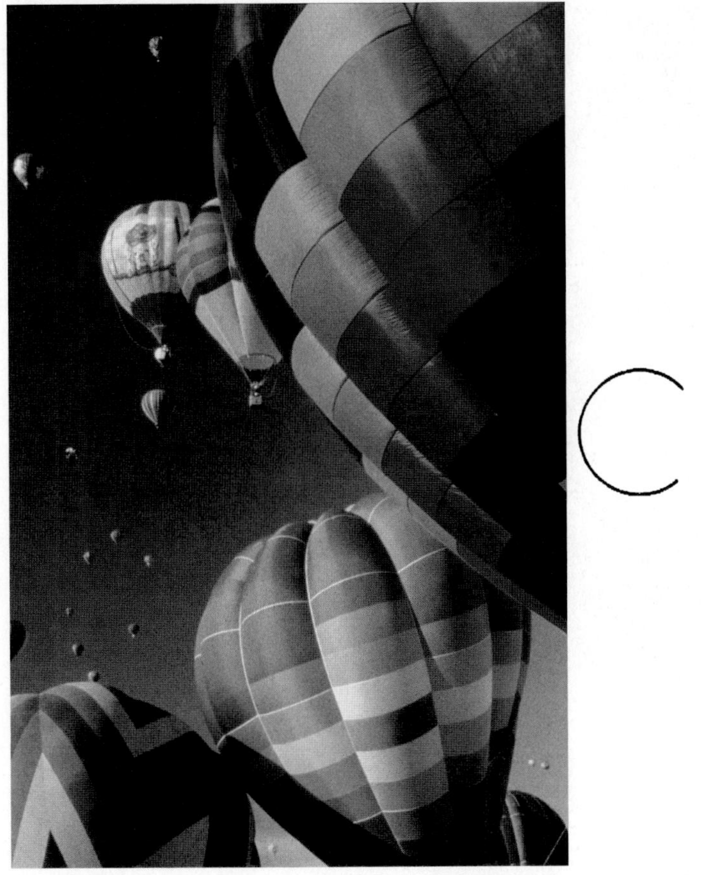

12◆21

J. Sohm. ALBUQUERQUE BALLOON FESTIVAL. The alignment of balloons creates a reversed "C". *Photographer: Joe Sohm/Chromasohm. Photo Researchers, NY.*

12◆23

Gary Faigin, AMONG THE FALLING; DROP ZONE, 1995. Oil on canvas, 60″ × 30″. Gary Faigin. *Courtesy of Gary Faigin, Seattle Academy of Fine Art.*

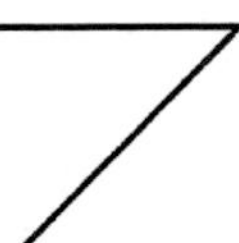

12◆22

Skip Lawrence. VIEW FROM THE STUDIO. 1995. Watercolor. 28″ × 40″. *Courtesy: Skip Lawrence.*

12◆24

Mark Mehaffey, WHERE THE HAWK PREYS. 1985. Transparent watercolor. 26″ × 35″. *Courtesy: Mark E. Mehaffey, Williamston.*

12◆25

Oneida Silversmiths. *Satin Edge* design. Stainless steel tableware. Advertisement. *Source: Oneida Ltd., Silversmiths. Oneida, Ltd. All rights reserved.*

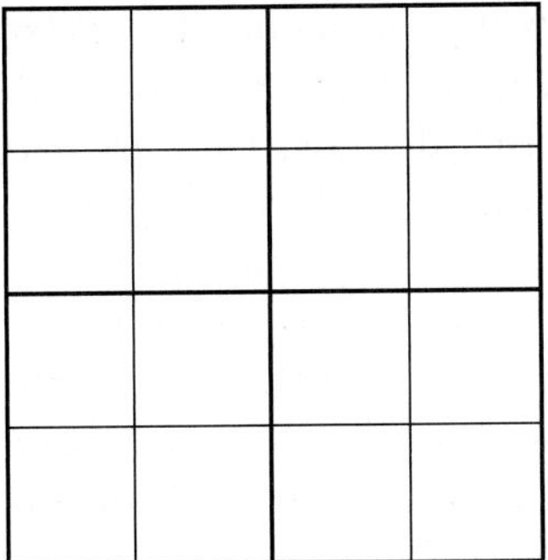

12◆29

Diagram: Grid.

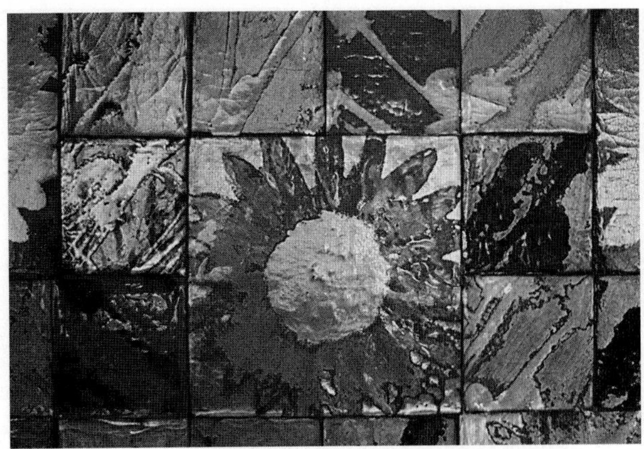

12◆31

Craig Ruwe, SUNFLOWER STUDY. Vitreous enamel on board. *Source: Craig Ruwe.*

12◆30

Advertisement for Oakwood Credit Union by Cuna and Affiliates. Madison, Wisconsin. *Source: CUNA Mutual Group and Affiliates.*

ements may be placed in such a way that the *implication* of space division is perceived.

Grids are extremely handy in unifying very diverse subject matter. As we mentioned in explaining UNIFICATION, repetition is a means of unifying—and a grid does just that. We are all familiar with designs based on the grid, but, like the element of LINE, they are so common that we don't stop to consider them for our own use.

Pattern. Pattern is a natural follow-up to grids. A grid is the repetition of squares in a regular sequence and could be accepted as a basic **pattern.** The simple, functional quilts stitched together by pioneer women to provide warm bed covers involved the piecing, or sewing together, of many squares of one size. These squares were not of the same fabric or color but a variety of both. Alteration of the exact grid effect came about because there were not enough scraps to make a new square identical to all the others, so smaller pieces were sewed together to make a square of the original size. These variations of sizes, and the interplay of shapes and colors, started some of our earliest traditional quilt patterns.

12◆32

Quilt design based on common grid: same-size squares sewn together.

12◆33

Smaller available pieces of fabric dictated changes in design. Some of our traditional quilt designs evolved from early piecing together of fabrics.

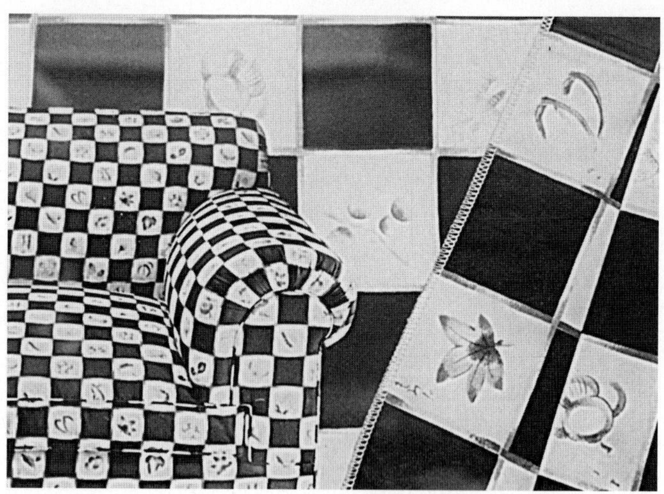

12◆34

Kazumi Yoshida, PETITE JAPONERIE, for Clarence House. Fabric design. *Courtesy: Clarence House.*

Pattern is repetition. A certain type of behavior—positive or negative—repeated over and over is called a "behavior pattern." In designing, we may contrive patterns as a way to establish variation, as well as movement or rhythm.

A shape, or a variation of that shape, used in an irregular way is called a **random pattern.**

These patterns exist everywhere, especially in nature. Look back at figure 8–12. The repetition of the

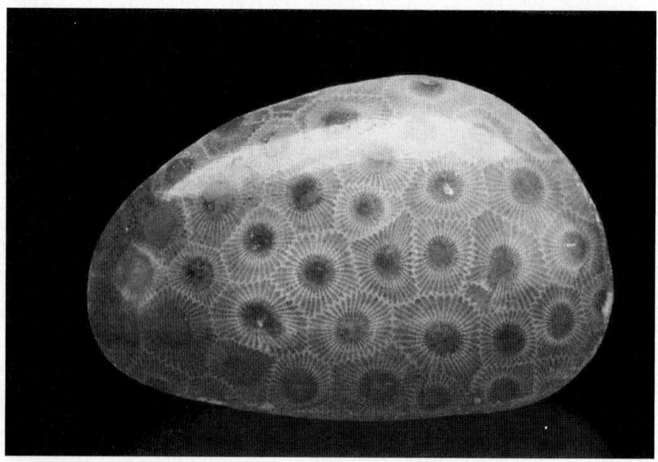

12◆35

C. D. Winters, PETOSKY STONE. The varied repetition of similar shapes in an irregular way gives us a *random* pattern. *Photographer: Charles D. Winters. Photo Researchers.*

varied, but same-to-similar shape (the cottonwood leaf), in an irregular way creates a RANDOM PATTERN.

An **all-over pattern** is usually created by a **motif.** A motif is a distinctive recurring shape (or a combination of shapes). It is used in a planned or predictable way to make an all-over pattern.

The concept of the pattern, like the grid, can help us solve our design problem.

It can be structured as an approach to designing a painting. Figure 12–39 shows the space divided into three distinct areas by linear shapes. These areas are divided again by more linear shapes that sometimes make abstracted triangular shapes that are repeated also. The elephants are the major images (the emphasis), and they too are repeated but each in a somewhat different pose. Other images are repeated in predictable placement, like the flower and leaf shapes, the seed pods, and several less important, miscellaneous small shapes. Colors are also repeated, which you see as

12◆36

A motif.

12◆37

Wallpaper design. A motif repeated in a specific or predictable way creates an *all-over* pattern. *Courtesy: Warner Wallcoverings, Chicago.*

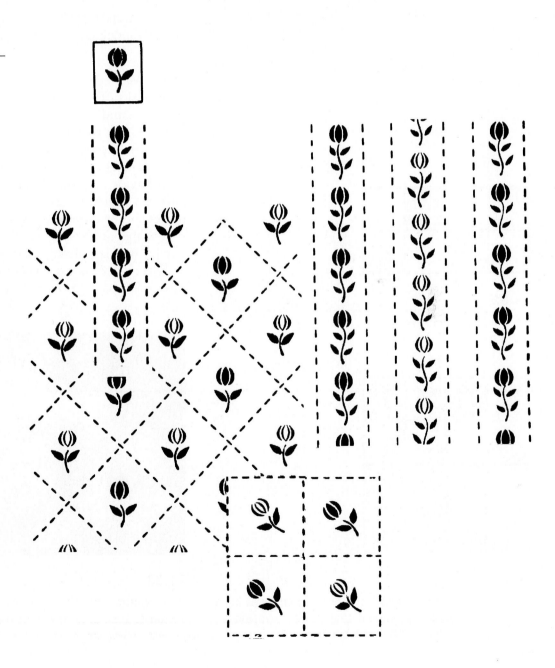

12◆38

M. Borchi, Detail of Mosaic ruins in Oaxaca, Mitla, Mexico. A predictable pattern. *Photo by Massimo Borchi. Photo Researchers.*

12◆39

Shirl Brainard, MAKING ELEPHANT TOOTHPICKS. 1996. Watercolor 20″ × 29″. *Source: S. Brainard.*

black to white values. The balance is approximate symmetry.

The various ways that we can use to strengthen our designs are, once more, a matter of CONTRAST. We often undermine the strength of contrast. We've talked about it in the chapter on value; we discussed it throughout the chapters on principles; and now we have seen that it is a factor in assembling our designs using some of the extra ways or devices. All contrasts are ways to compare, to show differences, to make the viewer SEE WHAT WE WANT HIM OR HER TO SEE!

◆ Ideas to Try

Use six of your cut-out, valued geometric shapes or make more. Again, remember line.

Manipulate your shapes and create a "working" relationship between the shapes.

Create a seventh shape as a negative shape.

Use more shapes. TRY:

overlapping shapes

touching shapes

almost touching

tension

DID YOU HAVE A PROBLEM WITH "TENSION"?

DID YOU END UP WITH ALL OF YOUR SHAPES DOING ALL OF THESE THINGS AT ONCE? WAS IT TOO MUCH?

◆ Now Try the Following . . .

Move your shapes around and create various RHYTHMIC PATHS.

Move your shapes around and create an UPBEAT mood.

Reassemble and create a quiet, tranquil mood.

Create a GRID. Can you make a grid with no lines?

Create a MOTIF. Create a PATTERN with your motif.

Create a pattern with simulated TEXTURE.

◆ Review

device ◆ A trick or way for effecting a purpose.

scale ◆ The size of one shape or image compared to another or to the space it occupies.

proportion ◆ The relative measurements or dimensions of parts or a portion of the whole.

placement ◆ Location, situation, or juxtaposition of elements.

touch ◆ To contact, adjoin.

crop ◆ To cut off a portion of a shape.

tension ◆ Opposing forces; push-pull, yin-yang.

rhythmic devices ◆ Systems of alignments in which to place elements to create a "visual path."

grid ◆ A network of usually straight lines placed at regular intervals.

pattern ◆ Repetition of a motif in either a predictable or random placement.

random pattern ◆ A pattern effect that is achieved through a repeated shape or motif that is scattered or not controlled. Less formal.

all-over pattern ◆ The pattern created when a shape or motif is used in a planned, predictable way.

motif ◆ A distinctive, recurring shape (or combination of shapes).

13

Analysis of Designs

- A Design Analysis
- Defining the Principles
- Can You Do These . . . ?

Now it's your turn to analyze a painting. Figure 13–2 is James McNeill Whistler's *Arrangement in Grey and Black*, commonly known as *Whistler's Mother*, a portrait of his mother done in 1871. The public and critics rejected it completely. It was "too simple"—a "side-view" hadn't been done in portraiture! Therefore, it was considered "avant-garde." Let's look at it.

What is the *format* of the space?
What kind of *shapes* are used?
Are there defined *lines*?
How many different simulated *textures* do you see?
Can you identify *how* the space is broken?
Can you identify *what balances* what?
What is *repeated*?
What is *varied*?
What kind of "emotional" *rhythm* is represented?
Was a *rhythmic device* or shape alignment used?
What is the focal point or *emphasis*?
Is anything *cropped*?
Is there any obvious *tension*? Where?
How do *you* feel about this painting?
Can you diagram the painting?

13◆2

James Abbott McNeill Whistler, (American 1834–1903) ARRANGEMENT IN GREY AND BLACK NO. 1: THE ARTIST'S MOTHER. 1871. Oil on canvas, 56″ × 64″. *The Louvre Museum, Paris. Source: Art Resource/Reunion des Musees Nationaux RMN.*

◆ Can You Do These . . .?

If you want to test yourself, here are some figures in this book for you to analyze!

8–10 VALUES ON COLORS
8–13 WOOD/PAINTING
8–23 JAPANESE GARDENS
12–17 MAHAFFEY/PAINTING
12–26 HOMER/PAINTING
12–27 FAIGIN/PAINTING
12–28 SCHLICTING/PAINTING

14

Three-Dimensional Design

Three-Dimensional Design

Throughout the book, we have seen references to **three-dimensional design,** or **3-D** design, as opposed to two-dimensional or 2-D design. In this chapter we will use the common abbreviations 3-D and 2-D as we examine the basics of 3-D design. How is it different from 2-D design? How is it similar?

How Is It Different?

SPACE. First and foremost, 3-D design differs from 2-D design in the *occupation of space.* As we learned in Chapter 3, a 2-D design occupies a given length and width of space, whereas a 3-D design occupies not only length and width of a space but also DEPTH. In that same chapter it was mentioned, however, that a 3-D work could be designed on a 2-D surface.

You can only look at a 2-D work from the front or upside down and the images stay the same, even if they are perceived differently when upside down. It is still only width and length. It is possible, however, to walk around a 3-D piece or hold it in your hand and turn it

14◆1B

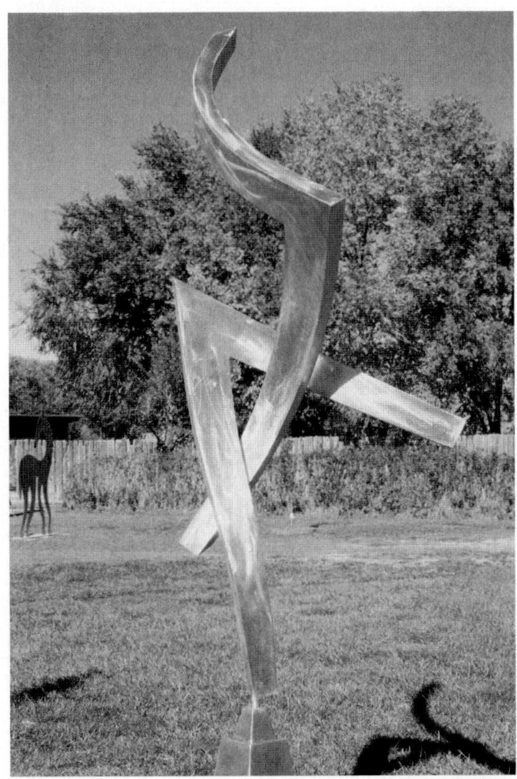

14◆1A-C

Bruce A. Niemi, ESSENCE OF DANCE IV. Stainless steel. Figures 14–A, B, and C gives us three views of the same figure. *Photographer: S. Brainard. Courtesy: Bruce A. Niemi.*

14◆1C

over and around; it may even surround you, like a building. The positive and negative shapes you see will seem to change.

Remember we talked about "designing ourselves"? When we dress, we are not flat, paper-doll figures. We have three dimensions. People can walk around us. We look different from various views. Think about the last time you had a haircut. Didn't the stylist turn you around as she or he cut your hair?

CONSTRUCTION. The second way the two differ is that in 2-D design a medium such as paint, graphite, paper, ink, thread, and so on is applied—spread on or printed on—by various means and *put on top of* a 2-D support surface such as canvas, paper, fabric or other surface. The result is still a two-dimensional, relatively flat piece.

In a 3-D design, the *basic* medium, such as wood, stone, or metal, is constructed, built, or *formed* by a number of diverse methods. Unlike 2-D design, it is necessary to at least introduce you to some methods used to create the 3-D design.

14◆2

Michelangelo Buonarroti (1475–1564), DAVID. Galleria dell' Academia, Florence, Italy. *Gala/SuperStock, Inc.*

14◆3

EGYPT, TUTANKHAMUN TREASURES. GODDESS OF SERKET. An example of sculpture "in the round" as well as low-relief work. *B. Brake, Photo. Photo Researchers, Inc.*

The first we identify with as children is the **subtractive method.** Remember taking a bar of Ivory soap in school or an activities program and making it into an "elephant"? You carved away chips and pieces. Of course, Michelangelo used the same method in his creation of *David* except that he used marble. This method of chipping away the basic material is one of the oldest in human history. The making of spear points or other tools by primitive man was "flintnapping," or flaking away the original material. The result is called "in-the-round" or "full-round."

Incising, or cutting into a material, was another subtractive or taking-away method. This is often called "low relief" (or bas-relief). Many times the depth was minimal. This was how early man decorated bone, ivory, and horn for decorative or ceremonial pieces. Another example is carving into the face of rock, called "petroglyphs." Or think of the "hieroglyphics" of the Egyptians, or other indigenous peoples. This has always been a popular and useful method, especially for smaller, decorative purposes.

14◆4

Low relief on wooden spoons from Mexico. *S. Brainard, Photo.*

"High relief" is similar to low relief but the amount of depth is greater, often amounting to carvings that are half or more of the natural material's depth. High relief doesn't necessarily mean it was produced by the subtractive method. It could have been built up by some means.

Many of these high relief forms are created by carving, chiseling, or sculpting the solid material into another form. Thus, these forms are usually called "sculpture," or pieces having a "sculptured effect."

Sculpture as an art form of 3-D design is not confined to the subtractive method. The second method we should become familiar with is called the **additive method.** This is a method in which a work—whether an art form or architecture, or other, is created by the process of building up one or more materials. These materials may be "found" (materials originally not intended for the purpose now used) or "intrinsic," such as wood, clay, metal, fiber, and so on. Sometimes an inner skeleton or armature is made that supports heavier materials and helps give form to the projected work. A building can have an inner beam structure of wood or steel that serves the same purpose.

There are many other methods used to create a 3-D design. Think of common carpentry and the construction of a table or a building.

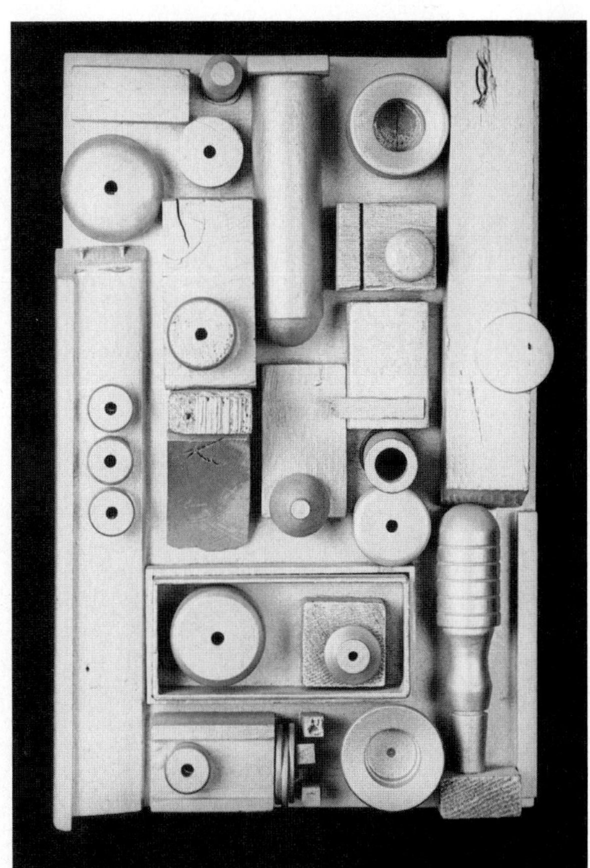

14◆5

Shirl Brainard, TO LOUISE. An example of high-relief assemblage. *Pat Berret, Photo.*

14◆6

George Manus PRAIRIE SCHOONER. 1993. 7′9″ H × 10′3″ W × 4′3″ D. Illustrates "Found" materials. *S. Brainard, Photo. Courtesy: George Manus.*

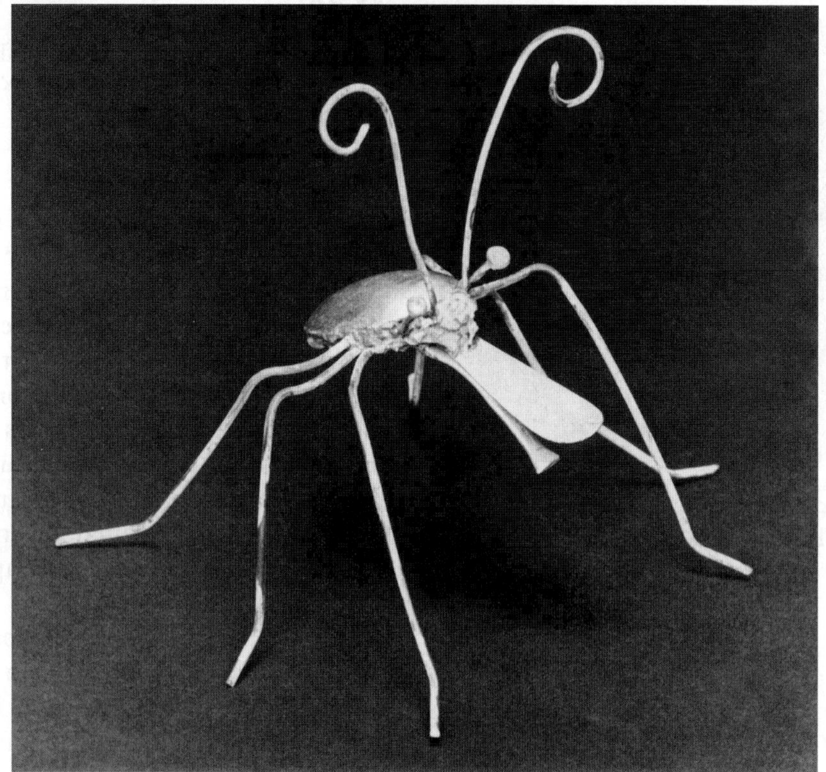

14◆7

GENEVIEVE THE SPOON BUG. Copper wire/silver-plated spoon.
Courtesy: Roger Evans. Pat Berret, Photo.

a performance of dance theater, or an exhibition. The occupants—shapes, either human or not—may be changing constantly, as in dance, or periodically, as in the articles displayed in a museum exhibit. Other examples could be the assemblage for a window display or an installation in an art gallery. The curator/choreographer/designer must give thought to the space in order to invite the viewer to explore and to react, but especially to give attention to the presentation.

Time is as important as perspective. How much time will it take for a viewer to look at, say, a kinetic (moving) sculpture? Will the viewer perceive it as the artist wished? Will the viewer watching a play witness the nuance of a scene in the short time the actors move about the set?

SO FAR, SO GOOD... We have been introduced to the

14◆12

Use of temporary space. Geneva Ballet Company, Switzerland. *SuperStock, Inc.*

main differences between 3-D design and 2-D design. The one thing we must remember is that this other dimension, DEPTH, makes us stop and consider new things in our design.

Sometimes it's difficult to label a design as either 2-D or 3-D. A textured fabric wall hanging, a collage, or perhaps a low-relief carving may be considered 3-D because of its depth, which may be relatively shallow. Because it may have a flat back and because of the way a piece may be presented, it may be *viewed* as two-dimensional. There is often a very fine line between the two.

We have looked at many architectural and art forms in this discussion of 3-D design. In reality, there are probably more 3-D designs for consumer or industrial products. There are scooters, stoves, footwear, helmets, motorcycles, watches, light fixtures, chairs . . . everything around us, including the kitchen sink! They are all 3-D designs.

14◆13

Man in hard hat with computer screen. Examples of various 3-D designs. How many can you count? *Rob Bartee SuperStock, Inc.*

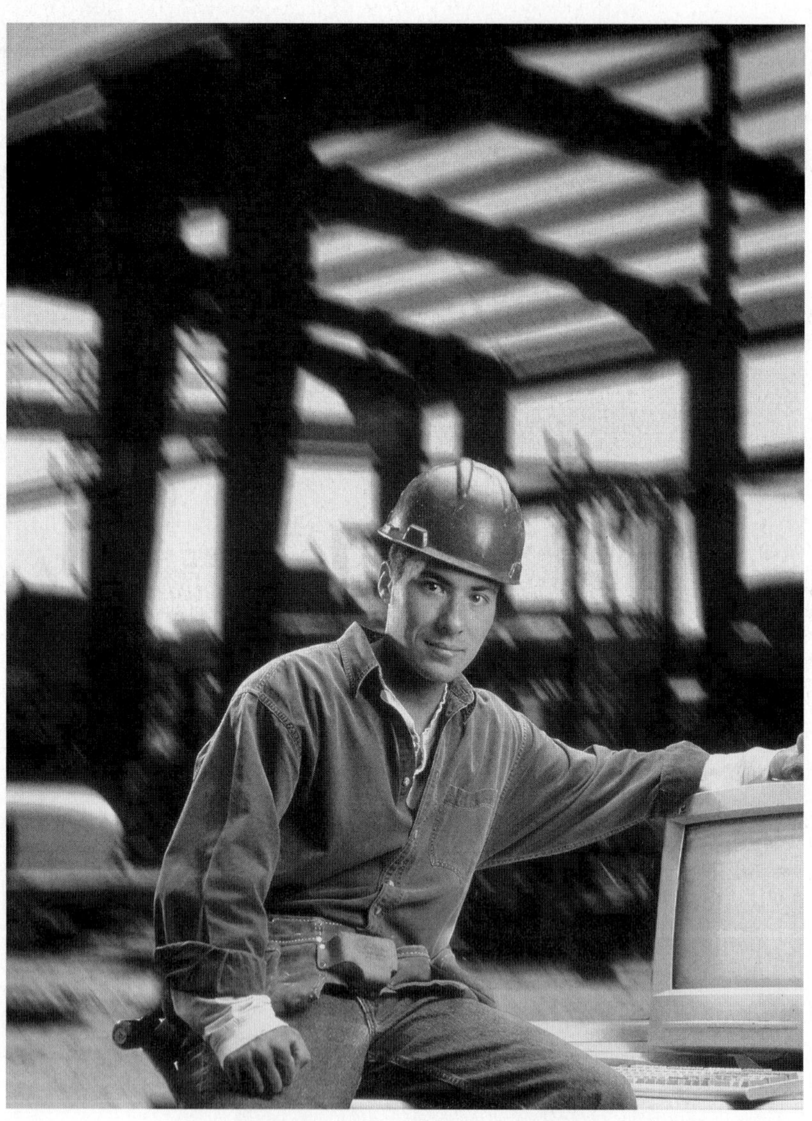

14◆14

NATURAL AND GEOMETRIC SHAPES Peter Woytuk, CONSTRUCTION WITH SIX CANS AND FOUR APPLES, 2000. Bronze, edition of 30. 12″ H × 13″ W × 15″ D. Natural and geometric shapes are present in this sculpture. *Courtesy: Owings-Dewey Fine Art Sculpture Gallery, Santa Fe, NM.*

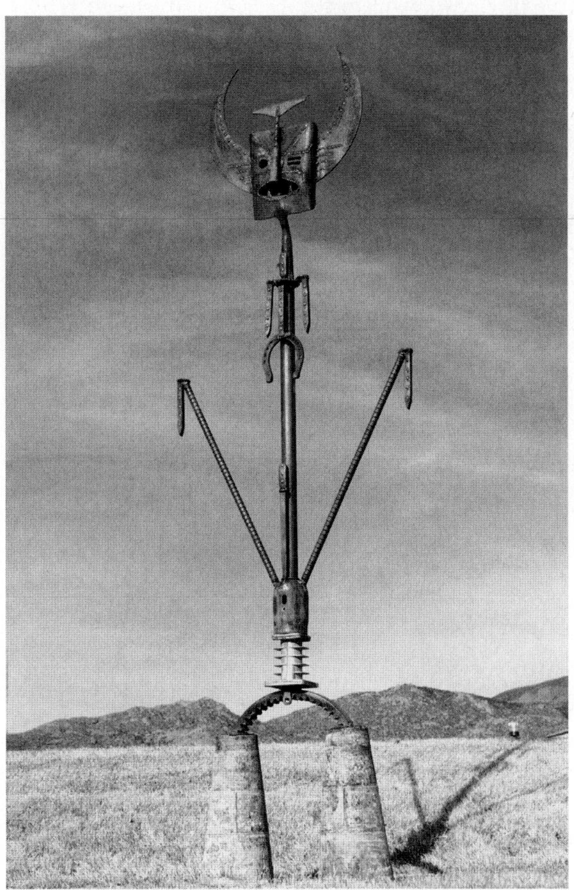

◆ How Is It the Same?

To quote sculptor Deborah Butterfield: "Sculpture (three-dimensional design) is just a different way of thinking from painting" (two-dimensional design).

As we look at examples of 3-D design, we can easily recall the *elements* of design. It's possible to identify all of the kinds of SHAPES, and we will see LINE.

Materials, as in 2-D design, may determine the TEXTURE and may play a part in the design itself. Light—natural or artificial—may affect how VALUE and/or COLOR may appear at different times or in different environments. We may want to refer back to figures 8–54, 8–55, and 8–56.

When we think of the *principles*, BALANCE is probably the most crucial. We need balanced buildings,

14◆15

ABSTRACT SHAPE George Manus, ISCARIOT. Found media. 6′10″ × 18 1/2″ × 29″. Abstract shapes in sculpture. *Courtesy: George Manus.*

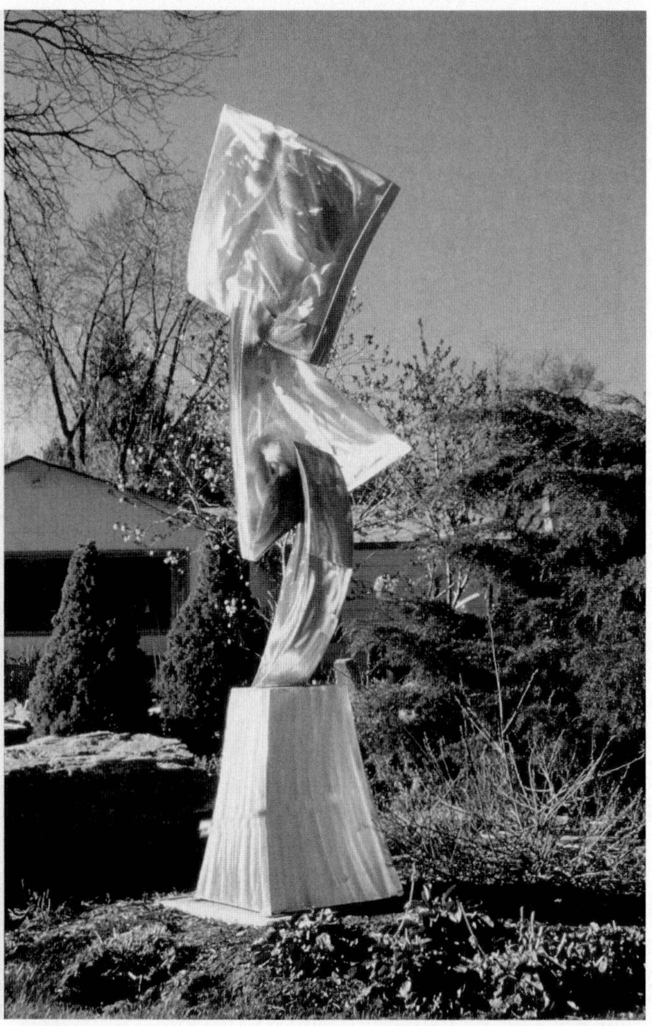

14◆16

Kevin Robb, TOY BLOCKS II. Sculpture—Stainless steel. 121″ × 40″ × 32″. This sculpture uses nonobjective shapes. Value is another important element, as it changes with different light or angles. *Courtesy: Kevin Robb.*

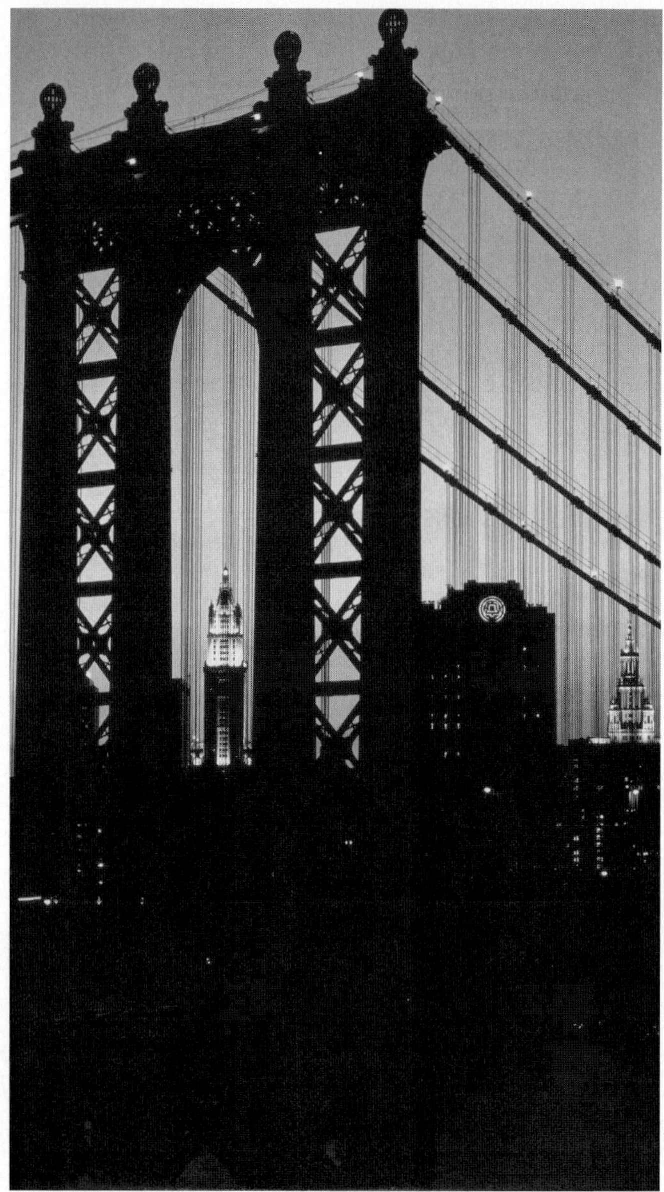

14◆17

NEW YORK MANHATTAN BRIDGE AT SUNSET. Line in 3-D design. *Courtesy: Photo Researchers, Inc. Ken Cavanaugh, Photo.*

14◆18

Texture is the element and emphasis of this vase of wood. It also shows formal balance. *Pat Berret, Photo.*

14◆19

The principle of balance is shown in this desk and chair design by John Wesley Williams. Bird's Eye Maple Wood and Wenge. *Jim Osborn, Photo. Courtesy of John Wesley Williams.*

furniture, and autos, not only visually but also structurally.

The components of UNITY—repetition, variety, and rhythm—are present in most 3-D designs but are most obvious visually in architecture, auto, and furniture design. EMPHASIS may be seen readily in architecture as an entrance, but a handle on a door may be the focal point in a utilitarian design. A statue of a person standing alone presents itself as a strong focal point.

SCALE and PROPORTION need to be observed in the case of consumer design, but in a fine art sculpture they may be grossly exaggerated.

Our DEVICES often play a significant role in the 3-D design process. We will still think of SHAPE RELATIONSHIPS and their placement. TENSION (see figure 14–16) or a RHYTHMIC DEVICE (see figure 14–14) may be introduced. A repetition of windows or columns in a building may create a PATTERN (see figure 14–20).

We have now seen the similarities and the differences between 3-D and 2-D design. Yes, just another way of thinking.

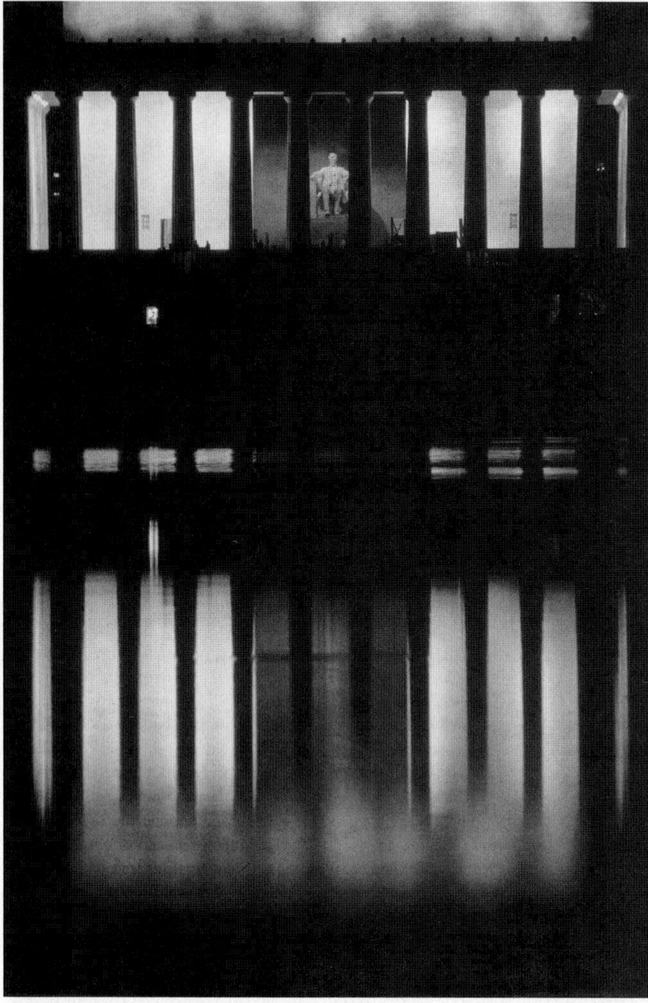

14◆20

Sunset at the Lincoln Memorial in Washington, D.C., is an example of repetition, variety, and rhythm. The statue is obviously the emphasis or focal point. *Photographer: Joseph Sohm. Source Photo Researchers, Inc.*

14◆21

William S. Arms, THE PITCHER. 72″ H × 66″ W × 52″ D. These painted steel 2-D pieces are joined to form 3-D life-size figures. Rhythm and excitement are evident. *On loan to Ted Turner Stadium, Atlanta, GA. Source: William S. Arms.*

◆ Let's Think About 3-D Design . . .

Does format affect a 3-D design?

Would you use any division of space?

Could you use a 2-D space to design something in 3-D?

Does scale make a difference?

Can you use all of the balance systems?

Can you analyze any of the illustrations?

Keyword to remember: DEPTH—the added dimension with height and width.

◆ What Can You Do to Create a 3-D Design?

Carve away material.

Add on material.

Make it BIG.

Make it SMALL.

WHAT ELSE?

◆ Can You Identify . . .?

Which of the following are 2-D designs? Which are 3-D designs?

DOLL	TOMBSTONE	HANDKERCHIEF
PAPER CUP	ROAD MAP	WRAPPING PAPER
BOX	CEREAL BOWL	ALBUM/CD COVER
$1 BILL	BOOK COVER	PHOTOGRAPH
GLOBE	MURAL	A BEAD

◆ Ideas to Try with 3-D Design

Try again with a bar of soap.

Use an empty box to create a fantasy 3-D interior (i.e., illustrate a scene in a book; or one of your own dreams).

Study one or several buildings. How many kinds of geometric shapes can you identify? Can you reconstruct this building two-dimensionally using shapes as in figure 10–16?

Can you analyze any of the 3-D illustrations using methods in Chapter 13?

AND SOMETHING TO REMEMBER—A CAKE IS THREE-DIMENSIONAL!

◆ Review

three-dimensional (3-D) ◆ Having height, width, and DEPTH in a given space.

subtractive method ◆ A process of taking away original material, by various means, to give form.

additive method ◆ A process of building up or combining materials to give form.

Form ◆ The mass or volume—apparent density—of a 3-D work or the illusion of volume in a 2-D work.

temporary space ◆ Actual 3-D space used only for a defined length of time.

15

Problems & Solutions

- **Problem-Solving Procedure**
- **Materials**
- **Tools**
- **The Emergence of Style . . . and You!**
- **Choice**
- **Connections**
- **Passion**
- **Review**

◆ Problem-Solving Procedure

We understand that a design is a solution to a problem. So far, we have looked at the elements and principles common to all designs. Now it is time to consider other things about designs.

Let's return to our cake. We want to make a cake. That is the problem to solve. What KIND of cake? What will it be made of? HOW will we make it? Let's start by looking at cake recipes. We choose one. We see the ingredients or materials needed. We decide whether we need to use a spoon, a mixer, or a food processor to mix it. Then we pop it in the oven!

What we have done is use a **problem-solving** procedure: DEFINED the problem; looked at our POSSIBILITIES or OPTIONS; DECIDED on a tool to mix it; and BAKED it.

We'll look at this process more closely. Then we will take a look at some of the materials and tools that can help us solve our design problems.

DEFINING THE PROBLEM. What *exactly* do you have to design? A refrigerator? A man's suit? A painting of a sunset? Different areas of design may have specific requirements. For example, the size of a car must be only so wide and so long to fit into existing garages and onto existing highways. Perhaps a requirement will arise because of a societal requirement for an article such as a gold-plated toothbrush. Perhaps only people with disabilities will use your product; maybe it is seasonal, or it may be regionally oriented for very specific utilitarian purposes (there are still *real* cowboys who really do wear cowboy boots!). A production cost factor may be a limitation. The list is endless, but so are the *possibilities*.

POSSIBILITIES. Any thought that may contribute to the solution of the problem should be jotted down and a sketch made. This is a brainstorming process that puts the initial idea into visual form. One idea may activate another, and the more ideas there are, the better the choices that can be made toward the solution. There may also be a mental incubation period, in which an idea is mulled over, thought about, and turned over. Haven't you ever faced a seemingly insoluble problem and suddenly awakened in the night with a plausible answer?

As we begin the selection or choice process toward a solution, we may have to do some research. Materials must be considered; cost factors may prohibit a marvelous idea; someone else may have already come up with your idea; individual interpretations of the problem may lose sight of the main objective. After all, just because *your* personal preference is to make a refrigerator look like an igloo doesn't mean that General Electric will agree.

PRODUCTION. After considering all the positive and negative information you have gathered, the choices begin to narrow and a clear view of the solution begins to emerge. If this occurs, you should probably put some of the better choices into more detailed thumbnails, layouts, or pasteups that you may present to your teacher, client, or employer for approval. On the other hand, if no approval is granted, this could be the time where the saying "back to the drawing board" originated!

15◆1A–D

Bob Kuhn, NORTH COUNTRY. Sketches. The problem of how to represent the bear as a wildlife portrait is being solved in this series of compositional sketches. *Courtesy: Bob Kuhn.*

15◆1B

(Continued)

15◆1C

15◆1D

FINALIZATION. This last step in problem solving comes when we finalize the choices we have made into a visual statement. We may have elaborated or minimized in order to define our solution. We have used our professional expertise to make decisions about the critical play of our elements and principles. We have remembered that the more focused the design, the more effective it will be to its audience. We have used our best technical abilities to present the design, and yet we have tried to maintain our own personal integrity and identity that becomes our style.

Problem-Solving Procedure.

PROBLEM DEFINITION
POSSIBILITIES
PRODUCTION
FINALIZATION

◆ Materials

As mentioned, your **materials** or media are what you use to make your design. Your present choice of media may not be what you'll use later. You wouldn't be the first to change design careers because of materials alone. I know an illustrator who was a landscape architect but liked doing the drawing better than the actual landscape project. I know a doll-maker turned potter and another architect turned sculptor.

The choice of materials may be based on your personal, physical, or aesthetic tendencies. Your choice

15◆2

Bob Kuhn, NORTH COUNTRY. Acrylic. 24″ × 36″. *Private collection. Courtesy: Bob Kuhn. Photographer: Kristine Kenner.*

will also influence the design itself. Common sense tells us that clay doesn't work as well as a pigmented medium to create a painting, but it does make a great bowl! Your aesthetics may make you choose fibers or fabrics over wood or steel because you like the feel of them better. Physical characteristics of materials may be what you like. You may want a medium that can be pounded, hammered, rolled, cut, folded, heated, cast, carved, bent, or twisted.

We may have to be concerned with a material's durability or longevity. We may have to ask if it will endure the weather. Will it rust? Will it be impervious to acid rain? What about climatic changes? Will it fade? Will it fall apart? These are a few of the questions to ask when choosing media.

We usually begin with materials on a two-dimensional surface, like coloring with crayons. We may then advance to various paints. We learn about different media; we experiment. This important exploration is paramount to our development as designers and is a never-ending journey.

◆ Tools

Earlier we spoke of how we were going to mix our cake. A spoon? A mixer? A food processor? Whatever we choose, one of these tools will help us mix our cake better than using our hands. Tools help solve problems. Every profession has its tools and each material may require different tools. The weaver, the bricklayer, the potter, the dentist, the carpenter, the chef—all have specific tools.

15◆3

Cake-Making Tools. Mixing bowl with whisk, spoon, and spatula balanced across the top. *S. Brainard, Photo.*

What is a tool? A **tool** is a contrivance, or something that can do work. A spoon is used to stir. A tool performs a function. Technology is ever in the process of giving us more sophisticated tools. Let's take a brief look at only two of the most used tools in the design field today.

CAMERA. The camera is a basic tool. It's a tool whose result is considered a medium: photography. Sometimes the two overlap. For example, as a tool a pencil is used for writing, but it is also a medium for drawing.

The camera has been used by artists as far back as da Vinci's time. Surprised? It was called a *camera obscura,* the forerunner of the old-fashioned box camera.

There are many types of cameras used by artists: video, digital, the common compact, and so on. A camera may be used to record our family's growth,

15◆4

The camera: A handy tool for many chores. Man holding an old flash camera. *SuperStock, Inc.*

document a crime scene or historical event, or create a visual catalog of information. Most conscientious artists keep a slide file of their work for portfolio presentation, juried exhibitions, and their individual business history. Many keep a print file of subject matter; some "still life" painters use photography as a means of "preserving" perishables, like fruit or flowers. Photography is used extensively as an advertising and illustration medium. Photography has become an art in itself.

The digital camera can do all of the above but uses no film, needs no developing, and stores the wanted images while deleting the rest. These images can be viewed on your computer or printed for use as posters, business cards, or even low-cost art prints.

The photographer Dorothea Lange said that "the camera is an instrument that teaches people how to see without a camera."

COMPUTER. We are still in the digital revolution! Did you know that it took 18 years before 50 million people tuned into radio compared to the *four* years that it took 50 million people to become computer users?

The computer is a versatile general-purpose machine with thousands of uses. It is an electronic apparatus that computes and stores information. It is, again, a tool and a medium at the same time. It is used in product and industrial design, the film industry, publishing, fine art—you name it, it can help you do it ! Robert S. McNamara said, "A computer does not substitute for judgment anymore than a pencil substitutes for literacy. But writing without a pencil is of no particular advantage." This quote sums up the help that digital techniques can offer, such as moving elements around in a given space in a two-dimensional design, giving the designer the options of viewing, making corrections, or deciding to begin anew. For an accurate representation of a three-dimensional object, be it a building or a sculpture, the computer can give us "virtual" views simultaneously of all sides of the object. This is different from a design composed on a two-dimensional surface, which is capable of showing us only *one* view (or side) at a time. Fed with pertinent information, the computer can calculate the dimensions of width, depth, and length and then enlarge the design. I personally imagine that the Egyptian pyramid builders would have loved them!

There are more and more software applications being developed for the design field. And we must not overlook computer-generated fine art. Here is an area that has taken two-dimensional art to a new boundary. Self-publishing artists can use digital printmaking to make a few prints or many. It is economical as well as space saving.

These tools have changed our perspective . . . and we have no idea what the limits are!

15◆5

The computer can do magical things. Computer with gloved hand and sparkles.
SuperStock, Inc.

15◆6

A new image based on da Vinci's early work. Design based on Leonardo da Vinci's Proportions of the Human Figure. *Digital photo art by Jesse Ceballos. Galleria dell' Academia, Venice/SuperStock.*

◆ The Emergence of Style . . . and You!

As we ended the problem-solving sequence, I mentioned the designer's "style." I like to think that an artist's style evolves from several sources. One is the individual's trend of "personal choice" of, or leaning toward, certain elements or principles over others, as well as the individual's selection of materials. These choices often become our visual signature.

◆ Choice

I remember seeing a documentary on television about Buckminster Fuller, who designed buildings based on the triangle, as was the geodesic dome. When he was a child, he loved the shape of triangles; he drew them; cut them from paper and cardboard; made constructions of them; and in reality, finally built a designing career from them.

Perhaps your personal choice is red over blue. Maybe you like to maximize shape before line, and the like. It is whatever the artist is comfortable with. It may happen that one device works exceptionally well for one artist and not at all for another; so, of course, it is to the advantage of the artist to use what he or she *knows* will be more successful. This does NOT mean that the artist is caught and cannot expand upon the chosen "system" that is working for him or her.

To quote our friend Robert Henri once more, he told students, "Find out what you really like, if you can. Find out what is really important to you. Then sing your song. . . ."

◆ Connections

Style emerges from how we look at our problem and HOW we go about solving it; HOW we interpret our solution in a creative way. Often, this may mean looking for our solution from a different angle in order to gain our desired effect. A measure of common sense, a little risk, willingness to explore possibilities, and a dose of playfulness are all assets that will help you pursue your style.

15◆7

Buckminister Fuller's geodesic dome in the U.S. Pavilion, Canadian EXPO 1967. *Bernard P. Wolff, Photography. Photo Researchers, Inc.*

15◆8

Shirl Brainard, ROSE CONTAINERS. 2002. Watercolor/paper collage. 18″ × 24″. *Private collection.*

15◆9

Goldfish in a plastic bag. *Laurence Dutton, Photo. Source: Getty Images, Inc.*

15◆10

Shirl Brainard, DIANA. 2000. Mixed water media/collage. 20″ × 24″. *Source: S. Brainard.*

Here are some ideas and examples of how to start *connecting* ideas, by using different identifications, opposites, unexpected combinations, or similar associations:

This work (Figure 15–8) was for an art exhibition entitled "Containers." Defining "container" was the first step, followed by exploring the kinds of containers that may be fun to paint. The usual boxes, vases, or sacks were out. But an empty "Pepsi" can is *also* a container. What would one put in an empty drink can? What *wouldn't* one put in it? Roses? The idea was incongruous; it was great!

Obviously, pet goldfish (Figure 15–9) go in a "goldfish bowl" once they're home . . . but how do you transport a goldfish home? Another look at containers, even though this photo wasn't in the above art exhibit. But, think! HOW would you depict two goldfish looking at one another?

Figure 15–10 is a portrait of a fellow artist who does a lot of oriental calligraphy with her monotypes and often introduces the image of a raven into her work. The painting evolved from a sketch, later developed into the portrait after the association of her and the elements in the work she does. (See figure 15–11.)

"Creative license" is another way of connecting ideas. You've heard of someone taking "artistic" or "poetic license." It usually means taking liberties or deviating from an original written, audio, or visual work. Forms of humor, such as cartoons or parodies (Figure 15–12), are means of associating with an original idea without abusing the original.

15◆11

Diana Stetson, RAVEN GIVES A JUMP. Monotype. *Source: Diana Stetson.*

A famous chef was interviewed about his culinary expertise, and one of his final statements concerned style, which, he said, "is like painting or music. You can take the same colors, the same ingredients and interpret them to reflect and express your personality."

So, you can add chocolate chips to your chocolate cake and that can be YOUR interpretation of CHOCOLATE CAKE!

◆ Passion

And last, but maybe the most important of all: PASSION. Your PASSION for your work! Your all-encompassing love for what you do! I will never forget hearing Gerald Brommer say in a workshop, "If you don't love what you're doing, quit bothering the paper!"

15◆12

Shirl Brainard, WHISTLER'S MOM. (a.k.a. "The Big Bad Wolf.") *Source: S. Brainard.*

◆ Review

problem-solving ◆ A sequence of strategies for finding a solution to a problem.

Materials ◆ Media (singular: *medium*).

Tool ◆ A contrivance that can do work.

creative license ◆ Same as "artistic license"; the designer's choices interpret the problem's solution without abusing the original problem-solving requirements.

16

Conclusion

- **A Concluding Thought**
- **A Chocolate Cake Recipe!**

◆ A Concluding Thought

We have now concluded our conversational exploration of the fundamental concepts of design. You have gained some helpful ideas to fall back on for extra help, seen a way to use this information in order to analyze a design, and learned how to solve a design problem using a logical procedure. There are more ideas we could talk about, but these are the basics. These are the ones to master in the beginning.

The theory of design is just theory until you start your own exploration and experimentation with your own design problems. Experiments are practice, as are class projects, and all are learning experiences. Some will be good, and some will be terrible. NO DESIGNER is successful ALL of the time! And that is what designing is—continual, endless practice. Each new design is a fresh experiment—and each new solution, a revelation. It is exciting that you can use the same elements, the same principles, and even the same problems, yet the end result will always be different, the solutions endless, and the search a forever frustrating but rewarding experience.

We'll end with one more quote from our friend and teacher Robert Henri: "Keep a bad drawing (design) until by study you have found out why it is bad." THEN MOVE ON . . .!

HAPPY DESIGNING AND CAKE BAKING!

◆ A Chocolate Cake Recipe (Using "Creative License")

This is a delicious, moist chocolate cake, put together quickly without a single bowl to wash! It is economical, and perfect for today's health-conscious world, because it is almost FAT FREE! And, YES!, you really do need the vinegar . . . it sharpens the flavor.

Preheat oven to 375°.

Space: 9″ square baking pan (spray with nonstick cooking spray)

Elements (ingredients):

- 1 cup sugar
- 1 1/2 cups flour (over *5,000′* altitude, add 1 1/2 tablespoons more)
- 1/3 cup cocoa
- 1 teaspoon baking soda
- 1/2 teaspoon salt
- 2 teaspoons vanilla extract
- 1/3 cup applesauce (the "creative license") OR 1/2 cup vegetable oil
- 1/2 cup cold water
- 2 tablespoons vinegar

Principles: (Method) Measure all ingredients, except vinegar, directly into cake pan. Mix all thoroughly, then add vinegar and stir quickly to blend. Immediately place in preheated oven. There must be no delay in baking after vinegar is added. Bake 20–25 minutes or until center puffs slightly and sides of cake begin to pull away from pan. Cool. May sprinkle top with powdered sugar.

Glossary

A

abstract shape A recognizable image that has been distorted or simplified.

actual space The real space we have to fill with our design. This space has defined dimensions.

additive color mixture The result of diffracted light reflected to our eye from a surface; color produced by light.

additive method A process of building up or combining materials to give form.

aesthetic A personal response to what we consider beautiful, often based on cultural or educated experience.

all-over pattern The pattern created when a shape or motif is used in a planned, predictable way.

analogous "Alike" hues; three to five (or more) hues lying next to one another on the color wheel.

anomaly Something that is noticed because it differs from its environment.

approximate symmetry A balance system in which our first impression is that of symmetry. Weight may be identical but not mirror image.

asymmetrical balance (Informal balance)—A balance system in which the visual weight of the elements on both sides of the implied axis is equal. Most often, the elements cross over the axis.

B

balance Positive and negative shapes distributed in space by apparent visual weight to create harmony.

boundary line A line that confines our visual attention. It may serve to separate areas.

C

color interaction The relative differences between colors as they react to one another in different environs.

color systems (Schemes, harmonies)—Synonymous with "simultaneous contrast."

color wheel A reference chart for colors.

complement The color directly opposite a selected color on the color wheel.

complex design Complicated as opposed to simple. Many elements are used so it is harder to design and comprehend.

composition The way the parts are arranged.

content The message created by the artist. May be functional for consumer purposes; iconography.

contour line A line depicting the outer edge of a shape or group of shapes.

contrast The result of comparing one thing to another and seeing the difference.

creative license Same as "artistic license"; the designer's choices interpret the problem's solution without abusing the original requirements.

crop To cut off a portion of a shape.

D

design A visual, creative solution to a functional or decorative problem.

device A tool, trick, or way used for effecting a purpose.

directional line A line or lines that direct our visual attention in a specific direction.

division space Breaking up space by use of positive and negative shapes.

E

elements The parts, or components, of a design.

emphasis The main element or focal point; what the viewer's eye should see first.

environmental design Functional designs considering natural surroundings.

F

form The mass or volume—apparent density—of a 3-D work or the illusion of volume in a 2-D work.

formal balance (Symmetrical balance)—Technically, a mirror image: Elements on either side of the implied axis have precisely the same shape, but in reverse, and have the same visual weight.

format The shape and direction of our working or actual space. May be horizontal, vertical, round, or the like.

functional design Design that is utilitarian; necessary.

G

geometric shape Usually man-made shapes that are precise, exact. Triangles, squares, circles, and the like.

graphic design Visual communication design for commercial purposes.

grid A network of usually straight lines placed at regular intervals.

H

hue A family of color; the pure state of a color.

I

implied axis A "mental," psychological division of space. Usually centered or perceived bilaterally.

implied line A perceived continuation of images or symbols that implies a line.

informal balance (Asymmetrical balance)—A balance system in which the visual weight of the elements on both sides of the implied axis is equal. Elements often cross the axis.

intensity The relative purity of a color; brightness or dullness.

intent What the designer or artist intended with the design; may not have content or message.

intermediate colors (Tertiary)—Colors produced by mixing a primary and secondary color.

L

line A mark longer than it is wide and seen because it differs in value, color, or texture from its background.

linear shape An elongated shape that reminds us of a line.

M

mass Having volume or depth; takes up three-dimensional space.

medium The kind of material(s) one is working with, such as pigments, film, fabric, pencil, steel, and the like (plural: media).

monochromatic One hue with value and/or intensity changes.

motif A distinctive, recurring shape (or combination of shapes).

N

natural shape Shapes found in nature; sometimes called organic.

negative shape The implied shape produced after two or more positive shapes are placed in a negative (empty) space.

negative space Completely empty actual or working space.

neutral The color resulting after two complements have been mixed to the point that neither color is evident.

nonfunctional design Design that is decorative or aesthetic. It is not strictly necessary for the functioning of a culture.

nonobjective shape A shape often made accidentally or invented from another source. There is no recognizable object involved.

O

original A primary, inventive form of producing an idea, method, performance, and so on.

P

pattern The repetition of a motif in either a predictable or random placement.

perception The individual response to the sensations of stimuli. Often cultural.

perspective The drawing technique of creating receding or diminishing objects of a three-dimensional nature on a two-dimensional surface.

pictorial space The illusion of depth or distance on a two-dimensional space.

placement Location, situation, or juxtaposition of elements.

positive shape A shape or line placed in a negative or empty space.

primary colors Colors that cannot be produced by mixing other colors. Theoretically, all other colors can be produced from the primaries.

principles Ways the parts or elements are used, arranged, or manipulated to create the composition of the design; how to use the parts.

problem solving A sequence of strategies for finding a solution to a problem.

product design The design of necessary, functional items in a society.

proportion The relative measurements or dimensions of parts or a portion of the whole.

R

radial balance Created by repetitive equilibrium of elements radiating from a center point.

random pattern A pattern effect because it is a repeated shape or motif but can be scattered or not controlled as in an all-over pattern. Less formal.

relativity The degree of comparison of one thing to another. How does *a* compare to *b;* then what is the comparison of *a* to *c?*

repetition The result of repeating or doing the same thing over and over.

rhythm A recurrence of movement. A "visual path" for the eye to follow; a "visual beat."

rhythmic devices Systems of alignments in which to place elements to create a "visual path."

S

scale The size of one shape or image compared to another or to the space it occupies.

secondary colors Colors produced by mixing two primaries.

shade A dark value of a color.

shape An image in space.

simultaneous color contrast Contrasting colors as defined by Michel-Eugène Chevreul using the traditional color wheel.

simple design Few elements used in the space and in the composition. Not difficult for a viewer to comprehend.

simulated texture The real quality of a tactile surface being copied or imitated.

space An empty, negative area where our design will fit.

space division Space divided by the use of positive and negative shapes.

split-complement Three hues; one hue and the hues on *either* side of its complement hue.

subtractive color mixture The result of pigments mixed together and exerting their force upon one another.

subtractive method A process of taking away material, by various means, to give form.

symbolic line A line or combination of lines that stands for, or reminds us of, something within our realm of knowledge.

symmetrical balance (Formal balance)—Technically a mirror image. Elements on either side of the implied axis have precisely the same shape, *but in reverse,* and have the same visual weight.

T

temperate colors The apparent psychological or emotional state of warmth or coolness of colors.

temporary space Actual 3-D space used only for a defined length of time.

tension Opposing forces, push-pull, yin-yang.

tertiary colors (Intermediate colors)—Colors produced by mixing a primary and a secondary color.

texture The quality of being tactile, or being able to *feel* a rough or smooth type of surface.

theory The examination of information that often ends in a plausible assumption or conclusion.

time and motion The planning for *actual* space to be used in bodily movement OR the anticipated illusion of movement in time.

three-dimensional (3-D) Having height, width, and DEPTH in a given space.

tint A light value of a color.

tones Neutrals of colors; relative neutral scale.

touch To contact, adjoin.

triad Three hues *equal* distance from one another on the color wheel.

U

unity The effect of all the principles being in harmony with one another, creating the feeling of wholeness.

V

value The range of possible lightness or darkness within a given medium.

variety The changing of the original character of any element; diversity.

W

working space The space that reflects the actual space. The two *may,* but not always, be the same space. This is the space we use to solve our design problem.

Further Research for Your Enjoyment

GENERAL

Robert Henri, *The Art Spirit*. New York: Harper & Row, 1984.

Rollo May, *The Courage to Create*. Des Plaines, IL: Bantam Books, 1975.

GENERAL DESIGN:

ID, The International Design Magazine. Cincinatti, OH: Faw Publications.

COLOR:

Jenny Balfour-Paul, *Indigo*. London: British Museum Press, 1998.

Victoria Finlay, *COLOR: A Natural History of the Palette*. New York: Ballantine 2002.

Simon Garfield, *Mauve*. London: W. W. Norton, 2001.

◆ Some Interesting Websites:

stevekline.com
jamesmcgulpin.com
mehaffeygallery.com
vebjorn-sand.com/thebridge.htm
satava.com
michaelschlicting.com
susanweeks.com
aletapippin.com
quillergallery.com
johnwesleywilliamfurniture.com
pantonecolor.com
unibz.it.com

Bibliography

Chapters 1–12

Albers, Josef, *The Interaction of Colors* (New Haven, CT: Yale University Press, 1975).

Arnheim, Rudolph, *Art and Visual Perception* (Berkeley, CA: University of California Press, 1954).

Behrens, Roy R., *Design in the Visual Arts* (Englewood Cliffs, NJ: Prentice Hall, 1984).

Bevlin, Marjorie, *Design Through Discovery* (New York: Holt, Rinehart & Winston).

Birren, Faber, *Color and Human Response* (New York: Van Nostrand Reinhold, 1978).

———, *Creative Colors* (New York: Van Nostrand Reinhold, 1961).

———, *History of Color in Painting* (New York: Van Nostrand Reinhold, 1965).

Cheatham, Frank, Jane Cheatham, and Sheryl Haler, *Design Concepts and Application* (Englewood Cliffs, NJ: Prentice Hall, 1983).

Chevreul, M. E., *The Laws of Harmony and Contrast* (New York: Van Nostrand Reinhold, 1981).

Edwards, Betty, *Drawing on the Right Side of the Brain* (Boston: Houghton Mifflin, 1979).

Ellinger, Richard G., *Color Structure and Design* (New York: Van Nostrand Reinhold, 1980).

Elliot, Sheila and John Elliot, "Painting an Upbeat Mood," *The Artist's Magazine* (July 1986).

Itten, Joannes, *Design and Form* (New York: Van Nostrand Reinhold, 1975).

———, *Elements of Color* (New York: Van Nostrand Reinhold).

———, *The Art of Color* (New York: Van Nostrand Reinhold, 1973).

James, Jane H., *Perspective Drawing* (Englewood Cliffs, NJ: Prentice Hall, 1981).

Johnson, Mary Frisbee, *Visual Workouts* (Englewood Cliffs, NJ: Prentice Hall, 1983).

Lauer, David A., *Design Basics* (New York: Holt, Rinehart & Winston, 1985).

Leland, Nita, *Exploring Color* (Cincinnati, OH: North Light Publishers, 1985).

Mante, Harold, *Color Design in Photography* (New York: Van Nostrand Reinhold, 1978).
Mendelowitz, Daniel, *A Guide to Drawing* (New York: Holt, Rinehart & Winston, 1976).

Ocvirk, Bon, et al., *Art Fundamentals, Theory and Practice* (New York: W.C. Brown).
Osborn, Ray, *Light & Pigments: Color Principles for Artists* (New York: Harper & Row, 1980).

Pfeiffer, John E., "Cro-Magnon Hunters Were Really Us, Etc.," *Smithsonian* (October 1986).
Pile, John F., *Design Purpose, Form and Meaning* (New York: W. W. Norton, 1979).
Proctor, Richard M., *Principles of Patterns for Craftsmen and Designers* (New York: Van Nostrand Reinhold, 1969).

Sargeant, Walter, *The Enjoyment and Use of Color* (New York: Charles Scribner's Sons, 1923). Revised Edition (New York: Dover Publishing, 1964).
Shell, Ellen Ruppel, "With the Right Package, You Can Sell Anything," *Smithsonian* (April 1996) p. 54.
Spencer, Patricia W., "Roses Are Red, White, Yellow, Pink . . . ," *Natural History* (Englewood Cliffs, NJ: June–July 1976).
Sullivan, Louis H., "The Tall Office Building Artistically Considered," *Lippencott's* (March 1896).

Zelanski, Paul, *Color* (Englewood Cliffs, NJ: Prentice Hall, 1989).
Zelanski, P. & Mary Pat Fisher, *Design: Principles and Problems* (New York: Holt, Rinehart & Winston, 1984).

◆ Chapter 16

Coke, Van Deren, *The Painter and the Photograph* (Albuquerque, NM: University of New Mexico Press, 1965).

Leslie, Jacques, "Computer Visions, The Good, The Bad and the Unknown," *Modern Maturity* (November–December 1998).

McCormick, Tracy, "What's Hot," *U.S. Art Gallery* (November 2000).

◆ Miscellaneous

Baker, Kenneth, "Museum or Monument," *Connoisseur* (February 1988), p. 128.

Doherty, M. Steven, *Dynamic Still Lifes in Watercolor* (New York: Watson Guptill, 1983), p. 23.

"Expo," "Risky Biscuits." *ID, The International Design Magazine* (April 2004), p. 27.

Fichner-Rathus, Lois, *Understanding Art* (Englewood Cliffs, NJ: Prentice Hall, 1986).
Fischl, Eric with Jerry Saltz, ed., *Sketchbook with Voices* (New York: Alfred van der Marck Editions, 1986), p. 28.

Henri, Robert, *The Art Spirit,* compiled by Margery A. Ryerson (New York: Harper & Row, Icon Editions, 1984).
Hines, Jack, "Creative Process," *Southwest Art* (April 1996), p. 44; (May 1996), p. 42.

Jones, Ronald, "Breuer Beyond Bauhaus," *ID, International Design Magazine* (April 2004), p. 88.

May, Rollo, *The Courage to Create* (New York: W. W. Norton, 1975).
Merriam-Webster, Inc. *Dictionary of Quotations* (Springfield, MA: Merriam-Webster, 1992).
Merriam-Webster, Inc. *Thesaurus.*

Norman, Donald A., *The Psychology of Everyday Things* (New York: Basic Books, 1988).

Pfeiffer, John E., *The Creative Explosion: An Inquiry into the Origins of Art and Religion* (New York: Harper & Row, 1982).
Pleshette, Ann, "A Chef's Chef," *Food and Wine* (July 1982).

Samulson, Jerry and Jack Stoops, *Design Dialogue* (Worcester, MA: Davis, 1983).

Scanlon, Jessie, "Big Business," *ID, The International Design Magazine* (April 2004), p. 61.

Sides, Dorothy Smith, *Decorative Art of the Southwest Indians* (New York: Dover, 1961).

Sinclair, Cameron, "Speak No Drivel," *ID, The International Design Magazine* (April 2004), p. 33.

Underhill, Ruth, *Pueblo Crafts* (Washington, DC: U.S. Department of the Interior, 1944).

Section II

The following selection is taken from *Photoshop® Classic Effects,* by Scott Kelby. Only the content intended for use in this course has been provided. There is no CD accompanying this selection, however there is a website with free downloads if you want to try the projects using the same photos used in this section. Please download these files from http://www.scottkelbybooks.com/classicphotos. The low-resolution images are zipped files so be sure to right click and Save the files to your desktop rather than simply opening the files.

The Tutorial to End All Tutorials

On these next six pages, I will reveal the single most-asked-for, most-talked-about, most-highly-sought-after Photoshop classic effect in the history of all Photoshop effects. Once you learn this technique, you can basically "name your price" and write your own ticket to fame and fortune. Ready? Let's begin.

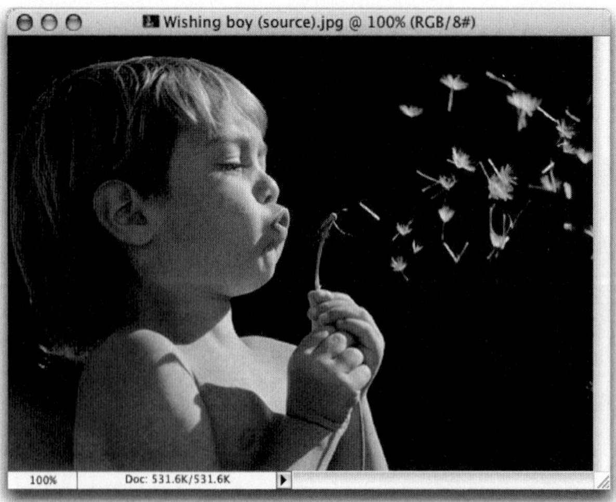

Step One:

Look, I've got to be straight with you right off the bat. This isn't a tutorial. Okay, I know it looks like a tutorial (that's the whole idea), but I just made it look like a tutorial because I know that if I did, you'd read it. But the sad truth is—this is actually the book's introduction. Whoa! Wait—don't turn the page. I know, I know—you want to skip the introduction and get to the tutorials (don't feel bad, statistics show that virtually no one reads a book's introduction. Okay, there's this one guy in Bozeman, Montana, who does, but outside of him, it's just about nil).

Step Two:

So why did I pull this "fake tutorial" stunt on you? I had to. Of all the introductions I've ever written, this one is the most important. If you skip this brief introduction (meaning the introduction has something to do with underwear), you may wind up getting frustrated and disoriented (meaning, you'll be removed from Asia. Get it? Dis-oriented? Man, I hope these jokes get better). In all seriousness, there are some things you'll want to know to make this book work for you, to understand why I did certain things the way I did. You'll also learn about something new that I've done to make things faster and easier for you, so go on to Step Three, and I'll fill you in as we go along.

Continued

Step Three:

First, you're probably wondering what those screen captures are over to the left. Those are part of my "fake tutorial," so you can just ignore them, but if you want to learn how to blend two images and add noise like that, check out the Blending Two Images tutorial. Now here's what this book is about. In the world of Photoshop special effects, there are really two categories of effects: classic effects and new effects.

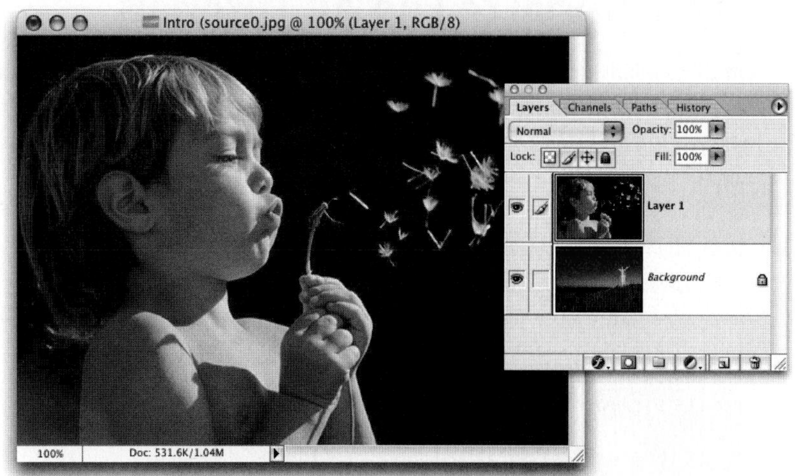

Step Four:

The "classics" are those tried-and-true effects that you see every day—every time you pick up a newspaper, a magazine, turn on the TV, or visit a website. You see these effects at work. They're everywhere—and a lot of people literally make a living using them. They're so popular, and so effective (no pun intended), that these effects have literally become classics, much in the same way certain songs have become classics, or certain food recipes have become classics. For example, if you bought a book titled *Classic Recipes*, you'd expect that it would include some kick-butt recipes for spaghetti sauce, apple pie, buttermilk pancakes, meatloaf, tomato soup, and a wide range of classic dishes, right? Right.

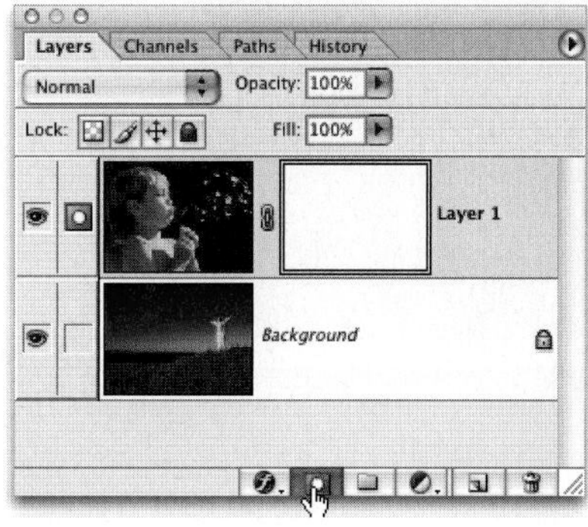

Step Five:

So, would you expect to find some wild new culinary explorations from Wolfgang Puck in a classic recipes book? Not a chance. Instead, you'd find the "meat-and-potatoes" recipes that are used every day by great cooks all over the world. Well, my friends, that's what you're holding—a book of the "meat-and-potatoes" special effects; the same ones used by great Photoshop artists, photographers, and designers all over the world. It's not the wild stuff, it's not the weird stuff—it's the stuff you can really use, the stuff clients ask for and expect that you'll know. But there's more.

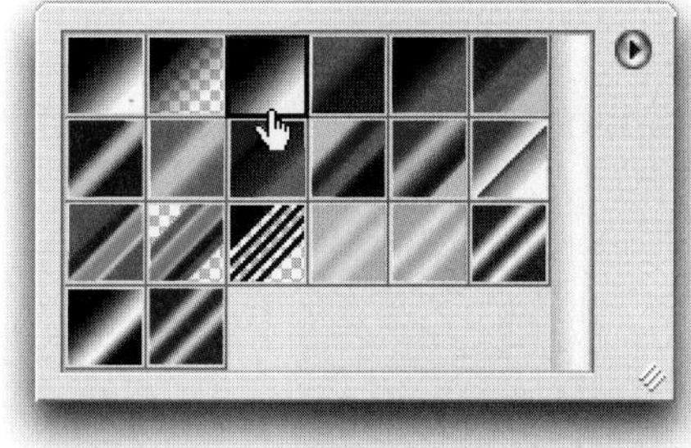

Step Six:

I didn't just want to say, "Here's the effect—have a nice day." I really wanted to teach you these effects by using them in the context they're used in today, by the industry's leading professionals. For example, torn-edge effects have been around for years, but they're used differently today than they were just three or four years ago. I wanted to create a book that has you create not just the simple effect but an entire real-world project that incorporates the effect. That way, not only will you see it in the context of today's effects, you'll use it in the right context, too!

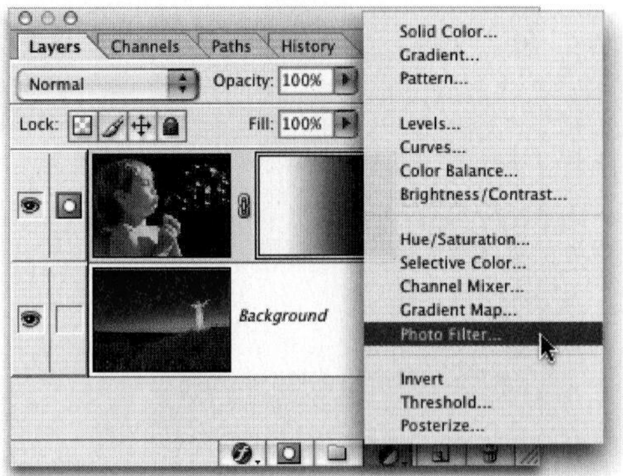

Step Seven:

So, are these effects just for beginners? Some are, some clearly aren't, but even the very simplest effects are still used every day by the biggest ad agencies, the leading Web developers, and the hottest video houses. It doesn't have to be hard or overly complicated to be good. These are the classics—they've been around a while because they're that good.

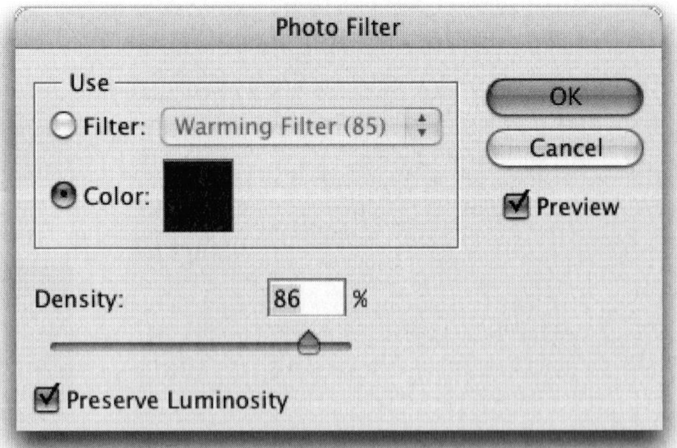

Step Eight:

Here's the thing: If your client is MTV, you can go out and do all the latest, wildest, weirdest effects and they'll love it (like the cutting-edge effects that are in my *Photoshop CS Down & Dirty Tricks* book). But what if your client is CBS or CNN? Try that stuff and they'll show you the door. They need a professional, clean look, and they'll expect you to know the classics and how they're used today. That's what this book is all about—teaching you the handy bag of tricks that you can use again and again to make your clients sing and your cash register ring.

Continued

Step Nine:
So that's how you'll learn—by building complete projects that go from blank page to final image—all within just a few pages—and within that project will be the classic effect. The bonus is, of course, that you'll learn much, much more than just the effect. You'll learn to lay out pages, create your own designs, and do things in Photoshop you never thought you could do by replicating what today's pros are doing. I think it's the best, and certainly the most fun way to learn Photoshop special effects.

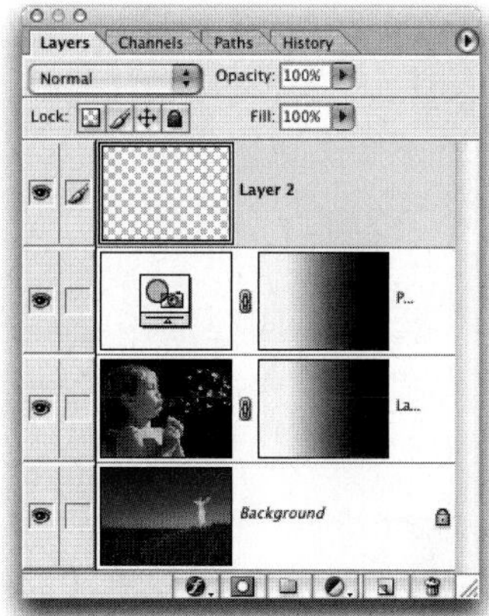

Step Ten:
By the way, for every classic effect in the book, you'll see a "Cut to the Chase" logo followed by a page number. This is that new idea I mentioned earlier. Here's what it's based on: I figure that when you get this book, you'll try all the projects that interest you, and really spend some time getting your hands dirty learning all these classic special effects. That's great while you have the time, but let's say that four months down the road you're working on tight deadline and you need to add, say…a scan lines effect to your project.

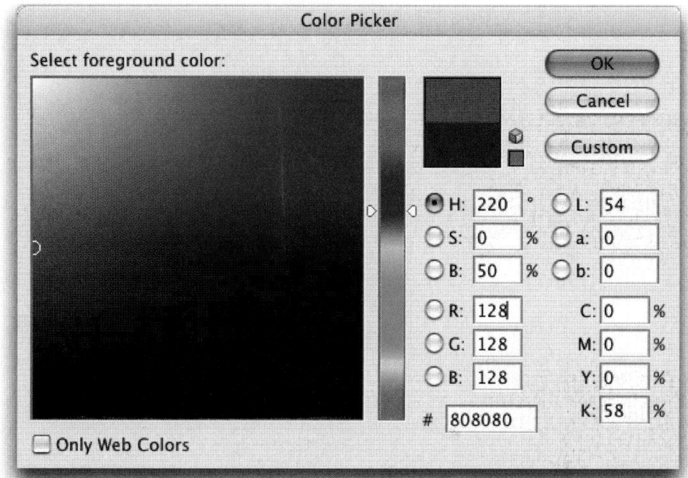

Step Eleven:
Do you have to go back and rebuild the entire Army TV ad project just to get the scan lines effect? Nope. You can "Cut to the Chase" and jump to the page number that appears within the logo. On that page is a simple three-step instruction on how to add the TV scan lines effect in a hurry. It's short, sweet, and to the point. No extra stuff—just the scan lines effect. Think of this as an appendix, a bonus chapter, whatever—just use it when you really need to "Cut to the Chase."

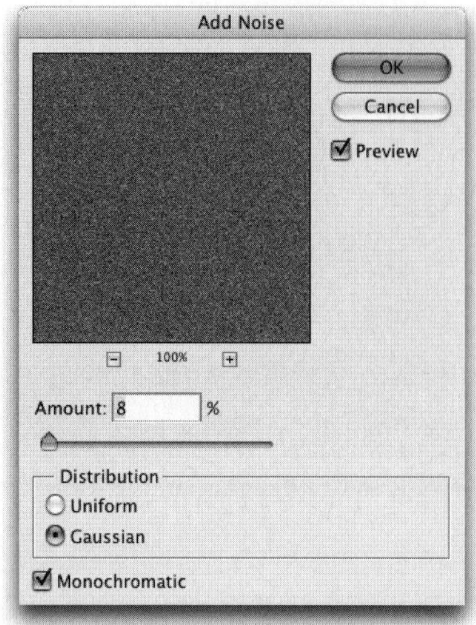

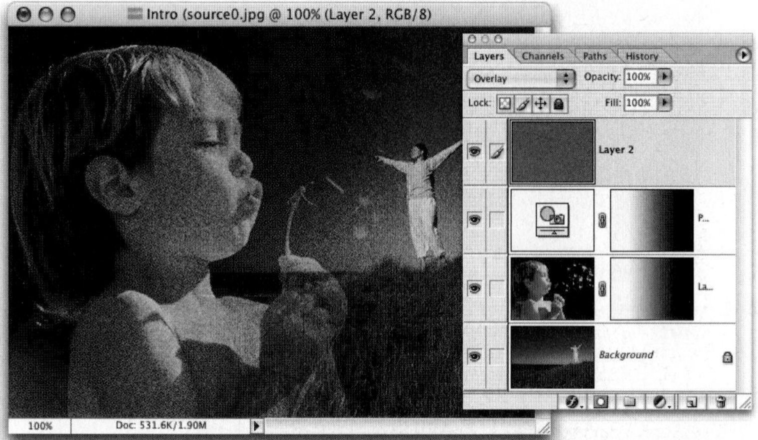

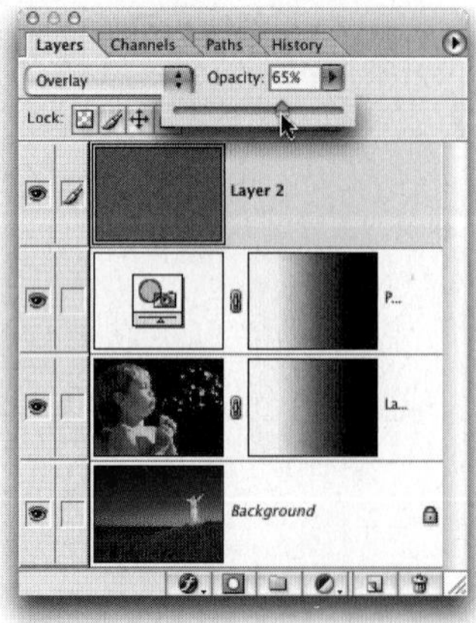

Step Twelve:

If you want to try these projects using the same photos as I used in the book, you're in luck. The wonderful people at Brand X Pictures have graciously enabled us to make low-res images available for you to download free so you can follow along. You can download these only from www.scottkelbybooks.com/classicphotos/. By the way, I chose Brand X Pictures royalty-free images for a reason—I think they offer the best, and most complete royalty-free stock images out there, bar none. Check out thousands of their images at www.brandx.com and you'll see what I mean.

Step Thirteen:

A few final things: I have no way of knowing whether you're a beginner, or an intermediate, or advanced Photoshop user, so I pretty much lay everything out from soup to nuts. For example, in each tutorial the first time I tell you to do something, I tell you the entire technique, so the first time it appears in a tutorial…

Step Fourteen:

…instead of just saying "create a new layer," I'll say: "Create a new layer by clicking on the Create a New Layer icon at the bottom of the Layers palette." If I need you to create another layer in that same tutorial, as I just laid it all out, I might then just say "create another new layer," assuming all the while that you don't have a serious short-term memory problem. So if you're a more advanced user, don't let it throw you that I spell everything out—I have to do this because I want this book to be accessible to as many users as possible. Also, Photoshop is identical on both the Mac and Windows platforms, but the keyboards on a PC and Mac are different, so I give both keyboard shortcuts every time.

Continued

Step Fifteen:

Another thing is this—you can jump in anywhere you want and start trying the effects. There's no "Photoshop Basics" chapter or anything like that that you have to start with first. And since I spell everything out for you, you can start anywhere you like, so don't feel like you have to start at the beginning and work your way through. Find a classic effect that interests you and have at it.

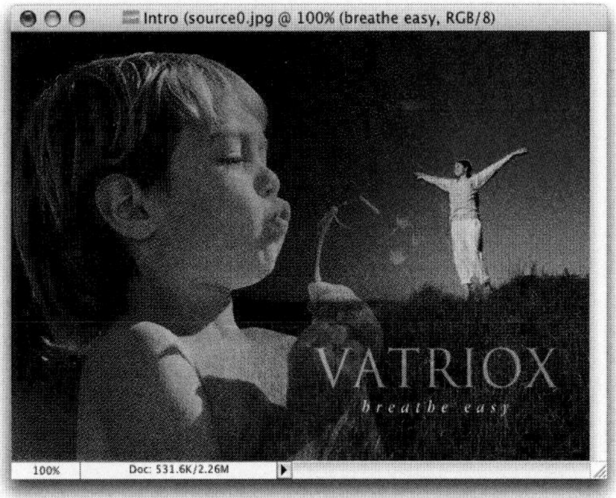

Step Sixteen:

Also, because we're doing complete projects, I used a lot of type and different typefaces (fonts) along the way. Most of the fonts I use either come with Photoshop CS, or they're so common (like Helvetica) that there's a 99% chance you already have them loaded on your system. Occasionally, I used a specialty font, but I always give you the name, and often where to buy it if you so desire, but feel free to substitute your own fonts—if you see I'm using a tall, thick font, choose one of your tall, thick fonts as well.

Step Seventeen:

Okay, now you've learned how to use the book, where to download the photos, how to deal with fonts, and how to "Cut to the Chase." You can see why I had to pull the whole "tutorial scam." These are important aspects of learning from this book, and even if I had to trick you into reading what is ostensively the introduction, now that you've read it, don't you feel an overwhelming sense of self-accomplishment and pride? No? Rats! Oh well, it was only a few short pages, right? Now get on with it. Go have some fun and cook up some yummy effects (and huge invoices).

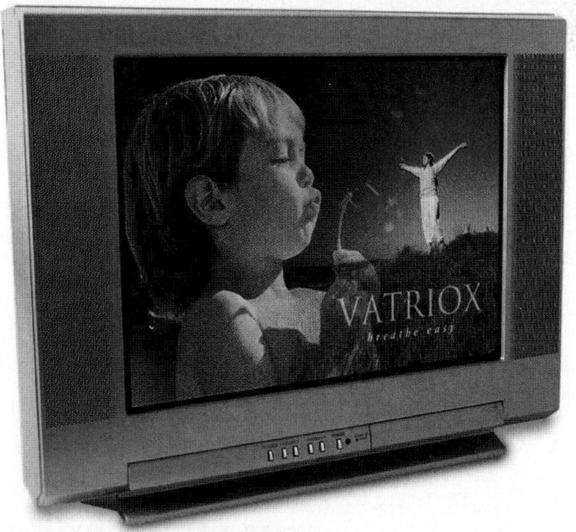

Photo Tinting

Tinting a color photo with a solid color is very popular and fairly easy—once you know how. That's why in this tutorial, I not only show you how to tint a photo but also how to take that tinted print and add some simple elements to create a full-size poster. What I really like about this technique is that it lets you take a fairly boring photo and turn it into something artistic quickly and easily.

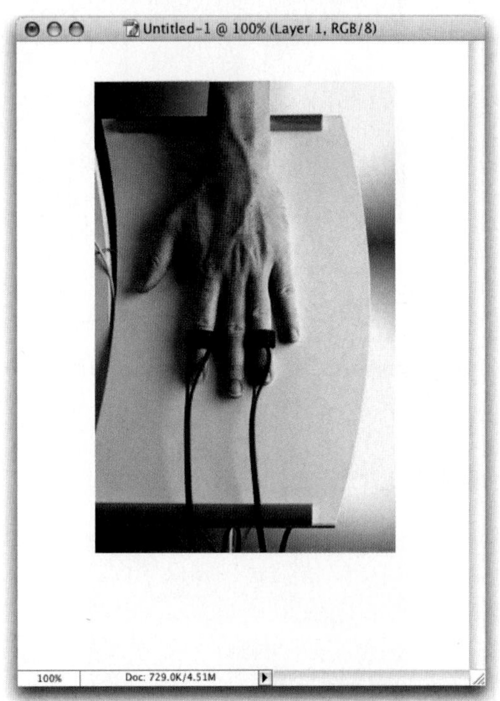

Step One:

Open the photo you want to apply a tint effect to. Create a new blank document (File>New) that's larger than the photo, then press the letter "v" to switch to the Move tool and drag-and-drop your photo onto this larger document (as shown here). We're doing this because we're not only going to tint the photo, but create a poster with the tinted photo (of course, the tinting is the technique—the poster part is to expand the technique by creating a real-world project using the tinted image).

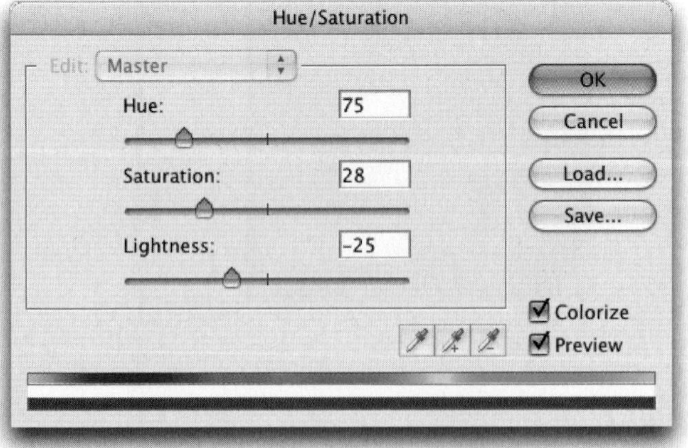

Step Two:

Command-click (PC: Control-click) on the photo's thumbnail in the Layers palette to put a selection around the image. Choose Hue/Saturation from the Create New Adjustment Layer pop-up menu (it's the fourth icon from the left) at the bottom of the Layers palette. When the dialog appears, click on the Colorize checkbox. Then move the Hue slider to choose your tint (in this case, move the Hue slider to 75). Then, because this photo has large areas of lighter tones, you'll need to darken the image a bit by lowering the Lightness slider to -25. Click OK and a greenish tint is applied to the image. Easy enough, eh? Now on to the rest of the poster project.

Continued

Step Three:

Let's add a stroke—choose Stroke from the Create a Layer Style pop-up menu at the bottom of the Layers palette. When the dialog appears, click on the Color swatch and change the stroke color to black. Increase the Size to 8 and change the Position pop-up menu to Inside so the stroke doesn't have rounded corners. Click OK to apply the stroke.

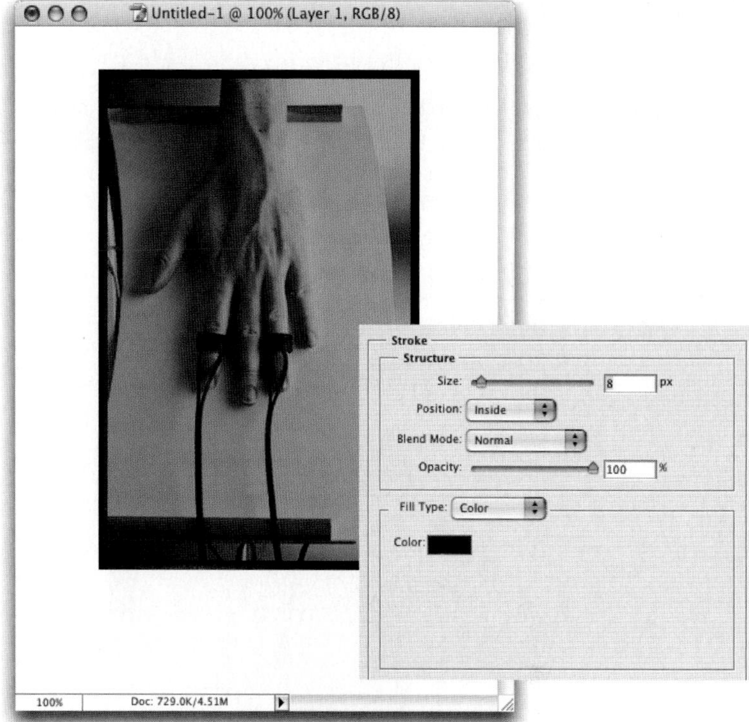

Step Four:

Now, we'll add two of the three "high-tech" elements we learned in the "high-tech" tutorial earlier in this chapter. Add two small paragraphs using the Type tool set to white, setting the font as Helvetica at 3 points in the Character palette, and drop in a couple of larger plus signs (+). And maybe a deep thoughtful line of text, like "Where does one find the truth?" set in Helvetica in all caps. Lower the Opacity of the Type layers in the Layers palette.

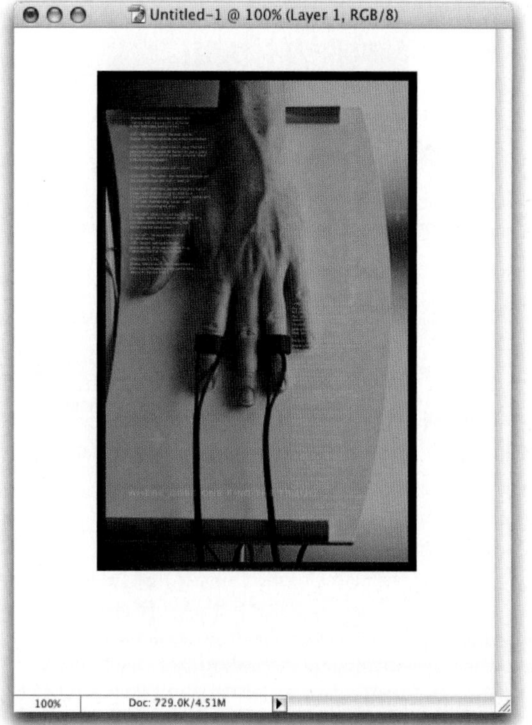

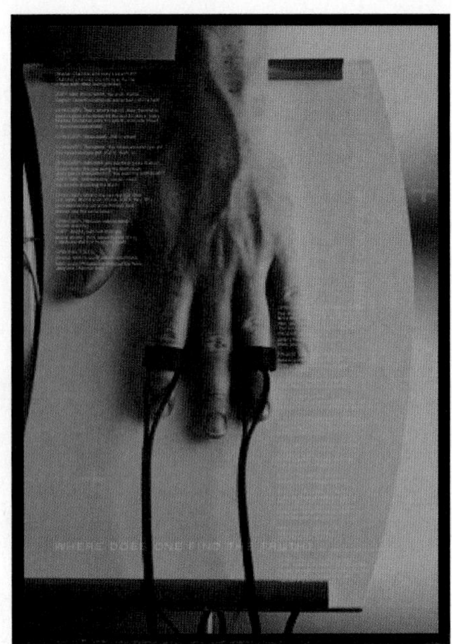

Step Five:
To finish the poster, you can add some text below the image (as shown here). The words "truth in advertising" are set in Helvetica Regular. The type directly below that is set in Copperplate Gothic Regular. The fictitious gallery name is set in Trajan Pro (which comes with Photoshop CS), and that completes the project.

Clipping Mask Effect

If you've ever wanted to know how to fit (or clip) a photo inside a specific shape so that none of the photo extends beyond that shape—this is how. The project we're building here was inspired by an AMC Entertainment Card that was in my wallet (got it as a stocking stuffer). The AMC card makes great use of this technique.

Step One:

Our clipping project will be a gift card for a fictitious record store, so start by creating a new document (File>New) that's 7x5" set at 72 ppi, then add a new layer by clicking on the Create a New Layer icon at the bottom of the Layers palette. Press "d" to set your Foreground color to black, then get the Rounded Rectangle tool from the Toolbox (as shown). Go up to the Options Bar and in the group of three icons on the left, click on the third icon from the left (as shown) so the tool will create pixels, rather than a path or a shape layer. While you're in the Options Bar, set the Radius (the roundness of the corners) to 10 pixels. Now use the tool to drag out a rounded rectangle in the shape of a credit card (as shown here).

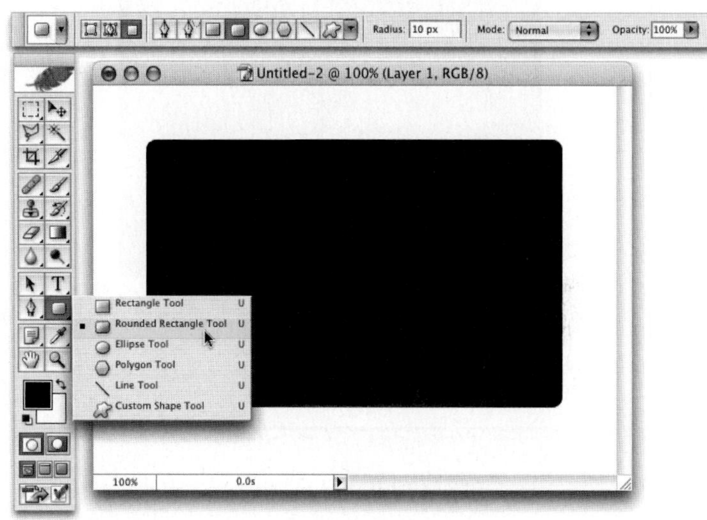

Step Two:

You're going to need to mark the horizontal center of this credit card shape. This is an easy three-step process: (1) Press Command-T (PC: Control-T) to bring up the Free Transform bounding box around your shape. (2) Press Command-R (PC: Control-R) to make your rulers visible. (3) Click directly on the top ruler and drag down a guide until it reaches the Free Transform's center point. (Note: If you have Snap turned on in the View menu, the guide will "snap" to the center point.) Now that Free Transform has helped you find the center, you don't need it anymore, so press the Escape key.

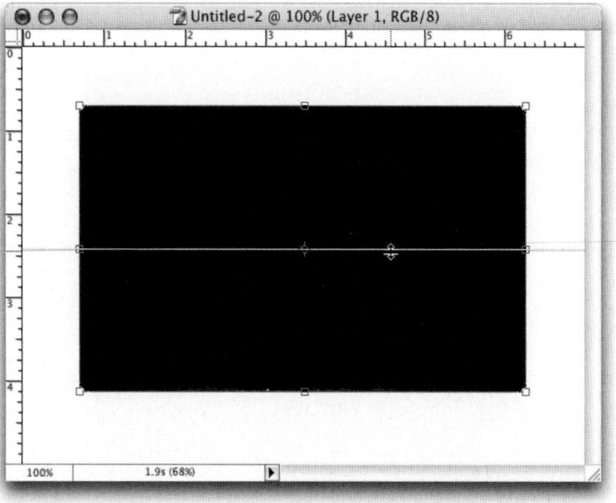

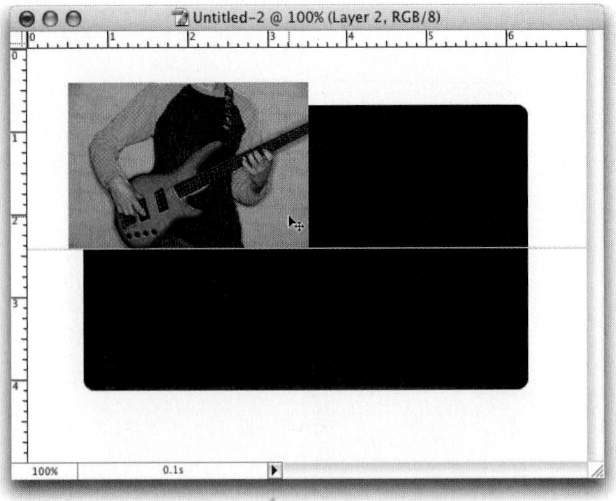

Step Three:

Open the first photo you want to "clip" into your credit card shape. Press the letter "v" to switch to the Move tool and drag the image over onto your credit card shape, and position it where you want it to appear (as shown here). If you need to resize your image, press Command-T (PC: Control-T) to bring up the Free Transform command. Use the guide to line up the bottom of the photo to the center half of the card.

Step Four:

To clip your photo inside the black credit card shape, just press Command-G (PC: Control-G) and the photo will fit neatly inside the shape (as shown here). Once it's clipped inside, if you need to reposition it, just use the Move tool. (The image will stay within the boundaries of the shape, which is one of the coolest things about clipping groups.) So that's how it's done. Now, on to the rest of the project.

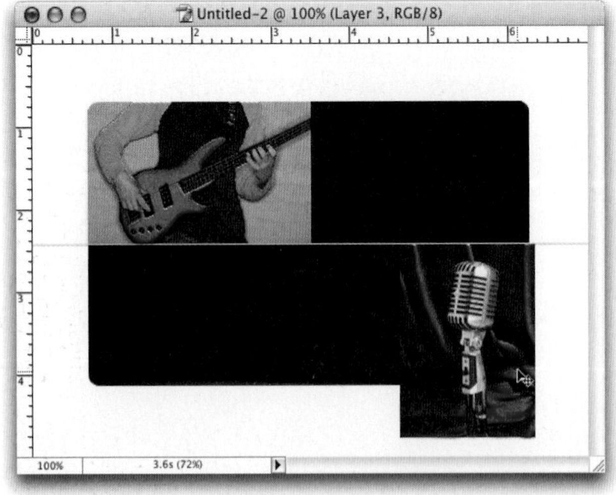

Step Five:

Open another image that you want clipped and use the Move tool to drag it over onto your credit card shape and position it approximately where you want it to appear within the card (as shown here). Use the guide to line up the top of the photo to the center half of the card. Again, if you need to resize your image, use the Free Transform command.

Continued

Step Six:

Press Command-G (PC: Control-G) and the photo will now be clipped inside the shape. Later, we'll want to add a tint to this one image, but for now let's just remove the color by going under the Image menu, under Adjustments, and choosing Desaturate so the image appears in black and white (as shown here).

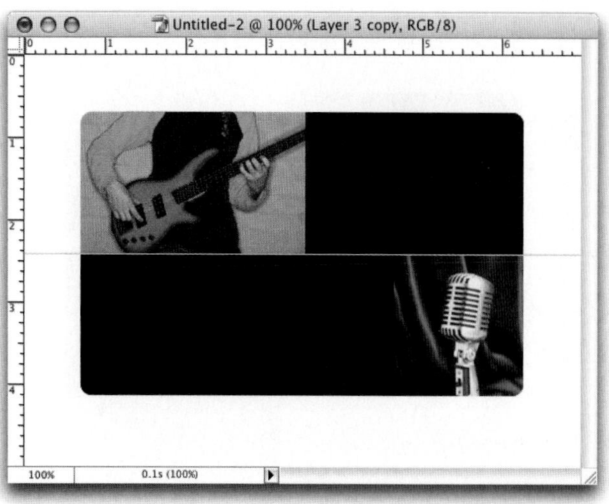

Step Seven:

Now we'll add a strip of color to the bottom of the card to the left of the microphone image. Go to the Layers palette and click the Create a New Layer icon. Press the letter "i" to switch to the Eyedropper tool, and click one of the tiny blue areas in the bass guitar strap to make that blue your Foreground color (you may need to use the Zoom tool from the Toolbox for a better view). Now press the letter "m" to switch to the Rectangular Marquee tool and drag a rectangular selection over the open area to the left of the microphone and below the bass player (as shown here). Fill that area with blue by pressing Option-Delete (PC: Alt-Backspace). Now you can deselect by pressing Command-D (PC: Control-D). Press Command-G (PC: Control-G), and the blue rectangle will now be clipped inside the shape (as shown here).

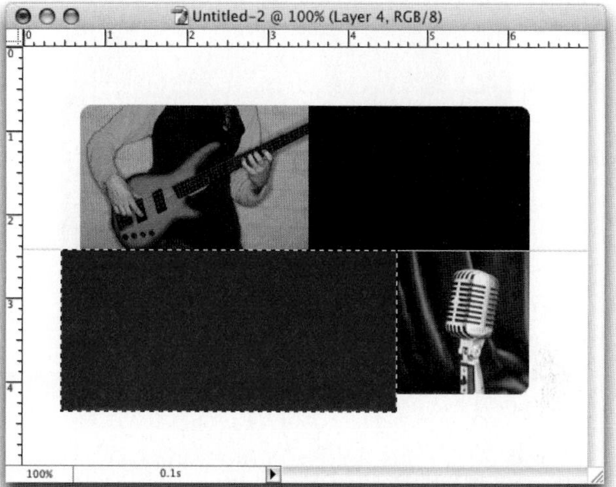

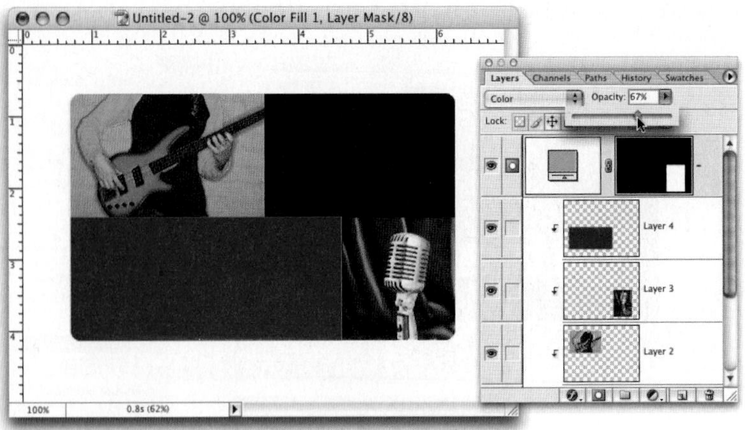

Step Eight:

Now we'll add the tint that I mentioned earlier to the microphone image. Go to the Layers palette and click on the microphone layer to make it active. Hold the Command key (PC: Control key) and click on the microphone layer to put a selection around it. Then choose Solid Color from the Create New Adjustment Layer pop-up menu at the bottom of the Layers palette (it's the fourth icon from the left). When the Color Picker appears, move your cursor outside the dialog and click on the yellow in the bass player's sleeves to make that your Foreground color. Click OK, then in the Layers palette change the blend mode of this Solid Color layer from Normal to Color. Lastly, lower the Opacity to 65% so it doesn't look so saturated.

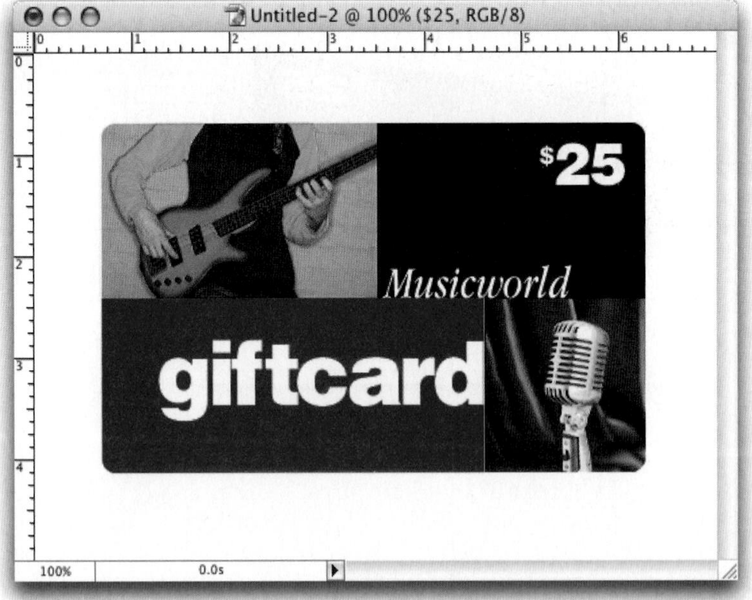

Step Nine:

It's time to add some white type with the Type tool. Click on your blue rectangle layer in the Layers palette, then press the letter "d" then "x" to set your Foreground to white. Press "t" to switch to the Type tool, then click on the image to add your type. The word "Musicworld" is set in Garamond Condensed Italic, and the word "giftcard" is set in Helvetica Black.

Continued

Step Ten:

We'll add a perspective effect to finish the project, but before we can apply the perspective, we have to get the card on a single layer. Go to the Layers palette and hide the Background layer from view by clicking on the Eye icon to the left of the Background layer. Then, go to the palette's flyout menu and choose Merge Visible (as shown here) to merge all the card layers into one single layer.

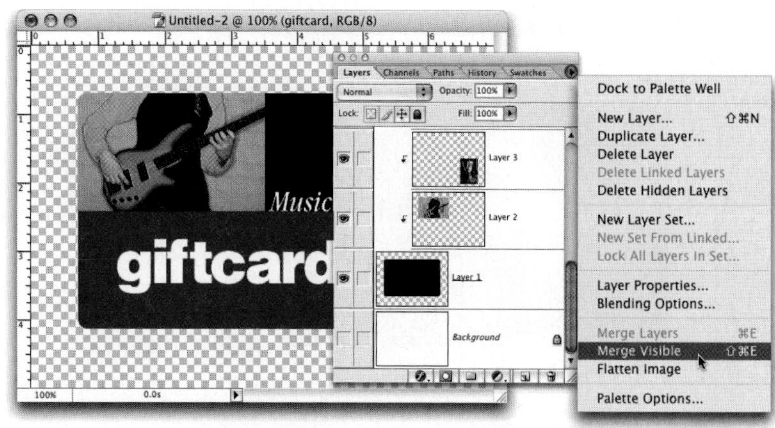

Step Eleven:

Now that the card is on one layer, press Command-T (PC: Control-T) to bring up the Free Transform command. Hold Shift-Option-Command (PC: Shift-Alt-Control), then click on the top-left transform handle and drag straight downward to create a perspective effect (as shown here). The card looks fairly stretched and distorted, but you'll fix that in the next step.

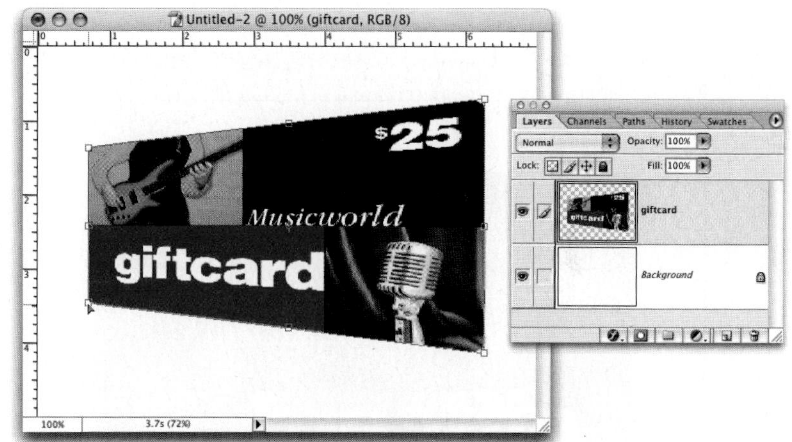

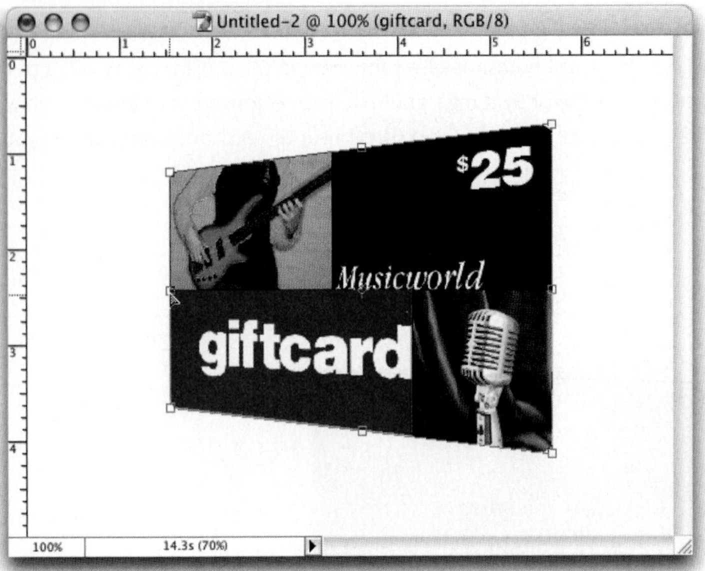

Step Twelve:

Release the keys you were holding, then click on the left-center transform handle and drag to the right to remove the stretched effect and make the card look normal again—just with a little perspective. Don't press Return (PC: Enter) quite yet.

Step Thirteen:

Now just move your cursor outside the Free Transform bounding box to the right, and click-and-drag downward to rotate the card just a little. Press Return (PC: Enter) to lock in all your Free Transform changes, completing the effect (as shown here).

Sepia Tone Effect

The sepia tone effect (popular many decades ago) has been a staple Photoshop effect for years. In the project you're going to do here (creating a CD cover for a fictitious band), you get an added twist by using a gradient map to convert your image to grayscale, which gives you a more "contrasty" grayscale conversion. Once again, the sepia part is near the end, but along the way you'll learn some other cool tricks as you build the project.

Step One:

Open the image you want to apply the sepia tone effect to.

Step Two:

After we apply the sepia tone effect later in this project, we'll use the image for a CD cover, so we'll need to set that up in the next two steps. Press the letter "m" to switch to the Rectangular Marquee tool, hold the Shift key, and draw a large perfectly square selection in the image, leaving plenty of room around the shack (as shown here).

Step Three:

Create a new blank document (File>New) that is larger than your shack selection. Then, press the letter "v" to switch to the Move tool, go back to the shack photo, and drag the selected area onto your new, larger document (as shown here).

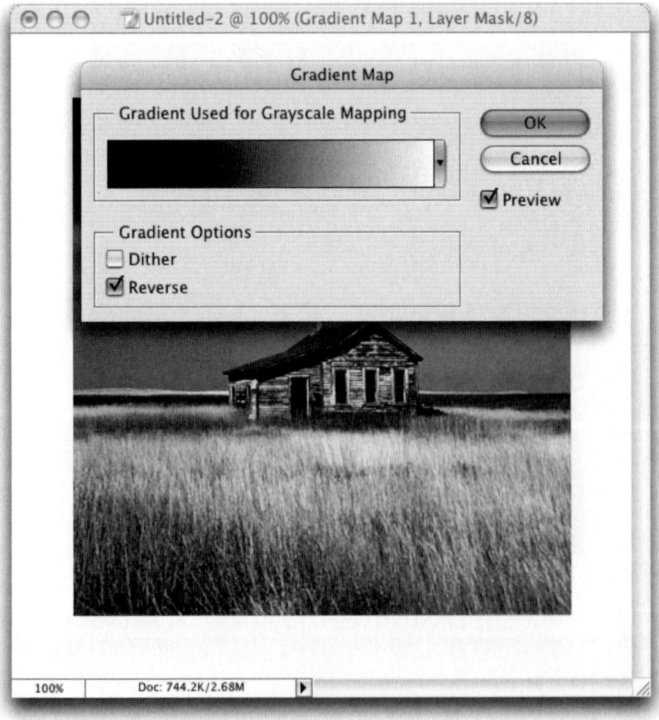

Step Four:

We're going to convert the photo to black-and-white (okay, grayscale), but we're going to do that using a gradient map so the conversion has more contrast. Set your Foreground to black by pressing the letter "d". Choose Gradient Map from the Create New Adjustment Layer pop-up menu at the bottom of the Layers palette. When the dialog appears, it immediately makes the photo look black-and-white, so just click OK. Next you'll add the sepia tone color over your black-and-white image.

Continued

Step Five:

Go under the Create New Adjustment Layer pop-up menu again, but this time choose Solid Color. When the Color Picker appears, click on the Custom button (it's right under the Cancel button). This brings up the Custom Colors dialog. In the Book pop-up menu, choose PANTONE Solid Coated and pick the color you want for your sepia tone (I chose Pantone 142) and click OK.

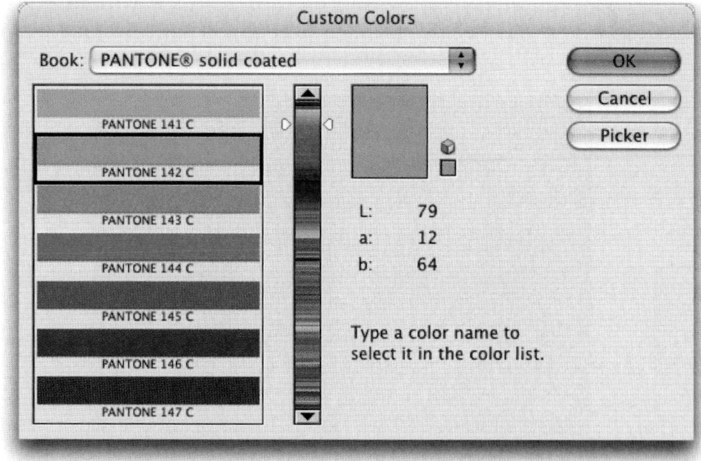

Step Six:

Once you click OK, you'll have just a solid block of color, so in the Layers palette change the layer blend mode of the Color Fill adjustment layer from Normal to Color, and you'll see the sepia tone effect shown here. Next, press the letter "m" to switch to the Rectangular Marquee tool, hold the Shift key, and draw a selection that's slightly larger than the shack photo (as shown here).

Step Seven:

Now that this selection is in place, you can add a thin stroke outside your photo. Click on the Background layer in the Layers palette to make it active, then go under the Edit menu and choose Stroke. When the Stroke dialog appears, choose black as your stroke color by clicking on the Color swatch to bring up the Color Picker, then choose 1 pixel for Width and Center for Location. Click OK to apply the stroke you see here.

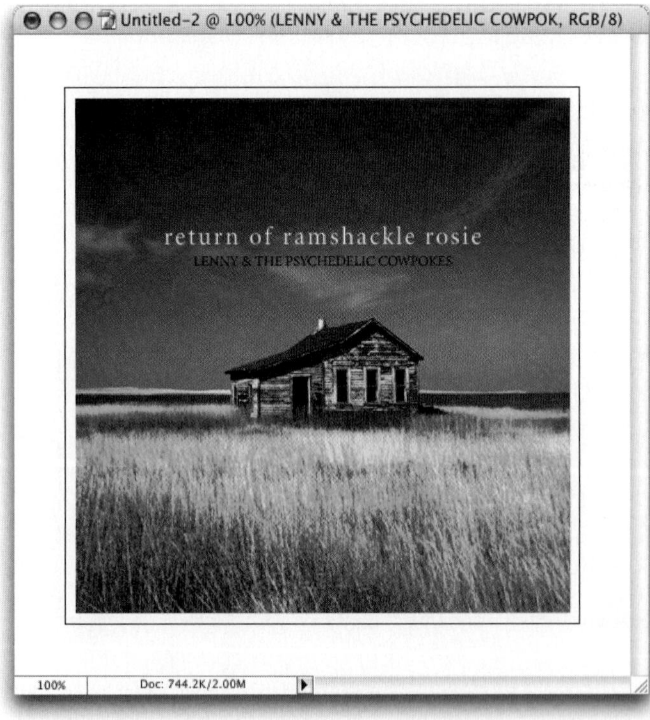

Step Eight:

To finish up the project, just add some text. Both the CD's name (all lowercase) and the band's name beneath it (all caps) are set in Minion.

Lightning Effect

This is about the quickest, easiest, time-tested way to add a lightning effect to your photo without having to draw a bunch of paths or jump through a lot of time-consuming hoops. In our project, we're going to add some lightning to a TV news weather-watch screen against a backdrop of a city at night.

Step One:

Create a new document (File>New) that's 7x5" at 72 ppi in RGB mode, then create a new blank layer by clicking on the Create a New Layer icon at the bottom of the Layers palette. Press Shift-M until you have the Elliptical Marquee tool, hold the Shift key, and draw a large circular selection (like the one shown here). Press "d" to set your Foreground color to black, then fill your selection with black by pressing Option-Delete (PC: Alt-Backspace). Press Command-D (PC: Control-D) to deselect.

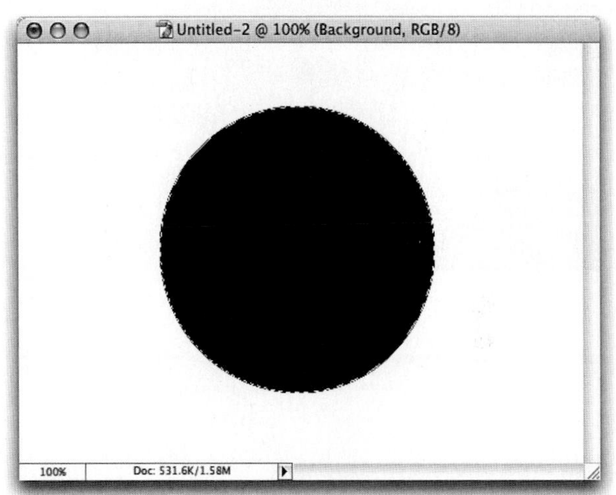

Step Two:

You need to mark the exact center of this circle, so press Command-T (PC: Control-T) to bring up the Free Transform bounding box around your circle. Press Command-R (PC: Control-R) to make your rulers visible, then click directly on the top ruler and drag a guide down until it reaches Free Transform's center point, and then release. Drag another guide to the center from the left ruler. Where these two guides cross is the exact center of your circle.

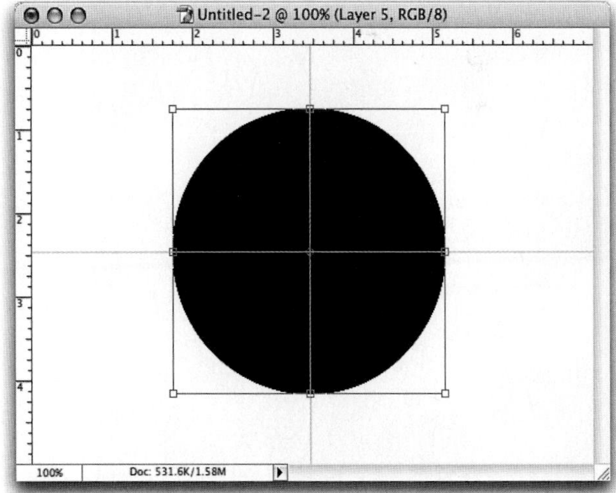

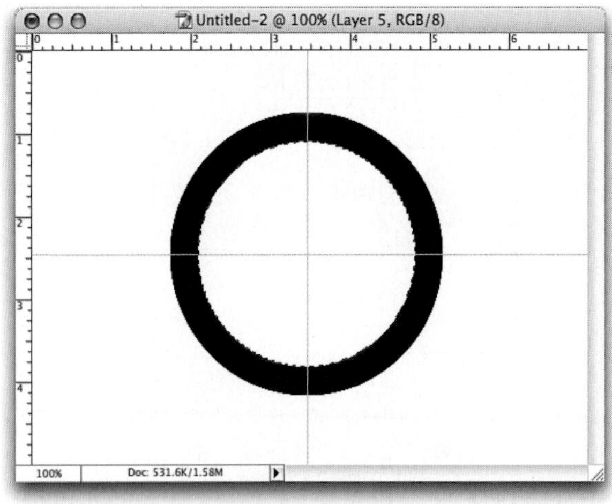

Step Three:

Now that the center point is marked with guides, you don't need Free Transform any longer, so press the Escape key. Hold Shift-Option (PC: Shift-Alt) and click the Elliptical Marquee tool directly on the point where those two guides cross and drag outward to create a smaller concentric circle (like the one shown here). Press Delete (PC: Backspace) to knock a hole out of your black circle (as shown), and press Command-D (PC: Control-D) to deselect. You're done with the guides, so you can remove them by going to View>Clear Guides.

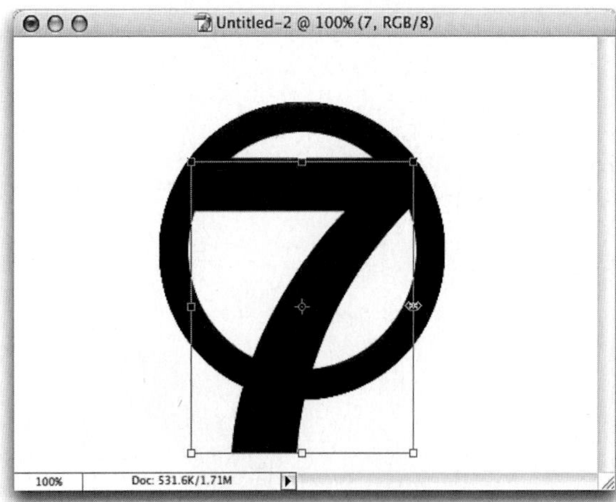

Step Four:

Press the letter "t" to switch to the Type tool, click on your document, and type the number "7" (the font shown here is Helvetica Bold, but any thick, sans serif typeface will do). Click on the Move tool in the Toolbox, and press Command-T (PC: Control-T) to bring up the Free Transform command. Hold the Shift key, grab a top-corner point of the bounding box, and drag upward until the top of the 7 extends from the left side of the circle to the right. If you need to make it wider, release the Shift key, grab the right-center point (as shown) and drag to the right. Don't press Return (PC: Enter) yet.

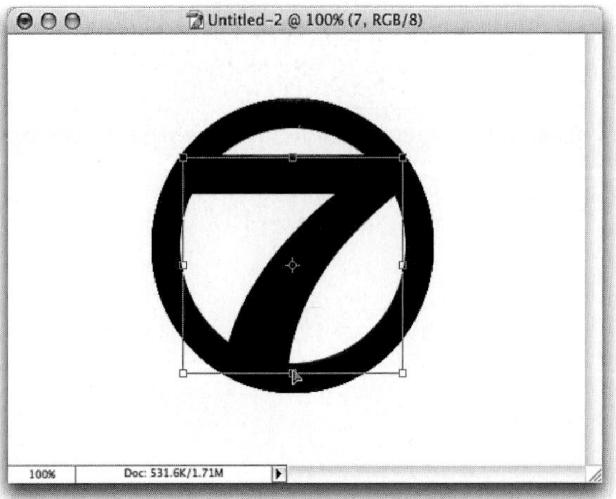

Step Five:

Once the width is right (and the top of the 7 touches both sides of the circle), you'll have to fix the part of the number that extends below the circle (you can see the problem in the previous step). Just grab the bottom-center point of the bounding box and drag upward until the bottom of the number is tucked up into the black circle (as shown here). Now press Return (PC: Enter) to lock in your transformation.

Continued

Step Six:
Now press Command-E (PC: Control-E) to merge your "7" layer with the black circle layer directly beneath it, creating just one layer (as shown here) for the logo. In the Layers palette, click on the first icon to the right of the word "Lock" to lock the transparent pixels on this layer. (You need to do this because in the next step you'll add a gradient to your logo. If you don't lock the transparent pixels, the Gradient tool will fill your entire layer with a gradient, not just the logo.)

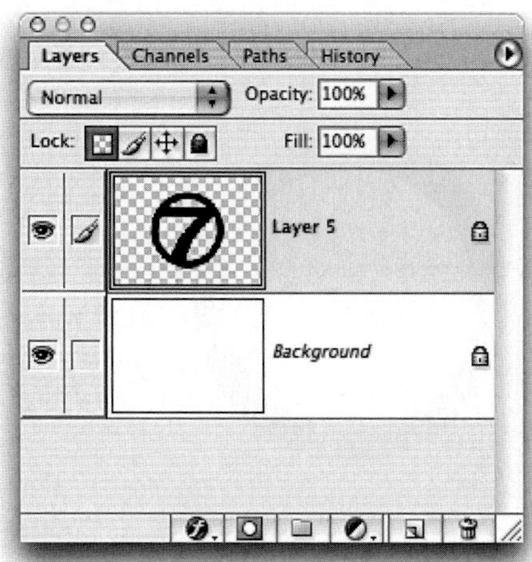

Step Seven:
Press the letter "g" to switch to the Gradient tool, then click on the down-facing arrow next to the gradient thumbnail in the Options Bar to bring up the Gradient Picker. From the Picker's flyout menu, choose Metals. Click the Append button in the resulting dialog to add the Metallic set of gradients to your default set of gradients. Once loaded, click on the Silver gradient in the Picker, then take the Gradient tool and drag diagonally through the logo (as shown).

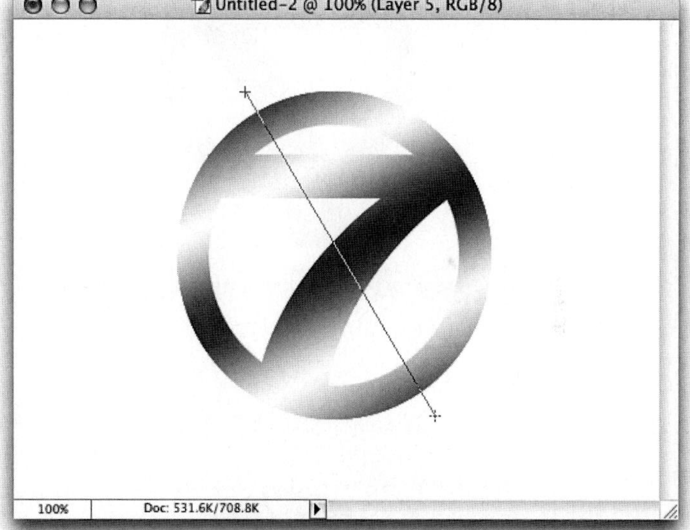

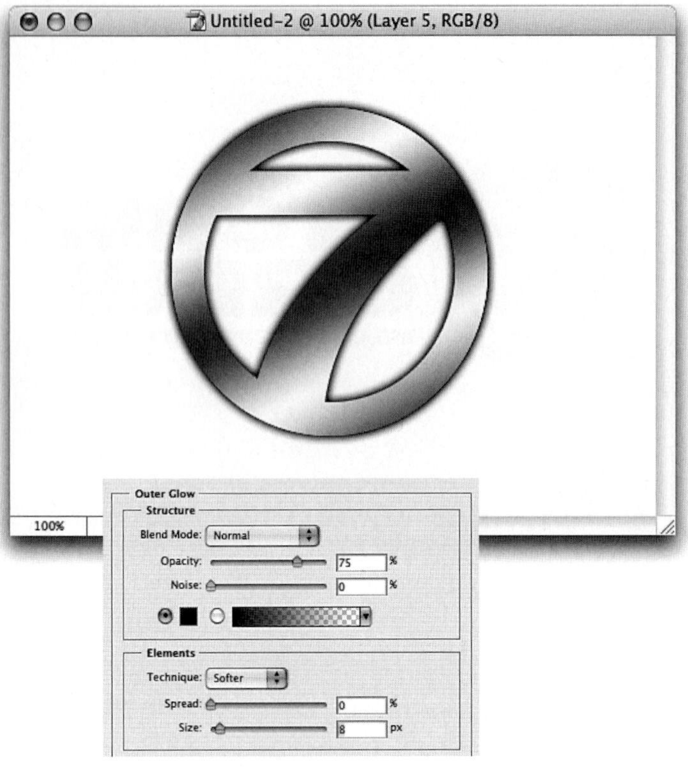

Step Eight:

Choose Outer Glow from the Add a Layer Style pop-up menu at the bottom of the Layers palette (it's the first icon from the left). Change the Blend Mode pop-up menu from Screen to Normal, then click on the beige color swatch and change the glow color to black in the Color Picker. Lastly, increase the Size to 8 and click OK to add a black glow around your logo (as shown here).

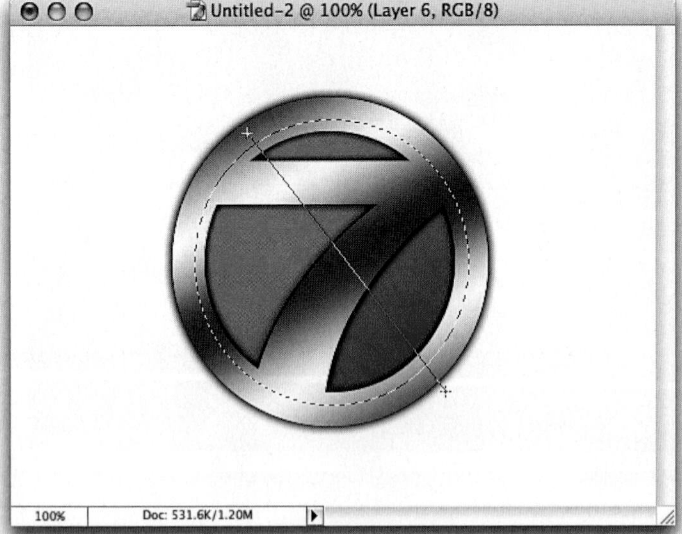

Step Nine:

Go to the Layers palette, hold the Command key (PC: Control key) and click on the Create a New Layer icon to create a new blank layer directly beneath your circle layer. Get the Elliptical Marquee tool, hold the Shift key, and draw a selection that's just a bit larger than the inner part of the circle (as shown here). (Tip: To position your selection as you draw, press-and-hold the Spacebar, move your selection, release the Spacebar, and continue to drag out your selection.) Click on the Foreground color swatch in the Toolbox and choose a bright red in the Color Picker, and then change your Background color to a darker red. Get the Gradient tool, open the Gradient Picker from the Options Bar, choose the first gradient in the default set (Foreground to Background), and drag the Gradient tool diagonally through your selection (as shown here). Deselect by pressing Command-D (PC: Control-D).

Continued

Step Ten:

Now we need to add some room for text. Go under the Image menu and choose Canvas Size. In the dialog, turn on the Relative checkbox, enter 4 inches for Width, click on the left-center square in the Anchor grid, choose White in the Canvas Extension Color pop-up menu, and click OK to add 4 inches of white canvas space to the right of your logo. Press the letter "d" to set your Foreground color to black, then switch to the Type tool and enter your type. The font shown here is Helvetica Black with the horizontal scaling set to 130% in the Character palette for the word "Storm"; 160% for the word "Crew"; and only 105% for the tag line below it. Now go to the Layers palette, and click in the second column beside the logo layer, the red gradient layer, and all your Type layers to temporarily link them together.

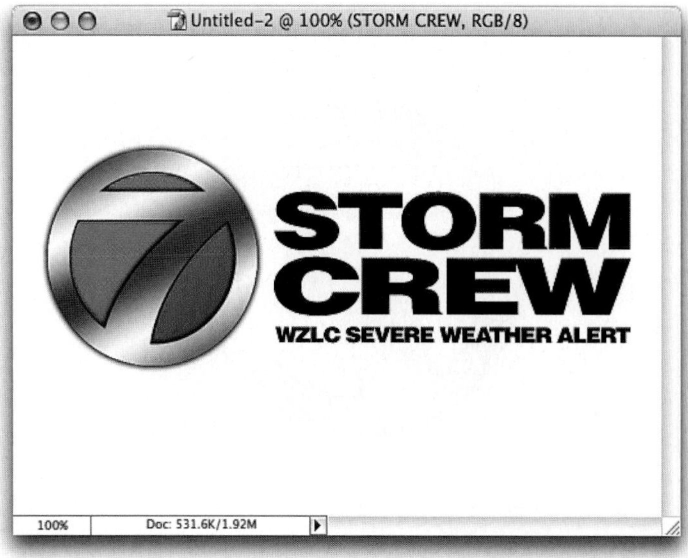

Step Eleven:

Open the photo you want to use as your background (in this case, a photo of a city at night). Go back to your logo document, press the letter "v" to switch to the Move tool, click directly on your logo, and drag it right onto your city photo. All the other linked layers will come right along with it. Note: If your logo is too large, resize it by pressing Command-T (PC: Control-T) to bring up Free Transform. Now, double-click directly on the Type layer's thumbnail (it has a "T" on it) in the Layers palette to highlight your type and to switch to the Type tool at the same time. In the Options Bar, click on the black color swatch and choose white in the Color Picker to change your copy to white. Click OK in the Color Picker and then press Enter to lock in your color change. Do this on all Type layers. Now we'll add the lightning to your project.

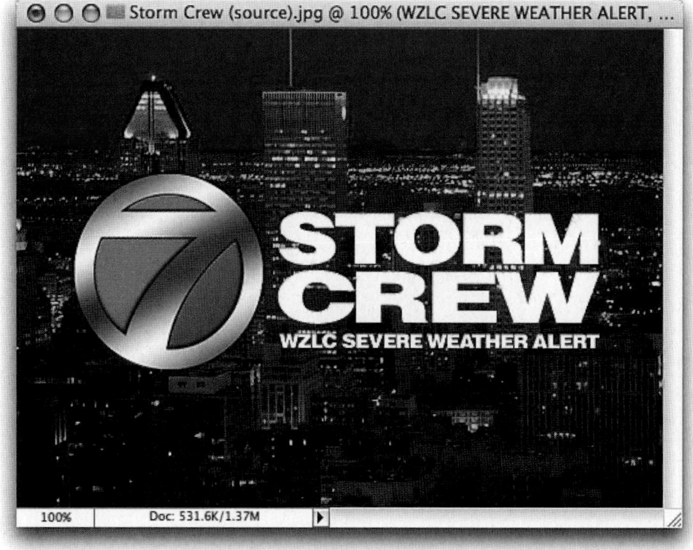

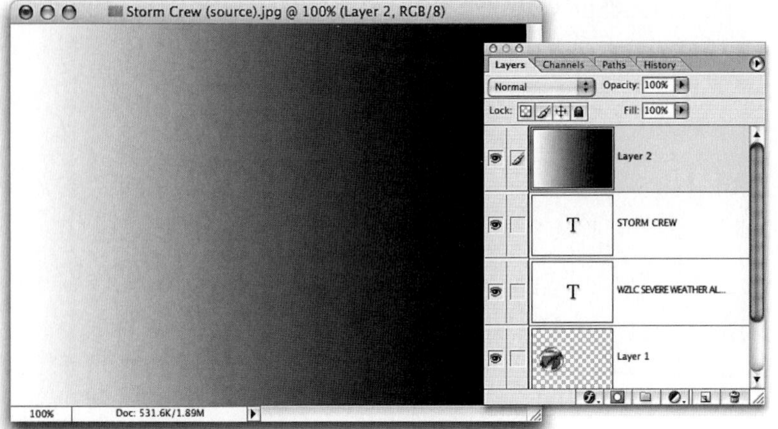

Step Twelve:

Press "d" then "x" to set your Foreground color to white and your Background color to black. Go to the Layers palette and click on the Create a New Layer icon to add a new blank layer and drag it to the top of the stack of layers (as shown here). Get the Gradient tool, bring up the Gradient Picker from the Options Bar, and choose the Foreground to Background gradient (it's the first gradient in the Picker). Drag the Gradient tool from the left side of your image area all the way to the right.

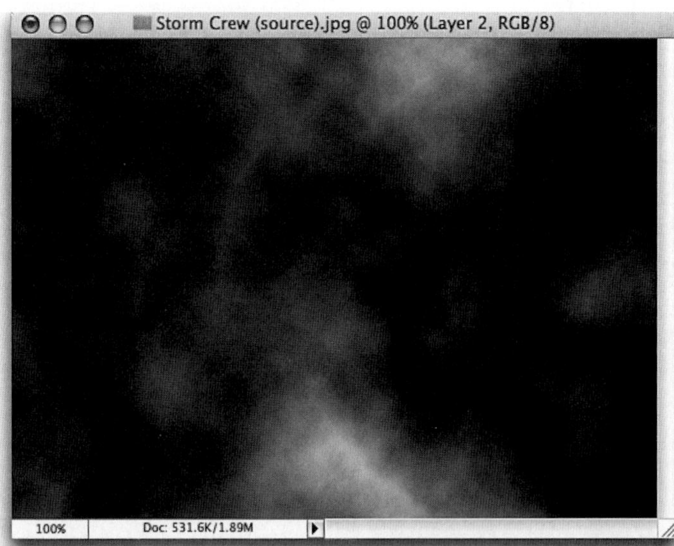

Step Thirteen:

Now go under the Filter menu, under Render, and choose Difference Clouds to apply a random cloud pattern over your gradient (as shown here). *Note:* Each time you apply this filter, you get a different look, so if you don't like the way your lightning looks in Step Fifteen, just go back to this step, and try applying Difference Clouds again or even try applying it two or three times until you come up with a lightning pattern that looks better.

Continued

Step Fourteen:

Press Command-I (PC: Control-I) to invert your clouds (as shown here).

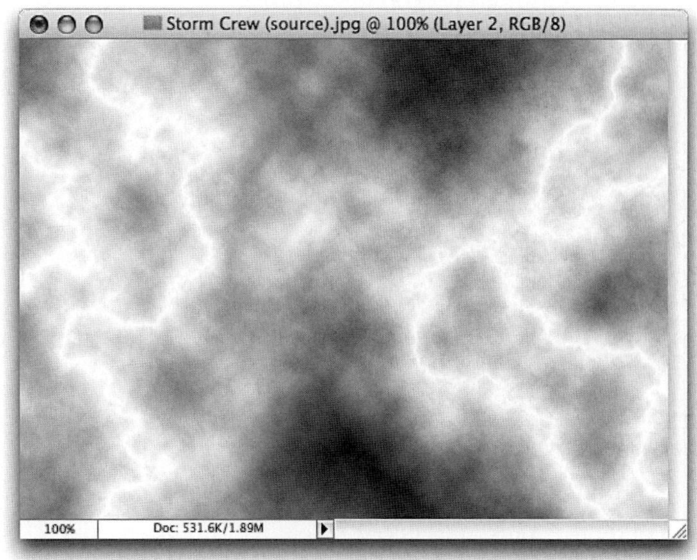

Step Fifteen:

Press Command-L (PC: Control-L) to bring up the Levels dialog. Grab the top-center Input Levels slider (the midtones slider) and drag it to the right. When you're almost all the way to the right, you'll see your lightning appear (as shown here). Click OK.

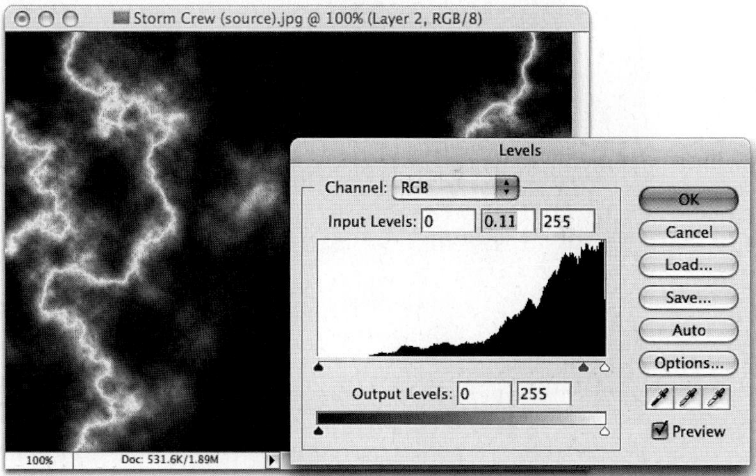

Step Sixteen:

To make your lightning blend in with your photo, go to the Layers palette and change the blend mode of your lightning layer from Normal to Screen (as shown here).

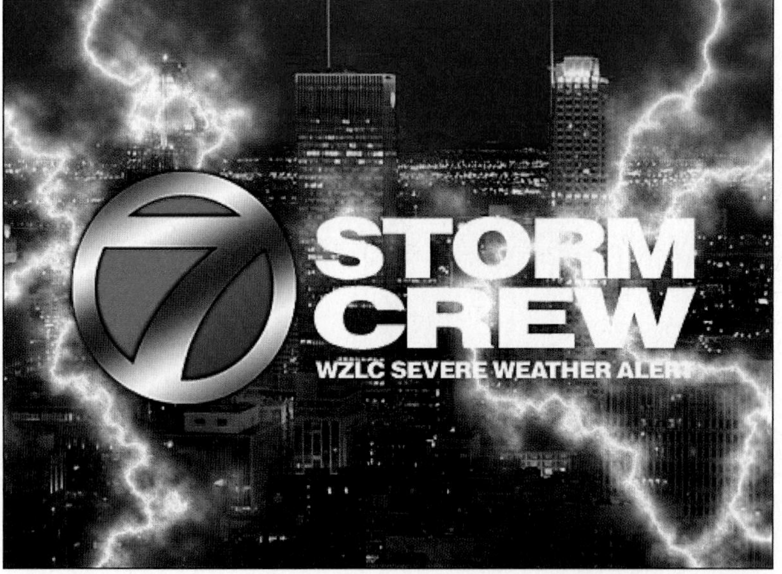

Step Seventeen:

The lightning goes right over the logo, but if you don't want that, you can do this: Hold Shift-Command (PC: Shift-Control) and in the Layers palette click once on both the logo layer (don't change layers, just click on it) and the red gradient layer to put a selection around your logo. Now press Delete (PC: Backspace) to erase the lightning that appears over the logo (you're basically knocking a round hole out of the lightning layer), then press Command-D (PC: Control-D) to deselect, which completes the effect.

Blending Two Images

For years, blending images together has been one of the single most-requested Photoshop techniques. In our project here, we're not only going to blend from one image to another, but we're also going to show how the technique is used in Hollywood to create movie posters (plus, you get to learn some other cool tricks along the way).

Step One:

This first part isn't necessary for blending two images, but since we're doing a whole project (a movie poster), go ahead and create a new document (File>New) that's 6x8" at 72 ppi. Click on the Foreground color swatch in the Toolbox and choose a dark brown color in the Color Picker (I used R=92, G=59, B=1). Fill the Background layer with this dark brown by pressing Option-Delete (PC: Alt-Backspace).

Step Two:

Open the first image you want to use in your two-image blend. Press the letter "v" to switch to the Move tool, then click-and-drag the image onto your brown background, and position it as shown here. You may need to use Command-T (PC: Control-T) to bring up the Free Transform command to size your image.

Step Three:

Open the second photo you want to use in your two-image blend. Using the Move tool, drag this image on top of your first image. At the bottom of the Layers palette, click on the Add a Layer Mask icon (it's the second icon from the left) as shown here.

Step Four:

Press the letter "x" until your Foreground color is black. Press the letter "b" to switch to the Brush tool. In the Options Bar, click on the icon next to the word "Brush" and choose a large (200-pixel), soft-edged brush from the Brush Picker. Move over your photo, and begin painting (as shown), and as you paint, the photo beneath it (the three soccer players) will be revealed. Because you're using such a large, soft-edged brush, the blend is very smooth.

Continued

Step Five:

Continue painting with this large, soft-edged brush to reveal as much of the photo as you want (as shown here, where the top is softly blended into the other image, and the rest of the photo is revealed).

Step Six:

Now that the two photos are blended, you can blend the bottom photo right into the brown background. Go to the Layers palette, click on Layer 1 (the three soccer players) to make it active, then click on the Add a Layer Mask icon (as shown). Go up to the Brush Picker and lower the size of your 200-pixel brush to a 100-pixel brush (you'll need this smaller brush in the next step).

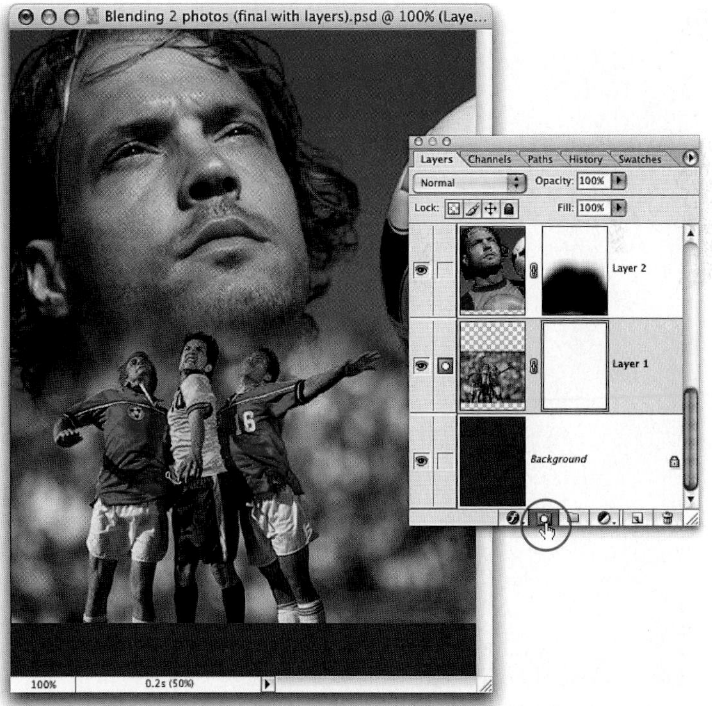

Step Seven:

Take the 100-pixel brush and paint a line along the bottom of your image of the three soccer players. This blends the bottom edge with the brown background (as shown here).

Step Eight:

Now to add a classic movie poster effect to your blended images: First, in the Layers palette click on the top layer (Layer 2) to make it active, then go under the Image menu, under Adjustments, and choose Desaturate to remove all the color from this top image. Then, go under the Filter menu, under Noise, and choose Add Noise. When the dialog appears, for Amount choose 4%, for Distribution choose Gaussian, and click on the Monochromatic checkbox (it's very important to turn on the Monochromatic checkbox so the noise is black and white, rather than colored dots). Click OK.

Continued

Step Nine:

In the Layers palette, click on Layer 1 to make it active. Just as we did in the previous step, desaturate this layer (remove the color) and apply the exact same Add Noise settings by choosing Filter>Noise>Add Noise.

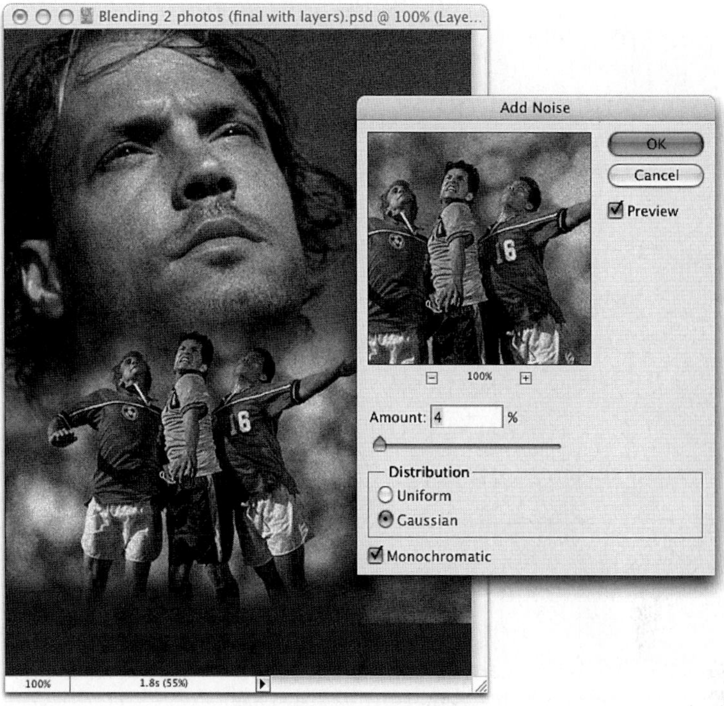

Step Ten:

Now you'll add a brown tint to the entire image. In the Layers palette, click on the top layer (Layer 2), and choose Solid Color from the Create New Adjustment Layer pop-up menu (it's the fourth icon from the left at the bottom). When the Color Picker appears, set it to the same brown color that we used in Step One, then click OK. This creates a solid brown color on top of your layers, so to get this color to blend in with your other layers, change the layer blend mode from Normal to Color in the Layers palette (as shown here).

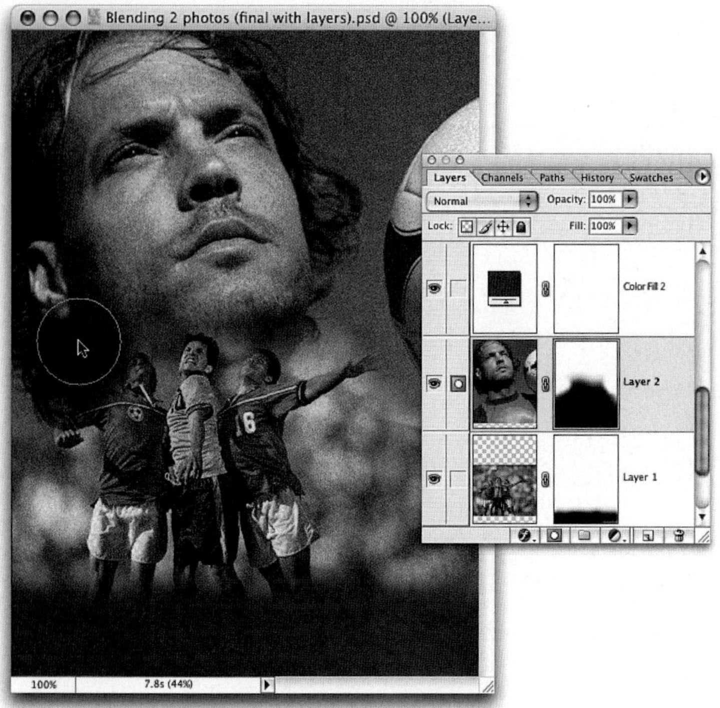

Step Eleven:

Now a little touch-up work: Click directly on the Layer 2 layer mask thumbnail to make it active. Press "x" until you've set your Foreground color to white, then paint over the entire soccer ball to make it visible. In the example shown here, I also switched to a smaller brush and painted over the right ear of the large soccer player to make it fully visible. Then I switched back to Layer 1, clicked on its layer mask thumbnail, pressed "x" until I changed the Foreground color to black, and painted another stroke inside the bottom of the photo to give me more room to add text.

Step Twelve:

Here's the image with type added. The actor's name and the name of the fictitious movie are set in Trajan Pro with the horizontal scaling set to 150% in the Character palette. The "IN THEATERS..." text is set in Helvetica Regular with the horizontal scaling set to 120%. That's it!

Cut to the Chase

Tinting a Photo

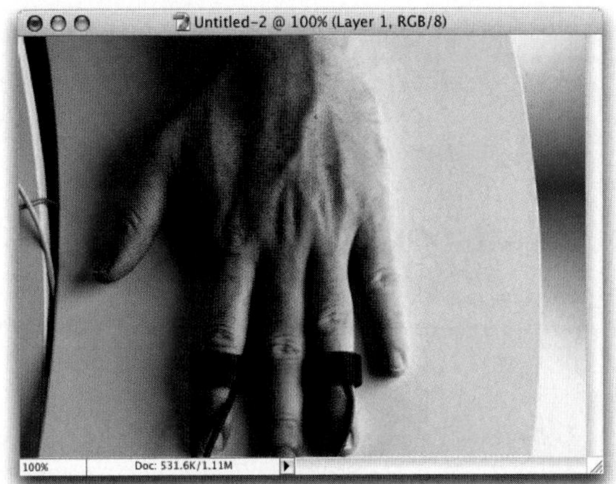

Step One:

Open the photo you want to tint.

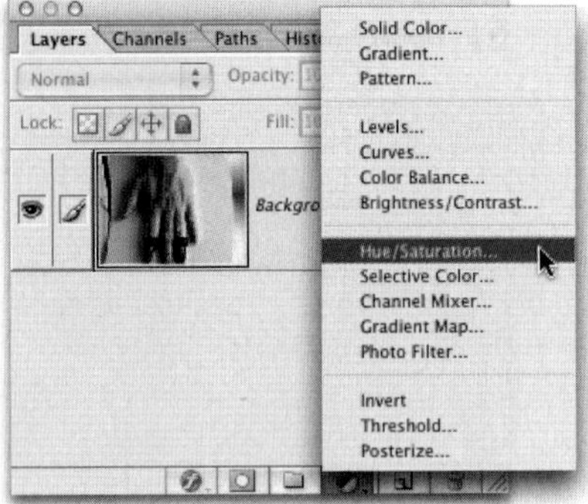

Step Two:

At the bottom of the Layers palette, choose Hue/Saturation from the Create New Adjustment Layer pop-up menu (as shown here).

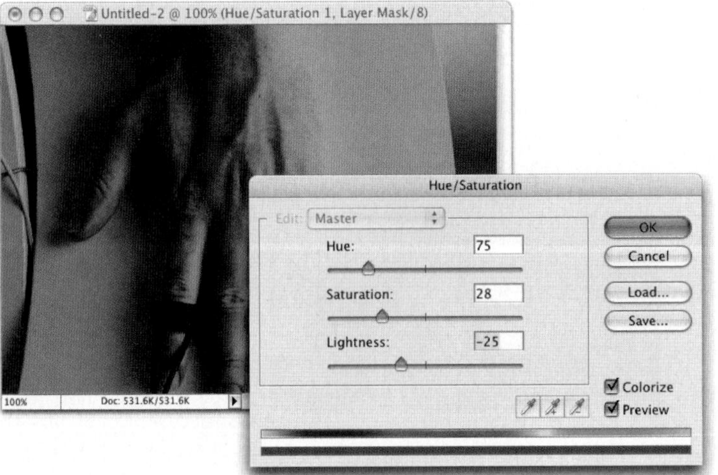

Step Three:

When the Hue/Saturation dialog appears, turn on the Colorize checkbox, then move the Hue slider until you see the color you want for your tint. To make the color more intense, drag the Saturation slider to the right. To darken the image, drag the Lightness slider to the left, or to lighten the image drag it to the right. When the tint looks good to you, click OK to apply the tint effect to your image (as shown here).

Clipping into a Shape

Step One:

Create a new document, then click the Create a New Layer icon at the bottom of the Layers palette. Set black as your Foreground color, then get the Rounded Rectangle tool (it's one of the Shape tools). Go up to the Options Bar and click on the third icon from the left so the tool will create pixels, rather than a path or a shape layer. In the Options Bar, set the Radius (the roundness of the corners) to 10 pixels. Now use the tool to drag out a rounded rectangle in the shape of a credit card.

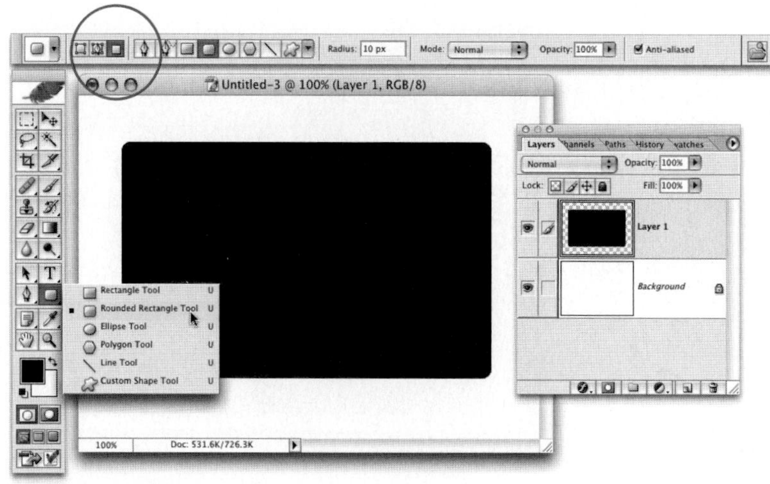

Step Two:

Open the first photo you want to "clip" into your credit card shape, get the Move tool, and drag-and-drop the image onto your credit card shape, positioning it where you want it to appear.

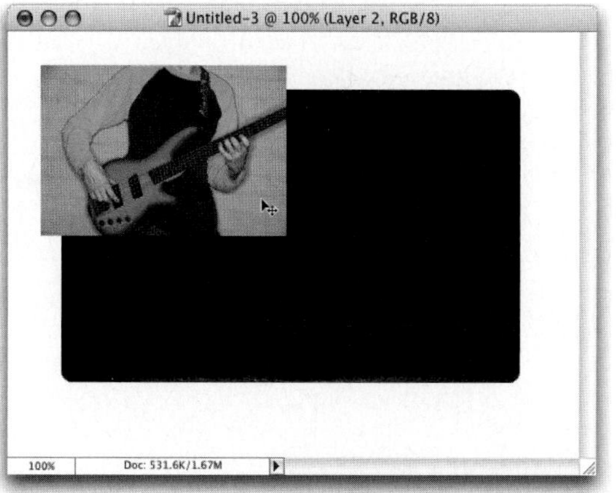

Step Three:

Press Command-G (PC: Control-G), which is the shortcut for Create Clipping Mask, and the photo will fit neatly inside the shape. Once it's clipped inside, if you need to reposition the image, just use the Move tool to position it where you want it, and it will stay within the boundaries of the shape.

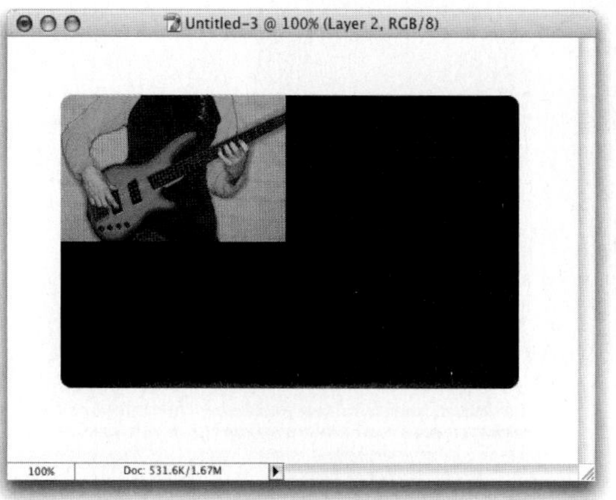

Sepia Tone Effect

Step One:

Open your image. You'll want to convert your photo into a black-and-white image with added contrast, so choose Gradient Map from the Create New Adjustment Layer pop-up menu at the bottom of the Layers palette.

Step Two:

When the Gradient Map dialog appears, click on the down-facing arrow next to the gradient thumbnail to bring up the Gradient Picker, and select the Black to White gradient. Click OK so the gradient is mapped over your photo, giving it a very "contrasty" black-and-white effect.

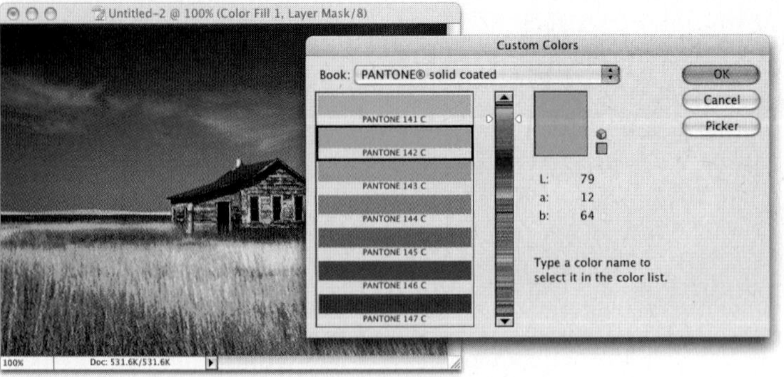

Step Three:

Choose Solid Color from the Create New Adjustment Layer pop-up menu at the bottom of the Layers palette. When the Color Picker appears, click on the Custom button to bring up the Custom Colors dialog. Choose the color you want, then change the layer blend mode from Normal to Color in the Layers palette to apply the sepia tone effect to your photo.

Instant Lightning Effect

Step One:

Open the photo you want to apply a lightning effect to. Go to the Layers palette and add a new blank layer. Press "d" to set your Foreground/Background colors to their default. Get the Gradient tool from the Toolbox, press Return (PC: Enter) to bring up the Gradient Picker, and choose the Foreground to Background gradient. Then click-and-drag the Gradient tool from the left side of your image area all the way to the right.

Step Two:

Go under the Filter menu, under Render, and choose Difference Clouds to apply a random cloud pattern over your gradient. Press Command-I (PC: Control-I) to invert your clouds. Reapply this step as needed until you get the lightning effect you desire.

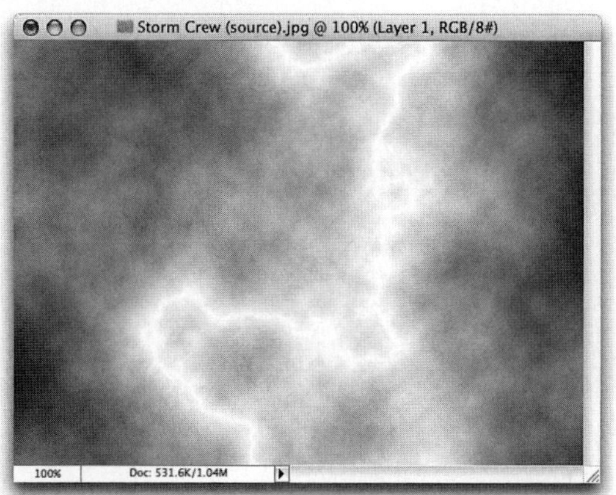

Step Three:

In the Layers palette, change the blend mode of your layer from Normal to Screen so the lightning will blend in with your photo. Press Command-L (PC: Control-L) to bring up Levels. Grab the center Input Levels slider (the midtones slider) and drag it almost all the way to the right to see the lightning effect appear within your photo.

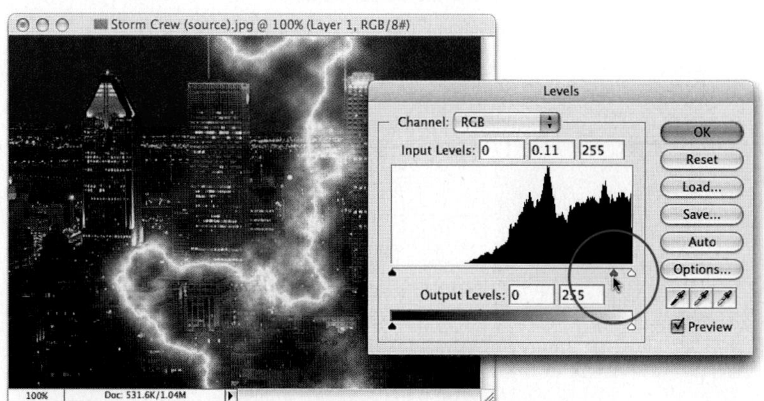

Blending Two Images

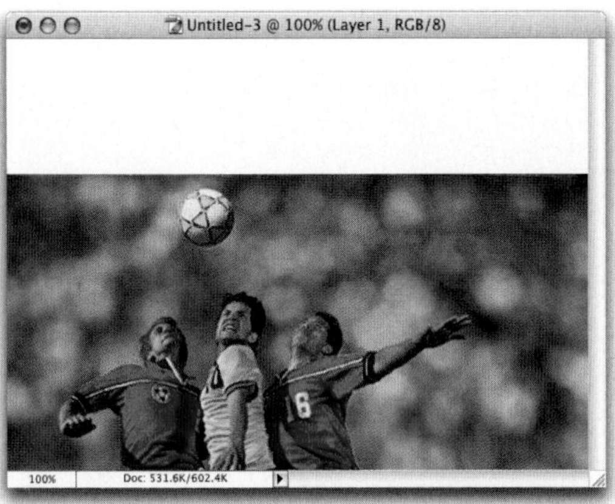

Step One:

Open the first image you want to use in your two-image blend.

Step Two:

Open the second photo you want to use in your two-image blend. Get the Move tool and drag-and-drop this image on top of your first image. Click on the Add a Layer Mask icon at the bottom of the Layers palette, then press "x" until you've set your Foreground color to black.

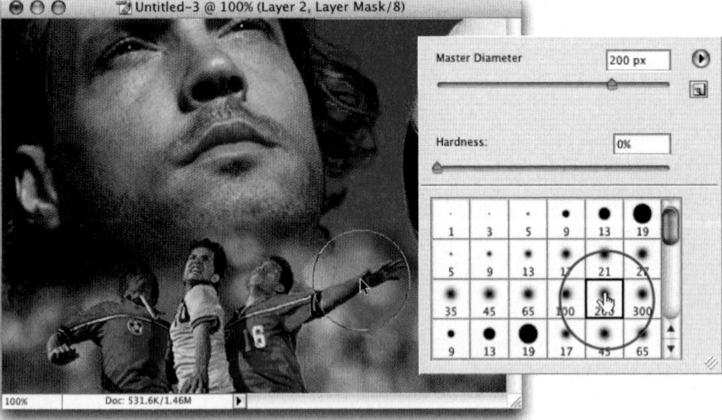

Step Three:

Get the Brush tool, and choose a large (200-pixel), soft-edged brush from the Brush Picker in the Options Bar. Begin painting over your photo, and as you paint, the photo beneath it (the soccer players) will be revealed. Because you're using such a large, soft-edged brush, the blend is very smooth. If you make a mistake, just switch your Foreground color to white, paint over the mistake, then switch back to black and continue painting.

Section III

The following section is taken from *The Complete Typograher,* Second Edition, by Will Hill. Only the content intended for use in this course has been provided.

Working with Type

In talking about typography, we are talking about the arrangement of positive shapes from which we construct readable meanings. Within these shapes, there is information about the internal workings of language, about texts and subtexts, about histories, systems, and cultures.

This discipline is an amalgam of several kinds of knowledge. Effective typography depends as much upon our awareness of design history as a mastery of technology, as much upon our understanding of language as our sense of visual aesthetics, and as much upon problem analysis as upon creativity.

This section introduces the terminology of typeface design, the fundamentals of page layout, the linguistic and grammatical conventions of typographic usage, and aspects of display, new media, and environmental typography.

THE TYPEFACE

The term typeface traditionally refers to any full set of standardized letterforms designed for reproduction through print. In recent years, this has also encompassed faces designed specifically for digital screen use. Although the terms typeface and font have increasingly been used as though they were interchangeable, a font is in fact a single character set comprising all uppercase and lowercase letters, numerals, and standard punctuation marks.

ABCDEFGHIJKLMNOPQRSTUVWXYZ &!?(),:;'
abcdefghijklmnopqrstuvwxyz 1234567890

ABCDEFGHIJKLMNOPQRSTUVWXYZ &!?(),:;'
abcdefghijklmnopqrstuvwxyz 1234567890

ABCDEFGHIJKLMNOPQRSTUVWXYZ &!?(),:;'
abcdefghijklmnopqrstuvwxyz 1234567890

Futura typeface comprising roman, italic, and bold fonts

Type families

A typeface normally includes a number of separate fonts, including roman, italic, and at least one variant weight, normally described as bold. The typeface may, in turn, belong to a larger type family, including condensed and extended versions and display faces. These are commonly seen as distinct but related. As a general but not universal rule, those variants that share a common width and proportion are seen as part of the same face, whereas related forms of differing width are more likely to be described as different faces within the same type family.

Some typefaces, such as Adrian Frutiger's Univers, were originally conceived as a system working across an extended range of weights and widths. In other instances, additional weights were introduced after the publication of the original face, sometimes drawn by other designers, as in the later weights of Paul Renner's Futura. The extreme display weights of Gill Sans were produced reluctantly in response to commercial demand, and, as a consequence, lack the integrity of form that characterizes the two original weights.

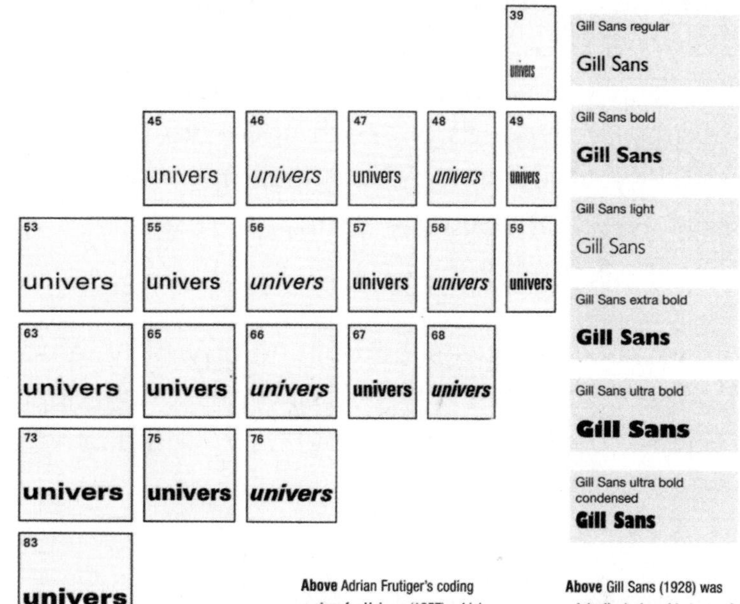

Above Adrian Frutiger's coding system for Univers (1957), which had 21 variations, was an attempt to avoid the varying and confusing typeface names used within the industry, such as light, medium, bold, extra bold, heavy, and so on.

Above Gill Sans (1928) was originally designed in two weights: regular and bold. The light, extra bold, ultra bold, and condensed forms were later additions to the family. The ultra bold and condensed forms in particular compromise the proportion and integrity of Gill's original letters.

What does a typeface contain?

All text typefaces can be expected to include a regular or roman form, a bold, italic, and a bold italic. It should be noted that the last, in particular, is a fairly recent convention. As a consequence, the design of bold italic forms for historic typefaces has often taken place at a much later date and been achieved with varying degrees of sensitivity.

The relationships between the italic and the roman, or upright, form vary considerably between one typeface and another. The italic forms of classic Humanist and Garalde faces are essentially distinct alphabets, revealing a greater influence from handwritten script than is evident in the roman form, and often a narrower set width. The convention that every typeface should be designed with an italic version is a slightly later development in type history, and many 19th- and 20th-century typefaces in these idioms actually draw upon different but contemporaneous sources for their italics.

By comparison, many sans serif typefaces have an italic that is little more than an inclined version of the upright form. Notable exceptions can be found in the italic forms of Goudy Sans or the understated elegance of the Gill Sans italics.

Tennis
Tennis

Bembo roman and italic

Tennis
Tennis

Gill Sans roman and italic

Tennis
Tennis

Goudy Sans roman and italic

Tennis
Tennis

Rockwell roman and italic

Above The original medieval roman type of Francesco Griffo, upon which Bembo is based, had no italic form. Bembo pairs these letters with an italic based upon a face designed by Ludovico degli Arrighi in the 1520s and later known as Blado. Frederic Goudy's Goudy Sans takes on a distinctive decorative fluidity in its italic form.

Above Gill Sans italic is a subtle and gracefully adapted form of the roman. Rockwell italic is a largely mechanical oblique variant—a sloped version of the upright letter.

DESCRIPTIVE TERMINOLOGY

In order to make informed decisions in the observation, analysis, selection, and use of type, we need to understand something of the vocabulary used to describe it. This vocabulary reflects some 500 years of typographic history, and remains essential if we are to communicate observations, identify preferences, and provide accurate instructions in the use of type.

The parts of the letter

An understanding of the basic anatomy of the letterform allows us to describe its characteristics in detail and to identify the defining features that distinguish one typeface from another. This provides the means for the recognition of typefaces and the vocabulary for describing their particular qualities.

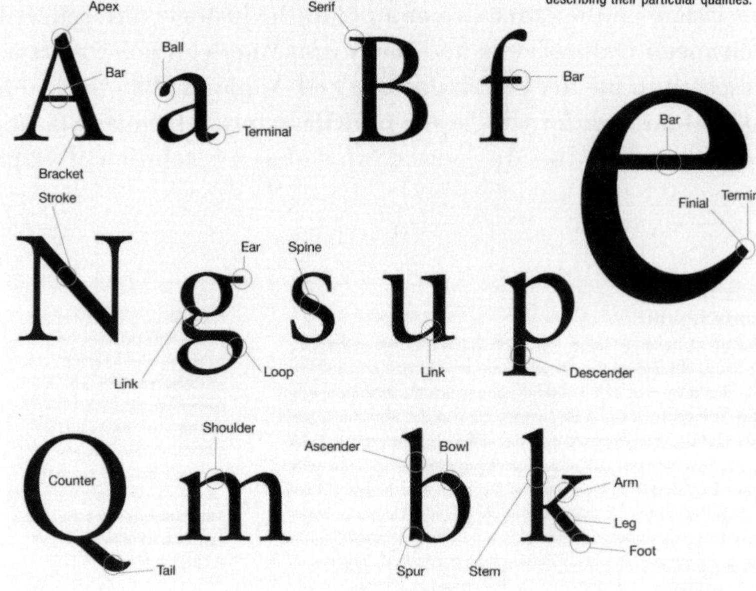

Stress

The term stress is used to describe the angle of variation between thick and thin stroke width. It could be seen as equivalent to the angle at which the letterer or calligrapher holds a broad-edged pen or brush. Vertical or angled stresses are characteristic of certain categories of type. The move from an inclined to a vertical stress follows a steady historical progression from the Humanist types of the late 15th century, in which there is a pronounced inclined stress, to the Didones of the late 18th century, in which the stress is vertical.

Color

The term color is used to describe both the tonal density and texture created by type when set as continuous running text upon the page (qualities also sometimes described in terms of gray value), and more specifically to describe the degree of variation or contrast in weight between its thick and thin strokes. This variation ranges from monoline designs that have a consistent weight of line at all points, and therefore minimal color, to the pronounced color resulting from the extremes of contrasting stroke width in the Didone faces of the late 18th century.

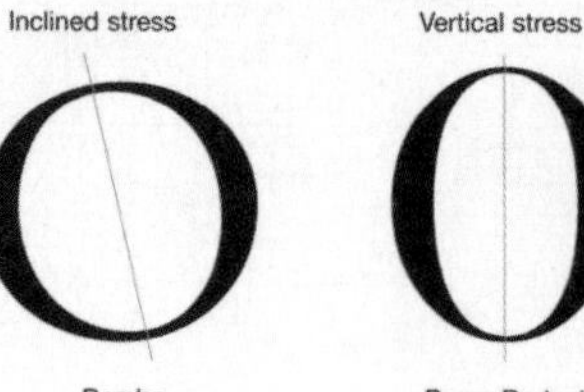

Bembo

Bauer Bodoni

Monoline stroke width

Contrasting stroke widths

Bell Gothic

DeVinne

THE POINT SYSTEM

The size of type is measured in points. While there have in the past been national variations in the exact size of a point, the historic differences between the European Didot system and the Anglo-American point system were effectively resolved in the decision by Adobe and Apple in 1985 to establish a point of exactly 1/72 of an inch for the Adobe page description language PostScript. This corresponds to the Mac screen, which has a resolution of 72 pixels to the inch.

Body height

Like most type terminology, the point system is based in the traditions of hand-set metal type, and the point size originally referred to the size of the "body" upon which the letterform was cast. This body was of a height to accommodate both the highest ascender and the deepest descender in the alphabet, and to leave some additional body clearance necessary to prevent ascenders and descenders from touching. For this reason, a 12-point (12pt) capital letter is not 12 points in height, and 12pt letters in some typefaces may appear considerably larger than in others, despite being the same point size. This variation is due to differences in body clearance and, primarily, to differences in x-height.

Below left The point size describes the size of the body upon which the type was cast—a height incorporating the tallest and deepest elements of letters in the font. Within this overall height a typeface will have a consistent baseline, x-height, and cap height.

Below right Adjustments to leading will increase or reduce the amount of interlinear white space.

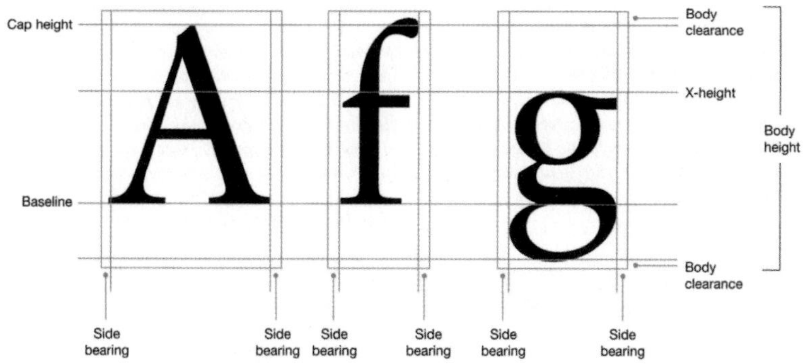

Cap height

Baseline

A f g

Body clearance

X-height

Body height

Body clearance

Side bearing

Side bearing

Side bearing

Side bearing

Side bearing

Side bearing

X-height

The x-height is the median line that defines the top of the lowercase letters—specifically, the height of the lowercase x. A typeface with shorter ascenders, and therefore a higher x-height, allows for a larger lowercase letter relative to the body size. Some typefaces are traditionally set on a generous body, giving larger body clearance space and a correspondingly smaller character size.

Baseline and cap height

The baseline is the line upon which the base of the letter sits. The cap height refers to the height of the uppercase letters, frequently a little lower than the full extent of the ascender.

Leading

As well as describing the size of type, the point system is used to specify the depth of space between lines (sometimes known as the pitch or line feed). Originally referring to the strips of lead inserted between lines of type, leading is the measurement in

This text is set 18/28pt.
There is plenty of space
between each line of type.

This text is set 18/18pt, known as set solid. There is little space between each line of type.

points from one baseline to the next. This allows for both size and leading to be combined within a concise specification—for instance, 12pt type on 18pt leading, sometimes abbreviated to 12/18. Type set with no additional leading is described as set solid.

Digital and photoset type may be set with the space between lines reduced to less than would be created by the body height of the letters; this is described as minus leading. When type is minus leaded, ascenders and descenders may overlap one another or even cross the baseline or x-height of adjacent lines. Minus leading is specified in the same way as the size/leading, but in these cases the leading will be less than the type size—12/10 or 12/8, for example.

When your type is minus leaded, in this case 30/24pt, the ascenders and descenders of the letters may overlap one another.

Line measure

The point system can be used to specify line measure, the column width, or maximum line length of type. This length is commonly expressed using the pica, a measurement of 12 points, giving 6 picas to the inch. This is also sometimes referred to as a pica em, or simply an em. While it is now increasingly common for column widths to be expressed in millimeters, pica ems remain in use as a system of line measure and the example below might be described as being set 9/12 to a column width of 21 pica ems (3½ inches/85mm).

There are 6 picas to the inch. This is also sometimes 12pt
referred to as a pica em, or simply an em. While it is now 12pt
increasingly common for column widths to be expressed 12pt
in millimeters, pica ems remain in use as a system of line 12pt
measure and this example might be described as being 12pt
set 9/12 to a column width of 21 ems (3½ inches/85mm). 12pt

1 2 3 4 5 6 7 8 9 10 11 12 13 14 15 16 17 18 19 20 21 ems

Em-square 72pt M 72pt

Em-square 12pt M 12pt

64 units 72pt M 72pt

The em

In the context of line measurement, the term em refers to a 12pt em (a pica), but the expression is more broadly used to describe a measure equal to the body height of the type at any size (based upon the square proportions of a classical capital M). A 30pt em is therefore 30 points in width. Both the em (a measure equal to the body height) and the en (a measure that is half the body height) are used to describe the width of dashes and spaces.

The unit

The em is subdivided into units. This is a term used for specifying in detail the individual widths of letters and the spaces between them, based upon the division of the em into fractions. Until relatively recently, it was common for this to be expressed through division of the em into anything between 18 and 64 units. However, depending on the software used, current PostScript technology uses a division of 1,000, giving 1,000 units to the em.

Set width

The resulting measurement allows for the description of the set width of each letter—that is, the individual measurement of each letter's width. It also provides a means of describing the space between letters, which can be increased or decreased unilaterally (letter spacing) or adjusted between individual letters (kerning).

Unlike the point, the unit is not a fixed measure, but a proportional measurement based upon the size of the type used: 10pt type is measured in units of 1,000th of 10 points; 36pt type in units of 1,000th of 36 points. Any adjustment to unit values can therefore be applied consistently across a range of type sizes. Letter spacing adjustments are specified in different ways by different typesetting systems, but the 1,000-unit em has allowed for unprecedented precision in the adjustment of letter and word space.

Many current software programs also allow for adjustments to set width—extending or condensing the proportions of the character itself. This should be used sparingly, because any change to the proportions of the letter is in effect a redesign of the font.

Above left & center The em is a variable square measurement equal in width to the body size of the type. A 72pt em is 72 points in width; a 12pt em is 12 points in width.

Above Detailed calculations of character width and spacing are specified in units. These are subdivisions of the em, which used to be divided into 18 to 64 units, but is now divided into 1,000 units using current PostScript technology.

Below The vertical proportion or set width of letters can be modified digitally. This creates extended or condensed versions of the original, and should be used sparingly and with care.

Set width: 100%

Set width: 120%

Set width: 80%

SPACING

Professional typesetting programs allow the designer to make detailed adjustments to the space between letters. The term letter spacing refers to modification of intercharacter space applied over an entire text, whereas the term kerning refers to separate adjustments in the spaces between individual pairs of letters.

Below The pairing of certain letters creates disproportionate amounts of white space between them, requiring the use of kerning pairs in the design of the typeface. This process automatically introduces special adjustments to the side bearings each time the pairing of these letters occurs.

Ta	Ta	VA	VA
Unkerned	Kerned	Unkerned	Kerned

Letter spacing

Adjustments to letter spacing may be made necessary by a number of factors. Some typefaces tend to lose clarity of intercharacter space at smaller sizes, and an increase in the space around letters may make their form more easily readable. At larger sizes, the intervals between letters may be made more harmonious by a reduction in the spaces between them. Where whole words or sentences have been set in capitals, additional letter spacing is often necessary for optical balance and readability. Adjustments to letter spacing can radically alter the appearance of a body of text and the performance of a typeface, so they should be applied consistently throughout a document.

Manual kerning

Manual kerning is the adjustment of individual intercharacter spaces to achieve a more consistently balanced spacing. Display type and titling, in particular, often benefit from manual kerning. However, it would be impractical to apply this process to continuous text.

Kerning

The design of text faces incorporates inbuilt automatic adjustments to the spacing of particular letter pairs that would otherwise create disproportionate spaces: VA and Ta, for example. These are known as kerning pairs. The quality and extent of kerning pairs within a font illustrate the attention to detail that characterizes high-quality typefaces that may, in many cases, include thousands of kerning pairs. The necessity for this degree of detailed kerning varies widely according to the stylistic qualities of the typeface. A monospace typeface, in which every letter is designed to sit upon a consistent body width, involves no kerning at all, whereas the digitization or adaptation of classic serif typefaces may require a great deal of kern adjustment and therefore a large number of kern pairs. Effective kerning ensures a consistent rhythm of intercharacter space, which enhances legibility and readability.

Word spacing

The space between words has traditionally been based upon a space equivalent to the body width of a lowercase i. This space can be adjusted manually for display and title setting. In text setting, it can be specified either as a constant—in the case of flush, or ranged, type—or as a maximum and minimum—in the case of justified type (see pages 216–219). The majority of digital type media give a generous space between words, and the appearance and readability of text can in many cases be improved by reducing the word spacing, giving greater continuity and less interruption to the flow of the sentence.

Space between words makes a noticeable difference to the readability of the text.

Space between words makes a noticeable difference to the readability of the text.

Space between words makes a noticeable difference to the readability of the text.

Above The word spacing in the top example has been reduced to the point at which differentiation becomes difficult but is still distinct. The middle example is ideal for the width and openness of the type, while the lower is too wide, and interrupts the continuity of the text.

Auto letter spacing

FLORAL

Adjusted close letter spacing

F L O R A L

Adjusted wide letter spacing

Left Increasing the letter spacing serves to balance the irregularities of a geometric face and the otherwise intrusive effect of the large counter of the circular O.

LIGATURES

A ligature is a single form incorporating two or more letters, parts of which might otherwise touch or overlap—for instance, fi or fl. This typographic refinement can be seen in the earliest printed books, and continues to be incorporated within professional-quality typefaces. Digital type design has allowed for unprecedented development in the range of ligatures available within certain typefaces. Some typefaces do not require ligatures at all, because their letterforms have been designed to minimize those problems that make ligatures necessary.

Standard ligatures

Many typefaces incorporate a small number of standard ligatures. Most common among these are the f ligatures. These address the problems caused by the overhanging drop of the lowercase f when followed by i, l, or f—fi, fl, ffi, or ffl (sometimes also including the less common fj). These ligatures are included in many serif faces and also in those sans serifs that feature significant overhang to the f.

Set without standard ligatures (Sabon)

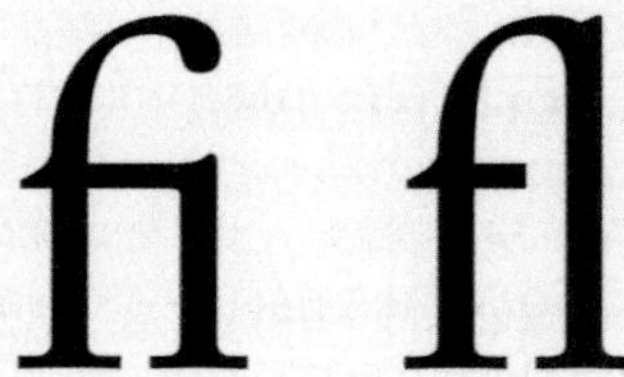

Set with standard ligatures (Sabon)

Archaic ligatures

Some specialist revival typefaces include a number of additional ligatures joining consonants, such as ct and st. These were in common use in printing up to the 18th century and would now normally only be used in instances where reference is being made to an appropriate historical period.

fb tt cti fh ffh tfr fi fk fj
ffj ttfr ffk stfr te sfr stfl
sty tf ta sp stfi stfj tti ttr
ctr str sfi sfy sh sk sp sf
sta ste ch ffb ttf tte tta
cty stf sti cta ctf ctfi cte
fr fk fti ftr fty ffl ffy fta

Left A typeface with an exceptionally extensive font of ligatures, incorporating up to four letters and using the archaic linking strokes on the s and c forms (Hoefler Requiem).

Special ligatures

Some typefaces include a large range of ligatures, in a few instances dedicating entire fonts to them, as in Hoefler Requiem. Where a typeface contains an extended family of ligatures, they may be used selectively for variation and visual effect. In particular, typefaces based upon script or calligraphic form may include a wide range of different ligatures and alternate letters, allowing the designer an extended palette of visual variations. A dramatic example of this can be found in Herman Zapf's Zapfino.

Diphthongs

A diphthong is a single form incorporating two vowel letters for specific phonetic reasons—such as ae and oe—rather than for the optical/aesthetic reasons that govern the design of ligatures.

Œ œ Æ æ ß

Above Diphthongs have a specific phonetic function, used largely in words derived from classical Latin (Hoefler Requiem).

Above Archaic ligatures, reviving a typographic device originally found in historic metal types (Hoefler Text).

ALTERNATE FONTS

Many special characters that are not supplied with the basic font can be obtained as a separate package called an expert set. These may include alternate versions of certain letters. For example, several type designs offer variants of the capitals R, K, and Q, allowing the designer to select either a descending stroke that sits on the baseline or one that descends below it. Similarly, some typeface families include alternate "beginner" and "ender" letters, to be used at the beginning and end of words. These may also be included within swash fonts.

Above A selection from the extended range of 58 ampersands available in Robert Slimbach's Poetica.

Swash characters

Some typefaces include fonts of swash characters. These are letters of greater decorative extravagance than those of the main face, and are designed for selective use. They may be used in titling and display, or as initial capitals to identify the beginning of a section of text. A swash font may also incorporate alternate lowercase letters and other decorative variant forms, such as ornaments and fleurons.

Below Typefaces that are derived from calligraphic forms, such as Poetica, offer particular scope for the design of swash alternates, adding color and variety and offering the designer an extended range of choices.

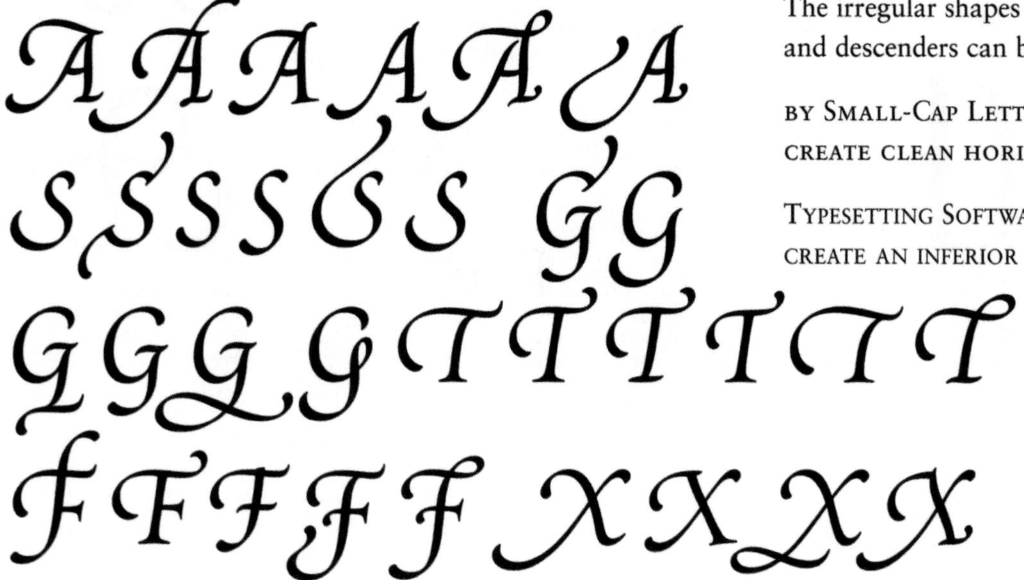

Small caps

Many high-quality typefaces include a small-cap font, for use in those instances where capital letterforms are used to set whole words and sequences of words. The substitution of a smaller size of capital letterform in place of lowercase letters is an established typographic tradition, perhaps most commonly associated with chapter openings.

The irregular shapes created by ascenders and descenders can be replaced

BY SMALL-CAP LETTERS DESIGNED TO CREATE CLEAN HORIZONTALS.

TYPESETTING SOFTWARE CAN BE USED TO CREATE AN INFERIOR SMALL-CAP SETTING.

Above Comparison between the two small-cap examples reveals the shortcomings of false small caps. The lower example shows less harmonious character spacing and an unacceptable variation in stroke width between the two sizes of capital.

Small-capital letters may be used for emphasis, differentiation, or in subtitles and running heads, where clean horizontals may be preferable to the irregular shapes created by ascenders and descenders. The small-cap letters are designed specifically for this purpose. Their weight, color, and stroke width all correspond to that of the full caps in their size, while their proportions are usually wider, corresponding more closely to those of the lowercase letter. The side bearings are more generous, and are designed to give balanced character spacing between capital forms. By comparison, words and phrases set using ordinary capital forms generally require both general and specific adjustment to spacing.

Professional typesetting software allows the designer automatically to create an inferior version of small-cap setting, through the crude substitution of capitals of a smaller point size. The visual shortcomings of this process serve to demonstrate the importance of a well-designed small-cap font, because the false small caps substituted in this way will be lighter in weight and stroke width, and will lack the considerations of set width, letter spacing, and kerning that characterize the well-designed small-cap font.

Old-style numerals

The small-cap font or expert set usually also contains old-style numerals. These are also known as non-lining or proportional numerals. They might usefully be described as lowercase numerals, because the forms align to the x-height rather than the cap height of the face, and have ascending and descending strokes. They are particularly valuable in those instances where there is a large amount of numerical information within the running text.

Standard lining or tabular numerals that correspond to the cap height may create an unintended visual emphasis, equivalent to that which occurs when a word is set in capitals. This interrupts the visual consistency of the text and the ease of reading. By comparison, old-style numerals correspond to the profiles and proportions of lowercase letters, and are therefore better integrated within running text.

Ornaments and other non-alphabet forms

In addition to the letters of the alphabet, punctuation marks, and other standard glyphs, digital fonts include a variety of non-alphabetical forms. These include ornaments, symbols, and other graphic icons. Historical forms, such as the dagger and double dagger, are included within the main font for most traditional typefaces. Other sets of non-alphabetical forms are associated with specific typefaces but occupy whole fonts. Many of these are adaptations of historical decorative forms, referred to as fleurons or printers' flowers. These may be used as paragraph markers and text endings, or may also be used to form continuous decorative borders or fields of repeated pattern. There are also fonts designed specifically to create borders and frames.

Right Tabular numerals (Sabon) and non-lining numerals (Sabon Old Style).

1234567890

1234567890

Right Ornaments and fleurons (Hoefler Text Ornament).

Right An informal miscellany of abstract and figurative symbols (Zapf Dingbats).

Right In Gill Sans Dual Greek, the outward characteristics of Gill's classic sans serif forms are applied to the different requirements of the Greek alphabet.

ΤΨΔΩΓΛΠΞαβγδεζηθικλ

μνξοπρστυφχψως

Some non-alphabetic fonts are not specific to any typeface or typographic genre, but are freestanding miscellanies including both functional and ornamental elements. These are commonly known as dingbats, wingdings, or sorts. Some fonts include graphic informational symbols. These are designed for more specific uses, including cartographic, mathematical, and scientific functions.

Other alphabets

Digital technology has led to major improvements in the availability of compatible Cyrillic and Hellenic alphabets. In the past, the coordinated design of typefaces across more than one alphabet was a relative rarity, limited to a few widely used faces, such as Times or Gill Sans, while the process of adapting the characteristics of existing Western faces and styles into different alphabets was achieved with only limited success. The development of Unicode and OpenType offers the prospect of far more effective typographic integration, allowing the incorporation of multiple alphabets or scripts within a single font.

SELECTING TYPE

In choosing a typeface for the setting of text, our first impulse is, understandably, to look at the letterforms themselves. Do they attract us visually? What associations do they possess? What values do they suggest? What responses do they evoke? However, this impulse is, if not misguided, an incomplete basis for choice.

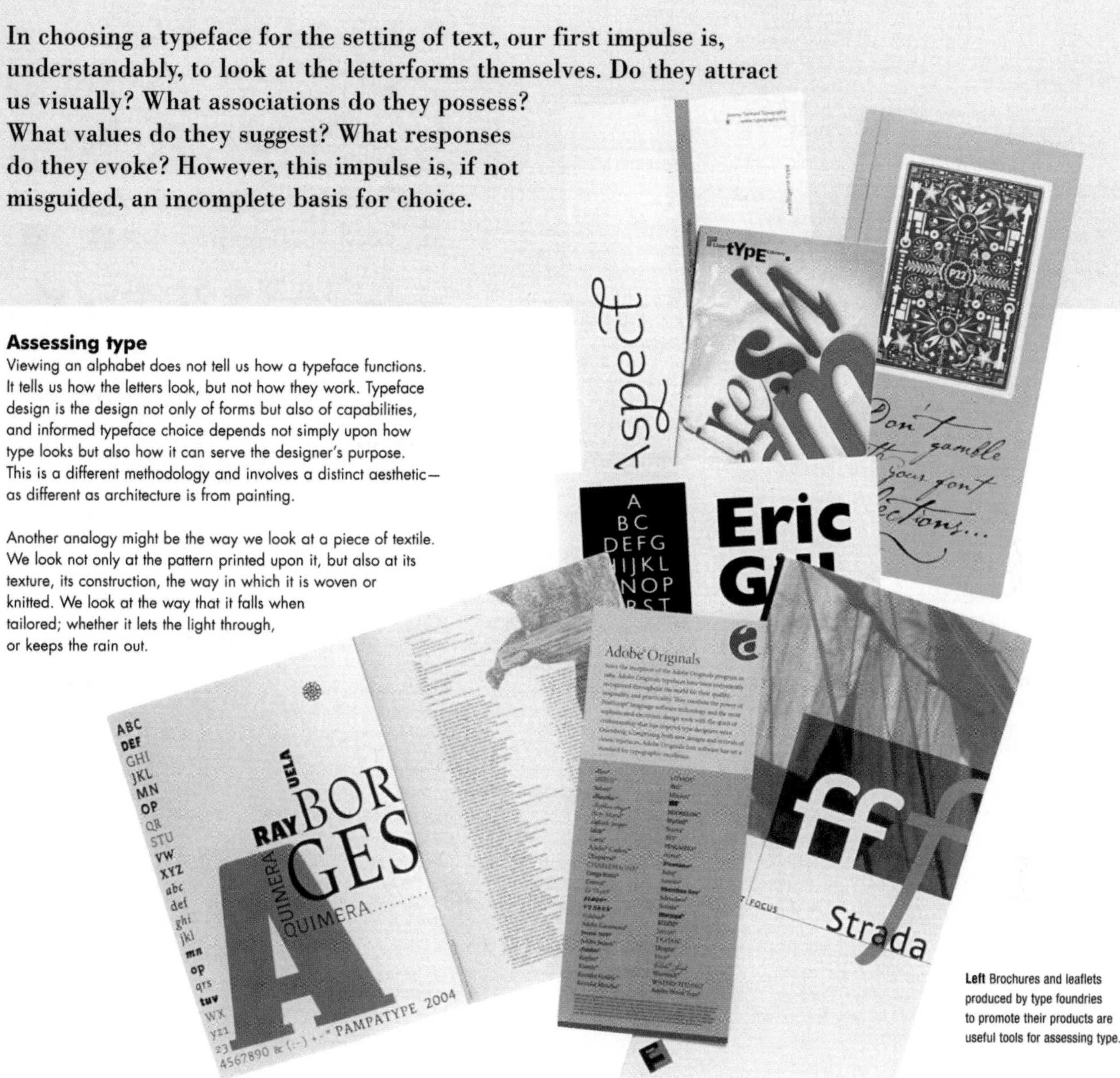

Assessing type

Viewing an alphabet does not tell us how a typeface functions. It tells us how the letters look, but not how they work. Typeface design is the design not only of forms but also of capabilities, and informed typeface choice depends not simply upon how type looks but also how it can serve the designer's purpose. This is a different methodology and involves a distinct aesthetic—as different as architecture is from painting.

Another analogy might be the way we look at a piece of textile. We look not only at the pattern printed upon it, but also at its texture, its construction, the way in which it is woven or knitted. We look at the way that it falls when tailored; whether it lets the light through, or keeps the rain out.

Left Brochures and leaflets produced by type foundries to promote their products are useful tools for assessing type.

WHAT DO WE WANT THE TYPEFACE TO DO?

The questions we might ask of a typeface will depend upon the job we wish it to do. The quality of our decisions will depend upon the intelligence we bring to this question. Relevant questions might include:

- How extensive is the range of fonts available as part of this face or family? For instance, what range of weights is available, and is the design equally satisfactory across the range of weights?

Weight *Weight*
Weight **Weight**
Weight **Weight**

- Are its historical references and antecedents appropriate to the context and structure of the product?

Context ***Context***
CONTEXT **CONTEXT**
CONTEXT **CONTEXT**

- Does it include fractions and non-lining numerals, which may be an important consideration if the job involves the use of numerals such as dates within the running text?

123456 *123456*
123456 *123456*
½ ⅛ ⅜ *½ ⅛ ⅜*

- Does it have related variants for display use? Does it include small caps and other expert set features?

Variants *Variants*
Variants *Variants*
VARIANTS *VARIANTS*
VARIANTS VARIANTS
VARIANTS VARIANTS

- Does it form part of a family of related faces? This might include condensed or extended versions and display variants, allowing the same typeface or family to be maintained across text and display uses.

Roman Text Face
Black Text Face
Swash Titling Face
ENGRAVED FACE
LIGHT SMALL-CAPS
ITALIC SWASH SMALL-CAPS

Legibility is probably best viewed as a body of knowledge, research, and opinion to which designers refer selectively, rather than a subject governed by any single unified theory or categorical law. There is a range of provisional truths, but the designer's own response to the text may still be the best point of reference. It is useful, however, to keep the following points in mind:

- The eye registers the shapes of words, reading as a whole the profiles of all words with which the reader is familiar. It is only when encountering a word that is new to us that we trace it letter by letter.
- Ascenders and descenders aid differentiation (distinguishing j from i, a from d). Lowercase forms are therefore more legible than capitals of equivalent size.
- Lower and more clearly defined junctions, as in the join of the stem to the curve of a lowercase n, will aid legibility. Open and well-defined counters are also a characteristic of the most legible typefaces.

Legibility

The analysis of legibility involves a range of factors, perspectives, and methodologies. While any of these may be relevant and illuminating in a particular context, it remains a study that resists absolute rules or categorical statements. For the experienced designer, legibility is largely addressed intuitively or, more accurately, through accumulated knowledge and experience. It may vary radically with the context of the work, with the use of negative space, leading, and line measure, and cannot be identified solely with the typeface itself.

Legibility depends upon the ease with which the eye can identify letters, and distinguish them from one another. It therefore depends as much upon the relationship of letters in the font as upon the design of the individual letters. An i that might appear perfectly legible when viewed in isolation will be compromised if the j is insufficiently differentiated from it. A geometric lowercase d appears highly legible until one considers how easily it may be mistaken for an o tight-spaced to an l. One might mistakenly assume that the relatively unadorned forms of geometric sans serifs, with their clear, or "clean," lines, would make such typefaces supremely legible. However, this clarity of form results in a lack of differentiation between letters.

We should also recognize that legibility is determined not only by formal and physiological influences, but also by the cultural norms and expectations of the time. John Baskerville's typefaces, models of legibility by present-day standards, were criticized in their time as unreadable due to the brilliance of their contrast. Blackletter type, which remained the norm for long text setting and book work in Germany until the 1940s, is now regarded as difficult to read. Certain typefaces can be identified as giving exceptional "page economy," providing a greater number of legible words per column inch than their competitors, but this is a partial and rather reductive measure of legibility.

Letter spacing that is too tight impairs legibility.

The correct amount of letter spacing enhances legibility.

Letter spacing that is too loose impairs legibility.

Above If letter spacing is too tight or too loose, it will impair legibility. The correct amount of letter spacing depends upon the characteristics of the typeface being used.

Legibility *Legibility*

Above A formal type design is more legible than a decorative one.

Legibility Legibility

Above Serif type is more legible than monoline sans serif.

Legibility LEGIBILITY

Above Lowercase letterforms are more legible than capitals.

Legibility Legibility Legibility

Legib

Above Very small or large type tires the reader and reduces legibility.

Legibility

Legibility

Legibility

Left A medium-weight type is more legible than a light or bold face.

Legibility Legibility

Above Black on white is generally more legible than other color combinations.

Readability

Readability and legibility are interdependent but distinct. Legibility concerns the recognition and differentiation of letters and the resulting word shapes that they form. Readability concerns the manner and ease with which the reading eye traces, connects, and absorbs these words as coherent and continuous sentences and paragraphs.

Line length, word spacing, and leading all crucially affect the readability of text. Short lines create repeated interruptions in the reading process, breaking sentences into dislocated fragments. Unduly long lines require the reader to scan more widely, and make it difficult for the eye to track accurately back to the succeeding line. A character count of 60–66 characters per line is widely held to be an optimum. In those circumstances where longer lines are unavoidable, their effect upon readability can be compensated by increases in leading.

Word spacing is also a key factor in readability. While too little space between words may make it difficult to distinguish one word from the next, the majority of digital type suffers from the other extreme, because the default settings insert excessive space between words. This causes unnecessary interruption to the readability of the text as well as introducing excessive white space into the overall texture of the column.

TEXTURE AND COLOR

The choice of typeface, type size, leading, word spacing, and line measure affects the texture and color (tonal value) of text setting. In these examples, the Clarendon creates a strong horizontal emphasis, while Bauer Bodoni has a pronounced vertical stress. The abrupt contrast of stroke widths in Bodoni produces a much richer texture than the monotone appearance of Helvetica. Text set in Baskerville italic has a more close-knit texture than text set in Baskerville roman. Note also the changes in color and texture achieved by increasing the leading.

9/11½pt Clarendon light

The purpose of typographic design is to arrange all the component parts of a piece of text into a harmonious and cohesive whole. This can be achieved either through the unity of similar design elements or by contrasting values.

10/11½pt Bauer Bodoni

The purpose of typographic design is to arrange all the component parts of a piece of text into a harmonious and cohesive whole. This can be achieved either through the unity of similar design elements or by contrasting values.

9/11½pt Baskerville

The purpose of typographic design is to arrange all the component parts of a piece of text into a harmonious and cohesive whole. This can be achieved either through the unity of similar design elements or by contrasting values.

9/11½pt Baskerville italic

The purpose of typographic design is to arrange all the component parts of a piece of text into a harmonious and cohesive whole. This can be achieved either through the unity of similar design elements or by contrasting values.

9/9pt Helvetica

The purpose of typographic design is to arrange all the component parts of a piece of text into a harmonious and cohesive whole. This can be achieved either through the unity of similar design elements or by contrasting values.

9/14pt Helvetica

The purpose of typographic design is to arrange all the component parts of a piece of text into a harmonious and cohesive whole. This can be achieved either through the unity of similar design elements or by contrasting values.

9/9pt Helvetica italic

The purpose of typographic design is to arrange all the component parts of a piece of text into a harmonious and cohesive whole. This can be achieved either through the unity of similar design elements or by contrasting values.

9/14pt Helvetica italic

The purpose of typographic design is to arrange all the component parts of a piece of text into a harmonious and cohesive whole. This can be achieved either through the unity of similar design elements or by contrasting values.

9/9pt Helvetica

The purpose of typographic design is to arrange all the component parts of a piece of text into a harmonious and cohesive whole. This can be achieved either through the unity of similar design elements or by a more dynamic composition of contrasting values.

9/14pt Helvetica

The purpose of typographic design is to arrange all the component parts of a piece of text into a harmonious and cohesive whole. This can be achieved either through the unity of similar design elements or by contrasting values.

9/14pt Helvetica italic

The purpose of typographic design is to arrange all the component parts of a piece of text into a harmonious and cohesive whole. This can be achieved either through the unity of similar design elements or by contrasting values.

ALIGNMENT

Lines of continuous text—also referred to as running text or long text—may be arranged upon the page according to any one of four main forms of alignment. While some are suitable for a wider range of purposes than others, it is important to recognize that no form of alignment is intrinsically better than another; their suitability is determined by the context in which they are to be used.

Using flush, or ranged, text

Flush type is seen as informal and its asymmetry may be used as a positive element in the design of a page. It may be set in narrow columns of as few as four or five words per line, and the consistent word spaces make flush type more readable and visually harmonious than the variable word spacing of justified type. Hyphenation can be kept to a minimum, or in some cases eliminated altogether. Frequently used in page layouts utilizing two or more columns, and in smaller documents, it is rarely used for single-column book pages, though arguments have been made, notably by Eric Gill, for the adoption of flush text in this context.

Hyphenation and word spacing: flush type

Flush type should be the preferred option when using basic programs that do not allow for detailed modifications of setting, but it can nevertheless benefit from the adjustments to hyphenation and word spacing provided by professional typographic software.

FLUSH-LEFT TEXT—PROS AND CONS

Each form of alignment has its characteristic qualities, advantages, and disadvantages. Decisions on the alignment of continuous text are ultimately governed by considerations of type size and column width. It is the relationship of these three interdependent factors that ultimately determines the appearance of printed text.

What is it?
Type set to an even left margin, giving an uneven or ragged right margin.
Other names
Also called ranged left or ragged right.
Key characteristic
Asymmetry.

The typographer's first duty is to the text
itself. An intelligent interpretation of the
text will not only ensure readability, but
will also reflect its tone, its structure, and
its cultural context. The typographer's
analysis illuminates the text, like the
musician's reading of a score.

Right Flush-left type, creating an irregular right-hand margin.

The typographer's first duty is to the text itself. An intelligent interpretation of the text will not only ensure readability, but will also reflect its tone, its structure, and its cultural context. The typographer's analysis illuminates the text, like the musician's reading of a score.

Above Type flush left to standard spacing defaults, showing unneccessarily wide word spacing.

12pt Classical Garamond
14pt leading
Word spacing—standard default: opt 110%
Hyphenation—none

The typographer's first duty is to the text itself. An intelligent interpretation of the text will not only ensure readability, but will also reflect its tone, its structure, and its cultural context. The typographer's analysis illuminates the text, like the musician's reading of a score.

Above Type flush left with word spacing reduced, to give a tighter line and improved readability.

12pt Classical Garamond
14pt leading
Word spacing—adjusted: opt 85%
Hyphenation—none

Since one of the main virtues of flush setting is that it minimizes the need for hyphenation, it is logical to hyphenate only where absolutely necessary. It may also be argued that the more pronounced raggedness of the resulting right-hand column makes a positive feature of its asymmetry, where a flush text that has been extensively hyphenated may result in nearly even lines.

The majority of typefaces and default settings allow more space than is strictly necessary between words, and the appearance of flush text setting can often be improved by fine-tuning the word spacing. While word spacing is traditionally equivalent to the body width of a lowercase i, in practice the designer's eye is the best guide in optimizing word space for ease of reading.

Advantages
- The space between words remains consistent. This is important to the readability of the text—the ease with which the reader's eye traces the progression from one word to the next. It also ensures an even texture to a column of type, maintaining an even "gray value" from line to line.
- It is not necessary to hyphenate words. Strictly speaking, it need not be necessary to hyphenate any words at all within flush text; in practice, it may be useful to specify hyphenation of extremely long words to avoid an excessively ragged right margin.
- It can be set across narrow columns.

Disadvantages and limitations
- Asymmetry—the ragged right margin may disturb the balance of an otherwise symmetrical page layout. However, this might equally be listed as an advantage, since asymmetry can be the basis for dynamic typographic compositions.

CENTERED TEXT—PROS AND CONS

What is it?
Type set on a central axis, with even word spacing and ragged left and right margins.
Other names
Also called ragged left and right.
Key characteristic
Symmetry.
Advantages
- Although seldom used for the setting of large quantities of continuous text, centered type can be extremely effective in the design of single pages in formal contexts (such as title pages).

Disadvantages and limitations
- Reduced readability—the absence of an even left margin makes it more difficult for the reader's eye to identify the beginning of the next line. This may be addressed by increasing the leading.

The typographer's first duty is to the text itself. An intelligent interpretation of the text will not only ensure readability, but will also reflect its tone, its structure, and its cultural context. The typographer's analysis illuminates the text, like the musician's reading of a score.

FLUSH-RIGHT TEXT—PROS AND CONS

What is it?
Type set to an even right margin, giving an uneven or ragged left margin.
Other names
Also called ranged right or ragged left.
Key characteristic
Asymmetry
Advantages
- Flush-right text is rarely used for text of any length. It can, however, be extremely effective for setting small bodies of text, captions, and so on within asymmetrical layouts, where a ragged left column may create or resolve dynamic tension within the composition of the page.

Disadvantages and limitations
- Reduced readability—the absence of an even left margin makes it more difficult for the reader's eye to identify the beginning of the next line. This may be addressed by increasing the leading.

The typographer's first duty is to the text itself. An intelligent interpretation of the text will not only ensure readability, but will also reflect its tone, its structure, and its cultural context. The typographer's analysis illuminates the text, like the musician's reading of a score.

JUSTIFIED TEXT—PROS AND CONS

What is it?
The space between the words is adjusted in each line, giving even margins both left and right.
Other names
Also called flush left and right.
Key characteristic
Symmetry.
Advantages
- Even margins left and right, giving a neat rectangular text area.

Disadvantages and limitations
- The space between words will necessarily vary from one line to the next, because each is adjusted to fill the same column width. This requires detailed adjustments to specification in order to avoid excessive spaces between words.
- Requires hyphenation.
- Requires wide columns/larger number of characters per line.

The typographer's first duty is to the text itself. An intelligent interpretation of the text will not only ensure readability, but will also reflect its tone, its structure, and its cultural context.

Above Justification involves automatic variations in word spacing to create a clean right-hand margin.

Using justified text

Justification creates balanced formal columns of text, providing visual symmetry and clean margins. It remains the accepted form of alignment for traditional single-column book pages, providing clean inner and outer margins. The feasibility of justified setting will depend upon the number of words per line. This is determined by two factors: the size of the type and the width of the column.

If type has to be fitted into a narrow, predetermined column width, at optimum size, this may result in a character count too small for justification to be feasible. If the nature of the job gives some measure of control over the column width, the designer may determine an optimum column width based on considerations of readability.

The optimum type size will be determined by the nature of the document, and may be affected by questions of economy and the need to achieve a given number of words per page. The smaller the character count, the fewer words per line, resulting in an increasingly noticeable variation of word spacing when justified. A column width giving an average of four or five words per line will show marked and intrusive variations of space that will not occur in a column of ten to twelve words per line.

Hyphenation and word spacing: justified type

Justification should not be attempted unless using a program or setting system that allows for detailed adjustments to hyphenation and justification (H&Js). Some degree of hyphenation is essential to justified setting. It is the designer's role to specify how far hyphenation is applied. This is expressed in terms of: the smallest word to be hyphenated, the minimum number of words before a hyphen, and the minimum number of words after a hyphen. While some clients may have a predetermined house style covering such questions, it is frequently left to the designer. The fine-tuning of H&Js can reflect a general aesthetic preference or be used to address specific justification problems.

Justification settings allow the designer to specify the minimum, optimum, and maximum spaces between words. The majority of typefaces and default settings allow more space than is strictly necessary between words, and the appearance of text setting can often be improved by fine-tuning the word spacing. Justification settings also allow for additional spacing to be introduced between letters where necessary. This last capability should be used sparingly, if at all, because even minimal increases in letter spacing can create lines that appear inconsistent with the rest of the text.

12pt Classical Garamond
14pt leading
Word spacing—standard default:
min 85%, opt 110%, max 250%
Hyphenation—standard default:
Shortest word 6
Minimum before 3
Minimum after 2

The typographer's first duty is to the text itself. An intelligent interpretation of the text will not only ensure readability, but will also reflect its tone, its structure, and its

The typographer's first duty is to the text itself. An intelligent interpretation of the text will not only ensure readability, but will also reflect its tone, its structure, and its cultural context. The typographer's analysis illuminates the text, like the musician's reading of a score.

Left Without adjustment to settings, there are very noticeable rivers in the text.

12pt Classical Garamond
14pt leading
Word spacing—adjusted
min 50%, opt 70%, max 90%
Hyphenation—standard default:
Shortest word 6
Minimum before 3
Minimum after 2

The typographer's first duty is to the text itself. An intelligent interpretation of the text will not only ensure readability, but will also reflect its tone, its

The typographer's first duty is to the text itself. An intelligent interpretation of the text will not only ensure readability, but will also reflect its tone, its structure, and its cultural context. The typographer's analysis illuminates the text, like the musician's reading of a score.

Left Reduced minimum and optimum settings improve the readability and the density of the type.

12pt Classical Garamond
14pt leading
Word spacing—adjusted
min 50%, opt 70%, max 70%
Hyphenation—standard default:
Shortest word 6
Minimum before 3
Minimum after 2

The typographer's first duty is to the text itself. An intelligent interpretation of the text will not only ensure readability, but will also reflect its tone, its structure, and its cultural context. The typographer's analysis illuminates the text, like the musician's reading of a score.

Left Where type is justified across a longer measure, the irregularities of word spacing are reduced.

RESOLVING JUSTIFICATION PROBLEMS

The most common problem of justification is the appearance of excessive spaces between words, creating what are called "rivers" within a column or page of type. This may be resolved by any of the following measurements:

- Adjusting the H&Js—to reduce the maximum word space and increase the incidence of hyphenation.
- Reducing type size—this will give a greater character count per line.
- Increasing leading—greater space between lines will compensate visually for pronounced word spaces; tighter leading will make the rivers more apparent.

The typographer's first duty is to the text itself. An intelligent interpretation of the text will not only ensure readability, but will also reflect its tone, its structure, and its cultural context. The typographer's analysis illuminates the text, like the musician's reading of a score.

Above Rivers in justified type.

DIFFERENTIATION

Any piece of typographic design is likely to contain several different kinds of information. It is an important part of the designer's role to ensure that these are prioritized and clearly differentiated visually. Differentiation may be achieved through: position, scale, weight, italicization, case, and mixing typefaces.

Position

Different types of information may be identified visually by their position on the page. Designated spaces within the page layout may, for instance, be allocated to running footnotes, captions, or timelines, as well as to recurring elements such as page numbers and running heads.

Scale

Content may be differentiated through the scale of type, by increases in point size. A title or subtitle, an introductory paragraph, or pull-quote may be differentiated from the main text by being set in a larger size. In some cases, specific words or phrases within continuous text may be set in larger sizes for emphasis. As a general rule, any such increase should be of at least 2 points; a single point difference is likely to look like an error rather than a deliberate decision.

Weight

Typefaces customarily include a choice of weights, from the single bold variant common to most text faces to intermediate weights, such as book, medium, and demi; or extremes, such as black or ultra bold. Among those typefaces that have only two weights, the interval between weights varies widely from one face to the next. As a consequence, the mixing of weights in one typeface may constitute a more "colorful" variation than in others. Because a typeface is designed in a different weight or width, a number of considerations inform the new design. An increase in stroke width will necessitate modifications of form, requiring particular attention to the junctions of strokes and in some cases significant changes to the design of letters.

Some type categories lend themselves naturally to variations of weight and width. In particular, the characteristic qualities

MULTIPLE MASTER TECHNOLOGY

Since the late 20th century, several typefaces have been designed in an extended range of weights using multiple master technology. The resulting range of options should nevertheless be used sparingly. A limited number of weights should be selected and careful consideration given to the amount of difference between them.

Bliss Light	Bliss Caps Light
Bliss Light Italic	*Bliss Caps Light Italic*
Bliss Regular	Bliss Caps Regular
Bliss Italic	*Bliss Caps Italic*
Bliss Medium	Bliss Caps Medium
Bliss Medium Italic	*Bliss Caps Medium Italic*
Bliss Bold	**Bliss Caps Bold**
Bliss Bold Italic	***Bliss Caps Bold Italic***
Bliss Extra Bold	**Bliss Caps Extra Bold**
Bliss Extra Bold Italic	***Bliss Caps Extra Bold Italic***
Bliss Heavy	**Bliss Caps Heavy**
Bliss Heavy Italic	***Bliss Caps Heavy Italic***

Left Multiple master fonts are available in an extended range of weights—24 of the 160 versions of Bliss are shown here.

of Didone types, in which there is pronounced contrast between horizontal hairlines and vertical strokes, can be maintained across a wide range of weights and dramatically condensed or extended variants.

Care should be observed when introducing bold type in digital setting. Some typesetting and word-processing software will respond to a "bold" command by introducing an automatically emboldened version of the face, rather than accessing the correct bold font. This false bold will invariably be inferior in form and detailing. For this reason, it is good practice always to specify the bold through making a specific font selection.

Italicization

Italic forms may be used to create emphasis or differentiation within continuous text. Their use can denote the stresses in speech, and indicate the introduction of words from other languages or idioms. Italic form also has a more general association with the spoken word, and may therefore be used for the setting of extended sections of quotation or reported speech. Italics may be adopted as the main text font for continuous setting, but it should be remembered that this will in turn create the need for some alternative form of differentiation where words within the text would otherwise have been italicized.

Case

Capital forms may be used within continuous text for visual differentiation or, sparingly, for emphasis. Where capital letters are to be set as "strings" to create whole words or sentences, the designer should consider the use of a small-cap font if one is available. If using the standard capitals from the main text font, particular attention must be given to letter spacing. Strings of capitals almost invariably benefit from general adjustments to letter spacing, and may also require the individual manual kerning of letter pairs at larger sizes.

Mixing typefaces

Many typefaces or typeface families contain within them a wealth of inbuilt variation, offering a range of weights and widths, display variants, small-cap fonts, and other characteristics, allowing the designer many forms of differentiation while using only one face. There will, however, be instances where the use of more than one type family is appropriate. Care should be taken to ensure both a well-defined contrast and an underlying affinity between the faces used.

It may be preferable to make positive use of the contrasts between serif and sans serif, rather than using two serif or two sans serif faces. (It is particularly difficult to combine different categories of sans serif successfully.) If contrasting typefaces are to be used in such a way that they occur within the same line, care should be taken to ensure that the two faces have a consistent x-height. Sans serif and serif faces can work together particularly well if there is a similarity in the underlying proportions of the letterforms. For this reason, Humanist Sans typefaces combine particularly happily with Romanesque serif letters, because they share a common model of proportion, both being modeled upon the classic Roman capital.

By comparison, Geometric and Neo-Grotesque faces are less suitable for combining with faces from other categories, because their forms and proportions reflect specific phases in the development of type. The historical and stylistic associations of such typefaces may render them unsuitable for combining with others.

TYPOGRAPHIC VARIATION

Typographic variation, whether in the use of differing typefaces, weights, and sizes, the introduction of bold, italic, or small-cap fonts, should serve to clarify visually for the reader specific kinds of emphasis and prioritization, and to establish consistent distinctions between different kinds of content. It separates the design of the page into levels or layers, simultaneously visible but distinct, clarifying for the reader the relationships between several related kinds of information. While this has the effect of visually enlivening the page, this is a consequence of the designer's analysis of the copy and the brief, rather than an outcome in itself.

Below A wide variety of weights and sizes has been used in this spread from *Fitréttir*, a newsletter for the Icelandic Association of Graphic Designers, by Einar Gylfason.

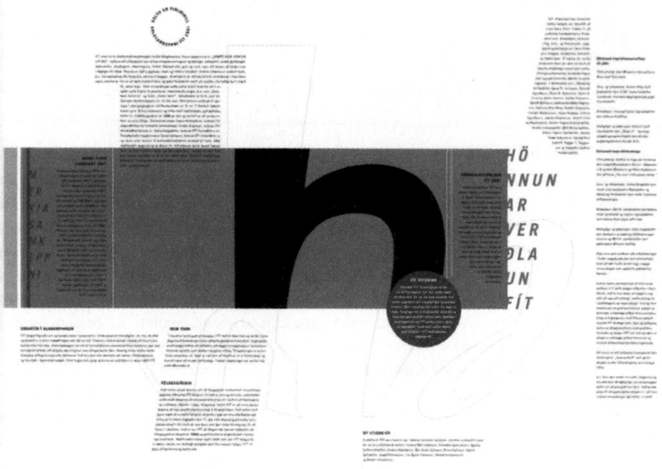

PAGE LAYOUT

The design of the page involves both the composition of the columns and margins that form the page grid, and decisions governing the size, weight, and leading of text, subheads, and titling. Page design is likely to involve both practical considerations, such as the amount of text on the page, its legibility and ease of use, and aesthetic or expressive factors, such as impact, differentiation, and visual appeal.

The choice of typeface and the structure of the page are closely linked and interdependent decisions, each of which may influence or determine the other. For example, an initial decision to compose a page along asymmetrical principles, using short columns of flush, or ranged, type, will in turn suggest certain typefaces as appropriate to this strategy, and rule out others as being either historically or visually unsuitable. Conversely, the page design may be driven by the choice of a particular typeface that then suggests certain characteristics of layout. These will be determined by both the functionality of that typeface and its associations within typographic history.

Many 20th-century sans serif faces have strong associations with the prevailing design philosophies of their time. For example, 20th-century Neo-Grotesques of the Swiss school belong to a tradition of typographic minimalism in which variation and differentiation is achieved primarily through scale and composition rather than variations of typographic form.

Text setting

The appearance of a column of type is determined by several distinct but closely interrelated factors. As well as the choice of typeface and alignment already discussed, the size of the type, the width at which it is set, and its leading must all be considered in relation to one another.

Type size

Text for the printed page is generally set at between 9 and 12 points. Variation in the x-heights of text faces means that it may be feasible to set in smaller sizes when using typefaces of exceptionally generous x-height, while typefaces with unusually pronounced ascenders may need to be set larger to achieve the optimum legibility.

Line length/column width

The width of a column may be determined by the amount of space available within a predetermined page, but wherever possible attention should be given to achieving an appropriate number of words per line. Lines that are too short impair readability by constantly interrupting the text; lines that are too long make it difficult for the reader's eye to return to the margin and identify successive lines. A character count of around 60–66 characters is generally accepted as providing an optimum point between these extremes. In some cases, longer lines may be unavoidable, in which case the effect upon readability can be compensated by an increase in leading.

Leading

The amount of leading necessary for a balanced and legible column of type will depend upon the typeface, and, in particular, the body clearance and x-height. Typefaces with long ascenders and descenders will, as a rule, require less additional leading than those with a greater x-height.

Below The long ascenders of Bauer Bodoni (left) create a greater volume of white space between the lines of lowercase letters than the high x-height of Swiss 721 (right), a Helvetica derivative.

Typefaces with long ascenders and descenders will as a rule require less additional leading than typefaces with a generous x-height.

Typefaces with generous x-height will as a rule require more additional leading than typefaces with long ascenders and descenders.

Text-setting styles

Many documents require a number of text-setting styles for the differentiation of distinct types of information or, in some cases, simply for visual variety, such as between different features in a magazine. This may introduce variations in type color, column width, and the size, weight, or typeface. Distinct and consistent styles also need to be established for the setting of captions, footnotes, and any other content that is not included within the running text.

Introduction styles

The point at which a text begins on the opening page of a chapter or the introduction to a magazine feature may be signposted visually in a number of ways. It may be necessary to make clear to the reader that the text is not a continuation from a previous page, or to bridge the otherwise abrupt transition from a space that may involve images and display typography into the continuum of running text.

This transition may be achieved by the use of a drop-cap: an initial letter set at a larger size than that used in the main text, either positioned on the first line or recessed into the text by being set to align with the second, third, or fourth line, depending upon its size. This may in turn be followed by additional words of the first sentence set in small caps at a size corresponding to the text, before moving into the established text style for the book. Introductory paragraphs may be identified by being set in a larger size, a heavier weight, or even a different typeface from the subsequent text.

Right Four different approaches to signaling paragraphs: moderate and deep indents, hanging exdents, and ornamental paragraph marks.

The designer has a number of typographic options for indicating the beginnings and ends of paragraphs. This is both an aid to readability and a means to introducing some visual variation into large sections of continuous text.

The first line of a new paragraph may be indented—that is, set in from the margin by a fixed measure.

The designer has a number of typographic options for indicating the beginnings and ends of paragraphs. This is both an aid to readability and a means to introducing some visual variation into large sections of continuous text.

The first line of a new paragraph may be indented—that is, set in from the margin by a fixed measure.

The designer has a number of typographic options for indicating the beginnings and ends of paragraphs. This is both an aid to readability and a means to introducing some visual variation into large sections of continuous text.

Very occasionally, there are instances where the opening of the paragraph is set outside the column margin.

❁ The designer has a number of typographic options for indicating the beginnings and ends of paragraphs. This is both an aid to readability and a means to introducing some visual variation into large sections of continuous text. ❁ Paragraphs may be indicated by graphic devices, removing the need to begin a paragraph on a new line.

Below The use of an initial drop capital signals the beginning of a chapter and provides a visual transition to the running text.

footprints on the sand | Gareth Watkins

The Snail
and the Grain of Salt

SINCE BEING BROUGHT TOGETHER mysteriously after a particularly heavy rainstorm, the snail and the granule of salt had become friends. The granule had ridden on the snail's back for some time now and they had become accustomed to each other's company. It was the month of April, rainstorms were frequent, and the poor granule, being a soluble salt, dwindled in size after every shower. "Please remove your shell for the moment so that I can get inside and shelter from the rain" called the grains to the snail, now fearful for their safety. Being an easygoing sort, the snail obliged and the grateful grains nestled down in the snail's soft skin. No sooner had he done so than the snail withered away and died.❦

Paragraph and indent styles

The designer has a number of typographic options for indicating the beginnings and ends of paragraphs. This is both an aid to readability and a means to introducing some visual variation into large sections of continuous text.

The first line of a new paragraph may be indented—that is, set in from the margin by a fixed measure. While traditional convention sets the optimum indent as one em (giving an indent equivalent to the point size of the type), there are many instances where a deeper indent may be appropriate, particularly if the column itself has an unusually long measure and word count. There are few instances where one would wish to indent by less than an em, since a poorly defined indent can appear as an error or inconsistency rather than a deliberate aspect of the design.

Very occasionally, there are instances where the opening of the paragraph is set outside the column margin. Sometimes rather clumsily termed an outdent, exdent, or hanging indent, this device is effective for highlighting paragraph openings within smaller documents, but creates an exaggerated differentiation between paragraphs and would seldom be used throughout a book.

The end of paragraphs may, in some cases, be indicated by additional line spacing. This is more common within smaller printed documents than in books, where considerations of page

economy and the effect on readability are likely to make this approach inappropriate. If an additional space is to be inserted, the space should be related to the leading of the text, as a line space or half-line space.

Paragraphs may be indicated by other graphic devices, removing the need to begin a paragraph on a new line. The book designs of William Morris for the Kelmscott Press draw upon medieval examples in using a fleuron for paragraphing, giving an unbroken right margin to the justified page.

Subheads
Many documents involve the use of subheads—secondary titles that may occur within the column of running text. The weight given to these headings depends both upon editorial and aesthetic considerations.

Subheads
Many documents involve the use of subheads—secondary titles that may occur within the column of running text. The weight given to these headings depends both upon editorial and aesthetic considerations.

SUBHEADS
Many documents involve the use of subheads—secondary titles that may occur within the column of running text. The weight given to these headings depends both upon editorial and aesthetic considerations.

Subheads
Many documents involve the use of subheads—secondary titles that may occur within the column of running text. The weight given to these headings depends both upon editorial and aesthetic considerations.

Subheads
Many documents involve the use of subheads—secondary titles that may occur within the column of running text. The weight given to these headings depends both upon editorial and aesthetic considerations.

Above, from top left The subheads in the first three examples are the same point size as the main text. The first uses a bold version of the same font (Futura), the second a serif bold font of similar x-height (Walbaum), and the third the same roman font as the main text but all caps. The final two examples use Futura bold and Walbaum bold italic, but at a larger size than the main text and with leading adjusted.

Subheads
Many documents involve the use of subheads—secondary titles that may occur within the column of running text. The weight given to these headings depends both upon editorial and aesthetic considerations. The content of the text itself and the preferences of the author or editor may indicate how much emphasis is appropriate, while the designer's own visual judgment will determine how far the subhead visually interrupts the continuity of the column. It may be that the subhead can be indicated without any change to type size or leading, by using a heavier weight or capital form of the typeface used in the text, or another typeface of equivalent size.

However, a subhead may involve the use of one or more different sizes of type, necessitating increased space both before and after the subhead. Care must be taken over the size and leading of subheads, to ensure that the total depth around the subhead relates to the leading of the running text, typically occupying a depth equal to one, two, or three lines of text. This ensures that the text following the subhead continues to align with text on adjacent columns.

MAINTAINED LEADING

In some instances, a page involves two different sizes of text. A consistent visual relationship can be maintained by basing the leading of larger type upon common multiples of the text leading.
10/12pt

A consistent relationship can be maintained by basing the leading of larger type upon common multiples of the text leading.
11/15pt

A consistent relationship can be maintained by basing the leading of larger type upon common multiples of the text leading.
12/18pt

Care should be taken to ensure that the lines of type on adjacent pages or columns align properly to one another. Where both columns are uninterrupted by subheads or the intrusion of any other form of additional space, this should occur automatically. The consistent leading of all the text will ensure that, as long as the top lines are correctly aligned, all subsequent lines will also align and each column will end at the same baseline across the double-page spread. If, however, any additional space is to be introduced between lines, this space should be designed so that the position of the following line of text returns to alignment with the lines on the adjacent column. The total leading of the subhead should therefore always be a multiple of the leading of the text.

In some instances, a page involves two different sizes of text; introductions or standfirsts may typically be several points larger than the main running text. In such cases, it may not be possible to maintain the same leading as the text. A consistent visual relationship, however, can still be maintained by basing the leading of the larger type upon common multiples of the text leading. If the text is set on 12pt leading, a larger introductory text may be set upon a leading of 18pt, allowing alignment of every fourth line of text (three lines to four), or 15pt, allowing alignment of every fifth line (four lines to five).

Even in layouts where the strict alignment of text may not be a consideration, recurrent mathematical relationships of this kind serve to reinforce the underlying coherence of the design and the sense that each of the elements belongs to a common scheme.

Although there are variations, the majority of books are structured according to the following conventions.

The prelims

Within the traditionally structured book, there are a number of preliminary pages that precede the main text:

Half-title

This is an initial title page that faces the endpapers (the inside of the front cover). It customarily gives the book title only.

Frontispiece/title page

The full-title page, including title, subtitles, author, and publisher, may fall on the right (recto) page, facing a frontispiece illustration on the left (verso). It may, alternatively, run across the whole double-page spread.

Imprint or biblio page

The verso page following the title normally contains the publishing details of the book: publisher, printer, edition, typeface/foundry, copyright dates, and so on. Alternatively, this information may appear on the verso page preceding the frontispiece or on the last page of the book.

Dedication

If the book is to have a dedication, it customarily falls on the recto, facing the biblio page.

Contents

This customarily falls on the next recto page, though in some circumstances there may be reason to run it across the whole spread.

List of illustrations, acknowledgments, preface, introduction

The book may require any or all of these, which commonly fall in the order shown above, although the first two items frequently also appear at the end of the book.

Part-titles

Where a book divides into several parts, with chapters within them, each part may be preceded by a part-title page. This is a form of page divider between the parts and commonly occurs on the recto page. The preceding verso page may also be incorporated into the design of the part-title.

Chapter titles

If the parts of the book are subdivided into chapters, the chapter title may occur on the same page as the opening text of the chapter or on the previous page. It may be designed as a single- or double-page spread, referred to as a chapter opener.

Footnotes, appendices, index

These are usually listed at the end of the book. Footnotes may also appear at the base of the page to which they refer.

Left Half-title page, featuring the title of the book.

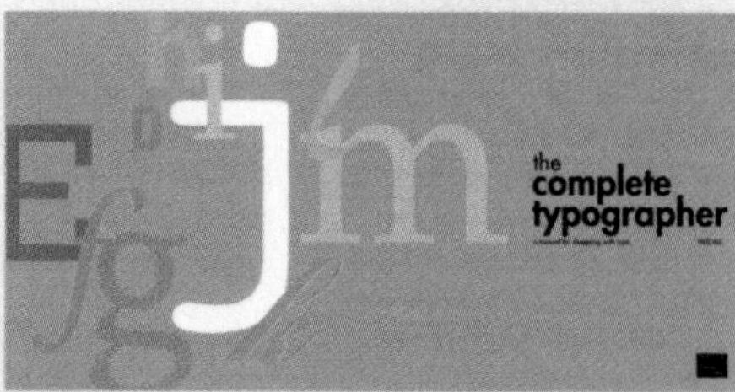

Left Title spread, featuring the title, subtitle, author, and publisher.

Left Imprint and contents spread.

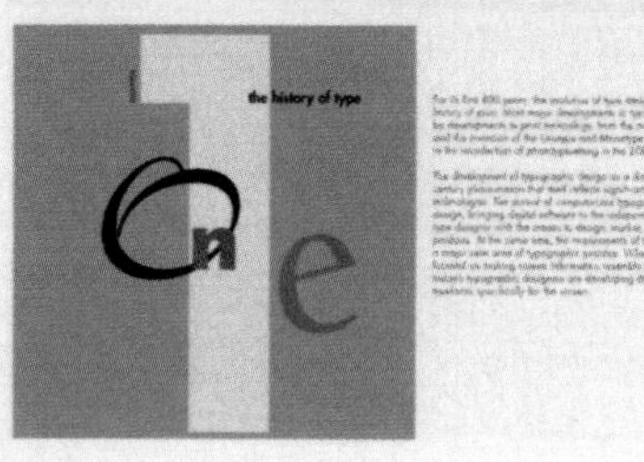

Left Chapter opener spread, featuring the chapter number and title with some introductory text.

Left Index.

The grid

The positioning of the columns of text upon the page spread is determined by the grid—a way of describing a fixed relationship of measurements applied throughout the document. The simplest page grid comprises the four lines used to define the left and right margins, the top line, and the baseline of the text area of each page. This is then repeated on the facing page, allowing for the design of the page spread as a whole. The grid also determines and defines the positioning of page numbers, running heads, and any other elements outside the text area that are to recur throughout the document (titling, section headings, and so on).

Magazines, newspapers, and large-format books use grids of far greater complexity, designed to allow flexibility and variation of page layout while maintaining an underlying consistency of structure. Within a multiple-column grid, the type may be set across two or more columns, giving the designer a range of column-width options. A six-column grid, for example, allows for a wide range of permutations: two columns of three-columns width; three columns of two-columns width; one column of four, and one of two. This flexibility of structure also allows for variation in the scale and positioning of illustrations and photographs, which may be set across any width from a single column to the entire text area, while still conforming to the grid structure.

Fielded grids

Some grids involve the horizontal division of the text area, creating a grid of smaller rectangular "fields" of consistent proportion. While this may be useful or aesthetically satisfying in some cases, it is not necessary in itself as long as the grid clearly establishes all the recurring horizontal elements within the design.

Asymmetrical grids

Some pages may use a grid based around two differing widths of column. This asymmetry may then either be reflected, keeping the narrower column at the outside or in the gutter of the spread, or duplicated, placing the narrower column at the same side of both recto and verso pages.

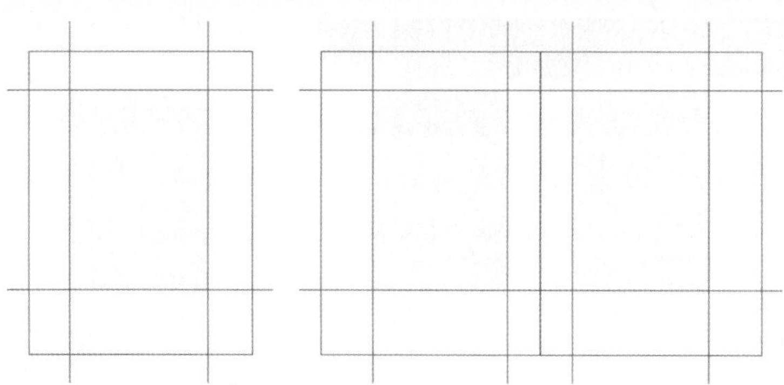

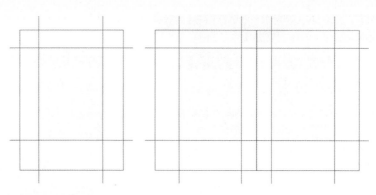

Above The basis of the grid: four lines that define the position of the text area upon the page.

Above A double-page grid, showing the text area and the "gutter" where pages join at the spine of the book.

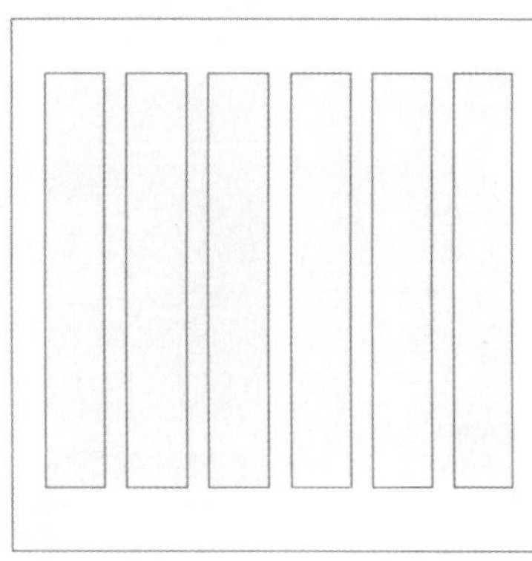

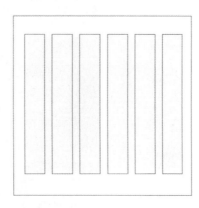

Above A six-column grid divided into two columns.

Above A six-column grid divided into three columns.

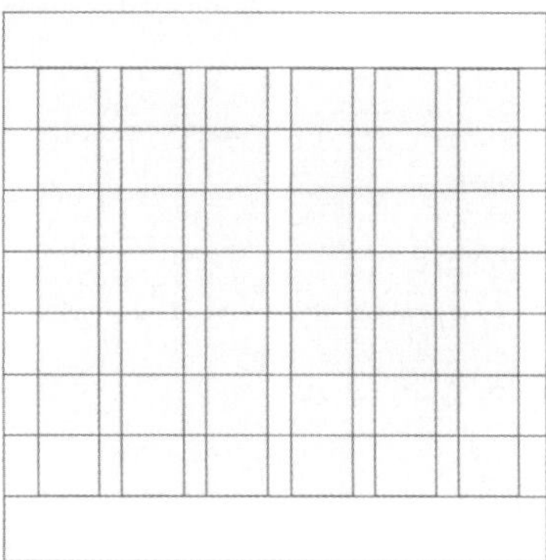

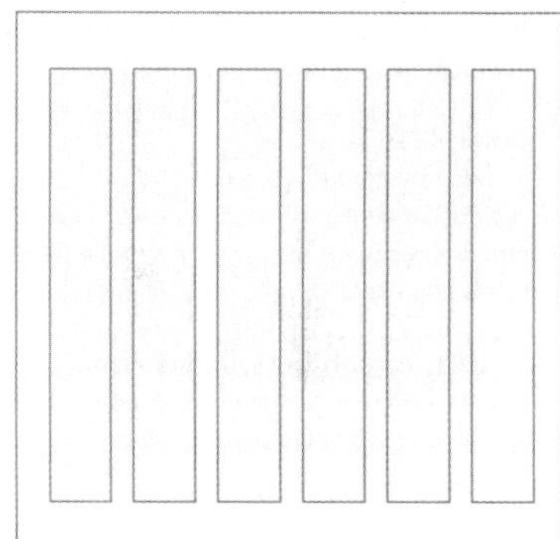

Right A six-column grid using regular horizontal intervals to create fields.

Far right An asymmetrical grid using one wide and one narrow column.

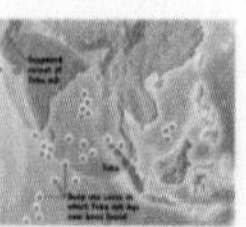

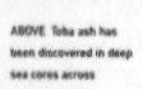

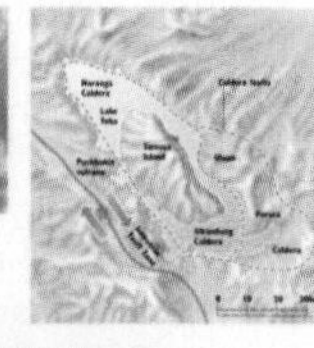

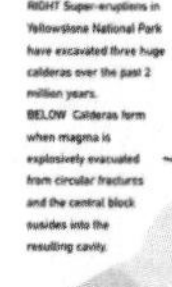

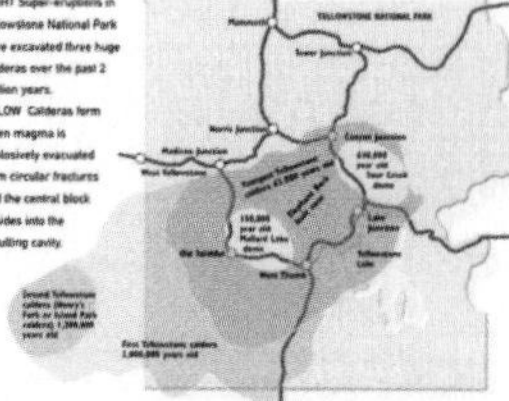

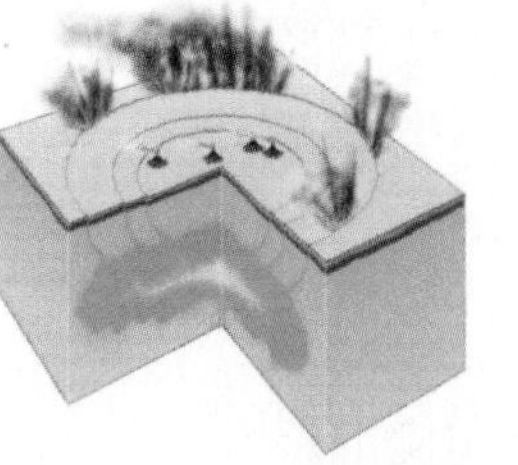

Restless giants
>>>The legacy of the Toba super-eruption is a spectacular lake-filled caldera over 62 miles (100km) long, which is almost matched in size—at 50 miles (80km)—by the largest of the three, giant Yellowstone calderas.
Certain obliteration
VOLCANOES 79

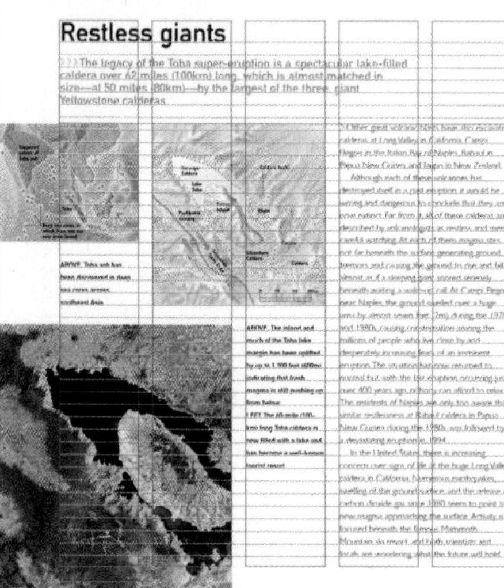

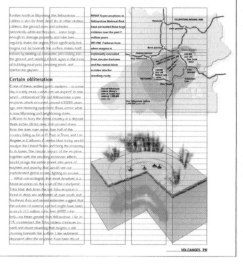

Top A complex grid allows the designer to create considerable compositional variation and to introduce a range of image formats into the spread, while maintaining a consistent underlying structure.

Above The superimposed grid shows the underlying structure to which the page layout conforms.

RULES AND BORDERS

Rules, frames, and borders may be used for purposes of differentiation and decoration. They are particularly effective where it is necessary to make clear the distinction between two different texts on the same page. Professional typographic programs offer a range of styles of rule, the width of which is specified in point sizes. Forms of rule include the traditional Oxford rule, composed of a thick and thin line, along with more elaborate variations.

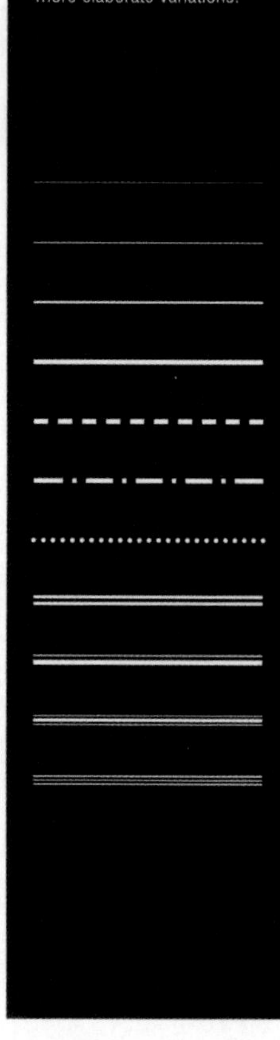

Constructing the grid

While the term grid may suggest restriction, and grid-free design has at times been thought to allow greater scope for creative expression, the intelligent use of a well-designed grid can allow for wide and colorful variation of page content while retaining an underlying visual continuity. In this sense, the most effective grid is the one that renders its presence imperceptible.

Relationship of text area to page

Most digital programs encourage the designer to define the dimensions of the margins and columns at the outset. It is, however, advisable to explore this through experimentation first, either through layout drawings on paper or by moving the position of the text columns on screen. This enables the designer to determine the relationship of the text area to the page spread visually, rather than letting this occur as the result of a series of decisions on margin width.

The page of a bound document is unlikely to require equal margins to left and right of each page. The outer margin should allow comfortable space for the reader to hold the pages open without obscuring the text. The space required for the inner or gutter margin will, to some extent, be determined by the size and binding of the document, because extra provision may need to be made at the gutter for the curve of the page toward the spine of the book. After any such factors have been taken into consideration, the designer should consider the relationship between the outer margins and the total inner margin space between the text areas of the two pages. To give each page an equal left and right page margin would result in a central margin area twice the width of the outer margins—a disproportionate white space that isolates the two page layouts from one another, rather than creating a unified spread.

A harmonious relationship between the inner rectangles of type areas and the outer rectangle of the page spread may be established by the use of diagonals. Studies of historic manuscripts and early printed books reveal the long history of this method, and it remains an effective way of determining the position and proportions of the text area. Diagonal lines drawn from corner to corner of the page and of the spread are used to determine the points at which margins intersect with baseline and topline.

Intercolumn space

The space necessary between adjacent columns depends upon a number of factors: the length of the lines, the size of the type, and particularly, the amount of leading. It may be necessary to allow for vertical rules to be inserted between columns, either as a general pattern or to distinguish one feature or section from another.

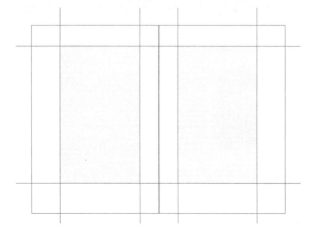

Above A double-page spread requires greater space at the outer margins than the inner. When the effect of the gutter has been taken into consideration, the spread should show a space between the two text areas roughly equal to the outer margins.

Below The proportions of the type area and its relationship to the page margins may be established by the use of diagonal lines.

COMPONENTS OF THE PAGE

In addition to the main running text, most pages include the following recurrent elements.

Folios

Page numbers are referred to as folios. Odd numbers are traditionally the recto or right-hand page, and even numbers the verso or left-hand page. Folios may be aligned to the main text in a number of ways: at the top or the base of the page or partway up. They may range to the same column margin as the text, or be set outside the column, aligned to the baseline of the first or last line. Traditionally, the introductory pages of a book (prelims) were numbered in Roman numerals (i, ii, iii, iv, v, vi, and so on) so that the numerals 1, 2, 3 began with the first chapter of the book itself, although this convention has fallen out of use in many areas of publishing.

Running heads

Running heads are the small headings repeated on each page. They may be used in a number of ways, according to the nature and requirements of the book. Examples include:

Verso	**Recto**
Book title	Chapter title
Part-title	Part of book (as in introduction, notes)

Other elements

The page may also include images for which a consistent caption style must be established, and other items of text such as pull-quotes, footnotes, attributions, and box items.

DISPLAY TYPOGRAPHY

The term display typography is generally used to describe those forms of typographic work that involve the use of fewer words at larger scale, and to distinguish this work from editorial typography and the setting of continuous text. Examples include corporate identity, book jackets, packaging, fascias, and motion graphics. Display typography may involve the interpretive, decorative, or illustrative use of letterforms, providing opportunity for the associative values and the formal characteristics of letters to be explored and exploited to deliberate effect.

Display typefaces

Many typefaces are defined as display faces. This term denotes a face based around particular associative and decorative values, but also indicates that the face would be impractical for use at small scale or in the setting of continuous text. Display typefaces draw upon a wide and colorful range of sources and idioms, and are not constrained by the considerations of legibility and page economy that inform the design of text faces. They are frequently overt statements of creative intent, rather than neutral carriers of content.

The accessibility of digital type design media has led to a proliferation of idiosyncratic or eccentric letters, as well as the revival of many historic display faces. Display type reflects a wide range of vernacular sources, including signwriting, woodletter type, script and calligraphic traditions, and the many forms of the hand-rendered letter. A number of digital typefaces have been designed to replicate distorted or distressed finishes, creating type that appears chipped or blurred and evokes a sense of physical history. The patterns of low-resolution pixelation have been stylistically incorporated into the design of a number of explicitly digital fonts.

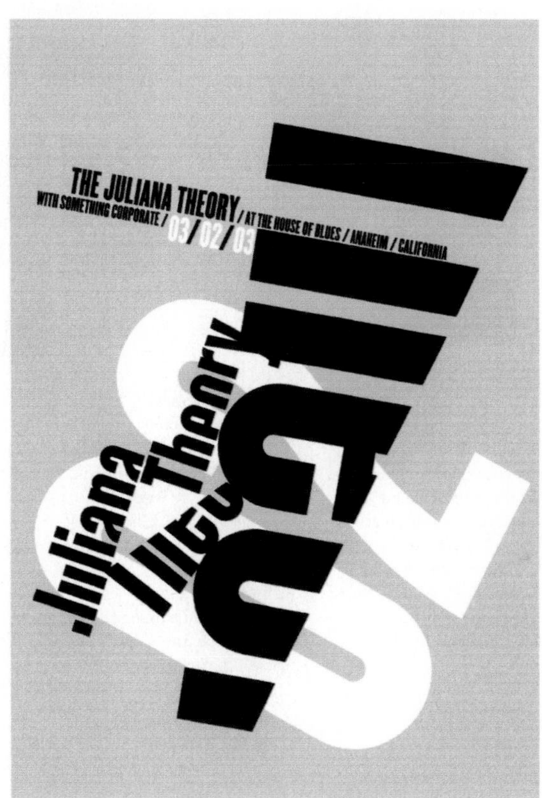

Right A robust sans serif type is set on a diagonal axis to create a dynamic composition of positive and negative forms in this poster by Sterotype Design. The cropped letters demonstrate the principle that lowercase letters are recognized primarily by their upper section.

USING TEXT FACES FOR DISPLAY

It should be noted that many text faces can be effectively used in display contexts, which can serve to draw attention to the intrinsic beauty of individual letterforms more commonly encountered within running text. Some faces based upon Venetian or Aldine models reveal particular elegance of form when viewed at large sizes. Their suitability for use at larger scale is determined to some extent by the quality of the digitization and, in particular, the optical mastering that has been applied in the design of the larger sizes.

Priorities of information

Variations of scale, tonal value, weight, color, and positioning may be necessary to establish the relationships between several different types of display information. Effective design prioritizes these elements visually within a single unified composition. Within the design of a book jacket, for example, the elements would typically be: title, author, image, publisher (in the case of high-profile authors, the first two elements may be reversed). Within the design of a poster or other event promotion, the elements would include: title/event, date, time, location, and booking information.

Tone

Digital media allow the designer to modify the tonal density of type or background. Used with sensitivity, tonal modulation can extend the depth and visual complexity of a monochrome design. The contrast and prominence of a large title may be moderated by printing in a percentage tint rather than a solid. Some care should be taken when applying this capability for type because it may affect the clarity of letterforms. Percentage screening lightens the tonal value of the type by introducing a fine pattern of white dots into the solid letterform. The effect upon the clarity and definition of the type may be imperceptible at larger sizes, but pale tints and coarse screening will reveal irregular edges to the letterforms that will be more intrusive at smaller sizes.

Radio Radio

Radio Radio

Above Type at four different tonal densities. Increased scale can offset the diminished legibility of pale or reversed type, increasing the dynamic palette available to the designer.

The effectiveness of percentage screening is also affected by the quality of paper that is to be used. This determines the size of dot screen that it is feasible for the printer to use; a coarse or absorbent paper requires a coarser screen composed of larger, and therefore more visible, dots. If the budget allows, any moderation in the tonal density of text should be achieved by running a special color printing.

Reversed type

Type may be "reversed out" of a background color, resulting in letterforms composed of un-inked rather than inked space. While this may be extremely effective when using robust typefaces at appropriate sizes, it will affect the legibility of letters, and may in some cases lead to problems in reproduction.

We are accustomed to viewing type as positive form upon a lighter background. While reversed type may create impact and visual variety upon the page, it is measurably less legible. High-contrast reversed lettering may be difficult or even painful to read. This need not be a consideration when setting titling or headlines of a few words, but is a strong argument against using reversed type for substantial amounts of continuous text. Typefaces are designed as positive inked forms, rather than negative forms to be surrounded by ink. Reversal can lead to loss of definition or detail in some typefaces; in particular, delicate hairlines and finely pointed serifs are prone to breaking or filling-in when reversed, fracturing or blunting the letterform. The quality of printing and the absorbency and roughness of the paper can also contribute to these problems.

Color

Color may be used to create emphasis, heighten contrast, evoke emotional responses, or provide informational color coding within a complex document. Some of the most effective display typography utilizes a limited range of specific colors rather than the full spectrum. A single additional printing may open up a range of possibilities, allowing the designer to use both positive and negative letterforms, duotone images, and a range of percentage tints in both of the two printed colors.

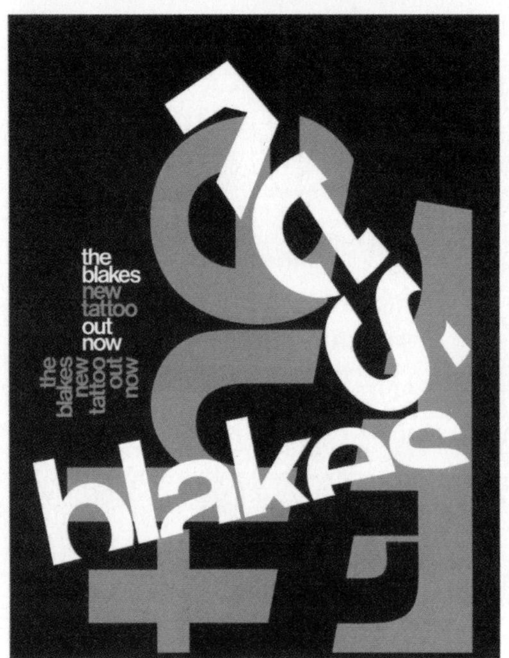

Right Vertical and diagonal elements and a complex use of negative space animate this subtle two-color poster by Stereotype Design.

COLOR PRINTING

Four-color process printing uses the four process colors: cyan, magenta, yellow, and black. The initial letters of these colors form the color mode CMYK (the German word *kohl* is used for black), which should always be specified when producing digital artwork for print reproduction. A color image such as a photograph or illustration is reproduced through the successive overprinting of dot-screened images in each of these four colors. These are called color separations. Colored type printed by four-color process is therefore composed of very fine dots of the four process colors.

Although quality printing will render this almost imperceptible to the eye, the result does not compare with the evenness of surface and clarity of outline achieved when the type is printed as a special ink—an ink actually mixed to a specified color. Because this requires a separate printing from an additional plate, adding one or more specials to a four-color job has serious cost implications, but is justified where large areas of color or colored type are to be used. Special spot colors are specified using the Pantone system, a universal system of color specification.

Type and image

Digital media have given designers increased control over the introduction of type into an image space, to the extent that this has become an accepted norm within many design contexts. The ease with which type can be laid over or reversed out of a photographic image or illustration in turn raises a number of potential problems.

To place type upon any tonally varied background either impairs its legibility overall or creates variations of legibility and contrast, making some letters or words more prominent than others and, at worst, rendering some parts illegible. The widespread practice of attempting to correct this by the introduction of drop-shadow is at best a crude solution to problems that should have been avoided at their source. The loss of legibility associated with variations of background tone may in turn necessitate the use of larger or bolder type than would otherwise be necessary, sacrificing subtlety and flexibility in the design.

Some programs allow the designer to fill the type from an image source. Provided that the typeface is appropriately robust and has sufficient weight, this can be an extremely effective graphic device.

Right A range of basic digital effects applied to type. These digitally mimic the effects of different physical processes and phenomena.

Below Type is positioned at the center of the image, and composed of graduated tints from the same color range.

Bottom An image is used to fill the positive space of the type.

blur

shadow

spin

zoom

warp

Effects

Digital programs offer a wide range of effects that can be applied to type. Many of these are essentially illusionistic, designed to replicate the effects of light. This may involve casting shadow as though the type were raised (drop-shadow), or creating the effect of three-dimensional embossed or recessed letterforms. Effects can replicate reflective surfaces such as chrome or glass, or luminous media, such as neon.

These effects are of varying use to the serious designer and should be used sparingly and with caution; a novelty effect may be as likely to distract the viewer from the message as it is to enhance it. Any effect should be integrated into the overall composition of the design. Illusions of three-dimensionality can be extremely effective in establishing a sense of depth, allowing the designer to organize multiple levels of information.

SPECIAL FINISHES

Designers have at their disposal a range of specialized processes and treatments that can enhance and enliven typographic products. Many of the following processes are not handled in-house by commercial printers but put out to more specialized finishers.

Spot UV varnishes

Varnishes and laminations may be used simply to protect the inked surface, to heighten the richness of color, or to provide a uniformity of gloss or matte texture. Varnish may, however, be more imaginatively used as a graphic medium in itself. Most varnishes are printed using essentially the same press technology as that used for color printing, and can be viewed as a special print run, much as one might view a special or spot color. The varnish may be printed onto the type alone or onto illustrations, or used as a visually independent level of artwork in which some elements are printed in varnish only. Varnishes are available in a wide range of finishes from high gloss to matte, and include colored and metallic variants.

Metallic inks

Wide ranges of metallic inks are available. While the quality of metallic print technology has improved considerably in recent years, it should be kept in mind that metallic inks normally have a fairly flat and granular finish.

Foil blocking

Reflective metallic finishes are best achieved through foil blocking—a relief printing process whereby a very fine layer of pressed metal is fused to the paper surface. Foil blocking can be carried out in a wide range of colored metallic finishes and matte colors, and is frequently combined with an embossing process.

Embossing

Type may be embossed in a number of different ways. Relief processes using both a positive and negative block can be used to create raised type; cushion embossing creates a gently curved relief surface over larger areas. Type can be impressed into a surface using relief-printing processes in combination with either metal foil or inks. Type may be embossed using no color at all—a process described as blind embossing. Relief-printing methods are particularly valuable when printing onto rough-textured materials, because the pressure of the press impresses the type, flattening the paper surface.

Above Silver foil blocking animates a gestural, calligraphic title on this book jacket.

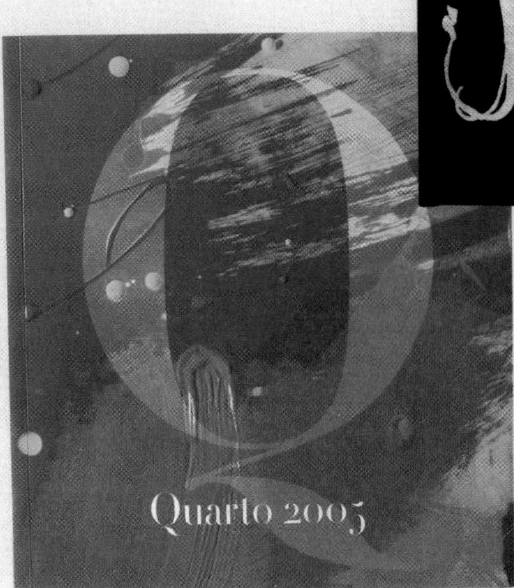

Left Matte laminate, spot varnish, and embossing create a complex interplay of layers and textures on this publishing company's catalog.

Die cutting

Letterforms and other graphic shapes may be cut out of paper or cardboard. In the past, this required the use of complex metal dies; recently, laser technology has allowed for more complex and versatile use of cutout forms.

Screen printing

Designs involving pale opaque printings upon darker paper stocks require special printing processes, because commercial lithographic inks are relatively transparent. Letterpress foil blocking may be used, but, for short print runs, it can be more economical to use screen printing. Screen-printing inks range from extreme transparency to colors with enough body to print vivid, densely opaque colors onto darker backgrounds.

Letter spacing for display type

Display typography is an illustrative, interpretive form that can draw upon a wide range of nuances and typographic effects. The range of possible approaches to the spacing of letters is therefore far broader and more varied than in editorial typography. In general terms, larger sizes of type often benefit from a tightening of letter spacing and leading, while smaller sizes may gain legibility from having the letter spacing and leading increased. The setting of titles and headlines allows the designer to concentrate more attention on individual letter pairs and manual kerning than would be practical across complex documents.

Display typography may employ extremes of spacing for deliberate typographic effect. Type may be set so close as actually to touch or overlap, creating unexpected graphic forms that the viewer traces and decodes. Extremely open letter spacing may be used to create a sense of deliberation and purpose, implying the gravity of the subject by requiring the reader to slow down and savor the information. Both approaches invite the readers' participation rather than dictating their response through "impact."

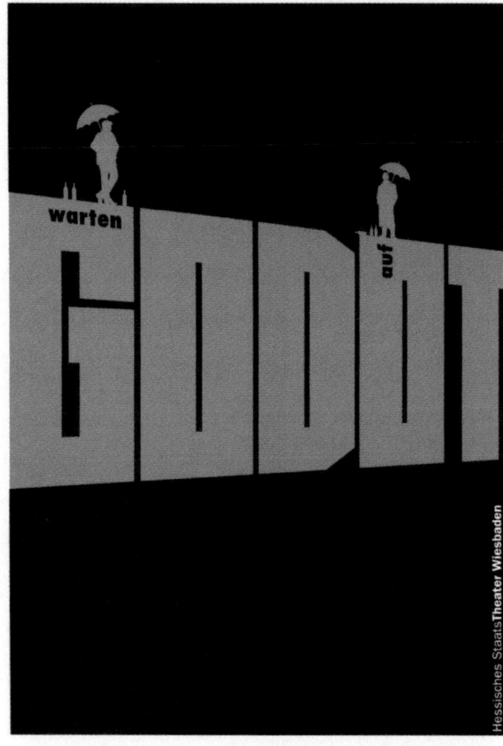

Left The dramatic composition and dimensionalized angle of the type create a sense of monumental scale in this theater poster designed by Günter Rambow.

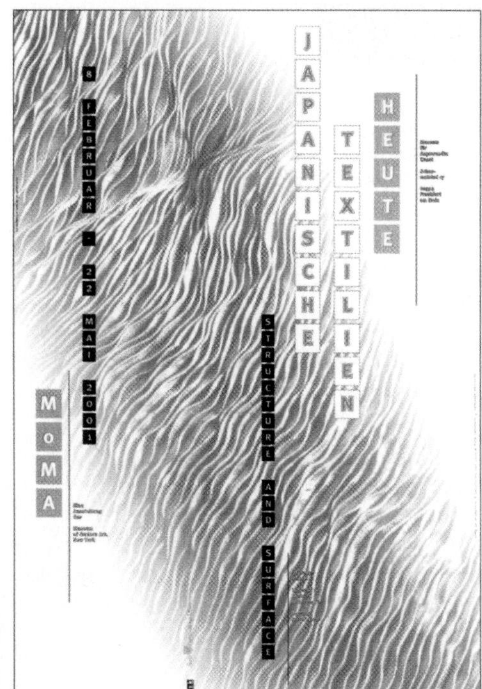

Left The use of a highly legible typeface such as Meta allows designers Büro für Gestaltung to stack the letters vertically without impairing legibility. Placing each letter in a square of the same width prevents the different widths of the letters from disrupting the design.

Many approaches to type that would be inappropriate in text setting can be utilized as positive qualities in display work. Discordant and fragmented forms may be appropriate in the context of the design; irregular spacing may be used to create fractured rhythms, incompatible typefaces may be deliberately juxtaposed, and legibility itself may be purposely reduced or obscured. We should judge the outcomes not by general typographic conventions, but by their effectiveness as an appropriate response to the content.

Grids in display typography

While the structured page grid belongs more specifically to editorial typography, display typography usually involves consideration of the alignments between its elements. Finding a common vertical axis for two or more elements of the design will bring cohesion and visual continuity, allowing us to make visual connections from larger to smaller sizes of type. Such alignments may develop through the design of the layout to form a kind of organic or asymmetrical grid.

The nature of display typography allows for type to be positioned upon more than one axis. This may involve a disciplined use of both horizontal and vertical type, a range of diagonal alignments, or an entirely free-form composition. As well as extending the visual dynamic of a design, the use of more than one axis can be an effective means of differentiating orders of information.

When type is set to a vertical, it is almost always more effective to turn the entire line upon its side than to attempt to stack horizontal letters in a vertical line. The natural variation of letter width creates a vertical line of varying width that is both visually unsatisfactory and difficult to read. If the design absolutely requires the vertical alignment of letters, the typeface should be broad and of substantial weight.

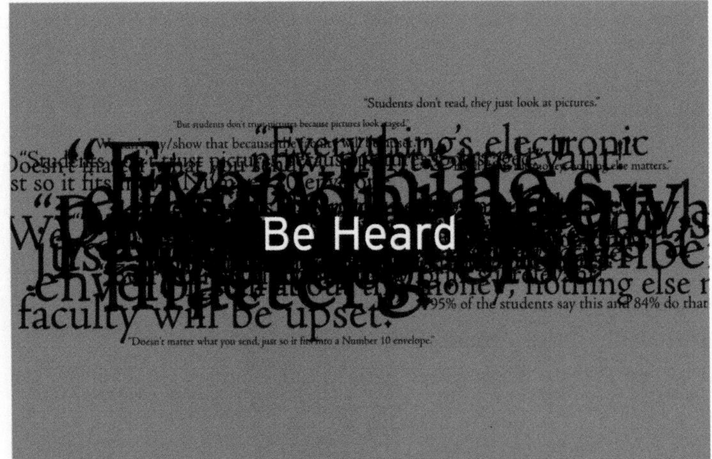

Left The clarity of reversed sans serif type is effectively juxtaposed with the "visual noise" of overlaid serif letters in this self-promotional booklet for design group Robert Rytter & Associates.

Below The strong diagonal emphasis of the abstract calligraphic forms is dramatically offset by the arrangement of information closely aligned to the top-left margin.

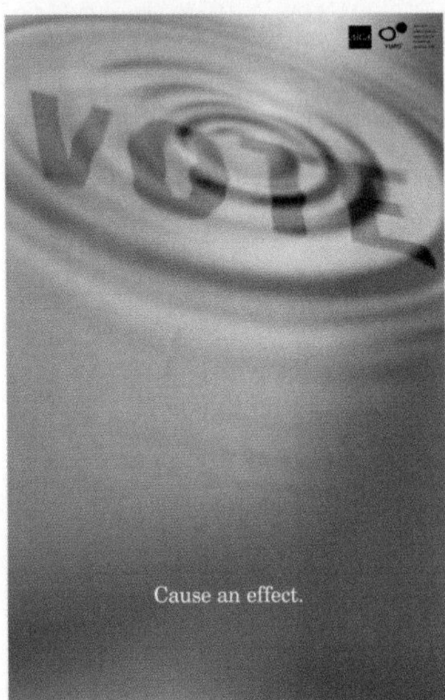

Above A simple phrase is given depth and resonance by its position within a large open space, echoing the visual metaphor of the ripple in this poster by Doyle Partners.

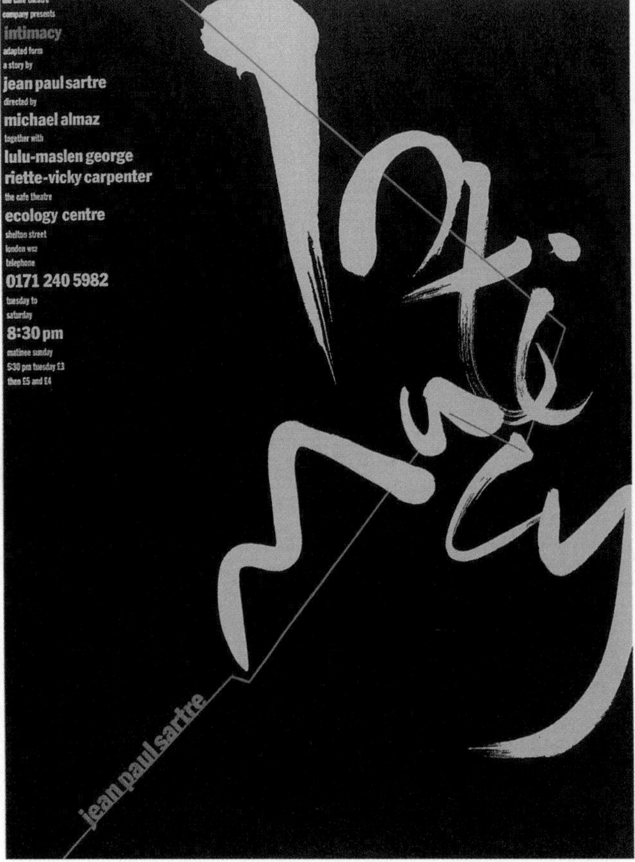

the cafe theatre
company presents
intimacy
jean paul sartre
michael almaz
lulu-maslen george
riette-vicky carpenter
ecology centre
0171 240 5982
8:30 pm
jean paul sartre

EVOKING RESPONSES THROUGH TYPE

Display setting frequently focuses upon the associative values of type, and the manner by which it evokes particular responses. At its simplest, the focus may be on subjective or abstract values: the response to the letterforms themselves (as curvaceous or angular, dominant or reticent, loud or soft, formal or informal, animated or static). More significant, however, is the range of associations type can evoke through reference to period, history, and tradition. Complex subtexts can be embedded in a design through the designer's awareness of cultural context and design history.

Titles themselves may provide starting points for their design, from within the specific shapes created by the words. Experimentation with different groupings and line-breaks will reveal patterns of ascenders and descenders, or other prominent graphic elements, that may be developed toward a setting of the title as a considered graphic unit.

NEW MEDIA TYPOGRAPHY

Applications such as web design, interactive CD-ROM, and any other outcomes designed to be viewed on screen involve certain considerations that are particular to new media. This does not, however, place them outside the broad principles of typographic practice and information design. Issues of legibility, readability, and a logical navigational structure are equally crucial to the screen and the printed page.

The layout may create variations in the alignment between the letterform and the grid of pixels that make up the screen. The process of anti-aliasing is designed to compensate for this loss of clarity, smoothing the contours of the letterform by introducing intermediate tones to selected pixels.

CD-ROM, screen, and broadcast graphics may use any digital typeface, but their clarity upon the screen can vary widely. Certain typefaces have been specifically designed for screen use, and it is best to use these wherever possible, particularly when working at smaller sizes, in order to ensure optimum legibility.

Above Digital effects such as embossing and drop-shadow can be incorporated into type when it is saved as a graphic. This transforms the type into an image that cannot then be edited.

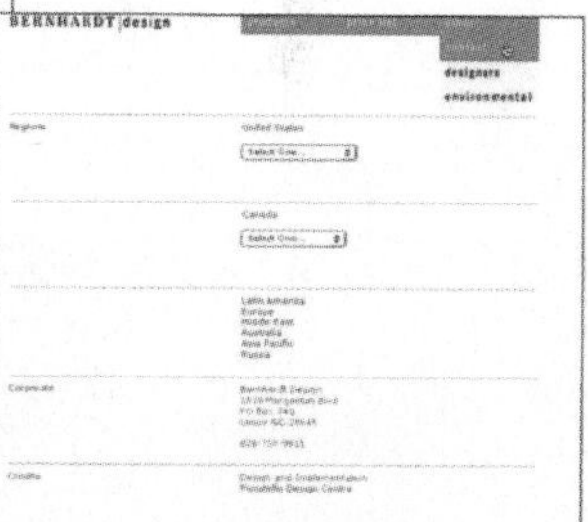

Above & right Intelligent use of negative space focuses the viewer's attention upon key navigation categories, making the use of the site clear and unambiguous (www.bernhardtdesign.com by Piscatello Design Center).

Web design

The design of text for the web raises particular problems for the typographer, and offers less control over the appearance of the final outcome than any other area of graphic reproduction. It remains the case that the text in a web page will appear in the fonts available on the end user's machine, rather than necessarily remaining consistent to the face in which it was designed. This presents the designer with a range of options. The simplest is to use the most widely available fonts for all running text, or to use a preferred font in which the body sizes and proportions correspond reasonably closely to a commonly used default. While it should be possible to embed fonts within the web page,

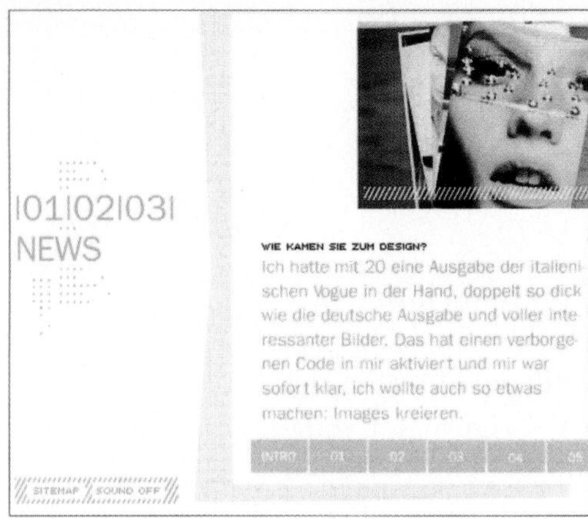

Left & above The design of a web page must take into consideration ease of reading and effective navigation. Intelligent structure and visual interest combine to retain the user's attention. Type is selected for on-screen quality, and navigational elements are clearly identified typographically (www.rocholl-projects.de by KearneyRocholl).

this will have an adverse effect upon download times, and also contravenes copyright. As with other screen-based applications, particular care should be taken at small sizes to ensure that the alignment of the letters with the pixel screen does not compromise or obscure their form. Wherever possible, the designer should use a typeface specifically designed for screen use.

In the design of display graphics for web, the designer can ensure that typographic material retains its intended form by saving headings, titles, and so on as graphics. This allows them to open without significant delay, but they will not be editable. Web type will be viewed upon monitors of varying size and quality, and should always be designed to function effectively at the lowest resolution at which it is likely to be seen. While this may seem to present an unacceptable set of limitations on the designer, and to diminish control over the quality of the final outcome, the best strategy will incorporate these constraints into the overall design rather than working in spite of them.

Below Color-coded pages identify different aspects of a photographer's portfolio, designed on a simple but effective three-column grid (www.dixonphotography.com by Paone Design Associates).

ENVIRONMENTAL TYPOGRAPHY

The design of lettering for the built environment has historically drawn upon different traditions, skills, and media than the design of type for print. Though these histories frequently overlapped or informed one another, the application of lettering to traditional building materials was seen as part of the craft of the stonemason or the signwriter, much as the layout of type was, until relatively recently, seen as the craft of the printer. Digital technology has to some extent brought about convergence of these areas of practice.

Architectural typography

Architectural typography needs to function effectively at scale, to be readable from a range of angles and distances. It must communicate to the moving viewpoint of the pedestrian or motorist, harmonize with the materials and proportions of the building, and reflect the values of both the architect and the institution or organization it houses. Faces designed for print may appear both ill-proportioned and visually crude if they are simply enlarged to the scale necessary for a building or monument. The designer needs to consider the action of light, and the manner in which the letters interact with the building materials. This may include the possibility of three-dimensionality: type that is raised, incised, or recessed. The conditions may require illuminated signage, presenting a wide range of options for type to be lit from within, behind, above, or below.

Opposite left, above & below Three-dimensional relief lettering used in a public art project based upon oral histories, designed by Bettina Furnee.

Left Sans serif type set on a raised circular frame uses the effect of light to provide dimensional depth and integrate the type within the architecture.

Below Lettering by Richard Kindersley carved directly into a brick fascia reflects the particular sensitivity involved in the design of letterforms for architectural scale.

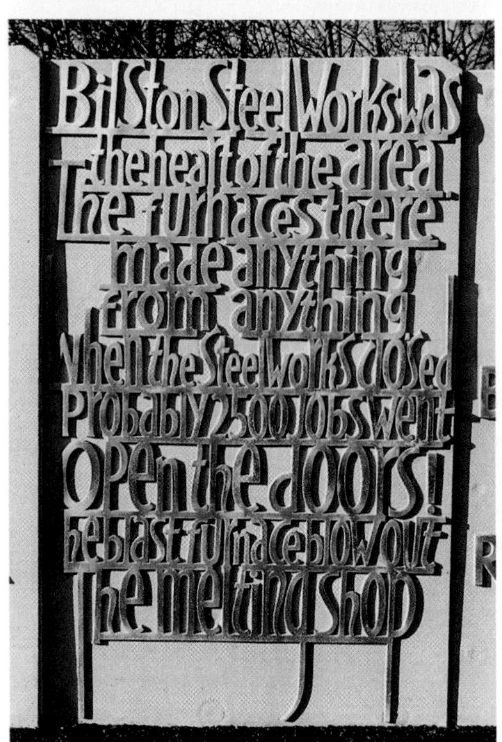

Informational signage

In the context of informational signage, legibility may be not only a matter of design aesthetics but also of life and death. It is therefore in this area that some of the most sustained and objective studies of legibility have taken place. Information on highways, hospitals, and airports may be crucial to safety, and the legibility of the type is therefore paramount.

In particular, the differentiation of letters within the typeface must be explicit, ensuring that no letter or numeral can be confused with any other. The legibility of letters for use in these contexts depends, in particular, upon well-defined counters and junctions.

Words that may be viewed from an angle or while in motion require greater space between characters than words designed to be viewed at a fixed reading distance. Sufficient space must be allowed between the words and any additional graphic forms, such as directional arrows, symbols, or schematic mapping.

Below center A contemporary sans serif type, Parisine, was designed by Jean-François Porchez specifically for the French RATP transit system. It improves significantly upon the Helvetica type previously used in their informational signage.

Below & bottom right Poulin + Morris's environmental graphic and wayfinding sign program for the newly renovated interior space at the New York Public Library for the Performing Arts at the Lincoln Center, consisting of public reading rooms, galleries, auditorium, and preservation lab.

GLOSSARY

Aldine Types derived from the types used by Aldus Manutius from punches by Francesco Griffo at the end of the 15th century.

Alignment The arrangement of lines of continuous text to a fixed margin or axis: flush (ranged), justified, or centered.

Ampersand Glyph used in place of the word "and," derived from contraction of the French *et*.

Application A computer program that performs a specific function, such as layout, image manipulation, and font design.

Arabic numerals The figures 0 through 9, as distinct from Roman numerals.

Ascender The part of the lowercase letter that rises above the x-height.

Assymetrical type Type arranged to multiple margins or alignments, producing an irregular composition on the page.

Baseline The notional horizontal line upon which the base of the letters is positioned.

Bezier A form of curve established by computer-determined control points, used in defining outlines in digital type.

Binary code The basis for digital data, made up of two distinct characters: 0 and 1.

Bit A contraction of "binary" and "digit"; the primary unit of digital information.

Bitmap The image on the monitor in which each pixel is mapped to a specific bit in the computer memory.

Black A term used to denote an extra bold weight of type.

Blackletter Germanic script based upon manuscript forms; variants include Textura, Rotunda, Bastarda, and Fraktur.

Bleed Any part of a design that extends beyond the cropped edge of the page.

Body Originally the metal block on which the print surface of the type letter was positioned, the body has come to denote the overall area within which each digital letter or glyph is contained.

Body size The size of type, expressed using the point system.

Body type Type of a size suitable for the setting of continuous text, normally between 6 and 14 points.

Bold The heavier weight variant of a regular typeface; also demi bold, ultra bold.

Borders Solid, multiple, or broken lines used to separate, enclose, or underline type. Borders may be composed of repeat typographic glyphs or specified as continuous linear forms.

Bracketing The curve from the letter stem or main stroke to the serif. Serifs that join at a sharp angle are described as unbracketed.

Calligraphic type Type based upon hand-rendered script letterforms.

Caps A common abbreviation of capital or uppercase letters.

Case The tray or drawer containing metal type that gave the name to upper and lowercase letters.

Casting Typesetting by the mechanical casting of lines of type or individual letters from molten metal. See also hand casting.

Centered Lines of type set with equal ragged margins left and right, to a central axis.

Chapter head Title and/or number set on the opening page of a chapter.

Chase Rectangular metal frame into which hand-set type and illustrations are locked for printing.

Cicero A European unit of measurement roughly equivalent to the pica.

Composition A traditional term for the arrangement and assembly of type for print.

Condensed Narrow type, normally a reduced variant of a regular width.

Copy The original raw text to be typeset.

Counter The enclosed spaces within letters, such as the bowls of b, p, and o.

Crosshead A heading that crosses more than one column of text.

Cursive Sloped type, normally based upon handwriting but not linked.

Dagger/double dagger Additional footnote reference marks, used in a similar manner to asterisks.

Descender The descending stroke, tail, or loop of a lowercase letter that falls below the baseline.

Didot A historic European system of point measurement.

Display type Type designed for use at larger sizes for titling and headlining. Display types may not contain all the glyphs or font variants found in a text face.

Drop-cap An initial display letter of larger size than the text into which it is set.

Egyptian Originally a term used to denote the antique qualities of sans serif, the term Egyptian was later adopted to denote an unbracketed slab serif.

Ellipsis Three dots used to indicate an omission.

Em A square measure of a width equal to the body height of the type, also described as an em-quad in metal setting.

Em-dash A dash of one em in width.

Em-space Intercharacter space of one em in width.

En A measure of width equal to half the body height of the type.

En-dash A dash of one en in width.

En-space Intercharacter space of one en in width.

Extended Wide type, normally a wider variant of a regular width. Also described as expanded.

Face The print surface of metal type, and the style of that form: the typeface.

Family A group of related typefaces, sometimes including condensed and extended versions, titling sizes, and additional alphabets.

Film setting Photosetting onto photographic film or paper for reproduction.

Flush The alignment of type to a single straight margin, also known as ranged.

Folios The name traditionally given to page numbers.

Font/fount A full set of characters of one particular typeface in one style.

Foot The base of the letterform, which normally sits upon the baseline.

Foundry type Metal type cast for hand setting and repeated use.

Fraktur Broken script; a form of Blackletter.

Galley A metal tray in which metal type was held prior to locking in chases for printing.

Galley proofs Type set from metal or photosetting, produced for checking prior to final assembly.

Glyph Term used to describe each graphic form within a digital font, including letters, punctuation, ligatures, and diacritics.

Gothic A term variously used to describe Blackletter types in Europe and sans serifs in the US.

Grid The arrangement of common vertical and horizontal rules that govern the positioning of type and illustrations on the page.

Grotesque Term used in Britain for the description of early sans serif typefaces. See also Gothic.

Hairline A term for a fine line, referring both to the finest available weight of rule and the fine serifs of Didone types.

Hand casting The casting by hand of individual letters of type from matrices.

H&J A common abbreviation for hyphenation and justification: the adjustment and specification of hyphenation and word spacing for justified type.

Hanging indent Style in which the first line of a paragraph is set outside the margin used for the remainder of the copy. Also called an exdent.

Hot metal The mechanical casting of type from molten metal.

Humanist Early types, also known as Venetian, in which the roman letterform replaces the Textura.

Humanist Sans Sans serif types based upon classical proportions.

Hung initial Display initial letter set outside the margin used for the remainder of the copy.

Imposition The arrangement of multiple pages for commercial printing from large plates.

Incunabula A term used for examples of early printing, particularly books from the 15th century.

Indent The practice of indicating the beginning of a new paragraph by insetting the first word, frequently by an em-space.

Initial Opening letter of a chapter or paragraph, sometimes set in a larger contrasting face for decoration or emphasis.

Italic Sloping letters, originally typefaces based upon Renaissance handwritten forms, later paired with roman fonts.

Justification The adjustment of word space to create regular left and right margins in running text.

Kern The part of a metal letter that overhangs the body, typically the loop of the f.

Kerning The adjustment of space between individual characters.

Kern pairs In-built adjustment to the spacing of problematic letter pairs, incorporated in the design of the font.

Latin Letterforms derived from Roman sources.

Latin script The Western European alphabet.

Leading The space between lines of type, specified as the measurement in points from one baseline to the next.

Letterpress Relief printing from metal or wood types; the principal method of printing from the 15th to the mid-20th century.

Letter spacing The amount of space between letters in a text, adjusted unilaterally rather than individually.

Ligature A compound form combining two letters to overcome visual problems of overhanging letters, such as occur in the letter pairs fi and fl.

Linotype A mechanical composition system designed to cast whole lines, or slugs, of metal type.

Lithography Printing process using chemical separation to create inked areas on a metal plate or stone. See also offset lithography.

Lowercase The small letters derived from minuscule written forms, as distinct from the capital uppercase letters.

Majuscule The handwritten or calligraphic basis for uppercase letters.

Margin The negative space between the type and the page edge. The term margin is also used to describe the line that defines the outer edge of the type area.

Matrix The mold from which metal type was cast, created by the impression made from a steel punch. Also used to describe photographic negative images of type used in photosetting.

Measure The length of a line or column of type.

Minuscule The handwritten or calligraphic basis for lowercase letters.

Modern Term used to describe the Didone faces of the late 18th century.

Monotype Mechanical composition system designed to cast each letter as a separate unit or sort.

Non-lining figures Also known as old-style figures, non-lining figures correspond to the lowercase letters and have ascenders and descenders, rather than being aligned to the height of the capitals.

Oblique Characters slanted to the right. The term oblique is sometimes used to distinguish sloped letters from true cursive or italic forms.

Offset lithography Commercial printing from a photosensitized lithographic plate. The printed areas are created by a process of chemical separation and transferred (offset) to a printing roller.

OpenType A new font format based upon the Unicode standard and allowing for dramatically increased glyph sets.

Outline face Typeface with only outline printing.

Pagination The numbering of pages in consecutive order.

Paragraph mark The use of a typographic element or symbol to indicate the beginning of a new paragraph.

Photosetting The setting of type by mechanically exposing photographic paper or film to a light projected through a sequence of letterforms.

Pica Also known as a pica em: a horizontal measure of 12 points.

Pixel An abbreviation of "picture element," used to describe a single square of the computer screen.

Point Unit of typographic measurement used to define the size of type and leading. One point equals 1/72 of an inch.

PostScript A page description language developed by Adobe in 1983.

Printer font The digital font containing the information that determines the form of the printed letter.

Punch The original forms from which the casting matrices were struck. Originally cut in steel by hand, punches were created mechanically from the late 19th century.

Ragged Term used to describe the irregular margin created by unjustified or flush type.

Ranged See flush.

Recto The right-hand page of a page spread. Page 1 and subsequent odd-numbered folios always fall on the recto page.

Resolution The accuracy of visual definition, determined by the number of pixels on either monitor or output device.

Reversed copy Type set to print out wrong-reading.

Reversed type Type set to read in white or a lighter color out of a printed surround.

Roman Upright letterform as distinct from italic, or the regular weight as distinct from the bold. Also used to describe the serif letter.

Romanesque Based upon the roman form of the Humanist bookhand, as distinct from the Textura forms of Blackletter.

Roman numerals Numerals set using the Roman system based on the use of I, V, L, X, C.

Rules Printed lines used to decorate or differentiate areas of type and image. Rules may be single, double, or broken.

Running head Repeated title and chapter heading occurring on each page of a book.

Running text Text set as a continuous sequence of words.

Sans serif Type without serifs; also variously described as Grotesque or Gothic.

Screen font The digital font that determines the display of type on the screen. Screen fonts are paired with printer fonts that contain more detailed information.

Script The term script is used to describe different alphabets such as Latin, Cyrillic, Greek, or Hebrew, particularly where these are contained within a single type family.

Script typefaces Script types are based upon handwritten letterforms that may be either formal or informal. The term script usually denotes linked letters rather than unlinked cursive letters.

Serif The broadening or triangular forms at the terminals of letters, derived from Roman inscriptional lettering.

Set width The width of the body of the letter.

Side bearing The space at either side of the letter, on the body of metal types or in the specification of digital fonts.

Slab serif Broad serifs with a squared end, either unbracketed or bracketed.

Slugs Solid lines of type cast by the Linotype mechanical composition system.

Small caps The use of a smaller size of capital forms in place of lowercase. Properly size-adjusted small capitals are a feature of expert set fonts.

Sorts Originally the term for individual pieces of cast type; sorts was later used to describe special characters outside the standard alphabet, such as symbols and dingbats.

Swash Decorative letters with long flourishes, tails, and ascenders. Usually produced as a variant or alternate font.

Text The main body of continuous copy on the page, as distinct from titling and headings.

Text typeface Typeface suitable for setting continuous text at sizes from 6 to 14 points.

Textura A form of Blackletter characterized by condensed lowercase letters and angular form.

Tiff Tagged image file: a method of storing images as bitmaps.

Tracking A term used to describe general letter spacing of a text or sentence (as distinct from individual kerning adjustments).

Transitional A category of type marking the transition from the Old Style or Garalde forms to the Modern or Didone.

TrueType A page description language introduced for use on the Macintosh computer.

Typeface A specific design of type available in a range of sizes. A text typeface customarily includes a number of fonts, including bold, italic, and bold italic.

U&lc An abbreviation of upper and lowercase.

Unicode An international character set proposed in 1997 to contain all the world's languages. The computer code system forms the basis for OpenType.

Unit A variable measurement of width based upon the division of the em into equal increments to describe the widths of letters, side bearings, and word spacing. Current professional systems use increments of a thousand units to the em.

Unit value The width of individual characters expressed in units.

Unjustified type Type in which the word spacing has not been adjusted to produce even margins. See also flush.

Uppercase The capital letter forms in a font.

Venetian See Humanist.

Verso The left-hand page, facing the recto. Page 2 and subsequent even-numbered folios always fall on the verso page.

Vox classification System for classifying typefaces devised in 1954 by Maximillien Vox.

Weight The density and stroke width of the letters within a typeface. Typefaces customarily include a bold weight and may include additional light, black, or ultra bold fonts.

Widow An unacceptably short line at the end of a column or paragraph.

Word spacing The space between words, ideally equivalent to the width of a lowercase i.

Wrong-reading Type reading in reverse mirror image, as found on punches, metal type, or negatives.

X-height The height of lowercase letters within a typeface, specifically the height of the lowercase x.

Index*

*Page numbers in italics refer to illustrations

C

D

E

F

G

H

I

J

K

L

M

N

O

P

Q

R

S

T

U

V

W

Y

Z

ITT TECHNICAL INSTITUTE-CANTON
30002031

ABOUT THE SHOPFLOOR SERIES

Put powerful and proven improvement tools in the hands of your entire workforce!

Progressive shopfloor improvement techniques are imperative for manufacturers who want to stay competitive and to achieve world class excellence. And it's the comprehensive education of all shopfloor workers that ensures full participation and success when implementing new programs. The Shopfloor Series books make practical information accessible to everyone by presenting major concepts and tools in simple, clear language and at a reading level that has been adjusted for operators by skilled instructional designers. One main idea is presented every two to four pages so that the book can be picked up and put down easily. Each chapter begins with an overview and ends with a summary section. Helpful illustrations are used throughout.

Books currently in the Shopfloor Series include:

TPM for America

What It Is and Why You Need It

Herbert R. Steinbacher and Norma L. Steinbacher

As much as 15 to 40 percent of manufacturing costs are attributable to maintenance. With a fully implemented TPM program, your company can eradicate all but a fraction of these costs. Co-written by an American TPM practitioner and an experienced educator, this book gives a convincing account of why American companies must adopt TPM if they are to successfully compete in world markets. Includes examples from leading American companies showing how TPM has changed them into more efficient and productive organizations.
ISBN 1-56327-044-7 / 169 pages / $25.00 / Order TPMAM-B241

Visual Control Systems

Nikkan Kogyo Shimbun (ed.)

Every day, progressive companies all over the world are making manufacturing improvements that profoundly impact productivity, quality, and lead time. Case studies of the most innovative visual control systems in Japanese companies have been gathered, translated, and compiled in this notebook. No other source provides more insightful information on recent developments in Japanese manufacturing technology. Plant managers, VPs of operations, and CEOs with little spare time need a concise and timely means of staying informed. Here's a gold mine of ideas for reducing costs and delivery times and improving quality.
ISBN 1-56327-143-5 / 189 pages / $30.00 / Order VCSP-B241

The Visual Factory

Building Participation Through Shared Information

Michel Greif

If you're aware of the tremendous improvements achieved in productivity and quality as a result of employee involvement, then you'll appreciate the great value of creating a visual factory. This book shows how visual management can make the factory a place where workers and supervisors freely communicate and take improvement action. It details how to develop meeting and communication areas, communicate work standards and instructions, use visual production controls such as kanban, and make goals and progress visible. Includes more than 200 diagrams and photos.
ISBN 0-915299-67-4 / 305 pages / $55.00 / Order VFAC-B241

Kaizen for Quick Changeover

Going Beyond SMED

Kenichi Sekine and Keisuke Arai

Especially useful for manufacturing managers and engineers, this book describes exactly how to achieve faster changeover. Picking up where Shingo's SMED book left off, you'll learn he process even further to reduce changeover time and optimize staffing at the same time.
ISBN 0-915299-38-0 / 315 pages / $75.00 / Order KAIZEN-B241

Kanban and Just-In-Time at Toyota

Management Begins at the Workplace

Japan Management Association / Translated by David J. Lu

Toyota's world-renowned success proves that with kanban, the Just-In-Time production system (JIT) makes most other manufacturing practices obsolete. This simple but powerful classic is based on seminars given by JIT creator Taiichi Ohno to introduce Toyota's own supplier companies to JIT. It shows how to implement the world's most efficient production system. A clear and complete introduction.
ISBN 0-915299-48-8 / 211 pages / $45.00 / Order KAN-B241

Manufacturing Strategy

How to Formulate and Implement a Winning Plan

John Miltenburg

This book offers a step-by-step method for creating a strategic manufacturing plan. The key tool is a multidimensional worksheet that links the competitive analysis to manufacturing outputs, the seven basic production systems, the levels of capability and the levers for moving to a higher level. The author presents each element of the worksheet and shows you how to link them to create an integrated strategy and implementation plan. By identifying the appropriate production system for your business, you can determine what output you can expect from manufacturing, how to improve outputs, and how to change to more optimal production systems as your business needs change.
ISBN 1-56327-071-4 / 391 pages / $45.00 / Order MANST-B241

Poka-Yoke

Improving Product Quality by Preventing Defects

Nikkan Kogyo Shimbun Ltd. and Factory Magazine (ed.)

If your goal is 100 percent zero defects, here is the book for you—a completely illustrated guide to poka-yoke (mistake-proofing) for supervisors and shop-floor workers. Many poka-yoke devices come from line workers and are implemented with the help of engineering staff. The result is better product quality—and greater participation by workers in efforts to improve rocesses, your products, and your company as a whole.
ISBN 0-915299-31-3 / 295 pages / $65.00 / Order IPOKA-B241

A Revolution in Manufacturing

The SMED System

Shigeo Shingo

The heart of JIT is quick changeover methods. Dr. Shingo, inventor of the Single-Minute Exchange of Die (SMED) system for Toyota, shows you how to reduce your changeovers by an average of 98 percent! By applying Shingo's techniques, you'll see rapid improvements (lead time reduced from weeks to days, lower inventory and warehousing costs) that will improve quality, productivity, and profits.
ISBN 0-915299-03-8 / 383 pages / $75.00 / Order SMED-B241

Corporate Diagnosis

Setting the Global Standard for Excellence

Thomas L. Jackson with Constance E. Dyer

All too often, strategic planning neglects an essential first step and final step-diagnosis of the organization's current state. What's required is a systematic review of the critical factors in organizational learning and growth, factors that require monitoring, measurement, and management to ensure that your company competes successfully. This executive workbook provides a step-by-step method for diagnosing an organization's strategic health and measuring its overall competitiveness against world class standards. With checklists, charts, and detailed explanations, Corporate Diagnosis is a practical instruction manual. The pillars of Jackson's diagnostic system are strategy, structure, and capability. Detailed diagnostic questions in each area are provided as guidelines for developing your own self-assessment survey.
ISBN 1-56327-086-2 / 115 pages / $65.00 / Order CDIAG-B241

Implementing a Lean Management System

Thomas L. Jackson with Karen R. Jones

Does your company think and act ahead of technological change, ahead of the customer, and ahead of the competition? Thinking strategically requires a company to face these questions with a clear future image of itself. Implementing a Lean Management System lays out a comprehensive management system for aligning the firm's vision of the future with market realities. Based on hoshin management, the Japanese strategic planning method used by top managers for driving TQM throughout an organization, Lean Management is about deploying vision, strategy, and policy to all levels of daily activity. It is an eminently practical methodology emerging out of the implementation of continuous improvement methods and employee involvement. The key tools of this book build on multiskilling, the knowledge of the worker, and an understanding of the role of the new lean manufacturer.
ISBN 1-56327-085-4 / 182 pages / $65.00 / Order ILMS-B241

Introduction to TPM

Total Productive Maintenance

Seiichi Nakajima

Total Productive Maintenance (TPM) combines preventive maintenance with Japanese concepts of total quality control (TQC) and total employee involvement (TEI). The result is a new system for equipment maintenance that optimizes effectiveness, eliminates breakdowns, and promotes autonomous operator maintenance through day-to-day activities. Since it was first introduced in Japan, TPM has caused a worldwide revolution in plant maintenance. Here are the steps involved in TPM and case examples from top Japanese plants.
ISBN 0-915299-23-2 / 149 pages / $45.00 / Order ITPM-B241

JIT Factory Revolution

A Pictorial Guide to Factory Design of the Future

Hiroyuki Hirano

The first encyclopedic picture-book of Just-In-Time, using photos and diagrams to show exactly how JIT looks and functions in production and assembly plants. Unprecedented behind-the-scenes look at multi-process handling, cell technology, quick changeovers, kanban, andon, and other visual control systems. See why a picture is worth a thousand words.
ISBN 0-915299-44-5 / 218 pages / $50.00 / Order JITFAC-B241

Books from Productivity, Inc.

Productivity, Inc. publishes books that empower individuals and companies to achieve excellence in quality, productivity, and the creative involvement of all employees. Through steadfast efforts to support the vision and strategy of continuous improvement, Productivity delivers today's leading-edge tools and techniques gathered directly from industry leaders around the world.

The 5S System:
Workplace Organization and Standardization (video)

Tel-A-Train and the Productivity Development Team (eds.)

5S is a method front-line workers can really use to improve workplace safety, reduce waste, simplify work processes, improve equipment maintenance and troubleshooting, and ensure product quality. It's the basis for any on-the-floor improvement activity. Now, using learn-while-doing training techniques, workshop teams can follow this step-by-step video training at their own pace, and implement 5S in their own target area. This complete video training program introduces you to each of the 5S activities and its rationale, and powerfully leads your team through implementation.
Includes seven video tapes (90 min. total), facilitator's guide, and participant's guide.
$1,995.00 / Order 5SV7-B241
Introductory tape only / $495.00 / Order 5SV1-B241

20 Keys to Workplace Improvement

Iwao Kobayashi

This easy-to-read introduction to the "20 keys" system presents an integrated approach to assessing and improving your company's competitive level. The book focuses on systematic improvement through five levels of achievement in such primary areas as industrial housekeeping, small group activities, quick changeover techniques, equipment maintenance, and computerization. A scoring guide is included, along with information to help plan a strategy for your company's world class improvement effort.
ISBN 0-915299-61-5 / 252 pages / $45.00 / Order 20KEYS-B241

Becoming Lean
Inside Stories of U.S. Manufacturers

Jeffrey Liker

Most other books on lean management focus on technical methods and offer a picture of what a lean system should look like. Some provide snapshots of before and after. This is the first book to provide technical descriptions of successful solutions and performance improvements. The first book to include powerful first-hand accounts of the complete process of change, its impact on the entire organization, and the rewards and benefits of becoming lean. At the heart of this book you will find the stories of American manufacturers who have successfully implemented lean methods. Authors offer personalized accounts of their organization's lean transformation, including struggles and successes, frustrations and surprises. Now you have a unique opportunity to go inside their implementation process to see what worked, what didn't, and why. Many of these executives and managers who led the charge to becoming lean in their organizations tell their stories here for the first time!
ISBN 1-56327-173-7 / 350 pages / $35.00 / Order LEAN-241

Cover images: *Deborah Doubting* by Thomas Barron, *Boston* by George Herman, *Pinks, Series 2, #7* by Atoinette M. Winters.

Taken from:

A Design Manual, Fourth Edition
by Shirl Brainard

Published by Pearson Prentice Hall
Upper Saddle River, New Jersey 07458

The Complete Typographer, Second Edition
by Will Hill

Published by Pearson Prentice Hall

Photoshop® Classic Effects
by Scott Kelby

Published by Peachpit Press
A division of Pearson Education
Berkeley, California 94710

This special edition is published in cooperation with Pearson Custom Publishing.

Printed in the United States of America

10 9 8 7 6 5 4 3 2 1

ISBN 0-536-35322-0

2006420358

EM

Please visit our web site at *www.pearsoncustom.com*

PEARSON CUSTOM PUBLISHING
75 Arlington Street, Suite 300, Boston, MA 02116
A Pearson Education Company

Visual
DESIGN THEORY

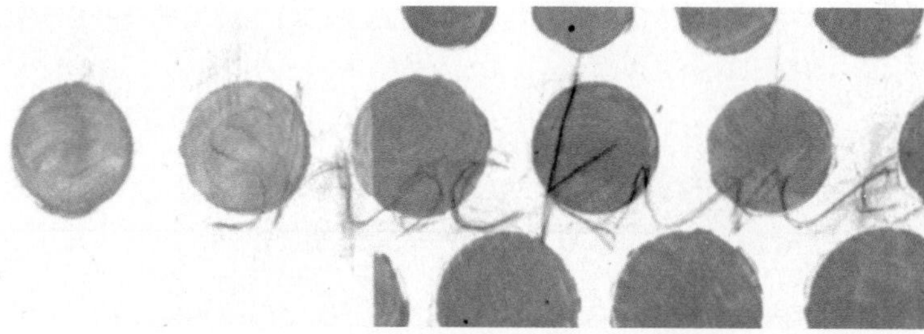

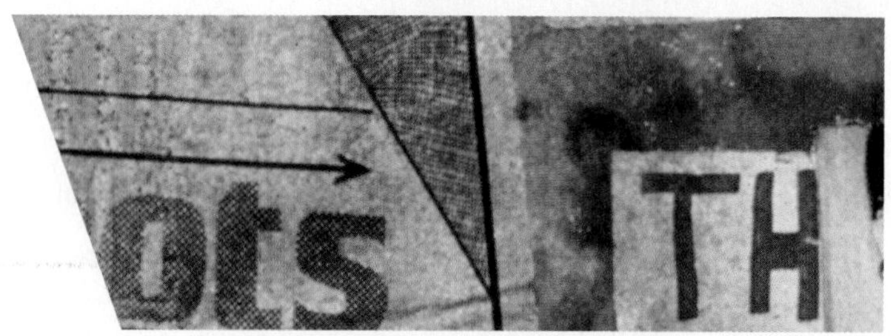

Taken from:

A Design Manual, Fourth Edition
by Shirl Brainard

The Complete Typographer, Second Edition
by Will Hill

Photoshop® Classic Effects
by Scott Kelby

CHAPTER FIVE

Screening and Assessment 123

With M. J. LaMontagne

CHAPTER SIX

Natural Environments for Infants and Toddlers and Preparing for Transitions 157

CHAPTER NINE

Models of Collaboration for Early Intervention: Laying the Groundwork 259

Virginia Buysse and Patricia W. Wesley

CHAPTER TEN

FOREWORD

Working with and caring for infants and toddlers is different from working with and caring for preschoolers. This fact has been obvious for years to early childhood professionals, but its implications still seem to elude the public and many operators of early child care programs. Recent research provides compelling evidence that the quality of child care programs for infants and toddlers is generally poorer than that of child care programs for preschoolers. This gap reflects in part a lack of societal commitment to our youngest citizens, in part a belief that what happens to an infant is not really so important in the grand scheme of things, and in part a lack of knowledge about what constitutes appropriate caregiving for infants and toddlers.

When infants and toddlers have or are at risk for disabilities, working with and caring for them poses an even more complex set of challenges. Professionals entering the field who want to work with very young children with disabilities need a broad range of exposure to topics as well as specific skills if they are to be adequately prepared. In this text, Patricia M. Blasco has identified much of the complexity underlying infant intervention programs and has presented this information in a readable and understandable fashion.

First, the text recognizes that professionals need a fundamental grounding in normal infant development. However, this is not the traditional view of development in terms of the attainment of specific milestones, but rather a portrayal of development that captures its interactive nature and the underlying goals that the infant is trying to achieve as he or she progresses through these milestones. Second, the text acknowledges the complex and multiple settings in which infants are cared for and in which services are provided. Hospitals, homes, and child care centers are probably the most common settings, and the roles that professionals will play in each setting will differ considerably. Third, the text emphasizes the importance of research in the biological realm, and that an understanding of both behavior and biology is essential in order to design appropriate interventions. Finally, the text establishes the importance of intervention in the context of families and family caregiving.

Throughout the text, Dr. Blasco has provided numerous examples of situations or events that help to bring points to life. Though brief, these "snapshots" give us insights into the unique experiences of children, families, and infants as they grow, live, and interact with various service systems. They show us the very real challenges faced by both families and professionals and remind us of the importance of an early intervention system that is both comprehensive and personal.

No single text will be sufficient to prepare individuals for work with infants and their parents. These skills ultimately will need to be developed and refined in the context of ongoing relationships and experiences. The present text, however, provides the necessary foundation in both information and insights into the world of practice. Blasco's efforts are a real contribution to the field and should help ensure that the next generation of practitioners is ready for the inevitable challenges it will face.

Don Bailey

PREFACE

The inspiration and motivation for this book came from my years of work with bright, competent service providers who for a variety of reasons return to pursue their education in graduate school. We were engaged in a mutual learning experience as we tried to understand the many new issues and trends in working with very young children and their families. In teaching these students, I was often frustrated by the lack of a teaching textbook that adequately linked research and practice in the field of early services and intervention.

This text combines a firm theoretical/philosophical orientation to both normal and atypical development of infants and toddlers with practical ideas for teaching and working with families. I worked with several assumptions while preparing this book:

- Service providers need a firm foundation in typical child development before they can understand and develop programs for children who have unique needs.
- Family members must be acknowledged as partners in making decisions about all aspects of their children's education
- Sensitivity to diversity must be addressed in all aspects of early intervention (e.g., referral, service delivery, curriculum, and evaluation).
- Children with disabilities are best served in their natural environments.
- A team, including family members and service providers, is jointly responsible for designing and implementing services for young children with disabilities.
- Ethical standards must be upheld and maintained by the team and related service providers.
- Service providers must be advocates for children and their families.

Many graduate students in the field of early childhood intervention come from a variety of backgrounds, including education, special education, nursing, occupational and physical therapy, and treatment of communication disorders. Many of these professionals have been prepared within the limited scope of their fields and often feel the need to expand their general knowledge about infants, toddlers, and families.

Service providers work in a variety of settings as team members, but dwindling resources can affect the ability of the team to function appropriately. Service providers may need to engage in more role releasing and job sharing. Textbooks currently available tend to represent the literature from one or two disciplines, but rarely include work from all applied fields. This approach makes it difficult for students to understand the underlying premises that guide each discipline. By reflecting more than one philosophical approach, this text offers students the opportunity to think critically about practices and to make decisions regarding appropriate interventions.

This book was written to integrate research with actual practice in the field of early intervention. In my classes, students would challenge me by asking questions such as, "We know what mastery motivation is, but how do we encourage it on a home visit?" In this text, I answer this and similar questions.

EARLY INTERVENTION SERVICES

The focus of this book is on providing services to infants and toddlers with disabilities and their families. I deliberately introduce the term *early intervention services* because of the multiple meanings of *early intervention* in today's society. For example, it has also been used to describe interventions for young, first-time offenders in our penal system. Furthermore, although early childhood services are available for children from birth to age eight, the focus of this textbook is on birth to age three. In textbooks that span the period from birth to age eight, there tends to be greater emphasis on the later years, and the information on birth to age three is not represented in depth across the many disciplines serving young children and their families. In addition, most textbooks continue to divide chapters according to developmental domains of early childhood (e.g., cognitive, social-emotional, motor). But the organization of this text follows the currently recommended practice of teaching across domains to enhance the holistic development of the child rather than concentrate on isolated skills.

CHAPTER ORGANIZATION

The first chapter presents a historical perspective on the programs serving young children that formed the present framework for service delivery. In this chapter, a family-centered approach to services is emphasized. Chapters 2 through 4 examine development from prebirth through year three. These chapters discuss typical development as well as the major disabilities that are often diagnosed during those years. The remaining chapters focus more directly on service delivery. Chapter 5 explores screening and assessment for infants and toddlers with disabilities. The importance of understanding standardized assessment protocols and methods of reliability and validity is underscored. This chapter highlights the current trend toward naturalistic and observational methods of gathering data. Chapter 6 addresses service delivery for young children in the natural environment. Chapter 7 considers strategies for teaching along with the curriculum guidelines currently used in the field of early intervention. Chapter 8 focuses on the medical issues prevalent among infants and young children who are referred for services. Chapter 9 discusses models of collaboration for service providers working in many different agencies. Chapter 10 addresses the use of assistive technology for young children with disabilities.

ACKNOWLEDGMENTS

I would like to thank all the students who have helped with this book through their ideas and insights into early intervention practices, particularly Asha Lateef Williams, Tara Layne, and Nigel Pierce. Many of these students were graduate students at the University of St. Thomas in St. Paul, Minnesota, as well as students at Bowie State University in Bowie, Maryland. I would also like to acknowledge the following reviewers: Virginia Buysse, University of North Carolina at Chapel Hill; Amy G. Dell, Trenton State College; Rebecca R. Fewell, University of Miami School of Medicine; Marie F. Fritz, Indiana State University; and Phillip L. Safford, Case Western Reserve University.

In addition, I would like to thank Don Bailey for his willingness to write the foreword and Sharon Walsh for her assistance with Part C of IDEA.

Some of the photographs in this text were contributed by Dan Grogan and Deborah Kravik. Many thanks.

My appreciation goes to Kimberly Brown, Danielle King, Naomi Mimnaugh, Halili Thompson, and A. Tasa Lehman from Portland State University for their assistance with typing the multiple revisions to this book. I would also like to thank my colleagues who patiently waited for this book to be completed after two cross-continental moves by the author. Thanks also to Deborah Brown of Allyn and Bacon and Joe Barron of P. M. Gordon Associates for shepherding the manuscript through production.

Finally I would like to thank my children, Margaret and Peter, who were my most important focus of attention for the past eight years, and my husband, Peter, whose support, in addition to his writing and editing, was instrumental in the completion of this book.

CHAPTER ONE

AN EVOLUTIONARY PERSPECTIVE ON EARLY SERVICES

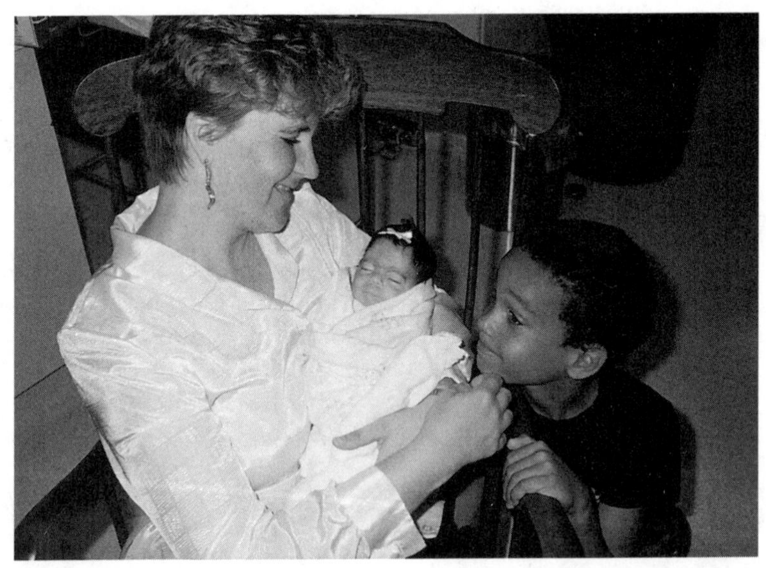

OBJECTIVES

- To provide a philosophical framework of early education and services for young children from birth to age three and their families
- To provide an understanding of the evolution of family-guided services for young children from birth to age three
- To provide insight into the response of families experiencing the birth and recent diagnosis of a child with a disability
- To describe the Individualized Family Service Plan (IFSP) through the experiences of one family
- To describe service coordination and the importance of coordinating services across disciplines
- To view early intervention within an ecological framework
- To discuss the efficacy of early intervention services
- To discuss the future of early intervention services

PHILOSOPHICAL FRAMEWORK

Many authors will argue that there are inherent philosophical differences between early childhood education and early childhood special education, but both fields share a common origin: the pursuit of better education for all young children. Early childhood education in this country can be traced to European roots. There are many people who helped shape the future of early childhood education, and a comprehensive review of all contributors is beyond the scope of this book. However, contributions of several key persons will be discussed.

In the eighteenth century the French philosopher Jean-Jacques Rousseau (1712–1778) argued that young children would benefit from an integrated curriculum that enhanced all the natural senses. He also believed children learned differently from adults by experiencing developmental stages (Essa, 1999).

Rousseau in turn influenced Friedrich Froebel, who in the early 1800s developed the concept of a kindergarten or "children's garden," where children could play and develop under the supervision of nurturing adults, an idea that forms the basis for recommended practices in early childhood today. As Froebel's beliefs became a part of the practice in American kindergartens, new voices argued for a more progressive approach to education led by John Dewey (1859–1952) and his colleagues. Early educators such as Dewey believed that children learned through both intrinsic motivation from within themselves and external motivation from the environment. Dewey's progressive approach to education continues to be reflected today through recommended practices by organizations such as the National Association for the Education of Young Children (NAEYC) and the Division for Early Childhood (DEC). His belief in the tandem process of intrinsic and external motivation is echoed in the works of Jean Piaget (1896–1980) and Lev Vygotsky (1896–1934).

Maria Montessori (1870–1952) was the first Italian woman to receive a doctorate in medicine. She was primarily interested in children and influenced by the work of Jean-Marc-Gaspard Itard and his student, Edouard Séguin. Both of these men believed that children learn through the senses. Their seminal work, *The Wild Boy of Aveyron,* is the account of a boy who grew up with little human contact and never learned to talk. Séguin and Itard developed a series of didactic materials that Montessori adapted when she opened her first school, Casa dei Bambini (The Children's House), to serve young children from disadvantaged areas of Rome. (Most publications list the opening of *Casa dei Bambini* as 1907, but some believe it was established in 1906.) Montessori also had an interest in helping children with mental disabilities. She believed that all children need to explore the world through their senses and that the teacher's role was primarily that of an observer/facilitator (Essa, 1999).

Montessori believed in a "prepared environment" where everything has a purpose and where materials are placed on shelves in specific order of difficulty, from simple to complex. She made the analogy between a sponge absorbing liquid and a child's mind absorbing learning. It is easy to see in Montessori's ideas the origin of many practices in special education today, particularly with children who have sensory impairments. With today's renewed emphasis on the plasticity of the human brain during the first three years of life, we can appreciate the importance of her original work.

Early education in the United States was established through nursery schools that promoted Dewey's philosophy in terms of exploratory learning and social engagement. These nursery schools primarily served children ages three to five from middle- and upper-income families who could afford the tuition. Infants and toddlers, by contrast, were studied behaviorally, in psychology laboratories associated with universities, as early as the 1880s (Rosenblith, 1992). These studies provided the foundation for understanding infant growth and development.

Although nursery schools for upper-class and middle-class children flourished, it was not until the 1960s and the federally declared War on Poverty that care for infants and toddlers outside the home was promoted. One of the most influential programs to advance early education for young children at risk was Project Head Start, founded in 1965 to remove children from the "cycle of poverty."

Educational and child development experts believed that prekindergarten education for disadvantaged children would lead to successful entry into formal education. An assumption behind the Head Start program was that children from impoverished environments were at risk for intellectual growth due to factors such as poor nutrition, lack of stimulation, and lack of educational opportunities.

Head Start also established a precedent for federal assistance to programs for young children and their families. In 1972, the Economic Opportunity Amendments (PL 92-424) required Head Start to reserve 10 percent of its enrollment slots for children with disabilities. As of 1998, 13 percent of children enrolled in Head Start had diagnosed disabilities. In 1994, the reauthorization of the Head Start Act established a new Early Head Start program for low-income families with infants and toddlers. Today, 600 projects provided Early Head Start child development and family support services for 35,000 children under the age of three. These projects include partnerships with early intervention services (Head Start Bureau, 1999). For a comprehensive history of the Head Start Program, see Zigler and Muenchow (1992).

The Head Start Bureau provides training and assistance to ensure program quality. Through its efforts, child-to-adult ratios, group size, average daily attendance, and percent of teachers with degrees have improved significantly. In 1998, Head Start was reauthorized by Congress. The current goals include establishing a seamless program from birth to compulsory school age and strengthening Early Head Start to meet the developmental needs of the youngest children (National Head Start Association, 1999).

CHILDREN WITH DISABILITIES

Programs that serve infants and toddlers with disabilities have been available to families in the United States for several decades. Early residential facilities for children and adults who were deaf and/or blind were established as early as 1800. For example, the Perkins Institute for the Blind founded by Samuel Gridley Howe in the 1800s (Peterson, 1987) continues to serve as a resource for early intervention.

Early programs for children with disabilities were also linked to local Associations for Retarded Citizens (ARC) or mental health agencies, but they were developed and run on shoestring budgets. Federal assistance to the parents of such children started as early as 1965, when PL 89-313, the amendment to the Elementary and Secondary Education Act (ESEA), gave states supplementary funds that could be applied to programs for children ages birth to five. In 1968, PL 90-538, the Handicapped Children's Early Education Assistance Act (HCEEAA), created the Handicapped Early Education Program (HCEEP) to provide federal assistance in developing experimental programs for young children with disabilities. Under the HCEEP Model Demonstration Programs, federal grants were distributed to model projects throughout the United States for a period of three years (Peterson, 1987). Today, this program operates under the auspices of the Office of Special Education and Rehabilitative Services (OSERS) at the U.S. Department of Education.

Many of these early programs involved parents as teachers of their children. The goal of early intervention was to teach the child developmental skills, and parents were often expected to carry out instructional objectives with their children at home. This service delivery model did not fully take into account the realities of the family setting, and parents were often overwhelmed by the expectations of service providers. Today parents and professionals work in partnership to provide the best services for the family. Families and service providers have joined together to bring about an awareness of the importance of early childhood in the field of special education. These efforts have included the creation of the Division for Early Childhood (DEC), a division of the Council for Exceptional Children (CEC), in 1973.

One of the most important steps by the federal government in support of children with disabilities was the passage of the Education for All Handicapped Children Act of 1975 (PL 94-142), now known as the Individuals with Disabilities Education Act. This law mandated free, appropriate public education for all school-age children with disabilities. Incentives were provided for preschool-aged children that formed the basis for the comprehensive services for this group that came in the 1980s and 1990s.

In the 1980s, service providers acknowledged that the family, and particularly the caregivers, were the most influential people in a child's life, while service providers may be transient in the child's life. Thus in 1986, through the grassroots efforts of families and service providers, PL 99-457 amended PL 94-142. This law established early intervention services for preschool children age 3 to 5 years and promised federal incentives for states to establish comprehensive, coordinated services for young children from birth to age three. In 1990, PL 101-476 reauthorized the federal law and changed its name to the Individuals with Disabilities Education Act (IDEA), extending the original intent of PL 94-142. A year later, in 1991, PL 102-119 was added as an amendment to IDEA. This law specified services that were to be made available to infants, toddlers, and their families. It also strengthened the role of the family in the education of young children.

All states receiving federal funds are required to develop and implement comprehensive, interagency plans for service delivery to infants, toddlers with disabilities, and their families. Under this agreement, the governor of the state names the lead agency that administers and monitors the early intervention system with the coooperation of the State Interagency Coordinating Council (SICC). The SICC is composed of parents, service providers, and members of various agencies (including those that deal with early intervention, preschool, health insurance, Head Start, and child care, as well as personnel education and state legislature) involved in services for young children with disabilities. Some states may include a representative from the Bureau of Indian Affairs or tribal council. There are also community ICCs at the local level.

Each state is also required to provide a central directory and a comprehensive child-find system to locate and refer children with disabilities (Brunim, 1990). The plan must include timelines and provision for participation by primary referral sources. Many states have implemented a central referral system that utilizes a single point of entry for accessing services. This central directory includes information on services and resources, including research and demonstration projects being conducted in the state. States are also required to have a comprehensive system of personnel development, to ensure an assessment process, and to oversee the Individualized Family Service Plan (IFSP) meeting, which documents the working relationship between families and service providers.

In the early stages of developing the IFSP, the National Early Childhood Technical Assistance System (NECTAS) and the Association for the Care of Children's Health (ACCH) developed guidelines that set out the underlying principles of the IFSP, principles which remain as pertinent today as they were during the initial development of federal policy:

PRINCIPLES UNDERLYING THE IFSP PROCESS

- Infants and toddlers are uniquely dependent on their families for their survival and care.
- States and programs should define "family" to reflect the diversity of family patterns and structures.
- Each family has its own structure, roles, values, beliefs, and coping styles.
- Respect for family autonomy, independence, and decision-making means that families should participate in determining not only the level and nature of services but also the duration and intensity of involvement in early intervention.
- Families and professionals participate as partners in designing, implementing, and evaluating the success of the early intervention program.
- Early intervention services should be flexible, accessible, and responsive to family's identified issues and concerns.
- Early intervention services should be provided according to the normalization principle—that is, families should have access to services provided in a reasonable way and in natural environments. Environments should promote the inclusion of both the child and family within the community.
- Cultural differences are recognized as strengths, not concerns, and choices that reflect a family's beliefs, priorities, and concerns should be respected.
- No one agency or discipline can meet the needs of families with diverse and complex concerns. A team approach that includes the efforts of family members is necessary to plan and implement the IFSP process.

Adapted from M. J. McGonigel, R. K. Kaufmann, and B. H. Johnson (Eds.), 1991, *Guidelines and Recommended Practices for the Individualized Family Service Plan,* 2nd ed., Bethesda: Association for the Care of Children's Health.

In 1990, the Individuals with Disabilities Education Act (IDEA) (PL 101-476) replaced the earlier Education for the Handicapped Act (EHA) of 1986. In 1991 amendments to IDEA were passed including, PL 102-119, Part H, legislation. The new law included provisions for a seamless transition to service delivery for preschool-age children; it also strengthened the role of families. The IFSP process, which included assessment of family resources, priorities, and concerns, was to be family-directed.

In 1997, Congress reauthorized IDEA and added some changes to the original legislation. The reauthorization created IDEA with four parts: Part A, General Provisions; Part B, Assistance for Education of All Children with Disabilities, Part C, Infants and Toddlers with Disabilities; and Part D, National Activities to Improve Education of Children with Disabilities. It is not within the scope of this book to cover all of the changes to IDEA; however, the changes affecting infants and toddlers and their families are important considerations. The Internet Web site (www.ideapractices.org, maintained by the federally funded IDEA Partnership project) contains the full text as well as summaries of the law.

Under Part A, General Provisions: option for use of "developmental delay" at state and local discretion was added to the definition of disability for children between three and nine years old. In addition, the new legislation added "orientation and mobility services" to the definition of "related services."

Part C (formerly known as Part H) states the purpose of federally funded early intervention programs, including:

- Maintain and implement a statewide, comprehensive, coordinated, multidisciplinary, interagency system of early intervention services for infants and toddlers with disabilities and their families;
- Facilitate the coordination of payment for early intervention services from Federal, State, local, and private sources (including public and private insurance coverage);
- Enhance the States' capacity to provide quality early intervention services and expand and improve existing early intervention services being provided to infants and toddlers with disabilities and their families; and
- Enhance the capacity of State and local agencies and service providers to identify, evaluate, and meet the needs of historically underrepresented populations, particularly minority, low-income, inner-city, and rural populations.

Early Intervention Program (1999), § 303.1

States are also encouraged to expand opportunities for children under the age of three who would be at risk of having substantial developmental delay if they did not receive early intervention services. States that do not provide services for at-risk infants and toddlers may now use funds to strengthen this statewide system by establishing or strengthening ties with community-based programs and agencies to help identify and evaluate infants and toddlers at risk (Early Intervention Program, 1999, § 303.3).

Under the new law, a transition plan arranged by the designated lead agency will ensure a smooth transition for children receiving early intervention services. A description of how the families will be included in the transition plan is also required.

State eligibility has been revised to allow states that have adopted a policy for appropriate early intervention services for all eligible children and their families to apply for federal funds. In this area, a major change has been made to allow states to establish policies and procedures to ensure that early intervention services are provided in a child's natural environments, whenever possible. According to the law, "natural environments means settings that are natural or normal for the child's age peers who have no disabilities" (Early Intervention Program, 1999, § 303.18). Services provided in a setting other than a natural environment occur only when early intervention cannot be achieved satisfactorily in a natural environment. In addition, justification must be indicated in the IFSP if early intervention services will not be provided in a natural environment.

In a position statement, the DEC (1998) endorsed the natural environments policy.

> DEC supports the rights of all children, regardless of their diverse abilities, to participate actively in natural environments within their community. A natural environment is one in which the child would spend time if he or she did not have

special needs. Family-centered and community-based care means that service providers not provide support for children, but they provide support to families and those in the community as well. Service providers must be able to facilitate parent-to-parent connections that link young children and their families to community-based natural supports such as babysitters, play groups and libraries. Instead of providing direct supports and services only to young children and their families, service providers must also serve as consultants, advocates, facilitators, and team members with community providers.

Changes to service delivery under Part C of IDEA may not be easy to implement at the local level. For example, fiscal restraints may prevent some service providers from changing their present direct-service delivery system. As one occupational therapist working in a center-based program for children with disabilities said, "We are not reimbursed for travel time to children's homes or their community." Another service provider questioned the definition of natural environments. In the inner city, community settings such as parks and fast food restaurants may not be safe places for families.

ENTERING THE SYSTEM

According to federal statute, infants and toddlers from birth to age 2, inclusive, are eligible for early intervention services if they are experiencing developmental delays. Service providers must document eligibility through the use of appropriate diagnostic instruments and procedures in one or more developmental areas: cognitive, physical, communication, social and emotional, or adaptive behavior. The child is also eligible if he or she has a diagnosed physical or mental condition that has a high probability of resulting in developmental delay. Infants and toddlers who are at risk of having substantial developmental delay may receive services at the state's discretion (Early Intervention Program, 1999, § 303.16). See Chapter 5 for a complete description of eligibility requirements.

All states must have criteria for entry into early intervention systems. Because various agencies work together in identifying and referring children with disabilities, services begin soon after diagnosis. Although the waiting period has decreased for many families who did not know how to access the early intervention system. For families who have just learned about a diagnosis, or are bringing a newborn home from an extended hospital stay, immediate service delivery can be intrusive. All new families need privacy to adjust to their new schedule and lifestyle, and this is certainly true when a child has a disability. The law is flexible in allowing a family time to adjust. For example, with parental consent, the team may provide services prior to completion of the assessment.

The age range of children entitled to services under Part C includes ages birth to three years (the entire second year is included). Many programs serving infants and toddlers provide home-based intervention until age three, when the child is transitioned to center-based services. With an increase in out-of-home child care for children under the age of three, service providers may see children both in the home and in other settings. Therefore, service providers should be trained to work successfully in a variety of environments (see Chapter 6).

The hallmark of Part C legislation is the Individualized Family Service Plan (IFSP). The key elements of the plan include:

- A statement of the child's present developmental status (based on appropriate assessment of the developmental domains: cognitive, communication, social/emotional, and adaptive)
- A statement of family's resources, priorities, and concerns related to enhancing the development of the child
- A statement of major outcomes expected to be achieved for the child and family (including criteria, procedures, and timelines used to determine the degree of progress toward those outcomes)
- A list of specific early intervention services and supports needed, and plan for service coordination (including frequency, intensity, and method of service delivery)
- A statement of the natural environments in which services will be provided (including justification, if necessary, to the extent that services will not be provided in the natural environment)
- The projected dates for service initiation and the anticipated duration of services
- The name of a qualified, appropriate service coordinator who will be responsible for coordinating services and implementing the plan
- Transition plans to support the child and family as they move on to preschool or other appropriate services
- The provisions for ongoing review, evaluation, and revision of the plan

Early Intervention Program (1999), § 303.344

PARTNERSHIPS WITH FAMILIES

The IFSP was developed for families to work in partnership with service providers in implementing early intervention services. An assumption underlining the plan is that service providers must understand the family from a systems perspective. Relationships within a family are driven by interacting subsystems (Minuchin, 1988; Turnbull & Turnbull, 1990). Different members within the family make up several subsystems that are mutually influential. For example, the marital subsystem is composed of the interaction of two primary caregivers (traditionally the parents). Other subsystems include the parent/child, sibling, and extended family.

Understanding the influence of these interacting subsystems will help service providers work with families in a more effective way. All families follow rules of interaction that are embedded in the individual cultural and ideological beliefs of the family (Blasco & Pearson, 1995). It is important to acknowledge family rules and boundaries established to delineate membership within a subsystem. Boundaries may either keep service providers outside of family interaction or let agencies into the inner core of the family. Families may respond differently to service providers at different times in their history. For example, when a family is in crisis, boundaries may be confused, inconsistent, or nonexistent (Minuchin, 1988). Thus, a service provider may be closed out of the family at a time when services could be most helpful. This scenario can be very frustrating to a service provider who feels he or she is doing everything possible to engage the family. Acknowledgment of the family's wishes and a willingness to follow the family's lead will help to establish the trust necessary for a continued working relationship.

The emotional bond that holds the family together is called *family cohesion* (Olson et al., 1989). Family cohesion occurs along a continuum of behavior ranging from enmeshment to disengagement. Healthy families tend to fall in the middle of the continuum. Enmeshment occurs when the boundaries between subsystems become confused or weak. Turnbull and Turnbull (1990) gave the example of the parent of a child with a disability who has devoted all of his or her time and energy to that child, at the expense of other family members. A family who is disengaged may forget about a home visit or miss several appointments with service providers.

Family adaptability refers to the ability of the family to change its power structure, role relationships, and rules in response to events that occur over a lifetime (Olson et al., 1989). Like cohesion, adaptability exists along a behavioral continuum, from rigidity to chaos. Families characterized as rigid may have too many rules that are not adaptable to a specific situation. Families that are chaotic may have few or inconsistent rules. Inconsistent or nonexistent rules can be very confusing for young children who developmentally are comforted by parental expectations and routines. Consider Vignette 1.1, from an inner-city child care center.

VIGNETTE 1.1 DAILY ROUTINES

Debbie is a child care worker at an inner-city child care center. In the morning the children enter the room and are greeted by the adults, who place themselves strategically within the room. Marietta is greeting children and parents at the door. Several parents arrive as a result of a court order to participate in parenting classes. Many of the children with disabilities arrive by bus.

Several of the children have histories of living in violent environments. Three of the children were exposed prenatally to cocaine, and two children have diagnosed attachment disorders. One child has fetal alcohol syndrome. Debbie and Marietta realize that routines and predictability are key ingredients for these children and for their families. After a brief free-play session, they ask children and parents who are present to join them in some singing. After a few get-together songs, Debbie goes over the morning schedule and reminds everyone of the events for that day, including daily routines. One of the parents, Tanya, asks, "It is a nice day, why don't they just stay outside on the playground all morning?" Debbie tries to explain that they want to follow the plan so the children know what to expect every day. Tanya replies, "At home, we just do what feels good. If they don't like what we're doing and fuss, I whoop them good and they come around." There is an embarrassed silence as Debbie and Marietta look at each other. Finally, one of the other parents, Akira, says, "They don't understand why you hit them if they don't know what they are supposed to do."

In Vignette 1.1, Tanya has difficulty understanding the need for routines. Tanya herself was an abused child, and her parents gave inconsistent messages regarding discipline. Akira's comment was well timed and probably helpful because it came from another parent, who has also experienced difficulty with parenting.

Flexibility is characteristic of families who can adapt to new situations, stresses, and demands appropriately (Minuchin, 1988). Families that have established open communication are more likely to engage in decision-making and conflict resolution with service providers. Positive communication skills such as reflective listening, clarification, and supportive comments help families and service providers engage in meaningful dialogue. Negative communication skills such as criticism, scolding, and judging are likely to disrupt or delay successful dialogue.

It is important to remember that a family systems approach, while helpful in providing a framework for understanding families, also requires a team effort in clinically describing a family and their behavior. Service providers should rely on the expertise of mental health and social service professionals when working with families. It is also important to acknowledge that all families may experience extreme behavior at different times in their development. However, many families eventually achieve a healthy balance. When the family is unable to find a balance, professionals in family therapy need to guide the intervention.

Supporting Families in Early Intervention

Figure 1.1 demonstrates how formal and informal support can be available to the family through service provision (Turnbull & Turnbull, 1990). The concentric lines at times may be either open or closed, depending on how the family is functioning at that particular time in their life cycle.

Life cycle refers to the family's developmental trajectory. Every family goes through a series of transitions that produce stress. For example, the birth of a child, though considered a joyous occasion, produces stress in the form of demands for new routines, challenges, and changes in living habits. The birth of a child with a disability may exacerbate such stress and leave the family feeling out of control.

Family Response to Disability

In the past, service providers often made judgments about families based on research conducted in the medical field. Drotar et al. (1975) published a study based on a questionnaire assessing parental perceptions, feelings, and attachment

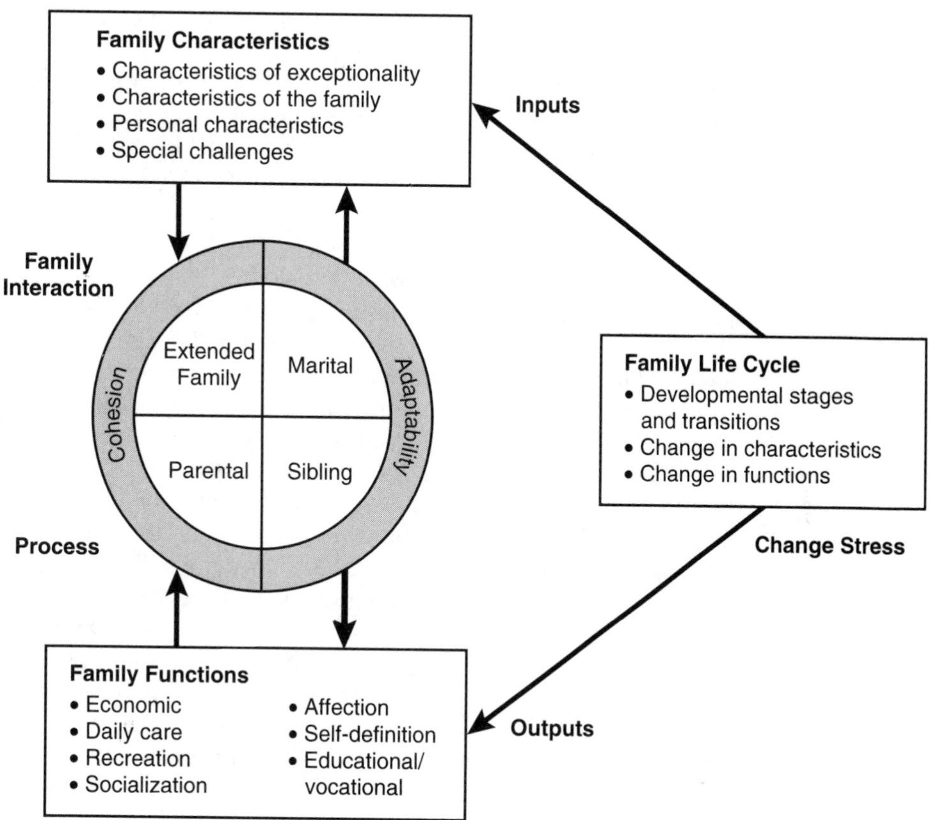

FIGURE 1.1 Family Systems Conceptual Framework

Source: From *Working with Families with Disabled Members: A Family Systems Approach*, by A. P. Turnbull, J. A. Summers, and M. J. Brotherson, 1984, Lawrence: University of Kansas, p. 60. Adapted by permission.

to their child with a disability. They developed a linear model that showed parents following a progression of feelings starting with shock and filtering through denial and anger until the parent comes to a point of reorganization, when parents are ready to deal with the responsibilities of their child.

In the 1980s many of these theories were disputed by researchers who stated that this kind of categorizing of feelings does families a disservice (Blacher, 1984). Families will respond differently to crises based on individual resources and support and previous coping strategies for dealing with difficult situations (Farran, Metzger, & Sparling, 1986). For example, a family can draw from religious or ideological beliefs to develop acceptance and love. Other families may receive support and guidance from another family member or friend who also has a child with a disability. The social and political influence of our society toward persons with disabilities will also affect a family's reaction. The more information is available to families, the better they can make the decisions necessary to move forward. Bailey and Blasco (1990) identified the need for information as one of the most important services that providers can give to families.

The Guzman family expressed their need for information early on as a way of dealing with the diagnosis of Cornelia deLange syndrome in their daughter, Alex. At the time of Alex's birth, Lori had a five-year-old son, Shawn, from a previous marriage. George, her husband, missed Alex's birth but arrived shortly after and was told "the news," as vignette 1.2 reveals.

VIGNETTE 1.2 INITIAL DIAGNOSIS

I knew right away something was wrong. They wouldn't let me see Alex and they kept asking me when would my husband arrive. The doctor finally came in and said he had to tell me some bad news about my child. They still needed to do some tests but they thought she had a syndrome of some type. Within a few days, they confirmed that she had Cornelia deLange syndrome. The medical team spent hours explaining the syndrome and its characteristics to us. I don't remember anything they said. They told me she would be severely retarded, possibly deaf and blind. Only one characteristic stood out in my mind that day. The physician said her hair would not grow beyond her ears. I remember thinking what a ridiculous thing to say to a parent. Years later when Alex had her school picture taken with hair well beyond her shoulders, I thought of sending a copy of that picture to the physician.

A concept that has recently resurfaced in the literature is that of *chronic sorrow,* a condition first described by Solnit and Stark (1961). Many families of children with disabilities describe their emotional state as a roller coaster ride. There are highs and lows, yet families never lose the sense of sadness that their child has a disability that will affect their lives forever. Events may reignite the sense of sadness, which can lead to depression and despair. In the literature, researchers pointed out that milestones, such as the beginning of school or the child's first birthday, can inspire chronic sorrow (Turnbull & Turnbull, 1990). Again, it is important to realize that each family is unique and, depending on cultural differences and beliefs, will vary in their responses to all aspects of raising a child with a disability.

During initial diagnosis of a child's disability, service providers can help families by listening to their concerns and issues. Providing an empathetic ear will allow families the time to sort through the multiple feelings and sense of confusion that accompany any time of change.

UNDERSTANDING THE IFSP PROCESS FOR ONE FAMILY

When Alex Guzmán was born with a disability in 1988, she was eligible for early intervention services at home. At that time, the IFSP process was relatively new in her state. At first, Lori and George Guzmán were frustrated by the thought of completing yet another long, complicated form. They had already completed an Individualized Education Plan (IEP), an Individualized Support Plan (ISP), and a nursing care plan. The early intervention team moved quickly, however, to involve the family in the IFSP process. Lori and George learned that the IFSP could combine all of the best aspects of the former care plans, the positive aspects of Alex's abilities, and the family's concerns, priorities, and resources as they related to Alex.

According to Lori,

> The IFSP process allows the family to identify what it needs to support the child, and to help the child achieve his or her outcomes. The family can identify its concerns and assign each a priority. Our family felt that getting more information about our child's syndrome was more important than getting an audiology report. (Guzmán & Guzmán, 1992, p. 1)

Figure 1.2 shows the part of the plan as written by the mother, Lori; the father, George; and brother, Shawn.

In many families, individuals have different opinions of and concerns for the child with disabilities. For example, George was more concerned about receiving information on Cornelia deLange syndrome and medical provisions for his daughter. While Lori too was eager for more information on medical procedures, she also needed help balancing her work schedule with the new demands of caring for Alex, and wanted to see Alex gain weight and to learn how to communicate with her. Since the Guzmáns are a dual-income family, Lori was worried about the financial costs of caring for Alex and the potential loss of her income. She was also concerned about Shawn and his needs for care and attention. Shawn wanted to see his sister become more like other children. Finally, Lori mentioned that there was some concern for the grandparents, who spoke Spanish and had difficulty understanding all the medical issues.

Bailey, Blasco, and Simeonsson (1992) found significant differences in the concerns expressed by mothers and fathers regarding social and family support and child care. All family members should have the opportunity to express their feelings and understanding during the IFSP process. From a family systems perspective, this approach will help ensure that services are understood and that all family members who wish to be included are participating to the fullest extent in the intervention plan.

Another important component of the IFSP is the flexibility in defining both child and family outcomes. For example, Lori was quite concerned with the loss of a connection with her neighbors as a result of the time and energy needed to care for Alex.

> The family was so involved with the medical procedures and the efforts of simply keeping our child alive that we missed every neighborhood picnic and gathering during the first year-and-a half of Alex's life. We became completely detached from our neighbors and friends, not by choice, but by circumstance. The IFSP not only allows for inclusion of neighbors and friends on the IFSP team, but also allows for them to be included in carrying out the actual plan. (Guzmán & Guzmán, 1992, p. 1)

Child's Name *Alexandra Guzmán*

Family Considerations for the Individual Family Service Plan

5-1-92
by Lori (mother)

1. Please describe how you see your child (what you like most, any concerns or needs).
   Likes: Long eyelashes, dark eyes, dark hair – her Mexican heritage shows.
   Concerns: apparent inability to gain weight; bouts of apnea + breathing difficulties; the diagnosis of severe mental retardation; will she ever walk?

2. What type of help would you want for your child and family in the months or year ahead?
   How to get mom back to work; Alex to gain weight – more instruction on how to care for her medically; how to get away; how to help brother feel okay; how to change retardation level from severe to mild; how to help pay for medical bills; how do we communicate with her.

3. Which of the following do you or other family members feel are important concerns or areas about which you would like more information?

for your child

- ___ getting around
- ✓ communicating
- ✓ learning
- ✓ feeding, nutrition
- ___ having fun with other children
- ___ challenging behaviors or emotions
- ___ equipment or supplies
- ✓ health or dental care
- ___ pain or discomfort
- ✓ vision or hearing
- ___ other

for your family . . .

- ___ meeting other families whose child has similar needs
- ___ finding or working with doctors or other specialists
- ___ coordinating, making appointments, dealing with agencies
- ✓ coordinating your child's medical care
- ___ finding out more about how different services work or how they could work better for you
- ✓ planning or expectations for the future
- ✓ more information about what resources might be available
- ___ transportation
- ✓ child care
- ___ finding a support group
- ✓ finding or working with people who can help you in your home or care for your child so you can have a break
- ___ housing, clothing, jobs, food, telephone
- ✓ information or ideas for brothers, sisters, friends, relatives, others
- ✓ information about the disability or diagnosis
- ___ money for extra costs of child's special needs
- ___ help with insurance
- ___ recreation
- ✓ other – *talking to another parent*

notes:

4. What else do you think would be helpful for others to know about your child?
   We are tired of being protected from the truth about our daughter's diagnosis + needs.

5. . . . about your family? *Grandparents speak Spanish; difficulty understanding her needs.*

Page 2

FIGURE 1.2 Sample Individual Family Service Plan

Child's Name Alexandra Guzmán

Family Considerations for the Individual Family Service Plan

5-1-92
by George (father)

1. Please describe how you see your child (what you like most, any concerns or needs).

   Little, Fighter

2. What type of help would you want for your child and family in the months or year ahead?

   Info on syndrome, what medical options are out there

3. Which of the following do you or other family members feel are important concerns or areas about which you would like more information?

for your child

- ✓ getting around
- ✓ communicating
- ✓ learning
- ✓ feeding, nutrition
- ___ having fun with other children
- ___ challenging behaviors or emotions
- ___ equipment or supplies
- ___ health or dental care
- ✓ pain or discomfort
- ✓ vision or hearing
- ___ other

for your family . . .

- ___ meeting other families whose child has similar needs
- ___ finding or working with doctors or other specialists
- ___ coordinating, making appointments, dealing with agencies
- ___ coordinating your child's medical care
- ___ finding out more about how different services work or how they could work better for you
- ___ planning or expectations for the future
- ✓ more information about what resources might be available
- ___ transportation
- ✓ child care
- ___ finding a support group
- ✓ finding or working with people who can help you in your home or care for your child so you can have a break
- ___ housing, clothing, jobs, food, telephone
- ___ information or ideas for brothers, sisters, friends, relatives, others
- ✓ information about the disability or diagnosis
- ___ money for extra costs of child's special needs
- ✓ help with insurance
- ✓ recreation
- ___ other

notes:

4. What else do you think would be helpful for others to know about your child?

5. . . . about your family?

Page 2

FIGURE 1.2 Continued

Child's Name Alexandra Guzmán

Family Considerations for the Individual Family Service Plan

5-1-92
by Shawn (brother) age 8

1. Please describe how you see your ~~child~~ sister (what you like most, any concerns or needs).

Small and soft

2. What type of help would you want for your ~~child~~ sister and family in the months or year ahead?

Get better do things that other kids could do go out side - take her for walks to be able to do things other kids could do.

3. Which of the following do you or other family members feel are important concerns or areas about which you would like more information?

for your child

- ✓ getting around
- ___ communicating
- ___ learning
- ___ feeding, nutrition
- ✓ having fun with other children
- ___ challenging behaviors or emotions
- ___ equipment or supplies
- ___ health or dental care
- ✓ pain or discomfort
- ✓ vision or hearing
- ___ other

for your family . . .

- ___ meeting other families whose child has similar needs
- ___ finding or working with doctors or other specialists
- ___ coordinating, making appointments, dealing with agencies
- ✓ coordinating your child's medical care
- ✓ finding out more about how different services work or how they could work better for you
- ___ planning or expectations for the future
- ___ more information about what resources might be available
- ✓ transportation
- ✓ child care
- ___ finding a support group
- ✓ finding or working with people who can help you in your home or care for your child so you can have a break
- ___ housing, clothing, jobs, food, telephone
- ___ information or ideas for brothers, sisters, friends, relatives, others
- ___ information about the disability or diagnosis
- ✓ money for extra costs of child's special needs
- ___ help with insurance
- ___ recreation
- ___ other

notes:

4. What else do you think would be helpful for others to know about your child?

5. . . . about your family?

Page 2

FIGURE 1.2 Continued

Child's Name Alexandra Guzmán

Agenda for the IFSP meeting. (After reviewing the Family Considerations (page 2).) The family and Facilitator create an agenda for the IFSP team meeting. (List the topics, questions and information to share; decide what sequence to follow and how much time will be needed.)

1. Introductions – how we got acquainted
2. Info about Alex – pictures (page 5)
3. Family issues (page 2)
4. Review page 6 – update, additions
5. Specify who will work on outcomes
6. Decide about next meeting – (where, when) and ongoing communication
7. Assign service coordinator

things to bring
nametags
flip chart
form
photos

IFSP Team Membership Selection - possibilities to consider for team members which will be helpful or supportive to child and family outcomes/issues/tasks

Family/Community:
- (*) parents
- other family members, relatives, friends
- community, civic, disability or parent groups
- respite, child care providers
- advocates
- legal representation
- ministry, other support source
- other: another parent

Social Services:
- (-) developmental disabilities case worker
- income maintenance/economic assistance
- mental health
- child welfare
- social worker
- other private providers

Health Care:
- primary physician
- other physician
- private home health care
- primary nurse

—— = considered
○ = invited

* must attend to meet IEP requirements

Health Care continued
- other hospital staff
- (-) public health nursing
- community health services habilitation providers (private therapy)
- Services for Children with Handicaps
- mental health providers
- personal care attendants
- other:

Education
- (*) administrator or designee
- (*) Early Childhood Special Education
- school nurse
- Early Childhood Family Education
- Head Start
- Community Education
- early childhood programs (e.g., nursery school, child care)
- kindergarten-regular/special educators, related services
- occupational therapy
- physical therapy
- speech therapy
- other:

SCHEDULING IFSP MEETING

Settings and times convenient to family to ensure that they will be able to attend.

M or T late afternoon (after 3:00)
F any time/ prefer only 5-6 people

at parents' home — $1\frac{1}{2}$ - 2 hrs. length

* Tues June 9 3 - 5 p.m.

Fill in details of team members on next page. Page 3

FIGURE 1.2 Continued

Child's Name Alexandra Guzmán

Summary of Child's Present Levels of Performance (To be completed by the IFSP Team. Draw from description of the child, additional assessments and observations, for each category. Include needs and functioning in context of daily routine settings. Address all areas listed.) DOB: 2-29-92

1. Current health and medical status
2. Basic senses including hearing and vision
3. Communication: speech and language development
4. Social/emotional/behavioral development
5. Physical/motoric development
6. Cognitive development
7. Self-help skills
8. Academic Performance (when appropriate)

Present Levels of Performance	Child's Needs
Alex is awake a lot. She likes to swing and play with her hands in front of her face. ^ She likes music on the tape recorder by her head ^ She's usually hot – don't use blankets much. She tolerates holding but cries if you hold her too tight. Her cry has a low growling sound.	
Alex's arms appear shorter than they should be; hands and fingers are extremely small. Her arms are bent up and her neck and legs seem stiff.	
Alex has had trouble breathing – gagging or apnea spells occur 1-2 x/day. When mucus collects and suctioned out Alex becomes frantic and cries; sometimes she turns blue because her heart has slowed down or stopped.	to breathe steadily and independently
Alex is fed through a gastrostomy tube; she has trouble with sucking and swallowing. Low birth weight, slow weight gain.	to gain weight to drink from a bottle/eat by mouth

Page 5

FIGURE 1.2 Continued

Child's Name Alexandra Guzmán

Initial Team List of IFSP Outcomes/Tasks/Issues

(An outcome is a statement of the changes family members want to see for their child, or for themselves, related to their ability to enhance their child's development.)

Priority #	Outcome/Issue/Task	People who can help with this outcome (to assess, plan, commit resources, and/or carry out the plan).	Additional Assessment Needed* ✓ INITIAL	FURTHER	NO
7 in process–	extended family fears and concerns (cultural) support for older brother	facilitator — local church — parents – cultural resources – sibling support group — ARC Hennepin			✓
2 done by day 30	more info about CdL syndrome – what will future bring?	MDH literature search by PHN another parent – Pilot Parent or CdL Syndrome Foundation			✓
(4) checked day care– no answers application pending MA • SS	help in home to care for Alex - – possibly day care or respite options	Soc. Serv. for respite possibilities PHN for MA options, home care or respite options	✓ ✓		
3 CPR done by day 30	training on medical procedures etc. for family including grandparents and friends	PHN, hospital staff, parents programs e.g. CPR			✓
6 school assess. cmpltd. by day 30	communication - hearing	school staff parents audiologist	✓		
(5) school assess. cmpltd. by day 30 ROM	minimize level and effect of mental retardation; reduce contractures at elbows; improve hip range of motion	school staff parents hospital OT/PT	✓		✓

*Attach assessment permits as needed

Page 6

FIGURE 1.2 Continued

Child's Name Alexandra Guzmán

Initial Team List of IFSP Outcomes/Tasks/Issues

(An outcome is a statement of the changes family members want to see for their child, or for themselves, related to their ability to enhance their child's development.)

	Priority #	Outcome/Issue/Task	People who can help with this outcome (to assess, plan, commit resources, and/or carry out the plan).	Additional Assessment Needed* ✓ INITIAL	FURTHER	NO
(8)	MA pending	help with medical bills	Soc. Services/Employment + Economic Assistance PHN	✓		
(1)	in process– ongoing	basic health concerns – apnea, breathing weight gain	doctor parents PHN			✓

*Attach assessment permits as needed

Page 6

FIGURE 1.2 **Continued**

Although the plan requires more documentation of child and family strengths and concerns than its predecessors, it does not have to be a labor-intensive process. Documents that only add more paperwork discourage both families as well as service providers. In fact, many states are working on flexible documentation that can be completed in a variety of settings, including a Neonatal Intensive Care Unit (NICU). Many have computerized the IFSP to make recording more efficient and less time-consuming.

SERVICE COORDINATION

One of the most important provisions of Part C of the IDEA is the inclusion of a service coordinator to help streamline early intervention services. Services are provided to infants and toddlers and their families by different professionals working together as a team. In Chapter 9, the varied approaches to teaming are discussed. The team is typically composed of parents and qualified personnel, including early childhood special education teacher, early childhood teacher or child care provider, speech and language clinician, occupational therapist, physical therapist, nurse or public health nurse, nutritionist, physician, social worker, audiologist, and psychologist. The role of the service coordinator is to coordinate and integrate the multiple agencies serving individual families. According to federal law, the service coordinator is responsible for seven main activities: coordinate evaluations and assessments; facilitate the development, implementation, and evaluation of the IFSP; assist families in the identification of service providers; coordinate and monitor the delivery of services; coordinate medical and health care; and facilitate the transition plan to preschool services.

Service coordination, although a new term, has been in existence in many fields allied with education services. For example, social workers are often assigned to a family as case managers (Bailey, 1989). This model of intervention focused on the family's problems. In other words, the family was viewed as a client and services addressed the "dysfunctional" aspect of the family. From a family systems perspective, social workers are assigned to families who are clinically in need of intervention. According to this model, families need help before they can be self-reliant.

Following a family empowerment model, Dunst and Trivette (1989) suggested that parents and professionals work together to secure and maximize services. These authors emphasized the importance of promoting the competencies of the family. There are basic strategies for working with families in partnerships, including:

- Working with the family from a systems perspective
- Helping to identify family issues and concerns
- Using reflective listening skills
- Engaging in constructive conflict and negotiating needs
- Locating and referring to community, state, and national resources

With the IDEA, the term service coordination replaced case management. The shift to service coordination reflects a change not only in terminology but also in attitude. Families are no long viewed as "cases" to be "managed" by experts. Rather, service coordination is more reflective of the involvement of families as partners in their child's intervention program (Hausslein, Kaufmann, & Hurth, 1992). Indeed, in some situations, families drive the process of making services work for their child.

In many states, the position of the service coordinator is still evolving. According to federal standards, service coordinators must have an understanding of eligibility requirements for infants and toddlers, Part C regulations, and early intervention services in their state. It is up to the state, and in many cases local agencies, to define the role of service provider within their community. Thus the lead agency within a state may view service coordination differently in different locations. For example, if the lead agency is education, some school districts may assign a service coordinator to a family once that family enters the early intervention system. Other school districts allow the families to chose from a menu of options for service coordination. That may include a service coordinator who is a parent, someone not connected with any of the agencies, or a familiar team member.

The use of parents as service coordinators can help ease the family's entry into a sometimes difficult system (Glisczinski, 1995). According to one parent coordinator:

> A seasoned early intervention parent can point new parents in the right direction—they know the ins and outs of paperwork and can provide helpful hints for accessing "the system" and working through loopholes. They know, for example, that the social worker with the brown glasses in the second room on the left is far more accommodating than the other social worker in the same room without glasses. (p. 40)

Whatever the particular job description, it is imperative that a service coordinator have excellent "people" skills as well as expertise in early intervention. That is, the service coordinator must be able to keep the lines of communication open between various agencies and the family. The coordinator may act as a troubleshooter for the family, because he or she is the person in whom the family have placed the most trust and belief. A good service coordinator is an empathetic listener who can also move families and agencies toward mutual agreement.

Dinnebeil and Rule (1994) surveyed families and service coordinators. They found that, according to parents, the important characteristics of service providers include strong skills in rapport building and in gathering and synthesizing resources, as well as a positive, concerned attitude. Finally, the service coordinator helps the family transition from the birth-to-three program to the preschool program. This transition may include stressful separation issues for all involved. Families not only experience anxiety for their child, who may be entering a center-based program for the first time, but also must prepare themselves for dealing with a new team and, in many situations, a new setting. Transition strategies are described in Chapter 7.

THEORETICAL APPROACHES

The Medical Model

Services to young children and their families have been influenced by the theoretical approaches of different delivery systems. For example, the diagnosis of a disability for children under the age of three often occurs within a medical setting. The *medical model* of service delivery is frequently characterized as a difficult system for families to negotiate. Health care personnel assume the role of the expert whose main purpose is to cure or fix the problem, but families have provided abundant stories about insensitive doctors and other professionals in these settings. Medical training has not provided trainees with the skills necessary to implement family-centered care. As one physician stated:

> Medical students' success is measured almost exclusively on how they perform on standardized tests of knowledge. Deductive reasoning and problem-solving is not always taught formally. Students trained in this particular scientific/data paradigm approach a child or a parent using the perspectives they were taught: collect data and use it to make a diagnosis, then recall the accepted therapeutic interventions and apply them. (Sharp & Lohr, p. 75)

Fortunately, many medical training programs have now added family-centered care as part of their training curriculum. The American Academy of Pediatrics has issued guidelines for physicians participating in the Individualized Family Service Plan. Today, many health care workers also participate on the statewide Interagency Coordinating Council (ICC).

The Developmental Perspective

The training received by service providers in both education and the allied health professions in early intervention is based on theories of the stages of development. Arnold Gesell, a psychologist in the early part of the twentieth century, linked the growth of physical and cognitive abilities to the stages in a linear model of development (Gesell & Amatruda, 1941).

Piaget (1962) followed with a model that also showed children gaining increasingly complex cognitive concepts in stages. In the early years, those stages are the sensorimotor stage (birth to 18 months) and the preoperational stage (1½ to 4½ years). Piaget believed that the infant learned through exploration and play. His work formed the basis for much of the research on the sensorimotor period.

The developmental perspective is reflected in recommended practices in early childhood today. Children are viewed as active learners who gather knowledge from physical, social, and cultural experiences to construct their understanding of the world around them (NAEYC, 1996).

Most of the curriculum that has been subsequently developed for infants and toddlers applies developmental milestones in the development of activities for young children. These milestones are further discussed in Chapters 3 and 4. Although milestones are very useful for describing typical development and form the basis for understanding atypical development, they should not be rigidly applied to instruction for every infant and toddler. In Vignette 1.3, Michelle teaches her service providers a lesson along these lines.

VIGNETTE 1.3 LEARNING FROM MICHELLE

Michelle was a 15-month-old with biliary atresia. Michelle had learned to sit at the age of 12 months and showed an interest in standing at 15 months. Following a developmental milestone guide, the occupational therapist and the teacher thought it would be a good idea to help Michelle learn to crawl. However, whenever Michelle was placed in a crawl position she would cry out in pain and agitation. One day, Michelle was playing on a mat when she saw a toy of interest on a low shelf. The teacher observed Michelle's attempts to pull herself to a stand (a higher skill on the milestone chart). In the next team meeting, the teacher and the occupational therapist realized that due to her illness, Michelle was never likely to crawl, but she could pull herself up to stand and cruise. Within a month, Michelle was standing at the low shelf and cruising to retrieve toys placed slightly out of reach.

The Behavioral Perspective

Special educators are most familiar with the behavioral approach, largely through the work of B. F. Skinner (1904–90) on operant conditioning, which continues to be used today. According to this approach, the service provider examines the antecedent events and the consequences related to a behavior, and then applies direct instruction and reinforcement to change the behavior (Zirpoli & Melloy, 2001).

The different approaches to early childhood are reflected by comparing the orientation of professionals who work in regular and special early childhood education. For example, service providers working with children in early childhood centers provide services that are typically more child-oriented and follow the child's lead. On the other hand, children in early childhood special education may experience a more structured approach to instruction based on behavior modification.

For infants and toddlers, these diverse practices may be less of an issue than for older preschool-age children, particularly in segregated, center-based programs. However, it is important to realize that service providers may have philosophical differences in both training and practice.

The Ecological Perspective

Greenspan and Meisels (1995) have provided the following explanation of the theoretical basis of the ecological perspective of development:

> Related to the interactivity among areas of development is the fact that both biological and environmental influences operate to support, facilitate, or impede the development of infants and young children. (p. 2)

Bronfenbrenner (1979) introduced an ecological model for understanding the influences that shape human development. He identified four systems that interact to affect the family both positively and negatively: the microsystem, the mesosystem, the exosystem, and the macrosystem. The *microsystem* consists of the child's immediate environment. For the young child, this would include people, objects, and events in his or her natural environment, including family members, peers, neighbors, etc. The microsystem lends support to the child in meeting his or her physical, cognitive, and emotional needs. Consider the story of Mariam Wright Edelman in the following vignette:

VIGNETTE 1.4 COMMUNITY SUPPORT

I went everywhere with my parents and was under the watchful eye of members of the congregation and community who were my extended parents. They kept me when my parents went out of town, they reported on and chided me when I strayed from the straight and narrow of community expectations, and they basked in and supported my achievements when I did well. (Edelman, 1992, p. 4)

For Edelman, her family and her community provided the safety net she needed to develop as a child. Think of all the children who have no safety net; these may include many children with developmental disabilities.

When the microsystem is unable to meet the needs of the child, for whatever reason, it becomes a source of developmental risk. Researchers have identified several factors that put a young child at risk developmentally, including caregiver mental health, attitude and anxiety, education and occupation, and reduced family support (Sameroff & Fiese, 1990; Sameroff & Seifer; Werner & Smith, 1989). For example, consider the recent research that indicates children prenatally exposed to substance abuse are additionally at risk due to ongoing environmental factors such as continued substance abuse, domestic violence, and poverty (Griffith, Azuma, & Chasnoff, 1994).

The *mesosystem* is composed of the interactions between various microsystems, for example, the interactions between the home and child care setting, or the home and community settings. Interactions that are positive and supportive, such as frequent, supportive contact between the family and service providers, will help the child grow in all developmental areas. Interactions that are negative or confusing for the family will have a negative impact on the infant or toddler.

The *exosystem*—settings that indirectly influence the child—can have a positive or negative impact on the child's microsystems and mesosystems (Zirpoli, 1995). For example, when a parent's workplace provides on-site child care that is a nurturing environment and meets the family needs, the child will also experience a positive sense of well-being that fosters growth and development.

Finally, the *macrosystem* is represented by the ideological and institutional beliefs of a particular society. Today our society increasingly values and supports persons with disabilities. It is now more common to see such individuals in all aspects of modern life (e.g., in the media, in advertisements, etc.). Not long ago, our society did not value persons who were different from the mainstream. Many with a disability or mental illness were institutionalized and not seen in the public arena. The macrosystem influences all of the other interaction systems, and can change as society and values change.

SUMMARY

This chapter introduced the field of early intervention for infants and toddlers. Over the last two decades, federal and state legislation has ensured quality early intervention services, as the emphasis on the role of the family and service coordination has led to many changes in service delivery. The interagency collaboration in birth-to-three services has made this field unique in its approach to comprehensive family-centered care.

An understanding of the family from a systems perspective will enable service providers to approach families as partners in the education and development of their young children. Flexibility is the key in working with families who are experiencing stress. It is also an attribute of families who can adapt to new stresses and demands in an appropriate way. Open communication with families will allow professionals to understand the family dynamics and individual differences that are part of each family. Families who are supported are more likely to respond to intervention services in a meaningful way.

Families experiencing a new diagnosis or the birth of a child with a disability respond differently to the situation. Some rely on prior coping strategies for dealing with a crisis. Some pull together; others fall apart. Families also vary in their initial response to services from the early intervention team. It may be helpful to give families more time before introducing services, but this should be a family decision. Eligibility requirements vary in each state, although general guidelines are required through federal legislation.

The IFSP is the hallmark of recent legislation in early intervention. This document is family-centered and includes information given by the family on what they perceive to be the priorities for services. The IFSP must include a statement by the family that addresses what they see as strengths and concerns relating to the development of the child. However, it may be that families do not wish to complete this statement, and they should have the opportunity to refuse to do so. Due to prior negative experiences with authorities or other service providers, some families may need time before a sense of trust is established. A service coordinator can help the family organize the many different services and agencies that will play a role in their lives. Characteristics of helpful service coordinators include the ability to build rapport, gather information, and maintain a positive proactive attitude. Service coordinators provide the link between the early intervention program, other agencies, and the transition to early childhood classrooms.

An important consideration in times of budget cuts and shrinking resources is whether early intervention is effective. The field of early intervention remains divided on whether early intervention is effective for all children. Much of the current legislation was passed without a substantial research basis. One issue in the research is whether it makes sense to look beyond statistical analysis for evidence of positive effects. More and more researchers are using qualitative analysis, including interviews and observations, to address questions of efficacy in early intervention.

When providing early intervention services, we should be aware of the influence of environmental benefits and constraints on the child and family. Bronfenbrenner's (1979) model enables us to view the child and family within the framework of both internal and external influences.

REFERENCES

Bailey, D. B. (1989). Case management in early intervention. *Journal of Early Intervention, 13,* 120–134.

Bailey, D. B., & Blasco, P. M. (1990). Parents' perspectives on a written survey of family needs. *Journal of Early Intervention, 14,* 196–203.

Bailey, D. B., Blasco, P. M., & Simeonsson, R. (1992). Needs expressed by mothers and fathers of young children with disabilities. *American Journal on Mental Retardation, 97,* 1–10.

Blacher, J. (1984). Sequential stages of adjustment to the birth of a child with handicaps/Fact or artifact? *Mental Retardation, 22,* 55–68.

Blasco, P. M., & Pearson, J. (1995). Working with families. In T. J. Zirpoli (Ed.), *Understanding and affecting the behavior of young children* (pp. 219–241). Englewood Cliffs, N.J.: Merrill.

Bronfenbrenner, U. (1979). *The ecology of human development.* Cambridge, Mass.: Harvard University Press.

Brunim, I. A. (1990). *Strengthening the roles of families in states' early intervention systems: Policy guide to procedural safeguards for infants, toddlers, and their families.* Washington, D.C.: Mental Health Law Project, and Reston, Va.: Division for Early Childhood of the Council for Exceptional Children.

Dinnebeil, L. A., & Rule, S. (1994). Variables that influence collaboration between parents and service coordinators. *Journal of Early Intervention, 18,* 349–361.

Division for Early Childhood, Council for Exceptional Children. (1998). *Position statement on services for children birth to age eight with special needs.* Denver, Colo.: Author.

Drotar, D., Baskiewicz, A., Irvin, N., Kennell, J., & Klaus, M. (1975). The adaptation of parents to the birth of an infant with a congenital malformation: A hypothetical model. *Pediatrics, 56,* 710–716.

Dunst, C. J., & Trivette, C. M. (1989). An enabling and empowerment perspective of case management. *Topics in Early Childhood Special Education, 8,* 87–102.

Early Intervention Program for Infants and Toddlers with Disabilities, 34 C.F.R. 303 (1999, July 1).

Edelman, M. W. (1992). *The measure of our success: A letter to my children and yours.* Boston, Mass.: Beacon Press.

Essa, E. (1999). *Introduction to early childhood education* (3rd ed.). Albany, N.Y.: Delmar.

Farran, D. C., Metzger, J., & Sparling, J. (1986). Immediate and continuing adaptations in parents of handicapping children. In J. Gallagher & P. Vietze (Eds.), *Families of handicapped persons* (pp. 143–163). Baltimore: Paul H. Brookes.

Gesell, A., & Amatruda, C. (1941). *Developmental diagnosis.* New York: Harper.

Glisczinski, C. P. (1995). *Family-focused early intervention: One family's experience.* Unpublished master's thesis. St. Paul, Minn.: University of St. Thomas.

Greenspan, S. I., & Meisels, S. (1995). Toward a new vision for the developmental assessment of infants and young children. *Zero to Three, 14,* 1–8.

Griffith, D. R., Azuma, S. D., & Chasnoff, I. J. (1994). Three-year outcome of children exposed prenatally to drugs. *Journal of the American Academy of Child and Adolescent Psychiatry, 33,* 20–27.

Guzmán, G., and Guzmán, L. (1992, June). Reflecting on the strengths of the IFSP. *Arc Light: A publication of the Association for Retarded Citizens* (pp. 1–3).

Hausslein, E., Kaufmann, R., and Hurth, J. (1992, February). From case management to service coordination: Families, policymaking, and Part H. *Zero to three,* 3, 10–13.

Head Start Bureau. (1999, November 19). *1999 Head Start fact sheet* [On-Line]. Available: http://www2.acf.dhhs.gov/programs/hsb/research/99_hsfs.htm

Lynch, E. W., and Hanson, M. J. (Eds.). (1992). *Developing cross-cultural competence: A guide for working with young children and their families.* Baltimore: Paul H. Brookes.

McGonigel, M. J. (1991). Philosophy and conceptual framework. In M. J. McGonigel, R. K. Kaufmann, & B. H. Johnson (Eds.), *Guidelines and recommended practices for the individualized family service plan* (pp. 7–14). Bethesda: Association for the Care of Children's Health.

Minuchin, P. (1988). Relationships within the family: A systems perspective. In R. A. Hinde & J. Stevenson-Hinde (Eds.), *Relationships within the families* (2nd ed., pp. 7–26). New York: Oxford University Press.

NAEYC (1996). *Position statement on developmentally appropriate practice in early childhood programs serving children from birth through age 8.* Washington, D.C.: Author.

National Head Start Association. (1999). *Head Start* [On-line]. Available: www.nhsa.org.

Olson, D. H., McCubbin, H. I., Barnes, H., Larsen, A., Muxem, M., & Wilson, M. (1989). *Families: What makes them work* (2nd ed.). Los Angeles: Sage.

Peterson, N. L. (1987). *Early intervention for handicapped and at-risk children.* Denver: Love.

Piaget, J. (1962). *Play, dreams, and imitation in childhood.* New York: Norton.

Rosenblith, J. F. (1992). *In the beginning: Development from conception to age two* (2nd ed.). Newbury Park, Calif.: Sage.

Sameroff, A. J., & Fiese, B. H. (1990). Transactional regulation and early intervention. In S. J. Meisels & J. P. Shonkoff (Eds.), *Handbook of early childhood intervention* (pp. 119–149). New Rochelle, N.Y.: Cambridge University Press.

Sameroff, A. J., & Seifer, R. (1990). Early contributors to developmental risks. In J. Roth, A. S. Masten, D. Cicchetti, K. H. Nuechterlein, & Weintaub, S. (Eds.), *Risk and protective factors in the development of psychopathology* (pp. 52–60). New York: Cambridge University Press.

Schweinhart, L. J., & Weikert, D. P. (1981). Effects of the Perry Preschool Program on youths through age 15. *Journal of the Division for Early Childhood, 4,* 29–39.

Shackelford, J. (1998). *State and jurisdictional eligibility definitions for infants and toddlers with disabilities under IDEA.* Chapel Hill, N.C.: NECTAS.

Sharp, M. C., & Lohr, J. A. (1994). The nature of teaching hospitals. In S. L. Hostler (Ed.), *Family-centered care: An approach to implementation* (pp. 71–88). Charlottesville: University of Virginia, Kluge Children's Rehabilitation Center.

Solnit, A., & Stark, M. (1961). Mourning and the birth of a defective child. *The Psychoanalytic Study of the Child, 16,* 523–537.

Turnbull, A. P., Summers, J. A., & Brotherson, M. J. (1984). *Working with families with disabled members: A family systems approach.* Lawrence, Kans.: University of Kansas.

Turnbull, A. P., & Turnbull, H. R. (1990). *Families, professionals, and exceptionality: A special partnership* (2nd ed.). Columbus, Ohio: Merrill.

Werner, E. E., & Smith, R. S. (1989). *Vulnerable but invincible: A longitudinal study of resilient children and youth.* New York: Adams, Bannister, & Cox.

Zigler, E., & Muenchow, S. (1992). *Head Start: The inside story of America's most successful educational experiment.* New York: Basic Books.

Zirpoli, T. J. (1995). Framework for understanding and affecting behavior. In T. J Zirpoli (ed.), *Understanding and affecting the behavior of young children* (pp. 2–33). Englewood Cliffs, N.J.: Merrill.

Zirpoli, T. J. & Melloy, K. J. (2001). *Behavior managment: Applications for teachers* (3rd ed.). Upper Saddle River, N.J.: Merrill.

CHAPTER TWO

THE PRENATAL PERIOD: BEGINNING THE JOURNEY

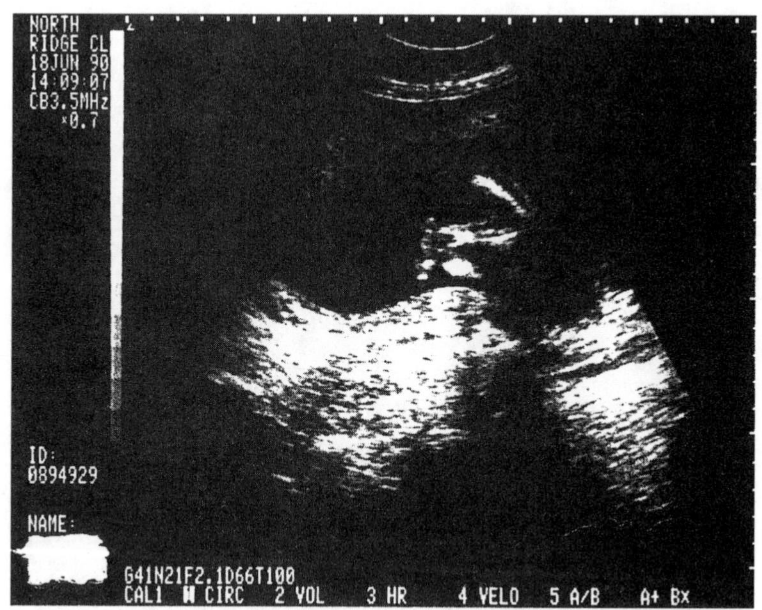

OBJECTIVES

- To understand the process of conception and development during the prenatal period
- To discuss the importance of prenatal development in terms of behavioral state and future development
- To understand the influence of the prenatal environment and the consequences for future development
- To understand the role of parents/caregivers during pregnancy
- To understand the process of prenatal diagnosis and the implications for families expecting a child with disabilities
- To explore the advent of gene therapy and implications of genetic engineering in the twenty-first century
- To discuss intervention strategies during the prenatal period, including planning for a difficult birth and dealing with grief and loss
- To understand ethical issues involving prenatal diagnosis

THE PRENATAL PERIOD

In recent years, there has been a growing interest in the impact of the fetal environment on later development (Graves, 1989). The hypothesis that fetuses prepare themselves for the next environment is not new. However, the increasing number of research articles demonstrating the competence of the newborn has refueled the issue in the last decade. During prebirth growth and development, first the embryo and then the fetus begins a process of growth and development analogous to life after birth.

In an attempt to understand this process, O'Leary (1992) related the prenatal experience to the neurological stages of development across the lifespan, as originally described by Gesell, which can be applicable to behavior. Beginning with conception, the fetus's development follows an orderly progression, with each stage achieving a new level of maturation. The end product of this process (the baby) is the result of the continuing reciprocity between the influences of nature (genetic endowment) and nurture (the prenatal environment).

During the prenatal period, the fetus moves through six stages of equilibrium and disequilibrium. The *smooth stage* prepares the intrauterine environment for conception as well as the birth. The *break-up stage* is characterized by the formation of all body cells in the fetus. At this point, the mother is undergoing tremendous psychological and physical changes. In the *sorting-out stage,* the fetus begins to move through flexion and extension and to explore the uterine environment. For example, by 20 weeks the fetus can hear sounds transmitted through the uterus and recognizes auditory stimuli. The mother is thinking about changes in her lifestyle. She might consider changes in her work, social life, and home life. The fetus settling into a mutually reciprocal relationship with the

TABLE 2.1 Developmental Cycles of Parenting During "Normal" Pregnancy

PHASES OF CYCLE	SMOOTH CONCEPTION	BREAK-UP BLASTOCYTE–12 WEEKS	SORTING OUT 12–24 WEEKS
Caplan's psychological tasks		Acceptance of Pregnancy Emotional affiliation with baby	
Fetal physiology	Conception	All organ systems forming & differentiate Most vulnerable to adversity	Rapid growth Placental functions in relationship with mother
Fetal behavior baby	Potential	**Energy:** Baby forming into who she is; reflex actions more differentiated **Mouth:** Opens; jaws snap rapidly **Fingers:** Close incompletely **Body:** Generalized movement **Extremity:** Isolated arm or leg movement **Eyes:** Move	Grasp with hands Sucks and swallows Coordinated hand to mouth movements Reacts to sounds Limb movements both reciprocal & symmetric Breathes
Maternal physiology	Ovulation & conception	Implantation HCG rises Progesterone, estrogen rise Breast size increases Fatigue	Quickening Placenta functions Becomes used to pregnancy Looks pregnant Fewer disruptive symptoms
Behavior and psychosocial partner and family	Calm, satisfied, & in harmony with body & environment Uncertain, variable	Oppositional At odds with self and environment Emotional roller coaster Ambivalence Own family background resurfaces	Temporary What fits? Seeking out other people & support Discover & explore Problem solving Time of questioning Mother sorts uterine contractions from baby movements Prepare financially Dream Prenatal Testing

From "The Parenting Process in the Prenatal Period: A Developmental Theory" by J. O'Leary, 1992, *Pre & Perinatal Psychology*, 7(2), 113–123. Reprinted by permission.

INWARDIZING 24–32 WEEKS	EXPANSION 32 WEEKS LABOR/BIRTH	"NEUROTIC" FITTING TOGETHER PP–4 WEEKS
	Perception of baby as separate individual	
Baby assumes fetal position Growth spurt Fetal heart rate (FHR) reacts to activity	Lungs mature Settles into mother's pelvis	Transition from fetal circulation to extrauterine life re: resp, HR, temp
Movements strong Pattern of movement Grasp nearly sufficient to support baby	Consciousness more closely defined after 38 weeks Sleep/awake cycles; awake longer Stretch & extend limbs with contractions Hearing more acute Much more aware of intrauterine life Competence increases	Copes with gravity; still flexed and mobile Shuts down if unfamiliar sounds Needs soft light Slow pace to see & hear together Movements more purposeful & less reflexive
Abdominal size & weight increase Notices fetal movements, uterine contractions	Uterine contractions, blood volume increase Cervical ripening Labor and birth	Involution Lochia Lactation Maternal hormones decrease
Restriction of view Work with parts to create new whole Introspective Concentrates energy on child within Can feel left out May distance self Seek help to affiliate with baby Fewer people around, not future oriented	New energy burst "Nesting" Prepares for birth, ready for birth class, ready to release baby to outside Seeks safe place & people to birth with	Emotional Sleep deprived Identity change: "Mom" & "Dad", not couple Let baby lead into roles

intrauterine environment characterizes the *inwardizing stage.* The fetus continues to gain weight and moves down toward the pelvis. The parent(s) start childbirth classes, and may decrease their social and work activities. During the *expansion stage,* the fetus becomes more active by stretching and expanding its body and, in turn, helps the uterus prepare for the impending birth, when the baby pushes and expands as she moves through the birth canal. (The mother who has a cesarean section experiences the expansion stage prior to the actual birth.) Finally, in the "neurotic," or fitting-together stage, the baby learns to adapt to external stimuli through six stages of consciousness. She is ready to eat, having practiced sucking and, in many cases, swallowing in utero. She learns to adjust to seeing and hearing in this new environment. The mother experiences the emotional impact of the baby who seeks out her parents with her eyes and knows their voices.

As this framework demonstrates, the baby takes the lead in the interactive ballet at the beginning of life. The pattern appears to be the same for all fetuses, regardless of later disability or medical complication (O'Leary, 1992). Although all families also experience these stages, one must consider individual differences and recognize that different families respond differently to similar events.

THE BEGINNING OF THE BIRTH PROCESS

From the very beginning, as a fertilized egg forms into a human being, the sequenced steps that occur are important for understanding the many disabilities that are possible as well as preventable. Basic to understanding conception is the fact that the male sperm contains 23 chromosomes that combine with the 23 chromosomes from the female. Therefore, the fertilized egg contains 46 chromosomes. Except for the sex chromosomes (X and Y), all other chromosomes are paired. The single-cell egg undergoes a process of successive cell divisions, and certain mishaps may occur when the cell divides. For example, if there is an extra number 21 chromosome, the child will have Down syndrome. With a procedure known as karyotyping, scientists are able to determine when cell division has been problematic by observing under a microscope the characteristics of chromosomes in terms of size, shape, and banding pattern (Batshaw, 1997).

INFLUENCES OF THE PRENATAL ENVIRONMENT ON DEVELOPMENT: TERATOGENS

Teratogens are agents such as infections, drugs, radiation, environmental pollutants, and chronic illness in the mother that lead to disruptions in fetal development (Graham & Morgan, 1997). Table 2.2 lists a number of teratogenic agents. The degree to which the fetus is affected depends on the timing and intensity of

TABLE 2.2 Teratogenic Agents

TERATOGEN	EXAMPLES
Drugs	Thalidomide, valproic acid, phenytoin
Environmental chemicals	Mercury
Radiation	X rays
Viruses	Rubella
Mechanical pressure	Amniotic band syndrome
Immobility (i.e., paralysis from a variety of causes)	Arthrogryposis multiplex congenita
Intrauterine environmental factors	Maternal phenylketonuria (PKU) Maternal diabetes Maternal fever

Courtesy of Peter A. Blasco, Oregon Health Sciences University, Portland.

contact. Since most of the human organs are formed between 10 and 60 days postconception, this is generally the most vulnerable time for the fetus (Batshaw, 1997). In addition, teratogens are one of the leading causes for developmental disabilities, particularly mental retardation, hearing loss, and vision loss (Graham & Morgan, 1997; Roizen & Johnson, 1996).

Infectious Diseases

While parents may devote time and resources to providing a prenatal environment conducive to optimal growth and development, no one can be absolutely certain that the fetus is safe from viral infection. Viral diseases usually affect approximately 5 percent of pregnant women (Rosenblith, 1992). A woman can contract a disease while she is pregnant or become pregnant when she is already infected. In the past, the most common congenital infections of the fetus and the newborn were known as the "TORCHS": *TO*xoplasmosis, *R*ubella, *C*ytomegalovirus, *H*erpes, and *S*yphilis. The number of disorders has expanded, as outlined below, but this acronym is often used by health care workers as an abbreviation for any or all congenital infections. (See Table 2.3.)

Toxoplasmosis. *Toxoplasma gondii* is a fairly common parasite that can produce the disease known as toxoplasmosis, which is asymptomatic in adults but is devastating to a developing fetus (Batshaw, 1997). The disease can be transmitted to the adult through eating raw eggs or meat and by unprotected exposure to cat or horse feces (Roizen & Johnson, 1996). Pregnant women may thus want to find a volunteer to change the kitty litter or purchase a self-cleaning litterbox. If the fetus

TABLE 2.3 Congenital Infections

INFECTIOUS DISEASE SYNDROME	CAUSATIVE AGENT	DURATION OF ACTIVE INFECTION	INFECTIVITY RISK TO:	
			Children	*Personnel*
Congenital Toxoplasmosis	Toxoplasma gondii	Ceases with treatment	– (never excretes oocysts) –	
Congenital Rubella Syndrome	Rubella virus	Months postnatal	+	– (should be vaccinated)
Cystomegalic Inclusion Disease	Cytomegalo-virus	? Up to 7 years	+	+/– (See text)
Neonatal Herpes Types 1 and 2	Herpes simplex virus	Indefinite, mostly latent	+ when active lesions present	+/– (requires impossibly intimate contact for type 1 virus)
Congenital Syphilis	Treponema pallidum	Ceases with treatment	+ until treated	+ until treated but requires intimate contact
Varicella Embryopathy	Varicella zoster virus	Lifelong, mostly latent	+	– (should be immune)
HIV Embryopathy	HIV	Lifelong	+/– (requires intimate contact)	

+, high infection risk; –, no infection risk.

becomes infected during the first trimester, the resulting complications are more severe than if the infection occurs in the third trimester.

At birth, there is no obvious sign of the disease in 90 percent of the infants infected with toxoplasmosis. In addition, according to Freij and Sever (as cited in Roizen & Johnson, 1996), a thorough examination yields positive results in only one-third of the infected infants. For those infants who are symptomatic, signs of toxoplasmosis include hydrocephalus, microcephaly, microphthalmia, visual impairment, and central nervous system damage (Roizen & Johnson). Other systemic conditions can include anemia, fever, liver damage, and respiratory distress.

According to Roizen and Johnson, without prenatal or postnatal treatment, 90 percent of those infants who manifested systemic or neurological signs of toxoplasmosis by the first year of life will have residual auditory, cognitive, and/or motor impairments. Treatment prenatally is very promising although controversial. In one study, 35 pregnant women were screened and suspected to be carrying the infection. One woman decided to have an abortion. The fetuses were treated in utero with antibotics (given via the mother) and followed after birth by the medical team. Only one child had symptoms by two months of age (Ghidini, Sirtori, Spelta, & Vergani, 1991); all the other children had typical development.

Rubella. Rubella, also known as German measles, is an infection that is capable of penetrating the placenta. In the 1960s investigators discovered that when the mother contracted rubella in the first trimester, 15–25 percent of all fetuses would have congenital deafness (Rosenblith, 1992). The time of infection is important in terms of the consequences for the fetus. If the mother contracts rubella within the first 60 days of pregnancy, the fetus is likely to develop cataracts; if she contacts it during the first 11 weeks, heart defects and deafness are likely. In the second trimester, deafness and retina involvement can also occur, but only 10 percent of fetuses are affected (Rosenblith, 1992). Today, most women are vaccinated against rubella; however, a disproportionate number of women from multicultural backgrounds may be at increased risk (Kaplin, Cochi, Edmonds, Zell, & Prelud, 1990).

Cytomegalovirus (CMV). Cytomegalovirus (CMV) is the most common cause of congenital infection in this country (Grose and Weiner, 1990). Most infected women are unaware that they have the virus. It typically affects the mother's cervix, breasts, and urinary tract (Rosenblith, 1992). The infant most commonly contracts the virus when passing through the birth canal. The leading cause of mental impairment and congenital deafness, CMV resulting in permanent disability occurs in 1 in 5,000 to 1 in 20,000 births (Batshaw, 1997).

Herpes Simplex Virus (HSV). Herpes simplex virus (HSV) is another infection that is most commonly (85 percent) contracted as the baby moves through the birth canal, although in some cases it is acquired after birth (10 percent) or in utero (5 percent) (Connelly & Stanberry, 1995). Growth delay, skin lesions, retinal abnormalities, and microcephaly are considered warning signs for HSV (Graham & Morgan, 1997). In addition, Roizen and Johnson (1996) believe seizures and fever may be indicative of HSV in infancy. With early detection and treatment, the infant will survive. Unfortunately, of those infants who do survive, half will develop microcephaly, cerebral palsy, seizures, deafness, and blindness.

Recognition of maternal HSV infection prior to delivery is the key to early identification of the at-risk infant and prevention of perinatal (at birth) transmission of the infection. If the medical team suspects maternal HSV, the baby can be delivered via caesarean section in order to avoid exposure to the virus (Roizen & Johnson, 1996).

Varicella Zoster. The varicella zoster virus is the causative agent of chicken pox. It can persist silently in the host (known as a latent infection) for decades and then reappear as a localized eruption referred to as shingles. Very rarely, the fetus of a woman with active varicella or active zoster can become infected with resultant congenital deformities, usually of the limbs. This is known as the fetal varicella syndrome (Alkalay, Pomerance, & Rimoin, 1987).

Human Immunodeficiency Virus (HIV). The human immunodeficiency virus (HIV) causes a devastating, progressive, and almost always fatal illness. Until very recently, a pregnant woman with the HIV infection had a 20 percent chance of transmitting the infection to her newborn (Newell & Peckman, 1993; Peckham and Gibb, 1995). In the past five years treatment of the mother with newly developed antiretroviral drugs (Conner et al., 1994) and additional strategies to shield the baby during and after delivery (Rogers & Shaffer, 1999) have decreased the risk of transmission to 5 percent or less. The odds are worse, however, for babies born in underdeveloped countries.

Syphilis. The agent that causes syphilis (known as a spirochete) can cross the placenta and is likely to infect the fetus in the later stage of pregnancy, after 16 to 18 weeks. It causes injury to many organs and can produce permanent damage. For example, lesions on the cornea can produce scarring and blindness. The infant born with syphilis is likely to be small for gestational age and have chronic liver problems, peritonitis (inflammation of the lining of the abdomen), anemia, and damage to the nervous system (Rosenblith, 1992). For children over two, late indicators of congenital syphilis include Hutchinson teeth (peg-shaped) and blurred vision (Roizen & Johnson, 1996).

If an infected mother is identified during pregnancy, congenital syphilis can be prevented with prenatal antibiotic treatment. However, as with rubella, women from low socioeconomic groups may not receive proper prenatal care, and are at a higher risk for the infection (Roizen & Johnson, 1996).

Radiation

One reason we know that radiation will cause birth defects is that women who had survived the nuclear bombing of Hiroshima and Nagasaki gave birth to children with multiple congenital abnormalities. Again, as with any teratogen, the amount of radiation exposure received during pregnancy makes a significant impact on the degree of disability. Women who were within one and one-quarter miles of the bombing had infants with microcephaly, but those who were outside a two-mile radius had apparently healthy infants, although years later, some developed leukemia (Graham & Morgan, 1997).

At present, scientists are not certain how much radiation is damaging to the fetus. The major concern, of course, is exposure to medically diagnostic X rays. Studies suggest that pregnant women can obtain a routine medical X ray (less than 5 rads) without harming the fetus (Graham & Morgan, 1997). The timing as well as the amount of radiation will determine the fetal effect. During the first month postconception, the embryo will either die as a result of exposure or survive to be a healthy infant. During the second and third months of pregnancy, when the fetus is very sensitive to teratogens, growth retardation is likely to occur. During the fourth and fifth months, the fetus is less sensitive but may still develop microcephaly and eye abnormalities (Graham & Morgan, 1997).

Exposure to radiation has led to concerns among expectant families as well as physicians about other medical procedures and about environmental radiation.

Ultrasound, sound waves that produce a moving image of the fetus, is often used during pregnancy and has proved to be essentially risk free (Blasco, Blasco, and Zirpoli, 1994). Today, most expectant parents carry an ultrasound picture of their future baby or babies to show to friends and family. Similarly, exposure to microwave ovens, radar, radio waves, and emissions from computer screens is apparently harmless (Graham & Morgan, 1997).

Medication and Chronic Illness

One of the most well-known examples of how medication used during pregnancy can affect a fetus occurred with the drug thalidomide, which was prescribed to pregnant women in Europe in the late 1950s and early 1960s to control nausea. Once again, the timing of the exposure resulted in different outcomes. If the mother took the drug between 21 and 35 days postconception, the infant was born with shortened or missing arms. If the drug was taken between days 21 and 30, the infant was born with shortened or missing legs as well as arms. If the mother took the drug more than 35 days postconception, the infant was born healthy (Graham & Morgan, 1997).

Other maternal medications that can affect the fetus include anticonvulsant drugs. For example, women who are on medication for seizure control may risk having children with fetal malformations, particularly cleft lip and palate. Not all women using antiepileptic drugs have children with congenital malformations (only 10–20 percent of children are affected). Women should work with their primary health care provider to determine whether a low dose of the medication is appropriate. Discontinuing medication during pregnancy could put both the mother and child at risk for convulsions (Graham and Morgan, 1997). When treating expectant mothers who require such medication, the medical team must balance the need to control her seizures with the necessity of minimizing possible harm to the fetus (Yerby, 1994).

Vignette 2.1 presents two cases of teratogenic syndromes, one due to a virus and the other to a drug effect.

VIGNETTE 2.1 PRENATAL EVENTS

Alicia was born at 38 weeks gestation to a primigravida woman (her first pregnancy) who had a mild illness in the second month of the pregnancy.

Alicia's mother had developed a rash, low-grade fever, malaise, and some joint aches, lasting 9–10 days. At birth the baby weighed 4 pounds, 3 ounces, and had a small head and a congenital heart defect. Later, it was determined she was deaf, and she had cataracts as well as retinal abnormalities. Developmentally, she made very slow progress and eventually was diagnosed with cerebral palsy, mental retardation, deafness, and visual impairment.

Peter is a three-year-old born at full term to a woman with epilepsy who took the anticonvulsant drug phenytoin (Dilantin)

> throughout her pregnancy. Peter is proportionally small and has coarse, dark hair. He also has a number of musculoskeletal anomalies, most notably, small fingers with dysplastic nails. Developmentally, he has been consistently delayed to a mild degree with developmental quotients (DQs) in the 60–70 range.

Alicia shows a classic clinical picture of the congenital rubella syndrome, and this diagnosis was confirmed by a blood test that revealed high levels of antibody to the rubella virus. Her mother's illness was typical of German measles; either she had never been vaccinated or had been a vaccine failure. Peter's mother, on the other hand, was required to stay on medication during her pregnancy because of the severe nature of her seizures, although she knew her baby had about a 10 percent risk of acquiring the fetal hydantoin syndrome, which he did develop.

The number of teratogenic syndromes and their clinical manifestations are myriad. The early interventionist, when working with a child with a known syndrome diagnosis, should consult the literature for specific information. The single best resource is *Smith's Recognizable Patterns of Human Malformation* (Jones, 1996). Another superb resource for professionals, and especially for parents, are diagnosis-specific parent support groups, which can be accessed through *Exceptional Parent* magazine.

EMBRYOLOGY AND STRUCTURAL ABNORMALITIES

As discussed earlier, embryology is the study of the formation and development of the embryo, when spectacular changes take place as the single-celled being (known as a zygote) matures until ready for birth. Along the way, damaging events occur that, depending on their timing and nature, can lead to wide-ranging and severe or quite focal and mild structural abnormalities, referred to as malformations, disruptions, and deformations.

Dysmorphology

Physical features that do not conform to standard norms for physical development are referred to as dysmorphisms or anomalies. The condition known as Down syndrome, for example, is associated with multiple dysmorphic features. (In fact, 29 signs have been recognized in the disorder and were the sole basis for diagnosis before chromosome analysis became available (see Jackson, North, & Thomas, 1976). Major malformations are defined as those that require modification, in terms of either ongoing care, or specific surgical or medical intervention, and that will likely alter the child's and family's life in significant ways. Major malformations occur in 2 percent of all newborn infants (Jones, 1996). Usually, they are isolated, such as a hole between the ventricles of the heart (ventricular septal defect).

In contrast, minor anomalies or malformations are morphologic features that are unusual but of no serious medical or cosmetic consequence (Jones, 1996). They are much more common, a single one occurring in 13–27 percent of all individuals. Rarely are they of any functional consequence. Very few children will have more than one minor malformation (1.5 percent), and as the number of minor anomalies increases to three or beyond, the likelihood of associated major anomalies becomes extremely high. The analysis of dysmorphic features falls to the specialties known as genetics and dysmorphology. These categories are discussed in detail in Chapter 8.

Syndromes

When a collection of malformations, major and minor, appear repeatedly together, the particular pattern is referred to as a syndrome. Examples would include Down syndrome, the congenital rubella syndrome noted above, and so on. Syndromes are considered to have a single, specific cause. Numerous specific syndromes have been identified. Many, but not all, have been named and each year new ones are added to the list.

Cellular and Molecular Genetics

In contrast to teratogens, which produce damage in what otherwise would have been a normal structure, some structural anomalies evolve naturally as a consequence of missing, altered, or even excessive genetic material in our cells. Thus, abnormal genes provide the code for the features of a given disorder. The best-known "inherited" genetic syndromes are those associated with extensive chromosome abnormalities: Down syndrome (chromosome 21 trisomy), Turner syndrome (X chromosome monosomy), and cri du chat syndrome (chromosome 5 partial deletion). Large numbers of genes are involved in these disorders.

Single-gene disorders involve only a tiny, localized portion of a chromosome and are generally inherited according to certain principles, known as Mendel's laws. Most disorders are either recessive or dominant in terms of their inheritance pattern. Since 44 of our 46 chromosomes are paired (the X and Y chromosomes that determine sex are a mismatch), each gene is represented twice in a normal cell—once on a maternally derived chromosome and once on the complementary paternally derived chromosome. If a defective gene is transmitted in a recessive fashion, it is merely silent, with the gene from the other parent supplying adequate amounts of whatever protein is needed. Recessive genes generally code for enzymes, and only one gene will produce enough enzyme for the cellular machinery to work. For the occurrence of the disorder, *both* recessive genes, that is, one from each parent, must be defective. In contrast, dominant genes usually code for a structural protein. In that case, some proportion of the body cell structure will contain protein derived from the defective gene, and, therefore, those areas will be weakened or disrupted. This is likely to have clinical consequences, sometimes severe, sometimes mild. Examples of dominatingly inherited disorders would include the Marfan syndrome, achondroplasia, and neurofibromatosis.

VIGNETTE 2.2 GENETIC TRAITS

At the turn of the twentieth century, the ruling family of Russia were the Romanovs, headed by Tsar Nicholas II and Tsarina Alexandra. Alexandra's grandmother was Queen Victoria of England, who carried the gene for hemophilia. Alexandra was one of eight children born to Victoria; her older sister was also a carrier, and one brother had the disease. Nicholas and Alexandra produced five children: four girls and one boy, Alexis, who is perhaps the most famous hemophiliac in history. It was Alexis's disease that brought his mother under the spell of the unscrupulous Rasputin, to whom she turned for spiritual guidance. His influence on Alexandra and the rest of the royal family was one of the key factors leading to the Russian Revolution and the end of the Russian monarchy in the early 1900s.

Genes located on the X chromosome constitute a special situation. Since males only have one X chromosome, a "recessive" gene abnormality on that chromosome would actually be expressed in males, because they, unlike women, have no second X to supply a functional gene. These disorders are referred to as X-linked (or sex-linked) conditions (see Vignette 2.2). The defective gene must come from the mother (who supplies the X for her sons, with the Y coming from the father). The mother, as a rule, is a silent carrier of X-linked recessive conditions. Since she has two X chromosomes, one normal and one with the gene that is defective, each male offspring has a 50-50 chance of having the disorder, whereas each female offspring has a 50-50 chance of being a carrier. Dominant X-linked conditions are generally fatal in males, with death occurring during gestation or very soon after birth. Females with dominant X-linked conditions may express them to a mild degree (and, therefore, be able to reproduce) or to a severe degree.

Many genetic phenomena, however, are not explained by Mendelian inheritance. These mechanisms of non-Mendelian genetic inheritance—mosaicism, uniparental disomy, genomic imprinting, and others—get quite complicated. Blizzard (1993) and Austin and Hall (1992) provide concise reviews of genetic textbooks. In many diseases (e.g., pyloric stenosis, diabetes mellitus) and some syndromes and birth defects (e.g., spina bifida, cleft palate), genes play a partial role in concert with other noninherited (i.e., environmental) factors. This situation is commonly referred to as multifactorial inheritance.

Prenatal diagnosis, which is discussed in greater depth later in the chapter, takes advantage of the known genetic facts about a given situation and applies them to the unborn fetus in an effort to predict abnormalities. Recent developments in the use of prenatal diagnosis have the potential to affect the incidence of certain genetic disorders, the psychological well-being of future parents, and the social and moral standards of society.

THE FUNCTIONING FETUS

The sequence of events that occur once the embryo is formed continues to have implications for the fetus. Although we expect a pregnancy to follow a certain developmental progression, few viewed the fetus as an active partner in that progression. Examining the role of the fetus as a functioning, sensory organism is a new critical frontier in early development. One week after conception, the fertilized egg attaches itself to the uterine wall in a process known as implantation (Batshaw, 1997). The uterine wall provides nutritional support for the developing embryo (Rosenblith, 1992). By three weeks, a primitive placenta develops and increases the flow of nutrition to the embryo. At three weeks to one month, the embryo begins to develop a nervous system when the outermost layer of cells, the primitive neurectoderm, folds over on itself to form the neural tube. A defect in this process may result in an opening in the spine. Myelomeningocele occurs when the spinal column and surrounding membranes form a pouch extending from the opening in the spine (Wolraich, 1992). The medical and educational implications of this condition and related conditions will be discussed in Chapter 8.

Around the fifth week, the heart begins to form and limb buds are formed. At eight to ten weeks, the six pharyngeal arches in the facial structure will join to form the lips, palate, and mandible. If these arches do not completely fuse, the child will have cleft lip and/or cleft palate. By the second month, the embryo begins to look like a human being. The term *fetus* is now used to describe the growing baby. The heart is beating and blood is circulating through the body and muscles. This is a period of rapid brain growth. Between three and six months the fetus continues to grow and develop. By week 35 of pregnancy, the fetus can tell the difference between dark and light. At this stage, 50 percent of fetuses have mature lungs. During weeks 35 and 36, the fetus is busy gaining weight. The eyes are open, and the irises are a deep blue. The fingernails reach to the ends of the fingers. The baby will attempt to descend into the pelvis area and fit its head snugly into the birth channel. From weeks 37 to 40, the baby continues to put on weight, sometimes up to an ounce a day. The fingernails have surpassed the fingertips and will need to be cut after delivery. Figure 2.1 provides an overview of fetal growth from conception to birth.

Fetal Movement

Most pregnant women will experience the first fetal movement, called quickening, by the sixteenth week of gestation. However, the fetus is able to show reflexive movement between 10 and 11 weeks gestation. For example, a fetus will respond to a touch stimulus in the palm of the hand; these early reflexive movements continue into postnatal life. By 15–16 weeks, the fetus will respond orally to stimulation similar to the postnatal sucking reflex. The fetus will move and change position frequently between 10 and 15 weeks. By the fifth month of pregnancy, almost all mothers will feel the movement of the fetus regularly. Over the

AGE weeks	LENGTH cm. C-R	LENGTH cm. Tot.	WT. gm.	GROSS APPEARANCE	CNS	EYE, EAR	FACE, MOUTH	CARDIO-VASCULAR	LUNG
$7\frac{1}{2}$	2.8				Cerebral hemisphere; Infundibulum, Rathke's	Lens nearing final shape	Palatal swellings; Dental lamina, Epithel.	Pulmonary vein into left atrium	
8	3.7				Primitive cereb. cortex; Olfactory lobes; Dura and pia mater	Eyelid; Ear canals	Nares plugged; Rathke's pouch detach.; Sublingual gland	A-V bundle; Sinus venosus absorbed into right auricle	Pleuroperitoneal canals close; Bronchioles
10	6.0				Spinal cord histology; Cerebellum	Iris; Ciliary body; Eyelids fuse; Lacrimal glands; Spiral gland different	Lips, nasal cartilage; Palate		Laryngeal cavity reopened
12	8.8				Cord-cervical & lumbar enlarged, Cauda equina	Retina layered; Eye axis forward; Scala tympani	Tonsillar crypts; Cheeks; Dental papilla	Accessory coats, blood vessels	Elastic fibers
16	14				Corpora quadrigemina; Cerebellum prominent; Myelination begins	Scala vestibuli; Cochlear duct	Palate complete; Enamel and dentine	Cardiac muscle condensed	Segmentation of bronchii complete
20						Inner ear ossified	Ossification of nose		Decrease in mesenchyme; Capillaries penetrate linings of tubules
24		32	800		Typical layers in cerebral cortex; Cauda equina at first sacral level		Nares reopen; Calcification of tooth primordia		Change from cuboidal to flattened epithelium; Alveoli
28		38.5	1100		Cerebral fissures and convolutions	Eyelids reopen; Retinal layers complete; Perceive light			Vascular components adequate for respiration
32		43.5	1600	Accumulation of fat		Auricular cartilage	Taste sense		Number of alveoli still incomplete
36		47.5	2600						
38		50	3200		Cauda equina, at L-3; Myelination within brain	Lacrimal duct canalized	Rudimentary frontal maxillary sinuses	Closure of: foramen ovale, ductus arteriosus, umbilical vessels, ductus venosus	
First postnatal year +					Continuing organization of axonal networks; Cerebrocortical function, motor coordination; Myelination continues until 2-3 years	Iris pigmented, 5 months; Mastoid air cells; Coordinate vision, 3-5 months; Maximal vision by 5 years	Salivary gland ducts become canalized; Teeth begin to erupt 5-7 months; Relatively rapid growth of mandible and nose	Relative hypertrophy left ventricle	Continue adding new alveoli

FIGURE 2.1 Fetal Development

From *Recognizable Patterns of Human Malformation,* 3rd ed., by D. W. Smith & K. L. Jones, 1982, Philadelphia: W. B. Saunders, inside front cover. Reprinted by permission.

course of the next four months, family members and others may be encouraged to feel for the baby.

Although fetal movement patterns vary from individual to individual, all fetuses demonstrate movement throughout the latter stages of pregnancy (Loman, 1994). Researchers who have studied fetal movements describe the rhythms and flow of movement as outlined below:

Tension-flow Rhythms. Patterns of tension that may be frequent or infrequent and serve to satisfy the baby's needs. Several of the behaviors observed at birth and during the first year of life, including sucking, biting, twisting, straining, and swaying have roots in prenatal movement (Loman, 1994).

Tension-flow Attributes. Attributes that are related to an individual's temperament, characteristics of arousal, and the ability to calm oneself, which Sossin and Loman (1992, p. 21) have described as qualities of intensity (see Table 2.4).

The quality of parental recognition of and attunement to fetal movement may be a predictor of the later parent-infant attachment. Expectant parents can learn to understand the flow of fetal movement. In one parenting class, mothers drew visual representations of their fetuses' movement on paper. In Vignette 2.3, one mother of twins describes her experience with tuning into her babies.

VIGETTE 2.3 WHERE ARE YOU?

I saw so many ultrasounds that I knew exactly where both twins were and who had all the room. Andrew, my son, was head down, snugly heading for the birth canal, and his movements were usually long and slow. Caitlin, my daughter, was squished on the left side, and her movements were rapid, quick, and short in duration. When I

TABLE 2.4 Attributes of Tension Flow

1. **Even-flow:** Tension in the fetus is regulated at the same level, suggesting rest, steadiness, and an even temperament.
2. **Flow-adjustment:** Tension in the fetus will adjust to new situations, suggesting an accommodating temperament.
3. **High intensity:** Tension in the fetus becomes extreme, suggesting intense feelings such as joy or anger; indicative of an excitable temperament.
4. **Low intensity:** Tension stays at a moderate level, suggesting low-key behavior and a mild temperament.
5. **Abrupt:** Tension varies rapidly, suggesting impulsivity, impatience, and alertness.
6. **Gradual:** Tension varies but at a slow pace, suggesting patience and endurance.

Adapted from "Attuning to the Fetus and the Young Child: Approaches from Dance Movement Therapy" by S. Loman, 1994, *Zero to Three, 15,* 21.

> was placed on bed rest, the nurse would tell me to lie on my left side. Although I knew my position would not affect the babies, I felt like Caitlin was being squished and pushed by her brother. My suspicions were confirmed when they were born; Caitlin weighed one and a half pounds less than her brother did. My obstetrician imitated her arrival into the world by mimicking, "I am here, and I am sick and tired of not having any room and less food, and now you're all going to pay for this!" Caitlin had to stay in the hospital an extra three weeks, as she was born at 3 pounds, 9 ounces. She seemed to be gaining weight steadily and quickly became a favorite with the Newborn nurses. One morning we received a call from the resident on duty. He was very concerned that Caitlin had necrotizing enterocolitis (NEC), a condition that severely damages the small intestine. They would do some tests, but would have to stop all feedings for Caitlin. I arrived to visit her with her brother in his infant seat. She had been screaming all morning and her face was close to purple. She had lost the full cheeks she had gained in the last few days and I was very frightened for her health. I was not allowed to feed her, so I sat and rocked her. She continued to cry and look at me as if to say, "How could you do this to me?" That night, the test showed that she was okay and she could continue to eat again. She has been a feisty, spirited child ever since!

Many parents express knowledge of their baby's environment prior to birth. The enhanced and regular use of ultrasound and other medical technologies has led to an increased parental awareness of the prenatal environment. More and more parents use yoga, music, and sensory inputs in hopes of enhancing later child development. To date, there is no scientific evidence of a link between these methods and later development. However, we know that a prenatal environment free of stress and toxic agents (e.g., drugs, alcohol) is essential for a healthy outcome.

Early Sensory Behaviors

While it may be premature to record with certainty the existence of fetal emotional expression (e.g., crying, facial expressions), early sensory behaviors of the fetus may be indicative of the prenatal roots of ego functions that emerge later in the developed child (Graves, 1989). Facial expressions of happiness, sadness, anger, and disgust are observable very early in life. This has led researchers to believe that they have a strong biological connection to the fetal origins of neural structure (Campos, Barrett, Lamb, Goldsmith, & Stenberg, 1983; Izard & Malatesta, 1987). Research continues to expand our knowledge of fetal neurobehavioral development with the hopes of gaining knowledge of later behavioral development (DiPietro, Hodgson, Costigan, & Hilton, 1996). Whatever the outcome, we know that the newborn enters the world prepared for social contact (Lally et al., 1997).

Maternal and Paternal Contributions

The fetus's nine months of growth is also a time of anxious anticipation and growth for the parents. As mentioned in Chapter 1, society influences the role parents assume as they prepare for the birth of a child. Years ago, most fathers did not actively assist the mother through childbirth. Women often delivered under anesthesia and were pleased to wake up and find the perfect baby waiting for them. Fathers paced in the hospital corridors and passed out cigars with blue or pink bands to announce the birth. All of that changed in the 1970s for the majority of families experiencing childbirth. The revolution toward mutual partnering in childbirth had controversial beginnings, however. In 1976, Klaus and Kennell developed the theory that there is a "critical period" during which the newborn and the mother must bond in order to ensure a healthy developmental future for the baby. Basing their information on a study of mothers and their babies immediately after birth, they claimed that mothers who had more contact time with their infants demonstrated better "mothering skills" than mothers who had less time with their infants. But several researchers disputed these findings, and in 1982 the authors amended their position to extend bonding experiences to fathers and to mothers whose infants were unavailable immediately after birth (e.g., infants in a special care unit) (Klaus & Kennell, 1982).

Despite the controversy over their findings, the researchers' work was very fruitful in that they precipitated an enormous increase in opportunities for parental access to their newborns. Updated birthing rooms, equipped to produce a relaxed environment, replaced sterile maternity units. Families were given the opportunity to be together and to participate in the birth process (Blasco & Pearson, 1995). Unfortunately, with the increase in managed health care and the decrease in the amount of time families can stay in the hospital after the birth of a child, some of these practices may become a thing of the past.

In order to prepare for the event, many parents attend childbirthing classes that help them to understand the changes in both the mother and baby over the nine months of pregnancy. These classes vary in methodology, but generally teach parents breathing exercises and what to do and expect during the delivery. For parents who are anticipating the birth of a child with a disability, these classes may be emotionally difficult, since they are geared toward a typical birth. Also, parents who have had a child with a disability and are expecting the birth of another child may need extra support at this time.

PRENATAL DIAGNOSIS

Years ago, parents were unaware that their child had a disability until birth or during the early childhood years. Now, expectant parents can be largely assured that their developing baby does not have a genetic disorder during the early months of pregnancy (Blasco, Blasco, & Zirpoli, 1994). And if a disability does exist, the ability to have a prenatal diagnosis may give expectant parents more time to seek information and services relating to their child's impairment prior to birth.

Families have a choice of continuing ending the pregnancy after prenatal diagnosis. Whatever the family's decision, service providers should be aware that they need continuing support. If the family decides to end the pregnancy, they may experience feelings similar to those families who suffer the loss of a child. If the parents decide to continue the pregnancy, they will need assistance in preparing for the birth and in locating appropriate community services (Blasco et al., 1994). Because the termination of a pregnancy is considered a medical risk, families may be hurried by the medical team to arrive at a decision in a few days. This kind of pressure can increase stress for all family members. Pauker and Pauker (1994) advocated the use of a decision tree to help families evaluate risks and attitudes toward miscarriage, elective termination, and the birth of a child with a known disability.

Diagnostic Screening

Diagnostic procedures have been refined over the last decade. Yet despite this improvement, expectant couples receive a diagnosis only of the disability, not of its severity. For example, a couple may be told that their expected child will have Down syndrome; however, the extent of the disability, including mental impairment, is not known at the time of the diagnosis. In addition, many known disabilities have several secondary disabilities related to the original disorder (Batshaw, 1997). The extent to which related disabilities may be involved is mostly unknown at the time of initial diagnosis.

Expectant parents who are viewed medically as a high-risk group are likely to be referred for genetic counseling and subsequent prenatal diagnosis. Issues surrounding the invasiveness of screening for parents has not been addressed in the literature. Some parents may not wish to undergo screening because they are considered high risk. In addition, many families are delaying childbirth for personal, financial, and professional reasons. Women over 35 are routinely offered prenatal diagnosis, usually amniocentesis, because of the increased risk for genetic defects in the fetus with increasing maternal age (Haddow, Polomaki, & Knight, 1992). However, many women and their partners are electing to have their first child in their forties and do so without complications. As a result, more and more physicians are questioning the age of 35 as a "magic number" for routine screening (Pauker & Pauker, 1994). In other words, some physicians do not believe maternal age should be the only criterion for prenatal testing.

Prenatal Screening Techniques

Several types of prenatal screening measures are now used on a routine basis. Amniocentesis, usually performed between 14 and 17 weeks of gestation, is probably the most widely known test. The technique involves the insertion of a needle through the abdominal wall into the amniotic fluid surrounding the fetus. Ultrasound is always used during amniocentesis to guide the needle into the uterus. The fluid can be used for specific biochemical tests, and the viable cells floating in it are cultured for chromosomal and DNA studies. Results are available in a few days to a few weeks, depending on the test being done (Batshaw, 1997).

Over 250 genetic disorders can be identified by analyzing amniotic fluid. The risk of miscarriage following this procedure is 0.5 percent, which is the same rate for fetal loss at the same point in gestation (Blasco et al., 1994). Other risks include fetal damage from needle puncture, leakage of amniotic fluid, maternal infection, and premature labor, but these complications are extremely rare.

Chorionic villus sampling (CVS) is a procedure performed between 9 and 11 weeks of gestation. Many families prefer CVS to amniocentesis because it is done earlier in the pregnancy and results are available within a few days. During this procedure, a catheter is inserted through the vagina and threaded into the uterus to the developing placenta using ultrasound guidance. A small sample of placental tissue is removed and placed into culture. Since the cells do not have to grow in a culture for several weeks, preliminary results are usually available in 48 to 72 hours (Blasco et al., 1994). The risk of miscarriage directly related to the CVS procedure (i.e., over and above the expected spontaneous loss rate) has been estimated to be 1 percent or less (Rhoads et al., 1989).

A new avenue for obtaining fetal cells is through the maternal blood (Bianchi, 1995). At present, it is still difficult to distinguish between fetal cells and maternal cells in a blood sample, but as fetal cell isolation techniques are advanced and perfected, the fetal genome will be easily detected (Bianchi, 1995). Fetal cell isolation has advantages over the commonly used procedures because of reduced risk and cost. As more and more women and families are requesting prenatal diagnosis regardless of their risk category, science attempts to keep pace.

Maternal serum alpha fetoprotein (AFP) is a screening test that may be completed prior to amniocentesis, between 16 and 18 weeks gestation. In fact, many physicians are recommending the use of this simple blood test over more invasive procedures if the mother is not high risk (Haddow et al., 1992; Bianchi, 1995). AFP can be measured in the maternal serum or in the amniotic fluid. High levels of AFP in the maternal serum suggest the possibility of a neural tube defect. Approximately 85 percent of such defects and some abdominal wall defects can be found with this simple blood test (Schnatterly, Hogge, and Felder, 1990). A low serum AFP level may be indicative of Down syndrome (Schoenfeld-DiMaio et al., 1987; Hershey, Crandall, & Perdue, 1986) and trisomy 18 (Simpson et al., 1986). Further diagnostic testing is almost always recommended when a positive result is found, because fewer than 10 percent of women with an abnormal serum AFP level are carrying a fetus with a disability (Batshaw, 1997). For example, a high serum AFP level may simply indicate that the mother is carrying twins.

Because AFP levels rise between 13 and 32 weeks, the precise period of gestation must be determined to interpret the results correctly. An over- or underestimated gestation will provide false comparison levels and potentially incorrect findings. The importance of adjusting AFP levels based on maternal weight in order to assign accurate risk status has been emphasized as well (Macri, Kasturi, Krantz, & Koch, 1986). Newer maternal serum markers for chromosome abnormalities are currently being developed and offer promise for much greater diagnostic sensitivity and specificity when combined with maternal serum AFP (Haddow, Palomaki, & Knight, 1992; Bianchi, 1995).

Ultrasound is a commonly known screening technique that can be used as early as two to three weeks conceptional age to identify a successful pregnancy. This procedure transposes reflected sound waves into images of the fetus on a computerlike screen. It is considered to be relatively risk free to both the mother and the fetus. In high-risk cases, it is not uncommon for women to have multiple ultrasound examinations during the course of a pregnancy.

Ultrasound is used for its own diagnostic value and also as a tool in other prenatal procedures. For example, it can be used to measure the length of the fetal femur, which is an excellent indicator of gestational age (Abramowicz, Jaffe, & Warsof, 1989). Ultrasound is used to guide needle insertion during amniocentesis as well as during intrauterine transfusion into an umbilical vessel (Charrow, 1985). It can successfully guide instruments during fetal surgery as well. Ultrasound is also used to identify tubal pregnancy, twins, some disabilities, and gender of the fetus.

Parents who do not want to undergo an invasive procedure that carries some risk, such as CVS or amniocentesis, can have an ultrasound examination between 18 and 22 weeks to confirm obvious structural abnormalities such as microcephaly, hydrocephalus, anencephaly, limb deformity, and spina bifida. Thorp and Bowes (1989) reported that ultrasound examination detected 90 percent of open neural tube defects among a group of parents who would not consider abortion. Another advantage of this procedure is that feedback is instantaneous. Ultrasound has also been used to detect more subtle malformations of internal organs such as cardiac abnormalities, fetal tumors, and fetal hernia (Campbell & Pearce, 1983).

Another technology available for prenatal diagnosis is DNA analysis. For example, developments in gene cloning and gene mapping have resulted in new tests for carrier detection of Mendelian, or monogenic (single-gene) defects (Ostrer, 1989). The first important contribution of prenatal DNA analysis came with the clarification of the gene that causes sickle cell disease (Chueh & Golbus, 1990). Other disorders that can be detected through DNA analysis include cystic fibrosis, Duchenne and Becker muscular dystrophy, myotomic dystrophy, Huntington disease, phenylketonuria (PKU), and Tay-Sachs disease, with the list expanding at a rapid rate. Within the next 15 years, molecular genetic techniques will likely be available for detecting most monogenic disorders (D'Alton & De-Cherney, 1993).

Commercial and university-based laboratories offer diagnosis using DNA techniques. Prior to the test, genetic counseling is advised so that a complete pedigree can identify family members who are at risk. Genomic DNA from any tissue is suitable for analysis. Parents are often requested to provide whole-blood samples (in which case the white cells are utilized) from themselves and their children. A disadvantage of this procedure is that it often requires analysis from multiple individuals to obtain a result. In addition, mothers need to undergo CVS or amniocentesis to provide a sample of cells from the fetus. Research directed at separating fetal cells circulating in the maternal bloodstream may eventually make it possible to substitute a simple maternal venipuncture for the much more invasive procedures (Simpson & Elias, 1993). This will enhance the availability and timeliness of sampling, since special on-site expertise and technology will no longer be necessary.

In Table 2.5, the most common types of prenatal diagnosis are summarized.

Preimplantation Sampling

The latest technique in prenatal screening involves sampling cells from early embryos prior to uterine implantation. With the establishment of in vitro fertilization as a routine technique, it has been demonstrated that it is possible to extract several cells from the developing embryo at the blastomere stage (where no cell differentiation has yet taken place). Rapid DNA amplification and the newest diagnostic techniques can then be applied to these few cells (literally one or two) (Simpson & Carson, 1992). Once the status of several embryos has been determined, the normal ones can be selected for introduction into the mother's uterus in time for implantation. Handyside, Lesko, Tarin, Winston, and Hughes (1992) have reported the successful application of this technique in a family in which both parents were carriers of the gene deletion for cystic fibrosis.

TABLE 2.5 Common Prenatal Screening and Diagnostic Procedures

PROCEDURE	TIMING	RESULTS	RISK	PURPOSE
Ultrasound	Anytime	Immediate	None	Observe fetal structure and growth, placenta and cord
Chorionic villus sampling (CVS)	9–11 weeks	2–3 days	<1%	Chorionic cell analysis
Amniocentesis	14–18 weeks	Fluid 2–3 days Cells 3–4 days	<1%	Amniotic fluid and fetal cell analysis
Maternal serum alpha fetoprotein (AFP)	16–18 weeks	2–3 days	None	Identify possible deformities and chromosome aberrations
DNA analysis (completed after CVS or amniocentesis)	9–18 weeks	Variable*	None	Identify specific genetic disorders
Maternal fetal circulating cells	Anytime	3–4 days	None	Fetal cell analysis (experimental; difficult to separate maternal from fetal cells)

*Results depend on number of family members involved and type of disease

Adapted from "Prenatal Diagnosis: Current Procedures and Implications for Early Interventionists Working with Families" by P. M. Blasco, P. A. Blasco, & T. J. Zirpoli, 1994, *Infants and Young Children, 7*(2), 33–42.

PRENATAL INTERVENTION

One advantage of early detection is the possibility of intervention directed at the developing fetus. The field of fetal surgery is not new but has continued to grow as more sophisticated equipment and techniques become available. The advantages of fetal rather than newborn surgery include: (1) early correction of a defect that could result in death, (2) lower rejection rate of early allogenic grafts by the immature immune system, and (3) quicker postoperative healing in the uterine environment. Procedures currently in use largely focus on life-threatening problems and include fetal blood sampling and transfusion, intrauterine shunting for hydrocephalus, repair of lung and diaphragm anomalies, and correction of urinary tract obstruction (Lorenz, Adzick, & Harrison, 1993; Estes, MacGillivray, Hedrick, Adzick, & Harrison, 1992).

One example of such surgery is the correction of fetal hydrocephalus. During surgery, ultrasound is used to insert a plastic shunt catheter into the fetal skull. The shunt is left in place, with the distal end in the mother's amniotic fluid. During birth, a cesarean section is carried out to avoid compression of the fetal head and bacterial infection of the shunt (Bland, Nelson, Meis, Weaver, & Abramson, 1983). At a later date, the original catheter is replaced with a ventriculoperitoneal shunt. Intrauterine shunting, however, has been somewhat disappointing in terms of outcome. For example, many professionals are concerned with the poor prognosis of patients regardless of treatment (Glick, Harrison, Nakayama et al., 1984; Drugan et al., 1989). The poor prognosis is likely related to other associated anomalies. Those babies who do have isolated progressive hydrocephalus will have varying needs for postnatal shunting (Evans, Drugan, Manning, & Harrison, 1989).

Open fetal surgery is still experimental and performed at only a few research centers. With technical advances employing fetoscopic techniques, open uterine surgery, which is riskier, can be avoided and earlier intervention for nonlife-threatening malformations can be considered (Estes et al., 1992). In a recent situation, a baby was diagnosed with an open heart defect in utero. An infant heart donor was found, and within several hours, the baby with the heart defect was delivered and then received the heart transplant.

Until now, more than 90 percent of children with spina bifida required a shunt to drain fluid off the brain. Fetal surgery for spina bifida is intended to decrease the disabilities associated with the condition. Researchers have found that the procedure apparently affects the way the brain develops in utero, allowing specific malformations of the brain, typically associated with spina bifida, to correct themselves (Adzick, Sutton, Crombleholme, & Flake, 1998). Promising research indicates that among infants who have had fetal surgery for spina bifida the need for a shunt is reduced by 33 to 50 percent (Bruner, Richards, Tulipan, & Arney, in press). As with any new procedure, fetal surgery for spina bifida is not risk free for either the mother or fetus. There are also ethical considerations, which will be discussed later in the chapter.

Drug Interventions

Other prenatal interventions that are effective include treating HIV-positive pregnant women with the drug azidothymidine (AZT), which can inhibit the replication of HIV and prohibits the lengthening of the viral DNA (Mueller & Pizzo, 1992). Although this treatment has reduced the likelihood of viral transmission to the developing fetus, it remains controversial for two reasons: (1) no one knows at what point during gestation transmission occurs; (2) only one out of three infants actually develops the infection (Mueller & Pizzo, 1992).

Gene Therapy

The most hopeful and potentially ameliorative technique for the prevention of developmental disabilities is gene therapy. At the same time, the implications of this treatment and the ethical and moral dilemmas surrounding it will be debated over the next few decades. Physicians now have the techniques for removing a defective gene and replacing it with a normal one, thus decreasing morbidity and mortality (de la Cruz & Friedmann, 1995).

In 1990, the first gene therapy experiment was federally approved and begun on a four-year-old girl with adenosine deaminase deficiency (ADA), which caused her to have a poor immune system that led to numerous potentially fatal illnesses and infections. As one can imagine, her life was far from typical for a four-year-old child. A safe, modified viral vector was used to carry a normal copy of the ADA gene (Fletcher, 1995). After the gene therapy, her immune system began to improve steadily.

Scientists still have a long way to go in understanding the potential benefits as well as the drawbacks of gene therapy. Currently, only single-gene disorders that cause severe mental disabilities are likely to have treatment with such means (Moser, 1995). These individuals account for less than 20 percent of persons with mental disabilities. In terms of the general population, only 0.3 to 0.6 percent of the population have single-gene disorders, such as Down syndrome or fragile-X syndrome (Moser, 1995).

Gene therapy raises many ethical and moral questions that have not been addressed by our society. As by Fletcher (1995) stated, "Experimental gene therapy for mental retardation will require heightened ethical sensitivity because it will be done with young children and infants, who are among the most vulnerable research subjects"(p. 8). Most hospitals have ethical review boards that are active in helping both physicians and families make such decisions.

WORKING WITH FAMILIES DURING PRENATAL DIAGNOSIS

Given the increase in the use of prenatal screening and technology in diagnosing and treating abnormalities prior to birth, families are faced with situations that never arose 10 years ago. Research shows that not all prospective parents receive all the information necessary to make informed decisions regarding a pregnancy (Heidrich & Cranley, 1989). In fact, couples or family members may be advised "not to waste time" with the fetus and they may instead be presented with a "therapeutic abortion" as the only option (Hassed et al., 1993). Some families consider themselves only "temporarily pregnant" as they wait for the results of prenatal diagnosis.

To date, prenatal testing is not included under services provided through the Individual with Disabilities Education Act (IDEA). Many families from improverished backgrounds do not seek prenatal care (including prenatal diagnosis) and in fact may be more at risk for prenatal problems such as poor nutrition and use of substances. These families tend to underutilize prenatal services (Arcia & Gallagher, 1993).

Prospective parents who do undergo prenatal diagnosis are learning to add their voice to the decision-making process, even when the diagnosis is terminal. In one study in which a lethal condition was diagnosed prenatally, 43 families (33 percent) elected to continue rather than terminate the pregnancy (Kaplan, 1993). In Vignette 2.4, one parent discusses her feelings regarding the choice to give birth to her son.

VIGNETTE 2.4 THE BIRTH OF A CHILD WITH A TERMINAL DIAGNOSIS

> I remember being scared for my baby. I knew his short life would come to an end soon. My labor was long because of my baby's syndrome. I didn't know what was happening or how to work with the contractions. At the time, I acted like a parent soothing my little baby. I remember being shocked at his appearance and panicked when he tried to take a breath. Those few moments with my son were worth all of the pain and sorrow I had felt in the previous months.

In terms of decision making during pregnancy, most families are given some support from the medical team, but, despite being well informed by physicians and genetic counselors, families may be missing important information that can be supplied only at birth. For example, when parents are told that they are carrying a child with Down syndrome, they have little or no information regarding the number or severity of defects. As with most disabilities, the range of severity is great. One child with Down syndrome may have mild mental impairments, while another may have several severe mental and/or multiple medical concerns.

In the case of a life-threatening situation, families cannot make these decisions alone. Ethical review boards, which make recommendations regarding institutional policies and national guidelines, may offer families help with the decision-making process but, at times, may advise against the parent's wishes. The committees act in an advisory capacity to help families weigh the benefits and concerns of treatment. When physicians, families, and consultants cannot agree upon a course of action, legal services are used to settle the situation. In Table 2.6, landmark cases in this area are outlined according to the ethical dilemma and the legal outcome.

TABLE 2.6 Legal Decisions Regarding Ethical Dilemmas of Newborns

CASE	YEAR	CONDITION	OUTCOME
Baby Houle	1974	Congenital malformations, including no left eye and suspected brain damage. Parents refused to consent for surgery.	Judge ordered surgery to protect the newborn from "neglect."
Baby Doe	1982	Down syndrome and correctable gastrointestinal malformation. Parents refused to consent for surgery.	Parents' right of refusal upheld by Indiana Supreme Court. Department of Health and Human Services issued new regulations known as "Baby Doe Directives."*
Baby Jane Doe	1983	Myelomeningocele, microcephaly, and hydrocephalus. Parents wanted conservative treatment but not surgery.	Ruled that these decisions should be made in private by parents and medical team, without government interference.
Baby K	1992	Anencephaly. Mother wanted the child treated; physicians wanted to discontinue life support.	Judge ruled in favor of mother. Hospital took the case to an appeals court, where similar decision was rendered.

*These directives required hospitals to place notices stating that failure to provide nutrition or medically beneficial treatment to an infant because of a disability was a violation of the federal Rehabilitation Act of 1973.

In 1984, Congress passed amendments to the Child Abuse and Neglect Prevention and Treatment Act (PL 98-457), establishing that withholding medically indicated treatment from a newborn or infant was a form of child abuse and neglect (Hastings Center Report, 1987). This legislation required states to comply with a set of regulations to handle cases of medical neglect, which was defined as withholding medically indicated treatment from disabled infants with life-threatening conditions. Treatment of life-threatening conditions includes appropriate nutrition, hydration, and medication. Treatment does not have to be administered if the following conditions apply:

1. The infant is irreversibly comatose;
2. Such treatment would merely prolong dying, or not result in ameliorating or correcting all of the infant's life-threatening conditions, or otherwise be futile in terms of the survival of the infant; or
3. Such treatment would be futile in terms of the survival of the infant and the treatment itself under such circumstances would be inhumane (PL 98-457, Section 121[3], cited in Hastings Center Report, 1987, p. 9).

PRINCIPLES OF ETHICS IN PRENATAL DIAGNOSIS

Ethics is not the only way to look at what is right and wrong. We understand ethics as a way to understand a situation that provides common ground for people who have different cultural backgrounds, different religious beliefs, and different personal experiences. Because health care is the shared effort of many people, it is helpful to have at least some way of understanding a situation that provides a system of looking at things which doesn't depend on individual, religious, or cultural group beliefs, but at the same time makes room for those beliefs.

—Brunnquell, 1993

Beauchamp and Childress (1989) outlined four principles used by most hospital review committees and apply to questions of ethics. These include:

1. *Respect for autonomy*: Each person should decide what is best for himself or herself. Individuals should have an opportunity to give "informed consent." In order to do this, one must have complete, unbiased information about a situation.
2. *Nonmaleficence*: The first premise in health care is to "do no harm." There are, however, times when some amount of harm may be inflicted in order to reap larger benefits, such as saving life. It stands to reason that different individuals will disagree on what measures constitute harm. Therefore, it is an important role of review committees to help make decisions regarding these controversies.
3. *Beneficence*: This principle supports the benefits of medical intervention. What constitutes a benefit is controversial. From a family systems perspective, one must look at the multiple effects of benefits. Who decides the definition of benefit? Is the recipient of the benefit the infant, the family, or society as a whole (Brunnquell, 1993)? All benefits have some drawbacks that must be addressed by the committee.
4. *Justice*: To ensure that everyone has been heard in ethical dilemmas, fairness to the various individuals should be evaluated. For example, one has to examine what is beneficial not only for the expectant family but also for society at large. This principle supports investigating the allocation of resources within our society. When expectant parents of a child with anencephaly decide to harvest their child's organs for the future of science, an ethical review committee must decide if this is really being done for the good of the community (see Vignette 2.5).

VIGNETTE 2.5 BABY GABRIELLE

Controversial issues were raised when an infant known to have anencephaly (a condition where most of the brain is missing) was kept alive on a respirator so her heart could be transplanted into another infant. One hospital, the Loma Linda Medical Center, adver-

> tised plans to accept babies born with anencephaly so that the organs could be harvested for transplant. Many parents who knew their babies would be born with anencephaly willingly offered their children because they wanted something good to come of their pregnancy and their child.

Ethicists, including Arthur Caplan, former Chair of the Bioethics Program at the University of Minnesota (1988), expressed concerns about infants' being placed on life support for the sole reason of harvesting their organs. Ethical questions include the length of time an infant is placed on a respirator and the use of technology to prolong an unsustainable life simply for the viable organs (Blakeslee, 1987). Such dilemmas will continue to be a concern during the twenty-first century.

SUMMARY

Years ago, society believed that infants entered the world as helpless individuals with no personality or abilities. Today, we know that they begin their development long before they enter the world. We are also learning more and more about the impact of the prenatal environment on later infant development.

O'Leary (1992) related the prenatal experience to Gesell's neurological stages of development. Beginning with conception, development follows an orderly progression, with each stage achieving a new level of maturation. Most pregnant women experience the first fetal movement, called quickening, by the sixteenth week of gestation. The quality of parental recognition of and parental attunement to fetal movement may be a precursor of later parent-infant attachment. Expectant parents may learn to understand the flow of fetal movement.

Early sensory behaviors of the fetus may be indicative of the prenatal roots of the egocentric phase that emerges later in the child. In vitro, facial movements such as opening and closing of the lips, thumb sucking, wrinkling of the brow and forehead, and turning of the head have all been observed. Therefore, we know that infants, after nine months in utero, enter the world preprogrammed to interact with and have an impact on the environment.

The prenatal period is the current frontier in research into developmental disabilities. For example, scientists recently discovered the gene for fragile X, one of the major causes of mental retardation. Prenatal diagnosis allows expectant families to know whether their unborn child is developing typically or if he or she will have a disability. Understanding the impact of prenatal diagnosis on families of children with disabilities is essential for service providers today. Often these families are viewed by medical personnel as being "at risk" and are thus targeted for prenatal diagnosis.

Preventing developmental disabilities is another result of prenatal diagnosis. Teratogens, including infections, radiation, and chronic illness in the mother, can affect the fetus, depending on the timing and intensity of exposure. Mothers who are aware of these risks can take precautions that may prevent future developmental disabilities in their child.

Finally, as science and technology become increasingly sophisticated, the ethical and moral dilemmas raised by gene therapy and genetic planning will increase. It is estimated that the number of genetic tests being administered will increase significantly over the next 10 years (Rennie, 1994). As a result, questions will be raised regarding family privacy and decision-making in high-risk populations. Will genetic testing cause expectant couples to lose jobs or insurance benefits? Will parents who decide to continue a pregnancy, despite the high probability of a genetic defect, be ostracized by society? These are just a few of the questions our society will need to address in the near future.

REFERENCES

Abramowicz, J. S., Jaffe, R., & Warsof, S. L. (1989). Ultrasonographic measurement of fetal femur length in growth disturbances. *American Journal of Obstetrics and Gynecology, 161,* 1137–39.

Adzick, N. S., Sutton, L. N., Crombleholme, T. M., & Flake, A. W. (1998). Successful fetal surgery for spina bifida. *Lancet, 352*(9141), 1675–1676.

Alkalay, A. L., Pomerance, J. J., & Rimoin, D. L. (1987). Fetal varicella syndrome. *Journal of Pediatrics, 3,* 320–323.

Arcia, E., & Gallagher, J. J. (1993). Who are the underserved by early intervention? Can we tell? *Infant-Toddler Intervention, 3,* 93–100.

Austin, K. D., & Hall, J. G. (1992). Nontraditional inheritance. *Pediatric Clinics of North America, 39,* 335–348.

Batshaw, M. L. (1997). *Children with disabilities* (4th ed.). Baltimore: Paul H. Brookes.

Beauchamp, T., & Childress, J. (1989). *Principles of biomedical ethics* (3rd ed.). New York: Oxford University Press.

Bianchi, D. W. (1995). Prenatal diagnosis by analysis of fetal cells in maternal blood. *Journal of Pediatrics, 127,* 847–856.

Blakeslee, S. (1987, December 14). New attention focused on infant organ donors. *New York Times,* p. 18.

Bland, R. S., Nelson, L. H., Meis, P. J., Weaver, R. L., & Abramson, J. S. (1983). Gonococcal ventriculitis associated with ventriculoamniotic shunt placement. *American Journal of Obstetrics and Gynecology, 147,* 781–784.

Blasco, P. M., Blasco, P. A., & Zirpoli, T. J. (1994). Prenatal diagnosis: Current procedures and implications for early interventionists working with families. *Infants and Young Children,* 7(2), 33–42.

Blasco, P. M., & Pearson, J. A. (1995). Working with families. In T. J. Zirpoli (Ed.), *Understanding and affecting the behavior of young children* (pp. 218–241). Englewood Cliffs, N.J.: Merrill.

Blizzard, R. M. (1993). Genetics and growth: New understanding. *Pediatric Rounds, 2* (2), 1–4.

Boyer, P. J., Dillon, M., Navaic, M., Deveikis, A., Keller, M., O'Rourke, S., & Bryson, Y. J. (1994). Factors predictive of maternal-fetal transmission of HIV-1: Preliminary analysis of zidovudine given during pregnancy and/or delivery. *Journal of the American Medical Association, 271,* 1925–1930.

Bruner, J. P., Richards, W. O., Tulipan, N. B., & Arney, T. L. (in press). Endoscopic coverage of fetal myelomeningocele in utero. *American Journal of Obstetrics & Gynecology.*

Brunnquell, D. (1993). *Ethical principals and analysis: A brief guide.* Unpublished manuscript, Minneapolis Children's Medical Center.

Campbell S., & Pearce, J. M. (1983). Ultrasound visualization of congenital malformations. *British Medical Bulletin, 39,* 322–331.

Campos, J. J., Barrett, K. C., Lamb, M. E., Goldsmith, H. H., & Stenberg, C. (1983). Socio-emotional development. In M. M. Haith and J. J. Campos (Eds.), *Infancy and developmental psychobiology* (4th ed., pp. 784–857). New York: Wiley.

Charrow, J. (1985). Prenatal diagnosis and management of endocrine and metabolic disorders. *Special Topics in Endocrinology Metabolism, 7,* 131–174.

Chueh J., & Golbus, M. S. (1990). Antenatal diagnosis by DNA analysis. *Contemporary Obstetrics/Gynecology, 35,* 1–96.

Connelly, B. L., & Stanberry, L. R. (1995). Herpes simplex virus infections in children. *Current Opinion in Pediatrics, 7,* 19–23.

Connor, E. M., Sperling, R. S., Gelber, R., Kiselev, P., Scott, G., O'Sullivan, M. J., VanDyke, R., Rey, M., Shearer, W., & Jacobson, R. L. (1994). Reduction of maternal-infant transmission of human immunodeficiency virus type 1 with zidovudine treatment. *New England Journal of Medicine, 331,* 1173–1180.

D'Alton, M. E, & DeCherney, A. H. (1993). Prenatal diagnosis. *New England Journal of Medicine, 328(2),* 114–120.

de la Cruz, F., & Friedmann, T. (1995). Editorial: Prospects for human gene therapy in mental retardation and developmental disabilities. *Mental Retardation and Developmental Disabilities Research Review, 1,* 2–3.

DiPietro, J. A., Hodgson, D. M., Costigan, K. A., & Hilton, S. C. (1996). Fetal neurobehavioral development, *Child Development, 67,* 2553–2567.

Drugan, A., Krause, B., Canady, A., Zador, I. E., Sacks, A. J., & Evans, M. I. (1989) The natural history of prenatally diagnosed cerebral ventriculomegaly. *Journal of the American Medical Association, 261,* 1785–1788.

Estes, J. M., MacGillivray, T. E., Hedrick, M. H., Adzick, N. S., & Harrison, M. R. (1992). Fetoscopic surgery for the treatment of congenital anomalies. *Journal of Pediatric Surgery, 27,* 950–954.

Evans, M. I., Drugan, A., Manning, F. A., & Harrison, M. R. (1989). Fetal surgery in the 1990's. *American Journal of Disabled Children, 143,* 1431–1436.

Fletcher, J. C. (1995). Gene therapy in mental retardation: Ethical considerations. *Mental Retardation and Developmental Disabilities Research Review, 1,* 7–13.

Gesell, A., & Amatruda, C. (1941). *Developmental diagnosis.* New York: Harper.

Ghidini, A., Sirtori, M., Spelta, A., & Vergani, P. (1991). Results of a preventive program for congenital toxoplasmosis. *Journal of Reproductive Medicine, 36*(4), 270–273.

Glick, P. L., Harrison, M. R, Nakayama, D. K., et al. (1984) Management of ventriculomegaly in the fetus. *Journal of Pediatrics, 105,* 97–105.

Graham, E. M., & Morgan, M. A. (1997). Growth before birth. In M. L. Batshaw (Ed.), *Children with disabilities* (4th Edition, pp. 53–69). Baltimore: Paul H. Brookes.

Graves, P. L. (1989). The functioning fetus. In S. I. Greenspan & G. H. Pollack (Eds), *The course of life. Volume 1: Infancy* (pp. 433–464). Madison, Wisc.: International University Press.

Grose, C., & Weiner, C. P. (1990). Prenatal diagnosis of congenital cytomegalovirus infection: Two decades later. *American Journal of Obstetrics & Gynecology, 163,* 447–450.

Haddow, J. E., Palomaki, G. E., Knight, G. J. (1992). Prenatal screening for Down syndrome with use of maternal serum markers. *New England Journal of Medicine, 327,* 588–593.

Handyside, A. H., Lesko, J. G., Tarin, J. J., Winston, R. M. L., & Hughes, M. R. (1992). Birth of a normal girl after in vitro fertilization and preimplantation testing for cystic fibrosis. *New England Journal of Medicine, 327,* 905–909.

Harrison, M. R., Adzick, N. S., Longaker, M. T., et al. (1990). Successful repair in utero of a fetal diaphragmatic hernia after removal of herniated viscera from the left thorax. *New England Journal of Medicine, 332,* 1582–1584.

Hassed, S. J., Miller, C. H., Pope, S. K., Murphy, P., Quirk, J. G., & Curnmiff, C. (1993). Perinatal lethal conditions: The effects of diagnosis on decision making. *Obstetrics & Gynecology, 82,* 37–42.

Hastings Center Report. (1987, December). *Imperiled infants.* New York: Author.

Heidrich, S. M., & Cranley, M. S. (1989). Effect of fetal movement, ultrasound scans, and amniocentesis on maternal-fetal attachment. *Nursing Research, 38*(2), 81–84.

Hershey, D. W., Crandall, B. F., & Perdue, S. (1986). Combining maternal age and serum alpha-fetoprotein to predict the risk of Down syndrome. *Obstetrics and Gynecology, 68 (2),* 177–180.

Iosub, S., Bamji, M., Stone, R. K., Gromisch, D. S., & Wasserman, E. (1987). More on human immunodeficiency virus embryopathy. *Pediatrics, 80,* 512–516.

Izard, C. E., and Malatesta, C. Z. (1987). Perspectives on emotional development: Differential emotions theory of early emotional development. In J. D. Osofsky (Ed.), *Handbook of infant development* (2nd ed., pp. 494–554). New York: Wiley.

Jackson, J. F., North, E. R., and Thomas, J. G. (1976). Clinical diagnosis of Down syndrome. *Clinical Genetics, 9,* 483–487.

Jones, K. L. (1996). *Smith's recognizable patterns of human malformation* (5th ed.). Philadelphia: W. B. Saunders.

Kaplan, D. (1993). Prenatal screening and its impact on persons with disabilities. *Clinical Obstetrics & Gynecology, 36*(3), 605–612.

Kaplan, K. M., Cochi, S. L., Edmonds, L. D., Zell, E. R., & Prelud, S. R. (1990). A profile of mothers giving birth to infants with congenital rubella syndrome: An assessment of risk factors. *American Journal of Diseases of Children, 144,* 118–123.

Klaus, M., & Kennell, J. (1976). *Maternal-infant bonding: The impact of early separation or loss on family development.* St. Louis: Mosby.

Klaus, M., & Kennell, J. (1982). *Parent-infant bonding.* St. Louis: Mosby.

Klein, S. D. (1993). The challenge of communicating with parents. *Journal of Developmental and Behavioral Pediatrics, 14,* 184–191.

Lally, R., Griffin, A., Fenichel, E., Segal, M., Szanton, E., & Weissbourd, B. (1997). Developmentally appropriate practice for infants and toddlers. In S. Bredekamp & C. Copple (Eds.), *Developmentally appropriate practice in early childhood programs serving children birth through age 8* (pp. 55–94). Washington, D.C.: NAEYC.

Loman, S. (1994). Attuning to the fetus and the young child: Approaches from dance movement therapy. *Zero to Three, 15,* 20–26.

Lorenz, H. P., Adzick, N. S., & Harrison, M. R. (1993). Open human fetal surgery. *Advances in surgery, 26,* 259–273.

Macri, J. N., Kasturi,R. V., Krantz, D. A., & Koch, K. E. (1986). Maternal serum alpha-fetoprotein screening, maternal weight, and detection efficiency. *American Journal of Obstetrics & Gynecology, 155,* 758–760.

Moser, H. W. (1995). A role for gene therapy in mental retardation. *Mental Retardation and Developmental Disabilities Research Review, 1,* 4–6.

Mueller, B. U., & Pizzo, P. A. (1992). Medical treatment of children with HIV infection. In A. C. Crocker, H. J. Cohen, & T. A. Kastner (Eds.), *HIV infection and developmental disabilities: A resource for service providers* (pp. 63–73). Baltimore: Paul H. Brookes.

Newell, M. L., & Peckham, C. (1993). Risk factors for vertical transmission of HIV-1 and early markers of HIV-1 infection in children. *AIDS, 7,* Supp: S91–S97.

NICHD National Registry for Amniocentesis Study Group. (1976). Midtrimester amniocentesis for prenatal diagnosis: Safety and accuracy. *Journal of the American Medical Association, 236,* 1471–1476.

Nilsson, L. (1977). *A child is born.* New York: Dell.

O'Leary, J. (1992). The parenting process in the prenatal period: A developmental theory. *Pre- and Perinatal Psychology Journal, 7,* 113–123.

O'Leary, J., & Torwick, C. (1993) Parenting during pregnancy: The infant as the vehicle for intervention in high risk pregnancy. *International Journal of Prenatal Perinatal Psychological Medicine, 5(3),* 303–310.

Ostrer, H. (1989) Prenatal diagnosis of genetic disorders by DNA analysis. *Pediatric Annals, 18*(11), 701–713.

Pauker, S. P., & Pauker, S. G. (1994). Prenatal diagnosis: Why is 35 a magic number? *New England Journal of Medicine, 330,* 1151–1152.

Peckham, C., & Gibb, D. (1995). Mother-to-child transmission of the human immunodeficiency virus. *New England Journal of Medicine, 333,* 298–302.

Rennie, J. (June 1994). Grading the gene tests. *Scientific American, 270,* 88–97.

Rhoads, G. G., Jackson, L. G., Schlesselman, S. E., de la Cruz, F. F., Desnick, R. J., Golbus, M. S., Ledbetter, D. H., Lubs, H. A., Mahoney, M. J., & Pergament, E. (1989). The safety and efficacy of chorionic villus sampling for early prenatal diagnosis of cytogenetic abnormalities. *New England Journal of Medicine, 320,* 609–617.

Rogers, M. F., & Shaffer, N. (1999). Reducing the risk of maternal-infant transmission of HIV by attacking the virus. *New England Journal of Medicine, 341,* 441–442.

Roizen, N. J., & Johnson, D. (1996). Congenital infections. In A. J. Capute & P. J. Accardo (Eds.), *Developmental disabilities in infancy and childhood* (pp. 175–193). Baltimore: Paul H. Brookes.

Rosenblith, J. F. (1992). *In the beginning: Development from conception to age two.* Newbury Park, Calif.: Sage.

Schnatterly P., Hogge, W. A., & Felder, R. (1990). *AFP (Alpha fetoprotein): A helpful test in pregnancy.* Charlottesville: University of Virginia Press.

Schoenfeld-DiMaio, M., Baumgarten, A., Greenstein, R. M., Saal, H. M., & Mahoney, M. J. (1987). Screening for fetal Down syndrome in pregnancy by measuring maternal serum alpha-fetoprotein levels. *New England Journal of Medicine, 316,* 342–346.

Simpson, J. L., Baum, L. D., Marder, R., Elias, S., Ober, C., & Martin, A. O. (1986). Maternal serum alpha-fetoprotein screening: Low and high values for detection of genetic abnormalities. *American Journal of Obstetrics & Gynecology, 155,* 593–597.

Simpson, J. L., & Carson, S. A. (1992). Preimplantation genetic diagnosis. *New England Journal of Medicine, 32,* 951–953.

Simpson, J. L., and Elias, S. (1993). Isolating fetal cells from maternal blood: Advances in prenatal diagnosis through molecular technology. *Journal of the American Medical Association, 270*(19), 2357–2361.

Sossin, K., & Loman, S. (1992). Clinical applications of the Kestenberg Movement Profile. In S. Loman & R. Brandt (Eds.), *The body mind connection in human movement analysis.* Keene, N.H.: Antioch New England Graduate School.

Thorp, J. M., & Bowes, W. A. (1989). Prenatal diagnosis for couples who would not consider abortion. *American Journal of Obstetrics & Gynecology, 74,* 828–829.

Yerby, M. S. (1994). Pregnancy, teratogenesis, and epilepsy. *Neurologic Clinics, 12*(4), 749–771.

Wolraich, M. (1992). Myelomeningocele. In J. Blackman (Ed.), *Medical aspects of developmental disabilities in children birth to three* (pp. 159–165). Rockville, Md.: Aspen.

CHAPTER THREE

LIVING IN OUR WORLD: THE FIRST YEAR

WITH JOLENE PEARSON

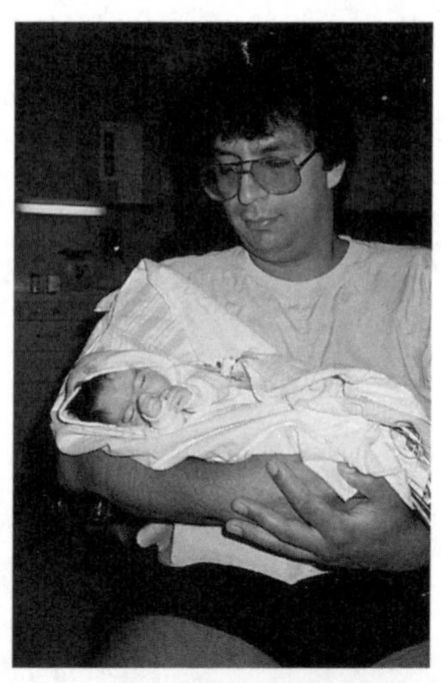

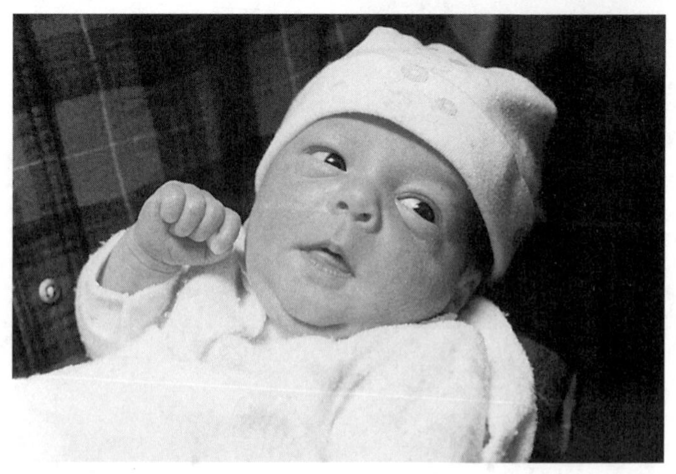

OBJECTIVES

- To provide an overview of the infant's development in terms of competencies and skill acquisition during first year of life
- To give an appreciation and understanding of the individual infant's developmental style and temperament
- To provide an understanding of the evolution of the study of infant development and the role of parenting
- To provide insight into the complexities of the parent-infant relationship
- To provide insight into the concerns and questions parents typically express during the first year of their child's life
- To explore the implications of prematurity on the child's and family's development
- To explore the implications of multiple births on the child's and family's development
- To explore the implications of disabilities on the child's and family's development
- To define and discuss ethical issues and their effects on infants and families

GETTING ACQUAINTED: THE NEWBORN

In the previous chapter, we explored the concepts of development and parenting in the prenatal period. In this chapter, our focus is on life after birth through the first year. The first year of life presents many rewards and challenges for the infant and the family. It is during the first year that many families will find out that something is not quite right with their baby. Some families will be told immediately that their child has a syndrome or medical condition, if they had not learned this prenatally. This was the situation for the Guzman family, introduced in Chapter 1. In this chapter, we look at specific disabilities that are identified during the prenatal, perinatal, and neonatal periods. However, in order to understand the development of infants and toddlers with disabilities, service providers also need a firm understanding of typical development in infants and toddlers.

Starting from the Beginning

The birth process and physical immaturity explain why newborns do not look the way their parents had anticipated. For example, almost all babies arrive having some molding or distortion of their head shape from the birth itself. Such molding is normal, and most infants' heads return to their naturally round shapes within 24–48 hours. Babies born by cesarean section or breech deliveries generally do not have skull molding. In the case of prolonged or difficult labor, infants may also arrive with a *caput succedaneum,* a swelling of the scalp caused by the pressure of the baby's head on the dilating cervix (Tappero & Honeyfield, 1993). This gradually disappears in the first 12 to 24 hours. Another common mark is a *cephalhematoma,* a bruise caused by blood vessels breaking. These bruises can be quite large and are almost always the result of a difficult labor. No treatment is required, but the bruises should be monitored for swelling and evidence of healing. This condition can take up to six months to resolve (Tappero & Honeyfield, 1993).

Physical Growth and Development

Birthweight helps set the stage for growth and development. Recording and following an infant's growth pattern provides a baseline for understanding both prenatal and future development. For example, if the mother had eclampsia (toxemia of pregnancy), the infant may be small for gestational age or premature (Forouzan, Morgan, & Batshaw, 1997). The average weight of a full-term baby (38–40 weeks of gestation) is 7 pounds, 3 ounces. There is, however, wide variation due to many factors, including genetic predisposition and nutrition during pregnancy.

It is important to differentiate between premature infants and those who have *low birth weight* (LBW), which is defined as less than 5 pounds, 8 ounces, or 2,500 grams. *Very low birthweight* is defined as less than 1,500 grams (Allen, 1996). Another important parameter is *small for gestational age* (SGA), which occurs when infants have suffered *intrauterine growth retardation* (IUGR). Tests are widely used by the medical team to determine the gestational age of an infant at birth (Dubowitz, Dubowitz, & Goldberg, 1970; Dubowitz, 1995). It is possible for an infant to be both premature and small for gestational age, or premature and large for gestational age.

The Apgar Scoring System

Within the first minutes of life the status of the new baby is quickly evaluated to determine if any intervention is needed. This is routinely done using a screening tool, developed by Virginia Apgar in 1953, and used in hospitals throughout the United States and in many other parts of the world. Administration involves rating each of five traits, at 1 minute after birth and again at 5 or 10 minutes, with a score of 0 if the trait is absent, 1 if the trait is observable, and 2 if the trait has an optimal condition (see Table 3.1).

It is rare for an infant to have a score of 10, yet parents are sometimes concerned if their infant's rating is not optimal. A low Apgar score is a red flag that the infant is in immediate distress and warrants close monitoring and possible further investigation. The rating does not indicate that the child will have a developmental disability. Apgar scores have been found to have varying degrees of correlation to other studies of fetal heart rate, intelligence, neonatal mortality, and maternal medication during childbirth (Self & Horowitz, 1979).

Again, it is important to note that in and of itself the Apgar score is not predictive, although it serves as a useful descriptor of how an infant began life outside of the uterus. Apgar scores are routinely noted in the birth history and become part of the child's pediatric health history.

TABLE 3.1 Apgar Screening Tool

	SCORES		
	0	*1*	*2*
Heart rate	Absent	<100	>100
Breathing	Absent	Irregular	Normal Crying
Muscle tone	Limp	Some Flexion	Active Movement
Gag Reflex	No response	Grimace	Sneeze; Cough
Color	Blue	Pink with blue Extremities	Pink all over

From "A Proposal for a New Method of Evaluation of the Newborn Infant" by V. Apgar, 1953, *Current Research in Anesthesia and Analgesia, 32,* 260–265.

THE NEONATAL PERIOD

Transition from Womb to the World

As discussed in the previous chapter, the neonate enters the world able to feel, hear, see, smell, and move. However, adapting to the external environment brings new ways to experience life. In the uterus, movement was limited by the boundaries of the uterine walls. The fetus assumed a flexed position with hands close by the face in easy reach for sucking. In contrast, birth means the loss of those comfortable boundaries, and when the infant moves he often sets off startles and tremors that surprise him.

Additionally, after birth, infants are placed in extended rather than flexed positions, and for the first time, they must learn to adapt. Lying on their backs, exposed and vulnerable, is new to them and initially causes them stress. Sound is no longer filtered through the uterine wall, and infants must adjust to the varied sounds in this new world. They have visual capabilities at 34 weeks and can see from the moment of birth. But the typical bright overhead lighting found in hospitals makes it difficult for infants to demonstrate their developed visual capacities. Lowering the lights often supports a quiet, alert state where babies can lock onto and follow parents with their eyes. This is but one of the amazing capabilities of the human newborn. Vignette 3.1 provides one mother's view of what occurred after the birth of her twins.

VIGNETTE 3.1 WELCOME TO OUR WORLD

The birth of twins continues to be somewhat more risky than that of singletons. I had made up my mind that I wouldn't go kicking and screaming into the operating room if the doctor felt a cesarean (C-section) was necessary. I was already diagnosed with preeclampsia and respected my doctor's opinion.

> Still, I was given the opportunity to try for a vaginal delivery. My husband and I were working hard on breathing through the contractions, when the nurse frowned and left the room. I knew immediately that something was wrong. My doctor came into the room to tell us the problem. I would have to have a C-section; my son was not breathing right and she didn't want to take a risk. She did tell us there would be time for an epidural (spinal anesthesia) so I could be awake during the birth.
>
> I waited with anticipation as my son was pulled from my womb. The doctor held him up for me to see before passing him to a nurse. My daughter was next, less than one minute after my son, but this time, the doctor did not hold her up for me to see. She was handed over to the neonatologist standing by. By this time, my husband had our son in his arms and was holding him toward me. I couldn't touch him because I had an electrode taped to my finger, but I reached for him anyway. He look like a content, relaxed baby with his eyes closed and snug in my husband's arms. I was reassured by his calm presence.
>
> Then the neonatologist brought my daughter over. She weighed 3 pounds, 4 ounces, and had been small for gestation age, had an ineffective placenta, and was born two weeks early. The doctor held her while he told me she was doing fine. She stared at me as if to say, "I haven't figured this out yet but I'm sure you had something to do with it." It was an expression I never forgot, despite the fact that the delivery led to full-blown eclampsia and I became extremely ill. It was three more days before I saw my twins again. I thought then that my daughter would be a spirited, intelligent child and today, at age five, she has shown that I was right. My son remains a calm, sensitive child who often helps his sister channel her extra energy.

Understanding the complexities and subtleties of newborn behavior and development has been the lifelong work of pediatrician and researcher T. Berry Brazelton. Brazelton, along with his colleagues, developed a systematized way to evaluate newborns both to understand the individual behavior of particular infants and to compare groups of infants for research purposes. This tool, the Neonatal Behavorial Assessment Scale (NBAS) (Brazelton & Nugent 1995), was first published in 1974 and revised in 1984 and again in 1995. The NBAS offers several important concepts that give us insight not only into the infant but also into the developing relationship between the infant and the parents. The NBAS as an assessment tool will be discussed in Chapter 6.

During the neonatal evaluation of newborns, their states of consciousness (Table 3.2) must be taken into consideration in order to interpret their responses (Brazelton, 1992).

Important Signals

Newborns are quite competent in developing a series of signals to help adults become aware of their emotional needs and desires. When a newborn has become overstim-

TABLE 3.2 Behavioral States

Deep sleep: The infant engages in regular breathing and is world around him. The infant's eyes are closed, and he is mo legs curled up in a flexed position, except for startled or je intervals.

Light, or REM (rapid eye movement), sleep: The infant's this state, he might startle once or twice and is more susceptib to the outside world. If he is aroused, he may become drowsy or struggle to get back into a deep sleep. Eye movements are observed under closed lids.

Drowsy, or semi-alert. Eyes may be open or closed. He may become active if aroused, but the degree of activity will vary.

Quiet alert state: The infant adapts to his surrounding. If he is excited by an object or person, he will breathe deeply. His movements seem organized and he can follow an adult's face or an object such as a rattle. He can also gaze intently at a person or object.

Fussy, wide-awake state: The infant's eyes are open, and he engages in considerable motor activity. He is not able to control himself.

Fussy, crying state: The infant's breathing is again irregular. His movements become jerky, and he will thrash about, trying to reorganize or gain control of himself. This is a difficult state for parents to accept and understand as part of development. The parents will often attempt to calm the baby down. When the baby does not respond to calming, the parents may feel ineffective too.

Reprinted from Understanding the Emotional and Behavioral Development of Young Children: Birth to 3 Years by P. M. Blasco, 1995, in T. J. Zirpoli (Ed.), *Understanding and Affecting the Behavior of Young Children*, Englewood Cliffs, N.J., Merrill, p. 42.

ulated, for example, she may close her eyes, sneeze, or turn her head away from the stimuli. Brazelton (1992) suggested that spit-ups and bowel movements may be a sign of stress from overstimulation. The caregiver should interpret this behavior as a red flag if it seems the newborn has been subjected to overwhelming stimulus.

Newborns are also adept at calming themselves after a stressful event by placing a thumb or fist in their mouths, or by pulling all of their limbs into a flexed position. In this way, the newborn takes control over her environment. Her ability to experience the environment through her senses and to begin to regulate that environment is the foundation of emotional development (Greenspan & Thorndike-Greenspan, 1985).

Table 3.3 describes some key points in the arrival of a newborn. Although the families discussed are typical of most, the responses of newborns vary widely according to individual resources, cultural differences, and sources of support.

MOTOR DEVELOPMENT

As the infant is learning to engage the caregiver, she is also busy learning to engage the world around her. She learns that by kicking and waving her arms, the mobile

TABLE 3.3 Full-Term Babies and Their Families

- Parents have gone through a full forty-week pregnancy and hopefully are psychologically ready to have their baby. This may also include practical preparations, such as completing birthing classes, preparing the nursery, and gathering clothing for the baby. This process is often referred to as *nesting*. Mothers-to-be, who early in the pregnancy were concerned about the physical process and discomforts of birth, are now "ready to get this baby out!"
- The infant is ready to be born and comes into the world prepared to stabilize herself physiologically. The baby possesses all the wonderful beginning capabilities that allow her to take in the world and communicate.
- Parents have a surge of emotion, a combination of relief, that they had a healthy baby and safe delivery, and amazement at their accomplishment. Predominant feelings are of success, achievement, and fulfilled expectations.
- Parents leave the hospital with their baby and thus begin the great adventure of learning to read their baby's cues, satisfying her nutritional needs, and providing all of the normal caregiving their baby needs. Parents and infants are nearly inseparable in these early days. Although new parents may not feel confident immediately, their confidence grows quickly through the opportunities they have to interact with one another and be successful.

over her crib will tinkle and even turn. Movements become increasingly sophisticated compared to the primitive reflexes she demonstrated as a newborn. The infant learns to grasp objects with the entire hand and bring objects into midline for further visual inspection. The infant will turn her head to sounds and hold it steady for brief periods. If the infant is placed on a mat facedown, she will turn from side to side and lift her head for brief periods.

Primitive Reflexes

In the past 20 years, neurodevelopmentalists have begun to establish the precise clinical importance of persistent primitive reflexes, delay in postural reaction evolution, and the more subtle qualitative and quantitative aspects of each. Capute, Accardo, and Vining (1978) emphasized the distinction between primitive reflexes and postural reactions. While both represent patterns of movement, primitive reflexes are true reflexes in the sense that they are highly stereotyped and are elicited by specific sensory stimuli (Blasco, 1994). The neurological connections necessary are located at a subcortical level in the brain stem (Capute, Shapiro, & Accardo, 1982). The maturation of cortical connections appears to override the brain stem primitive reflex generators to alter their intensity and eventually leads to their "disappearance" (some prefer the term *integration*) with age.

Primitive reflexes begin to make their appearance prior to term in the normal fetus, as early as 25 weeks of gestation, and they remain visibly evident through the first three to six months of life (Allen & Capute, 1986) (see Figure 3.1). In children who are developing typically, almost all primitive reflexes have visibly disappeared after six months. The symmetric toxic neck reflex (STNR) and the Galant reflex (primitive trunk incurvation from paraspinal pressure) remain the only exceptions. The Galant reflex persists the longest, and is visibly present in 50 percent of infants between 12 and 18 months of age (Blasco, 1994). The STNR has a history of subtlety in the newborn and becomes apparent in only a fraction of babies after term birth, but then disappears (Blasco, 1994).

When cortical integration is jeopardized prenatally or neonatally, primitive reflex responses persist beyond the usual age of disappearance and are visibly exaggerated. In the situation of later acquired brain injury, these reflexes often reappear (Haley, Baryza, Troy, Geckler, & Schoenberg, 1991). For example, a three-year-old who receives a head injury as a result of a car accident will often demonstrate these reflexes in the early stages of recovery. A posture is considered obligatory when the child becomes fixed or stuck in the primitive reflex posture, or in other words, "obligated" to remain there until the stimulus is removed (Blasco, 1994).

Postural reactions, unlike primitive reflexes, typically are not present in the newborn. They begin to make their functional appearance with lateral head-righting at two to three months of age in the full-term infant. Postural mechanisms are not true reflexes, because they are based on multiple, interacting, input modalities that require cortical integrity (Blasco, 1994). In the infant with brain damage, postural mechanisms appear later than usual, if at all, and are less effective. These mechanisms serve a functional purpose in the typically developing infant, as the names of their descriptive subgroups indicate: righting, protection, and equilibrium leading to the evolution of motor-skill development.

For children with physical disabilities such as cerebral palsy, the disappearance of primitive reflexes and the evolution of postural reactions form the basis for locomotor prognosis. Cerebral palsy is defined as a nonprogressive disorder of movement caused by a single or multiple lesions of the brain that affect motor development. Persistence of obligatory primitive reflexes beyond 12 months of age carries an unfavorable prognosis for eventual walking (Blasco, 1994). Table 3.4 lists typical gross and fine motor skills from birth through three years.

In the absence of early intervention, infants and young children with motor impairments will retain primitive reflexes and develop atypical movement patterns, which may lead to muscle tightness, joint contractures, and musculoskeletal deformities (Harris, 1997). See Chapter 4 for a detailed description of interventions for infants and toddlers with motor impairments.

INFANTS BORN PREMATURELY

Deciding if an infant is premature has to do with gestational age—or the amount of time the baby spent in the womb. A full-term baby develops in utero for 38–42 weeks. If born before 38 weeks, infants do not necessarily display the same

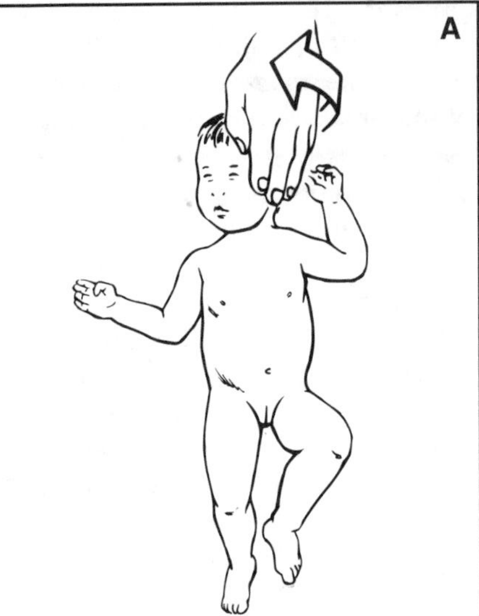

The sensory limb of the ATNR probably involves cervical proprioceptors. With either active or passive head turning to the side, the baby *reflexively* extends the fingers, arm, and leg on the face side and flexes the extremities on the occiput side. There is also some mild paraspinous muscle tightening on the occiput side, often producing subtle trunk curvature.

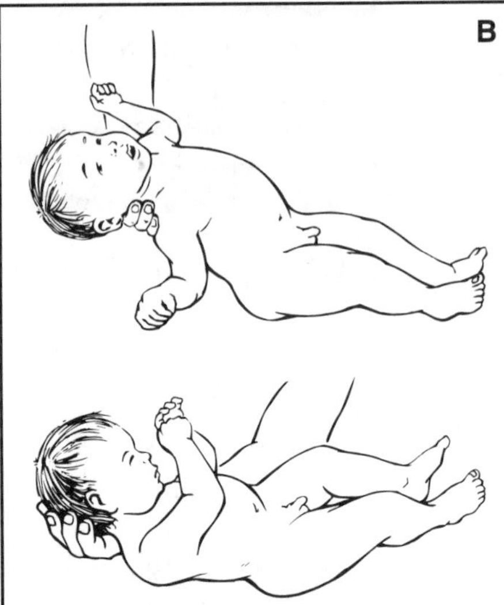

In the supine position, the baby's head is mildly extended (about 45 degrees) by gentle support under the shoulders. This yields relative extension of the legs and retraction of the shoulders, producing the upper extremity "surrender posture". With active or passive neck flexion (ideally to 45 degrees above the plane of the body) the arms come forward to the midline and the legs flex.

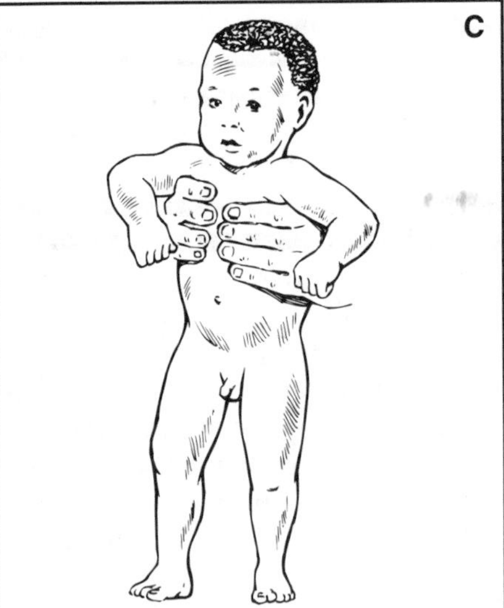

With support around the trunk, the child is suspended and lowered to pat the feet gently on a flat surface. This stimulus produces reflex extension at the hips, knees, and ankles so the baby stands straight. Often children may go up on their toes initially, but should come down flat within 20 to 30 seconds before sagging back down toward a sitting position.

The examiner has suspended the child horizontally by the waist and lowered him face down toward a flat surface. The arms extend in front, slightly abducted at the shoulders, and the fingers spread as if to break a fall.

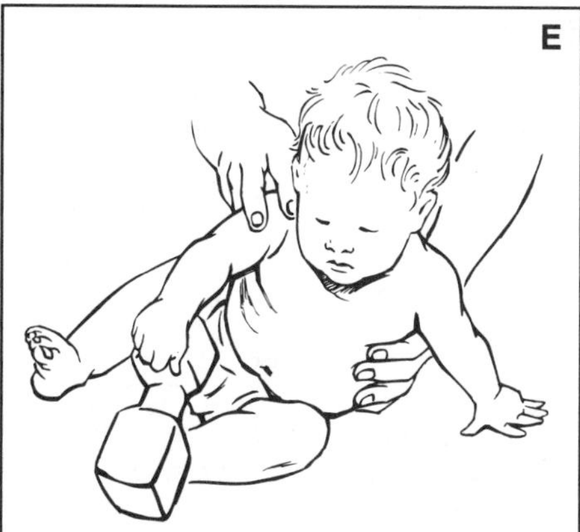

The infant is comfortably seated, supported about the waist (if necessary) and distracted by a toy or parent. The examiner gently tilts the child to one side, noting deviation of the head back toward the midline (head-righting), lateral extension of one arm toward the side of the fall (protection), and upward counter movements of the arm and leg (equilibrium reactions).

FIGURE 3.1 Primitive Reflexes and Postural Reactions. A, Asymmetric tonic neck reflex. **B,** Tonic labyrinthine reflex. **C,** Positive support reflex. **D,** Normal parachute reaction. **E,** Postural mechanisms.

Source: From "Normal and Abnormal Motor Development" by P. A. Blasco, 1992, *Pediatric Rounds, 1*(2), 4–5.

behavioral competencies and skills as their full-term peers. The earlier the baby is born, the more important it is to understand the behavior and organization of the premature infant. Als (1982) has proposed a framework for understanding the premature infant, known as the synactive theory of development, based on the infant's reactivity and threshold for disorganization and stress in response to environmental stimuli. An important issue here is the ability of the infant born prematurely to self-regulate to maintain or regain a balanced state (Rosenblith, 1992). The tool used to document this process is the Assessment for Preterm Infant Behavior (APIB) (Als, Lester, Tronick, & Brazelton, 1982). The work of Als and her colleagues has led to changes in the developmental care of premature and high-risk infants (Als & Gilkerson, 1995).

It is important to understand the keen differences between the experiences of giving birth to a full-term infant and one who is premature or high-risk. All families wish for a healthy, term delivery. Even when parents anticipate an early baby, they are not planning for the complications and sometimes the uncertain

TABLE 3.4 Gross and Fine Motor Development

GROSS MOTOR DEVELOPMENT		FINE MOTOR DEVELOPMENT	
Gross Motor Milestone	*Age*	*Motor Milestone*	*Age*
PRONE POSITION (ON STOMACH)		Retain ring	1 month
		Hand unfisted	3–4 months
Head up	1 month	Reach	3–4 months
Chest up	2 months	Hands to midline	3–4 months
Up on elbows	3 months	Transfer	5 months
Up on hands	4 months	Take one-inch cube	5–6 months
		Take pellet (crude grasp)	6–7 months
ROLL		Immature pincer	7–8 months
Front to back	3–5 months	Mature pincer	10 months
Back to front	3–5 months	Release	12 months
SIT			
With support	5 months		
Without support	7 months		
Come to sit	8 months		
Pull to stand	8–9 months		
Cruise	9–10 months		
WALK			
With 2 hands held	10 months		
With 1 hand held	11 months		
Walk alone	12 months		
Run (stiff-legged)	15 months		
Walk up stairs (with rail)	21 months		
Jump in place	24 months		
Pedal tricycle	30 months		
Walk down stairs, alternating feet	3 years		

Adapted from "Normal and Abnormal Motor Development" by P. A. Blasco, 1992, *Pediatric Rounds, 1*(2), 1, 3.

future facing their child. Table 3.5 discusses some of the experiences of parents of infants who are premature.

There have been remarkable advancements in techniques for caring for infants born prematurely, including the use of surfactants, which has led to the survival of infants born at 23 to 24 weeks of gestation (Allen, Donohue, & Dusman, 1993). Although some of these infants live healthy, typical lives, others will have chronic medical conditions. Because the medical technological advances have come so rapidly and because these very early-born infants are newcomers to researchers, it is not possible to make generalized statements about their develop-

TABLE 3.5 Infants Who Are Premature and Their Families

- Parents have not gone through a full, 40-week pregnancy. At the point they deliver, they may not be able to focus on the baby; their focus may be, rather, the loss of the pregnancy and/or guilt and confusion as to why the baby came early.
- Parents will need time and support to process the feelings of loss and at the same time develop a relationship with their baby. Attachment takes time and experience with the baby, just as it does with a full-term experience.
- The baby enters the world before she is ready and may need intensive medical care to survive. During this time she is less alert and available for interaction with parents. Because of the early arrival and subsequent medical complications, it may be weeks before parents are able to hold the infant. Interactions are limited and the infant's responses may be more indicative of stress than pleasure. It can be a frustrating time for the new parents, as the staff have more access to the infant than the parents.
- Parents may have surges of emotion that include shock, anger, and grief. Depression is not uncommon at this time. Parents often have a sense of the loss of a dream. Friends and family may be hesitant to offer congratulations because of the uncertain future. This can add to the parents' sense of loss.
- Parents may not leave the hospital with their baby, which mothers have said was the most difficult part of the experience. After carrying the baby for nine months, the parents are left with a sense of emptiness and lack of reciprocity with the baby they were getting to know through kicks and movements. Experiences in the NICU that can help families reunite with the infant are very important.
- Parents often feel at a disadvantage in understanding treatment alternatives or differences of opinion among physicians. They may feel they are being given "half-truths" or vague statements.
- Parents may feel excluded from the decision-making process due to the life-threatening nature of their newborn's situation.

Adapted from *Premature Babies: A Different Beginning* by W. A. H. Sammons and J. M. Lewis, 1985, St. Louis: Mosby; and "Ethical Issues in Family-Centered Neonatal Care" by H. Harrison, 1998, in A. H. Widerstrom, B. A. Mowder, and S. R. Sandall (Eds.), *Infant Development and Risk,* 2nd ed., 1998, Baltimore: Paul H. Brookes, pp. 175–196.

mental potential. For parents this can be frustrating, as they are on a unique journey with their child (Klaus, 1993). Vignette 3.2 describes one family's experience when their baby was born prematurely.

VIGNETTE 3.2 PREMATURITY: A DIFFERENT BEGINNING

Sara was born at 24 weeks of gestation. A year before her birth, her parents, Katherine and Michael, had a miscarriage at 20 weeks. Therefore, Sara's birth was seen as a miracle. But her survival also meant weeks and months of medical treatment and anxiety for the family.

Katherine was alert to the signs of premature labor. When she began to suspect that once again she was in early labor, she went immediately to the doctor's office. She was admitted to the hospital and placed on medication (magnesium sulfate) to arrest the labor. In addition, injections of betamethasone were administered to speed the maturity of the fetal lungs in the event that the baby was early. After two days, Katherine's water broke. Because she had a slight fever, it was suspected she might have an infection and all medication was stopped. Within six hours, baby Sara was born, weighing 1 pound, 3 ounces. In the delivery room a neonatal team was in place and ready to treat the baby. They were able to stabilize her for transport to the Neonatal Intensive Care Unit. The neonatal team had spoken with parents prior to the delivery and explained that Sara's chances were about 50-50. Michael and Katherine said that they would like all measures taken to keep their baby alive.

After the birth, Katherine caught a glimpse of Sara and saw that she had blond hair. Although this is a small detail, it was important for Katherine, as she would not be able to accompany her baby to intensive care. She held in her mind an image of a very tiny baby with a head of blond hair. Michael, although confused about whether to stay to support his wife, accompanied the baby to the intensive care unit. This was not at all how the parents envisioned the circumstances around birth. It seemed that the joy of the birth was greatly overshadowed by the fear they felt upon seeing their tiny, fragile daughter intubated and whisked off to newborn intensive care.

The next three months were an emotional roller coaster for the family. While they were able to touch Sara through the portholes of the isolette, it would be three and a half weeks before they were able to hold her for even a few minutes. At that point, the family struggled to understand all of the medical terminology and highly technical equipment. They felt there was little they could actually do to help Sara. They came each day and sat near her isolette. The nurses gave them information and whenever possible showed them how to administer some of Sara's care. Changing a diaper was never such a challenging or triumphant event! Sara initially did well, but at two weeks of age became ill with an infection. There were a number of times during this period when they thought she might not live through the night. Once this was resolved, Sara gradually was weaned off the ventilator. The following weeks were tense for the family. Sara's immature nervous system was susceptible, and she often exhibited apnea (forgetting to breathe) and bradycardia (slowed heart rate). It was especially terrifying when she had an apnea spell while Katherine was holding her.

After the third month of hospitalization, the parents were able to use "kangaroo care" with Sara. This is a way of holding the baby on the parent's chest with as much skin-to-skin contact as possible. In this position, Sara would sleep deeply, never had an apnea or bradycardia spell, and when she was alert seemed more robust and focused. Both the parents looked forward to their kangaroo care sessions with Sara. Katherine, who felt cheated out of her full pregnancy, found kangaroo care a way to feel like she and Sara were together again. It also helped with Sara's breast-feeding, by allowing her to nuzzle the breast.

Finally the day came when Sara would be going home. This brought the parents both joy and concern. They wondered if they would be able to care for their "high-tech" baby at home. While Sara was in the hospital, they had come to rely on the expertise of the nurses, who were always close by and very supportive. Going home meant doing it on their own! With mixed emotions, Katherine and Michael said their farewells and embarked on another milestone in their experience of parenthood: becoming a family at home.

Despite the difficult journey experienced by the family described in Vignette 3.2, once Sara was home, they soon assumed a more typical experience. Sara received early intervention services through home visits from an occupational therapist. She was seen by the medical team in follow-up clinic for two years until they decided she no longer needed services. Today, Sara is a bright, happy child who attends family child care.

Research highlights the changes in both the mortality and morbidity in the population of infants born prematurely. Professionals and parents should use caution when using previous findings to try to see into the future of a particular child. Research, by its very nature, is often somewhat outdated by the time it is published. This is particularly true of longitudinal studies of infants born prematurely (Allen, 1996). Longitudinal studies often do not include many of the earliest-born infants, and older studies do not account for participants who have been the recipients of current therapies and treatments. However, technological advancements and new treatments such as surfactants have greatly improved the potential for such a child's development.

INFANTS AS PARTNERS

As stated, current practices reflect the viewpoint of the infant as an organized, interacting partner as opposed to a passive being. Each newborn enters the world endowed with a personality and characteristics to which parents and caregivers must respond. In that way the infant brings her own special qualities to the developing relationship between parent and child (Worobey & Brazelton, 1990).

When an infant is born with sensory impairments such as visual impairment or deafness, communication must rely on interpretation of different responses (Chen, 1996). According to Chen, parents must adapt their expectations and communicative style in order to identify and respond to their infant's signals. Similarly, when a child has a motor impairment such as cerebral palsy, the parents must adapt their behavior to understand the signals given by the child. For example, the newborn may arch away from the parents rather than cuddle into their arms. This experience can be both frightening and disappointing for the new parents, who have visualized holding their newborn baby during the many months of preparation for birth.

The service provider must be able to work well with the infant to elicit the behaviors in the infant that reflect her best performance (Nugent, 1985; Brazelton & Nugent, 1995). By doing this, service providers can help parents in turn articulate and recognize the individual communicative style of each child, as the experience described in Vignette 3.3 demonstrates.

VIGNETTE 3.3 KEITH AND HIS SMILE

Many parents view the first smile as one of the most easily remembered and important milestones for their baby. Keith was born with a facial cleft that extended from his eyes to his chin. Both his nose and mouth were misplaced on his face, and Keith would need extensive surgery over the next ten years. Keith was a playful three-month-old but confined to a hospital crib without much opportunity for movement. He was unable to bring his hands to midline, as two splints kept him from pulling at the surgical sutures from his first surgery. The hospital teacher would visit and bring a musical mobile that Keith could bat at and reach without having to flex his arms. When playing together, the teacher noted Keith smiling with his eyes. She exclaimed, "Oh, look at Keith smile." His mother seemed surprised at first, and then laughed and said, "He is smiling. I didn't think he could smile, but look at his eyes."

For many parents of a child with a disability, the day-to-day interaction in the home helps them discover the baby's special cues and interactive patterns. However, in Vignette 3.3, the family was still dealing with the intensity of a hospital setting and a medical future that seemed overwhelming. The opportunity to see her child playing with another adult helped the mother realize that he wanted to play just like other children, despite the obstacles he faced.

Bonding and Attachment

Once the birth is over both parents tend to feel that they need time to recover their equilibrium, to think and talk about it and to rest. But the birth resulted in a baby. The presence of that baby usually means no recovery period for either parent. They must somehow struggle straight from giving birth to caring for the baby. There is no time to think about the amazing business of becoming a parent because being one starts straight away.

—Leache, 1987, p. 3

As discussed in Chapter 2, Klaus and Kennell (1976) first described the concept of *bonding*. The media focus on the concept resulted in its popularization and perhaps went beyond the bounds of the original studies, which claimed that a few hours of contact between mother and infant in the immediate postpartum period produced a bonding experience that was necessary for the development of a successful mother-infant attachment and a healthier infant (Klaus & Kennell, 1976). The extra early contact that occurs for some families may indeed be important and may be influential in the growth of attachment. It has not been found, however, to be the magic point at which relationships are made or broken. Attachment is a lifelong process that continues even into adulthood.

The positive contributions of the concept of bonding include increased parent participation in labor and delivery as well as after the birth in the form of rooming-in with the baby and demand feeding. The negative influences, however, have been to raise the anxiety of parents who are not able to have the extra physical contact with their infant or infants after birth because the baby or the mother needs special medical care. Their sense of loss and the fear that they will never have a "bonding" experience should be allayed. No study to date has demonstrated that extra contact after birth is necessary for parents and infants to develop a rich and positive attachment.

To address the ongoing need for information and support on the issue of attachment, Abbott Northwestern Hospital, a large perinatal center in Minneapolis, Minnesota, joined with the local Early Childhood Family Education Program to form the New Parent Connection, a group designed to assist parents in the weeks and months following their baby's birth. Table 3.6 presents the Parent Connection philosophical framework.

The purpose of the joint program between the hospital and the local education service is to help all parents understand their new roles. Many families from middle-class backgrounds spend a great deal of time and energy on how-to books on parenting. Families from low-income communities may not have the same opportunity. It is important for community service agencies to understand these families as they try to adjust to their new experiences. Vignette 3.4 describes one family as viewed through the eyes of a service provider.

VIGNETTE 3.4 COMING TOGETHER

I was looking forward to participating in the New Parent Connection. I had heard a great deal about this important program and the service it provided for new families. Jolene, the facilitator, had invited several colleagues to observe her class. On this night, she was working with one family. Mom was 19 years old and this was her first baby. She was European-American, and accompanied by the father and her mother. The father was an 18-year-old African American wearing a large earring in one ear. I felt a rush of misgivings as I looked at this new family. How could they afford to take care of this baby? They weren't married and they were too young to have a child. Is Grandma going to raise this child?

Then I watched Jolene go to work. She talked about the baby's alertness. She demonstrated how the baby would turn first to the

TABLE 3.6 The Parent Connection

- With shortened hospital stays, there is little time to recover after childbirth, and parents leave exhausted, having slept little due to the excitement of giving birth. While much information is offered in the hospital, many parents are not able to absorb what is taught, as they are too overwhelmed and have not had much opportunity to interact with their newborn yet. The questions come later when they are at home on their own.
- Many new mothers have arranged leave from work and are committed for a specific number of weeks or months. What seemed like a good plan prior to the birth of the baby makes many mothers (especially) feel a great deal of pressure trying to meet both mothering and work demands. They discover there are many things to learn about their baby. Some parents discover they are uncomfortable putting their child in the care of others. (Some parents find it very difficult even to find child care.)
- Parents are surprised to discover their old routines completely altered by the needs of the new baby. One very common experience is that it is hard to find time to brush your teeth or shower! Many breast-feeding mothers need to make an extra effort to eat well and drink fluids. What was taken for granted before the baby came has now become the focus of regaining a new equilibrium.
- Couples discover their relationship is undergoing transition. Not only must they continue to work together as a couple, but they must integrate this with the baby, who is now a part of their family. This process may be perceived by mothers and fathers differently, and it can become the source of new tension and conflict if not addressed.
- Parents discover they have different ways of doing things, based on values from their family of origin. Old patterns and rituals must be evaluated and at times new ones must be instituted. This is a process that also takes time.
- Infants change so quickly! Our motto is, "Just when you think you've figured your baby out, she will grow and change, moving into new routines and with new needs." Parenting is an ongoing adjustment to the age and developmental stage of the child. This often is surprising to new parents who hoped to find "the way" to handle each situation, such as feeding and sleep.
- Infants are unique individuals. What works for one baby may not work for another. Most new parents receive so much advice that they are overwhelmed with ideas. This advice is usually offered in a way meant to be helpful, but it often challenges the parents' confidence in their process of discovery and competence in taking care of their infant. It is the process of finding out what works for the baby that builds the confidence and skills of new parents.

mother's voice and then to the father's voice. I watched the faces of these young parents as she held their baby and demonstrated all the competencies of this child born less than 24 hours ago. They were concerned, proud parents. The father's eyes sparkled as his new daughter turned to find his voice. I felt a sense of relief; these parents would love and cherish their baby. They knew how to access both informal and formal sources of support. I also learned how easy it is to let our biases interfere with our perceptions when working with families.

Early Stages of Parent-Infant Interaction

Brazelton and Cramer (1990) have developed a theoretical model to help us understand the stages of relationship building (see Table 3.7). They are important indicators of the emotional well-being of the growing and changing relationship between parents and their infants. While Brazelton and Cramer have written

TABLE 3.7 Early Caregiver Interaction

Synchrony: In this phase of attachment, nurturing from adults is critical. The first step is for parents and caregivers to adjust themselves to the baby's rhythms and attend to the baby's needs. Cries for attention are indeed a reflection of real need. As adults meet these needs, the infant comes to know them as reliable and responsive people in their lives. As adults and caregivers, in turn, see that they can help babies become more alert and soothe them when they are irritable, they begin to feel competent as nurturers. This synchrony set the stage for the next step.

Symmetry: As the parent has learned to help the infant remain in control and has begun to learn the language of the infant's behavior, the parent learns ways to draw out the baby's attention. Time is spent in mutual gaze and study of one another.

Contingency: As the growing relationship moves into the next phase, infants are able to vocalize, smile, and cry in response to interaction with their caregivers. Alert babies as young as four to six weeks of age can signal their caregivers to come and play with them. Parents and caregivers learn what "works" in this stage and usually enjoy making the baby smile.

Play: At three to four months of age, infants and caregivers who have mastered synchrony, symmetry, and contingency interactions move into play. In this phase, either the caregiver or infant will begin the interaction. In addition to smiling, infants may coo, look away, increase or decrease motor behavior. Caregivers and infants may imitate and model each other. This is an important milestone for infants as they are learning how to maintain an interaction. For parents/caregivers, we learn to help infants pay attention and respond in a variety of ways.

Autonomy and Flexibility: By about five months of age, infants enjoy these play interactions very much. In this phase parents/caregivers begin to notice the infant is more often initiating the play or stopping it. Infants at this stage often enjoy smiling or cooing at strangers. This stage also occurs at the same point the infant is becoming more developed visually, auditorially, and motorically.

Adapted from *The Earliest Relationship* by T. B. Brazelton and B. G. Cramer, 1990, Reading, Mass.: Addison-Wesley, pp. 121–128.

specifically about parents and infants, it is reasonable to assume that infants with caregivers other than parents may follow a similar progression in establishing a relationship.

ATTACHMENT IN INFANTS

Bowlby (1982) developed a theory of attachment based on both ethology and psychoanalysis that stated that infants' demonstration of need for the proximity of the mother was an adaptive behavior similar to imprinting in birds. Bowlby believed that some mothers were nurturing in their interactions with their children, while others deprived their children of nurturing interactions and responded by withholding care or using negative punishment. His writings influenced many psychologists who studied maternal deprivation and separation. Ainsworth (1969) was influenced by Bowlby and spent some time working with his researchers in the early years of her career. Her initial study of infants in Uganda used direct observation in the natural environment. She noted that the mother provided a secure base from which the infant was free to explore and return for safety. Her name has become synonymous with the concept of the "strange situation," a series of eight types of separation and reunion between mother and child that evaluate the attachment relationship. These episodes classify individual differences according to five interactive categories: proximity seeking, contact maintaining, proximity and interaction avoidance, contact and interaction resistance, and distance interaction. Infants are then categorized according to their behavior as either securely attached, anxious-avoidant, and ambivalent-attached infants.

In her research, Main (cited in Main & Solomon, 1990) noted that some infants did not fit into Ainsworth's categories, and described them as disorganized and/or disoriented. An infant described as disorganized showed a contradiction in movement pattern that related to an inferred contradiction in intention or plan. An infant described as disoriented displayed "a lack of orientation to the immediate environment" (Main & Solomon, 1990, p. 133).

It is equally important to understand the parental contributions to interactive behavior. Achieving synchrony in the parent-infant relationship is one of the first steps in building attachment. Between three and six months, infants demonstrate an understanding of the relationship between themselves and others. They will employ a variety of behaviors, including crying to gain the attention of adults (Zirpoli, 1997). Stroufe (1996) believed that young infants rely on the primary caregiver to help them regulate their emotions. As the infant gets older, he becomes better at expressing his needs. Reciprocally, the adult reinforces appropriate behaviors and redirects others.

An important milestone occurs between seven and eight months, when the infant experiences stranger anxiety. The child may cling and cry for the primary caregiver. This is typical behavior at this age, and parents should not be concerned. As the child grows he should separate more easily from the primary caregiver. Stranger anxiety should not be confused with an attachment disorder, which is a consistent, predictable diagnostic disorder that requires treatment from qualified professionals. Most children will grow out of the stranger anxiety stage. A secure attachment is the foundation from which the infant will grow, separate, and flourish.

Children with disabilities may be at risk in forming secure attachments due to unresolved feelings in the caregiver about the diagnosis. In one study of 91 mothers of children from 15 to 50 months of age, Pianta, Marvin, Britner, and Borowitz (1996) found that approximately half of the mothers were classified as unresolved in terms of their child's diagnosis. For the mothers in the resolved group, cognitive strategies were frequently used to resolve their feelings about the disability.

TEMPERAMENT AND DEVELOPMENT

The first three months of life are a period of tremendous growth and change. Infants learn to communicate with their environment through physical and vocal attempts to engage caregivers. Interpreting the infant's behavior continues to be complex but less stressful as the caregiver learns the infant's signals and routines. For example, although crying may indicate that the infant is experiencing hunger, discomfort, fatigue, or sensory overload, it may also be that the infant simply needs to let off some steam (Brazelton, 1992).

Infants exert a great deal of energy in figuring out their new environment and the caregivers who play an important role in their first three months. One theory regarding infant intelligence has been that there is discontinuity between scores on infants' sensorimotor tests and their later scores on intelligence tests. This theory has been challenged in studies that showed that infants have a visual preference for novel stimuli (Fagan, 1984). For example, researchers have found that infants with Down syndrome showed decreased sensitivity to novel stimuli, which caused them to perseverate in response to the stimulis (Fagan, 1984; Ganiban, Wagner, & Cicchetti, 1990).

In other studies infants showed facial discrimination for the mother over a strange adult (Field, Cohen, Garcia, & Greenberg, 1984; Pascalis et al., 1995). According to Fagan (1984), "The discovery that intelligence is continuous from infancy also has implications for understanding the contribution of genetic endowment and environmental circumstance to intellectual functioning" (p. 5). The question of how much human capability is genetic versus environmentally influenced continues to raise debates among experts and researchers.

Although it is difficult to sort out the nature versus nurture contributions to behavior (Emde et al., 1992), it is evident that infants develop their own way of coping and interacting. Temperament has been defined as individual differences in behavioral style (Thomas & Chess, 1977). Buss and Plomin (1975) defined three distinct characteristics of temperament: emotionality, activity, and sociability. Emotionality relates to the infant's ability to soothe himself or to be soothed once he is upset or irritable. Activity refers to both the tempo and vigor of the infant's behavior. Sociability refers to the infant's response to caregivers and strangers.

One of the first milestones in the early infant's behavioral repertoire is the social smile. Parents will readily tell you the first time their infant smiled and name the recipient of this honor. There are times when a newborn may appear to be smiling due to reflexes. The difference between a reflexive smile and a social smile is that the reflexive smile involves muscles around the mouth and lower face, while the social smile involves both mouth and eye muscles. In Vignette 3.5, a two-and-a-half-year-old infant sends mixed messages to his mother.

VIGNETTE 3.5 THE FIRST THREE MONTHS OF LIFE

Gwen and her son Alexander began attending the New Parents Connection group when Alexander was three weeks of age. Gwen expressed relief that she was not the only mother unsure of herself and "tired day in and day out." Gwen felt her baby was responsive to her, but her husband felt the baby was "unresponsive." In the group, Gwen noted that many of the other babies were smiling and cooing. She thought her husband would be more excited about the baby if he smiled. We asked the other mothers in the group to share when they noticed their babies begin to smile. We used the "expert" opinions of the group members, as it reinforces the notion that they can learn by watching their baby. Gwen learned that it not only would probably be a few more weeks, but that within the group there was quite a bit of variation from one baby to the next. We shared the idea that smiling at and talking to your baby was a way to encourage the baby to smile and talk to you.

In the next months, Gwen became one of the parent "experts" about very young babies. Alexander had "joined the group," as he looked at people who spoke and smiled when spoken to. Gwen came to a session when he was two and a half months old and raised new questions and concerns. Alexander was beginning to stick out his lower lip and whimper if Gwen could not be right in front of him interacting. She was very concerned that he was now spoiled. Her husband agreed that Alexander loved being the center of attention. Gwen was asked to recall how Alexander had begun to smile and coo and how much fun it had been. We asked parents in the group with older babies to describe times when their babies demanded attention. It was clear that there is a time developmentally when babies have learned the fun and enjoyment of interaction with their parents and just can't get enough of it. Parents felt this had been a challenging time for them too and shared the strategies they used to satisfy their baby and still get work done around the house. We shared the importance of the baby's getting to this stage and how it indicated that Alexander was discriminating and attaching to their special relationship. Gwen had not thought of it in that way. As she remembered her previous concern about Alexander's not smiling, she said, "You're right, he really does know us and likes to play!"

In the vignette, the service providers blended information and support to create an empowerment model of parent development. New parents need to enjoy strategies that work for them, based on their best knowledge of the situation. Parents in the group who served as sources of information for other parents increased their own understanding of how much they had learned. Including the whole group allowed for the individuality of both parents and babies to be expressed. It not only helped parents learn an important lesson about parenting their young baby, but also laid the foundation for information gathering and problem-solving all along the way.

During the first three months of life, the infant gradually decreases fussiness and increases alertness. She delights in play involving gentle touch. With increasing awake periods, the infant shows greater interest in the social environment. She will attempt to engage the caregiver in reciprocal play through visual, physical, and vocal engagement. The infant will reach toward a familiar face and respond physically to familiar objects such as a mobile or bottle. By one month, most infants can fixate on a moving object held at 12 inches, and follow the object across 180 degrees both vertically and horizontally. She will study her own hand and use hand movements to swat at objects. Although crying and fussing are the main forms of communication, she will occasionally express other sounds, including vowel sounds in response to social interaction.

Infants learn quickly how to engage their caregivers. Most infants will cuddle when held and prefer the caregiver's voice to that of a stranger. Infants with disabilities may not be able to give these cues to caregivers. For example, infants with cerebral palsy may arch or stiffen when picked up by an adult. This reaction may be interpreted by the adult as a rejection to interactive play. Service providers can help parents interpret their babies' behavior by listening to the parents' concerns, offering suggestions, and modeling appropriate responses.

MASTERY MOTIVATION

The infant shows an increasing interest in objects and persons during the next three months of life. He will actively use his hands to mouth and manipulate objects. He will continue a conversation by "talking" with the adult. Infant talk at this age consists of vowel sounds and raspberries. As he reaches six months, he may make consonant-vowel sounds after imitating an adult. By six months, the infant loves to engage in games such as peekaboo and pat-a-cake. He can sit alone for brief periods of time and roll over. Mobility increases the infant's ability to explore the environment. The innate interest in exploration at this time in the infant's life is referred to as mastery motivation.

Mastery motivation is a theoretical construct that can be related to both cognitive and social competence in the young child (Blasco, 1994). It is most often measured as the child's persistence in challenging goal-directed tasks. White (1959) is credited with applying Piagetian notions of cognitive change to understanding motivational theory. He characterized children's focused attention, exploration, and organizational actions toward the environment as reasonable indicators of their motivation. This behavior is observed in the selected, directed, and persistent attempts of the child to master her environment. Motivation to interact with the environment is one of the earliest processes observed in the infant.

During the first year of life infants learn that they can influence and control their environment through cause and effect. A baby kicking her feet and waving her arms causes the mobile over her head to move slightly. Prior to the beginning of the second year, toddlers are able to complete tasks in order to reach a goal and manipulate objects to create a novel effect.

Mastery During Infancy

The first attempt to study mastery motivation in infancy was made by Yarrow and his colleagues (Yarrow, Morgan, Jennings, Harmon, & Gaiter, 1982; Yarrow et al., 1983; Messer et al., 1986, MacTurk, McCarthy, Vietze, & Yarrow, 1987). In many of these studies an emphasis was placed on the relationship between persistence and cognitive development, and the influence of environmental factors on the development of mastery motivation. Persistence was defined as the percentage of time the child remained engaged in task-oriented behavior. Competence was also assessed by counting the number of times the infant was successful at producing an effect, combining objects, or securing the goal object. Finally, the child's affect during tasks was assessed. This last dimension of mastery was known as mastery pleasure.

Mastery in Play

In addition to its measurement with structured tasks, mastery motivation has also been measured during exploratory play (Belsky & Most, 1981; Belsky, Garduque, & Hrncir, 1984; Jennings, Harmon, Morgan, Gaiter, & Yarrow 1979; Hrncir, Speller, & West, 1985). These researchers believed that infants' exploratory competence is a reasonable indicator of their mastery motivation. Exploration increases the child's knowledge of the environment because the relationship between the infants and their environment is reciprocal in nature (Jennings et al., 1979; Sameroff, 1985).

In response to the child's mastery attempts, the environment provides both feedback and reinforcement, thereby refining the child's acquisition of new skills and leading to more complex manipulations and explorations. Belsky suggested that accurate and meaningful appraisals of children's competence can be made from careful observation of everyday interactions in natural life settings (Jennings et al., 1979; Belsky et al., 1984; Blasco, Bailey, & Burchinal, 1993).

Infants thus have established the ability both to master their environment and to persist at a goal before their second birthday. Many experiences during the period from birth to two years can enhance or inhibit mastery behaviors. Enhancing experiences include being successful at mastery attempts, receiving unobtrusive help to succeed in mastery attempts, having freedom to explore the environment and effect changes, and having a responsive environment early in life.

The Relationship Between Mastery and Environmental Influences

Given the importance of environmental feedback for children's mastery attempts and developmental competencies, parents play a fundamental role in providing experiences that can enhance or undermine mastery motivation. Jennings et al. (1979) found that maternal prohibition in the home was inversely related to infants' persistence and to cognitively mature play. Other studies have focused on the attitudes of parents toward their infants' mastery attempts. Jennings, Connors, Stegman, Sankaranarayan, and Mendelsohn (1985) observed that mothers of children with physical handicaps perceived their children as more dependent on adults than mothers of children without special needs. It follows that parents' attitudes and behaviors may influence the involvement of their children in mastery behavior. In preliminary work, Seifer and Vaughn (1995) also found that the quality of mothers' assistance or the degree to which mothers effectively structured, timed, and formulated their assistance was related to the extent of the child's exploration. Scaffolding, a process by which the parent or caregiver supports the expression of cognitive competence during interaction, has been examined in relation to mastery behavior by a number of researchers (Maslin, Bretherton, & Morgan, 1986; Blasco, Hrncir, & Blasco, 1990). Belsky, Good, and Most (1980) found that family influences on infant exploratory competence appeared to develop best when both parents frequently engaged their toddlers in highly arousing and positively affective social interaction. Studies showed that children whose mothers encouraged autonomy were more likely to be successful at mastery—both nonrisk children (Frodi, Bridges, & Grolnick, 1985) and children with disabilities (Blasco, Hrncir, & Blasco, 1990; Hauser-Cram, 1996).

Children with Disabilities

In a study of exploratory behavior, MacTurk, Hunter, McCarthy, Vietze, and McQuiston (1985) examined the sequences of object manipulations of infants with Down syndrome and of infants developing normally, matched at a mental age of six months. The goal of the study was to discover the distribution of behaviors in both groups during exploratory play in order to identify the similarities and differences in organizational patterns. Although the two groups of children did not vary in the total amount of behavior, they differed widely in the distribution of behavior. MacTurk and his colleagues found that children with Down syndrome had more difficulty discerning social cues (i.e., seeking social reinforcement) than their peers. The infants with Down syndrome who displayed more social responsiveness were more likely to stay on task.

Schwethelm and Mahoney (1986) measured the development of motivation in infants diagnosed with mental disabilities. They utilized the Yarrow paradigm and specifically focused on task persistence as a measure of mastery behavior. The children (ages 12 to 36 months) exhibited persistent behavior with tasks that were in their range of competence and engaged in more exploratory behavior if the tasks were slightly challenging or difficult. The findings indicated that children with mental disabilities were less motivated than their peers to approach and solve challenging tasks. Thus children with mental disabilities may benefit from receiving assistance to succeed in more challenging mastery attempts.

Jennings et al. (1985) studied aspects of mastery motivation in both structured-task and free-play settings among preschoolers with and without physical handicaps. They found that preschoolers with physical handicaps were less likely to engage in mastery tasks than their peers but that they were just as curious. These authors also concluded that the presence of a physical handicap may decrease experiences that facilitate mastery attempts and lead to learned helplessness.

Blasco et al. (1990) examined aspects of mastery behavior in toddlers with cerebral palsy and found that a measure of spontaneous mastery was a better indicator of the child's true developmental abilities than a standardized developmental quotient. In general the research has pursued two fundamentally important questions: (1) what is mastery behavior and how can it be measured? and (2) what factors influence mastery behavior?

Scholars have argued that qualitative differences are observed in the mastery attempts of children with special needs (Jennings et al., 1985; Krakow & Kopp, 1982; MacTurk, Vietze, McCarthy, McQuiston, & Yarrow, 1985; Blasco et al., 1990). For example, a child who is unable to physically manipulate an object may engage his environment through visual attention, vocalization, and/or social interaction.

Another issue in examining mastery motivation in infants and toddlers with disabilities is that developmental age plays a role in the definition of mastery. For example, a one-year-old child with Down syndrome may explore toys the same way as a typical six-month-old. Therefore, pushing a toy to make it turn might be a mastery behavior for this child but not a very challenging task for a typical 12-month-old (Blasco, Bailey, & Burchinal, 1993).

Table 3.8 indicates many of the developmental milestones that are achieved during the first twelve months. It is important to realize that children vary widely in the acquisition of these milestones. In general, the milestones provide a starting point for typical development. For children with disabilities, the type of disability will affect the achievement of milestones. For example, we know that children with Down syndrome often achieve the same milestones as children who are typically developing but at a slower rate. Therefore a one-year-old with Down syndrome may be gaining skills at the six- to eight-month level. A child with autism would have a more scattered profile across domains of development and therefore

TABLE 3.8 Important Milestones: Birth to Twelve Months

BEHAVIOR	AGE OF ONSET RANGE (MONTHS)
Responds positively to feeding and comforting	B–1
Regards person momentarily	B–1
Shows social smile	1.5–3
Quiets with sucking	1.5–3
Shows distress and excitement	1.5–3
Responds with vocal sounds when talked to	1–6
Discriminates mother	1–5
Laughs	3–5
Aware of strange situation	3–6
Discriminates strangers	3–6
Interested in mirror image	5–7
Laughs at games (peekaboo)	5–7
Cooperates in games	5–12
Resists having a toy taken away	5–12
Plays pat-a-cake	5–12
Imitates facial expressions	7–9
Shows stranger anxiety	8–10
Tugs at adult to gain attention	8–12
Offers toy to adult	12–16
Shows affection toward people, pets, or possession	12–17
Enjoys playing with other children	12–17
Engages in tantrums	12–18
Demonstrates mastery pleasure	12–24

would be unlikely to achieve milestones in any consistent pattern (Pat Pulice, personal communication, November 4, 1996).

ALTERNATIVE EXPLORATION

Children explore their environment both mentally and physically. Children with physical and visual disabilities may need to develop alternative methods for exploring their environment. As discussed in Chapter 10, assistive technology is a great equalizer in allowing children with physical limitations to explore and discover through cause and effect.

Alternative methods for children's exploratory behavior motivated physical therapists to question traditional, hierarchical motor theories. For example, the theory that control of movement progressed from proximal to distal control has been challenged as researchers showed through studies of infant reaching that proximal and distal control developed at the same time. These challenges to traditional theory have led to the adoption of a new theory of motor development called dynamic systems theory (Horak, 1991), which conceptualizes the human body as comprising many subsystems that interact to produce coordinated movement (Scalise-Smith & Bailey, 1992).

According to this theory, the infant takes a more active role in solving motor problems rather than simply learning movement patterns. Rather, a motor skill develops out of a need to master the environment. However, the therapist needs to see if the movement solves the motor problem and then help to plan strategies for generalization (Schmidt, 1991). Movement gives the infant an opportunity to explore all aspects of her environment and to learn how her body will support her in acquiring new physical skills such as pulling to stand and walking. For children who are immobile, adaptive equipment and assistive technology help provide the same opportunities their peers enjoy. For example, an infant can activate a single switch to turn a radio on and off. When an infant is positioned properly, he is more likely to show interest in learning activities. Promising practice for the provision of physical therapy includes a transdisciplinary approach to teaching that fully integrates physical therapy within the infant's natural environment (York, Rainforth, & Giangreco, 1990; Eliason, 1995).

FEEDING AND NUTRITION

Infants between the ages of birth and three months are very busy learning how to receive nutrition from an external source, in many cases a bottle. The reflexes of rooting, sucking, swallowing, and gagging are present at birth. Rooting occurs when the infant turns toward the source of food after being stimulated around the corners of the mouth or along the upper and lower lips (Murphy & Caretto, 1999). Sucking is the primary mechanism the infant uses to receive nutrition and plays a role in helping the infant to become calm and later on to explore new materials and objects (Wolf & Glass, 1992). Infants who have difficulty with the sucking reflex may have an anatomic defect (e.g., cleft lip), poor muscular control (e.g., caused by cerebral palsy), or oral pain (e.g., caused by thrush or lesions). Swallowing is a more complex motor sequence that involves the coordination of muscles in the mouth, pharynx, larynx, and esophagus (Wolf & Glass, 1992). Swallowing difficulty may also be due to anatomic or neuromuscular abnormalities. Gastroesophageal reflux occurs when the infant is unable to keep milk in the stomach, and the milk and gastric contents return up the esophagus. This behavior may be symptomatic of failure to thrive, apnea, respiratory disease, or esophageal irritation (Wolf & Glass, 1992).

The gag reflex protects the infant from choking on food or materials dangerous to swallow (Murphy & Caretto, 1999). Prior to four months of age, the infant may gag if given even pureed food. Between four and six months, the infant can handle pureed foods much better. The infant at this age will recognize a bottle and hold her mouth open in anticipation of food. In concert with the exploratory stage, the infant will begin to finger-feed himself and attempt to hold his own bottle. Between 10 and 15 months, the infant will be able to bite soft food and hold a cup to drink liquids. Some infants develop an abnormal bite called the tonic bite reflex, which is manifested by a sudden tense bite with little or no release. The reflex has been observed in infants who experience sensory stimulation around the teeth and gums. The service provider can use a rubber-coated spoon to avoid touching the teeth and gums (Lowman, 1999). After 15 months of age, the infant develops strong lip closure, allowing her to drink and chew with little or no spillage. For most infants and toddlers, eating is a pleasurable experience that awakens the senses and leads to discovery of new tastes and textures. By the age of two, most children can hold their own cup with one hand and drink without spilling.

NEW RESEARCH ON BRAIN DEVELOPMENT

As exciting new advances in neurobiology continue to unfold, greater understanding of the human brain will be a major scientific achievement in the twenty-first century. Researchers and scientists now have imaging tools for viewing the brain from prebirth to adulthood, which have led to a better understanding of the mechanics of memory and learning.

Learning takes place through construction of neural networks. Neurons are the basic functional units of the nervous system. At birth, the brain has its full complement of neurons (close to 100 billion) (Shore, 1997). The weight of the newborn's brain is 25 percent of its adult weight, and by age two, it is 75 percent of its adult weight (Rosenblith, 1992). Sometime between the ages of three and five years, 95 percent of adult brain weight is achieved (Capone, 1996).

The brain is organized developmentally by a series of complex molecular, biochemical, and cellular mechanisms that occur in various regions of the brain (Capone, 1996). These developmental events take place between three and four weeks of gestation and five years of age, emphasizing the importance of the early childhood years. For children with neurodevelopmental disorders, significant research efforts to study the brain and the neurotransmitters that affect behavioral performance may lead to successful treatment and, in some situations, amelioration of a disability. For a complete review of early brain development see Capone (1996) and Shore (1997).

SUMMARY

This chapter examined the first year of life, beginning with the newborn. An important consideration is the role of the newborn in early interaction with caregivers. The infant enters the world endowed with a personality and characteristics to which parents and caregivers must respond. In this way she brings her own special qualities to the developing relationships with her parents and caregivers.

The newborn infant develops a series of signals to help adults become aware of her emotional needs and desires. When a newborn has become overstimulated, he may close his eyes, sneeze, or turn his head away from the stimuli. Newborns calm themselves from stressful events by placing a thumb or fist in their mouths, or by pulling all their limbs into a flexed position. For those infants born early, many of these responses are the same, but there are some differences. For example, infants who are born premature may need many medical interventions to stay alive. During this time they may be less alert and less available for interaction with their parents. In some cases, it may be weeks before parents are able to hold their infant. Because interactions are limited, the infant's responses are more indicative of stress than of pleasure. It may be weeks before both the infant and parents can participate in the reciprocal interactions that form attachment.

Bowlby (1982) defined *attachment* as a warm, continuous relationship with a mother or maternal substitute. Ainsworth (1969), who was influenced by him and his researchers in the early years of her career, has become identified with the concept of the "strange situation," a series of eight types of separation and reunion between the mother and child that evaluate the attachment relationship. These episodes classify individual differences according to five interactive categories.

Temperament has been defined as individual differences in behavioral style (Thomas & Chess, 1977). Emotionality relates to infants' ability to soothe themselves or to be soothed once they are upset or irritable. Activity refers to both the tempo and vigor of the infant's behavior. Sociability refers to the infant's response to caregivers and strangers.

Mastery motivation is a theoretical construct that can be related to both cognitive and social competence in the young child. It is most often measured as the child's persistence in challenging goal-directed tasks. Mastery motivation may be observed through the infant's exploratory behavior. For example, an infant who pushes a toy and activates the musical chime is engaged in a mastery task.

One issue in examining mastery motivation in infants and toddlers with disabilities is that developmental age plays a role in the definition of mastery. For example, a one-year-old child with Down syndrome may explore toys in the same way as a typical six-month-old. Therefore, what may be a mastery task for one child may not be challenging for another. Service providers must combine their skills of observation and knowledge of the developmental level of the child in order to evaluate mastery behavior. Children who have accomplished a mastery task will often smile or sigh in response to successful completion.

Infants who are unable to explore their environment visually or physically will find alternative ways to develop sensorimotor skills that are similar to those of typically developing infants. Caregivers learn to match their interactive style with the unique needs of their infants. With the help of service providers, infants also explore the world through eating and tasting. Good nutrition is essential for optimal growth and development. Learning self-help skills for eating leads a child toward a sense of independence and success.

This chapter examined the first year of life as seen through some key concepts for understanding young children. It provided a lens for understanding individual differences within this period. The complexity of parenting is often increased when a child has a disability. A firm understanding of the parenting process is necessary in order to help with parental concerns during the first year of life.

REFERENCES

Ainsworth, M. D. S. (1969). Object relations, dependency and attachment: A theoretical review of the infant-mother relationship. *Child Development, 40,* 969–1025.

Allen, M. C. (1996). Prematurity. In A. J. Capute & P. J. Accardo (Eds.), *Developmental disabilities in infancy and childhood, Vol. 1: Neurodevelopmental diagnosis and treatment* (2nd ed., pp. 159–173). Baltimore: Paul H. Brookes.

Allen, M. C., & Capute, A. J. (1986). The evolution of primitive reflexes in extremely premature infants. *Pediatric Research, 20,* 1284–1289.

Allen, M. C., Donohue, M. S., & Dusman, A. E. (1993). The limit of viability: Neonatal outcome of infants born at 22 to 25 weeks' gestation. *New England Journal of Medicine, 329,* 1597–1601.

Als, H. (1982). Towards a synactive theory of development: Promise for the assessment of infant individuality. *Infant Mental Health Journal, 3,* 229–243.

Als, H., & Gilkerson, L. (1995). Developmentally supportive care in the neonatal intensive care unit. *Zero to Three, 15(6),* 1–9.

Als, H., Lester, B. M., Tronick, E. Z., & Brazelton, T. B. (1982). Manual for the assessment of preterm infants' behavior (APIB). In H. E. Fitzgerald, B. M. Lester, & M. W. Yogman (Eds.), *Theory and research in behavioral pediatrics,* pp. 35–63. New York: Plenum.

Apgar, V. (1953). A proposal for a new method of evaluation of the newborn infant. *Current Research in Anesthesia and Analgesia, 32,* 260–265.

Batshaw, M. L., & Shapiro, B. K. (1997). Mental retardation. In M. L. Batshaw (Ed.), *Children with disabilities* (4th ed., pp. 335–339). Baltimore: Paul H. Brookes.

Bayley, N. (1993). *The Bayley Scales of Infant Development.* San Antonio, Tex.: Psychological Corporation.

Belsky, J., Garduque, L., & Hrncir, E. (1984). Assessing performance, competence, and executive capacity in infant play: Relations to home environment and security of attachment. *Developmental Psychology, 20,* 406–417.

Belsky, J., Good, M., & Most, R. (1980). Maternal stimulation and infant exploratory competence: Cross-sectional correlational and experimental analyses. *Child Development, 51,* 1163–1178.

Belsky, J., & Most, R. K. (1981). From exploration to play: A cross-sectional study of infant free play behavior. *Developmental Psychology, 17,* 630–639.

Blasco, P. A. (1992). Normal and abnormal motor development. *Pediatric Rounds, 1(2),* 1–6.

———. (1994). Primitive reflexes: Their contribution to the early detection of cerebral palsy. *Clinical Pediatrics, 33,* 388–397.

Blasco, P. M., Bailey, D. B., & Burchinal, M. A. (1993). Dimensions of mastery in same-age and mixed-age integrated classrooms. *Early Childhod Research Quarterly, 8,* 193–206.

Blasco, P. M., Hrncir, E. J., & Blasco, P. A. (1990). The contribution of maternal involvement to mastery performance in infants with cerebral palsy. *Journal of Early Intervention, 14,* 161–174.

Bottos, M. (1986). Clues in neonatal behavior of severely handicapped infants and young children. *Infant Mental Health Journal, 7(4).*

Bowlby, J. (1982). *Attachment.* New York: Basic Books.

Brazelton, T. B. (1992). *Touchpoints: The essential reference.* Reading, Mass.: Addison-Wesley.

Brazelton, T. B., & Cramer, B. G. (1990). *The earliest relationship.* Reading, Mass.: Addison-Wesley.

Brazelton, T. B., & Nugent, J. K., (1995). *Neonatal Behavioral Assessment Scale* (3rd ed.). London: MacKeith Press.

Brownell, C. A. (1990). Peer social skills in toddlers: Competencies and constraints illustrated by same-age and mixed-age interaction. *Child Development, 61,* 838–848.

Bruner, J. S. (1973). Organization of early skilled action. *Child Development, 44,* 1–11.

Buss, A. H., & Plomin, R. (1975). *A temperament theory of personality development.* New York: Wiley.

Capone, G. T. (1996). Human brain development. In A. J. Capute & P. J. Accardo (Eds.), *Developmental disabilities in infancy and childhood* (2nd ed., pp. 25–75). Baltimore: Paul H. Brookes.

Capute, A. J., & Accardo, P. J. (1996). *Developmental disabilities in infancy and childhood.* Baltimore: Paul H. Brookes.

Capute, A. J., Accardo, P. J., & Vining, E. P. G. (1978). *Primitive reflex profile.* Baltimore: Paul H. Brookes.

Capute, A. J., Shapiro, B. K., and Accardo, P. J. (1982). Motor functions: associated primitive reflex profiles. *Developmental Medicine and Child Neurology, 24,* 662–669.

Chen, D. (1996). Parent-infant communication: Early intervention for very young children with visual impairment or hearing loss. *Infants and Young Children, 9,* 1–12.

D'Apolito, K. (1991). What is an organized infant? *Neonatal Network, 10*(1), 97–105.

Dubowitz, L. M. S., Dubowitz, V., & Goldberg, C. (1970). Clinical assessment of gestational age in the newborn infant. *Journal of Pediatrics, 77*(1), 1–10.

Dubowitz, V. (1995). Chaos in the classification of SMA: A possible resolution. *Neuromuscular Disorder, 5*(1), 3–5.

Eliason, L. (1995). The physical management of students with disabilities: Training for school personnel. Masters project. St. Paul, Minn.: University of St. Thomas.

Emde, R. N., Plomin, R., Robinson, J., Corley, R., DeFries, J., Fulker, D. W., Reznick, J. S., Campos, J., Kagan, J., & Zahn-Waxler, C. (1992). Temperament, emotion, and cognition at fourteen months: The MacArthur longitudinal twin study. *Child Development, 63,* 1437–1455.

Fagan, J. F. (1984). The intelligent infant: Theoretical implications. *Intelligence, 8,* 1–9.

Field, T. M., Cohen, D., Garcia, R., & Greenberg, R. (1984). Mother-stranger face discrimination by the newborn. *Infant Behavior and Development, 7,* 19–25.

Forouzan, I., Morgan, M. A., & Batshaw, M. (1997). In M. Batshaw (Ed.), *Children with disabilities* (4th ed., pp. 71–91). Baltimore: Paul H. Brookes.

Frodi, A., Bridges, L., & Grolnick, W. (1985). Correlates of mastery-related behavior: A short-term longitudinal study of infants in their second year. *Child Development, 56,* 1291–1298.

Ganiban, J., Wagner, S., & Cicchetti, D. (1990). Temperament and Down syndrome. In D. Cicchetti & M. Beeghly (Eds.), *Children with Down syndrome* (pp. 63–100). New York: Cambridge University Press.

Greenspan, S., & Thorndike-Greenspan, N. (1985) *First feelings: Milestones in the emotional development of your baby and child.* New York: Penguin.

Haley, S. M., Baryza, M. J., Troy, M., Geckler, C., & Schoenberg, S. (1991). In M. Lister (Ed.), *Contemporary management of motor control problems: Proceedings of the II-STEP Conference* (pp. 237–245). Alexandria, Va.: Foundation for Physical Therapy.

Harris, S. R. (1997). The effectiveness of early intervention for children with cerebral palsy and related motor disabilities. In M. J. Guralnick (Ed.), *The effectiveness of early intervention* (pp. 327–347). Baltimore: Paul H. Brookes.

Harrison, M. J. (1990). A comparison of parental interactions with term and preterm infants. *Research in Nursing and Health, 13,* 173–179.

Harter, S. (1975). Developmental differences in the manifestation of mastery motivation on problem-solving tasks. *Child Development, 46,* 370–378.

Harter, S., & Zigler, E. (1974). The assessment of effectance motivation in normal and retarded children. *Developmental Psychology, 10,* 169–180.

Hauser-Cram, P. (1996). Mastery motivation in toddlers with developmental disabilities. *Child Development, 67,* 236–248.

Heriza, C. B., & Sweeney, J. K. (1994). Pediatric physical therapy: Part 1. Practice scope, scientific basis, and theoretical foundation. *Infants and Young Children, 7,* 20–32.

Horak, F. B. (1991). Assumptions underlying motor control for neurological rehabilitation. In M. J. Lister (Ed.), *Contemporary management of motor control problems* (pp. 11–27). Alexandria, Va.: Foundation for Physical Therapy.

Hrncir, E. J., Speller, G. M., & West, M. (1985). What are we testing? *Developmental Psychology, 21,* 226–232.

Hunt, J. (1965). Intrinsic motivation and its role in psychological development. *Nebraska Symposium on Motivation, 13,* 189–282.

Hupp, S. C., & Abbeduto, L. (1991). Persistence as an indicator of mastery motivation in young children with cognitive delays. *Journal of Early Intervention, 15,* 219–225.

Jennings, K. D., Connors, R. E., Stegman, C. E., Sankaranarayan, P., & Mendelsohn, S. (1985). Mastery motivation in young preschoolers: Effect of a physical handicap and implications for educational programming. *Journal of the Division of Early Childhood, 9,* 162–169.

Jennings, K. D., Harmon, R. J., Morgan, G. A., Gaiter, J. L., & Yarrow, L. J. (1979). Exploratory play as an index of mastery motivation: Relationship to persistence, cognitive functioning, and environmental measures. *Developmental Psychology, 15,* 386–394.

Klaus, M., (1993). Prematurity and serious medical illness in infancy: Implications for development and intervention. In C. J. Zeanah (Ed.), *Handbook of infant mental health* (pp. 105–130). New York: Guilford.

Klaus, M. H., & Kennell, J. H. (1970). Mothers separated from their newborn infants. *Pediatric Clinics of North America, 17,* 1015–1037.

Klaus, M. H., & Kennell, J. H. (1976). *Maternal infant bonding.* St. Louis: Mosby.

Klaus, M. H., & Kennell, J. H. (1982). *Bonding: The beginnings of parent-infant bonding.* St. Louis: Mosby.

Krakow, J. B., & Kopp, C. B. (1982). Sustained attention in young Down syndrome children. *Topics in Early Childhood Special Education, 2*(2), 32–42.

Leach, P. (1987). *Babyhood.* New York: Alfred A. Knopf.

Lester, T. M. (1985). Data analysis and prediction. In T. B. Brazelton (Ed.), *Neonatal Behavioral Assessment Scale, (*2nd ed., pp. 85–91). London: Spartica International.

Levy, J. (1993). *Mother-infant bonding: A scientific fiction.* New Haven, Conn.: Yale University Press.

Lowman, D. K. (1999). Adaptive equipment for feeding. In D. K. Lowman & S. M. Murphy (Eds.), *The educator's guide to feeding children with disabilities* (pp. 141–154). Baltimore: Paul H. Brookes.

MacTurk, R. H., Hunter, F., McCarthy, M., Vietze, P., & McQuiston, S. (1985). Social mastery motivation in Down syndrome and nondelayed infants. *Topics in Early Childhood Special Education, 4,* 93–103.

MacTurk, R. H., McCarthy, M. E., Vietze, P. M., & Yarrow, L. J. (1987). Sequential analysis of mastery behavior in 6- and 12-month-old infants. *Developmental Psychology, 23,* 199–203.

MacTurk, R. H., Vietze, P. M., McCarthy, M. E., McQuiston, S., & Yarrow, L. J. (1985). The organization of exploratory behavior in Down syndrome and non-delayed infants. *Child Development, 56,* 573–581.

Main, M., & Hesse, E. (1990). Parents' unresolved traumatic experiences are related to infant disorganized attachment status: Is frightened and/or frightening parental behavior the linking mechanism? In M. T. Greenberg, D. Cicchetti, & E. M. Cummings (Eds.), *Attachment in the preschool years: Theory, research, and intervention* (pp. 161–182). Chicago: Chicago University Press.

Main, M., & Solomon, J. (1990). Procedures for identifying infants as disorganized/disoriented during the Ainsworth strange situation. In M. T. Greenberg, D. Cicchetti, & E. M. Cummings (Eds.), *Attachment in the preschool years: Theory, research, and intervention* (pp. 121–160). Chicago: Chicago University Press.

Maslin, C. A., Bretherton, I., & Morgan, G. A. (1986, April). *The influence of attachment security and maternal scaffolding on toddler mastery motivation.* Paper presented at the Fifth International Conference on Infant Studies, Los Angeles.

Messer, D. J., McCarthy, M. E., McQuiston, S., MacTurk, R. H., Yarrow, L. J., & Vietze, P. M. (1986). Relation between mastery behavior in infancy and competence in early childhood. *Developmental Psychology, 22,* 336–372.

Murphy, S. M., & Caretto, V. (1999). Anatomy of the oral and respiratory structures made easy. In D. K. Lowman & S. M. Murphy (Eds.), *The educator's guide to feeding children with disabilities* (pp. 35–64). Baltimore: Paul H. Brookes.

Nickel, R. E., & Widerstrom, A. H. (1997). Developmental disorders in infancy. In A. H. Widerstrom, R. A. Mowder, & S. R. Sandall (Eds.), *Infant development and risk* (2nd ed., pp. 89–121). Baltimore: Paul H. Brookes.

Nugent, K. J. (1985). *Using the NBAS with infants and their families.* White Plains, N.Y.: March of Dimes Foundation.

——— (1989). Preventive intervention with infants and families: The NBAS model. *Infant Mental Health Journal, 10*(2), 84–99.

Pascalis, O., de Schonen, S., Morton, J., Deruelle, C., & Fabre-Grenet, M. (1995). Mother's face recognition by neonates: A replication and an extension. *Infant Behavior and Development, 18,* 79–85.

Piaget, J. (1952). *The origins of intelligence in children.* New York: International University Press.

Pianta, R. C., Marvin, R. S., Britner, P. A., & Borowitz, K. C. (1996). Mothers' resolution of their children's diagnosis: Organized patterns of caregiving representations. *Infant Mental Health Journal, 17*(3), 239–256.

Redding, R. E., Morgan, G. A., & Harmon, R. J. (1988). Mastery motivation in infants and toddlers: Is it greatest when tasks are moderately challenging? *Infant Behavior and Development, 11,* 419–430.

Rosenblith, J. F. (1992). *In the beginning: Development from conception to age two* (2nd ed.). Newbury Park, Calif.: Sage.

Sameroff, A. J. (1985). Environmental factors in the early screening of children at risk. In W. K. Frankenburg, R. N. Emde, & J. W. Sullivan (Eds.), *Early identification of children at risk: An international perspective* (pp. 21–44). New York: Plenum Press.

Scalise-Smith, D., & Bailey, D. (1992). Facilitating motor skills. In D. B. Bailey & M. Wolery (Eds.), *Teaching infants and preschoolers with disabilities* (pp. 407–440). New York: Merrill.

Schmidt, R. A. (1991). Motor learning principles for physical therapy. In M. J. Lister (Ed.), *Contemporary management of motor control problems* (pp. 49–63). Alexandria, Va.: Foundation for Physical Therapy.

Schwethelm, B., & Mahoney, G. (1986). Task persistence among organically-impaired mentally retarded children. *American Journal of Mental Deficiency, 90,* 432–439.

Seifer, R., & Vaughn, B. E. (1995). Mastery motivation within a general organizational model of competence. In R. H. MacTurk & G. A. Morgan (Eds.), *Mastery motivation: Origins, conceptualizations, and applications, Vol. 12: Advances in applied developmental psychology* (pp. 95–115). Norwood, N.J.: Ablex Publishing.

Self, P. A., & Horowitz, F. D. (1979). The behavioral assessment of the neonate: An overview. In J. Osofsky (Ed.), *The handbook of infant development* (pp. 127–133). New York: Wiley.

Shore, R. (1997). *Rethinking the brain: New insights into early development.* New York: Families and Work Institute.

Smilansky, S. (1968). *The effects of socio-dramatic play on disadvantaged preschool children.* New York: Wiley.

Stroufe, L. A. (1996). *Emotional development: The organization of emotional life in the early years.* New York: Cambridge University Press.

Tappero, E., & Honeyfield, M. E. (1993). *Physical assessment of the newborn: A comprehensive approach to the art of physical examination.* Petaluma, Calif.: NICU Publications.

Thomas, A., & Chess, S. (1977). *Temperament and development.* New York: Bruner/Mazel.

Wachs, T. D. (1987). Purdue free play mastery motivation manual. Department of Psychological Sciences. West Lafayette, Ind.: Purdue University.

Wachs, T. D. (1987). Specificity of environmental action as manifest in environmental correlates of infant's mastery motivation. *Developmental Psychology, 23,* 782–790.

White, R. W. (1959). Motivation reconsidered: The concept of competence. *Psychological Review, 66,* 297–333.

Wolf, L. S., & Glass, R. P. (1992). *Feeding and swallowing disorders in infancy: Assessment and management.* Tucson, Arizona: Communication Skill Builders.

Worobey, J. and Brazelton, T. B. (1990). Newborn assessment and support for parenting: The neonatal behavioral assessment scale. In E. D. Gibbs, & D. M. Teti (Eds.), *Interdisciplinary assessment of infants, A guide for early intervention professionals* (pp. 33–41). Baltimore: Paul H. Brookes.

Yarrow, L. J., McQuiston, S., MacTurk, R. H., McCarthy, M. E., Klein, R. P., & Vietze, P. M. (1983). Assessment of mastery motivation during the first year of life: Contemporaneous and cross-age relationships. *Developmental Psychology, 19,* 159–171.

Yarrow, L. J., Morgan, G. A., Jennings, K. D., Harmon, R. J., & Gaiter, J. L. (1982). Infants' persistence at tasks: Relationship to cognitive functioning and early experience. *Infant Behavior and Development, 5,* 131–141.

York, J., Rainforth, B., & Giangreco, M. (1990). Transdisciplinary teamwork and integrated therapy: Clarifying the misconceptions. *Pediatric Physical Therapy, 2,* 73–79.

Zirpoli, S. (1997). Issues in early childhood behavior. In T. J. Zirpoli & K. J. Melloy (Eds.), *Behavior management: Applications for teachers and parents* (2nd ed., pp. 383–417). Upper Saddle River, N.J.: Merrill.

CHAPTER FOUR

TODDLERS: THE SECOND AND THIRD YEARS

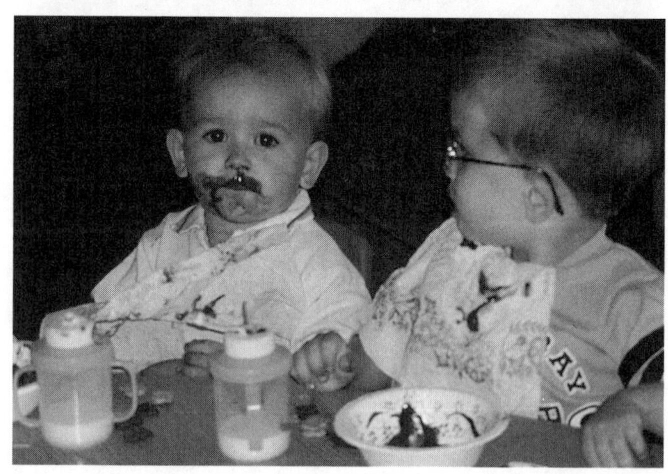

OBJECTIVES

- To introduce the theoretical approaches to learning in infants and toddlers with and without disabilities
- To understand social development, including social mastery motivation and social competence, and the impact of social development on all developmental domains
- To understand pretend play and its role in development for all toddlers, including children at risk
- To understand prosocial behavior and the expression of feelings during the toddler years
- To understand the impact of language and alternative communication systems for toddlers
- To understand the impact of motor development and new approaches to understanding motor development in toddlers
- To understand the impact of risk status on young children

EXPLORATION THROUGH MENTAL AND PHYSICAL PROCESSES

The second year of life is a time of challenges for the child and challenging behavior for the adults. The busy life of the toddler can readily be observed in all areas of development: the physical, the emotional, language, and cognition. Providing children with the supports they need to grow and learn will promote self-esteem and independence. Cognitive psychologists see thinking and learning as an interactive process between a person and her environments. Over the last three decades, knowledge of child development and, particularly, intellectual development had been greatly influenced by the writings of Piaget (1960).

According to Piaget, from birth to approximately 18 months, children progress through the sensorimotor period. During this period the child is actively engaged in exploring the environment through the sensory modalities of speech and hearing, and touch. Children between the ages of 12 to 18 months often exhibit the following characteristics:

- Engages in trial and error (attempts various methods to gain a response)
- Activates a novel toy after a demonstration
- Understands object permanence (knows when a toy is concealed under a cover)
- Practices placing and removing objects in a container
- Combines actions to complete a task or goal

Children with disabilities also go through the sensorimotor period but may do so at different rates, depending on the disability. For example, data showed that children with Down syndrome progressed through the same stages of sensorimotor development, yet complex competencies were demonstrated at a later age (Dunst, 1990).

Wishart (1995) argued that infants with Down syndrome engage in specific exploration behaviors that are counterproductive to learning. For example, many children with Down syndrome engage in repetitive activities with objects. Currently researchers are exploring the possibility that such repetition may be a step in the process of acquiring knowledge (Lender, Goodman, & Linn, 1998). According to Batshaw and Shapiro (1997), children with severe cognitive impairments do not progress beyond the sensorimotor period.

Children with physical disabilities experience sensorimotor development through the use of technology and with the physical assistance of adults. The application of technology is discussed in detail in Chapter 10. In Vignette 4.1, a child with cerebral palsy communicates his need for help to his mother.

VIGNETTE 4.1 JUSTIN AND HIS MOM

Justin is an 18-month-old with hemiplegic cerebral palsy. He is playing with a Fisher-Price garage toy and he needs assistance bringing the car up in the elevator and releasing it onto the "down" ramp. His mother watches as Justin pushes the car into the elevator. He touches the crank and then gazes at his mother to request help. Justin's mother asks, "Should we raise the elevator?" and waits for a verbal or physical response (often he will raise his eyebrows and vocalize "ah" for yes). She then places her hand over Justin's hand to try the crank. When the elevator reaches the top floor, the car is released down the ramp. Justin laughs as he watches the car speed across the floor.

Although Justin's mother gave physical assistance when requested, she did not complete the task for him. This strategy is referred to as partial participation, and is discussed further in Chapter 7. It is important to give Justin the opportunity to succeed at a task involving problem-solving, despite his physical limitations. In the past, parents of children with disabilities were rated by practitioners and researchers as being more directive in their interactions with their children (Jennings, Connors, Stegman, Sankaranarayan, & Mendelsohn, 1985). However, service providers may have inadvertently contributed to this interactive style by requiring parents to set goals and attain them before the next home visit. Recent studies have shown that the parents' behavior may also be reflective of their attempt to adapt the environment so their child may be more successful (Blasco, Hrncir, & Blasco, 1990; Marfo, 1991; Hauser-Cram, 1996). In any event, current trends in services would include supporting parent/caregiver–child interaction by helping parents and caregivers interpret and change their or their child's behavior. As McCollum (in McCollum & Hemmeter, 1997) stated, with this approach the parent becomes an observer, interpreter, and hypothesizer.

Piaget described the period between the ages of two to seven as the preoperational stage, when children gain skills in problem-solving. This is the time when all six layers of the cortex and of the structures that link the two hemispheres of the brain mature (Batshaw & Shapiro, 1997). Children engage in pretend play on an increasingly sophisticated level. They can begin to sort and match objects. For many children, this is a time for language explosion. For children with disabilities and at-risk children, language delay can have serious repercussions in all other areas of development.

A hallmark of Piagetian theory is that the growth of the young child's cognitive skills is gradual and continuous. Each period of development builds on the previous one in a process Piaget called "the growth of mental structures." Finally, Piaget believed that the toddler is engaged in constructing a plan. The concept of "intentionality" gradually emerges as the child selects objects, plays with them, repeats actions on them, and finalizes a plan for interacting with them (Gonzalez-Mena & Widmeyer Eyer, 1993).

THE BEHAVIORAL APPROACH TO LEARNING

A second approach to understanding early conceptual development in toddlers is reflected in the work of Skinner (1953), which formed the basis for the behavioral approach to learning. These scholars believed that behavior was conditioned or learned. Under this approach, the adult manipulates the environment to change the child's behavior. Skinner (1953) believed that overt behaviors are measurable using direct observation. His work formed the foundation for the use of operant conditioning and reinforcement contingencies in working with children with disabilities. Operant conditioning emphasizes the relationship between specific events in the environment and changes in a target behavior (Zirpoli & Melloy, 2001). Antecedent events precede a specific behavior, and consequences are events that occur after the event. For example, when a caregiver brings a spoon of food toward the toddler's mouth, the toddler will open his mouth to receive it. The consequences of opening his mouth are the taste of the food and the response of the caregiver. When a child refuses to accept the food, the antecedent behavior may need to be evaluated and changed. The consequences can be negative for both the child and the caregiver (the child is undernourished, and the caregiver is stressed). Special educators are traditionally taught a behaviorist approach to managing behavior as part of their training program: that is, most behavior is learned and stimulus-specific. Treatment involves teaching specific strategies to chance behavior. This approach may be viewed as narrowly focused when compared with a more developmental or sociocultural theory of learning that commonly provides the foundations for early childhood education.

SOCIAL LEARNING

Recently, scholars have challenged the argument advanced by both behavioral theory and Piagetian theory that children's conceptual development is more dependent on the development of insights or skills that are domain, task, and context specific than on the development of sequential, logical structures (Case, Okamoto et al., 1996). Following Vygotsky's (1962) view that children's thought development is more influenced by external sources and social interaction, some researchers believe that cognitive abilities are dependent on both linguistic and conceptual frameworks that children inherit from their culture and the physical and social principles associated with these frameworks (Case, Okamoto et al. 1996).

The hallmark of Vygotskian theory is that children learn in the "zone of proximal development," which is defined as "a phase of mastery created in the course of social interaction in which the child has partially acquired a skill but can successfully apply it only with the assistance and supervision of an expert partner (Berk & Winsler, 1995, p. 108).

By exploring familiar environments, children engage in problem-solving through the use of their senses. Although they do need some guidance from adults to explore these environments, the caregivers must understand the children's agenda and make decisions aimed at supporting them within the context of learning and appropriate interactional play. As Berk and Winsler (1995) have written, "the social environment is the necessary scaffold, or support system, that allows the child to move forward and continue to build new competencies" (p. 26).

SOCIAL DEVELOPMENT

Social Mastery Motivation

In Chapter 3, we discussed the importance of mastery motivation for infants who are typically developing as well as for infants with disabilities. Mastery motivation continues to be a key developmental framework for understanding the young child. However, as a child enters the second year of life, explorations take on a more social component. During the second year, the infant expands on relationships with others and engages in increasingly sophisticated social behavior. Social mastery motivation is defined as engagement in appropriate social interaction with adults and/or peers by initiation of contact and appropriate response to others (Blasco, 1995a). It is demonstrated by the child's "motivation to generate, maintain, and influence the course of social interaction" (MacTurk, Hunter, McCarthy, Vietze, & McQuiston, 1985, p. 94). According to Boat (1995), social mastery motivation reflects the child's ability to engage in goal-directed social behavior and is nontask specific. Guralnick (1994) pointed out that although the process of developing meaningful and constructive relationships continues throughout the life cycle, the early years are critical if children are to develop the skills that are essential for their daily routines.

Children with disabilities may have difficulty engaging in social interactions as a result of either innate and/or environmental influences (Blasco et al., 1990; Hauser-Cram, 1996). For example, a child with a seizure disorder may have a hard time interacting with his environment due to the high levels of medication necessary to control the seizures (Hauser-Cram, 1996).

Studies have pointed out that as children with disabilities grow into the preschool years, they need more than proximity to other children in order to engage in appropriate social interactions (Odom, McConnell, & McEvoy, 1992). It is imperative that caregivers (both parents and service providers) help scaffold the child's early attempts at social mastery motivation. In two previously published studies, researchers found that caregivers could directly affect on the child's ability to engage in mastery motivation through scaffolding the child's play (see Blasco et al., 1990; Hauser-Cram, 1996).

Social Competence

The roots of peer interaction are now observable as the toddler starts to move from parallel play to complementary and reciprocal play. This behavior occurs sequentially after the toddler has developed the ability to engage in symbolic (pretend) play (Howes, 1988). Complementary play may include give-and-take activities and turn-taking. The child's ability to sustain her own wants and needs in order to share with others begins to increase as the child reaches her second birthday. Although the toddler is now engaging in reciprocal play, that play is typically directed toward one or two children within a group or toward a familiar adult.

Howes (1988) developed a construct for understanding early social competence by describing it as being composed of two independent but related dimensions: social interaction skills and friendship. Social interaction skills include, but are not limited to, the ability to join a play group, play with peers, and demonstrate affective expressions. Friendships are defined as stable, interactive relationships that demonstrate reciprocity and shared positive affect (Howes & Farver, 1987). Table 4.1 demonstrates the sequence of development in terms of social competence with peers.

THE EMERGENCE OF PRETEND PLAY IN INFANTS AND TODDLERS

Between the second and third year, young children continue to expand their interactional capacities toward others. Piaget (1960) described this period (which for many children starts around 18 months), as the preoperational stage. Characteristics of this stage include increased use of language and increasingly sophisticated pretend play. Toddlers now have the ability to store mental images, and they have increased their memory capacity.

This tendency toward reaching out is precipitated by increasing skills in all developmental domains, particularly in the area of language development. For children with disabilities, an inability to attain or gain communication skills can inhibit all areas of development and the achievement of independence. When an

TABLE 4.1 Constructs Representing Social Competence with Peers

AGE	SOCIAL INTERACTION	FRIENDSHIP FORMATION
13–24 months	Imitative	Beginning friendship
	Complementary and reciprocal play	All social overtures directed to same child
25–36 months	Communication of meaning (cooperative friendships, social pretend play)	Flexibility of friendship (in choice of partner)

Adapted from *Peer Interaction in Young Children* by C. Howes, 1988, Monographs of the Society for Research in Child Development, 53 (1, Ser. No. 217), p. 94; and "Toddler's Emerging Ways of Achieving Social Coordinations with a Peer" by C. O. Eckerman, C. C. Davis, & S. M. Didow, 1989, *Child Development, 60,* 440–453.

infant or toddler has not developed the social skills needed to become engaged in appropriate interactions with others, she is at risk for further developmental delay.

Pretend play develops from the simple manipulation of objects during the first year of life. Vondra and Belsky (1989) found that simple manipulative play declined significantly from 12 to 13 months of age in typically developing children. At the same time, there was a substantial increase in the pretend play of these children. In addition, unfocused play decreased in children from 18 to 24 months, while complex pretend play increased. In contrast, Blasco, Bailey, and Burchinal (1993) found that children with disabilities tended to engage in less sophisticated play at one, two, and three years of age. Thus the inability to engage in increasing levels of pretend play puts children with disabilities at a disadvantage. To complicate the matter further, File (1994) found that teachers in early intervention programs were more likely to support cognitive play than social play in classroom settings.

Play behavior in typical developmental milestones for infants and toddlers was derived by theorists such as Gesell (1925) and Piaget (1960). These milestones provide a basis for understanding typical behavior. For children with disabilities, however, skills may be scattered in terms of developmental level, and it is often difficult to interpret their play. Thus it is important for the team to evaluate and document such children's play behavior through a combination of observations, anecdotal records, and family interviews. In Table 4.2 play behavior is documented by age.

Children with disabilities generally learn to play in the same ways as their typically developing peers but at different rates. However, there is a noticeable dif-

TABLE 4.2 Play Behavior During Infancy and Toddlerhood

AGE	PLAY BEHAVIOR	ACTIVITIES
B–12 months	Sensorimotor/perceptual	mouthing, looking, banging, locating, localizing
12–24 months	Sensorimotor/exploratory	simple manipulation, stacking, imitating simple gestures
24–36 months	Exploration becomes integrated with constructive play and dramatics	simple pretend play, substitutes objects
36–48 months	Familiar fantasy themes	role play, planned play activities
48–60 months	Complex themes	multiple planned sequences, substitutions, simple board games

Adapted from "Play-Based Assessment" by P. M. Blasco & M. LaMontagne, 1996, in L. J. Johnson, M. J. LaMontagne, P. M. Elgas, & A. M. Bauer (Eds.), *Early Childhood Education: Blending Theory, Blending Practice,* Baltimore: Paul H. Brookes.

ference in the ability of children with disabilities to engage in more sophisticated levels of play that involve social roles (Blasco, 1995a). In other to understand the social components of play, service providers should utilize a categorical hierarchy of play behavior. Although developed in 1932, Parten's categories of social play continue to provide the standard for evaluating dimensions of social play. Table 4.3 lists the categories of social play.

Children with disabilities tend to play alone or engage in parallel play (Blasco et al., 1993; Bailey, McWilliam, Ware, & Burchinal, 1992). It is important for caregivers and service providers to realize that children with disabilities may need help in reaching more sophisticated levels of social play.

If a toddler or young child is in a center-based program, service providers should observe that child as well as other children to determine the level of play encouraged in the setting. Child care centers should have toys, materials, and dress-up clothes to encourage social play.

The caregiver can provide the scaffolding needed to help the child engage in social play. For example, if the child offers the adult a cup, the caregiver can pretend to drink from the cup and talk about the contents. "Yum, milk! I love to drink my milk in the morning. Thank you, may I have more milk?" As the child pretends to pour more milk for the caregiver, the caregiver could say, "Timmy [another child] might like to have some milk too. Can you ask Timmy if he would like some milk?"

By observing all children in the setting, the level of play most children engage in can be determined. If children in the setting are not encouraged to move

TABLE 4.3 Parten's Categories of Play

TYPE	BEHAVIOR
Unoccupied	Distracted, looking all around the room.
Solitary	Plays alone and independently with toys. Pursues own interests despite others playing nearby.
Onlooker	Watches the play of others. May talk to other children but makes no attempt to join play.
Parallel	Plays independently but activity is like others' activity. May use same toys as another child but in a different way.
Associative	Plays with other children. May exchange toys and comments, but there is no organization to the play.
Cooperative	Play is organized to make a product or to attain a goal, such as games.

Adapted from "Social Participation among Preschool Children" by M. Parten, 1932, *Journal of Abnormal and Social Psychology, 27,* 243–269.

beyond parallel or solitary play, the early intervention team may want to implement some changes. Vignette 4.2 describes one family's experience with the day care center attended by their son, who was diagnosed with autism.

VIGNETTE 4.2 DON'T ASK, DON'T TELL

Max had been attending a neighborhood child care center. At first, Max's parents were delighted and optimistic about the program, but with time they became increasingly frustrated with his lack of progress. They said that the teachers and children did not interact with Max. When they came to school to pick him up, the teachers would say he had a great day. Eventually, the parents came to realize that a great day occurred when Max did not "disrupt the class." Max's father felt that the teachers were not prepared to work with children with disabilities, so they simply ignored him.

Many service providers have a better opportunity than family members to see a child's progress or lack of progress over time in center-based programs. If the child's needs are not being met, the service provider should encourage the family to make a visit and advocate for a better placement.

Interventions aimed at helping children develop pretend skills and providing means of communication can serve as preventive measures for future failures. For example, young children who cannot express themselves or engage in play with others are less likely to be successful in inclusive environments.

Children acquire the skills to engage in pretend play after they have practiced imitating simple actions that they have observed others performing. For example, a child sees an adult comb his hair. The child picks up the comb and brings it toward his hair. Later, as the child matures and develops pretend skills, he will repeat the action by brushing a doll's hair or by offering to brush Mommy's or Daddy's hair. Vignette 4.3 shows how an 18-month-old with cerebral palsy demonstrated his sophisticated knowledge of pretend play.

VIGETTE 4.3 JASON AND HIS DOLL

Jason was lying on the floor in his favorite play position. He has spastic dyplegia, which affects both his legs and one arm. He uses his right hand to reach for a small doll. He finds a baby bottle and feeds the baby using the bottle. He follows this interaction by feeding himself from the bottle. Jason looks around at his toys and finds a bed for his doll. He puts the doll into bed and places a sponge on top of the doll as a substitute for a blanket. The sponge falls off the doll and Jason looks around and finds a piece of felt cloth to cover the doll. He then pats the baby and says, "Ni-ni."

Jason thus demonstrated that he could use sequence pretend play and substitution, which are appropriate for his age. Yet his degree of cerebral palsy makes it difficult for him to show his abilities on typical measures of development. His strong demonstration of successful pretend play will help others know Jason's capabilities as well as his disabilities.

TABLE 4.4 Intervention Strategies to Promote Symbolic Play

- Observe and then identify experiences that the child enjoys in daily events or activities and use toys to represent these events or activities.
- Respond to the child with pretend actions. For example, when the child lies down on the floor, cover her with a blanket, say "night-night," and sing a lullaby.
- Encourage representation of family members. Use play sets that are culturally sensitive and represent the world the child lives in.
- Substitute one object for another. Use a block for a bed. Use a washcloth or napkin for a blanket.
- Elaborate on the child's pretend play. If he gets into a car, ask, "Where are the keys? Can you turn the motor on? Do we have enough gas?"
- Make use of "breakdowns" by using symbolic solutions to fix things or deal with frustration or anger (e.g., a doctor's kit to make things better).
- Uses cues to prompt an action using a least intrusive to most intrusive strategy. For example, "uh-oh" to "you better turn it around."
- Let the child lead the action and follow her lead.
- Pay attention to the starting and ending of pretend sequences. Let the child decide when and how to end a sequence or begin a new theme.

Adapted from "Creating Connections: Intervention Guidelines for Increasing Interaction with Children with Multisystem Developmental Disorder (MSDD)" by S. Wieder, 1997, *Zero to Three, 17*, 19–29.

Opportunities for pretend play with others help young children develop the prerequisite skills for engaging others. As toddlers gain independence through motor skills (e.g., walking, picking up items, climbing), they become more willing to separate from the caregiver and play near other toddlers. Toddlers engage in parallel play when they play next to other children, using materials and toys that may be similar, but do not interact with one another. In Chapter 5, the various types of play are discussed as part of the exploration of the assessment process. Table 4.4 presents intervention strategies designed to promote symbolic pretend play.

THE EMERGENCE OF PROSOCIAL AND UNDESIRABLE BEHAVIOR

All children learn both positive and undesirable or oppositional behaviors that are a natural part of development. Adults smile and acknowledge the toddler who hugs a sibling or a crying child. Conversely, they frown at or punish the child who bites or hits another child in a play situation. It is important that both positive and oppositional behaviors are acknowledged and that alternative methods for dealing with undesirable behaviors are found and demonstrated.

The Division for Early Childhood's (DEC) position paper on discipline stated that many young children engage in challenging behaviors in the course of early development. In order for all young children to participate in the least restrictive environment with their typically developing peers, the DEC recommends:

- Designing environments and activities to prevent challenging behavior and to help all children develop appropriate behavior
- Utilizing effective behavioral interventions that are positive and addressing the form and function of a young child's challenging behavior
- Adopting curriculum modification and accommodation strategies designed to help young children control their behavior
- Accessing consultation and technical assistance or additional staffing when necessary

It is particularly important for adults to model appropriate behavior toward children and other adults in order to effectively influence children's positive behaviors. All too often, we have seen child care workers speak negatively to groups of two- and three-year-olds or to other adults in front of young children. Children will imitate the behaviors that they observe and that are covertly or overtly reinforced by adults.

Beginning Feelings

Young children's ability to demonstrate sympathetic feelings or caring is an exciting developmental milestone. Radke-Yarrow and Zahn-Waxler (1975) pioneered research in sympathetic behavior. They found that children as young as 14 months would try to do something to alleviate the distress of others. These behaviors might include stopping an activity and observing, patting the person in distress, or bursting into tears. It may be that the demonstration of sympathetic behavior emerges after children have acquired the ability to imitate.

Sympathetic behavior appears to be related not only to the child's developmental level, but also to individual differences among children and the physical and social setting in which young children are placed (Barclay-Murphy, 1992). In a day care setting, where mishaps are common, children will have opportunities to engage in sympathetic behavior. The attitudes and actions of the staff will influence a child's willingness to demonstrate sympathy. Teachers and parents who model and display affection and caring and reinforce affection and caring in young children will more likely make a difference.

Fear is another behavior that takes on new meaning during the toddler years. Although children exhibit fear in infancy by demonstrating stranger anxiety or startling and crying to a loud noise, the cause of fear changes as the child enters the toddler years. At this point the child is more likely to exhibit fears of imaginary creatures or physical harm. Brazelton (1992) observed that even a somewhat familiar person can induce fear in the toddler. For example, a relative visiting from out of state or a newcomer to a day care center may produce a quiet response in the toddler. If that person gets too close or speaks too loudly, the child may burst into uncontrollable tears.

The two-year-old begins the third year in relative peace. His newly acquired language skills have gained him some control over his emotions (Lally, Provence, Szanton, & Weissbourd, 1987). However, at two and two and a half, the child continues to exhibit mood swings that are difficult to trace to specific antecedent events (Brazelton, 1992). He frequently displays aggressive behaviors toward others. The traces of sharing noted as he approaches his second year seem to be gone again. Everything is a definite *"mine"*. The feelings of fearfulness discussed above increase, and night terrors may be noted. Brazelton (1992) described night terrors as out-of-control screaming and thrashing, sometimes accompanied by sweating. The child typically calms down when an adult comes to his rescue and will return to sleep after some cuddling. Night terrors could be reflective of a "bad" or stressful day and may be one way the child works off emotional steam.

The two- to three-year-old is capable of empathic behavior. Her feelings of empathy grow as she observes that others have feelings too. As stated, language helps the child to express her feelings of empathy toward others. In child care settings, children ranging in age from 16 to 33 months will respond to signals of distress 93 percent of the time. However, in order for empathy to exist, the child must have developed a clear sense of self in relationship to others and the cognitive ability to understand that another person is experiencing distress or pain (Barclay-Murphy, 1992; Campos et al., 1983; Howes & Farver, 1987). Lewis (1987) stated that both ecocentric thought (the use of self to infer actions and feelings of others) and decentered thought (the ability to consider that all selves are not like oneself) need to develop before the child is capable of demonstrating and maintaining empathy and sharing.

Other emotions that arise during the two- to three-year age span include guilt, shame, and pride (Lewis, 1992). Similar to empathy, these emotions emerge concurrently with more sophisticated cognitive thought processes and are contingent on socialization practices. As previously mentioned, Lewis described the child's ability to evaluate his own actions, thoughts, and feelings as a prerequisite for demonstrating many of these feelings. In addition, the child must evaluate his performance according to some precondition or standard that is either met or failed.

According to Lewis, shame and hubris (pridefulness) are the result of global self-evaluation, whereas guilt and pride are the result of attribute-specific self-evaluation. With the former, the child decides that she is bad because of the things she does; with the latter, the child decides that she should have said "no" instead of hitting Dashay when she took her car.

Given the complexity of feelings and emotions that the two- to three-year-old is capable of experiencing, the ability to express those feelings in functional ways is of vital importance. The increasing sophistication of language allows the child to express his feelings, but sometimes caregivers must rely on body signals, as when a child withdraws from a group snack after spilling his milk. Observing children and their facial and body responses to situations will help caregivers be more in tune with their emotional responses, particularly if the children are not comfortable vocalizing their feelings.

Modeling empathic behavior is also a way to encourage children to demonstrate some of their own feelings. For example, if a child falls in the block area and cries, a reassuring hug and gentle encouragement from an adult will create a more positive influence than ignoring the child or telling her not to cry. Although this may seem like common sense, in a busy classroom it is only too easy to ignore children's expression of emotions unless they are disruptive to the entire group. Helping children find ways to vent their feelings in a positive way can lead to successful future interactions for both the caregiver and the child.

COMMUNICATION IN TODDLERS

The ability to communicate effectively can be enhanced or defeated during the second year of life. During this time young children learn the power of words and use them to let the adult know what they want and how they may feel (Blasco, 1995b). Communication skills are interrelated with all domains of development: social, cognitive, motor, and adaptive. However, in terms of toddler behavior, communication and the social domain seem to be inseparable. Crais and Roberts (1996) stated, "communication is a social act, the function of which is interaction with another living being" (p. 336). Researchers have found that facilitating communication skills in the early years may prevent or ameliorate future learning problems, including emotional/behavioral issues (Wetherby & Prizant, 1993).

Development of Gestures

Infants and toddlers learn to communicate their needs and desires through preverbal aspects of language, in particular gestures and symbolic play. Infants exhibit behaviors that are labeled "communicative intent" prior to the use of actual verbal communication and words. These gestures are purposeful movements that can communicate meaning to a caregiver (Blake, McConnell, Horton, & Benson, 1992).

Reaching is one of the first gestures to come under the infant's control, at around four months of age. The infant then develops a gesture that pairs movement with reaching. Gradually she develops this gesture into pointing, which serves its purpose for obtaining and showing objects. Pointing at pictures in a book begins at about nine months (Sweeney, 1996). Blake et al. (1992) found that the development of gestures appeared to be an indicator of the later nonreferential as well as referential words that develop about six months later. Gestures are often combined with spoken words to form the first true two-word symbol utterances, which occur before verbal two-word combinations are heard (Kennedy, Sheridan, Radlinski, & Beeghly, 1991).

Language and Speech

When a toddler wants a drink, she may point at the refrigerator and make sounds. If the caregiver asks, "What do you want? Would you like some juice?," the toddler may respond with an approximation of the word *juice*. This dialogue continues until the toddler can say "juice" and then expands the request by saying "more juice" and "more juice, please."

So the toddler has developed the ability to use language as a means of communication. This language is particular to the child. Children who are deaf learn to communicate using sign language. In order to acquire language, children must learn a fairly complex system of rules that govern sounds, grammar, meanings, and uses (Crais & Roberts, 1996).

According to the American Speech-Language-Hearing Association (1993):

> a language disorder is impaired comprehension and/or use of spoken, written and/or other symbol systems. The disorder may involve (1) the form of language (phonology, morphology, syntax), (2) the content of language (semantics), and/or (3) the function of language in communication (pragmatics) in any combination. (p. 40)

The components of the form of language are defined as follows:

- Phonology, the rules for the formation of sounds and sound combinations. Phonemes are sounds that join together to form words. This is demonstrated when the child says, "See."
- Morphology, the rules for the structure of words and the construction of word forms. This is demonstrated when the child says, "Mommy, help."

- Syntax, the rules for combining words to form sentences and for establishing the relationships among the components within a sentence. This is demonstrated when the child says, "Help me."

Semantics refers to the rules for meanings of words and sentences. This is demonstrated when a caregiver pushes a ball toward a toddler who then says, "Ball Go." Pragmatics refers to the rules for combining language components into functional and socially appropriate communication. For infants, pragmatic components of language include eye contact, turn-taking, and verbal interchange. From 12 to 15 months, toddlers begin to use words to state their desires. These words are typically single-word utterances that the child has learned from previous feedback. When the child wants to go outside to play, she may say "go" or "out." From 18 to 24 months, toddlers begin to use word combinations such as "go out." Toddlers approximately 18 months of age know about 50 words and comprehend around 300 words (Crais & Roberts, 1996). In Chapter 5, instruments for evaluating communication skills are listed.

Although there is a lack of research on the timing of intervention for language delays with very young children, approximately one-fourth of young children who are eligible for early intervention services are identified as having a communication disorder (McLean & Cripe, 1997). Children with communication concerns may have specific disabilities that are the primary cause of their disorder. On the other hand, some children exhibit no deficits in other developmental areas.

Hearing Loss

It is particularly important that the early intervention team rule out hearing loss as a source or contributor to language delay. Young children may experience a common childhood infection known as otitis media. Otitis media with effusion may include fluid in the middle ear that can lead to a mild to moderate hearing loss (American Academy of Audiology, 1988; Roberts, Burchinal, Davis, Collier, & Henderson, 1991). During the first year of life, the infant develops skills in localizing, recognizing, discriminating, and categorizing sounds (Peck, 1995). The results of these efforts include increased speech during the second year. We know from recent research on the brain that human communication develops at a rapid rate between birth and 36 months of age.

The importance of early detection and identification of hearing loss cannot be overestimated. One study of 203 young children referred for early intervention services found that 35 percent had some degree of hearing loss (Anderson, 1996). One concern is that children with hearing loss sometimes go unidentified or they are referred instead for communication or behavioral issues. In the United States, the delay between the time a hearing loss is suspected by the parents or service providers and confirmed by a hearing test is usually one year (American Academy of Audiology, 1988).

It is important to remember that communication skills go hand in hand with other areas of development. In planning interventions and activities for the child, the service provider should include activities to enhance all areas of development. Although parents may suspect autism when a child is turning two, most children with autism and other multisensory disorders are diagnosed in the second to third year.

ALTERNATIVE METHODS OF COMMUNICATION

Children who are unable to utilize expressive language skills due to a disability can learn alternative communication methods at an early age. For example, the toddler with Down syndrome who is nonverbal can learn to use sign language to communicate with his family, service providers, and peers. Very young children can also use assistive devices such as push-button communicators and computers for expressive language. These devices are discussed in Chapter 10.

TODDLERS WHO EXPERIENCE DIFFICULTY IN COMMUNICATION AND SOCIAL INTERACTIONS

For children diagnosed with autism or an autism-spectrum disorder, the pretend-play activities that are an integral part of toddler development may appear to be delayed or nonexistent. Lifter, Sulzer-Azaroff, Anderson, and Cowdery (1993) found that young children with autism were more likely to learn and generalize pretend-play activities when they matched their developmental level. Some researchers found that a direct instruction approach using modeling and imitation increased the frequency of and/or duration in which the child will play with objects (Rettig, 1994). Toys that inspire social interaction between the adult and child or between the child and a peer are more likely to lead to increases in social behavior, particularly modeling and imitation (Martin & Brady, 1991). Social toys would include dramatic-play toys, puppets, toy vehicles, and balls. In contrast, isolative toys would include puzzles, pegboards, and stacking toys.

MOVEMENT FOR TODDLERS

Parents will remember the first time their child walked, including the details surrounding the main event. Children who are typically developing begin to walk sometime between 11 and 15 months (*Bayley Scales*, 1993). When parents of a newborn or very young child just diagnosed with a disability discuss expectations for their child, one of the first questions is, "Will he walk?" (Blasco & Johnson, 1996). The ability to become mobile facilitates the child's exploratory skills and leads to independence. The child's ability to produce and control a wide range of movements is related to the child's ability to engage in problem-solving (Wood, 1995). Movement also allows the toddler to experiment with separating from the primary caregiver for brief periods that increase over time.

When a child has a disability that impedes movement, it is crucial to find alternative methods that promote her active exploration of her environment and provide opportunities for independence. The literature on motor development has recently changed its recommended practices for young children with motor delays. In the past, movement ability was said to develop in a predictable sequence that followed a hierarchical model (Scalise-Smith & Bailey, 1992). Motor control was seen as developing in a cephalocaudal direction (head to feet).

However, new theories emerged with the advancement of technology that monitored muscle behavior and the nervous system (VanSant, 1991). Therapists became increasingly aware of the complex interactions between the individual and the environment. This led to decreased emphasis in hands-on manipulation of the child and an increased emphasis on problem-solving to determine the expectations, constraints, and support available for functional movement (Heriza & Sweeney, 1994).

NEW THEORIES ABOUT MOTOR DEVELOPMENT

The contemporary view of motor development focuses on the belief that motor development is determined by multiple factors (Thelen, 1995). A dynamic systems approach to understanding motor development is a process-oriented theory that addresses the development, learning, and control of behavior (Heriza & Sweeney, 1994). At the core of this theory is the view that behavior develops from the dynamic interaction and coordination of many subsystems, including the cognitive, biomechanical, neuromotor, environmental, maturational, and social. Heriza (1991) outlined six basic principles of the dynamic systems theory:

- Multiple systems cooperate to produce useful motor patterns such as walking.
- New forms of movement result when changes in the body occur over time or with a particular task or in a particular environment.
- Movement patterns adapt to the demands of the task and the environment.
- Coordinated movement patterns use less energy as they become preferred movement patterns.
- Children develop comfortable patterns of movement.
- The variables that influence the shift from one form of movement to another change over time.

Intervention using this approach emphasizes the practice of functional tasks within a natural environment. Outcomes are designed to achieve these functional tasks. A child's ability to produce and control a wide range of movements is related to his or her ability to practice problem-solving skills. As a result, motor problem-solving should involve cognitive, perceptual, and motor skills in a variety of functional, environmental situations (Higgins, 1991). Table 4.5 compares traditional versus contemporary theories of motor development, learning, and control.

Another similar approach to motor intervention was described by Horn, Warren, & Jones (1995). Neurobehavioral motor intervention combines behav-

TABLE 4.5 Comparison of Traditional and Contemporary Theories of Motor Development, Learning, and Control

TRADITIONAL	CONTEMPORARY
Central nervous system is hierarchical	Cooperative interaction of subsystems heterarchical (distributed among subsystems)
Movement patterns hard-wired Movement for movement's sake	Movement patterns adaptable to task Movement functionally outcome-directed
Passive motor learning with little emphasis on other systems	Active motor learning with emphasis on other systems and problem-solving

Adapted from "Pediatric Physical Therapy. Part II: Approaches to Movement Dysfunction" by C. B. Heriza & J. K. Sweeney, 1995, *Infants and Young Children,* 7(2), 20–32.

ioral modification with neuromotor intervention strategies. In this approach, service providers identify the movement components missing from the child's repertoire, identify functional skills and activities requiring the ability to use these movements, and then develop intervention strategies that use both behavior and neurodevelopmental programming.

There are many different types of equipment that can help children with motor impairments to function successfully in the environment. Several studies have shown that positioning in adaptive seating devices has improved functional skills such as eating and drinking (Hulme, Shaver, Acher, Mullette, & Eggert, 1987), pulmonary function (Nwaobi & Smith, 1986), and visual tracking and grasping (Hulme, Gallagher, Walsh, Niesen, & Waldron, 1987). Other researchers have found higher test scores for preschoolers with cerebral palsy who were positioned properly (Miedaner & Finuf, 1993).

In addition, the use of inhibitive ankle-foot orthoses (AFOs) for young children with cerebral palsy increased the duration of their standing balance and improved the symmetry of their weight bearing in standing (Harris & Riffle, 1986). Children who use four-wheeled posterior rolling walkers rather than two-wheeled rolling walkers had improved ambulation (Levangie, Chimera, Johnston, Robinson, & Wobeskya, 1989). When children without locomotor abilities were provided with power mobility, they showed increased activity, curiosity, exploratory play, and child-initiated behaviors (Butler, 1986).

SUBSTANCE ABUSE AND ITS LONG-TERM IMPLICATIONS FOR TODDLERS

In 1989, the National Association for Perinatal Addiction Research and Education (NAPARE) published a survey of 36 hospitals nationwide and reported that approximately 11 percent of women who delivered babies tested positive for substance abuse. However, for poor women in inner-city neighborhoods, the levels are even higher. For example, 70–75 percent of the mothers of 200 children followed in an East Baltimore clinical study continued to test positive for substance abuse (personal communication, Dr. Harolyn Belcher, October 15, 1997).

The debate over the impact on long-term development of in utero exposure to substances other than alcohol continues to raise questions about long-term effects. Most studies reporting two- to three-year outcomes of children prenatally exposed to cocaine and other drugs showed little difference in their scores on developmental or behavioral outcome measures compared to children who weren't exposed (Carta et al., 1994; Hurt et al. 1995; Hurt et al., 1996).

The findings of studies on the effect of prenatal exposure to substance abuse on children's play are mixed. In a controlled study, Hurt et al. (1996) found no difference in the play behavior at 18 and 24 months between toddlers exposed to cocaine prenatally and a matched group of unexposed toddlers. Other researchers found that toddlers prenatally exposed to substance abuse showed less age-appropriate play and more irritability during play than controls (Metosky & Vondra, 1995).

A more immediate concern for the infant or toddler is the ongoing environmental effects of living with adults who continue to engage in substance abuse. These families may have fewer resources to deal with the stresses of everyday life. They may not trust service providers who represent a different culture or economic group. For many of these families, the delivery of services must be individually tailored and may not reflect the typical procedures of the agency. These families will need attention to basic needs before they can follow a plan to help their child (Coles, 1995).

Striessguth (1997, p. 11) describes the protective environmental factors that are associated with better outcomes for children exposed to substance abuse:

1. A stable and nurturing home
2. Fewer changes in living arrangements or family membership
3. A home free of domestic violence
4. Recipient of early intervention
5. Diagnosis prior to age six

Substance abuse can also affect the parent-child relationship. When mothers and fathers continue to abuse substances, the consequences for the young child can be devastating. Young children are often the innocent bystanders to family and community violence. The parents may also be affected by mental health issues that go largely untreated. Thus, it is important to consult with members of the team who deal with mental health issues so they can follow up on referrals for mental health care. In Chapter 5, criteria for assessing the effects of violence on young children are discussed in detail.

Service providers need a firm understanding of parent-child relationships in order to help families who need external support and guidance. Positive relationships enable the adult to model, guide, and emotionally support the child (Poulson, 1995), and help the toddler to develop a sense of self that is vitally important in becoming able to persist at difficult tasks (mastery motivation), learn delayed gratification, and develop skills to handle both internal and external frustrations (Poulson, 1995).

MENTAL HEALTH ISSUES

Many service providers working in inner-city environments are increasingly finding that infants and toddlers who qualify for early intervention services due to a language delay also have mental health issues. The service providers often feel unprepared for assisting these children and their families based on their training in either special education or a related field.

One of the best resources for understanding mental health issues in infants and toddlers is the Zero to Three organization, which publishes a newsletter on topics that often deal with mental health (see the references in this book).

Traumatic stress disorder provides an umbrella term for a continuum of symptoms exhibited by children who have experienced a single traumatic event or chronic stress (Wieder, 1994). Children who are experiencing traumatic stress disorder may exhibit aggressive and agitated behavior or socially withdrawn behavior. In Chapter 5, we discuss procedures for evaluating children who may be experiencing the syndrome. It is important to seek qualified help for a diagnosis and to keep ongoing records of the child's daily behavior in all possible settings. The effect on the child's behavior should be understood within the following framework:

- The impact of the trauma
- The child's temperament and personality
- The parent's or guardian's ability to help the child understand and cope with the situation
- The need for protection and safety
- The possibility for working through the experience (Wieder, 1994, p. 19)

MALTREATMENT OF INFANTS AND TODDLERS WITH DISABILITIES

Child maltreatment is a general term used to describe neglect, physical and sexual abuse, and emotional and psychological abuse by caregivers. Of children who are the victims of physical abuse, one-third are estimated to be less than one year of age. Pianta, Egeland, and Erickson (1989) have suggested that some children under the age of three are the victims of multiple forms of abuse.

Risk factors that are related to child maltreatment include both parental/caregiver and child characteristics and environmental influences. In terms of parental risk factors, the following characteristics have been perceived to be associated with child maltreatment:

- Negative maternal attitude toward the pregnancy
- High levels of perceived social stress
- Social violence modeled within families over generations
- Ongoing substance abuse
- Maternal mental health issues
- Absence of social support and social isolation

Environmental characteristics that may contribute to child maltreatment include low socioeconomic status, homelessness, and unemployment. However, no one should assume that families facing these environmental pressures are likely to abuse their children. Child characteristics, including difficulty in feeding, poor sleeping patterns, and challenging behavior are also consider risk factors. For parents who do not have the resources or support to parent or who are not ready to be parents, the child's characteristics may exacerbate an already volatile situation (Pianta et al., 1989). No one risk factor will lead to child maltreatment. It is the combination of the multiple factors cited above that leads to the problem.

SUMMARY

Increased mobility, a beginning understanding of cause and effect, and initial control over expressive language characterize the second year of life. Emotional and behavioral development is largely influenced by development in three areas (physical, cognitive, and language). The toddler learns that he can control his environment and the sequence of events with an emphatnic "No!" The once placid infant will now squirm and turn during a diaper change or get up and walk away. The toddler spends his time engaging in activities he determines to be important.

This is also a very frustrating time for the child because, although she understands a great deal, she is limited in her ability to communicate and often will revert to screeching or lying on the floor when she cannot effectively express herself. Expressive communication typically occurs through facial expression, pointing or gesturing, and one-word statements such as "more" or "bye-bye."

During the second year of life there is an explosion in language development as well as in the ability to move around freely in many environments. For children with disabilities, the lack of language skills and motoric ability may place them at a disadvantage in learning new skills as well as in engaging in pretend play, which is crucial in helping children to gain the cognitive and social skills that will allow them to be more successful in future relationships.

Children who are at risk and children who have been abused may exhibit the inability to engage in simple play activities. They may need help in utilizing play as a tool for learning. Service providers may find that the parents of at-risk children may not have learned to play as children. In addition, children who have disabilities may experience maltreatment. Many early childhood centers provide opportunities for parents and children to play together.

In this chapter, we discussed the changes that occur in children during the toddler years that equip them with both the cognitive and social skills they need to form relationships with others.

REFERENCES

American Academy of Audiology. (1988). *Audiologic guidelines for the diagnosis and treatment of otitis media in children* (Position Statement).

American Speech-Language-Hearing Association. (1993). Definition of communication disorders and variations. *Asha, 35* (Suppl. 10), 40–41.

Anderson, G. (1996, April). Hearing loss in children referred to early childhood special education. Paper presented at the American Academy of Audiology, Salt Lake City, Utah.

Bailey, D. B., McWilliam, R. A., Ware, W. B., & Burchinal, M. A. (1993). The social interactions of toddlers and preschoolers in same-age and mixed-age play groups.

Barclay-Murphy, L. (1992). Sympathetic behavior in very young children. *Zero to Three, 12,* 1–5.

Batshaw, M. L., & Shapiro, B. K. (1997). Mental retardation. In M. L. Batshaw (Ed.), *Children with disabilities* (4th ed., pp. 335–359). Baltimore: Paul H. Brookes.

Bayley Scales of Infant Development (BSID II) (1993). San Antonio, TX: Psychological Corporation.

Beckman, P. J., & Lieber, J. (1992). In S. L. Odom, S. R. McConnell, & M. A. McEvoy (Eds.), *Social competence of young children with disabilities* (pp. 65–92). Baltimore: Paul H. Brookes.

Berk, L. E., & Winsler, A. (1995). *Scaffolding children's learning: Vygotsky and early childhood education.* Washington, D.C.: National Association of Education for Young Children.

Blake, J., McConnell, S., Horton, G., & Benson, N. (1992). The gestural repertoire and its evolution over the second year. *Early Development, 24,* 127–136. *Journal of Applied Developmental Psychology, 14,* 261–276.

Blasco, P. A., & Johnson, C. P. (1996). Supports for parents of children with disabilities. In A. J. Capute & P. J. Accardo (Eds.), *Developmental disabilities in infancy and childhood* (2nd ed, pp. 443–464). Baltimore: Paul H. Brookes.

Blasco, P. M. (1995a). *Community-based service models: For children with and without disabilities.* Minneapolis: Minnesota Department of Health.

Blasco, P. M. (1995b). Understanding the emotional and behavioral development of young children: Birth to 3 years. In T. J. Zirpoli (Ed.), *Understanding and affecting the behavior of young children* (pp. 35–59). Englewood Cliffs, N.J.: Merrill.

Blasco, P. M., Bailey, D. B., & Burchinal, M. A. (1993). Dimensions of mastery in same-age and mixed-age integrated classrooms. *Early Childhood Research Quarterly, 8,* 193–206.

Blasco, P. M., Hrncir, E. J., & Blasco, P. (1990). The contributions of maternal involvement to mastery performance of infants with cerebral palsy. *Journal of Early Intervention, 14,* 161–174.

Blasco, P. M., Lynch, E., Trimbach, K., & Scheel, C. (1994). *Community-based service models for young children with disabilities: Final report.* St. Paul: Minnesota Department of Children, Families, and Learning.

Boat, M. (1995). *Defining social mastery motivation in young children with or without disabilities.* Unpublished doctoral dissertation. University of Minnesota.

Brazelton, T. B. (1992). *Touchpoints: The essential reference.* Reading, Mass.: Addison-Wesley.

Butler, C. (1986). Effects of power mobility on self-initiated behaviors of very young children with locomotor disability. *Developmental Medicine and Child Neurology, 28,* 3325–3332.

Campos, J. J., Barrett, K. C., Lamb, M. E., Goldsmith, H. H., & Stenberg, C. (1983). In M. M. Haith & J. J. Campos (Eds.), *Infancy and development psychobiology* (4th ed., pp. 784–857). New York: Wiley.

Carta, J. J., Sideridis, G., Rinkel, P., Guimaraes, S., Greenwood, C., Baggett, K., Peterson, P., Atwater, J., McEvoy, M., & McConnell, S. (1994). Behavioral outcomes of infants and young children prenatally exposed to illicit drugs: Review and analysis of the experimental literature. *Topics in Early Childhood Special Education, 14*(2), 184–216.

Case, R., Okamoto, Y., et al. (1996). Introduction: Reconceptualizing the nature of children's conceptual structures and their development in middle childhood. In R. Case & Y. Okamoto (Eds.), *The role of central conceptual structures in the development of children's thought* (pp. 1–130). Chicago: Monographs of the Society for Research in Child Development.

Cole, P. M., Barrett, K. C., & Zahn-Waxler. (1992). Emotion displays in two-year-olds during mishaps. *Child Development, 63,* 314–324.

Coles, C. D. (1995). Children of parents who abuse drugs and alcohol. In G. H. Smith, C. D. Coles, M. K. Poulson, & C. K. Cole (Eds.), *Children, families, and substance abuse* (pp. 3–23). Baltimore: Paul H. Brookes.

Crais, E. R., & Roberts, J. E. (1996). Assessing communication skills. In M. Mclean, D. B. Bailey, & M. Wolery (Eds.), *Assessing infants and preschoolers with special needs* (2nd ed., pp. 334–397). Englewood Cliffs, N.J.: Merrill.

Dawson, G., & Osterling, J. (1997). Early intervention in autism. In M. J. Guralnick (Ed), *The effectiveness of early intervention* (pp. 307–326). Baltimore: Paul H. Brookes.

Division for Early Childhood. (1998). *Position statement on interventions for challenging behavior.* Denver: Author.

Dunst, C. J. (1990). Sensorimotor development of infants with Down syndrome. In D. Cicchetti & M. Beeghly (Eds.), *Children with Down syndrome: A developmental perspective.* Cambridge: Cambridge University Press.

Eckerman, C. O., Davis, C. C., & Didow, S. M. (1989). Toddlers' emerging ways of achieving social coordination with a peer. *Child Development, 60,* 440–453.

File, N. (1994). Children's play, teacher-child interactions, and teacher beliefs in integrated early childhood programs. *Early Childhood Research Quarterly, 9,* 223–240.

Gesell, A. (1925). *The mental growth of the preschool child: A psychological outline of normal development from birth to the sixth year, including a system of developmental diagnosis.* New York: MacMillan.

Gonzalez-Mena, J., & Widmeyer Eyer, D. (1993). *Infants, toddlers, and caregivers.* (3rd ed.). Mountain View, Calif.: Mayfield.

Greenspan, S. I. (1992). Reconsidering the diagnosis and treatment of very young children with autistic spectrum or pervasive developmental disorder. *Zero to Three, 13,* 1–9.

Guralnick, M. J. (1994). Social competence with peers: Outcome and process in early childhood special education. In P. L. Safford, B. Spodek, & O. N. Saracho (Eds.), *Yearbook in early childhood education: Early childhood special education* (Vol. 5, pp. 45–71). New York: Teachers College Press.

Haas, L., Baird, S. M., McCormick, K., & Reilly, A. (1994). Infant behaviors interpreted by their mothers. *Infant-Toddler Intervention: The Transdisciplinary Journal,* pp. 203–220.

Harris, S. R., & Riffle, K. (1986). Effects of inhibitive ankle-foot orthoses on standing balance in a child with cerebral palsy: A single-subject design. *Physical Therapy, 66,* 663–667.

Hauser-Cram, P. (1996). Mastery motivation in toddlers with developmental disabilities. *Child Development, 67,* 236–248.

Heriza, C. B. (1991). Motor development: Traditional and contempory theories. In M. J. Lister (Ed.), *Contemporary management of motor control problems.* (pp. 99–126). Alexandria, Va.: Foundation for Physical Therapy.

Heriza, C. B., & Sweeney, J. K. (1994). Pediatric physical therapy: Part 1. Practical scope, scientific basis, and theoretical foundation. *Infants and Young Children,* 7(2), 20–32.

Higgins, S. (1991). Motor skill acquisition. In J. M. Rothstein (Ed.), *Movement Science* (pp. 64–180). Alexandria, Va.: American Physical Therapy Association.

Horn, E. M., Warren, S. F., & Jones, H. A. (1995). An experimental analysis of a neurobehavioral intervention. *Developmental Medicine and Child Neurology, 37,* 697–714.

Howes, C. (1987). *Peer interaction of young children.* Monographs of the Society for Research in Child Development, 53 (1, Ser. No. 217).

Howes, C., & Farver, J. (1987). Social pretend play in 2-year olds: Effects of age of partner. *Early Childhood Research Quarterly, 2,* 305–314.

Hulme, J. B., Gallagher, K., Walsh, J., Niesen, S., & Waldron, D. (1987). Behavioral and postural changes observed with use of adaptive seating by clients with multiple handicaps. *Physical Therapy, 67,* 1060–1106.

Hulme, J. B., Shaver, J., Acher, S., Mullette, L., & Eggert, C. (1987). Effects of adaptive seating devices on the eating and drinking of children with multiple handicaps. *The American Journal of Occupational Therapy, 4,* 81–89.

Hurt, H., Brodsky, N. L., Betancourt, L., Braitman, L. E., Belsky, J., & Giannetta, J. (1996). Play behavior in toddlers with in utero cocaine exposure: A prospective, masked, controlled study. *Developmental and Behavioral Pediatrics, 17,* 373–379.

Hurt, H., Brodsky, N. L., Betancourt, L., Braitman, L. E., Malmud, E., & Giannetta, J. (1995). Cocaine-exposed children: Follow-up through 30 months. *Developmental and Behavioral Pediatrics, 16*(1), 29–35.

Jennings, K. D. Connors, R. E., Stegman, C. E., Sankaranarayan, P., & Mendelsohn, S. (1985). Mastery motivation in young preschoolers: Effect of a physical handicap and implications for educational programming. *Journal of the Division of Early Childhood, 9,* 162–169.

Kennedy, M., Sheridan, M., Radlinski, S., & Beeghly, M. (1991). Play-language relationships in young children with developmental delays: Implications for assessment. *Journal of Speech and Hearing Research, 34,* 112–122.

Lally, R., Provence, S., Szanton, E., & Weissbourd, B. (1987). Developmentally appropriate care for children birth to age 3. In S. Bredekamp (Ed.), *Developmentally appropriate practice in early childhood programs serving children from birth through age 8.* Washington, D.C.: NAEYC.

Lender, W. L., Goodman, J. F., & Linn, M. I. (1998). Repetitive activity in the play of children with mental retardation. *Journal of early Intervention, 21*(4), 308–322.

Levangie, P. K., Chimera, M., Johnston, M., Robinson, R., & Wobeskya, L. (1989). The effects of posterior rolling walkers *vs* the standard rolling walker on gait characteristics of children with spastic cerebral palsy. *Physical and Occupational Therapy in Pediatrics, 9,* 1–17.

Lewis, M. (1987). Social development in infancy and early childhood. In J. Osofsky (Ed.), *Handbook of Infant Development* (2nd ed., pp. 419–493). New York: Wiley.

Lewis, M. (1992). Shame, the exposed self. *Zero to three: Bulletin of National Center for Clinical Infant Programs, 12,* 6–10.

Lifter, K., Sulzer-Azaroff, B., Anderson, S. R., Cowdery, G. E. (1993). Teaching play activities to preschool children with disabilities: The importance of developmental considerations. *Journal of Early Intervention, 17*(2), 139–159.

McCollum, J. A. (1991). At the crossroad: Reviewing and rethinking interaction coaching. In K. Marfo (Ed.), *Early intervention in transition: Current perspectives on programs for handicapped children* (pp. 137–176). New York: Praeger.

McCollum, J. A., & Hemmeter, M. L. (1997). Parent-child interaction intervention when children have disabilities. In M. J. Guralnick (Ed.), *The effectiveness of early intervention.* Baltimore: Paul H. Brookes.

McLean, L. K., & Cripe, J. W., (1997). The effectiveness of early intervention for children with communication disorders. In M. J. Guralnick (Ed.), *The effectiveness of early intervention* (pp. 349–428). Baltimore: Paul H. Brookes.

MacTurk, R. H., Hunter, F., McCarthy, M., Vietze, P., & McQuiston, S. (1985). Social mastery motivation in Down Syndrome and nondelayed infants. *Topics in Early Childhood Special Education, 4,* 93–103.

MacTurk, R. H., Vietze, P. M., McCarthy, M. E., McQuiston, S., & Yarrow, L. J. (1985). The organization of exploratory behavior in Down syndrome and non-delayed infants. *Child Development, 56,* 573–581.

Marfo, K. (1991). The maternal directiveness theme in mother-child interaction research: Implications for early intervention. In K. Marfo (Ed.), *Early intervention in transition: Current perspectives on programs for handicapped children* (pp. 177–203). New York: Praeger.

Martin, S., & Brady, M. (1991). Effects of toys on social behavior of preschool children in integrated and nonintegrated groups: Investigation of a setting event. *Journal of Early Intervention, 15,* 153–161.

Metosky, P., & Vondra, J. (1995). Prenatal drug exposure and play and coping in toddlers: A comparison study. *Infant Behavior and Development, 18,* 15–25.

Miedaner, J., & Finuf, L. (1993). Effects of adaptive positioning on psychological test scores for preschool children with cerebral palsy. *Pediatric Physical Therapy, 5,* 177–182.

Nickel, R. E., & Widerstrom, A. H. (1997). Developmental disorders in infancy. In A. H. Widerstrom, B. A. Mowder, & S. R. Sandall (Eds.), *Infant development and risk* (2nd Ed., pp. 89–121). Baltimore: Paul H. Brookes.

Nwaobi, O. M., & Smith, P. D. (1986). Effect of adaptive seating on pulmonary function of children with cerebral palsy. *Developmental Medicine and Child Neurology, 28,* 351–354.

Odom, S. L., McConnell, S. R., & McEvoy, M. A. (1992). *Social competence of young children with disabilities: Issues and strategies for intervention.* Baltimore: Paul H. Brookes.

Peck, J. E. (1995). Development of hearing: Part III. Postnatal development. *Journal of the American Academy of Audiology, 6,* 113–123.

Piaget, J. (1960). *Psychology of intelligence.* Totowa, N.J.: Littlefield, Adams.

Pianta, R., Egeland, B., Erickson, M. F. (1989). The antecedents of maltreatment: Results of the mother-child interaction project. In D. Cicchetti, & V. Carlson (Eds.), *Child maltreatment: Theory and research on the cause and consequences of child abuse and neglect* (pp. 203–253). New York: Cambridge University Press.

Poulson, M. K. (1995). Building resilience in infants and toddlers at risk. In G. H. Smith, C. D. Coles, M. K. Poulson, & C. K. Cole (Eds.) *Children, families, and substance abuse* (pp. 95–119). Baltimore: Paul H. Brookes.

Radke-Yarrow, M., & Zahn-Waxler, C. (1975). *The emergence and functions of prosocial behavior in young children.* Washington, D.C.: National Institute of Health.

Rettig, M. (1994). Play behaviors of young children with autism: Characteristics and interventions. *Focus on Autistic Behavior, 9,* 1–6.

Roberts, J., Burchinal, M., Davis, B., Collier, A., & Henderson, F. (1991). Otitis media in early childhood and later language. *Journal of Speech and Hearing Research, 34,* 1158–1168.

Rosetti, L. (1990). *The Rosetti Infant-Toddler Language Scale.* East Moline, Ill.: LinguiSystems Inc.

Scalise-Smith, D., & Bailey, D. B. (1992). Facilitating motor skills. In D. B. Bailey & M. Wolery (Eds.), *Teaching infants and preschoolers with disabilities* (pp. 407–440). New York: Macmillian.

Skinner, B. F. (1953). *Science and human behavior.* New York: Free Press.

Streissguth, A. (1997). *Fetal alcohol syndrome: A guide for families and communities.* Baltimore: Paul H. Brookes.

Sweeney, C. (1996). *The development of gestures and their relations to communication in infants and toddlers.* Unpublished paper. St. Paul, Minn.: University of St. Thomas.

Thelen, E. (1995). Motor development: a new synthesis. *American Psychologist, 50*(2), 79–95.

VanSant, A. (1991). Motor control, motor learning, and motor development. In P. Montgomery & B. Connolly (Eds)., *Motor control and physical therapy* (pp. 13–27). Hixson, Tenn.: Chattanooga Group, Inc.

Vondra, J., & Belsky, J. (1989). Infant play at one year: characteristics and early antecedents. In J. Lockman & A. Hazen (Eds.). *Action in a social context: Perspectives on early development* (pp. 173–206). New York: Plenum Press.

Vygotsky, L. S. (1962). *Thought and language* (E. Hanfmann & G. Vaker, Trans.). Cambridge: Massachussetts Institute of Technology Press.

Wetherby, A. M., & Prizant, B. M. (1993). Profiling communication and symbolic abilities in young children. *Journal of Childhood Communication Disorders, 15*(1), 23–32.

Wieder, S. (1994). *Diagnostic classification of mental health and developmental disorders of infancy and early childhood. Diagnostic Classification: 0–3.* Arlington, Va.: Zero to Three/National Center for Clinical Infant Programs.

Wishart, J. G. (1995). Cognitive abilities in children with Down syndrome: Developmental instability and motivational deficits. In C. Epstein, T. Hassold, I. T. Lott, L. Nadel, & D. Patterson (Eds.), *Etiology pathogenesis of Down syndrome* (pp. 57–92). New York: Wiley.

Wood, S. (1995). *Dynamic systems theory and motor learning.* Unpublished master's thesis. St. Paul, Minn.: Unversity of St. Thomas.

Zirpoli, T. J. (1995). Introduction: A framework for understanding and affecting the behavior of young children. In T. J. Zirpoli (Ed.), *Understanding and affecting the behavior of young children* (pp. 1–33). Englewood Cliffs, N.J.: Merrill.

Zirpoli, T. J., & Melloy, K. J. (2001). *Behavior management: Applications for teachers* (3rd ed.). Upper Saddle River, N.J.: Merrill.

CHAPTER FIVE

SCREENING AND ASSESSMENT

WITH M. J. LAMONTAGNE

OBJECTIVES

- To understand eligibility requirements for early intervention services and child-find for screening young children
- To understand the theoretical approaches to assessment of young children with disabilities
- To become familiar with issues regarding measurement of young children and their families, including the reliability and validity of assessment instruments
- To understand the utility of alternatives to standardized assessments, including play-based and curriculum-based instruments
- To develop rapport skills in order to discuss assessment results with families in a sensitive and appropriate manner
- To understand the dynamics of caregiver-child interaction and how these relationships influence learning and development
- To understand the approach to assessment with preterm infants
- To become familiar with alternative assessment instruments for specific populations (e.g., children with autism, children exposed to violence)

"Assessment is a generic term that refers to the process of gathering information for the purpose of making a decision"

—McLean, 1996, p. 12.

This definition offers a global interpretation of a very complex task. Assessment is used to make multiple decisions regarding the diagnosis, placement, continuing evaluation, and programmatic strengths and needs of individual young children with disabilities.

Service providers are required by law to document the assessment of children referred for services. The federal government, under the reauthorization of IDEA (Individuals with Disabilities Education Act of 1996, PL 101–476) implemented in July 1998, has enacted Part C legislation, which includes a general definition for eligibility of infants and toddlers. The Part C lead agency in each state is responsible for defining the diagnostic procedures to be used.

The 1997 amendments to IDEA provided that states may include, at their discretion, an "at-risk" infant or toddlers in their definition of "infant or toddler with a disability." This change to the law has led to a reexamination of the eligibility criteria used by states that do not offer funding to children at risk. States that do provide services for infants and toddlers at risk must describe those services in their applications for federal funds. Table 5.1 presents eligibility definitions mandated in Part C.

According to the law, evaluation means documentation, by qualified personnel using appropriate procedures, of the need for services by an infant or toddler

TABLE 5.1 Eligibility under IDEA

(a) As used in this part, infants and toddlers with disabilities means individuals from birth through age 2, who need early intervention services because they—

1) Are experiencing developmental delays, as measured by appropriate diagnostic instruments and procedures in one or more of the following areas:
   (i) Cognitive development
   (ii) Physical development
   (iii) Communication development
   (iv) Social or emotional development
   (v) Adaptive development; or
2) Have a diagnosed physical or mental condition that has a high probability of resulting in developmental delay.

(b) The term may also include, at the State's discretion, children from birth through age 2 who are at risk of having substantial developmental delays if early intervention services are not provided.

The phrase "a diagnosed physical or mental condition that has a high probability of resulting in developmental delay," as used in paragraph (a)(2) of this section, applies to a condition if it typically results in developmental delay. Examples of these conditions include chromosomal abnormalities; genetic or congenital disorders; severe sensory impairments, including hearing and vision; inborn errors of metabolism; disorders reflecting disturbance of the development of the nervous system; congnital infections; disorders secondary to exposure to toxic substances, including fetal alcohol syndrome; and severe attachment disorders.

With respect to paragraph (b) of this section, children who are at risk may be eligible under this part if a State elects to extend services to that population, even though they have not been identified as disabled.

Under this provision, States have the authority to define who would be "at risk of having substantial developmental delays if early intervention services are not provided." In defining the "at risk" population, States may include well-known biological and environmental factors that can be identified and that place infants and toddlers "at risk" for developmental delay. Commonly cited factors include low birth weight, respiratory disress as a newborn, lack of oxygen, brain hemorrhage, infection, nutritional deprivation, and a history of abuse or neglect. It should be noted that "at risk" factors do not predict the presence of a barrier to development, but they may indicate children who are at higher risk of developmental delay than children without these problems.

Early Intervention Program for Infants and Toddlers with Disabilities, 34 C.F.R. § 303.16 (July 1, 1999).

and his family. Moreover, early intervention services must be provided by qualified personnel, including:

- Audiologists
- Family therapists
- Nurses

- Nutritionists
- Occupational therapists
- Orientation and mobility specialists
- Pediatricians and other physicians
- Physical therapists
- Psychologists
- Social Workers
- Special educators
- Speech and language pathologists

Early Intervention Program (1999), § 303.12

This list is not exhaustive. Qualified personnel may also include such personnel as vision specialists, paraprofessionals, and parent-to-parent support personnel.

All commercially available measurement tools recommend qualifications for users in order to maintain the validity and reliability of the instrument. For example, the Bayley Scales of Infant Development (1993) recommend that examiners have formal instruction in administering standardized assessments in a graduate or professional training program. Other tests list qualified personnel by professional field and may include trained educational assistants. This and other instruments must be administered in the native language of the parent. Service providers must use multiple procedures for determining eligibility, including observation. States require observation in the natural environment along with the use of standardized assessments and other procedures. In many states, informed clinical judgment as well as standardized results help determine eligibility.

A full comprehensive assessment is required for the following reasons:

1. To identify and diagnose children for program eligibility according to federal and state guidelines.
2. To plan programs and provide appropriate services as required by the Individualized Family Service Plan.
3. To monitor the child's progress on an ongoing basis. Although used for different purposes, both evaluation and assessment are critical parts of service delivery. Assessment refers to the actual procedures used to develop the Individualized Family Service Plan, including periodic review (McLean, 1996). Part C regulations for the IFSP require the evaluation and assessment of the child along with documentation of family resources, priorities, and concerns.

Part C legislation also mandates that state and local lead agencies actively seek infants and toddlers who may qualify for services. Through this mandate, service providers structure a series of evaluation procedures to provide developmental information to families, health care providers, human services professionals, and education interventionists known as child-find activities.

CHILD-FIND

Child-find is a state-regulated system of locating children who are eligible or may be eligible for early intervention services (McLean, 1996). Children with known disabilities such as cerebral palsy or Down syndrome are typically easier to find because of referrals from medical and other agencies. Children who may have a disability that is not as obvious in infancy and during the toddler years or who are at risk for developmental delay are harder to identify. Providing families with guidelines for typical development often helps caregivers who are unsure if their child has a delay. Many states have created multiple ways for identifying hard-to-find children. A common procedure is to place brochures or ads in settings families are likely to visit (e.g., a doctor's office, school, or mall). Some states use television and radio advertisements to help families who may have questions about their child's development.

SCREENING

Many local early intervention services have a central telephone number that accepts referrals and assigns a service provider to do initial screening. Related to the assessment process, screening is a brief and inexpensive method of identifying children who may need further and more extensive evaluation. Screening usually takes 10 to 20 minutes, and can be done with a formal screening instrument, such as the *Denver II* (formerly the *Denver Developmental Screening*) (Frankenburg et al., 1990), or an informal screening examination completed by the child's physician or another professional.

As a result of federal and state requirements for the identification and evaluation of all children with disabilities, mass screening is offered by many local school systems. These are collaborative community events (including multiple agencies such as Head Start, Early Childhood Special Education, social services, and public health) using advanced advertisements in the local media (newspapers, radio, and television). Many states offer screening for children three years of age and older prior to entering kindergarten. In some states screening is mandatory before the child attends kindergarten. During the screening process, children and their families go from one assessment area to another in order to identify developmental issues, vision problems, and hearing concerns. In addition, some programs include questionnaires or interview formats to elicit family concerns regarding the child's health or developmental status (Wright & Ireton, 1995). Parents play an important role in screening, because they can provide more reliable information about their child's behavioral characteristics than an abbreviated screening instrument (Diamond & Squires, 1993).

Tracking is a part of comprehensive child-find system that provides continuous monitoring of infants and toddlers who are at risk for developing disabilities (Blackman, 1986). An example of this type of service is the premature infant follow-up clinic. Several states have implemented statewide systems. Iowa, for example, has developed a statewide screening and tracking system for infants with biological risk factors. This system represents a cooperative effort by many state agencies, including the University of Iowa and child health specialty clinics. Infants with medical records indicative of neonatal risk factors, including very low birth weight, hypotonia, or seizures, are referred for screening at 4, 9, 18, and 20 months of age. The infants undergo a series of screening and assessment measures, including the *Denver Developmental Screening (DDST) II,* a physical and neurological examination, and an unstructured assessment of psychosocial behaviors and environmental conditions.

THEORETICAL APPROACHES TO ASSESSMENT

The development of assessments for young children is guided by three overlapping theoretical approaches to assessment. The first is the developmental approach. The Gesell Developmental Schedules (Gesell, 1925) established the importance of milestones in the developing child. Over the next two decades Bayley continued to refine this approach and first published the *Bayley Scales of Infant Development* in 1969. This test was renormed in 1992, but continues to be plagued by problems, and though the Bayley Scales continue to be used, no one has ever replicated her work.

The second approach to testing young children is the behavioral approach, which examines the behavioral responses of the child in relation to the environment. The Bayley Scales was one of the developmental scales that examined the child's behavioral repertoire during assessment. Another example of a behavioral assessment is the Brazelton Neonatal Assessment Scale (BNAS) (Brazelton & Nugent, 1995). A primary goal of the BNAS is to demonstrate the newborn's capabilities in terms of the caregiving environment.

The third type of approach to assessment is the ecological approach, which examines the child's abilities and needs in terms of the multiple environments in which the child interacts on a daily basis. The Assessment, Evaluation, and Programming System (AEPS) (Bricker, 1993) is an example of an ecological assessment tool. This approach recognizes the importance of child and family variables that affect development and learning. It also takes into consideration the connection between the child, family, community, and society. By using this approach, the assessment team can probe environmental factors that the family perceives as important (Bricker, 1993).

Standardized assessments generally follow the developmental milestones approach that include specific guidelines for administration, scoring, and interpretation of test results. The instruments are developed using sampling procedures to ensure that all children within a certain age group are represented across race, sex, geographic location, and (in some cases) socioeconomic status. These tests are also called norm-referenced tests because they compare the child's performance to that of a normative group.

Criterion-referenced assessments may also follow a developmental milestone approach, but they measure the child's performance according to a certain level of mastery rather than to a normative group.

Curriculum-based assessment may incorporate all three approaches to assessment. In addition, the assessment is directly linked to a curriculum so that intervention plans can be drawn from the results. The Transdisciplinary Play-Based Assessment (Linder, 1993) is an example of a curriculum-based assessment.

For many service providers working in the field, play has always provided the best window into viewing a child's capacity.

For years, service providers have struggled with federal and state requirements to use standardized assessments with infants and toddlers because these instruments continued to penalize children with disabilities (Blasco, 1989). However, with the passage of Part C, many states have added the requirement of observation-based assessment in the natural environment, and some states do not require standardized assessment at all. However, since many states continue to require a formal assessment procedure, service providers must be familiar with scoring and interpreting these tests.

STANDARDIZED ASSESSMENT

Standardized assessment of young children has been used in this country since the 1930s. The California First Year Mental Scale (Bayley, 1933) was the precursor to the Bayley Scales of Infant Development (BSID) (Bayley, 1993). Standardized measures adhere to required protocols, materials, and procedures for scoring and interpretation (Bailey & Nabors, 1996). As stated, these tests give normative data on children who fall into the age range specified by their developers, who administered the test to a sample population. Such norm-referenced tests can therefore give developmental age scores, developmental quotients, standard scores, and percentile ranks. It is important to realize that some assessments give information on developmental age that is not based on a normative sample. The information in the guidelines or preface to the test should be read carefully to ensure that it is norm-referenced.

Developmental age scores indicate the average age at which 50 percent of the children in the sample population received a particular raw score on the test. A problem with this measurement is that it relies on the raw score and does not differentiate the child's performance on specific items. For example, if one child scored a 2 on three of five items and a 1 on the last two items, and another child scored a 1 on the first two items and a 2 on the last three items, they would have the same score but different needs for learning and skill acquisition. Bailey and Nabors (1996) also pointed out that although a child may exhibit skills typical of an 18-month-old, there is wide variability in the abilities of an 18-month-old, and thus the information is not very helpful in planning intervention.

A developmental quotient (DQ) can be computed by dividing the child's developmental age (DA) by her chronological age (CA), and multiplying by 100. For example, the DQ of an 18 month-old toddler who scores developmentally at 18 months would be as follows:

$$\frac{18 \text{ months (DA)}}{18 \text{ months (CA)}} \times 100 = 100$$

Many physicians use the developmental quotient because it is easy to deliver a small sample of items (Peter A. Blasco, personal communication, March 3, 1996).

Some researchers, however, believe it is problematic because of the disparity between a child's DQ at different ages (Bailey & Nabors, 1996), which, unlike an IQ score, is likely to change as the child grows older. There continues to be a great deal of debate regarding infant assessments that attempt to predict later intelligence. However, infant assessments with items that assess memory, discrimination, or attention correlate highly with intelligence tests given at later ages (Siegel, 1999).

The assessment of infants can be influenced by the temperament of the child and his response to the examiner and to the items. For example, children with difficult temperaments score lower than children with easier temperaments. In addition, infants and toddlers vary greatly in their mood depending on the time of day, their energy level, and their nutritional status. Parents can also influence the child's performance on a standardized assessment. If the parent is overly anxious, the child may sense this and become distraught. It is important for the examiner to establish rapport not only with the child (to overcome any stranger anxiety) but also the parent. Parents may need reassuring from time to time, especially if the child is failing items. In Vignette 5.1, a father expresses his concern about his daughter's performance.

VIGNETTE 5.1 SHE CAN DO BETTER THAN THAT!

Gary and Mary brought 18-month-old Gina in for her assessment after she failed on a preschool screening exam. Gina was born eight weeks prematurely and had developed bronchopulmonary dysplasia while in the Neonatal Intensive Care Unit (NICU). Both parents were anxious about the outcome of this assessment, although they knew they would gain access to services for Gina. Sara, the examiner, pointed out Gina's successes and smiled at both parents to reassure them. After about 10 minutes, Gina was not able to perform many of the items. Her father had played pat-a-cake with her many times, but the examiner could not get her to play the game. Then she tried to get Gina to play peekaboo. She still was unsuccessful, and it was obvious that this item would not be scored as a pass. Gary was furious, for he had seen Gina play both games many times. He began to move about in his seat restlessly and made several comments about the inadequacy of the test. Gina sensed something was wrong and began to cry. She wouldn't take any interest in the items and wanted to be held. The examiner suggested that Mary give her a hug to help her calm down. Gary said, "No, I'll take her." This action only increased Gina's anxiety. The examiner suggested that they continue the assessment on another day.

Although the situation in Vignette 5.1 does not occur frequently, it is likely that parental anxiety will be heightened during testing. In the above situation, the examiner could have explained beforehand that the assessment required her to continue even after the child began to fail items, or she could have commented that children don't always perform during assessments as they would in a less strange situation. Unfortunately, given the nature of many standardized assessments, families do not participate as equal partners in the assessment process. For example, although a parent report is included on the BSID II, it cannot be used for scoring purposes. It is important for families to have equal status in the assessment process in order to establish a sense of trust (McLean & Crais, 1996). Most curriculum-based and play-based assessments include a parent report as part of the assessment process.

In a perfect world, assessments would occur at the optimal time for both children and parents. But this can be impractical in some situations, especially for the examiner who feels he has an overburdened caseload and does not have time to reschedule assessments. Thus, examiners may be cutting corners to complete an assessment as scheduled, particularly if they are more experienced with assessing older children and do not understand the needs of infants and toddlers.

UNDERSTANDING STATISTICAL PROPERTIES

In order to use all assessment measures correctly, service providers should have a firm background in measurement. Service providers who do not understand procedures are likely to make both administration and scoring errors. In one study, Bailey, Vandiviere, Delinger, and Munn (1987) found that out of 79 teachers, only 11 (14.5 percent) had no scoring errors on the Battelle Developmental Inventory (BDI), a widely used assessment instrument (Newborg, Stock, Wnek, Guidubaldi, & Svinicki, 1984).

There is no replacement for the study of a thorough text on test and measurement. However, at the very least, a few key terms should be reviewed before using assessments in early intervention. Most assessments in early childhood use a standard score for interpreting the overall performance on a test. A standard score provides a mean and standard deviation that is represented on a normal bell-shaped curve that provides a model for the theoretical distribution of scores. Any introductory textbook on statistics will provide an example of the bell curve. With a standardized assessment, most children will score near the mean. A standard deviation provides numeric information on how far a child's score deviates from the mean.

Many states use standard deviations for determining eligibility for special education services. For example, to receive early childhood special education services in Minnesota, a child must receive a score 1.5 standard deviations below the mean on a standardized developmental assessment, or, if the child is younger than 18 months old, a motor score 2.0 standard deviations below the mean.

In addition, the state requires systematic observation in the routine environment and a developmental history and medical history. Percentile ranks are also used to compare a child's score with a population (Bailey & Nabors, 1996). If a child has a percentile score of 70, this would indicate that she scored higher than 69 percent of the normative population.

Reliability and Validity

The developers of a standardized test must supply information regarding its reliability and validity. Reliability refers to the extent to which individual differences are measured consistently. Reliability is the ratio of true variance divided by obtained variance. When the ratio is 1, then reliability is perfect.

There are several types of reliability. Stability, also known as test-retest reliability, examines the relationship of an individual's score on the first administration of the test to her score on the second administration of the same test. A coefficient of stability is reported. For example, for the BSID II, test-retest scores are reported for the mental, motor, and behavior scales as well as for several subscales. The testing was completed on a sample of infants (N = 48) at 12 months of age. The two tests were administered within one to 16 days, with a median retest date of four days. The stability coefficient was .83 for the mental scale and .77 for the motor scale (Bayley, 1993). One concern with test-retest reliability is the influence of practice and memory. Tests scheduled close together give the child opportunities to practice items that were similar.

Another type of reliability examines the internal consistency within the test. Split-half reliability assesses two halves (such as all odd-numbered items and all even-numbered items) by correlating the scores obtained in the comparison of the two halves for each individual. Two statistical procedures for computing internal consistency are the Spearman-Brown and Kuder-Richardson formulas. Interrater (interobserver) reliability examines the relationship between items passed or failed, using percentage of agreement between two independent observers. One problem in using interrater reliability with rating scales is that it does not indicate the discrepancy between two scores. For example, one scorer gave a child a 5 and the other scorer a 1 on the same item. However, when the total was calculated, the observers agreed more than disagreed, so the reliability was high. One solution is to use a statistical procedure called the G-coefficient that also takes into account the variability within the scores between observers.

Validity is the degree to which a test measures what it is supposed to measure. Very few assessments give an indication of their face validity, or their attractiveness to the user. But, as one psychologist pointed out, face validity can make or break an assessment. "I've seen tests where the staff just didn't like the looks of it. They could never give a good explanation for why they didn't like the test, but you can be certain it ended up in a closet collecting dust!"

Content validity measures the intended content area of the test. One question to ask is whether the items on the test correspond to its objectives. All standardized tests include information on their content.

Construct validity measures an intended hypothetical construct. For example, Sell, Figueredo, and Wilcox (1995) completed a confirmatory factor analysis to validate behavioral domains on the Assessment of Preterm Infants' Behavior (APIB). With a sample of 145 infants who required neonatal intensive care, they confirmed six behavioral constructs: overall modulation of behavior, availability for examination, motor competency, sociability, habituation, and reactivity.

Criterion validity relates performance on the test to performance on another criterion. For example, Siegel, Cooper, Fitzhardinger, and Ash (1995) compared a subtest of expressive language items on the Bayley Scales of Infant Development with the Reynell Developmental Language Scales (RDLS-R), using 137 low-birth-weight preterm infants at two years of age. Both tests were scored both with age correction for prematurity and with no correction by using the child's chronological age (corrected scores implies full correction for age). The correlations were .66 for uncorrected comprehension scores and .79 for uncorrected expressive scores. The correlations were .67 for corrected comprehensive scores and .80 for corrected expressive scores.

ALTERNATIVES TO STANDARDIZED ASSESSMENTS

Assessment for early intervention is not a test-based process, primarily; early childhood assessment is a flexible, collaborative decision-making process in which teams of parents and professionals repeatedly revise their collective judgments and reach consensus about the changing developmental, educational, medical, and mental health service needs of young children and their families.

—Bagnato & Neisworth, 1991, p. xi

Recommended practice in both early intervention and early childhood education recognizes the importance of a link between assessment and curriculum in order to ensure program content is meeting the needs of the child and the concerns of the family (Bagnato, Neisworth, & Munson, 1997; Bredekamp & Rosegrant, 1995; Bricker, 1993). No single assessment can make that link. It is the responsibility of the team, including the parents, to make the decisions that affect the child's learning experience. In Chapter 9, we discuss in depth the role of the team in early intervention and the ways in which teams are formed. Over the past decade, teams have found formal assessments to be inappropriate for program planning based on individual needs. As a result, there has been a shift away from the use of formal assessments and toward the use of informal assessments. This has meant increased reliance on criterion-referenced assessments, which focus on mastery of specific skills, rather than making a comparison to a norm sample (Benner, 1992). These types of assessments can be simple checklists that provide a baseline for program planning as well as ongoing evaluation. Although such a checklist can be useful for planning IFSP outcomes, service providers should be cautious about "teaching to the test," since IFSP outcomes should reflect the child's needs as well as the family's priorities.

There are many curriculum-based assessments for infants and toddlers on the market. These tools are designed to link assessment and curriculum. The items on the assessment protocol follow a typical developmental progression. The curriculum activities that correspond to test items teach functional skills related to the identified needs of the individual child. Many of these measures are introduced in Chapter 7. The Carolina Curriculum for Infants and Toddlers with Special Needs (Johnson-Martin, Jens, Attermeier, & Hacker, 1991), for example, provides developmental markers for assessing infants and toddlers across developmental domains. The Carolina Curriculum also provides suggestions for modifying test items for children with motor or sensory impairments. Similarly, the Hawaii Early Learning Profile (HELP) provides developmental assessment for infants and toddlers from birth to three. In addition to curriculum activities, HELP at Home provides activity sheets for parents across the developmental domains (Parks et al., 1992).

The AEPS (Bricker, 1993) was designed as an intervention model that links assessment, intervention, and evaluation processes. According to Bricker (1993):

> Assessment refers to the process of establishing a baseline or entry level measurement of the child's skills and desired family outcomes. The assessment process should produce the necessary information to select appropriate and relevant intervention goals and objectives. Intervention refers to the process of arranging the physical and social environment to produce the desired growth and development specified in the formulated intervention plan for the child and family. Evaluation refers to the process of comparing the child's performance on selected intervention goals and objectives before and after intervention, and comparing the family's progress toward established family outcomes. (p. 12)

Curriculum-based assessment provides the team with an opportunity to plan outcomes for each individual child based on the results of the assessment. Both practitioners and families find this approach to assessment more functional and meaningful in meeting the needs of the child. Because play is such an integral part of the curriculum for very young children, play-based assessment can help to identify the learning needs of children regardless of disability.

PLAY-BASED ASSESSMENT

We suggest that the motivation/competence relationship can be measured in spontaneous play because in spontaneous play children are free to show or not show their most sophisticated behaviors.

—Hrncir, Speller, & West, 1985, p. 227

The dynamic nature of infants and toddlers with disabilities has presented many challenges to interventionists charged with the task of assessing their skills, abilities, and behaviors. Young children exhibit characteristics that are often not compatible with standardized assessments (Linder, 1993; McLean, 1996; Peterson, 1988; Fewell, 1983). Infants and toddlers appropriately display anxiety and fear in the presence of strangers who are structuring interactions with them. Unfamiliar settings can create an atmosphere of discomfort for the infant or toddler, resulting in refusal and avoidance behaviors. An assessment environment that is not responsive to the daily routine of a child may impose misjudgments of an infant or toddler who is ready for a nap or a feeding rather than interactions with an adult. In addition, the field of early intervention has become more attentive to infant and toddler characteristics that frame the performance of a skill. The understanding of characteristics such as temperament, states of arousal, motivation, engagement, interactional patterns, and interests has proved to be valuable for designing and implementing individual family service programs. There is also recognition that the interdependence of developmental systems is a major characteristic of infancy that must be addressed if a complete understanding of infant functioning is to be obtained (Teti & Gibbs, 1990).

Acknowledging the limitations of using standardized assessment instruments with infants and toddlers has led to the development of alternative approaches to identifying present levels of functioning in this population. Campbell (1991) concisely articulated the challenge by defining the purpose of assessment as identifying the unique needs of the infant or toddler with disabilities, with the understanding that these needs are constantly changing due to the child's status as an infant or toddler. A particularly effective means of achieving this is through the use of play-based assessment, which has evolved from a transdisciplinary assessment process developed by the United Cerebral Palsy Association (1976) to gather information to use in planning programs for individuals with moderate or severe cerebral palsy.

This transdisciplinary approach transforms the assessment process to a more supportive environment that accesses the competencies and identifies the needs of the infant or toddler with disabilities and her family. In play-based assessment, a single individual interacts with the infant or toddler, while professionals and family members observe the child's performance of skills (Linder, 1993). The observers become active participants as they request the elicitation of specific behaviors during the play session. Play-based assessment is thus a systematic method of viewing a young child's skills and abilities through the medium of play (Blasco & LaMontagne, 1996; Lifter, 1996; Linder, 1993; Woodruff, 1980).

Components of Play-Based Assessment

The five basic components of a play-based assessment (Blasco & LaMontagne, 1996; Linder, 1993; Woodruff, 1980) are described in Table 5.2.

Each of these components contributes to the successful implementation of a play-based assessment. Team membership should reflect the concerns presented by the family during the intake or referral process. A transdisciplinary approach requires that all of the professionals and family members involved assume the various roles in the assessment. If possible, the facilitator should be an individual familiar with the family so that she can gather information from and support the family during the entire procedure. Regardless of the specific format or approach, assessment is stressful for families, and having a familiar facilitator can help to alleviate some of the tension. It is best if the play facilitator is someone who is known to the child and/or who is skilled in working with infants and toddlers in order to be able to follow the child's lead and interests, and be responsive and flexible as the interactions change and as the child's temperament and personality are revealed. In addition, the play facilitator should be comfortable interacting while sitting on the floor or playing at the sand or water table. This person also should be able to provide exaggerated facial responses and to sing or use differing voice tones to engage the child's attention, which are often necessary when interacting with infants and toddlers.

TABLE 5.2 Play-Based Assessment Components

COMPONENTS	ACTIONS
1. Team selection based on child and family characteristics; team members (to include parents if they so choose) define purpose of assessment	Identify and assign roles (e.g., facilitator, play facilitator)
2. Information about priorities, resources, and concerns disseminated to team members; review previous results	Gather information related to child and family background,
3. Selection of appropriate assessment materials	Identify written observation format Identify and develop activities to support the child's demonstration of skills
4. Conduct assessment	Structure environment in child- and family-friendly manner Review assessment purpose Review team member roles Play facilitator presents activities to the child and/or allows the child to lead the interactions Facilitator supports family members during the assessment and/or gathers additional information from family Team members make suggestions for additional activities Team members record descriptive information on observation forms and record demonstration of behaviors on developmental checklists
5. Assessment staffing	Include family as team member Review past assessment data Review information gathered during play-based assessment Brainstorm insights and recommendations Develop group consensus in relation to IFSP goals and outcomes Generate IFSP and/or assessment report

It is important that information about the family and child be disseminated to team members prior to the assessment. This will reduce the length of the assessment and reduce redundancy in gathering data. Such information will also help the team select the appropriate assessment materials. For a play-based assessment to be successful in gathering information needed for program planning, the play facilitator must prepare a series of activities that will allow the infant or toddler to demonstrate his skills and abilities. In many instances, the play facilitator will be able to follow the child's lead, and these preplanned activities may not be needed. However, it is important that activities be available when a team member requests that a specific skill be elicited. For some play-based assessments, team members may want to record demonstration of skills across developmental domains on developmental checklists, with descriptive information logged in available space. For others, observation forms that provide a format for recording running observations of the child throughout the assessment process may be more appropriate.

Conducting the play-based assessment is the most involved component of the process and requires attention to several steps (Blasco & LaMontagne, 1996; Linder, 1993; Woodruff, 1980), as identified in Table 5.3.

TABLE 5.3 The Play-Based Assessment Process

Step 1. Orient the child and family to the team members and the environment. Let the child hear the voices of the team members so that they will be familiar when heard during the assessment. Introduce the family members to any unknown team member. Allow the family to choose where they would like to sit, and allow the infant or toddler to explore the environment.

Step 2. Have team members sit around the perimeter of the assessment area so that each has an observational field of the child and play facilitator. Ensure that the environment is child- and family-friendly. Use child-size furniture when appropriate. Have age- and developmentally appropriate toys, including large motor equipment, such as rocking boats, slides, bikes, and push/pull toys. Place a blanket or mat on the floor so that the infant or toddler is comfortable when crawling or lying down.

Step 3. As the play facilitator engages the child, observers record information on observation forms. Additional information can be gathered from the family as the assessment progresses. When appropriate, observers may request activities and demonstration of specific child skills from the play facilitator. When necessary, observers may talk quietly among themselves but must be careful not to distract the infant or toddler.

Step 4. If possible, structure the play-based assessment time to include the following interactions: child-family, child-peer, child-sibling, and child-adult. Also include opportunities for the infant or toddler to have a snack or lunch in order to observe self-help/adaptive and feeding skills.

Step 5. Whenever possible, allow the infant or toddler to dictate the pace, the materials, and the interactions. If the child appears disinterested, ask family members for suggestions for engaging her attention. Use planned activities when requested by team members or when the child is hesitant about initiating an interaction with the play facilitator.

Step 6. Continue the play-based assessment until: the allotted time is up; the child becomes tired, irritable, or otherwise nonengaged; the observers have acquired all the information of interest; or the family expresses a desire to stop.

It is critical for the family and child to feel comfortable in this assessment environment. As much attention as possible should be paid to creating a relaxed and supportive atmosphere. Refreshments such as coffee or soft drinks often serve to relieve anxiety. Using a room that is bright and cheerful can ease the tension for many families. Reviewing the assessment purpose and reminding participants that this is an opportunity for the child to play and "strut his stuff" takes the emphasis off the concept of right or wrong responses and focuses attention instead on the competencies and abilities of the child. During the assessment, the child should be given the opportunity to interact with peers, siblings, and family members in order to obtain insights into the child's social, communicative, and adaptive skills. Scheduling a short snack not only reenergizes the infant or toddler for further play, but also provides a view of mealtime routines and interactions. Throughout the assessment period, observers should focus on what skills the child performs and how the child demonstrates those skills (i.e., what sustained the child's interest, preference, motivation, learning style, and perseverance). Table 5.4 lists areas that can be observed during the assessment. The play-based assessment should continue until the child, family, or team indicates a need for termination.

After the play-based assessment is completed, the team members meet to discuss and integrate all of the child and family information gathered. Family members are an important part of this reflective process, as they are the professionals' guide to the validity of the results. During this team meeting, past information is reviewed and the data gathered from the play-based assessment are examined. It is at this stage that issues related to teaming become meaningful. All teams go through stages of development: forming, storming, norming, performing, and adjourning (Tuckman & Jensen, 1977). As play-based assessment teams form, they identify their membership and discuss their reason for participating on this team. Next comes the storming phase, where roles and responsibilities are negotiated. During this stage, conflict resolution and mediation strategies are critical as team members struggle to present opposing perspectives. It is important to remember that on most play-based assessment teams, each member has her own view of what is in the best interest of the particular child and family. In order for the team to reach consensus, individuals must negotiate, compromise, and collaborate with each other. The performing stage is characterized by the actions needed to complete the play-based assessment, the staffing, and the development of the IFSP. The goals and outcomes documented on the IFSP are generated at the team meeting and reflect the child and family data derived from the assessment. At the successful completion of these tasks, the team adjourns until the next infant or toddler with disabilities and his family is referred for assessment.

Categories of Play

Because play-based assessment uses play to evoke an infant's or toddler's skills and abilities across developmental domains, team members need an understanding of

TABLE 5.4 Observing an Individual Child

BODY MOVEMENTS AND USE OF BODY

Movements are usually quick or slow

Seems at ease with physical self

Small and large muscle skills and movements are about equally developed or one area is more developed than the other area

FACIAL EXPRESSIONS

Uses face to express feelings (e.g., smiles, frowns, neutral)

Reacts to experiences occurring around her/him

Shows intense feelings most of the time

Shows neutral or "deadpan" expression most of the time

SPEECH

Uses tone of voice to express feelings

Raises voice or yells when upset

Uses speech as primary communication method

Uses alternative communication (e.g., gestures, adaptive equipment)

Can imitate songs, chants, verbal expressions

Uses fluent, articulate (easy-to-understand) speech

EMOTIONAL REACTIONS

Method of exhibiting emotional reactions (e.g., smiles when happy, cries when angry)

Good balance in controlling feelings

Responds appropriately to adults/to other children

PLAY ACTIVITIES

Frequent and favorite activities

Play initiation skills, and patterns of play (e.g., how play progresses and next event)

Persistence during activities or flits from one activity to another

Avoidance of certain activities (e.g., sensory materials like clay or glue)

Evidence of mastery pleasure in completing an activity

Evidence of frustration with activities

Tempo or pace of play remains even or too slow or fast. Under what circumstances?

Plays alone. Under what circumstances?

Engages in pretend play (indicate with self or partner)

Engages in dramatic play (list roles)

Tries new things

Shows curiosity about the environment, including materials, equipment, and people

Prefers to play in certain areas (list areas or indoor *vs.* outdoor)

Special skills in one area (e.g., music, art, etc.)

BASIC NEEDS

Typical response to food

Natural bowel and bladder control

Appropriate sexuality

Seems well rested most of the time

Adapted from *A Guide to Observing and Recording Behavior* by W. Bentzen, 1993, Albany, N.Y.: Delmar.

the categories associated with play. There are several hierarchical models of play behavior; perhaps the most familiar in early childhood is Parten's (1932) categories of social play (see Table 4.3). The first level in this taxonomy is unoccupied behavior. On this level the child shows no sustained attention to any material or person. The second level is solitary play, when a child plays by herself with materials unlike those used by other children in the play area. At the onlooker level, the child observes other children at play and will even converse with them without actually engaging in the play routine. In the fourth stage, parallel play, the child plays next to other children, using materials and toys that may be similar. Associative play occurs when the child exchanges materials with other children, discusses the ongoing actions of the play, and invites others to the play situation, yet remains independent in choice and action. The final stage of Parten's social play is cooperative play. At this level, children are organizing, directing, assigning roles, dividing labor, and working together for some purpose.

Belsky and Most (1981) have identified categories of play activities that focus on how the infant or toddler uses objects. Their first category is mouthing, which is categorized by the haphazard mouthing of objects. Simple manipulation occurs when the infant or toddler intentionally moves or turns objects or materials. In the next stage, functional, the manipulation becomes appropriate to the object or material. When an infant or toddler demonstrates a relational play activity, he brings two unrelated objects together in an action; and when the infant or toddler combines objects or materials in an appropriate fashion, the activity becomes functional-relational. Enactive naming is a behavior that approaches pretend use of objects or materials. For example, a child may bring a telephone receiver or flip-phone up to her shoulder but does not bring it to her ear and say, "Hello." On the next level, the toddler engages in pretend play. Pretend self-play is characterized by behavior directed toward the self, such as picking up a spoon and eating pretend food. Pretend external play is characterized by behavior directed toward another, such as feeding a doll or offering to feed an adult. Substitution happens when the child creatively uses an object or material to give it new meaning. For example, the child may substitute a stick for a baby bottle or a sponge for a blanket.

Next in the hierarchical progression are play behaviors related to sequence. The first, sequence pretend, is displayed when the child links different pretend schemes together, and the second, sequence pretend substitution, occurs when the child makes a substitution in one of the pretense schemes he is linking. An example of sequence pretend is when the child pours pretend milk in a cup and then takes a drink; an example of sequence pretend substitution is when the child places a baby doll in a bed and covers it with a sponge that serves as the blanket. In the final level of play behavior, double transformation, the child uses two substitute materials in a single act. An example is when the child substitutes a stick for a baby doll, places the stick in a bed, covers it with a sponge, and says, "Night-night."

Blasco and LaMontagne (1996) have summarized play behaviors with associated activities and ages to provide an easier framework for using play as the medium for assessment (see Chapter 4). When assessing a young child with a disability through a play-based approach, the play facilitator must have an understanding of what to expect from the child during play interactions and what types of play activities will entice the child into interactions with their environment (e.g., materials, objects, and people). If the play assessment team is observing a 24-month-old infant with suspected developmental delays, then planned activities will include sensorimotor and exploratory activities. In addition, the play facilitator will need to have a few activities that represent more integrated exploration (the next level) in order to challenge the toddler's upward movement to more complex play behaviors. If the assessment is for a 24-month-old infant whose past evaluations indicate a 12-month-old developmental level, then planned activities will focus on sensorimotor/perceptual and/or beginning sensorimotor/exploratory play.

Advantages of Play-Based Assessment

Many of the advantages of play-based assessment are related to the particular characteristics of infants and toddlers. A play-based approach is less intrusive to the child and provides an interactive and engaging format that capitalizes on an infant's or toddler's natural curiosity, exploration, and interests. Play-based assessment has an inherent flexibility and responsiveness that match the child's activity level, temperament, and states of arousal. With this approach, all children, regardless of disability level or age can be assessed. Team members observe the child's interactions and gain insight into his skills and abilities, while family members are available to comment and expand on their child's performance of developmental behaviors. Play-based assessment reduces redundancy, as the play facilitator elicits child behaviors for every team member to observe. Because such assessment focuses on the child's demonstration of abilities, stress is reduced for the child and the family, since there is no right or wrong answer in play. Through observations, team members record the assessment events, and triangulation of data collection is achieved when three or more observers document the same child behavior. This validation of observations strengthens the integrity of the play-based assessment results. The transdisciplinary foundation of play-based assessment brings a richness to the process not found in standardized assessments. The sharing of information before, during, and after the play-based assessment integrates information in an extensive and holistic manner and creates a base of knowledge from which to generate a meaningful and realistic individualized family service program.

Disadvantages of Play-Based Assessment

Although it is an innovative approach to assessing infants and toddlers with disabilities, play-based assessment has certain limitations. As discussed, team-building and consensus can make or break the process. The degree to which individual team members perceive this approach as a valid and reliable method for assessing this population and are committed to the process has a direct impact on the success of the team. The use of specialized jargon that is specific to a discipline can contribute to communication barriers and confusion. Arranging the schedules of various professionals and family members so they can all be in the same place at the same time can be a monumental task. Time commitment is another potential limitation, especially for beginning teams. A play-based assessment can take from one to two hours to complete, depending on the child's age and level of disability, and the presenting concerns of the family. Furthermore, the objectivity of observational data is often questioned, since biased interpretations of play-based assessment events can be recorded as factual. Recognizing the limitations of this observational approach provides early interventionists with a clear view of the potential barriers that may interfere w implementation.

ASSESSING FAMILY ISSUES AND CONCERNS

Sharing Sensitive Information—Saving the Messenger

Most service providers can tell horror stories about their attempts to deliver a diagnosis to parents. In the traditional medical model, the idea was to spill the beans and run out the door. Medical education programs that concentrated on disease but provided little or no training in community resources, human service agencies, or home visiting (Sharp & Lohr, 1994) reinforced this approach. Although medical education is changing with the incorporation of training in community-based and home-visiting programs (Blasco, Kohen, & Shapland, 1999), the push for shorter hospital stays and denial of insurance coverage for certain medical visits make it difficult to practice family-centered care. Families of children with disabilities may find that the first contacts who have time to listen to them are the early intervention team members.

In terms of recommended practice, there is an emphasis on delivering news that is accurate yet respectful of families (Kroth, Olson, & Kroth, 1986). Blasco, O'Leary, Engstrom, Calvin, and Ferski (1996) presented a simple formula for giving news to families—be brief, be gentle, be quiet, and be there. Families often need time to assimilate a child's diagnosis. They may need time to be alone and think things through as a family. However, it is important that service providers be available to answer questions. It is also a good idea to let families know where they can reach you if they have any questions once they return home.

Allowing families to determine their involvement in the assessment process has been advocated as best practice in early intervention (Kjerland & Kovach, 1990; McGonigel, Kaufmann, & Johnson, 1991; McLean & Crais, 1996; Winton & Bailey, 1997). A true family-centered approach to services includes respect for individual decisions. Some families may want to take a very active role in the assessment, while others may be more passive and look to other team members for decision-making. Some families may be less involved in the initial stages and more involved in the implementation and evaluation of services.

It is equally important to realize that family involvement will change over time. Service providers who encounter a family taking a less active role in their early interactions are often surprised when that family wants to be more involved once other resources are in place and needs have been met. Likewise, some families may at times need a break from decision-making or advocacy and rely on professionals to take the lead. If we are to be truly family-guided, then we need to respect family decisions in terms of their involvement. Table 5.5 lists tips for family-guided assessment suggested by the National Center for Clinical Infant Programs.

TABLE 5.5 Tips For Family-Guided Assessment

- Young children should not be separated from their parents during an assessment procedure, if possible. The child may respond to separation by becoming more anxious and cannot give an optimal performance under these conditions.
- Standardized tests should not be the only measurement used with young children. Most standardized tests are designed for children with typical development and will not reflect the abilities and needs of a child with disabilities.
- Other assessment procedures should include parental report and observation of the child and the parent-child relationship.
- Parents should bring an advocate to the child's IFSP meeting. It helps to have the support of a friend or someone who knows the child as well as the parent to offer collaboration and support.
- Parents have a right to disagree, make changes, or ask for clarification in terms of their child's outcomes.

Adapted from S. J. Meisels and E. Fenichel, (Eds.), 1996, *New Visions for the Developmental Assessment of Infants and Young Children*, Arlington, Va.: Zero to Three/National Center for Infant Programs.

Assessing Family Concerns

The IFSP is a document that includes an assessment or inventory of family aspirations for and concerns about their child (Bailey, 1996). Part C of IDEA strengthened the family's role in the assessment process. Families should decide if they think an assessment of their own resources, priorities, and concerns is necessary in order to improve services to the child. Any formal or informal method for gathering information from family members should include the families' own description of these areas. Families will vary in the way they wish to share this information. Some families will prefer checklists or survey options to more informal personal interviews (Bailey & Blasco, 1990).

In order to effectively include family feedback into the process, the service provider should be proficient in both verbal and nonverbal listening skills. Good listening skills include the following:

- Using clarification to restate the content of what a person says in a brief and concise manner
- Using effective questions, both open-ended and closed-ended, as needed
- Reflecting on the feelings expressed by the speaker and demonstrating appropriate empathy and understanding (Winton, 1988; Winton & Bailey, 1993). In addition, nonverbal skills, such as sitting close to the speaker, leaning forward, nodding one's head, and establishing eye contact when appropriate help to keep the conversation going (Winton, 1988; Winton & Bailey, 1993).

In Vignette 5.2, one parent experiences an initial interview with a examiner new to the team. A school psychologist, whose previous work had been with school-age children, the examiner was not used to having parents present during an assessment and was not yet comfortable with this approach.

VIGNETTE 5.2 HE MIGHT AS WELL BE STEVEN

Michael and Ann had brought Shawn, 13 months, in for assessment after a recommendation from the pediatrician, who was concerned that Shawn was showing global developmental delays; he had already ruled out vision or hearing problems. Ann and Michael's first child, Shawn had been born two months prematurely. Both were very anxious about the outcome of the assessment. When the assessment was completed, the examiner said she would score it later and discuss it with them. She asked them to complete an initial interview form for the early intervention program. She said, "Tell me about [she paused to check the name on the folder] Shawn." As she spoke, she continued to write in a folder. Michael and Ann were surprised. They weren't sure what to say. After a brief time, the examiner looked up and said, "What does he like to do, you know . . . play with?" Ann began to talk about his favorite toys, when the telephone rang. The examiner picked up the phone and began talking to someone. She kept looking at her watch and alternatively back at Ann, expecting her to continue. Ann and Michael heard her tell someone that she would be late for the next appointment and to hold the family there until she arrived. The examiner put down the phone and said, "Okay, what are your concerns about Steven?" Both Ann and Michael corrected her at the same time: "His name is Shawn." The examiner offered a brief apology and makes a comment referring to her workload of cases. Ann and Michael took turns talking about the issues raised by the pediatrician and observed by them at home. The examiner seemed to be writing what the parents were reporting, but she was also looking through another file on the desk as if she had misplaced something. When Ann and Michael finished, there was silence as she continued to write in her file. Then she suddenly looked up and said, "Good," and closed the file. She stood up and said, "Someone will be getting back to you soon. It was nice meeting you and Shawn."

In the above vignette, the examiner gave the impression that she was too busy to give her full attention to this family. She was more concerned with completing her paperwork and getting to her next appointment. Although this example paints a dramatic picture that we hope has not occurred in reality, it is intended to underscore the importance of practicing good verbal and nonverbal listening skills with families. It is very easy for overburdened service providers to slip into a pattern of nonlistening when they are in a hurry and overwhelmed. As one psychologist said, "I know all of this sounds like it should come naturally, but it doesn't.

It's just not as easy as it sounds" (Frank Kaufman, School Psychologist, Baltimore City Schools, February 13, 1997).

PARENT-CHILD INTERACTION

Another assessment domain that is included with the birth to three population in particular is parent-child interaction. Many of the well-known measures of this dimension were developed in the late 1970s to mid-1980s, and consisted of either binary checklists or rating scales. The Nursing Child Assessment Feeding Scale (NCAFS) (Barnard, 1978a) examined interaction during feeding, including sensitivity to cues, response to distress and social-emotional and cognitive development, using a binary checklist (yes or no). The Nursing Child Assessment Teaching Scale (NCATS) (Barnard, 1978b) examined these areas when the parent was asked to teach the child. Hauser-Cram (1996) used the NCATS with mothers of toddlers who had developmental disabilities. She found that toddlers whose caregivers gave clear directions and both verbal and nonverbal support and praise while teaching tasks demonstrated more mastery motivation than toddlers whose caregivers did not show these behaviors.

The Parent-Caregiver Involvement Rating Scale (PCIS) (Farran, Kasari, Comfort, & Jay, 1986) examined not only the amount of interaction but also qualitative aspects of the interaction and the appropriateness of the parent/caregiver's behavior along 11 dimensions: physical involvement, verbal involvement, responsiveness of caregiver to child, play interaction, teaching behavior, control activities, directives and demands, relationship among activities, positive statements, negative statements, and goal setting. Professionals trained in the use of the instrument rated these behaviors. In one study, Blasco, Hrncir, and Blasco (1990) used the PCIS with 30 mothers of 18-month-old infants who were diagnosed with cerebral palsy. They found that the mothers scaffolded their children's play behavior by providing appropriate and nonintrusive cues.

In the past, parents (and particularly mothers) of infants and toddlers were consistently rated by researchers to be lacking in their interactions with their children. This research has been challenged by current work that focuses on qualitative aspects of parent-child interaction and evaluation of that interaction when parents/caregivers participate in the evaluation. (see Haas, Baird, McCormick, & Reilly, 1994).

Parent-child interactions may be difficult due to a variety of reasons, including a mismatch in temperaments or the lack of family resources and support. When families are not included as partners in the evaluation process, it is all too common for professionals to make judgments about them that may be inaccurate or misguided. The play-based assessment process allows both professionals and families to observe and evaluate parent-child interaction without the subjectivity of a rating scale or behavioral checklist.

ASSESSMENT WITH SPECIFIC POPULATIONS OF INFANTS AND TODDLERS

Preterm Infants

During the past two decades, medical technology has led to an increase in the number of infants surviving premature birth at earlier and earlier gestational ages. More than 50 percent of infants born prematurely are likely to be referred for early intervention services. For example, Collin et al. (1991) found that 40 to 64 percent of the infants born prematurely qualified for special education. In the past, assessment instruments provided no guidelines for assessing premature infants, because they were developed using a population of full-term infants. When preterm infants are developmentally compared using assessments normed on full-term populations, the results are biased.

Today, several standardized assessments include guidelines for correcting or adjusting age due to premature birth (Bayley II). However, the rationale for these guidelines has not been standardized across instruments. In addition, the length of time to continue age correction has not been clearly defined (Blasco, 1989). There are no state or federal guidelines indicating the best or most accurate procedure. These inconsistencies serve to frustrate families and practitioners as the struggle to provide appropriate services to this population of infants continues.

Allen and Alexander (1990) examined gross motor development in premature infants and believed that full age correction would lead to overdiagnosis of motor delays. Allen (1994) recommended adjusting for prematurity until at least two years of age. In a review of the literature, Blasco (1989) concluded that either full correction or no correction could lead to incorrect diagnosis. He recommended half-correction for the first 6 months of life. After 6 months, partial correction should be made for language skills and visual motor skills. For children with motor delays, full correction should be used after 6 months. However, correction was not necessary after 18–24 months (depending on the degree of prematurity).

Several researchers recommended reporting separate scores for motor development and cognitive/mental development. When these scores are combined into an overall score, motor problems would lower the result (Tvete, 1995). However, many standardized mental assessments for infants are heavily dependent on motor ability. For example, although the Bayley Scales offer a separate motor and mental form, motor skills are used to demonstrate most of the cognitive items on the mental form. Blasco (1989) found that upper dexterity was required to complete 45 percent of the items on the mental form. For infants older than 12 months, several items are scored according to the amount of time needed to complete the task, which would be affected by motor ability.

Infants and Toddlers with Visual Impairments

Infants use their vision to seek out their environment. The newborn's visual system involves the eye, optic nerve, optic radiation, and cerebral cortex. During the first year of life, the focusing power of the cornea and lens becomes very precise and the number of connections between the optic nerves and visual cortex increases significantly. Young children reach levels of 20/20 (adult level) between 3 and 5 years of age (Menacker & Batshaw, 1997).

Most newborns will close their eyes in response to a bright light and will fix their gaze on a person's face when held close to the adult. By two months of age, their ability to focus their attention on a person's face is well developed, and they will follow objects across a vertical and horizontal plane. Between three and six months, infants' unsteady eye movements become smooth.

Infants who have difficulty fixating on an object or who continue to have unsteady eye movements should be referred for further evaluation. In most states, a child must have a medically verified visual impairment that interferes with acquisition of knowledge or interaction with the environment to be eligible for services. A licensed teacher of the visually impaired usually conducts a functional assessment of visual abilities. Children who are legally blind (20/200 or less) will likely have some functional vision. For example, children with less than 20/400 vision may recognize hand movement and light projection (Hoon, 1996).

Infants who display behavioral or physical characteristics that may indicate a visual concern should also be referred for further evaluation. Although these characteristics may be unrelated to the visual impairment, they should serve as a red flag for the early interventionist. Consultation with a vision specialist would be appropriate for any of the following:

- Eyes are crossed or misaligned
- Encrusted lids, red and watery eyes
- Swollen or dropped eyelids
- Frequent styes
- Eyes that move independently of each other

The interventionist should refer the infant for vision evaluation if any of the following behaviors are observed:

- Shows sensitivity to light
- Squints at near and/or distant objects
- Blinks frequently when fixating on an object
- Turns or tilts the head
- Rubs the eyes excessively
- Is unable to locate and pick up small objects that have been dropped
- Stares at light for long periods

Adapted from a checklist used by Intermediate District 287, Minneapolis Public Schools

Infants and toddlers with visual impairments generally receive services from vision experts after initial diagnosis, typically during the first year of life.

Nearsightedness, or *myopia,* occurs when the refractive power of the cornea and lens is too strong, so the individual can see well "near" but has blurred distance vision. Farsightedness, or *hyperopia,* occurs when the refractive power is too weak and the image is focused behind the retina, so near vision is the problem and distance vision is good. *Astigmatism* is the irregularity in the shape of the cornea or lens and not all of the image is sharply focused on the retina (Nickel & Widerstrom, 1997). *Strabismus* is a result of an imbalance of the eye muscles causing one eye or both eyes to turn out. It is often a secondary diagnosis for children with disabilities (Menacker & Batshaw, 1997). *Esotropia* occurs when the eye turns in, and *exotropia* occurs when the eye turns out.

Retinopathy of prematurity (ROP) occurs when there is scarring and detachment of the retina. This condition was a result of too much oxygen being administered to premature newborns. Today, hospitals monitor the use of oxygen closely to avoid ROP (Nickel & Widerstrom, 1997). *Glaucoma* is typically the result of genetic disorder or congenital infection (Menacker & Batshaw, 1997). Fluid builds up in the eye and causes pressure on the retina and damage to the nerve fibers. *Cortical blindness* occurs when there is damage to the visual cortex. This type of blindness is associated with other primary diagnoses such as cerebral palsy (Nickel & Widerstrom, 1997).

Infants and toddlers with visual impairments may be delayed in other areas as well. However, interventions for infants and toddlers have demonstrated a positive impact on increasing developmental skills despite vision impairment.

In order to optimize learning, it is very important that a thorough assessment of visual ability is conducted when the team suspects a problem. Parents and professionals work collaboratively throughout the assessment process to ensure functional outcomes for the young child with visual impairments. Parents will need assistance in learning about the multiple types of evaluations and in interpreting results from ophthalmologists and optometrists (Chen, 1997).

Behavioral Assessment of Infants and Toddlers

Today, more and more children are being referred for services because of behavioral concerns. This trend is not limited to older children. The increase may reflect two societal changes:

1. A better understanding of and more sophisticated instruments to test for behavioral differences
2. An estimated 3.3 million children per year who are exposed to and witness to domestic violence, ranging from verbal abuse to physical assaults with guns (Jaffe, Wolfe, & Wilson, 1990)

Given the age of the child, it is often difficult to tell if the behavior is the sign of a problem or if it is merely a developmental stage. Evaluations for infants and toddlers should include ruling out physical health problems as the cause. As a rule of thumb, there is reason for concern if:

- After four months of age, the infant does not smile or show signs of pleasure when approached or cuddled
- The infant is inconsolable for long periods of time, but this is not related to colic or other physical distress

- After one year of age, the infant does not appear to differentiate between strange and familiar persons
- The infant or toddler has difficulty acquiring typical developmental milestones
- The toddler exhibits self-stimulation behaviors such as hand waving, rocking, or head banging
- The toddler appears sad and shows no appropriate signs of pleasure, fear, anger, or happiness
- The toddler frequently engages in inappropriate behaviors, including hitting or biting, and shows an inability to follow directions or participate in listening activities, even for a brief period (Minnesota Department of Human Services, 1995)

It is important to realize that all infants and toddlers may exhibit the above signs from time to time. It is the frequency and duration of such behavior should be monitored. Another consideration is the environments in which the child spends most of his time. If the child is the victim of or witness to violence or domestic abuse, he may show symptoms of posttraumatic stress syndrome (PTSD) (Scheeringa et al., cited in Gaensbauer, 1996).

For many of the children referred, the concern is that autism or persuasive developmental delay (PDD) may be present. Service providers use a combination of standardized assessments and clinical judgement that follow criteria guidelines outlined by the state in accordance with federal guidelines. In addition, the National Center for Clinical Infant Programs, Zero to Three, has developed a guide for identifying infants and young children who may be presenting mental health concerns (Diagnostic Classification of Mental Health and Developmental Disorders of Infancy and Early Childhood, 1994).

Although children with autism spectrum are often diagnosed by a medical team, following a complete medical and neurological exam, service providers may need to provide functional assessments that facilitate educational placement and individualized programs (Falco, Arick, & Hanzen, 1991). The Autism Screening Instrument for Educational Placement (Krug, Arick, & Almond, 1993) was developed to assist service providers in the identification of children with autism and to develop functional, appropriate learning opportunities. The tool consists of five separate standardized subtests: The Autism Behavior Checklist, The Sample of Vocal Behavior, Interaction Assessment, Educational Assessment, and Prognosis of Learning Rate. These subtests were developed for children between the ages of three months to 49 months (Krug, Arick, & Almond, 1993). The authors provide information on the standardization process for each subtest in the manual. The Child Behavior Checklist & Profile (Auchenbach, 1992) is a three-point rating scale that examines 99 behaviors that can be identified as problematic in two- to three-year-olds. Normed on a sample of 368 typically developing children, this checklist has been used both as a tool to help qualify a child for services and as part of the ongoing evaluation. As with any behavioral assessment, it is important to involve all members of the team, including mental health professionals who are trained to clinically recognize emotional disturbance, when using the checklist. In addition, a checklist adds one source of information, and information gathered from a variety of sources should supplement the findings obtained from any one instrument (Wittmer, Doll, & Strain, 1996). Finally, many behavioral checklists were developed and standardized on children from white, middle-class backgrounds. Some of the items are not appropriate in terms of cultural differences or diversity (e.g., sexual orientation).

Children Exposed to Violence

Infants and young children with disabilities are often the target of physical violence (Zirpoli, 1997). They may also be in homes where poverty and crime impair the abilities of their caregivers. Infants and toddlers who are exposed to or experience personal violence may experience long-term psychological distress (Zeanah & Scheeringa, 1996). Service providers of young children are increasingly baffled by the number of children who are being removed from one child care center to another and referred for special education services due to their aggression or out-of-control behavior as toddlers. One service provider claimed she had a child who was moved from three child care centers in six months because the staff couldn't handle her.

Recent awareness of the influence of domestic violence on young children has led to a new approach to evaluation and subsequent treatment of aggressive, disruptive behavior in infants and toddlers. According to Zeanah and Scheeringa (1996), it is important to assess the antecedent events (both in a child care setting and at home) that preceded the aggressive behavior. For children who have a history of chronic domestic violence, the diagnosis of posttraumatic stress disorder (PTSD) should be considered. Although it takes a qualified team member to make this diagnosis, all members of the team can help in identifying this disorder by the observation and recording of consistent behavioral concerns.

Young children who are affected by traumatic stress disorder may show a numbing of responsiveness. They may lose recently acquired skills, especially in areas such as expressive language and toileting. Children may also show signs of avoidance of adults who remind them of an abuser. They may exhibit increased irritability and temper tantrums that were not observed prior to the experience. Since many children at this age exhibit temper tantrums now and then, it is important that service providers not make assumptions based solely on their observations. Many families experience temporary difficulties, and young children may show signs of distress at such times. Service providers can offer support and assistance to families. Sometimes just listening and acknowledging the difficulties of family life in our society may serve the purpose. However, if there are persistent, ongoing family issues that are unresolved, and if the child exhibits persistently difficult behavior or seems chronically depressed, a complete evaluation of the child and the family situation by qualified professionals should be pursued.

According to Zeanah (1994), the following issues should be addressed in the evaluation of young children who have experienced traumatic events:

1. Ensure that the child is currently living in a safe and stable environment. If the child is not removed from the traumatic situation, intervention and treatment will be more difficult.
2. Consider the developmental skills of the child prior to and after the traumatic event. Knowledge of the child's previous developmental level will help the team understand her perceptions of the event.
3. Review the quality of the pretrauma caregiving environment and the impact of the event on the environment.
4. Examine the nature of the event. Was it acute or chronic in terms of ongoing events? For example, if a caregiver is the victim of ongoing domestic abuse, the situation would be considered chronic.
5. Find out the child's proximity to the event, particularly if a caregiver was involved. An example is a child's presence during a police raid for illicit drugs.
6. Construct a picture of the child's symptoms that appeared after the event.
7. Utilize the strengths and protective factors, especially in terms of relationships, that may help a child deal with a traumatic experience. For example, a grandmother may provide nurturing support.

It is also important to explore how the caregiver responds to violent events (Lewis, 1996). He may think the child is too young to remember what happened. According to Osofsky, Wewers, Hann, and Fick (cited in Lewis, 1996), another concern is the level of intensity of the violence experienced by the child. The child could be either a victim (e.g., sexually abused) or a witness to a violent scene (e.g., gunfire and a corpse in the street).

Finally, a multisystems approach is critical in working with children exposed to violence (Groves, 1996). Because crisis intervention is often necessary, police, the courts, the local crisis nursery, and temporary foster placement may be involved to handle the immediate needs of the situation. Service providers may find themselves working with a whole new team in trying to continue to provide support and services.

SUMMARY

This chapter addressed issues of the screening and assessment of infants and toddlers and their families. Service providers are required by law to document the assessment of children referred for services. The federal government, under the reauthorization of IDEA, enacted Part C legislation, which included a general definition for eligibility of infants and toddlers. Part C regulations also require the evaluation and assessment of the child, along with documentation of family resources, priorities, and concerns, in developing the individualized family service plan.

Child-find is a state-regulated system of locating children who are eligible for or may be eligible for early intervention services (McLean, 1996). Many local early intervention services have a central telephone number that accepts referrals and assigns a service provider to do the initial screening, which is a brief and inexpensive method of identifying children who may need further and more extensive evaluation.

The development of tests for young children is guided by three overlapping theoretical approaches to assessment. The first is the developmental milestones approach, generally followed by standardized tests, which include specific guidelines for administration, scoring, and interpretation of the results. Another approach is the behavioral approach, which assesses the behavioral responses of the child in relation to the environment. The third type of approach to assessment is the ecological approach, which examines the child's abilities and needs in terms of the multiple environments in which the child interacts on a daily basis.

Acknowledging the limitations of using standardized assessment instruments with infants and toddlers has led to the development of alternative means of identifying levels of functioning in this population. In play-based assessment, a single individual interacts with the infant or toddler, while professionals and family members observe the child's performance of skills (Linder, 1993). Such an approach is less intrusive to the child and provides an interactive and engaging format that capitalizes on an infant's or toddler's natural curiosity, exploration, and interests. Play-based assessment also has an inherent flexibility and responsiveness that match the child's activity level, temperament, and states of arousal. The degree to which individual team members perceive this approach as a valid and reliable method for assessing this population, and their commitment to the process, have a direct impact on the success of the play-based assessment team.

Another assessment process that is used with the birth-to-three population in particular is parent-child interaction. In the past, parents (and particularly mothers) of infants and toddlers were consistently rated by researchers to be lacking in their interactions with their children. This research has been challenged by current work that focuses on qualitative aspects of parent-child interaction and parent evaluation of these interactions.

For some, parent-child interactions may be difficult due to a variety of reasons, including a mismatch between their temperaments and lack of family resources and support. When families are not included as partners in the evaluation process, it is all too common for professionals to make judgments about families that may be inaccurate or misguided.

Other assessment procedures relate to special populations of children. Infants who are born preterm may have both medical and later developmental complications that should be addressed through early intervention. Similarly, children with challenging behavior and those children exposed to violence are presenting one of the growing categories of children at risk. Strategies for both prevention and intervention should be addressed from a mental health framework, as outlined in this chapter.

Assessment in early intervention is used for the purposes of eligibility, ongoing evaluation, and annual evaluation. As stated by Bagnato et al., 1997, "most conventional, norm-referenced, standardized materials developed through psychometric procedures do not meet standards for acceptable assessment in early intervention" (p. 3). Many service providers and families rely on curriculum-based and other informal means (e.g., play, parent report) as ways to assess young children. The use of curriculum-based assessments is important for establishing a link between the assessment and intervention. Bagnato and his colleagues provide an excellent guide to identification of assessments that provide this link for children birth to three (see Bagnato et al., 1997).

REFERENCES

Allen, M. C. (1994). Neurodevelopmental follow-up of the preterm infant. *Pediatric Rounds, 3,* 1–4.

Allen, M. C., & Alexander, G. R. (1990). Gross motor milestones in preterm infants: Correction for degree of prematurity. *Journal of Pediatrics, 116,* 955–999.

Auchenbach, T. M. (1992). *Manual for the Child Behavior Checklist/2–3 age and 1992 profile.* Burlington: University of Vermont.

Bagnato, S. J., & Neisworth, J. T. (1991). *Assessment for early intervention: Best practices for professionals.* New York: Guilford Press.

Bagnato, S. J., Neisworth, J. T., & Munson, S. M. (1993). Sensible strategies for assessment in early intervention. In D. M. Bryant & M. A. Graham (Eds.), *Implementing early intervention: From research to effective practice.* New York: Guilford Press.

Bagnato, S. J., Neisworth, J. T, & Munson, S. M. (1997). *LINKing assessment and early intervention: An authentic curriculum-based approach.* Baltimore: Paul H. Brookes.

Bailey, D. B. (1996). Assessing family resources, priorities, and concerns. In M. McLean, D. B. Bailey, & M. Wolery (Eds.), *Assessing infants and toddlers with special needs* (2nd ed., pp. 203–233). Englewood Cliffs, N.J.: Merrill/Prentice Hall.

Bailey, D. B., & Blasco, P. M. (1990). Parents' perspectives on a written survey of family needs. *Journal of Early Intervention, 14,* 196–203.

Bailey, D. B., & Nabors, L. A. (1996). Tests and development. In M. McLean, D. B. Bailey, & M. Wolery (Eds.), *Assessing infants and preschoolers with special needs* (2nd ed., pp. 23–45). Englewood Cliffs, N.J.: Merrill/Prentice Hall.

Bailey, D. B., Vandiviere, P., Delinger, J., & Munn, D. (1987). The Battelle Developmental Inventory: Teacher perceptions and implementation data. *Journal of Psychoeducational Assessment, 3,* 217–226.

Baird, S. M., Peterson, J., & Reilly, A. (1995). Patterns of specific infant behavior interpretation. *Infant-Toddler Intervention: The Transdisciplinary Journal, 5*(3), pp. 255–276.

Barnard, K. E. (1978a). *Nursing child assessment feeding scale.* Seattle: University of Washington.

Barnard, K. E. (1978b). *Nursing child assessment teaching scale.* Seattle: University of Washington.

Barrera, M. E., Rosenbaum, P. L., & Cunningham, C. E. (1987). Corrected and uncorrected Bayley scores: Longitudinal developmental patterns in low and high birth weight infants. *Infant and Behavior Development, 10,* 337–346.

Bayley, N. (1933). *The California first-year mental scale.* Berkeley: University of California Press.

Bayley, N. (1969). *Bayley Scales of Infant Development.* New York: Psychological Corporation.

Bayley, N. (1993). *Bayley Scales of Infant Development—II.* San Antonio, TX: Psychological Corporation.

Belsky, J., & Most, R. K. (1981). From exploration to play: A cross-sectional study of infant free-play behavior. *Developmental Psychology, 17,* 630–639.

Benner, S. M. (1992). *Assessing children with special needs: An ecological perspective.* New York: Longman.

Bernbaum, J. C., & Hoffman-Williamson, M. (1991). *Primary care of the preterm infant.* St. Louis: Mosby.

Blackman, J. A. (1986). *Warning signals: Basic criteria for tracking at-risk infants and young children.* Washington, D.C.: Zero to Three: National Center for Clinical Infant Programs.

Blasco, P. A. (1989). Preterm birth: To correct or not to correct. *Development Medicine and Child Neurology, 21,* 174–177.

Blasco, P. A., Kohen, H., & Shapland, C. (1999). Parents as teachers: Design and establishment of a training programme for paediatric residents. *Medical Education, 33,* 695–701.

Blasco, P. M. (1989). *Comparison of the Bayley Scales and a measure of mastery in infants with cerebral palsy.* Poster presented at the conference of the American Academy for Cerebral Palsy and Developmental Medicine, San Francisco.

Blasco, P. M., Hrncir, E. J., & Blasco, P. A. (1990). The contribution of maternal involvement to mastery motivation performance in infants with cerebral palsy. *Journal of Early Intervention, 14,* 161–174.

Blasco, P. M., & LaMontagne, M. J. (1996, September). *Play-based assessment.* Paper presented at the conference of the American Academy for Cerebral Palsy and Developmental Medicine, Minneapolis.

Blasco, P. M., O'Leary, J., Engstrom, B., Calvin, S., & Ferski, G. (1996, December). *Postconference workshop on prenatal diagnosis.* Presented at the Conference of the International Division for Early Childhood, Phoenix.

Brazelton, T. B., & Nugent, J. K. (1995). *Neonatal behavioral assessment scale* (3rd. ed.). London: MacKeith Press.

Bredekamp, S., & Rosegrant, T. (Eds.). (1995). *Reaching potentials: Transforming early childhood curriculum and assessment.* Washington, D.C.: National Association for the Education of Young Children.

Bricker, D. (1993). *AEPS: Measurement for birth to three years.* Baltimore: Paul H. Brookes.

Campbell, P. H. (1991). Evaluation and assessment in early intervention for infants and toddlers. *Journal of Early Intervention, 15*(1), 36–45.

Chen, D. (1997). What can baby see? Vision tests and interventions for infants with multiple disabilities [videotape and viewers' guide]. New York: AFB Press.

Collin, M. F., Halsey, C. L., & Anderson, C. L. (1991). Emerging developmental sequelae in the "normal" extremely low birth weight infant. *Pediatrics, 88,* 115–119.

Cripes, J., & Bricker, D. (1992). *AEPS: Curriculum for birth to three years.* Baltimore: Paul H. Brookes.

Diagnostic Classification of Mental Health and Developmental Disorders of Infancy and Early Childhood. (1999). Arlington, Va.: Zero to Three/National Center for Clinical Infant Programs.

Diamond, K. E., & Squires, J. (1993). The role of parental report in the screening and assessment of young children. *Journal of Early Intervention,* 17, 107–115.

Early Intervention Program for Infants and Toddlers with Disabilities, 34 C.F.R. 303 (1999, July 1).

Falco, R., Arick, J., & Hanzen, J. (1991). *Quality education services training: Project QUEST.* Portland, Ore.: Portland State University.

Farran, D., Kasari, C., Comfort, M., & Jay, S. (1986). *Parent/Caregiver Involvement Scale.* Nashville, Tenn.: Vanderbilt University.

Fewell, R. (1983). Assessing handicapped infants. In S. Garwood & R. Fewell (Eds.), *Educating handicapped infants.* Rockville, Md.: Aspen.

Frankenburg, W. K., Dodds, J., Archer, P., Bresnick, B., Marshka, P., Edelman, N., & Shapiro, H. (1990). *Denver II.* Denver: Denver Developmental Materials.

Furuno, S., O'Reilly, K., Hosaka, C. M., Inatsuka, T. T., Zeisloft-Falbey, B., & Allman, T. (1994). *Revised HELP checklist: Birth to three years.* Palo Alto, Calif.: Vort.

Gaensbauer, T. (1996). Developmental and therapeutic aspects of treating infants and toddlers who have witnessed violence. *Zero to Three, 16,* 15–20.

Gesell, A. (1925). *The mental growth of the preschool child: A psychological outline of normal development from birth to the sixth year, including a system of developmental diagnosis.* New York: MacMillan.

Groves, B. M. (1996). Children without refuge: Young witnesses to domestic violence. *Zero to Three, 16,* 29–34.

Haas, L., Baird, S. M., McCormick, K., & Reilly, A. (1994). Infant behaviors interpreted by their mothers. *Infant-Toddler Intervention: The Transdisciplinary Journal,* 203–220.

Hauser-Cram, P. (1996). Mastery motivation in toddlers with developmental disabilities. *Child Development, 67,* 236–248.

Hoon, A. H. (1996). Visual impairments in children. In A. J. Capute & P. J. Accardo (Eds.), *Developmental disabilities in infancy and childhood* (2nd ed., pp. 461–478). Baltimore: Paul H. Brookes.

Hrncir, E. J., Speller, G. M, & West, M. (1985). What are we testing? *Developmental Psychology, 21,* 226–232.

Jaffe, P. G., Wolfe, D. A., & Wilson, S. K. (1990). *Children of battered women.* Newbury Park, Calif.: Sage.

Johnson-Martin, N., Jens, K., Attermeier, S., & Hacker, B. (1991). *The Carolina curriculum for infants and toddlers with special needs* (2nd ed.). Baltimore: Paul H. Brookes.

Kjerland, L., & Kovach, J. (1990). Family-staff collaboration for tailored infant assessment. In E. Gibbs & D. Teti (Eds.), *Interdisciplinary assessment of infants: A guide for early intervention professionals* (pp. 287–298). Baltimore: Paul H. Brookes.

Kroth, R. L., Olson, J., & Kroth, J. (1986). Delivering sensitive information, or please don't kill the messenger. *Counseling and Human Development, 18,* 1–11.

Krug, D. A., Arick, J. R., Almond, P. J. (1993). ASIEP—2: *Autism screening instrument for educational planning* (2nd ed.). Austin, Tex.: Pro-ed.

Lewis, M. L. (1996). Trauma reverberates: Psychosocial evaluation of the caregiving environment of young children exposed to violence and traumatic loss. *Zero to Three, 16,* 21–28.

Lifter, K. (1996). Assessing play skills. In M. McLean, D. B. Bailey, & M. Wolery (Eds.), *Assessing infants and preschoolers with special needs* (2nd ed., pp. 435–461). Englewood Cliffs, N.J.: Merrill.

Linder, T. (1993). *Transdisciplinary play-based assessment: A functional approach to working with young children* (2nd ed.). Baltimore: Paul H. Brookes.

McGonigel, M. J., Kaufmann, R., & Johnson, B. (1991). *Guidelines and recommended practices for the individualized family service plan* (2nd ed.). Bethesda: Association for the Care of Children's Health.

McLean, M. (1996). Assessment and its importance in early intervention/early childhood special education. In M. McLean, D. B. Bailey, & M. Wolery (Eds), *Assessing infants and preschoolers with special needs* (2nd ed., pp. 1–22). Englewood Cliffs, N. J.: Merrill.

McLean, M., & Crais, E. R. (1996). Procedural considerations in assessing infants and preschoolers with disabilities. In M. McLean, D. B. Bailey, & M. Wolery (Eds.), *Assessing infants and preschoolers with special needs* (pp. 46–68). Englewood Cliffs, N.J.: Prentice-Hall.

Meisels, S. J., & Fenichel, E. (Eds.) (1996). *New visions for the developmental assessment of infants and young children.* Arlington, Va.: Zero to Three/National Center for Clinical Infant Programs.

Meisels, S. J., & Provence, S. (Eds.). (1996). Screening and assessment: Guidelines for identifying young disabled and developmentally vulnerable children and their families [Special issue]. *Zero to Three.*

Menacker, S. J., & Batshaw, M. L. (1997). Vision: Our window to the world. In M. L. Batshaw (Ed.), *Children with disabilities* (4th ed., pp. 211–239). Baltimore: Paul H. Brookes.

Minnesota Department of Human Services. *Children and youth at risk of emotional disturbance* (1995). St. Paul, Minn.: Mental Health Division.

Newborg, J., Stock, J. R., Wnek, L., Guidubaldi, J., & Svinicki, J. (1988). *The Battelle Developmental Inventory (BDI).* Dallas, Tex.: DLM Teaching Resources.

Nickel, R. E., & Widerstrom, A. H. (1997). Developmental disorders in infancy. In A. H. Widerstrom, B. A. Mowder, & S. R. Sandall (Eds.), *Infant development and risk* (2nd ed.). Baltimore: Paul H. Brookes.

Parks, S., et al. (1992). *Help at home: Activity sheets for parents.* Palo Alto, Calif.: Vort.

Parten, M. (1932). Social participation among preschool children. *Journal of Abnormal and Social Psychology, 27,* 243–269.

Peterson, N. (1988). *Early intervention for handicapped and at-risk children.* Denver: Love.

Reynell, J. (1985). Reynell Developmental Language Scales. Los Angeles, Calif.: Webster Psychological Services.

Scheeringa, M., Zeanah, C. H., Drell, M., & Larrieu, J. (1995). Two approaches to the diagnosis of post-traumatic stress disorder in infancy and early childhood. *Journal of the American Academy of Child and Adolescent Psychiatry, 34,* 191–200.

Sell, E. J., Figueredo, A. J., & Wilcox, T. G. (1995). Assessment of preterm infants' behavior (APIB): Confirmatory factor analysis of behavioral constructs. *Infant Behavior and Development, 18,* 447–457.

Sharp, M. C., & Lohr, J. A. (1994). The nature of teaching hospitals. In S. L. Hostler (Ed.), *Family-centered care: An approach to implementation* (pp. 72–88). Charlottesville: Children Rehabilitation Center, University of Virginia.

Siegel, D. J. (1999). *The developing mind: Toward a Neurobiology of interpersonal experience.* New York: Guilford Press.

Siegel, L. S., Cooper, D.C., Fitzhardinger, P. M., Ash, A. J. (1995). The use of the mental developmental index of the Bayley Scale to diagnose language delay in 2-year-old high-risk infants. *Infant Behavior and Development, 18,* 483–486.

Teti, D. M., & Gibbs, E. D. (1990). Infant assessment: Historical antecedents and contemporary issues. In E. D. Gibbs & D. M. Teti (Eds.), *Interdisciplinary assessment of infants: A guide for early intervention professionals* (pp. 3–13). Baltimore: Paul H. Brookes.

Tuckman, B. W., & Jensen, M. A. C. (1977). Stages of small group development revisited. *Group and Organization Studies, 2,* 419–427.

Tvete, J. M. (1995). *When and how long to adjust for prematurity? Assessment of premature infants for early childhood special education.* Unpublished manuscript. St. Paul, Minn.: University of St. Thomas.

United Cerebral Palsy Association. (1976). *Staff development handbook: A resource for the transdisciplinary process.* New York: Author.

Winton, P. J. (1988). The family-focused interview. A mechanism for collaborative goal-setting with families. *Journal of the Division for Early Childhood, 12,* 195–207.

Winton, P. J., & Bailey, D. B. (1993). Communicating with families: Examining practices and facilitating change. In J. Paul & R. J. Simeonsson (Eds.), *Children with special needs: Family, culture, and society* (pp. 210–230). Baltimore: Paul H. Brooks.

Winton, P. J., & Bailey, D. B. (1997, February). Family-centered care: The revolution continues. *Exceptional Parent,* 16–20.

Wittmer, D., Doll, B., & Strain, P. (1996). Social and emotional development in early childhood: The identification of competence and disabilities. *Journal of Early Intervention, 20,* 299–318.

Woodruff, G. (1980, June). Transdisciplinary approach for preschool children and parents. *Exceptional Parent,* 13–16.

Wright, A., & Ireton, H. (1995). Child development days: A new approach to screening for early intervention. *Journal of Early Intervention, 19,* 253–263.

Zeanah, C. H. (1994). The assessment and treatment of infants and toddlers exposed to violence. In J. D. Osofsky & E. Fenichel, (Eds.). *Caring for infants and toddlers in violent environments: Hurt, healing, and hope.* Arlington, Va.: Zero to Three: National Center for Clinical Infant Programs.

Zeanah, C. H., & Scheeringa, M. (1996). Evaluation of posttraumatic symptomatology in infants and young children exposed to violence. *Zero to Three, 16,* 9–14.

Zirpoli, S. (1997). Issues in early childhood behavior. In T. J. Zirpoli & K. J. Melloy (Eds.), *Behavior management: Applications for teachers and parents* (2nd ed., pp. 383–417). Upper Saddle River, N.J.: Merrill.

CHAPTER SIX

NATURAL ENVIRONMENTS FOR INFANTS AND TODDLERS AND PREPARING FOR TRANSITIONS

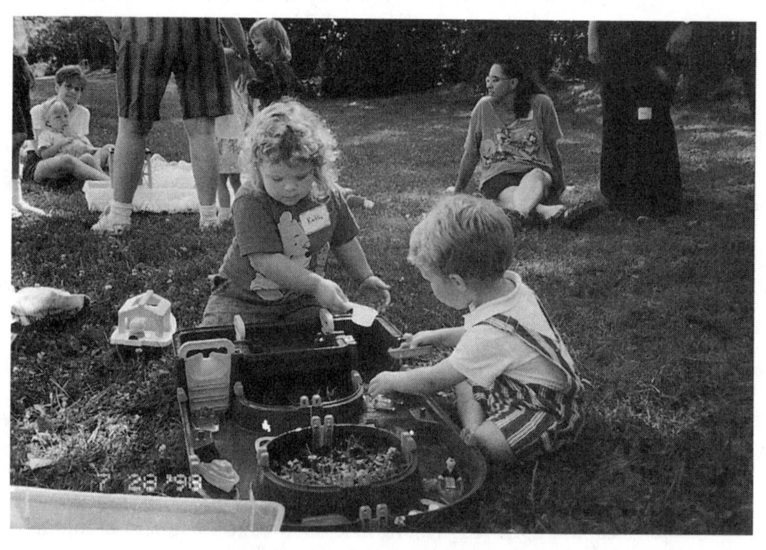

OBJECTIVES

- To understand the importance of service provision in a variety of natural environments for infants and toddlers
- To present a framework for a family-centered approach within these environments (e.g., home, center-based, community-based)
- To consider the interventionist's role in home visiting, especially with regard to ethical and cultural issues in working with families
- To apply knowledge of the use of outdoor space for all children to promote growth and learning
- To apply knowledge of the transition process from early intervention services to school-aged services, and to understand its effect on the child, family, and service providers

This chapter was written, in tandem with a graduate seminar, with Betsy May, Dolly Lastine, Debra Bomberg, Katherine Eldevik, and Stacy Rovick. The chapter contains more vignettes than the other chapters do, and these vignettes reflect the experiences of these service providers as they worked in early intervention.

Today, more than ever, service providers are working with infants, toddlers, and their families in many different environments. Historically, services for infants and toddlers were primarily provided in the family's home. Most often service providers worked with the mother or father (or both parents) and child for a set period of time every week. This model of service provision falls short in our present society, where 60 percent of all women with children under the age of six are in the workforce (Children's Defense Fund, 1999).

Given the increase in the number of households with both parents working, early intervention services are often provided outside the home in center-based programs such as child care or family home care settings. In addition, the increase of children identified as "at risk" (National Center on Child Abuse and Neglect, 1988) may require visits in other settings, including foster homes and shelters. One service provider reported that a family came to her office because they were living in their car. The purpose of this chapter is to discuss the many environments currently utilized by service providers in the field of early intervention. *Parent* will be used to refer to the primary caregiver, who may or may not be a biological parent. In addition, the impact of transition from early intervention services to school-aged services will be discussed.

In Chapter 1, we looked at the addition of the "natural environments" clause in Part C of the Individual with Disabilities Education Act (IDEA). That is, to the maximum extent appropriate, early intervention services must be provided in natural environments, including the home and community settings in which children without disabilities participate. This law expands systems of support for infants and toddlers and their families in natural environments. Research studies suggest that toddlers with disabilities who are served in inclusive settings do as well as those who are served in segregated settings (Bruder, 1998). Challenges in meeting the requirement of the law include finding quality child care settings and designing a statewide system of training for child care staff. Bruder (1998) also pointed out that time constraints, staff turnover, children with diverse needs, and a lack of fiscal resources in some states may affect the transition from segregated settings to inclusive settings. Chapter 9 discusses the importance of training service providers in collaboration skills as states move toward the use of natural environments.

SERVICES PROVIDED IN THE HOME SETTING

Home visiting programs function within a context shaped by both their underlying theory and their organization.

—Powell, 1993, p. 24

McWilliam and Bailey (1993) defined three philosophical tenets that are characteristic of home-based family-centered services: (1) recognizing differences among families; (2) using a family systems approach; and (3) respecting the family's priorities. Today, the very definition of the word *family* implies diversity. A family can range from a single parent and a child to extended multigenerational caregivers who are raising a child. Recognizing the diversity of family units is necessary for professionals working in the home environment (Lynch & Hanson, 1998). As discussed in Chapter 1, just as family function is related to individual uniqueness, there is no single way to raise a child. Values, roles, and priorities differ in each family. Strategies for service provision should meet the family's particular styles of functioning within the child's natural environments.

From a family systems approach, the interventionist must believe that every family has strengths. These strengths may not be easy to recognize from one's own perspective. The family's values may differ radically from the mainstream concepts of a strong family unit, and it may be easier to focus only on the family's needs and deficits. Their strengths may also be overshadowed by unemployment, lack of resources, lack of educational opportunities, or other societal factors. In a world of increasing cultural diversity, service providers should examine their own beliefs and values and how they might be inadvertently projecting them onto families.

When visiting in the home, autonomy of the family should also be respected. According to federal law, families have the right to determine their priorities and needs to the extent that they are willing and able. It is up to the service provider to help the family explore options, to advocate for the family, to mediate, and to consult with other professionals. The family should be able to decide what is important not only for their child but also for the whole family system. Some families may be ready and eager to accept services and make changes, while others may need more time to ponder options. Still others may not want services at all or may discontinue services for a variety of reasons. The service provider, therefore, must tailor the services to meet the family's concerns and resources (Kjerland & Corrigan Eide, 1990). Vignette 6.1 demonstrates a situation that requires flexibility on the part of the service provider.

VIGNETTE 6.1 IS ANYBODY HOME?

In my first home visit with an isolated rural family, I had been told that this family rarely left the home. They had four preschoolers whom a doctor had thought were nonverbal. So, although I had spoken with the mother very briefly on the phone to set up the visit, I was still surprised when she just opened the door a crack and didn't make eye contact with me as we spoke. I saw three little faces peering at me through an upstairs screen as I approached the house. There was complete silence as I stood vainly attempting to establish some kind of rapport with the mother. She didn't invite me in and when I asked if I could meet the children, she hesitated and said, "They're kind of shy. We've only had their grandparents come to our house before; Virgil [the father] goes to the store when we need something." I arranged to come back the next week and said I hoped I could meet the children. I left a list of a few activities for her do with the children as well as some toys that they could borrow until the next visit.

Although those first visits were extremely short, they were very intense for both the mother and myself because of the family's extreme social isolation. Over the course of the next several months, I was able to get the children to come into the same room with me and to very tentatively explore the toys. By the year's end, I had built a trusting relationship with the family. The two eldest preschoolers were happily enrolled in a preschool and their mother had started volunteering in their classroom.

In Vignette 6.1, the service provider was able to make a breakthrough with the family over an extended period of time. This type of experience may not be valued by an administrator who wants the child assessed and then enrolled in a center-based program for a variety of reasons. Service providers are often left to use their own initiative in handling a difficult situation. It is a good idea to get feedback from team members and to know the policies of the agency in which you are employed before making a decision.

Goals of Family-Centered, Home-Based Programs

In recent years the frequency of the question "Who is the client?" has reflected the shift from a child focus to a family focus and from an individual focus to a family systems focus (Wasik, Bryant, & Lyons, 1990; Roberts, Akers, & Behl, 1996; Roberts, Behl, Akers, & 1996). The purpose of family support is to enhance the ability of families to work toward their own goals and deal effectively with their own concerns. Advocates of self-determination believe that persons with disabilities and their family members should strive to attain the goals of independence and self-efficacy despite societal setbacks (Mike Ward, personal communication, October 2, 1999).

Because complex interactions exist among members of a family, a change in any family member will affect other relationships within the family (Blasco, 1995).

A family-centered focus means that the client may change as different needs emerge among family members. Programs centered on the broader base of parent, family, and environmental factors that directly or indirectly influence outcomes for the child are more likely to experience success. In Table 6.1, home visiting from a family's point of view was captured by staff at Project Dakota.

In a comprehensive review of the experimental literature on the effectiveness of various types of home visiting programs, Olds and Kitzman (1993) concluded that clarifying the purpose and goals of a particular program was an important requisite for successful outcomes. This sense of mission is exemplified by the broadening focus of existing programs.

Likewise, as Bronfenbrenner (1979) indicated, a shift toward looking at the family in the context of the larger web of extended family, neighborhood, and community is necessary. Because changes in the larger system may also affect the family, awareness of the full extent of the family's involvement and dependence upon the larger community is crucial. An effective program will enable families to recognize their strengths, to make decisions that benefit their family unit, and to provide an optimal environment for their children. Many interventionists find themselves wearing more than one hat, including that of the advocate who helps the family deal with the day-to-day stress received from a variety of sources.

Role of the Interventionist in the Home Environment

When PL 99-457 was passed in 1986, it held strong implications for interventionists already serving families in their homes. Service providers reexamined their

TABLE 6.1 A Family's View of a Good Home Visit

- Be clear about agenda and roles.
- Give choices in scheduling that are convenient and flexible.
- Provide a record of the visit using writing, pictures, or toys.
- Give ideas for activities, then help parents brainstorm.
- Be flexible with the family's daily schedule: pitch in, change agenda, and reschedule.
- Don't use jargon, and let the family know it's okay to ask questions.
- Use modeling and reminding; don't overload with information.
- Explain what you are doing and why.
- Include others, e.g., siblings, grandparents, etc., in activities and conversations.
- Explain paperwork and point out progress/changes that are made.
- Be sensitive to the family's need for someone to take over.
- Be courteous; call if you are going to be late, absent, etc.
- Respect the family's values; don't judge.
- Be prepared; don't waste the family's time and energy.
- Be honest with the family.

Adapted by permission from Project Dakota Outreach, Training and Consultation Services, Eagan, Minn.

traditional roles and the way in which they implemented services to promote mutual respect and a partnership with families. Dunst, Trivette, and Deal (1988) were clearly ahead of their time when they defined the multiple roles of service providers described in Table 6.2.

Establishing Rapport with Families. Opening lines of communication with parents and families is a necessary first step toward fulfillment of these roles. Building a trusting relationship with a family means showing mutual respect and a willingness to share ideas, feelings, and information. A way to begin this process is to drop one's preconceived ideas about the family and to begin with an optimistic focus. As Turnbull and Turnbull (1988) noted, "being open to new views allows one to expand their repertoire of skills and creativity." (p. 4)

Well-meaning colleagues may wish to advise us on what to expect from a family, but such comments only serve to ignite negative feelings. Instead, emphasizing the family's strengths rather than weaknesses can focus attention where it can best benefit both the family and the interventionist.

VIGNETTE 6.2 JOHN

John was a three-year-old boy in my early childhood special needs classroom who had physical and visual impairments. As I read his school records, I discovered that John had been a normally developing, healthy child until his young mother with limited resources had attempted to smother him. I felt enormous revulsion at this act. I knew that I was obligated to make home visits, but it was very difficult for me. I had to leave my own values on the doorstep and try to see John's mother as a person who desperately needed support.

TABLE 6.2 Primary Helping Roles

ROLE	CHARACTERISTICS
Empathetic listener	Listens active and reflectively
Teacher/therapist	Instructs and intervenes
Consultant	Offers information and opinions in response to family requests
Resource person	Provides information about support resources and services
Enabler	Helps family acquire competencies they need to mobilize resources to meet their needs
Mobilizer	Mobilizes resources and support services
Mediator	Acts as an intermediary between family and others
Advocate	Provides knowledge and skills for proactive advocacy

Adapted from *Enabling and Empowering Families: Principles and Guidelines for Practice* by C. J. Dunst, C. Trivette, & A. Deal, 1988, Cambridge, Mass.: Brookline Books, pp. 91–94.

A person who is hurting, either physically or emotionally, needs care and support. When working with families, it may be very obvious that the parent is the one most acutely in need of care, as Vignette 6.2 demonstrates. Relying on other team members and/or other agencies in the mental health field is important for home visitors. An interventionist must be responsive to the immediate needs of a family member. At the same time, it is important to provide an appropriate learning opportunity for the child. As Ramey and Ramey (1993) stated, "limiting the focus in home visiting programs to supporting the family first, without special efforts to target the child's early development as well, may be self defeating." (p. 133)

Gathering Information. Because the interventionist's role is dependent upon the input of the families, establishing expectations early in the relationship is paramount. This can be accomplished by an informal, preliminary discussion or through a formal checklist or assessment (Winton, 1988). Whatever method is used, the crucial ingredient is that the expectations should be two-way: what the interventionist can expect of the family and what the family can expect of the interventionist. Families should have an opportunity to select the method of sharing information (Bailey & Blasco, 1990). Some families prefer written surveys, whereas others prefer informal interviews.

Some interventionists like to use an open-ended questionnaire that can be filled in as each item is discussed and that includes very general categories. A benefit of this approach is that it not only serves as a vehicle for opening communication with the family, but it also will be a written communication that the parent can discuss with family members who may not be present for the home visit. For those families who have never had a service provider work in their home, the use of an open-ended interview can help to establish trust and ease the uncertainty about having an unfamiliar person visit. In Vignette 6.3, one parent recollects the first home visit she received.

VIGNETTE 6.3 COMPANY COMING

I spent hours cleaning my house before the home teacher came. I didn't know if she'd stay in the living room or want to see Nathan's room. I made coffee and cookies, but she said she'd just eaten. She said she'd come for an hour, but by the time she finished with all the paperwork it was closer to two hours, and I'd forgotten half of what she said. Nathan was fussy and ready for his nap, and my three-year-old had just interrupted us for the umpteenth time. I wasn't sure that home visits were going to be such a good idea.

For this mother, it was obvious that the interventionist had her own agenda and was not sensitive to the family's priorities. Winton (1988) suggested that service providers can reduce parental anxiety by reconfirming the allotted time for the visit before arriving. This interventionist could have asked the mother if she should continue or if she should reschedule the visit for another time.

Practical Aspects and Scheduling

Flexibility is a key factor in providing services to families on a least intrusive schedule for visits (Wasik, Bryant, & Lyons, 1990). The timing of the interventionist's visit needs to reflect the child's own schedule as well as the schedule of the family. If the child has a difficult time with feeding, the most efficient time for a visit would be during the child's naturally occurring feeding schedule. Modeling the activity for the parent and responding with feedback are more beneficial when the child is actually hungry. However, a home visit may hinder communication and optimal collaboration with the parent if, for example, it's scheduled during the parent's scheduled recreation activity, or when the parent is preparing dinner in the late afternoon. Finding the best time is not always easy and may necessitate compromise on the part of the service provider and the family. Service providers should yield to family preference when possible. Many early intervention programs allow for flexible working hours so that service providers can meet family timelines.

Another aspect to consider is the family's working schedule during the day. Families that work may prefer evening visits or, conversely, may be too exhausted for an interventionist to come to their home after they have been working all day. Creative scheduling may include a home visit in the morning, before the parent goes to work, or a visit in the child's child care setting with the parent present during his or her lunch hour or in the evening. Vignette 6.4 describes an evening visit to one family's home.

VIGNETTE 6.4 NIGHT VISITS

Jean was a single mother of four children ages two to seven. She was planning to return to work and was worried about having to forgo home visits for her two-year-old son, Ronald, who had developmental delays and nonorganic failure to thrive diagnosed at 15 months. Jean, a recovered addict who had been separated from her children for extended periods of time, found the visits not only beneficial for her son but organizing for herself as well. We discussed how visits may be hard after a long day for the children and herself. We chose shorter visits every other week with a phone call in between to discuss Ronald's child care and developmental concerns.

The frequency and length of home visits must reflect the needs of the child and family. It may be necessary to come once a week or bimonthly to exchange ideas and find out what is working with the child. In planning the visit, the interventionist must consider the family's circumstances, the energy level of the child, the focus of the parent, and unforeseen events that may happen in the home. In one situation, the parent spent the entire visit setting limits for her two-and-a-half-year-old. The one-hour visit was too stressful for him and his mother. The interventionist shortened her visit to a half hour, and the toddler was much less oppositional.

Table 6.3 offers several tips to keep in mind when visiting a family in their home. Compiled from several sources, they are based on the practical skills that service providers have found useful over the years.

Clearly, it is essential to try to follow the recommendations given in Table 6.3 when working with families. However, the interventionist will need to have Plan B ready in case Plan A does not work. The schedule may not go as planned due to a crisis in the home, an illness with a child, the parent's focus on another issue, or an activity that isn't working with the child. Therefore, flexibility is crucial when considering the child's schedule, the family's schedule, and the professional schedule of the interventionist.

Materials

Many homes contain an amazing array of possible teaching tools for infants and toddlers, yet many interventionists continue to rely on store-bought educational toys. In doing so they may inadvertently give the parents the message that in order to help their child, they must spend a lot of money and buy a wide variety of toys. On the other hand, when an interventionist brings in a homemade rattle, or, better yet, shows the parent how to make one, she is modeling resourcefulness. Sim-

TABLE 6.3 Suggestions for Home Visitors

- Greet each family member or day care provider as well as other children.
- Confirm the allotted time and discuss the plan for the visit.
- Begin and end the home visit on time.
- Prepare an activity for the siblings or include siblings and other children in day care in the activity.
- Take time to acknowledge pets, favorite toys, or household items.
- Confirm information with the parent about recent or upcoming medical or other appointments.
- Share developmental information and review developmental progress.
- Evaluate suggested activities.
- Discuss and model activities.
- Encourage parents to show how they ordinarily interact or play with their child.
- Listen to parents' concerns and offer support.
- Share problem-solving strategies.
- Share a sense of humor.
- Locate community resources.
- Schedule and discuss the next visit.
- Remain calm and focused despite distractions.
- Be flexible if the activity is not working with the child.

Adapted from "The Art of Home Visiting," by G. Calvello, 1990, in F,. Otto (Ed.), *Parents and Visually Impaired Infants,* Louisville, Ky.: American Printing House for the Blind; "Learning Together: A Parent Guide to Socially Based Routines for Visually Impaired Infants" by D. Chen, C. T. Friedman, and G. Cavello, 1990, in F. Otto (Ed.), *Parents and Visually Impaired Infants;* and *Adapting Early Childhood Curricula for Children in Inclusive Settings* by R. E. Cook, A. Tessier, & M. D. Klein, 2000, Englewood Cliffs, N.J.: Merrill/Prentice-Hall.

ple items found at home can be turned into valuable teaching tools. If one of the parents' goals for the toddler is that he learn to match objects, the interventionist and parents might consider functional objects around the house that could be used for this purpose (socks, shoes, etc.).

When items commonly found in the home are used in teaching, they can be easily incorporated in the family's routine and can make learning a natural occurrence. By suggesting that the child sort laundry, find matching socks, or place all the boxes of macaroni and cheese on the same shelf, parents are enriching the experiences for their children as well as providing a sense of self-determination. In addition, toddlers who are frustrated or tired often delight in an activity that they can do together with a parent. The activity helps them refocus their energy into a productive task.

Family Routines

Calvello (1990) emphasized the importance for the interventionist to spend time and observe the child during naturally occurring routines in the home environment. Such observations offer an insight into the family's life and routines and allow the interventionist to provide services within that framework. When working collaboratively with the parent during routines that are not taken out of context, a natural opportunity for learning will occur. Likewise, if the parent provides the child with learning experiences during everyday routines (e.g., meals, play, bath, bedtime), the activities will have more meaning to the child (Bricker, Pretti-Frontczak, & McComas, 1998; Chen, Friedman, & Calvello, 1990).

Siblings

Siblings or playmates in the child's child care are invaluable teachers. They are able to engage in repetitive games with the child to encourage social interaction in a natural setting. The interventionist should, with the parents, plan activities to occupy the siblings or playmates, or, more important, to design strategies to include the other children in the visit. Vignette 6.5 describes how one service provider accomplished this goal.

VIGNETTE 6.5 GO PLAY

Katie is a one-year-old with a severe visual impairment, who attends a family day care setting. Jane (the child care provider) expressed concern about the amount of time she spent with Katie alone and felt guilty about telling her two-year-old daughter, Kara, to go play while she worked with Katie. The interventionist had brought toys and materials to facilitate Katie's development, and Jane wanted to spend time working with Katie doing the activities. The interventionist explained how Kara would be a wonderful role model and playmate for Katie and could help in developing Katie's play skills. The interventionist developed play strategies with Jane to include her daughter and other children in playing with Katie.

Meyer and Vadasy (1994) reported that when siblings are involved in their brother's or sister's intervention, the entire family benefits. With planning from the interventionist and parent, the sibling can assume an active role in the child's intervention at home. The interventionist needs to view the family as a system and understand that all family members are influenced by events affecting one member of the family (Wasik, Bryant, & Lyons, 1990).

Environmental Intrusions

Many home visits follow a smooth schedule, as described in the previous examples. However, the service provider needs to be prepared for challenging intrusions and then must either adapt to the changes or develop strategies with which to handle them. These intrusions can take innumerable forms, ranging in seriousness from a blaring television set to an act of violence during a home visit. Vignette 6.6 portrays a crisis in one home.

VIGNETTE 6.6 TELL ME WHAT'S REALLY IMPORTANT!

A referral from the public health nurse was received to assess the developmental skills of Erik. After numerous tries to contact the parent to schedule a convenient time to visit, his mother finally agreed to a date scheduled in the later part of an afternoon. Upon arriving at their home, Erik's mother, Jody, was busy feeding her eight-week-old daughter. Erik was asleep on the sofa because he had been up all night after choking on a piece of candy. The phone rang and it was the phone company informing Jody of their intent to disconnect her phone. Jody told the phone company that her check was in the mail and begged them not to disconnect the phone. After her phone call, Jody stated that she was moving to another apartment soon. We set up a time the following week to see Erik and Jody. The day before we were scheduled to come, we tried to call Jody. Her phone had been disconnected.

Eventually the assessment team did contact Jody through the mail and set up another date to come and see Erik. After completing the assessment and sharing the results, Jody decided that she did not want any services for Erik and she would take care of his needs.

Although Jody and Erik would benefit from services, it was difficult for this mother to reach out for help. She was preoccupied with providing the most basic needs for her family. Perhaps when her living situation is more stable, she will see the importance of getting services for Erik. At this point, does the service provider have other options for the family? Possibly the public health nurse could continue to contact or visit the family to establish rapport and trust to encourage some form of communication regarding Jody and Erik's situation. The assessment team could try to reassess Erik in six months and offer services again.

Often situations cannot be changed and instead need to be adapted for a successful home visit. Some intrusions are a necessary part of the child's daily routine.

Consider Vignette 6.7, which illustrates medically related intrusions for one child and her family.

VIGNETTE 6.7 OLIVIA

Olivia is a three-year-old with a significant birth history: born premature at 24 weeks. She spent six months in NICU and three additional months in the infant critical care unit before discharge. Medically she has been followed for bronchopulmonary dysplasia, tracheostomy with ventilator assistance, and retinopathy of prematurity. Olivia was weaned from mechanical ventilation at two and a half years. Just recently, at age three, she had successful surgery for decannulation and now has a stable airway.

Olivia has had many environmental intrusions. Each day, she requires nebulizing treatments every four hours for respiratory difficulties (at times, they can be every two hours), feedings through a gastrostomy tube, and medication. Home visits are scheduled when Olivia is most rested and does not need medical therapy or medication. Her mother, Cheryl, is also affected by intrusions, which may include the home health nurse's own agenda and phone calls from the pediatrician or pulmonologist, from the home health care agency to reschedule or inform Cheryl of changes in nursing staff, and from friends who call during Olivia's therapy to chat or make plans.

Developmentally, Olivia is ready to interact and play with other children. However, her pediatrician has recommended that she not participate in a play group or preschool program for at least one year due to the possibility of a respiratory infection. Cheryl feels that the medical demands and the threat for illness with a medically at-risk child have led to a very isolating experience for Olivia and her family. Olivia's parents are pursuing play groups with other medically at-risk children whose parents understand what precautions are needed to allow the children to play together.

Although Olivia's environmental intrusions are very necessary, Cheryl has coordinated Olivia's schedule so that Olivia has opportunities to explore and learn in her environment with minimal interruptions. Therapists, nurses, doctors, and friends have been asked not to call during Olivia's home visits with the interventionist. Communication, collaboration, and flexibility are key factors in working around the many environmental intrusions on families in order to facilitate successful home visits (Wasik, Bryant, & Lyons, 1990).

Advocacy

Families can become their child's best advocate. With advocacy skills, families are better able to help their child obtain appropriate resources and intervention services (Turnbull & Turnbull, 1990). In Vignette 6.7, Cheryl shared how she coordinated and communicated with all professionals involved in Olivia's medical and educational needs. When asked how she advocates for Olivia, Cheryl chuckled and said, "I'm a bully." Seriously, Cheryl and her husband, Steve, continue to ask questions of doctors, nurses, therapists, and other parents. They research information to help them be more knowledgeable in making informed decisions about Olivia's medical and educational needs.

Many families feel intimidated and may not be comfortable communicating to professionals their particular issues regarding intervention or medical services. It may be helpful for the family to compile a running list of questions or concerns and then share it at an appropriate time (for example, during a home visit, at an IFSP meeting, or in the doctor's office). Families need to be encouraged to ask questions, request additional information, and positively assert their needs as a family (Armenta, 1993).

Networking

Families can be a valuable resource to other families. Networking may help them to identify with other families whose child has a similar disability, offer or gain support, create additional resources, establish a friendship, lessen the sense of isolation, and provide opportunities to learn from each other (Armenta, 1993). Informal or formal networking may occur through the interventionist, the pediatrician, and local or national organizations.

However, families with few supports often have difficulty negotiating the system independently. The process of getting the appropriate social services is very time-consuming and bureaucratic. Likewise, the process of finding child care, transportation, housing, and a job can be very complicated. Some parents may question why they should even attempt to become more self-sufficient when struggling with so many demands and expectations. In Vignette 6.8, a parent loses her job and gives up hope.

VIGNETTE 6.8 NO HOPE LEFT

Mary had lost her job due to her inability to transport herself to her job site. The loss of her job meant she had to apply for housing assistance and food stamps. It also meant the loss of a child care subsidy, which had paid for the majority of the child care for Jason, who is autistic. With no car, no child care, and mounting worries about providing shelter and sustenance for her family, she contemplated whether or not to try to find a job. The stress of this situation caused increased frustration for Jason. Because she had lost her child care, she was taking him along to apply for assistance and jobs. Jason was unable to sit and wait with her. He would scream and cry and try to run from the room. Mary often had to leave the office before completing the application.

This is an all-too-familiar story in the lives of many families. If Mary had access to reliable transportation, she might have been able to prevent her situation from deteriorating. What is particularly frustrating is that Mary's son was not getting his needs met. How can the early interventionist help parents function more autonomously? Providing opportunities and encouraging parents to network with others are essential in promoting independence. Doss and Hatcher (1996) discussed the importance of being involved in parent organizations. They found that these organizations helped parents learn the latest philosophies guiding services and supports for their children. Many parents find that making a connection with others who have similar experiences is empowering as well as validating in that they are able to hear the success stories.

ETHICAL ISSUES IN HOME VISITING

Home visiting gives the early interventionist another opportunity to enhance the quality of life for a child. Working outside the professional domain of classroom or clinic presents many situations in which a skilled home visitor must be able to operate independently. By allowing professionals into their home, families are giving up a considerable amount of privacy and may view home visits as invasive. The situation places them in a vulnerable position that may require a significant amount of adjustment. Some parents may feel inadequate about providing a home for their child or be worried that the professional will discover some negative information about the family, such as drug abuse or domestic violence. Building a strong, trusting relationship with the family can help the home visitor provide appropriate services. Critical in this process is establishing the boundaries that are necessary for home visiting to take place (Powell, 1993).

Most professional organizations provide a set of ethical guidelines that members are encouraged to follow. The American Psychiatric Association (APA) and the National Association of Social Workers (NASW) are examples of helping professions that have adopted a set of standards to be applied when situations of an ethical nature arise in servicing clients. These standards outline appropriate conduct and rules for the delivery of services. The Council for Exceptional Children (CEC) has developed a Code of Ethics, and requires compliance by all members. Early interventionists should follow these guidelines when serving children and their families. Compliance will help professionals provide support for the actions they may take in serving clients.

Table 6.4 is drawn from a number of sources in order to provide a comprehensive view of the major ethical issues for home visitors. Reamer (1982) developed guidelines more specific to situations that may involve conflict or require a judgment call. These guidelines were further elaborated on by Wasik, Bryant, and Lyons (1990) for home visitors. Additional guidelines were added to address other current issues in home visiting, such as the client's legal rights and your rights as a professional.

It is important to follow and understand safety procedures established by the service organization. In many states, early intervention agencies have worked closely with police and others to ensure the safety of home visitors. Some of the

TABLE 6.4 Ethical Issues in Home Visiting

- Rules against basic harms to necessary preconditions (e.g., life, health, food, safety) take precedence over rules against lying or revealing confidential information. In other words, a professional may lie about the whereabouts of a mother and child to an abusing spouse who may be threatening him or her.
- An individual's right to basic well-being takes precedence over another individual's right to freedom. If a parent is engaged in self-destructive behavior, they may do so without interference from the professional unless someone else's well-being is at stake.
- An informed individual's rights to choose an unsafe action takes precedence over his or her own right to basic well-being. A home visitor may provide resources, information, and even transportation to a mental health agency for a parent with a mental illness, but the parent has the right to refuse assistance. The visitor should enlist other family members and mental health professionals in determining a solution.
- The obligation to obey laws, rules, and regulations that the home visitor has voluntarily consented to takes precedence over one's right to engage in actions that conflict with these laws, rules, and regulations. Thus, home visitors must abide by the rules and regulations stipulated by their agency.
- An individual's right to well-being may take precedence over laws, rules, regulations of the agency in a case of conflict. It may be an agency rule to wait for police before taking a family to a shelter. However, if the family is in immediate danger, the home visitor may need to take faster action.
- The obligation to prevent basic harms such as starvation, and promote public education, assistance, and adequate housing overrides the right to keep one's property. Home visitors often face the dilemma of using their own resources to assist the families they are working with. They try to find a balance between providing resources and disempowering families.
- Home visitors must demonstrate cultural sensitivity and adaptation of visiting goals to diverse family ecologies.

Adapted from *Ethical Dilemmas in Social Service* by F. G. Reamer, 1982, New York: Columbia University Press, pp. 72–79; *Home Visiting: Procedures for Helping Families* by B. H. Wasik, D. M. Bryant, & C. M. Lyons, 1990, Newbury Park, Calif.: Sage, pp. 203–206; "Home Visiting Programs and the Health and Development of Young Children" by C. T. Ramey & S. L. Ramey, 1993, in R. E. Behrman (Ed.), *The Future of Children: Home Visiting,* Los Altos, Calif.: Center for the Future of Children, David and Lucille Packard Foundation, p. 134.

strategies used by programs include the use of cellular phones for all home visitors, required reporting of arrival and departure times at the agency, teaming up for visits in questionable neighborhoods, using reliable, safe transportation, and leaving valuables in the trunk or at the agency.

Data Privacy

Another important issue in serving families with special needs is how information is used and shared among those involved in delivering services. Special care must be taken to uphold client confidentiality and respect their privacy. Medical information, environmental considerations, personal history, and families' goals and issues must be considered confidential and only shared with permission by parents. It is important that the information shared is pertinent to the professional who is receiving it. However, there are times when confidentiality guidelines should be bypassed (Corey, Corey, & Callanan, 1993). If the professional is concerned for the safety of an individual, confidentiality may be overlooked. For example, professionals are mandated by law to report suspected cases of abuse or neglect of a child.

Child Abuse and Neglect

Maltreatment of children is one of the most complex issues faced by professionals working with families. Children with disabilities are at an increased risk of abuse because of the stress that exceptionality may create in families (T. J. Zirpoli, 1986, 1995). Other risk factors include the child's temperament; maternal and paternal variables such as age, socioeconomic status, race, marital status, and education level; social isolation; and environmental stressors (Willis, Holden & Rosenberg, 1992). Home visiting is a valuable tool in prevention of child abuse. Research supports the positive impact early intervention can have in the home (Olds, Henderson, Chamberlain, & Tatelbaum, 1986). Visitors should be knowledgeable about the indicators of abuse and the correct procedures in reporting cases to child welfare and law enforcement. Information for each state should be available from the respective state department of human services.

Cultural Diversity and Sensitivity

Effective communication is the basis for working across cultures. A home interventionist will convey many messages, not only through words but also with body language, gestures, eye contact, and facial expressions. Researchers have outlined strategies to enhance communication with families from diverse cultures, as summarized in Table 6.5.

TABLE 6.5 Cross-Cultural Effectiveness

- Acknowledging one's own cultural heritage and its impact on your work.
- Investigating the cultural norms and traditions of specific groups through literature and a community inventory.
- Recognizing differences in communication styles within various cultures.
- Recognizing nonverbal communication styles.
- Showing respect and openness toward other cultures.
- Being willing to tolerate ambiguity.
- Approaching others with a desire to learn.

Adapted from *Developing Cross-Cultural Competence: A Guide from Working with Young Children and Their Families* by E. W. Lynch & M. J. Hanson, 1998, Baltimore: Paul H. Brookes; and *Strategies for Working with Culturally Diverse Communities and Clients* by E. Randall-David, 1989, Washington, D.C.: Association for the Care of Children's Health.

Even if communication is optimized, differences in basic beliefs may need to be addressed. For example, one of the main assumptions of early intervention programs is that change is not only possible but also valued (Hanson, 1992). Thus, families from diverse cultures immediately come up against mainstream values about change and action. In some cultures, changes may be viewed as undesirable or unnecessary. Families may prefer to take a "wait and see" approach. An early interventionist who moves ahead with inquiries and assumes that the family will actively participate may find that those good intentions are not in accordance with the family's dynamics and beliefs, thus alienating the family from the start.

Table 6.6 illustrates how beliefs that are an everyday part of the mainstream Anglo-American psyche may be extremely different from those of other cultural groups.

The values listed in Table 6.6 are such an integral part of a person's being that daily actions and interactions are unconsciously guided by them. When working with families from cultures dissimilar to our own, it is prudent to pause and question these assumptions. For example, if the interventionist is from the mainstream culture, it might seem natural to assume that informal attire is appropriate for home visits because, more than likely, one may end up on the floor working with a child. Yet some cultural groups might take this as a sign of disrespect, because for them more formal attire is appropriate when entering another person's home.

VIGNETTE 6.9 THE LEE FAMILY

Louise knocked politely on the door of the Lee family's apartment. Upon entering, she introduced herself to the family, and shook hands

TABLE 6.6 Contrasting Beliefs, Values, and Practices

DIVERSE CULTURAL VALUES	ANGLO-AMERICAN VALUES
Fate	Personal control over environment
Tradition	Change
Human interaction dominates	Time dominates
Hierarchy/rank/status	Human equality
Group welfare	Individualism/privacy
Birthright inheritance	Self-help
Cooperation	Competition
Past orientation	Future orientation
"Being" orientation	Action/goal/work orientation
Formality	Informality
Indirectness/ritual/"face"	Directness/openness/honesty
Idealism/theory	Practicality/efficiency
Spiritualism/detachment	Materialism

Adapted from "Cross-Cultural Counseling: A Guide for Nutrition and Health Counselors" United States Department of Agriculture & United States Department of Health and Human Services, 1986, Washington, D.C.: Author, p. 3.

with Mr. Lee, Mrs. Lee, and Mr. Lee's father. She was offered both food and drink; but declined, saying she had eaten just before coming. She felt slightly uneasy with this new family, and because the Lees seemed so reserved and quiet, Louise tried to fill in the uncomfortable pauses with animated questions and talk. Louise's queries were politely answered, but she felt she was somehow not connecting with the family.

If Louise had attempted to understand and respect the family's cultural background, she probably would have been more successful in her first visit. But she inadvertently offended the family numerous times in her ignorance of their cultural customs, which dictate that shoes be taken off at the door, that women typically do not shake hands with men or anyone significantly older than themselves, that food or a beverage is always graciously accepted, and that laughter, informality, and personal questions are inappropriate when initially meeting someone (Chan, 1998).

On the other hand, just because a family has roots in another culture or is of a different race, this doesn't necessarily mean that they adhere to the customs and values typical of that culture. Several generations of a family might live in a mainstream culture without ever acculturating to it, while other, recently immigrated families may immediately embrace the new ways and values even though they may not speak the language.

Wayman, Lynch, and Hanson (1991) developed a comprehensive set of guidelines that address in detail the family's structure, childrearing practices, language and communication systems, and attitudes and that can be extremely helpful in determining the concerns, priorities, and resources of a family (see Table 6.7). These guidelines can serve to ease the process toward understanding a family's perspective.

TABLE 6.7 General Guidelines for Cultural Sensitivity in Home Visiting

- Don't overgeneralize about members of any specific cultural group.
- Realize that cultural differences as well as similarities are common.
- Find out about the culture and the family's degree of acculturation before you make your first contact.
- Use resources written by members of the culture.
- Be respectful of the family's belongings and ask where they would like you to sit, work with the child, etc.
- Be especially sensitive to social structure and hierarchy.
- Accept food or drink graciously, even if only a token amount.
- Be aware that the family's childrearing practices may be directly at odds with mainstream norms.
- Use reflective listening often to check if you are hearing what the family intended to communicate, as language differences may impair communication.

Adapted from "Home-Based Early Childhood Services: Cultural Sensitivity in a Family Systems Approach" by K. Wayman, E. Lynch, & M. Hanson, 1991, *Topics in Early Childhood Special Education, 10,* 65–66.

SERVICES IN OTHER SETTINGS

Infants and toddlers expend much of their energy adjusting to the behavioral styles of their primary caregivers (Blasco, 1995). Research shows that both the infant and the adult are active partners who affect each other's behavior over time (Sameroff & Fiese, 1990). For the infant or toddler with disabilities, this interactive dance often becomes difficult and frustrating for both partners. Given the increase in out-of-home care, infants and toddlers with disabilities must learn to interpret and respond to a variety of behavioral characteristics of those who care for them in many different settings (Belsky, 1988). Therefore, it is important to understand and evaluate the quality of attachment and the care that young children receive outside the home.

Bowlby (1982), and Ainsworth (in Ainsworth, Blehar, Waters, & Wall, 1978) were pioneers in developing attachment theory and highlighting its importance in the field of child development. Their efforts have resulted in attention to attachment issues in caregiving situations outside the home. Belsky (1988) looked at the amount of time infants spent in child care and its impact on infant-parent attachment. Using the "strange situation" method developed by Ainsworth, he found that infants who were in nonparental care for more than 20 hours per week showed higher rates of insecure attachment behaviors when reunited with parents.

Further studies indicate the importance of secure parental attachment for success in child-caregiver relationships (Barnas & Cummings, 1994; Howes & Hamilton, 1992). "When children are distressed, attachment figures can serve as an effective source of security, and in routine play they may facilitate functioning by serving as a secure base for infants' explorations" (Barnas & Cummings, p. 141).

From a practical standpoint there are three critical factors in determining whether a child care situation is going to be a positive social and emotional experience for a child: (1) daily transitions of departing and reuniting, (2) the quality of the child's emotional experiences in the course of the day, and (3) the quality of the parent's relationship with the caregiver (Lieberman, 1993, p. 203).

All these are important regardless of the setting—in-home care, center care, or family home care. Family home care is defined as care provided for a child by someone other than the parent in the other adult's home. It is a form of care for infants and toddlers highly used in the United States. Until recently, it also was the least supported and regulated type of care for children. Typically, family day care is a mixed-age setting with one caregiver responsible for the well-being of all children in her care. States have implemented licensing guidelines for family day care operations that help to ensure safe environments for children, but these guidelines are inconsistent (Adams, 1995). There are many family day care settings that are operating without frequent inspections. Parents may choose those settings due to their low cost or proximity to work (Bryant & Graham, 1993).

Although developmentally appropriate practices are paramount for family day care, the environment differs from the atmosphere of a center. "Toys and equipment are available for children, but children's interactions, rather than explicit planning and involvement of the provider, form the core of the day's activities" (Jones & Meisels, 1987, p. 2). Family day care providers should be trained and experienced in child development and should have the opportunity to build skills and network with other providers on a continuous basis. Providers need to have firm guidelines and limits, which parents should follow in regard to hours of service, sickness policies, and payment.

Among the barriers to quality child care that social policy needs to address are training and qualification standards of providers, networking and support systems for providers, and financial assistance for parents and providers (NAEYC, 1999). Another area for growth would be increasing training and support for family day care.

Staff Qualifications

In an ideal world, infants, toddlers, and their families could find child care staffed by individuals who are highly skilled and knowledgeable about typical and atypical development and family structure. Currently, there is much interest in developing a career ladder in early childhood education that extends from technical colleges providing child care certificates to institutions of higher education preparing students on the baccalaureate, master, and doctoral levels. The National Association for the Education of Young Children (NAEYC) and the Division for Early Childhood (DEC) have developed specific guidelines and recommended practices for teachers working with young children. These guidelines offer specific recommendations regarding the following core content: child development and learning, curriculum, family and community partnerships, assessment and evaluation, practical and field experiences, and diversity (Bredekamp, 1995; Odom & McLean, 1993). Field experiences to demonstrate competency include but are not limited to child care environments, including center-based and home-based education. Working professionals receive continuing education through local and state sponsored in-services and training efforts. One way that professionals can keep current in their field is through affiliation with organizations such as the NAEYC and DEC. Both of these provide service providers with current knowledge of the best practice and networking opportunities.

The American Speech and Hearing Association (ASHA), the American Occupational Therapy Association (AOTA), the Physical Therapy Association, and the American Medical Association (AMA) have all developed guidelines for their disciplines regarding practice with families and young children.

Staff-to-child ratios are a critical factor in the quality of care. The NAEYC recommendations for classes of typical developing children are 1:3 for infants, 1:6 for toddlers (24–36 months), and 1:8 for 3-year-olds (Bredekamp, 1993). DEC recommendations suggest that ratios provide the highest quality care possible to meet the safety, health, and educational goals of the specific group of children (Odom & McLean, 1993). Group size may vary depending on the needs of children and individual state guidelines. However, a small-group approach for toddlers has been shown to foster independent choice-making, self-worth, and conflict resolution (Elgas & Barber Peltier, 1998). The small-group format used in many programs today is modeled on the Reggio Emilia approach to learning. The philosophical basis for this approach was mentioned in Chapter 1. Important components of this approach include self-determination, relationship-based learning, and emergent curriculum (Rinaldi, 1993).

Appropriate Materials and Curriculum

The use of materials and curriculum for child care centers is discussed in Chapter 7. However, it is important to consider curriculum within the context of the environment. As previously mentioned, developmentally appropriate practice (DAP) (Bredekamp & Copple, 1998) provides guidelines to meet children's individual developmental needs. DAP is implemented through planned curriculum and design of the environment. "Infants and toddlers learn by experiencing the environment through their senses by physically moving around and through social interaction" (Bredekamp, 1993, p. 5). DAP recommendations include encouragement of cognitive learning and healthy social emotional development, in part by service providers and parents providing appropriate play experiences in a safe, nurturing environment.

Children with disabilities may require more structure and guidance in their play from the caregiver. Fox, Hanline, Vail, and Galant (1994) pointed out that early intervention programs focus on the remediation of skills and the prevention of future developmental problems. These programs tend to emphasize developing individualized goals for children and designing learning activities to achieve those goals. Incorporating recommended practices with DAP is appropriate for children with disabilities. "This best practice is echoed in the Early Childhood Special Education (ECSE) literature in that teaching through routines and in natural contexts is promoted as a functional approach that will yield generalized responding. A developmentally appropriate curriculum provides ample opportunity for child-directed play with objects and peers, during which specific skills can be targeted for young children with special needs" (Fox et al., 1994, p. 244).

Designing Environments for Child Care

The overall environment of a child care center can set the stage for optimal growth and learning by young children. McEvoy, Fox, and Rosenberg (1991) pointed out that there are two important considerations in designing the environment: in addition to establishing a social environment, the physical layout of the center needs to be considered very carefully to include all children. In the past, child care centers have had to take what they could get in terms of physical space. Although centers must meet certain legal requirements for their buildings and grounds, many struggled to meet the bare minimum. Because of the need for quality child care, there has been a vast improvement in the design of child care centers.

According to Bailey and Wolery (1992, p. 200), a responsive environment should incorporate the following teaching strategies:

- Provide opportunities for children to use appropriate materials for problem-solving and mastery;
- Provide opportunities for children to understand and respond to verbal and nonverbal signals from other children as well as adults;
- Encourage autonomy through appropriate adaptive equipment, assistive technology, and child-size furniture.

Child care centers should provide children with separate active and quiet spaces. Quiet activities such as storytelling or "reading" (looking at a book) should be located near other quiet activities. The block area should be in a distant part of the room, perhaps near the dress-up area to encourage symbolic play within these two sections (S. B. Zirpoli, 1995). With very young children, it is important to consider how each area will be utilized so that appropriate behavior occurs. For example, hanging a mobile or placing bright color pictures on the ceiling in the diaper-changing area can create opportunities for conversation and avoid the battles that may arise during a change. The aisle in the room should be wide enough for a wheelchair but not so wide that it creates a runway for toddlers. It is a good idea to define spaces using tables, shelving, or furniture. Different areas and materials can be identified with picture and name labels. A good physical layout of a center for toddlers is illustrated in Figure 6.1.

Adaptive equipment allows a child with a physical disability to participate in typical center routines. For example, a corner chair or a floor seat can be used to position a toddler during group time. Wedges and prone standers can be useful when the child is looking at books or participating in table activities. The team should spend time making sure the equipment is used properly and not for an overextended period. To use the previous example, young children may have difficulty staying in a straight-leg position during group time. Children should be monitored for head, back and trunk stability when sitting in a group (Nwaobi & Smith, 1986). Lofts and platforms are very popular in child care centers today, yet one must consider the difficulty that children with disabilities encounter in negotiating such spaces. A good rule is to plan ahead with the team (including parents, of course) to make the optimal use of the space for all children.

Outdoor Environments

The opportunity for play in a safe outdoor environment is very important for all children. Rivkin (1995) noted the lack of available, appropriate space for young children in many center-based programs.

Most centers begin by taking stock of what is available and deciding what are the priorities in meeting children's needs. Outdoor play should provide lots of opportunity for children to engage in large muscle activities, and also serve to increase their exploratory behavior by using interesting materials and equipment.

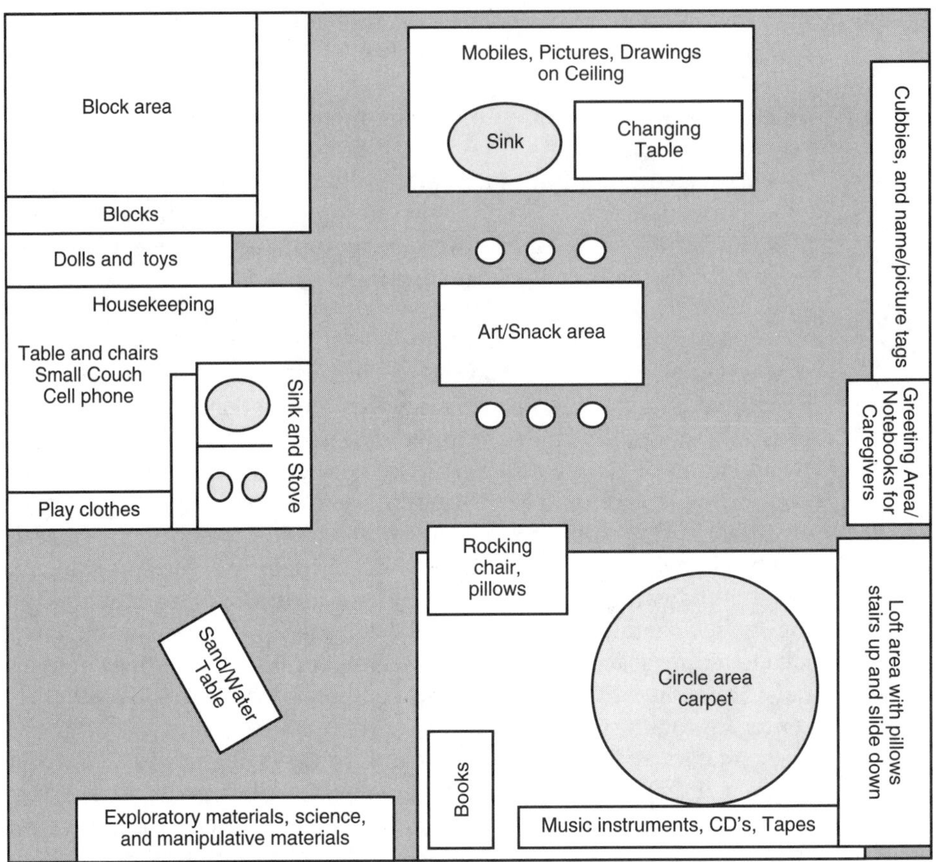

FIGURE 6.1 Toddler Room

Source: From "Designing Environments for Optimal Behavior" by Susan B. Zirpoli, 1995, in T. J. Zirpoli (Ed.), *Understanding and Affecting the Behavior of Young Children,* Englewood Cliffs, N.J.: Merrill, pp. 122–150.

Such equipment should be of appropriate size for toddlers and should include adaptive devices for children with physical disabilities. Tricycles and pull wagons can be modified to hold adaptive seating. It is important to consider access to a play area for children with disabilities. For example, Levangie, Brouwer, McKeen, Parker, and Shelby (1989) found that posterior rolling walkers helped children with motor impairments to walk with close to a normal gait. Young children are encouraged to use their walkers to negotiate hallways and playgrounds. Because many centers do not have a stable walkway leading to the play area, the team needs to problem-solve a way to get the child to these areas as independently as possible.

Another consideration for making the most of outdoor play is the role of staff, including assistants, all of whom must stay actively involved with the children. Outdoor time is not a "break time" for adults. S. B. Zirpoli (1995) offered suggestions to manage behavior on the playground:

- Separate play areas for younger and older preschoolers. (In some states, this is now required by law.) Toddlers need especially close supervision and should play on equipment designed for them.
- Allow for adequate monitoring and supervision. For example, an extra adult should be available to take children indoors when necessary for toileting or other needs.
- Make sure there is adequate equipment to go around. Otherwise, limiting the number of children on the playground may eliminate waiting for a turn on the swing or slide.
- Teach children how to use the playground equipment. For example, showing children the correct way to walk around swings and other hazards will decrease injuries and conflicts. (p. 133)

TRANSITIONS IN NATURAL ENVIRONMENTS

Transitions within early childhood environments are used to move children to and from various locations (Dee-Tourdot, 1995). Researchers have found that preschool-age children spend as much as 20 to 30 percent of time in center-based programs moving from one activity to another (Sainato, Strain, Lefebvre, & Rapp, 1987). Too many transitions within a classroom may be frustrating for very young children. When activities are structured and planned appropriately, they can provide opportunities for very young children to learn and develop self-management skills (Dee-Tourdot, 1995). Elements that promote smooth transitions include: an organized and easily accessed environment, staff planning and preparation, and routine timing and procedure (Larson, Henthorne, & Plum, 1994). For example, toddlers can get their blankets from cubbies in preparation for napping if the cubbies are at their height level.

When not planned, transitions can increase disruptive behavior and decrease the effective use of instructional time (Carta et al., 1992). "Down" time occurs when children are waiting or nonengaged in appropriate activities. Vignette 6.10 shows how this behavior, coupled with ambiguous instructions, creates a chaotic atmosphere.

VIGNETTE 6.10 CHANGES AND STAGES

Martha's class of older toddlers was required to stand in line by the sink to wash hands after outdoor play. The children had difficulty maintaining the line and staying within their own space. The transition was trying for both the children and staff. Martha's solution was to have another staff member help the children wash hands in small groups of two or three while the others were seated for a short singing activity. The stress was greatly reduced by this change in the routine.

Much of the research on transitions within the classroom focused on decreasing "down" time and increasing independence. Strategies to improve transitions within the classroom include organization of the environment to enhance learning and specific instructional strategies (Sainato & Lyon, 1989).

As an example, S. B. Zirpoli (1995) listed physical elements of a center-based program that can facilitate organization and structure including the following:

- Separating active and quiet activity spaces
- Providing obvious boundaries of all play spaces, using furniture and/or space dividers
- Labeling activity areas with word labels and picture symbols
- Limiting the number of children per activity area (e.g., through use of chairs, tickets, activity necklaces, carpet squares, and pictures noting how many children are allowed in the area)
- Using child-size furniture and bathroom fixtures to promote independence.

In Vignette 6.11, one child humorously illustrates his knowledge of a two-person area.

VIGNETTE 6.11 TWO-PERSON AREA

Joey has a great understanding of how many children are allowed to play in each area of the classroom. Recently, Joey went on a class field trip to the History Center. At the center, he saw an exhibit involving a large model cow. All of the children were crowding in awe around the cow. Joey reminded everyone that it was "a two-person cow!"

Classroom Schedule

A critical component for a smooth transition is an effective and predictable schedule (Dee-Tourdot, 1995). The daily schedule includes the times of various activities and events throughout the day. It is helpful to include information on where events will be held and which staff members will be responsible for different activities (Sainato, 1990). Daily schedules can promote learning across content areas (e.g., language, preacademics, gross motor) by sequencing high- and low-activity periods, grouping by skill components, and building reliance on established routines (Ostrosky, Skellenger, Odom, McConnell, & Peterson, 1994).

Defining the responsibilities of staff in relation to the schedule will help to eliminate confusion. The "zone" procedure assigns staff to specific areas within the classroom, while the children are free to move around the room. In the "man-to-man" procedure, children must wait until everyone has completed an activity before moving on to another area. The zone method was more effective in decreasing the time children spent in transitions and increasing their level of engagement in planned activities (Zirpoli, 1995).

When developing strategies for classroom transitions, the team must consider what is developmentally appropriate for the child. Linking transition plans with the child's individual education program (IEP) or individual family service plan (IFSP) is an effective way to build successful transitions within the classroom.

HELPING FAMILIES WITH CHILD CARE

Most centers follow state guidelines in meeting standards for child care. However, parents sometimes feel forced to choose between quality child care and less expensive or more convenient services. It is often difficult for service providers who are working with children as consultants to see them placed in a questionable setting. Several options exist in these situations. You may want to offer suggestions or share strategies and curriculum ideas with the child care center. If this does not help, you may want to visit the center with the parents and indicate areas that need improvement. There are several tools available to assess quality in child care programs and environments for infants and toddlers. The Family Day Care Rating Scale (Harms & Clifford, 1989), The Infant/Toddler Environment Rating Scale (Harms, Cryer, & Clifford 1990), and *Barriers and Supports to Early Childhood Inclusion* (Wesley & Buysse, 1994a) are three such instruments that assess environments by looking at all domains of child development, interactions with parents, and general structure of routines. These tools are applicable to inclusive settings and match current guidelines on quality care.

TRANSITION FROM PROGRAM TO PROGRAM

In most states, when children turn three years of age, they are often "moved" from early intervention services to early childhood special education. The difference in approach to services between the two forms may reflect more than a change from the IFSP to the IEP. For one thing, families no longer have access to a service coordinator. As mandated by federal law, the early intervention program staff will help them with the transition to a preschool program. This can be a joyous but also stressful time for families and their young children. It is also sometimes difficult for service providers who have to let go of a child and family after three years of building a relationship.

A successful transition is a primary goal for service providers working with young children and their families. PL 99-457, Part H (1986), placed a spotlight on the transition process for young children. When the Individuals with Disabilities Education Act (IDEA), Part C, was passed in 1991 and reauthorized in 1997, states were required to define how they will assure a smooth transition for the family when applying for federal funds for early intervention programs.

To secure a smooth transition, the law states that an Individual Education Plan (IEP) must be developed and implemented by the child's third birthday. In states that have adopted the IFSP (Individualized Family Service Plan) through age five, such as Oregon, the new program uses the IFSP unless an annual review is due. A description of the family's role in the transition process must be included in the documentation. At least 90 days before the child's third birthday, a meeting between the sending and receiving personnel and the family must occur (Rosenkoetter, Hains, & Fowler, 1994). The trend in early childhood services is to collaborate within the community and become family-centered. Furthermore, state and local agencies need to service families and their children in natural and least intrusive environments (Rosenkoetter et al., 1994).

Transition is a time of change that can lead to growth and at the same time add stress in families' lives. Planning successful transitions leads to positive experiences (Odom & McLean, 1993). Rosenkoetter and colleagues suggested several key ideas for bridging the transition process, including (1) ensuring program continuity by using developmentally appropriate curriculum for all age levels in all settings; (2) maintaining ongoing communication and cooperation between staff at both programs; and (3) helping children and families prepare for the transition (Rosenkoetter et al., 1994).

Parents have legal rights to be involved in the decisions made regarding the IFSP and ensuring that adequate steps are made in the transition process. Information should be given to the parents about future placements, educational options, and training. Families have many concerns regarding transitions. Table 6.8 lists some of these concerns.

In addition, families need to evaluate philosophies and practices in the new program that may be different from those in the previous program. For example, moving from a teacher who may work as a member of a transdisciplinary team to a single contact person who represents the other members of the team involves a change in philosophies. A trusting relationship with a particular service coordinator/ provider may have evolved, and in a transition, the family is forced to form a new relationship. To open the lines of communication, the child, the parents, and the new teacher may choose to hold informal meetings, thus giving everyone the opportunity to share information and visit the future environment (Rosenkoetter et al., 1994).

TABLE 6.8 Families' Concerns Regarding Transitions

- Changes in service delivery, including focus, types, and coordination of services
- Differences in service personnel
- Eligibility for services
- Labeling
- Social acceptance
- Transportation issues
- No or fewer home visits
- Schedule/routine changes
- Change from family-centered to child-centered environment

Adapted from *Bridging Early Services for Children with Special Needs and Their Families: A Practical Guide for Transition Planning* by E. S. Rosenkoetter, H. A. Hains, and A. S. Fowler, 1994, Baltimore: Paul H. Brookes.

The degree to which families are involved in the decision-making process during the transition may differ from family to family and from situation to situation. Some families may choose to advocate strongly for their child, while other parents may prefer to take a backseat in the process. In any case, educators need to be sensitive to the families' preferences and concerns by providing them with information and support during the transition (Rosenkoetter et al., 1994). Families can also provide valuable information about their child and should be considered an equal member of the transition team (Odom & McLean, 1993). Summers (cited in Rosenkoetter et al., 1994) stated that "professionals need to remember, however, that families may not always be *ready* to hear, understand, or accept some information, but it should be available for later use." (p. 88)

Through collaborative efforts, agencies should establish a timeline to ensure that policies and procedures have been followed. By providing a continuum of services for children and families, duplication can be avoided. A plan should define fiscal responsibilities, guidelines, and constraints of each agency. This plan should include both formative and summative evaluation (Rosenkoetter et al., 1994).

Transition means change, which is a part of life. To provide positive experiences with change, professionals need to be sensitive to strategies that families and children can use to cope with the transitions. Children need to be prepared for environments that are structured differently and to be taught functional skills that can be integrated into the new setting (Odom & McLean, 1993). For families, leaving the child at child care, joining a new play group, and meeting new friends are all steps that promote successful transitions in the future.

Rosenkoetter and colleagues (1994) have suggested strategies, presented in Table 6.9, to help prepare children and families for transitions.

Transitioning from program to program can be a challenge. However, with collaboration on the part of administrators, teachers, and the sending and receiving programs, it can be done with success. Interagency planning is necessary to develop working agreements between agencies, form the transition team, and allocate a timeline to accomplish transition tasks. In addition, team responsibilities must be assigned and carried out. Intraagency planning is necessary to designate the responsibilities of the service coordinators/providers and to allow adequate time to plan a successful transition (Odom & McLean, 1993).

It is important to evaluate the transition process from the family's perspective. Were support services coordinated throughout the process? Families can be extremely helpful in identifying what worked and what needs to be improved for future transitions. Formal and informal means of collecting information from families regarding the transition process have been used. Questionnaires and observations are a few tools used in developing the evaluation plan. The evaluation team may consist of families, staff members, and agency representatives. Eliminating any biases while forming and implementing the evaluation plan will lead to an accurate outcome. Communicating the evaluation findings to the appropriate persons in various programs is vital to implementing change for future transitions (Rosenkoetter et al., 1994).

TABLE 6.9 Preparing Children for Transition from Program to Program

- Help the child anticipate the situation by talking about the new program, providing concrete experiences, and providing opportunities for the child to ask questions and express emotions.
- Read picture books about children undergoing changes in their environment that may be stressful.
- Volunteer to visit the new program with the parent or, if preferred by the parent, alone.
- Review changes in routines and schedules and the impact on all family members.
- If possible, videotape a new situation for viewing by the child. For example, videotape group time if the child hasn't sat in a group before, and let them watch the videotape as often as they like.
- Discuss separation from parents and other caregivers who may have been involved with the child.
- Facilitate social skills so the child is comfortable with social initiations and interactions with peers.
- Target new skills that can be learned in natural situations and easily transferable to a new environment (e.g., carrying a backpack to the library).
- Practice familiar skills in multiple settings.
- Assist the family with the preparation of the child's paperwork and portfolio.

Adapted from *Bridging Early Services for Children with Special Needs: A Practical Guide for Transition Planning* by S. E. Rosenkoetter, A. H. Hains, and S. A. Fowler, 1994, Baltimore: Paul H. Brookes, pp. 129–146.

SUMMARY

This chapter highlighted the many environments in which infants and toddlers grow and develop. Traditionally, children under three received services in the home. The teacher or other staff member worked with the parent in developing goals and objectives for the child. Today, the involvement of all family members in every stage of early intervention from planning to implementation reflects recommended practice. Families can be as involved as they want to be. However, there is an emphasis on helping them achieve independent problem-solving skills and a sense of self-determination.

Service providers working with families in the home must be trained in helping skills, including the ability to access resources, provide empathic listening, and act as a mediator and advocate for the family. Service providers should be flexible and willing to adjust schedules to fit the family's concerns. Another area of concern is environmental intrusions that interfere with the provision of regular services. These intrusions can range from minor ones, such as the use of loud entertainment devices during home visits, to life-threatening ones, such as domestic abuse. A successful home visitor uses communication strategies, collaboration skills, and flexibility in dealing with environmental intrusions. The home visitor should be aware of each agency's policy on ethical dilemmas and act quickly if a family or family member is viewed as being in danger. It is important to be respectful of cultural differences when visiting in a family's home and to respect and protect the integrity of the family. Ethical decisions during home visiting may become a necessity, and service providers should be aware of state reporting procedures regarding child abuse and neglect.

An increasing number of infants and toddlers are receiving care outside of the home. Given this increase, infants and toddlers must learn to interpret and respond to a variety of behavioral characteristics of those who care for them in many different settings (Belsky, 1988). This effort may be compounded when the infants and toddlers have disabilities.

Service providers may assist families in locating quality early childhood centers in their communities. Both the NAEYC and the DEC offer guidelines on best practices in early childhood intervention. Parents should be aware of regulations regarding staffing and staff qualifications. There may be occasions when a family chooses a child care setting that is not the best environment for the child but may be convenient to the family's home or work. In such situations, the service provider offers consultation or technical assistance. If the environment continues to be a poor match for the child's needs, the service provider may want to document his or her concerns and share them with the family.

The structure of the environment and the daily schedule are important considerations in observing and evaluating center-based programs. In addition, young children may have difficulty when there are no established routines or no clear method for handling transitions to and from activities or other environments, such as outdoor play. Several suggestions were given for helping young children make smooth transitions within early intervention or preschool programs.

Another type of transition to consider for young children is the movement from birth-to-three services to preschool services when the child turns three. This transition can present new challenges to the family and to the service providers. It is helpful when service providers inventory the future setting to assess the necessary skills the child will need. It is also a good idea to have the receiving service provider (usually a teacher) visit in the home or the child care center.

Often the process is further complicated because the agency currently working with the child may be different from the receiving agency. For example, the public health nurse may have been the primary service provider and now the child will receive services through the school system. Agencies must coordinate their efforts to help the child and the family move through the stages of transition as smoothly as possible. Finally, all stakeholders, including the family, should engage in the evaluation of the process to ensure satisfaction and implement any changes necessary for future transitions.

It is important to remember that both families and service providers may need time to say good-bye. Many families will have worked with a primary caregiver and/or service provider for three years. Families may have feelings of anger and frustration at having to develop new relationships. They may need time to build a sense of trust with the new agency and its representatives. Service providers can help families accept the changes and move on to the new program. Service providers who have not recognized their own need to say good-bye may inadvertently undermine the transition by making it more difficult for the new staff to step in. By keeping the concerns of the child and family as the primary focus of transitions, service providers can balance their loss with the family's gains.

REFERENCES

Adams, G. (1995). *How Safe? The status of state efforts to protect children in child care.* (ERIC Document Reproduction Service No. ED 406059).

Ainsworth, M. D. S., Blehar, M., Waters, E., & Wall, E. (1978). *Patterns of attachment: A psychological study of the strange situation.* Hillsdale, N.J.: Erlbaum.

Armenta, F. (1993). The family. In *First steps: A handbook for teaching young children who are visually impaired* (pp. 35–56). Los Angeles: Blind Children's Center.

Bailey, D. B., & Blasco, P. M. (1990). Parent's perspectives on a written survey of family needs. *Journal of Early Intervention, 14,* 196–203.

Bailey, D. B., & Wolery, M. (1992). *Teaching infants and preschoolers with disabilities* (2nd ed.). New York: Macmillan.

Barnas, M. V., & Cummings, E. M. (1994). Caregiver and toddlers' attachment-related behavior towards caregivers in day care. *Infant Behavior and Development 17,* 141–147.

Belsky, J. (1988). Infant day care and socioemotional development: The United States. *Journal of Child Psychology and Psychiatry, 29,* 397–406.

Blasco, P. M. (1995). Understanding the emotional and behavioral development of young children: Birth to three years. In T. J. Zirpoli (Ed). *Understanding and affecting the behavior of young children* (pp. 34–59). Englewood Cliffs, N.J.: Merrill.

Bowlby, J. (1982). *Attachment and loss.* New York: Basic Books.

Bredekamp, S. (1993). *Developmentally appropriate practice in early childhood programs serving children from birth through age 8.* Washington, D.C.: National Association for the Education of Young Children.

Bredekamp, S., (1995). What do early childhood professionals need to know and be able to do? *Young Children, 50*(2), 67–69.

Bredekamp, S., & Copple, C. (1998). Developmentally appropriate practice in early childhood programs (rev. ed.). Washington, D.C.: National Association for the Education of Young Children.

Bricker, D., Pretti-Frontczak, K., & McComas, N. (1998). *An activity-based approach to early intervention* (2nd ed.). Baltimore: Paul H. Brookes.

Bronfenbrenner, U. (1979). *The ecology of human development: Experiments by nature and design.* Cambridge: Harvard University Press.

Bruder, M. B. (1998). A collaborative model to increase the capacity of child care providers to include young children with disabilities. *Journal of Early Intervention, 21,* 177–186.

Bruder, M. B., & Staff, I. (1998). A comparison of the effects of type of classroom and service characteristics on toddlers with disabilities. *Topics in Early Childhood Special Education, 18*(1), 26–37.

Bryant, D. M., and Graham, M. A. (1993) *Implementing early intervention.* New York: Guilford Press.

Calvello, G. (1990). The art of home visiting. In F. Otto (Ed.), *Parents and visually impaired infants* (10 pp.). Louisville, Ky.: American Printing House for the Blind.

Carta, J., Elliot, M., Orth-Lopes, L., Scherer, H., Schwartz, I., & Atwater, J. (1992). *Skills for learning independence in diverse environments: Project SLIDE.* Lawrence, Kans.: The University of Kansas Juniper Gardens Children's Project.

Chan, S. (1998). Families with Asian roots. In E. W. Lynch and M. J. Hanson (Eds.), *Developing cross-cultural competence: A guide for working with young children and their families* (pp. 251–344). Baltimore: Paul H. Brookes.

Chen, D., Friedman, C. T., & Calvello, G. (1990). Learning together: A parent guide to socially based routines for visually impaired infants. In F. Otto (Ed.), *Parents and visually impaired infants* (29 pp.). Louisville, Ky.: American Printing House for the Blind.

Children's Defense Fund. (1999). *The state of America's children yearbook.* Washington, D.C.: Author.

Cook, R. E., Tessier, A., & Klein, M. D. (2000). *Adapting early childhood curricula for children in inclusive settings* (5th ed.). Englewood Cliffs, N.J.: Merrill.

Corey, G., Corey, M. S., & Callanan, P. (1993). *Issues and ethics in the helping professions* (4th ed.). Pacific Grove, Calif.: Brooks/Cole.

CEC standard for professional practice in special education (1994). Reston, Va.: Council for Exceptional Children.

Dee-Tourdot, D. S. (1995). *Classroom transition strategies in early childhood.* Unpublished master's thesis. St Paul, Minn.: University of St. Thomas.

Doss, B., & Hatcher, B. (1996). Self-determination as a family affair: Parents' perspectives on self-determination. In D. J. Sands & M. L. Wehmeyer (Eds.), *Self-determination across the lifespan* (pp. 51–63). Baltimore: Paul H. Brookes.

Dunst, C. J., Trivette, C., & Deal, A. (1988). *Enabling and empowering families: Principles and guidelines for practice.* Cambridge, Mass.: Brookline Books.

Elgas, P. M., & Barber Peltier, M. B. (1998). Jimmy's journey: Building a sense of community and self-worth through small group work. *Young Children, 53*(2), 17–21.

Fox, L., Hanline, M. F., Vail, C. O., & Galant, K. R. (1994). Developmentally appropriate practice: Applications for young children with disabilities. *Journal of Early Intervention, 18*(3), 243–257.

Fraiberg, S. H. (1959). *The magic years.* New York: Charles Scribner's Sons.

Greenman, J. (1988). *Caring spaces, learning places: Children's environments that work.* Redmond, Wash.: Exchange Press.

Hanson, M. J. (1992). Ethnic, cultural, and language diversity in intervention settings. In E. W. Lynch & M. J. Hanson (Eds.), *Developing cross-cultural competence: A guide for working with young children and their families.* Baltimore: Paul H. Brookes.

Harms, T., & Clifford, R. M. (1989). *The Family Day Care Rating Scale (FDCRS).* New York: Teachers College Press.

Harms, T., Cryer, D., & Clifford, R. M. (1990). *Infant/Toddler Environment Rating Scale (ITERS).* New York: Teachers College Press.

Howes, C., & Hamilton, C. E. (1992). Children's relationships with caregivers: Mother and child care teachers. *Child Development, 63,* 859–866.

Jones, S. N., & Meisels, S. J. (1987). Training family day care providers to work with special needs children. *Topics in Early Childhood Special Education* 7(1), 1–11.

Kjerland, L., & Corrigan Eide, K. (1990). *Project Dakota: Early intervention tailor-made.* Eagan, Minn.: Project Dakota Outreach.

Larson, N., Henthorne, M., & Plum, B. (1994). *Transition magician: Strategies for guiding young children in early childhood programs.* St. Paul, Minn.: Redleaf Press.

Levangie, P. K., Brouwer, J., McKeen, S. H., Parker, K. L., & Shelby, K. A. (1989). The effects of the standing rolling walker and two posterior rolling walkers on gait variables of normal children. *Physical and Occupational Therapy in Pediatrics, 9,* 1–17.

Lieberman, A. F. (1993). *The emotional life of the toddler.* New York: Free Press.

Lynch, E. W., & Hanson, M. J. (1998). *Developing cross-cultural competence: A guide from working with young children and their families.* Baltimore: Paul H. Brookes.

McEvoy, M. A., Fox, J. J., & Rosenberg, M. S. (1991). Organizing preschool environments: Suggestions for enhancing the development/learning of preschool children with handicaps. *Topics in Early Childhood Education, 11*(2), 18–28.

McWilliam, P. J. & Bailey, D. B. (1993). *Working together with children and families.* Baltimore: Paul H. Brookes.

Meyer, D. J., & Vadasy, P. F. (1994) *Sibshops: Workshops for siblings of children with special needs.* Baltimore: Paul H. Brookes.

National Association for the Education of Young Children (NAEYC). (1999). *Developing and implementing effective public policies to promote early childhood and school-age care program accreditation* [On-line]. Available: www.naeyc.org/accreditation/position/htm

National Center on Child Abuse and Neglect (1988). *Study of national incidence and prevalence of child abuse and neglect: 1988.* Washington, D.C.: U.S. Department of Health and Human Services.

Nwaobi, O. M., & Smith, P. D. (1986). Effect of adaptive seating on pulmonary function of children with cerebral palsy. *Developmental Medicine and Child Neurology, 28,* 351–354.

Odom, L. S., & McLean E. M. (1993). DEC recommended practices: Indicators of quality in programs for infants and young children with special needs and their families (pp. 96–103). Reston, Virg.: Division for Early Childhood of the Council for Exceptional Children.

Olds, D., & Kitzman, H. (1993). Review of research on home visiting for pregnant women and parents of young children. In R. E. Behrman (Ed.), *The future of children: Home visiting* (pp. 53–94). Los Altos, Calif.: Center for the Future of Children, David and Lucille Packard Foundation.

Olds, D. L., Henderson, C. R., Chamberlin, R., & Tatelbaum, R. (1986). Preventing child abuse and neglect: A randomized trial of nurse home visitation, *Pediatrics, 78,* 65–78.

Ostrosky, M., Skellenger, A. C., Odom, S. L., McConnell, S. R., & Peterson, C. (1994). Teachers' schedules and actual time spent in activities in preschool special education classes. *Journal of Early Intervention, 18*(1), 25–33.

Powell, D. R. (1993). Inside home visiting programs. In R. E. Behrman (Ed.), *The future of children, 3* (3) (pp. 23–38). Los Altos, Calif.: Center for the Future of Children, David and Lucille Packard Foundation.

Ramey, C. T., & Ramey, S. L. (1993). Home visiting program and the health and development of young children. In R. E. Behrman (Ed.), *The future of children: Home visiting* (pp. 127–139). Los Altos, Calif.: Center for the Future of Children, David and Lucille Packard Foundation.

Randall-David, E. (1989). *Strategies for working with culturally diverse communities and clients.* Washington, D.C.: Association for the Care of Children's Health.

Reamer, F. G. (1982). *Ethical dilemmas in social service.* New York: Columbia University Press.

Rinaldi, C. (1993). The emergent curriculum and social constructivism. In C. Edwards, L. Gandini, & G. Forman (Eds.), *The hundred languages of children* (pp. 101–111). Greenwich, Conn.: Ablex.

Rivkin, M. S. (1995). *The great outdoors: Restoring children's right to play outside.* Washington, D.C.: National Association for the Education of Young Children.

Roberts, R. N., Akers, A. L., & Behl, D. D. (1996). Family-level service coordination within home visiting programs. *Topics in Early Childhood Special Education, 16*(3), 279–301.

Roberts, R. N., Behl, D. D., & Akers, A. L. (1996). Community-level service integration within home visiting programs. *Topics in Early Childhood Special Education, 16*(3), 302–321.

Roberts, R. N., and Wasik, B. H. (1990). Home visiting programs for families with children birth to three: Results of a national survey. *Journal of Early Intervention, 14*(3), 274–284.

Rosenkoetter, E. S., Hains, H. A., Fowler, A. S. (1994). *Bridging early services for children with special needs and their families. A practical guide for transition planning.* Baltimore: Paul H. Brookes.

Sainato, D. M. (1990). Classroom transitions: Organizing environments to promote independent performance in preschool children with disabilities. *Education and Treatment of Children, 13,* 288–297.

Sainato, D. M., & Lyon, S. R. (1989). Promoting successful mainstreaming transitions for handicapped preschool children. *Journal of Early Intervention, 13,* 304–314.

Sainato, D. M., Strain, P. S., Lefebvre, D., & Rapp, N. (1987). Facilitating transition times with handicapped preschool children: A comparison between peer mediated and antecedent prompt procedures. *Journal of Applied Behavior Analysis, 20,* 285–292.

Sameroff, A. J., & Fiese, B. H. (1990). Transactional regulation and early intervention. In S. J. Meisels & J. P. Shonkoff (Eds.), *Handbook of early childhood intervention* (pp. 119–149). Cambridge: Cambridge University Press.

Turnbull, A. P., & Turnbull, H. R. (1988) Toward great expectations for vocational opportunities: Family-professional partnerships. *Mental Retardation, 26*(6), 337–342.

Turnbull, A. P., & Turnbull, H. R. (1990). *Families, professionals, and exceptionality: A special partnership* (2nd ed.). Columbus, Ohio: Merrill.

Wasik, B. H., Bryant, D. M., & Lyons, C. M. (1990). *Home visiting: Procedures for helping families.* Newbury Park, Calif.: Sage.

Wayman, K., Lynch, E., & Hanson, M. (1991). Home-based early childhood services: Cultural sensitivity in a family systems approach. *Topics in Early Childhood Special Education, 10,* 65–66.

Wesley, P., Buysse, V. (1994a). *Barriers and supports to early childhood inclusion.* Chapel Hill, N.C.: Frank Porter Graham Child Development Center.

Wesley, P., & Buysse, V. (1994b). *Self-assessment for child care professionals.* Chapel Hill, N.C.: Frank Porter Graham Child Development Center.

Willis, D. J., Holden, E. W., & Rosenberg, M. (1992). *Prevention of child maltreatment, Developmental and ecological perspectives.* New York: Wiley.

Winton, P. J. (1988). The family-focused interview: An assessment measure and goal-setting mechanism (pp. 185–205). In D. B. Bailey & R. J. Simeonsson (Eds.), *Family assessment in early intervention.* Columbus, Ohio: Merrill.

Zirpoli, S. B. (1995). Designing environments for optimal behavior. In T. J. Zirpoli (Ed.), *Understanding and affecting the behavior of young children* (pp. 122–151). Englewood Cliffs, N.J.: Merrill.

Zirpoli, T. J. (1986). Child abuse and children with handicaps. *Remedial and Special Education,* 7(2), 39–48.

Zirpoli, T. J. (1995). *Understanding and affecting the behavior of young children.* Englewood Cliffs, N.J.: Merrill.

CHAPTER SEVEN

CURRICULUM AND TEACHING STRATEGIES IN EARLY INTERVENTION

OBJECTIVES

- To apply knowledge of curriculum-recommended practices from both the Division for Early Childhood (DEC) and National Association for the Education of Young Children (NAEYC)
- To understand emergent curriculum and its implication for children with disabilities
- To understand individually appropriate skills and activities across ages for children with disabilities
- To understand the role of parents in designing and implementing curriculum objectives
- To be knowledgeable about the most current curriculum guides for infants and toddlers
- To understand the importance of skill acquisition, fluency, generalization, and maintenance
- To understand the use of milieu teaching strategies as well as prompting and modeling techniques to increase skill acquisition
- To understand the implementation of IFSP outcomes through functional curricula across settings (e.g., home, child care)
- To maintain ethical standards for instruction as specified by the Council for Exceptional Children (CEC) and the National Association for the Education of Young Children (NAEYC)

The behavior of children cannot be fragmented into isolated segments since play, exploration, and a variety of other activities continuously flow from one another.

—Hughes, 1991, p. 46

One of the most important aspects of service provision is supplying young children and their families with appropriate, functional activities that promote optimal growth and development for each child. It is important that service providers and families work together to identify outcomes that have meaning and relevance within the child's real-life environment of home and community (Cook, Tessier, & Klein, 2000; Kaiser, Hester, Harris-Solomon, & Keitiz, 1994). Young children are active learners and benefit from activities that promote multiple learning opportunities across developmental domains.

The statements above reflect the thrust of the theoretical beliefs as well as the policy that guide the development of curriculum in early intervention (Spodek & Brown, 1993). In order to meet the need of coordinated services for young children with disabilities and their families, professional organizations developed and refined standards for practice in early intervention (McLean & Odom, 1993; Odom, McLean, Johnson, & LaMontagne, 1995). The Division for Early Childhood (DEC) of the Council for Exceptional Children (CEC) offered recommended practices for curriculum and intervention (McLean and Odom, 1993) that include the following:

- Support and encouragement of family values and participation
- Responsiveness to infants'/childrens' interests, preferences, motivation, interactional styles, developmental status, learning histories, cultural variables, and level of participation
- Ability to integrate information and strategies from different disciplines
- Provision of structured learning activities in all relevant environments
- Ability to select a balance between child- and adult-initiated/directed activities
- Ability to integrate skills from various domains within routine activities in the classroom
- Ability to design a plan for the acquisition (initial learning, fluency, proficiency), maintenance (retention), and generalization (application, utilization across settings) of important outcomes or goals

As stated in Chapter 6, given the number of families with both parents (over 60 percent) in the workforce (Children's Defense Fund, 1999), and the emphasis on inclusion practice for children in child care settings, it is important to consider curriculum designed for all young children in these settings. The National Association for the Education of Young Children (NAEYC) has established guidelines for curricula that promote recommended practice for all young children, including the following:

- Address a broad range of content that is relevant, engaging, and meaningful to children.
- Respect and support individual, cultural, and linguistic diversity.
- Support and encourage positive relationships with children's families.
- Provide conceptual frameworks for children so that their mental constructions based on prior knowledge and experience become more complex over time.
- Focus on a particular topic or content while allowing for integration across traditional subject-matter divisions by planning around themes and/or learning experiences that provide opportunities for rich conceptual development.
- Provide for development across domains—physical, emotional, social, cognitive, and psychological—through an integrated approach.
- Strengthen children's sense of competence and enjoyment of learning by providing experiences for them to succeed from their point of view.
- Enable teachers to adapt to individual children or groups. (Bredekamp & Rosegrant, 1995, p. 16)

EMERGENT CURRICULUM

Curriculum that develops when exploring what is "socially and culturally relevant, engaging, and important to a young child is referred to as emergent curriculum" (Gestwicki, 1999). In the field of early education, this type of curriculum is considered recommended practice. Ideas for curriculum emerge from interactions within a particular environment, by a particular group of children and adults. Although children's interests are followed, the values and concerns of all those involved (including staff and parents) help to form the classroom culture (Cassidy & Lancaster, 1993). Thus a service provider or parent may follow up on a child's ideas by introducing new materials to sustain his or her interest and engagement.

Infants and toddlers with disabilities may require more flexibility and adaptability on the part of service providers when using curricula (Wolery, Werts, & Holcombe, 1994). Ongoing opportunities for young children to learn and practice skills should be available at intervals throughout the day during naturally occurring routines (Bricker, Patti-Frontczak, & McComas, 1998). Outcomes should be incorporated into all daily activities, as specified by the family (Cook et al., 2000).

ENVIRONMENTAL CONSIDERATIONS

In Chapter 6, we discussed the impact of the environment on young children's learning. For infants and toddlers, this environment is typically the home, a child care center, or a family day care arrangement. Providing services in natural environments that are effective, efficient, and nonintrusive follows the original intent of normalization (Bailey & McWilliam, 1990). The normalization principle promotes services that build on naturally occurring routines and events in the child's life. All routines have a beginning (preparation stage), middle (participation stage), and end (termination stage) (Stremel, Matthews, Wilson, & Holston, 1992). Functional, developmentally appropriate activities can be naturally grouped into each stage. In Vignette 7.1, an interactive game between a father and his eight-month-old son demonstrates all three stages.

VIGNETTE 7.1 PEEK-A-BOO

Tony was born 10 weeks premature after a difficult labor. By three months of age, his parents knew that something was not right. Tony was very stiff and hard to hold. He was diagnosed with cerebral palsy after a visit to the local pediatrician and a follow-up visit to a developmental clinic. Tony and his parents began to receive services from an early intervention program in the home. As part of the IFSP, Susan (the occupational therapist), and the family wanted to try simple interaction games. Gary, the dad, liked to play peek-a-boo with Tony because when he smiled his entire face lit up. Today, Gary was in a hurry to get to work, but as he approached Tony, who was still lying in his crib, he looked down and smiled. Tony focused on his father's face in anticipation of interaction. Gary slowly brought his tie up to cover his eyes and said, "Peek-a-boo!" Tony instantly smiled and shrieked, ready to enter the game. He batted at the tie each time Gary brought it to his face. When the game was over, his father said gently, "All done. Daddy has to go to work. Bye-bye, big boy."

In this vignette, the simple interaction between Tony and Gary had a stage-setting time, a play time, and an ending. Although the activity was brief, it occurred in a natural setting when both Tony and Gary would be highly interested in a successful interaction. Service providers can help families realize that activities and learning experiences do not have to be regimented for most young children. Learning should be fun and conducted at a time that is convenient and natural for the family.

Today there are many commercial curriculum guides that promote functional and individually appropriate activities for young children from birth to three (Johnson-Martin, Jens, Attermeier, & Hacker, 1991; Linder, 1993; Bricker, 1993). These curricula provide excellent assistance with designing intervention strategies, but, as with other products, the user must be aware of individual differences and responses. Curriculum guides are most useful when the users can adapt the activities to reflect the individual preferences of the child and family. As Sandall (1993) stated, "Curricular sequences help interventionists to organize and plan intervention, but rigid adherence to particular sequences may be counterproductive" (p. 137).

Table 7.1 summarizes the various curricula available today.

When purchasing a curriculum, it is important to consider the long-term benefits of using the materials with children and families. Curriculum books are increasingly expensive and many require that assessment tools and videos be purchased as a package. Table 7.2 provides a guide for deciding which curriculum best fits your program and team needs.

Whether services are provided in the home or in a center-based program, planning for effective, efficient learning opportunities is important. Several steps should be taken before implementing an intervention program. The team should:

- Determine the child's present level of performance
- Identify the child's strengths, interests, and concerns
- Identify family priorities and concerns
- Inventory the child's routines and daily schedule
- Identify multiple learning opportunities throughout the day and across settings
- Identify teaching strategies and materials, making sound decisions regarding curriculum implementation
- Identify team members who can help with implementation
- Implement the intervention and monitor its effectiveness with the team

Adapted from Bailey & Wolery, 1992; Bricker, Pretti-Frontczak, & McComas, 1998.

The IFSP provides a framework for developing lesson plans based on the above components. The team, including the family, should gather ideas for activities based on the outcomes identified in the IFSP. Vignette 7.2 sets the stage for the lesson plan, which is presented in Box 7.1.

TABLE 7.1 Curriculum Guide for Early Services

TITLE	AUTHOR	DATE	PUBLISHER	AGES	PARENTS AS PARTNER	DOMAINS	STRATEGIES	ASSESS LOG
AEPS Curriculum for Birth to Three Years	Cripe, Sluntz, & Bricker	1993	Paul H. Brookes	birth–3	yes	all domains	yes	yes; separate book; also progress charts
Active Learning for Infants, Ones, Twos, and Threes	Cryer, Harms, & Bourland	1987	Addison-Wesley	birth–3	yes	communication, physical/creative	yes	no
Carolina Curriculum for Infants and Toddlers with Special Needs	Johnson-Martin, Jens, Attermier, & Hacker	1991	Paul H. Brookes	birth–3	yes	all domains	yes	yes; separate protocol; also progress charts
Creative Play Activities*	Morris & Schulz	1989	Human Kinetics Books	birth–8	yes	senses, movement, outdoor play	yes	no
Help at Home	Parks et al.	1991	Vort	birth–3	yes	all domains	yes	yes
Instructional Activities for Children at Risk	Dolimar, Boser, and Holm	1994	DLM	2–6	no	all domains	yes	no
Teaching Young Children Using Themes	Kostelnik et. al.	1991	Goodyear Books	2–6	no	themes: social science, numbers, language	no	no
Transdisciplinary Play-Based Intervention	Linder	1993	Paul H. Brookes	birth–5	yes	all domains, including mastery motivation	yes	yes; separate assessment book

*For children with disabilities

TABLE 7.2 Choosing a Curriculum

QUESTION	YES	NO
Is the curriculum developmentally and age appropriate?	_____	_____
What strategies for modeling does the curriculum use?	_____	_____
Can the curriculum be used with various group sizes?	_____	_____
Can the curriculum be implemented by parents/caregivers?	_____	_____
Is the curriculum culturally sensitive to all families?	_____	_____
Are assessment procedures included?	_____	_____
Does the curriculum include supportive, instructive materials such as a videotape or CD-ROM?	_____	_____
Are strategies that promote generalization and maintenance of skills included?	_____	_____
Is the cost of the curriculum reasonable?	_____	_____

Adapted from "Social Skills Curriculum Analysis" by J. Carter and G. Sugai, 1989, *Teaching Exceptional Children, 22*(1), 36–39.

VIGNETTE 7.2 JOHN AND MOMMA

John is a 13-month-old with Klippel-Feil syndrome. He has congenital fusion of the first through fourth cervical vertebrae. This results in very limited range of motion of his neck. Associated conditions include a soft cleft palate and maldevelopment of the inner ear. Thus John was also diagnosed with a severe sensorineural hearing loss and now has a body-mounted hearing aid. John's use of the body aid is inconsistent due to his activity as an infant. He is starting to pull to a stand and uses his hands to manipulate toys. He uses pointing, head nodding, and natural gestures to get his needs met. He has learned a few signs, including "Mom," "Dad," and "bird" (the family pet).

The service provider and John's family planned some activities that could easily be implemented at home, in a child care center, or in the community. Since both parents work full-time, the service provider gave them a copy of the plan so the family day care provider could also try it.

The lesson plan was designed to enhance both infant and family participation. The service provider used visual and auditory cueing as well as a natural game between participants. The activity is easy to implement across environments and results in a pleasurable interaction for both the mother and the child. In addition, the materials used are generally found in the home and are not costly or difficult to obtain. Service providers should always consider both cost and familiarity of use when choosing materials for young children and families.

BOX 7.1

LESSON PLAN FOR JOHN AND HIS FAMILY

Outcome: To help John notice and turn to auditory, visual, and tactile events.

Name of activity: Where is Momma?

Purpose of the activity: To improve the child's orientation to auditory, visual, and tactile stimuli in order to comprehend and develop verbal language and/or sign language.

Materials: rattles, drum, music box, squeeze toys

Procedures:

1. Position the child on the floor on his tummy (prone) or back (supine), sitting or in an infant seat.
2. Mother presents a noisemaking object (i.e., bell, rattle, squeeze toy, drum) close to child and within visual range (approximately three feet).
3. Mother holds the object up to her face and encourages the child to make eye contact through use of vocal cues: "Where's Momma?"
4. After the child makes eye contact, verbally praise the child, nod head, and then touch the child's hands or feet.
5. Allow the child to touch the object and demonstrate to the child how to make the object produce a sound.
6. Incorporate a song to the tune of "Thumbkin," using different voice intonations and pitch to encourage play.

    Where is Momma?
    Where is Momma?
    Here I am.
    Here I am.
    Shake the rattle for me.
    Shake the rattle for me.
    Give it to John.

Variations:

1. The caregiver approaches the child from behind or to the side and calls his name. A noisemaking toy can be used as an additional auditory stimulus.
2. The caregiver moves into the child's line of sight while saying, "Where's Momma?"

For children with severe to profound hearing loss, use a vibrating tactile cue, for example, knocking on the wall, stamping your foot on each step while calling his name and using sign language.

Contributed by Diane Dee-Tourdot, Minneapolis, Minn.: Minneapolis Public Schools, Birth-to-three team.

Other considerations for selecting materials include the following:

- Do they focus on functional behaviors and skills that the child needs to be successful in multiple environments (home, community, center-based program)?
- Are they multipurpose and adaptable? Do they elicit a range of developmentally appropriate responses?
- Do they promote social interaction with either a caregiver or other children?
- Do they promote the efficient learning of important outcomes?
- Are they culturally sensitive and relevant to the individual child?

(Adapted from Bailey & McWilliam, 1990; Rettig, Kallam, & McCarthy-Salm, 1993)

All intervention strategies should result in skill acquisition, fluency, maintenance, and generalization. Skill acquisition refers to the learning of new skills. Fluency refers to a smooth demonstration of the new skill at each observation (Bailey & Wolery, 1992). Once the child has learned the skill, he or she needs to show that the skill can be used in other situations with other people. Maintenance refers to the degree of change in behavior over time following skill acquisition (Zirpoli & Melloy, 1996). Generalization refers to the degree of change in behavior that transfers to other settings, situations, and materials. Maintenance and generalization may not occur spontaneously and must be included in the design of an instructional strategy. The service provider can provide natural opportunities for generalizing in other settings and to other persons or materials.

TEACHING STRATEGIES TO ENHANCE CURRICULUM DEVELOPMENT

In order to establish generalization and maintenance, teaching strategies have been developed to prompt and reinforce the behavior of young children. According to Wolery, Werts, and Holcombe (1994), "although a balance should be maintained between the child- and teacher-initiated activities, the value of teacher-guided learning is especially important for young children with disabilities." (p. 7) This statement seems applicable to all service providers working with young children with disabilities and their families. For many children with disabilities, strategies that include behavioral dimensions such as intermittent reinforcement, variable stimuli, and trials to increase skill acquisition may be necessary. Service providers can provide a scaffold to help the child maximize his or her potential across developmental domains. As discussed in Chapter 4, Vygotsky (1962) advocated the "zone of proximal development" as the window in which the child can learn and continue to grow. If we encourage the child to perform at a level too far above or too far below his or her ability, we miss this window of learning opportunity.

Direct Instruction Versus Naturalistic Teaching Approaches

The direct instruction method tends to be adult-directed and offers little room for flexibility in terms of instructional objectives. However, many of the more recent activity-based interventions combine strategies from direct instruction with strategies for early childhood (Bricker et al., 1992). These strategies include various prompting systems and other methods for eliciting appropriate responses. It is important when choosing strategies to apply the most naturalistic approach with young children. Naturalistic teaching approaches occur in the natural environment, can be child- or adult-initiated, and use natural consequences (Kaiser, Ostrosky, & Alpert, 1993).

System of Least Prompts

The system of least prompts is a response-prompting procedure that is effective in teaching a variety of skills linked together through a series of events (Wolery, Ault, & Doyle, 1992). This technique consists of a target stimulus, a prompt hierarchy of least-to-most assistance, an opportunity to respond independently at each level of the hierarchy, and an opportunity for positive reinforcement (Wolery et al., 1992).

An example of the least prompt system is described in Vignette 7.3.

VIGNETTE 7.3 HOLD YOUR HEAD UP

During a home visit, Mary, the occupational therapist, worked with Vicki, the mother, to help Kenisha hold her head up when lying on her tummy (prone). Mary would place a bright red toy apple in front of Kenisha. Then she gently shook the apple so it would make a soft chime. Kenisha showed signs of alertness but did not pick up her head. Mary shook the apple again while Vicki said, "Kenisha, look at my apple." When Kenisha still did not move, Mary waited 10 seconds and then placed her hands gently on Kenisha's shoulders, repeating, "Kenisha, look at my apple." She waited another 10 seconds for a response, then she gently applied pressure to Kenisha's shoulders and guided her head up. Once Kenisha had lifted her head, Mary placed one hand on her bottom to help maintain stability in the head-up position.

This strategy can be used with a task analysis so that an outcome objective can be broken down into a series of simple steps. The number of steps and the difficulty of each step are individually tailored to the needs of the child. In Vignette 7.3, Mary used a system of prompts, starting with a simple auditory cue (the least prompt), then adding a verbal cue, and finally providing physical assistance, to achieve the objective. During this task, the least intrusive prompt was used first. In other prompt systems, the most intrusive prompt may be used first and then faded over time. Finally, the task was a natural, pleasurable activity for Kenisha and her mother.

Simultaneous Prompting

Another natural teaching strategy that can fit into a natural sequence of events is simultaneous prompting (MacFarlane, Smith, Schuster, & Stevens, 1993), in which the service provider presents a prompt simultaneously with the target stimulus. The child is given an opportunity to respond and a correct response is reinforced. At other times, the service provider presents the target stimulus without the prompt to examine the child's response.

Violation of Expectancy

Another strategy that has been used successfully with young children is called violation of expectancy. The service provider may do something incorrectly or out of order for a routine (Bailey & Wolery, 1992), such as helping a toddler to put on a coat by holding the coat upside down. The adult might say, "Is this where your coat goes?" Toddlers will recognize the game and happily join in the fun. This is an excellent way to teach self-help skills. You can easily continue the game by asking, "Where do you put your [hat, gloves, etc.]?"

For this strategy to work, the child needs a solid cognitive understanding of the task. It will not work with a child who does not have the cognitive capability to understand change in routines and should not be used with children who are easily upset by a change in routine. For example, a child with autism may become confused and upset rather than participate in a learning opportunity.

Graduated Guidance

This strategy is more intrusive than some of the other strategies discussed above. However, graduated guidance has been used to teach children with autism to follow a photo schedule and remain on task for longer periods of time (MacDuff, Kasntz, & McClannahan, 1993). This procedure may require much assistance in the beginning. The amount of help is determined by observing the child's response (Noonan & McCormick, 1993). An infant with low muscle tone or poor muscle strength may need help holding a rattle. The service provider might bring the rattle into view and wait to see if the infant will reach for it. If the infant is unable to reach for the toy, the service provider may then use a physical prompt by placing her hand under the infant's elbow to move the hand forward. If the infant is unable to grasp the rattle, she may help the infant hold it by closing her hand over the infant's hand. As the infant becomes stronger, the amount of assistance is decreased.

MILIEU TECHNIQUES

Milieu teaching is a naturalistic approach that encompasses three types of teaching strategies: incidental teaching, mand (task or request)-model, and time delay. Intervention includes teaching opportunities that are infused into typical conversations that follow the child's interest (Warren, 1992). Milieu strategies have been used to teach parents methods of instruction for their infants and toddlers with language delays (Alpert & Kaiser, 1992; Kaiser, Hemmeter, Ostrosky, Alpert, & Hancock, 1995; Simser, 1993) and with children who have disabilities (Warren, Yoder, Gazdag, Kim, & Jones, 1993). Service providers trained in using environmental strategies with milieu teaching that incorporate augmentative communication systems have observed increases in total communication and the use of targets in three preschool-age children (Kaiser, Ostrosky, & Alpert, 1993). Although some parent training programs have been successful, it is important to include family-guided decision-making when designing any intervention program, and especially when developing strategies for use in daily routines (Stremel et al., 1992).

Milieu strategies that have been used to increase social interactions among infants and toddlers with disabilities include those designed to:

- use duplicate toys to encourage parallel play and modeling (imitation)
- use "social" toys (dolls, blocks, bells)
- use words to describe children's play
- use a peer model to demonstrate a play or interaction skill
- facilitate helping relationships among children

Adapted from Wittmer & Peterson, 1992.

Incidental Teaching

Hart and Risley (1975) originally described incidental teaching as the mutual interaction between an adult and a child that arises naturally within the context of a situation and/or setting. The interaction is child-initiated with the adult responding to the child's interest and cues.

Mand-Model

In this strategy the adult initiates a mand (task or request) related to something of interest to the child. The strategy builds on the child's focus of attention to guide the interaction. For example, a toddler is playing with a red truck by pushing it around a play town set up on the floor. The caregiver approaches and observes the child as she imitates a motor sound. The child looks up and continues to make motor noises. The caregiver smiles and says, "Oh, I see you are playing with something." The child responds by saying, "Car." The caregiver says, "That's right, car," and then expands the conversation: "You have a red car, I have a blue car. Where shall we go today?" If the child does not respond to the initial request, the teacher models the appropriate response. This strategy differs slightly from incidental teaching because the adult does not wait for the child to initiate the interaction (Noonan & McCormick, 1993).

Time Delay

This strategy can be used to increase the amount of time between the introduction of the stimulus and a cue. A cue is a type of prompt that gives a specific command. For example, a parent may say to his toddler, "Eat your food, please." He then waits five seconds before guiding the child's hand to pick up the food. For a child with a severe physical disability, a task analysis can be used to guide him through the steps necessary to bring food to his mouth (see Table 7.3).

When implementing a plan, the team needs to decide the amount of time between each step, and a method for handling correct and incorrect responses. By increasing the amount of time before the prompt is introduced, the service provider can gradually reduce the level of assistance (Bailey & Wolery, 1992; Snell,

TABLE 7.3 Task Analysis for a Toddler with Motor Difficulties

James will bring food to his mouth.

1. Give a verbal cue: *James, pick up the banana.*
2. Physically assist James as he picks up the food.
3. Give a verbal cue: *James, eat your food.*
4. Physically guide James's hand with the food to his mouth.
5. Give a verbal cue: *James, eat your food.*
6. Physically guide James's hand with the food to open his lips.
7. Give a verbal cue: *James, chew your food.*

1987). With infants and toddlers, verbal praise that specifies the correct response is a natural reinforcer. For example, the service provider or parent might say, "Good for you! You put the top on the box." If the child does not perform a step within a predetermined period of time, the adult provides assistance, either verbal, physical, or both, and then continues with the next step.

Naturalistic Time Delay. Time delay can be used to increase the amount of time between a natural prompt and a teaching prompt (Bailey & Wolery, 1992). For example, a toddler wants more milk and bangs her cup against the table. Her mother says, "Do you want more milk? Say, 'More.' " At the next occasion the child bangs her cup on the table, and the mother waits five seconds before introducing the prompt, "Say 'More.' " She continues to increase the time by five seconds until the toddler says, "More" by herself to the request "Do you want more milk?"

Whatever strategy is used, the team should plan for inappropriate responses. Although reinforcement is a powerful tool for teaching new behaviors, very young children do not have the ability to understand the meaning of withholding of reinforcement for inappropriate behavior. Service providers and parents may instead redirect the child from an inappropriate behavior. For example, a toddler who hits another toddler at the snack table may need to be reminded, "No, hitting, hitting hurts," and then be redirected toward a more constructive activity with a statement such as "Let's pour more milk for Amber."

PROMPTING STRATEGIES TO INCREASE PLAY BEHAVIOR

Strategies that can be used to increase play behavior include pointing to a toy, placing a toy in front of the child and removing other materials, offering the toy, and restructuring the toy's configuration (e.g., if the toy is upside down, turning it right side up). If the child does not respond actively, the adult can model a use for the toy, then ask the child to do it, or activate a toy partially and then let the child complete the task (this is called partial participation) (Lifter, 1993).

ACTIVITY-BASED INTERVENTION

Activity-based intervention is a curriculum approach that was adapted from the instruction of children with severe disabilities (Bruder, 1997). Bricker, Pretti-Frontczak, and McComas (1998) designed activity-based strategies that (1) promote active involvement of the learner; (2) facilitate learning through routines and natural opportunities; and (3) enhance learning through meaningful and functional activities. In addition, activity-based intervention utilizes a behavioral approach by defining antecedents and consequences of behavior and collecting data on a weekly, quarterly, and annual basis.

FAMILY-CENTERED CURRICULUM

Bailey (1997) described an adult-centered view of curriculum content. He suggested that curriculum activities are based on what the adult does or what the environment provides. Alternatively, a child-centered view focuses on what the child perceives or experiences. Bruder (1997) emphasized the importance of the family role in curriculum. A family-centered curriculum would include what the child and family members perceive or experience.

PARENTS AS PARTNERS

Most curricula designed for early intervention are child-centered. The tasks and outcomes designed in these curricula are focused on increasing the child's skills across developmental domains. However, if parents and other caregivers are to be included as partners in early intervention, then curricula should include the family as part of the intervention plan.

A part of curricula unique to early intervention are materials that include parent-child interaction. Since Bell's (1968) seminal paper on parent-infant reciprocity, both researchers and practitioners have recognized the importance of the partnership between the parent and the child during interaction. There needs to be a match between parental intent and the child's response or vice versa for a successful interaction (Sameroff & Fiese, 1990). The transactional model of development described the parent and child as active participants who continue to affect one another's behaviors and renegotiate the partnership (Sameroff & Chandler, 1975; Sameroff & Fiese, 1990).

Early research on parent-child interactions and on children with disabilities often described parents as ineffective partners who could not "read" their child's behaviors and interactive style. However, more recent studies have shown that many parents are able to match their interactive behavior to the needs of their child despite the disability (Baird, Haas, McCormick, Carruth, & Turner, 1992; Blasco, Hrncir, & Blasco, 1990; Hauser-Cram, 1996). The assessment of parent-child interaction was discussed in Chapter 5.

In reviewing the extensive literature on parent-child interaction, it is evident that parents' education and socioeconomic status (SES) are related to levels of appropriate developmental play for children at risk, including children who were born premature and had low birthweight (Bailey, 1997; Fewell, Casal, Glick, Wheeden, & Spiker, 1996). The impact of prenatal (e.g., substance abuse, smoking) and postnatal risk factors (attachment issues) were discussed in Chapters 2, 3, and 4 respectively.

Families will vary in how they use both formal and informal resources and in how they define their concerns to other members of the intervention team. In addition, cultural differences may dictate interactive behavior that may not be viewed as appropriate by members of the mainstream culture.

Thus targeting family members for intervention remains controversial in the early intervention field. As members of the team, should parents determine to what extent they want to be involved directly in intervention? This question is asked as teams are struggling to meet both child and family outcomes. An additional concern is that some team members do not receive training in parent-child interaction and attachment theory. Thus it is important to seek the help of qualified personnel who have had training in both adult learning theory and family-child interaction.

Despite the controversy, service providers working with families cannot ignore a mismatch in parent-child interactive styles. Baird and colleagues (1992) used videotaping to help parents to examine their own interactive style and to identify those behaviors they would like to change and those behaviors of their child that are causing concerns. This strategy gives the interventionist the opportunity to provide recommendations without giving unsolicited advice about the partnership.

There is very little research on the impact of parent-child interaction on curricula. However, several commercial products are available that are geared toward helping parents work with their babies. These include the Partners for Learning (Sparling & Lewis, 1984); Help at Home (Parks et al., 1998); and Best Beginning (Hussey-Gardner, 1999). Both of these curriculum guides offer suggestions and guidelines for understanding the infant's behavior.

CURRICULUM INVENTORY

Even when you have found a curriculum that seems tried and true, it is important to evaluate it periodically to see what the child and family have gained from the experience. Some good questions to think about include:

- What are the features or sensory modalities of the materials that interest and sustain the attention of this child?
- What are the features or sensory modalities that do not attract or sustain the attention of this child?
- Are you currently using verbal or physical prompts to support appropriate problem-solving and engagement in activities? Should you fade support or add support in some areas?
- What level of mastery motivation is exhibited by the child? Does the child persist at problem-solving tasks, give up easily, or become frustrated when he cannot complete a task?
- Does the child exhibit "mastery pleasure" when a task is completed?
- Does the child ask for help (either verbal or physical) when appropriate?
- Does the family find the materials and tasks to be meaningful and appropriate?
- Do the materials and strategies reflect culturally responsive and developmentally appropriate content?

The information needed for a curriculum inventory can be gathered through multiple methods of observation. Examples of informal observation methods include the use of photographs, video, tape recordings, and anecdotal records. In Chapter 5, the various methods of using observations as assessment tools were discussed. These methods include checklists, rating scales, observation narratives (including anecdotal records), informal and formal assessment tools, and samples of children's work (portfolio).

In addition, many curriculum guides have assessment packets that include daily and long-term evaluation of skill acquisition. It is equally important to develop a generalization and maintenance plan. No skill is truly learned unless the child can generalize to other settings, behaviors, and persons. The following strategies promote generalization and maintenance of new behaviors:

- Provide learning opportunities within settings where the behavior is likely to occur and across multiple settings; avoid artificial and isolated teaching of skills.
- Implement learning opportunities among all caregivers who have regular contact with the child.
- Use natural stimuli that occur in the child's natural environment.
- Reinforce generalization and maintenance by telling the child when you notice generalization has occurred. For example, say, "That's right, you use the cup to drink."

All curricula and materials should be evaluated by the team on a continuing basis. This can be done by using formative evaluation, that is, data collected on a daily basis regarding progress of the individual child using a specific curriculum. Service providers should also collect summative evaluation information. This information looks at the overall effectiveness of the curriculum with groups of children. Both forms of evaluation will help the team make informed decisions regarding curriculum.

In providing services, professionals should be careful to offer only those services for which they are trained (Wasik, Bryant, & Lyons, 1990). This ethical standard also applies to implementing curricula. This is not to say that service providers should not engage in role release but that they should be well trained before implementing an activity.

When working in the home, such situations are inevitable, and professionals must be prepared for them (Wasik et al., 1990). Each service provider must be familiar with state and federal regulations regarding children's welfare. It is also helpful to meet with team members trained in crisis intervention. Every team should have a social worker and/or psychologist available for consultation. The impact of ethical issues and standards for ethical conduct were discussed in Chapter 6. It is important to apply these same standards to curricula and materials.

Service providers need to be aware of cultural differences and adapt curricula and materials accordingly. There are several resources available that address cultural diversity in curriculum. One important resource is CLAS (Cultural and Linguistically Appropriate Services, Early Childhood Research Institute, Office of Special Education Programs). This federally funded project provides descriptions and reviews of current early childhood materials and the potential usefulness of these materials with culturally and linguistically diverse children and families. Information is easily accessed through the Web site at *http://www.uius.edu/clas.* Some suggested questions for service providers include:

- How closely does the community you serve resemble those for whom the material was developed?
- Is the material based on assumptions, beliefs, or values that are agreeable to most members of the community you serve?
- Are the family or child roles described in the material consistent with those found in the community you serve?
- If the material is presented in a language other than English, does the language style and dialect match that of the community to be served?

Questions for family members include the following:

- How closely does your family or child resemble those for whom the material was developed?
- If you see many differences, how important are these differences to you?
- Does the material contain assumptions, beliefs, or values that are similar to those of your family?
- Does the language style and dialect match what your family uses?
- Does the material describe provider, family, or child roles that are similar to those in your family?
- Do you have the time, skills, and resources to use this material?

From CLAS (Culturally & Linguistically Appropriate Services) Web site.

TABLE 7.4 Culturally Sensitive Services

1. Reflect on your own cultural heritage and how it influences your life and work.
2. Build on your awareness of other cultures through literature, the media, community events.
3. Meet community leaders of various cultural groups and seek out friends from diverse cultural backgrounds.
4. Conduct a community inventory of the institutions (e.g., churches, food stores, clinics) that are utilized by families from culturally diverse backgrounds.
5. Learn to understand the communicative style of various cultures but don't overgeneralize.
6. Listen to families and respect their choices.
7. Help others see cultural differences as strengths, not weaknesses.
8. Ask questions when you are unsure or unclear. Families will forgive you for not knowing everything.
9. Seek out interpreters with a good understanding of early childhood development.
10. Learn to interpret both verbal and non-verbal communication.

Information from *Developing Cross-Cultural Competence: A Guide for Working with Young Children and Their Families,* 2nd ed., by E. W. Lynch and M. J. Hanson, 1998, Baltimore: Paul H. Brookes; and *Strategies for Working with Culturally Diverse Communities and Clients,* by E. Randall-David, 1992, Bethesda: The Association for the Care of Children's Health.

Table 7.4 provides cultural-sensitivity suggestions for service providers. These strategies help one to become comfortable with his or her own cultural identity.

Although most curricula designed today advocate culturally sensitive material and activities, it is still possible to find materials that are insensitive to different cultural groups or family definitions. This is particularly true when choosing computer software for very young children. Most software is developed for traditional Caucasian, middle-class families, and these programs can inadvertently be insensitive to cultural differences. For example, service providers in one Midwestern town were unable, due to a schoolwide policy, to use software they purchased to teach language skills because there were no culturally diverse role models in the program. It is a good idea to preview materials before using them with families.

SUMMARY

This chapter examined current practices in developing curricula for service providers working with young children and their families. In order to make an impact on a child's individual learning styles, curricula must be flexible, functional, and adaptable. Organizations that support the education of young children, including NAEYC and DEC, offer guidelines on curricula. Whether new to the field or practicing for several years, service providers need to be aware of recommended practices and keep current with changing curricula trends. As pointed out by Cook, Tessier, & Klein (2000), early intervention and early childhood special education are evolving fields. Each decade brings new challenges and new ideas for curriculum development.

Today, many commercial curriculum guides promote functional and individually appropriate activities for young children from birth to age three. It is important to be flexible and adapt materials and activities to individual needs. Service providers should involve family members in planning and implementing services as stipulated by federal law. The IFSP is a document that is family-driven. There should be a match between IFSP-identified outcomes and the choice of curriculum materials.

Service providers should continue to reflect on their own teaching strategies to see if they are meeting the needs of each child and family. Intervention strategies should be recorded through one or several methods of observation. Record keeping and reevaluation are important for meeting the changing needs of children and their families.

Service providers should be mindful of ethical standards within their affiliated organizations, as well as state and federal guidelines. They should also attend to cultural differences when choosing activities and materials. Planning ahead with the family will help avoid potentially embarrassing sessions in which activities and materials are deemed culturally offensive by a family. Using activities and materials that are culturally sensitive and individually appropriate provides current recommended practices in the field today.

REFERENCES

Alpert, C., & Kaiser, A. (1992). Training parents as milieu language teachers. *Journal of Early Intervention, 16,* 31–52.

Bailey, D. B. (1997). Curriculum alternatives for infants and preschoolers. In M. J. Guralnick (Ed.),. *The effectiveness of early intervention* (pp. 227–247). Baltimore: Paul H. Brookes.

Bailey, D. B., & McWilliam, R. A. (1990). Normalizing early intervention. *Topics in Early Childhood Special Education, 10,* 33–47.

Bailey, D. B., McWilliam, R. A., Ware, W. B., & Burchinal, M. A. (1993). The social interactions of toddlers and preschoolers in same-age and mixed-age play groups. *Journal of Applied Developmental Psychology, 14,* 261–276.

Bailey, D. B., & Wolery, M. (1992). *Teaching infants and preschoolers with disabilities* (2nd ed.). Columbus, Ohio: Merrill.

Baird, S. M., Haas, L., McCormick, K., Carruth, C., & Turner, K. D. (1992). Approaching an objective system for observation and measurement: Infant-parent social interaction code. *Topics in Early Childhood Special Education, 12,* 544–571.

Bell, R. Q. (1968). A reinterpretation of the direction of effects in studies of socialization. *Psychological Review, 75,* 1171–1190.

Berk, L. E., & Winsler, A. (1995). *Scaffolding children's learning: Vygotsky and early childhood education*. Washington, D.C.: National Association for the Education of Young Children.

Blasco, P. M., Bailey, D. B., & Burchinal, M. A. (1993). Dimensions of mastery in same-age and mixed-age integrated classrooms. *Early Childhood Research Quarterly, 8,* 193–206.

Blasco, P. M., Hrncir, E., & Blasco, P. B. (1990). The contribution of maternal involvement to mastery performance in infants with cerebral palsy. *Journal of Early Intervention, 14,* 161–174.

Bredekamp, S. (1993). The relationship between early childhood education and early childhood special education: Healthy marriage or family feud? *Topics in Early Childhood Special Education, 13,* 258–273.

Bredekamp, S., & Rosegrant, T. (Eds.). (1995). *Reaching potentials: Transforming early childhood curriculum and assessment* (Vol. 2). Washington, D.C.: National Association for the Education of Young Children.

Bricker, D. (1993). *Assessment, evaluation, and programming system for infants and young children* (Vol. 1). *AEPS measurement for birth to three.* Baltimore: Paul H. Brookes.

Bricker, D., Pretti-Frontczak, K., & McComas, N. (1998). *An activity-based approach to early intervention* (2nd ed.). Baltimore: Paul H. Brookes.

Bruder, M. B. (1997). Curriculum for children with disabilities. In M. Guralnick (Ed.), *The effectiveness of early intervention* (pp. 523–548). Baltimore: Paul H. Brookes.

Cassidy, D., & Lancaster, C. (1993, September). The grassroots curriculum: A dialogue between children and teachers. *Young Children, 48*(5), 47–51.

Children's Defense Fund. (1999). *The state of America's children yearbook.* Washington, D.C.: Author.

Cook, R. E., Tessier, A., & Klein, M. D. (2000). *Adapting early childhood curricula for children in inclusive settings* (5th ed). Englewood Cliffs, N.J.: Merrill.

Cripe, J., Slentz, K., & Bricker, D. (1993). *Assessment, evaluation, and planning system for infants and children: Curriculum for birth to three years.* Baltimore: Paul H. Brookes.

Dolinar, K., Boser, C., & Holm, E. (1994). *Learning through play: Curriculum and activities for the inclusive classroom.* Albany: Delmar.

Doyle, P., Gast, D., Wolery, M., Ault, M., & Farmer, J. (1990). Use of constant time delay in small group instruction: A study of observational and incidental learning. *Journal of Special Education, 23,* 369–385.

Fewell, R. R., Casal, S. G., Glick, M. P., Wheeden, C. A., & Spiker, D. (1996). Maternal education and maternal responsiveness as predictors of play competence in low birth weight, premature infants: A preliminary report. *Developmental and Behavioral Pediatrics, 17,* 100–104.

Fox, L., & Hanline, M. (1993). A preliminary evaluation of learning within developmentally appropriate early childhood settings. *Topics in Early Childhood Special Education, 13,* 308–327.

Gestwicki, C. (1999). *Developmentally appropriate practice: Curriculum and development in Early Education* (2nd ed.). Albany, N.Y.: Delmar.

Hanson, M. J., & Lynch, E. W. (1989). *Early intervention: Implementing child and family services for infants and toddlers who are at-risk or disabled.* Austin, Tex.: Pro-ed.

Hart, B., & Risley, T. (1975). Incidental teaching language in the pre-school. *Journal of Applied Behavior Analysis, 8,* 411–420.

Hauser-Cram, P. (1996). Mastery motivation in toddlers with developmental disabilities. *Child Development, 67,* 236–248.

Hughes, F. P. (1991). *Children, play, and development.* Boston: Allyn & Bacon.

Hussey-Gardner, B. (1999). *Best beginning: Helping parents make a difference through individualized anticipatory guidance (Birth to three).* Palo Alto, Calif.: Vort.

Johnson-Martin, N., Jens, K., Attermeier, S., & Hacker, B. (1991). *The Carolina curriculum for infants and toddlers with special needs* (2nd ed.). Baltimore: Paul H. Brookes.

Kaiser, A. P., Hemmeter, M. L., Ostrosky, M. M., Alpert, C. L., & Hancock, T. B. (1995). The effects of group training and individual feedback on parent use of milieu teaching. *Journal of Childhood Communication Disorders, 16,* 39–48.

Kaiser, A., Hester, P., Harris-Solomon, A., & Keitiz, A. (June, 1994). *Enhanced milieu teaching: An analysis of applications by interventionists and classroom teachers.* Paper presented at the 118th Annual Meeting of the American Association on Mental Retardation, Boston, Mass.

Kaiser, A. P., Ostrosky, M. M., & Alpert, C. L. (1993). Training teachers to use environmental arrangement and milieu teaching with nonvocal preschool children. *Journal of the Association for Persons with Severe Handicaps, 18*(3), 188–199.

Lifter, K., Sulzer-Azaroff, B., Anderson, S., & Cowdery, G. (1993). Teaching play activities to preschool children with disabilities: The importance of developmental considerations. *Journal of Early Intervention, 2,* 139–159.

Linder, T. (1993). *Transdisciplinary play-based intervention: Guidelines for developing a meaningful curriculum for young children.* Baltimore: Paul H. Brookes.

Lynch, E. W., & Hanson, M. J. (1998). *Developing cross-cultural competence: A guide for working with young children and their families* (2nd ed.). Baltimore: Paul H. Brookes.

MacDuff, G., Kasntz, P., & McClannahan, L. (1993). Teaching children with autism to use photographic activity schedules: Maintenance and generalization of complex response chains. *Journal of Applied Behavior Analysis, 26* (1), 89–97.

MacFarlane-Smith, J., Schuster, J., & Stevens, K. (1993). Using simultaneous prompting to teach expressive object identification to preschoolers with developmental delays. *Journal of Early Intervention, 17,* 50–60.

McCollum, J. A., & Stayton, V. D. (1985). Infant/parent interaction: Studies and intervention guidelines based on the SIAI model. *Journal of the Division of Early Childhood, 9,* 125–135.

McLean, M. E, & Odom, S. L. (1993). Practices for young children with and without disabilities: A comparison of DEC and NAEYC identified practices. *Topics in Early Childhood Special Education, 13*(3), 274–292.

Noonan, M. J., & McCormick, L. (1993). *Early intervention in natural environments: Methods and procedures.* Belmont, Calif.: Brooks/Cole.

Odom, S. L., McLean, M. E., Johnson, L. J., & LaMontagne, M. J. (1995). Recommended practices in early childhood special education: Validation and current use. *Journal of Early Intervention, 19*(1), 1–17.

Parks, S., Furuno, S., O'Reilly, K., Hosaka, C., Inatsuka, T., & Zeisloft-Talby, B. (1998). *Hawaii early learning profile at home.* Palo Alto, Calif.: Vort.

Rettig, M., Kallam, M., McCarthy-Salm, K. (1993). The effect of social and isolate toys on social interactions of preschool-aged children. *Education and Training in Mental Retardation, 28,* 258–256.

Sameroff, A. J., & Chandler, M. J. (1975). Reproductive risk and the continuum of caretaking casualty. In F. D. Horowitz, M. Hetherington, S. Scarr-Salapatek, & G. Siegel (Eds.), *Review of child development literature* (pp. 187–244). Chicago: University of Chicago Press.

Sameroff, A. J., & Fiese, B. H. (1990). Transactional regulation and early intervention. In S. J. Meisels & J. P. Shonkoff (Eds.), *Handbook of early childhood intervention* (pp. 119–149). Cambridge: Cambridge University Press.

Sandall, S. (1993). Curricula for early intervention. In W. Brown, S. K. Thurman, & L. F. Pearl (Eds.), *Family-centered early intervention with infants and toddlers: Innovative cross-disciplinary approaches* (pp. 129–151). Baltimore: Paul H. Brookes.

Simser, J. (1993). Auditory-verbal intervention: Infants and toddlers. *Volta-Review, 95*(3), 217–229.

Snell, M. E. (1987). *Systematic instruction of persons with handicaps.* Columbus, Ohio: Merrill.

Sparling, J., & Lewis, I. (1984). *Partners for learning.* Lewisville, N.C.: Kaplan Press.

Spodek, B., & Brown, P. C. (1993). Curriculum alternatives in early childhood education. A historical perspective. In B. Spodek (Ed.), *Curriculum alternatives in early childhood education: A historical perspective* (pp. 91–104). New York: Macmillan.

Stremel, K., Matthews, P., Wilson, R., Holston, J. (December, 1992). *Facilitating infant/toddler skills in family-child routines.* Paper presented at the Division for Early Childhood Conference, Washington, DC.

Vygotsky, L. S. (1962). *Thought and language* (E. Hanfmann & G. Vaker, Trans.) Cambridge: Massachusetts Institute of Technology Press.

Warren, S. F. (1992). Facilitating basic vocabulary acquisition with milieu teaching procedures. *Journal of Early Intervention,* 16(3), 235–251.

Warren, S. F., Yoder, P. J., Gazdag, G. E., Kim, K., & Jones, H. A. (1993). Facilitating prelinguistic communication skills in young children with developmental delay. *Journal of Speech and Hearing Research, 36,* 83–97.

Wasik, B. H., Bryant, D. M., & Lyons, C. M. (1990). *Home visiting: Procedures for helping families.* Newbury Park, Calif.: Sage.

Wittmer, D., & Peterson, S. (1992). Social development and integration: Facilitating the prosocial development of typical and exceptional infants and toddlers in group settings. *Zero to Three, 12,* 14–20.

Wolery, M., Ault, M. J., & Doyle, P. M. (1992). *Teaching students with moderate to severe disabilities: Use of response prompting strategies.* White Plains, N.Y.: Longman.

Wolery, M., Werts, M., & Holcombe, A. (1994). Current practices with young children who have disabilities: Placement, assessment, and instructional issues. *Focus on Exceptional Children, 26*(6), 1–12.

Zirpoli, T. J., & Melloy, K. J. (2001). *Behavior management: Applications for teachers* (3rd ed.). Upper Saddle River, N.J.: Merrill.

CHAPTER EIGHT

MEDICAL CONSIDERATIONS

PETER A. BLASCO, M.D.

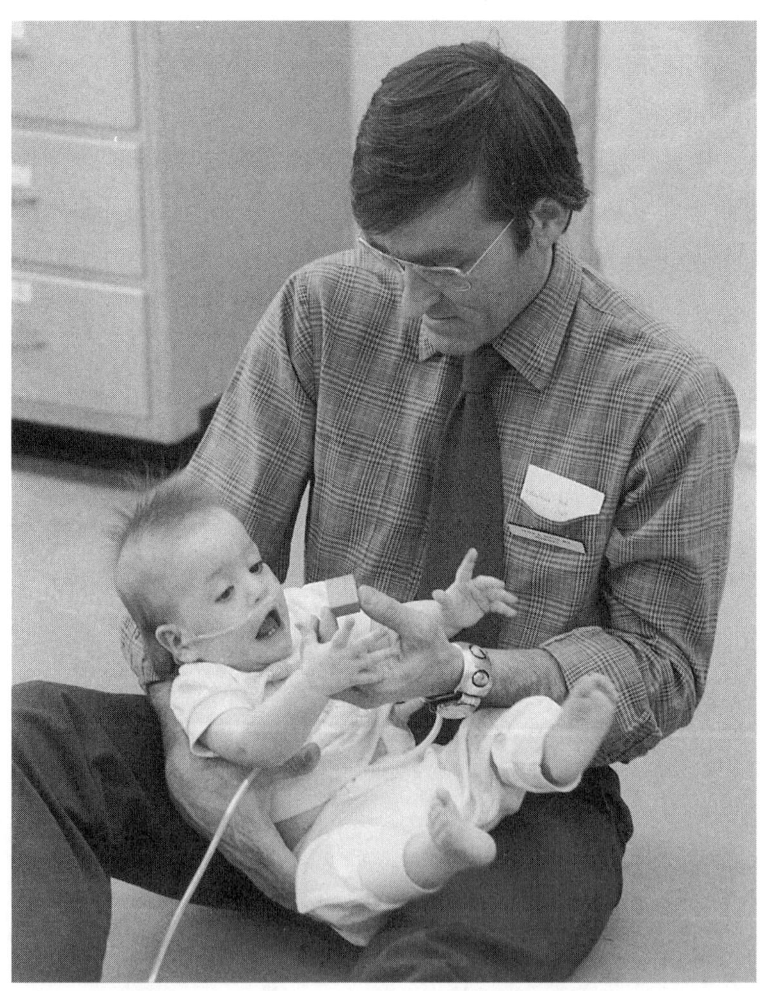

OBJECTIVES

- To recognize the different patterns of growth deficiency and their implications
- To review the spectrum of neurodevelopmental disabilities
- To review in depth the problem of cerebral palsy as a prototype for neurodevelopmental disability in general
- To understand the diagnostic approach to the enormous number of causes of disabilities
- To identify and define specific conditions unique to high-risk infants
- To understand aspects of medical assistive technology
- To review emergency first aid interventions relevant to children with disabilities
- To review important infectious disease considerations
- To go over some issues related to professional communication, including do not resuscitate (DNR) orders

Personnel working in early childhood programs are often faced with children and family issues that are distinctly different from those that primary school teachers are accustomed to with their special education students. The latter group traditionally comes to the attention of educational professionals because of learning and/or behavior problems. These older children with high-prevalence but low-severity disorders tend to have a minimum of medical needs. Diagnostically many of these children have the milder developmental disabilities (e.g., learning disabilities and attention deficit hyperactivity disorder [ADHD]), acquired emotional and behavioral problems, and to a lesser extent chronic medical conditions that by school age are almost always stable. Service providers working with the birth-to-three range, however, see a very different population of children.

Children who are identified early (i.e., during infancy) as being in need of intervention are likely to have neurodevelopmental problems that are more severe and more pervasive than those found in children who present later. In thinking about the medical issues that confront early intervention personnel, the contrast between low-prevalence/high-severity disorders and high-prevalence/low-severity disorders is an important consideration. The infant group often involves children with rare or uncommon conditions that tend to be both complex and severe in their manifestations. Hence, symptoms and signs appear and tend to be identified early. Medical complications and neurodevelopmental problems are prominent features and may even be life-threatening. They are often extremely difficult to manage. Minor acute illnesses, such as a simple upper respiratory infection (a routine "cold"), may severely affect the child's ability to perform or greatly disrupt otherwise stable health functions, such as breathing. Feeding problems and nutritional deficits may be primary factors that are most difficult to treat. These medical issues add an additional level of challenge for the early intervention team and may, indeed, be quite intimidating and anxiety-provoking. In addition, families of such children are typically facing a diagnosis for the first time and have had no prior experience with or even awareness of early intervention services.

The main intent of this chapter is to address the many medical considerations as they pertain to the natural environments of infants and toddlers (e.g., the home, child care center, and community) and to provide some structure for thinking about complex medical problems. A second goal is to provide information about and approaches to accessing and utilizing resources in the medical community that will enhance the relationship between service provider and health care professional and thereby improve everyone's ability to work with children who have various low-prevalence/high-severity disorders, and with their families. All of the case illustrations are real, although some are blended histories. The names of the children and families have all been changed to ensure confidentiality.

GROWTH AND DEVELOPMENT

When thinking about child development in the broadest terms, one usually begins under the encompassing umbrella of "growth and development":

1. Physical growth is precisely measured using standard parameters: height, weight, and head circumference. Occasionally additional measures are of significance, such as the ratio between the upper and lower body segments and skin-fold thickness. The conformation of the body is also examined, and abnormalities are described in terms of dysmorphic features (dysmorphisms).
2. Behavioral development is measured in terms of Gesell's traditional four streams: language, problem-solving, motor, and psychosocial (or affective) sequences of neurobehavioral maturation (Knobloch & Pasamanick, 1974).

The separation of physical growth and development from behavioral growth and development and the further splitting of behavior into four streams, or areas, are representative of the "medical model." This conceptual approach is applied widely in the medical neurodevelopmental world. It provides a very useful construct for logically approaching the child who is brought to the physician because he is viewed as being different in some way (delayed, small, unusual looking, etc.).

Measurement

In general, physical growth milestones are predictable, although they must be viewed within the context of each child's specific genetic and ethnic background. It is essential to plot the child's growth on gender and age-appropriate charts. Fetal weight gain is greatest during the third trimester. There is a continuation of this rapid growth during the first few months of life, after which growth decelerates. Whereas birth weight doubles by four to five months, height does not double until between three and four years of age (Hamill et al., 1979). Head growth during the first five or six months is due to continued neuronal cell division and is remarkably rapid. Later, increasing head size is due to neuronal cell growth and support tissue proliferation, and the rate of head growth decelerates.

Large and small head size are both relative red flags for developmental problems. Microcephaly, or small head size, is associated with an increased incidence of mental retardation, but there is no straightforward relationship between small head size and depressed intelligence. As a reflection of normal variation, microcephaly is not associated with structural pathology of the nervous system or with low intelligence. Furthermore, microcephaly can be seen with above average cognitive capability. Microcephaly associated with genetic or acquired disorders reflects cerebral pathology and almost always carries cognitive implications. Macrocephaly, or large head size, may be due to hydrocephalus, which has an increased incidence of cognitive deficits, especially learning disabilities. Macrocephaly without hydrocephalus, far from being a predictor of advanced intelligence, is also associated with a higher prevalence of cognitive deficits. It may be due to metabolic and/or anatomic abnormalities. About 50 percent of the time, macrocephaly is familial, in which case the implications are benign in terms of intellect. When evaluating infants with isolated macrocephaly, the finding of a large head size in one or both parents is reassuring.

Body size follows the same logic. While the majority of individuals with below or above average size are otherwise normal, there is an increased prevalence of developmental disabilities in these two subpopulations. Many genetic syndromes are associated with short stature; large stature syndromes are less common. Again, in evaluating deviation from the norm in a specific child, family characteristics must be taken into consideration. Knowing the size of the biological parents is useful in determining whether a given child's size is appropriate for his or her familial growth pattern.

VIGNETTE 8.1 DARLENE

Darlene is a 14-month-old who was born at 31 weeks of gestation and weighed 1.29 kilograms (kg). She spent nine weeks in the neonatal intensive care unit. Her course in the unit was relatively benign, but she did experience an intraventricular hemorrhage (IVH). She was identified as motor delayed by nine months of age and was referred for early intervention services at 10 months. At 13 months, a diagnosis of spastic diplegic cerebral palsy was made. At this time, her height is 71.5 centimeters (cm), her weight is 8.7 kg, and her head circumference is 46.5 cm. Her mother is worried because Darlene is small and tends to be a picky eater.

Is this child described in Vignette 8.1 growing adequately? The answer can only be determined by graphing the measured growth parameters (Figures 8.1A and 8.1B). Obviously all preterm babies will be small relative to full-gestation birth heights and weights. Growth parameters at birth are plotted for gestational age on special growth charts developed for premature infants, and, indeed, Darlene's birth weight of 1.29 kg was perfectly appropriate for her gestational age of 31 weeks (not shown). As the child ages, by convention the full number of months preterm is subtracted from the child's chronologic age for the purpose of plotting on the standard growth chart. Because Darlene was born nine weeks early (almost exactly two months), her height and weight are plotted at 12 months rather than 14 months to correct for her degree of prematurity. Plotting these points reveals that she is in the 10th to 25th percentile for both height and weight. This indicates that her height and weight are within the normal range and are relatively proportionate. She is a little below average in terms of size for a 12-month-old, and if her mother is comparing Darlene to 14-month-olds, then it is easy to see why she might perceive her daughter as too small (Figure 8.1B). To help with the assessment of body proportion, weight is plotted against height. On that chart, Darlene ranks at the proper level, in the 50th percentile.

Darlene's head looks a little bit large clinically, and its circumference plots at the 75th percentile. This indicates some body disproportion. Does this child have hydrocephalus? Because she has a motor disability, we know that she sustained a brain injury. We also know that she had an IVH, so hydrocephalus is a real concern. Could it be contributing to her disability or limiting her response to therapy?

The answer is that we don't know from the information given. However, many preterm babies tend to have heads that are relatively large compared to their bodies, without having genuine obstructive hydrocephalus. Most infants who experience an intracranial hemorrhage do not go on to develop hydrocephalus. Nonetheless, an IVH can lead to obstructive hydrocephalus. The two most important additional pieces of information that should be already available are prior head circumference measurements, to document how the head has grown over time, and clinical symptoms. If the *rate* of head growth is increasing, then progressive hydrocephalus is a serious possibility and must be tested for. A neurodiagnostic study of the cranium itself would need to be done to see whether the ventricular fluid spaces are enlarged, which would indicate hydrocephalus. This would most easily be done through a head ultrasound study. A cranial computerized tomogram (head CT) or magnetic resonance imaging (MRI) scan would provide a much more sophisticated and more detailed picture of the brain than the head ultrasound, but would not help answer the question much more accurately. Darlene's ultrasound study was normal, arguing against progressive hydrocephalus.

Failure to Thrive (FTT)

The term *failure to thrive* (FTT) is often applied generically and rather loosely to any situation in which a child is not growing adequately. Precise definitions of failure to thrive have varied in the medical literature. Currently, most growth experts use the term to refer only to those of individuals who are underweight for their height. Older literature tended to use FTT more broadly to encompass individuals who demonstrated generalized growth deficits and behavioral abnormalities.

Regardless of which definition one prefers, the diagnosis of failure to thrive is, once again, absolutely dependent upon accurately measured growth parameters plotted on appropriate growth charts. It is worth noting that growth failure tends to fall into several patterns, the recognition of which can help differentiate the most likely underlying cause of the growth retardation.

VIGNETTE 8.2 TOMMY

Tommy is a 24-month-old who is developmentally delayed, somewhat slow and lethargic in his general demeanor, and small. He was born at full term and was of average size at birth. His current height is 79 cm (less than 5th percentile), and his weight is 11.1 kg (10th percentile) (Figure 8.2A). His head circumference is 48.5 cm (25th percentile) (Figure 8.2B). By inspection of the growth curves alone, one would anticipate that this boy is perhaps a bit on the chubby side. In other words, he is short but appears far from malnourished. Inspection of the weight-for-height chart confirms that he is indeed above average, plotting just over the 50th percentile (Figure 8.2B).

In the scenario described in Vignette 8.2, organic etiologies are high on the list of the causes of Tommy's condition, the most likely being endocrine abnormalities or disturbances of skeletal growth that are causing retardation in linear growth but have no effect on appetite or weight gain. It turns out Tommy had acquired thyroid deficiency. This was easily diagnosed by a blood test, and, when he was treated with thyroid hormone, his linear growth returned to a normal rate. His state of alertness and developmental profile also improved, although he was left with some mild permanent cognitive deficits.

Another growth pattern seen in the broad category of failure to thrive includes children who are small for both height and weight. If their head circumferences are normal and their development is appropriate, these tend to be simply normal, small children. This pattern usually has a familial basis and is sometimes referred to as constitutional or familial short stature. On the other hand, if the head circumference is below the 5th percentile and/or the child is developmentally delayed, this pattern represents a subgroup that will often fall into the category of a syndrome diagnosis, especially if some dysmorphic features are also present.

VIGNETTE 8.3 PETER

Peter is a 12-month-old who is small and developmentally delayed. He was born at 38 weeks of gestation (considered full term). Recently, he has been placed in foster care with his aunt, having been abandoned by his biological mother. At the time of placement his height was 75 cm (25th percentile) and his weight was 7.8 kg (below the 5th percentile) (Figure 8.3A). His head circumference was 47 cm (50th percentile) (Figure 8.3B). His weight-for-height measurement is well below the 5th percentile.

A

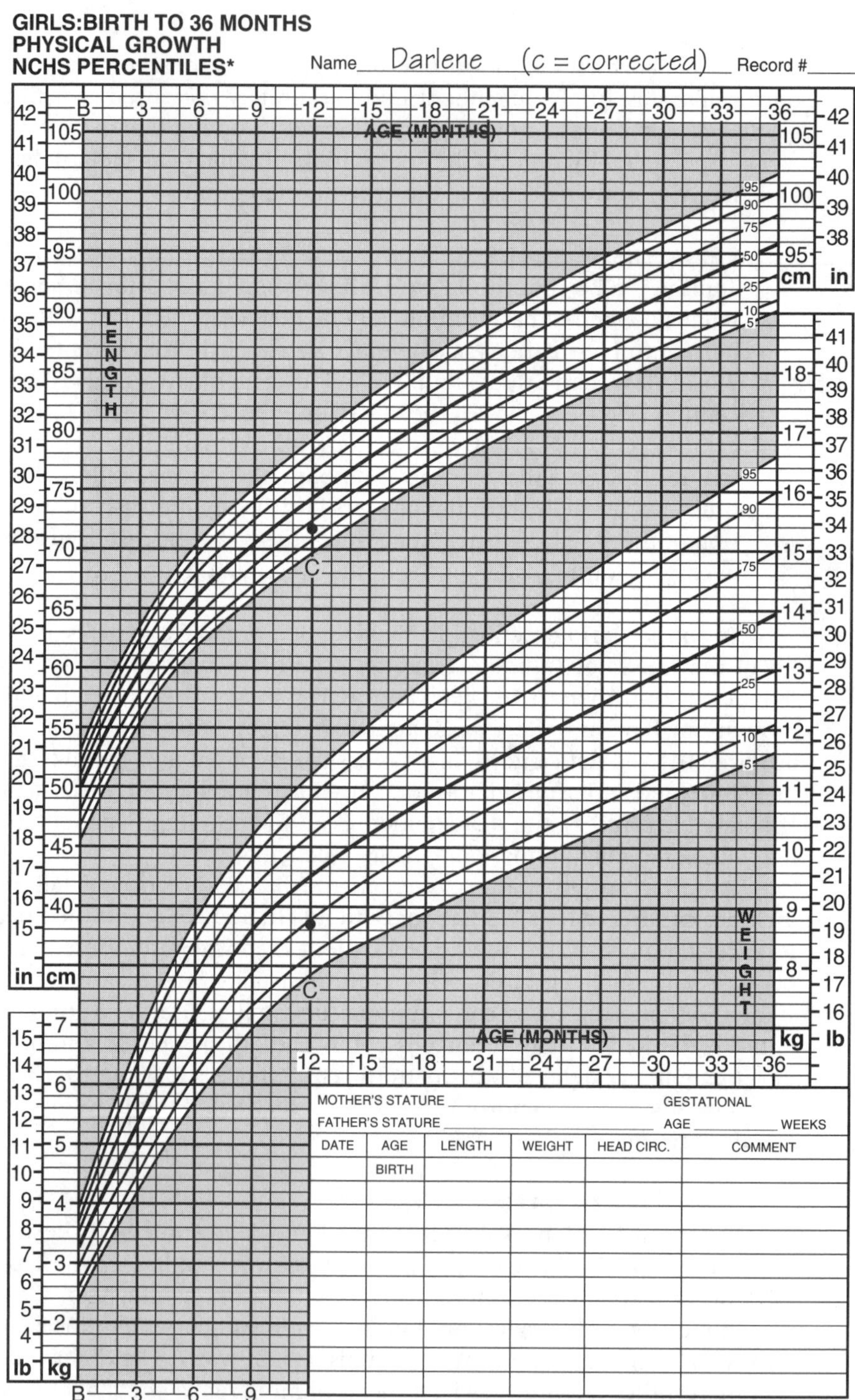

FIGURE 8.1 Case 1: Darlene. Standard infant girl growth chart plotted at Darlene's corrected age (12 months). **A,** Height = 71.5 cm, weight = 8.7 kg. **B,** Head circumference = 46.5 cm, height = 71.5 cm, weight = 8.7 kg.

B

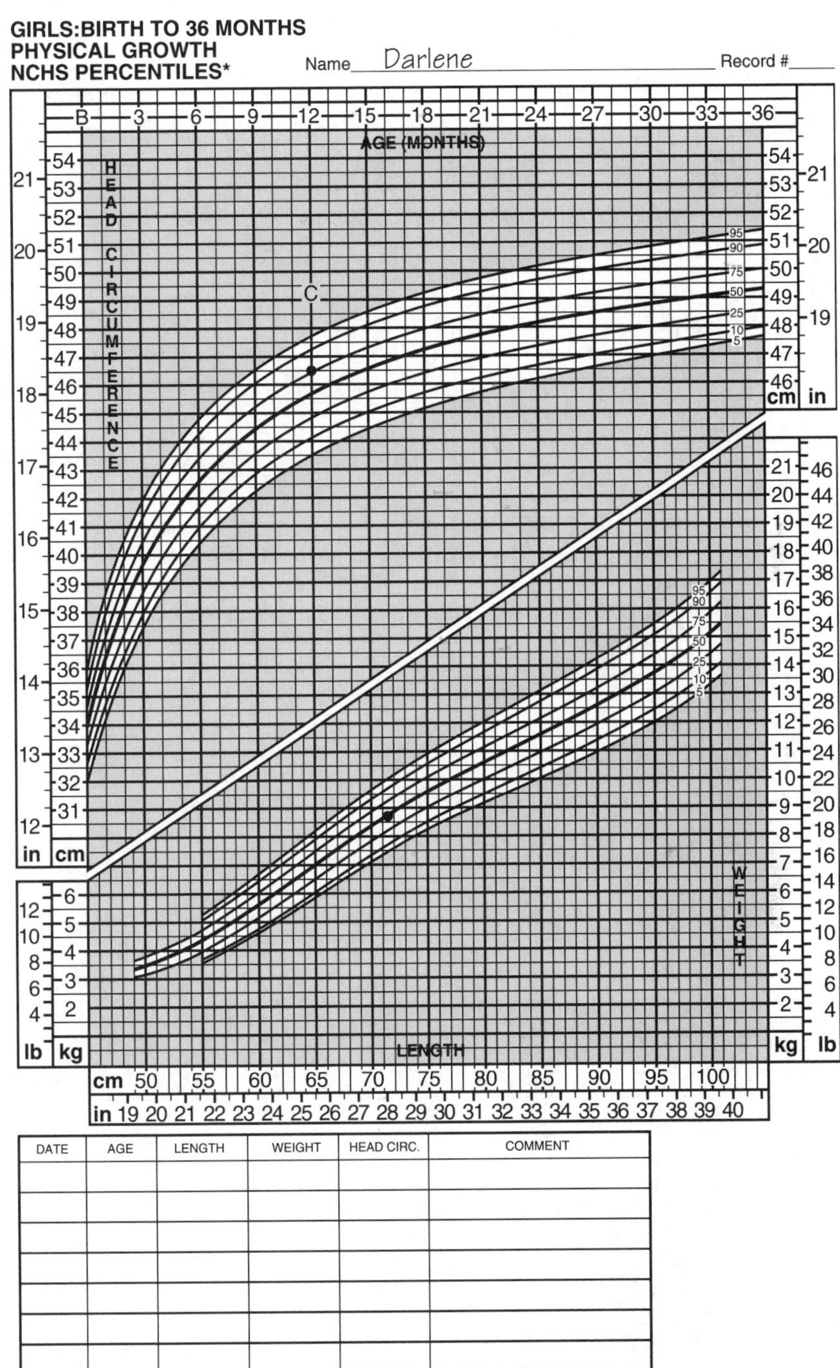

DATE	AGE	LENGTH	WEIGHT	HEAD CIRC.	COMMENT

Source: From "Physical Growth: National Center for Health Statistics Percentiles" by P. V. V. Hamill, T. A. Drizd, C. L. Johnson, R. B. Reed, A. F. Roche, and W. M. Moore, 1979, *American Journal of Clinical Nutrition, 32,* 607–629. Data from the Fels Longitudinal Study, Wright State University School of Medicine, Yellow Springs, Ohio. Copyright 1982 Ross Products Division, Abbott Laboratories. Adapted by permission.

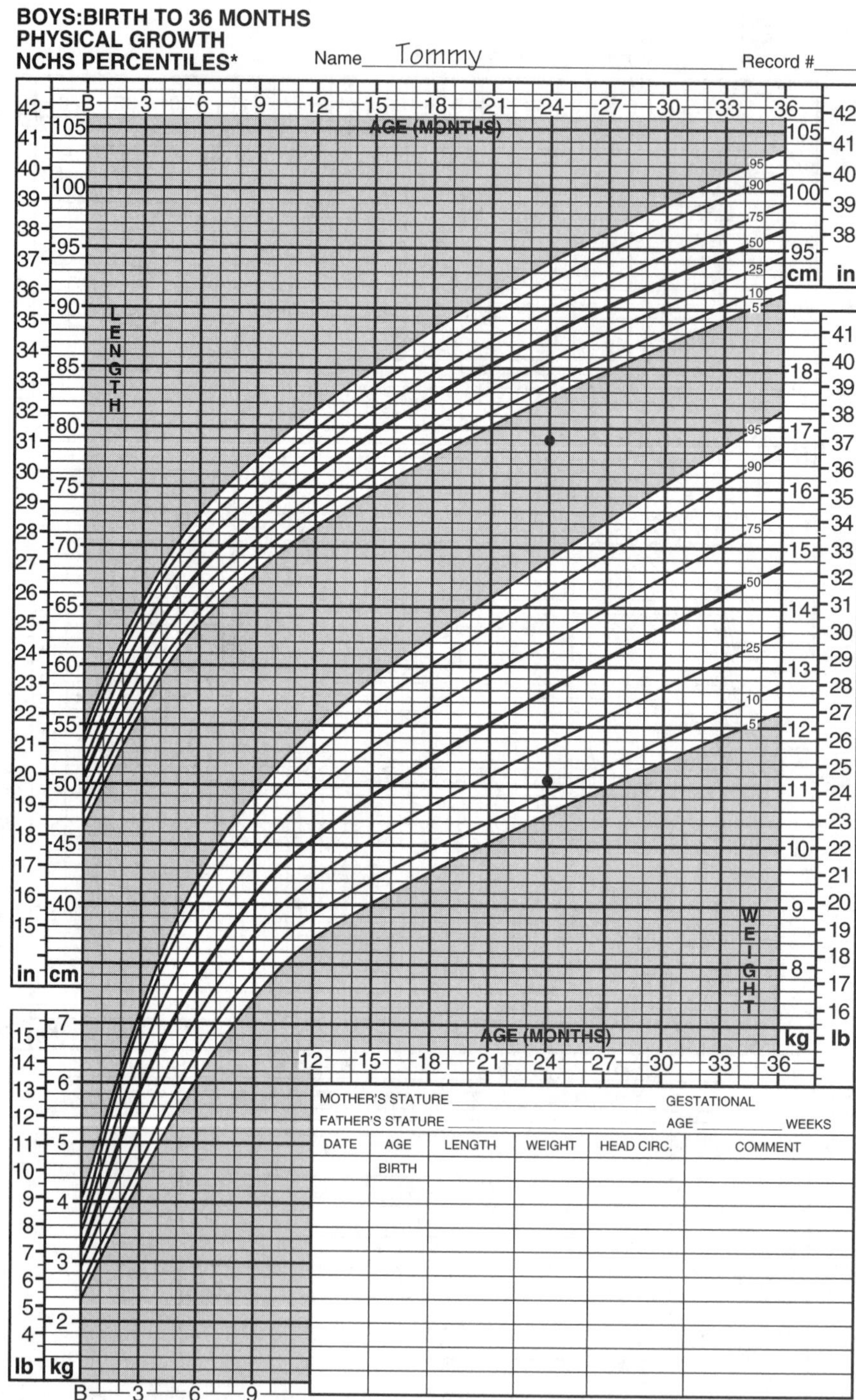

FIGURE 8.2 **Case 2: Tommy.** Standard infant boy growth chart plotted at Tommy's chronologic age (24 months). **A,** Height = 79 cm, weight = 11.1 kg. **B,** Head circumference = 48.5 cm, height = 79 cm, weight = 11.1 kg.

B

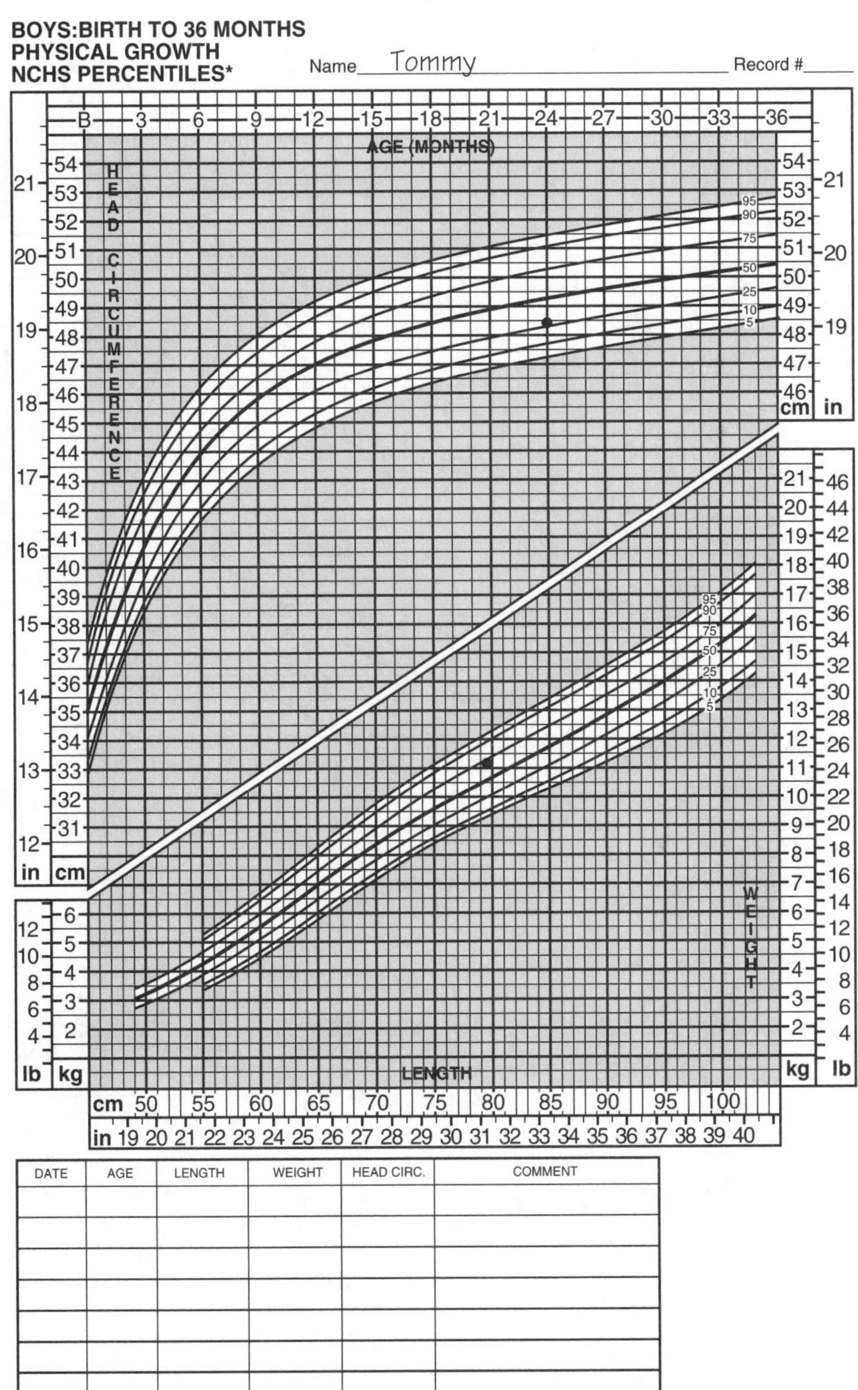

DATE	AGE	LENGTH	WEIGHT	HEAD CIRC.	COMMENT

Source: From "Physical Growth: National Center for Health Statistics Percentiles" by P. V. V. Hamill, T. A. Drizd, C. L. Johnson, R. B. Reed, A. F. Roche, and W. M. Moore, 1979, *American Journal of Clinical Nutrition, 32,* 607–629. Data from the Fels Longitudinal Study, Wright State University School of Medicine, Yellow Springs, Ohio. Copyright 1982 Ross Products Division, Abbott Laboratories. Adapted by permission.

A

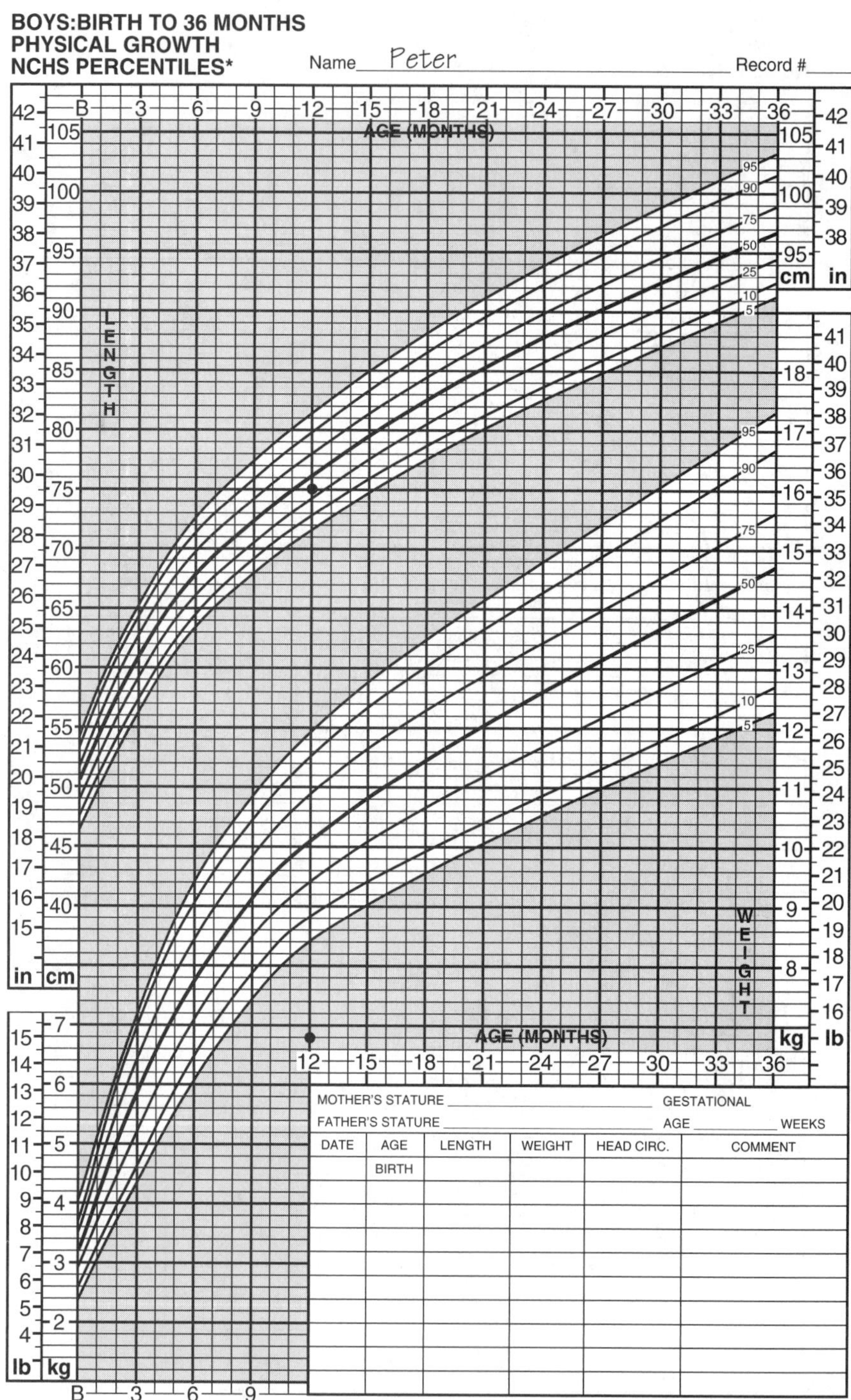

FIGURE 8.3 Case 3: Peter. Standard infant boy growth chart plotted at Peter's chronologic age (12 months). **A,** Height = 75 cm, weight = 7.8 kg. **B,** Head circumference = 47 cm, height = 75 cm, weight = 7.8 kg.

B

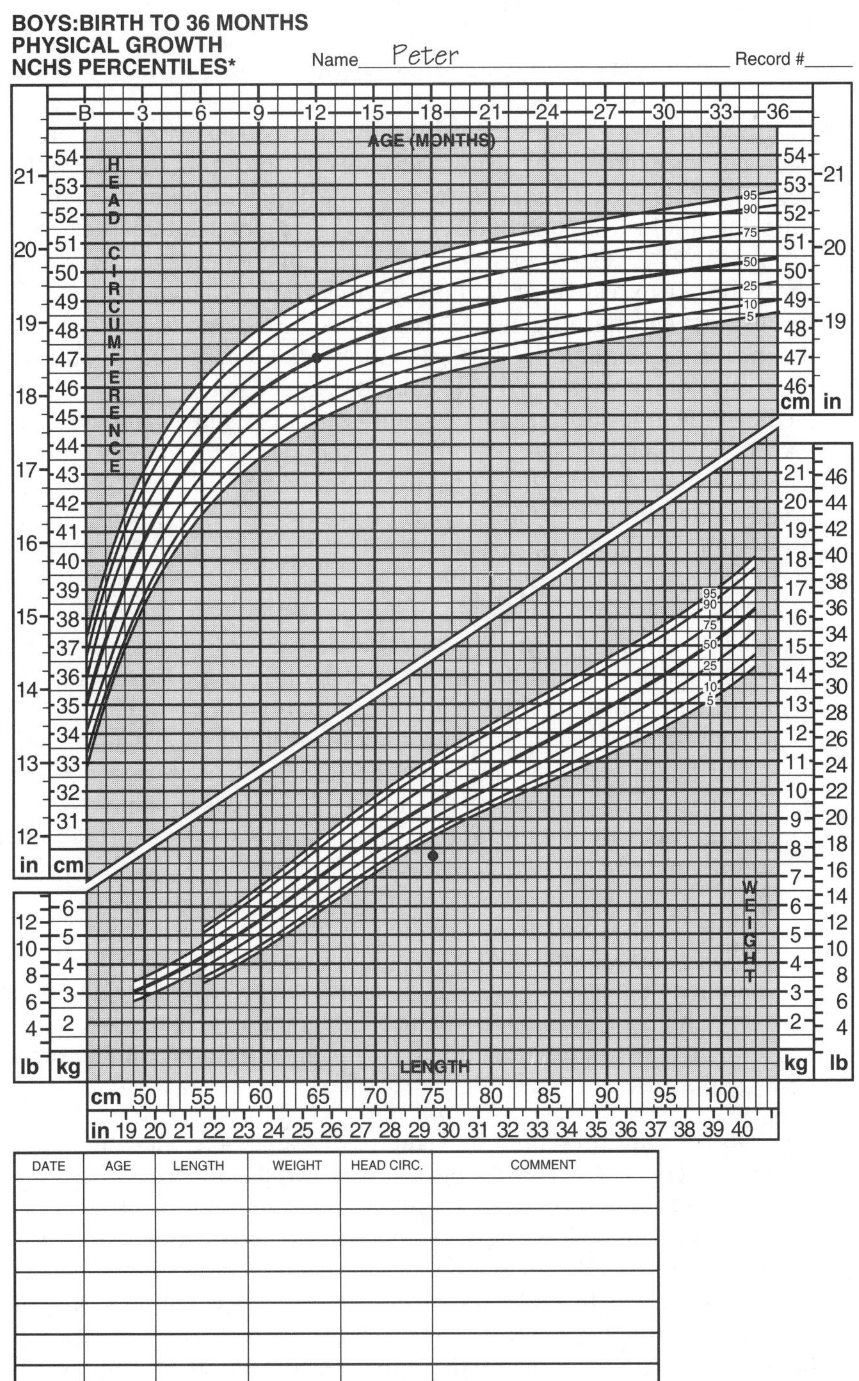

Source: From "Physical Growth: National Center for Health Statistics Percentiles" by P. V. V. Hamill, T. A. Drizd, C. L. Johnson, R. B. Reed, A. F. Roche, and W. M. Moore, 1979, *American Journal of Clinical Nutrition, 32,* 607–629. Data from the Fels Longitudinal Study, Wright State University School of Medicine, Yellow Springs, Ohio. Copyright 1982 Ross Products Division, Abbott Laboratories. Adapted by permission.

In the situation presented in Vignette 8.3, simple inspection of the height and weight graphs (Figures 8.3A and 8.3B) would lead one to expect to see a thin infant, which was indeed true clinically. If we also performed some measure of body fat, for example, by using the skin-fold thickness test, it would have been below normal as well. In this case we are dealing with genuine malnutrition. Malnutrition results from one of three processes: (1) inadequate intake of calories and nutrients, (2) excessive loss of calories and nutrients (such as occurs with diarrhea), or (3) excessive or ineffective utilization of absorbed nutrients (such as results from chronic lung disease, congenital heart disease, and other medical conditions). In this situation, Peter was simply not being fed adequately in the home. Most cases of failure to thrive are caused by inadequate intake due to parent-child feeding difficulties that are not organic in nature, which is the source of the often-used term *nonorganic failure to thrive* (NOFTT). Peter rapidly and dramatically gained weight when his home environment was altered and he was fed an appropriate diet by his foster family. NOFTT is a troubling and complex disorder with many difficult, long-term social and behavioral subissues. For a thorough review of the subject, see Stevenson (1992).

The last group is composed of those children who are close to or below the lower limit for height, usually below the margin for weight, and far below the 5th percentile for head circumference. The lack of head growth, out of proportion to body growth, is usually a reflection of substantial brain damage, and these children typically have severe associated neurodevelopmental deficits that are permanent. The brain dysfunction may be the result of a malformation of the nervous system or an acquired injury to the developing nervous system. There may also be a superimposed component of undernutrition related to oral motor dysfunction and resultant difficulty with feeding and swallowing.

VIGNETTE 8.4 EDDIE

Eddie is a 15-month-old born at full term with Down syndrome and congenital heart disease, which is believed to be relatively mild. However, he is a slow feeder and has been gaining weight slowly. His height is 69 cm and his weight is 7.4 kg, both under the 5th percentile on the growth curves (Figure 8.4A).

Do the data presented in Vignette 8.4 suggested that Eddie is undernourished? This boy's height and weight are both well below the 5th percentile, which is not in itself too surprising, given that we know he has a genetic syndrome. Could his heart condition be causing additional growth deficiency? Determining whether or to what degree he is undernourished requires looking at the appropriateness of his weight for his particular height. Inspecting the weight-for-height curve reveals that he is, in fact, doing reasonably well and is proportionate (Figure 8.4B). This should be apparent from visual inspection as well. Will feeding him more help his growth? On the contrary, Eddie is adequately nourished, and increasing his calorie intake may lead to greater weight gain but is unlikely to increase his linear growth, which is deficient as a consequence of his genetic constitution, not as a consequence of malnutrition and/or heart disease.

Could there be other factors at play? If one has the advantage of following Eddie's growth over time, a consistent pattern of slow but steady, proportionate length and weight increments would most likely be seen. Children with Down syndrome do, however, have a high rate of thyroid deficiency, something the astute pediatrician would be routinely screening for with blood tests done at regular intervals. As an added assist, a number of syndrome-specific growth charts have been developed to allow comparisons against more appropriate norms (for example, for Down syndrome, see Cronk et al., 1988; for Prader-Willi syndrome, see Butler & Meaney, 1991). When plotted on such a chart, Eddie's height and weight are roughly in the 10th percentile, which is within the average range (Figure 8.5).

In summary, the approach to determining adequacy of growth is straightforward and depends on accurate measurement of growth parameters for height, weight, and head circumference, followed by careful plotting on the appropriate growth curves. The weight-for-height curve is exceedingly valuable in helping to determine adequacy of nutrition. For the child who is failing to grow at an appropriate rate in any (or all) parameters, the pattern of deficiency and the presence of additional factors (developmental deficits, dysmorphisms, etc.) help direct the clinician toward an etiologic explanation for the growth problem.

DEVELOPMENTAL DIAGNOSIS

VIGNETTE 8.5 DANIEL

Daniel is a 13-month-old referred for developmental delay, mainly because he is not sitting independently. His mother had been worried about him since he was about four to five months old because "he just didn't seem right." The family doctor believed Daniel would "grow out of" his delays. He was a first child.

On examination the child is quite hypotonic (floppy). Developmentally he is close to sitting while propped and has a gross motor level of four to five months. His fine motor, problem-solving, and language levels are all in the same range, indicating severe delays in motor and cognitive domains. Additionally, he has a number of subtle dysmorphic facial features and some unusual palmar increases noted on physical examination.

Based on the history of slow developmental progress, this seemed most likely to be a case of static encephalopathy. A salient feature was that Daniel's mother had experienced approximately 15 spontaneous abortions. During the etiologic workup, the child's chromosome analysis showed a translocation of genetic material between two chromosomes. His mother's chromosomes revealed a "balanced" translocation of the same genetic material, permitting her to be normal but making all of her ova either nonviable or characterized by a severe abnormality. The translocation coupled with Daniel's clinical features did not conform to a known syndrome.

A

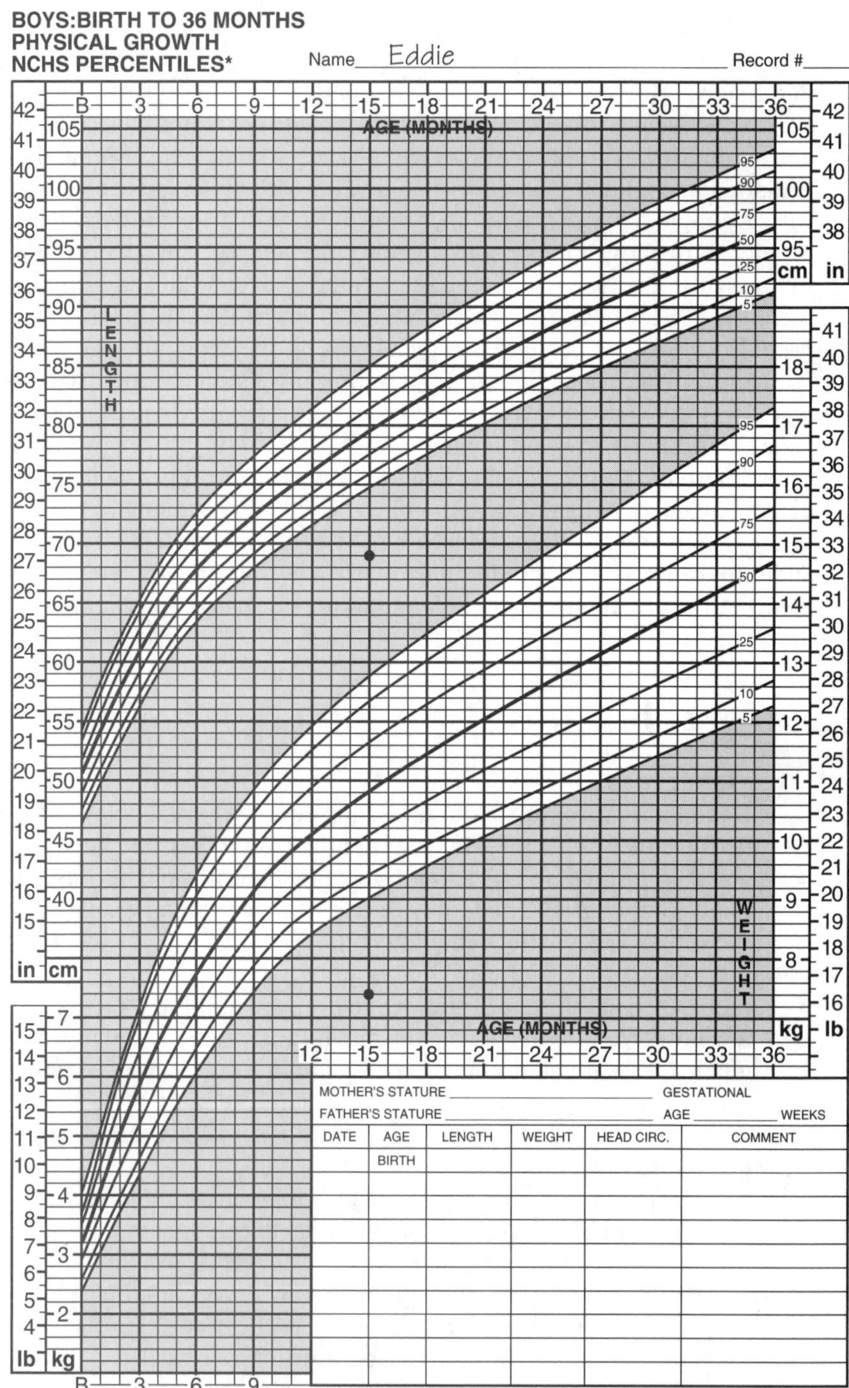

FIGURE 8.4 Case 4: Eddie. Standard infant boy growth chart plotted at Eddie's chronologic age (15 months). **A,** Height = 69 cm, weight = 7.4 kg. **B,** Height = 69 cm, weight = 7.4 kg.

B

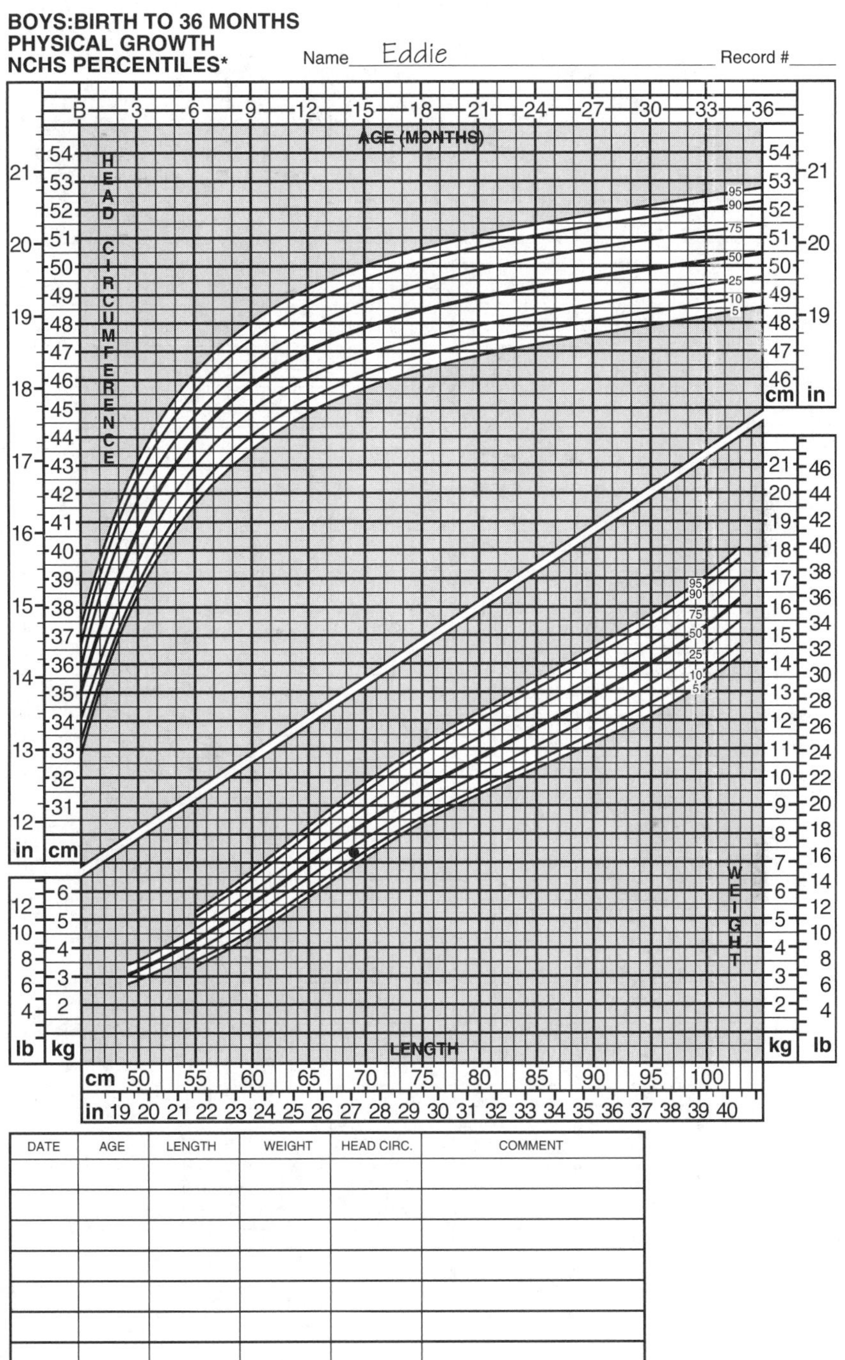

DATE	AGE	LENGTH	WEIGHT	HEAD CIRC.	COMMENT

Source: From "Physical Growth: National Center for Health Statistics Percentiles" by P. V. V. Hamill, T. A. Drizd, C. L. Johnson, R. B. Reed, A. F. Roche, and W. M. Moore, 1979, *American Journal of Clinical Nutrition, 32,* 607–629. Data from the Fels Longitudinal Study, Wright State University School of Medicine, Yellow Springs, Ohio. Copyright 1982 Ross Products Division, Abbott Laboratories. Adapted by permission.

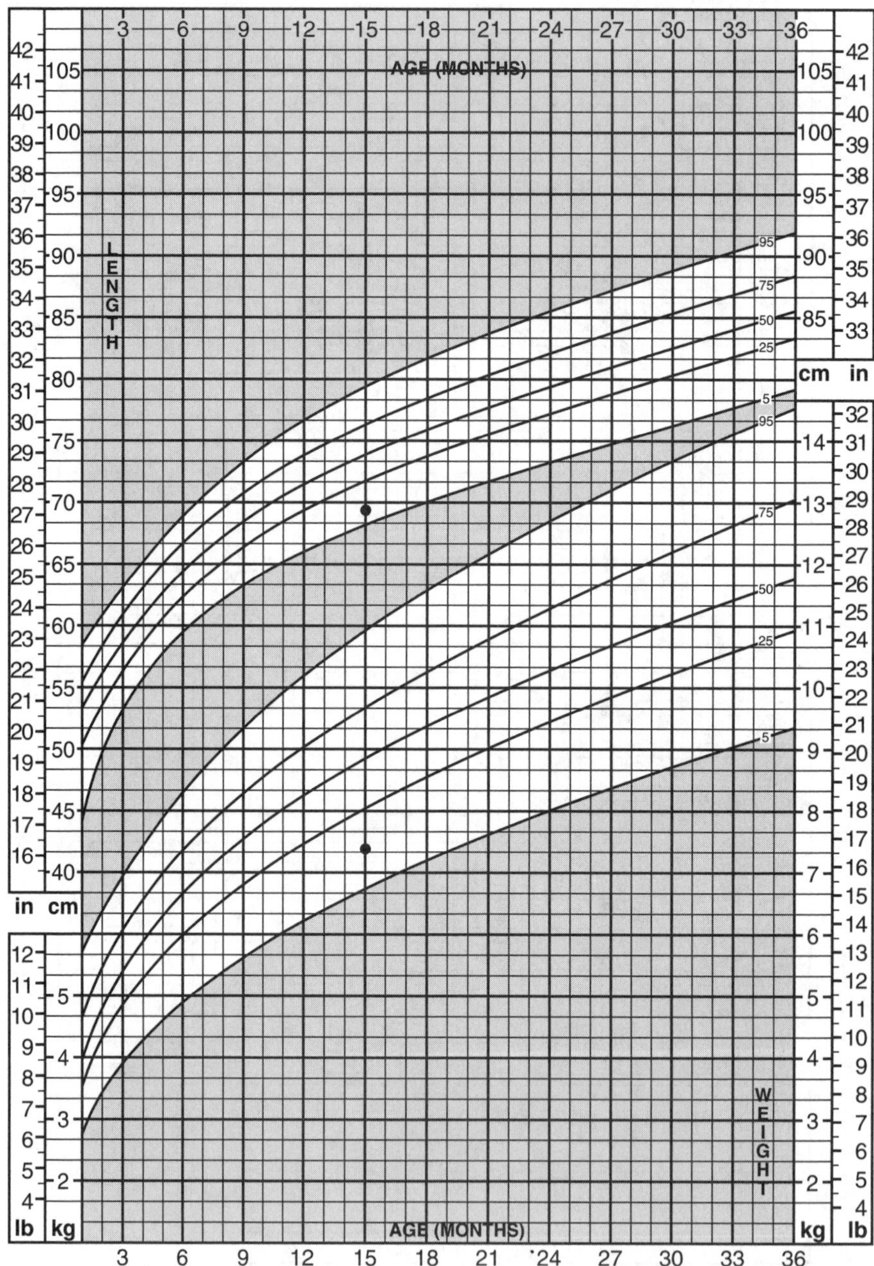

FIGURE 8.5 **Case 4: Eddie.** Eddie's weight (7.4 kg) and height (69 cm) plotted on a Down syndrome growth chart for boys.

Source: From "Growth Charts for Children with Down Syndrome: 1 Month to 18 Years of Age" by C. Cronk et al., 1988, *Pediatrics, 81,* 102–110. Reprinted by permission.

Developmental disabilities include a spectrum of disorders whose underlying substrate is the presence of chronic and nonprogressive neurological impairment at a cerebral level, clinically known as a static encephalopathy as illustrated in Vignette 8.5 (Capute & Palmer, 1980). Such cerebral dysfunction can exist on the basis of a central nervous system (CNS) that has not developed properly right from the start, referred to as a central nervous system anomaly, or, alternatively, can be the consequence of an injury to a developing nervous system that, up to the point of the insult, was normal. The neurodevelopmental disabilities are presented in Table 8.1. Cerebral palsy refers to *significant* motor dysfunction due to a nonprogressive cerebral insult. The definition indicates nothing about intellectual function. Mental retardation refers to significantly below average general intellectual ability, likewise due to cerebral dysfunction.

Communication disorders span a spectrum of primary language disorders that may be congenital or acquired. Among the congenital communication disorders, which are usually very subtle in their early symptoms, the severe end of the spectrum is autism. The acquired disorders are commonly referred to as aphasias and are rarely subtle in their onset. In the past the low-severity spectrum of dysfunction was known as minimal brain dysfunction or minimal cerebral dysfunction and now is more specifically referred to as learning disability (LD) and/or attention hyperactivity deficit disorder syndromes. Blindness and deafness are self-explanatory. For most of these conditions, an essential criterion for the diagnosis is the fact that the nervous system lesion is static, that is to say, not progressive in nature.

Hence, as a broad group these conditions are referred to as the static encephalopathies. In violation of this general principle, however, we do tend to use the terms *blindness* and *deafness* regardless of whether the underlying process is static or, as it is in a minority of cases, progressive in nature. However, progressive cognitive

TABLE 8.1 Developmental Disabilities

Cerebral palsy
Mental retardation
Communication disorders
Autism
Aphasia
Learning disabilities/ADHD
Blindness
Deafness
Chronic childhood neurological disorders (which may *masquerade as* developmental disabilities) (e.g., seizures, degenerative CNS disease, myopathies)

deficit and progressive motor deficit should never be referred to as mental retardation or cerebral palsy. (Progressive mental deterioration is termed *dementia.*) Many slowly progressive neurological conditions are notorious for masquerading as static encephalopathies, but the implications are vastly different for progressive (also known as degenerative) disorders. The neurodevelopmental clinician must always be alert to the possibility of mistaking a progressive disorder for a static one and must be certain to reaffirm that the condition is not one of deterioration over time. Seizure disorders are very common among individuals with developmental disabilities, but by convention seizures are not classified among the developmental disabilities. Seizures do not *of necessity* affect development. They also have a wide variety of causes, some static and some progressive.

Prevalences of the neurodevelopmental disabilities vary (Table 8.2). The LD/ADD/ADHD complex is most common, found in 5–7 percent of all school-aged children. Mental retardation, by statistical definition, must occur in a little over 2.5 percent of the population, and empirically it is present in roughly 3 percent of individuals. There is considerable debate (especially in the education profession) about this number, which may be as low as 1 percent. In any case, the distribution is greatly skewed toward the mild end of the spectrum. What the lay public commonly thinks of in terms of mental retardation is not the mildly impaired individual but rather the 10–15 percent of the retarded population that falls in the moderate, severe, and profound range.

Diagnostic Levels

An area of confusion for nonmedical professionals and the lay public often centers around the issue of diagnosis. It is important to keep in mind that diagnosis occurs on two separate conceptual planes. Problem diagnosis, the first level of developmental diagnosis, relates to the problem at hand. Cerebral palsy, for example, is a disorder of movement and posture; in other words, it is a motor function problem.

The second level of diagnosis relates to etiology; or is the cause of the neurologic dysfunction. An extraordinary number of conditions—basically anything that can affect the brain or brain development—can cause any type of developmental disability (Table 8.3).

TABLE 8.2 Prevalence of Developmental Disabilities

DISABILITY	PERCENT
Learning disabilities/ADD syndromes	5–7
Mental retardation	3
Cerebral palsy	.2–.5
Deafness	.1
Blindness	.05
Autism	.04

TABLE 8.3 Causes of Developmental Disabilities

CONGENITAL	ACQUIRED
▪ Genetic (e.g., Down syndrome, neurocutaneous syndromes, dyslexia) ▪ Infectious (e.g., TORCHS) ▪ Toxic/metabolic (e.g., maternal PKU, maternal iodine deficiency, fetal alcohol syndrome) ▪ Other (e.g., unexplained CNS malformations)	▪ Perinatal (e.g., hypoxic-ischemic insult, prematurity) ▪ Head trauma ▪ Spinal cord injury ▪ Infectious (e.g., encephalitis, or secondary effect on CNS, as with sepsis and shock or pneumonia and hypoxia) ▪ Toxic/Metabolic (e.g., inborn errors of metabolism; hypothyroidism; lead poisoning) ▪ Neoplastic ▪ Other diseases (e.g., vascular accidents [strokes], nutritional deficiency, collagen vascular disease)

The causes of any given developmental disability (for example, cerebral palsy) are innumerable, and any given insult (for example, meningitis) can in general result in almost any developmental disability. A broad classification of cause categories, with a few more common specific examples, is presented here. Etiologic investigation in these conditions can be extremely difficult and not infrequently unrewarding. The medical workup for etiology relies heavily on the history and the physical and neurological examinations. Finding a cause cannot depend on completing an all-inclusive laboratory investigation for every child. There are too many possibilities to rule out every one with a test. The approach is, rather, to rely on clues that point toward a specific etiology.

Age

How early can one make a specific developmental diagnosis? The neurodevelopmental disabilities are not recognized and diagnosed as early as we would all like. Cerebral palsy is diagnosed at a mean age of 12 months. Disorders that are heralded by communicative dysfunction are referred for evaluation and diagnosed considerably later—closer to two and a half years for mental retardation and even later for learning disabilities and autism (Table 8.4).

These data come from a community with a long and strong history of exceptional developmental teaching in the local medical schools and pediatrics residencies. Hence, the pediatricians in the area are probably more attuned to neurodevelopmental problems than most. The numbers may be worse in other communities. The most flagrant example of delay in developmental diagnosis is

TABLE 8.4 Mean Age of Presentation (Referral) of Developmental Disabilities

DISABILITY	AGE
Cerebral palsy	12 months
Mental retardation	27 months
Communication disorder	32 months
Attention deficit disorder	7 years
Learning disability	9½ years

From "Age of Presentation of Developmental Disabilities" by T. H. M. Lock, B. T. K. Shapite, A. Ross, and A. J. Capute, 1986, *Journal of Developmental and Behavioral Pediatrics, 7,* 340. Adapted by permission.

deafness. Most deafness is inherited and therefore congenital. However, the mean age of diagnosis of congenital deafness ranges from 20 to 27 months and has not changed for four decades (deSchweinitz, Miller, & Miller, 1959; Robinson, Willits, & Benson, 1965; Shah, Chandler, & Doll, 1978; Coplan, 1987; Drews, Yeargin-Allsopp, Murphy, & Decoufle, 1994).

Cerebral Palsy

From an academic and conceptual standpoint, cerebral palsy (CP) represents the prototypical developmental disability, because it encompasses the entire spectrum of cerebral dysfunction. For that reason it is singled out for a more detailed review as an illustration of the nature of this entire class of disorders. As noted previously, the diagnosis of CP refers to a group of motor dysfunctions arising from a nonprogressive cerebral insult. The motor disability is subclassified based on pattern of involvement diplegia, hemiplegia, and certain qualitative neurological features, spasticity and ataxia (cf. Baird & Gordon, 1983; Batshaw, 1997). The majority of children with CP have additional problems, referred to as associated deficits (Table 8.5).

The hallmarks of the primary motor dysfunction are abnormalities of muscle tone, imbalance of various muscle groups, and aberrant movement patterns. These abnormalities generate forces on developing muscles and bones that were never meant to be, and as a result frequently produce deformities of the soft tissues (muscles and tendons), the bones themselves, and the joints. These alterations produce mechanical disadvantages that further interfere with functional ability and in addition can result in substantial pain, not to mention cosmetic deformity. More than half of the children with CP have cognitive dysfunction (mental retardation and learning disabilities). Oral-motor involvement can lead to a broad spectrum of serious impairments: poor speech intelligibility due to articulation problems, feeding difficulty leading to nutritional deficits, and swallowing dysfunction with drooling and/or aspiration. Blindness, deafness, and seizures will be much more common in children with CP than in the general population. Both

TABLE 8.5 Cerebral Palsy: Associated Disorders

Orthopedic deformities
- Muscle/tendon contracture
- Bone deformity/malalignment
- Joint dislocation and degeneration
- Scoliosis
- Osteoporosis and fracture

Cognitive deficits
- Mental retardation
- Learning disability

Oral-motor performance impairments
- Speech dysfunction
- Feeding and swallowing problems
- Drooling
- Malnutrition

Special sensory losses
- Hearing impairment
- Visual impairment

Seizures

Peripheral sensory impairment

Behavioral/emotional problems
- Organic
- Acquired

innate behavioral disorders (i.e., ADHD) and acquired behavioral/emotional disturbances are also more prevalent.

Evaluation of the child with CP, of necessity, must be quite comprehensive and, to be efficient, ought to be highly interdisciplinary. Just as communication among the professionals involved is critical, so is communication with the family, particularly at the time of initial diagnosis. Counseling parents at this sensitive time is a difficult process and a learned skill (Klein, 1993; Krahn, Hallum, & Kime, 1993). A family-centered approach to care should ideally be the governing principle for all interactions (Brewer, McPherson, Magrab, & Hutchins, 1989; Blasco & Johnson, 1996).

Treatments covering the primary disorder and the multitude of associated problems in some children may be very extensive and exceedingly complex. Treatment approaches for the motor disorder alone can be classified into five types of intervention (Table 8.6).

Counseling refers to providing information to the parents, as well as to the involved child and siblings. Written materials can be a tremendous adjunct to this process (see Kraft, 1985), but one needs to be discerning in their selection (Blasco, Baumgartner, & Mathes, 1983). The hands-on therapies include occupational,

TABLE 8.6 Interventions for Children with Cerebral Palsy

Counseling

Hands-on Therapy
- Physical Therapy
- Occupational Therapy
- Speech Therapy
- Recreational Therapy

Equipment
- Braces
- Adaptive Devices
- Electronics

Drugs

Surgery

physical, and speech therapy. Often short-changed on the list are the recreational therapists and their close counterparts, adaptive physical education professionals. Recreational activities can have the advantage of providing treatment while building self-esteem; for example, sitting astride a horse is beneficial for stretching one's adductor and hamstring muscles, but it also represents a powerful mastery experience for a young child.

An extensive—in truth, bewildering—array of equipment is available to help the disabled child function better. These can be grouped into braces and splints, whose purpose is to provide mechanical stability and prevent deformity; adaptive equipment, such as wheelchairs, seating systems, potty and bath chairs, etc.; and electronic devices, from the simplest mercury switch for activating a toy to the most sophisticated computerized augmentative communication systems (see Chapter 10). Medications have a role in the treatment of muscular hypertonus and movement disorders. Although there are a huge number to choose from, they are often rather unpredictable in terms of effects and side effects. Different drops are administered by different routes to achieve the best effect: orally (most drugs; see Pranzatelli, 1996), into the muscle itself (botulinum toxin; see Koman, Mooney, & Smith, 1996), or even into the spinal canal (intrathecal baclofen; see Albright, Cerri, & Singletary, 1991). Surgical interventions encompass an extensive array of orthopedic operations (Bleck, 1987) and a smaller group of neurosurgical procedures, with the most currently popular being dorsal rhizotomy (Peacock, Arens, & Berman, 1987). The surgical goals are always first and foremost to facilitate function and prevent deformity. Once a deformity has already developed, surgical outcomes are destined to achieve less and expectations are more limited: to correct deformity (as much as possible), to relieve discomfort, and to enhance care. Cosmesis is occasionally a consideration but is never primary.

Individuals unfamiliar with developmental disabilities, both lay and professional, often mistakenly assume that treatments are undertaken in a hierarchical fashion. In other words, one begins with talk therapy and progresses to physical therapy, occupational therapy, and so on. If those are unsuccessful, one moves on to braces and other equipment. The next intervention would be drugs, and one would look to surgery only as a last resort. Of course, this is not at all the case. The key to management of the child with any type of physical disability is applying the right treatment at the right time. When, for example, surgery is indicated to promote a function, then it is time to intervene surgically, regardless of what treatment has or has not preceded it. In many instances, surgery can be viewed as a necessary precursor to intensive hands-on therapy. The clinical experience and expertise of the interdisciplinary habilitation team are critical to arriving at these timely judgments.

MEDICAL DIAGNOSIS

The causes of developmental disabilities are numerous and include basically anything that can do injury to the brain, the eyes, or the ears. Table 8.3 outlined the broad spectrum of potential causes and offered a few examples. As noted, the search for the cause (etiology) of a particular developmental problem must be somehow narrowed for the process to be an efficient exercise. The diagnostic approach is outlined in Table 8.7. Such a list is, of necessity, incomplete, presenting only some of the more common tests.

TABLE 8.7 Medical Approach to Etiological Diagnosis Developmental Disabilities

CLINICAL ASSESSMENT	LABORATORY DIAGNOSTIC STUDIES	
■ History	*Blood tests*	*X-ray/imaging studies*
■ Physical examination	■ CBC, diff, plt, smear	■ Hips
■ Neurodevelopmental examination	■ SMAC	■ Skull
■ Consults	■ LFTs	■ Spine
■ Other	■ Amino Acids	■ Long bones
	■ Lead/FEP	■ Bone age
	■ Chromosomes	■ CT scan
	■ Thyroid and other endocrine tests	■ MRI
	■ CK, other muscle enzymes	*Other neurodiagnostic studies*
	■ Antibody titers, TORCH, HIV	■ EEG
	■ Drug levels	■ EMG
	Urine tests	■ NCV
	■ Urinalysis	■ SSEP
	■ Amino acids (also mother)	■ BAER
	■ Metabolic screen	■ VEP
	■ Organic acids	■ PET scan
	■ Culture (esp. virus)	

A fundamental truth of etiologic investigation in the developmental disabilities is that one does not always arrive at an answer. For cerebral palsy, for example, this occurs about 20 percent of the time—a disconcerting circumstance for clinicians and a frustrating one for parents. Another general truth is that the greater the severity of disability, the more likely one is to find an etiology. Thus, most of the time mild mental retardation goes unexplained (and is often referred to as "idiopathic"), whereas severe and profound degrees of retardation will almost always have some identifiable organic pathology.

Another key point for parents is that arriving at an etiology very often does not mean that one can do anything about the condition. Nonetheless, just knowing the cause provides some degree of satisfaction and perhaps relief. There may also be important genetic and prognostic implications that come with a specific etiologic diagnosis.

VIGNETTE 8.6 MICHAEL

Michael is an 18-month-old referred to a child neurologist by his pediatrician because of a four-month history of gradually increasing irritability and a two-week history of repeated bouts of vomiting. The child is extremely irritable at times without obvious reason, and has otherwise been listless with no interest in food and little interest in play. He frequently holds or hits his head. Among other things, the examination shows a head circumference that is barely at the 5th percentile in a child who is in the 50th percentile for height and the 25th percentile for weight. The head shape is elongated in the anterior-posterior dimension.

Neurodiagnostic tests measure some aspect of neuroanatomic structure or neurophysiologic function. Neuroimaging studies are those that provide a neuroanatomic picture. The simplest such example would be a skull X ray, which gives a picture not of the brain directly but of the box enclosing it. This provides indirect information about the contents by indicating whether the skull is for example too big or too small (although you could get similar information by simply inspecting and measuring the head circumference). Skull X rays can also help explain neurological symptoms (e.g., irritability, vomiting, or a misshapen skull). In Vignette 8.6, skull X rays showed stenosis (premature closure) of the child's skull bones along the sagittal suture line, known as craniosynostosis. Because this event limits growth directed laterally, the skull is elongated in the anterior-posterior direction (known as scaphocephaly or dolichocephaly). Despite the growth that does take place, there is still encroachment on the rapidly growing brain with resulting symptoms of increased intracranial pressure, which could have caused Michael's irritability and vomiting, and probably made his head ache. The treatment for this condition is fairly urgent surgical splitting of the involved sutures.

The head ultrasound (HUS) test can provide a very crude picture of brain anatomy by bouncing sound waves off different surfaces, such as the fluid-filled ventricles and the skull. Because the HUS requires a "window" through the bony skull, its greatest utility is in neonates and infants who still have open fontanels. The ultrasound machine is portable and can be brought to the patient, a great advantage when one is dealing with small, fragile, premature infants. The HUS could not be done with Michael because his fontanels were closed. Indeed, it would not have been very useful anyway, because in his case the skull bones themselves were of primary interest. Pictures of brain anatomy are best supplied by magnetic resonance imaging and computed tomography scans. Computed cranial tomography (CT scan) of the head would have shown the same thing as the skull X rays as well as some of the compression effects going on in the brain. The CT scan involves a large series of X rays that are computer analyzed and reconstructed to give a three-dimensional picture of the brain and skull. It provides much more information than does a simple skull X ray but also involves a much greater exposure to radiation. MRI scanning takes advantage of the ability of an extremely high-powered magnet to alter the orientation of tissue water molecules. When the magnet's electronic field is changed, the molecules change orientation in space and then flip back, releasing energy in the process. This energy can be captured and converted to create a picture. The anatomic detail of the brain shown by an MRI is superior to that of a CT (in most respects), and it has the added advantage of no radiation exposure. While both are capable of producing very refined pictures of brain (and other organ) anatomy, they do not tell us everything. The great disadvantage of both the MRI and the CT is that the patient needs to hold perfectly still for about 15 minutes, which means that young children must be well sedated.

The electroencephalogram (EEG) measures electrical activity generated by brain neurons at multiple points along the scalp. It provides very little information about structure and is a fairly crude test of neurophysiologic function. Its greatest utility is in determining the presence and subtype of seizure disorders, but even here it has limitations (Lewis & Freeman, 1977). Variations on the EEG are used to gather information on visual pathway integrity (VER, or visual evoked response) and on auditory function (AEP, auditory evoked potential, and BAER, brainstem audiometric evoked response). Cortical evoked potentials, both visual and auditory, have fairly limited utility in young children. Brain stem audiometry is particularly helpful in screening for or documenting hearing levels in subjects with limited or no ability to cooperate with earphone or behavioral testing.

Other neurodiagnostic tests provide increasingly sophisticated information about brain metabolism and blood flow (NMR spectroscopy, nuclear magnetic resonance, and PET, positron emission tomography scanning, respectively,) but are not widely available and are never first-line investigative tools.

The electromyogram (EMG) and nerve conduction velocity (NCV) studies specifically define the electrophysiology of muscles and peripheral nerves. Innumerable blood and urine tests for normal and abnormal chemical constituents can provide clues in the diagnosis of metabolic disorders, infectious exposures, and genetic makeup. These tests are too numerous to review here and are only undertaken when a specific, small category of diagnoses or a single diagnosis is being sought.

SPECIFIC MEDICAL CONSIDERATIONS

High-Risk Infants

The baby born prematurely is at extremely high risk to experience complications while in the neonatal intensive care unit (NICU) and to acquire a broad spectrum of clinical problems. These complications will at times be fatal, and among survivors long-term, sometimes lifelong, problems can result. The chronic disorders associated with preterm birth fall into four domains: medical problems, growth deficits, neurodevelopmental disabilities, and emotional/behavioral issues.

The service provider who has reviewed a discharge summary from the NICU may be confronted by a cryptic "alphabet soup" of diagnoses (IVH, BPD, ROP, CP, NEC, etc.). Organizing one's thoughts about these problems and understanding a little about their nature can greatly assist the provider in terms of realistic program planning, hands-on activities for the child, and coordination of services for the family.

Medical Problems

Neonates who are sick can develop chronic conditions involving any organ system, but most typically it is the lungs. In the immature lung, respiratory insufficiency results from inadequate surfactant coating the surface of the pulmonary alveoli (where respiratory gas exchange between the inspired air and the circulating blood takes place). This acute condition is known as the respiratory distress syndrome (RDS), aptly describing the clinical appearance of these very sick babies. Without surfactant, the alveoli tend to collapse and cannot easily snap back open during inspiration. As a result, the neonate must work extremely hard to breathe and even with great effort may still inadequately oxygenate her blood, causing a bluish color to the skin and lips (cyanosis). Surfactant replacement treatment has become widely available in recent years and greatly ameliorates the situation. Nonetheless, most of these infants need to be treated with oxygen, and some need to be mechanically ventilated. Under conditions of high inspired oxygen concentration, high ventilation pressures, and prolonged need for ventilator assistance, damage accumulates in the lung tissue, resulting in bronchopulmonary dysplasia (BPD), the chronic lung disease of infancy. Although an occasional child will succumb early to RDS or later to BPD, or at any time to other conditions, especially infection, the ultimate outlook is quite good. Home cardiac and respiratory monitoring and home oxygen use will be necessary for many months in some children. The illness itself and to some extent these additional devices restrict activities, limit stamina, and interfere with growth, especially weight gain. Children with BPD are more likely to become ill, even critically ill, with what would otherwise be a mild respiratory infection in the healthy infant.

Even those infants who leave the hospital without pulmonary sequelae are at increased risk for acute respiratory illness, especially during the first winter at home. They are more likely to wheeze with an upper respiratory infection, more likely to experience a moderate-to-severe respiratory syncytial virus infection, and more likely to come down with pneumonia. As many as 45 percent of infants with birthweight less than 1,500 grams who required mechanical ventilation in the neonatal period will be rehospitalized in the first year. Family members, physicians, and service providers should be vigilant about early signs and symptoms of respiratory illness. Because of the inevitable greater exposure to infectious agents, there is good reason to think twice about center-based early intervention programming, especially for infants with known BPD. Everyone around the infant should be counseled about passive smoke exposure, be diligent about hand washing, and try to decrease the infant's exposure to adults and children during the cold/influenza season.

An acute gastrointestinal problem commonly encountered in the preterm baby is necrotizing enterocolitis (NEC). Providing nutrition to the sick preterm infant is an enormous clinical challenge. One of the pitfalls associated with introducing feeding is the development of NEC, which is linked to a large number of factors centered around exposing the immature gut to food. In severe cases, NEC results in death of portions of the bowel. This requires surgical excision of the necrotic tissue and aggressive treatment of the accompanying massive infection. If enough small intestine is involved, the baby may survive with little or no ability to absorb nutrients. Such a child could be dependent on complicated tube feedings given by slow drip and/or intravenous feeding for years, potentially indefinitely. Chronic heart disease, liver problems, bone or joint damage, and palatal and dental problems are also among the problems that can plague the high-risk neonate.

Many premature infants, especially those with very low birthweight (VLBW), defined as less than 1,500 grams, develop moderate to severe anemia. In the first six to eight weeks of life, this usually represents anemia of prematurity, a poorly understood delay in bone marrow responsiveness. The hematocrit may drop to very low levels, but most infants tolerate anemia well. Others may present with symptoms of poor feeding, poor weight gain, or apnea, and require blood transfusions. After two months of age, the infant may become iron deficient, further worsening anemia.

Umbilical and inguinal hernias are common in premature infants. Rarely will an umbilical hernia require surgical correction. Inguinal hernias, on the other hand, pose a significant risk of incarceration. Once recognized, timely referral for surgical repair is important due to this risk.

Growth Deficits

Most infants will have demonstrated adequate weight gain as a condition for discharge from the neonatal unit. Some preterm infants, however, remain too small. They grow poorly, for reasons that are not well understood. It is not unusual for the infant with extremely low birthweight (ELBW), defined as less than 1000 grams, to gain weight and length at a pace below the 5th percentile and to parallel that curve through the first 18 to 24 months of life. This may be a "normal" pattern of growth for some premature infants, who, due to illness and/or relatively poor nutrition at a critical period of life, have lost some growth potential. As long as the infant's growth rate and caloric intake are appropriate, no additional therapy or investigation is necessary.

Occasionally, premature infants will demonstrate a growth curve that begins to drop across percentiles or falls further below the 5th percentile. Poor weight gain may result from the infant's inability to keep up with increased caloric requirements due to ongoing respiratory problems, thermal instability, malabsorption secondary to necrotizing enterocolitis, or feeding difficulty consequent to neurodevelopmental deficits. Often the failure to thrive is complicated by problems that are behavioral in nature and need to be addressed with a consistent behavior management program (Singer et al., 1996).

Premature infants, especially VLBW and ELBW infants, have nutritional needs beyond those of the full-term infant. The premature infant should receive a daily multivitamin supplement until he is consuming at least 28 to 32 ounces of formula each day. The infant also requires iron supplementation. Some neonatal nutritionists recommend continuing the premature infant on a special premature infant formula, with its increased mineral, vitamin, and protein content, at least until the infant is approximately 40 weeks postconception.

Breast-feeding is strongly encouraged for the premature infant. Many of these infants will leave the hospital fully breast-fed. Some, however, will be making the transition from bottle to breast, while a few will remain dependent on some formula supplementation for several weeks or months. The breast-fed premature infant requires both multivitamin and iron supplementation, and the breast-feeding mother may require additional support and encouragement during this period. Service providers can be extremely helpful in this regard, even by simply promoting the benefits of breast-feeding and acknowledging the priority of a "good meal" (be it at the breast, bottle, or table) in an intervention session. Mothers receive valuable assistance from lactation support groups, lactation consultants, and other mothers of premature babies.

Neurodevelopmental Disabilities

The brain of the premature baby is extremely fragile and is routinely exposed to hypoxic stresses, rapid metabolic events, and wide swings in intracranial blood pressures that would virtually never be experienced in the uterus. What is perhaps most remarkable about high-risk preterm infants is that any of them survive neurologically intact. Major neurodevelopmental deficits (CP, mental retardation, blindness, deafness) occur in roughly 20–25 percent of surviving ELBW infants. Minor dysfunctions (learning disability, ADHD, lesser vision and hearing problems) probably occur in close to 50 percent, leaving the remainder, approximately 25 percent, apparently entirely normal and presumably having suffered no ill effects from their preterm birth (Allen, 1994; Halsey, Collin, and Anderson, 1996).

The prototypical neurodevelopmental deficit in the preterm infant is cerebral palsy. Sorting out what may be minor deficits or insignificant motor delays from CP in the first 12–18 months can be clinically difficult, and early intervention may be desirable before a firm diagnosis can be established. Mental retardation as a consequence of perinatal cerebral insult almost always occurs in concert with CP. It is quite uncommon to see significant cognitive impairment without equal or greater motor impairment unless there is some other explanation (e.g., a syndrome). In the mid-1950s, there was an epidemic of blindness in this country related to the use of high concentrations of life-saving oxygen in premature infants with RDS. The blindness was due to damage to the developing retina, then called RLF (retrolental fibroplasia). Oxygen toxicity is one of a number of factors that can contribute to this condition, which we now term ROP (retinopathy of prematurity). ROP still occurs, but with much less frequency, and generally only in the smallest and sickest premies. Since the link to oxygen was discovered back in the 1950s, blood oxygen levels have been monitored with great attention in order to keep them down to safe levels.

All premature infants who weighed less than 1,500 grams at birth (or any baby receiving oxygen therapy in the newborn period) should have an ophthalmologic examination for ROP at five to seven weeks of age and at least once again, due to the unpredictable course of ROP. In addition, premature infants are at increased risk, independent of the history of retinopathy, for strabismus and myopia. Careful evaluation of the eyes and the infant's vision is a part of routine well-child care, and service providers need to document their observations on how the infant uses his eyes in the intervention/play setting.

Published studies estimate a 1–5 percent incidence of hearing loss in preterm infants, especially in association with specific risk factors—birth weight less than 1,500 grams, intracranial hemorrhage, persistent fetal circulation (PFC), also called persistent pulmonary hypertension, or PPH exposure to ototoxic drugs, and meningitis. Many newborn units routinely screen infants falling into these risk categories. All preterm infants should have an audiologic screening evaluation prior to discharge. An abnormal screen may indicate an immature central nervous system or may be secondary to transient and reversible conductive deficits. Repeat evaluation is often necessary. As with vision, attention to and documentation of auditory performance by early intervention providers are most helpful.

Emotional/Behavioral Issues

Almost all parents will attest that the birth of one's child is a special, emotionally charged event. Surrounding this impression has risen a large and at times contentious literature related to these process of attachment, also known as "bonding" (Chess & Thomas, 1982; Lamb, 1982; Minde, 1986). The process is enormously disrupted by the birth of a sick and/or premature infant. High-risk infants have more developmental and behavioral problems as children, and the contribution of disrupted bonding to long-term behavioral/emotional disturbances is unknown. Anecdotally many parents seem strongly attached to their sick babies despite prolonged separations, and as these babies grow they seem equally attached to their parents (Chang et al., 1982). But for some more vulnerable parents, especially the younger, poorer, and less socially supported, interventions to foster attachment may have an extremely important effect on the attachment process (Anisfeld & Lipper, 1983)

Technology Assistance

Any apparatus that augments or replaces a bodily function is considered medical assistive technology. Many are internal (e.g., a shunt for hydrocephalus or a pacemaker). This section will address only the more common external devices, the vast majority of which are related to breathing or feeding functions.

Intravenous Lines. Fluids, nutrients, or medications that must be delivered by direct infusion require an intravenous (IV) access route. IV catheters may be placed peripherally, whereby the tip of the catheter is in an extremity, or centrally, in which case the catheter is actually in the heart or in a major vein directly adjacent to it. Infection involving intravenous lines, especially central lines, is a major hazard. Therefore meticulous care is required to avoid contamination. These lines should be manipulated only by those specifically trained to do so.

Suctioning. Children with severe oral motor dysfunction will have difficulty handling their own secretions. In this instance, feeding may be fraught with difficulty and may even be hazardous. Suctioning secretions from the mouth is intended to clear the airway and make breathing easier. Suctioning can be accomplished in easily accessible portions of the mouth and nose using the standard rubber bulb syringe. Deep suctioning to reach secretions that are in the back part of the mouth (the pharynx) requires a longer and relatively firm but not stiff tube and an electrically driven suction machine. Deep suctioning will almost always cause the patient to gag and can do damage to the throat if the tube is too stiff and is handled too vigorously. Suctioning is done as often as necessary, which may vary tremendously from child to child and will always increase when a child has an upper respiratory illness.

Tube Feeding. For children who are unable to maintain adequate nutrition by oral feeding, the use of feeding tubes becomes a necessity. Tubes that are passed into the stomach through the nose (nasogastric) or mouth (orogastric) are generally employed for relatively short durations of time. These types of tubes are common in neonatal intensive care units, where the infant is expected to eventually acquire the ability to suck and swallow and sustain herself by the oral route. Gastrostomy tubes, on the other hand, should be considered in situations where longer-term oral feeding inadequacy is anticipated. The tube itself goes directly through the abdominal wall and through the stomach wall, where it is secured by means of a small, soft balloon. Feeding is accomplished directly into the stomach, bypassing the mouth and esophagus entirely. The gastrostomy tube (g-tube) itself is cumbersome; it gets in the way of prone activities, and it is at risk to be accidentally pulled out. After a relatively short period of time (usually 6–12 weeks), it can almost always be replaced with a gastrostomy button device that acts as a sealable port into which a feeding tube can be intermittently passed and then withdrawn. Button devices avoid the problems with positioning and prone activities. Often, children have gastrostomies performed in combination with a gastric fundoplication. This is a procedure designed to inhibit the reflux of stomach contents up the esophagus, with resultant vomiting and sometimes aspiration. Gastroesophageal reflux (GER) is particularly common in children with more severe neurodevelopmental problems. Care and management of the g-tube or button is influenced by whether the child has also had a fundoplication. A superb gastrostomy care manual for parents and other caretakers has been developed by clinicians at the University of Virginia (Paarlberg, Atkinson, Bella, & Kocher, 1991).

Monitors. Monitoring devices are used to continuously measure breathing or heart rate performance in children who are prone to have respiratory or cardiac events that may be life-threatening. Monitors generally rely on sensitivity to the respiratory rate, the pulse rate, or a measure of blood oxygen content (oximetry) through a sensor located on the skin, usually the earlobe or the fingertip. These devices are often mechanically troublesome because the wires and body attachments involved can easily become detached and may produce frequent false alarms. They are used almost exclusively during sleep and, therefore, should not interfere with active intervention programming.

Oxygen. Many children with chronic respiratory failure require supplemental oxygen in order to maintain an oxygen saturation in their blood at a level adequate for growth and well-being. Room air contains 21 percent oxygen; additional oxygen may be administered by a nasal cannula (a tube with short prongs inserted into the nostrils), face mask, oxygen tent or hood, or an artificial airway, such as a tracheostomy. A child requiring oxygen can go to school or to a therapy program with an oxygen source and delivery system.

There is a common misconception that oxygen is explosive. Oxygen itself is not combustible, but it is essential to support the combustion of other materials. Hence, a higher concentration of oxygen will make any fire burn *faster* (and therefore hotter), but oxygen itself does not explode in the presence of a flame.

Ventilators. Mechanical ventilation becomes necessary when, for any reason, the thoracic cage is unable to move air adequately into and out of the lungs, or when the lung tissue itself is diseased to such a point that oxygen and carbon dioxide cannot be effectively exchanged. An example of the latter would be the respiratory distress syndrome outlined previously. An example of the former situation would a high spinal cord injury paralyzing the respiratory muscles of the rib cage and/or diaphragm. For almost all purposes, mechanical ventilation involves delivering positive pressure through the airway, although negative pressure can be used (and was extremely important back in the days of the "iron lung" respirator for polio). Air can be pumped through the natural airway (via a mask), or, in a more invasive fashion, it can be delivered directly into the trachea via a tube inserted through the mouth, the nose, or a tracheostomy opening created surgically.

The tracheostomy incision is made in the cartilage of the trachea just below the larynx ("Adam's apple"). A tracheostomy is by far the most likely artificial ventilation system that a teacher would need to learn to deal with in the classroom. The tube is secured with adhesive or foam-padded strings around the neck. This open airway is then attached to a small mask, a ventilator machine, or a continuous pressure device with tubing that provides humidified air alone or mixed with extra oxygen. The tracheostomy permits access for suctioning secretions or removing of other obstructions, accomplished easily by disconnecting the ventilator tubing from the tracheostomy tube.

A blocked tracheostomy tube must be replaced or unobstructed immediately. A dislodged tube must be correctly repositioned immediately. This is especially true for children with narrowed tracheas who are at extra risk for a catastrophe because they have less (or no) natural airway passage to fall back on if the tube is blocked or dislodged. Children with tracheostomies should be closely observed and electronically monitored when human surveillance is limited (i.e., when sleeping). It is helpful for classroom personnel to be aware of the specifics of the child's airway in order to know the degree of response urgency needed.

The ventilator itself contains an alarm system that sounds under conditions of low or high pressure. The most common reason for a low-pressure alarm is accidental disconnection of the tracheostomy tube from the ventilator tubing. A high-pressure alarm most commonly sounds because something is obstructing the flow of gas into the child. The cause may be external to the child (e.g., kinked or obstructed tubing), or it may be within the child (e.g., mucus plugging the tracheostomy tube). Mucus plug formation is usually prevented by humidifying the gas mixture that passes through the tubing. If there is a mucus plug, it requires removal by suctioning. Ventilators typically are powered via standard wall socket electricity; they also have their own built-in power source (a battery) for emergency and temporary-use situations. The alarm system also will go off when there are electrical problems, when the battery is low, and so on.

Developmental complications of long-term mechanical ventilation include language deficits and behavior and feeding problems. A number of studies have pointed to deficits in language production, syntax, and articulation related to the presence of a tracheostomy during the period of early language development (Simon, Fowler, & Handler, 1983; Singer, et al., 1989). A speech-language pathologist should provide alternative methods of communication that are developmentally appropriate for the child. These include sign language and the use of medical or nonmedical technology assistance, such as a speaking tracheostomy valve or an augmentative communication system (e.g., picture board, language board, or computer).

Ventilator-dependent children may have behavior problems. The absence of audible speech leads to frustration in attempts at communication and may result in aggressive or acting-out behavior. Noncompliance and attention-getting behaviors (such as intentionally disconnecting the ventilator hose from the tracheostomy tube) can appear as well. All these issues should be managed in a formal way with an emphasis on consistency of approach in the school, home, and any other environments where they occur.

EMERGENCIES AND FIRST AID

Fifth-grade teacher: "Kevin, how do you define 'first aid'?"
Kevin: "First aid is what you can do for yourself before the doctor gets a hold of you."

This section of the chapter will provide a quick overview of how to react to certain situations that are *more likely* to arise among children with neurodevelopmental disabilities. Teachers in any classroom setting need to be prepared to respond to any and all pediatric/childhood emergency situations. For a concise, wonderfully illustrated resource, see the *Baby and Child Emergency First Aid Handbook* (Einzig, 1992).

All personnel working with medically fragile children should be trained in the performance of cardiopulmonary resuscitation (CPR). In fact, it is highly desirable for *all* day care, preschool, and early childhood professionals to be trained and to maintain proficiency in CPR. Respiratory arrest almost always precedes cardiac arrest in children. This fact cannot be stressed enough, because the ease and likelihood of successful resuscitation and the outlook following successful resuscitation are all tremendously more optimistic with children than with adults. Proper technique for mouth-to-mouth and bag-and-mask resuscitation is an essential skill for early interventionists and caretakers. With a little practice, the techniques become quite easy and unforgettable (like riding a bicycle).

Infant or young child CPR should be initiated as soon as someone becomes aware that a child is not breathing. As with all emergencies, the single most important factor is keeping one's equanimity when panic is the usual immediate reaction. The "ABC" (*airway*, rescue *breathing*, cardiac chest *compression*) basics and the need to call for help should be heeded, and will become automatic with regular recertification. For further details, the reader is encouraged to review guidelines for the performance of CPR (see American Heart Association, 1980, or other resources) and to become officially certified in the technique.

Allergic Reactions/Latex Allergy

Allergic reactions to medications and environmental allergens are common in children and are generally minor. Rashes, areas of swelling, flushing, sneezing, and running eyes and noses are the most common symptoms and are uncomfortable but never life-threatening.

More serious reactions include vomiting, wheezing, respiratory distress, and even cardiovascular shock. While these are exceedingly rare, they can be life-threatening. All caretakers and intervention personnel need to be aware that certain subgroups of special needs children, most notably those with spina bifida, are at very high risk to have serious allergic reactions to an extremely common substance—rubber (Cotter et al., 1996; Landwehr & Boguniewicz, 1996). This is the problem of latex allergy. Children with spina bifida are exposed repeatedly to latex-containing hospital supplies (catheters, rubber gloves, etc.) in an invasive manner. Many become sensitized, and once sensitized they can experience a life-threatening response to what would seem a trivial exposure (i.e., a toy balloon). The problem is so widespread and so serious that medical personnel treat all children with spina bifida under the assumption that they are latex allergic. School personnel should do the same. Table 8.8 provides an incomplete list of the innumerable common objects that contain latex.

As with children known to have anaphylactic reactions to insect stings (venom allergy), children known to have severe reactions to latex should carry an epinephrine administration device (Epi-Pen) for immediate injection. Caregivers and intervention personnel should be trained in its use. The records and health-information forms of such children should be conspicuously labeled. Also note that a recent report emphasizes that there is strong cross-reactivity between latex allergen and avocado proteins (Ahlroth et al., 1995).

Choking

Infants have frequent minor bouts of choking and gagging, usually on food. Children with neuromotor abnormalities are more likely to experience choking episodes, and

TABLE 8.8 Latex*-Containing Objects

MEDICAL SUPPLIES	CLASSROOM AND PLAYGROUND ITEMS
Adhesives	Art supplies: paints, glues
Bandages and dressings	Balloons
Catheters	Clothing: appliqués, elastic
Crutch tips and pads	Diapers, nipples, and pacifiers
Diapers, nipples, pacifiers	Dishwashing gloves
Elastic wraps and cuffs	Erasers
Enemas	Inner tubes
Gloves	Newspaper, coupons
Reflex hammers	Numerous toys (e.g., car wheels)
Syringe stoppers	Playground surfaces (shredded tires)
Tubing	Pool gear (e.g., goggles, thongs)
	Shoe soles
	Sports equipment (e.g., balls, handle grips)
	Stretch toys

NB: *Cross-reaction with banana, kiwi, and avocado can occur.

The Spina Bifida Association updates an exhaustive list of latex-containing and latex-free materials on a yearly basis. For a copy write to:

SBAA, Suite 250
4590 MacArthur Blvd. NW
Washington, DC 20007

some will be less able to spontaneously clear the obstruction on their own. If a significant choking episode appears to be under way, the key things to remember are:

1. Do not be too aggressive if the child can still cough, breathe, or cry.
2. Get help (call 911).
3. Avoid reaching in for the obstructing object.
4. Initiate CPR beathing, if necessary, *after* the airway has been cleared (cf. Einzig, 1992).

Fractures

Children who do not bear weight on their bones (e.g., the nonambulatory child with cerebral palsy or myelodysplasia), who are malnourished, or who have metabolic bone disorders (e.g., osteogenesis imperfecta) are at risk to break bones under circumstances that would usually be considered mildly traumatic or nontraumatic. These breaks can be relatively silent—accompanied by relatively mild discomfort and only minor swelling and/or a barely perceptible deformity. Additionally, a child may not be able to clearly express degree of pain or its localization.

School personnel need to be aware of children under their care who have had recurrent fractures or who are osteoporotic (have weakened, poorly calcified bone structure) and, therefore, are at risk for fracture. Basic splinting and immobilization techniques are useful to know and employ when a probable or definite fracture is recognized. Immobilization with a splint will greatly decrease pain and also limit additional tissue damage, bleeding, and swelling.

Drug Effects and Overdose/Poisoning

Every medication produces both beneficial and undesirable effects. Drug effects refer to the desirable, hoped-for benefits that prompted initiation of the medication. The measure of how well any given medication is accomplishing this is the objective (at least as much as possible) change in the target symptom, such as a decrease in muscle tone or increase in hand coordination from being placed on diazepam (Valium), or a decrease in seizure frequency from an anticonvulsant. Documentation of effects by nurses (who check, e.g., blood pressure), therapists (who check, e.g., tone and positioning, articulation), teacher (who checks, e.g., seizures, tone, positioning, attention span, etc.), parents, and other caregivers, and timely communication of these data are critical if the physician is to make a well-informed decision about changes in drug dosage.

The side effects of drugs are those signs and symptoms that are not the intended reason for using the medication and are usually (although not always) undesirable. Most side effects are predictable or at least can be somewhat anticipated; some will be unexpected. Their presence and severity (once again, well documented) must be balanced against the benefits of the medication in determining which way to go with dosing.

Some parents and many nonmedical professionals like to use the *PDR* (*Physicians' Desk Reference*) to help them understand a medication, anticipate its undesirable effects, and get a feel for its safety; however, a word of caution is in order. For the nonphysician, nonnurse, or nonpharmacist, a very limited amount of information about drug usage and drug effects is accessible in the *PDR*. On the other hand, an enormous amount of side effect information is presented without discrimination. Basically, every drug can produce multiple damaging effects on every organ system, a very large number of which are potentially life-threatening. The same litany of deathly consequences is more or less repeated for every drug in the compendium. This aspect of the information is virtually useless. What is of importance in decision-making is the discrimination of which side effects are most likely to occur, how persistent or transient they typically are when they appear, and how much of a problem they might cause the particular patient. Additionally, one needs to know how frequently the truly serious, life-threatening side effects are known to occur.

Children with cognitive deficits may be more likely to ingest medication or other harmful substances as a result of pica (the tendency to mouth and eat nonfood objects). More commonly, the child who is taking medication (e.g., anticonvulsant drugs for seizures) may gradually become toxic due to rising blood levels of the drug, even without any change in the dose. This phenomenon can occur due to changes in drug metabolism resulting from drug interference (from another medication), an unrecognized *brand* change, or a minor illness. A dose change (intentional or accidental) is also distinctly possible. The only indication of drug toxicity may be behavioral change in the classroom, once again pointing out the importance of knowing a child's baseline and making note of observed changes therefrom.

Head Injury

Head trauma in special needs children should be managed as it would be for any other child. Minor injuries can be treated with cold compresses, pressure for bleeding, cleaning, and covering for abrasions. More severe injuries that require possible suturing or have associated neurological symptoms will require medical attention.

Seizures

A seizure is the clinical manifestation of paroxysmal electrical activity in the brain. Seizures may be extremely subtle, as with *petit mal* epilepsy (characterized by very brief staring and/or perhaps a few rapid blinks), or frighteningly explosive, as with *grand mal* epilepsy (typified by falling to the ground, rigidity and violent shaking, stridorous breathing, and/or cyanosis).

Children with neurodevelopmental disorders are at much higher risk than the general population to experience an isolated seizure or to have epilepsy (repeated seizures). The two key factors in the classroom are observation and basic first aid. Observation is important in order to report the duration, frequency, and exact clinical features of a seizure or seizures as accurately as possible. First aid is important to protect the child from doing further harm to himself as a result of striking the head or limbs or biting the tongue. The old recommendation to put a stick, spoon, billfold, or heaven-knows-what in the mouth so the child does not swallow his tongue is incorrect. Loosening clothing, removing eyeglasses, keeping the child (especially the head and extremities) out of harm's way, and positioning the child on his side are the basic measures to be followed. Many children who experience "hard" seizures for more than two or three minutes will turn blue, but as this occurs the seizure tends to lessen and their breathing will improve. When the seizure finally ceases, they usually resume normal breathing, often with a deep sigh or two. If good breathing and improved skin color do not return, then the CPR sequence (ABC, with special attention to A) should be initiated.

For children with a known seizure disorder, having reliable knowledge of the usual type and frequency of seizures is essential if the teacher is to be able to respond appropriately to a spell that is out of the ordinary. As a rule, any first seizure requires urgent medical attention. In a child with known seizures, a spell that lasts five minutes or more generally deserves medical evaluation. This guideline may be too short for some individuals known to typically have slightly longer seizures. On the other hand, even four minutes may be troubling in a child whose usual pattern is much briefer. This also reemphasizes the importance of observational data on seizures in a child with epilepsy that differ in their manifestations or frequency from that child's usual pattern, which may be a warning that something new or different is going awry (e.g., with a shunt, a metabolic condition, or an anticonvulsant drug). These observations warrant diligent reporting and are extremely useful to the physician treating the child.

AIDS

The human immunodeficiency virus (HIV) is almost always acquired by infants and toddlers from their HIV-infected mother at the time of birth. Recent medical advances in drug therapy for HIV have substantially reduced the chance of transmission from mother to infant. At the time of this writing, if the mother is placed on a special regimen of zidovudine medication and if other general precautions are observed, the risk of transmission from mother to newborn is as low as 5 to 10 percent (American Academy of Pediatrics [AAP] Committee on Pediatric AIDS, 1997).

HIV multiplies in certain cells of the immune system, eventually depleting them and rendering the child almost defenseless against numerous infections, some of which can transform other cells into cancers. Once the child begins to acquire infections, the problem is referred to as the acquired immunodeficiency syndrome (AIDS). Although the various infections can be suppressed or successfully treated with appropriate medications for years, ultimately infection and/or cancer are fatal for the great majority of people with AIDS.

Needless to say, the presence of an HIV-infected child in school and day care settings can be the cause of extreme anxiety for parents, children, health care providers, and educators. HIV is not transmitted through casual contact (sharing toys, food, and eating utensils; hugging; kissing; etc.) nor by contact in the environment with urine, stool, saliva, or vomitus. Under extremely rare circumstances, direct contact of HIV-infected blood with broken skin can produce infection. Because of this possibility, preschoolers and developmentally disabled children who might bite are viewed as a theoretical transmission hazard. Actual transmission of HIV through biting in a day care setting has never been reported. There is one reported "possible" (unconfirmed) case of a sibling being infected at home from the bite of an infected toddler (Shirley & Ross, 1989).

Communities should emphasize their own state and national guidelines in designing school placement policies for HIV-infected children (Table 8.9).

State agencies (e.g., the Virginia Department of Health, 1995a, 1995b), the American Academy of Pediatrics (AAP Task Force on Pediatric AIDS, 1992), and others (Crocker & Cohen, 1990; Santelli, Birn, & Linde, 1992) have prepared guidelines in regard to developmental services and school and day care attendance for children with HIV infection and AIDS. Policies work best in the context of a comprehensive program incorporating AIDS education and care (Santelli et al, 1992).

TABLE 8.9 National Guidelines Regarding School Placement for Human Immunodeficiency Virus (HIV)-Infected Children*

1. In general, infected school-age children should be allowed to attend school in an unrestricted setting. The benefits of school attendance outweigh the remote possibility of transmission occurring in school.
2. Some children, such as preschoolers and children with neurologic impairments, with open skin lesions, or with behavior problems such as biting, may need a more restricted setting.
3. In determining an individual educational placement, a team approach should be employed using representatives of health and education departments as well as family members.
4. Staff knowledge about a child's HIV status should be based on a "need to know." The child's and family's right to privacy should be respected.
5. Universal hygiene precautions should be adopted by schools.
6. Mandatory or universal screening is not warranted.
7. Education about HIV/AIDS should be encouraged for parents, students, and educational staff.

*Based on recommendations of the American Academy of Pediatrics and the Centers for Disease Control.

From "School Placement for HIV-Infected Children: The Baltimore Experience" by J. H. S. Santelli, A. E. Birn, and J. Linde, 1992, *Pediatrics, 89,* 843–848. Adapted by permission.

Hepatitis

Hepatitis (inflammation of the liver) can result from a number of causes. As a primary disease, it is most commonly caused by one of several viruses, which are designated by letters (A, B, C, etc.); less commonly, another infection or a toxic agent can be involved. It can be an associated problem of other infections (e.g., infectious mononucleosis). It can be a toxic side effect of therapeutic drugs (e.g., anticonvulsants) or a direct effect of environmental toxins or drug overdoses (e.g., acetaminophen, iron). In the years before the deinstitutional movement began, infectious hepatitis was rampant in institutions for the mentally retarded. Hepatitis A virus is highly communicable by the fecal-oral route. The other hepatitis viruses are more difficult to transmit and usually require blood (via transfusions or contaminated needles) or other intimate exchange. Hepatitis can easily be transmitted from an infected mother to her newborn at birth.

In the early intervention setting, the infant or toddler who has active hepatitis could transmit the infection to staff and to other children as well as to family members. There are two key considerations to understanding the risks and the precautions. First, most people who acquire viral hepatitis resolve the infection and become immune to it. They carry hepatitis *antibody* in their blood indicating a past infection, and they *cannot* transmit the disease. (In fact, they no longer have the disease.) Individuals who are still infected (and therefore potentially infectious) carry hepatitis *antigen* in their blood. The first order of business is to learn whether the child is a "carrier," that is to say, positive for the antigen. The second issue is to learn which viral type is involved. Hepatitis B is not generally transmitted by casual contact, but hepatitis A can be.

COMMUNICATION AMONG PROFESSIONALS

Doctors and the IFSP

Part C of the Individuals with Disabilities Education Act (see Chapter 1) deals with financial incentives offered to states to develop their own comprehensive services for infants and toddlers who are disabled. The services are to be family-centered and truly coordinated among agencies. The IFSP (individualized family service plan) required by Part C reflects a broad and comprehensive human services approach to structuring an efficient array of supports, taking into account all aspects of family life and dynamics. The American Academy of Pediatrics has strongly encouraged pediatricians to participate in the IFSP process (AAP, Committee on Children with Disabilities,1992).

Pediatricians, however, have often felt left out by the language employed in federal legislation that limits medical services to diagnosis and evaluation only. The Committee on Children with Disabilities has promoted a much broader role for pediatricians, which includes program planning and monitoring, medical supervision, and other aspects of management as well (Purvis, 1991).

Regardless of these language deficiencies at the policy level, at the local level individual school personnel have urged increased pediatrician input into the process. Children who come to light in the under-three age range are likely to have considerable medical needs, as noted. In addition to major medical and neurodevelopmental problems (seizures, technology dependency, etc.), a proportion of them have infectious or related etiologies (e.g., congenital infections, AIDS) that can be highly anxiety-provoking for early interventionists, caretakers, and parents of other children in the same program, as noted in many of the above vignettes.

A cooperative relationship between team members is fundamental to achieving the goal of coordinated family-centered care. Developmental pediatricians and general pediatricians with a special interest in chronic conditions should be key collaborators in the care for young children. The goal is to see that the best supports are made available to the parents of children with any chronic illness or disability. The "medical home" philosophy has dominated new directives adopted by the American Academy of Pediatrics (AAP, Task Force on the Definition of the Medical Home, 1992) and federal funding policies. It implies the essential importance of quality community services in order to achieve successful family-centered care. While medical center–based interdisciplinary clinics will still be needed for comprehensive evaluations, academic pediatricians must better address the need for continuing education programs for community professionals that are up-to-date, comprehensive, and practical.

DNR Orders

If a child has an untoward event that results in the cessation or compromise of respiratory or cardiac function, the immediate response by professional, paraprofessional, and lay observers should be to resuscitate (see the section on CPR above). Do not resuscitate (DNR) orders represent specific instructions, written by a licensed physician, either to not initiate or to limit the extent of resuscitation efforts. There are many children who have DNR orders in place while receiving care in the hospital or at home. Some of these individuals will be in center-based school programs.

Obviously the decision to establish a DNR order must be a carefully considered exercise involving the child (to the extent she is capable), the parents, the attending physician, and other relevant members of the family and the health care team. DNR orders are legally binding! A clear delineation of actions that should or should not be carried out needs to be communicated verbally and in writing to all relevant parties. The health care team doctors, nurses, emergency medical technicians, and so on are clearly implicated. It is less clear how directly these wishes and orders apply to school personnel. Many school administrators have simply declared it to be "school policy" that DNR orders cannot be carried out in school settings, which is probably more a reflection of avoiding the issue than of thoughtfully considering the ethical implications. In the author's discussions with teachers, nurses, and therapists about the topic, it seems that the uneasiness expressed about DNR orders comes down to three issues:

1. The acute psychological distress occasioned by "not doing something"
2. The fear that a simple and easily remediable event could be missed (e.g., choking on thick saliva)
3. The effect on other children in the vicinity

The first issue is one that everyone has to deal with—parent, doctor, teacher, and others. It has a lot to do with understanding death as a natural and necessary end point and with being able to acknowledge that when the time has come, it is permissible to allow death to happen. This viewpoint runs strongly counter to most people's instincts. Thus, the determination *not* to intervene must be a premeditated conclusion arrived at in each individual case. When the decision to limit intervention has been carefully thought out in advance, carrying it out in a palliative, supportive manner is much easier than trying to make such a decision in a crisis mode or intervening in a way or to a degree that one senses is wrong.

The second issue can be broken down into two parts: following explicit orders and being reasonable. A sample set of DNR orders, taken from a current hospital chart, is presented in Table 8.10. These orders are simply and clearly stated and are unequivocal. They are a model for the type of clarity desired. In this particular instance, they allow for examining the patient and "doing something" in the case of a remediable situation. In a different case, where, for example, assisted ventilation were *not* endorsed, it would still be *reasonable* for a classroom aide (or whoever) to check the mouth for an obstruction or to suction the airway of a child who has suddenly and unexpectedly stopped breathing, even if not specified in the orders. (It is hard to imagine suctioning being explicitly prohibited in a child with or at risk for respiratory compromise.) On the other hand, for a teacher, an emergency medical technician, or a physician to initiate and persist with mouth-to-mouth resuscitation and cardiac chest compressions in the face of written DNR orders prohibiting these measures amounts to unreasonable (and disrespectful) behavior.

TABLE 8.10 Sample DNR Orders

The following advanced directive is to be honored per the wishes of the parents (or legal guardians) of ____________________ (name of patient). In the event of cardiorespiratory dysfunction or arrest:

1. *Support* with assisted ventilation.
2. *Support* with parenteral medications for control of blood pressure or arrhythmias.
3. Do *not* administer intracardiac drugs.
4. Do *not* initiate chest compressions.
5. Do *not* administer electroshock cardioversion.

The final issue is an important one that takes into account the well-being of other children and demands careful consideration. The key to all three issues is advance planning and a willingness to collaborate on a plan that will fairly serve all parties the involved child, parents, school staff, other children, and bystanders. For the benefit of the latter two groups, some effort at comforting and segregating (not hiding) the "patient"; maintaining a calm, controlled, and professional atmosphere; and rendering some type of appropriate explanation all need to be accomplished.

Case managers are central to this entire process, and the county medical examiner needs to be notified *in advance* that a death may occur in the community, be it at home, in school, or in another setting. Otherwise, unnecessary police and/or medical examiner investigations may be imposed on an already difficult situation.

In summary, early interventionists are very likely to encounter children with substantial medical needs, even medical fragility, in their case loads. Early childhood service providers need general medical background information and need support from the medical community with regard to specific issues about each child they are working with. The intent of this chapter has been to provide some of that background and to offer some insights on when and how to effect collaboration and communication among medical and educational professionals.

REFERENCES

Ahlroth, M., Alerius, H., Turjanmaa, K., Makinen-Kiljunen, S., Reunala, T., & Palusno, T. (1995). Cross-reacting allergens in natural rubber latex and avocado. *Journal of Allergy and Clinical Immunology, 96,* 167–173.

Albright, A. L., Cerri, A., & Singletary, J. (1991). Intrathecal baclofen for spasticity in cerebral palsy. *Journal of the American Medical Association, 265,* 1418–1422.

Allen, M. C. (1994). Neurodevelopmental follow-up of the preterm infant. *Pediatric Rounds, 3*(1), 1–4.

Allen, M. C., & Alexander, G. R. (1990). Gross motor milestones in preterm infants: Correction for degree of prematurity. *Journal of Pediatrics, 116,* 955–959.

American Academy of Pediatrics Committee on Children with Disabilities (1992). Pediatricians' role in the development and implementation of an individual education plan (IEP) and/or an individual family service plan (IFSP). *Pediatrics 89,* 340–342.

American Academy of Pediatrics Task Force on Definition of the Medical Home (1992). The medical home. *Pediatrics, 90,* 774.

American Academy of Pediatrics Task Force on Pediatric AIDS (1988). Pediatric guidelines for infection control of human immunodeficiency virus (acquired immunodeficiency virus) in hospitals, medical offices, schools, and other settings. *Pediatrics, 82,* 801–807.

American Academy of Pediatrics Task Force on Pediatric AIDS (1992). Guidelines for human immunodeficiency virus (HIV)-infected children and their foster families (1992). *Pediatrics, 89,* 681–683.

American Academy of Pediatrics Committee on Pediatric AIDS (1997). Evaluation and medical treatment of the HIV-exposed infant. *Pediatrics, 99,* 909–917.

American Heart Association (1980). *Cardiopulmonary resuscitation: CPR.* (2nd ed.) Tulsa: CPR Publishers.

Anisfeld, E., & Lipper, E. (1983). Early contact, social support, and mother-infant bonding. *Pediatrics, 72,* 79–83.

Austin, K. D., & Hall, J. G. (1992). Nontraditional inheritance. *Pediatric Clinics of North America, 39,* 335–348.

Baird, H. W., & Gordon, E. C. (1983). *Neurological evaluation of infants and children* (Clinics in Developmental Medicine No. 84/85). Philadelphia: J. B. Lippincott.

Batshaw, M. L. (1997). *Children with disabilities* (4th ed.). Baltimore: Paul H. Brookes.

Blasco, P. A. (1989). Preterm birth: To correct or not to correct. *Developmental Medicine and Child Neurology, 31,* 816–821.

Blasco, P. A. (1992). Normal and abnormal motor development. *Pediatric Rounds, 1*(2), 1–6.

Blasco, P. A., Baumgartner, M. C., & Mathes, B. C. (1983). Literature for parents of children with cerebral palsy. *Developmental Medicine and Child Neurology, 25,* 642–647.

Blasco, P. A., & Johnson, C. P. (1996). Supports for parents of children with disabilities. In A. J. Capute & P. J. Accardo (Eds.), *Developmental disabilities in infancy and childhood,* 2nd ed. (pp. 443–472) Baltimore: Paul H. Brookes.

Blasco, P. M., Blasco, P. A., & Zirpoli, T. J. (1994). Prenatal diagnosis: Current procedures and implications for early interventionists working with families. *Infants and Young Children, 7,* 33–42.

Bleck, E. E. (1987). *Orthopedic management in cerebral palsy* (Clinics in Developmental Medicine No. 99/100). Philadelphia: J. B. Lippincott.

Blizzard, R. M. (1993). Genetics and growth: New understanding. *Pediatric Rounds, 2*(2), 1–4.

Brewer, E. J., McPherson, M., Magrab, P. R., & Hutchins, V. L. (1989). Family-centered, community-based, coordinator care for children with special health care needs. *Pediatrics, 83,* 1055–1061.

Butler, M. G., & Meaney, F. J. (1991). Standards for selected anthropometric measurements in Prader-Willi syndrome. *Pediatrics, 88,* 853–860.

Capute, A. J., & Accardo, P. J. (1996) *Developmental disabilities in infancy and childhood* (Vols. I & II, 2nd ed.). Baltimore: Paul H. Brookes.

Capute, A. J., & Palmer, F. P. (1980). A pediatric overview of the spectrum of developmental disabilities. *Journal of Developmental and Behavioral Pediatrics, 1,* 66–69.

Capute, A. J., Shapiro, B. K., Palmer, F. P., Ross, A., & Wachtel, R. C. (1985). Normal gross motor development: The influence of race, sex, and socio-economic status. *Developmental Medicine and Child Neurology, 27,* 635–643.

Chang, P. N., Thompson, T. R., & Fisch, R. O. (1982). Factors affecting attachment between infants and mothers separated at birth. *Journal of Developmental and Behavioral Pediatrics, 3,* 96–98

Chess, S., & Thomas, A. (1982). Infant bonding: Mystique and reality. *American Journal of Orthopsychiatry, 52,* 213–222.

Coplan, J. (1987). Deafness: Ever heard of it? Delayed recognition of permanent hearing loss. *Pediatrics, 79,* 206–213.

Cotter, C. M., Burbach, C., Boyer, M., Engelhardt, M., Smith, M., & Hubka, K. (1996). Latex allergy and the student with spina bifida. *Journal of School Nursing, 12,* 14–18.

Crocker, A. C., & Cohen, H. J. (1990). *Guidelines on developmental services for children and adults with HIV infection.* Silver Spring, Md.: AAUAP for Persons with Developmental Disabilities.

Cronk, C., Crocker, A. C., Pueschel, S. M., Shea, A. M., Zackai, E., Pickens, G., & Reed, R. B. (1988). Growth charts for children with Down syndrome: 1 month to 18 years of age. *Pediatrics, 81,* 102–110.

deSchweinitz, L., Miller, C. A., & Miller, J. B. (1959). Delays in the diagnosis of deafness among preschool children. *Pediatrics,* 24, 462–468.

Drews, C. D., Yeargin-Allsopp, M., Murphy, C. C., & Decoufle, P. (1994). Hearing impairment among 10-year-old children: Metropolitan Atlanta, 1985 through 1987. *American Journal of Public Health, 84,* 1164–1166.

Einzig, M. J. (1992). *Baby and child emergency first aid handbook.* New York: Meadowbrook.

Erhardt, R. P. (1994). *Developmental hand dysfunction: Theory, assessment, treatment* (2nd ed.). San Antonio: Therapy Skill Builders.

Halsey, C. L., Collin, M. F, & Anderson, C. L. (1996). Extremely low-birth-weight children and their peers: A comparison of school-age outcomes. *Archives of Pediatrics and Adolescent Medicine, 150,* 790–794.

Hamill, P. V. V., Drizd, T. A., Johnson, C. L., Reed, R. B., Roche, A. F., & Moore, W. M. (1979). Physical growth: National Center for Health Statistics percentiles. *American Journal of Clinical Nutrition, 32,* 607–629.

Jackson, J. F., North, E. R., III, & Thomas, J. G. (1976). Clinical diagnosis of Down's syndrome. *Clinical Genetics, 9,* 483–487.

Jones, K. L. (1996). *Smith's recognizable patterns of human malformation* (5th ed.). Philadelphia: W. B. Saunders.

Kaminer, R. K., & Jedrysek, E. (1983). Age of walking and mental retardation. *American Journal of Public Health, 73,* 1094–1096.

Klein, S. D. (Ed.) (1977). National resources for specific disabilities and conditions. *Exceptional Parent* (Annual Resource Guide), *27,* 9–39.

Klein, S. D. (1993). The challenge of communicating with parents. *Journal of Developmental and Behavioral Pediatrics, 14,* 184–191.

Knobloch, H., & Pasamanick, B. (1974). *Gesell and Amatruda's develpomental diagnosis* (3rd ed.). Hagerstown, Md.: Harper and Row, pp. 3–15.

Koman, L. A., Mooney, J. F., & Smith, B. P. (1996). Neuromuscular blockade in the management of cerebral palsy. *Journal of Child Neurology, 11* (Suppl.1), S23–S28.

Kraft, M. (1985). *A child's guide to cerebral palsy.* Charlottesville: University of Virginia, Kluge Children's Rehabilitation Center.

Krahn, G. L., Hallum, A., & Kime, C. (1993). Are there good ways to give "bad news"? *Pediatrics, 91,* 578–582.

Lamb, M. E. (1982). Early contact and maternal-infant bonding: One decade later. *Pediatrics, 70,* 763–768.

Landwehr, L. P., & Boguniewicz, M. (1996). Current perspectives on latex allergy. *Journal of Pediatrics, 128,* 305–312.

Lewis, D. V., & Freeman, J. M. (1977). The electroencephalogram in pediatric practice: Its use and abuse. *Pediatrics, 60,* 324–330.

Lipkin, P. H. (1996), Epidemiology of the developmental disabilities. In A. J. Capute & P. J. Accardo (Eds.), *Developmental disabilities in infancy and childhood* (Vol. I, 2nd ed.) (pp. 137–156). Baltimore: Paul H. Brookes.

Liptak, G. S., Keller, B. B., Feldman, A. W., & Chamberlin, R. W. (1983). Enhancing infant development and parent-practitioner interaction with the Brazelton Neonatal Assessment Scale, *Pediatrics, 72,* 71–78.

Lock, T. M., Shapiro, B. K., Ross, A., & Capute, A. J. (1986). Age of presentation of developmental disabilities. *Journal of Developmental and Behavioral Pediatrics, 7,* 340–345.

Minde, K., (1986). Bonding and attachment: Its relevance for the present day clinician. *Developmental Medicine and Child Neurology, 28,* 803–813.

Myers, B. J. (1982). Early intervention using Brazelton training with middle-class mothers and fathers of newborns. *Child Development, 53,* 462–471.

Nolan, C. (1987). *Under the eye of the clock.* New York: St. Martin's.

Paarlberg, J., Atkinson, W., Bella, D., & Kocher, A. (1991). *Guide to gastrostomy tubes and their care: A parent instruction manual.* Charlottesville: University of Virginia, Kluge Children's Rehabilitation Center.

Peacock, W. J., Arens, L. J., & Berman, B. (1987). Cerebral palsy spasticity: Selective posterior rhizotomy. *Pediatric Neuroscience, 13,* 61–66.

Peckham, C., & Gibb, D. (1995). Mother-to-child transmission of the human immunodeficiency virus. *New England Journal of Medicine, 333,* 289–302.

Physicians' desk reference (51st ed.). (1997). Montvale, N.J.: Medical Economics Data Production.

Pranzatelli, M. R. (1996). Oral pharmacotherapy for the movement disorders of cerebral palsy. *Journal of Child Neurology, 11* (Suppl. 1), S13–S22.

Purvis, P. (1991). The public laws for education of the disabled: The pediatrician's role. *Journal of Developmental and Behavioral Pediatrics, 12,* 327–339.

Remington, J. S., & Klein, J. O. (Eds.). (1995). *Infectious diseases of the fetus and newborn* (4th ed.). Philadelphia: W. B. Saunders.

Robinson, C. G., Willits, R. E. & Benson, K. I. G. (1965). Delayed diagnosis of congenital hearing loss in preschool children. *Public Health Reports, 80,* 790–796.

Santelli, J. S., Birn, A.-E., & Linde, J. (1992). School placement for HIV-infected children: The Baltimore experience. *Pediatrics, 89,* 843–848.

Shah, C. P., Chandler, D., & Doll, R. (1978). Delay in referral of children with impaired hearing. *Volta Review, 80,* 206–215.

Shirley, L. R., & Ross, S. A. (1989). Risk of transmission of human immunodeficiency virus by bite of infected toddler. *Journal of Pediatrics, 114,* 425–427.

Simon, B. M., Fowler, S. M., & Handler, S. D. (1983). Communication development in young children with long-term tracheostomies: Preliminary report. *International Journal of Pediatric Otolaryngology, 6,* 37–50.

Singer, L. T., Davillier, M., Preuss, L., Szekely, L., Hawkins, S., Yamashita, T., & Baley J., et al. (1996). Feeding interactions in infants with very low birth weight and bronchopulmonary dysplasia. *Journal of Developmental and Behavioral Pediatrics, 17,* 69–76.

Singer, L. T., Kercsmar, C., Legris, G., Orlowski, J. P., Hill, B. P., & Doershurk, C. (1989). Developmental sequelae of long-term infant tracheostomy. *Developmental Medicine and Child Neurology, 31,* 224–230.

Stevenson, R. D. (1992). Failure to thrive. In D. E. Greydanus & M. L. Wolraich (Eds.), *Behavioral pediatrics* (pp. 298–313). New York: Springer-Verlag.

Virginia Department of Health (1995a). *Recommendations for day care center attendance.* Richmond: Author.

Virginia Department of Health. (1995b). *Recommendations for school attendance.* Richmond: Author.

Widmayer, S. M., & Field, T. M. (1981). Effects of Brazelton demonstrations for mother on the development of preterm infants. *Pediatrics, 67,* 711–714.

CHAPTER NINE

MODELS OF COLLABORATION FOR EARLY INTERVENTION

Laying the Groundwork

VIRGINIA BUYSSE

PATRICIA W. WESLEY

OBJECTIVES

- To describe the expanding roles of early intervention professionals in the context of a changing field
- To apply the concept of quality to early intervention practice as a foundation for identifying consumers and evaluating the effectiveness of services
- To understand the similarities and distinctions among various models of collaboration, including technical assistance, consultation, teaming, training, and supervision and mentorship
- To develop strategies for evaluating the effectiveness of existing collaborative approaches and envisioning new methods for working together in the future.

Most of us operate in a small central area of the role which we can call a "zone of comfort." Within this zone of comfort we feel quite safe because we are very sure of our ground and it is a low-risk area. Once we step outside this comfort zone the ground is considerably less firm underfoot. These swampy areas are at the boundary of our expertise, professional knowledge, authority and confidence.

—Dimock, 1993, p. 45

The field of early intervention has changed and continues to change rapidly. As described in previous chapters, parents and professionals have witnessed the adoption of a family-centered orientation, the unification of early education and early intervention, and the move to serve young children with disabilities in inclusive and natural environments. In addition, a corresponding paradigm shift has occurred in the way early intervention services are designed and delivered from a stimulation or remediation model to one that promotes competence and supports full inclusion and participation in the community through multiagency collaboration. These and other innovations have created new professional roles for early interventionists and redefined the ways in which parents and professionals work together (Buysse & Wesley, 1993).

This paradigm shift has also resulted in a move from direct services to indirect services. Kontos and File (1993) pointed out that "when children with disabilities are placed in integrated community programs, even for part of a day, early interventionists are no longer the only educators working with the children, and, in many instances, the responsibilities of the early interventionist evolve from those of direct service to those of indirect service to the children." (p. 176)

Indirect services are primarily adult-oriented and consist of consultation and collaboration, rather than direct instruction, which focuses on the child. The shift from direct to indirect services requires that early interventionists learn new roles and extend the boundaries of their professional comfort by expanding their partnerships to include not only family members but child care providers, therapists, health care professionals, administrators, social workers, and others with whom children and families interact in a variety of community settings.

The purpose of this chapter is to familiarize the reader with state-of-the-art models of collaboration for early intervention. The specific professional roles and models that have been identified to enhance collaborative work relationships emanate from the fields of business, organizational development, international politics, education, community mental health, and psychology. These include technical assistance, consultation, teaming, training, and supervision and mentorship. Our intent in this chapter is to lay the groundwork to equip early interventionists with the skills to work effectively with parents and adults who serve children and families. In addition to a theoretical framework, each of the collaborative models presented in this chapter contains practical suggestions, as well as a discussion of the process and tools needed to build relationships, communicate effectively, identify and respond to technical assistance needs, and plan strategically for the future. We begin by discussing the concept of quality as it relates to consumers of early education and intervention, and then distinguish among various models of collaboration that promote quality services for young children and families. We conclude with a framework that can be used to integrate and evaluate these approaches.

APPLYING THE CONCEPT OF QUALITY TO EARLY INTERVENTION PRACTICE: WHO ARE THE CONSUMERS?

Sometimes it is difficult to remember that collaboration is a means to an end, not an end in itself. We seek better methods of working together for one basic reason: to improve the quality of our services for young children and families. The focus on improving quality among the human service professions can be viewed as part of a growing quality movement across many institutions throughout the world today. Quality is a term that is, at the same time, both easy to understand and difficult to define. What do we mean by quality services, and what are some benchmarks for measuring it?

Total Quality Management (TQM), which originated in business and manufacturing, offers one approach for understanding ideas related to quality. The ideas inherent in TQM were introduced by Demming, Juran, and others in the 1930s and 1940s, but were not widely accepted in the United States until recently (Sallis, 1993). TQM is a philosophy and a methodology for managing institutional change with the goal of improving quality (Sallis, 1993). The main idea behind the concept is quite simple: quality is a function of customer satisfaction. To assess whether our customers are satisfied, we must first determine who the customer is and then decide what the product is. As mentioned earlier, the consumers of early intervention are young children and their families, as well as a growing number of professionals and assistants from a variety of settings: homes, child care centers, preschool classrooms, family child care homes, hospitals, and clinics. The product is more difficult to define. Drawing a distinction between human services and other types of products, Sallis (1993) noted that human services are both intangible and relationship-based, making quality an even more challenging notion to define and measure.

One concept from TQM that has implications for improving the quality of early education and intervention services is the assessment of the organizational structure of early education and intervention programs. Programs that rely too heavily on top-down, hierarchical management structures may find it difficult to involve families in decision-making, to create leadership roles for families, or to promote interdisciplinary collaboration through teamwork, which is an essential element of TQM. Developing leadership potential to create a vision and communicate this vision effectively to others is another TQM concept that could be applied in our work with families and other professionals. Creating effective team leaders, supervisors, and program administrators through leadership training and other methods represents an important step in developing high-quality programs and services. Finally, we must embrace teamwork at every level as a building block for improving quality and implementing strategic planning to address current and future needs of young children and families.

In programs that serve young children and their families, the concept of quality must be applied broadly across all aspects of planning, delivering, and evaluating services. National professional organizations have described recommended practices and guidelines to help practitioners and families define and apply notions of quality across each of these areas. As part of the process of improving quality, professionals face particular challenges in developing ways to involve family members and create leadership roles for them. Most professionals now recognize the value of family involvement, but have found it difficult to find ways to encourage broad-based parental participation on boards and planning teams and to promote family decision-making at every level. Another important challenge in making quality improvements lies in developing an awareness of the influence of cultural diversity on collaborative processes. Many programs serving young children and families were influenced by a cultural perspective that is different from that of the clients they serve (Nugent, 1994). Viewing the early childhood fields from different cultural perspectives challenges professional assumptions about child development, raises questions about the appropriateness of program goals and practices, and reveals the rich diversity of child-rearing patterns and beliefs among various ethnic and cultural groups. Although there is general consensus that programs serving young children and their families should be community-based, family-centered, and culturally sensitive, most programs continue to struggle to achieve a balance.

TECHNICAL ASSISTANCE

As community child care and early intervention organizations redefine their mission, target population, and methods of service delivery, it is easy to recognize a need for support and guidance. Technical assistance (TA) can provide helpful tools to programs experiencing these kinds of changes as they reexamine the way they relate to each other and the rest of the community.

Although definitions of TA vary, a common feature is the transfer of "information, methods, tools, and support" (Sullivan, 1991, p. 290) or "specialized knowledge, skills, information, and technologies" (Richman & Clifford, 1980, p. 13) from one system to another that perceives a need for change. Although the terms *in-service training* and *consultation* are often equated with TA, Trohanis

(1982) pointed out that "TA involves the provision of quality content and/or process expertise via a responsive, continuous, and external system to assist clients and their organization to change or improve for the better." (p. 120) Based on this definition, consultation and training are but two strategies that may be employed in a carefully designed sequence of activities to promote systems change. Technical assistance offers a system of strategies that can be used to effect changes that require more intensive and extensive assistance than can be provided through materials, training, or consultation alone (Loucks-Horsley & Mundry, 1991).

As early interventionists expand their collegial networks to include persons who traditionally have been outside the special education field, they can be valuable resources to programs undergoing some of the systems changes described in this chapter. In Vignette 9.1, Julie encounters someone eager to take advantage of her expertise.

VIGNETTE 9.1 BRIGHT BEGINNINGS AND FUTURE NEEDS

Julie is an early interventionist who has been visiting 15-month-old Jorge at Bright Beginnings child care for nearly six weeks, ever since she went with Jorge and his mother to visit the program prior to enrollment. Jorge has cerebral palsy, and his new teacher, Ann, was especially glad to have Julie in the classroom on Tuesday and Thursday mornings. Ann had many questions about how best to adapt routines and activities for Jorge, and about his health and physical condition. But Ann also had questions about toddlers in general, since this was the first year the center had opened a toddler class. Julie made a few suggestions for making more toys and materials accessible to the children by rearranging some low shelves in the room. On a recent visit, Ann told Julie about the center's toddler waiting list. Ann was on a staff committee at the center to look into expanding in the spring—perhaps adding another toddler class and an infant class. She knew Julie also saw an infant in a family child care home in the neighboring county, and she wondered about what other types of programs were available for infants and toddlers, including those with special needs. What did Julie think were the challenges and benefits of serving younger children? What steps could they take to make sure a new class would be appropriate for children with special needs? Ann also had lots of questions about training resources and opportunities for herself and the other staff at the center. She wondered if Julie could do a workshop about child development in the near future for the whole center. She also wanted to learn more about how to work with parents of very young children.

We can imagine how overwhelmed Julie may have felt after this visit. She was comfortable answering the questions Ann had about Jorge, and she was glad to offer suggestions about room arrangement. She wasn't prepared, however, to provide consultation about program expansion or to take on training the whole staff. Julie knew that she would have to draw from a range of resources to be able to help Ann, and that there were some services Ann needed that she could not personally provide. What Julie and Ann both needed was the support of multiple TA services focusing on early childhood issues. In the absence of a formal system of resources and support, Julie would do the best she could to find such assistance for Ann. She could refer Ann and the expansion committee to a child care program in the neighboring county that had expanded its infant-toddler program the previous year. She could loan them a videotape series about child development from her office, and mention their need for a workshop to the nurse who provides training as a part of the public health department's well child clinic. She could also refer Ann to a staff person at the local child care resource and referral agency who was aware of what types of licensed and registered child care centers and family child care homes were operating across their local tricounty area. Finally, Julie and some of her colleagues at the office had just been talking about the challenges of collaborating with parents to meet the needs of their young children. Perhaps they would all benefit from sitting down with someone like Ann and sharing ideas.

Strategies like the ones described above illustrate how flexible TA must be to respond to the diverse needs that arise in early intervention and child care today. Technical assistance providers must draw from a range of options to be effective in a variety of contexts. Some states have responded to the needs of practitioners like Julie and Ann and to the corresponding needs of families by creating statewide systems of TA to support early childhood programs. In other states, regional teams provide support to local communities. In many instances, however, early interventionists find themselves in a position much like Julie's, where their role evolves to include providing TA in specific situations. It is useful to be aware of resources in the community that can help. For example, perhaps a local university sponsors a TA project or offers in-service training on a particular topic, or a mental health agency or child care resource and referral agency may offer a lending library of training materials and other resources. Ways to locate resources include talking with professional colleagues in the community, attending regional and state conferences, and conducting a search on the Internet.

Whether the focus of TA is on facilitating change at the state, regional, community, program, classroom, or individual child or family level, the process involves common goals based on what we know about how change occurs. In the following sections, we will see how these broad goals might apply to Julie and Ann's situation, and we will examine the roles and process of technical assistance.

Goals

Technical assistance providers first must understand and help the people with whom they are working to understand the barriers and facilitators of change in specific situations (Peck, Furman, & Helmstetter, 1993). For example, when programs like Ann's begin to serve children with disabilities, it is necessary to examine program policies, personnel preparation practices, and the adequacy of resources such as special education consultation to determine what obstacles and supports exist for the innovation. Similarly, although the attitudes of the staff at the child care program may be supportive of early childhood inclusion, there may be families of children with and without disabilities who are not comfortable with the idea. Only when these critical issues are examined can change be implemented in an effective way.

Second, TA builds support and commitment for innovation by encouraging the broad participation of all stakeholders in planning, and by creating opportunities for them to listen to and understand the unique perspective that each brings to the process. At Bright Beginnings, a staff committee has been formed to talk about expanding the center to serve more infants and toddlers in the community. If Julie agrees to provide TA during this process, one of her roles might be to help the committee identify who else might have a stake in the center's expansion and to bring them to the table. For example, there may be parents or other early intervention professionals whose experiences and interests would be valuable contributions to the committee's work.

Third, TA provides expertise to help clients develop their vision of what changes are needed and to translate that vision into a written plan of action. In other words, it enhances both content and process. Ann and the committee at Bright Beginnings have a broad vision of serving younger children, including those with special needs. Julie can help link them to the resources they need to fine-tune their vision and long-range plan. Such resources might represent a variety of content areas: child care rules and regulations regarding infant/toddler classrooms, service coordination for young children with special needs, the critical components of quality inclusive infant/toddler care, and building strong relationships with families. Technical assistance could also help the committee identify and implement a step-by-step planning process.

Fourth, TA utilizes and promotes multiple services and methods of working with others that help the client implement the plan of action: consulting on site, coordinating or delivering training and staff development, providing print and audiovisual materials or other self-instructional resources, linking people to others with similar interests and needs, and offering short-term advice and information. The methods and services selected are determined by the unique needs and characteristics of the clients, and will change over time depending on what outcomes are desired (Trohanis, 1986). For example, some services are intended to transmit information. Others, such as consultation, are better suited to assisting in problem-solving or in the development of products and procedures. In-service training and print and audiovisual materials are used to develop new knowledge and skills. Lasting change stems from variety in TA alternatives and a flexibility that allows the TA and client system to adapt to one another (McLaughlin, 1991). Ann has asked Julie for a combination of services, including information and training. If we imagine TA continuing through the opening of the new classes, we can see how providing on-site consultation and pairing

Ann with other infant/toddler teachers for continued professional development would also be relevant.

A final goal of TA is to build the capacity of the client to evaluate and sustain changes and to identify and solve problems in the future. This is accomplished by engaging the client from the beginning in activities that promote the transfer of responsibility from the external assistance provider to the client staff (Loucks-Horsley & Mundry, 1991). The TA provider encourages the client to compare outcomes with the action plan throughout the TA process. When major systems changes such as the implementation of family-centered practices or early childhood inclusion are involved, TA can support clients as they establish or modify policies, identify funding, design continuing staff development and orientation, or participate in other activities that support the institutionalization of the change. Ongoing support and follow-up are also provided once the initial changes have been implemented.

Let's imagine Julie one year later. She has continued to work with Bright Beginnings as they enroll the infants and toddlers for the new classes, including two of the new children on her early intervention caseload. She has also discovered that Ann is not the only child care provider she is visiting who needs assistance. Because no formal TA system is available in Julie's community, she and the speech and language, physical therapy, and occupational therapy specialists at her agency, along with a consultant from the local child care resource and referral agency, have agreed to work as an informal TA team. Since they are present in the programs on a regular basis to provide services and consultation related to children with special needs, they are in a good position to field a variety of requests related to program-level changes from both center- and home-based child care providers. Their continued presence and support have enhanced the effectiveness of major changes, such as expansion of classes and smaller changes like those related to room arrangement or staff development. Julie realizes that she and her colleagues on the early intervention team enhance their own knowledge and skills when they collaborate with early childhood professionals. Table 9.1 outlines the goals of technical assistance.

TABLE 9.1 Goals of TA

- To help clients clarify their vision of what changes are needed and begin to understand the barriers to and facilitators of change
- To build support for change by encouraging broad participation of community stakeholders in planning
- To help clients translate their vision of what changes are needed into an action plan
- To provide multiple services to support the implementation of the action plan
- To build the capacity of clients to evaluate and sustain the changes

Roles

The above examples clearly illustrate the diverse roles of TA. Crandall (cited in Loucks-Horsley & Mundry, 1991) described a TA provider as a person who must have specialized skills to play various roles and be able to play them in a variety of contexts. A person providing TA may function as an assessor of needs and resources, facilitator, broker or linker, teacher or trainer, helper or coach, capacity-builder, information specialist, regulator or monitor, relationship-builder, morale-booster, communicator or translator, diagnostician, planner, visionary, coordinator, problem-solver, expert, and evaluator (Dimock, 1981; Trohanis, 1986; Loucks-Horsley & Mundry, 1991; Kanter, Stein, & Jick, 1992; Buckley & Mank, 1994). Care should be taken in choosing the appropriate role or combination of roles, depending on the specific needs of the client and the TA relationship. For example, although the client may request assistance from the TA system to evaluate a program or service system, it would not be appropriate for the TA provider to suggest such a role in the early stages of getting to know the client and establishing trust. It is also helpful to consider how directive or nondirective a role may be; the roles of expert or regulator may be less collaborative than those of capacity-builder, linker, or coach. Table 9.2 gives an example of TA roles.

Process

The TA process is not unlike any consultation or strategic planning process in which lasting changes depend on collaboration and ongoing support. Several

TABLE 9.2 TA Roles

Needs assessor: identifies discrepancy between current and desired practice

Capacity builder: encourages clients to identify problems and resources for solving them

Facilitator: assists clients to collaborate and solve problems

Broker: links clients with resources and coordinates the assistance they need

Trainer: teaches new knowledge and skills

Information specialist: gathers and organizes new information and makes it accessible to clients

Helper: delivers services that support the client in making changes

Relationship builder: helps clients build trust and identify effective roles in working together

Morale booster: helps clients feel confident and recognize positive aspects of change

process models have been described in the literature and can be used to deliver in-depth, long-term or short-term TA (Havelock, 1973; Trohanis, 1982; Loucks-Horsley & Mundry, 1991; Kanter et al., 1992). Typically, the following steps are included: (1) establish first contact and build trust with stakeholders; (2) assess attitudes and needs related to change; (3) develop a written plan specifying methods and timelines for change; (4) deliver TA to support implementation of the plan and solve problems along the way; (5) evaluate the outcomes; and (6) consider a plan for ongoing support. These steps may overlap. For example, the TA provider and clients may assess attitudes throughout the process; clients may go back and modify the action plan after implementation has begun; and problem-solving often occurs as soon as Step 2. The trusting relationship that begins at the beginning of the TA process becomes the foundation for subsequent steps toward change and is as important in contributing to effective outcomes as the intrapersonal competencies and personal qualities of the TA provider.

Challenges and Opportunities

Given the complexity of the early intervention and early childhood systems today, it is critical that TA providers recognize the developmental nature of collaboration. Early interventionists who provide community TA in addition to direct services to children and families are challenged to find the time to facilitate a planning process like the one described above. Participants themselves at first may want "quick fixes" and may need help in seeing the benefits of learning strategies for working together to solve their own problems. These skills, however, are of increasing value in the early intervention community as multiple agencies and programs work together to implement early childhood inclusion and improve services for all children and families.

Another challenge of providing TA is the need for participants to develop understanding and respect for each others' diverse perspectives. By utilizing training and awareness activities that build upon the experiences of participants and stimulate discussions about value judgments, TA providers can promote such understanding and identify sources of resistance to change. Personal qualities such as the ability to "speak the language" of the TA participants are also important ingredients for success.

CONSULTATION

The term *consultant* is used so frequently today that there is some danger that people will embrace the title without fully comprehending implications for theory and practice (Hansen, Himes, & Meier, 1990). This is complicated by the fact that consultation is an emerging body of knowledge, and unfortunately, theory and research have not kept pace with practice. Consultation is broadly defined as an indirect service delivery model in which consultant (e.g., physical therapist, speech-language pathologist, early interventionist) and a consultee (e.g., parent, general early childhood educator, child care provider) work together to address a common goal (Brown, Pryzwansky, & Schulte, 1998; Coleman, Buysse, Scalise-Smith, & Schulte, 1991; Buysse, Schulte, Pierce, & Terry, 1994; Wesley, 1994).

According to Hansen et al. (1990), three aspects of this definition distinguish consultation from other types of helping relationships. First, consultation involves any activity in which an expert provides assistance to someone who lacks expertise in a particular area; however, the nature of this interaction differs from the way in which knowledge is transferred through other methods such as supervision, teaching, or counseling. Second, consultation is defined in terms of process. While the process may vary depending on the particular model of consultation that is employed, the stages of consultation generally involve building rapport and establishing a relationship with a consultee; identifying the nature of the problem or defining a common goal; and identifying, implementing, and evaluating strategies to address these needs. Figure 9.1 describes each stage in the consultation process in more detail. Finally, unlike other forms of collaboration, consultation is defined by its triadic nature. The consultant and consultee work together to address a mutually identified goal that benefits the client (e.g., infant with special needs and his or her family).

Various approaches to consultation exist in the consultation literature (Bergan & Kratochwill, 1990; Caplan, 1970). Table 9.3 displays four models of consultation that vary primarily in the expected roles of the consultant and consultee at various stages in the consultation process.

Two other consultation models are worth noting. The *organizational consultation* addresses complex problems and potential solutions from a systems perspective (Conyne & O'Neil, 1992). Any organization, such as an early intervention or child care program, consists of interrelated and interactive components. An organizational consultant might focus on problems within a single component of the program, such as staffing patterns and caseloads, supervision and service delivery, or on the system as a whole. The *process model* of consultation places less emphasis on content knowledge and more emphasis on facilitating problem-solving or serving as a catalyst for change. Thus, the process consultant frequently functions as a coach, encouraging consultees to draw upon their own knowledge, skills, and areas of expertise.

Wesley (1994) described yet another model of consultation that was developed and tested specifically for early intervention to enhance the quality of child care programming. This approach involved a collaborative relationship between trained professionals (e.g., those with a master's degree in early childhood education or early childhood special education) and child care teachers who lack experience or training in serving young children with disabilities. During a series of visits over a four- to six-month time span, the consultant collects data on the concerns, needs, and resources of the staff and provides hands-on assistance as needed. Key components of the model include:

- Providing effective strategies for meeting the needs of children with disabilities in inclusive settings;

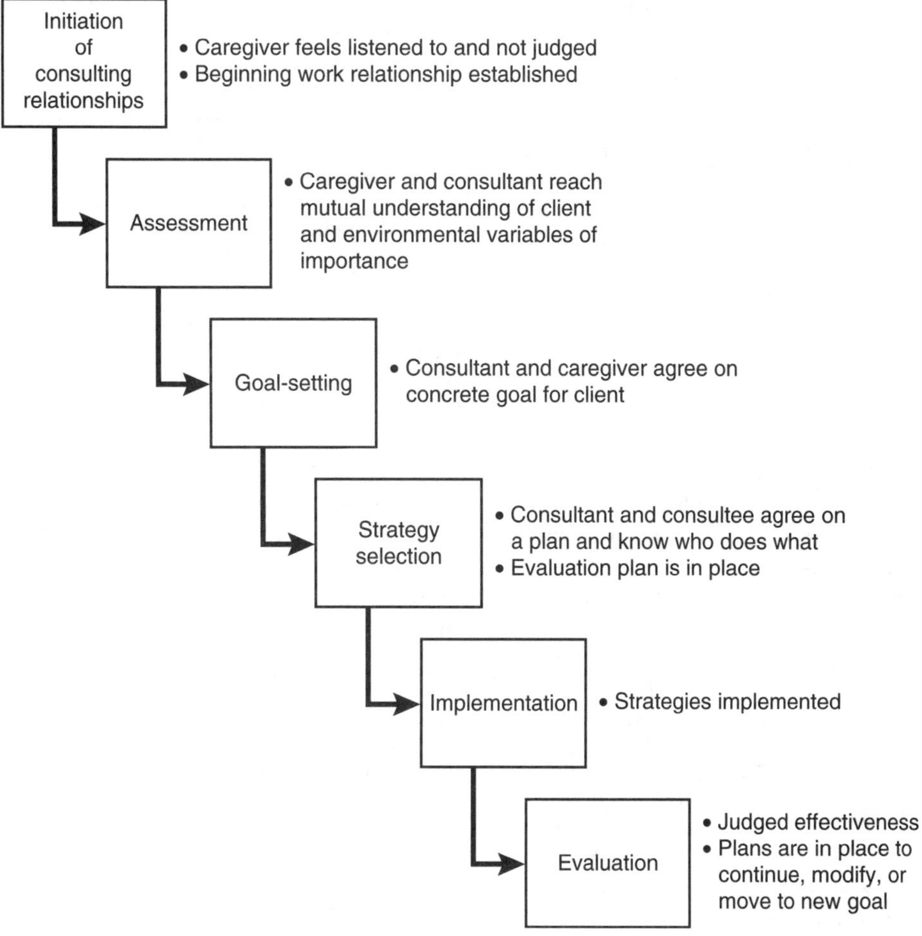

FIGURE 9.1 Stages of Consultation

Source: From *Information from Psychological Consultation: Introduction to Theory and Practice,* 3rd ed., by D. Brown, W. B. Pryzwansky, and A. C. Schulte, 1998, Boston: Allyn & Bacon.

- Completing a joint assessment using the Infant/Toddler Environment Rating Scale (Harms, Cryer, & Clifford, 1997);
- Identifying specific consultation goals and empowering goal-related activities;
- Evaluating both the changes made and the consultation process itself.

The on-site model offers multiple resources to support collaborative consultation. These include providing print and audiovisual materials, helping to arrange visits to exemplary inclusive programs, and working with child care staff to make improvements in the physical and social environment (Wesley, 1994).

TABLE 9.3 Models of Consultation

	COLLABORATION	MENTAL HEALTH	MEDICAL	EXPERT/ BEHAVIORAL
Consultant goal	Work with consultee to identify problem, plan and carry out recommendations	Increase consultee's ability to deal with similar problem in future	Identify problem and develop recommendations for consultee to carry out	Plan and carry out recommendations for problem identified by consultee
Problem identification	Both consultee and consultant identify problem	Consultant helps consultee identify problem by clarifying his/her perceptions of it	Consultant identifies problem	Consultant identifies problem
Intervention recommendations	Consultee and consultant suggest intervention recommendations	Consultee plans intervention with consultant acting as facilitator	Consultant offers recommendations for consultee to implement	Consultant plans intervention which he/she will implement
Implementation of recommendations	Consultee and consultant may each implement some recommendations	Consultee implements recommendations he/she developed	Consultee implements recommendations developed by consultant	Consultant implements his/her recommendations
Nature and extent of follow-up	Consultee and consultant engage in continuous follow-up to modify intervention if necessary	Further consultation may be initiated at request of consultee	Consultant may offer further advice to consultee	None

Reprinted with permission from "Models of Consultation: Preferences of Educational Professionals at Five Stages of Service" by N. L. Babcock and W. B. Pryzwansky, 1983, *Journal of School Psychology, 21,* 359–366.

Because these approaches vary on a number of dimensions (e.g., theoretical underpinnings, goals, intervention strategies), Gallesich (1985) proposed a framework for unifying these dimensions by developing three broad categories to encompass all consultation models. In the *scientific-technological* model, the consultant's goal is to address knowledge deficits of the consultee through training and knowledge dissemination (e.g., a care provider is taught clean intermittent catheterization techniques); whereas the *human development* model emphasizes the consultee's needs for human growth and professional development (e.g., a care provider and a consultant work together to create a professional development plan), and the *social-political* model is concerned with facilitating change within the consultee's organization or work orientation (e.g., a consultant introduces a team-building model to all early intervention personnel). To further elucidate the similarities among various consultation models, Gallesich (1982, 1985) identified characteristics that are common to most consultation practice:

- Consultants have expertise or content knowledge that the consultee lacks;
- Consultants focus primarily on the consultee's work-related problems or goals;
- Consultants work directly with consultees, and only indirectly with clients;
- Consultants are frequently external to the consultee's organization;
- Consultation typically involves collaboration between peers whose areas of responsibility and expertise differ;
- Consultation is governed by philosophies, ideologies, or values;
- Consultation involves a set of processes by which consultation goals can be accomplished; and
- Consultees are free to accept or reject the advice offered by consultants and have primary responsibility for implementing the consultant's suggestions.

File and Kontos (1992) suggested that there is "no one right model of consultation." (p. 226.) However, a number of studies have shown that service providers and other professionals have a preference for a collaborative approach to consultation, one that involves direct help-giving in the form of offering specific strategies to parents and care providers, as well as facilitation of the consultation process (Buysse et al., 1994; Babcock & Pryzwansky, 1983; Schulte, Osborne, & Kauffman, 1993; West, 1985). This means that effective consultation should stress content (e.g., knowledge of infant development, recommended practices regarding assessment and selection of curriculum materials) as well as process (e.g., relationship building, conflict resolution, facilitative communication).

Service providers who function as consultants to parents and other professionals wear a number of different hats, depending on the particular consulting roles that they assume. It is important to note that these roles are apt to change throughout the consultation process. What are the various roles that consultants play and how do they select the appropriate role for each stage of consultation? Figure 9.2 presents some options for selecting a consulting role. These roles are constructed along two axes. The *X* axis presents a continuum of roles designed to help the consultee grow professionally. The *Y* axis displays roles designed to help the consultee obtain positive results for the client. To illustrate, if the goal of consultation is to provide more opportunities for a toddler with delays to interact successfully with her environment, the consultant may choose to model strategies for arranging the environment or demonstrate methods for adapting toys. On the other hand, if the consultant's goal is to increase the caregiver's capacity to perform these functions independently, the consultant may elect to serve as a facilitator or a coach.

Vignette 9.2 presents a typical scenario for consultants in early intervention. In this vignette, the consultant must consider the human and professional needs

To help consultee grow professionally ↑

Counselor "You do it; I will be your sounding board."	**Coach** "You did well; you can add this next time."	**Partner** "We will do it together and learn from each other."
Facilitator "You do it; I will attend to the process."	**Teacher** "Here are some principles you can use to solve problems of this type."	**Modeler** "I will do it; you watch so you can learn from me."
Reflective observer "You do it; I will watch and tell you what I see and hear."	**Technical adviser** "I will answer your questions as you go along."	**Hands-on expert** "I will do it for you; I will tell you what to do."

To help consultee obtain positive results for client →

FIGURE 9.2 Consulting Role Grid

Source: From "Choosing a Consulting Role" by D. P. Champion, D. H. Kiel, and J. A. McLendon, March 1990, *Training and Development Journal,* 66–69. Copyright March 1990, Training & Development, American Society for Training & Development. Reprinted with permission. All rights reserved.

of the teacher as well as appropriate and effective intervention strategies to address the social-emotional goals for the child.

VIGETTE 9.2 ORLANDO

Marianna watched in horror as one of her two-year-old charges, Orlando, reached out and pulled the hair of another toddler, who was playing with blocks. "Get out of his hair," Marianna demanded. Orlando did not acknowledge his teacher's reprimand, nor did he appear to notice the loud protests of his most recent victim. Marianna walked quickly across the classroom and pulled Orlando away from the other child. "Don't pull hair," she repeated firmly. But Orlando only squirmed out of her arms and retreated to the other side of the classroom, where he joined a group of toddlers on the climbing structure.

Later, as she watched how effortlessly a parent volunteer organized snacktime and led a story-time activity, Marianna confided in an early intervention consultant who had been observing Orlando's

> behavior in the classroom. Why, she wondered, did Orlando respond so well to other adults? The consultant listened sympathetically. She had been working with Marianna to help her deal more appropriately with Orlando's challenging behaviors in the infant-toddler classroom. Up until now, this involved regular weekly meetings to talk about some specific behavior problems and several strategies for dealing with them. Today, after observing Orlando and listening to Marianna, the consultant was considering a different approach.

In light of this dilemma, how should the consultant proceed? To answer this question, it is useful to examine the roles and verbal processes that a consultant might use at each stage of the consultation process. The types of consulting roles and stages in the consultation process were presented earlier. Table 9.4 outlines verbal processes or communication strategies used by skilled consultants to transfer knowledge and to elicit information from the consultee.

During the initial stages of consultation with Marianna, the consultant was concerned primarily with gaining rapport and establishing a relationship with her,

TABLE 9.4 Communication Strategies for Early Intervention Consultants

STRATEGY	GOAL	EXAMPLE
ACKNOWLEDGING	Indicates that the consultant is listening, interested, and nonjudgmental	Leaning toward the speaker, maintaining eye contact, nodding, and simple verbal messages such as "Yes," "Right," or "Mmm-hmm."
PARAPHRASING	Provides feedback to speakers about the essence of what was said	"You're not sure if you have the training or experience to work with him."
REFLECTING	Focuses on the speaker's feelings	"This situation makes you uncomfortable."
CLARIFYING	Seeks to ascertain the speaker's message	"Is that right?"
ELABORATING	Embellishes what the speaker says by adding detail	"Her ability to talk, both to reduce her frustration and to help her relate more successfully with others, is an important goal right now."
SUMMARIZING	Integrates and synthesizes all of the relevant information presented by the speaker.	"Well, for now, you'd like to see her move independently and play with her toys and work toward walking later."

Information from *Collaboration in the Schools: An Inservice and Preservice Curriculum for Teachers, Support Staff, and Administrators* by J. F. West, L. Idol, and G. Cannon, 1989, Austin, Tex.: Pro-ed.

so she functioned as a reflective observer or a facilitator (e.g., "You're not sure if you're doing the right things with Orlando."). Later on, after several consultation sessions, the consultant's role remained facilitative, but the emphasis changed to focus more specifically on identifying the nature of the problem and on determining the goals of consultation (e.g., "Tell me more about what Orlando does during circle time," or "It sounds like one of our goals might be to help Orlando understand the consequences of his behaviors. Is that right?"). Once several strategies had been identified to address common goals, the consultant's role and communication strategies centered around implementation issues (e.g., "What happened when you tried redirecting him as we discussed?"). During implementation, the consultant may play various roles, depending on the consultee's knowledge and skills and the nature of the problem. The consultant could begin by observing implementation in the classroom, but quickly move into another role—that of a technical adviser, modeler, or trainer. The final stage of consultation consists of evaluating the effectiveness of the intervention strategies that were implemented. During this phase, the consultant may return to roles that are more reflective and facilitative (e.g., "You handled Orlando beautifully during snacktime today."), or he or she may attempt to redirect or refine the intervention strategy (e.g., "Tomorrow, let's think about giving Orlando several choices during snacktime.").

Overcoming Consultation Constraints

Because consultation is an emerging service delivery model in early intervention, consultants frequently face barriers at many different levels, including state and local systems, programs, and individual classrooms (File & Kontos, 1992). Although many service providers now receive some form of training in consultation, putting these skills into practice may prove challenging. The challenges include both pragmatic issues such as caseload size, lack of time to consult, and funding patterns, as well as conceptual barriers that spring from different professional assumptions about the best way to organize and deliver services for young children. To overcome these barriers, File and Kontos (1992) suggested that future personnel preparation efforts be extended to include both early education professionals and service providers, as well as other consumers of consultation services. Moreover, all professionals involved in consultation should seek organizational support for consultation services from their administrators and develop a plan to grow professionally in consultation practice through supervision or peer mentorship.

TEAMING

Teaming is fundamental to the provision of services. The team approach, which achieves shared decision-making among parents and professionals and creates a wholesome system of checks and balances, is an important, underlying principle of federal legislation pertaining to early intervention and special education (Individuals with Disabilities Education Act, 1999). Furthermore, the team-based model of service delivery is widely recognized as a recommended practice in early intervention (Division for Early Childhood Task Force on Recommended Practices, 1993), largely because no one agency or discipline can meet the complex needs of young children with disabilities and their families.

A team usually consists of a child's parents or caregivers and professionals representing two or more disciplines (Rosin, Whitehead, Tuchman, Jesien, & Begun, 1993). The functions of the early intervention team are to provide cross-disciplinary evaluation and assessment, develop the Individualized Family Service Plan (IFSP), and implement and evaluate intervention and support services. Many authors have described the team approach as well as various models of team functioning, such as multidisciplinary, interdisciplinary, and transdisciplinary (Antoniadis & Videlock, 1991; Bailey, 1984; Bailey, McWilliam, & Winton, 1992; Briggs, 1993; McGonigel, Woodruff, & Roszmann-Millican, 1994; Maple, 1987; Rosin et al., 1993). The primary contribution of these models is to describe different ways in which team members relate to one another. Absent from these descriptions, however, are strategies to assist teams in achieving more effective functioning or a process by which they might move from one stage of development to the next. Moreover, these models may be less relevant today as a result of the shift to community-based programming, as child care providers, program administrators, and other human service professionals are now more likely to be part of the early intervention team. Second, early childhood special educators and other specialists may not be housed together under one roof or within a single organization. As a result, service providers face significant challenges in determining how to involve a key player who may not recognize his or her role as a team member, is unfamiliar with principles and practices related to teaming, or is unable to attend team meetings due to time or staffing constraints.

Recent changes in the field provide an opportunity for service providers to reexamine team functioning in view of expanding community contexts, the addition of multiprogram and multiagency team players, and the increasingly important role of families as active team members. The following sections present two team models. The first, the seven-stage model of team development (Drexler, Sibbet, & Forrester, 1992), is typical of the approach being used extensively in business and the corporate world to enhance team functioning. The second team model, the team-based model for change, was developed and tested by Bailey and his colleagues (Bailey et al., 1992; Winton, McWilliam, Harrison, Owens, & Bailey, 1992). This approach was designed specifically for the field of early intervention, as a method for promoting family-centered practices among members of these teams. Both approaches hold promising implications for community-based teaming in early intervention.

A Seven-Stage Model for Building Effective Teams

The seven-stage model for building effective teams (Drexler et al., 1992) is a process for bringing people together to form a team and help them to define a common ground for envisioning, implementing, and evaluating a strategic plan. In addition to achieving common goals related to a specific content area (e.g., becoming family-centered, implementing community-based services, increasing professionals' cultural sensitivity), the primary outcome of this process is to function more effectively as a team. This is an important outcome, since early intervention teams often have unstated, informal goals related to increasing their smooth functioning (Maple, 1987).

The seven stages of the Drexler, Sibbet, and Forrester approach are presented in Table 9.5, along with some of the issues a team must address at each stage. The process represents developmental stages of team formation, beginning with getting to know team members (i.e., orientation), and progressing to the development of a shared vision and common goals (i.e., trust building, goal and role clarification, commitment), and finally, implementing and evaluating a plan. At each stage of development, the team must address a key question (e.g., "Why am I here?"). The goal is to move the team from an unresolved to a resolved state. The seventh stage, renewal, is designed to help team members grow both personally and professionally and to renew their commitment to team ideals.

Team-Based Model for Change

The team-based model for change (Bailey et al., 1992; Winton et al., 1992) was developed to involve family members in early intervention teams and help them serve in meaningful ways. The model is based on the following assumptions about how change among team members occurs:

- Change is a difficult process.
- Change is a gradual, long-term process.
- Change is more likely to occur in small steps that blend new and existing ideas.

TABLE 9.5 Seven-Stage Team Building Model

Stage 1.	*Orientation:* "Why am I here?"
Stage 2.	*Trust Building:* "Who are you?"
Stage 3.	*Goal/Role Clarification:* "What are we doing?"
Stage 4.	*Commitment:* "How will we do it?"
Stage 5.	*Implementation:* "Who does what, when, where?"
Stage 6.	*Evaluation:* "How are we doing?"
Stage 7.	*Renewal:* "Why continue?"

Adapted from "The Team Performance Model," in *Team Building: Blueprints for Productivity and Satisfaction* (booklet) by A. Drexler, D. Sibbett, and R. Forrester, 1992, Alexandria, Va.: NTL Institute and University Associates.

TABLE 9.6 Moving a Team from an Unresolved to a Resolved State

STAGE	UNRESOLVED	RESOLVED
Orientation (Why am I here?)	■ Disorientation ■ Uncertainty ■ Fear	■ Purpose ■ Personal fit ■ Membership
Trust-building (Who are you?)	■ Caution ■ Mistrust ■ Façade	■ Mutual regard ■ Forthrightness ■ Spontaneous interaction
Goal/role clarification (What are we doing?)	■ Apathy ■ Explicit assumptions ■ Façade	■ Clear, integrated goals ■ Identified goals
Commitment (How will we do it?)	■ Dependence ■ Resistance	■ Shared vision ■ Allocated resources ■ Strategies/tools identified
Implementation (Who does what, when, where?)	■ Conflict/confusion ■ Nonalignment ■ Missed opportunities	■ Clear processes ■ Alignment ■ Effective execution
Evaluation (How are we doing?)	■ Who are stakeholders? ■ Who evaluates? ■ Who needs results?	■ Multiple strategies ■ Criteria for success ■ Results used for planning
Renewal (Why continue?)	■ Boredom ■ Burnout?	■ Recognition ■ Personal/professional development ■ Staying power

Adapted from "The Team Performance Model," in *Team Building: Blueprints for Productivity and Satisfaction* (booklet) by A. Drexler, D. Sibbett, and R. Forrester, 1992, Alexandria, Va.: NTL Institute and University Associates.

- Training to promote change should focus on the entire team, not on the individual.
- Training to promote change should empower team members to identify their own change strategies and solutions.
- Parents and other consumers should have input about changes that will affect them.

The team-based model for change relies on an intensive four-day workshop format in which people work together within their existing teams to describe current practices and identify strategies for change with respect to family involvement. The process is guided by a facilitator who encourages self-reflection and shared decision-making through case studies and small- and large-group discussions. Over the course of the training session, six key questions are addressed:

1. What is our philosophy?
2. How will we involve families in child assessment?
3. How will we assess family needs and resources?
4. How will we involve families in team meetings and decision-making?
5. How will we write family goals and the IFSP?
6. How will we implement the IFSP and provide service coordination?

The outcome of the workshop is a specific plan developed by the early intervention team that includes goals, resources, and strategies for implementing family-centered practices upon return to their early intervention programs. To ensure success with this particular method of team training, Bailey and colleagues suggest that training organizers stress a shared decision-making approach and that administrators and family members be involved in team training efforts.

Challenges and Opportunities of the Team-Based Approach

Parents and professionals who serve on teams are presented with both challenges and opportunities. Common challenges include ensuring maximum participation from all team players and reducing negative effects when team members are absent from team meetings (Winton et al., 1992). To transform these challenges into opportunities, some early intervention teams have found it useful to alter their meeting places and times. For example, an IFSP meeting could take place at a child care center during naptime or during arrival and departure times to allow parents, child care teachers, and directors to attend the meetings.

Another challenge of creating effective teams in early intervention is identifying strong leadership potential (Brill, 1976; Friend & Cook, 1996). Leadership is necessary to give the team momentum and to monitor and guide the work of the team. In situations where a single leader has not emerged, it is sometimes useful to implement a system in which the leadership is rotated among some or all of the team members.

Another significant challenge to effective teaming occurs when there is dissatisfaction from one or more team members, but not the entire team, regarding team goals, roles, or process. In this case, the dissatisfaction of individual team members about how the team works can be turned into opportunities for self-reflection and an assessment of current team functioning and ideal practices. This process might begin by examining qualities of effective teams, as listed in Table 9.7.

To examine individual roles and styles of early intervention teams, an instrument such as the Parker Team Player Survey (Parker, 1991) may be administered. This survey provides a guideline for examining the style of team members, as shown in Table 9.8.

TABLE 9.7 Qualities of Effective Intervention Teams

1. Clear mission, purpose, and goals
2. Sufficient resources
3. Qualified team members
4. Open communication
5. Sufficient time devoted to team meetings
6. Effective problem-solving and conflict resolution strategies
7. Evaluation of individual and team performance
8. A climate of trust and support
9. Strong leadership
10. Organizational support

From "Team Talk: Communication Skills for Early Intervention Teams" by M. H. Briggs, 1993, *Journal of Childhood Communication Disorders, 15*(1), 33–40.

TABLE 9.8 Styles of Team Members

Contributor: Task oriented—trainer, mentor, disseminator of technical knowledge

Collaborator: Goal oriented—cheerleader, encourager, synthesizer of information

Communicator: Process oriented—monitor, consensus builder, listener, interdictor

Challenger: Values oriented—questioner, risk taker, seeker of creative solutions

Information from *Team Players and Teamwork* by G. M. Parker, 1991, San Francisco: Jossey Bass.

Team functioning and effectiveness can be further assessed through an examination of aspects of team culture, such as roles and rituals, and team artifacts such as IFSPs and assessment reports (Westby & Ford, 1993). Table 9.9 gives an example of questions for examining team structure.

Team members should look for evidence of clarity of mission, group cohesion, and parent participation in their team practices and products. Finally, from time to time, all teams must deal with basic differences among team members regarding philosophies, professional assumptions, and communication styles. These challenges, too, can be transformed into opportunities when team members realize that change is gradual and that it requires patience and a commitment to improving team functioning through team development activities.

TABLE 9.9 Questions for Evaluating Team Structure

- Who communicates most and how?
- Who has power and how is it exhibited?
- Who likes whom and what are the effects?
- How do team members' roles affect each other?
- How does work flow among members?
- What are peoples' status in relation to others?

Information from *Working in Teams* by M. Payne, 1982, London: Macmillan Press.

TRAINING

Training is a basic tool for improving the knowledge and skills of staff in order to ensure quality services for children and families. As communities continue to implement the Americans with Disabilities Act and the Individuals with Disabilities Education Act, local agencies increasingly view service providers as vital resources in planning and delivering training. In Vignette 9.1, we saw how child care providers may ask early interventionists to provide technical assistance, and how training is one strategy for building knowledge and skills. Community colleges also seek consultation and training from service providers as they expand their early childhood programs to address special education concerns. In many community colleges, service providers teach courses about children with special needs or co-teach early childhood courses. Local child care resource and referral agencies are another source of training for practitioners serving young children with disabilities and their families.

Within their own agencies, professionals may be team members, mentors, or supervisors, who provide training to colleagues, including those who are newly hired and others who may be taking on additional responsibilities or roles. In some places, early interventionists are members of interdisciplinary and multiagency community planning teams that coordinate services in the early intervention/early childhood system. These teams make recommendations to reduce gaps and duplications in services and to make efficient use of scarce resources.

In some communities, community planning teams also plan and implement training opportunities for practitioners and families concerned with young children with and without special needs. In fact, it may be helpful to consider training as an ongoing process that starts prior to and continues throughout employment.

Under Part C of the Individuals with Disabilities Education Act, each state is required to have a Comprehensive System of Personnel Development (CSPD) that encourages interagency coordination and collaboration in training. Training has been viewed traditionally as a process that focuses on individuals from the same discipline or agency who are presumed to need the same set of competencies to do their jobs (Buckley & Mank, 1994). Yet, to be effective, training must do more than concentrate solely on the education of individuals or homogeneous groups. Training methods and content should instead address the multiple settings, agencies, funding sources, and stakeholders who work together in early intervention. Ideally, training promotes and is guided by the creative collaboration of families, professionals from various disciplines, community organizations, agencies, and universities.

What's missing in the way training is typically provided? In Vignette 9.3, one community's experiences provides a glimpse of how staff development often occurs.

VIGETTE 9.3 ALLEN COUNTY'S EXPERIENCE

Families and professionals in Allen County depend on a hodgepodge of training opportunities to develop and maintain their knowledge and skills in early education and early intervention. For example, every March the local Child Care Coalition sponsors a Day for Day Care, when child care providers attend workshops at the community college. Child care training credit is offered for participation in sessions led by local child care directors or teachers. The topics are chosen based on needs assessments completed the year before, and often include behavior management, developmentally appropriate practice, and resources for children with special needs. Although anyone can attend Day for Day Care, publicity is limited to the county child care network, and center- and home-based providers are usually the only participants.

The early interventionists in the county attend a two-day state conference every year. There they receive infant specialist licensure credit for sessions on many of the same topics offered at Day for Day Care. The topics are chosen by the conference's organizing committee based on the availability of speakers. The majority of participants are early childhood special educators who provide direct services to children and families, with only 10 percent being administrators. Therapists also go to the state conference, but are more likely to attend state and national meetings of their own discipline's professional organizations.

Allen County's elementary schools sponsor three days of in-service training for teachers seeking certificate renewal credit. Although the topic this year was early childhood inclusion, the sessions were not publicized or open to persons who are not school personnel. Following the teacher training, the schools hold a monthlong Spring Fling of weekly workshops for parents of children three to eight years old. This spring, the teacher-led sessions focused on home-school communication. A community college instructor from the Early Childhood Department was asked to lead a session, but the Spring Fling schedule conflicted with a night course she was teaching on early childhood curriculum.

> The community college course provides one of several preservice opportunities available locally. There are two major universities within a 45-mile radius of Allen County offering birth-kindergarten teacher licensure programs that reflect an inclusive focus on early childhood education. Interestingly, although more inclusive practicum sites are needed, the universities do not place students in Allen County, and have not explored the potential of developing sites there.
>
> P. J. Winton, J. A. McCollum, and C. Catlett (Eds.), 1997, *Reforming Personnel Preparation in Early Intervention: Issues, Models, and Strategies,* Baltimore: Paul H. Brookes Publishing Company, p. 54.

As is the case with the vast majority of in-service training, the staff development activities available to Allen County are not conducted in accordance with known components of effective training. The experiences of early intervention personnel and families illustrate a pattern of separating persons who seek staff development according to agency, discipline, job description, and whether they are engaged in preservice or in-service training. There is some history in Allen County of clustering events in the spring, but a system-wide view of training that is responsive to ongoing local needs is absent. Although training needs are similar among child care providers, early interventionists, and teachers, needs assessment is not coordinated across agencies, and training opportunities are not jointly sponsored. There is a lack of variety in training, resulting in only brief exposures to topics through onetime workshops that prove inadequate to support the implementation of changes at the local level. Although coordination with the community college is attempted, there seems to be no dialogue between community agencies and the nearby universities about either one's needs regarding personnel preparation. A critical shortcoming of Allen County's experience is the lost opportunity for diverse professionals and families to come together through staff development to create and sustain meaningful changes where they live and work.

A Plan for Staff Development

If community programs for children and families are to be viable, they must have an ongoing plan for recruiting and maintaining qualified and motivated staff. Edelman (1994) recommended nine survival skills for providers. These are:

1. Being able to think in terms of systems by seeing the process, rather than functions, and interrelationships, as opposed to linear cause-and-effect
2. Being a team player who shares respect, dialogue, vision, commitment, and language
3. Understanding the interrelationship between services and complex issues facing families and communities (e.g., violence, substance abuse, isolation)
4. Supporting families as caregivers and engaging families to shape programs
5. Acknowledging the power and influence of culture and honoring diversity in families

6. Providing professional skills within the framework of parent-directed decision-making and nurturing collaborative relationships to implement change
7. Sharing information and valuing information from other disciplines
8. Assuming the role of advocate for children and families
9. Becoming a change agent by recognizing the transformation of services, challenging the status quo, sharing visions, and working in partnerships

Training Challenges and Suggestions

We face numerous challenges as we consider how best to prepare and maintain a qualified workforce. Program staff are likely to be at various stages of career development. They have different experiences, learning styles, and goals for obtaining new knowledge and skills. They may have varying requirements and credit systems for training according to their discipline or agency. Training at the local and state levels often seems fragmented and seems to have little relevance to needs that arise in daily practice. The availability of resources, such as distance learning or trainers competent to address audiences from diverse disciplines and backgrounds, varies. Similarly, challenges in scheduling and locating space in which to provide training and conduct follow-up activities may seem overwhelming. Early interventionists and other professionals can use the following guidelines when providing training to others or selecting options for themselves:

- Emphasize training in early intervention that reflects the content and philosophical assumptions outlined in personnel preparation standards presented in the position statement by the Division for Early Childhood Task Force on Recommended Practices (1993). These include: (1) the uniqueness of early childhood as a developmental phase; (2) the significant role of families in early education; (3) the role of developmentally and individually appropriate practice; (4) the preference for service delivery in inclusive settings; (5) the importance of culturally competent professional behavior; and (6) the importance of collaborative interpersonal and interprofessional actions.
- Develop a system of ongoing collaboration across community agencies to assess training needs of staff and to plan for meeting them.
- Utilize multiple training formats and strategies based on adult learning theory. These may include university or community college coursework, correspondence courses, traditional workshops, on-site seminars, interactive video or self-instructional media packages, teleconferences, resource fairs, short- or long-term intensive institutes, study tours, lectures, panel presentations, question-and-answer sessions, or many other small- or large-group interactive formats.
- Provide joint training opportunities for staff from various agencies, disciplines, and levels of management, and emphasize participation by teams who work together.

- Obtain approval in advance to offer as many different kinds of training credit as possible, so that persons from various disciplines and agencies will be motivated to participate.
- Provide for the development of relationships among participants while emphasizing content and process, collaboration, and practical problem-solving. Require learners to make decisions and act rather than to just sit and think.
- Utilize participant journals, self-assessments or personal inventories, and written action plans to help participants evaluate the relevance of the information to themselves and develop plans for applying what they are learning.
- Provide time during the training to discuss what participants will do differently back in the community as a result of the training.
- Reflect and promote cross-cultural sensitivity.
- Employ real-life examples and case studies.
- Provide follow-up after the training to help participants transfer what they have learned to daily practice.

(See the appendix for a further discussion of innovative training models.)

Supervision and Mentorship

Tell me what you did, and how you felt about what you did.

Let me tell you what that suggests to me and then you can think it over and see what occurs to you. Okay?

That must have been really hard to take. They remind me of a father who cursed me out at the top of his lungs when I told him I had missed sending out an insurance reimbursement form.

Here's what I see as your strengths. . . . And these are the areas to work on. . . . Tell me what you think of what I've said, and if it makes sense to you, how do you think we could work on those areas?

—Shanok, 1991, pp. 16–19

What is supervision and mentorship? Most early education and intervention practitioners are unfamiliar with the term supervision as it relates to professional development. They may think of supervision as simply monitoring an individual's work performance. For professionals from medicine and the mental health fields, clinical supervision occurs naturally and has a very different meaning. The term mentor may be more familiar to most educators and more closely approximates the meaning of supervision as a method of collaboration. In the words of Pawl (1995): "Clinical supervision is a very special environment for teaching, created by the interaction between the supervisor and the supervisee. Just like any relationship, it always bears the stamp of each contributor and just like any relationship where one person bears greater responsibility than the other, the supervisor assumes the greater responsibility for the quality of what passes between them and for the basic parameters of the relationship." (p. 22)

Gallacher (1997) distinguishes between mentoring—a relationship between a more knowledgeable, experienced mentor and a less knowledgeable, less experienced mentee—and supervision, a relationship in which professional development is only one aspect of guidance in accomplishing organizational goals. In the majority of early education and intervention programs, however, it may be difficult to separate practices related to supervision and mentorship. Administrators of early childhood programs and experienced personnel frequently serve as both mentors and supervisors to less experienced staff members.

Roles of the Supervisor and Supervisee. Practiced correctly, supervision is beneficial to both the supervisor and the supervisee (Pawl, 1995). In other words, the "special environment for teaching" (p. 5) creates a relationship for learning that is bidirectional. This means that, no matter how seasoned a veteran professional may be, the potential to gain another perspective about a particular issue or to enlarge one's view of the world always exists. Supervision and mentorship may be particularly beneficial in helping professionals develop complex skills requiring problem-solving, critical thinking, and creativity (Gallacher, 1997). According to Fenichel (1991), experienced educators and administrators who function as supervisors are provided with opportunities to:

- Model a mutually respectful, collaborative relationship that parallels the professional-family relationship;
- Offer information and instruction in areas that are relevant and appropriate to the supervisee's needs;
- Support the supervisee, particularly as she deals with the more stressful aspects of work with young children and families; and
- Create and maintain a climate of intellectual inquiry, open communication, empathy, and support for long-term professional development.

For novice professionals, supervision and mentorship provide opportunities to:

- Deepen and broaden knowledge and skills;
- Reflect on professional experiences and practices;
- Develop a sense of professional identity and style through increased self-understanding;
- Examine the philosophy that underlies the policies and practices of a professional discipline or service system;
- Learn from an experienced professional who discusses successes and failures in the context of her own professional development (Fenichel, 1991).

Essential Features of Supervisory and Mentoring Relationships. What are the essential features of supervision and mentorship? The Zero to Three work group on Learning through Supervision and Mentorship identified three critical features of supervision that have evolved from various disciplines and traditions, and are relevant to the early education and intervention fields: reflection, collaboration, and regularity (Fenichel, 1991). Reflection requires the early interventionist to stand back from her work to examine its implications for young children and families as well as for her own professional identity. As part of this process, a supervisor offers an enlarged perspective, challenging the supervisee to consider the values and principles underlying her practices by asking, "What were you thinking about when you met with the family?" Reflection helps the novice interventionist understand the feelings associated with her work and to develop a "tolerance for ambiguity" (Fenichel, 1991), the realization that some problems pose human dilemmas that cannot be fully solved nor explained. In the course of supervision, an effective supervisor encourages reflection and responds in a variety of ways: by directing a supervisee to resource materials, by sharing reflections on her own professional experiences, by role-playing situations, or by providing instruction on specific strategies and techniques.

Collaboration could be considered the foundation of supervision and mentorship. The collaboration between novice and expert is based on shared power, on the recognition of the authority of the early intervention professional's own work experience, and on clear mutual expectations that delineate the boundaries and responsibilities of each participant in the supervisory relationship (Fenichel, 1991). Regularity, the third essential element of supervision and mentorship, requires a commitment on the part of the participants to meet on a regular basis. At the same time, it is important to note that supervision and mentorship may take different forms: a supervisor and supervisee may discuss how best to address a family's concern about their child over a cup of coffee, a group of preservice students may share their practicum experiences with an experienced field site supervisor, or staff may meet weekly with an infant mental health specialist to explore and reflect on home visiting practices. Ideally, professionals in early education and intervention will be introduced to the essential elements of supervision and mentorship as part of their field experiences in their preservice training programs. Once students enter the field as professionals, the practice of supervision and mentorship should continue throughout their careers to enhance professional development and improve the quality of services for young children and families.

Final Notes on Supervision and Mentorship The relationship between the supervisor and supervisee based on collaboration, mutual respect, and safety parallels the professional-family partnership found in effective practice. The notion that the supervisory relationship can set the tone for how professionals, in turn, relate to young children and families has been referred to as *parallel process*

(Fenichel, 1991; Pawl, 1995). Thus, because experiences and insights gained through supervision and mentorship directly affect consumers of early intervention services, supervisors bear a particular responsibility for ensuring that the supervisee develops an acute understanding of how relationships are the "medium through which all services are given" (Pawl, 1995, p. 22). Underscoring this important point is mounting evidence suggesting that the quality of supervision is tied to the quality of caregiving practices and the relationships between professionals and their clients (Pawl, 1995).

INTEGRATING AND EVALUATING COLLABORATIVE PROCESSES

Similarities and Distinctions Among Collaboration Models

Table 9.10 summarizes the key elements of each of the collaboration models presented in this chapter. At a glance, it is easy to identify the common elements of each of the models, as well as some unique features that distinguish them. Common to each is the notion that collaboration is a long-term, if not a lifelong, proposition. Professional development does not begin and end in graduate school. The need to work in a collaborative fashion with others continues as long as early education and intervention services are provided by professionals from a variety of backgrounds, disciplines, and agencies—with the ultimate goal of creating a coordinated and integrated system that is consumer-oriented, family-driven, and community-based. In addition, while the various collaborative roles and processes vary to some extent, building collaborative work relationships generally involves the following steps: getting to know someone and building trust, identifying goals for change, developing and implementing a plan, and evaluating these efforts. To make the collaborative process work, professionals must rely on a repertoire of roles (e.g., teacher, evaluator, coach) that change in response to client needs and the particular stage of the collaborative process (e.g., establishing rapport, assessing needs, suggesting different strategies).

The similarities among collaboration models help to explain why terms for these models often are used interchangeably. In actual practice, the models of collaboration frequently overlap. For example, a member of an early intervention team might serve as a consultant to another team member. As part of supervision, a director of an early intervention program might decide to implement training activities on a particular topic. Yet each of these models has evolved from different disciplines and traditions, and each has a slightly different purpose. To distinguish among the various approaches, it is useful to determine the recipient of collaboration, the specific goals for change, and available personnel and resources to address these needs. For example, if the recipient is a child care provider who needs classroom assistance in working with a child with disabilities,

TABLE 9.10 Key Elements of Collaboration Models

MODELS	DESCRIPTION	GOALS	PROVIDER ROLES	PROCESS
Technical assistance	An array of information and technology resources transferred by a specialist through a variety of methods, including dissemination, consultation, and training	Help clients identify areas in which change is needed; assist in implementing change; build capacity to sustain change over time	Evaluator Capacity-builder Facilitator Broker Educator Information specialist Helper Friend	1. Build trust 2. Assess needs 3. Develop a plan 4. Implement services 5. Evaluate 6. Amend plan
Consultation	Consultant and consultee working together to address a mutually identified goal for a client	Address client goals; increase consultee's capacity to solve problems independently in the future	Counselor Coach Partner Facilitator Teacher Modeler Observer Technical advisor Hands-on expert	1. Initiate consulting relationship 2. Assess needs 3. Set goals 4. Select strategies 5. Implement strategies 6. Evaluation
Teaming	Group consisting of a child's parent(s) or guardians and professionals from two or more disciplines	Promote shared decision-making regarding evaluation and assessment, development of the IFSP, and implementation and evaluation of interventions	Contributor Collaborator Communicator Challenger	1. Orientation 2. Building trust 3. Goal and role clarification 4. Commitment 5. Implementing a plan 6. Evaluation 7. Renewal
Training	Tools for improving knowledge, attitudes, and skills of early education/intervention professionals	Identify participant needs; provide opportunities for observation, practice, and structured feedback	Educator Evaluator Mentor Train-the-trainer	1. Preservice 2. Start-up support 3. Maintenance of effort 4. Periodic review and feedback 5. Transition
Supervision and mentorship	A special environment for leaning created by interactions between a supervisor and supervisee	Recognize, understand, and cope with professional challenges	Reflector Collaborator Mentor Catalyst	1. Establish a mentor relationship 2. Develop regular meeting times 3. Reflect on professional experiences and practices

consultation or technical assistance, rather than teaming or training, may be the most appropriate forms of collaboration. In addition to making these distinctions, professionals should strive for precision in the language they use to label collaborative processes in order to facilitate communication about these various approaches.

A Framework for Evaluating Collaboration

How can professionals determine if they have been successful in their efforts to collaborate? Like all good evaluations, a plan for evaluating collaboration should address the purpose of the evaluation, the audience for the evaluation results, and a set of criteria for determining if collaboration efforts were successful (Branham, 1992; Trohanis, 1986; Strata & Bricker, 1996). Articulating the specific goals of collaboration and the purpose of documenting its effectiveness should be viewed as essential first steps in any attempt to evaluate it. Specific evaluation strategies can then be incorporated into an evaluation framework consisting of three components: monitoring and accountability, documenting the processes, and outcomes related to collaboration. Monitoring is a useful tool for documenting the extent to which people actually participated in collaborative efforts and for projecting future needs. Examples of monitoring activities include documenting the number and nature of requests for training and technical assistance or tracking the number of consultative sessions or supervisory meetings one attends. Documenting the process of collaboration can be achieved by keeping a written log regarding the stages and phases of collaboration. Finally, a comprehensive evaluation must address the impact of collaboration on a variety of levels (program, professional, services for children and families). Again, the specific methods and instruments used to evaluate collaboration outcomes will depend, in large measure, on the goals of collaboration. The primary objectives should be to document consumer satisfaction with a particular form of collaboration (technical assistance, consultation, teaming, training, supervision and mentorship), along with specific aspects of collaboration that contributed to consumer satisfaction (training content, a skilled facilitator, a resource lending library). More challenging to document are the systemic changes resulting from collaboration efforts that influence the services and infrastructure of programs as well as human outcome—improvements for children and families (Kagan, Goffin, Golub, & Pritchard, 1995). Documenting these and other important outcomes of collaboration should be carried out in conjunction with ongoing, comprehensive program evaluation efforts.

FUTURE DIRECTIONS

As we approach the twenty-first century, we may see new forms of collaboration emerge or a refinement of those already in existence. Many of these ideas regarding forms of collaboration have their origin in the field of organizational transformation, a relatively new area of theory and practice designed to help organizations transform their purposes, structures, cultures, and strategies (Fletcher, 1990). The emphasis on organizational transformation is beginning to change our thinking about how to view the purposes of collaboration—from diagnosing the problem to envisioning the future, from improving services to reinventing services, from identifying goals and objectives to creating a mission statement, from making minor changes to implementing a major paradigm shift, from improving the organization to empowering the people who work there.

To support future collaborative efforts in early education and intervention, it is necessary to

- Educate students and professionals about various models of collaboration and the roles, goals, and processes associated with each;
- Test models of collaboration with people from other cultural groups and backgrounds and make adaptations to enhance the relevance and acceptability of these approaches;
- Obtain administrative support for early education and intervention personnel who must balance the need to collaborate with the direct service demands of their jobs;
- Create opportunities for family members and other nontraditional stakeholders, including individuals from historically underrepresented groups and diverse cultures, to participate actively in collaboration efforts;
- Conduct research to document outcomes related to particular forms of collaboration and to identify factors associated with the success or failure of these efforts;
- Identify leaders who can assist programs in making the necessary transformations to envision and create an ideal system of services for young children, families, and the professionals who work collaboratively to serve them.

REFERENCES

Antoniadis, A., & Videlock, J. L. (1991). In search of teamwork: A transactional approach to team functioning. *Infant-Toddler Intervention, 1*(2), 157–167.

Babcock, N. L., & Pryzwansky, W. B. (1983). Models of consultation: Preferences of educational professionals at five stages of service. *Journal of School Psychology, 21*, 359–366.

Bailey, D. B. (1984). A triaxial model of the interdisciplinary team and group process. *Exceptional Children, 51*, 17–25.

Bailey, D. B., McWilliam, P. J., & Winton, P. J. (1992). Building family-centered practices in early intervention: A team-based model for change. *Infants and Young Children, 5*(1), 73–82.

Bergan, J. R., & Kratochwill, T. R. (1990). *Behavioral consultation and therapy.* New York: Plenum.

Branham, L. A. (1992). An update on staff development evaluation. *Staff Development Practices, 13*(4), 24–28.

Briggs, M. H. (1993). Team talk: Communication skills for early intervention teams. *Journal of Childhood Communication Disorders, 15*(1), 33–40.

Brill, N. I. (Ed.). (1976). The internal life of the team, III. In *Team-work: Working together in the human services* (pp. 83–102). Philadelphia: J. B. Lippincott.

Brown, D., Pryzwansky, W. B., & Schulte, A. C. (1998). *Psychological consultation: Introduction to theory and practice* (3rd ed.). Boston: Allyn & Bacon.

Buckley, J., & Mank, D. (1994). New perspectives on training and technical assistance: Moving from assumptions to a focus on quality. *Journal of the Association for Persons with Severe Handicaps, 19*(3), 223–232.

Buysse, V., Schulte, A. C., Pierce, P. P., & Terry, D. (1994). Models and styles of consultation: Preferences of professionals in early intervention. *Journal of Early Intervention, 18*(3), 302–310.

Buysse, V., & Wesley, P. P. (1993). The identity crisis in early childhood special education: A call for professional role clarification. *Topics in Early Childhood Special Education, 13,* 418–429.

Caplan, G. (1970). *The theory and practice of mental health consultation.* New York: Basic Books.

Coleman, P. P., Buysse, V., Scalise-Smith, D. L., & Schulte, A. C. (1991). Consultation: Applications to early intervention. *Infants and Young Children, 4*(2), 41–46.

Conyne, K., & O'Neil, J. M. (1992). *Organizational consultation: A casebook.* Newbury Park, Calif.: Sage.

Dimock, H. G. (1981). *Intervention and collaborative change.* Guelph, Ontario: Centre for Human Resource Development.

Dimock, H. G. (1993). *Intervention and collaboration: Helping organizations to change.* San Diego: Pfeiffer.

Division for Early Childhood Task Force on Recommended Practices. (1993). *DEC recommended practices: Indicators of quality in programs for infants and young children with special needs and their families.* Reston, Va.: Author.

Drexler, A., Sibbet, D., & Forrester, R. (1992). The team performance model. In W. B. Reddy & Kaleel Jamieson (Eds.), *Team building: Blueprints for productivity and satisfaction.* Alexandria, Va.: NTL Institute and University Associates.

Edelman, L. (August, 1994). *Preparing learning for the present: Change and emerging roles.* Presentation at the Midwestern Consortium for Faculty Development. Minneapolis, Minn.: University of Minnesota.

Fenichel, E. (1991). Learning through supervision and mentorship to support the development of infants, toddlers, and their families. *Zero to Three, 12*(2), 1–8.

File, N., & Kontos, S. (1992). Indirect service delivery through consultation: Review and implications for early intervention. *Journal of Early Intervention, 16,* 221–233.

Fletcher, B. R. (1990). *Organization transformation theorists and practitioners.* New York: Praeger.

Friend, M., & Cook, L. (1996). *Interactions: Collaboration skills for school professionals.* White Plains, N.Y.: Longman.

Gallacher, K. K. (1997). Supervision, mentoring, and coaching: Methods for supporting personnel development. In P. J. Winton, J. A. McCollum, & C. Catlett (Eds.), *Reforming personnel preparation in early intervention: Issues, models, and practical strategies* (pp. 191–214). Baltimore: Paul H. Brookes.

Gallesich, J. (1982). *The profession and practice of consultation: A handbook for consultants, trainers of consultants, and consumers of consultation services.* San Francisco: Jossey-Bass.

Gallesich, J. (1985). Toward a meta-theory of consultation. *The Counseling Psychologist, 13,* 336–362.

Hansen, J. C., Himes, B. S., & Meier, S. (1990). *Consultation: Concepts and practices.* Englewood Cliffs, N.J.: Prentice Hall.

Harms, T., Cryer, D., & Clifford, R. M. (1997). *Infant/toddler environment rating scale* (rev. ed.). New York: Teachers College Press.

Havelock, R. (1973). *The change agent's guide to innovation in education.* Englewood Cliffs, N.J.: Educational Technology Publications.

Individuals with Disabilities Education Act, 20 U.S.C. §1400 *et seq.* (1999, January 5).

Kagan, S. L., Goffin, S. G., Golub, S. A., & Pritchard, E. (1995). *Toward systemic reform: Service integration for young children and their families.* Falls Church, Va.: National Center for Service Integration.

Kanter, R. M., Stein, B. A., & Jick, T. D. (1992). *The challenge of organizational change: How companies experience it and leaders guide it.* New York: The Free Press.

Kontos, S., & File, N. (1993). Staff development in support of integration. In C. A. Peck, S. L. Odom, & D. D. Bricker (Eds.), *Integrating young children with disabilities into community programs: Ecological perspectives on research and implementation* (pp. 169–186). Baltimore: Paul H. Brookes.

Loucks-Horsley, S., & Mundry, S. (1991). Assisting change from without: The technical assistance function. In J. R. Bliss, W. A. Firestone, & C. E. Richards (Eds.), *Rethinking effective schools: Research and practice* (pp. 112–127). Englewood Cliffs, N.J.: Prentice Hall.

Maple, G. (1987). Early intervention: Some issues in cooperative teamwork. *Australian Occupational Therapy Journal, 34*(4), 145–151.

McGonigel, M. J., Woodruff, G., Roszmann-Millican, M. (1994). The transdisciplinary team: A model for family-centered early intervention. In L. J. Johnson, R. J. Gallagher, & M. J. LaMontagne (Eds.), *Meeting early intervention challenges: Issues from birth to three* (2nd ed., pp. 95–131). Baltimore: Paul H. Brookes.

McLaughlin, M. W. (1991). The Rand change agent study: Ten years later. In A. R. Odden (Ed.), *Education policy implementation* (pp. 143–155). Albany: State University of New York.

Nugent, J. K. (1994). Cross-cultural studies of child development: Implications for clinicians. *Zero to Three, 15*(2), 1–8.

Parker, G. M. (1991). *Parker team player survey.* Tuxedo, N.Y.: Xicom.

Pawl, J. H. (1995). On supervision. In L. Eggbeer & E. Fenichel (Eds.), Educating and supporting the infant/family work force: Models, methods, and materials. *Zero to Three, 15*(3), 21–29.

Payne, M. (1982). *Working in teams.* London: Macmillan.

Peck, C. A., Furman, G. C., & Helmstetter, E. (1993). Integrated early childhood programs: Research on the implementation of change in organizational contexts. In C. A. Peck, S. L. Odom, & D. D. Bricker (Eds.), *Integrating young children with disabilities into community programs: Ecological perspectives on research and implementation* (pp. 187–205). Baltimore: Paul H. Brookes.

Richman, H., & Clifford, R. M. (1980). Toward a model of technical assistance. In R. M. Clifford & P. L. Trohanis (Eds.), *Technical assistance in educational settings* (pp. 13–18). Columbus, Ohio: Ohio State University.

Rosin, P., Whitehead, A., Tuchman, T., Jesien, G., & Begun, A. (1993). *Partnerships in early intervention: A training guide on family-centered care, team building, and service coordination.* Madison, Wisc.: Waisman Center.

Sallis, E. (1993). *Total quality management in education.* Philadelphia: Kogan Page.

Schulte, A. C. Osborne, S. S., & Kauffman, J. M. (1993). Teacher responses to two types of consultative special education services. *Journal of Educational and Psychological Consultation, 4*(1), 1–27.

Shanok, R. S. (1991). The supervisory relationship: Integrator, resource, and guide. *Zero to Three, 12*(2), 16–19.

Strata, E., & Bricker, D. (1996). Building a collaborative team. In D. Bricker & A. Widerstrom (Eds.), *Preparing personnel to work with infants and young children and their families* (pp. 321–345). Baltimore: Paul H. Brookes.

Sullivan, W. P. (1991). Technical assistance in community mental health: A model for social work consultants. *Research on Social Work Practice, 1*(3), 289–305.

Trohanis, P. L. (1982). Technical assistance and the improvement of services to exceptional children. *Theory into Practice, 21*(2), 119–128.

Trohanis, P. L. (1986). *Improving state technical assistance programs.* Chapel Hill: Frank Porter Graham Child Development Center, University of North Carolina at Chapel Hill.

Wesley, P. W. (1994). Providing on-site consultation to promote quality in integrated child care programs. *Journal of Early Intervention, 18*(4), 391–402.

West, J. F. (1985). *Regular and special educators' preferences for school-based consultation models: A statewide study* (Tech. Rep. No. 101). Austin: The University of Texas at Austin, Research and Training Institute on School Consultation.

West, J. F., Idol, L., & Cannon, G. (1989). *Collaboration in the schools: An inservice and preservice curriculum for teachers, support staff, and administrators.* Austin, Tex.: Pro-ed.

Westby, C. E., & Ford, V. (1993). The role of team culture in assessment and intervention. *Journal of Educational and Psychological Consultation, 4*(4), 319–341.

Winton, P. J., McWilliam, P. J., Harrison, T., Owens, A. M., & Bailey, D. B. (1992). Lessons learned from implementing a team-based model for change. *Infants and Young Children, 5*(1), 49–57.

CHAPTER TEN

TECHNOLOGY AND THE FUTURE

DEBORAH J. KRAVIK

OBJECTIVES

- To understand the use of assistive technology for young children with disabilities
- To understand the importance of exploratory behavior for infants and toddlers with disabilities and the outlet provided by adaptive toys, augmentative communication devices, and computers
- To apply the use of assistive technology to home and classroom situations for young children with disabilities
- To assess young children with disabilities for assistive technology needs
- To assess the environment of children with disabilities for specific technology needs
- To assist families in the selection of equipment, software, and other technologies for their children
- To locate and access services via technology for families of children with disabilities
- To understand and utilize computerized Individualized Family Service Plans
- To understand the impact of long distance learning relative to young children and families as well as service providers

ASSISTIVE TECHNOLOGY: DEFINITION, THE LAW, AND PHILOSOPHICAL BASIS

Assistive technology refers to the simple adaptation of toys and materials as well as the more complex development of sophisticated technical devices. A definition of assistive technology first appeared in the law in the Technology-Related Assistance for Individuals with Disabilities Act (PL 100-407), signed by President Ronald Reagan in 1988. PL 100-407 defined assistive technology as "any item, piece of equipment, or product system, whether acquired commercially off the shelf, modified, or customized, that is used to increase, maintain, or improve functional capabilities of children with disabilities" (Early Intervention Program, 1999, § 303.12).

The 1990 revision of the Individuals with Disabilities Education Act (IDEA) mandated responsibility to schools to provide assistive technology devices as well as services when appropriate. PL 100-407 and IDEA defined an assistive technology service as:

> Any service that directly assists an individual with a disability in the selection, acquisition, or use of an assistive technology device, including:
>
> - the evaluation of needs of an individual with a disability, including a functional evaluation of the individual's customary environment;
> - purchasing, leasing, or otherwise providing for the acquisition of assistive technology devices by individuals with disabilities;
> - selecting, designing, fitting, customizing, adapting, applying, maintaining, repairing, or replacing assistive technology devices;

- coordinating and using other therapies, interventions, or services with assistive technology devices, such as those associated with existing education and rehabilitation plans and programs;
- training or technical assistance for an individual with disabilities or the family, and for professionals (including individuals providing education and rehabilitation services), employers, or other individuals who provide services to, employ, or are otherwise substantially involved in the major life functions of individuals with disabilities.

—"New Federal Support," 1989, p. 3

In 1997 IDEA was reauthorized. It required consideration of assistive technology needs and services every time a new Individualized Education Plan (IEP) is written (Lance, 1998). As families and birth-to-three service providers participate on the IEP team, the child's current use of assistive technology as well as training requirements for users and staff should be considered during the transition to the new program.

Traditionally, children with disabilities have had more exposure to assistive technology than their typically developing peers. This is because technology has been used to serve as an equalizer. Parents and professionals have seen the effectiveness of assistive technology as a compensation mechanism for children with disabilities (Pierce, 1994). "Disabilities which limit mobility or cause developmental delays affect the physical, intellectual, social and emotional growth of a child" (Enders & Hall, 1990, p. 171). Every facet of a child's life is potentially affected by a limitation in mobility, whether it be physically based or cognitively based, because such limitations hinder the opportunity to explore the environment. The use of assistive technology devices has provided mobility, communication, and access to children with disabilities so that they might participate equally with their nondisabled peers. Switch toys allow a child to manipulate and explore the qualities of toys. Computers assist a child to engage in exploratory play. Wheelchairs or mobility devices may allow a child to move about to explore the same things nondisabled peers explore. Communication devices allow a child to have a voice to express needs and wants as well as to converse.

Armstrong and Jones (1994) acknowledge the current paradigm shift from viewing assistive technology as a useful tool for individual training based on a hierarchy of technology skill development to seeing it as "an effective tool to help children to be more active participants in typical routines" (p. 1). The shift has been toward viewing technology as an ongoing strategy to facilitate play and learning instead of as a device to be mastered. Assistive technology devices can be used in the home, in center-based programs, and in the community as a means to provide learning, communication, and social opportunities.

Play and Learning

An understanding of how infants and young children learn is essential to any discussion involving technology with children with disabilities. As Piaget's stages of development indicate, appropriate environmental experiences play a large role in cognitive development (Garwood & Fewell, 1983). Children's exploration of the environment facilitates learning. Play is the medium through which infants and toddlers experience their world (Bailey & Wolery, 1984; Enders & Hall, 1990; Linder, 1990; Musselwhite, 1986). It influences all domains of development (e.g., cognitive, social-emotional, communication, and motor).

It stands to reason that a child who is unable to explore and manipulate objects can now do so using technology. In Vignette 10.1, Dominic explored the effects of participating in his own birthday party and interacting with the other children.

VIGNETTE 10.1 DOMINIC AND HIS FRIENDS

Dominic is a two-year-old boy with multiple disabilities. He is involved in a home-based birth-to-three program and receives special instruction, occupational therapy, and physical therapy services. He requires round-the-clock nursing care, provided by a combination of home care nurses and his parents. He has three siblings: two brothers and a sister, ages five, four, and one, and will soon have another brother or sister. Dominic is gavage-fed, requires supplemental oxygen at times, and has a tracheostomy. It is unclear how well Dominic can see and hear, but he loves music and interaction with his parents and siblings. He likes to explore some textures. He is unable to sit unsupported and has limited control of his extremities. Dominic communicates by smiling, crying, and softly humming. He can roll from his back to his side while he is lying on the floor, and he sometimes rolls away to communicate his desire to discontinue an activity. Dominic is unable to actively participate in most family activities, and he reaches a state of overload quite easily.

This summer, Dominic's sister and brothers and their friends played outside frequently, and Dominic spent more time either alone or with a nurse. He missed the other children, and his face would visibly brighten when they came in to play with him. While working on the goals that were written by Dominic's mom, he and his teacher began to prepare for his upcoming birthday. During learning sessions, Dominic would touch, smell, and manipulate modeling clay and form it into a "cake." Magic candles that relight after they are blown out were placed in the "cake" and lit. Dominic already knew how to turn an adapted fan on and off with his switch to blow gentle breezes on himself at will. By pressing his switch, he now used the fan to blow out the candles again and again. He also practiced using the fan to blow pinwheels, which could later be given to all children as party favors. As Dominic became proficient at blowing out candles with the switch, the other children were invited in to play "birthday party" with him. With practice, as the children sang "Happy Birthday" to him, Dominic learned to blow the candles out at the appropriate time.

When the actual birthday arrived, a morning practice party was held to refresh Dominic's skills for his real party. As friends and family gathered around and sang "Happy Birthday" to him, Dominic blew out his own candles by activating the switch-adapted fan at the appropriate time in the song! The other children all clapped and cheered as Dominic smiled and hummed. Dominic was also able to participate in a weekend party with his relatives, taking an active role in his own birthday.

Typical and Atypical Development

For the infant and toddler, motor skills are the "primary vehicle for learning socialization" (Butler, 1988, p. 66). Piaget's theory of intellectual development was based on the belief that although the environment exerts an influence on the child, that influence occurs in the process of a child's actions upon the environment. "Piaget's central theme is that the infant is active; that is, he seeks contact with the environment. His curiosity does not let him wait for environmental events to happen; rather he searches them out and seeks increased levels of stimulation and excitement" (Ginsburg & Opper, 1979, p. 67). The child has a natural curiosity. It is in his nature to explore, participate in, and interact with his environment.

Disabilities in any area of development affect the manner in which the child plays and learns. Without opportunities to affect her world, a child may be severely limited in cognitive development as well as language development (Enders & Hall, 1990). How can the child with a disability seek out increased levels of stimulation? How can this child satisfy her curiosity? The child who has cerebral palsy may not be able to move around freely to explore. The child who views the world from a supine position gains a different understanding of events than the child who is able to view it from an upright position. The infant with a visual impairment may not be able to use visual cues in the same way another child can. Her perspective of the world may not include as large an area of exploration as that of another child. The child with a hearing impairment will not have the same opportunities to develop and engage in language as the typical child. The child with cognitive delays may not interpret cues from the environment or develop language in the typical fashion. Research has demonstrated quantitative and qualitative differences in the play of children with disabilities and children without disabilities (Linder, 1990). Limited access to the world of play deprives a child of crucial developmental opportunities.

Technology as a Learning Tool

One way to facilitate play in children with disabilities is to make toys and materials accessible to them. This is the role of adaptive switch devices, simple communication devices, and appropriate computer software and peripherals. Switches can provide access to toys, computers, augmentative communication devices, the daily living environment, leisure activities, and the social world. Infants and toddlers can be enticed to explore, interact, and be engaged through the creative use of adaptive equipment.

Using a computer-monitored adapted toy program Sullivan and Lewis (1993) gathered data that supported the use of technology in a systematic contingency curriculum. They suggested that switch-toy technology is developmentally appropriate for 2 -to-12-month-olds, based on the accepted Piagetian model of development and infant contingency learning research. Learned helplessness can be prevented by providing opportunities for control that can promote an attitude of expectancy of control over the environment, which in turn facilitates mastery motivation. "If motivation, attention, and fostering of engagement of the physical environment are considered important goals for the disabled infant, then switches, adapted toys, and other currently available technologies are the tools for achieving these goals and can be introduced at levels of cognitive functioning as early as 2 to 3 months" (Sullivan and Lewis, 1993, p. 75). Kinsley and Langone (1995) reviewed four studies that addressed the use of switch-adapted activities with young children with disabilities. In these studies, the researchers use adapted switch toys as contingent reinforcers. Such target behaviors as "increasing movement patterns" (p. 319) were identified. Although further replication of these studies is necessary, each supported the use of adapted switch toys as "powerful motivators for children who have disabilities" (p. 319).

Technology is a "means to provide new methods of access to play, language, and socialization, the primary developing domains of young children" (Behrmann, Jones, & Wilds, 1989, p. 68). When adaptations and technology are included creatively as intervention strategies, new opportunities are provided to facilitate play and learning. The development of these strategies should include typical children in natural settings. For example, computers or communication devices can provide a means of helping the child with disabilities to engage in activities with her typically developing peers.

Technology should be the tool or the strategy, rather than the goal. It is appropriate for a range of assistive technology options, rather than a single all-purpose device, to be considered to meet a child's current and future needs. For the child with a cognitive, physical, or sensory impairment or a developmental delay, the use of adaptive switches, communication devices, and/or a computer can provide the experience of influence over her world, fostering expectancy of participation and success. In the following sections, a variety of assistive technology devices will be discussed.

TYPES OF ASSISTIVE TECHNOLOGY

The most common types of assistive technology that are useful with the birth-to-three population are switches and switch toys, simple augmentative communication devices, and adapted computers. All can provide opportunities for the development of a sense of control and autonomy, language development, cognitive development, creative play, social interaction, and full participation in the physical and social environment (Burkhart, 1993; Hutinger et al., 1990; Musselwhite, 1986; Robinson, 1986). While more sophisticated devices are available, many are not appropriate for the very young child.

Switches

An adaptive switch is a device that allows alternative access to a battery-operated or electrical item. The switch provides an "interface between the child and a reinforcing device, so that the child can activate the device independently" (Musselwhite, 1986, p. 51). Switches can provide easier access to toys, augmentative communication devices, computers, mobility devices, tools, environmental controls, electrical devices, recreational equipment, items in the daily living environment, and more (Burkhart, 1987; Church & Glennen, 1992; Goossens', Crain, & Elder, 1994; Reichle, York, & Sigafoos, 1991).

Many types of switches can be constructed or purchased commercially, with a variety of activation methods (Church & Glennen, 1992; Goossens' & Crain, 1992; Musselwhite, 1986; Reichle et al., 1991). Some of the types of switches commonly used are listed in Table 10.1; several commercial versions are described in Table 10.2.

Appropriate switch selection depends on "the child's abilities, switch sensitivity, switch size, feedback, durability, and placement" (Hutinger, Johanson, Robinson, & Schneider, 1992, p. 19). Commercially available switches vary in sensitivity, or in the amount of pressure and/or movement required for activation. A knowledge of the child's physical abilities as they relate to the sensitivity of the switch will assist in selection.

Feedback refers to sound, light, or tactile information that is provided by the switch itself when it is activated. It may click, buzz, vibrate, light up, or play music as a signal that activation has occurred. These can be very useful features for children who have sensory or cognitive impairments. On the other hand, the feedback

TABLE 10.1 Types of Switches

Button switch
Pressure switch
Wobble switch
Sip-and-puff switch
Shadow switch
Joystick
Plate switch
String switch
Mercury switch
Grip switch
Sound-voice-activated switch
Infrared-beam switch

TABLE 10.2 Switches and Accessories

DEVICE	PRICE	VENDOR	DESCRIPTION
Battery Device Adapter	$8	AbleNet 1-800-322-0956 *www.ablenet.com*	An adapter that, when inserted in a device's battery compartment, allows activation of the device with a switch. For AA, C, or D batteries. Specify battery size when ordering.
Big Red Switch	$42	AbleNet 1-800-322-0956 *www.ablenet.com*	A durable, sensitive switch that is pressure-sensitive across its entire surface. 5" diameter.
Grip and Puff Switch	$46	Enabling Devices 1-800-832-8697 *www.enablingdevices.com*	A pneumatic switch that is activated by squeezing a vinyl grip
Jelly Bean Switch	$42	AbleNet 1-800-322-0956 *www.ablenet.com*	A 2½"-diameter version of the Big Red Switch
Joy Stick Switch	$50	Enabling Devices 1-800-832-8697 *www.enablingdevices.com*	A switch that can activate four different devices by pushing in four different directions
Judy Lynn Software Adaptor	$27	Judy Lynn Software 732-390-8845 *www.castle.net/judylynn*	A switch adapter for use with Judy Lynn software
L. T. Switch	$48	Don Johnston, Inc. 1-800-999-4660 *www.donjohnston.com*	A light-touch switch requiring limited strength for activation
PowerLink 2	$159	AbleNet 1-800-322-0956 *www.ablenet.com*	A control unit that allows a user to operate electrical appliances by switch activation. The PowerLink allows control in three modes: direct (when switch is operated); timed (at preset intervals of 1 to 60 seconds); or latch (with one-touch on and one-touch off).
Pull Switch	$25	Enabling Devices 1-800-832-8697 *www.enablingdevices.com*	A switch that activates a device by pulling on a wooden ball (specify ¼" or ⅛" jacks and plugs)
Rocking Plate Switch	$36 (large, 4 × 12") $27 (small, 1½ × 5")	Enabling Devices 1-800-832-8697 *www.enablingdevices.com*	A switch that can activate two devices separately (specify ¼" or ⅛" jacks and plugs)

(continued)

TABLE 10.2 Continued

DEVICE	PRICE	VENDOR	DESCRIPTION
Roller Switch Music Box	$33	Enabling Devices 1-800-832-8697 *www.enablingdevices.com*	A switch that plays music and/or activates a device by movement of a roller bar
Series Adaptor	$13	AbleNet 1-800-322-0956 *www.ablenet.com*	An adaptor that requires switches to be activated by two children simultaneously to operate a device
Slide Projector Control	$21	AbleNet 1-800-322-0956 *www.ableNet.com*	A control that advances slides on most Kodak carousels through single-switch operation
Specs Switch	$45	AbleNet 1-800-322-0956 *www.ablenet.com*	A 1⅜"-diameter version of the Big Red Switch
Vertical Wobble Switch	$41	Enabling Devices 1-800-832-8697 *www.enablingdevices.com*	A switch that activates a device through any swiping motion (specify ⅛" or ¼" jacks and plugs)
Vibrating Pillow Switch	$26	Enabling Devices 1-800-832-8697 *www.enablingdevices.com*	A soft pillow switch that vibrates. Can be used alone or connected to another device.

may be so stimulating to some children that they are distracted from the reinforcer and unable to focus on the intended activity. Instead, such children may get all the reinforcement they need from the switch click. A knowledge of the child and the switch will help determine how much feedback is reasonable and acceptable. Additional feedback, such as movement, light, sound, vibration, or any combination of these, is provided by the device being activated by the switch.

Durability of the switch is a necessary consideration when it is being used by young children. The switch may be dropped, thrown, stepped on, drooled on, or mouthed. It needs to be durable enough to be used in a variety of environments by a variety of children.

Choosing the appropriate size and placement of the switch and the device it will activate, and providing a comfortable and nondemanding position for the child, are critical elements in successfully providing access to an activity.

Switch Toys

Switch-adapted toy play offers a range of possibilities to children with varying skill levels. The development of an understanding of cause and effect can be facilitated through switch toys. Exploration of the properties of toys—sound, movement, color, light, and texture—can occur. Motor manipulation, visual tracking, motor development, choice selection, turn-taking, communication, imitation, matching, problem-solving, language development, social interaction, independent play, and concept development can be facilitated with switch-adapted toys (Hutinger et al., 1990; Musselwhite, 1986). The concepts of cause and effect, imitation, and turn-taking are vital pieces in the development of language. Activating switches can provide auditory, visual, tactile, and sensory stimulation. Using a variety of switches will aid in generalizing skills and will provide opportunities for higher skill development (Behrmann et al., 1989). Strategies should be individualized for each child, depending on her particular ability, interests, limitations, developmental level, and goals (Robinson, Rauschert & Schneider, 1988).

When a battery-operated toy is adapted with a switch, the child can easily control its action. For exampls, a six-month-old child can make the train go by activating the switch and can practice his motor skills naturally by crawling after the train. The switch toy becomes the means to entice movement while giving opportunities to explore cause and effect. To move beyond cause and effect, or if the same action becomes too repetitive to hold the child's interest, switch toy can become a "new" toy that emphasizes new concepts by being covered with a puppet (King-DeBaun, 1995). Play will now have a new focus. Stories and play activities can be built around the new toy, and the child can direct appropriate action with the switch.

In Vignette 10.2, Dominic chooses one of two activities via technology.

VIGNETTE 10.2 THE POWER OF CHOICES

As Dominic became more proficient with switch activation and was ready to move beyond cause and effect, a method of indicating choices was needed. A choice switch was adapted with real objects so that he could indicate which of two activities he wanted. Two very different activities were selected initially. One side of the switch was connected via a battery interrupter to a toy bird that waddled, then stopped and squeaked, opening and shutting its beak as long as the switch was activated. Attached to the other side was a felt cutout of a character in the story "Brown Bear, Brown Bear." If Dominic chose that activity, a page of the story was read to him. Each activation resulted in another page being read. Often he would choose to hear several pages and then was ready for a break. He seemed to delight in his newfound power and would frequently change to the other activity as if to test whether his teacher would respond to his choice. Once he was confident that his selections would be honored, he stayed with a chosen activity for longer periods of time.

In this vignette, Dominic can be seen exerting influence over people, activities, and interactions. As they began to realize his abilities, his family and his nurses were also able to give him more opportunities to communicate his wishes and exercise choice. This is an important opportunity for a child whose disabilities are so severe that he constantly endures procedures being performed on his body.

A child's self-esteem can be enhanced by providing opportunities for his participation, control over the environment, and decision-making. In all cases, the child should play an active rather than a passive role. Access to switch-adapted toys can and should provide multisensory experiences with objects and people in the environment. The goal is access to play, not switch activation. Switch activation is the strategy that provides opportunities for play.

Augmentative Communication Devices

An augmentative communication device can be as simple as a picture that aids language expression or as complex as a multilevel electronic communication device. At the infant and toddler level, there are many single-message and 2–16-message devices available. They can be as inexpensive as an adapted talking picture frame. Most commonly used with young children are single-switch devices such as the BIGmack (Ablenet) and 4–8-message devices such as the talkPad (Frame Technologies) or the Cheaptalk (Enabling Devices) (see Table 10.3). The messages are quickly and easily recorded into the device, then activated when the child presses the message cell or a switch connected to it. King-Debaun (1995) described adapting a peekaboo book with simple vocal output to enable a child who is nonverbal or who is physically handicapped to participate with her parent in early reading experiences by pressing the page to activate the message. Simple communication devices can be used in a variety of play activities and can be changed in seconds. To make these developmentally appropriate, pictures should be attached to the cells so the child has a visual representation of the message inside.

Participation in small-group activities by all children can be enhanced through adapted play and communication devices. The young child's natural curiosity can be a catalyst for turn-taking and social interaction when an activity is set up appropriately. Play can be equalized and inclusion fostered with voice output. All children, with and without disabilities, should have the opportunity to communicate with the device. It is only then that the child who needs it can see that it truly can be used to communicate. The communicative intent of all who use it should be honored and responded to.

Play can be a means of building communication and direction-following concepts by using a simple communication device. Messages can easily be recorded to say "Build it up," "More blocks," "Uh-oh," "Crash," "My turn," and so on. Repetitive lines from stories or finger plays can be recorded for the child to play/say at the appropriate time.

In Vignette 10.3, Jackson uses a communication device to participate in a play group.

VIGNETTE 10.3 JACKSON TALKS TO HIS FRIENDS

Jackson, a two-and-a-half-year-old with Down syndrome and cerebral palsy, loved his friends at play group. He was usually one of the first to arrive with his dad. Jackson had a strong attachment to his

TABLE 10.3 Communication Devices

DEVICE	PRICE	VENDOR	DESCRIPTION
Alphatalker	$1595	Prentke-Romich 1-800-262-1990 *www.prentkeromich.com*	A communication device that allows for up to 32 messages on one board. Multiple boards with chained messages can convey a variety of messages. Accessed by direct selection, switches, or scanning.
BIGmack	$86	AbleNet 1-800-322-0956 *www.ablenet.com*	A single-message communication device that is activated with any switch
Cheap Talk 4 Direct*	$79	Enabling Devices 1-800-832-8697 *www.enablingdevices.com*	A communication device that allows the user to activate a choice of four prerecorded phrases (up to five seconds each)
Cheap Talk 8 Direct*	$95	Enabling Devices 1-800-832-8697 *www.enablingdevices.com*	Same as Cheap Talk 4 but with eight choices.
Dial Scan	$195	Don Johnston 1-800-999-4660 *www.donjohnston.com*	A rotary-scanning communication device that is activated by a switch. Speed and direction of scan can be set.
Shadow Talker	$110	Enabling Devices 1-800-832-8697 *www.enablingdevices.com*	A four-choice communication device that is activated by any body movement that creates a shadow over a choice station. Messages are prerecorded.
Voice-in-a-Box	$150	Wisconsin Assistive Technology Initiative 1-800-831-6391 *www.wati.org*	A 16-message communication device that is accessed by direct selection or a switch. Also available in 24- and 40-message models, and a 6-level/16-messages per level model.
talkPad	$99	Frame Technologies (920) 869-2979	A 4-message communication device that is easily recorded with human voice. In a lightweight, brightly colored, durable case.
One-Step Communicator	$99	AbleNet 1-800-322-0956 *www.ablenet.com*	A single-message communication aide that holds up to 20 seconds of memory.

*Cheap Talk 4 and Cheap Talk 8 are also available in scan versions or as switch modules.

father, and currently experienced intense separation anxiety whenever his dad moved away from him. As the other children drifted in one by one, Jackson would silently wave to greet them, but he rarely was able to get their attention. They would walk past him to find toys with which to play. Jackson was not able to walk, and he could only say a few words. He needed a way to greet his friends that would get their attention and entice them to come over to play with him.

A Cheap Talk 8 was on loan to Jackson's birth-to-three program. The teacher decided to program it for greetings. The messages "Hi, Buddy!," "See you later," and "I want to read a book now" (Jackson's favorite activity) were recorded, and the remaining message cells were hidden from view with a cardboard cutout. After modeling by his dad and the teacher, Jackson waved and pressed the cell for "Hi, Buddy!" when Kaila came in the door. At first, he did not get her attention. He continued to wave and activate the message "Hi, Buddy!" Finally, Kaila heard and saw Jackson, and she immediately came over and sat down to play with him and the new toy! Jackson was thrilled as he and Kaila looked at each other and took turns talking to each other with the aid of the Cheap Talk. After a little while, Jackson, seemingly satisfied, pressed the messages "See you later" and "I want to read a book now," waved to his dad, and crawled over to the book corner! This was Jackson's first exposure to any communication device.

In this vignette, Jackson was given a way to communicate very simple social messages to a variety of people. With his new power, he was able to more easily separate from his father. He now had his own way of talking to his peers and became less dependent on his father to facilitate the interaction. Jackson also began to use this device in his childcare setting at home with his brother and parents.

Technology is a "means to provide new methods of access to play, language, and socialization, the primary developing domains of young children" (Behrmann et al., 1989, p. 68). When adaptations and technology are included creatively as intervention strategies, new opportunities are provided to facilitate play and learning. The development of these strategies should include typical children in natural settings. Adapted toys, communication devices, and computers can provide a means of helping the child with disabilities to engage in activities with her typically developing peers.

Computers

The ability to operate simple switches is a prerequisite to computer access for young children. Computers can be used at early developmental levels with single-switch programs. The same type of switches used to operate toys can be used with computer software. Early switch-toy games were the precursors of more complex methods of accessing computers (Robinson, 1986, 1986–87). Computers can provide the next step in establishing a child's autonomous interaction with the environment. They are effective tools that, when included in the developmentally appropriate activities, can promote a child's ability to play, interact, communicate, problem-solve, and learn in many other ways. Even outdated Apple IIe and IBM computers can be useful with this age population. These can be acquired very inexpensively or for free as schools and companies upgrade their computers. By using public domain software, play activities can easily be adapted for very young children for home- or center-based use for less than $100 (the cost of a switch and a switch interface).

In Vignette 10.4, Kelsey gains a sense of self through her use of technology.

VIGNETTE 10.4 KELSEY AT PLAY

An outdated IBM computer had been donated by a local bank to 18-month-old Kelsey, who has muscular dystrophy, Because she has little strength in her extremities and is not able to scoot, crawl, or walk, she was unable to explore objects in her environment in typical ways. She was able to say some words or approximations, but was difficult to understand. Because of her limited strength, she was unable to pick up and play with toys that had any weight to them. When Kelsey's teacher made a home visit and brought her the Judy Lynn Software version of Fundamental Concepts to try for the first time, Kelsey greeted her by asking for the "pu" (computer). Kelsey was placed in her high chair in front of the computer. A Jelly Bean Switch (AbleNet) was plugged into a switch adapter (available from Judy Lynn Software), and the adapter was plugged into the joystick port in the back of the computer. The Jelly Bean Switch was small enough for Kelsey's tiny hands and for her high chair tray. A baby doll and a washcloth were also placed on her tray. "PeekaBoo" was selected from the software menu. The teacher first attempted to engage Kelsey in a game of peekaboo with the washcloth and the doll, and then with her own face. Kelsey was not interested and repeated "pu" in a demanding voice. She said "ba" for button, and the switch was given to her. As she pressed the switch, a screen slowly opened to reveal a face. Kelsey recognized the sing-song of the word "peekaboo" and repeated three nondescript syllables in the same intonation. Her delight was evident in her smile, and she clapped for herself when she uncovered the face by pushing her button. When Kelsey bored of this activity, she chose to color. Markers and paper were brought out and the game "Coloring" from the same software was used to color pictures. The same color markers that she chose on the computer were used by her teacher.

This vignette shows that, with the use of a switch and the computer, Kelsey was able to experience concepts that were developmentally appropriate for her age, despite the fact that she was so motorically challenged.

Lepper and Milojkovic (1986) identified instructional advantages of using the computer. With the computer, learning is interactive. Responses from the computer are immediate. Learning can be individualized, and responses can be given in a variety of modes, depending on the needs and learning style of the child. On the computer, the child can independently explore developmentally appropriate concepts. The computer, however, should not be substituted for interaction with adults or peers.

Research is emerging on the use of computers with children with disabilities who are under the age of three. The applications that have been reported so far are of three types: direct training of sensorimotor skills, contingency awareness, and communication and socialization (Butler, 1988). Butler (1988) reported the combined use of adaptive switches and computers to train "contingency awareness or cause-effect relationships in children as young as 3 months who had mentally retarding conditions such as Down syndrome" (p. 71). This understanding of cause and effect resulted in increased interest and involvement in their environment.

In Vignette 10.5, Emily learns to activate a switch to cause a change in the action on screen.

VIGNETTE 10.5 EMILY MAKES IT GO

The children trickled into the play-group room. On the floor, in the quiet corner, an Apple IIe computer was set up with the Dump Truck program on the Cause and Effect public domain software from Colorado Easter Seals. On the monitor appeared a dump truck, a hill, and a pile of dirt. The keyboard was completely hidden with a cardboard box covered with plain white adhesive-backed plastic. In the center was an AbleNet Big Red Switch attached to the box with Velcro. The switch was plugged into a switch adapter (Don Johnston, Inc.), which was then plugged into the game port in the back of the computer. On top of the monitor was a toy dump truck and a pile of cotton balls. It was the first time the computer had been available in the room.

Fourteen-month-old Emily, who has Down syndrome, was working on the motor objective "pulling to stand" and the communication objective "imitating sounds." She entered the room and immediately crept over to the computer. She studied the picture on the monitor with great interest, and slowly pulled herself up to stand by the cardboard box. She tapped the monitor several times and watched. Nothing happened. The teacher then showed Emily how to press the switch to cause the truck to dump its load and return for another load. Emily watched with fascination, then began tapping the switch. The teacher then "drove" the toy dump truck down to Emily's level and dumped the load of cotton balls while making a voiced lip-fluttering sound to emulate a truck noise. The teacher and Emily alternated between the activity on the computer and the toy play. Emily visibly made the connection between her switch activation and the movement on the monitor. She then became more interested in the toy play and began to push the truck along while imitating the teacher's truck sounds. Other children joined Emily in this activity as they arrived.

This vignette demonstrates Emily's awareness of the concept of cause and effect, her beginning imitation skills, and her interest in concrete objects. The visual action on the computer monitor provided a highly motivating activity that enticed Emily to pull to stand, to engage in turn-taking and imitation, and to produce environmental sounds.

Computer Access

Use of the regular keyboard with very young children is not developmentally appropriate. Alternative access to the computer for infants and toddlers can be achieved through a switch, a mouse, a trackball, the Muppet Learning Keys (Sunburst), the TouchWindow (Edmark), and IntelliKeys (IntelliTools). These operate in place of the standard keyboard and are more developmentally suited to young children (see Table 10.4). Some require software designed specifically for use with the particular alternative keyboard, while others work with overlays and can be programmed for activities individualized to the child's abilities and needs. Newer computers will be needed to run the more powerful animated software. The same factors must be considered when selecting an alternative keyboard as those considered when selecting switches (sensitivity, size, durability, feedback, and placement).

In Vignette 10.6, children use a TouchWindow to explore bubbles.

VIGNETTE 10.6 BUBBLE PLAY

At Playgroup, the day's theme revolved around bubbles. The children blew bubbles with wands and with switch-adapted bubble blowers, and played in whipped bubbles. The sensory pool contained a variety of items, including see-through balls, bubble-foam padding, and bubble pillows. For a gross motor activity, the children sat, crawled, walked, or jumped on bubble packing. They also reached way up high to catch the bubbles floating by. For language, all the activities focused on the words "pop," "bubble," and "my turn." Symbols (Mayer-Johnson) for these words were posted by every activity area. The Macintosh computer was loaded with Bubble Castle from the Reader Rabbit's Toddler CD (The Learning Company), an activity that allowed the children to engage in two-dimensional bubble play. The TouchWindow was attached to the monitor. Two-year-old Trevor and one-year-old Johnathan were busy touching the bubbles that floated around on the screen. As each bubble was touched, it popped and an animal dropped down to enter the castle. Trevor and Johnathan looked at each other excitedly when the bubbles popped.

TABLE 10.4 Computer Peripherals and Alternative Keyboards

DEVICE	PRICE	VENDOR	DESCRIPTION
Big Red Switch	$42.00	AbleNet 1-800-322-0956 *www.ablenet.com*	With a Computer Switch Interface, can be used to access single-switch software
Computer Switch Interface—Apple	$36.00	AbleNet 1-800-322-0956 *www.ablenet.com*	An adapter that allows a single switch to be connected to an Apple computer
Computer Switch Interface—Mac	$135.00	Don Johnston, Inc. 1-800-999-4660 *www.donjohnston.com*	An adapter that allows a single switch to be connected to a Mac computer
Computer Switch Interface—IBM	$99.00	Don Johnston, Inc. 1-800-999-4660 *www.donjohnston.com*	An adapter that allows a single switch to be connected to an IBM computer
IntelliKeys	$395.00	IntelliTools, Inc. 1-800-899-6687 *www.intellitools.com*	A light-touch keyboard that can be used with any standard keyboard software. Self-authoring software allows individualization for particular needs.
IntelliKeys with Mac Access Pac	$650.00	IntelliTools, Inc. 1-800-899-6687 *www.intellitools.com*	Includes the software Overlay Maker, IntelliPics, ClickIt!, and IntelliTalk
Microsoft EasyBall	$44.00	Don Johnston, Inc. 1-800-999-4660 *www.donjohnston.com*	Easy-to-use stationary mouse with a single button for click function. The child rolls the ball to move the cursor, then pushes the button.
Muppet Learning Keys	$129.95 (Apple II) $199.95 (Mac) $149.95 (DOS)	Sunburst 1-800-321-7511 *www.sunburst.com*	A touch-sensitive input device that allows users to access the computer without using the keyboard. Requires an Echo card and a color monitor.
Rollerball	$295.00	Don Johnston, Inc. 1-800-999-4660 *www.donjohnston.com*	Rolling ball replaces the mouse or cursor movement. Separate buttons perform click functions.
TouchWindow	$335.00	Edmark 1-800-426-0856 *www.edmark.com*	A touch-sensitive alternative input device. Software programs with overlays transform the surface into game boards and talking word boards. Requires an Apple IIe emulator card and works only with Mac software.

In this vignette, two boys explore a concept in a variety of ways. Using the computer with the TouchWindow allows direct selection that is developmentally appropriate for their ages and abilities.

The IntelliKeys is an user-friendly alternative keyboard that works with any software and can be used with switches, on either a Macintosh- or an IBM-compatible computer. Visual and auditory scanning with switch selection or direct selection is available. Commercial software or self-authored software can be run. There are many preprinted overlays for popular software programs for younger children with automatic setups for IntelliKeys and setups for printing overlays for Ke:nx. Easy-to-use authoring programs that allow individualized programming and overlay designing are also available.

Software for Very Young Children

Just as toys or communication devices provide the reinforcer with switches, software provides the reinforcer in computer activities. Software can provide the opportunity for exploratory play, interactive play, language development, storytelling, painting, and a variety of skills development (see Table 10.5). Careful software selection matched to the child's abilities, interests, and needs can provide a new avenue of access to the world.

Computer software for very young children has various functions, from exploration to more complex skill development. Many programs can be used with children at a variety of developmental levels. It is critical to consider the child's individual goals when selecting and planning computer activities. Skills and concepts can be introduced and reinforced, but the use of computers for drill and practice is not recommended (Hutinger, Robinson, & Schneider, 1995). Rather, activities and software should be implemented and utilized as one part of a comprehensive, integrated plan of intervention.

Computer games and activities may be designed specifically for development of an understanding of cause and effect at the simplest level, or they may involve fairly complex problem-solving at a much higher level. Behrmann (1984) identified three levels of learning for young children in which the computer is a useful strategy: cause and effect, choice-making, and matching. More recently, professionals report a wide range of goals that have successfully been addressed through computer activities, including exploration, communication, choice-making, play skills, cooperation, early math concepts, prereading skills, beginning problem-solving, cause and effect, attending skills, concept development, listening skills, classifying, object identification, picture identification, vocabulary development, fine motor skills, eye-hand coordination, visual motor skills, motor planning, social skills, and basic skill development (Church & Glennen, 1992; Hutinger et al., 1995; Fallon & Wann, 1994; Kinsley & Langone, 1995; Musselwhite, 1986). A recent survey of research replication sites in preschools reported that communication skill development is the most commonly cited use of computer activities with young children (Hutinger et al., 1995). Similar research with infants and toddlers is needed.

TABLE 10.5 Software for Young Children

DEVICE	PRICE	VENDOR	DESCRIPTION
Animals Coloring Book	$49.95	IntelliTools, Inc. 1-800-899-6687 *www.intellitools.com*	Colors are chosen by Intelli-Keys, a switch, or the mouse. The colors for the animal pictures are named as they are chosen. Creations can be printed.
Animated Toys	$35.00	Judy Lynn Software 732-390-8845 *www.castle.net/judylynn*	Single-switch access provides cause-and-effect and early scanning experiences
Arump!	$25.00	Creative Communicating 801-645-7737 *www.creativecomm.com*	A familiar rhyme provides the platform for practicing targeting skills using Touch Window, IntelliKeys, or the mouse
Baby Bear Nursery Series	$75.00	Creative Communicating 801-645-7737 *www.creativecomm.com*	Activities combine nursery rhymes, counting, and farm animal sounds with animation and colorful graphics
Baby Bear Series	$75.00	Creative Communicating 801-645-7737 *www.creativecomm.com*	Includes "Baby Bear's Bubble Bath," "Baby Bear Goes to School," and "Baby Bear Plays Outside"
Best of KidTECH	$59.00	Creative Communicating 801-645-7737 *www.creativecomm.com*	Includes one verse from six children's songs, including "Five Green and Speckled Frogs" and "I'm Bringing Home a Baby Bumble Bee"
BoardMaker	$399.00	Mayer-Johnson Co. 619-550-0084 *www.mayer-johnson.com*	Computerized library of picture communication symbols for creating overlays and communication displays
Circletime Tales Deluxe	$59.00	Don Johnston, Inc. 1-800-999-4660 *www.donjohnston.com*	Interactive nursery rhymes and activities in early literacy, counting, opposites, and directionality
ClickIt!*	$99.95	IntelliTools, Inc. 1-800-899-6687 *www.intellitools.com*	Software for customizing popular software to provide hotspots and scanning capabilities
Creature Antics	$85.00	Laureate 1-800-562-6801 *www.LaureateLearning.com*	Colorful animation and lively sounds by silly characters, accessible by keyboard, switch, mouse, or TouchWindow
Early Play	$30.00	Linda J. Burkhart 410-795-8834	Includes balloon play, clay, and blocks (requires IntelliPics software)
Eensy and Friends	$45.00	Don Johnston, Inc. 1-800-999-4660 *www.donjohnston.com*	Cause-and-effect activities that introduce concepts and early literacy
Five Green and Speckled Frogs	$95.00	Creative Communicating 801-645-7737 *www.creativecomm.com*	Activities involving cause and effect, numbers, number words, directionality, and beginning substitution

TABLE 10.5 Continued

DEVICE	PRICE	VENDOR	DESCRIPTION
Five Little Ducks	$59.00	Creative Communicating 801-645-7737 *www.creativecomm.com*	Cause-and-effect and beginning scanning activities teach 10 action verbs
Holidays Coloring Book	$49.95	IntelliTools, Inc. 1-800-899-6687 *www.intellitools.com*	Colors are chosen by IntelliKeys, a switch, or the mouse. The colors are named as they are chosen. Holiday theme creations can be printed.
Humpty Dumpty and Friends	$45.00	Don Johnston, Inc. 1-800-999-4660 *www.donjohnston.com*	Activities involving cause and effect, early exploration, opposites, and directionality
HyperStudio	$120.00– $130.00	Roger Wagner Publishing 1-800-497-3778 *www.hyperstudio.com*	Users can create and individualize programs in multimedia formats with text, sound, graphics, and video
IntelliPics*	$99.95	IntelliTools, Inc. 1-800-899-6687 *www.intellitools.com*	Creates activities from pictures by adding motion and sound
IntelliTalk*	$39.95 (Mac) $49.95 (Win)	IntelliTools, Inc. 1-800-899-6687 *www.intellitools.com*	Adds talking word processing to activities
JumpStart Baby	$20.00	Knowledge Adventure 1-800-542-4240 *www.knowledge*	Activities are filled with colors, sound, and music. Children can play hide-and-seek, sing nursery rhymes, do puzzles, and perform dressing activities.
JumpStart Toddler	$24.95	Knowledge Adventure 1-800-542-4240 *www.knowledge*	Enticing activities that introduce concepts in an exploratory manner
Just Grandma and Me	$40.00	Broderbund 1-800-474-8840 *www.broderbund.com*	Interactive software presenting early literacy experiences
KidPix Studio Deluxe	$69.96	Broderbund 1-800-474-8840 *www.broderbund.com*	Drawing, painting, and animation software for children's art projects. Includes colorful graphics and sound.
Little People Discovery Farm (CD-ROM)	$20.00	Fisher Price & Davidson 1-800-545-7677 *www.fisherprice.com*	Exploratory play featuring the little people from Fisher Price toys
Make It Go	$59.00	Creative Communicating 801-645-7737 *www.creativecomm.com*	Combines causes and effect with beginning scanning so children can play hide-and-seek, blow bubbles, find a puppy, etc.
Monkey's Jumping on the Bed	$95.00	Creative Communicating 801-645-7737 *www.creativecomm.com*	Activities involving cause and effect, colors, numbers, and matching

(continued)

TABLE 10.5 Continued

DEVICE	PRICE	VENDOR	DESCRIPTION
Old MacDonald's Farm	$75.00	Creative Communicating 801-645-7737 *www.creativecomm.com*	Children choose the animal that MacDonald sings about
Overlay-Maker*	$69.95 (Mac) $99.95 (Win)	IntelliTools, Inc. 1-800-899-6687 *www.intellitools.com*	Software for designing and customizing overlays for use with IntelliKeys and the computer. Can also design low-tech communication displays.
Press to Play Series	$45.00 each	Don Johnston, Inc. 1-800-999-4660 *www.donjohnston.com*	Cause-and-effect, exploratory play, and humorous multicultural activities
Reader Rabbit Playtime for Baby	$30.00	The Learning Company 1-800-543-9778 *www.learningco.com*	With parent's guidance, child can use mouse, keyboard, or TouchWindow to explore faces and feelings; play hide-and-seek, peek-a-boo, music, and imitation games; and listen to rhymes and stories
Reader Rabbit Toddler	$19.95	The Learning Company 1-800-543-9778 *www.learningco.com*	Early exploratory play using music, bubbles, animals, and other toddler activities
Ready for School Toddler (CD-ROM)	$20.00	Fisher Price & Davidson 1-800-545-7677 *www.fisherprice.com*	Concepts are explored using Fisher Price characters
Seasonal Activities I & II	$75.00 each	Creative Communicating 1-801-645-7737 *www.creativecomm.com*	The mouse, TouchWindow, or a switch can be used to explore seasonal activities.
Sesame Street Baby and Me	$30.00	The Learning Company 1-800-543-9778 *www.learningco.com*	With parent's guidance, child can interact with Sesame Street characters. Enlarged keyboard and hand-over-hand mouse movement facilitate typical early play and learning experiences.
Singalongs—volume I (CD-ROM)	$20.00	Fisher Price & Davidson 1-800-545-7677 *www.fisherprice.com*	Child can select familiar songs to hear and sing.
Songs and Play	$30.00	Linda J. Burkhart 410-795-8834	Includes "The Spider Song," "Five in a Bed," and "Big/Small/Fast/Slow" (requires IntelliPic software)
Storytime Just for Fun!	$125.00	Creative Communicating 801-645-7737 *www.creativecomm.com*	Digitized speech, colorful graphics, and animation provide interactive story experiences using IntelliKeys and IntelliPics (based on Pati King-Debaun's book of same title).

*Bundle price for all four software programs: Mac—$280.00, Win—$310.00; or Access Pac including all four software programs and IntelliKeys: Mac—$650.00, Win—$680.00.

In Vignette 10.7, Evelyn tries two programs for the first time.

VIGNETTE 10.7 EVELYN DISCOVERS HER VOICE

One-and-a-half-year-old Evelyn and her family have a Macintosh computer at home. Evelyn was born 12 weeks early and is doing quite well despite her complicated medical history. She is a quiet little girl who loves books but wants them read to her constantly. Otherwise, she has trouble focusing on activities for any length of time. Her mother is interested in expanding Evelyn's interests, increasing her vocalizations, and improving her ability to play with toys. Because Evelyn's mother is very interested in using the computer to capitalize on Evelyn's strength in attending to books, the TouchWindow was brought and set up with the program Old MacDonald's Farm (kidTECH). Evelyn is so tiny that her mom removed the keyboard from the computer desk, and Evelyn sat on the desk in the keyboard area with her mom behind her. As the program began, Evelyn's eyes got very big. When she saw the horse she exclaimed, "Oh!" When she saw the pig, she said, "pi." As the music played, Evelyn bounced up and down. When it stopped, she touched an animal to restart an activity.

Evelyn's mom then tried the exploratory program KeyWack (Stoneware Software). It can be used with a switch, the keyboard, or the TouchWindow. Whenever Evelyn touched the screen, she produced bright shapes and silly sounds. This led to lots of vocalizations, and Evelyn remained interested for far longer periods than she had before.

In this vignette, Evelyn demonstrates awareness of cause and effect, exploratory play, imitation, attending skills, choice-making, picture identification, communication, and eye-hand coordination skills on her computer at home. The computer activities provide motivation and reinforcement through graphics and animation. Any preschool skill can be reinforced by designing activities using carefully selected software. Speech synthesizer activities and vocal output foster language development. Problem-solving skills can be enhanced utilizing planning and sequencing programs (Robinson et al., 1988). Augmentative communication can be trained with software designed for that purpose. Authoring programs allow for the development of individualized overlays.

Technology and software development for infants and very young children, though still in its infancy, is rapidly expanding, and its possibilities are endless. More and more developmentally appropriate software for infants and toddlers is becoming available. Simple cause-and-effect software programs are being expanded to include exploratory play. For software to be appropriate, it must be multisensory and must address typical play of infants and toddlers. Linda T. Burkhart's programs, Early Play and Songs and Play, engage children in balloon play, clay exploration, block-building, and finger-play songs and actions. The kidTECH/SoftTouch software programs engage children in interactive songs frequently sung with very young children ("Five Green and Speckled Frogs," "Five Little Ducks," "Old MacDonald's Farm," "I'm Bringing Home a Baby Bumble Bee," etc.). Pati King-Debaun's Storytime Just for Fun! and Storytime Songbook include familiar songs and early literacy activities appropriate for 12-month-olds. Elaine Clark Center produces very simple and engaging software designed with infants and toddlers in mind. The Baby Bear Series follows Baby Bear in daily activities such as playing in the bath or the sandbox. The Baby Bear Nursery Series allows children to practice animal sounds or to expand concepts from the song "If You're Happy and You Know It." Most of this software is available with overlays for use with IntelliKeys. It can be used with a single switch or a TouchWindow.

The CD, or compact disk, is read by the computer without the necessity of storing the software on the computer's hard drive. While allowing interactive play on the computer, CD-ROM software does not use internal memory. This type of software can also be used in combination with switches and alternative access devices such as the TouchWindow and IntelliKeys. Commercially available software that is available on a disk or CD-ROM includes Ready for School Toddler, JumpStart Baby, and Reader Rabbit's Toddler in which toddlers can explore such activities as popping bubbles, singing songs, counting, sorting, matching shapes, and participating in stories. The Living Books Series provides opportunities for young children to explore stories interactively while experiencing them visually and auditorally. Software that is suitable for infants and toddlers is emerging at a rapid pace.

TECHNOLOGY ASSESSMENTS

A variety of technology assessment guides are available, and assessment techniques can be found in topical books and guides (Carl, Mataya, & Zabala, 1994; Church & Glennen, 1992; Goossens' & Crain, 1992; Hutinger et al., 1992; Levin & Scherfenberg, 1990; Wisconsin Assistive Technology Initiative, 1997). Ranging from interest surveys to formal assessment tools, they vary in many ways. Many resources that deal with implementation strategies also include informal strategies for assessing the child's needs and matching those needs to adaptive equipment (Burkhart, 1982; Goossens' & Crain, 1992; Musselwhite, 1986; Ray & Timms, 1993; Wright & Nomura, 1985).

In addition to defining assistive technology devices and services, PL 100-407 provided funding for states to develop comprehensive programs of assistive technology service delivery. States were to develop systems to provide a link between people with disabilities and assistive technology, and address the need to provide training to professionals, the users of assistive technology, and their families. Evaluation was also considered a major factor in providing quality assistive technology programs. As part of the training function, many states developed or adapted assessment guides for their service delivery programs that were then used statewide. In a study of professionals working with the early childhood special education population, ineffective assessment procedures were cited as a primary cause of abandonment or lack of implementation of assistive technology (Lesar, 1998).

The Assessment Team

Assessment of the use of technology involves a team approach, with the child and family as primary members in the decision-making process. The structure of the team is dictated by the child's physical and developmental needs, as well as the goals of intervention (Carl et al., 1994; Hutinger et al., 1992; Reed & Bowser, 1991; Wisconsin Assistive Technology Initiative, 1997). It is useful to include individuals who have sufficient knowledge of the child's abilities, needs, and communication skills. The nonverbal child may use very subtle cues to indicate pleasure, discomfort, interest, and disinterest. A person who has knowledge of these subtle indicators is a valuable team member. Again, the key to a good technology assessment is to consider the child first, then the device.

A team approach to the selection of equipment is essential for the success of the intervention. Table 10.6 lists candidates for inclusion on the team. At the very minimum, the team should include the child and the family, a child development specialist/teacher, and someone familiar with the technology. The latter may be someone chosen solely for this function or one of the other specialists who is also

TABLE 10.6 Technology Team Members

Child
Family
Occupational therapist
Child development specialist/teacher
Speech therapist
Assistive technology consultant
Family services coordinator
Administrator
Day care provider
Recreational therapist
Orientation and mobility specialist
Teacher of students with hearing impairments
Teacher of students with visual impairments
Therapist
Psychologist
Nurse
Advocate
Paraprofessional
Equipment vendor
Audiologist
Social worker
Funding representative

familiar with the technology. Other members are added as dictated by the child's and family's needs.

Assessing Individual Needs

The primary issue when assessing for possible technology use is the individual child (Hutinger et al., 1992), whose strengths, needs, interests, and motivation are to be addressed within the framework of the family and environments in which the child is expected to function. Choosing a piece of equipment is not a goal. Rather, determining the child's expectations in what environments and under what conditions is what leads the assessment process (Carl et al., 1994). The assessment team should focus on the following questions. What skills does the child have? What is the child having difficulty doing as well as her typical peers? What is hindering her performance? When and where does she need to demonstrate these abilities? under what conditions? What creative strategies can be implemented to address these difficulties? The choice of a piece of equipment is the last step in the process. Simple adaptations of materials and activities may be all that is needed in some cases.

Once it is determined that the goals of the child and the family can best be met by using assistive technology as a strategy, selection of the equipment begins. In this portion of the assessment, the determination of the best types of equipment to address the needs of the child occurs by carefully looking at the child's physical requirements, cognitive abilities, communication skills, motivation and interest levels, attention span, and movement patterns. Positioning of the child should guarantee that he is comfortable, is able to move independently, and has access to the reinforcer being activated by the switch. The child should not have to exert an excess amount of energy to maintain a stable position. His position should free him to engage in the desired activity. The inclusion of a physical and/or occupational therapist on the team is critical at this point.

Reliable movements that can be used to activate switches involve various body parts, such as the finger, hand, arm, trunk, leg, knee, foot, toe, head, chin, mouth, eyes, and facial muscles. Movements can be made on the right or left side of the body. They may consist of squeezing, pressing, waving, pulling, lifting, pushing, sucking, blowing, leaning, blinking, tilting, turning, flexing, or extending. Eye gaze may be the easiest reliable movement for one child. Consideration of the child's medical condition may preclude the use of certain pieces of equipment or reinforcers (i.e., some seizures are induced by flashing lights). Switches that are activated by reflex movements or controlled abnormal movements should never be selected. The movement chosen should be controlled by the child. It should involve an appropriate, voluntary, normal movement pattern (Goossens' & Crain, 1992).

Assessing the Environment

Careful assessment of all environments in which the child will be expected to use technology devices should be included in the assessment process. A child in a birth-to-three program may be served primarily in the home, at a center, at a day care, or at any combination of these settings. Awareness of the opportunities, limitations, and expectations in each setting is important in planning strategies for facilitating participation and generalization. For a child who participates in a center-based program or who attends a local day care center, selection and placement of equipment, positioning, and implementation strategies planned with an awareness of all the children in the setting will facilitate social interaction. In group settings, equipment will be used by all the children in the setting, not just the target child.

In Vignette 10.8, all the children help make the juice through the use of technology.

VIGNETTE 10.8 MAKING JUICE TOGETHER

On a hot summer day at Playgroup, the parents and children were preparing to have a snack. A blender was plugged into an AbleNet PowerLink2 and an AbleNet Big Red Switch was plugged into the PowerLink2. The teacher began to talk the children through the juice-making preparations. First she poured the frozen concentrated juice into the blender, and then added water from a pitcher. The older, more verbal children made comments about the process and the appearance of the juice in the blender. To help make the juice, each child took a turn mixing it by pressing the switch. The switch was passed from one child to another and placed on the table in a secure position in front of each one. As it was pressed, the children could see the change in color, hear the sound of the blender, and feel its vibration. Afterward, they tasted the juice. The typical children in the group spontaneously kept track and made sure each child had a turn, and were particularly concerned that those who had more difficulty calling attention to themselves for a turn were not excluded.

In this vignette, instead of simply drinking juice, all the children were invited to participate in the preparation. The switch and the power control unit provided the means by which they could participate while experiencing the multisensory properties of the activity. In a functional activity, each child exercised autonomy and productivity.

SELECTING MATERIALS

Material selection should only occur after a comprehensive technology assessment. Consideration of the purpose of the activity and the child's cognitive and physical abilities is important in selecting the switch. The appropriateness of a system for a particular child, whether it be for switch-toy play, communication, mobility, or computer play, involves examination of the unique needs of the child (Harrymann & Warren, 1992; Jensen & Bergman, 1992; Robinson, 1986; Wright & Nomura, 1985; York & Wiemann, 1991).

The selection of a switch and the switch-accessed activity should be made with the entire picture in mind. Do the switch system and activity invite participation and interaction with peers? How does the system fit in the family situation? Is the system easily accessible whenever the child wishes to use it or whenever it is appropriate to use it? How appropriate are the size, color, sensitivity, and feedback from the switch? Does the durability match its intended uses? These questions must be carefully answered within each setting in which the child will be using the switch system and activities: in the home, in peer groups, and in the community.

To maintain a holistic approach to the child and intervention, focus should be on the selection of toys and programs that provide auditory, visual, and tactile interaction as well as motor training. An important measure of effectiveness lies in the image of engagement and joy evidenced by the child.

Selection and placement of switches and reinforcers, and positioning of the child in the home setting must address the family's routines, preferences, goals, and space arrangements and limitations in order to promote family interaction and participation. Success should be assured for the child. When constructing a system, every attempt should be made to use developmentally appropriate materials and to provide as normal an appearance as possible.

Learning is experiential. Activities should be multisensory and developmentally appropriate, and should invite interaction with the toys, other children, and the facilitator. Design activities and create opportunities for guided exploration and play through switch access. Consider technology options to assist the infant to do what all children do in order to learn: see, hear, feel, taste, hold, bat, push, drop, and throw.

One of the benefits of using assistive technology with infants and toddlers is helping them learn "that they can play, communicate, interact, control their world, and do what all children their age can do" (Armstrong & Jones, 1994, p. 1). Infants and toddlers examine and explore toys through their senses. They see them, touch them, hold them, hear them, taste them, smell them, drop them, throw them, bat them, and manipulate them. Each toy has a unique input into the sensory system. Babies learn about objects by bringing them to their mouths and exploring their taste and texture. Older infants learn about contingency by throwing objects on the floor and then gesturing and/or vocalizing to persuade someone to interact and pick them up.

IMPLEMENTATION STRATEGIES

The use of adaptive devices and computers should never be a substitute for social interaction. Careful planning should ensure that the implemented strategies provide comprehensive experiences to effectively capture the exploratory nature of infants' and young children's play and learning. The role of the adult is to facilitate the child's opportunities to interact with the environment in as many ways as possible.

When using the computer as an avenue for providing experience, it is also important to offer three-dimensional, interactive experiences to accompany the computer activities (Hutinger et al., 1990). A variety of off-computer activities can be planned that reinforce and extend the experiences on the computer. The more exposure the child has in a variety of settings, the greater the chance for generalization of skills or concepts. In Vignette 10.5, Emily demonstrated skills both during computer play and during off-computer activities with the toys.

Social interaction opportunities should be built into switch-toy and computer activities at all levels. The goal of inclusion in community settings should be planned for at the very earliest stages of intervention, whether that intervention is in the home, in a child care setting, or a center. The facilitator may be the parent, the teacher or therapist, or an older sibling.

Switch Toys

In home or at a center, the switch and toy may be placed on the child's tray or high chair, on a table, or, as is often the case for infants and nonambulatory toddlers, on the floor. Securing the switch with Velcro to a surface is a quick and easy adaptation that provides stability. Many surfaces can be prepared with Velcro so that the switch can be easily transferred from location to location throughout the day and in different settings. Additional stabilizing aides include Blue-Tac and UltraStik, both from AbleNet, dycem, and pieces of nonslip drawer liner. It is useful to have more than one switch available to avoid excess setup time between activities. For instance, if a child uses a switch-activated voice output device to engage in conversation at the breakfast table, a family may find it easier to have another switch available in the play area for battery toys.

Subtle changes in presentation can be made for age appropriateness. Goossens' and Crain (1992) described a bib switch-mounting system constructed of terry cloth and Tempo Loop Display Fabric (Lockfast, Inc.). Burkhart (1987) described head mounts made of barrettes and headbands.

GUIDELINES FOR SUCCESSFUL TECHNOLOGY USE

Select battery-operated toys to which a baby or toddler might typically be attracted, remembering to engage as many senses as possible without overloading the child. Ensure that the child can reach the toy as well as the switch. Allow the infant or toddler to explore the toy visually, tactilely, orally, and auditorally, both with and without switch activation. Discuss attributes of the toy and its action (soft/hard, big/little, slow/fast, up/down, happy/sad, blue/red, hungry/thirsty, empty/full, etc.). Identify its parts or attributes such as color, texture, smell, or taste. A battery-operated black-and-white cow can be fun to play with as either a quiet, nonmoving toy or a walking, mooing, tail-swishing animal! Burkhart (1994) has suggested using cookie tin lids of varying sizes or hula hoops to contain moving toys so that they do not immediately "escape" from the child. Cafeteria trays, shoe-box lids, and many other household materials can accomplish the same task.

Much more can be addressed in switch-toy activities than just the concept of cause and effect. Functional goals including visual tracking, object permanence, play skills such as object play, relation of objects to each other, pretend play, sound production, labeling, motor and verbal imitation, turn-taking, choice-making, problem-solving, and communication skills can all be developed through switch-toy play in natural settings. For example, the moving cow may go into the barn and partially disappear as an activity in object permanence, or she may come out to eat from a bowl as the child visually tracks her progress. Identification of body parts may be addressed. Matching of animals to their sounds, counting skills, color matching, identification of actions, problem-solving, cooperative play, and many more skills can be effectively developed through well-designed activities utilizing switch toys as a strategy. Two or more children can engage in a block-building activity. As one child builds the blocks up high, counting each block as it is stacked, another child can activate the switch that drives the truck that knocks them down.

Augmentative Communication Devices

The speech therapist is essential in designing activities and selecting vocabulary for augmentative communication devices. Vocabulary should be chosen that is fun and invites interaction. Activities should be designed to provide both the need and the motivation to speak. Toddlers who are learning to pretend may enjoy playing a game in which they take turns with Mom or Dad pretending to fall asleep. The nonverbal child can "wake" snoring Dad by activating a single-message switch programmed to say, "Wake up!" With a four-message device, the game can be extended to include directives and messages with social comments such as "That's silly," "My turn," and "Nighty-night."

It is important that the communication devices be functionally used by both parties in the interaction so that the child understands that use of the device will be respected as communication. The adult models the use of the device and responds to the message the child conveys. In a play-group setting all the children, both verbal and nonverbal, should have the opportunity to communicate using the device. The communication, rather than the device, is the important feature. Sign language may also be used in conjunction with the device, just as it would be with voice.

Whenever possible, messages on communication devices should be programmed with a child's voice. Using lots of comments typically used by peers is a good motivator. "That's yucky!" or "Cool!" or "Mine!" are developmentally and socially appropriate comments that can be included on communication devices. Carefully listening to typical verbal infants and toddlers can give lots of clues for designing messages that are developmentally and socially appropriate.

Computers

As with switch toys, computers can be used with very young children as one part of a comprehensive strategy to develop a wide range of skills. The key to any well-designed plan is to provide access to activities in multiple, integrated settings using a variety of strategies and materials to expose a child to opportunities to learn. The child should be an active participant in the learning process. Computer activities for birth-to-three-year-olds should also involve a variety of related off-computer activities to provide opportunities to practice new skills (Hutinger et al., 1990).

Whenever possible, computers should be placed on the floor to ensure that the infant or toddler has easy access. Only the essential components of the computer need to be accessible to the child: the switch or alternative keyboard and the monitor. All other components can be removed or hidden from the child. If the computer is on a table, it should be a child-sized table, and appropriate child-sized seating should be available. If the regular keyboard is not detachable, a cardboard cover can easily be constructed, and the switch or alternate keyboard can be secured on the cardboard cover. If a TouchWindow is used, only the monitor with the window attached need be available to the child. All connecting cables should be removed from sight, and access to them should be prevented. The equipment should be stable, and specific positioning needs for each child should be addressed. Software should be loaded and ready to use. In addition to the computer and equipment setup, materials to reinforce activities on the computer should be available. If the activity portrayed on the monitor involves a baby, a baby doll should be available. If cars and blocks are involved, cars and blocks should be available during the computer activity. Babies and toddlers love to manipulate objects. Abstract concepts on the computer should be reinforced with manipulatives that resemble the pictured objects on the computer as closely as possible. The toys can duplicate actions that occur on the monitor. Visual attention, motor imitation skills, and concepts can be expanded by duplicating the action that occurred on the monitor with the toys that are available for the activity. Software is available that allows the user to print out the pictures that appear on the monitor. The printed material can be used for a wide variety of activities including coloring, painting, making a book, making a t-shirt, and making characters for youngsters to hold during story time. Books that reinforce the concepts from the computer activity should be available to the child. Toys that appear in the program can be used to expand play. With switch toys and computers as strategies for learning, every effort should be made to facilitate play in as natural a manner as possible. Young children should be enticed to participate in many activities that reinforce a concept and that provide opportunities for repetition and practice.

ISSUES AND CONCERNS AROUND TECHNOLOGY USE

As new horizons in technology open new paths for enhancing development, it is necessary to be cognizant of some critical cautions. Each use of an adaptive device or system should be examined for its ability to provide maximum opportunity in the most natural manner possible. Each device or system should be usable by peers in inclusive settings and promote interaction. Use of the simplest, most natural techniques that promote independence should take precedence over more complex technology. Opportunities for socialization and skill development should be provided in a variety of situations using a repertoire of strategies. The primary aim of computer technology for young children with disabilities should be "to allow [them] access to the assistive technology which will be the most appropriate for their needs and to provide for the maximum participation of the young child in social and educational environments" (Wilds, 1989, p. 6).

Adaptive devices should be viewed as a means to an end rather than as a goal. They should enhance development rather than infringe on independence. Solutions utilizing technology should be innovative techniques to equip, entice, and encourage a child to interact with her environment, thereby promoting development to her fullest potential.

The home environment is also a major consideration for infants. Because the home is often the natural setting for birth-to-three-year-olds, utmost consideration should be given to the families' preferences when planning adaptations. The families should be included in the decision-making process from the very beginning.

FAMILIES AND TECHNOLOGY

In Vignette 10.9, Dominic and his family share some special times at home.

VIGNETTE 10.9 DOMINIC AND HIS MOM SHARE QUALITY TIME

Dominic's mother, Rita, reported that she was able to spend some quality time with him each night after the other children were in bed. Dominic's sleeping patterns are irregular, and he often has his days and nights mixed up. A string of Christmas lights was strung along his crib rail, and he was able to turn them on and off at will with a Big Red Switch and a PowerLink2. A tape player was added so that he could also turn music on and off at will. Each evening, Dominic's mother would spend some quiet time with him, talking and singing to him softly. It was during this time that Dominic would smile and hum and turn the lights off and on in a turn-taking activity with his mother. In addition to this beautiful time together for Rita and Dominic, a goal of participation in the family Christmas celebration was intended. As the family gathered around the Christmas tree, Dominic could actively participate by turning the tree lights on.

This vignette shows the importance of the family's priorities. In a household where other children are able to verbalize their needs, desires, and feelings, it is essential to provide opportunities for quality interaction time and strategies for participation for the child who cannot speak out.

Particularly in a home-based program, the family's comfort level with the technology will dictate the frequency of usage. How the technology is implemented to address the family's goals should be detailed in a clear manner. Just as the child may need to be enticed, the family may need to be engaged. Often, the family's intended use of technology may be for social and emotional purposes, rather than for the achievement of cognitive goals (Hutinger, 1994). The family's goals should take precedence and should be reflected on the Individualized Family Service Plan (IFSP). When excitement is transferred to the family, all will benefit. Siblings are wonderful instructional partners, and many welcome the shared responsibility as well as the interaction. Careful planning for implementation by the family is critical.

Professionals' goals for children often center around cognitive and motor development, while parents' goals for their children reflect goals that are social and emotional in nature (Hutinger, 1994). During this early time in their child's life, the family is often dealing with intricate grief feelings and is engaged in a period of great adjustment. Their hopes and dreams for their child must change as they come to an awareness that she will have difficulties that they had not anticipated or planned for. When asked what their dreams for their child are, they may respond that they really want her to have friends and to be able to play with other children. This dream should not be taken lightly by the professional. It is not necessarily inconsistent with the cognitive, communication, and motor goals that guide the teacher. The focus of all the goals can be functionally incorporated and may be well served using assistive technology as a strategy.

In Vignette 10.10, Kyle and his teacher use the computer to work on imitation, communication, and switch training as well as the social goals of the family by using eye contact to request the restart of an activity.

VIGNETTE 10.10 KYLE

Kyle is an adorable two-and-a-half-year-old boy who loves books and music. He is nonverbal and attempts to teach him to sign simple words have met with inconsistent results. He avoids eye-contact and interactive games, preferring to climb on a stool and watch the patterns of the sun through the leaves on the trees. His parents said it hurts them that Kyle doesn't look or smile at them. He enjoys rough play and can't seem to get enough. His parents feel that this is the only way Kyle is able to interact wih them meaningfully. They spend a lot of time swinging and bouncing him as he laughs and laughs. Usually, the adults wear out before he does!

During a home visit, Kyle's teacher set up an donated Apple IIe computer with a switch and the Laureate software program Creature Antics. The teacher held Kyle in her arms. She pressed the switch and the creature on the monitor bounced up and down. She then bounced up and down with Kyle. He laughed and tried to get her to bounce more by bouncing himself in her arms. Instead, she guided his hand to press the switch and pointed to the creature bouncing on the screen. When the creature bounced, so did they. If the creature wiggled or blinked, so did they. Next, the teacher guided Kyle's vision from the monitor to her face, using her index finger to point from the

> screen to her eyes. When Kyle briefly looked at her, she smiled and they repeated the activity from the monitor. Kyle picked this up fairly quickly, and soon began to press the switch and then request the physical movement by looking at his teacher.

In this vignette, the teacher is working on the cognitive goals of imitation and turn-taking. At the same time, she is also working on the family's priority of engaging in visual interaction with Kyle. The activity was repeated with Kyle's mom so she could experience his visual attention to her.

Assistive technology in the Birth to Three program and in the home can offer families "a degree of hope that their children can become active participants in society" (Hutinger et al., 1990, p. 7). In Vignette 10.3, Jackson engaged in cognitive, motor, communicative, social, and emotional behavior. His dad was thrilled to hear him say, "Hi, Buddy!" with a voice output device. What was even more thrilling was to watch other children come over and play with him. The interactions that flowed from a single, simple greeting were priceless. This incident became the springboard for Jackson's family's tireless pursuit to find a way for Jackson to communicate verbally.

Families may be hesitant to entertain the thought of using assistive technology with their child. It may connote for them a vision of helplessness and disability and thus, a picture of a child who is more severely disabled than they perceive their own child to be. Their child is a baby, after all, and may not have severe needs. Nor may their child's needs be visible to the eye. Technology may be viewed as necessary only for children with severe disabilities. While it is easier to comprehend the need for assistive technology for children with more involved disabilities, it is helpful for families to see how technology can be used with all young children and how it can facilitate play. Seeing a group of children playing at the computer or with a switch toy can help allay parents' fears that their child will become "technology dependent." Siblings are often natural demonstrators of how enticing adapted toys can be.

Parents and grandparents may fear that the use of a communication device will prevent a child from developing verbal speech. They need to know that when a child is able to experience the power of using a voice output device, speech will be facilitated rather than impeded.

Another roadblock to acceptance of technology use is the mystery behind it. Parents may not be sure what assistive technology is. The words may mean little without seeing what is meant by the term. Demonstrating what a switch is and how it works with a toy to engage their child and entice her to play and explore will give the words far more meaning than will an explanation. Actually seeing a variety of children playing with adapted toys will aid in understanding that assistive technology is a strategy that can facilitate play, interaction, learning, and active participation in the environment. An additional point that may encourage parents' acceptance and excitement is the fact that computers are used with younger and younger children in schools and preschools. Switch use, when seen as a forerunner to computer use, and adapted computer use, when seen as a means of providing a head start for a child with special needs, become vehicles for excitement rather than fear.

Families will feel more comfortable about assistive technology use if they have opportunities to see it in action. They may understand how technology can foster inclusion when they see all the children use a communication device in a play group. At home, when they see their child use a single-message switch to help read a story, acceptance and understanding of its value can be personally experienced.

SERVICE PROVIDERS AND TECHNOLOGY

Teachers and therapists may also share fears similar to parents'. Perhaps the greatest concern is how to make the technology work and how to incorporate it into intervention beyond the cause-and-effect level. The simplest way to overcome the fear is to attend a workshop or training session that includes, at the very least, demonstrations of devices. Opportunities to use the devices will be very helpful. Often, workshop presenters provide lists of resources that offer support at local, state, and national levels. In addition, other service providers who attend the same training become sources of support.

In Lesar's (1998) study, on-site workshops and consultation and technical support by specialists were cited as the most helpful training methods for professionals working with preschool children. Conferences and in-service courses were also listed as helpful. However, her study did not include early intervention specialists in Birth to Three programs because of the diversity of service delivery models.

The abundance of technical information and the variety of assistive technology devices on the market can be overwhelming to anyone! It is important from the start to recognize how rapidly the field of assistive technology advances and to realize that no one person is ever fully aware of all that is available. Everyone, even the expert, has gaps in information. It is impossible to keep abreast of all the new information about assistive technology. It is an ever-changing field. This can be a very comforting realization, as it removes a huge burden of responsibility from the individual service provider in the field. What is important is to focus on the information that is useful for a particular child or program and to follow best practice guidelines. It is not necessary to use state-of-the-art devices when simpler ones will do. Although a particular computer may be outdated, it may be quite functional for the purpose of the child being served.

Although a bigger and better device may be available tomorrow, today's version (or even yesterday's version) may be perfectly suitable. Low-end technology may be preferable to high-end technology. It is the child, the family, the goals, and the strategies that are most important.

Since the first step in assistive technology use is usually the most threatening for everyone, choosing a simple device, perhaps a basic switch toy, to incorporate into intervention is likely to be the most rewarding and successful. As Musselwhite (1997) is fond of saying, "We must eat the elephant in small bites!" Once some success has been experienced, a comfort level will follow. Capitalizing on a simple success can broaden awareness and comfort levels. Making plans to gradually add more technology into the Birth to Three program will ensure continued personal and program growth. Before spending program money to purchase devices, borrowing adapted toys from a toy lending library could provide necessary experience and avoid potentially costly mistakes and wasted money. State birth-to-three administrators are good resources for locating contact people at the local level who can share their experiences and suggestions. Service providers who are using assistive technology in their interventions can be great sources of information and support. Many states have assistive technology training opportunities in place.

THE COMPUTER AS A RESOURCE

In addition to facilitating learning opportunities for children, the computer is helpful to families and professionals in a variety of ways. Instant access to information, opportunities for communication, service plan development strategies, and continued participation in education are available through the computer.

Information and Communication

The Internet is a connection of computers and computer networks that allows users to share information. It includes networks of computer systems all over the world. In addition to sharing written information, the Internet provides the ability to send and receive e-mail messages, copy programs and data, use remote computers, and view information with text, pictures, sound, and video. Less expensive access to the Internet via the television screen, which will avoid the cost of a full computer system, will soon be available to more families.

A vast and rapidly expanding source of information for services providers and families is available on the Internet. Service providers who have access to the Internet can search for information on a particular disability from a medical, educational, or intervention standpoint. Local, national, and international resources can be accessed. Active discussions can be held with others from all over the world who have an interest in the same subject area. Experiences, strategies for intervention, and brainstorming can be shared among service providers, families, or any other interested individuals. Families can communicate directly with medical specialists, support organizations, and other parents, in addition to accessing information on their child's particular disability. New information is posted daily. Medical personnel, families, support organizations, research groups, and service providers can present queries about rare disabilities in an attempt to locate others with similar symptoms.

A very useful and comprehensive resource on the Internet for information specific to families of people with disabilities is the Family Village Web site. The address is http://www.familyvillage.wisc.edu/. This site is of particular value for those involved in Birth to Three programs. It offers the opportunity to find information, to locate resources, to receive training, to identify other families with similar needs, to learn how to access health care, and to chat with others. The Family Village is updated frequently and additions can be suggested by those who visit this site.

Individualized Family Service Plans

Computerized Individualized Family Service Plans can assist the service provider and the family to develop an appropriate, comprehensive plan for the family and child.

Distance Education

Distance education can be presented as interactive television, two-way audio, or one-way video at a central site. Online classes are available in the home or workplace. Students can earn graduate degrees or undergraduate credits. Colleges offer in excess of 30,000 courses via distance education ("Distance Education," 1998). Distance education can be a convenient way for those who work well independently to receive preservice and continuing course credit. More advanced courses may not be offered locally, and this technology allows access without the need for geographic proximity.

SUMMARY

This chapter provides information about the use of technology with and for infants and toddlers with disabilities and their families. Young children learn through play—through movement and active exploration and manipulation of objects in their environment—a learning strategy that is often unavailable to children with disabilities. Structuring the learning environment to include adaptations that provide access to exploration and manipulation can maximize a child's potential to become an active participant in her world. The use of technology can facilitate play and foster a sense of a capable self, as well as assist in the development of skills in every domain.

Inclusion of children with disabilities can be facilitated through the use of technology. Adapted devices can level the playing field by providing the ability and the means for a child to participate. They can provide a means of communicating with peers. Often, because the adapted toys are very attractive in terms of feedback, they tend to entice typical children to play with their disabled peers.

Careful assessment of the learner, the environments, and the tasks expected of the child within each environment will provide a firm basis for selecting possible technology devices to use. Assessment is a team process that is ongoing and should include the family. Implementation strategies include the provision of opportunities to learn new concepts in a variety of settings with a variety of materials.

Technology use should be planned as one part of a comprehensive strategy of facilitating play and learning. In all activities that include adaptations using technology, the device should be viewed as a tool to entice and encourage interactions with the toys and other children. This should be the primary focus of activities that provide multisensory, comprehensive experiences. Infants and toddlers should be viewed holistically with attention to the various aspects of their lives: at home, in the community, in peer groups, in therapy, and at school if intervention is center-based.

Families' stated goals for their child may differ from those of the service providers. The family may focus on social goals while the professional focuses on cognitive or communication goals. These goals are not mutually exclusive, and the goals identified by the parents should be primary. The use of technology can facilitate all these goals simultaneously.

Technology changes daily, and no individual can possible be aware of all the technology that is available at any one time. Everyone is continually learning. A variety of trainings are available to address particular needs and interests. Service providers and families can and should take advantage of the trainings that fit their particular needs at a given time. Just as the information and technology change, so do the needs.

Information and resources are readily available for service providers and families on the Internet. Families can access information and software, as well as communicate with others throughout the world who have similar issues. Service providers can access information that may be useful in intervention in addition to locating resources and information for families.

The future holds great promise for creative technology use with infants and toddlers. Providing alternative opportunities for learning and mastering the environment for infants and young children with disabilities can maximize their potential in exciting new ways, opening many new doors that were previously closed to those with disabilities. The early use of computers, augmentative communication devices, and adapted toys by young children can help provide them with opportunities for physical, cognitive, and social experiences on a level playing field.

The use of technology with very young children with disabilities can change others' perspectives of them. Rather than allowing a disability to limit a child, technology can maximize his potential. The earlier it is taken advantage of, the more far-reaching the results can be. Not only can the child's skills be addressed, but the family's and service provider's needs as well. Technology is useful for the child with the disability; for the family who needs and wants information, resources, software, and a parent network; and for the service provider who needs access to information, professional resources, and software.

RESOURCES

PROFESSIONAL ORGANIZATIONS

Council for Exceptional Children (CEC)
1920 Association Drive
Reston, VA 22091
Phone (888) 232-7733
Fax (703) 264-9494
www.cec.sped.org
Annual dues vary by state:
professional—$74.00–$85.00;
student—$32.50–$33.00
Publishes:
Exceptional Children
Teaching Exceptional Children

Technology and Media Division (TAM) of CEC
(address same as above)
Phone (800) 486-5773
www.tamcec.org
Annual subdivision dues (in addition to CEC dues): professional—$20.00; student—$10.00
Publishes:
Journal of Special Education Technology
The TAM Newsletter

NEWSLETTERS

ACTTive Technology
Project ACTT—Macomb Projects
College of Education
27 Horrabin Hall
Western Illinois University
Macomb, IL 61455
Phone (309) 298-1634
Annual dues: $16.00

Closing the Gap
P.O. Box 68
Henderson, MN 56044
Phone (612) 248-3294
www.closingthegap.com
Annual dues: $31.00—(6 issues plus the *Resource Directory*)
Publishes:
Closing the Gap Resource Directory ($14.95 plus shipping)

REFERENCES

ACTT outreach training module 2: Birth to three component. (1992). (Available from Project ACTT, College of Education, Western Illinois University, Macomb, IL 61455)

Armstrong, J. S., & Jones, K. (1994, August–September). Assistive technology and young children: Getting off to a great start! *Closing the Gap, 13*(3), 1, 31–32.

Bailey, D., & Wolery, M. (1984). *Teaching infants and preschoolers with handicaps.* Columbus, Ohio: Merrill.

Baumgartner, L., Brassfield, J., Cooper, L., LeHew, S., Muller, L., & Shores, S. (1992, October). *Switches: Under construction.* (Available from Steven Shores, 201 Seventh Avenue N W, Puyallup, WA 98371)

Behrmann, M. M. (1984). A brighter future for early learning through high tech. *The Pointer, 28*(2), 23–26.

Behrmann, M. M., Jones, J. K., & Wilds, M. L. (1989). Technology intervention for very young children with disabilities. *Infants and Young Children, 1*(4), 66–77.

Burkhart, L. J. (1980). *Homemade battery-powered toys and educational devices for severely handicapped children.* Eldersburg, Md.: Author.

Burkhart, L. J. (1982). *More homemade battery devices for severely handicapped children with suggested activities.* Eldersburg, Md.: Author.

Burkhart, L. J. (1987). *Using computers and speech synthesis to facilitate communicative interaction with young and/or severely handicapped children.* Eldersburg, Md.: Author.

Burkhart, L. J. (1993). *Total augmentative communication in the early childhood classroom.* Eldersburg, Md.: Author.

Burkhart, L. J. (1994, October). *Augmentative communication and adaptive play for infants and toddlers.* Workshop conducted at the Closing the Gap conference, Minneapolis, Minn.

Butler, C. (1988). High tech tots: Technology for mobility, manipulation, communication, and learning in early childhood. *Infants and Young Children, 1*(2), 66–73.

Carl, D., Mataya, C., & Zabala, J. (1994). *What's the big IDEA? 1994: Assistive technology issues for teams in school settings.* (Available from Region IV Education Service Center, 7145 Tidwell Road, Houston, TX 77092)

Church, G., & Glennen, S. (1992). *The handbook of assistive technology.* San Diego: Singular.

Distance education: A learning tool for professionals and students. (1998). *CEC Today, 5,* (1), 1, 5, 15.

Early Intervention Program for Infants and Toddlers with Disabilities, 34 C.F.R. 303 (1999, July 1).

Enders, A., & Hall, M. (Eds.). (1990). *Assistive technology sourcebook.* Washington, DC: Resna.

Fallon, M. A., & Wann, J. A. S. (1994). Incorporating computer technology into activity-based thematic units for young children with disabilities. *Infants and Young Children, 6*(4), 64–69.

Federal laws strengthen: The core of current rights. (1991). *NICHCY News Digest, 1,* 4–9.

Garwood, S. G., & Fewell, R. R. (1983). *Educating handicapped infants.* Rockville, Md.: Aspen.

Ginsburg, H., & Opper, S. (1979). *Piaget's theory of intellectual development.* Englewood Cliffs, N.J.: Prentice Hall.

Goossens', C., & Crain, S. S. (1992). *Utilizing switch interfaces with children who are severely physically challenged.* Austin, Tex.: Pro-ed.

Goossens', C., Crain, S. S., & Elder, P. (1994). *Engineering the preschool environment for interactive symbol communication.* Birmingham, AL: Southeast Augmentative Communication Conference Publications.

Harrymann, S. E., & Warren, L. R. (1992). Positioning and power mobility. In G. Church & S. Glennen, *The handbook of assistive technology* (pp. 55–92). San Diego: Singular.

Hutinger, P. L. (1994). *Effective use of technology to meet educational goals of children with disabilities* (PR No. 180R10020, CFDA 84.180R). Macomb: Western Illinois University, Technology, Educational Media, and Materials for Individuals with Disabilities Program.

Hutinger, P. L., Clark, L., Flannery, B., Johanson, J., Lawson, K., Perry, L., Robinson, L., Schneider, C., & Whitaker, K. (1990). *Building ACTTive futures: ACTT's curriculum guide for young children and technology.* Macomb, Ill.: Macomb Projects.

Hutinger, P. L., Johanson, J., Robinson, L., & Schneider, C. (1992). *The technology team assessment process.* Macomb, Ill.: Macomb Projects.

Hutinger, P. L., Robinson, L., & Schneider, C. (1995). Annual survey of ACTT sites indicates common technology practices. *ACTTive Technology, 10*(1), 1, 3.

Jensen, A. S., & Bergman, J. S. (1992). Positioning the child for viable switch access. In C. Goossens' & S. S. Crain, *Utilizing switch interfaces with children who are severely physically challenged* (pp. 17–37). Austin, Tex.: Pro-ed.

King-DeBaun, P. (1995, October–November). Babes in bookland. *Closing the Gap, 14*(4), 1, 7, 36–38.

Kinsley, T. C., & Langone, J. (1995). Applications of technology for infants, toddlers, and preschoolers. *Journal of Special Education Technology, 12,* 312–324.

Lahm, E. A. (1989). Tools for a lifetime. *Exceptional Parent, 9,* 26–30.

Lance, D. (1998). Legal issues in assistive technology. *Closing the Gap, 17*(3), 1, 14, 19.

Lepper, M. R., & Milojkovic, J. D. (1986). The "computer revolution" in education: A research perspective. In P. Campbell & G. Fein (Eds.), *Young children and microcomputers* (pp. 12–23). Englewood Cliffs, N.J.: Prentice Hall.

Lesar, S. (1998). Use of assistive technology with young students with disabilities: Current status and training needs. *Journal of Early Intervention, 21*(2), 146–149.

Levin, J., & Scherfenberg, L. (1990). *Selection and use of simple technology in home, school, work, and community settings.* Minneapolis: Ablenet.

Linder, T. W. (1990). *Transdisciplinary play-based assessment.* Baltimore: Paul H. Brookes.

Malouf, D. B., Jamison, P. J., Kercher, M. H., & Carlucci, C. M. (1991). Computer software aids effective instruction. *Teaching Exceptional Children, 23,* 56–58.

Morris, K. J. (1989). Alternative computer access methods for young handicapped children. *Closing the Gap, 7,* 1, 15.

Musselwhite, C. R. (1986). *Adaptive play for special needs children.* Austin, Tex.: Pro-ed.

New federal support for technology services. (1989). *OSERS News in Print, 2,* 2–3.

Pierce, P. L. (1994). Technology integration into early childhood curricula: Where we've been, where we are, where we should go. In D. Bailey, V. Buysse, and P. Peirce, *Research synthesis on early intervention practices* [On-line]. Available: http://idea.uoregon.edu/~ncite/documents/techrep/tech11.html

Ray, J., & Timms, J. (1993, November). *A guide to computers and software for young children with disabilities.* (Available from Carolina Computer Access Center, 700 East Second Street, Charlotte, NC 28202)

Reed, P., & Bowser, G. (1991). The role of the occupational and physical therapist in assistive technology. In *Tech use guide: Using computer technology.* Reston, Va.: The Council for Exceptional Children.

Reichle, J., York, J., & Sigafoos, J., with invited contributors (1991). *Implementing augmentative and alternative communication: Strategies for learners with severe disabilities.* Baltimore: Paul H. Brookes.

Robinson, L. (1986). Designing computer intervention for very young handicapped children. *Journal of the Division for Early Childhood, 10,* 209–215.

Robinson, L. (1986–87, December–January). Computers provide solid learning base for preschool children. *Closing the Gap, 5*(5), 1, 18, 25.

Robinson, L. (1992a). From the editors. *ACTTion News, 7,* 2.

Robinson, L. (1992b). Integrating technology into birth to three programs. In *ACTT outreach training module 2: Birth to three component.* (Available from Project ACTT, College of Education, Western Illinois University, Macomb, IL 61455)

Robinson, L., Rauschert, M., & Schneider, C. (1988). Computer technology as a tool for preschool handicapped children. *Closing the Gap, 7,* 26–29.

Sullivan, M. W., & Lewis, M. (1993). Contingency, means-end skills, and the use of technology in infant intervention. *Infants and Young Children, 5*(4), 58–77.

Taber, F. M. (1986). Adaptive devices and the computer. *The Exceptional Parent, 6,* 29–30.

Wilds, M. L. (1989). Effective use of technology with young children. *NICHCY News Digest, 13,* 6–7.

Wisconsin Assistive Technology Initiative. (1997). *Assessing Students' Needs for Assistive Technology: A Resource Manual for School District Teams.* Amherst, Wisc.: Author.

Wright, C., & Nomura, M. (1985). *From toys to computers: Access for the physically disabled child.* San Jose: Author.

York, J., & Wiemann, G. (1991). Accommodating severe physical disabilities. In J. Reichle, J. York, & J. Sigafoos, with invited contributors, *Implementing augmentative and alternative communication* (pp. 239–255). Baltimore: Paul H. Brookes.

INDEX